SOCIOLOGY OF EDUCATION

This comprehensive and bestselling reader examines the most pressing topics in sociology and education while exposing students to examples of sociological research on schools. Drawing from classic and contemporary scholarship, noted sociologist Alan R. Sadovnik has chosen readings that examine current issues and reflect diverse theoretical approaches to studying the effects of schooling and society. The second edition provides students with seven new readings from some of the best theorists and researchers in education including James S. Coleman, Madeleine Arnot, and Claudia Buchman. Through full, rather than excerpted primary source readings, students have the opportunity to read sociological research as it is written and engage in critical analyses of readings in their entirety. Including comprehensive section introductions, questions for reflection and discussion, and suggested readings, *Sociology of Education* will stimulate student thinking about the important roles that schools play in contemporary society and their ability to solve fundamental social, economic, and political problems.

Alan R. Sadovnik is Professor of Education, Sociology, and Public Affairs at Rutgers University, Newark, New Jersey.

SOCIOLOGY OF EDUCATION

A CRITICAL READER

Second Edition

Edited by Alan R. Sadovnik

Routledge
Taylor & Francis Group

NEW YORK AND LONDON

First edition published 2007
by Routledge
270 Madison Ave, New York, NY 10016

This second edition published 2011
by Routledge
270 Madison Ave, New York, NY 10016

Simultaneously published in the UK
by Routledge
2 Park Square, Milton Park, Abingdon, Oxon OX14 4RN

Routledge is an imprint of the Taylor & Francis Group, an informa business

© 2011 Taylor and Francis

Typeset in Helvetica Neue and Minion Pro by Prepress Projects Ltd, Perth, UK

Printed and bound in the United States of America on acid-free paper by Sheridan Books, Inc.

Library of Congress Cataloging in Publication Data
Library of Congress Cataloging-in-Publication Data
Sociology of education : a critical reader / edited by Alan R. Sadovnik. — 2nd ed.
p. cm.
1. Educational sociology. 2. Educational sociology—United States. I. Sadovnik, Alan R.
LC191.2.S632 2010
306.43—dc22
2010023372

British Library Cataloguing in Publication Data
A catalogue record for this book is available from the British Library

ISBN 13: (hbk) 978-0-415-80369-4
ISBN 13: (pbk) 978-0-415-80370-0

For Mags

We're working on it!

Contents

Acknowledgments

This book would not have been possible without the help of a number of important individuals. At Rutgers, Lachone McKenzie and her work-study students provided essential secretarial support. My graduate assistants, Elizabeth Morrison and Tara Davidson, provided important administrative support; and Princeton University intern, Ralph Schaefer, provided excellent technical and administrative support.

At Routledge, my editors Catherine Bernard and Georgette Enriquez provided helpful support and advice at all stages of the project. For the first edition, Lynn Goeller and Judith Simon, and for the second edition, Andrew Davidson provided helpful assistance and advice during production.

My wife and collaborator on many other scholarly projects, Susan F. Semel, provided effective and cheerful assistance in proofreading the final page-proofs. Mags Semel provided helpful assistance in the final stages of production.

This book is dedicated to Mags Semel, my developmentally disabled stepdaughter, who has taught me what living up to one's potential really means.

Introduction

The sociology of education has provided important insights into the ways in which schools affect individuals and groups. Through an examination of the relationships among societal factors such as political, economic and cultural systems and schools, sociologists have uncovered how educational processes affect the way people think, live and work, their place in society, and their chances for success or failure. From the famous Coleman Report, *Equality of Educational Opportunity* in 1966, research in the sociology of education has attempted to understand whether educational systems and their practices provide opportunities for all children to achieve based on their merits or whether they reproduce existing social inequalities. From the beginning of the twenty-first century, with educational policy in the United States emphasizing the concurrent themes of standards and equity and the reduction of the achievement gap among groups, based on social class, race, ethnicity, gender, and disability, sociologists of education continue to provide important empirical findings on the effects of education.

Theory and research in the sociology of education seek to understand, in Christopher Hurn's (1993) words, "the limits and possibilities of schooling." In a country that has placed enormous faith in the power of schools to ameliorate all types of social problems, including poverty, and has viewed schools as the central institutions for social mobility, the sociology of education provides evidence about the extent to which schools can solve social problems.

The discipline of sociology developed at the end of the nineteenth century amid the promise and problems of industrialization, urbanization, and a developing belief in education in Europe and the United States. During this period, more and more children were required to go to school and sociologists began to examine the relationship between school and society. As schooling became more available to increased numbers of children, many believed that schools would be critical to a modern era where merit, talent, and effort would replace privilege and inheritance as the most significant factor for social and occupational mobility (Sadovnik, Cookson, and Semel, 2006, p. 20).

Until the 1960s, sociologists for the most part shared this optimism about the role of education in a modern society. They examined important themes, including how children are socialized for adult roles, the school as a social organization, and the effects of schooling on students' life chances. Beginning in the 1960s, sociologists of education began to doubt that schools, by themselves, could solve social problems, especially problems of economic and social inequality. These sociologists questioned whether schools were or could be, in the words of the U.S. nineteenth-century educational reformer Horace Mann, "the great equalizer" (Sadovnik, Cookson, and Semel, 2006, p. 20).

Sociologists of education continued to believe that they could improve education through the application of scientific theory and research. Because of their scientific orientation, they are more likely to ask *what is* rather than *what ought to be*, although sociological research has been the basis for trying to improve and change schools. They want to discover what occurs inside schools and what the effects of schooling are on individuals and groups. The distinctive feature of the sociology of education is empiricism, or the collection and analysis of empirical data within a theoretical context in order to construct a logical set of conclusions (Sadovnik, Cookson, and Semel, 2006, p. 20).

Thus, the sociology of education relies on empirical methods to understand how schools are related to society, how individuals and groups interact within schools, and what the effects of schooling are for individuals and groups of children. Its findings are based on an attempt to be objective and scientific. It examines individuals and groups in their social context and examines the social forces that affect them. The sociological approach to education is crucial because it provides conclusions based on focused and tested observations. Without such an analysis, one cannot know *what is*; and without knowing *what is*, one cannot make *what ought to be* a reality (Sadovnik, Cookson, and Semel, 2006, p. 20).

In his important book *The Sociological Imagination* (1959), C. Wright Mills argued that the sociological imagination was vital for understanding society. The sociological imagination, according to Mills, allows individuals to transcend the often narrow boundaries of their lives and to see the world from the larger context of history and society. Using the sociological imagination allows individuals to relate their own lives to the social, cultural, and historical factors that have affected them, and ultimately enables individuals to understand how and why these forces are crucial in shaping our lives (Sadovnik, Cookson, and Semel, 2006, p. 5). Based on this, the relationship between school and society is at the heart of the sociology of education. Without an understanding of how the components of society fit together, it is impossible to understand how schools work and their effects within a particular society. In an increasingly multi-ethnic and multi-racial society, the need for such a sociological perspective remains as important as ever.

In her book *Education and Inequality* (1977), Caroline Persell provided a model for understanding the relationship between school and society through four interrelated levels of sociological analysis. These include the societal, institutional, interpersonal, and intrapsychic levels (for the complete model, see Sadovnik, Cookson, and Semel, 2006, p. 111). The *societal* level encompasses the most general structures of society, including its political and economic systems, its level of development, and its system of social stratification (or institutionalized levels of inequality). The *institutional* level includes a society's main institutions, including the family, the schools, churches, synagogues, and mosques, business and government agencies, and the media, all of which play an essential part in the socialization of children into adult roles and responsibilities. The *interpersonal* level includes the processes, symbols, and interactions that occur within institutional settings. These include language, dress, face-to-face interactions, gestures, and rituals, which make up everyday life. The *intrapsychic* level includes individual thoughts, beliefs, values, and feelings, which are to a large extent shaped by a society's institutions and interactions. For sociologists of education, the degree to which external forces determine individual actions or whether individuals are capable of freely shaping the world is a crucial dialectic. A sociological perspective, although recognizing the human capacity for free will, stresses the power of external forces in shaping individual choices and how these are often related to group differences within the stratification system. As you will see in Part I, functionalism is concerned with the societal, institutional, and interpersonal processes that create what Emile Durkheim termed the collective conscience (society internalized in the individual). Conflict theory is concerned with the ways in which social, political, cultural, and economic differences among groups at the societal level produce conflict that often results in change (Sadovnik, Cookson, and Semel, 2006, p. 111).

In order to understand these issues, *The Sociology of Education: A Critical Reader* provides some of the most important readings in the field. The reader is designed for advanced undergraduate and graduate students in the sociology of education and related courses. It is organized into six parts. Part I examines theory and method in the sociology of education. Through both classic and contemporary readings, you will explore the major theoretical and methodological issues in the field. Part II examines school organization and processes through an exploration of teaching, learning, and curriculum. Although the majority of the book focuses on education in the United States, Part III examines international education in order to analyze the similarities and differences in educational systems throughout the world, how schools reflect national character and culture, and the degree to which schooling as an institution has become a worldwide phenomenon, with far more similarities than differences among national systems. Part IV examines higher education in the United States and focuses on issues related to access and opportunity. This section explores whether American higher education has become more democratic and meritocratic or if it remains highly stratified according to race, social class, and gender. Within this context, it analyzes access and opportunity in different sectors of the higher educational system, two- and four-year colleges and universities, both public and private. Part V examines arguably the most important area in the field: the relationship between education and inequality. It examines the role of schools in reproducing existing inequalities or in providing opportunities for mobility for students from lower socio-economic backgrounds. Further, it examines the effects of educational processes such as tracking and ability grouping. Finally, it analyzes the effects of education on different groups, including African Americans, Latinos, Asian Americans, Native Americans, women and men, different social classes, and students with disabilities. Part VI examines educational policy and reform by examining the limits and possibilities of various policies, including district- and school-based reforms, standards-based reforms, school choice, and the No Child Left Behind Act (2001). This section provides an important insight into the extent to which school reform alone can ameliorate the effects of factors outside the schools, including poverty and families.

Selecting twenty-six articles for inclusion was no easy task, given the hundreds that are suitable for inclusion in this reader. They are in no way meant to be exhaustive or to cover all the important topics in the field. In addition, unlike many readers that include edited selections of articles and can include many more, this reader includes articles in their entirety. The reason for this is to ensure that advanced undergraduate and graduate students have the opportunity to read sociological research as it is written and to engage in critical analyses of full texts. Obviously what is gained in depth is lost in breadth. My criteria for selection included the following:

1   With a small number of exceptions, sociologists or researchers closely associated with the sociology of education have written all of the articles. Although there have been many important articles written by economists, political scientists, anthropologists, and historians of education, a reader in the sociology of education ought to include work done mostly by sociologists.

2   The article applies a sociological perspective to the study of education. Such a sociological perspective views schools and schooling as part of the larger social order, examines the effects of schooling on individuals and groups, and analyzes the factors external to the individual that affect individual and group behavior.

3   The article makes an important theoretical and/or research contribution to our understanding of the main issues and problems in the sociology of education. Within this context, the selections include various theoretical perspectives and methodological approaches.

4   The articles represent either classical or contemporary approaches to the sociology of education.

5   The article is written in a language that is understandable to advanced undergraduate and graduate students. Although this is the case for most of the articles, some are theoretically and/or methodologically difficult and are included because they represent an essential contribution to the field.

6   For the articles following Part I, the article provides empirical evidence on a problem in the sociology of education and illustrates the power of the sociology of education for understanding educational problems.

7   The articles as a whole are representative of the diversity of researchers and problems in the field, with respect to race, ethnicity, and gender. Although there was no quota used to ensure that a diversity of authors and topics were included (the reader does not include equal representation), I attempted to choose articles that represented such diversity.

The readings in *Sociology of Education: A Critical Reader* are meant to stimulate your thinking about the important roles that schools play in contemporary society and their ability to solve fundamental social, economic, and political problems.

References

Coleman, J., Campbell, E. Q., Hobson, C. J., McPartland, J., Mood, A. J., Weinfeld, F. D., and York, R. L. (1966). *Equality of educational opportunity*. Washington, DC: U.S. Government Printing Office.

Hurn, C. (1993). *The limits and possibilities of schooling*. Needham Heights, MA: Allyn and Bacon.

Mills, C. W. (1959). *The sociological imagination*. New York: Oxford University Press.

Persell, C. H. (1977). *Education and inequality*. Glencoe, IL: Free Press.

Sadovnik, A. R., Cookson, P. W., and Semel, S. F. (2006). *Exploring education: An introduction to the foundations of education* (3rd ed.). Boston: Allyn and Bacon.

Suggested Readings

The following texts are excellent sources for all of the sections of the reader:

Ballantine, J. H. and Hammack, F. M. (2009). *The sociology of education: A systematic analysis* (6th ed.). Saddle River, NJ: Prentice Hall.

Ballantine, J. H. and Spade, J. Z. (Eds.) (2007). *Schools and society: A sociological approach to education*. Newbury Park, CA: Pine Forge Press.

Brint, S. (1998). *Schools and society*. Thousand Oaks, CA: Pine Forge.

Hallinan, M. (2000). *Handbook of the sociology of education*. New York: Kluwer.

Halsey, A. H., Lauder, H., Brown, P., and Wells, A. S. (1997). *Education: Culture, economy, society*. New York: Oxford.

Hurn, C. (1993). *The limits and possibilities of schooling*. Needham Heights, MA: Allyn and Bacon.

Karabel, J. and Halsey, A. H. (1977). *Power and ideology in education*. New York: Oxford.

Levinson, D., Cookson, P. W., and Sadovnik, A. R. (2001*). Sociology and education: An encyclopedia*. New York: Routledge/ Falmer.

Riordan, C. (2003). *Equality and achievement: An introduction to the sociology of education* (2nd ed.). Boston: Allyn and Bacon.

Sadovnik, A. R., Cookson, P. W., and Semel, S. F. (2006). *Exploring education: An introduction to the foundations of education* (3rd ed.). Boston: Allyn and Bacon.

Theory and Method in the Sociology of Education

Part I provides some of the most important theoretical readings in the sociology of education. They examine the development of theory and research in the sociology of education.

Chapter 1, "Theory and Research in the Sociology of Education" by the Rutgers University sociologist Alan R. Sadovnik, provides an overview of classical and contemporary theories and quantitative, qualitative, and mixed-methods approaches in sociological and educational research.

Chapter 2, "On Education and Society" by the classical nineteenth-century sociologist Emile Durkheim, provides the foundation for the development of functionalist theories in the sociology of education, popularized in the mid-twentieth century by Talcott Parsons.

Chapter 3, "Functional and Conflict Theories of Educational Stratification" by the University of Pennsylvania sociologist Randall Collins, provides a comparison of functionalist and conflict theories in the sociology of education and the foundation of his status-competition theory of educational expansion.

Chapter 4, "Broken Promises: School Reform in Retrospect" from their classic book *Schooling in Capitalist America* (1976) by the University of Massachusetts political economists Samuel Bowles and Herbert Gintis, applies their neo-Marxist correspondence theory to the history of school reform in the United States.

Chapter 5, "On Understanding the Processes of Schooling: The Contributions of Labeling Theory" by the sociologist Ray C. Rist, provides an overview of the contributions of interactionist theory in general and labeling theory in particular to understanding the processes of schooling.

Chapter 6, "The Forms of Capital" by the late French sociologist Pierre Bourdieu, provides a conflict analysis of the role of different types of capital (human, economic, cultural, and social) in reproducing social class advantages.

Chapter 7, "Social Capital in the Creation of Human Capital" by the late sociologist James S. Coleman, provides a functionalist analysis of the role of social capital in providing individuals and society with the human capital required for a cohesive and productive social order.

Chapter 8, " Class and Pedagogies: Visible and Invisible" by the late British sociologist Basil Bernstein, uses functionalist (Durkheimian), conflict (neo-Marxist and Weberian), and interactionist approaches to analyze the relationship between social class and educational practices and how they manifest themselves in different pedagogic practices in the classroom.

Chapter 9, "The Effects of Education as an Institution" by the Stanford University sociologist John W. Meyer, provides the foundation for institutional theory as developed by Meyer and his colleagues since the 1980s. Institutional theory argues that mass public education as an institution has been a worldwide phenomenon and examines comparative and international similarities and differences among educational institutions as they have developed in different countries since the nineteenth century.

Questions for Reflection and Discussion

1   How do functionalist and conflict theorists differ in their assessment of the role of schools in helping to change societies?

2   How does interactionist theory differ in its focus from functionalist and conflict theories? Can it complement one or both of the other theories?

3   Is research in the sociology of education scientific? Should it be? What do you think of trying to make educational research similar to medical or pharmaceutical research?

4   What did Emile Durkheim see as the major functions of schools? Can you give some contemporary examples of these functions in the twenty-first century?

5   How do Bowles and Gintis view the potential for educational reforms to reduce poverty and to provide economic mobility for low-income children?

6   How would Randall Collins view proposals to require a master's degree as the entry-level credential to become a teacher or a nurse?

7   How does Ray Rist analyze the classroom processes that result in the maintenance of social class–based inequalities? How is this article an example of both conflict and interactionist theories?

8   How do social class differences in pedagogic practices, which Bernstein identifies through visible and invisible pedagogies, affect working-class and middle-class students? In the 1970s, Basil Bernstein was criticized as a cultural deprivation theorist; that is one who argued that low-income children do less well in school because their culture is deficient compared with middle-class and upper-class children. Do you agree with this criticism and why? Do you think that Bourdieu's theories of cultural and social capital are examples of cultural deprivation theory? What are the similarities and differences between Bourdieu's and Bernstein's theories? What are the similarities and differences between Bourdieu's and Coleman's theories?

9   Many economists argue that mass public educational systems developed around the world to meet the increasing demands of technology and the high level of skills required by technological societies. How would John Meyer respond to this argument? How would Randall Collins? How would Bowles and Gintis?

1

Theory and Research in the Sociology of Education[1]

ALAN R. SADOVNIK

The sociology of education has mirrored the larger theoretical debates in the discipline of sociology. From its roots in the classical sociology of Karl Marx, Max Weber, and Emile Durkheim to the contemporary influences of symbolic interactionism, postmodernism, and critical theory, sociology of education research has been influenced by a number of different theoretical perspectives. This chapter provides an overview of the major theoretical perspectives in the sociology of education—functionalism, conflict theory, and symbolic interactionism—as well as contemporary theoretical approaches: the code theory of Basil Bernstein, the cultural capital theory of Pierre Bourdieu, the status-competition theory of Randall Collins, the institutional theory of John Meyer, and postmodern critical theory.

Functionalist Theory[2]

Functionalist sociologists begin with a picture of society that stresses the interdependence of the social system; these researchers often examine how well parts are integrated with each other. Functionalists view society as a kind of machine, in which one part articulates with another to produce the dynamic energy required to make society work. Most importantly, functionalism emphasizes the processes that maintain social order by stressing consensus and agreement. Although functionalists understand that change is inevitable, they underscore the evolutionary nature of change. Further, although they acknowledge that conflict between groups exists, functionalists argue that, without a common bond to unite groups, society would disintegrate. Thus, functionalists examine the social processes necessary to the establishment and maintenance of social order.

Functionalist theories of school and society trace their origins to the French sociologist Emile Durkheim's (1858–1917) general sociological theory. At its center, Durkheim's sociology (1947, 1954) was concerned with the effects of the decline of traditional rituals and community during the transition from traditional to modern societies. Durkheim's analysis of the differences between mechanical and organic solidarity in *The Division of Labor* (1947) and his concept of anomie in *Suicide* (1951) examined the need for societies to create rituals and institutions to provide for social cohesion and meaning. Like Ferdinand Tönnies's (1957) analysis of Gemeinschaft and Gesellschaft, Durkheim provided a sociological analysis of the effects of modernity on community.

For Durkheim, the processes of industrialization, urbanization, and modernization led to the breakdown of traditional rituals and methods of social control, which in turn led to the breakdown of social solidarity and cohesion. In *Suicide* (1951), he demonstrated empirically how the breakdown in traditional community resulted in the decline of collective conscience and the rise of individualism. Such a breakdown lead to what Durkheim called anomie, the condition of normlessness in individuals and society.

As the bonds that connected individuals to each other and to society became unhinged, modern societies faced disintegration from within. Durkheim, however, was not a reactionary; he did not

3

believe that the solution to social disintegration was a return to the past, with its strict forms of social control and regulation. Rather, he believed that modern societies had to develop new forms of social control and cohesion that would allow for the newly developed individualism of modernity to exist within a cohesive modern society. Such a society, what Durkheim called organic solidarity, would allow for a balance between individualism and community.

Durkheim was the first sociologist to apply sociological theory to education. His major works on education include *Moral Education* (1962), *The Evolution of Educational Thought* (1977), and *Education and Sociology* (1956). Although Durkheim recognized that education had taken different forms at different times and in different places, he believed that, in virtually all societies, education was of critical importance in creating the moral unity necessary for social cohesion and harmony. For Durkheim, moral values were the foundation of society.

Durkheim's emphasis on values and cohesion set the tone for how present-day functionalists approach the study of education. Functionalists tend to assume that consensus is the normal state in society and that conflict represents a breakdown of shared values. In a highly integrated, well-functioning society, schools socialize students into the appropriate values and sort and select students according to their abilities. From a functional point of view, then, educational reform is supposed to create structures, programs, and curricula that are technically advanced and rational and that encourage social unity. It should be evident that most American educators and educational reformers implicitly base their reform suggestions on functional theories of schooling. When, for example, *A Nation at Risk*, a government report on U.S. schools, was released in 1983, its authors argued that our schools were responsible for a whole host of social and economic problems. There was no suggestion that perhaps education might not have the power to overcome deep social and economic problems without changing other aspects of American society.

Functionalism is concerned with the functions of schooling in the maintenance of social order. Whereas conflict theory (see the next section) argues that schools function in the interests of the dominant groups in a society, functionalism sees schools as functioning in the interests of the majority of citizens, at least within democratic societies. Therefore functionalists examine the specific purposes of schooling and the role of schools in society. These purposes or functions are intellectual, political, social, and economic (Bennett and LeCompte, 1990, pp. 5–21) and refer to their role within any existing society. Functionalists, however, are most concerned with the role of schools in modern, democratic societies.

The intellectual purposes of schooling include the following: to teach basic cognitive skills such as reading, writing, and mathematics; to transmit specific knowledge, for example, in literature, history, and the sciences; and to help students acquire higher-order thinking skills such as analysis, evaluation, and synthesis.

The political purposes of schooling are to inculcate allegiance to the existing political order (patriotism); to prepare citizens who will participate in this political order (for example, in political democracies); to help assimilate diverse cultural groups into a common political order; and to teach children the basic laws of the society.

The social purposes of schooling are to socialize children into the various roles, behaviors, and values of the society. This process, referred to by sociologists as socialization, is a key ingredient in the stability of any society; it enables members to help to solve social problems; and, by participating in socialization, schools work, along with other institutions such as the family, and the church or synagogue, to ensure social cohesion.

The economic purposes of education are to prepare students for their later occupational roles and to select, train, and allocate individuals into the division of labor. Whereas the degree to which schools directly prepare students for work varies from society to society, most schools have at least an indirect role in this process.

Sometimes these purposes contradict each other. For example, the following question underscores the clash between the intellectual and political purposes of the school. If it is the intellectual purpose of the school to teach higher-order thinking skills such as critical thinking and evaluation, then can the school simultaneously engender patriotism and conformity to society's rules?

Modern functionalist theories of education have their origin in the work of Talcott Parsons (1959). Parsons (1902–1979) believed that education was a vital part of a modern society, a society that differed considerably from all previous societies. From this perspective, schooling performs important functions in the development and maintenance of a modern, democratic society, especially with regard to equality of opportunity for all citizens. Functionalists such as Kingsley Davis and Wilbert Moore (1945) argued that inequality was functional and necessary in all societies, as it ensured that the most talented individuals would fill the functionally most important positions. Nonetheless, modern democratic societies differ from previous, traditional agrarian societies because they are meritocratic; that is, talent and hard work should determine the allocation of individuals to positions, rather than accidents of birth. Thus, in modern societies education becomes the key institution in a meritocratic selection process.

This democratic-liberal functionalist perspective views education as a vital institution in a modern capitalist society defined by its technocratic, meritocratic, and democratic characteristics (Hurn, 1993, pp. 44–47). Although considerable inequality remains, society in this framework is characterized by the evolutionary movement from ascription to achievement, with equal educational opportunity the crucial component. According to this perspective, the historical pattern of academic failure by minority and working-class students was a blemish on the principles of justice and equality of opportunity expounded by a democracy. This educational pattern necessitated the formulation of reform programs to ensure equality of opportunity. Whereas functionalist theorists disagreed on the causes of academic failure, they vigorously believed that the solutions to both educational and social problems were possible within the capitalist social structure. As Diane Ravitch argued:

> It is indisputable that full equality has not been achieved, but equally indisputable in the light of the evidence is the conclusion that a democratic society can bring about effective social change, if there is both the leadership and the political commitment to do so. To argue, against the evidence, that meaningful change is not possible is to sap the political will that is necessary to effect changes (1977, pp. 114–115).

The central distinction made by the functionalist perspective was between equality of opportunity and equality of results. A democratic society is a just society, according to this tradition, if it generates the former. Therefore, functionalist theory rested on a positive view of meritocracy as a laudable goal, with education viewed as the necessary institutional component in guaranteeing a fair competition for unequal rewards. The just society, then, is one in which each member has an equal opportunity for social and economic advantages, and individual merit and talent replace ascriptive and class variables as the most essential determinants of status. Education is thus the vehicle in ensuring the continual movement toward this meritocratic system.

In addition to its role in a meritocratic society, education plays a significant function in the maintenance of the modern democratic and technocratic society. In a political democracy, schools provide citizens with the knowledge and dispositions to participate effectively in civic life. In an ever increasingly technical society, schools provide students with the skills and dispositions to work in such a society. Although schools do teach specific work skills, they also teach students how to learn so they may adapt to new work roles and requirements.

Functionalist theory was the dominant paradigm in sociology and the sociology of education until the 1960s. In the 1960s, conflict theory emerged as a significant critique and alternative to functionalism. Conflict theorists argued that schools functioned in the interests of dominant groups, rather than everyone, and that functionalists confused what is with what ought to be. According to this critique, whereas schools ought to be democratic and meritocratic, the empirical evidence did not support the functionalist contention that they were. Although the specific nature of conflict theory is developed in the next section, it is important to note some of the problems with functionalism. First, conflict theorists argue that the relationship between schooling, skills, and jobs is far less rational than functionalists suggest (Hurn, 1993, pp. 50–52). Second, conflict theorists point out that the role of schools in providing equality of opportunity is far more problematic than functionalists suggest (Hurn, 1993, pp. 52–54). Third, large-scale empirical research on the effects of schooling casts significant doubt on the functionalist assertion that the expansion of schooling brings about an increasingly just and meritocratic social order (Hurn, 1993, pp. 54–55).

Conflict Theory[3]

As suggested above, not all sociologists of education believe that society is held together by shared values and collective agreement alone, rather than the ability of dominant groups to impose their will on subordinate groups through force, cooptation, and manipulation. In this view the glue of society is economic, political, cultural, and military power. Ideologies or intellectual justifications created by the powerful are designed to enhance their position by legitimizing inequality and the unequal distribution of material and cultural goods. One argument, for instance, is that differences are an inevitable outcome of biology or history. Clearly, conflict sociologists see the relation between school and society as problematic. Whereas functionalists emphasize cohesion in explaining social order, conflict sociologists emphasize struggle. From a conflict point of view, schools are similar to social battlefields, where students struggle against teachers, teachers against administrators, and so on. These antagonisms, however, are most often muted for two reasons: the authority and power of the school and the achievement ideology. In effect, the achievement ideology convinces students and teachers that schools promote learning and sort and select students according to their abilities, not according to their social status. In this view, the achievement ideology disguises the "real" power relations within the school, which, in turn, reflect and correspond to the power relations within the larger society (Bowles and Gintis, 1976).

Although Karl Marx (1818–1883) did not write a great deal about education specifically, he is the intellectual founder of the conflict school in the sociology of education. His analytic imagination and moral outrage were sparked by the social conditions found in Europe in the late nineteenth century. Industrialization and urbanization had produced a new class of workers—the proletariat—who lived in poverty, worked up to 18 hours a day, and had little, if any, hope of creating a better life for their children. Marx believed that the class system, which separated owners from workers and workers from the benefits of their own labor, made class struggle inevitable. He believed that, in the end, the proletariat would rise up and overthrow the capitalists, and in doing so, establish a new society where men and women would no longer be "alienated" from their labor. Marx's powerful and often compelling critique of early capitalism has provided the intellectual energy for subsequent generations of liberal and leftist thinkers who believe that the only way to a more just and productive society is the abolition or modification of capitalism and the introduction of socialism. The political economists Samuel Bowles and Herbert Gintis, in their book *Schooling in Capitalist America* (1976), use a Marxist perspective for examining the growth of the American public school. To their minds, there is a direct "correspondence" between the organization of schools and the organization of society; and, until society is fundamentally changed, there is little hope of real school reform. Other conflict sociologists of education, however, argue that traditional Marxism is too deterministic and overlooks the power of culture and human agency in promoting change. That is, they suggest that Marxism places too much emphasis on the independent effects of the economy and not enough on the effects of cultural, social, and political factors.

An early conflict sociologist who took a slightly different theoretical orientation when viewing society was Max Weber (1864–1920). Like Marx, Weber was convinced that power relations between dominant and subordinate groups structured societies, but, unlike Marx, Weber believed that class differences alone could not capture the complex ways human beings form hierarchies and belief systems that make these hierarchies seem just and inevitable. Thus, Weber examined status cultures as well as class position. Status is an important sociological concept because it alerts us to fact that people identify their group by what they consume and with whom they socialize. Weber also recognized that political and military power could be exercised by the State, without direct reference to the wishes of the dominant classes. Moreover, Weber had an acute and critical awareness of how bureaucracy was becoming the dominant type of authority in the modern state and how bureaucratic ways of thinking were bound to shape educational reforms. Weber made the distinction between the "specialist" and the "cultivated man." What should be the goal of education: training individuals for employment or for thinking? Or are these two goals compatible?

The Weberian approach to studying the relation between school and society has developed into a compelling and informative tradition of sociological research. Researchers in this tradition tend to analyze school organizations and processes from the point of view of status competition and organizational constraints. One of the first American sociologists of education to use these concepts was Willard Waller. In his book *The Sociology of Teaching* (1965), Waller portrays schools as autocracies in a state of "perilous equilibrium." Without continuous vigilance, schools would erupt into anarchy because students are essentially forced to go to school against their will. To Waller's mind, rational models of school organization only disguise the inherent tension that pervades the schooling process. Waller's perspective is shared by many contemporary conflict theorists who see schools as oppressive and demeaning and portray student non-compliance with school rules as a form of resistance.

Contemporary conflict theory includes a number of important approaches. First, a major research tradition that has emerged from the Weberian school of thought is represented by Randall Collins (1978). He believes that educational expansion is best explained by status group struggle. He argues that educational credentials, such as college diplomas, are primarily status symbols, rather than indicators of actual achievement. The rise of "credentialism" indicates not that society is becoming more expert but that education is increasingly used by dominant groups to secure more advantageous places in the occupational and social structure for themselves and their children.

A second school of conflict theory, called institutional theory, is based on the work of the Stanford sociologist John Meyer and his collaborators. Meyer argues that the expansion of education worldwide has been due not to functional requirements or labor market demands but rather to the worldwide process of citizenship and the democratic belief that educational development is a requirement of a civil society. Like Collins, Meyer believes that such expansion is a proof not of democracy, but rather of the belief that educational expansion is necessary. Through comparative, historical, and institutional analysis Meyer and his colleagues (Meyer and Rowan, 1977, 1978; Meyer, Ramirez, and Soysal, 1992; Rubinson, 1986) demonstrate that educational expansion often preceded labor market demands and that educational expansion is legitimized by institutional ritual and ceremony rather than actual practices.

Third, a variation of conflict theory, referred to as the "new sociology of education" (Young, 1971) began in France and England during the 1960s. Unlike most Marxists, who tend to emphasize the economic structure of society, social and cultural reproduction theorists argued that school processes reflect the interests of cultural and social elites. The "new sociologists of education" attempted to link micro and macro processes into a comprehensive theory of school and society. Pierre Bourdieu (1931–2002) examined how cultural capital (particular forms of culture, such as knowledge of music, art, and literature) is passed on by families and schools (1977). The concept of "cultural capital" is important because it suggests that, in understanding the transmission of inequalities, we ought to recognize that the cultural characteristics of individuals and groups are significant indicators of status and class position. There is a growing body of literature that suggests schools pass on to graduates specific social identities that either enhance or hinder their life chances. For example, a graduate from an elite prep school has educational and social advantages over many public school graduates in terms of acceptance to elite colleges and occupational mobility. This advantage has very little to do with what prep school students learn in school and a great deal to do with the power of their schools' reputations for educating members of the upper class. Bourdieu's theories extend the work of other sociologists who have argued persuasively that human culture cannot be understood as an isolated and self-contained object of study but must be examined as part of a larger social and cultural structure. To understand the impact of culture on the lives of individuals and groups we must understand the meanings that are attributed to cultural experiences by those who participate in them (Mannheim, 1936).

Another social reproduction theorist, Basil Bernstein (1924–2000) synthesized macro- and microsociological approaches, primarily using a conflict perspective (1990a,b,c,d). He argued that the structural aspects of the educational system and the interactional aspects of the system reflect each other and must be viewed holistically. He examined how speech patterns reflect students' social class backgrounds and how students from working-class backgrounds are at a disadvantage in the school setting because schools are essentially middle-class organizations. Bernstein combined a class analysis with an interactional analysis, which links language with educational processes and outcomes. Bernstein demonstrated empirically how school processes at the micro level result in the reproduction of social stratification at the macro level. Later in the chapter, the work of Bernstein, Bourdieu, and Collins will be examined in more detail.

Interactionist Theory[4]

In general, interactionist theories about the relation of school and society are critiques and extensions of the functionalist and conflict perspectives. The critique arises from the observation that functionalist and conflict theories are very abstract and emphasize structure and process at a societal (macro-sociological) level of analysis. Although this level of analysis helps us to understand education in the "big picture," macro-sociological theories hardly provide us with an interpretable snap-shot of what schools are like on an everyday level. What do students and teachers actually do in school? Interactionist theories attempt to make the "commonplace strange" by turning on their heads everyday taken-for-granted behaviors and interactions between students and students and between students and teachers. It is exactly what most people do not question that is most problematic to the interactionist. For example, the processes by which students are labeled "gifted" or "learning disabled" are, from an interactionist point of view, important to analyze because such processes carry with them many implicit assumptions about learning and children. By examining the micro-sociological or interactional aspects of school life, we are less likely to create theories that are logical and eloquent, but without meaningful content.

Interactionist theory has its origins in the social psychology of the early twentieth-century sociologists George Herbert Mead (1863–1931) and Charles Horton Cooley (1864–1929). Mead and Cooley examined the ways in which the individual is related to society through ongoing social interactions. This school of thought, known as symbolic interactionism, viewed the self as socially constructed in relation to social forces and structures and the product of ongoing negotiation of meanings. Thus, the social self is an active product of human agency rather than a deterministic product of social structure. This more existential perspective, with its origins in the school of philosophy known as phenomenology (Giddens, 1975), stresses what the sociologists Peter Berger and Thomas Luckmann (1963) called the social construction of reality.

Interactionist theory is usually combined with functionalism and/or conflict theory to produce a more comprehensive theory of society. One of the most influential interactionist theorists was the Canadian-born sociologist Erving Goffman, whose work examined the micro sociology of everyday life and the functions of interaction rituals in holding society together. Trained as an anthropologist in the functionalist tradition of Emile Durkheim and A. R. Radcliffe-Brown, Goffman was interested in how everyday taken-for-granted patterns of interactions serve to hold society together. Goffman's brand of interactionism was functionalist, as he viewed social interaction patterns as rituals that served to maintain society through an invisible micro-social order. Although Goffman did not directly study education, his writings on mental hospitals in *Asylums* (1961a), on the labeling of so-called deviant behavior in *Stigma* (1963a), and of patterns of interpersonal behavior in *The Presentation of Self in Everyday Life* (1959), *Encounters* (1961b), *Behavior in Public Places* (1963b), and *Interaction Ritual* (1967) have provided a rich tapestry of concepts for sociologists of education, particularly through the use of labeling theory, which has been applied to the study of teacher expectations (Persell, 1977), ability grouping and tracking (Oakes, 1985), and the study of schools as total institutions (Cookson and Persell, 1985).

Ray Rist has provided some of the most important insights on the ways in which school processes affect educational achievement. Rist's (1970, 1973, 1977) research into the everyday processes of schooling in an inner-city school provided an understanding of how school practices, such as labeling and ability grouping, contribute to the reproduction of educational and social inequalities. In his classic essay, "On understanding the processes of schooling: the contributions of labeling theory" (1977), Rist argued that interactionism has provided important understandings of the way in which the everyday workings of schools (including teacher and student interactions), labeling, and linguistic discourse are at the root of unequal educational outcomes. Drawing upon labeling theory, originally a key approach in the sociology of deviance, Rist demonstrated how teacher expectations of students based on categories such as race, class, ethnicity, and gender affect student perceptions of themselves and their achievment. In another classic essay, "Student social class and teacher expectations: the self fulfilling prophecy in ghetto education" (1970), Rist reported findings from his ethnographic study of a St. Louis elementary school, consisting of primarily African-American students. Rist demonstrated how African-American teacher labeling of students based on their different social class backgrounds resulted in low-income students being placed in lower-ability reading groups and middle-class students in higher-ability groups, independent of ability. These labels became "life sentences" that had profoundly negative effects on the achievement of the low-income students, who remained in low-ability groups throughout their careers. Rist concludes that the interactional processes of the school resulted in educational inequality mirroring the larger structures of society. He concluded that "the system of public education in reality perpetuates what it is ideologically committed to—eradicating class barriers which result in inequality in the social and economic life of the citizenry" (Rist, 1970: 449). Combined with the findings of conflict theory, Rist's interactionist approach provides an empirical documentation of how schools reproduce inequality.

Contemporary Approaches in the Sociology of Education

Code Theory: Basil Bernstein's Contribution to Understanding Education[5]

Code theory is the term used to describe the theoretical and empirical project of the British sociologist Basil Bernstein. This approach is concerned with how the macro level (social, political, and economic structures and institutions) is dialectically related to the way in which people understand systems of meaning (codes). For over three decades, Bernstein was one of the centrally important and controversial sociologists, whose work influenced a generation of sociologists of education and linguists. From his early works on language, communication codes, and schooling to his later works on curriculum and pedagogy (teaching methods), Bernstein attempted to produce a theory of social and educational codes (meaning systems) and their effect on social reproduction. Although structuralist in its approach, Bernstein's sociology drew on the essential theoretical orientations in the field—Durkheimian, Weberian, Marxist, and interactionist—and provided the possibility of an important synthesis.

Bernstein's early work on code theory was highly controversial because it discussed social class differences in language that some labeled a deficit theory. Nonetheless, the work raised crucial questions about the relationships among the social division of labor, the family, and the school and explored how these relationships affected differences in learning among social classes. His later work (1977) began the difficult project of connecting macro power and class relations to the micro-educational processes of the school. Whereas class reproduction theorists such as Bowles and Gintis (1976) offered an overtly deterministic view of schools, viewing education as exclusively influenced by the economy without describing or explaining what goes on in schools, Bernstein's work promised to connect the societal, institutional, interactional, and intrapsychic levels of sociological analysis. In doing so, it presented an opportunity to synthesize the classical theoretical traditions of the discipline: Marxist, Weberian, and Durkheimian.

The concept of code is central to Bernstein's structural sociology. From the outset of its use in his work on language (restricted and elaborated codes), the term refers to a "regulative principle which underlies various message systems, especially curriculum and pedagogy" (Atkinson, 1985, p. 136). Bernstein's early work on language (1958, 1960, 1961a,b) examined the relationship between public language, authority, and shared meanings (Danzig, 1995, pp. 146–147). By 1962, Bernstein began to develop code theory through the introduction of the concepts of restricted and elaborated codes (1962a,b). In *Class, Codes, and Control*, Volume 1 (1973), Bernstein's sociolinguistic code theory was developed into a social theory examining the relationships between social class, family, and the reproduction of meaning systems.

For Bernstein, there were social class differences in the communication codes of working-class and middle-class children, differences that reflect the class and power relations in the social division of labor, family, and schools. Based upon empirical research, Bernstein distinguished between the restricted code of the working class and the elaborated code of the middle class. Restricted codes are context-dependent and particularistic, whereas elaborated codes are context-independent and universalistic. For example, when asked to tell a story describing a series of pictures, working-class boys used many pronouns, and their stories could be understood only by looking at the pictures. Middle-class boys, on the other hand, generated descriptions rich in nouns, and their stories could be understood without the benefit of the pictures (Bernstein, 1970). Although Bernstein's critics (see Danzig, 1995) argued that his sociolinguistic theory represented an example of deficit theory (alleging that he was arguing that working-class language was deficient) Bernstein consistently rejected this interpretation (see Bernstein, 1996, pp. 147–156). Bernstein argued that restricted codes are not deficient, but rather are functionally related to the social division of labor, whereby context-dependent language is necessary in the context of production. Likewise, the elaborated code of the middle class represents functional changes necessitated by changes in the division of labor and, as a result, by the middle class's new position in reproduction rather than production. That schools require an elaborated code for success means that working-class children are disadvantaged by the dominant code of schooling, not deficient. For Bernstein, difference becomes deficit in the context of macro-power relations.

In the third and fourth volumes of *Class, Codes, and Control* and in *Pedagogy, Symbolic Control and Identity* (1977, 1990a, 1996), Bernstein developed code theory from its sociolinguistic roots to examine the connection between communication codes and curriculum and teaching methods. In this respect, code theory became concerned with the processes of schooling and how they related to social-class reproduction. Bernstein analyzed the significant differences between different forms of educational transmission and suggested that social-class differences in curriculum and pedagogy are related to inequalities of educational achievement between working-class and middle-class students. Schools that serve middle-class students have different curricula and teaching methods from schools that serve working-class students, and these differences result in educational inequality. Through a careful and logical consideration of the inner workings of the dominant forms of educational practice, Bernstein contributed to a greater understanding of how the schools (especially in the United Kingdom and United States) reproduce what they are ideologically committed to eradicating: social-class advantages in schooling and society. Bernstein's analysis of the social-class assumptions of pedagogic practice is the foundation for linking micro-educational processes to the macro-sociological levels of social structure and class and power relations.

Despite the criticisms that Bernstein's work is sometimes complex and difficult, it is undeniable that it represented one of the most sustained and powerful attempts to investigate significant issues in the sociology of education. Over 35 years ago, Bernstein began with a simple but overwhelming issue: how to find ways to "prevent the wastage of working-class educational potential" (1961a, p. 308). Taken as a whole, Bernstein's work provided a systematic analysis of the relationship between society, schools, and the individual and of how schooling systematically reproduces social inequality.

Cultural Capital and Symbolic Violence: The Contributions of Pierre Bourdieu

Like Bernstein, Pierre Bourdieu (Bourdieu and Passeron, 1977; Bourdieu, 1973, 1977, 1984) attempted to test empirically a theory of society, culture, and education that synthesizes Durkheim and Marx (Swartz, 1997). As the director of the Centre de Sociologie Européenne in Paris, Bourdieu, with his research colleagues, provided a theoretical and empirical understanding of culture and stratification. As Collins (Collins and Makowsky, 1993, p. 259) notes, for Bourdieu:

> culture itself, is an economy. . . . Stratification in the cultural economy and in the material economy are reciprocally related. For Bourdieu, culture is a realm of power struggle, related to the struggle over the means of violence that characterizes the realm of politics.

Thus, Bourdieu's central concepts of cultural capital and symbolic violence, which were developed in Bourdieu and Passeron's *Reproduction in Education, Society and Culture* (1977), are used to understand how schooling is part of a symbolic process of cultural and social reproduction. Symbolic violence is "power which manages to impose meanings and to impose them as legitimate by concealing the power relations which are the basis of its force" (Collins and Makowsky, 1993, p. 259). This type of power is found not only in schooling but also in other educational realms, including such arenas as child rearing, museums, and musical and artistic institutions. Although schools appear to be neutral, they actually advantage the upper and middle classes through their symbolic representations. These classes possess cultural capital, or symbolic representations of cultural domination, such as language, ideas, and knowledge of music, art, and literature, all of which have important exchange value in the educational and cultural marketplace.   •

Drawing upon the functionalism in the sociology of Durkheim and the anthropology of Lévi-Strauss, Bourdieu, like Bernstein, provided more of a conflict, neo-Marxist dimension that demonstrates that cultural capital reproduces social classes and that schooling reproduces cultural capital unevenly among social classes. Schooling corresponds to the dominant interests of society; as a result, upper- and middle-class forms of cultural capital become codified in the school's curriculum. Unlike functionalists, Bourdieu and Bernstein viewed these patterns as leading not to social cohesion and agreement but rather to class domination.

Bourdieu was not without his critics. According to Collins (Collins and Makowsky, 1993, p. 264):

> Bourdieu's theory is completely closed. It is totally cynical, totally pessimistic. We are eternally doomed to stratification. . . . We cannot get outside our skins; we can only change places inside an iron circle.

This view, as Collins suggests, fails to point out the intense organizational and societal conflicts that often result in some reshaping of social stratification (p. 265). Nevertheless, Collins (Collins and Makowsky, 1993) includes Bourdieu as among the most influential European sociologists of the late twentieth century.

Understanding Unequal Educational Outcomes: The Contributions of James Coleman

James Coleman's contributions to the sociology of education included theoretical, empirical, theoretical and policy dimensions. Coleman spent most of his career at Johns Hopkins University and the University of Chicago and was best known for his important work *Equality of Educational Opportunity* (Coleman et al., 1966). Completed for the United States government and based on statistical analysis of large data sets, the Coleman Report argued that school-based factors such as school funding, resources, and teacher quality explained little of the differences between black and white, and low-income and more affluent students. Rather, Coleman found that external factors such as peer groups, community, and family—that is, student background and socio-economic status—had a greater impact on educational achievement. Coleman suggested that given these factors, low-income black students would benefit from racially integrated school settings. This resulted in the controversial policy in the 1960s and 1970s of school busing for racial integration, which often led to violent opposition. By 1975, Coleman argued that busing had led to "white flight" to the suburbs and that busing had failed. This position led to an unsuccessful attempt by some members of the American Sociological Association to revoke his membership. Nevertheless, in 1991, he became its President.

By the 1980s, Coleman changed his position on the effects of schools on student achievement. In two important books (Coleman, Hoffer and Kilgore, 1982; Coleman and Hoffer, 1987), Coleman argued that students in private schools (independent and Catholic) had higher achievement than students in public schools, controlling for student background and socio-economic status. This argument became the foundation for what was termed the "Catholic School effect," which influenced school choice and voucher proponents in the coming years. Coleman's conclusions were criticized on methodological and policy grounds, with critics arguing that he and his coauthors did not adequately control for family background variables, selection bias associated with parental choices to send their children to private schools, and the fact that private schools, unlike public schools, could expel students for academic and behavioral reasons. Despite these criticisms, their argument that families and the school communities play an important role in educational achievement continues to be an essential part of sociological explanations of unequal educational achievement.

In addition to Coleman's sociology of education, he made significant contributions to social science methodology and sociological theory. His early work on mathematical sociology (Coleman, 1964) provided the foundation for the use of mathematical modeling and large-scale data sets in social science research. His classic book *Foundations of Social Theory* (1990) applied the rational choice theories of classical economics to social behavior by integrating social factors such as peer group influence, social status, and social capital into a more sociologically informed theory. This approach built upon his analysis of social capital (1988), which became one of the most important concepts in the sociology of education. Coleman defined social capital as the social networks that individuals belong to and proposed that these networks enable individuals, and especially groups, to marshal resources for educational and social benefits. Along with his concept of intergenerational closure, which referred to the ties between parents and children that affect educational achievement, Coleman's work provided a more functionalist analysis than Bourdieu's. Whereas Bourdieu argued that social and cultural capital reproduced class inequalities, Coleman argued that social capital provided both the basis for group cohesion and a mechanism for social mobility.

Despite the often vociferous criticism of his work, there is little doubt that Coleman's sociology of education influenced the field for four decades.

Status Competition and Interaction Ritual: The Contributions of Randall Collins

Like Bourdieu and Bernstein in Europe, the U.S. sociologist Randall Collins has attempted to synthesize Marx, Weber, and Durkheim, as well as the micro-sociologist Erving Goffman, into an overall conflict theory of society. The role of education is central to his theory.

In *Conflict Sociology* (1975), Collins outlined a theory of sociology as an explanatory science, and tested a series of propositions about the nature of social order and change. In it, Collins, although rooted in a Weberian conflict perspective, attempted to synthesize the sociologies of Marx, Weber, Durkheim, and Goffman. Beginning in this ambitious volume, Collins argues that the role of sociology is to understand scientifically the relationship between macro power relations and micro social processes. From Durkheim and Freud, Collins argues that the world is held together by non-rational as well as rational factors and, from Weber, that conflict between social groups over wealth, power, and status are the fuel of social life. Collins (1978) distinguishes between productive and political labor within organizations: Productive labor represents the rational and functional processes that are related to goals and objectives; political labor represents the often non-rational processes related to status competition and group domination and advantage. Although most groups argue that their work in organizations is functional and productive, it is often non-rational and used as a means to legitimize control and domination by dominant groups. Unlike Marxists, who see dominant groups as defined largely by economic forces, Collins provides a Weberian analysis that sees group formation as defined by cultural and political forces as well.

Collins's work on education began with his important article "Functionalist and conflict theories of educational stratification" (1971), which provided a critique of functionalist theories of social stratification. Unlike functionalists, who viewed the expansion of education as a result of an ongoing expansion of democracy, meritocracy, and technology, Collins argued that educational expansion was far less rational. Rather than seeing the expansion of educational systems in democratic-liberal societies as a rational response to democratic processes of equality of opportunity and meritocratic ideology, and as a result of the rise in requirements for expert knowledge in a highly technological society, Collins (1978) argues that the rise in credentials cannot be explained by the demands of political process or the needs of the labor market.

In *The Credential Society* (1978), Collins suggests that the expansion in educational credentials has been a result of status competition among groups who engage in symbolic conflict over scarce cultural, political, and economic rewards. For example, elevation of the college degree over the high school degree as an entry-level requirement is not, as functionalists argue, the result of the higher skills and knowledge required in an increasingly technological society. Rather, Collins argues, the competition for good positions, combined with the expansion of opportunities in higher education in response to democratic claims for equality of opportunity made by historically marginalized groups, has raised the stakes for all groups. As groups who historically had not attended college gained access, advantaged groups did not sit by idly, waiting for them to catch up. Rather, through professional organizations they raised the entry-level requirements for professions by using a rational-functional argument that such credentials were necessitated by increased skills of the professions.

Based on a historical and empirical analysis of the requirements of different professions, Collins demonstrated that educational credentials have increased far in excess of an increase in occupational skills and requirements. For example, whereas pharmacists now need a five-year college program rather than the apprenticeship program of the 1930s, the actual knowledge and skills of the profession have not increased dramatically. In fact, in the 1930s pharmacists were called chemists because they made medication from scratch. Today, most pharmacists distribute manufactured medications from bottles and use computer programs to prevent harmful drug interactions. Certainly medical knowledge has increased; however, the requirements of the profession have not increased to a level that justifies the increase in educational requirements.

A second example is the rising educational requirements for nurses. Although it is still possible to become a registered nurse through a two-year community college associate degree program, the movement to require a four-year bachelor's degree is becoming the norm. Proponents of the Bachelor of Science in Nursing argue that the explosion of medical knowledge, combined with the need for a liberally educated nurse who can think on her feet, necessitates elevating the requirement. Collins, however, suggests that there is little empirical evidence to support these claims or that nurses with baccalaureate degrees are more effective than those with degrees in Associate Arts and Sciences. Rather, the movement for increased credentials is an attempt by nurses to raise their own status, especially in relation to doctors, through increased educational levels. Likewise, the increased educational credentials required by pharmacists is viewed as their attempt to raise their own status and income. Similar movements are now occurring for teachers, whereby teacher-educators and policymakers are arguing that a master's degree should be the minimum entry-level requirement rather than the baccalaureate because of the increased knowledge required to teach children. Although this argument is presented as a rational and functional requirement, there is little evidence to suggest that teachers who enter teaching with master's degrees are more effective.

The rise of credentials, according to Collins, is a result of middle-class professional attempts to raise their status—and to raise the stakes. As historically marginalized groups struggle to catch up, advantaged groups use professional organizations not only to raise their own status but also to increase their advantage in the competition for professional positions. Since they already possess higher credentials, they can continue to distance themselves from competitors who do not have them.

Critics of Collins suggest that his view is too cynical and non-rational and often denies the important functional aspects of educational expertise and the need for increased education. Although these critics are correct in suggesting that, given rising technological demands, increased education is sometimes important, it is also the case that the dramatic increase in credentials cannot be explained by functional demands alone.

Institutional Theory: The Contributions of John Meyer

The work of John Meyer and his colleagues on the development of mass systems of public education worldwide has been an important theoretical approach in the sociology of education since the 1970s. In what is called institutional theory, Meyer argues that schools are global institutions and have developed similarly throughout the world since the nineteenth century. Although schools do reflect national cultures and there are differences among national school systems, Meyer and his colleagues have argued that mass educational systems have developed as part of international patterns of democratization and globalization. Meyer argues that all over the world mass systems of public education have developed, giving access to more and more people. At the institutional level, schools develop formal and informal rituals and processes that legitimize their existence and functions in society. Meyer, like Collins, does not believe that educational expansion is predominantly caused by the needs of the labor market. Rather, it is the belief in education in a democratic civil society that fuels demands for mass schooling. Finally, Meyer and his colleagues have applied institutional theory internationally and comparatively to provide a global analysis of educational systems. Critics have argued that:

Meyer's emphasis on consensual societal beliefs about the meaning and efficacy of education, and the legitimating functions of schooling, are devoid of attention to the social bases for those beliefs, and for the ways those beliefs legitimate domination and inequality (Olneck, 2007).

David Baker and Gerald LeTendre (2005) have applied institutional theory to a comparative analysis of international educational systems and processes. Based on Meyer's theory, they argue that there is a number of related themes in the development of worldwide educational systems. These include "the worldwide success of mass schooling," that "schooling is an institution," and that "educational change is institutional change" (Baker and LeTendre, 2005, pp. 6–12). They argue that there is a fundamental set of beliefs that have influenced the development of mass schooling, including that all children should be educated; that nations should invest in schooling; that education functions for the collective good of society; that children should receive early and ongoing schooling; that the types of cognitive skills learned in schools are good for individuals and society; and that one's social, economic, or racial status should not limit access to schooling (Baker and LeTendre, 2005, pp. 7–8). Although these are similar to the democratic-liberal functions of schooling outlined by functionalists, institutional theorists also see how conflict between groups over access and opportunity to mass schooling has affected educational institutions. According to Baker and Letendre:

> Over a thirty-year research program with colleagues, institutional theorist and comparative sociologist John Meyer has convincingly established a strong case for thinking about schooling as a product of a world culture that renders education as a resilient and powerful institution in modern society (see, as examples, Baker, 1999; Meyer, 1977; Ramirez and Boli, 1987; Meyer, Ramirez and Soysal, 1992; Fuller and Rubinson, 1992). They have shown that mass schooling takes similar forms throughout the world, and that there are common beliefs in what schooling can and should do for society. This process, they argue, has to a large degree been driven by a dynamic world culture (Baker and LeTendre, 2005, p. 10).

Although Meyer and colleagues believe that national differences are important, they stress the commonalities among educational institutions and the worldwide belief that mass schooling is important.

Postmodernism and Critical Theory[6]

Postmodernism developed out of a profound dissatisfaction with the modernist project of enlightenment and reason. Beginning with the poststructural writings of Jacques Derrida (1973, 1981, 1982) and Jean Baudrillard (1981, 1984), social theorists, particularly in France, questioned the appropriateness of modernist categories for understanding what they saw as a postmodern world, a world that transcended the economic and social relations of the industrial world that modernist thought had sought to understand. In particular, the work of Jean Francois Lyotard (1984) rejected the Marxist perspective and the Enlightenment and modernist assumptions underlying Marxist theory and sought to create a different theory for the late twentieth century.

Postmodernist thought consists of many interrelated themes. First, postmodernism insists on what Lyotard (1984) has labeled the rejection of all metanarratives. By this, Lyotard meant that modernist preoccupation with grand, total, or all-encompassing explanations of the world needs to be replaced by localized and particular theories. Second, postmodernism stresses the necessary connection between theory and practice as a corrective to the separation of them in much modernist thought. Third, postmodernism stresses the democratic response to authoritarianism and totalitarianism. In particular, Stanley Aronowitz and Henry Giroux (1991), Giroux (1991), and Peter McLaren and R. Hammer (1989) call for a democratic, emancipatory, and antitotalitarian theory and practice, with schools seen as sites for democratic transformation. Fourth, postmodernism sees modernist thought as Eurocentric and patriarchal. Giroux (1991), Patricia Lather (1991), Elizabeth Ellsworth (1989), and others provide an important critique of the racism and sexism in some modernist writings and of the failure of modernism to address the interests of women and people of color. Fifth, postmodernist theorists believe that all social and political discourses are related to structures of power and domination. Sixth, postmodernism stresses what Nicholas Burbules and Susan Rice (1991) term "dialogue across differences." Recognizing the particular and local nature of knowledge, postmodern theorists call for the attempt to work through differences rather than to see them as hopelessly irreconcilable. Thus, postmodern theories of education call for teachers and students to explore the differences between what may seem like inherently contradictory positions in an effort to achieve understanding, respect, and change.

Although much of postmodern theory developed as a critical theory of society and a critique of modernism, it quickly became incorporated into radical writings on education that are often called critical theory. Critical educational theory, which over the past two decades has involved an interdisciplinary mixture of social theory, sociology, and philosophy, has been profoundly affected by postmodernist thought. In particular, by the 1980s, critical theories of education, which from the late 1970s attempted to provide an antidote to the over-determinism of Bowles and Gintis (1976), regularly incorporated postmodern language and concerns. There have been numerous postmodern theories of education or applications of postmodernism to education, which will be referred to as postmodern-critical theory. Critical theories of education often draw heavily on the work of the Brazilian educator Paolo Freire (1972, 1985, 1987), whose influential work *Pedagogy of the Oppressed* (1972) became the foundation for critical educational theory in the United States (Kincheloe, 2008; Kincheloe and Steinberg, 1998; McLaren and Kincheloe, 2007; Steinberg and Kincheloe, 1998). Critical theories of education are similar to neo-Marxist theory with respect to curriculum and pedagogy. A school of thought called critical pedagogy (Kincheloe and Steinberg, 1998, chapter 1) stresses the classroom as a site for political action and teachers as agents of change. Finally, postmodern theories of education eschewed what they saw as the overly quantitative approach of traditional sociology of education research and instead argued for more qualitative, narrative, autobiographical approaches to research (Denzin and Lincoln, 2006).

Sadovnik (1995b) points out a number of problems with postmodern and critical theories of education. First, postmodern and critical theories of education often are written in a language that is difficult to understand. Although this is a problem for all academic work, it is more so for a theory that purports to provide an agenda for critique and change in the school. Second, they usually eschew empirical methods to study schools. As a result, they are sometimes long on assertion and short on evidence. Finally, and most importantly, postmodernist theories of education often fail to connect theory to practice in a way that practitioners find meaningful and useful. Although this does not suggest that postmodernists write exclusively for practitioners, if one of the stated aims of theorists such as Giroux is to develop teachers as transformative intellectuals and to provide a critical pedagogy for school transformation, then the problem of language is of central importance. How can we have dialogues across difference if teachers are excluded from the dialogue?

What separates postmodern and critical theories from the rest of the sociology of education is the frequent absence of empirical evidence. Although many of the sociological approaches discussed in this chapter are conceptual and theoretical, theory is the foundation for empirical research. For example, functionalist theory resulted in a rich empirical research project on the relationship between education, achievement, and mobility. Conflict theory resulted in a rich array of comparative, historical, and empirical research on the relationship between education and social reproduction, between educational expansion and labor market requirements, and on the beliefs in citizenship. Interactionist theory resulted in a rich variety of qualitative, ethnographic studies of schools and classroom practices, describing how school processes related to social stratification.

Postmodern and critical theory often does not provide sufficient empirical research to test its frequently tautological propositions. Therefore, although it represents an important social theory, it sometimes fails to live up to the promise of sociology: to develop a scientific, empirically tested set of propositions about how the social world works. The following section examines the different types of social scientific research employed by sociologists of education.

Feminist Theory

Beginning in the 1960s, feminists challenged what they viewed as the dominant patriarchal ideologies of society. In the political arena, this resulted in liberal feminists demanding social, economic, and sexual equality. In addition, they critiqued traditional gender roles, which to a significant degree were reproduced in the schools. Feminist educators and sociologists of education examined the ways in which schools perpetuated sexist attitudes and behaviors, as well as unequal educational outcomes based on gender. Radical feminist sociologists of education (Arnot, 2002) synthesized feminist and Marxist theory to link patriarchal gender relations to capitalist economic processes and argued that traditional gender roles were inexorably linked to the reproduction of economic inequalities.

Feminist educational theorists and sociologists of education examined a number of linked processes. First, they analyzed the role of schooling in the reproduction of gender roles (Thorne, 1993). Second, based on these analyses, feminist educational theorists proposed alternative feminist pedagogies to interrupt sexist gender socialization through gender-balanced curricula and pedagogic practices (Maher and Tetrault, 2001). Finally, feminist sociologists of education examined the role of schooling in reproducing a gender-based achievement gap, which until the 1990s favored males in terms of educational achievement and attainment. From the 1990s, as this gender gap closed, with females outperforming males in most subjects except mathematics and science, and with female high school graduation rates and college attendance rates outpacing males, sociologists of education often turned their attention to explaining the "boy problem" (Arnot, David, and Weiner, 1999).

The Rise of Empirical Sociology of Education: Methodological Approaches to Studying Educational Effects

Beginning in the 1960s, quantitative methods dominated research in the sociology of education. Large-scale data sets, such as High School Beyond, the National Educational Longitudinal Study, and the School and Staffing Surveys collected by organizations such as the National Opinion Research Center at the University of Chicago and the National Center for Educational Statistics, were mined using sophisticated statistical techniques, including multivariate analysis, hierarchical linear modeling, path analysis, and others. The purpose of this type of research was to examine the independent effects of schooling on educational and economic outcomes, while controlling for a series of independent variables, both inside and outside schools. Beginning with the Coleman Report in the 1960s (Coleman et al., 1966) and Jencks's analyses of family and school (Jencks et al., 1972; Jencks 1979), these quantitative analyses examined the explained and unexplained variation in academic achievement among different groups, based on race, social class, ethnicity, gender, age, disability, and other factors. This type of research also examined school effects on these groups by comparing different types of schools, including public, private, and charter schools, as well as the effects of school organization and processes, including ability grouping, tracking, and school and class size (Hallinan, 2000; Levinson, Cookson and Sadovnik, 2002).

Although this type of research provided important evidence on the effects of school organization and processes and the independent effects of factors outside schools, such as poverty, family, neighborhood, community, and peer groups, interactionist sociologists of education argued that research based on large-scale data sets often missed the reasons for these effects, as they did not examine school processes.

As an antidote to large data set quantitative research, qualitative researchers provided complementary approaches to understanding schooling using ethnographic methods. Based on the methods of the Chicago School of Sociology in the 1930s (Vidich and Lyman, 1994) researchers such as Annette Lareau (1989, 2004), Lois Weis (1990, 2004), and Michelle Fine (1992) provided important analyses of how school processes affect students from various backgrounds.

Some qualitative researchers have remained squarely in the scientific tradition of post-positivism, insisting on objectivity, rigorous research design, and examining causality (Maxwell, 2004). Others are more rooted within interpretive traditions, including symbolic interactionism, ethnomethodology, hermeneutics, postmodernism, feminism, critical theory, and cultural studies (Riehl, 2001, p. 116) and in varying degrees reject post-positivist notions of scientific rigor. As noted above, many of the postmodern critical studies prefer narrative and autobiographical approaches. Despite critiques of qualitative research as unscientific (see Denzin and Lincoln, 2006), qualitative research continues to be an important part of research in the sociology of education.

By the beginning of the twenty-first century, as a response to this critique of the unscientific nature of some qualitative educational research, policymakers and governmental officials at the U.S. Department of Education called for educational research to mirror the scientific methods of the natural sciences. Arguing that experimental research design with randomized trials, "the gold standard" of medical and pharmaceutical research, should be the preferred method in educational research, the U.S. Department of Education issued guidelines for funded educational research privileging experimental design in particular and quantitative methods in general. In addition, the Department of Education's policies, including the federal No Child Left Behind Act (2001) required scientific evidence for programs and curricula to appear on its What Works Clearinghouse list, or to be eligible for federal funds in Title I (high poverty) districts or for comprehensive school reform model grants. Although social science and educational research organizations such as the American Educational Research Association issued statements opposing this strict definition of scientific research and called for the inclusion of qualitative studies on an equal footing, federal policy and funding continues to privilege quantitative methods.

A number of researchers have argued that there are weaknesses in both quantitative and qualitative research methods and that mixed-method approaches make more sense (Chatterji, 2005; Johnson and Onwuegbuzie, 2004; Maxwell, 2004). Based upon these strengths and weaknesses, it is clear that both quantitative and qualitative methods should be an important part of sociology of education research. Riehl (2004) argues that qualitative research in the sociology of education has made valuable contributions to our understanding of educational problems and has offered policymakers useful data for school improvement. Large-scale data set analyses have provided essential evidence on the effects of schooling and have been invaluable to policymakers. In an age when educational research is dominated by the Institute of Education Sciences at the U.S. Department of Education labeling experimental research design and randomized field trials, modeled after the pharmaceutical and medical research communities, as the "gold standard" for evaluating what works, and recommending policy and programmatic interventions, it is imperative that both quantitative and qualitative research are recognized as an important tool for policymakers. Whether studies are totally quantitative or totally qualitative or part of a mixed-method approach that uses both quantitative and qualitative methods, sociology of education research provides important data for public policy. Chatterji (2005) argues convincingly that a mixed-method approach rich in qualitative methods must be part of extended-term mixed-method (ETMM) evaluation designs to ensure that researchers provide policy makers with the best evidence of what works in education, although this approach is difficult and costly.

Conclusion

The sociology of education originated in the concerns of classical sociology in the nineteenth and early twentieth centuries. It came of age from the 1960s onward and concentrated on the significant questions regarding meritocracy and equality. Contemporary theories in the sociology of education have attempted to synthesize the major theories in the field—functionalism, conflict theory, and interactionism—and have provided a rich theoretical foundation for empirical work. At the same time, the concern with educational inequalities has resulted in a preoccupation with empirical, mostly quantitative, investigations of school effects. Using large data sets such as High School and Beyond and the National Education Longitudinal Study, these investigations have focused on school processes such as tracking and their effects. Although these studies have provided important findings on educational outcomes and the independent effects of schooling, family, and other student background characteristics, they have often lacked theoretical sophistication.

Today, the sociology of education is at a crossroads. The twentieth century represented the attempt to refine and empirically test the theoretical insights of the classical sociology of the nineteenth century. Through sophisticated methodological approaches, sociologists of education provided important empirical evidence on the effects of education on different groups and have been an important source of data for discussions of the achievement gap. However, postmodern theorists and researchers, usually using qualitative methods, provided an alternative to what they perceived as the overly scientific, quantitative focus of much of the sociology of education research. For many sociologists of education, this response has weakened the scientific base of educational research. For others (Cookson, 1987; Hallinan, 1996), sociology of education of all types has been too removed from policy and practice. In the coming years, sociologists of education need to combine varied research methodologies, quantitative and qualitative, to examine the most important question common to functionalist and conflict theory: to understand why students from lower socio-economic backgrounds do less well in school and to provide pragmatic policy recommendations for successful school reform and to reduce the achievement gap. Although sociological theory in the sociology of education will continue to be an important part of this project, the separation of theory, research, and practice needs to be diminished.

Notes

1. Earlier versions of this chapter appeared in Sadovnik (2004) and Sadovnik (2001).
2. Adapted from Sadovnik and Cookson (2002).
3. This section is adapted from Sadovnik, Cookson, and Semel (2006).
4. This section is adapted from Sadovnik, Cookson, and Semel (2006).
5. This section is adapted from Sadovnik (1991). Reprinted by permission of the American Sociological Association.
6. This section is adapted from Sadovnik (1995).

References

Arnot, M. (2002). *Reproducing gender: Selected critical essays on educational theory and feminist politics.* London: Falmer.

Arnot, M., David, M., & Weiner, G. (1999). *Closing the gender gap: Postwar education and social change.* Cambridge: Polity.

Aronowitz, S. & Giroux, H. (1991). *Postmodern education: Politics, culture and social criticism.* Minneapolis: University of Minnesota Press.

Atkinson, P. (1985). *Language, structure and reproduction: An introduction to the sociology of Basil Bernstein.* London: Methuen.

Baker, D. P. (1999). Schooling all the masses: Reconsidering the origins of American schooling in the post-bellum era. *Sociology of Education*, 72(4), 197–215.

Baker, D. P. & LeTendre, G. K. (2005). *National differences, global similarities: World culture and the future of schooling.* Palo Alto, CA: Stanford University Press.

Baudrillard, J. (1981). *For a critique of the political economy of the sign* (Charles Leaven, Trans.). St. Louis, MO: Tellos Press.

Baudrillard, J. (1984). The precession of simulacra. In B. Wallis (Ed.), *Art after modernism: Rethinking representation* (pp. 213–281). Boston: David Godine.

Bennett, K. P. & LeCompte, M. D. (1990). *How schools work.* New York: Longman.

Berger, P. & Luckmann, T. (1963). *The social construction of reality.* Garden City, NY: Doubleday.

Bernstein, B. (1958). Some sociological determinants of perception: An enquiry into sub-cultural differences. *British Journal of Sociology*, 9, 159–174.

Bernstein, B. (1960). Language and social class: A research note. *British Journal of Sociology*, 11, 271–276.

Bernstein, B. (1961a). Social structure, language, and learning. *Educational Research*, 3, 163–176.

Bernstein, B. (1961b). Social class and linguistic development: A theory of social learning. In A. H. Halsey, J. Floud, & C. A. Anderson (Eds.), *Education, economy and society* (pp. 288–314). New York: Free Press.

Bernstein, B. (1962a). Linguistic codes, hesitation phenomena and intelligence. *Language and Speech*, 5, 31–46.

Bernstein, B. (1962b). Social class, linguistic codes and grammatical elements. *Language and Speech*, 5, 221–240.

Bernstein, B. (1970). Education cannot compensate for society. *New Society*, 387, 344–347.

Bernstein, B. (1973). *Class, codes, and control* (Vol. 1). London: Routledge & Kegan Paul. (Original work published 1971.)

Bernstein, B. (1977). *Class, codes, and control* (Vol. 3). London: Routledge & Kegan Paul. (Original work published 1975.)

Bernstein, B. (1990a). *Class, codes and control: Vol. 4: The structuring of pedagogic discourse*. London: Routledge.

Bernstein, B. (1990b). Social class and pedagogic practice. In B. Bernstein, *Class, codes, and control: Vol. 4: The structuring of pedagogic discourse* (pp. 63–93). London: Routledge.

Bernstein, B. (1990c). Elaborated and restricted codes: Overview and criticisms. In B. Bernstein, *Class, codes and control: Vol. 4: The structuring of pedagogic discourse* (pp. 94–130). London: Routledge.

Bernstein, B. (1990d). The social construction of pedagogic discourse. In B. Bernstein, *Class, codes, and control: Vol. 4: The structuring of pedagogic discourse* (pp. 165–218). London: Routledge.

Bernstein, B. (1996). *Pedagogy, symbolic control and identity: Theory, research, critique*. London: Taylor & Francis.

Bourdieu, P. (1973). Cultural reproduction and social reproduction. In R. Brown (Ed.), *Knowledge, education, and cultural change* (pp. 71–112). London: Tavistock.

Bourdieu, P. (1977). *Outline of a theory of practice*. Cambridge, UK: Cambridge University Press.

Bourdieu, P. (1984). *Distinction: A social critique of the judgment of taste*. Cambridge, MA: Harvard University Press.

Bourdieu, P., & Passeron, J. C. (1977). *Reproduction in education, society and culture*. London: Sage.

Bowles, S. & Gintis, H. (1976). *Schooling in capitalist America*. New York: Basic Books.

Burbules, N. & Rice, S. (1991). Dialogue across differences: Continuing the conversation. *Harvard Educational Review*, 61 (4), 393–416.

Chatterji, M. (2005). Evidence on "What Works": An argument for extended-term mixed-method (ETMM) evaluation designs. *Educational Researcher*, 34 (5), 14–24.

Coleman, J. S. (1964). *Introduction to mathematical sociology*. New York: Macmillan.

Coleman, J. S. (1987). *Public and private schools: The impact of communities*. New York: Basic Books.

Coleman, J. S. (1988). Social capital in the creation of human capital. *American Journal of Sociology*, 94, S95–S120.

Coleman, J. S. (1990). *Foundations of social theory*. Cambridge, MA: Harvard University Press.

Coleman, J. S., Campbell, E. Q., Hobson, C. J., McPartland, J., Mood, A. J., Weinfeld, F. D., & York R.L. (1966) *Equality of educational opportunity*. Washington: USGPO [The Coleman Report].

Coleman, J. S., Hoffer, T., & Kilgore, S. (1982). *High school achievement: Public, Catholic and private schools compared*. New York: Basic Books.

Collins, R. (1971). Functional and conflict theories of educational stratification. *American Sociological Review*, 36 (6), 1002–1019.

Collins, R. (1975). *Conflict sociology*. New York: Academic Press.

Collins, R. (1978). *The credential society*. New York: Academic Press.

Collins, R. & Makowsky, M. (1993). *The discovery of society*. New York: McGraw Hill.

Cookson, P. W. (1987). Closing the rift between scholarship and practice. *Educational Policy*, 1, 321–331.

Cookson, P. W., Jr. & Persell, C. H. (1985). *Preparing for power: America's elite boarding schools*. New York: Basic.

Danzig, A. (1995). Applications and distortions of Basil Bernstein's code theory. In A. R. Sadovnik (Ed.), *Knowledge and pedagogy: The sociology of Basil Bernstein* (pp. 145–170). Norwood, NJ: Ablex Publishing Corporation.

Davis, K. & Moore, W. (1945). Some principles of stratification. *American Sociological Review*, 10, 242–249.

Denzin, N. K. & Lincoln, Y. S. (2006). *Handbook of qualitative research* (3rd ed.). Thousand Oaks, CA: Sage.

Derrida, J. (1973). *Speech and phenomenon*. Evanston, IL: Northwestern University Press.

Derrida, J. (1981). *Positions*. Chicago: University of Chicago Press.

Derrida, J. (1982). *Of grammatology*. Baltimore, MD: Johns Hopkins University Press.

Durkheim, E. (1947). *The division of labor in society*. Glencoe, IL: Free Press. (Original work published 1893.)

Durkheim, E. (1951). *Suicide*. Glencoe, IL: Free Press. (Original work published 1897.)

Durkheim, E. (1954). *The elementary forms of religious life*. Glencoe, IL: Free Press. (Original work published 1915.)

Durkheim, E. (1956). *Education and sociology*. New York: Free Press.

Durkheim, E. (1962). *Moral education*. New York: Free Press.

Durkheim, E. (1977). *The evolution of educational thought* (P. Collins, Trans.). London: Routledge & Kegan Paul.

Ellsworth, E. (1989). Why doesn't this feel empowering? Working through the repressive myths of critical pedagogy. *Harvard Educational Review*, 59 (3), 297–324.

Fine, M. (1992). *Framing dropouts*. Albany, NY: SUNY Press.

Freire, P. (1972). *Pedagogy of the oppressed*. New York: Herder & Herder.

Freire, P. (1985). *The politics of education*. South Hadley, MA: Bergin & Garvey.

Freire, P. (1987). *A pedagogy for liberation*. South Hadley, MA: Bergin & Garvey.

Fuller, B. & Rubinson, R. (Eds.). (1992). *The political construction of education*. New York: Praeger.

Giddens, A. (1975). *The new rules of sociological method*. London: Cambridge University Press.

Giroux, H. (1991). *Postmodernism, feminism, and cultural politics: Redrawing educational boundaries*. Albany, NY: SUNY Press.

Goffman, E. (1959). *The presentation of self in everyday life*. Garden City, NY: Doubleday.

Goffman, E. (1961a). *Asylums*. Garden City, NY: Doubleday.

Goffman, E. (1961b). *Encounters*. Indianapolis, IN: Bobbs-Merrill.

Goffman, E. (1963a). *Stigma*. Englewood Cliffs, NJ: Prentice-Hall.

Goffman, E. (1963b). *Behavior in public places*. Garden City, NY: Doubleday.

Goffman, E. (1967). *Interaction ritual*. Garden City, NY: Doubleday.

Hallinan, M. T. (Ed.). (2000). *Handbook of sociology of education*. New York: Kluwer.

Hallinan, M. T. (1996). Bridging the gap between scholarship and practice. *Sociology of Education*, 69 (Extra Issue), 131–134.

Hurn, C. (1993). *The limits and possibilities of schooling*. Needham Heights, MA: Allyn & Bacon.

Jencks, C. (1979). *Who gets ahead.* New York: Basic Books.

Jencks, C. et al. (1972). *Inequality.* New York: Basic Books.

Johnson, R. & Onwuegbuzie, A. (2004). Mixed methods: A research paradigm whose time has come. *Educational Researcher,* 33 (7): 14–26.

Kincheloe, J. (2008). *Knowledge and critical pedagogy: An introduction.* New York: Springer.

Kincheloe, J. L. & Steinberg, S. R. (Eds.) (1998). *Unauthorized methods: Strategies for critical teaching.* New York: Routledge.

Lareau, A. (1989). *Home advantage.* New York: Routledge.

Lareau, A. (2004). *Unequal childhood: Class, race and family life.* Berkeley: University of California Press.

Lather, P. (1991). *Getting smart: Feminist research and pedagogy with/in the postmodern.* New York: Routledge.

Levinson, D. L., Cookson, P. W., & Sadovnik, A. R. (2002). *Encyclopedia of education and sociology.* New York: Routledge.

Lyotard, J. F. (1984). *The postmodern condition* (G. Bennington & B. Massumi, Trans.). Minneapolis: University of Minnesota Press.

Maher, F. & Tetrault, M. K. (2001, expanded edition). *The feminist classroom.* Lanham, MD: Rowman and Littlefield.

Mannheim, K. (1936). *Ideology and utopia.* New York: Harcourt & Brace.

Maxwell, J. (2004) Causal explanation, qualitative research and scientific inquiry in education. *Educational Researcher,* 33 (2), 3–11.

McLaren, P. & Hammer, R. (1989). Critical pedagogy and the postmodern challenge: Toward a critical postmodernist pedagogy of liberation. *Educational Foundations,* 3 (3), 29–62.

McLaren, P. & Kincheloe, J. (2007). *Critical pedagogy: Where are we now?* New York: Peter Lang.

Meyer, J. (1977). The effects of education as an institution. *American Journal of Sociology,* 83 (1), 55–77.

Meyer, J. & Rowan, B. (1977). The structure of educational organizations. In M. Meyer & Associates (Eds.), *Environments and organizations* (pp. 78–109). San Francisco: Jossey-Bass.

Meyer, J. & Rowan, B. (1978). Institutionalized organizations: Formal structure as myth and ceremony. *American Journal of Sociology,* 83, 340–363.

Meyer, J., Ramirez, F. & Soysal, Y. (1992). World expansion of mass education, 1870–1980. *Sociology of Education,* 65, 128–149.

Oakes, J. (1985). *Keeping track: How schools structure inequality.* New Haven: Yale University Press.

Olneck, M. (2007, September 10). Personal communication.

Parsons, T. (1959). The school as a social system. *Harvard Educational Review,* 29, 297–318.

Persell, C. H. (1977). *Education and inequality.* New York: Free Press.

Ramirez, F. & Boli, J. (1987). The political construction of mass schooling: European origins and worldwide institutionalization. *Sociology of Education,* 60, 2–17.

Ravitch, D. (1977). *The revisionists revisited.* New York: Basic Books.

Riehl, C. (2001). Bridging to the future: The contributions of qualitative research to the sociology of education. *Sociology of Education,* 74 (Extra Issue), 115–134.

Rist, R. (1970). Student social class and teacher expectations: The self fulfilling prophecy in ghetto education. *Harvard Educational Review,* 40, 411–451.

Rist, R. (1973). *The urban school: Factory for failure.* Cambridge, MA: MIT Press.

Rist, R. (1977). On understanding the processes of schooling: The contributions of labeling theory. In J. Karabel & A. H. Halsey, *Power and ideology in education* (pp. 292–305). New York: Oxford University Press.

Rubinson, R. (1986). Class formation, politics and institutions: Schooling in the United States. *American Journal of Sociology,* 92, 519–548.

Sadovnik, A. R. (1991). Basil Bernstein's theory of pedagogic practice: A structuralist approach. *Sociology of Education,* 64 (1), 48–63.

Sadovnik, A. R. (Ed.). (1995a). *Knowledge and pedagogy: The sociology of Basil Bernstein.* Norwood, NJ: Ablex Publishing Corporation.

Sadovnik, A. R. (1995b). Postmodernism and the sociology of education: Closing the rift among scholarship, research, and practice. In George Noblit & William Pink (Eds.), *Continuity and contradiction: The futures of the sociology of education.* Cresskill, NJ: Hampton Press.

Sadovnik, A. R. (2001). Theories in the sociology of education. In J. Ballantine and J. Spade (Eds.), *Schools and society: A sociological approach to education* (pp. 15–34). place: Wadsworth.

Sadovnik, A. R. (2004). Theories in the sociology of education. In J. Ballantine and J. Spade (Eds.), *Schools and society: A sociological approach to education* (2nd ed., pp. 7–26). place: Wadsworth.

Sadovnik, A. R. & Cookson, P. W., Jr. (2002). Functionalism. In *Education and sociology: An encyclopedia.* New York: Routledge,.

Sadovnik, A. R., Cookson, P. W., Jr., & Semel, S. F. (1994; 2001, 2006). *Exploring education: An introduction to the foundations of education.* Boston: Allyn and Bacon.

Steinberg, S. & Kincheloe, J. (1998). *Unauthorized methods: Strategies for clinical teaching.* New York: Routledge.

Swartz, D. (1997). *Culture and power: The sociology of Pierre Bourdieu.* Chicago: University of Chicago Press.

Thorne, B. (1993). *Gender play: Girls and boys in school.* New Brunswick, NJ: Rutgers University Press.

Tönnies, F. (1957). *Community and society.* New York: Harper. (Original work published 1887.)

U.S. Department of Education. (1983). *A nation at risk.* Washington, DC: U.S. Government Printing Office.

Vidich, A. J. & Lyman, S. M. (1994). Qualitative methods: Their history in sociology and anthropology. In N. K. Denzin & Y. S. Lincoln (Eds.), *Handbook of qualitative research* (1st ed., pp. 23–59). Thousand Oaks, CA: Sage Publications.

Waller, W. (1965). *The sociology of learning.* Chicago: University of Chicago Press.

Weis, L. (1990). *Working class without work.* New York: Routledge.

Weis, L. (2004). *Class reunion.* New York: Routledge.

Young, M. F. D. (Ed.). (1971). *Knowledge and control: New directions of the sociology of education.* London: Collier-Macmillan.

2

On Education and Society

ÉMILE DURKHEIM

Educational transformations are always the result and the symptom of the social transformations in terms of which they are to be explained. For a people to feel at any given moment the need to change its educational system, it is necessary that new ideas and needs have emerged for which the old system is no longer adequate. But these needs and ideas do not arise spontaneously; if they suddenly come to the forefront of human consciousness after having been ignored for centuries, it is necessarily the case that in the intervening period there has been a change and that it is this change of which they are an expression. Thus, in order to understand the educational achievement of the sixteenth century, we need as a preliminary to know in a general way what constituted the great social movement that historians call the Renaissance and of which a new educational theory was but one manifestation.

The essence of the Renaissance has often been identified with a return to the spirit of classical times; and indeed this is precisely the meaning of the word normally used to designate this period of European history. The sixteenth century is supposed to have been a period when man, abandoning the gloomy ideals of the Middle Ages, reverted to the gayer and more self-confident view of life which prevailed in the ancient pagan world. As to the cause of this change of direction, it allegedly consisted in the rediscovery of classical literature, the principal masterpieces of which were rescued during this period from the oblivion in which they had languished for centuries. On this view it was the discovery of the great works of classical literature that brought about this new change of outlook in the western European mind. But to speak of the Renaissance in this way is only to point in the most superficial way to its façade. If it were indeed true that the sixteenth century simply took up the classical tradition at the point it had reached when the Dark Ages arrived and temporarily blotted it out, the Renaissance would emerge as a movement of moral and intellectual reaction that would be hard to account for. We would have to assume that humanity had strayed from its natural path for fifteen centuries, since it had to retrace its steps back over a period of such length in order to embark upon a whole new stage in its career. Certainly progress does not proceed in a straight line; it makes turnings and detours; advances are followed by recessions but that such an aberration should be prolonged over a period of fifteen hundred years is historically incredible. It is true that this view of the Renaissance accords with the way in which the eighteenth-century-writers spoke of it. But just because they felt a kind of admiration for the simple life of primitive societies, are we to say that then social philosophy was an attempt to restore prehistoric civilization? Because the men of the Revolution thought that they were imitating the actions of the ancient Romans, are we to view the society that resulted from the Revolution as an imitation of the ancient city? People involved in action are the least well placed to see the causes that underlie their actions, and the way in which they represent to themselves the social movement of which they are a part should always be regarded as suspect and should by no means be thought of as having any special claim to credibility.

Besides, it is simply not true that classical literature was unknown during the centuries we have just been considering, that it was only discovered towards the beginning of the sixteenth century, and that it was this revelation that suddenly expanded the intellectual horizons of Europe. The fact is that there was not a single period during the whole of the Middle Ages when these literary masterpieces were not known; in every generation we find a few people sufficiently intelligent and sensitive to be able to appreciate their worth. Abélard, the hero of dialectic, was at the same time a literary scholar; Virgil, Seneca, Cicero, and Ovid were just as familiar to him as were Boethius and Augustine. During the twelfth century there was a famous school at Chartres which, inspired by its founder, Bernard de Chartres, offered a classical education similar to what would later be offered by the Jesuits. One could multiply examples of this type. It is true that these attempts to introduce classical literature into education remained isolated cases; they never succeeded in capturing the imagination of the Scholastics, who cast them back into obscurity. But they are nonetheless real, and they are sufficient to prove that if classical literature was not appreciated in the Middle Ages, if it played no part in education, this was not because people did not know of its existence. In short, the Middle Ages knew about all the main aspects of classical civilization, but it only retained what it regarded as important, what answered to its own needs. Its entire attention was caught by logic, and this eclipsed everything else. Thus, if everything changed in the sixteenth century, if suddenly Greek and Roman art and literature were recognized as being of incomparable educational value, this clearly must have been because at that moment in history, as a consequence of a change that had taken place in the public mind, logic lost its former prestige—while by contrast an urgent need was felt for the first time for a kind of culture that would be more refined, more elegant or literary. People did not acquire this taste because they had just discovered classical antiquity; rather, they demanded from the antiquity they already knew the means of satisfying the new taste they had just acquired. What we must seek, therefore, is an account of this change of direction in the intellectual and moral outlook of the European peoples, if we wish to understand the nature of the Renaissance insofar as it affected educational thought no less than scientific and literary thought. A people only modifies its mental outlook to such an enormous extent when very fundamental features of social life have themselves been modified. We can therefore be certain in advance that the Renaissance derives, not, I repeat, from the fortuitous fact that certain classical works were exhumed at this time, but rather from profound changes in the organization of European societies. I cannot, of course, attempt here to paint a complete and detailed picture of these transformations, but I should like at least to point out the most important of them so as to be able to relate the educational movement we shall be exploring to its social roots.

In the first place, there was a group of interrelated changes in the economic sphere. People had finally got away from the paltry life-style of the Middle Ages, when the general insecurity of relations paralyzed the spirit of enterprise, when the limited number of markets stifled great ambition, when only the extreme simplicity of their tastes and needs enabled men to live in harmony with their environment. Gradually order had been established; better government and more efficient administration had rallied people's confidence. Towns had proliferated and become more populous. Most important of all, the discovery of America and the trade route via the Indies had galvanized economic activity by opening up new worlds in which it could operate. Consequently, the general welfare had been increased; vast fortunes had been amassed; and the acquisition of wealth stimulated and developed a taste for the easy, elegant life of luxury....

However, if this transformation had been limited to the world of the aristocracy, it probably would not have had such extensive social consequences. But one of the effects of accrued wealth was to produce at the same time a narrowing of the gaps between social classes. Up till then the bourgeoisie had not even dared raise its eyes to look at the aristocracy across what it felt to be a great fixed gulf. And it found it natural to lead quite a different existence. But now that the bourgeoisie had become richer and consequently more powerful, it also became more ambitious and sought to narrow the gap. Its expectations had increased with its resources, making the life it had led up till then appear intolerable. It was no longer afraid to cast its gaze upwards and it wanted as well to live the life of the nobles, to imitate their style, their manners, their luxury. As one writer puts it: "Pride was reaching ever higher peaks in every section of the community. The bourgeoisie in the towns have started wanting to dress in the same way as the aristocracy…and the people from the villages in the same way as the bourgeoisie in the towns." According to another author, the bourgeois ladies grew bored with their life of obscurity; they now wanted to copy the great ladies. "One can scarcely distinguish any longer between a noble lady and a plebeian…one sees women who are worse than plebeian dressing in flowing robes embroidered in gold and silver…their fingers are loaded with emeralds and other precious stones … in the old days the practice of kissing a lady's hand in greeting was restricted to aristocrats, and noble ladies did not offer their hand to the first comer, let alone to anyone at all. Today men smelling of leather rush to kiss the hand of a woman whose escutcheon is exclusively aristocratic. Patrician ladies marry plebeian men, plebeian women marry patrician men; thus we are breeding hybrid creatures." It is easy to guess that so considerable a change in the way life was understood would inevitably be accompanied by a change in the way education was understood, and that instruction designed to produce a good bachelor of arts, versed in all the secrets of syllogism and argument, would be quite unsuited to the enterprise of producing an elegant and fluent nobleman able to hold his own in a salon and possessing all the social graces.

However, in addition to this transformation, there was another one, no less important, which took place in the world of ideas.

By the sixteenth century, the great nation states of Europe had been in large measure established. Whereas in the Middle Ages there had been but one Europe, one Christendom, which was united and homogeneous, there now existed great individual collectivities with their own intellectual and moral characters. England found its identity and its unity with the Tudors, Spain with Ferdinand of Castile and his successors. Germany with the Hapsburgs (albeit more vaguely), and France did so before any of the others under the Capetians. The old unity of Christendom had thus been definitively shattered. However much people continued to profess respect for the fundamental doctrines, which still appeared highly abstract, each of the groups which had thus been formed had its own special mode of thought and feeling, its own national temperament whose particular emphasis tended to affect the systems of belief that had been accepted until that time by the vast majority of the faithful. And since the great moral figures that had arisen could only develop their individual natures, since they could not organize their thoughts and beliefs according to their own lights unless they were granted the right to deviate from accepted beliefs, they claimed this right and in claiming it they proclaimed it; that is to say they claimed the rights of schism and of free inquiry—albeit only to a limited extent, and not as absolute rights, since such a thing would have been inconceivable at the time. It is here that we find the root cause of the Reformation, that other aspect of the Renaissance that was the natural result of the movement towards individualization and differentiation taking place at that time within the homogeneous mass of Europe. In one sense, of course, Scholasticism had paved the way for it. Scholasticism had taught reason to be more self-confident by confronting it with monumental questions and equipping it with a rigorous logical training so that it might make fresh conquests. However, between the audacities of Scholasticism, especially at the end of the fifteenth century, which were always relatively moderate—between the more or less bold claims made by a few thinkers whose voices were scarcely heard outside the schools, and the sudden explosion that was the Reformation and that shook the whole of Europe, there is clearly a radical break, which bears witness to the fact that new forces had come into play.

Here we have a new causal factor, which was to bring about a change in the theory and practice of education. The Christian faith had played too large a part in medieval education for the educational system not to be affected by the upheavals that faith was undergoing. Moreover, there were other ways in which the economic factor exercised a parallel influence. It is clear, in fact, that the aesthetic ideal of the Middle Ages was quite unsuited for pupils who had acquired a taste for luxury and the life of leisure. And since this aesthetic ideal was the ideal of Christianity, Christianity itself was affected by the same phenomenon. For it was not possible that the aversion felt henceforth for the old view of life should not be extended to the whole system of beliefs upon which that view of life was grounded. If, as we have argued, Christianity was accepted so readily by the barbarians, this was precisely because of its starkness, its indifference towards the products of civilization, its disdain for the joys of existence. But the same reasons that accounted for its triumph then were now to diminish its authority over people's minds. Societies that had learned to savor the joy of living could no longer put up with a doctrine that rendered sacrifice, self-denial, abstinence, and suffering in general the supreme objects of desire.

Individuals, sensing that this system ran counter to their deepest feelings and opposed the satisfaction of needs they regarded as quite natural, could only be disposed to cast doubt upon it, or at least to cast doubt upon the way it had been interpreted up to that time; for it is impossible to accept uncritically, unreservedly, and without sufficient reason a doctrine that in certain respects seems to go against nature. Without renouncing it completely, people came to feel the need to revise it, to interpret it afresh, in such a way that it would harmonize with the aspirations of the age. Now, any such revision and reinterpretation presuppose the right to revise, to inspect, and to interpret, in some sense the right to examine, which, however one looks at it, implies a diminution of faith....

Now, it is clear that there is nothing in Scholasticism that could have satisfied these new tastes: on the contrary, it was bound to be hostile to them. Since it attached no importance to form, it did not hesitate to twist language savagely in order to satisfy all the needs of thought, without regard to considerations of purity or harmony. As a result of the very great place it accorded to debate, it developed a taste not for ideas that were delicate, subtle, measured, but rather for opinions that were dogmatic and clear-cut and whose features stood out in such a way that conflicting opinions could be clearly contrasted. Moreover, the violent arguments that were born of these contrasts could only encourage a coarseness in manners comparable to what had been upheld for so long by the noble knights in their tourneys and similar practices. The student of the Middle Ages was primarily concerned with crushing his opponent beneath the weight of his arguments and did not care in the least whether his presentation was attractive. His unkempt appearance and his rustic deportment and manners were expressions of this same state of mind.

Here we have the explanation of why the men of the new generation were quite literally horrified by Scholasticism and its methods. The extreme virulence of their polemics seems at first sight to be out of place in a purely educational quarrel. But the fact is that the issue was really more wide-ranging. The sixteenth century did not accuse Scholasticism simply of having engaged in certain debatable or regrettable academic practices but rather of having constituted a school of barbarousness and coarseness. Hence the frequency with which the words *barbarus, stoliditas, rusticitas* recur in the writings of Erasmus. To these refined minds a Scholastic is quite literally a barbarian (remember the title of Erasmus's book *Antibarbaros),* who speaks a language scarcely human, crude-sounding, formally inelegant; who delights only in arguments, in deafening yells, in verbal and other battles; who is ignorant, in sum, of all the benefits of civilization, of everything that contributes to the charm of life. We can readily conceive of the feeling such an educational system would be capable of arousing in men whose aim was to render humanity more tender, more elegant, more cultivated.

The only way to succeed in ridding the human intellect of its coarseness, to polish and refine it, was to introduce it to and make it intimate with an elegant and refined civilization, so that it might become imbued with its spirit. Now, the only civilization that could satisfy this condition at that time was that of the classical peoples as it had been expressed and preserved in the works of their great writers, poets, and orators. It was thus quite natural that these should be seen as providing the schoolteachers needed by the young. "What then," says Erasmus, "what then could have guided these coarse men of the Stone Age towards a more human life, towards being more gentle of character and more civilized in morals? Was it not literature? It is literature that molds the mind, that mollifies passions, that checks the untamed outbursts of natural temperament." For this purpose there existed no other established and developed literatures apart from those of Rome and Greece.

With this in view, the moral milieu in which the child was to be molded had to be made up of all the extant elements of these literatures. Hence the enormous attention accorded by the public at this time to the masterpieces of Greco-Roman civilization. If people esteemed and admired them, if they sought to imitate them, this is not because they were exhumed at this moment in history and, by being discovered, suddenly inculcated in people a taste for literature. Quite the reverse: it was because a taste for literature, a taste for a new kind of civilization, had just been acquired that they suddenly became objects of enthusiastic veneration; for they appeared, and quite rightly so, as the only means available of satisfying this new need. If this vast body of literature had hitherto been neglected, this was not because nothing was known of it (we have already seen that the major works were known); rather, its virtues were not appreciated because they did not meet any contemporary need. If, by contrast, they were then regarded in the eyes of public opinion, or at least of a certain section of it, as being of incomparable value, this was because a new attitude of mind was in the process of developing and could only be fully realized in the school of the classics. And one may even wonder whether the greater frequency of the finds and exhumations that occurred at this period was not a result of the fact that since, henceforth, the value of these discoveries was fully appreciated people devoted more of their ingenuity to making them. To find, one must seek, and one only seeks in earnest when one attaches importance to what one hopes to find.

Thus the educational ideas of the humanists were not the result of simple accidents. They derived, rather, from a fact whose influence on the moral history of our country it is difficult to exaggerate; I refer to the establishment of polite society. If France did indeed become from the sixteenth century onwards a center of literary life and intellectual activity, this was because, at this same period, there had developed among us a select society, a society of intellectually cultivated people to whom our writers addressed themselves. It was the ideas and the tastes of this society that they communicated; it was for this society that they wrote and for it that they thought. It was here in this particular environment that the driving force of our civilization from the sixteenth century to the middle of the eighteenth century arose. And the object of education as Erasmus conceived of it was to prepare man for this special and restricted society.

Here too we can see the essential character and at the same time the radical flaw of this educational theory. It is the fact that it is essentially aristocratic in nature. The kind of society that it seeks to fashion is always centered around a court, and its members are always drawn from the ranks of the aristocracy or at least from the leisured classes. And it was indeed here and here alone that that fine flowering of elegance and culture could take place, the nurturing and development of which were regarded as more important than anything else. Neither Erasmus nor Vivès had any awareness that beyond this small world, which for all its brilliance was very limited, there were vast masses who should not have been neglected and for whom education could have brought about higher intellectual and moral standards and an improved material condition.

When such a thought did occur to them it disappeared again very quickly without their thinking it necessary to examine it at length. Since he realizes that this expensive education is not suitable for everyone, Erasmus wonders what the poor will do; his answer to this objection is utterly simple. "You ask," he says, "what the poor will be able to do. How will those who can scarcely feed their children be able to give them over a sustained period of time the right kind of education? To this I can only reply by quoting the words of the comic writer: 'You can't ask that what we are capable of achieving should be as great as what we would like to achieve.' We are expounding the best way of bringing up a child, we cannot produce the means of realizing this ideal." He restricts himself to expressing the wish that the rich will come to the help of those who are well-endowed intellectually but who would be prevented by poverty from developing their aptitudes. But he seems not to realize that even if this education were made available to everybody the difficulty would not be resolved, for this generalized education would not meet the needs of the majority. Indeed, for the majority the supreme need is survival, and what is needed in order to survive is not the art of subtle speech, it is the art of sound thinking, so that one knows how to act. In order to struggle effectively in the world of persons and the world of things more substantial weapons are needed than those glittering decorations with which the humanist educationalists were concerned to adorn the mind to the exclusion of anything else.

Think now how much Scholasticism, for all its abstractness, was imbued with a more practical, more realistic, and more social spirit. The fact is that dialectic answered real needs. Intellectual conflict, competition between ideas, constitutes a genuinely important part of life. Moreover, the strength and virility of thought which were acquired as a result of such arduous mental gymnastics could be used in the service of socially useful ends. Thus we must beware of thinking that the medieval schools served only to produce dreamers, seekers after quintessences, and useless pettifogging quibblers. The truth is quite the opposite. It was there that the statesmen, the ecclesiastical dignitaries, and the administrators of the day were brought up. This training, which has been so denigrated, created men of action. It was the education recommended by Erasmus that forms a totally inadequate preparation for life. In it, rhetoric supplants dialectic. Now, if rhetoric had good reason for featuring in the education of the classical world, where the practice of eloquence constituted not only a career but the most important career, this was by no means the case in the sixteenth century, when it played only a very small part in the serious business of life. A theory of education that made rhetoric the principal academic discipline could thus only develop qualities related to the luxuries of existence and not at all to its necessities....

In order to know what became of the educational theories of the Renaissance when they were translated into practice, it would thus seem that we have only to investigate how the University understood them and applied them. But what makes such a procedure impossible, what makes the whole question more complicated, is the great change that took place at this very moment in our academic organization. Up till that time the University had a complete monopoly on and sole responsibility for education, and consequently the future of any educational reforms was dependent upon the University and upon the University alone. However, towards the middle of the sixteenth century, over and against the University corporation there was established a new teaching corporation, which was to break the University's monopoly and which was even to achieve with quite remarkable rapidity a kind of hegemony in academic life. This was the corporation of the Jesuits.

The Jesuit order arose from the need felt by the Catholic Church to check the increasingly threatening progress of Protestantism. With extraordinary speed the doctrines of Luther and Calvin had won over England, almost the whole of Germany, Switzerland, the Low Countries, Sweden, and a considerable part of France. In spite of all the rigorous measures taken, the Church felt itself impotent and began to fear that its dominion in the world would collapse completely. It was then that Ignatius Loyola had the idea of raising a wholly new kind of religious militia the better to combat and, if possible to crush, heresy. He realized that the days were over when people's souls could be governed from the depths of a cloister. Now that people, carried by their own momentum, were tending to elude the Church, it was essential that the Church move closer to them so as to be able to influence them. Now that particular personalities were beginning to stand out from the homogeneous moral and intellectual mass that had been the rule in preceding centuries, it was essential for the Church to be close to individuals, to accommodate its influence over them to intellectual and temperamental diversities. In short, the vast monastic masses familiar to the Middle Ages, which, stationary at their post, had restricted themselves to repulsing such attacks as occurred, without, however, knowing how to take the offensive themselves, had to be replaced. An army of light troops would be established that would be in constant contact with the enemy and consequently well-informed about all his movements, but at the same time sufficiently alert and mobile to be able to go at the slightest signal wherever there was danger, and yet sufficiently flexible to be able to vary its tactics in accordance with the diversity of people and circumstances; its troops would do all this while always and everywhere pursuing the same goal and cooperating in the same grand design. This army was the Company of Jesus.

What was distinctive about it was that it was able to contain within itself two characteristics, which the Middle Ages had adjudged irreconcilable and contradictory. On the one hand, the Jesuits belong to a religious order in the same way as the Dominicans or the Franciscans; they have a head, they are all subject to one and the same rule, to a communal discipline; indeed passive obedience and unity of thought and action have never been carried to such an extreme degree in any militia whether secular or religious. The Jesuit is thus a regular priest. But, on the other hand, he simultaneously possesses all the characteristics of the secular priest; he wears his habit; he fulfills his functions, he preaches, he hears confessions, he catechizes; he does not live in the shadow of a monastery, he rather mingles in the life of the world. For him duty consists not in the mortification of the flesh, in fasting, in abstinence, but in action, in the realization of the goal of the Society. "Let us leave the religious orders," Ignatius Loyola used to say, "to outdo us in fasts, in watches, in the austerity of the regime and habit that, out of piety, they impose upon themselves." "I believe that it is more valuable, for the glory of Our Lord, to preserve and to fortify the stomach and other natural faculties rather than enfeebling them ... you should not assault your own physical nature, because if you exhaust it your intellectual nature will no longer be able to act with the same energy."

Not only must the Jesuit mingle with the world, he must also open himself up to the ideas that are dominant within it. The better to guide his age he must speak its language, he must assimilate its sports. Ignatius Loyola sensed that a profound change had taken place in manners and that there was no going back on this: that a taste for well-being, for a less harsh, easier sunnier existence had been acquired that could not conceivably be stifled or fobbed off; that man had developed a greater degree of pity for his own sufferings and for those of his fellowmen, that there was more sparing of pain, and consequently that the old ideal of absolute renunciation was finished. To prevent the faithful from drifting away from religion, the Jesuits devoted their ingenuity to divesting religion of its former austerity: they made it pleasant and devised all kinds of accommodating arrangements to make it easy to observe. It is true that in order to remain faithful to the mission they had assigned themselves, to avoid seeming to encourage the innovators against whom they were struggling by their own example, they had at the same time to stick to the letter of immutable dogma. It is well known how they extricated themselves from this difficulty and were able to reconcile these conflicting demands thanks to their casuistry, whose excessive flexibility and over ingenious refinements have frequently been pointed out. While maintaining in their sacred form the traditional prescriptions of Roman Catholicism, they were still able to place these within the scope not only of human weakness in general—there is no religion that has ever managed to escape this necessity—but of the elegant frivolousness of the leisured classes of the sixteenth century in particular; it was these leisured classes that it was so important to keep free from heresy and to preserve in the faith. And this is how, while they became essentially men of the past, defenders of the Catholic tradition, the Jesuits were able to exhibit towards the idea, the tastes, and even the defects of the time an attitude of indulgence for which they have often, and not without reason, been reproached. They thus had a dual identity as conservatives, even as reactionaries, on the one hand, and as liberals on the other: a complex policy the nature of which we needed to show here, for we shall encounter it again in the foundations of their educational theory.

But they very quickly came to realize that in order to achieve their end it was not enough to preach, to hear confession, to catechize: the really important instrument in the struggle for mastery of the human soul was the education of the young. Thus they resolved to seize hold of it. One fact in particular made them acutely aware of the urgent need for this; one would have had to be blind to all the evidence not to see that the new methods taking root in the schools could only have the effect of opening up the road to heresy. Indeed, the greatest minds of the time, the most illustrious of the humanists, had openly been converted to the new religion; this was the case with Dolet, with Ramus, with Mathurin Cordier, with the majority of teachers in the College de France, recently founded by Francois I. Thus humanism by its very nature constituted a threat to the fait. And indeed it is clear that an inordinate taste for paganism was bound to cause people's minds to dwell in a moral environment with absolutely nothing Christian about it. Accordingly, if the evil was to be attacked at it sources it would be necessary instead of abandoning the humanist movement to its own devices, to gain control of it and to direct it.

The aim of the Jesuits thus had nothing to do with getting the pupil acquainted with and able to understand classical civilizations; it was exclusively concerned with teaching them to speak and write in Greek and Latin. This explains the importance attributed to written assignments and the nature of these assignments. This is why in the grammar classes prose composition prevailed and was far more important than translation from Latin, which was scarcely practiced at all. This is why stylistic exercises were so numerous and so varied. This attitude even influenced the way the expositions were carried out. Father Jouvency has left us model expositions of Latin authors; one has only to read them to see that their main aim is to get the pupils to appreciate the author's Latin and his literary style, and to encourage them to imitate these same qualities.

Far from seeking to get their pupils to think again the thoughts of antiquity, far from wishing to steep them in the spirit of classical times, the Jesuits had precisely the opposite aim. Indeed, this was because they could see no other way of extricating themselves from the contradictory situation in which they had quite deliberately placed themselves. Because the fashion was for humanism, because classical letters were the object of a veritable cult, the Jesuits, always sensitive to the spirit of their age, professed, as we have just seen, a form of humanism—even quite an uncompromising one, since Greek and Latin alone were permitted entry into their colleges. But from another point of view, as we have said, they realized full well that humanism constituted a threat, that there was a real danger in wishing to fashion Christian souls in the school of paganism. How could these two contradictory needs be reconciled? How could the faith be defended and safeguarded as was required by the self-imposed mission of the Jesuits, while they simultaneously made themselves the apologists and exegetes of pagan literature?

There was only one way of resolving this antinomy: this was, in the very words used by Father Jouvency, to expound the classical authors in such a way "that they became, although pagan and profane, the eulogists of the faith." To make paganism serve the glorification and the propagation of the Christian ethic was a daring undertaking and, it would appear, remarkably difficult; and yet, the Jesuits had enough confidence in their ability to attempt it and to succeed in it. But in order to do this they had deliberately to denature the ancient world; they had to show the authors of antiquity, the men they were and the men they portray for us, in such a way as to leave in the shadows everything that was genuinely pagan about them, everything that makes them men of a particular city at a particular time, in order to highlight only those respects in which they are simply men, men as they are at all times and in all places. All the legends, all the traditions, all the religious ideas of Rome and Greece were interpreted in this spirit so as to give them a meaning any good Christian could accept.

Thus the Greco-Roman environment in which they made their pupils live was emptied of everything specifically Greek or Roman, so that it became a kind of unreal, idealized environment peopled by personalities who had no doubt historically existed but who were presented in such a way that they had, so to speak, nothing historical about them. They were now simply figures betokening certain virtues and vices and all the great passions of humanity. Achilles is courage; Ulysses is wily prudence; Numa is the archetype of the pious king; Caesar, the man of ambition; Augustus, the powerful monarch and lover of learning; etc. Such general and unspecific types could easily be used to exemplify the precepts of Christian morality.

Such disinheriting of antiquity was made easier for the Jesuits by the fact that, at least for a long time, all teaching of history was almost completely absent from their colleges. Even literary history was unknown. A writer's works were expounded without anyone's bothering to notice the physiognomy of the author, his manner, the way he related it to his age, to his environment, to his predecessors. His historical personality mattered so little that it was normal to study not an author, not even a work, but selected passages and extracts. How was it possible to form a picture of a specific man out of such sparse and disjointed fragments, among which his individuality was dispersed and dissolved? Each of these pieces could scarcely appear to be anything other than an isolated model of literary style, a sort of fair copy of exceptional authoritativeness.

We can now understand better how it came about that the Jesuits, and perhaps to a lesser extent so many other educators, tended to attribute to the past and especially to the distant past an educational value greater than that which they attributed to the present. This was because the past, at least at a time when the historical sciences have not advanced sufficiently to render it almost as precise and specific as the present—the past, because we see it from afar, naturally appears to us in vague, fluid, unstable forms, which are consequently all the easier to mold according to our will. It constitutes a more malleable and plastic substance that we can transform and present according to our fancy. It is thus easier to bend it for educational purposes. These people, these things from former times, we embellish without realizing we are deceiving ourselves in order to turn them into models for youth to imitate. The present, because it is before our very eyes, forces itself upon our attention and does not lend itself to this kind of reworking; it is virtually impossible for us to see it other than as it is with its ugliness, its mediocrity, its vices, and its failings; and this is why it seems to us ill-adapted to serve our educational ends. It was in this way that antiquity in the hands of the Jesuits could become an instrument for Christian education, whereas they would not have been able to utilize literature of their own age in the same way, imbued as it was with the spirit of rebellion against the church. In their desire to attain their goal, they had a powerful vested interest in fleeing from the moderns and taking refuge in antiquity....

But so far we have only studied the Jesuits' teaching. We must now consider their disciplinary structures. It is perhaps in this area that they showed the most art and originality and it is their superiority in this respect that best explains their success.

Their entire discipline was founded upon two principles.

The first was that there can be no good education without contact at once continuous and personal between the pupil and the educator—and this principle served a dual purpose. First, it ensured that the pupil was never left to his own devices. To be properly molded he had to be subjected to pressure that never let up or flagged; for the spirit of evil is constantly watchful. This is why the Jesuits' pupil was never alone. "A supervisor would follow him everywhere, to church, to class, to the refectory, to his recreation; in the living quarters and sleeping quarters he was always there examining everything." But this supervision was not intended only to prevent misconduct. It was also to enable the Jesuit to study at his ease "character and habits so that he might manage to discover the most suitable method of directing each individual child." In other words, this direct and constant intercourse was supposed not only to render the educational process more sustained in its effect but also to make it more personal and better suited to the personality of each pupil. Father Jouvency never stops recommending that a teacher not limit himself to exerting a general and impersonal influence on the anonymous crowd of pupils but rather graduate his influence and vary it according to age, intelligence, and situation. If he is conversing with a child in private, "let him examine the child's character so that he can mold what he says in accordance with it and, as they say, 'hook' his interlocutor with the appropriate bait." And the better to get the pupils to open their minds to him, he will need to make them open their hearts by endearing himself. Indeed there can be no doubt that in the course of the relationships thus cemented between teachers and pupils, bonds of friendship were frequently formed that survived school life. Thus Descartes remained very sincerely attached to his former teachers at La Flèche.

One can readily imagine how effective this system of continuous immersion must have been. The child's moral environment followed him wherever he went; all around him he heard the same ideas and the same sentiments being expressed with the same authority. He could never lose sight of them. He knew of no others. And in addition to the fact that this influence never ceased to make itself felt, it was also all the more powerful because it knew how best to adapt to the diversity of individual personalities, because it was most familiar with the openings through which it could slip and insinuate itself in the pupil's heart. By comparison with the style of discipline that had been practiced in the Middle Ages this represented a major revolution. The medieval teacher addressed himself to large and impersonal audiences, among which each individual, that is to say each student, was lost, drowned, and consequently abandoned to his own devices. Now, education is essentially an individual matter, and as long as the medieval teacher was dealing with vast masses he could obtain only very crude results. Hence the rowdy indiscipline of the students of the Middle Ages, which the establishment of the fully residential colleges was an attempt—never fully successful—to counter. For the colleges did not have at their disposal a staff of teachers and supervisors sufficiently numerous or perhaps sufficiently committed to the task of supervision to be able to exercise the necessary control and influence over each individual.

But in order to train pupils in intensive formal work, which was moreover pretty lacking in substance, it was not enough to surround them, to envelop them at close quarters with solicitude and vigilance; it was not enough to be constantly concerned to contain and sustain them; it was also necessary to stimulate them. The goad which the Jesuits employed consisted exclusively of competition. Not only were they the first to organize the competitive system in the colleges, they also developed it to a greater intensity than it has ever subsequently known.

Although today in our classrooms this system still has considerable importance, nevertheless it no longer functions without interruption. It is fair to say that with the Jesuits it was never suspended for a single moment. The entire class was organized to promote this end. The pupils were divided into two camps, the Romans on the one hand and the Carthaginians on the other, who lived, so to speak, on the brink of war, each striving to outstrip the other. Each camp had its own dignitaries. At the head of the camp there was an imperator, also known as dictator or consul, then came a praetor, a tribune, and some senators. These honors, which were naturally coveted and contested, were distributed as the outcome of a competition, which was held monthly. From another point of view, each camp was divided into groups consisting of ten pupils each ("decuries"), commanded by a captain (called the "decurion") who was selected from among the worthies we have just mentioned. These groups were not recruited at random. There was a hierarchy among them: the first groups were composed of the best pupils, the last groups of the weakest and least industrious of the scholars. Thus just as the camp as a whole was in competition with the opposite camp, so in each camp each group had its own immediate rival in the other camp at the equivalent level. Finally, individuals themselves were matched and each soldier in a group had his opposite number in the opposing group. Thus academic work involved a kind of perpetual hand-to-hand combat. Camp challenged camp; group struggled with group; pupils supervised one another, corrected one another, and took one another to task. On some occasions the teacher was not supposed to be afraid of pitting together two pupils of unequal ability. For example, an able pupil would have his work corrected by a less able pupil, says Father Jouvency, "so that those who have made mistakes may be the more ashamed and the more mortified by them." It was even possible for any pupil to do battle with a pupil from a higher group and, if victorious, to take his place.

It is interesting to note that these various ennoblements carried with them not only honorific titles but also active functions; and indeed it was these that constituted the prize. The captain enjoyed extensive powers. Seated opposite his group he was responsible for maintaining silence and attentiveness among his ten scholars, noting down absences, making the scholars recite their lessons, ensuring that assignments had been done with care and completed. The consuls exercised the same authority over the captains in their camp that these did over their own group members. Everyone was thus kept constantly in suspense. Never has the idea that the classroom is a small organized society been realized so systematically. It was a city-state where every pupil was a functionary. Moreover, it was thanks to this division of labor between the teacher and the pupils that one teacher was able without too much difficulty to run classes that sometimes numbered as many as two or three hundred pupils.

In addition to such regularly recurring competitions there were intermittent competitions too numerous to list. From time to time the best pieces of work were affixed to the classroom doors; the most noteworthy were read publicly in either the refectory or the Hall of Acts. Aside from the annual prize-giving, which took place solemnly to the sound of trumpets, prizes were given out spasmodically in the course of the year for a good piece of declamation, for a meritorious literary work, for a well executed dance, etc. From the second form onwards there was in each grade an Academy to which only the best pupils belonged. Then there were all kinds of public meetings in which the most brilliant pupils appeared and to which the families came to hear and applaud them. Thus an infinite wealth of devices maintained the self-esteem of the pupils in a constant state of extreme excitation.

Here again the Jesuits were effecting a revolution compared with what had gone before. We have seen that in the University and the colleges of the Middle Ages the system of competition was completely unknown; there were no rewards to recompense merit and induce effort, and exams were organized in such a way that for conscientious pupils they were little more than a formality. And here we have, quite suddenly, a totally different system, which not only establishes itself but which instantaneously develops to the point of superabundance. It is easier to understand now how the training given by the Jesuits managed to acquire the intensive character which we were recently remarking upon. Their entire system of discipline was organized towards this goal. The state of constant competition in which the pupils lived incited them to strain all the resources of their intelligence and will-power and indeed rendered this essential. At the same time the careful supervision to which they were subjected diminished the possibility of lapses. They felt themselves guided, sustained, encouraged. Thus everything induced them to exert themselves. As a result, within the colleges there was genuinely intense activity, no doubt flawed by being expended on the superficial rather than on the profound, but whose existence was incontestable.

However, now that we have noted the transformations that the Jesuits initiated in the realm of school discipline, we must seek their causes. Where did these two new principles come from? Did they derive exclusively from the particular aim the Jesuits were pursuing, from the very nature of their institution, from the mission they had assigned themselves, or were they not, by contrast, rather the effect of more general causes, were they not a response to some change that had occurred in public thought and ethics?

What must immediately rule out the first hypothesis is the fact that if the Jesuits were the first to realize these principles in academic practice, they had nevertheless been recognized and proclaimed already by the educational thinkers of the Renaissance. We remember Montaigne's protests against teachers unintelligent enough to wish to regiment the minds of all individuals in identical fashion. He too wants teachers to study the temperament of the pupil, to test him in order to understand him better, to make him, as he says, "run in front of himself" in order to be able to guide him in an enlightened way. And from another point of view, we have seen that the love of glory, the thirst for praise, and the sentiment of honor were for Rabelais and for Erasmus, as for the major thinkers of the sixteenth century, the essential motives for all intellectual activity and consequently for all academic activity. The Jesuits were thus on these two points, at least in principle, in agreement with their time. It is interesting to note that we know of at least one college where, before the time of the Jesuits, the competitive system was organized and practiced, moreover, in a form that in more than one respect resembled the one we have just described. This is the college at Guyenne, where Montaigne spent several years. The pupils in any one class were divided according to ability into sections that bore considerable resemblance to the Jesuits' groups of ten. Examinations took place frequently in which the pupils of one class were questioned by the pupils from a higher class or section. And here again we encounter competitions in public speaking, which took place before the assembly of all the classes.

It was the fact that a great change had taken place in the moral constitution of society that made this double change in the system of academic discipline necessary. In the seventeenth century the individual played a much greater part in social life than that which had hitherto been accorded to him. If, in the Middle Ages, teaching was impersonal, if it could be addressed diffusely to the indistinct crowd of pupils without any disadvantage, this was because at that time the notion of individual personality was still relatively undeveloped. The movements that occurred in the Middle Ages were mass movements carrying along large groups of human beings in the same direction, in the midst of which individuals became lost. It was Europe in its entirety that rose up at the time of the Crusades; it was the whole of cultivated European society that soon afterwards, under the influence of a veritable collective urge, flooded towards Paris to receive instruction. The didactic style of the time was thus in accord with the moral condition of society.

With the Renaissance, by contrast, the individual began to acquire self-consciousness; he was no longer, at least in enlightened circles, merely an undifferentiated fraction of the whole; in a sense, he was himself already a whole, he was a person with his own physiognomy who had and who experienced at least the need to fashion for himself his own way of thinking and feeling. We know that at this period there occurred, as it were, a sudden blossoming of great personalities. Now, it is quite clear that in proportion as people's consciousness becomes individualized, education itself must become individualized. From the moment it is required to exert its influence on distinct and heterogeneous individuals it cannot continue to develop in blanket fashion, homogeneously and uniformly. Thus education had to be diversified, and this was only possible if the educator, instead of remaining distant from the pupil, came close to him to get to know him better and to be able to vary his actions according to his individual nature.

But from another point of view, it is equally clear that an individual possessed of self-awareness, with his own set of beliefs and interests, cannot be motivated or trained to act by the methods applicable to an amorphous crowd. For the latter methods mighty shakings of the foundations are needed, powerful collective impressions of a rather vague and general kind, like those that sent tremors through the multitudes gathered around Abélard on the Montagne Sainte-Geneviève. By contrast, in proportion as each individual has his own particular moral life he must be moved by considerations specifically appropriate to him. Thus one must indeed appeal to self-esteem, to the sense of personal dignity, to what the Germans call *Selbstgefühl*. It is no accident that competition becomes more lively and plays a more substantial role in society as the movement towards individualization becomes more advanced. And so, since the moral organization of the school must reflect that of civil society, since the methods that are applied to the child cannot differ in essence from those that later on will be applied to the man, it is clear that the processes of the medieval disciplinary system could not survive; it is clear that discipline had to become more personal, to take greater account of individual feelings, and consequently to allow for a degree of competitiveness.

There was thus nothing intrinsically arbitrary about the two innovations the Jesuits introduced into the disciplinary system: the principle underlying them, at least, was well-grounded in the nature of things, that is to say in the condition of society in the sixteenth century. But if the principle was right, if it was to be retained, if it deserved to survive, the Jesuits applied it in the spirit of extremism that is one feature of their academic policy and, simply by doing this, they denatured it. It was good to keep close to the child in order to be able to guide him confidently; the Jesuits came so close to him that they inhibited all his freedom of movement. And in this way the method worked against the end it was meant to serve. It was wise to get to know the child well in order to be able to help in the development of his nascent personality. The Jesuits, however, studied him in order to stifle more effectively his sense of self—and this was a potential source of schism. At least, once they had recognized the value of rivalry and competitiveness, they made such immoderate use of them that the pupils were virtually at war with one another. How can we fail to consider immoral an academic organization that appealed only to egotistical sentiments? Was there then no means of keeping the pupils active other than by tempting them with such paltry bait?

Functional and Conflict Theories of Educational Stratification

RANDALL COLLINS

Education has become highly important in occupational attainment in modern America, and thus occupies a central place in the analysis of stratification and of social mobility. This paper attempts to assess the adequacy of two theories in accounting for available evidence on the link between education and stratification: a functional theory concerning trends in technical skill requirements in industrial societies; and a conflict theory derived from the approach of Max Weber, stating the determinants of various outcomes in the struggles among status groups. It will be argued that the evidence best supports the conflict theory, although technical requirements have important effects in particular contexts. It will be further argued that the construction of a general theory of the determinants of stratification in its varying forms is best advanced by incorporating elements of the functional analysis of technical requirements of specific jobs at appropriate points within the conflict model. The conclusion offers an interpretation of historical change in education and stratification in industrial America, and suggests where further evidence is required for more precise tests and for further development of a comprehensive explanatory theory.

The Importance of Education

A number of studies have shown that the number of years of education is a strong determinant of occupational achievement in America with social origins constant. They also show that social origins affect educational attainment, and also occupational attainment after the completion of education (Blau and Duncan, 1967:163–205; Eckland, 1965; Sewell et al., 1969; Duncan and Hodge, 1963; Lipset and Bendix, 1959:189–192). There are differences in occupational attainment independent of social origins between the graduates of more prominent and less prominent secondary schools, colleges, graduate schools, and law schools (Smigel, 1964:39, 73–74, 117; Havemann and West, 1952:179–181; Ladinsky, 1967; Hargens and Hagstrom, 1967).

Educational requirements for employment have become increasingly widespread, not only in elite occupations but also at the bottom of the occupational hierarchy (see Table 3.1). In a 1967 survey of the San Francisco, Oakland, and San Jose areas (Collins, 1969), 17% of the employers surveyed required at least a high school diploma for employment in even unskilled positions;[1] a national survey (Bell, 1940) in 1937–1938 found a comparable figure of 1%. At the same time, educational requirements appear to have become more specialized, with 38% of the organizations in the 1967 survey which required college degrees of managers preferring business administration training, and an additional 15% preferring engineering training; such requirements appear to have been virtually unknown in the 1920s (Pierson, 1959:34–54). At the same time, the proportions of the American population attending

Table 3.I Percent of Employers Requiring Various Minimum Levels of Employees, by Occupational Level

	Unskilled	Semiskilled	Skilled	Clerical	Managerial	Professional
National Survey, 1937–38						
Less than high school	99%	97%	89%	33%	32%	9%
High school diploma	1	3	11	63	54	16
Some college				1	2	23
College degree				3	12	52
	100%	100%	100%	100%	100%	100%
San Francisco Bay Area, 1967						
Less than high school	83%	76%	62%	29%	27%	10%
High School diploma	16	24	28	68	14	4
Vocational training beyond high school	1	1	10	2	2	4
Some college				2	12	7
College degree					41	70
Graduate degree					3	5
	100%	100%	100%	101%	99%	100%
	(244)	(237)	(245)	(306)	(288)	(240)

schools through the completion of high school and advanced levels have risen sharply during the last century (Table 3.2). Careers are thus increasingly shaped within the educational system.

The Technical-Function Theory of Education

A common explanation of the importance of education in modern society may be termed the technical-function theory. Its basic propositions, found in a number of sources (see, for example, B.

Table 3.2 Percentage Educational Attainment in the United States, 1869–1965

Period	High School graduates/ pop. 17 yrs. old	Resident college students/ pop. 18–21	B.A.s or 1st prof. degrees/ 1/10 of pop. 15–24	M.A.s or 2nd prof. degrees/ 1/10 of pop. 25–34	Ph.D.s 1/10 of pop. 25–34
1869–1870	2.0	1.7			
1879–1880	2.5	2.7			
1889–1890	3.5	3.0			
1899–1900	6.4	4.0	1.66	0.12	0.03
1909–1910	8.8	5.1	1.85	0.13	0.02
1919–1920	16.8	8.9	2.33	0.24	0.03
1929–1930	29.0	12.4	4.90	0.78	0.12
1939–1940	50.8	15.6	7.05	1.24	0.15
1949–1950	59.0	29.6	17.66	2.43	0.27
1959–1960	65.1	34.9	17.72	3.25	0.42
1963	76.3	38.0			
1965			19.71	5.02	0.73

Clark, 1962; Kerr et al., 1960), may be stated as follows: (1) the skill requirements of jobs in industrial society constantly increase because of technological change. Two processes are involved: (a) the proportion of jobs requiring low skill decreases and the proportion requiring high skill increases; and (b) the same jobs are upgraded in skill requirements. (2) Formal education provides the training, either in specific skills or in general capacities, necessary for the more highly skilled jobs. (3) Therefore, educational requirements for employment constantly rise, and increasingly larger proportions of the population are required to spend longer and longer periods in school.

The technical-function theory of education may be seen as a particular application of a more general functional approach. The functional theory of stratification (Davis and Moore, 1945) rests on the premises (A) that occupational positions require particular kinds of skilled performance; and (B) that positions must be filled with persons who have either the native ability, or who have acquired the training, necessary for the performance of the given occupational role.[2]

The technical-function theory of education may be viewed as a subtype of this form of analysis, since it shares the premises that the occupational structure creates demands for particular kinds of performance, and that training is one way of filling these demands. In addition, it includes the more restrictive premises (1 and 2 above) concerning the way in which skill requirements of jobs change with industrialization, and concerning the content of school experiences.

The technical-function theory of education may be tested by reviewing the evidence for each of its propositions (1a, 1b, and 2).[3] As will be seen, these propositions do not adequately account for the evidence. In order to generate a more complete explanation, it will be necessary to examine the evidence for the underlying functional propositions, (A) and (B). This analysis leads to a focus on the processes of stratification—notably group conflict—not expressed in the functional theory, and to the formalization of a conflict theory to account for the evidence.

Proposition (1a): *Educational requirements of jobs in industrial society increase because the proportion of jobs requiring low skill decreases and the proportion requiring high skill increases.* Available evidence suggests that this process accounts for only a minor part of educational upgrading, at least in a society that has passed the point of initial industrialization. Fifteen percent of the increase in education of the U. S. labor force during the twentieth century may be attributed to shifts in the occupational structure—a decrease in the proportion of jobs with low skill requirements and an increase in proportion of jobs with high skill requirements (Folger and Nam, 1964). The bulk of educational upgrading (85%) has occurred *within* job categories.

Proposition (1b): *Educational requirements of jobs in industrial society rise because the same jobs are upgraded in skill requirements.* The only available evidence on this point consists of data collected by the U. S. Department of Labor in 1950 and 1960, which indicate the amount of change in skill requirements of specific jobs. Under the most plausible assumptions as to the skills provided by various levels of education, it appears that the educational level of the U. S. labor force has changed in excess of that which is necessary to keep up with skill requirements of jobs (Berg, 1970:38–60). Over-education for available jobs is found particularly among males who have graduated from college and females with high school degrees or some college, and appears to have increased between 1950 and 1960.

Proposition (2): *Formal education provides required job skills.* This proposition may be tested in two ways: (a) Are better educated employees more productive than less educated employees? (b) Are vocational skills learned in schools, or elsewhere?

(a) *Are better educated employees more productive?* The evidence most often cited for the productive effects of education is indirect, consisting of relationships between *aggregate* levels of education in a society and its overall economic productivity. These are of three types:

(i) The national growth approach involves calculating the proportion of growth in the U. S. Gross National Product attributable to conventional inputs of capital and labor; these leave a large residual, which is attributed to improvements in skill of the labor force based on increased education (Schultz,

1961; Denison, 1965). This approach suffers from difficulty in clearly distinguishing among technological change affecting productive arrangements, changes in the abilities of workers acquired by experience at work with new technologies, and changes in skills due to formal education and motivational factors associated with a competitive or achievement-oriented society. The assignment of a large proportion of the residual category to education is arbitrary. Denison (1965) makes this attribution on the basis of the increased income to persons with higher levels of education interpreted as rewards for their contributions to productivity. Although it is a common assumption in economic argument that wage returns reflect output value, wage returns cannot be used to prove the productive contribution of education without circular reasoning.

(ii) Correlations of education and level of economic development for nations show that the higher the level of economic development of a country, the higher the proportion of its population in elementary, secondary, and higher education (Harbison and Myers, 1964). Such correlations beg the question of causality. There are considerable variations in school enrollments among countries at the same economic level, and many of these variations are explicable in terms of political demands for access to education (Ben-David, 1963–64). Also, the overproduction of educated personnel in countries whose level of economic development cannot absorb them suggests the demand for education need not come directly from the economy, and may run counter to economic needs (Hoselitz, 1965).

(iii) Time-lag correlations of education and economic development show that increases in the proportion of population in elementary school precede increases in economic development after a takeoff point at approximately 30–50% of the 7–14 years old age-group in school. Similar anticipations of economic development are suggested for increases in secondary and higher education enrollment, although the data do not clearly support this conclusion (Peaslee, 1969). A pattern of advances in secondary school enrollments preceding advances in economic development is found only in a small number of cases (12 of 37 examined in Peaslee, 1969). A pattern of growth of university enrollments and subsequent economic development is found in 21 of 37 cases, but the exceptions (including the United States, France, Sweden, Russia, and Japan) are of such importance as to throw serious doubt on any *necessary* contribution of higher education to economic development. The main contribution of education to economic productivity, then, appears to occur at the level of the transition to mass literacy, and not significantly beyond this level.

Direct evidence of the contribution of education to *individual* productivity is summarized by Berg (1970:85–104, 143–176). It indicates that the better educated employees are not generally more productive, and in some cases are less productive, among samples of factory workers, maintenance men, department store clerks, technicians, secretaries, bank tellers, engineers, industrial research scientists, military personnel, and federal civil service employers.

(b) *Are vocational skills learned in school, or elsewhere?* Specifically vocational education in the schools for manual positions is virtually independent of job fate, as graduates of vocational programs are not more likely to be employed than high school dropouts (Plunkett, 1960; Duncan, 1964). Most skilled manual workers acquire their skills on the job or casually (Clark and Sloan, 1966:73). Retraining for important technological changes in industry has been carried out largely informally on-the-job; in only a very small proportion of jobs affected by technological change is formal retraining in educational institutions used (Collins, 1969: 147–158; Bright, 1958).

The relevance of education for nonmanual occupational skills is more difficult to evaluate. Training in specific professions, such as medicine, engineering, scientific or scholarly research, teaching, and law can plausibly be considered vocationally relevant, and possibly essential. Evidences comparing particular degrees of educational success with particular kinds of occupational performance or success are not available, except for a few occupations. For engineers, high college grades and degree levels generally predict high levels of technical responsibility and high participation in professional activities, but not necessarily high salary or supervisory responsibility (Perrucci and Perrucci, 1970).

At the same time, a number of practicing engineers lack college degrees (about 40% of engineers in the early 1950s; see Soderberg, 1963:213), suggesting that even such highly technical skills may be acquired on the job. For academic research scientists, educational quality has little effect on subsequent productivity (Hagstrom and Hargens, 1968). For other professions, evidence is not available on the degree to which actual skills are learned in school rather than in practice. In professions such as medicine and law, where education is a legal requirement for admission to practice, a comparison group of noneducated practitioners is not available, at least in the modern era.

Outside of the traditional learned professions, the plausibility of the vocational importance of education is more questionable. Comparisons of the efforts of different occupations to achieve "professionalization" suggest that setting educational requirements and bolstering them through licensing laws is a common tactic in raising an occupation's prestige and autonomy (Wilensky, 1964). The result has been the proliferation of numerous pseudo-professions in modern society; nevertheless these fail to achieve strong professional organization through lack of a monpolizable (and hence teachable) skill base. Business administration schools represent such an effort. (See Pierson, 1959: 9, 55–95, 140; Gordon and Howell, 1959:1–18, 40, 324–337). Descriptions of general, nonvocational education do not support the image of schools as places where skills are widely learned. Scattered studies suggest that the knowledge imparted in particular courses is retained only in small part through the next few years (Learned and Wood, 1938:28), and indicate a dominant student culture concerned with nonacademic interests or with achieving grades with a minimum of learning (Coleman, 1961; Becker et al., 1968).

The technical-function theory of education, then, does not give an adequate account of the evidence. Economic evidence indicates no clear contributions of education to economic development, beyond the provisions of mass literacy. Shifts in the proportions of more skilled and less skilled jobs do not account for the observed increase in education of the American labor force. Education is often irrelevant to on-the-job productivity and is sometimes counter-productive; specifically, vocational training seems to be derived more from work experience than from formal school training. The quality of schools themselves, and the nature of dominant student cultures suggest that schooling is very inefficient as a means of training for work skills.

Functional and Conflict Perspectives

It may be suggested that the inadequacies of the technical-function theory of education derive from a more basic source: the functional approach to stratification. A fundamental assumption is that there is a generally fixed set of positions, whose various requirements the labor force must satisfy. The fixed demand for skills of various types, at any given time, is the basic determinant of who will be selected for what positions. Social change may then be explained by specifying how these functional demands change with the process of modernization. In keeping with the functional perspective in general, the needs of society are seen as determining the behavior and the rewards of the individuals within it.

However, this premise may be questioned as an adequate picture of the fundamental processes of social organization. It may be suggested that the "demands" of any occupational position are not fixed, but represent whatever behavior is settled upon in bargaining between the persons who fill the positions and those who attempt to control them. Individuals want jobs primarily for the rewards to themselves in material goods, power, and prestige. The amount of productive skill they must demonstrate to hold their positions depends on how much clients, customers, or employers can successfully demand of them, and this in turn depends on the balance of power between workers and their employers.

Employers tend to have quite imprecise conceptions of the skill requirements of most jobs, and operate on a strategy of "satisficing" rather than optimizing—that is, setting average levels of performance as satisfactory, and making changes in procedures or personnel only when performance falls noticeably below minimum standards (Dill et al., 1962; March and Simon, 1958:140–141). Efforts to predict work performance by objective tests have foundered due to difficulties in measuring performance (except on specific mechanical tasks) and the lack of control groups to validate the tests (Anastasi, 1967). Organizations do not force their employees to work at maximum efficiency; there is considerable insulation of workers at all levels from demands for full use of their skills and efforts. Informal controls over output are found not only among production workers in manufacturing but also among sales and clerical personnel (Roy, 1952; Blau, 1955; Lombard, 1955). The existence of informal organization at the managerial level, the widespread existence of bureaucratic pathologies such as evasion of responsibility, empire-building, and displacement of means by ends ("red tape"), and the fact that administrative work is only indirectly related to the output of the organization, suggest that managers, too, are insulated from strong technological pressures for use of technical skills. On all levels, wherever informal organization exists, it appears that standards of performance reflect the power of the groups involved.

In this light, it is possible to reinterpret the body of evidence that ascriptive factors continue to be important in occupational success even in advanced industrial society. The social mobility data summarized at the onset of this paper show that social origins have a direct effect on occupational success, even after the completion of education. Both case studies and cross-sectional samples amply document widespread discrimination against Negroes. Case studies show that the operation of ethnic and class standards in employment based not merely on skin color but on name, accent, style of dress, manners, and conversational abilities (Noland and Bakke, 1949; Turner, 1952; Taeuber *et al.*, 1966; Nosow, 1956). Cross-sectional studies, based on both biographical and survey data, show that approximately 60 to 70% of the American business elite come from upper-class and upper-middle-class families, and fewer than 15% from working-class families (Taussig and Joselyn, 1932:97; Warner and Abegglen, 1955:37–68; Newcomer, 1955:53; Bendix, 1956:198–253; Mills, 1963:110–139). These proportions are fairly constant from the early 1800s through the 1950s. The business elite is overwhelmingly Protestant, male, and completely white, although there are some indications of a mild trend toward declining social origins and an increase of Catholics and Jews. Ethnic and class background have been found crucial for career advancement in the professions as well (Ladinsky, 1963; Hall, 1946). Sexual stereotyping of jobs is extremely widespread (Collins, 1969:234–238).

In the traditional functionalist approach, these forms of ascription are treated as residual categories: carry-overs from a less advanced period, or marks of the imperfections of the functional mechanism of placement. Yet available trend data suggest that the link between social class origins and occupational attainment has remained constant during the twentieth century in America (Blau and Duncan, 1967:81–113); the proportion of women in higher occupational levels has changed little since the late nineteenth century (Epstein, 1970:7); and the few available comparisons between elite groups in traditional and modern societies suggest comparable levels of mobility (Marsh, 1963). Declines in racial and ethnic discrimination that appear to have occurred at periods in twentieth-century America may be plausibly explained as results of political mobilization of particular minority groups rather than by an increased economic need to select by achievement criteria.

Goode (1967) has offered a modified functional model to account for these disparities: that work groups always organize to protect their inept members from being judged by outsiders' standards of productivity, and that this self-protection is functional to the organizations, preventing a Hobbesian competitiveness and distrust of all against all. This argument re-establishes a functional explanation, but only at the cost of undermining the technological view of functional requirements. Further, Goode's conclusions can be put in other terms: it is to the advantage of groups of employees to organize so that they will not be judged by strict performance standards; and it is at least minimally to the advantage of the employer to let them do so, for if he presses them harder he creates dissension and alienation. Just how hard an employer *can* press his employees is not given in Goode's functional model. That is, his model has the disadvantage, common to functional analysis in its most general form, of covering too many alternative possibilities to provide testable explanations of specific outcomes. Functional analysis too easily operates as a justification for whatever particular pattern exists, asserting in effect that there is a proper reason for it to be so, but failing to state the conditions under which a particular pattern will hold rather than another. The technical version of job requirements has the advantage of specifying patterns, but it is this specific form of functional explanation that is jettisoned by a return to a more abstract functional analysis.

A second hypothesis may be suggested: the power of "ascribed" groups may be the *prime* basis of selection in all organizations, and technical skills are secondary considerations depending on the balance of power. Education may thus be regarded as a mark of membership in a particular group (possibly at times its defining characteristic), not a mark of technical skills or achievement. Educational requirements may thus reflect the interests of whichever groups have power to set them. Weber (1968:1000) interpreted educational requirements in bureaucracies, drawing especially on the history of public administration in Prussia, as the result of efforts by university graduates to monopolize positions, raise their corporate status, and thereby increase their own security and power vis-à-vis both higher authorities and clients. Gusfield (1958) has shown that educational requirements in the British Civil Service were set as the result of a power struggle between a victorious educated upper-middle-class and the traditional aristocracy.

To summarize the argument to this point: available evidence suggests that the technical-functional view of educational requirements for jobs leaves a large number of facts unexplained. Functional analysis on the more abstract level does not provide a testable explanation of which ascribed groups will be able to dominate which positions. To answer this question, one must leave the functional frame of reference and examine the conditions of relative power of each group.

A Conflict Theory of Stratification

The conditions under which educational requirements will be set and changed may be stated more generally, on the basis of a conflict theory of stratification derived from Weber (1968:926–939; see also Collins, 1968), and from advances in modern organization theory fitting the spirit of this approach.

A. *Status groups.* The basic units of society are associational groups sharing common cultures (or "subcultures"). The core of such groups is families and friends, but they may be etxended to religious, educational, or ethnic communities. In general, they comprise all persons who share a sense of status equality based on participation in a common culture: styles of language, tastes in clothing and decor, manners and other ritual observances, conversational topics and styles, opinions and values, and preferences in sports, arts, and media. Participation in such cultural groups gives individuals their fundamental sense of identity, especially in contrast with members of other associational groups in whose everyday culture they cannot participate comfortably. Subjectively, status groups distinguish themselves from others in terms of categories of *moral evaluation* such as "honor," "taste," "breeding," "respectability," "propriety," "cultivation," "good fellows," "plain folks," etc. Thus the exclusion of persons who lack the ingroup culture is felt to be normatively legitimated.

There is no *a priori* determination of the number of status groups in a particular society, nor can the degree to which there is consensus on a rank order among them be stated in advance. These are not matters of definition, but empirical variations, the causes of which are subjects of other developments of the conflict theory of stratification. Status groups should be regarded as ideal types, without implication of *necessarily distinct* boundaries; the concepts remain useful even in the case where associational groupings and their status cultures are fluid and overlapping, as hypotheses about the conflicts among status groups may remain fruitful even under these circumstances.

Status groups may be derived from a number of sources. Weber outlines three: (a) differences in life style based on economic situation (i.e., class); (b) differences in life situation based on power position; (c) differences in life situation deriving directly from cultural conditions or institutions, such as geographical origin, ethnicity, religion, education, or intellectual or aesthetic cultures.

B. *Struggle for Advantage.* There is a continual struggle in society for various "goods"—wealth, power, or prestige. We need make no assumption that every individual is motivated to maximize his rewards; however, since power and prestige are inherently scarce commodities, and wealth is often contingent upon them, the ambition of even a small proportion of persons for more than equal shares of these goods sets up an implicit counter-struggle on the part of others to avoid subjection and disesteem. Individuals may struggle with each other, but since individual identity is derived primarily from membership in a status group, and because the cohesion of status groups is a key resource in the struggle against others, the primary focus of struggle is between status groups rather than within them.

The struggle for wealth, power, and prestige is carried out primarily through organizations. There have been struggles throughout history among organizations controlled by different status groups, for military conquest, business advantage, or cultural (e.g., religious) hegemony, and intricate sorts of interorganizational alliances are possible. In the more complex societies, struggle between status groups is carried on in large part *within* organizations, as the status groups controlling an organization coerce, hire, or culturally manipulate others to carry out their wishes (as in, respectively, a conscript army, a business, or a church). Organizational research shows that the success of organizational elites in controlling their subordinates is quite variable. Under particular conditions, lower or middle members have considerable *de facto* power to avoid compliance, and even to change the course of the organizations (see Etzioni, 1961).

This opposing power from below is strengthened when subordinate members constitute a cohesive status group of their own; it is weakened when subordinates acquiesce in the values of the organization elite. Coincidence of ethnic and class boundaries produces the sharpest cultural distinctions. Thus, Catholics of immigrant origins have been the bulwarks of informal norms restricting work output in American firms run by WASPs, whereas Protestants of native rural backgrounds are the main "rate-busters" (O. Coffins *et al.,* 1946). Selection and manipulation of members in terms of status groups is thus a key weapon in intraorganizational struggles. In general, the organization elite selects its new members and key assistants from its own status group and makes an effort to secure lower-level employees who are at least indoctrinated to respect the cultural superiority of their status culture.[4]

Once groups of employees of different status groups are formed at various positions (middle, lower, or laterally differentiated) in the organization, each of these groups may be expected to launch efforts to recruit more members of their own status group. This process is illustrated by conflicts among whites and blacks, Protestants and Catholics and Jews, Yankee, Irish and Italian, etc. found in American occupational life (Hughes, 1949; Dalton, 1951). These conflicts are based on ethnically or religiously founded status cultures; their intensity rises and falls with processes increasing or decreasing the cultural distinctiveness of these groups, and with the succession of advantages and disadvantages set by previous outcomes of these struggles which determine the organizational resources available for further struggle. Parallel processes of cultural conflict may be based on distinctive class as well as ethnic cultures.

C. *Education As Status Culture.* The main activity of schools is to teach particular status cultures, both in and outside the classroom. In this light, any failure of schools to impart technical knowledge (although it may also be successful in this) is not important; schools primarily teach vocabulary and inflection, styles of dress, aesthetic tastes, values and manners. The emphasis on sociability and athletics found in many schools is not extraneous but may be at the core of the status culture propagated by the schools. Where schools have a more academic or vocational emphasis, this emphasis may itself be the content of a particular status culture, providing sets of values, materials for conversation, and shared activities for an associational group making claims to a particular basis for status.

Insofar as a particular status group controls education, it may use it to foster control within work organizations. Educational requirements for employment can serve both to select new members for elite positions who share the elite culture and, at a lower level of education, to hire lower and middle employees who have acquired a general respect for these elite values and styles.

Tests of the Conflict Theory of Educational Stratification

The conflict theory in its general form is supported by evidence (1) that there are distinctions among status group cultures—based both on class and on ethnicity—in modern societies (Kahl, 1957:127–156, 184–220); (2) that status groups tend to occupy different occupational positions within organizations (see data on ascription cited above); and (3) that occupants of different organizational positions struggle over power (Dalton, 1959; Crozier, 1964). The more specific tests called for here, however, are of the adequacy of conflict theory to explain the link between education and occupational stratification. Such tests may focus either on the proposed mechanism of occupational placement, or on the conditions for strong or weak links between education and occupation.

Education as a Mechanism of Occupational Placement. The mechanism proposed is that employers use education to select persons who have been socialized into the dominant status culture: for entrants to their own managerial ranks, into elite culture; for lower-level employees, into an attitude of respect for the dominant culture and the elite which carries it. This requires evidence that: (a) schools provide either training for the elite culture, or respect for it; and (b) employers use education as a means of selection for cultural attributes.

(a) Historical and descriptive studies of schools support the generalization that they are places where particular status cultures are acquired, either from the teachers, from other students, or both. Schools are usually founded by powerful or autonomous status groups, either to provide an exclusive education for their own children, or to propagate respect for their cultural values. Until recently most schools were founded by religions, often in opposition to those founded by rival religions; throughout the 19th century, this rivalry was an important basis for the founding of large numbers of colleges in the U. S., and of the Catholic and Lutheran school systems. The public school system in the U. S. was founded mainly under the impetus of WASP elites with the purpose of teaching respect for Protestant and middle-class standards of cultural and religious propriety, especially in the face of Catholic, working-class immigration from Europe (Cremin, 1961; Curti, 1935). The content of public school education has consisted especially of middle-class, WASP culture (Waller, 1932:15–131; Becker, 1961; Hess and Torney, 1967).

At the elite level, private secondary schools for children of the WASP upper class were founded from the 1880s, when the mass indoctrination function of the growing public schools made them unsuitable as means of maintaining cohesion of the elite culture itself (Baltzell, 1958:327–372). These elite schools produce a distinctive personality type, characterized by adherence to a distinctive set of upper-class values and manners (McArthur, 1955). The cultural role of schools has been more closely studied in Britain (Bernstein, 1961; Weinberg, 1967), and in France (Bourdieu and Passeron, 1964), although Riesman and his colleagues (Riesman, 1958; Jencks and Riesman, 1968) have shown some of the cultural differences among prestige levels of colleges and universities in the United States.

(b) Evidence that education has been used as a means of cultural selection may be found in several sources. Hollingshead's (1949:360–388) study of Elmtown school children, school dropouts, and community attitudes toward them suggests that employers use education as a means of selecting employees with middle-class attributes. A 1945–1946 survey of 240 employers in New Haven and Charlotte, N. C. indicated that they regarded education as a screening device for employees with desirable (middle-class) character and demeanor; white-collar positions particularly emphasized educational selection because these employees were considered most visible to outsiders (Noland and Bakke, 1949:20–63).

A survey of employers in nationally prominent corporations indicated that they regarded college degrees as important in hiring potential managers, not because they were thought to ensure technical skills, but rather to indicate "motivation" and "social experience" (Gordon and Howell, 1959:121). Business school training is similarly regarded, less as evidence of necessary training (as employers have been widely skeptical of the utility of this curriculum for most positions) than as an indication that the college graduate is committed to business attitudes. Thus, employers are more likely to refuse to hire liberal arts graduates if they come from a college which has a business school than if their college is without a business school (Gordon and Howell, 1959:84–87; see also Pierson, 1959:90–99). In the latter case, the students could be said not to have had a choice; but when both business and liberal arts courses are offered and the student chooses liberal arts, employers appear to take this as a rejection of business values.

Finally, a 1967 survey of 309 California organizations (Collins, 1971) found that educational requirements for white-collar workers were highest in organizations which placed the strongest emphasis on normative control over their employees.[5] Normative control emphasis was indicated by (i) relative emphasis on the absence of police record for job applicants; (ii) relative emphasis on a record of job loyalty; (iii) Etzioni's (1961) classification of organizations into those with high normative control emphasis (financial, professional services, government, and other public services organizations) and those with remunerative control emphasis (manufacturing, construction, and trade). These three indicators are highly interrelated, thus mutually validating their conceptualization as indicators of normative control emphasis. The relationship between normative control emphasis and educational requirements holds for managerial requirements and white-collar requirements generally, both including and excluding professional and technical positions. Normative control emphasis does not affect blue-collar education requirements.

Variations in Linkage between Education and Occupation

The conflict model may also be tested by examining the cases in which it predicts education will be relatively important or unimportant in occupational attainment. Education should be most important where two conditions hold simultaneously: (1) the type of education most closely reflects membership in a particular status group, and (2) that group controls employment in particular organizational contexts. Thus, education will be most important where the fit is greatest between the culture of the status groups emerging from schools, and the status group doing the hiring; it will be least important where there is the greatest disparity between the culture of the school and of the employers.

This fit between school-group culture and employer culture may be conceptualized as a continuum. The importance of elite education is highest where it is involved in selection of new members of organizational elites, and should fade off where jobs are less elite (either lower level jobs in these organizations, or jobs in other organizations not controlled by the cultural elite). Similarly, schools which produce the most elite graduates will be most closely linked to elite occupations; schools whose products are less well socialized into elite culture are selected for jobs correspondingly less close to elite organizational levels.

In the United States, the schools which produce culturally elite groups, either by virtue of explicit training or by selection of students from elite backgrounds, or both, are the private prep schools at the secondary level; at the higher level, the elite colleges (the Ivy league, and to a lesser degree the major state universities); at the professional training level, those professional schools attached to the elite colleges and universities. At the secondary level, schools which produce respectably socialized, nonelite persons are the public high schools (especially those in middle-class residential areas); from the point of view of the culture of WASP employers, Catholic schools (and all-black schools) are less acceptable. At the level of higher education, Catholic and black colleges and professional schools are less elite, and commercial training schools are the least elite form of education.

In the United States, the organizations most clearly dominated by the WASP upper class are large, nationally organized business corporations, and the largest law firms (Domhoff, 1967:38–62). Those organizations more likely to be dominated by members of minority ethnic cultures are the smaller and local businesses in manufacturing, construction, and retail trade; in legal practice, solo rather than firm employment. In government employment, local governments appear to be more heavily dominated by ethnic groups, whereas particular branches of the national government (notably the State Department and the Treasury) are dominated by WASP elites (Domhoff, 1967: 84–114, 132–137).

Evidence on the fit between education and employment is available for only some of these organizations. In a broad sample of organizational types (Collins, 1971), educational requirements were higher in the bigger organizations, which also tended to be organized on a national scale, than in smaller and more localistic organizations.[6] The finding of Penned and Perrucci (1970) that upper-class social origins were important in career success precisely within the group of engineers who graduated from the most prestigious engineering schools with the highest grades may also bear on this question; since the big national corporations are most likely to hire this academically elite group, the importance of social origins within this group tends to corroborate the interpretation of education as part of a process of elite cultural selection in those organizations.

Among lawyers, the predicted differences are clear: graduates of the law schools attached to elite colleges and universities are more likely to be employed in firms, whereas graduates of Catholic or commercial law schools are more likely to be found in solo practice (Ladinsky, 1967). The elite Wall Street law firms are most educationally selective in this regard, choosing not only from Ivy League law schools but from a group whose background includes attendance at elite prep schools and colleges (Smigel, 1964: 39, 73–74, 117). There are also indications that graduates of ethnically-dominated professional schools are most likely to practice within the ethnic community; this is clearly the case among black professionals. In general, the evidence that graduates of black colleges (Sharp, 1970:64–67) and of Catholic colleges (Jencks and Riesman, 1968:357–366) have attained lower occupational positions in business than graduates of white Protestant schools (at least until recent years) also bolsters this interpretation.[7]

It is possible to interpret this evidence according to the technical-function theory of education, arguing that the elite schools provide the best technical training, and that the major national organizations require the greatest degree of technical talent. What is necessary is to test simultaneously for technical and status-conflict conditions. The most direct evidence on this point is the California employer study (Collins, 1971), which examined the effects of normative control emphasis and of organizational prominence, while holding constant the organization's technological modernity, as measured by the number of technological and organizational changes in the previous six years. Technological change was found to affect educational requirements at managerial and white-collar (but not blue-collar) levels, thus giving some support to the technical-function theory of education. The three variables—normative control emphasis, organizational prominence, and technological change—each independently affected educational requirements, in particular contexts. Technological change produced significantly higher educational requirements only in smaller, localistic organizations, and in organizational sectors not emphasizing normative control. Organizational prominence produced significantly higher educational requirements in organizations with low technological change, and in sectors de-emphasizing normative control. Normative control emphasis produced significantly higher educational requirements in organizations with low technological change and in less prominent organizations. Thus, technical and normative status conditions all affect educational requirements; measures of association indicated that the latter conditions were stronger in this sample.

Other evidence bearing on this point concerns business executives only. A study of the top executives in nationally prominent businesses indicated that the most highly educated managers were not found in the most rapidly developing companies, but rather in the least economically vigorous ones, with highest education found in the traditionalistic financial and utility firms (Warner and Abegglen, 1955:141–143, 148). The business elite has always been highly educated in relation to the American populace, but education seems to be a correlate of their social origins rather than the determinant of their success (Mills, 1963:128; Taussig and Joslyn, 1932:200; Newcomer, 1955:76). Those members of the business elite who entered its ranks from lower social origins had less education than the businessmen of upper and upper-middle-class origins, and those businessmen who inherited their companies were much more likely to be college educated than those who achieved their positions by entrepreneurship (Bendix, 1956:230; Newcomer, 1955:80).

In general, the evidence indicates that educational requirements for employment reflect employers' concerns for acquiring respectable and well-socialized employees; their concern for the provision of technical skills through education enters to a lesser degree. The higher the normative control concerns of the employer, and the more elite the organization's status, the higher his educational requirements.

Historical Change

The rise in educational requirements for employment throughout the last century may be explained using the conflict theory, and incorporating elements of the technical-functional theory into it at appropriate points. The principal dynamic has centered on changes in the supply of educated persons caused by the expansion of the school system, which was in turn shaped by three conditions:

(1) Education has been associated with high economic and status position from the colonial period on through the twentieth century. The result was a popular demand for education as mobility opportunity. This demand has not been for vocational education at a terminal or commercial level, short of full university certification; the demand has rather focused on education giving entry into the elite status culture, and usually only those technically-oriented schools have prospered which have most closely associated themselves with the sequence of education leading to (or from) the classical Bachelor's degree (Collins, 1969:68–70, 86–87, 89, 96–101).

(2) Political decentralization, separation of church and state, and competition among religious denominations have made founding schools and colleges in America relatively easy, and provided initial motivations of competition among communities and religious groups that moved them to do so. As a result, education at all levels expanded faster in America than anywhere else in the world. At the time of the Revolution, there were nine colleges in the colonies; in all of Europe, with a population forty times that of America, there were approximately sixty colleges. By 1880 there were 811 American colleges and universities; by 1966, there were 2,337. The United States not only began with the highest ratio of institutions of higher education to population in the world, but increased this lead steadily, for the number of European universities was not much greater by the twentieth century than in the eighteenth (Ben-David and Zloczower, 1962).

(3) Technical changes also entered into the expansion of American education. As the evidence summarized above indicates: (a) mass literacy is crucial for beginnings of full-scale industrialization, although demand for literacy could not have been important in the expansion of education beyond elementary levels. More importantly, (b) there is a mild trend toward the reduction in the proportion of unskilled jobs and an increase in the promotion of highly skilled (professional and technical) jobs as industrialism proceeds, accounting for 15% of the shift in educational levels in the twentieth century (Folger and Nam, 1964). (c) Technological change also brings about some upgrading in skill requirements of some continuing job positions, although the available evidence (Berg, 1970:38–60) refers only to the decade 1950–1960. Nevertheless, as Wilensky (1964) points out, there is no "professionalization of everyone," as most jobs do not require considerable technical knowledge on the order of that required of the engineer or the research scientist.

The existence of a relatively small group of experts in high-status positions, however, can have important effects on the structure of competition for mobility chances. In the United States, where democratic decentralization favors the use of schools (as well as government employment) as a kind of patronage for voter interests, the existence of even a small number of elite jobs fosters a demand for *large-scale* opportunities to acquire these positions. We thus have a "contest mobility" school system (Turner, 1960); it produced a widely educated populace because of the many dropouts who never achieve the elite level of schooling at which expert skills and/or high cultural status are acquired. In the process, the status value of American education has become diluted. Standards of respectability are always relative to the existing range of cultural differences. Once higher levels of education become recognized as an objective mark of elite status, and a moderate level of education as a mark of respectable middle-level status, increases in the supply of educated persons at given levels result in yet higher levels, becoming recognized as superior, and previously superior levels become only average.

Thus, before the end of the nineteenth century, an elementary school or home education was no longer satisfactory for a middle-class gentleman; by the 1930s, a college degree was displacing the high school degree as the minimal standard of respectability; in the late 1960s, graduate school or specialized professional degrees were becoming necessary for initial entry to many middle-class positions, and high school graduation was becoming a standard for entry to manual laboring positions. Education has thus gradually become part of the status culture of classes far below the level of the original business and professional elites.

The increasing supply of educated persons (Table 3.2) has made education a rising requirement of jobs (Table 3.1). Led by the biggest and most prestigious organizations, employers have raised their educational requirements to maintain both the relative prestige of their own managerial ranks and the relative respectability of middle ranks.[8] Education has become a legitimate standard in terms of which employers select employees, and employees compete with each other for promotion opportunities or for raised prestige in their continuing positions. With the attainment of a mass (now approaching universal) higher education system in modern America, the ideal or image of technical skill becomes the legitimating culture in terms of which the struggle for position goes on.

Higher educational requirements, and the higher level of educational credentials offered by individuals competing for position in organizations, have in turn increased the demand for education by the populace. The interaction between formal job requirements and informal status cultures has resulted in a spiral in which educational requirements and educational attainments become ever higher. As the struggle for mass educational opportunities enters new phases in the universities of today and perhaps in the graduate schools of the future, we may expect a further upgrading of educational requirements for employment. The mobilization of demands by minority groups for mobility opportunities through schooling can only contribute an extension of the prevailing pattern.

Conclusion

It has been argued that conflict theory provides an explanation of the principal dynamics of rising educational requirements for employment in America. Changes in the technical requirements of jobs have caused more limited changes in particular jobs. The conditions of the interaction of these two determinants may be more closely studied.

Precise measures of changes in the actual technical skill requirements of jobs are as yet available only in rudimentary form. Few systematic studies show how much of particular job skills may be learned in practice, and how much must be acquired through school background. Close studies of what is actually learned in school, and how long it is retained, are rare. Organizational studies of how employers rate performance and decide upon promotions give a picture of relatively loose controls over the technical quality of employee performance, but this no doubt varies in particular types of jobs.

The most central line of analysis for assessing the joint effects of status group conflict and technical requirements are those which compare the relative importance of education in different contexts. One such approach may take organization as the unit of analysis, comparing the educational requirements of organizations both to organizational technologies and to the status (including educational) background of organizational elites. Such analysis may also be applied to surveys of individual mobility, comparing the effects of education on mobility in different employment contexts, where the status group (and educational) background of employers varies in its fit with the educational culture of prospective employees. Such analysis of "old school tie" networks may also simultaneously test for the independent effect of the technical requirements of different sorts of jobs on the importance of education. Inter-nation comparisons provide variations here in the fit between types of education and particular kinds of jobs which may not be available within any particular country.

The full elaboration of such analysis would give a more precise answer to the historical question of assigning weight to various factors in the changing place of education in the stratification of modern societies. At the same time, to state the conditions under which status groups vary in organizational power, including the power to emphasize or limit the importance of technical skills, would be to state the basic elements of a comprehensive explanatory theory of the forms of stratification.

Notes

1. This survey covered 309 establishments with 100 or more employees, representing all major industry groups.
2. The concern here is with these basic premises rather than with the theory elaborated by Davis and Moore to account for the universality of stratification. This theory involves a few further propositions: (C) in any particular form of society certain occupational positions are functionally most central to the operation of the social system; (D) the ability to fill these positions, and/ or the motivation to acquire the necessary training, is unequally distributed in the population; (E) inequalities of rewards in wealth and prestige evolve to ensure that the supply of persons with the necessary ability or training meshes with the structure of demands for skilled performance. The problems of stating functional centrality in empirical terms have been subjects of much debate.
3. Proposition 3 is supported by Tables 3.1 and 3.2. The issue here is whether this can be explained by the previous propositions and premises.
4. It might be argued that the ethnic cultures may differ in their functionality: that middle-class Protestant culture provides the self-discipline and other attributes necessary for higher organizational positions in modern society. This version of functional theory is specific enough to be subject to empirical test: are middle-class WASPs in fact better businessmen or government administrators than Italians, Irishmen, or Jews of patrimonial or working class cultural backgrounds? Weber suggested that they were in the initial construction of the capitalist economy within the confines of traditional society; he also argued that once the new economic system was established, the original ethic was no longer necessary to run it (Weber, 1930:180–183). Moreover, the functional explanation also requires some feedback mechanism whereby organizations with more efficient managers are selected for survival. The oligopolistic situation in large-scale American business since the late 19th century does not seem to provide such a mechanism; nor does government employment. Schumpeter (1951), the leading expositor of the importance of. managerial talent in business, confined his emphasis to the formative period of business expansion, and regarded the large, oligopolistic corporation as an arena where advancement came to be based on skills in organizational politics (1951:122–124); these personalistic skills are arguably more characteristic of the patrimonial cultures than of WASP culture.
5. Sample consisted of approximately one-third of all organizations with 100 or more employees in the San Francisco, Oakland, and San Jose metropolitan areas. See Gordon and Thal-Larsen (1969) for a description of procedures and other findings.
6. Again, these relationships hold for managerial requirements and white-collar requirements generally, both including and excluding professional and technical positions, but not for blue-collar requirements. Noland and Bakke (1949:78) also report that larger organizations have higher educational requirements for administrative positions than smaller organizations.
7. Similar processes may be found in other societies, where the kinds of organizations linked to particular types of schools may differ. In England, the elite "public schools" are linked especially to the higher levels of the national civil service (Weinberg, 1967:139–143). In France, the elite Ecole Polytechnique is linked to both government and industrial administrative positions (Crozier, 1964: 238–244). In Germany, universities have been linked principally with government administration, and business executives are drawn from elsewhere (Ben-David and Zloczower, 1962). Comparative analysis of the kinds of education of government officials, business executives, and other groups in contexts where the status group links of schools differ is a promising area for further tests of conflict and technical-functional explanations.
8. It appears that employers may have raised their wage costs in the process. Their behavior is nevertheless plausible, in view of these considerations: (a) the thrust of organizational research since Mayo and Barnard has indicated that questions of internal organizational power and control, of which cultural dominance is a main feature, take precedence over purely economic considerations; (b) the large American corporations, which have led in educational requirements, have

held positions of oligopolistic advantage since the late 19th century, and thus could afford a large internal "welfare" cost of maintaining a well-socialized work force; (c) there are inter-organizational wage differentials in local labor markets, corresponding to relative organizational prestige, and a "wage-escalator" process by which the wages of the leading organizations are gradually emulated by others according to their rank (Reynolds, 1951); a parallel structure of "educational status escalators" could plausibly be expected to operate.

References

Anastasi, Anne, 1967 "Psychology, psychologists, and psychological testing." *American Psychologist* 22 (April): 297–306.

Baltzell, E. Digby, 1958 *An American Business Aristocracy*. New York: Macmillan.

Becker, Howard S., 1961 "Schools and systems of stratification." Pp. 93–104 in A. H. Halsey, Jean Floud, and C. Arnold Anderson (eds), *Education, Economy, and Society*. New York: Free Press.

Becker, Howard S., Blanche Geer, and Everett C. Hughes, 1968 *Making the Grade: The Academic Side of College Life*. New York: Wiley.

Bell, H. M., 1940 *Matching Youth and Jobs*. Washington: American Council on Education.

Ben-David, Joseph, 1963– "Professions in the class systems of present-64 day Societies." *Current Sociology* 12:247–330.

Ben-David, Joseph and Awraham Floczower, 1962 "Universities and academic systems in modern societies." *European Journal of Sociology* 31:45–85.

Bendix, Reinhard, 1956 *Work and Authority in Industry*. New York: Wiley.

Berg, Ivar, 1970 *Education and Jobs*. New York: Praeger.

Bernstein, Basil, 1961 "Social class and linguistic development." Pp. 288–314 in A. H. Halsey, Jean Floud, and C. Arnold Anderson (eds), *Education, Economy, and Society*. New York: Free Press.

Blau, Peter M., 1955 *The Dynamics of Bureaucracy*. Chicago: University of Chicago Press.

Blau, Peter M. and Otis Dudley Duncan, 1967 *The American Occupational Structure*. New York: Wiley.

Bourdieu, Pierre and Jean-Claude Passeron, 1964 *Les Heritiers: Les Etudiants et la Culture*. Paris: Les Editions de Minuit.

Bright, James R., 1958 "Does automation raise skin requirements?" *Harvard Business Review* 36 (July–August):85–97.

Clark, Burton R., 1962 *Educating the Expert Society*. San Francisco: Chandler.

Clark, Harold F. and Harold S. Sloan, 1966 *Classrooms on Main Street*. New York: Teachers College Press.

Coleman, James S., 1961 *The Adolescent Society*. New York: Free Press.

Collins, Orvis, Melville Dalton, and Donald Roy 1946 "Restriction of output and social cleavage in industry." *Applied Anthropology* 5 (Summer): 1–14.

Collins, Randall, 1968 "A comparative approach to political sociology." Pp. 42–67 in Reinhard Bendix et at. (eds.), *State and Society*. Boston: Little, Brown.

———— 1969 Education and Employment. Unpublished Ph.D. dissertation, University of California at Berkeley.

———— 1971 "Educational requirements for employment: A comparative organizational study." Unpublished manuscript.

Cremin, Lawrence A., 1961 *The Transformation of the School*. New York: Knopf.

Crozier, Michel, 1964 *The Bureaucratic Phenomenon*. Chicago: University of Chicago Press.

Curti, Merle, 1935 *The Social Ideas of American Educators*. New York: Scribners.

Dalton, Melville, 1951 "Informal factors in career achievement." *American Journal of Sociology* 56 (March): 407–415.

———— 1959 *Men Who Manage*. New York: Wiley.

Davis, Kingsley and Wilbert Moore, 1945 "Some principles of stratification." *American Sociological Review* 10:242–249.

Denison, Edward F., 1965 "Education and economic productivity." Pp. 328–340 in Seymour Harris (ed.), *Education and Public Policy*. Berkeley: McCutchen.

Dill, William R., Thomas L. Hilton, and Walter R. Reitman, 1962 *The New Managers*. Englewood Cliffs: Prentice-Hall.

Domhoff, G. William, 1967 *Who Rules America?* Englewood Cliffs, New Jersey: Prentice-Hall.

Duncan, Beverly, 1964 "Dropouts and the unemployed." *Journal of Political Economy* 73 (April):121–134.

Duncan, Otis Dudley and Robert W. Hodge, 1963 "Education and occupational mobility: A regression analysis." *American Journal of Sociology* 68:629–644.

Eckland, Bruce K., 1965 "Academic ability, higher education, and occupational mobility." *American Sociological Review* 30:735–746.

Epstein, Cynthia Fuchs, 1970 *Woman's Place: Options and Limits in Professional Careers*. Berkeley: University of California Press.

Etzioni, Amitai, 1961 *A Comparative Analysis of Complex Organizations*. New York: Free Press.

Folger, John K. and Charles B. Nam, 1964 "Trends in education in relation to the occupational structure." *Sociology of Education* 38:19–33.

Goode, William J., 1967 "The protection of the inept." *American Sociological Review* 32:5–19.

Gordon, Margaret S. and Margaret Thal-Larsen, 1969 *Employer Policies in a Changing Labor Market*. Berkeley: Institute of Industrial Relations, University of California.

Gordon, Robert A. and James E. Howell, 1959 *Higher Education for Business*. New York: Columbia University Press.

Gusfield, Joseph R., 1958 "Equalitarianism and bureaucratic recruitment." *Administrative Science Quarterly* 2 (March):521–541.

Hagstrom, Warren O. and Lowell L. Hargens, 1968 "Mobility theory in the sociology of science." Paper delivered at Cornell Conference on Human Mobility, Ithaca, N.Y. (October 31).

Hall, Oswald, 1946 "The informal organization of the medical profession." *Canadian Journal of Economic and Political Science* 12 (February): 30–44.

Harbison, Frederick and Charles A. Myers, 1964 *Education, Manpower, and Economic Growth*. New York: McGraw-Hill.

Hargens, Lowell and Warren O. Hagstrom, 1967 "Sponsored and contest mobility of American academic scientists." *Sociology of Education* 40:24–38.

Havemann, Ernest and Patricia Salter West, 1952 *They Went to College*. New York: Harcourt, Brace.

Hess, Robert D. and Judith V. Torney, 1967 *The Development of Political Attitudes in Children*. Chicago: Aldine.

Hollingshead, August B., 1949 *Elmtown's Youth*. New York: Wiley.

Hoselitz, Bert F., 1965 "Investment in education and its political impact" Pp. 541–565 in James S. Coleman (ed.), *Education and Political Development*. Princeton: Princeton University Press.

Hughes, Everett C., 1949 "Queries concerning industry and society growing out of the study of ethnic relations in Industry." *American Sociological Review* 14:211–220.

Jencks, Christopher and David Riesman, 1968 *The Academic Revolution*. New York: Doubleday.

Kahl, Joseph A., 1957 *The American Class Structure*. New York: Rinehart.

Kerr, Clark, John T. Dunlop, Frederick H. Harbison, and Charles A. Myers, 1960 *Industrialism and Industrial Man*. Cambridge: Harvard University Press.

Ladinsky, Jack, 1963 "Careers of lawyers, law practice, and legal institutions." *American Sociological Review* 28 (February):47–54.

―――― 1967 "Higher education and work achievement among lawyers." *Sociological Quarterly* 8 (Spring):222–232.

Learned, W. S. and B. D. Wood, 1938 *The Student and His Knowledge*. New York: Carnegie Foundation for the Advancement of Teaching.

Lipset, Seymour Martin and Reinhard Bendix, 1959 *Social Mobility in Industrial Society*. Berkeley: University of California Press.

Lombard, George F., 1955 *Behavior in a Selling Group*. Cambridge: Harvard University Press.

March, James G. and Herbert A. Simon, 1958 *Organizations*. New York: Wiley.

Marsh, Robert M., 1963 "Values, demand, and social mobility." *American Sociological Review* 28 (August): 567–575.

McArthur, C., 1955 "Personality differences between middle and upper classes." *Journal of Abnormal and Social Psychology* 50:247–254.

Mills, C. Wright, 1963 *Power, Politics, and People*. New York: Oxford University Press.

Newcomer, Mabel, 1955 *The Big Business Executive*. New York: Columbia University Press.

Noland, E. William and E. Wight Bakke, 1949 *Workers Wanted*. New York: Harper.

Nosow, Sigmund, 1956 "Labor distribution and the normative system." *Social Forces* 30:25–33.

Peaslee, Alexander L., 1969 "Education's role in development." *Economic Development and Cultural Change* 17 (April): 293–318.

Perrucci, Carolyn Cummings and Robert Perrucci, 1970 "Social origins, educational contexts, and career mobility." *American Sociological Review* 35 (June):451–463.

Pierson, Frank C., 1959 *The Education of American Businessmen*. New York: McGraw-Hill.

Plunkett, M., 1960 "School and early work experience of youth." *Occupational Outlook Quarterly* 4:22–27.

Reynolds, Lloyd, 1951 *The Structure of Labor Markets*. New York: Harper.

Riesman, David, 1958 *Constraint and Variety in American Education*. New York: Doubleday.

Roy, Donald, 1952 "Quota restriction and goldbricking in a machine shop." *American Journal of Sociology* 57 (March):427–442.

Schultz, Theodore W., 1961 "Investment in human capital." *American Economic Review* 51 (March):1–16.

Schumpeter, Joseph, 1951 *Imperialism and Social Classes*. New York: Augustus M. Kelley.

Sewell, William H., Archibald O. Halter, and Alejandro Portes, 1969 "The educational and early occupational attainment process." *American Sociological Review* 34 (February):82–92.

Sharp, Laure M., 1970 *Education and Employment: The Early Careers of College Graduates*. Baltimore: Johns Hopkins Press.

Smigel, Erwin O., 1964 *The Wall Street Lawyer*. New York: Free Press.

Soderberg, C. Richard, 1963 "The American engineer." Pp. 203–230 in Kenneth S. Lynn, *The Professions in America*. Boston: Beacon Press.

Taeuber, Alma F., Karl E. Taeuber, and Glen G. Cain, 1966 "Occupational assimilation and the competitive process: A reanalysis." *American Journal of Sociology* 72:278–285.

Taussig, Frank W. and C. S. Joslyn, 1932 *American Business Leaders*. New York: Macmillan.

Turner, Ralph H., 1952 "Foci of discrimination in the employment of nonwhites." *American Journal of Sociology* 58:247–256.

―――― 1960 "Sponsored and contest mobility and the school system." *American Sociological Review* 25 (October):855–867.

Waller, Willard, 1932 *The Sociology of Teaching*. New York: Russell and Russell.

Warner, W. Lloyd and James C. Abegglen, 1955 *Occupational Mobility in American Business and Industry, 1928–1952*. Minneapolis: University of Minnesota Press.

Weber, Max, 1930 *The Protestant Ethic and the Spirit of Capitalism*. New York: Scribner's.

―――― 1968 *Economy and Society*. New York: Bedminster Press.

4

Broken Promises

School Reform in Retrospect

SAMUEL BOWLES AND HERBERT GINTIS

We shall one day learn to supercede politics by education.—Ralph Waldo Emerson

· · ·

Democracy and Technology in Educational Theory

The minds...of the great body of the people are in danger of really degenerating, while the other dements of civilization are advancing, unless care is taken, by means of the other instruments of education, to counteract those effects which the simplifications of the manual processes has a tendency to produce.—James Mill, 1824

Scholars abhor the obvious. Perhaps for this reason it is often difficult to find a complete written statement of a viewpoint which is widely accepted. Such is the case with modern liberal educational theory. Discovering its conceptual underpinnings thus requires more than a little careful searching. What exactly is the theory underlying the notion of education as "panacea"? In reviewing the vast literature on this subject, we have isolated two intellectually coherent strands, one represented by John Dewey and his followers—the "democratic school"—and the other represented by functional sociology and neoclassical economics—the "technocratic-meritocratic school." These approaches are best understood by analyzing the way they deal with two major questions concerning the limits of educational policy. The first concerns the compatibility of various functions schools are supposed to perform. The second concerns the power of schooling to perform these functions. We shall treat each in turn.

In the eyes of most liberal reformers, the educational system must fulfill at least three functions. First and foremost, schools must help integrate youth into the various occupational, political, familial, and other adult roles required by an expanding economy and a stable polity. "Education," says John Dewey in *Democracy and Education,* probably the most important presentation of the liberal theory of education, "is the means of [the] social continuity of life." We refer to this process as the "integrative" function of education.

Second, while substantial inequality in economic privilege and social status are believed by most liberals to be inevitable, giving each individual a chance to compete openly for these privileges is both efficient and desirable. Dewey is representative in asserting the role of the school in this process:

It is the office of the school environment...to see to it that each individual sets an opportunity to escape from the limitations of the social group in which he was born, and to come into living contact with a broader environment.[1]

Many liberal educational theorists—including Dewey—have gone beyond this rather limited objective to posit a role for schools in equalizing the vast extremes of wealth and poverty. Schooling, some have proposed, cannot only assure fair competition, but can also reduce the economic gap between the winners and the losers. We shall refer to this role of schooling in the pursuit of equality of opportunity, or of equality itself, as the "egalitarian" function of education.

Lastly, education is seen as a major instrument in promoting the psychic and moral development of the individual. Personal fulfillment depends, in large part, on the extent, direction, and vigor of development of our physical, cognitive, emotional, aesthetic, and other potentials. If the educational system has not spoken to these potentialities by taking individual development as an end in itself, it has failed utterly. Again quoting Dewey:

> The criterion of the value of school education is the extent in which it creates a desire for continued growth and supplies the means for making the desire effective in fact.... The educational process has no end beyond itself it is its own end.[2]

We refer to this as the "developmental" function of education.

For Dewey, the compatibility of these three functions—the integrative, the egalitarian, and the developmental—derives from basic assumptions concerning the nature of social life. First, he assumed that occupational roles in capitalist society are best filled by individuals who have achieved the highest possible levels of personal development. For Dewey, personal development is economically productive. Second, Dewey assumed that a free and universal school system can render the opportunities for self-development independent of race, ethnic origins, class background, and sex. Hence the integrative, egalitarian, and developmental functions of schooling are not only compatible, they are mutually supportive....

Dewey argues the necessary association of the integrative, egalitarian, and developmental functions of education in a democracy. A more recent liberal perspective argues only their mutual compatibility. This alternative view is based on a conception of the economy as a technical system, where work performance is based on technical competence. Inequality of income, power, and status, according to this technocratic-meritocratic view, is basically a reflection of an unequal distribution of mental, physical, and other skills. The more successful individuals, according to this view, are the more skillful and the more intelligent. Since cognitive and psychomotor development are vital and healthy components of individual psychic development and can be provided equally according to the "abilities" of the students upon their entering schools, the compatibility of these three functions of the educational system in capitalism is assured.

The popularity of the technocratic-meritocratic perspective can be gleaned from the policy-maker's reaction to the "rediscovery" of poverty and inequality in America during the decade of the 1960s. Unequal opportunity in acquiring skills was quickly isolated as the source of the problems.[3] Moreover, in assessing the efficacy of the educational system, both of preschool enrichment and of other school programs, measures of cognitive outcomes—scholastic achievement, for example—have provided the unique criteria of success.[4] Finally, the recent failure of educational policies significantly to improve the position of the poor and minority groups has, among a host of possible reappraisals of liberal theory, raised but one to preeminence: the nature-nurture controversy as to the determination of "intelligence."[5]

This technocratic-meritocratic view of schooling, economic success, and the requisites of job functioning supplies an elegant and logically coherent (if not empirically compelling) explanation of the rise of mass education in the course of industrial development. Because modern industry, according to this view, consists in the application of increasingly complex and intellectually demanding production technologies, the development of the economy requires increasing mental skills on the part of the labor force as a whole. Formal education, by extending to the masses what has been throughout human history the privilege of the few, opens the upper levels in the job hierarchy to all with the ability and willingness to attain such skills. Hence, the increasing economic importance of mental skills enhances the power of a fundamentally egalitarian school system to equalize economic opportunity....

The modern technocratic-meritocratic perspective avoids Mann's [Horace Mann was the father of the Common School movement in the 19th century who viewed schools as a great equalizer] class analysis but retains his basic assertions. According to the modern view, the egalitarianism of schooling is complemented by the meritocratic orientation of industrial society. Since in this view ability is fairly equally distributed across social class, and since actual achievement is the criterion for access to occupational roles, differences of birth tend toward economic irrelevance. Since whatever social-class based differences exist in an individual's "natural" aspirations to social status are minimized by the competitive orientation of schooling, expanding education represents a potent instrument toward the efficient and equitable distribution of jobs, income, and status. If inequalities remain at the end of this process, they must simply be attributed to inevitable human differences in intellectual capacities or patterns of free choice.

Thus as long as schooling is free and universal, the process of economic expansion will not only be consistent with the use of educational as an instrument for personal development and social equality; economic expansion, by requiring educational expansion, will necessarily enhance the power of education to achieve these ends. So the argument goes.[6]

If we accept for the moment the compatibility of various functions of education, we are confronted with a second group of questions concerning the power of education to counteract opposing tendencies in the larger society. If the educational system is to be a central social corrective, the issue of its potential efficacy is crucial to the establishment of the liberal outlook. Dewey does not withdraw from this issue:

> ...The school environment...establishes a purified medium of action.... As society becomes more enlightened, it realizes that it is responsible not to transmit and conserve the whole of its existing achievements but only such which make for a better future society. The school is its chief agency for the accomplishment of this end.[7]

But such generalizations cannot substitute for direct confrontation with the thorny and somewhat disreputable facts of economic life. In the reality of industrial society, can the school environment promote either human development or social equality? Self-development may be compatible with ideal work roles, but can education change the seamy realities of the workaday world? Equality may be compatible with the other functions of education, but can the significant and pervasive system of racial, class, and sexual stratification be significantly modified by "equal schooling"?

···

This approach became a fundamental tenet of educational reformers in the Progressive Era. Education, thought Dewey, could promote the natural movement of industrial society toward more fulfilling work, hence bringing its integrative and developmental functions increasingly into a harmonious union.

To complete our exposition of liberal theory, we must discuss the power of the educational system to promote social equality. For Dewey, of course, this power derives from the necessary association of personal growth and democracy—whose extension to all parts of the citizenry is a requisite of social development itself. In the technocratic version of liberal theory, however, the egalitarian power of the educational system is not automatically fulfilled. Were economic success dependent on race or sex, or upon deeply rooted differences in human character, the ability of schooling to increase social mobility would of course be minimal. But according to the modern liberal view, this is not the case. And where equal access is not sufficient, then enlightened policy may devise special programs for the education of the poor: job training, compensatory education, and the like.

Poverty and inequality, in this view, are the consequences of individual choice or personal inadequacies, not the normal outgrowths of our economic institutions. The problem, clearly, is to fix up the people, not to change the economic structures which regulate their lives. This, indeed, is the meaning of the "social power" of schools to promote equality.

Despite persistent setbacks in practice, the liberal faith in the equalizing power of schooling has dominated both intellectual and policy circles. Education has been considered not only a powerful tool for self-development and social integration; it has been seen, at least since Horace Mann coined the phrase well over a century ago, as the "great equalizer."

Education and Inequality

Universal education is the power, which is destined to overthrow every species of hierarchy. It is destined to remove all artificial inequality and leave the natural inequalities to find their true level. With the artificial inequalities of caste, rank, title, blood, birth, race, color, sex, etc., will fall nearly all the oppression, abuse, prejudice, enmity, and injustice, that humanity is now subject to. Lester Frank Ward, *Education* c. 1872

Much of the content of education over the past century and a half can only be construed as an unvarnished attempt to persuade the "many" to make the best of the inevitable. The unequal contest between social control and social justice is evident in the total functioning of U.S. education. The system as it stands today provides eloquent testimony to the ability of the well-to-do to perpetuate in the name of equality of opportunity an arrangement which consistently yields to themselves disproportional advantages, while thwarting the aspirations and needs of the working people of the United States. However grating this judgment may sound to the ears of the undaunted optimist, it is by no means excessive in light of the massive statistical data on inequality in the United States. Let us look at the contemporary evidence.

We may begin with the basic issue of inequalities in years of schooling. As can be seen in Figure 4.1, the number of years of schooling attained by an individual is strongly associated with parental socioeconomic status. This figure presents the estimated distribution of years of schooling attained by individuals of varying socioeconomic backgrounds, If we define socioeconomic background by a weighted sum of income, occupations, and educational level of the parents, a child from the ninetieth percentile may expect, on the average, five more years of schooling than a child in the tenth percentile.[8]

A word about our use of statistics is in order. Most of the statistical calculations which we will present have been published with full documentation in academic journals.... Those interested in gaining a more detailed understanding of our data and methods are urged to consult our more technical articles.

The data, most of which was collected by the U.S. Census Current Populations Survey in 1962, refers to "non-Negro" males, aged 25–64 years, from "non-farm" background in the experienced labor force.[9] We have chosen a sample of white males because the most complete statistics are available for this group. Moreover, if inequality for white males can be documented, the proposition is merely strengthened when sexual and racial differences are taken into account.

Additional census data dramatize one aspect of educational inequalities: the relationship between family income and college attendance. Even among those who had graduated from high school in the early 1960s, children of families earning less than $3,000 per year were over six times as likely *not* to attend college as were the children of families earning over $15,000.[10] Moreover, children from less well-off families are *both* less likely to have graduated from high school and more likely to attend inexpensive, two-year community colleges rather than a four-year B.A. program if they do make it to college.[11]

Not surprisingly, the results of schooling differ greatly for children of different social backgrounds. Most easily measured, but of limited importance, are differences in scholastic achievement. If we measure the output of schooling by scores on nationally standardized achievement tests, children whose parents were themselves highly educated outperform the children of parents with less education by a wide margin. Data collected for the U.S. Office of Education Survey of Educational Opportunity reveal, for example, that among white high school seniors, those whose parents were in the top education decile were, on the average, well over three grade levels in measured scholastic achievement ahead of those whose parents were in the bottom decile.[12]

Given these differences in scholastic achievement, inequalities in years of schooling among individuals of different social backgrounds are to be expected. Thus one might be tempted to argue that the close dependence of years of schooling attained on background displayed in the left-hand bars of Figure 4.1 is simply a reflection of unequal intellectual abilities, or that inequalities in college attendance are the consequences of differing levels of scholastic achievement in high school and do not reflect any additional social class inequalities peculiar to the process of college admission.

This view, so comforting to the admissions personnel in our elite universities, is unsupported by the data, some of which is presented in Figure 4.1. The right-hand bars of Figure 4.1 indicate that even among children with identical IQ test scores at ages six and eight, those with rich, well-educated, high status parents could expect a much higher level of schooling than those with less-favored origins. Indeed, the closeness of the left-hand and right-hand bars in Figure 4.1 shows that only a small portion of the observed social class differences in educational attainment is related to IQ differences across social classes.[13,14] The dependence of education attained on background is almost as strong for

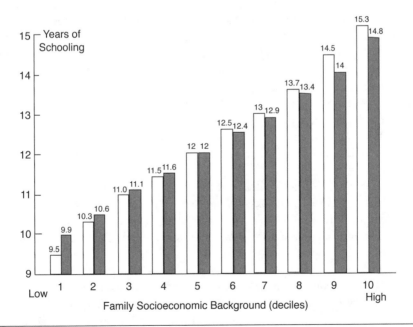

Figure 4.1 Educational attainments are strongly dependent on social background even for people of similar childhood IQs.

Notes: For each socioeconomic group, the left-hand bar indicates the estimated average number of years of schooling attained by all men from that group. The right-hand bar indicates the estimated average number of years of schooling attained by men with IQ scores equal to the average for the entire sample. The sample refers to "non-Negro" men of "nonfarm" backgrounds, aged 35–44 years in 1962.[14]

Source: Samuel Bowles and Valerie Nelson, "'The Inheritance of IQ,' and the Intergenerational Transmission of Economic Inequality," *The Review of Economics and Statistics,* Vol. LVI, No. 1. February 1974. Reprinted by permission.

individuals with the same IQ as for all individuals. Thus, while Figure 4.1 indicates that an individual in the ninetieth percentile in social class background is likely to receive five more years of education than an individual in the tenth percentile, it also indicated that he is likely to receive 4.25 more years schooling than an individual from the tenth percentile with the same IQ. Similar results are obtained when we look specifically at access to college education for students with the same measured IQ. Project Talent data indicates that for "high ability" students (top 25 percent as measured by a composite of tests of "general aptitude"), those of high socioeconomic background (top 25 percent as measured by a composite of family income, parents' education, and occupation) are nearly twice as likely to attend college than students of low socioeconomic background (bottom 25 percent). For "low ability" students (bottom 25 percent), those of high social background are more than four times as likely to attend college as are their low social background counterparts.[15]

Inequality in years of schooling is, of course, only symptomatic of broader inequalities in the educational system. Not only do less well-off children go to school for fewer years, they are treated with less attention (or more precisely, less benevolent attention) when they are there. These broader inequalities are not easily measured. Some show up in statistics on the different levels of expenditure for the education of children of different socioeconomic backgrounds. Taking account of the inequality in financial resources for each year in school and the inequality in years of schooling obtained, Jencks estimated that a child whose parents were in the top fifth of the income distribution receives roughly twice the educational resources in dollar terms as does a child whose parents are in the bottom fifth.[16]

The social class inequalities in our school system, then, are too evident to be denied. Defenders of the educational system are forced back on the assertion that things are getting better; the inequalities of the past were far worse. And, indeed, there can be no doubt that some of the inequalities of the past have been mitigated. Yet new inequalities have apparently developed to take their place, for the available historical evidence lends little support to the idea that our schools are on the road to equality of educational opportunity. For example, data from a recent U.S. Census survey reported in Spady indicate that graduation from college has become no less dependent on one's social background. This is true despite the fact that high-school graduation is becoming increasingly equal across social classes.[17] Additional data confirm this impression. The statistical association (coefficient of correlation) between parents' social status and years of education attained by individuals who completed their schooling three or four decades ago is virtually identical to the same correlation for individuals who terminated their schooling in recent years.[18] On balance, the available data suggest that the number of years of school attained by a child depends upon family background as much in the recent period as it did fifty years ago.

Thus, we have empirical reasons for doubting the egalitarian impact of schooling. But what of those cases when education has been equalized? What has been the effect. We will investigate three cases: the historical decline in the inequality among individuals in years of school attained, the explicitly compensatory educational programs of the War on Poverty, and the narrowing of the black/white gap in average years of schooling attained.

Although family background has lost none of its influence on how far one gets up the educational ladder, the historical rise in the minimum legal school-leaving age has narrowed the distance between the top and bottom rungs. Inequality of educational attainments has fallen steadily and substantially over the past three decades.[19] And has this led to a parallel equalization of the distribution of income? Look at Figure 4.2. The reduction in the inequality of years of schooling has not been matched by an equalization of the U.S. income distribution,[20] In fact, a recent U.S. Labor Department study indicates that as far as labor earnings (wages and salaries) are concerned, the trend since World War II has been unmistakably away from equality. And it is precisely inequality in labor earnings which is the target of the proponents of egalitarian school reforms.[21] But does the absence of an overall trend toward income

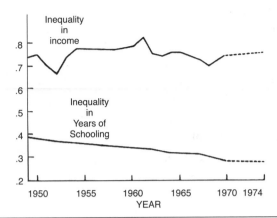

Figure 4.2 Equalization of education has not been associated with equalization of income.

Notes: The upper line shows the trend over time in the degree of inequality of income, as measured by the standard deviation of the natural logarithm of annual income of males aged twenty-five or older. The lower line shows the trend over time in the degree of inquality of years of schooling, as measured by the coefficient of variation (the standard deviation divided by the mean) of the years of schooling attained by males aged twenty-five and older. Data for 1970 to 1974 are estimates based on U.S. Census data.

Source: Barry Chiswick and Jacob Mincer, "Time Series Changes in Personal Income Inequality in the U.S.," *Journal of Political Economy,* Vol. 80, No. 3, Part II (May–June 1972).

equality mask an equalizing thrust of schooling that was offset by other disequalizing tendencies? Perhaps, but Jacob Mincer and Barry Chiswick of the National Bureau of Economic Research, in a study of the determinants of inequality in the United States, concluded that the significant reduction in schooling differences among white male adults would have had the effect—even if operating in isolation—of reducing income inequality by a negligible amount.[22]

Next, consider that group of explicitly egalitarian educational programs brought together in the War on Poverty. In a systematic economic survey of these programs, Thomas Ribich concludes that with very few exceptions, the economic payoff to compensatory education is low.[23] So low, in fact, that in a majority of cases studied, direct transfers of income to the poor would have accomplished considerably more equalization than the education programs in questions. The major RAND Corporation study by Averch came to the same conclusion.

Lastly, consider racial inequalities. In 1940, most black male workers (but a minority of whites) earned their livelihoods in the South, by far the poorest region; the education gap between nonwhites and whites was 3.3 years (38 percent of median white education).[24] By 1972, blacks had moved to more affluent parts of the country, and the education gap was reduced to 18 percent (4 percent for young men aged 25–34 years).[25] Richard Freeman has shown that this narrowing of the education gap would have virtually achieved black/white income equality had blacks received the same benefits from education as whites.[26] Yet the income gap has not closed substantially: The income gap for young men is 30 percent, despite an education gap of only 4 percent.[27] Clearly as blacks have moved toward educational (and regional) parity with whites, other mechanisms—such as entrapment in center-city ghettos and suburbanization of jobs, and perhaps increasing segmentation of labor markets—have intensified to maintain a more or less constant degree of racial income inequality. Blacks certainly suffer from educational inequality, but the root of the their exploitations lies outside of education, in a system of economic power and privilege in which racial distinctions play an important role.

The same must be concluded of inequality of economic opportunity between men and women. Sexual inequality persists despite the fact that women achieve a level of schooling (measured in years) equivalent to men.

We conclude that U.S. education is highly unequal, the chances of attaining much or little school-ing being substantially dependant on one's race and parents' economic level. Moreover, where there is a discernible trend toward a more equal educational system—as in the narrowing of the black educational deficit for example—the impact on the structure of economic opportunity is minimal at best. As we shall presently see, the record of the U.S. school system as a promoter of full human development is no more encouraging.

Education and Personal Development

While the educational practice of regimentation of children has persisted, the fundamentalist concep-tion of a child as immoral or savage has given way, through various stages, to a more appreciative view. To modern educators, the child appears as the primitive embodiment of the good and the natural—the noble savage, if you will. Children are spontaneous and joyful, unpredictable and trusting—traits to be cherished but sadly evanescent in the path toward maturity.[28]

At the same time, the educator's view of the family has changed. Once the trusted engine of moral training for youth, to which the school was considered a complement and ballast, the family increasingly appears in the writings of educators as the source of the child's inadequacy. Thus in the thought of the culture of poverty and cultural deprivation advocates, the school has been elevated to the status of family surrogate in the well engineered Society.[29] The social roots of this transformed concept of the family-school relationship have little to do with any alteration in family structure, and less to do with any heightening of the public morality. The impetus stems rather from the professional educator's profound mistrust of, and even fear of, the families of black and poor children, and in an earlier period, of Irish and other immigrant families.[30] Nor is this mistrust alien to the logic of social control. For all its nobility, the noble savage remains savage, and integration into the world of adults requires regimentation.

The most striking testimonial to the hegemony of the social-control ideology is perhaps its clear primacy even among those who opposed such obvious manifestations of the authoritarian classroom as corporal punishment and teacher-centered discussion. The most progressive of progressive educa-tors have shared the commitment to maintaining ultimate top-down control over the child's activities. Indeed, much of the educational experimentation of the past century can be viewed as attempting to broaden the discretion and deepen the involvement of the child while maintaining hierarchical control over the ultimate processes and outcomes of the educational encounter. The goal has been to enhance student motivation while withholding effective participation in the setting of priorities.

Hence, like the view of the child, the concept of discipline has itself changed. Two aspects of this change are particularly important. First, the once highly personalized authority of the teacher has become a part of the bureaucratic structure of the modern school. Unlike the teachers in the chaotic early nineteenth-century district schools, modern teachers exercise less personal power and rely more heavily on regulations promulgated by higher authorities. Although frequently prey to arbitrary inter-vention by parents and other community members, the nineteenth-century teacher was the boss of the classroom. The modern teacher is in a more ambiguous position. The very rules and regulations which add a patina of social authority to his or her commands at the same time rigidly circumscribe the teacher's freedom of action.

Second, the aim of discipline is no longer mere compliance: The aim is now "behavior modifica-tion." Prompt and obedient response to bureaucratically sanctioned authority is, of course, a must, But sheer coercion is out of keeping with both the modern educator's view of the child and the larger social needs for a self-controlled not just controlled-citizenry and work force. Discipline is still the theme, but the variations more often center on the "internalization of behavioral norms," on equipping the child with a built-in supervisor than on mere obedience to external authority and material sanctions.[31]

The repressive nature of the schooling process is nowhere more clearly revealed than in the system of grading, the most basic process of allocating rewards within the school. We will have gone some distance toward comprehending the school as it is—in going behind the educational rhetoric—if we can answer the question: Who gets what and why?

Teachers are likely to reward those who conform to and strengthen the social order of the school with higher grades and approval, and punish violators with lower grades and other forms of disapproval, independent of their respective academic and cognitive accomplishments. This fact allows us to investigate exactly what personality traits, attitudes, and behavioral attributes are facilitated by the educational encounter.

Outside of gross disobedience, one would suspect the student's exhibition of creativity and divergence of thought to be most inimical to the smooth functioning of the hierarchical classroom. For the essence of the modern educational encounter is, to use Paolo Freire's words, that teaching:

> ...becomes an act of depositing, in which the students are the depositories and the teacher is the depositor. Instead of communicating, the teacher issues communiques and makes deposits which the student patiently receive, memorize, and repeat. This is the "banking" concept of education.... The teacher teaches and the students are taught.... The teacher chooses and enforces his choice and the students comply. The teacher acts and the students have the illusion of acting through the action of the teacher.[32]

Others refer to this conception as the "jug and mug" approach to teaching whereby the jug fills up the mugs.

Thus the hostility of the school system to student behavior even approaching critical consciousness should be evident in the daily lives of students. Getzels and Jackson[33] have shown that high school students perceive this to be the case. They subjected a group of 449 high school students to an IQ test and a battery of exams which purport to measure creativity.[34] They found no appreciable correlation between measured IQ and measured "creativity." The top 20 percent in IQ on the one hand, and in creativity on the other, were singled out and asked to rank certain personality traits (a) on the degree to which they would like to have these traits, and (b) on the degree to which they believed teachers would like the student to have. There was virtually complete agreement by the high IQ and the high creatives on which traits are preferred by teachers; in other words, these students view the demands made upon them in a similar way. However, the two groups disagreed on what traits they themselves would like to have: The correlation between the two groups' ratings of the personality traits "preferred for oneself" was quite low.[35] Most striking of all, however, was the finding that, while the high IQs' "preferred traits" correspond closely to their perception of the teachers' values, the high creatives ranking of preferred traits was actually inversely related to the perceived teachers' ranking.[36] The high creatives do not fail to conform; rather they do not wish to conform.[37]

Getzel and Jackson's is but one of the many studies which link personality traits to school grades. We have undertaken a review of this literature, the results of which support the following interpretation.[38] Students are rewarded for exhibiting discipline, subordinancy, intellectually as opposed to emotionally oriented behavior, and hard work independent from intrinsic task motivation. Moreover, these traits are rewarded independently of any effect of "proper demeanor" on scholastic achievement.

Rather than plowing through this mass of data, we shall present the results of the most extensive of our sources. In the early 1960s, John L. Holland undertook a study of the determinants of high school success among a group of 639 National Merit Scholarship finalists—males for the most part in the top 10 percent of students in IQ and the top 15 percent in class rank.[39] Holland collected four objective measures of cognitive development from his subjects' College Entrance Examination Board tests.[40] In addition, he collected some sixty-five measures of personality, attitude, self-concept, creativity, and home life through testing the students, their parents, and obtaining various ratings from their teachers.[41]

We have extensively analyzed this massive body of data.[42] Our first conclusion is that, while the group's high academic rank is doubtless related to their above-average IQs, differences in scholastic achievement among them were not significantly related to their grades, despite a good deal of variation in both achievement and grades within the group. More telling, however, is the fact that many of the personality variables were significantly and positively related to grades. Most important were the teachers' ratings of the students' *Citizenship* and the students' self evaluation of *Drive to Achieve*.[43] Neither of these variables had any significant impact on actual achievement measures!

These results are not in themselves surprising. It is to be expected that students will be rewarded for their conformity to the social order of the school *(Citizenship)* as well as their personal motivation to succeed within the nexus of this social order *(Drive to Achieve)*. Only the most naive would expect school grades to depend on scholastic achievement alone.

But what do *Citizenship* and *Drive to Achieve* really reflect? In a liberated educational encounter, we would expect these traits to embody some combination of diligence, social popularity, creativity, and mental flexibility. Yet statistical analysis *of* the Holland data reveals a strikingly different pattern. Students who are ranked by their teachers as high on *Citizenship* and *Drive to Achieve* are indeed more likely to be diligent (e.g., they are high on such measures as *Deferred Gratification, Perseverance,* and *Control)* and socially popular (e.g., they are high on *Social Leadership* and *Popularity)*. But they are, in fact, significantly below average on measures of creativity and mental flexibility (e.g., they are low on such measures as *Cognitive Flexibility, Complexity of Thought, Originality, Creativity,* and *Independence of Judgment)*.[44] Moreover, further statistical analysis shows that these same traits of creativity and mental flexibility are directly penalized in terms of school grades, holding constant test scores, *Citizenship,* and *Drive to Achieve.*

The conclusions from this body of data seem inescapable. Conformity to the social order of the school involves submission to a set of authority relationships which are inimical to personal growth. Instead of promoting a healthy balance among the capacity for creative autonomy, diligence, and susceptibility to social regulation, the reward system of the school inhibits those manifestations of personal capacity which threaten hierarchical authority.

We have emphasized elements on the "hidden curriculum" faced in varying degrees by all students. But schools do different things to different children. Boys and girls, blacks and whites, rich and poor are treated differently. Affluent suburban schools, working-class schools, and ghetto schools all exhibit a distinctive pattern of sanctions and rewards. Moreover, most of the discussion here has focused on high-school students. In important ways, colleges are different; and community colleges exhibit social relations of education which differ sharply from those of elite four-year institutions. In short, U.S. education is not monolithic; our analysis will be expanded accordingly in future chapters.

Why do schools reward docility, passivity, and obedience? Why do they penalize creativity and spontaneity? Why the historical constancy of suppression and domination in an institution so central to the elevation of youth? Surely this is a glaring anomaly in terms of traditional liberal educational theory. The naive enthusiasm of the contemporary free-school movement suggests the implicit assumption that no one bad ever tried to correct this situation—that the ideal of liberated education is simply a new conception which has never been tried. Even sophisticated critics, such as Charles Silberman, tend to attribute the oppressiveness of schooling to simple oversight and irrationality:

> What is mostly wrong with public schools is not due to venality or indifference or stupidity but to mindlessness...It simply never occurs to more than a handful, to ask why they are

doing what they are doing to think seriously or deeply about the purposes or consequences of education.[45]

Yet, the history of the progressive-education movement attests to the intransigence of the educational system to "enlightened change" within the context of corporate capitalism.

Progressivism has been the keynote of modern educational theory embracing such pillars of intellect and influence as John Dewey, Charles W. Elliot, Alfred North Whitehead, William James, and G. Stanley Hall. The birth of the Association for the Advancement of Progressive Education in 1918 was merely the political codification of an already active social movement whose aim, in the words of its founder Stanwood Cobb, "...had little of modesty.... We aimed at nothing short of changing the entire school system of America."[46] Subscribing to Dewey's dictum that "... education is the fundamental method of social reform,...." the statement of principles of the Association for the Advancement of Progressive Education had its aim to be "...the truest and fullest development of the individual, based upon the scientific study of his mental, physical, spiritual, and social characteristics and needs."[47] However avant-garde today's liberal educationists feel themselves to be, they envision little more than did the Progressives in the dawning years of the century. Schooling was to provide the child with the freedom to develop "naturally" with a teacher as guide, not taskmaster. Intrinsic interest not external authority was to motivate all work. The leitmotif of the day was "taking the lid off kids," and the aim was to sublimate natural creative drives in fruitful directions rather than to repress them. Emotional and intellectual development were to hold equal importance, and activity was to be "real life" and "student directed."

The mass media dramatically attest to the ideological victory of the Progressives: Professional journals, education textbooks, and even the various publications of the U.S. Office of Education mouthed the rhetoric of Progressivism. As Lawrence A. Cremin, a foremost historian of the Progressive Movement in education, notes:

> There is a "conventional wisdom"... in education... and by the end of World War II progressivism had come to be that conventional wisdom. Discussions of educational policy were liberally spiced with phrases like "recognized individual differences," "personality development," "the whole child," "the needs of learners," "intrinsic motivation," "persistent life situations," "bridging the gap between home and school," "teaching children, not subjects," "adjusting the school to the child," "real-life experiences," "teacher pupil relationships," and "staff planning." Such phrases... signified that Dewey's forecast of the day when progressive education would eventually be accepted as good education had now finally come to pass.[48]

Yet the schools have changed little in substance.

Thus we must reject mindlessness along with venality, indifference, and stupidity as the source for oppressive education. A more compelling explanation of the failure to combat repression in U.S. schooling is simply that progressive education, though triumphant in educational theory, was never given a chance in practice. Indeed, this argument is often used by those adhering to the liberal perspective. Thus Raymond E. Callahan traces the failure of Progressivism to the growing preoccupation with order and efficiency in educational practice at the same time that progressive education was capturing hearts and minds in educational theory. Callahan argues that:

> ... Very much of what has happened in American education since 1900 can be explained on the basis of the extreme vulnerability of our schoolmen to public criticism and pressure and that this vulnerability is built into our pattern of local support and control.[49]

The direction the formal educational system took in this situation was dictated by the power of business interests and the triumphant ideology of "efficient management." Again Callahan:

> What was unexpected (in my investigation) was the extent not only of the power of the business-industrial groups, but of the strength of the business ideology. I had expected more professional autonomy and I was completely unprepared for that extent and degree of capitulation by administrators to whatever demands were made upon them.[50]

This vulnerability had great implications for student, teacher, and administrator alike. "Business methods" in schools meant that administrators were to be recruited from the ranks of politicians and especially businessmen, rather than professional educators, and their orientation was toward cost-saving and control rather than quality of education. Business methods also meant that the teacher was to be reduced to the status of a simple worker, with little control over curriculum, activities, or discipline, and whose accountability to the administrator again involved classroom authority rather than the quality of classroom experience. Lastly, the student was reduced to an "object" of administration, "busy-work," and standardized tests coming to prevail over play and self-development.

In short, the history of twentieth-century education is the history not of Progressivism but of the imposition upon the schools of "business values" and social relationships reflecting the pyramid of authority and privilege in the burgeoning capitalist system. The evolution of U.S. education during this period was not guided by the sanguine statements of John Dewey and Jane Addams, who saw a reformed educational system eliminating the more brutal and alienating aspects of industrial labor. Rather, the time motion orientation of Frederick Taylor and "Scientific Management," with its attendant fragmentation of tasks, and imposition of bureaucratic forms and top-down control held sway.

Thus there are some grounds for the opinion that the modern liberal view of the self-development capacities of schooling has not been falsified by recent U.S. experience; rather it has never been tried. A historian of Progressivism in U.S. education might well echo Gandhi's assessment of Western civilization: "It would be a good idea."

A Preface to the Critique of Liberal Educational Reform

> Ignorance is the mother of industry as well as of superstition. Reflection and fancy are subject to err; but a habit of moving the hand or the foot is independent of either. Manufacture, accordingly, prospers most where the mind is least consulted, and where the workshop may...be considered an engine, the parts of which are men.—Adam Ferguson, *An Essay on the History of Civil Society,* 1767

Decades of broken promises cast strong doubt on modern liberal educational theory. But the anomalies which arise when theory and practice are juxtaposed cannot lay it finally to rest. *As* Thomas Kuhn has noted, even in the physical sciences, only a recognizably superior alternative seals the fate of faulty but generally accepted dogma.[51]

All the more true is this observation in the social sciences. In the case of liberal educational theory, the failures of educational reform we have presented are by no means decisive. The "necessary connection" among the integrative, egalitarian, and developmental functions of education may appear only in the long run. Capitalism may still be young, and does seem to promote a rhetoric of tolerance and egalitarianism, as well as a supreme emphasis on individualism and human development. That this rhetoric is consistently thwarted in practice may simply represent a perverse institutional inertia. While educational policy has failed in the past, maturity and increased expertise may render it vastly more potent in the future. No one ever claimed reform to be easy—only ultimately possible with proper dedication. Finally, there may be tangible limits—technologically determined—to the degree of social mobility, due to inherent differences in mental ability. The possibility has been asserted forcefully by such writers as Arthur Jensen and Richard Herrnstein.[52]

In short, decent respect for liberal theory demands it be critiqued on theoretical grounds as well as in terms of the social outcomes it predicts, and, preferably with an alternative in mind. This will be our goal. While detailed presentation of our alternative will await future chapters, our argument may be summarized simply enough here: the failure of progressive educational reforms stems from the contradictory nature of the objectives of its integrative, egalitarian and developmental functions in a society whose economic life is governed by the institutions of corporate capitalism.

Both the democratic and technocratic versions of liberal education theory focus on the relationships into which individuals enter upon adulthood. In Dewey's democratic version, political life is singled out as central, while for the technocratic version, the technical aspects of production hold the honored position. Both have been blind to—or at least treated in quite unrealistic manner—the social relationships of capitalist production. Dewey's overall framework seems eminently correct. His error lies in characterizing the social system as democratic, whereas, in fact, the hierarchical division of labor in the capitalist enterprise is politically autocratic. Moreover, his central thesis as to the economic value of an educational system devoted to fostering personal growth is untrue in capitalist society. Dewey's view requires that work be a natural extension of intrinsically motivated activity. The alienated work of corporate life is inimical to intrinsic motivation.

In corporate capitalist society, the social relations of production conform, by and large, to the "hierarchical division of labor," characterized by power and control emanating from the top downward through a finely gradated bureaucratic order.[53] The social relationships of the typically bureaucratic corporate enterprise require special attention because they are neither democratic nor technical.

For Dewey, democracy is, in essence, "...a mode of conjoint communicative experience..." which "...repudiates the principle of external authority...in favor of voluntary disposition and interest." In this sense, the dominant forms of work for which the educational system prepares youth are profoundly antidemocratic. Under capitalism, work is characterized not by conjoint, but by hierarchical "communicative experience," and rigid patterns of dominance and subordinacy, where personal interaction is dictated primarily by rules of procedure set by employers: Dewey's "voluntary disposition" of the worker extends only over the decision to work or starve.

Dewey is of course aware of the undemocratic control of production in capitalist society; indeed, he refers explicitly to "...those in control of industry—those who supply its aims." But he avoids the fatal consequence of this admission for his theory by de-emphasizing democratic process and focusing on outcomes: the quality of the decision made by industrial aristocrats. The dehumanized nature of work in Dewey's time, exemplified by Taylorism and time-motion studies, and today, by the "human relations" school of organizational theory—is attributed to their "one-sided stimulations of thought," and hence responsive to liberal educational exposure. Here Dewey exhibits in raw form the liberal proclivity to locate the source of systemic failures in the shortcomings of individuals aim to propose "expert" solutions which respect—even reinforce—the top-down control of social life under corporate capitalism.[54] Surely he could not have been unaware of the forces in a market-oriented economy forcing managerial decision continually toward profit maximization to which end secure hierarchical authority and flexible control of the enterprise from the top are prime requisites.[55]

Similarly, the technocratic version of liberal educational theory suffers from an extremely partial characterization of the capitalist system. The major error in the technocratic school is its overemphasis on cognitive skills as the basic requirement of job adequacy. We shall show that cognitive requirements are by no means determinant, and indeed, can account for little of the association of education and economic success, Had the technocratic school looked at the social rather than the technical relations of production, it might have been more circumspect in asserting the compatibility of the integrative, egalitarian, and developmental functions of schooling. Indeed, it might have found that the way in which the school system performs its integrative function—through its production of stratified labor force for the capitalist enterprise—is inconsistent with its performance of either developmental or egalitarian functions. Focusing on cognitive variables, it cannot even entertain the idea that the correspondence between the social relations of production and the social relations of education—the essential mechanism of the integrative function of schooling—might preclude an egalitarian or truly humanistic education.

Thus the modern economy is a product of a social as well as a technical revolution. In the development of productive organization from precapitalist forms, through the relativity simple entrepreneur-worker relationship of the early factory system based on piecework, immediate supervision, and direct worker assessment to the modern complex, stratified, and bureaucratically ordered corporation or governmental organ, not simply the technical demands of work, but its social organization have changed drastically. Seen from the present, the Industrial Revolution may appear as a simple upgearing of the pace of technological change. From the point of view of those experiencing it, however, it constituted a thorough-going social upheaval involving not only radically new institutions in the governance of economic activity, but a radically different pattern of social interactions with demanding and pervasive requirements on the level of individual psychic functioning. Values, beliefs, modes of personal behavior, and patterns of social and economic loyalties were formed, transformed, and reproduced in the process of bringing the individual into line with the needs of capital accumulation and the extension of the wage labor system.

Conclusion

> Of manufactures, of commerce, of both individual and national prosperity, nay even of science itself, the extended and abundant increase tends to complete the fatal circle: and, by decay, convulsion, anarchy, and misery, to produce a new and renovated order of things. In an advanced state of society, where the meridian is attained or passes, nothing can prevent or even protract the evil day, except the revivifying influence of education.—Thomas Bernard, "Extract from an account of the Mendip Schools," *Report of the Society for the Better Condition of the Poor,* 1799

The record of actual successes and failures of education as reform is not sufficient either to accept or to reject the liberal outlook. But it must be a point of departure in any serious inquiry into its potential contribution to social improvement. The record, as we have shown, is not encouraging. First, despite the concerted efforts of progressive educators of three generations, and despite the widespread assimilation of their vocabulary in the United States, schools, by and large, remain hostile to the individual's needs for personal development. Second, the history of U.S. education provides little support for the view that schools have been vehicles for the equalization of economic status or opportunity. Nor are they today. The proliferation of special programs for the equalization of educational opportunity had precious little impact on the structure of the U.S. education, and even less on the structure of income and opportunity in the U.S. economy. It is clear that education in the United States is simply too weak an influence on the distribution of economic status and opportunity to fulfill its promised mission as the Great Equalizer. Schooling remains a meager instrument in promoting full participation of racial minorities in the United States—indeed, even the expensive pilot projects in this direction seem to have failed rather spectacularly.

The educational system serves—through the correspondence of its social relations with those of economic life—to reproduce economic inequality and to distort personal development. Thus under corporate capitalism, the objectives of liberal educational reform are contradictory: It is precisely because of its role as producer of an alienated and stratified labor force that the educational system has developed its repressive and unequal structure. In the history of U.S. education, it is the integrative function which has dominated the purpose of schooling, to the detriment of the other liberal objectives.

More fundamentally, the contradictory nature of liberal educational reform objectives may be directly traced to the dual role imposed on education in the interests of profitability and stability; namely, enhancing workers' productive capacities and perpetuating the social, political, and economic conditions for the transformation of the fruits of labor into capitalist profits. It is these overriding objectives of the capitalist class—not the ideals of liberal reformers—which have shaped the actuality of U.S. education, had left little room for the school to facilitate the pursuit of equality or full human development. When education is viewed as an aspect of the reproduction of the capitalist division of labor, the history of school reforms in the United States appears less as a story of an enlightened but sadly unsuccessful corrective and more as an integral part of the process of capitalist growth itself.

We cannot rule out the possibility that a future dramatic and unprecedented shift toward equality of educational opportunity might act as a force for equality. Nor do we exclude the possibility that open classrooms and free schools might make a substantial contribution to a more liberating process of human development. Indeed, we strongly support reforms of this type is part of a general strategy of social and economic transformation. But to consider educational change in isolation from other social forces is altogether too hypothetical. The structure of U.S. education did not evolve in a vacuum; nor will it be changed, holding other things constant. Education has been historically a device for allocating individuals to economic positions, where inequality among the positions themselves is inherent in the hierarchal division of labor, differences in the degree of monopoly power of various sectors of the economy, and the power of different occupational groups to limit the supply or increase the monetary returns to their services. Thus equalization of educational outcomes, rather than reducing inequality, would more likely simply shift the job of allocating individuals to economic positions to some other "institution." Similarly, a less repressive educational system will produce little more than the "job blues" unless it can make an impact upon the nature of work and the control over production.

This much, at least, we can say with some certainty: Repression, individual powerlessness, inequality of incomes, and inequality of opportunity did not originate historically in the educational system, nor do they derive from unequal and repressive schools today. The roots of repression and inequality lie in the structure and functioning of the capitalist economy. Indeed, we shall suggest in the next chapter that they characterize any modern economic system—including the socialist state—which denies people participatory control of economic life.

Notes

1. John Dewey, *Democracy and Education* (New York: The Free Press, 1966), p. 20.
2. *Ibid.*, pp. 50–53.
3. Theodore W. Schultz, "Investment in Poor People," Seminar on Manpower Policy and Programs, Office of Manpower Policy Evaluation Research, Washington: Department of Labor, 1966.
4. Harvey Averch *et al.*, "How Effective Is Schooling: A Critical Review and Synthesis of Research Findings" (Santa Monica: The Rand Corporation, 1972).
5. Samuel Bowles and Herbert Gintis, "IQ in the U.S. Class Structure," in *Social Policy*, November–December 1972 and January–February 1973.
6. Arthur A. Jensen, "How Much Can We Boost IQ and Scholastic Achievement?" *Havard Educational Review*, Vol. 39, No. 1, 1969; Richard Herrnstein, "IQ," *Atlantic Monthly*, Vol. 228, No, 3, September 1971; Edward C. Banfield, *The Unheavenly City* (Boston: Little, Brown and Company, 1968); Daniel P. Moynihan and Nathan Glazer, *Beyond the Melting Pot* (Cambridge, Mass.: MIT Press, 1970).
7. Dewey (1966), *op. cit.*, p. 20.
8. This calculation is based on data reported in full in Samuel Bowles and Valerie Nelson, "The 'Inheritance of IQ' and the Intergenerational Transmission of Economic Inequality," *The Review of Economics and Statistics*, Vol. LVI, No.1, February 1974. It refers to non-Negro males from non-farm backgrounds, aged 35–44 years. The zero-order correlation coefficient between socioeconomic background and years of schooling was estimated at 0.646. The estimated standard deviation of years of schooling was 3.02. The results tor other age groups are similar.
9. See Appendix A, footnote 14, in Chapter 4 and the following sources: Bowles and Nelson (1974), *op. cit.* Peter Blau and Otis D. Duncan, *The American Occupational Structure* (New York: John Wiley, 1967); Otis D. Duncan, D. C. Featherman, and Beverly Duncan, *Socioeconomic Background and Occupational Achievement, Final Report*, Project No, S-0074 (EO-191) (Washington, D.C.: Department of Health, Education and Welfare, Office of Education, 1968); Samuel Bowles, "Schooling and Inequality from Generation to Generation," *The Journal of Political Economy*, Vol. 80, No.3, Part II, May-

June 1972.

10. These figures refer to individuals who were high-schoo! seniors in October, 1965, and who subsequently graduated from high school. College attendance refers to both two- and four-year institutions, Family income is for the twelve months preceding October 1965. Data is drawn from U.S. Bureau of the Census, *Current Population Reports,* Series P-60, No. 183, May 1969.

11. For further evidence, see U.S. Bureau of the Census (1969), *op. cit.,* and Jerome Karabel, "Community Colleges and Social Stratification," *Harvard Educational Review,* Vol. 424, No. 42, November 1972.

12. Calculation based on data in James S. Coleman *et al., Equality of Educational Opportunity* (Washington, D.C.: U.S. Government Printing Office, 1966), and Bowles and Gintis (1972), *op. cit.*

13. The data relating to IQ are from a 1966 survey of veterans by the National Opinion Research Center; and from N. Bayley and E. S. Schaefer, "Correlations of Material and Child Behaviors with the Development of Mental Ability: Data from the Berkeley Growth Study," *Monographs of Social Research in Child Development,* 29, 6 (1964).

14. This figure is based on data reported in full in our Appendix A and in Bowles and Nelson (1974), *op. cit.* The left-hand bars of each pair were calculated using the estimated corrdation coefficient between socioeconomic background and education of 0.65. The results for other age groups were similar: 0.64 for ages 25–34 and 44–54, and 0.60 for ages 55–64 years. The right-hand bars were calculated from thc normalized regression coeficient on socioeconomic background from an equation using background and early childhood IQ to predict years of schooling, which was estimated at 0.54. The results for other age groups were similar: 0.54 for ages 25–34 and 45–54, and 0.48 for ages 55–64. Socioeconomic background is defined as normalized sum of father's education, father's occupational status, and parents' income. The mean and standard deviation of years of schooling were estimated at 11.95 and 3.02, respectively.

15. Based on a large sample of U.S. high-school students as reported in: John C. Flannagan and William. W. Cooley, *Project Talent, One Year Follow-up Study,* Cooperative Research Project, No. 2333, University of Pittsburgh: School of Education, 1966.

16. Christopher Jencks *et al., Inequality: A Reassessment of the Effects of Family* and *Schooling in America* (New York: Basic Books, 1972), p.48.

17. William L. Spady, "Educational Mobility and Access: Growth and Paradoxes," in *American Journal of Sociology,* Vol. 73, No. 3, November 1967; and Blau and Duncan, *op. cit.* (1967).

18. Blau and Duncan (1967), *op. cit.* See the reported correlations in Appendix A.

19. We estimate the coefficient of variation of years of schooling at about 4.3 in 1940 (relying on Barry Chiswick and Jacob Mincer, "Time Series Changes in Personal Income Inequality in the U.S." *Journal of Political Economy,* Vol. 80, No. 3, Part II [May–June 1972], Table 4 tor the standard deviation of schooling and the Decennial Census for the mean), and at 2.95 in 1969 (relying on Chiswick and Mincer [1972] Table B10).

20. Calculated from Table B1 and Table B10 in Chiswick and Mincer (1972), *op. cit.*

21. Peter Henle, "Exploring the Distribution of Earned Income," *Monthly Labor Review,* Vol. 95, No. 12, December 1972. Inequalities in income (profit, rent interest, and transfer payments plus labor earnings) may also have increased if the unmeasured income from capital gain and other tax shelters for the rich are taken into acount. See Jerry Cromwell, "Income Inequalities, Discrimination and Uneven Development," unpublished Ph.D. dissertation, Harvard University, May 1974.

22. Chiswick and Mincer (1972), op. *cit.*

23. Thomas I. Ribich, *Education and Poverty* (Washington, D.C.: Brookings Institution, 1968).

24. United States Bureau of the Census, *Current Population Reports,* Series P-60, October 1970, Table 75, p. 368.

25. United States Bureau of the Census, *Curren. Population Reports,* series P-60, November, 1972, Table 1, p. 14.

26. Michael Reich, *Racial Discrimination and the Distribution of Income,* Ph.D. dissertation, Harvard University, May 1973.

27. United States Bureau of the Census, *op. cit.* (Dccember 1973), Table 47, p. 114.

28. Whence e. e. cummings' sharp lines: "…the children knew, but only a few/ and down they forgot as up they grew." e. e. cummings, *Poems, 1923–1954* (New York: Harcourt, Brace and World, 1954), p. 370.

29. cf. Charles Valentine, *Culture and Poverty* (Chicago: University of Chicago Press, 1968). Early in the nineteenth century, Robert Dale Owen, the renowned utopian, had proposed that the interests of social equality dictated that the children of the poor be raised in public institutions.

30. Tyack (1967), *op. cit.;* Katz (1971), *op. cit.*

31. In Chapter 5 we will argue that both changes in the approach to discipline reflect the changing social relationships of production in the corporate capitalist economy.

32. Paulo Freire, *Pedagogy of the Oppressed* (New York: Herder and Herder, 1972), pp. 58–59.

33. J. W. Getzels and P. W. Jackson, "Occupational Choice and Cognitive Functioning," in *Journal of Abnormal and Social Psychology,* February 1960.

34. For a general discussion of the content and meaning of creativity tests, see Michael W. Wallach, *The Intelligence of Creativity Distinction* (New York: General Learning Corporation, 1971),

35. The exact correlation was r = 0.41.

36. The correlations between own and teacher's desired personality traits were r = 0.67 for the high IQs and r = 0.25 for the high creatives.

37. Both groups had similar scores on tests of achievement motivation—McClelland n-ach and Strodtbeck V-score,

38. Herbert Gintis, "Education, Technology, and the Characteristics of Worker Productivity," *American Economic Review,* May 1971.

39. John L. Holland, "Creative and Academic Performance Among Talented Adolescents," *Journal of Educational Psychology,* No. 52, 1961.

40. Verbal and Mathematical sections of the Scholastic Achievement Test, Humanities and Scientific Comprehension.

41. The interested reader should consult Holland (1961), *op. cit.* and Herbert Gintis, *Alienation and Power,* Ph.D. dissertation for Harvard University, May 1969.

42. Gintis (1969), *op. cit.* and (1971), *op. cit.*

43. Holland's personality measures will be presented in italics. Unless otherwise indicated, all are statistically significant at the 1 percent level.

44. In addition to the good citizenship—externally motivated student, a small portion of the high *Drive to Achieve* students exhibit a set of personality traits quite similar to those of the *Deviant Creatives* described in Getzel and Jackson's study, already presented. These students, high on *Artistic Performance and Creative Activities,* evidently reject the pressure to define their personal goals in terms compatible with high grades and teacher approbation, and their positive personality traits are uniformly penalized in terms of grades and teacher ratings for *Citizenship.*

45. Charles Silberman (1971), *op. cit.*

46. As quoted in Lawrence Cremin (1964), *op. cit., p.* 241.

47. *Ibid.,* pp. 240–241.

48. *Ibid.,* p. 328.

49. Raymond Callahan, *Education and the Cult of Efficiency* (Chicago; University of Chicago Press, 1962), preface.

50. *Ibid.*

51. Thomas S. Kuhn, *The Structure of Scientific Revolutions (Chicago:* The University of Chicago Press, 1962), p. 53.

52. Arthur A. Jensen, *Educability and Group Differences* (New York: Harper & Row, 1973); and Richard Herrnstein, *IQ in the Meritocracy* (Boston: Little, Brown and Company, 1973).

53. For a more complete discussion, see Richard C. Edwards, Michael Reich, and Thomas Weisskopf, *The Capitalist System* (Englewood Cliffs, NJ: Prentice-Hall, 1972); André Gorz, "Technical Intelligence and the Capitalist Division of Labor," *Telos,* Summer 1972; and Chapter 3.

54. Clarence Karier, *Shaping the American Educational State: 1900 to the Present* (New York: The Free Press, 1975); and Clarence Karier, Joel Spring, and Paul C. Violas (1973), *op. cit.*

55. Indeed, it has been pointed out to us by Dr. F. Bohnsack in a personal communication that Dewey did begin to revise his views, especially after World War I:

For this later time, at least, I would doubt whether we could say he characterized the social system as democratic. He saw and criticized the totalitarian features of existing society and the missing "… intrinsic growth orientation of education." As self development and equality of opportunity, to him, were inconsistent with preparing workers for existing [alienated] jobs, he criticized such a preparation and wanted to change existing industrial education as well as industrial work.

See A. G. Wirth, *The Vocational-Liberal Studies Controversy between John Dewey and Others (1900–1917)* (Washington, D.C., 1970), and John Dewey, "Education vs. Trade-training," *The New Republic,* Vol. 3, No. 15, May 1915.

As Virginia Held has pointed out to us, Dewey, in his mature work, *Art as Experience* (New York: Minton, Balch and Company, 1934), went further to claim:

The labor and employment problem of which we are so acutely aware cannot be solved by mere changes in wage, hours of work, and sanitary conditions. No permanent solution is possible save in a radical alteration, which affects the degree and kind of participation the worker has in the production and social disposition of the wares he produces. (p. 343)

5

On Understanding the Processes of Schooling

The Contributions of Labeling Theory

RAY C. RIST

There have been few debates within American education which have been argued with such passion and intensity as that of positing causal explanations of success or failure in schools.[1] One explanation which has had considerable support in the past few years, particularly since the publication of *Pygmalion in the Classroom* by Rosenthal and Jacobson (1968), has been that of the "self-fulfilling prophecy." Numerous studies have appeared seeking to explicate the mechanisms by which the teacher comes to hold certain expectations of the students and how these are then operationalized within the classroom so as to produce what the teacher had initially assumed. The origins of teacher expectations have been attributed to such diverse variables as social class, physical appearance, contrived test scores, sex, race language patterns, and school records. But from the flurry of recent research endeavors, there has emerged a hiatus between this growing body of data and any larger theoretic framework. The concept of the self-fulfilling prophecy has remained simply that—a concept. The lack of a broader conceptual scheme has meant that research in this area has become theoretically stymied. Consequently, there has evolved instead a growing concern over the refinement of minute methodological nuances.

The thrust of this [article] is to argue that there is a theoretical perspective developing in the social sciences which can break the conceptual and methodological logjam building up on the self-fulfilling prophecy. Specifically, the emergence of *labeling theory* as an explanatory framework for the study of social deviance appears to be applicable to the study of education as well. Among the major contributions to the development of labeling theory are Becker, 1963, 1964; Broadhead, 1974; Lemert, 1951, 1972, 1974; Douglas, 1971, 1972; Kitsuse, 1964; Loffland, 1969; Matza, 1964, 1969; Scheff, 1966; Schur, 1971; Scott and Douglas, 1972; and Rubington and Weinberg, 1973.

If the labeling perspective can be shown to be a legitimate framework from which to analyze social processes influencing the educational experience and the contributions of such processes to success or failure in school, there would then be a viable *interactionist* perspective to counter both biological and cultural determinists' theories of educational outcomes. While the latter two positions both place ultimate causality for success or failure *outside* the school, the labeling approach allows for an examination of what, in fact, is happening *within* schools. Thus, labeling theory would call our attention for example, to the various evaluative mechanisms (both formal and informal) operant in schools, the ways in which schools nurture and support such mechanisms, how students react, what the outcomes are for interpersonal interaction based on how these mechanisms have evaluated individual students, and how, *over time,* the consequences of having a certain evaluative tag influence the options available to a student within a school. What follows first is a summary of a number of the key aspects of labeling theory as it has been most fully developed in the sociological literature; second is an attempt to integrate the research on the self-fulfilling prophecy with the conceptual framework of labeling theory. Finally, the implications of this synthesis are explored for both future research and theoretical development.

Becoming Deviant: The Labeling Perspective

Those who have used labeling theory have been concerned with the study of *why* people are labeled, and *who* it is that labels them as someone who has committed one form or another of deviant behavior. In sharp contrast to the predominant approaches for the study of deviance, there is little concern in labeling theory with the motivational and characterological nature of the person who committed the act.

Deviance is understood, not as a quality of the person or as created by his actions, but instead as created by group definitions and reactions. It is a social judgment imposed by a social audience. As Becker (1963:9) has argued:

> The central fact of deviance is that it is created by society. I do not mean this in the way it is ordinarily understood, in which the causes of deviance are located in the social situation of the deviant, or the social factors, which prompted his action. I mean, rather, that social groups create deviants by making the rules whose infraction constitute deviance, and by applying those rules to particular people and labeling them as outsiders. From this point of view, *deviance is not the quality of the act the person commits, but rather a consequence of the application by others of rules and sanctions to an "offender." This deviant is one to whom the label has been successfully applied. Deviant behavior is behavior that people so label.* (emphasis added)

The labeling approach is insistent on the need for a shift in attention from an exclusive concern with the deviant individual to a major concern with the *process* by which the deviant label is applied. Again citing Becker (1964:2):

> The labeling approach sees deviance always and everywhere as a process and interaction between at least two kinds of people: those who commit (or who are said to have committed) a deviant act, and the rest of the society, perhaps divided into several groups itself.... One consequence is that we become much more interested in the process by which deviants are defined by the rest of the society, than in the nature of the deviant act itself.

The important questions, then, for Becker and others, are not of the genre to include, for example: Why do some individuals come to act out norm-violating behavior? Rather, the questions are of the following sort: Who applied the deviant label to whom? Whose rules shall prevail and be enforced? Under what circumstances is the deviant label successfully and unsuccessfully applied? How does a community decide what forms of conduct should be singled out for this kind of attention? What forms of behavior do persons in the social system consider deviant, how do they interpret such behavior, and what are the consequences of these interpretations for their reactions to individuals who are seen as manifesting such behavior? (See Akers, 1973.)

The labeling perspective rejects any assumption that a clear consensus exists as to what constitutes a norm violation—or for that matter, what constitutes a norm—within a complex and highly heterogeneous society. What comes to be determined as deviance and who comes to be determined as a deviant is the result of a variety of social contingencies influenced by who has the power to enforce such determinations. Deviance is thus problematic and subjectively given. The case for making the societal reaction to rulebreaking a major independent variable in studies of deviant behavior has been succinctly stated by Kitsuse (1964:101):

A sociological theory of deviance must focus specifically upon the interactions which not only define behaviors as deviant, but also organize and activate the application of sanctions by individuals, groups, or agencies. For in modern society, the socially significant differentiation of deviants from the nondeviant population is increasingly contingent upon circumstances of situation, place social, and personal biography, and the bureaucratically organized activities of agencies of social control.

Traditional notions of who is a deviant and what are the causes for such deviance are necessarily reworked. By emphasizing the processual nature of deviance, any particular deviant is seen to be a product of being caught, defined, segregated, labeled, and stigmatized. *This is one of the major thrusts of the labeling perspective—that forces of social control often produce the unintended consequence of making some persons defined as deviant even more confirmed as deviant because of the stigmatization of labeling. Thus, social reactions to deviance further deviant careers.* Erikson (1966) has even gone so far as to argue that a society will strive to maintain a certain level of deviance within itself as deviance is functional to clarifying group boundaries, providing scapegoats, creating out-groups who can be the source of furthering in-group solidarity, and the like.

The idea that social control may have the paradoxical effect of generating more of the very behavior it is designed to eradicate was first elaborated upon by Tannenbaum. He noted (1938:21):

The first dramatization of the "evil" which separates the child out of his group...plays a greater role in making the criminal than perhaps any other experience.... He now lives in a different world. He has been tagged.... The person becomes the thing he is described as being.

Likewise, Schur (1965:4) writes:

The societal reaction to the deviant, then, is vital to an understanding of the deviance itself and a major element in—if not the cause of—the deviant behavior.

The focus on outcomes of social control mechanisms has led labeling theorists to devote considerable attention to the workings of organizations and agencies which function ostensibly to rehabilitate the violator or in other ways draw him back into conformity. Their critiques of prisons, mental hospitals, training schools, and other people-changing institutions suggest that the results of such institutions are frequently nearly the opposite of what they were theoretically designed to produce. These institutions are seen as mechanisms by which opportunities to withdraw from deviance are sealed off from the deviant, stigmatization occurs, and a new identity as a social "outsider" is generated. There thus emerges on the part of the person so labeled a new view of himself which is one of being irrevocably deviant.

This movement from one who has violated a norm to one who sees himself as a habitual norm violator is what Lemert (1972:62) terms the transition from a primary to a secondary deviant. A primary deviant is one who holds to socially accepted roles, views himself as a nondeviant, and believes himself to be an insider. A primary deviant does not deny that he has violated some norm, and claims only that it is not characteristic of him as a person. A secondary deviant, on the other hand, is one who has reorganized his social-psychological characteristics around the deviant role. Lemert (1972:62) writes:

Secondary deviation refers to a special class of socially defined responses which people make to problems created by the societal reaction to their deviance. These problems...become central facts of existence for those experiencing them.... Actions, which have these roles and self-attitudes as their referents make up secondary deviance. The secondary deviant...is a person whose life and identity are organized around the facts of deviance.

A person can commit repeated acts of primary deviation and never come to view himself or have others come to view him as a secondary deviant. Secondary deviation arises from the feedback whereby misconduct or deviation initiates social reaction to the behavior which then triggers further misconduct. Lemert (1951:77) first described this process as follows:

> The sequence of interaction leading to secondary deviation is roughly as follows: 1) primary deviation; 2) societal penalties; 3) further primary deviation; 4) stronger penalties and rejections; 5) further deviations, perhaps with hostilities and resentments beginning to focus upon those doing the penalizing; 6) crisis reached in the tolerance quotient, expressed in formal action by the community stigmatizing of the deviant; 7) strengthening of the deviant conduct as a reaction to the stigmatizing and penalties; and 8) ultimate acceptance of deviant social status and efforts at adjustment on the basis of the associated role.

Thus, when persons engage in deviant behavior they would not otherwise participate in and when they develop social roles they would not have developed save for the application of social control measures, the outcome is the emergence of secondary deviance. The fact of having been apprehended and labeled is the critical element in the subsequent construction of a deviant identity and pursuit of a deviant career.

The Origins of Labeling: Teacher Expectations

Labeling theory has significantly enhanced our understanding of the process of becoming deviant by shifting our attention from the deviant to the judges of deviance and the forces that affect their judgment. Such judgments are critical, for a recurrent decision made in all societies, and particularly frequent in advanced industrial societies, is that an individual has or has not mastered some body of information, or perhaps more basically, has or has not the capacity to master that information. These evaluations are made periodically as one moves through the institution of school and the consequences directly affect the opportunities to remain for an additional period. To be able to remain provides an option for mastering yet another body of information, and to be certified as having done so. As Ivan Illich (1971) has noted, it is in industrial societies that being perceived as a legitimate judge of such mastery has become restricted to those who carry the occupational role of "teacher." A major consequence of the professionalization of the role of teacher has been the ability to claim as a near exclusive decision whether mastery of material has occurred. Such exclusionary decision-making enhances those in the role of "teacher" as they alone come to possess the authority to provide certification for credentials (Edgar, 1974).

Labeling theorists report that in making judgments of deviance, persons may employ information drawn from a variety of sources. Further, even persons within the same profession (therapists, for example) may make divergent use of the same material in arriving at an evaluative decision on the behavior of an individual. Among the sources of information available to labelers, two appear primary: first-hand information obtained from face-to-face interaction with the person they may ultimately label, and second-hand information obtained from other than direct interaction.

The corollary here to the activities of teachers should be apparent. Oftentimes, the evaluation by teachers (which may lead to the label of "bright," "slow," etc.) is based on first-hand information gained through face-to-face interaction during the course of the time the teacher and student spent together in the classroom. But a goodly amount of information about the student which informs the teacher's evaluation is second-hand information. For instance, comments from other teachers, test scores, prior report cards, permanent records, meetings with the parents, or evaluations from welfare agencies and psychological clinics are all potential informational sources. In a variation of the division between first-hand and second-hand sources of information, Johnson (1973) has suggested that there are three key determinants of teacher evaluations: student's prior performance, social status characteristics, and present performance. Prior performance would include information from cumulative records (grades, test scores, notes from past teachers or counselors, and outside evaluators) while social status and performance would be inferred and observed in the ongoing context of the classroom.

What has been particularly captivating about the work of Rosenthal and Jacobson (1968) in this regard is their attempt to provide empirical justification for a truism considered self-evident by many in education: School achievement is not simply a matter of a child's native ability, but involves directly and inextricably the teacher as well. Described succinctly, their research involved a situation where, at the end of a school year, more than 500 students in a single elementary school were administered the "Harvard Test of Inflected Acquisition." In actuality this test was a standardized, relatively nonverbal test of intelligence, Flanagan's (1960) Test of General Ability (TOGA). The teachers were told that such a test would, with high predictive reliability, sort out those students who gave strong indication of being intellectual "spurters" or "bloomers" during the following academic year. Just before the beginning of school the following fall, the teachers were given lists with the names of between one and nine of their students. They were told that these students scored in the top twenty percent of the school on the test, though, of course, no factual basis for such determinations existed. A twenty percent subsample of the "special" students was selected for intensive analysis. Testing of the students at the end of the school year offered some evidence that these selected children did perform better than the nonselected. The ensuing debate as to the validity and implications of the findings from the study will be discussed in the next section.

The findings of Deutsch, Fishman, Kogan, North, and Whiteman (1964); Gibson (1965): Goslin and Glass (1967); McPherson (1966); and Pequignot (1966) all demonstrate the influence of standardized tests of intelligence and achievement on teacher's expectations. Goaldman (1971), in a review of the literature on the use of tests as a second-hand source of information for teachers, noted: "Although some of the research has been challenged, there is a basis for the belief that teachers at all levels are prejudiced by information they receive about a student's ability or character." Mehan (1971, 1974) has been concerned with the interaction between children who take tests and the teachers who administer them. He posits that testing is not the objective use of a measurement instrument, but the outcome of a set of interactional activities which are influenced by a variety of contingencies which ultimately manifest themselves in a reified "test score." Mehan suggests (1971):

> Standardized test performances are taken as an unquestioned, non-problematic reflection of the child's underlying ability. The authority of the test to measure the child's real ability is accepted by both teachers and other school officials. Test results are accepted without doubt as the correct and valid document of the child's ability.

Characteristics of children such as sex and race are immediately apparent to teachers. Likewise, indications of status can be quickly inferred from grooming, style of dress, need for free lunches, information on enrollment cards, discussion of family activities by children, and visits to the school by parents. One intriguing study recently reported in this area is that by two sociologists, Clifford and Walster (1973:249). The substance of their study was described as follows:

> Our experiment was designed to determine what effect a student's physical attractiveness has on a teacher's expectations of the child's intellectual and social behavior. Our hypothesis was that a child's attractiveness strongly influences his teachers' judgments; the more attractive the child, the more biased in his favor we expect the teachers to be. The design required to test this hypothesis is a simple one: Teachers are given a standardized report card and an attached photograph. The report card includes an assessment of the child's academic performance as

well as of his general social behavior. The attractiveness of the photos is experimentally varied. On the basis of this information, teachers are asked to state their expectations of the child's educational and social potential.

Based on the responses of 404 fifth grade teachers within the state of Missouri, Clifford and Walster concluded (1973:255):

> There is little question but that the physical appearance of a student affected the expectations of the teachers we studied. Regardless of whether the pupil is a boy or girl, the child's physical attractiveness has an equally strong association with his teacher's reactions to him.

The variables of race and ethnicity have been documented, by Brown (1968), Davidson and Lang (1960), Jackson and Cosca (1974), and Rubovits and Maehr (1973), among others, as powerful factors in generating the expectations teachers hold of children. It has also been documented that teachers expect less of lower-class children than they do of middle-class children (cf. Becker, 1952; Deutsch, 1963; Leacock, 1969; Rist, 1970, 1973; Stein, 1971; Warner, Havighurst, and Loeb, 1944; and Wilson, 1963). Douglas (1964), in a large-scale study of the tracking system used in British schools, found that children who were clean and neatly dressed in nice clothing, and who came from what the teachers perceived as "better" homes, tended to be placed in higher tracks than their measured ability would predict. Further, when placed there they tended to stay and perform acceptably. Mackler (1969) studied schools in Harlem and found that children tended to stay in the tracks in which they were initially placed and that such placement was based on a variety of social considerations independent of measured ability. Doyle, Hancock, and Kifer (1971) and Palardy (1969) have shown teacher expectations for high performance in elementary grades to be stronger for girls than boys.

The on-going academic and interpersonal performance of the children may also serve as a potent source of expectations for teachers. Rowe (1969) found that teachers would wait longer for an answer from a student they believed to be a high achiever than for one from a student they believed to be a low achiever. Brophy and Good (1970) found that teachers were more likely to give perceived high achieving students a second chance to respond to an initial incorrect answer, and further, that high achievers were praised more frequently for success and criticized less for failure.

There is evidence that the expectations teachers hold for their students can be generated as early as the first few days of the school year and then remain stable over the months to follow (Rist, 1970, 1972, 1973; Willis, 1972). For example, I found during my three-year longitudinal and ethnographic study of a single, *de facto* segregated elementary school in the black community of St. Louis, that after only eight days of kindergarten, the teacher made permanent seating arrangements based on what she assumed were variations in academic capability. But no formal evaluation of the children had taken place. Instead, the assignments to the three tables were based on a number of socio-economic criteria as well as on early interaction patterns in the classroom. Thus, the placement of the children came to reflect the social class distinctions in the room—the poor children from public welfare families all sat at one table, the working class children sat at another and the middle class at the third. I demonstrated how the teacher operationalized her expectations of these different groups of children in terms of her differentials of teaching time, her use of praise and control, and the extent of autonomy within the classroom. By following the same children through first and second grade as well, I was able to show that the initial patterns established by the kindergarten teacher came to be perpetuated year after year. By second grade, labels given by another teacher clearly reflected the reality each of the three groups experienced in the school. The top group was called the "Tigers," the middle group the "Cardinals," and the lowest group, the "Clowns." What had begun as a subjective evaluation and labeling by the teacher took on objective dimensions as the school proceeded to process the children on the basis of the distinctions made when they first began.

Taken together, these studies strongly imply that the notion of "teacher expectations" is multi-faceted and multi-dimensional. It appears that when teachers generate expectations about their students, they do so not only for reasons of academic or cognitive performance, but for their classroom interactional patterns as well. Furthermore, not only ascribed characteristics such as race, sex, class, or ethnicity are highly salient, interpersonal traits are also. Thus, the interrelatedness of the various attributes which ultimately blend together to generate the evaluation a teacher makes as to what can be expected from a particular student suggests the strength and tenacity of such subsequent labels as "bright" or "slow" or "trouble-maker" or "teacher's little helper." It is to the outcomes of the student's having one or another of these labels that we now turn.

An Outcome of Labeling: The Self-Fulfilling Prophecy

W. I. Thomas, many years ago, set forth what has become a basic dictum of the social sciences when he observed, "If men define situations as real, they are real in their consequences." This is at the core of the self-fulfilling prophecy. An expectation which defines a situation comes to influence the actual behavior within the situation so as to produce what was initially assumed to be there. Merton (1968:477) has elaborated on this concept and noted: "The self-fulfilling phase is, in the beginning, a *false* definition of the situation evoking a new behavior which makes the originally false conception come true" (emphasis in the original).

Here it is important to recall a basic tenet of labeling theory—that an individual does not become deviant simply by the commission of some act. As Becker (1963) stressed, deviance is not inherent in behavior *per se,* but in the application by others of rules and sanctions against one perceived as being an "offender." Thus, the only time one can accurately be termed a "deviant" is after the successful application of a label by a social audience. Thus, though many persons may commit norm violations, only select ones are subsequently labeled. The contingencies of race, class, sex, visibility of behavior, age, occupation, and who one's friends are all influence the outcome as to whether one is or is not labeled. Scheff (1966), for example, demonstrated the impact of these contingencies upon the diagnosis as to the severity of a patient's mental illness. The higher one's social status, the less the willingness to diagnose the same behavioral traits as indicative of serious illness in comparison to the diagnosis given to low status persons.

The crux of the labeling perspective lies not in whether one's norm violating behavior is known, but in whether others decide to do something about it. Further, if a label is applied to the individual, it is posited that this in fact causes the individual to become that which he is labeled as being. Due to the reaction of society, the change in the individual involves the development of a new socialized self-concept and social career centered around the deviant behavior. As Rubington and Weinberg (1973:7) have written:

> The person who has been typed, in turn, becomes aware of the new definition that has been placed upon him by members of his groups. He, too, takes this new understanding of himself into account when dealing with them.... When this happens, a social type has been ratified, and a person has been socially reconstructed.

Rosenthal and Jacobson's *Pygmalion in the Classroom* (1968) created wide interest in the notion of the self-fulfilling prophecy as a concept to explain differential performance by children in classrooms. Their findings suggested that the expectations teachers created about the children randomly selected as "intellectual bloomers" somehow caused the teachers to treat them differently, with the result that the children really did perform better by the end of the year. Though the critics of this particular research (Snow, 1969; Taylor, 1970; Thorndike, 1968, 1969) and those who have been unsuccessful in replicating the findings (Claiborn, 1969) have leveled strong challenges to Rosenthal and Jacobson, the disagreements are typically related to methodology, procedure, and analysis rather than to the proposition that relations exist between expectations and behavior.

The current status of the debate and the evidence accumulated in relation to it imply that teacher expectations are *sometimes* self-fulfilling. The early and, I think, overenthusiastic accounts of Rosenthal and Jacobson have obscured the issue. The gist of such accounts have left the impression, as Good and Brophy (1973:73) have noted, that the mere existence of an expectation will automatically guarantee its fulfillment. Rather, as they suggest:

> The fact that teachers' expectations can be self-fulfilling is simply a special case of the principle that any expectations can be self-fulfilling. This process is not confined to classrooms. Although it is not true that "wishing can make it so," our expectations do affect the way we behave in situations, and the way we behave affects how other people respond. In some instances, our expectations about people cause us to treat them in a way that makes them respond just as we expect they would.

Such a position would be borne out by social psychologists who have demonstrated that an individual's first impressions of another person do influence subsequent interactions (Dailey, 1952; Newcomb, 1947) and that one's self-expectations influence one's subsequent behavior (Aronson and Carlsmith, 1962; Brock and Edelman, 1965; Zajonc and Brinkman, 1969).

The conditionality of expectations related to their fulfillment is strongly emphasized by labeling theorists as well. Their emphasis upon the influence of social contingencies on whether one is labeled, how strong the label, and if it can be made to stick at all, points to a recognition that there is a social process involved where individuals are negotiating, rejecting, accepting, modifying, and reinterpreting the attempts at labeling. Such interaction is apparent in the eight stages of the development of secondary deviance outlined above by Lemert. Likewise, Erikson (1964:17), in his comments on the act of labeling as a rite of passage from one side of the group boundary to the other, has noted:

> The common assumption that deviants are not often cured or reformed, then, may be based on a faulty premise, but this assumption is stated so frequently and with such conviction that it often creates the facts which later "prove" it to be correct. If the returning deviant has to face the community's apprehensions often enough, it is understandable that he, too, may begin to wonder whether he has graduated from the deviant role—and *so respond to the uncertainty by resuming deviant activity.* In some respects, this may be the only way for the individual and his community to agree as to what kind of person he really is, for it often happens that the community is only able to perceive his "true colors" when he lapses, momentarily into some form of deviant performance. (emphasis added)

Explicit in Erikson's quote is the fact of the individual's being in interaction with the "community" to achieve some sort of agreement on what the person is "really" like. Though Erikson did not, in this instance, elaborate upon what he meant by "community," it can be inferred from elsewhere in his work that he sees "community" as manifesting itself in the institutions persons create in order to help organize and structure their lives. Such a perspective is clearly within the framework of labeling theory, where a major emphasis has been placed upon the role of institutions in sorting, labeling, tracking, and channeling persons along various routes depending upon the assessment the institution has made of the individual.

One pertinent example of the manner in which labeling theory has been applied to the study of social institutions and their impact upon participants has been in an analysis of the relation of schooling to juvenile delinquency. There have been several works which suggest as a major line of argument that schools, through and because of the manner in which they label students, serve as a chief instrument in the creation of delinquency (Hirschi, 1969; Noblit and Polk, 1975; Polk 1969; Polk and Schafer, 1972; Schafer and Olexa, 1971). For example, Noblit and Polk (1975:3) have noted:

> In as much as the school is the primary institution in the adolescent experience—one that promises not only the future status available to the adolescent, but also that gives or denies status in adolescence itself—it can be expected that its definitions are of particular significance for the actions of youth. That is, the student who has been reported from success via the school has little reason to conform to the often arbitrary and paternalistic regulations and rules of the school. In a very real sense, this student has no "rational constraints" against deviance. It is through the sorting mechanisms of the school, which are demanded by institutions of higher education and the world of work, that youth are labeled and thus sorted into the situation where deviant behavior threatens little while providing some alternative forms of status.

It is well to reiterate the point—interaction implies behavior and choices being made by both parties. The person facing the prospect of receiving a new label imputing a systemic change in the definition of his selfhood may respond in any of a myriad number of ways to this situation. Likewise, the institutional definition of the person is neither finalized nor solidified until the end of the negotiation as to what precisely that label should be. But, in the context of a single student facing the authority and vested interests of a school administration and staff, the most likely outcome is that over time, the student will increasingly move towards conformity with the label the institution seeks to establish. Good and Brophy (1973:75) have elaborated upon this process within the classroom as follows:

1 The teacher expects specific behavior and achievement from particular students.
2 Because of these different expectations, the teacher behaves differently toward the different students.
3 This teacher treatment tells each student what behavior and achievement the teacher expects from him and affects his self-concept, achievement motivation, and level of aspiration.
4 If this teacher treatment is consistent over time, and if the student does not actively resist or change it in some way, it will tend to shape his achievement and behavior. High-expectation students will be led to achieve at high levels, while the achievement of low-expectations students will decline.
5 With time, the student's achievement and behavior will conform more and more closely to that originally expected of him.

The fourth point in this sequence makes the crucial observation that teacher expectations are not automatically self-fulfilling. For the expectations of the teacher to become realized, both the teacher and the student must move towards a pattern of interaction where expectations are clearly communicated and the behavioral response is consonant with the expected patterns. But as Good and Brophy (1973:75) also note:

> This does not always happen. The teacher may not have clear-cut expectations about a particular student, or his expectations may continually change. Even when he has consistent expectations, he may not necessarily communicate them to the student through consistent behavior. In this case, the expectation would not be self-fulfilling even if it turned out to be correct. Finally, the student himself might prevent expectations from becoming self-fulfilling by overcoming them or by resisting them in a way that makes the teacher change them.

Yet, the critique of American education offered by such scholars as Henry (1963), Katz (1971), Goodman (1964), or Reimer (1971) suggests the struggle is unequal between the teacher (and the institution a teacher represents) and the student. The vulnerability of children to the dictates of adults in positions of power over them leaves the negotiations as to what evaluative definition will be tagged on the children more often than not in the hands of the powerful. As Max Weber himself stated, to have power is to be able to achieve one's ends, even in the face of resistance from others. When that resistance is manifested in school by children and is defined by teachers and administrators as truancy, recalcitrance, unruliness, and hostility, or conversely defined as a lack of motivation, intellectual apathy, sullenness, passivity, or withdrawal, the process is ready to be repeated and the options to escape further teacher definitions are increasingly removed.

Postscript: Beyond the Logjam

This paper has argued that a fruitful convergence can be effected between the research being conducted on the self-fulfilling prophecy as a consequence of teacher expectations and the conceptual framework of labeling theory. The analysis of the outcomes of teacher expectations produces results highly similar to those found in the study of social deviance. Labels are applied to individuals which fundamentally shift their definitions of self and which further reinforce the behavior which had initially prompted the social reaction. The impact of the self-fulfilling prophecy in educational research is comparable to that found in the analysis of mental health clinics, asylums, prisons, juvenile homes, and other people-changing organizations. What the labeling perspective can provide to the study of educational outcomes as a result of the operationalization of teacher expectations is a model for the study of the *processes* by which the outcomes are produced. The detailing over time of the interactional patterns which lead to changes in self-definition and behavior within classrooms is sadly lacking in almost all of the expectation research to date. A most glaring example of this omission is the study by Rosenthal and Jacobson themselves. Their conclusions are based only on the analysis of a pre- and post-test. To posit that teacher expectations were the causal variable that produced changes in student performances was a leap from the data to speculation. They could offer only suggestions as to how the measured changes in the children's performance came about, since they were not in the classrooms to observe how assumed teacher attitudes were translated into subsequent actual student behavior.

To extend the research on the educational experiences of those students who are differentially labeled by teachers, what is needed is a theoretical framework which can clearly isolate the influences and effects of certain kinds of teacher reactions on certain types of students, producing, certain typical outcomes. The labeling perspective appears particularly well-suited for this expansion of both research and theoretical development on teacher expectations by offering the basis for analysis at either a specific or a more general level. With the former, for example, there are areas of investigation related to 1) types of students perceived by teachers as prone to success or failure; 2) the kinds of reactions, based on their expectations, teachers have to different students; and 3) the effects of specific teacher reactions on specific student outcomes. At a more general level, fruitful lines of inquiry might include 1) the outcomes in the post-school world of having received a negative vs. a positive label within the school; 2) the influences of factors such as social class and race on the categories of expectations teachers hold; 3) how and why labels do emerge in schools as well as the phenomenological and structural meanings that are attached to them; and 4) whether there are means by which to modify or minimize the effects of school labeling processes on students.

Labeling theory provides a conceptual framework by which to understand the processes of transforming attitudes into behavior and the outcomes of having done so. To be able to detail the dynamics and influences within schools by which some children come to see themselves as successful and act as though they were, and to detail how others come to see themselves as failures and act accordingly, provides in the final analysis an opportunity to intervene so as to expand the numbers of winners and diminish the numbers of losers. For that reason above all others, labeling theory merits our attention.

Note

1. The preparation of this paper has been aided by a grant (GS-41522) from the National Science Foundation—Sociology Program. The views expressed here are solely those of the author and no official endorsement by either the National Science Foundation or the National Institute of Education is to be inferred.

References

Akers, R. L. *Deviant Behavior: A Social Learning Approach.* Belmont, Cal.: Wadsworth, 1973.

Aronson, E., and Carlsmith, J. M. "Performance Expectancy as a Determinant of Actual Performance." *Journal of Abnormal and Social Psychology* 65 (1962):179–182.

Becker, H. S. "Social Class Variations in the Teacher–Pupil Relationship." *Journal of Educational Sociology* 25 (1952):451–465.

Becker, H. S. *Outsiders.* New York: The Free Press, 1963.

Becker, H. S. *The Other Side.* New York: The Free Press, 1964.

Broadhead, R. S. "A Theoretical Critique of the Societal Reaction Approach to Deviance." *Pacific Sociological Review* 17 (1974):287–312.

Brock, T. C., and Edelman, H. "Seven Studies of Performance Expectancy as a Determinant of Actual Performance." *Journal of Experimental Social Psychology* 1 (1965):295–310.

Brophy, J., and Good, T. "Teachers' Communications of Differential Expectations for Children's Classroom Performance: Some Behavioral Data." *Journal of Educational Psychology* 61 (1970):365–374.

Brown, B. *The Assessment of Self-Concept among Four Year Old Negro and White Children: A Comparative Study Using the Brown IDS Self-Concept Reference Test.* New York: Institute for Developmental Studies, 1968.

Claiborn, W. L. "Expectancy Effects in the Classroom: A Failure to Replicate." *Journal of Educational Psychology* 60 (1969):377–383.

Clifford, M. M., and Walster, E. "The Effect of Physical Attractiveness on Teacher Expectations." *Sociology of Education* 46 (1973):248–258.

Dailey C. A. "The Effects of Premature Conclusion upon the Acquisition of Understanding of a Person." *Journal of Psychology* 33 (1952):133–152.

Davidson, H. H., and Lang. G. "Children's Perceptions of Teachers' Feelings toward Them." *Journal of Experimental Education* 29 (1960): 107–118.

Deutsch, M. "The Disadvantaged Child and the Learning Process." in *Education in Depressed Areas,* edited by H. Passow. New York: Teachers College Press, 1963.

Deutsch, M., Fishman, J. A., Kogan, L., North, R., and Whiteman, M. "Guidelines for Testing Minority Group Children." *Journal of Social Issues* 20 (1964): 129–145.

Douglas. J. *The Home and the School.* London: MacGibbon and Kee, 1964.

Douglas, J. *The American Social Order.* New York: The Free Press, 1971.

Douglas, J. (ed.). *Deviance and Respectability.* New York: Basic Books, 1972.

Doyle, W., Hancock, G., and Kifer, E. "Teachers' Perceptions: Do They Make a Difference?" Paper presented at the meeting of the American Educational Research Association, 1971.

Edgar, D. E. *The Competent Teacher.* Sydney, Australia: Angus & Robertson, 1974.

Erikson, K. T. "Note on the Sociology of Deviance," in *The Other Side,* edited by H. S. Becker. New York: The Free Press, 1964.

Erikson, K. T. *Wayward Puritans.* New York: Wiley, 1966.

Flanagan, J. C. *Test of General Ability: Technical Report.* Chicago: Science Research Associates, 1960.

Gibson, G. "Aptitude Tests." *Science* 149 (1965):583.

Goaldman, L. "Counseling Methods and Techniques: The Use of Tests," in *The Encyclopedia of Education,* edited by L. C. Deighton. New York: Macmillan, 1971.

Good, T., and Brophy, J. *Looking in Classrooms.* New York: Harper and Row, 1973.

Goodmam, P. *Compulsory Mis-Education* New York: Random House, 1964.

Goslin, D. A., and Glass, D. C. "The Social Effects of Standardized Testing on American Elementary Schools." *Sociology of Education* 40 (1967): 115–131.

Henry, J. *Culture Against Man.* New York: Random House, 1963.

Hirschi, T. *Causes of Delinquency.* Berkeley: University of California Press, 1969.

Illich, I. *Deschooling Society.* New York: Harper and Row, 1971.

Jackson, G., and Cosca, C. "The Inequality of Educational Opportunity in the Southwest: An Observational Study of Ethnically Mixed Classrooms." *American Educational Research Journal* 11 (1974):219–229.

Johnson, J. *On the Interface between Low income Urban Black Children and Their Teachers during the Early School Years: A Position Paper.* San Francisco: Far West Laboratory for Educational Research and Development. 1973.

Katz, M. Class, *Bureaucracy and Schools.* New York: Praeger, 1971.

Kitsuse, J. "Societal Reaction to Deviant Behavior: Problems of Theory and Method," in *The Other Side,* edited by H. S. Becker. New York: The Free Press, 1964.

Leacock, E. *Teaching and Learning in City Schools.* New York: Basic Books, 1969.

Lemert, E. *Social Pathology.* New York: McGraw-Hill, 1951.

Lemert, E. *Human Deviance, Social Problems and Social Control.* Englewood Cliffs, N.J.: Prentice-Hall, 1972.

Lemert, E. "Beyond Mead: The Societal Reaction to Deviance." *Social Problems* 21 (1974):457–468.

Lofland, J. *Deviance and Identity.* Englewood Cliffs, N.J.: Prentice-Hall, 1969.

Mackler, B. "Grouping in the Ghetto." *Education and Urban Society* 2 (1969):80–95.

Matza, D. *Delinquency and Drift.* New York: Wiley, 1964.

Matza, D. *Becoming Deviant.* Englewood Cliffs, N.J.: Prentice-Hall, 1969.

McPherson, G. H. *The Role-set of the Elementary School Teacher: A case study.* Unpublished Ph.D. dissertation, Columbia University, New York, 1966.

Mehan, H. B. *Accomplishing Understanding in Educational Settings.* Unpublished Ph.D. dissertation, University of California, Santa Barbara, 1971.

Mehan, H. B. *Ethnomethodology and Education.* Paper presented to the Sociology of Education Association conference, Pacific Grove, California, 1974.

Merton, R. K. "Social Problems and Social Theory," in *Contemporary Social Problems,* edited by R. Merton and R. Nisbet. New York: Harcourt, Brace and World, 1968.

Newcomb, T. M. "Autistic Hostility and Social Reality." *Human Relations* 1 (1947):69–86.

Noblit, G. W., and Polk, K. *Institutional Constraints and Labeling.* Paper presented to the Southern Sociological Association meetings, Washington, D.C., 1975.

Palardy, J. M. "What Teachers Believe—What Children Achieve." *Elementary School Journal,* 1969, pp. 168–169 and 370–374.

Pequignot, H. "L'équation Personnelle du Juge." In *Semaine des Hopitaux* (Paris), 1966.

Polk, K. "Class, Strain, and Rebellion and Adolescents." *Social Problems* 17 (1969):214–224.

Polk, K., and Schafer, W. E. *Schools and Delinquency.* Englewood Cliffs, N.J.: Prentice-Hall, 1972.

Reimer, E. *School Is Dead.* New York: Doubleday, 1971.

Rist, R. C. "Student Social Class and Teachers' Expectations: The Self-fulfilling Prophecy in Ghetto Education." *Harvard Educational Review* 40 (1970):411–450.

Rist, R. C. "Social Distance and Social Inequality in a Kindergarten Classroom: An Examination of the 'Cultural Gap' Hypothesis." *Urban Education* 7 (1972):241–260.

Rist, R. C. *The Urban School: A Factory for Failure.* Cambridge, Mass.: The M.I.T. Press, 1973.

Rosenthal, R., and Jacobson, L. "Teachers' Expectancies: Determinants of Pupils' IQ Gains." *Psychology Reports* 19 (1966):115–118.

Rosenthal, R., and Jacobson, L. *Pygmalion in the Classroom.* New York: Holt, Rinehart and Winston, 1968.

Rowe, M. "Science, Silence and Sanctions." *Science and Children* 6 (1969):11–13.

Rubington, E., and Weinberg, M. S. *Deviance: The Interactionist Perspective.* New York: Macmillan, 1973.

Rubovits, P., and Maehr, M. L. "Pygmalion Black and White." *Journal of Personality and Social Psychology* 2 (1973):210–218.

Schafer, W. E., and Olexa, C. *Tracking and Opportunity.* Scranton, Pa.: Chandler, 1971.

Scheff, T. *Being Mentally Ill.* Chicago; Aldine, 1966.

Schur, E. *Crimes without Victims.* Englewood Cliffs, N.J.: Prentice-Hall, 1965.

Schur, E. *Labeling Deviant Behavior.* New York: Harper and Row, 1971.

Scott, R. A., and Douglas, J. C. (eds.). *Theoretical Perspectives on Deviance.* New York: Basic Books, 1972.

Snow, R. E. "Unfinished Pygmalion." *Contemporary Psychology* 14 (1969):197–199.

Stein, A. "Strategies for Failure." *Harvard Educational Review* 41 (1971):158–204.

Tannenbaum, F. *Crime and the Community.* New York: Columbia University Press, 1938.

Taylor, C. "The Expectations of Pygmalion's Creators." *Educational Leadership* 28 (1970):161–164.

Thorndike, R. L. "Review of Pygmalion in the Classroom." *Educational Research Journal* 5 (1968): 708–711.

Thorndike, R. L. "But Do You Have to Know How to Tell Time?" *Educational Research Journal* 6 (1969):692.

Warner, W. L.; Havighurst, R.; and Loeb, M.B. *Who Shall be Educated?* New York: Harper and Row, 1944.

Willis, S. *Formation of Teachers' Expectations of Student Academic Performance.* Unpublished Ph.D. dissertation, University of Texas, Austin, 1972.

Wilson, A. B. "Social Stratification and Academic Achievement," in *Education in Depressed Areas,* edited by H. Passow. New York: Teachers College Press, 1963.

Zajonc, R. B., and Brinkman, P. "Expectancy and Feedback as Independent Factors in Task Performance." *Journal of Personality and Social Psychology* 11 (1969):148–150.

6
The Forms of Capital
PIERRE BOURDIEU

The social world is accumulated history, and if it is not to be reduced to a discontinuous series of instantaneous mechanical equilibria between agents who are treated as interchangeable particles, one must reintroduce into it the notion of capital and with it, accumulation and all its effects. Capital is accumulated labor (in its materialized form or its 'incorporated,' embodied form) which, when appropriated on a private, i.e., exclusive, basis by agents or groups of agents, enables them to appropriate social energy in the form of reified or living labor. It is a *vis insita*, a force inscribed in objective or subjective structures, but it is also a *lex insita*, the principle underlying the immanent regularities of the social world. It is what makes the games of society—not least, the economic game—something other than simple games of chance offering at every moment the possibility of a miracle. Roulette, which holds out the opportunity of winning a lot of money in a short space of time, and therefore of changing one's social status quasi-instantaneously, and in which the winning of the previous spin of the wheel can be staked and lost at every new spin, gives a fairly accurate image of this imaginary universe of perfect competition or perfect equality of opportunity, a world without inertia, without accumulation, without heredity or acquired properties, in which every moment is perfectly independent of the previous one, every soldier has a marshal's baton in his knapsack, and every prize can be attained, instantaneously, by everyone, so that at each moment anyone can become anything. Capital, which, in its objectified or embodied forms, takes time to accumulate and which, as a potential capacity to produce profits and to reproduce itself in identical or expanded form, contains a tendency to persist in its being, is a force inscribed in the objectivity of things so that everything is not equally possible or impossible.[1] And the structure of the distribution of the different types and subtypes of capital at a given moment in time represents the immanent structure of the social world, i.e., the set of constraints, inscribed in the very reality of that world, which govern its functioning in a durable way, determining the chances of success for practices.

It is in fact impossible to account for the structure and functioning of the social world unless one reintroduces capital in all its forms and not solely in the one form recognized by economic theory. Economic theory has allowed to be foisted upon it a definition of the economy of practices which is the historical invention of capitalism; and by reducing the universe of exchanges to mercantile exchange, which is objectively and subjectively oriented toward the maximization of profit, i.e., (economically) *self-interested*, it has implicitly defined the other forms of exchange as noneconomic, and therefore *disinterested*. In particular, it defines as disinterested those forms of exchange which ensure the *transubstantiation* whereby the most material types of capital—those which are economic in the restricted sense—can present themselves in the immaterial form of cultural capital or social capital and vice versa. Interest, in the restricted sense it is given in economic theory cannot be produced without producing its negative counterpart, disinterestedness. The class of practices whose explicit purpose is to maximize monetary profit cannot be defined as such without producing the purposeless finality of cultural or artistic practices and their products; the world of bourgeois man, with his double-entry accounting, cannot be invented without producing the pure, perfect universe of the artist and the intellectual and the gratuitous activities of art-for-art's sake and pure theory. In other words, the constitution of a science of mercantile relationships which, inasmuch as it takes for granted the very foundations of the order it claims to analyze—private property, profit, wage labor, etc.—is not even a science of the field of economic production, has prevented the constitution of a general science of the economy of practices, which would treat mercantile exchange as a particular case of exchange in all its forms.

It is remarkable that the practices and assets thus salvaged from the 'icy water of egotistical calculation' (and from science) are the virtual monopoly of the dominant class—as if economism had been able to reduce everything to economics only because the reduction on which that discipline is based protects from sacrilegious reduction everything which needs to be protected. If economics deals only with practices that have narrowly economic interest as their principle and only with goods that are directly and immediately convertible into money (which makes them quantifiable), then the universe of bourgeois production and exchange becomes an exception and can see itself and present itself as a realm of disinterestedness. As everyone knows, priceless things have their price, and the extreme difficulty of converting certain practices and certain objects into money is only due to the fact that this conversion is refused in the very intention that produces them, which is nothing other than the denial (*Verneinung*) of the economy. A general science of the economy of practices, capable of reappropriating the totality of the practices which, although objectively economic, are not and cannot be socially recognized as economic, and which can be performed only at the cost of a whole labor of dissimulation or, more precisely, *euphemization*, must endeavor to grasp capital and profit in all their forms and to establish the laws whereby the different types of capital (or power, which amounts to the same thing) change into one another.[2]

Depending on the field in which it functions, and at the cost of the more or less expensive transformations which are the precondition for its efficacy in the field in question, capital can present itself in three fundamental guises: as *economic capital*, which is immediately and directly convertible into money and may be institutionalized in the form of property rights; as *cultural capital*, which is convertible, on certain conditions, into economic capital and may be institutionalized in the form of educational qualifications; and as *social capital*, made up of social obligations ('connections'), which is convertible, in certain conditions, into economic capital and may be institutionalized in the form of a title of nobility.[3]

Cultural Capital

Cultural capital can exist in three forms: in the *embodied state*, i.e., in the form of long-lasting dispositions of the mind and body; in the *objectified* state, in the form of cultural goods (pictures, books, dictionaries, instruments, machines, etc.), which are the trace or realization of theories or critiques of these theories, problematics, etc.; and in the *institutionalized* state, a form of objectification which must be set apart because, as will be seen in the case of educational qualifications, it confers entirely original properties on the cultural capital which it is presumed to guarantee.

The reader should not be misled by the somewhat peremptory air which the effort at axiomization may give to my argument.[4] The notion of cultural capital initially presented itself to me, in the course of research, as a theoretical hypothesis which made it possible to explain the unequal scholastic achievement of children originating from the different social classes by relating academic success, i.e., the specific profits which children from the different classes and class fractions can obtain in the academic market, to the distribution of cultural capital between the classes and class fractions. This starting point implies a break with the presuppositions inherent both in the commonsense view, which sees academic success or failure as an effect of natural aptitudes, and in human capital theories.

Economists might seem to deserve credit for explicitly raising the question of the relationship between the rates of profit on educational investment and on economic investment (and its evolution). But their measurement of the yield from scholastic investment takes account only of *monetary* investments and profits, or those directly convertible into money, such as the costs of schooling and the cash equivalent of time devoted to study; they are unable to explain the different proportions of their resources which different agents or different social classes allocate to economic investment and cultural investment because they fail to take systematic account of the structure of the differential chances of profit which the various markets offer these agents or classes as a function of the volume and the composition of their assets (see esp. Becker 1964b). Furthermore, because they neglect to relate scholastic investment strategies to the whole set of educational strategies and to the system of reproduction strategies, they inevitably, by a necessary paradox, let slip the best hidden and socially most determinant educational investment, namely, the domestic transmission of cultural capital. Their studies of the relationship between academic ability and academic investment show that they are unaware that ability or talent is itself the product of an investment of time and cultural capital (Becker 1964a: 63–6). Not surprisingly, when endeavoring to evaluate the profits of scholastic investment, they can only consider the profitability of educational expenditure for society as a whole, the 'social rate of return,' or the 'social gain of education as measured by its effects on national productivity' (Becker 1964b: 121, 155). This typically functionalist definition of the functions of education ignores the contribution which the educational system makes to the reproduction of the social structure by sanctioning the hereditary transmission of cultural capital. From the very beginning, a definition of human capital, despite its humanistic connotations, does not move beyond economism and ignores, *inter alia*, the fact that the scholastic yield from educational action depends on the cultural capital previously invested by the family. Moreover, the economic and social yield of the educational qualification depends on the social capital, again inherited, which can be used to back it up.

The Embodied State

Most of the properties of cultural capital can be deduced from the fact that, in its fundamental state, it is linked to the body and presupposes embodiment. The accumulation of cultural capital in the embodied state, i.e., in the form of what is called culture, cultivation, *Bildung*, presupposes a process of embodiment, incorporation, which, insofar as it implies a labor of inculcation and assimilation, costs time, time which must be invested personally by the investor. Like the acquisition of a muscular physique or a suntan, it cannot be done at second hand (so that all effects of delegation are ruled out).

The work of acquisition is work on oneself (self-improvement), an effort that presupposes a personal cost (*on paie de sa personne*, as we say in French), an investment, above all of time, but also of that socially constituted form of libido, *libido sciendi*, with all the privation, renunciation, and sacrifice that it may entail. It follows that the least inexact of all the measurements of cultural capital are those which take as their standard the length of acquisition—so long, of course, as this is not reduced to length of schooling and allowance is made for early domestic education by giving it a positive value (a gain in time, a head start) or a negative value (wasted time, and doubly so because more time must be spent correcting its effects), according to its distance from the demands of the scholastic market.[5]

This embodied capital, external wealth converted into an integral part of the person, into a habitus, cannot be transmitted instantaneously (unlike money, property rights, or even titles of nobility) by gift or bequest, purchase or exchange. It follows that the use or exploitation of cultural capital presents particular problems for the holders of economic or political capital, whether they be private patrons or, at the other extreme, entrepreneurs employing executives endowed with a specific cultural competence (not to mention the new state patrons). How can this capital, so closely linked to the person, be bought without buying the person and so losing the very effect of legitimation which presupposes the dissimulation of dependence? How can this capital be concentrated—as some undertakings demand—without concentrating the possessors of the capital, which can have all sorts of unwanted consequences?

Cultural capital can be acquired, to a varying extent, depending on the period, the society, and the social class, in the absence of any deliberate inculcation, and therefore quite unconsciously. It always remains marked by its earliest conditions of acquisition which, through the more or less visible marks they leave (such as the pronunciations characteristic of a class or region), help to determine its distinctive value. It cannot be accumulated beyond the appropriating capacities of an individual agent; it declines and dies with its bearer (with his biological capacity, his memory, etc.). Because it is thus linked in numerous ways to the person in his biological singularity and is subject to a hereditary transmission which is always heavily disguised, or even invisible, it defies the old, deep-rooted distinction the Greek jurists made between inherited properties (*ta patroa*) and acquired properties (*epikteta*), i.e., those which an individual adds to his heritage. It thus manages to combine the prestige of innate property with the merits of acquisition. Because the social conditions of its transmission and acquisition are more disguised than those of economic capital, it is predisposed to function as symbolic capital, i.e., to be unrecognized as capital and recognized as legitimate competence, as authority exerting an effect of (mis)recognition, e.g., in the matrimonial market and in all the markets in which economic capital is not fully recognized, whether in matters of culture, with the great art collections or great cultural foundations, or in social welfare, with the economy of generosity and the gift. Furthermore, the specifically symbolic logic of distinction additionally secures material and symbolic profits for the possessors of a large cultural capital: any given cultural competence (e.g., being able to read in a world of illiterates) derives a scarcity value from its position in the distribution of cultural capital and yields profits of distinction for its owner. In other words, the share in profits which scarce cultural capital secures in class-divided societies is based, in the last analysis, on the fact that all agents do not have the economic and cultural means for prolonging their children's education beyond the minimum necessary for the reproduction of the labor-power least valorized at a given moment.[6]

Thus the capital, in the sense of the means of appropriating the product of accumulated labor in the objectified state which is held by a given agent, depends for its real efficacy on the form of the distribution of the means of appropriating the accumulated and objectively available resources: and the relationship of appropriation between an agent and the resources objectively available, and hence the profits they produce, is mediated by the relationship of (objective and/or subjective) competition between himself and the other possessors of capital competing for the same goods, in which scarcity—and through it, social value—is generated. The structure of the field, i.e., the unequal distribution of capital, is the source of the specific effects of capital, i.e., the appropriation of profits and the power to impose the laws of functioning of the field most favourable to capital and its reproduction.

But the most powerful principle of the symbolic efficacy of cultural capital no doubt lies in the logic of its transmission. On the one hand, the process of appropriating objectified cultural capital and the time necessary for it to take place mainly depend on the cultural capital embodied in the whole family—through (among other things) the generalized Arrow effect and all forms of implicit transmission.[7] On the other hand, the initial accumulation of cultural capital, the precondition for the fast, easy accumulation of every kind of useful cultural capital, starts at the outset, without delay, without wasted time, only for the offspring of families endowed with strong cultural capital; in this case, the accumulation period covers the whole period of socialization. It follows that the transmission of cultural capital is no doubt the best hidden form of hereditary transmission of capital, and it therefore receives proportionately greater weight in the system of reproduction strategies, as the direct, visible forms of transmission tend to be more strongly censored and controlled.

It can immediately be seen that the link between economic and cultural capital is established through the mediation of the time needed for acquisition. Differences in the cultural capital possessed by the family imply differences first in the age at which the work of transmission and accumulation begins—the limiting case being full use of the time biologically available, with the maximum free time being harnessed to maximum cultural capital—and then in the capacity, thus defined, to satisfy the specifically cultural demands of a prolonged process of acquisition. Furthermore, and in correlation with this, the length of time for which a given individual can prolong his acquisition process depends on the length of time for which his family can provide him with the free time, i.e., time free from economic necessity, which is the precondition for the initial accumulation (time which can be evaluated as a handicap to be made up).

The Objectified State

Cultural capital, in the objectified state, has a number of properties which are defined only in the relationship with cultural capital in its embodied form. The cultural capital objectified in material objects and media, such as writings, paintings, monuments, instruments, etc., is transmissible in its materiality. A collection of paintings, for example, can be transmitted as well as economic capital (if not better, because the capital transfer is more disguised). But what is transmissible is legal ownership and not (or not necessarily) what constitutes the precondition for specific appropriation, namely, the possession of the means of 'consuming' a painting or using a machine, which, being nothing other than embodied capital, are subject to the same laws of transmission.[8]

Thus cultural goods can be appropriated both materially—which presupposes economic capital—and symbolically—which presupposes cultural capital. It follows that the owner of the means of production must find a way of appropriating either the embodied capital which is the precondition of specific appropriation or the services of the holders of this capital. To possess the machines, he only needs economic capital; to appropriate them and use them in accordance with their specific purpose (defined by the cultural capital, of scientific or technical type, incorporated in them), he must have access to embodied cultural capital, either in person or by proxy. This is no doubt the basis of the ambiguous status of cadres (executives and engineers). If it is emphasized that they are not the possessors (in the strictly economic sense) of the means of production which they use, and that they derive profit from their own cultural capital only by selling the services and products which it makes possible, then they will be classified among the dominated groups; if it is emphasized that they draw their profits from the use of a particular form of capital, then they will be classified among the dominant groups. Everything suggests that as the cultural capital incorporated in the means of production increases (and with it the period of embodiment needed to acquire the means of appropriating it), so the collective strength of the holders of cultural capital would tend to increase—if the holders of the dominant type of capital (economic capital) were not able to set the holders of cultural capital in competition with one another. (They are, moreover, inclined to competition by the very conditions in which they are selected and trained, in particular by the logic of scholastic and recruitment competitions.)

Cultural capital in its objectified state presents itself with all the appearances of an autonomous, coherent universe which, although the product of historical action, has its own laws, transcending individual wills, and which, as the example of language well illustrates, therefore remains irreducible to that which each agent, or even the aggregate of the agents, can appropriate (i.e., to the cultural capital embodied in each agent or even in the aggregate of the agents). However, it should not be forgotten that it exists as symbolically and materially active, effective capital only insofar as it is appropriated by agents and implemented and invested as a weapon and a stake in the struggles which go on in the fields of cultural production (the artistic field, the scientific field, etc.) and, beyond them, in the field of the social classes—struggles in which the agents wield strengths and obtain profits proportionate to their mastery of this objectified capital, and therefore to the extent of their embodied capital.[9]

The Institutionalized State

The objectification of cultural capital in the form of academic qualifications is one way of neutralizing some of the properties it derives from the fact that, being embodied, it has the same biological limits as its bearer. This objectification is what makes the difference between the capital of the autodidact, which may be called into question at any time, or even the cultural capital of the courtier, which can yield only ill-defined profits, of fluctuating value, in the market of high-society exchanges, and the cultural capital academically sanctioned by legally guaranteed qualifications, formally independent of the person of their bearer. With the academic qualification, a certificate of cultural competence which confers on its holder a conventional, constant, legally guaranteed value with respect to culture, social alchemy produces a form of cultural capital which has a relative autonomy vis-à-vis its bearer and even vis-à-vis the cultural capital he effectively possesses at a given moment in time. It institutes cultural capital by collective magic, just as, according to Merleau-Ponty, the living institute their dead through the ritual of mourning. One has only to think of the *concours* (competitive recruitment examination) which, out of the continuum of infinitesimal differences between performances, produces sharp, absolute, lasting differences, such as that which separates the last successful candidate from the first unsuccessful one, and institutes an essential difference between the officially recognized, guaranteed competence and simple cultural capital, which is constantly required to prove itself. In this case, one sees clearly the performative magic of the power of instituting, the power to show forth and secure belief or, in a word, to impose recognition.

By conferring institutional recognition on the cultural capital possessed by any given gent, the academic qualification also makes it possible to compare qualification holders and even to exchange them (by substituting one for another in succession). Furthermore, it makes it possible to establish conversion rates between cultural capital and economic capital by guaranteeing the monetary value of a given academic capital.[10] This product of the conversion of economic capital into cultural capital establishes the value, in terms of cultural capital, of the holder of a given qualification relative to other qualification holders and, by the same token, the monetary value for which it can be exchanged on the labor market (academic investment has no meaning unless a minimum degree of reversibility of the conversion it implies is objectively guaranteed). Because the material and symbolic profits which the academic qualification guarantees also depend on its scarcity, the investments made (in time and effort) may turn out to be less profitable than was anticipated when they were made (there having been a *de facto* change in the conversion rate between academic capital and economic capital). The strategies for converting economic capital into cultural capital, which are among the short-term factors of the schooling explosion and the inflation of qualifications, are governed by changes in the structure of the chances of profit offered by the different types of capital.

Social Capital

Social capital is the aggregate of the actual or potential resources which are linked to possession of a durable network of more or less institutionalized relationships of mutual acquaintance and recognition—or in other words, to membership in a group[11]—which provides each of its members with the backing of the collectivity-owned capital, a 'credential' which entitles them to credit, in the various senses of the word. These relationships may exist only in the practical state, in material and/or symbolic exchanges which help to maintain them. They may also be socially instituted and guaranteed by the application of a common name (the name of a family, a class, or a tribe or of a school, a party, etc.) and by a whole set of instituting acts designed simultaneously to form and inform those who undergo them; in this case, they are more or less really enacted and so maintained and reinforced, in exchanges. Being based on indissolubly material and symbolic exchanges, the establishment and maintenance of which presuppose reacknowledgment of proximity, they are also partially irreducible to objective relations of proximity in physical (geographical) space or even in economic and social space.[12]

The volume of the social capital possessed by a given agent thus depends on the size of the network of connections he can effectively mobilize and on the volume of the capital (economic, cultural, or symbolic) possessed in his own right by each of those to whom he is connected.[13] This means that, although it is relatively irreducible to the economic and cultural capital possessed by a given agent, or even by the whole set of agents to whom he is connected, social capital is never completely independent of it because the exchanges instituting mutual acknowledgment presuppose the reacknowledgment of a minimum of objective homogeneity, and because it exerts a multiplier effect on the capital he possesses in his own right.

The profits which accrue from membership in a group are the basis of the solidarity which makes them possible.[14] This does not mean that they are consciously pursued as such, even in the case of groups like select clubs, which are deliberately organized in order to concentrate social capital and so to derive full benefit from the multiplier effect implied in concentration and to secure the profits of membership—material profits, such as all the types of services accruing from useful relationships, and symbolic profits, such as those derived from association with a rare, prestigious group.

The existence of a network of connections is not a natural given, or even a social given, constituted once and for all by an initial act of institution, represented, in the case of the family group, by the genealogical definition of kinship relations, which is the characteristic of a social formation. It is the product of an endless effort at institution, of which institution rites—often wrongly described as rites of passage—mark the essential moments and which is necessary in order to produce and reproduce lasting, useful relationships that can secure material or symbolic profits (see Bourdieu 1982). In other words, the network of relationships is the product of investment strategies, individual or collective, consciously or unconsciously aimed at establishing or reproducing social relationships that are directly usable in the short or long term, i.e., at transforming contingent relations, such as those of neighborhood, the workplace, or even kinship, into relationships that are at once necessary and elective, implying durable obligations subjectively felt (feelings of gratitude, respect, friendship, etc.) or institutionally guaranteed (rights). This is done through the alchemy *of consecration*, the symbolic constitution produced by social institution (institution as a relative—brother, sister, cousin, etc.—or as a knight, an heir, an elder, etc.) and endlessly reproduced in and through the exchange (of gifts, words, women, etc.) which it encourages and which presupposes and produces mutual knowledge and recognition. Exchange transforms the things exchanged into signs of recognition and, through the mutual recognition and the recognition of group membership which it implies, reproduces the group. By the same token, it reaffirms the limits of the group, i.e., the limits beyond which the constitutive exchange—trade, commensality, or marriage—cannot take place. Each member of the group is thus instituted as a custodian of the limits of the group: because the definition of the criteria of entry is at stake in each new entry, he can modify the group by modifying the limits of legitimate exchange through some form of misalliance. It is quite logical that, in most societies, the preparation and conclusion of marriages should be the business of the whole group, and not of the agents directly concerned. Through the introduction of new members into a family, a clan, or a club, the whole definition of the group, i.e., its fines, its boundaries, and its identity, is put at stake, exposed to redefinition, alteration, adulteration. When, as in modern societies, families lose the monopoly of the establishment of exchanges which can lead to lasting relationships, whether socially sanctioned (like marriage) or not, they may continue to control these exchanges, while remaining within the logic of laissez-faire, through all the institutions which are designed to favor legitimate exchanges and exclude illegitimate ones by producing occasions (rallies, cruises, hunts, parties, receptions, etc.), places (smart neighborhoods, select schools, clubs, etc.), or practices (smart sports, parlor games, cultural ceremonies, etc.)

which bring together, in a seemingly fortuitous way, individuals as homogeneous as possible in all the pertinent respects in terms of the existence and persistence of the group.

The reproduction of social capital presupposes an unceasing effort of sociability, a continuous series of exchanges in which recognition is endlessly affirmed and reaffirmed. This work, which implies expenditure of time and energy and so, directly or indirectly, of economic capital, is not profitable or even conceivable unless one invests in it a specific competence (knowledge of genealogical relationships and of real connections and skill at using them, etc.) and an acquired disposition to acquire and maintain this competence, which are themselves integral parts of this capital.[15] This is one of the factors which explain why the profitability of this labor of accumulating and maintaining social capital rises in proportion to the size of the capital. Because the social capital accruing from a relationship is that much greater to the extent that the person who is the object of it is richly endowed with capital (mainly social, but also cultural and even economic capital), the possessors of an inherited social capital, symbolized by a great name, are able to transform all circumstantial relationships into lasting connections. They are sought after for their social capital and, because they are well known, are worthy of being known ('I know him well'); they do not need to 'make the acquaintance' of all their 'acquaintances'; they are known to more people than they know, and their work of sociability, when it is exerted, is highly productive.

Every group has its more or less institutionalized forms of delegation which enable it to concentrate the totality of the social capital, which is the basis of the existence of the group (family or a nation, of course, but also an association or a party), in the hands of a single agent or a small group of agents and to mandate this plenipotentiary, charged with *plena potestas agendi et loquendi*,[16] to represent the group, to speak and act in its name and so, with the aid of this collectively owned capital, to exercise a power incommensurate with the agent's personal contribution. Thus, at the most elementary degree of institutionalization, the head of the family, the *pater familias*, the eldest, most senior member, is tacitly recognized as the only person entitled to speak on behalf of the family group in all official circumstances. But whereas in this case, diffuse delegation requires the great to step forward and defend the collective honor when the honor of the weakest members is threatened, the institutionalized delegation, which ensures the concentration of social capital, also has the effect of limiting the consequences of individual lapses by explicitly delimiting responsibilities and authorizing the recognized spokesmen to shield the group as a whole from discredit by expelling or excommunicating the embarrassing individuals.

If the internal competition for the monopoly of legitimate representation of the group is not to threaten the conservation and accumulation of the capital which is the basis of the group, the members of the group must regulate the conditions of access to the right to declare oneself a member of the group and, above all, to set oneself up as a representative (delegate, plenipotentiary, spokesman, etc.) of the whole group, thereby committing the social capital of the whole group. The title of nobility is the form *par excellence* of the institutionalized social capital which guarantees a particular form of social relationship in a lasting way. One of the paradoxes of delegation is that the mandated agent can exert on (and, up to a point, against) the group the power which the group enables him to concentrate. (This is perhaps especially true in the limiting cases in which the mandated agent creates the group which creates him but which only exists through him.) The mechanisms of delegation and representation (in both the theatrical and the legal senses) which fall into place—that much more strongly, no doubt, when the group is large and its members weak—as one of the conditions for the concentration of social capital (among other reasons, because it enables numerous, varied, scattered agents to act as one man and to overcome the limitations of space and time) also contain the seeds of an embezzlement or misappropriation of the capital which they assemble.

This embezzlement is latent in the fact that a group as a whole can be represented, in the various meanings of the word, by a subgroup, clearly delimited and perfectly visible to all, known to all, and recognized by all, that of the *nobiles*, the 'people who are known', the paradigm of whom is the nobility, and who may speak on behalf of the whole group, represent the whole group, and exercise authority in the name of the whole group. The noble is the group personified. He bears the name of the group to which he gives his name (the metonymy which links the noble to his group is clearly seen when Shakespeare calls Cleopatra 'Egypt' or the King of France 'France', just as Racine calls Pyrrhus 'Epirus'). It is by him, his name, the difference it proclaims, that the members of his group, the liegemen, and also the land and castles, are known and recognized. Similarly, phenomena such as the 'personality cult' or the identification of parties, trade unions, or movements with their leader are latent in the very logic of representation. Everything combines to cause the signifier to take the place of the signified, the spokesmen that of the group he is supposed to express, not least because his distinction, his 'outstandingness', his visibility constitute the essential part, if not the essence, of this power, which, being entirely set within the logic of knowledge and acknowledgment, is fundamentally a symbolic power; but also because the representative, the sign, the emblem, may be, and create, the whole reality of groups which receive effective social existence only in and through representation.[17]

Conversions

The different types of capital can be derived from *economic capital,* but only at the cost of a more or less great effort of transformation, which is needed to produce the type of power effective in the field in question. For example, there are some goods and services to which economic capital gives immediate access, without secondary costs; others can be obtained only by virtue of a social capital of relationships (or social obligations) which cannot act instantaneously, at the appropriate moment, unless they have been established and maintained for a long time, as if for their own sake, and therefore outside their period of use, i.e., at the cost of an investment in sociability which is necessarily long-term because the time lag is one of the factors of the transmutation of a pure and simple debt into that recognition of nonspecific indebtedness which is called gratitude.[18] In contrast to the cynical but also economical transparency of economic exchange, in which equivalents change hands in the same instant, the essential ambiguity of social exchange, which presupposes misrecognition, in other words, a form of faith and of bad faith (in the sense of self-deception), presupposes a much more subtle economy of time.

So it has to be posited simultaneously that economic capital is at the root of all the other types of capital and that these transformed, disguised forms of economic capital, never entirely reducible to that definition, produce their most specific effects only to the extent that they conceal (not least from their possessors) the fact that economic capital is at their root, in other words—but only in the last analysis—at the root of their effects. The real logic of the functioning of capital, the conversions from one type to another, and the law of conservation which governs them cannot be understood unless two opposing but equally partial views are superseded: on the one hand, economism, which, on the grounds that every type of capital is reducible in the last analysis to economic capital, ignores what makes the specific efficacy of the other types of capital, and on the other hand, semiologism (nowadays represented by structuralism, symbolic interactionism, or ethnomethodology), which reduces social exchanges to phenomena of communication and ignores the brutal fact of universal reducibility to economics.[19]

In accordance with a principle which is the equivalent of the principle of the conservation of energy, profits in one area are necessarily paid for by costs in another (so that a concept like wastage has no meaning in a general science of the economy of practices). The universal equivalent, the measure of all equivalences, is nothing other than labor-time (in the widest sense); and the conservation of social energy through all its conversions is verified if, in each case, one takes into account both the labor-time accumulated in the form of capital and the labor-time needed to transform it from one type into another.

It has been seen, for example, that the transformation of economic capital into social capital presupposes a specific labor, i.e., an apparently gratuitous expenditure of time, attention, care, concern, which, as is seen in the endeavor to personalize a gift, has the effect of transfiguring the purely monetary import of the exchange and, by the same token, the very meaning of the exchange. From a narrowly economic standpoint, this effort is bound to be seen as pure wastage, but in the terms of the logic of social exchanges, it is a solid investment, the profits of which will appear, in the long run, in monetary or other form. Similarly, if the best measure of cultural capital is undoubtedly the amount of time devoted to acquiring it, this is because the transformation of economic capital into cultural capital presupposes an expenditure of time that is made possible by possession of economic capital. More precisely, it is because the cultural capital that is effectively transmitted within the family itself depends not only on the quantity of cultural capital, itself accumulated by spending time, that the domestic group possess, but also on the usable time (particularly in the form of the mother's free time) available to it (by virtue of its economic capital, which enables it to purchase the time of others) to ensure the transmission of this capital and to delay entry into the labor market through prolonged schooling, a credit which pays off, if at all, only in the very long term.[20]

The convertibility of the different types of capital is the basis of the strategies aimed at ensuring the reproduction of capital (and the position occupied in social space) by means of the conversions least costly in terms of conversion work and of the losses inherent in the conversion itself (in a given state of the social power relations). The different types of capital can be distinguished according to their reproducibility or, more precisely, according to how easily they are transmitted, i.e., with more or less loss and with more or less concealment; the rate of loss and the degree of concealment tend to vary in inverse ratio. Everything which helps to disguise the economic aspect also tends to increase the risk of loss (particularly the intergenerational transfers), Thus the (apparent) incommensurability of the different types of capital introduces a high degree of uncertainty into all transactions between holders of different types. Similarly, the declared refusal of calculation and of guarantees which characterizes exchanges tending to produce a social capital in the form of a capital of obligations that are usable in the more or less long term (exchanges of gifts, services, visits, etc.) necessarily entails the risk of ingratitude, the refusal of that recognition of nonguaranteed debts which such exchanges aim to produce. Similarly, too, the high degree of concealment of the transmission of cultural capital has the disadvantage (in addition to its inherent risks of loss) that the academic qualification which is its institutionalized form is neither transmissible (like a title of nobility) nor negotiable (like stocks and shares). More precisely, cultural capital, whose diffuse, continuous transmission within the family escapes observation and control (so that the educational system seems to award its honors solely to natural qualities) and which is increasingly tending to attain full efficacy, at least on the labor market, only when validated by the educational system, i.e., converted into a capital of qualifications, in subject to a more disguised but more risky transmission than economic capital. As the educational qualification, invested with the specific force of the official, becomes the condition for legitimate access to a growing number of positions, particularly the dominant ones, the educational system tends increasingly to dispossess the domestic group of the monopoly of the transmission of power and privileges—and, among other things, of the choice of its legitimate heirs from among children of different sex and birth rank.[21] And economic capital itself poses quite different problems of transmission, depending on the particular form it takes. Thus, according to Grassby (1970), the liquidity of commercial capital, which gives immediate economic power and favors transmission, also makes it more vulnerable than landed property (or even real estate) and does not favor the establishment of long-lasting dynasties.

Because the question of the arbitrariness of appropriation arises most sharply in the process of transmission—particularly at the time of succession, a critical moment for all power—every reproduction strategy is at the same time a legitimation strategy aimed at consecrating both an exclusive appropriation and its reproduction. When the subversive critique which aims to weaken the dominant class through the principle of its perpetuation by bringing to light the arbitrariness of the entitlements transmitted and of their transmission (such as the critique which the Enlightenment *philosophes* directed, in the name of nature, against the arbitrariness of birth) is incorporated in institutionalized mechanisms (for example, laws of inheritance) aimed at controlling the official, direct transmission of power and privileges, the holders of capital have an ever greater interest in resorting to reproduction strategies capable of ensuring better-disguised transmission, but at the cost of greater loss of capital, by exploiting the convertibility of the types of capital. Thus the more the official transmission of capital is prevented or hindered, the more the effects of the clandestine circulation of capital in the form of cultural capital become determinant in the reproduction of the social structure. As an instrument of reproduction capable of disguising its own function, the scope of the educational system tends to increase, and together with this increase is the unification of the market in social qualifications which gives rights to occupy rare positions.

Notes

1. This inertia, entailed by the tendency of the structures of capital to reproduce themselves in institutions or in dispositions adapted to the structures of which they are the product, is, of course, reinforced by a specifically political action of concerted conservation, i.e., of demobilization and depoliticization. The latter tends to keep the dominated agents in the state of a practical group, united only by the orchestration of their dispositions and condemned to function as an aggregate repeatedly performing discrete, individual acts (such as consumer or electoral choices).

2. This is true of all exchanges between members of different fractions of the dominant class, possessing different types of capital. These range from sales of expertise, treatment, or other services which take the form of gift exchange and dignify themselves with the most decorous names that can be found (honoraria, emoluments, etc.) to matrimonial exchanges, the prime example of a transaction that can only take place insofar as it is not perceived or defined as such by the contracting parties. It is remarkable that the apparent extensions of economic theory beyond the limits constituting the discipline have left intact the asylum of the sacred, apart from a few sacrilegious incursions. Gary S. Becker, for example, who was one of the first to take explicit account of the types of capital that are usually ignored, never considers anything other than monetary costs and profits, forgetting the nonmonetary investments (*inter alia*, the affective ones) and the material and symbolic profits that education provides in a deferred, indirect way, such as the added value which the dispositions produced or reinforced by schooling (bodily or verbal manners, tastes, etc.) or the relationships established with fellow students can yield in the matrimonial market (Becker 1964*a*).

3. *Symbolic capital*, that is to say, capital—in whatever form—insofar as it is represented, i.e., apprehended symbolically, in a relationship of knowledge or, more precisely, of misrecognition and recognition, presupposes the intervention of the habitus, as a socially constituted cognitive capacity.

4. When talking about concepts for their own sake, as I do here, rather than using them in research, one always runs the risk of being both schematic and formal, i.e., theoretical in the most usual and most usually approved sense of the word.

5. This proposition implies no recognition of the value of scholastic verdicts; it merely registers the relationship which exists in reality between a certain cultural capital and the laws of the educational market. Dispositions that are given a negative value in the educational market may receive very high value in other markets—not least, of course, in the relationships internal to the class.

6. In a relatively undifferentiated society, in which access to the means of appropriating the cultural heritage is very equally distributed, embodied culture does not function as cultural capital, i.e., as a means of acquiring exclusive advantages.

7. What I call the generalized Arrow effect, i.e., the fact that all cultural goods—paintings, monuments, machines, and any objects shaped by man, particularly all those which belong to the childhood environment—exert an educative effect by their mere existence, is no doubt one of the structural factors behind the 'schooling explosion,' in the sense that a growth in the quantity of cultural capital accumulated in the objectified state increases the educative effect automatically exerted by the environment. If one adds to this the fact that embodied cultural capital is constantly increasing, it can be seen that, in each generation, the educational system can take more for granted. The fact that the same educational investment is increasingly productive is one of the structural factors of the inflation of qualifications (together with cyclical factors linked to effects of capital conversion).

8. The cultural object, as a living social institution, is, simultaneously, a socially instituted material object and a particular class of habitus, to which it is addressed. The material object—for example, a work of art in its materiality—may be separated by space (e.g., a Dogon statue) or by time (e.g., a Simone Martini painting) from the habitus for which it was intended. This leads to one of the most fundamental biases of art history. Understanding the effect (not to be confused with the function) which the work tended to produce—for example, the form of belief it tended to induce—and which is the true basis of the conscious or unconscious choice of the means used (technique, colors, etc.), and therefore of the form itself, is possible only if one at least raises the question of the habitus on which it 'operated.'

9. The dialectical relationship between objectified cultural capital—of which the form *par excellence* is writing—and embodied cultural capital has generally been reduced to an exalted description of the degradation of the spirit by the letter, the living by the inert, creation by routine, grace by heaviness.

10. This is particularly true in France, where in many occupations (particularly the civil service) there is a very strict relationship between qualification, rank, and remuneration (translator's note).

11. Here, too, the notion of cultural capital did not spring from pure theoretical work, still less from an analogical extension of economic concepts. It arose from the need to identify the principle of social effects which, although they can be seen clearly at the level of singular agents—where statistical inquiry inevitably operates—cannot be reduced to the set of properties individually possessed by a given agent. These effects, in which spontaneous sociology readily perceives the work of 'connections,' are particularly visible in all cases in which different individuals obtain very unequal profits from virtually equivalent (economic or cultural) capital, depending on the extent to which they can mobilize by proxy the capital of a group (a family, the alumni of an elite school, a select club, the aristocracy, etc.) that is more or less constituted as such and more or less rich in capital.

12. Neighborhood relationships may, of course, receive an elementary form of institutionalization, as in the Bearn—or the Basque region—where neighbors, *lous besis* (a word which, in old texts, is applied to the legitimate inhabitants of the village, the rightful members of the assembly), are explicitly designated, in accordance with fairly codified rules, and are assigned functions which are differentiated according to their rank (there is a 'first neighbor,' a 'second neighbor,' and so on), particularly for the major social ceremonies (funerals, marriages, etc.). But even in this case, the relationships actually used by no means always coincide with the relationships socially instituted.

13. Manners (bearing, pronunciation, etc.) may be included in social capital insofar as, through the mode of acquisition they point to, they indicate initial membership of a more or less prestigious group.

14. National liberation movements or nationalist ideologies cannot be accounted for solely by reference to strictly economic profits, i.e., anticipation of the profits which may be derived from redistribution of a proportion of wealth to the advantage of the nationals (nationalization) and the recovery of highly paid jobs (see Breton 1964). To these specifically economic anticipated profits, which would only explain the nationalism of the privileged classes, must be added the very real and very immediate profits derived from membership (social capital) which are proportionately greater for those who are lower down the social hierarchy ('poor whites') or, more precisely, more threatened by economic and social decline.

15. There is every reason to suppose that socializing, or, more generally, relational, dispositions are very unequally distributed among the social classes and, within a given class, among fractions of different origin.

16. A 'full power to act and speak' (translator).

17. It goes without saying that social capital is so totally governed by the logic of knowledge and acknowledgment that it always functions as symbolic capital.

18. It should be made clear, to dispel a likely misunderstanding, that the investment in question here is not necessarily conceived as a calculated pursuit of gain, but that it has every likelihood of being experienced in terms of the logic of emotional investment, i.e., as an involvement which is both necessary and disinterested. This has not always been appreciated by historians, who (even when they are as alert to symbolic effects as E. P. Thompson) tend to conceive symbolic practices—powdered wigs and the whole paraphernalia of office—as explicit strategies of domination, intended to be seen (from below), and to interpret generous or charitable conduct as 'calculated acts of class appeasement.' This naively Machiavellian view forgets that the most sincerely disinterested acts may be those best corresponding to objective interest. A number of fields, particularly those which most tend to deny interest and every sort of calculation, like the fields of cultural production, grant full recognition, and with it the consecration which guarantees success, only to those who distinguish themselves by the immediate conformity of their investments, a token of sincerity and attachment to the essential principles of the field. It would be thoroughly erroneous to describe the choices of the habitus which lead an artist, writer, or researcher toward his natural place (a subject, style, manner, etc.) in terms of rational strategy and cynical calculation. This is despite the fact that, for example, shifts from one genre, school, or speciality to another, quasi-religious conversions that are performed 'in all sincerity,' can be understood as capital conversions, the direction and moment of which (on which their success often depends) are determined by a 'sense of investment' which is the less likely to be seen as such the more skillful it is. Innocence is the privilege of those who move in their field of activity like fish in water.

19. To understand the attractiveness of this pair of antagonistic positions which serve as each other's alibi, one would need to analyze the unconscious profits and the profits of unconsciousness which they procure for intellectuals. While some find in economism a means of exempting themselves by excluding the cultural capital and all the specific profits which place them on the side of the dominant, others can abandon the detestable terrain of the economic, where everything reminds them that they can be evaluated, in the last analysis, in economic terms, for that of the symbolic. (The latter merely reproduce, in the realm of the symbolic, the strategy whereby intellectuals and artists endeavor to impose the recognition of their values, i.e., their value, by inverting the law of the market in which what one has or what one earns completely defines what one is worth and what one is—as is shown by the practice of banks which, with techniques such as the personalization of credit, tend to subordinate the granting of loans and the fixing of interest rates to an exhaustive inquiry into the borrower's present and future resources.)

20. Among the advantages procured by capital in all its types, the most precious is the increased volume of useful time that is made possible through the various methods of appropriating other people's time (in the form of services). It may take the form either of increased spare time, secured by reducing the time consumed in activities directly channeled toward producing the means of reproducing the existence of the domestic group, or of more intense use of the time so consumed, by recourse to other people's labor or to devices and methods which are available only to those who have spent time learning how to use them and which (like better transport or living close to the place of work) make it possible to save time. (This is in contrast to the cash savings of the poor, which are paid for in time—do-it-yourself, bargain hunting, etc.) None of this is true of mere economic capital; it is possession of cultural capital that makes it possible to derive greater profit not only from labor-time, by securing a higher yield from the same time, but also from spare time, and so to increase both economic and cultural capital.

21. It goes without saying that the dominant fractions, who tend to place ever greater emphasis on educational investment, within an overall strategy of asset diversification and of investments aimed at combining security with high yield, have all sorts of ways of evading scholastic verdicts. The direct transmission of economic capital remains one of the principal means of reproduction, and the effect of social capital ('a helping hand,' 'string-pulling,' the 'old boy network') tends to correct the effect of academic sanctions. Educational qualifications never function perfectly as currency. They are never entirely separable from their holders: their value rises in proportion to the value of their bearer, especially in the least rigid areas of the social structure.

References

Becker, G. S. (1964a), *A Theoretical and Empirical Analysis with Special Reference to Education* (New York: National Bureau of Economic Research).

—— (1964b), *Human Capital* (New York: Columbia Univ. Press).

Bourdieu, P. (1982), 'Les rites d'institution', *Actes de la recherche en sciences sociales*, 43: 58–63.

Breton, A. (1962), 'The Economics of Nationalism', *Journal of Political Economy*, 72: 376–86.

Grassby, R. (1970), 'English Merchant Capitalism in the Late Seventeenth Century: The Composition of Business Fortunes', *Past and Present*, 46: 87–107.

Social Capital in the Creation of Human Capital[1]

JAMES S. COLEMAN

There are two broad intellectual streams in the description and explanation of social action. One, characteristic of the work of most sociologists, sees the actor as socialized and action as governed by social norms, rules, and obligations. The principal virtues of this intellectual stream lie in its ability to describe action in social context and to explain the way action is shaped, constrained, and redirected by the social context.

The other intellectual stream, characteristic of the work of most economists, sees the actor as having goals independently arrived at, as acting independently, and as wholly self-interested. Its principal virtue lies in having a principle of action, that of maximizing utility. This principle of action, together with a single empirical generalization (declining marginal utility) has generated the extensive growth of neoclassical economic theory, as well as the growth of political philosophy of several varieties: utilitarianism, contractarianism, and natural rights.[2]

In earlier works (Coleman 1986a,b), I have argued for and engaged in the development of a theoretical orientation in sociology that includes components from both these intellectual streams. It accepts the principle of rational or purposive action and attempts to show how that principle, in conjunction with particular social contexts, can account not only for the actions of individuals in particular contexts but also for the development of social organization. In the present paper, I introduce a conceptual tool for use in this theoretical enterprise: social capital. As background for introducing this concept, it is useful to see some of the criticisms of and attempts to modify the two intellectual streams.

Criticisms and Revisions

Both these intellectual streams have serious defects. The sociological stream has what may be a fatal flaw as a theoretical enterprise: the actor has no "engine of action." The actor is shaped by the environment, but there are no internal springs of action that give the actor a purpose or direction. The very conception of action as wholly a product of the environment has led sociologists themselves to criticize this intellectual stream, as in Dennis Wrong's (1961) "The Oversocialized Conception of Man in Modern Sociology."

The economic stream, on the other hand, flies in the face of empirical reality: persons' actions are shaped, redirected, constrained by the social context; norms, interpersonal trust, social networks, and social organization are important in the functioning not only of the society but also of the economy.

A number of authors from both traditions have recognized these difficulties and have attempted to impart some of the insights and orientations of the one intellectual stream to the other. In economics, Yoram Ben-Porath (1980) has developed ideas concerning the functioning of what he calls the "F-connection" in exchange systems. The F-connection is families, friends, and firms, and Ben-Porath, drawing on literature in anthropology and sociology as well as economics, shows the way these forms of social organization affect economic exchange. Oliver Williamson has, in a number of publications (e.g., 1975, 1981) examined the conditions under which economic activity is organized in different institutional forms, that is, within firms or in markets. There is a whole body of work in economics, the "new institutional economics," that attempts to show, within neoclassical economic theory, both the conditions under which particular economic institutions arise and the effects of these institutions (i.e., of social organization) on the functioning of the system.

There have been recent attempts by sociologists to examine the way social organization affects the functioning of economic activity. Baker (1983) has shown how, even in the highly rationalized market of the Chicago Options Exchange, relations among floor traders develop, are maintained, and affect their trades. More generally, Granovetter (1985) has engaged in a broad attack on the "undersocial-ized concept of man" that characterizes economists' analysis of economic activity. Granovetter first criticizes much of the new institutional economics as crudely functionalist because the existence of an economic institution is often explained merely by the functions it performs for the economic system. He argues that, even in the new institutional economics, there is a failure to recognize the importance of concrete personal relations and networks of relations—what he calls "embeddedness"—in generating trust, in establishing expectations, and in creating and enforcing norms.

Granovetter's idea of embeddedness may be seen as an attempt to introduce into the analysis of economic systems social organization and social relations not merely as a structure that springs into place to fulfill an economic function, but as a structure with history and continuity that give it an independent effect on the functioning of economic systems.

All this work, both by economists and by sociologists, has constituted a revisionist analysis of the functioning of economic systems. Broadly, it can be said to maintain the conception of rational action but to superimpose on it social and institutional organization—either endogenously generated, as in the functionalist explanations of some of the new institutional economists, or as exogenous factors, as in the more causally oriented work of some sociologists.

My aim is somewhat different. It is to import the economists' principle of rational action for use in the analysis of social systems proper, including but not limited to economic systems, and to do so without discarding social organization in the process. The concept of social capital is a tool to aid in this. In this paper, I introduce the concept in some generality, and then examine its usefulness in a particular context, that of education.

Social Capital

Elements for these two intellectual traditions cannot be brought together in a pastiche. It is necessary to begin with a conceptually coherent framework from one and introduce elements from the other without destroying that coherence.

I see two major deficiencies in earlier work that introduced "exchange theory" into sociology, despite the pathbreaking character of this work. One was the limitation to microsocial relations, which abandons the principal virtue of economic theory, its ability to make the micro–macro transition from pair relations to system. This was evident both in Homans's (1961) work and in Blau's (1964) work. The other was the attempt to introduce principles in an ad hoc fashion, such as "distributive justice" (Homans 1964, p. 241) or the "norm of reciprocity" (Gouldner 1960). The former deficiency limits the theory's usefulness, and the latter creates a pastiche.

If we begin with a theory of rational action, in which each actor has control over certain resources and interests in certain resources and events, then social capital constitutes a particular kind of resource available to an actor.

Social capital is defined by its function. It is not a single entity but a variety of different entities, with two elements in common: they all consist of some aspect of social structures, and they facilitate certain actions of actors—whether persons or corporate actors—within the structure. Like other forms of capital, social capital is productive, making possible the achievement of certain ends that in its absence would not be possible. Like physical capital and human capital, social capital is not completely fungible but may be specific to certain activities. A given form of social capital that is valuable in facilitating certain actions may be useless or even harmful for others.

Unlike other forms of capital, social capital inheres in the structure of relations between actors and among actors. It is not lodged either in the actors themselves or in physical implements of production. Because purposive organizations can be actors ("corporate actors") just as persons can, relations among corporate actors can constitute social capital for them as well (with perhaps the best-known example being the sharing of information that allows price-fixing in an industry). However, in the present paper, the examples and area of application to which I will direct attention concern social capital as a resource for persons.

Before I state more precisely what social capital consists of, it is useful to give several examples that illustrate some of its different forms.

1 Wholesale diamond markets exhibit a property that to an outsider is remarkable. In the process of negotiating a sale, a merchant will hand over to another merchant a bag of stones for the latter to examine in private at his leisure, with no formal insurance that the latter will not substitute one or more inferior stones or a paste replica. The merchandise may be worth thousands, or hundreds of thousands, of dollars. Such free exchange of stones for inspection is important to the functioning of this market. In its absence, the market would operate in a much more cumbersome, much less efficient fashion.

   Inspection shows certain attributes of the social structure. A given merchant community is ordinarily very close, both in the frequency of interaction and in ethnic and family ties. The wholesale diamond market in New York City, for example, is Jewish, with a high degree of intermarriage, living in the same community in Brooklyn, and going to the same synagogues. It is essentially a closed community.

   Observation of the wholesale diamond market indicates that these close ties, through family, community, and religious affiliation, provide the insurance that is necessary to facilitate the transactions in the market. If any member of this community defected through substituting other stones or through stealing stones in his temporary possession, he would lose family, religious, and community ties. The strength of these ties makes possible transactions in which trustworthiness is taken for granted and trade can occur with ease. In the absence of these ties, elaborate and expensive bonding and insurance devices would be necessary—or else the transactions could not take place.

2 The *International Herald Tribune* of June 21–22, 1986, contained an article on page 1 about South Korean student radical activists. It describes the development of such activism: "Radical thought is passed on in clandestine 'study circles,' groups of students who may come from the same high school or hometown or church. These study circles . . . serve as the basic organizational unit for demonstrations and other protests. To avoid detection, members of different groups never meet, but communicate through an appointed representative."

   This description of the basis of organization of this activism illustrates social capital of two kinds. The "same high school or hometown or church" provides social relations on which the "study circles" are later built. The study circles themselves constitute a form of social capital—a cellular form of organization that appears especially valuable for facilitating opposition in any political system intolerant of dissent. Even where political dissent is tolerated, certain activities are not, whether the activities are politically motivated terrorism or simple crime. The organization that makes possible these activities is an especially potent form of social capital.

3 A mother of six children, who recently moved with husband and children from suburban Detroit

to Jerusalem, described as one reason for doing so the greater freedom her young children had in Jerusalem. She felt safe in letting her eight year old take the six year old across town to school on the city bus and felt her children to be safe in playing without supervision in a city park, neither of which she felt able to do where she lived before.

The reason for this difference can be described as a difference in social capital available in Jerusalem and suburban Detroit. In Jerusalem, the normative structure ensures that unattended children will be "looked after" by adults in the vicinity, while no such normative structure exists in most metropolitan areas of the United States. One can say that families have available to them in Jerusalem social capital that does not exist in metropolitan areas of the United States.

4   In the Kahn El Khalili market of Cairo, the boundaries between merchants are difficult for an outsider to discover. The owner of a shop that specializes in leather will, when queried about where one can find a certain kind of jewelry, turn out to sell that as well—or, what appears to be nearly the same thing, to have a close associate who sells it, to whom he will immediately take the customer. Or he will instantly become a money changer, although he is not a money changer, merely by turning to his colleague a few shops down. For some activities, such as bringing a customer to a friend's store, there are commissions; for others, such as money changing, merely the creation of obligations. Family relations are important in the market, as is the stability of proprietorship. The whole market is so infused with relations of the sort I have described that it can be seen as an organization, no less so than a department store. Alternatively, one can see the market as consisting of a set of individual merchants, each having an extensive body of social capital on which to draw, through the relationships of the market.

The examples above have shown the value of social capital for a number of outcomes, both economic and noneconomic. There are, however, certain properties of social capital that are important for understanding how it comes into being and how it is employed in the creation of human capital. First, a comparison with human capital, and then an examination of different forms of social capital, will be helpful for seeing these.

Human Capital and Social Capital

Probably the most important and most original development in the economics of education in the past 30 years has been the idea that the concept of physical capital as embodied in tools, machines, and other productive equipment can be extended to include human capital as well (see Schultz 1961; Becker 1964). Just as physical capital is created by changes in materials to form tools that facilitate production, human capital is created by changes in persons that bring about skills and capabilities that make them able to act in new ways.

Social capital, however, comes about through changes in the relations among persons that facilitate action. If physical capital is wholly tangible, being embodied in observable material form, and human capital is less tangible, being embodied in the skills and knowledge acquired by an individual, social capital is less tangible yet, for it exists in the relations among persons. Just as physical capital and human capital facilitate productive activity, social capital does as well. For example, a group within which there is extensive trustworthiness and extensive trust is able to accomplish much more than a comparable group without that trustworthiness and trust.

Forms of Social Capital

The value of the concept of social capital lies first in the fact that it identifies certain aspects of social structure by their functions, just as the concept "chair" identifies certain physical objects by their function, despite differences in form, appearance, and construction. The function identified by the concept of "social capital" is the value of these aspects of social structure to actors as resources that they can use to achieve their interests.

By identifying this function of certain aspects of social structure, the concept of social capital constitutes both an aid in accounting for different outcomes at the level of individual actors and an aid toward making the micro-to-macro transitions without elaborating the social structural details through which this occurs. For example, in characterizing the clandestine study circles of South Korean radical students as constituting social capital that these students can use in their revolutionary activities, we assert that the groups constitute a resource that aids in moving from individual protest to organized revolt. If, in a theory of revolt, a resource that accomplishes this task is held to be necessary, then these study circles are grouped together with those organizational structures, having very different origins, that have fulfilled the same function for individuals with revolutionary goals in other contexts, such as the *Comités d'action lycéen* of the French student revolt of 1968 or the workers' cells in tsarist Russia described and advocated by Lenin ([1902] 1973).

It is true, of course, that for other purposes one wants to investigate the details of such organizational resources, to understand the elements that are critical to their usefulness as resources for such a purpose, and to examine how they came into being in a particular case. But the concept of social capital allows taking such resources and showing the way they can be combined with other resources to produce different system-level behavior or, in other cases, different outcomes for individuals. Although, for these purposes, social capital constitutes an unanalyzed concept, it signals to the analyst and to the reader that something of value has been produced for those actors who have this resource available and that the value depends on social organization. It then becomes a second stage in the analysis to unpack the concept, to discover what components of social organization contribute to the value produced.

In previous work, Lin (1988) and De Graf and Flap (1988), from a perspective of methodological individualism similar to that used in this paper, have shown how informal social resources are used instrumentally in achieving occupational mobility in the United States and, to a lesser extent, in West Germany and the Netherlands. Lin focused on social ties, especially "weak" ties, in this role. Here, I want to examine a variety of resources, all of which constitute social capital for actors.

Before examining empirically the value of social capital in the creation of human capital, I will go more deeply into an examination of just what it is about social relations that can constitute useful capital resources for individuals.

Obligations, Expectations, and Trustworthiness of Structures

If A does something for B and trusts B to reciprocate in the future, this establishes an expectation in A and an obligation on the part of B. This obligation can be conceived as a credit slip held by A for performance by B. If A holds a large number of these credit slips, for a number of persons with whom A has relations, then the analogy to financial capital is direct. These credit slips constitute a large body of credit that A can call in if necessary—unless, of course, the placement of trust has been unwise, and these are bad debts that will not be repaid.

In some social structures, it is said that "people are always doing things for each other." There are a large number of these credit slips outstanding, often on both sides of a relation (for these credit slips appear often not to be completely fungible across areas of activity, so that credit slips of B held by A and those of A held by B are not fully used to cancel each other out). The El Khalili market in Cairo, described earlier, constitutes an extreme case of such a social structure. In other social structures where individuals are more self-sufficient and depend on each other less, there are fewer of these credit slips outstanding at any time.

This form of social capital depends on two elements: trustworthiness of the social environment, which means that obligations will be repaid, and the actual extent of obligations held. Social structures differ in both these dimensions, and actors within the same structure differ in the second. A case that illustrates the value of the trustworthiness of the environment is that of the rotating-credit associations of Southeast Asia and elsewhere. These associations are groups of friends and neighbors who typically meet monthly, each person contributing to a central fund that is then given to one of the members (through bidding or by lot), until, after a number of months, each of the persons has made contributions and received one. As Geertz (1962) points out, these associations serve as efficient institutions for amassing savings for small capital expenditures, an important aid to economic development.

But without a high degree of trustworthiness among the members of the group, the institution could not exist—for a person who receives a early in the sequence of meetings could abscond and leave the others with a loss. For example, one could not imagine a rotating-credit association operating successfully in urban areas marked by a high degree of social disorganization—or, in other words, by a lack of social capital.

Differences in social structures in both dimensions may arise for a variety of reasons. There are differences in the actual needs that persons have for help, in the existence of other sources of aid (such as government welfare services), in the degree of affluence (which reduces aid needed from others), in cultural differences in the tendency to lend aid and ask for aid (see Banfield, 1967) in the closure of social networks, in the logistics of social contacts (see Festinger, Schachter, and Back, 1963) and other factors. Whatever the source, however, individuals in social structures with high levels of obligations outstanding at any time have more social capital on which they can draw. The density of outstanding obligations means, in effect, that the overall usefulness of the tangible resources of that social structure is amplified by their availability to others when needed.

Individual actors in a social system also differ in the number of credit slips outstanding on which they can draw at any time. The most extreme examples are in hierarchically structured extended family settings, in which a patriarch (or "godfather") holds an extraordinarily large set of obligations that he can call in at any time to get what he wants done. Near this extreme are villages in traditional settings that are highly stratified, with certain wealthy families who, because of their wealth, have built up extensive credits that they can call in at any time.

Similarly, in political settings such as a legislature, a legislator in a position with extra resources (such as the Speaker of the House of Representatives or the Majority Leader of the Senate in the U.S. Congress) can, by effective use of resources, build up a set of obligations from other legislators that makes it possible to get legislation passed that would otherwise be stymied. This concentration of obligations constitutes social capital that is useful not only for this powerful legislator but useful also in getting an increased level of action on the part of a legislature. Thus, those members of legislatures among whom such credits are extensive should be more powerful than those without extensive credits and debits because they can use the credits to produce bloc voting on many issues. It is well recognized, for example, that in the U.S. Senate, some senators are members of what is called "the Senate Club," while others are not. This in effect means that some senators are embedded in the system of credits and debits, while others, outside the "Club," are not. It is also well recognized that those in the Club are more powerful than those outside it.

Information Channels

An important form of social capital is the potential for information that inheres in social relations. Information is important in providing a basis for action. But acquisition of information is costly. At a minimum, it requires attention, which is always in scarce supply. One means by which information can be acquired is by use of social relations that are maintained for other purposes. Katz and Lazarsfeld (1955) showed how this operated for women in several areas of life in a midwestern city around 1950. They showed that a woman with an interest in being in fashion, but no interest in being on the leading edge of fashion, used friends who she knew kept up with fashion as sources of information. Similarly, a person who is not greatly interested in current events but who is interested in being informed about important developments can save the time of reading a newspaper by depending on spouse or friends who pay attention to such matters. A social scientist who is interested in being up-to-date on research in related fields can make use of everyday interactions with colleagues to do so, but only in a university in which most colleagues keep up-to-date.

All these are examples of social relations that constitute a form of social capital that provides information that facilitates action. The relations in this case are not valuable for the "credit slips" they provide in the form of obligations that one holds for others' performances or for the trustworthiness of the other party but merely for the information they provide.

Norms and Effective Sanctions

When a norm exists and is effective, it constitutes a powerful, though sometimes fragile, form of social capital. Effective norms that inhibit crime make it possible to walk freely outside at night in a city and enable old persons to leave their houses without fear for their safety. Norms in a community that support and provide effective rewards for high achievement in school greatly facilitate the school's task.

A prescriptive norm within a collectivity that constitutes an especially important form of social capital is the norm that one should forgo interest and act in the interests of the collectivity. A norm of this sort, reinforced by social support, status, honor, and other rewards, is the social capital that builds young nations (and then dissipates as they grow older), strengthens families by leading family members to act selflessly in "the family's" interest, facilitates the development of nascent social movements through a small group of dedicated, inward-looking, and mutually rewarding members, and in general leads persons to work for the public good. In some of these cases, the norms are internalized; in others, they are largely supported through external rewards for selfless actions and disapproval for selfish actions. But, whether supported by internal or external sanctions, norms of this sort are important in overcoming the public goods problem that exists in collectivities.

As all these examples suggest, effective norms can constitute a powerful form of social capital. This social capital, however, like the forms described earlier, not only facilitates certain actions; it constrains others. A community with strong and effective norms about young persons' behavior can keep them from "having a good time." Norms that make it possible to walk alone at night also constrain the activities of criminals (and in some cases of noncriminals as well). Even prescriptive norms that reward certain actions, like the norm in a community that says that a boy who is a good athlete should go out for football, are in effect directing energy away from other activities. Effective norms in an area can reduce innovativeness in an area, not only deviant actions that harm others but also deviant actions that can benefit everyone. (See Merton, 1968, pp. 195–203, for a discussion of how this can come about.)

Social Structure that Facilitates Social Capital

All social relations and social structures facilitate some forms of social capital; actors establish relations purposefully and continue them when they continue to provide benefits. Certain kinds of social structure, however, are especially important in facilitating some forms of social capital.

Closure of Social Networks

One property of social relations on which effective norms depend is what I will call closure. In general, one can say that a necessary but not sufficient condition for the emergence of effective norms is action that imposes external effects on others (see Ullmann-Margalit, 1977; Coleman, 1987). Norms arise as attempts to limit negative external effects or encourage positive ones. But, in many social structures where these conditions exist, norms do not come into existence. The reason is what can be described as lack of closure of the social structure. Figure 7.1 illustrates why. In an open structure like that of Figure 7.1a, actor *A,* having relations with actors *B* and *C,* can carry out actions that impose negative externalities on *B* or *C* or both. Since they have no relations with one another, but with others instead (*D* and *E*), then they cannot combine forces to sanction *A* in order to constrain the actions. Unless either *B* or *C* alone is sufficiently harmed and sufficiently powerful vis-à-vis *A* to sanction alone, *A*'s actions can continue unabated. In a structure with closure, like that of Figure 7.1b, *B* and *C* can combine to provide a collective sanction, or either can reward the other for sanctioning *A.* (See Merry, 1984, for examples of the way gossip, which depends on closure of the social structure, is used as a collective sanction.)

In the case of norms imposed by parents on children, closure of the structure requires a slightly more complex structure, which I will call intergenerational closure. Intergenerational closure may be described by a simple diagram that represents relations between parent and child and relations outside the family. Consider the structure of two communities, represented by Figure 7.2. The vertical lines represent relations across generations, between parent and child, while the horizontal lines represent relations within a generation. The point labeled *A* in both Figure 7.2a and Figure 7.2b represents the parent of child *B,* and the point labeled *D* represents the parent of child *C.* The lines between *B* and *C* represent the relations among children that exist within any school. Although the other relations among children within the school are not shown here, there exists a high degree of closure among peers, who see each other daily, have expectations toward each other, and develop norms about each other's behavior.

The two communities differ, however, in the presence or absence of links among the parents of children in the school. For the school represented by Figure 7.2b, there is intergenerational closure; for that represented by Figure 7.2b there is not. To put it colloquially, in the lower community represented by 7.2b the parents' friends are the parents of their children's friends. In the other, they are not.

The consequence of this closure is, as in the case of the wholesale diamond market or in other similar communities, a set of effective sanctions that can monitor and guide behavior. In the community in Figure 7.2b, parents *A* and *D* can discuss their children's activities and come to some consensus about standards and about sanctions. Parent *A* is reinforced by parent *D* in sanctioning his child's actions; beyond that, parent *D* constitutes a monitor not only for his own child, *C,* but also for the other child, *B.* Thus, the existence of intergenerational closure provides a quantity of social capital available to each parent in raising his children—not only in matters related to school but in other matters as well.

Closure of the social structure is important not only for the existence of effective norms but also for another form of social capital: the trustworthiness of social structures that allows the proliferation of

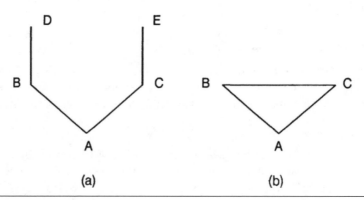

Figure 7.1 Network without (a) and with (b) closure.

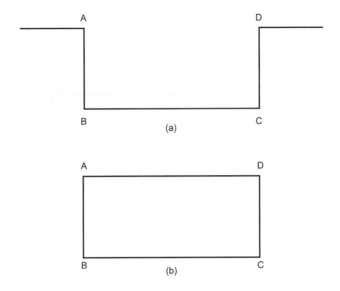

Figure 7.2 Network involving parents (A, D) and children (B, C) without (a) and with (b) intergenerational closure.

obligations and expectations. Defection from an obligation is a form of imposing a negative external-ity or another. Yet, in a structure without closure, it can be effectively sanctioned, if at all, only by the person to whom the obligation is owed. Reputation cannot arise in an open structure, and collective sanctions that would ensure trustworthiness cannot be applied. Thus, we may say that closure creates trustworthiness in a social structure.

Appropriable Social Organization

Voluntary organizations are brought into being to aid some purpose of those who initiate them. In a housing project built during World War II in an eastern city of the United States, there were many physical problems caused by poor construction: faulty plumbing, crumbling sidewalks, and other defects (Merton, n.d.). Residents organized to confront the builders and to address these problems in other ways. Later, when the problems were solved, the organization remained as available social capital that improved the quality of life for residents. Residents had resources available that they had seen as unavailable where they had lived before. (For example, despite the fact that the number of teenagers in the community was smaller, residents were *more* likely to express satisfaction with the availability of teenage babysitters.)

Printers in the New York Typographical Union who were monotype operators formed a Monotype Club as a social club (Lipset, Trow, and Coleman, 1956). Later, as employers looked for monotype operators and as monotype operators looked for jobs, both found this organization an effective em-ployment referral service and appropriated the organization for this purpose. Still later, when the Progressive Party came into power in the New York Union, the Monotype Club served as an organi-zational resource for the Independent Party as it left office. The Monotype Club subsequently served as an important source of social capital for the Independents to sustain the party as an organized opposition while it was out of office.

In the example of South Korean student radicals used earlier, the study circles were described as consisting of groups of students from the same high school or hometown or church. Here, as in the earlier examples, an organization that was initiated for one purpose is available for appropriation for other purposes, constituting important social capital for the individual members, who have available to them the organizational resources necessary for effective opposition. These examples illustrate the general point, that organization, once brought into existence for one set of purposes, can also aid others, thus constituting social capital available for use.

It is possible to gain insight into some of the ways in which closure and appropriable social organization provide social capital by use of a distinction made by Max Gluckman (1967) between simplex and multiplex relations.[3] In the latter, persons are linked in more than one context (neighbor, fellow worker, fellow parent, coreligionist, etc.), while in the former, persons are linked through only one of these relations. The central property of a multiplex relation is that it allows the resources of one relationship to be appropriated for use in others. Sometimes, the resource is merely information, as when two parents who see each other as neighbors exchange information about their teenagers' activities; sometimes, it is the obligations that one person owes a second in relationship X, which the second person can use to constrain the actions of the first in relationship Y. Often, it is resources in the form of other persons who have obligations in one context that can be called on to aid when one has problems in another context.

Social Capital in the Creation of Human Capital

The preceding pages have been directed toward defining and illustrating social capital in general. But there is one effect of social capital that is especially important: its effect on the creation of human capital in the next generation. Both social capital in the family and social capital in the community play roles in the creation of human capital in the rising generation. I will examine each of these in turn.

Social Capital in the Family

Ordinarily, in the examination of the effects of various factors on achievement in school, "family background" is considered a single entity, distinguished from schooling in its effects. But there is not merely a single "family background"; family background is analytically separable into at least three different components: financial capital, human capital, and social capital. Financial capital is approximately measured by the family's wealth or income. It provides the physical resources that can aid achievement: a fixed place in the home for studying, materials to aid learning, the financial resources that smooth family problems. Human capital is approximately measured by parents' education and provides the potential for a cognitive environment for the child that aids learning. Social capital within the family is different from either of these. Two examples will give a sense of what it is and how it operates.

John Stuart Mill, at an age before most children attend school, was taught Latin and Greek by his father, James Mill, and later in childhood would discuss critically with his father and with Jeremy drafts of his father's manuscripts. John Stuart Mill probably had no extraordinary genetic endowments, and his father's learning was no more extensive than that of some other men of the time. The central difference was the time and effort spent by the father with the child on intellectual matters.

In one public school district in the United States where texts for school use were purchased by children's families, school authorities were puzzled to discover that a number of Asian immigrant families purchased *two* copies of each textbook needed by the child. Investigation revealed that the family purchased the second copy for the mother to study in order to help her child do well in school. Here is a case in which the human capital of the parents, at least as measured traditionally by years of schooling, is low, but the social capital in the family available for the child's education is extremely high.

These examples illustrate the importance of social capital within the family for a child's intellectual development. It is of course true that children are strongly affected by the human capital possessed by their parents. But this human capital may be irrelevant to outcomes for children if parents are not an important part of their children's lives, if their human capital is employed exclusively at work or elsewhere outside the home. The social capital of the family is the relations between children and parents (and, when families include other members, relationships with them as well). That is, if the human capital possessed by parents is not complemented by social capital embodied in family relations, it is irrelevant to the child's educational growth that the parent has a great deal, or a small amount, of human capital.[4]

I will not differentiate here among the forms of social capital discussed earlier, but will attempt merely to measure the strength of the relations between parents and child as a measure of the social capital available to the child from the parent. Nor will I use the concept in the context of the paradigm of rational action, as, for example, is often done in use of the concept of human capital to examine the investments in education that a rational person would make. A portion of the reason for this lies in a property of much social capital not shown by most forms of capital (to which I will turn in a later section): its public goods character, which leads to underinvestment.

Social capital within the family that gives the child access to the adult's human capital depends both on the physical presence of adults in the family and on the attention given by the adults to the child. The physical absence of adults may be described as a structural deficiency in family social capital. The most prominent element of structural deficiency in modern families is the single-parent family. However, the nuclear family itself, in which one or both parents work outside the home, can be seen as structurally deficient, lacking the social capital that comes with the presence of parents during the day, or with grandparents or aunts and uncles in or near the household.

Even if adults are physically present, there is a lack of social capital in the family if there are not strong relations between children and parents. The lack of strong relations can result from the child's embeddedness in a youth community, from the parents' embeddedness in relationships with other adults that do not cross generations, or from other sources. Whatever the source, it means that whatever *human* capital exists in the parents, the child does not profit from it because the *social* capital is missing.

The effects of a lack of social capital within the family differ for different educational outcomes. One for which it appears to be especially important is dropping out of school. With the *High School and Beyond* sample of students in high schools, Table 7.1 shows the expected dropout rates for students in different types of families when various measures of social and human capital in the family and a measure of social capital in the community are controlled statistically.[5] An explanation is necessary for the use of number of siblings as a measure of lack of social capital. The number of siblings represents, in this interpretation, a dilution of adult attention to the child. This is consistent with research results for measures of achievement and IQ, which show that test scores decline with sib position, even when total family size is controlled, and that scores decline with number of children in the family. Both results are consistent with the view that younger sibs and children in large families have less adult attention, which produces weaker educational outcomes.

Item 1 of Table 7.1 shows that, when other family resources are controlled, the percentage of students who drop out between spring of the sophomore year and spring of the senior year is 6 percentage points higher for children from single-parent families. Item 2 of Table 7.1 shows that the rate is 6.4 percentage points higher for sophomores with four siblings than for those with otherwise equivalent family resources but only one sibling. Or, taking these two together, we can think of the ratio of adults to children as a measure of the social capital in the family available for the education of any one of them. Item 3 of Table 7.1 shows that for a sophomore with four siblings and one parent, and an otherwise average background, the rate is 22.6%; with one sibling and two parents, the rate is 10.1%—a difference of 12.5 percentage points.

Another indicator of adult attention in the family, although not a pure measure of social capital, is the mother's expectation of the child's going to college. Item 4 of the table shows that, for sophomores without this parental expectation, the rate is 8.6 percentage points higher than for those with it. With the three sources of family social capital taken together, item 5 of the table shows that sophomores with one sibling, two parents, and a mother's expectation for college (still controlling on other resources of

Table 7.1 Dropout Rates between Spring, Grade 10 and Spring, Grade 12 for Students Whose Families Differ in Social Capital, Controlling for Human Capital and Financial Capital in the Family

	Percentage Dropping Out	Difference in Percentage Points
1. Parents' presence:		
Two parents	13.1	6.0
Single parent	19.1	
2. Additional children:		
One sibling	10.8	6.4
Four siblings	17.2	
3. Parents and children:		
Two parents, one sibling	10.1	12.5
One parent, four siblings	22.6	
4. Mother's expectation for child's education:		
Expectation of college	11.6	8.6
No expectation of college	20.2	
5. Three factors together:		
Two parents, one sibling, mother expects college	8.1	22.5
One parent, four siblings, no college expectation	30.6	

Source: Estimates taken from logistic regression reported more fully in Hoffer (1986).

family) have an 8.1% dropout rate; with four siblings, one parent, and no expectation of the mother for college, the rate is 30.6%.

These results provide a less satisfactory test than if the research had been explicitly designed to examine effects of social capital within the family.

Social Capital outside the Family

The social capital that has value for a young person's development does not reside solely within the family. It can be found outside as well in the community consisting of the social relationships that exist among parents, in the closure exhibited by this structure of relations, and in the parents' relations with the institutions of the community.

The effect of this social capital outside the family on educational outcomes can be seen by examining outcomes for children whose parents differ in the particular source of social capital discussed earlier, intergenerational closure. There is not a direct measure of intergenerational closure in the data, but there is a proximate indicator. This is the number of times the child has changed schools because the family moved. For families that have moved often, the social relations that constitute social capital are broken at each move. Whatever the degree of interegenerational closure available to others in the community, it is not available to parents in mobile families.

The logistic regression carried out earlier and reported in table shows that the coefficient for number of moves since grade 5 is 10 times its standard error, the variable with the strongest overall effect of any variable in the equation, including the measures of human and financial capital in the family (socioeconomic status) and the crude measures of family social capital introduced in the earlier analysis. Translating this into an effect on dropping out gives 11.8% as the dropout rate if the family has not moved, 16.7% if it has moved once, and 23.1% if it has moved twice.

In the *High School and Beyond* data set, another variation among the schools constitutes a useful indicator of social capital. This is the distinctions among public high schools, religiously based private high schools, and nonreligiously based private high schools. It is the religiously based high schools that are surrounded by a community based on the religious organization. These families have intergenerational closure that is based on a multiplex relation: whatever other relations they have, the adults are members of the same religious body and parents of children in the same school. In contrast, it is the independent private schools that are typically least surrounded by a community, for their student bodies are collections of students, most of whose families have no contact.[6] The choice of private school for most of these parents is an individualistic one, and, although they back their children with extensive human capital, they send their children to these schools denuded of social capital.

In the *High School and Beyond* data set, there are 893 public schools, 84 Catholic schools, and 27 other private schools. Most of the other private schools are independent schools, though a minority have religious foundations. In this analysis, I will at the outset regard the other private schools as independent private schools to examine the effects of social capital outside the family.

The results of these comparisons are shown in Table 7.2. Item 1 of the table shows that the dropout rates between sophomore and senior years are 14.4% in public schools, 3.4% in Catholic schools, and 11.9% in other private schools. What is most striking is the low dropout rate in Catholic schools. The rate is a fourth of that in the public schools and a third of that in the other private schools.

Adjusting the dropout rates for differences in student-body financial, human, and social capital among the three sets of schools by standardizing the population of the Catholic schools and other private schools to the student-body backgrounds of the public schools shows that the differences are affected only slightly. Furthermore, the differences are not due to the religion of the students or to the degree of religious observance. Catholic students in public school are only slightly less likely to drop out than non-Catholics. Frequency of attendance at religious services, which is itself a measure of social capital through intergenerational closure, is strongly related to dropout rate, with 19.5% of public school students who rarely or never attend dropping out compared with 9.1% of those who attend often. But this effect exists apart from, and in addition to, the effect of the school's religious affiliation. Comparable figures for Catholic school students are 5.9% and 2.6% respectively (Coleman and Hoffer, 1987, p. 138).

The low dropout rates of the Catholic schools, the absence of low dropout rates in the other private schools, and the independent effect of frequency of religious attendance all provide evidence of the importance of social capital outside the school, in the adult community surrounding it, for this outcome of education.

A further test is possible, for there were eight schools in the sample of non-Catholic private schools

Table 7.2 Dropout between Spring, Grade 10, and Spring Grade 12, for Students from Schools with Differing Amounts of Social Capital in the Surrounding Community

(a)

	Public	Catholic	Other Private Schools
Raw dropout rates	14.4	3.4	11.9
2. Dropout rates standardized to average public school sophomore[a]	14.4	5.2	11.6

(b)

	Non-Catholic Religious	Independent
3. Raw dropout rates for students[b] from independent and non-Catholic religious private schools	3.7	10.0

Notes:

a The standardization is based on separate logistic regressions for these two sets of schools, using the same variables listed in n. 5. Coefficients and means for the standardization are in Hoffer (1986, tables 5 and 24).

b This tabulation is based on unweighted data, which is responsible for the fact that both rates are lower than the rate for other private schools in item 1 of the table, which is based on weighted data.

("other private" in the analysis above) that have religious foundations and over 50% of the student body of that religion. Three were Baptist schools, two were Jewish, and three from three other denominations. If the inference is correct about the religious community's providing intergenerational closure and thus social capital and about the importance of social capital in depressing the chance of dropping out of high school, these schools also should show a lower dropout rate than the independent private schools. Item 3 of Table 7.2 shows that their dropout rate is lower, 3.7%, essentially the same as that of the Catholic schools.[7]

The data presented above indicate the importance of social capital for the education of youth, or, as it might be put, the importance of social capital in the creation of human capital. Yet there is a fundamental difference between social capital and most other forms of capital that has strong implications for the development of youth. It is this difference to which I will turn in the next section.

Public Goods Aspects of Social Capital

Physical capital is ordinarily a private good, and property rights make it possible for the person who invests in physical capital to capture the benefits it produces. Thus, the incentive to invest in physical capital is not depressed; there is not a suboptimal investment in physical capital because those who invest in it are able to capture the benefits of their investments. For human capital also—at least human capital of the sort that is produced in schools—the person who invests the time and resources in building up this capital reaps its benefits in the form of a higher-paying job, more satisfying or higher-status work, or even the pleasure of greater understanding of the surrounding world—in short, all the benefits that schooling brings to a person.

But most forms of social capital are not like this. For example, the kinds of social structures that make possible social norms and the sanctions that enforce them do not benefit primarily the person or persons whose efforts would be necessary to bring them about, but benefit all those who are part of such a structure. For example, in some schools where there exists a dense set of associations among some parents, these are the result of a small number of persons, ordinarily mothers who do not hold full-time jobs outside the home. Yet these mothers themselves experience only a subset of the benefits of this social capital surrounding the school. If one of them decides to abandon these activities—for example, to take a full-time job—this may be an entirely reasonable action from a personal point of view and even from the point of view of that household with its children. The benefits of the new activity may far outweigh the losses that arise from the decline in associations with other parents whose children are in the school. But the withdrawal of these activities constitutes a loss to all those other parents whose associations and contacts were dependent on them.

Similarly, the decision to move from a community so that the father, for example, can take a better job may be entirely correct from the point of view of that family. But, because social capital consists of relations among persons, other persons may experience extensive losses by the severance of those relations, a severance over which they had no control. A part of those losses is the weakening of norms and sanctions that aid the school in its task. For each family, the total cost it experiences as a consequence of the decisions it and other families make may outweigh the benefits of those few decisions it has control over. Yet the beneficial consequences to the family of those decisions made by the family may far outweigh the minor losses it experiences from them alone.

It is not merely voluntary associations, such as a PTA, in which investment of this sort occurs. When an individual asks a favor from another, thus incurring an obligation, he does so because it brings him a needed benefit; he does not consider that it does the other a benefit as well by adding to a drawing fund of social capital available in a time of need. If the first individual can satisfy his need through self-sufficiency, or through aid from some official source without incurring an obligation, he will do so—and thus fail to add to the social capital outstanding in the community.

Similar statements can be made with respect to trustworthiness as social capital. An actor choosing to keep trust or not (or choosing whether to devote resources to an attempt to keep trust) is doing so on the basis of costs and benefits he himself will experience. That his trustworthiness will facilitate others' actions or that his lack of trustworthiness will inhibit others' actions does not enter into his decision. A similar but more qualified statement can be made for information as a form of social capital. An individual who serves as a source of information for another because he is well informed ordinarily acquires that information for his own benefit, not for the others who make use of him. (This is not always true. As Katz and Lazarsfeld, 1955, show, "opinion leaders" in an area acquire information in part to maintain their position as opinion leaders.)

For norms also, the statement must be qualified. Norms are intentionally established, indeed as means of reducing externalities, and their benefits are ordinarily captured by those who are responsible for establishing them. But the capability of establishing and maintaining effective norms depends on properties of the social structure (such as closure) over which one actor does not have control yet are affected by one actor's action. These are properties that affect the structure's capacity to sustain effective norms, yet properties that ordinarily do not enter into an individual's decision that affects them.

Some forms of social capital have the property that their benefits can be captured by those who invest in them; consequently, rational actors will not underinvest in this type of social capital. Organizations that produce a private good constitute the outstanding example. The result is that there will be in society an imbalance in the relative investment in organizations that produce private goods for a market and those associations and relationships in which the benefits are not captured—an imbalance in the sense that, if the positive externalities created by the latter form of social capital could be internalized, it would come to exist in greater quantity.

The public goods quality of most social capital means that it is in a fundamentally different position with respect to purposive action than are most other forms of capital. It is an important resource for individuals and may affect greatly their ability to act and their perceived quality of life. They have the capability of bringing it into being. Yet, because the benefits of actions that bring social capital into being are largely experienced by persons other than the actor, it is often not in his interest to bring it into being. The result is that most forms of social capital are created or destroyed as by-products of other activities. This social capital arises or disappears without anyone's willing it into or out of being and is thus even less recognized and taken account of in social action than its already intangible character would warrant.

There are important implications of this public goods aspect of social capital that play a part in the development of children and youth. Because the social structural conditions that overcome the problems of supplying these public goods—that is, strong families and strong communities—are much less often present now than in the past, and promise to be even less present in the future, we can expect that, ceteris paribus, we confront a declining quantity of human capital embodied in each successive generation. The obvious solution appears to be to attempt to find ways of overcoming the problem of supply of these public goods, that is, social capital employed for the benefit of children and youth. This very likely means the substitution of some kind of formal organization for the voluntary and spontaneous social organization that has in the past been the major source of social capital available to the young.

Conclusion

In this paper, I have attempted to introduce into social theory a concept, "social capital," paralleling the concepts of financial capital, physical capital, and human capital—but embodied in relations among persons. This is part of a theoretical strategy that involves use of the paradigm of rational action but without the assumption of atomistic elements stripped of social relationships. I have shown the use of this concept through demonstrating the effect of social capital in the family and in the community in aiding the formation of human capital. The single measure of human capital formation used for this was one that appears especially responsive to the supply of social capital, remaining in high school until graduation versus dropping out. Both social capital in the family and social capital outside it, in the adult community surrounding the school, showed evidence of considerable value in reducing the probability of dropping out of high school.

In explicating the concept of social capital, three forms were identified: obligations and expectations, which depend on trustworthiness of the social environment, information-flow capability of the social structure, and norms accompanied by sanctions. A property shared by most forms of social capital that differentiates it from other forms of capital is its public good aspect: the actor or actors who generate social capital ordinarily capture only a small part of its benefits, a fact that leads to underinvestment in social capital.

Notes

1 I thank Mark Granovetter, Susan Shapiro, and Christopher Winship for criticisms of an earlier draft, which aided greatly in revision. Requests for reprints should be sent to James S. Coleman, Department of Sociology, University of Chicago, Chicago, Illinois 60637.

2 For a discussion of the importance of the empirical generalization to economics, see Black, Coats, and Goodwin (1973).

3 I am especially grateful to Susan Shapiro for reminding me of Gluckman's distinction and pointing out the relevance of it to my analysis.

4 The complementarity of human capital and social capital in the family for a child's development suggests that the statistical analysis that examines the effects of these quantities should take a particular form. There should be an interaction term between human capital (parents' education) and social capital (some combination of measures such as two parents in the home, number of siblings, and parents' expectations for child's education). In the analysis reported, here, however, a simple additive model without interaction was used.

5 The analysis is carried out by use of a weighted logistic model with a random sample of 4,000 students from the public schools in the sample. The variables included in the model as measures of the family's financial, human, and social capital were socioeconomic status (a single variable constructed of parents' education, parents' income, father's occupational status, and household possessions), race, Hispanic ethnicity, number of siblings, number of changes in school due to family residential moves since fifth grade, whether mother worked before the child was in school, mother's expectation of child's educational attainment, frequency of discussions with parents about personal matters, and presence of both parents in the household. An analysis with more extensive statistical controls, including such things as grades in school, homework, and number of absences, is reported in Hoffer (1986, table 25) but the effects reported in Table 7.1 and subsequent text are essentially unchanged except for a reduced effect of mother's expectations. The results reported here and subsequently are taken from Hoffer (1986) and from Coleman and Hoffer (1987).

6 Data from this study have no direct measures of the degree of intergenerational closure among the parents of the school to support this statement. However, the one measure of intergenerational closure that does exist in the data, the number of residential moves requiring school change since grade 5, is consistent with the statement. The average number of moves for public school students is 0.57; for Catholic school students, 0.35; and for students in other private schools, 0.88.

7 It also true, though not presented here, that the lack of social capital in the family makes little difference in dropout rates in Catholic schools—or, in the terms I have used, social capital in the community compensates in part for its absence in the family. See Coleman and Hoffer (1987, ch. 5).

References

Baker, Wayne. 1983. "Floor Trading and Crowd Dynamics." Pp. 107–28 in *Social Dynamics of Financial Markets*, edited by Patricia Adler and Peter Adler. Greenwich, Conn.: JAI.

Banfield, Edward. 1967. *The Moral Basis of a Backward Society*. New York: Free Press.

Becker, Gary. 1964. *Human Capital*. New York: National Bureau of Economic Research.

Ben-Porath, Yoram. 1980. "The F-Connection: Families, Friends, and Firms and the Organization of Exchange." *Population and Development Review* 6:1–30.

Black, R. D. C., A. W. Coats, and C. D. W. Goodwin, eds. 1973. *The Marginal Revolution in Economics*. Durham, N.C.: Duke University Press.

Blau, Peter. 1964. *Exchange and Power in Social Life*. New York: Wiley.

Coleman, James S. 1986a. "Social Theory, Social Research, and a Theory of Action." *American Journal of Sociology* 91:1309–1335.

——. 1986b. *Individual Interests and Collective Action*. Cambridge: Cambridge University Press.

——. 1987. "Norms as Social Capital." Pp. 133–55 in *Economic Imperialism*, edited by Gerard Radnitzky and Peter Bernholz. New York: Paragon.

Coleman, J. S., and T. B. Hoffer. 1987. *Public and Private Schools: The Impact of Communities*. New York: Basic.

DeGraaf, Nan Dirk, and Hendrik Derk Flap. 1988. "With a Little Help from My Friends." *Social Forces,* vol. 67 (in press).

Festinger, Leon, Stanley Schachter, and Kurt Back. 1963. *Social Pressures in Informal Groups.* Stanford, Calif.: Stanford University Press.

Geertz, Clifford. 1962. "The Rotating Credit Association: A 'Middle Rung' in Development." *Economic Development and Cultural Change* 10:240–63.

Gluckman, Max. 1967. *The Judicial Process among the Barotse of Northern Rhodesia,* 2d ed. Manchester: Manchester University Press.

Gouldner, Alvin. 1960. "The Norm of Reciprocity: A Preliminary Statement." *American Sociological Review* 25:161–78.

Granovetter, Mark. 1985. "Economic Action, Social Structure, and Embeddedness." *American Journal of Sociology* 91:481–510.

Hoffer, T. B. 1986. *Educational Outcomes in Public and Private High Schools.* Ph.D. dissertation. University of Chicago, Department of Sociology.

Homans, George. 1974. *Social Behavior: Its Elementary Forms,* rev. ed. New York: Harcourt, Brace World.

Katz, E., and P. Lazarsfeld. 1955. *Personal influence.* New York: Free Press.

Lenin, V. I. (1902) 1973. *What Is To Be Done.* Peking: Foreign Language Press.

Lin, Nan. 1988. "Social Resources and Social Mobility: A Structural Theory of Status Attainment." In *Social Mobility and Social Structure,* edited by Ronald Breiger. Cambridge: Cambridge University Press.

Seymour, M. Trow, and J. Coleman. 1956. *Union Democracy.* New York: Free Press.

Merry, Sally, E. 1984. "Rethinking Gossip and Scandal." Pp. 271–302 in *Toward a General Theory of Social Control.* Vol. 1, *Fundamentals,* edited by Donald Black. New York: Academic.

Merton, Robert K. 1968. *Social Theory and Social Structure,* 2d ed. New York: Free Press.

——. n.d. "Study of World War Housing Projects." Unpublished manuscript. Columbia University, Department of Sociology.

Schultz, Theodore. 1961. "Investment in Human Capital." *American Economic Review* 51 (March): 1–17.

Ullmann-Margalit, Edna. 1977. *The Emergence of Norms.* Oxford: Clarendon.

Williamson, Oliver. 1975. *Markets and Hierarchies.* New York: Free Press.

——. 1981. "The Economics of Organization: The Transaction Cost Approach." *American Journal of Sociology* 87:548–77.

Wrong, Dennis. 1961. "The Oversocialized Conception of Man in Modern Sociology." *American Sociological Review* 26:183–93.

8

Class and Pedagogies

Visible and Invisible

BASIL BERNSTEIN

I shall examine some of the assumptions and the cultural context of a particular form of pre-school/infant school pedagogy. A form which has at least the following characteristics:

1 Where the control of the teacher over the child is implicit rather than explicit.
2 Where, ideally, the teacher arranges the *context* which the child is expected to re-arrange and explore.
3 Where within this arranged context, the child apparently has wide powers over what he selects, over how he structures, and over the time-scale of his activities.
4 Where the child apparently regulates his own movements and social relationships.
5 Where there is a reduced emphasis upon the transmission and acquisition of specific skills.[1]
6 Where the criteria for evaluating the pedagogy are multiple and diffuse and so not easily measured.

Invisible Pedagogy and Infant Education

One can characterize this pedagogy as an invisible pedagogy. In terms of the concepts of classification and frame, the pedagogy is realized through weak classification and weak frames. Visible pedagogies are realized through strong classification and strong frames. The basic difference between visible and invisible pedagogies is in the *manner* in which criteria are transmitted and in the degree of specificity of the criteria. The more implicit the manner of transmission and the more diffuse the criteria, the more invisible the pedagogy; the more specific the criteria, the more explicit the manner of their transmission, the more visible the pedagogy. These definitions will be extended later in the paper.

If the pedagogy is invisible, what aspects of the child have high visibility for the teacher? I suggest two aspects. The first arises out of an inference the teacher makes from the child's ongoing behaviour about the *developmental* stage of the child. This inference is then referred to a concept of *readiness*. The second aspect of the child refers to his external behaviour and is conceptualized by the teacher as busyness. The child should be busy doing things. These inner (readiness) and outer (busyness) aspects of the child can be transformed into one concept of 'ready to do'. The teacher infers from the 'doing' the state of 'readiness' of the child as it is revealed in his present activity and as this state adumbrates future 'doing'.

We can briefly note in passing a point which will be developed later. In the same way as the child's reading releases the child from the teacher and socializes him into the privatized, solitary learning of an explicit anonymous past (i.e. the textbook), so busy children (children doing) releases the child from the teacher but socializes him into an ongoing inter-actional present in which the past is invisible and

115

so implicit (i.e. the teacher's pedagogical theory) Thus a non-doing child in the invisible pedagogy is the equivalent of a non-reading child in the visible pedagogy. (However, a non-reading child may be at a greater disadvantage and experience greater difficulty than a 'non-doing' child.)

The concept basic to the invisible pedagogy is that of play. This is not the place to submit this concept to logical analysis, but a few points may be noted:

1   Play is the means by which the child exteriorizes himself to the teacher. Thus the more he plays and the greater the range of his activities, the more of him is made available to the teacher's screening. Thus, play is the fundamental concept with 'readiness' and 'doing' as subordinate concepts. Although not all forms of doing are considered as play (hitting another child, for example) most forms can be so characterized.

2   Play does not merely describe an activity, it also contains an evaluation of that activity. Thus, there is productive and less productive play, obsessional and free-ranging play, solitary and social play. Play is not only an activity, it entails a theory from which interpretation, evaluation and diagnosis are derived and which also indicates a progression: a theory which the child can never know in the way a child can know the criteria which are realized in visible pedagogy. Play implies a potentially all-embracing theory, for it covers nearly all if not all the child's doing and not doing. As a consequence, a very long chain of inference has to be set up to connect the theory with any one exemplar ('a doing' or a 'not doing'). The theory gives rise to a total—but invisible—surveillance of the child, because it relates his inner dispositions to all his external acts. The 'spontaneity' of the child is filtered through this surveillance and then implicitly shaped according to interpretation, evaluation and diagnosis.

3   Both the means and ends of play are multiple and change with time. Because of this, the stimuli must be, on the whole, highly abstract, available to be contextualized by the child, and so the unique doing of each child is facilitated. Indeed, play encourages each child to make his own mark. Sometimes, however, the stimulus may be very palpable when the child is invited to feel a leaf, or piece of velour, but what is *expected* is a *unique* response of the child to his own sensation. What is the code for reading the marks; a code the child can never know, but implicitly acquires. How does he do this?

4   The social basis of this theory of play is not an individualized act, but a personalized act; not strongly framed, but weakly framed encounters. Its social structure may be characterized as one of *overt* personalized organic solidarity, but covert mechanical solidarity. Visible pedagogies create social structures which may be characterized as *covert* individualized organic solidarity and *overt* mechanical solidarity.[2] (See later discussion.)

5   In essence, play is work and work is play. We can begin to see here the class origins of the theory. For the working class, work and play are very strongly classified and framed: for certain sub-groups of the middle class, work and play are weakly classified and weakly framed. For these sub-groups, no strict line may be drawn between work and play. Work carries what is often called 'intrinsic' satisfactions, and therefore is not confined to *one* context. However, from another point of view, work offers the opportunity of symbolic narcissism which combines inner pleasure and outer prestige. Work for certain sub-groups of the middle class is a personalized act in a privatized social structure. These points will be developed later.

Theories of Learning and Invisible Pedagogy

We are now in a position to analyse the principles underlying the selection of theories of learning which invisible pre-school/infant school pedagogies will adopt. Such pedagogies will adopt any theory of learning which has the following characteristics:

1   The theories in general will be seeking universals and thus are likely to be developmental and concerned with sequence. A particular context of learning is only of interest inasmuch as it throws light on a sequence. Such theories are likely to have a strong biological bias.

2   Learning is a tacit, invisible act, its progression is not facilitated by explicit public control.

3   The theories will tend to abstract the child's personal biography and local context from his cultural biography and institutional context.

4   In a sense, the theories see socializers as potentially, if not actually, dangerous, as they embody an adult-focused, therefore reified, concept of the socialized. Exemplary models are relatively unimportant and so the various theories in different ways point towards *implicit* rather than explicit hierarchical social relationships. Indeed, the imposing exemplar is transformed into a *facilitator*.

5   Thus the theories can be seen as interrupters of cultural reproduction and therefore have been considered by some as progressive or even revolutionary. Notions of child's time replace notions of adult's time, notions of child's space replace notions of adult's space; facilitation replaces imposition and accommodation replaces domination.

We now give a group of theories, which, despite many differences, fulfil at a most abstract level all or nearly all of the five conditions given previously:

Piaget	1	2	3	4	5
Freud	1	2	3	4	5
Chomsky	1	2	3	4	5
Ethological theories of critical learning	1	2	3		
Gestalt		2	3	4	5

What is of interest is that these theories form rather a strange, if not contradictory group. They are often selected to justify a specific element of the pedagogy. They form in a way the theology of the infant school. We can see how the crucial concept of play and the subordinate concepts of readiness and doing fit well with the above theories. We can also note how the invisibility of the pedagogy fits with the invisible tacit act of learning. We can also see that the pre-school/infant school movement from one point of view is a progressive, revolutionary, colonizing movement in its relationships to parents, and in its relationship to educational levels above itself. It is antagonistic for different reasons to middle-class and working-class families, for both create a deformation of the child. It is antagonistic to educational levels above itself, because of its fundamental opposition to their concepts of learning and social relationships. We can note here that as a result the child is abstracted from his family and his future educational contexts.

Of central importance is that this pedagogy brings together two groups of educationists who are at the extremes of the educational hierarchy, infant school teachers and university teachers and researchers. The consequence has been to professionalize and raise the status of the pre-school/infant school teacher; a status not based upon a specific competence, a status based upon a weak educational identity (no subject). The status of the teachers from this point of view is based upon a diffuse, tacit, symbolic control which is legitimized by a closed explicit ideology, the essence of weak classification and weak frames.

Class and the Invisible Pedagogy

From our previous discussion, we can abstract the following:

1   The invisible pedagogy is an interrupter system, both in relation to the family and in its relation to other levels of the educational hierarchy.
2   It transforms the privatized social structures and cultural contexts of visible pedagogies into a personalized social structure and personalized cultural contexts.
3   Implicit nurture reveals unique nature.

The question is what is it interrupting? The invisible pedagogy was first institutionalized in the private sector for a fraction of the middle class—the new middle class.[3] If the ideologies of the old middle class were institutionalized in the public schools and through them into the grammar schools, so the ideology of the new middle class was first institutionalized in private pre-schools then private/public secondary schools, and finally into the state system, at the level of the infant school. Thus the conflict between visible and invisible pedagogies, from this point of view, between strong and weak classification and frames, is an ideological conflict within the middle class. The ideologies of education are still the ideologies of class. The old middle class were domesticated through the strong classification and frames of the family and public schools, which attempted, often very successfully, cultural reproduction. But what social type was reproduced?

We know that every industrialized society produces organic solidarity. Now Durkheim, it seems to me, was concerned with only *one* form of such solidarity—the form which created individualism. Durkheim was interested in the vicissitudes of the types as their classification and framing were no longer, or only weakly, morally integrated, or when the individual's relation to the classification.and frames underwent a change. His analysis is based upon the old middle class. He did not foresee, although his conceptual procedures make this possible, a form of organic solidarity based upon weak classification and weak frames; that is, a form of solidarity developed by the new middle class. Durkheim's organic solidarity refers to *individuals* in privatized class relationships; the second form of organic solidarity refers to persons in privatized class relationships.[4] The second form of organic solidarity celebrates the apparent release, not of the individual, but of the persons and *new* forms of social control.[5] Thus, we can distinguish *individualized* and *personalized* forms of organic solidarity *within* the middle class, each with their own distinctive and conflicting ideologies and each with their own distinctive and conflicting forms of socialization and symbolic reality. These two forms arise out of developments of the division of labour within class societies. Durkheim's individualized organic solidarity developed out of the increasing complexity of the economic division of labour; personalized organic solidarity, it is suggested, develops out of increases in the complexity of the division of labour of cultural or symbolic control which the new middle class have appropriated. The new middle class is an interrupter system, clearly not of class relationships, but of the form of their reproduction. In Bourdieu's terms, there has been a change in habitus, but not in function. This change in habitus has had far-reaching effects on the selective institutionalization of symbolic codes and codings in the areas of sex and aesthetics, and upon preparing and repairing agencies, such as the family, school, and mental hospitals. In all these areas there has been a shift towards weak classification and frames.[6]

This conflict within the middle class is realized sharply in different patterns of the socialization of the young. In the old middle class, socialization is into strong classification and strong framing, where the boundaries convey, tacitly, critical condensed messages. In the new middle class, socialization is into weak classification and weak frames, which promote, through the explicitness of the communication code, far greater ambiguity, and drives this class to make visible the ideology of its socialization; crucial to this ideology is the concept of the *person* not of the *individual*. Whereas the concept of the *individual* leads to specific, unambiguous role identities and relatively inflexible role performances, the *concept* of the person leads to ambiguous personal identity and flexible role performances. Both the old and the new middle class draw upon biological theories, but of very different types. The old middle class held theories which generated biologically fixed types, where variety of the type constituted a threat to cultural reproduction. The new middle class also hold theories which emphasize a fixed biological type, but they also hold that the type is capable of great variety. This, in essence, is a theory which points towards social mobility—towards a meritocracy. For the old middle class, variety must be severely reduced in order to ensure cultural reproduction; for the new middle class, the variety must be encouraged in order to ensure interruption. Reproduction and interruption are created by variations in the strength of classifications and frames.[7] As these weaken, so the socialization encourages more of the socialized to become visible, his uniqueness to be made manifest. Such socialization is deeply penetrating, more total as the surveillance becomes more invisible. This is the basis of control which creates personalized organic solidarity. Thus the forms of socialization within these two conflicting factions of the middle class are the origins of the visible and invisible pedagogies of the school. We have a homologue between the interruption of the new middle class of the reproduction of the old and the interruption of the new educational pedagogy of the reproduction of the old; between the conflict within the middle class and the conflict between the two pedagogies: yet it is the conflict between the interruption of *forms* of transmission of class relationships. This point we will now develop. The new middle class, like the proponents of the invisible pedagogy, are caught in a contradiction; for their theories are at variance with their objective class relationship. A deep-rooted ambivalence is the ambience of this group. On the one hand, they stand for variety against inflexibility, expression against repression, the inter-personal against the inter-positional; on the other hand, there is the grim obduracy of the division of labour and of the narrow pathways to its positions of power and prestige. Under individualized organic solidarity, property has an essentially physical nature; however, with the development of personalized organic solidarity, although property in the physical sense remains crucial, it has been partly psychologized and appears in the form of ownership of valued skills made available in educational institutions. Thus, if the new middle class is to repeat its position in the class structure, then appropriate secondary socialization into privileged education becomes crucial. But as the relation between education and occupation becomes more direct and closer in time, then the classifications and frames increase in strength. Thus the new middle class take up some ambivalent enthusiasm for the invisible pedagogy for the early socialization of the child, but settle for the *visible* pedagogy of the secondary school. And they will continue to do this until the university moves to a weaker classification and a weaker framing of its principles of transmission and selection. On the other hand, they are among the leaders of the movement to institutionalize the invisible pedagogy in state preschools and often for its colonization of the primary school and further extension into the secondary school. And this can be done with confidence for the secondary school is likely to provide both visible and invisible pedagogies. The former for the middle class and the latter for the working class.

The Class Assumptions of the Invisible Pedagogy

We can now begin to see that because the invisible pedagogy had its origins within a fraction of the middle class, it pre-supposes a relatively long educational life. Inherent within this pedagogy is a concept of time—middle-class time.[8] Of equal significance because it originates within the middle class, it pre-supposes a communication code (an elaborated code) which orientates the child early towards the significance of relatively context independent meanings, whether these are in the form of speech or of writing. Thus the development of specific educational competencies can either be delayed because of the longer educational life, or the child will achieve them early because of the focus of the communication code. But this does not complete the class assumptions of the invisible pedagogy. We have so far suggested two: a long educational life, and an elaborated code. There is a third.

The shift from individualized to personalized organic solidarity changes the structure of family relationships, and in particular the role of the woman in the socializing of the child. Historically, under individualized organic solidarity, the mother was neither important as a transmitter of physical or of symbolic property. She was almost totally abstracted from the means of reproduction of either physical or symbolic property. The control of the children was delegated to others (nanny, governess, tutor). She was essentially a domestic administrator, and it follows that she could be a model only for her daughter. She was often capable of cultural reproduction, for often she possessed a sensitive awareness of the literature of the period. This concept of the abstracted maternal function perhaps re-appears in the concept of the pre-school assistant as a baby minder, and the governess as the teacher of elementary competencies. Thus individualized organic solidarity might generate two models for the pre-school or infant school:

1   The abstracted mother → nanny—baby minder.
2   The governess → teacher of elementary competencies.

Under personalized organic solidarity, the *role of the mother* in the rearing of her children undergoes a qualitative change. As we have noted earlier, with such solidarity, property has been partly psychologized and it arises out of forms of inter-action—forms of communication—which are initiated and developed and focused by the mother very early in the child's life. Thus the mother under personalized organic solidarity is transformed into a powerful and crucial agent of cultural reproduction who provides access to symbolic forms and who shapes the disposition of her children so that they are better able to exploit the possibilities of education. Thus as we move from individualized to personalized organic solidarity so the woman is transformed from an agent of physical reproduction to an agent of cultural reproduction. There is, however, a contradiction within her structural relationships. Unlike the mother in a situation of individualized solidarity, she is unable to get away from her children. For the weak classification and weak frames of her child-rearing firmly anchor her to her children; for her inter-action and surveillance is totally demanding and, at the same time, her own socialization into both a personal and occupational identity points her away from the family. These tensions can be partly resolved by placing the child early in a pre-school which faithfully reproduces the ambience for her own child-rearing. Thus the middle-class mother in a context of personalized organic solidarity provides the model for the pre-school infant school teacher. The pre-school, however, amplifies the messages, and wishes to extend them in time. Here we can see a second contradiction, for such an amplification brings the middle-class mother and the school into conflict. The public examination system is based upon a visible pedagogy as it is realized through strong classification and strong frames. It is this pedagogy which transmits symbolic property. If access to visible pedagogy is delayed too long, then examination success may be considered to be in danger.

We have now made explicit three assumptions underlying the invisible pedagogy. There is a fourth. The size of the class of pupils is likely to be small and the teacher–pupil ratio very favourable.

1   It pre-supposes a middle-class conception of educational time and space.
2   It pre-supposes an elaborated code of communication.
3   It pre-supposes a middle-class mother who is an agent of cultural reproduction.
4   It pre-supposes a small class of pupils.

Thus the social significance of the invisible pedagogy will be crucially different according to the social class of the child.

We started this section by abstracting the following points from our initial discussion of the invisible pedagogy:

1   The invisible pedagogy is an interrupter system both in relation to the home and in relation to other levels of the educational hierarchy.

2   It transforms the privatized social structure and cultural contents of visible pedagogies into a personalized social structure and personalized cultural contexts.

3   It believes that implicit nurture reveals unique nature.

We have argued that this pedagogy is one of the realizations of the conflict between the old and the new middle class, which in turn has its social basis in the two different forms of organic solidarity, individualized and personalized; that these two forms of solidarity arise out of differences in the relation to the division of labour within the middle class; that the movement from individualized to personalized interrupts the *form* of the reproduction of class relationships; that such an interruption gives rise to different forms of *primary* socialization within the middle class; that the form of primary socialization within the middle class is the model for primary socialization into the school; that there are contradictions within personalized organic solidarity which create deeply felt ambiguities; as a consequence, the outcomes of the form of the socialization are less certain. The contemporary new middle class are unique, for in the socialization of their young is a sharp and penetrating contradiction between a subjective personal identity and an objective privatized identity; between the release of the person and the hierarchy of class.

Whereas it is possible for school and university to change the basis of its solidarity from individualistic to personalized, i.e. to relax its classification and frames, it is more difficult for those agencies to change their privatizing function, i.e. the creation of knowledge as private property. It by no means follows that a shift to personalized organic solidarity will change the privatizing function. Indeed, even the shift in the form of solidarity is more likely to occur in that part of the educational system which either creates no private property, as in the case of the education of the lower working class, or in the education of the very young. We are then left with the conclusion that the major effects of this change in solidarity will be in the areas of condensed communication (sex, art, style) and in the form of social control (from explicit to implicit).

Transition to School

(a) Class Culture, Power and Conflict

The shift from visible to invisible pedagogies at the pre- and primary levels of education changes the relationships between the family and the school. We have already noted the ambiguous attitude of the middle class to such a shift. In the case of the working class, the change is more radical. The weak classification and the weak framing of the invisible pedagogy potentially makes possible the inclusion of the culture of the fanlily and the cornmunity. Thus the experience of the child and his everyday world could be psychologically active in the classroom, and if this were to be the case, then the school would legitimize rather than reject the class-culture of the family. Inasmuch as the pacing of the knowledge to be transmitted is relaxed and the emphasis upon early attainment of specific competencies is reduced, the progression is less marked by middle-class assumptions. In the case of visible pedagogies early reading and, especially, writing are essential. Once the child can read and write, such acts free the teacher, but, of more importance, once the child can read he can be given a book, and once he is given a book he is well on the way to managing the role of the solitary privatized educational relationship. The book is the preparation for receiving the past realized in the textbook. And the textbook in turn tacitly transmits the ideology of the collection code: for it epitomizes strong classification and strong frames. The textbook orders knowledge according to an explicit progression, it provides explicit criteria, it removes uncertainties and announces hierarchy. It gives the child an immediate index of where he stands in relation to others in the progression. It is therefore a silent medium for creating competitive relationships. Thus socialization into the textbook is a critical step towards socialization into the collection code. The stronger the collection code, that is the stronger classification and frames, the greater the emphasis on early reading and writing. The middle-class child is prepared for this emphasis, but this is not so in the case of the working-class child. The weakening of classification and frames reduces the significance of the textbook and transforms the impersonal past into a personalized present. It would appear that the invisible pedagogy carries a beneficial potential for working-class children. However, because the form we are discussing has its origins in a fraction of the middle class, this potential may not be actualized.

This point we will now develop. From the point of view of working-class parents, the visible pedagogy of the collection code at the primary level is immediately understandable. The basic competencies which it is transmitting of reading, writing, and counting, in an ordered explicit sequence, make sense. The failures of the children are the children's failures not the school's for the school is apparently carrying out impersonally its function. The school's form of social control does not interfere with the social control of the family. The infant school teacher will not necessarily have high status, as the competencies she is transmitting are, in principle, possible also for the mother. In this sense, there is symbolic continuity (or rather extension) between the working-class home and the school. However, in the case of the invisible pedagogy, there is possibly a sharp discontinuity. The competencies and their progression disappear, the form of social control may well be at variance with the home. The theory of the invisible pedagogy may not be known by the mother or be imperfectly understood. The lack of stress on competencies may render the child a less effective (useful) member of the family, e.g. running errands, etc. However, there is a more fundamental source of tension. The invisible pedagogy contains a different theory of transmission and a new technology, which views the mother's own informal teaching, where it occurs, or the mother's pedagogical values, irrelevant if not downright harmful. There are new reading schemes, new mathematics replace arithmetic, an expressive aesthetic style replaces one which aims at facsimile. If the mother is to be helpful, she must be re-socialized or kept out of the way. If it is the former or the latter, then the power relationships have changed between home and school: for the teacher has the power and the mother is as much a pupil as the pupil. This in turn may disturb the authority relationships within the home: this disturbance is further facilitated by the use of implicit forms of social control of the school. Even if the pedagogy draws its contents from the class culture, basic forms of discontinuity still exist. If the mother wishes to understand the theory of the invisible pedagogy, then she may well find herself at the mercy of complex theories of child development. Indeed, whichever way the working-class mother turns, the teacher has the power: although the mother may well be deeply suspicious of the whole ambience.[9]

Where, as in the case of the visible pedagogy there are, for the working class, relative to the middle class, implicit forms of discontinuity and explicit forms of inequality in the shape of the holding power of the school over its teachers, the size of class and possibly streaming: in the case of the invisible pedagogy, there is also an *explicit* symbolic discontinuity which may well go with inequalities in provision and quality of teaching staff. The teacher also has difficulties, because the invisible pedagogy presupposes a particular form of maternal primary socialization *and* a small class of pupils *and* a particular architecture. Where these are absent, the teacher may well find great difficulty. Ideally, the invisible pedagogy frees the teacher so that time is available for ameliorating the difficulties of any one child, but if the class is large, the socialization, from the point of view of the school, inadequate, the architecture inappropriate, then such individual assistance becomes infrequent and problematic. Here again we can see that such a pedagogy, if it is to be successfully implemented in its own terms, necessarily requires minimally the same physical conditions of the middle-class school. It is an *expensive* pedagogy because it is derived from an expensive class: the middle class.

From the point of view of the middle class, there is at least an intellectual understanding of the invisible pedagogy, if not always an acceptance of its values and practice. Further, if the middle-class child is not obtaining the basic competencies at the rate the mother expects, an educational support system can be organized through private coaching or through the mother's own efforts. The power relationships between the middle-class mother and the teacher are less tipped in favour of the teacher. Finally, the middle-class mother always has the choice of the private school or of moving near a state school of her choice. However, because of the middle-class mother's concept of the function of secondary education, she is likely to be anxious about the acquisition of basic competencies, and this will bring her into conflict with the school at some point.

Finally, inasmuch as age and sex statuses within the family are strongly classified and ritualized, it is likely that the acquisition, progression and evaluation of competencies obtained within the school will become part of the markers of age and sex status within the family. For example, there is a radical change in the status and concept of the child when he is transformed into a pupil. Now, to the extent that the infant/primary school fails to utilize age and sex as allocating categories *either* for the acquisition and progression of competencies *or* for the allocation of pupils to groups and spaces, the school is weakening the function of these categories in the family and community. Visible pedagogies not only reinforce age and sex classification, they also provide markers for progression within them. Invisible pedagogies are likely to weaken such classifications and inasmuch as they do this they transform the concept of the child and the concepts of age and sex status.

(b) Class, Pedagogy and Evaluation

Interesting questions arise over the system of evaluating the pupils. Where the pedagogy is visible, an 'objective' grid exists for the evaluation of the pupils in the form of (a) clear criteria and (b) a delicate measurement procedure. The child receives a grade or its equivalent for any valued performance. Further, where the pedagogy is visible, it is likely to be standardized and so schools are directly comparable as to their successes and failures. The profile of the pupil may be obtained by looking across his grades. The pupil knows where he is, the teacher knows where he is, and so do the parents. The parents have a yardstick for comparing schools. When children change schools they can be slotted into place according to their academic profile. Further, it is difficult for the parent to argue about the profile for it is 'objective'. Clearly, there are subjective elements in the grading of the children, but these are masked by the apparent objectivity of the grid. In the case of invisible pedagogies, no such grid exists. The evaluation procedures are multiple, diffuse and not easily subject to apparently precise measurement. This makes comparison between pupils complex, and also comparisons between schools.[10] First, the invisible pedagogy does not give rise to progression of a *group*, but is based upon progression of a person. Second, there is likely to be considerable variation between infant/pre-school groups *within* the general form of the pedagogy. There is less difficulty in slotting a child into a new school because there is no explicit slot for him. Thus the mother is less able to diagnose the child's progress and as a consequence she cannot *provide specific educational support*.[11] She would be forced into providing a general educational milieu in the home and this she might only be able to do if she had fully internalized the invisible pedagogy's theoretical basis. As we have previously argued, this is less likely to be the case where the parents are working-class. Thus these parents are cut off from the evaluation of their child's progress. More, they are forced to accept what the teacher counts as progress.

Because an apparently objective grid exists for the evaluation of the visible pedagogies, this grid acts selectively on those dispositions of the child which become candidates for labelling by the teacher. Clearly motivation and interest are probably relevant to any pedagogy, but their significance will vary with the pedagogy, and certainly their consequences. In the case of visible pedagogies, the behaviour of the child is focused on the teacher so that, in this case, attentiveness to, co-operation with, the teacher becomes relevant: persistence and carefulness are also valued by the teacher. Further, it is possible for there to be a conflict between the child's academic profile *and* the teacher's evaluation of his attitudes and motivation. These objective and subjective criteria may have different consequences for different class groups of pupils. Either criteria, irrespective of their validity, are likely to be *understood* by working-class parents. In the case of invisible pedagogy, as more of the child is made available, and, because of the theory which guides interpretation, diagnosis and evaluation, a different class of acts and dispositions of the child become relevant. In the case of visible pedagogies we have argued that the attention of the child is focused on the teacher; however, in the case of invisible pedagogies the attention of the teacher is focused on the *whole* child: in its total doing and 'not doing'. This can lead to discrepancies between the teacher's and the parents' view of the child unless the parents share the teacher's theory. Indeed, it is possible that the dispositions and acts which are subject to evaluation by the teacher may be considered by some parents as irrelevant or intrusive or inaccurate or all three. Where this occurs the child's behaviour is being shaped by conflicting criteria. From the point of view of the teacher, the child becomes an *innovating* message to the home. The invisible pedagogy is not only an interrupter system in the context of educational practice, but it also transforms the child, under certain conditions, into an innovating message to the family.

This pedagogy is likely to lead to a change in the school's procedures of evaluation, both objective and subjective. Where the pedagogy is visible, there is a profile which consists of the grading of specific competencies and a profile which consists of the grading of the child's motivation and work attitudes. It is likely that the latter will consist of rather short, somewhat stereotyped unexplicated judgments. In the case of invisible pedagogies, these highly condensed, unexplicated but *public* judgments are likely to be replaced by something resembling a dossier which will range across a wide variety of the child's internal processes and states *and* his external acts. Further, the connection between inner and outer is likely to be made *explicit*. In other words, there is likely to be an explicit elaborated account of the relationships between the child's internal states and his acts. It is now possible that the school will have a problem of secrecy. How much is to go into the dossier, where is it to be kept, how much of and in what way are its contents to be made available to parents or to others in the school and outside of it? Thus invisible pedagogies may also generate *covert* and *overt* forms and contents of evaluation. Such a system of evaluation increases the power of the teacher to the extent that its underlying theory is not shared by parents *and* even when it is shared.

Finally, the major analysis in this section has been of idealized pedagogies. If, however, the argument is correct, that there may be a disjunction in the forms of socialization between primary and secondary stages, *or* between secondary and tertiary stages, then behind weak classification and weak frames may well be strong classification [C] and strong frames [Fs]. Thus we can have a situation where strong Cs and Fs follow weak Cs and Fs, *or* where weak Cs and Fs follow strong Cs and Fs, as, possibly, in the case of the training of infant school teachers in England. It is important not only to understand continuity in the strength of classification and frames, but also *disjunction* and *when* the disjunction occurs. It is more than likely that if we examine empirically invisible pedagogies we shall find to different degrees a stress on the transmission of *specific* isolated competencies. Thus the 'hidden curriculum' of invisible pedagogies may well be, embryonically, strong classification, albeit with relatively weak frames. It becomes a matter of some importance to find out which children or groups of children are particularly responsive to this 'hidden curriculum'. For some children may come to see or be led to see that there are two transmissions, one overt, the other covert, which stand in a figure–ground relation to each other. We need to know for which teachers, and for which children, what is the figure and what is the ground. Specifically, will middle-class children respond to the latent visible pedagogy, or are they more likely to be selected as receivers? Will lower working-class children respond more to the invisible pedagogy or receive a weaker form of the transmission of visible pedagogy? The 'hidden curriculum' of invisible pedagogies may well be a visible pedagogy. However, the outcomes of the imbedding of one pedagogy in the other are likely to be different than they are in the case of the transmission of any *one* pedagogy. From a more theoretical standpoint, the crucial component of visible pedagogy is the strength of its *classification,* for in the last analysis it is this which creates what counts as valued property, and also, in so doing, regulates mental structures. Frame strength regulates the modality of the socialization into the classification. In the microcosm of the nursery or infant class, we can see embryonically the new forms of transmission of class relationships.

Let us take a concrete example to illustrate the above speculation. An infant school teacher in England may experience the following conjunctions or disjunctions in her socialization:

1   Between socialization in the family and between primary and secondary school.
2   Between secondary school and teacher training. The higher the qualifications required by the college of education, the more likely that the socialization in the later years of the secondary school will be through strong classification and frames. On the other hand, the socialization into the college of education may well be into classification and frames of varying strengths.

Transition between Stages of Education

We have examined aspects of the transition to school; there is also the question of transition between stages of education, from pre-school to primary, from primary to secondary. These transitions between stages are marked by three inter-related features:

1   An increase in the strength of classification and frames (initiation into the collective code).
2   An increase in the range of different teachers; that is, the pupil is made aware of the insulations within the division of labour. He also learns that the principle of authority transcends the individuals who hold it, for, as teachers/subjects change, his role remains the same.
3   The weak classification and frames of the invisible pedagogy emphasize the importance of *ways* of knowing, of constructing problems, whereas the strong classification and frames of visible pedagogies emphasize states of knowledge and received problems.

Thus there is a crucial change in what counts as having knowledge, in what counts as a legitimate realization of that knowledge *and* in the social context.

Thus the shift from invisible to visible pedagogies in one phrase is a change in code; a change in the principles of relation and evaluation whether these are principles of knowledge, of social relationships, of practices, of property, of identity.

It is likely that this change of code will be more effectively made (despite the difficulties) by the new middle-class children, as their own socialization within the family contains both codes—the code which creates the manifestation of the person and the code which creates private property. Further, as we have argued elsewhere, it is more likely that the working-class children will experience continuity in code between stages of education. The class bias of the collection code (which creates a visible pedagogy) may make such a transmission difficult for them to receive and exploit. As a consequence, the continuation of the invisible pedagogy in the form of an integrated code is likely for working-class children, and its later institutionalization for the same children at the secondary level.

We can now begin to see that the conditions for continuity of educational code for *all* children, irrespective of class, is the type of code transmitted by the university. Simply expanding the university, increasing differentiation within the tertiary level, equalizing opportunity of access and outcome, will not fundamentally change the situation at levels below. We will only have expanded the size of the cohort at the tertiary level. From another point of view, although we may have changed the organizational structure we have not changed the code controlling transmission; the process of reproduction will not be fundamentally affected. To change the code controlling transmission involves changing the culture and its basis in privatized class relationships. Thus if we accept, for the sake of argument, the greater educational value of invisible pedagogies, of weak classification and frames, the condition for their effective and total institutionalization at the secondary level is a fundamental change of code at the tertiary level. If this does not occur then codes and class will remain firmly linked in schools.

Finally, we can raise a basic question. The movement to invisible pedagogies realized through integrated codes may be seen as a superficial solution to a more obdurate problem. Integrated codes are integrated at the level of ideas, they do *not* involve integration at the level of institutions, i.e. between school and work. Yet the crucial integration is precisely between the principles of education and the principles of work. There can be no such integration in Western societies (to mention only one group) because the work epitomizes class relationships. Work can only be brought into the school in terms of the function of the school as a selective mechanism or in terms of social/psychological adustment to work. Indeed, the abstracting of education from work, the hallmark of the liberal tradition, or the linkage of education to leisure, masks the brutal fact that work and education cannot be integrated at the level of social principles in class societies. They can either be separated or they can *fit* with each other. Durkheim wrote that changes in pedagogy were indicators of a moral crisis; they can also disguise it and change its form. However, inasmuch as the move to weak classification and frames has the potential of reducing insulations in mental structures and social structures, has the potential of making explicit the implicit and so creating greater ambiguity but less disguise, such a code has the potential of making visible fundamental social contradictions.

Acknowledgments

This paper was written on the suggestion of Henri Nathan for a meeting on the effects of scholarization, itself a part of the International Learning Sciences Programme, CERI, OECD. I am grateful to Henri Nathan for his insistence on the need to understand the artefacts of learning.

The basis of this paper was written whilst I was a visitor to the École Pratique des Hautes Études (Centre de Sociologie Européenne under the direction of Pierre Bourdieu). I am very grateful to Peter Corbishley, graduate student in the Department of the Sociology of Education for his help in the explication of the concept of an 'interrupter system'. The definition used in this paper owes much to his clarification. Finally I would like to thank Gerald Elliot, Professor of Physics, Open University, who, whilst in no way ultimately responsible, assisted in the formal expression of 'object code'.

Notes

1   This raises a number of questions. We cannot consider skills abstracted from the context of their transmission, from their relationships to each other and their function in creating, maintaining, modifying or changing a culture. Skills and their relationship to each other are culturally specific competencies. The manner of their transmission and acquisition socializes the child into their contextual usages. Thus, the unit of analysis cannot simply be an abstracted specific competence like reading, writing, counting, but the *structure* of social relationships which produces these specialized competencies. The formulation 'where there is a reduced emphasis upon transmission and acquisition of specific skills' could be misleading, as it suggests that in the context under discussion there are few specialized repertoires of the culture. It may be better to interpret the formulation as indicating an emphasis upon the inter-relationships between skills which are relatively weakly classified and weakly framed. In this way any skill or sets of skills are referred to the *general features oj the socialization*.
2   This can be seen very clearly if we look at a school class.
3   We regard the new middle class as being represented by those who are the *new* agents of symbolic control, e.g. those who are filling the ever-expanding major and minor professional class, concerned with the servicing of persons. We are not saying that all occupants are active members of the new middle class, but that there is a structural change in the culture which is shaping their transmissions. It is a matter of empirical research to identify specifically which groups, concerned with what symbolic controls, who are active representatives. In earlier papers I suggested that there were two forms of an elaborated code, object/person and that these were evoked by different class-based forms of family socialization, positional and personal. It is now possible, at least theoretically, to show that such families vary as to the strength of their classification and frames and that such variation itself arises out of different forms of the transmission of class relationships and represents an ideological conflict *within* the middle class.
4   A shift from the production of differentiated types of individuals to a type of person.
5   It is a matter of some interest to consider changes in emphasis of research methodologies over recent decades. There has been a shift from the standardized closed questionnaire or experimental context to more unstructured contexts and relationships. It is argued that the former methodology renders irrelevant the subjective meanings of those who are the

object of study. In so doing, the researched offer their experience through the media of the researchers' imposed strong classification and strong frames. Further, it is argued that such a method of studying people is derived from a method for the study of objects, and therefore it is an outrage to the subjectivity of man for him to be transformed into an object. These arguments go on to link positivist methods with the political control of man through the use of the technology of social science. The new methodology employs apparently weak classification and weak frames, but it uses techniques (participant observation, tape-recordings, video tapes, etc.) which enable more of the researched to be visible, and its techniques allow a range of others to witness the spontaneous behaviour of the observed. Even if these public records of natural behaviour are treated as a means of dialogue between the recorded and the recorder, this dialogue is, itself, subject to the disjunction between intellectual perspectives which will shape the communication. The self-editing of the researcher's communication is different from that of the researched, and this is the *invisible* control. On the other hand, paradoxically, in the case of a closed questionnaire the privacy of the subject is safeguarded, for all that can be made public is a pencil mark which is transformed into an impersonal score. Further, the methods of this transformation must be made public so that its assumptions may be criticized. In the case of the new methodology, the principles used to restrict the vast amount of information and the number of channels are often implicit. One might say that we could distinguish research methodologies in terms of whether they created invisible or visible pedagogies. Thus the former give rise to a total surveillance of the person who, relative to the latter, makes public more of his inside (e.g. his subjectivity), which is evaluated through the use of diffuse, implicit criteria. We are suggesting that the structural origins of changes in the classification and framing of forms of socialization may perhaps also influence the selection of research methodologies. The morality of the research relationship transcends the dilemmas of a particular researcher. Research methodologies in social science are themselves elements of culture.

6   It is interesting to see, for example, where the invisible pedagogy first entered the secondary-school curriculum. In England we would suggest that it first penetrated the *non-verbal* area of *unselective* secondary schools; the area which is considered to be the least relevant (in the sense of not producing symbolic property) and the most strongly classified: the area of the art room. Indeed, it might be said that, until very recently, the greatest symbolic continuity of pedagogies between primary and secondary stages lay in the non-verbal areas of the curriculum. The art room is often viewed by the rest of the staff as an area of relaxation or even therapy, rather than a space of crucial production. Because of its strong classification and irrelevance (except at school 'show-off' periods) this space is potentially open to change. Art teachers are trained in institutions (at least in recent times) which are very sensitive to innovation, and therefore new styles are likely to be rapidly institutionalized in schools, given the strong classification of art in the secondary-school curriculum, and also the belief that the less able child can at least do something with his hands even if he finds difficulty with a pen. We might also anticipate that with the interest in such musical forms as pop on the one hand and Cage and Stockhausen on the other, music departments might move towards the invisible pedagogy. To complete the direction in the non-verbal area, it is possible that the transformation of physical training into physical education might also extend to movement. If this development took place, then the non-verbal areas would be realized through the invisible pedagogy. We might then expect a drive to integrate the three areas of sight, sound and movement; *three* modalities would then be linked through a common code.

7   We can clarify the issues raised in this paper in the following way. Any socializing context must consist of a transmitter and an acquirer These two form a matrix in the sense that the communication is regulated by a structural principle. We have suggested that the underlying principle of a socializing matrix is realized in classification and frames. The relationship between the two and the strengths show us the structure of the control and the form of communication. We can, of course, analyse this matrix in a number of ways: (1) we can focus upon the transmitter; (2) we can focus upon the acquirer; (3) we can focus upon the principles underlying the matrix; (4) we can focus upon a given matrix and ignore its relationship to other matrices; (5) we can consider the relationships between critical matrices, e.g. family, peer group, school, work.

We can go on to ask questions about the function of a matrix and questions about the change in the form of its realization, i.e. changes in the strength of its classification and frames. We believe that the unit of analysis must always be the matrix and the matrix will always include the theories and methods of its analysis (see note 5 on research methodology). Now any one matrix can be regarded as a reproducer, an interrupter, or a change matrix. A reproduction matrix will attempt to create strong classification and strong frames. An interrupter matrix changes the *form* of transmission, but not the critical relationship *between* matrices. A change matrix leads to a fundamental change in the structural relationship *between* matrices. This will require a major change in the institutional structure. For example, we have argued that within the middle class there is a conflict which has generated two distinct socializing matrices, one a reproducer, the other an interrupter. And these matrices are at work within education for similar groups of children up to possibly the primary stage, and different groups of pupils at the secondary stage. However, inasmuch as the structural relationship between school and work is unchanged (i.e. there has been no change in the basic principles of their relationship), then we cannot by this argument see current differences in educational pedagogy as representing a change matrix. In other words, the form of the reproduction of class relationships in education has been *interrupted* but not changed. We might speculate that ideological conflict within the middle class takes the form of a conflict between the symbolic outcomes of reproduction and interruption matrices. If one takes the argument one stage further, we have to consider the reproduction of the *change* in the form of class relationships. In this case, the reproduction of an interrupter matrix is through weak classification and weak frames. However, it is possible that such a form of reproduction may at some point evoke its own interrupter, i.e. an increase in either classification or frame strength, or both.

8   It pre-supposes a middle-class concept of space. Invisible pedagogy cannot be realized in a small space per person.

9   This does *not* mean *all* teachers wish to have the power or use it.

10   Paradoxically, this situation carries a potential for increasing competitiveness.

11   She can offer, of course, elements of a visible pedagogy.

References

Bernstein, B. (1967), 'Open schools, open society?' *New Society*, 14 September. Reprinted as Chapter 3 of the present volume.

Bernstein, B. (1971), *Class, codes and control*, Vol. 1, Part III, Routledge & Kegan Paul.

Bernstein, B., Elvin, L. and Peters, R. (1966), 'Ritual in education'. *Philosophical Transactions of the Royal Society of London*, Series B, 251, No. 772.

Blyth, W. A. L. (1965), *English Primary Education*, Vols. 1 and 2, Routledge & Kegan Paul.

Boltansky, L. (1969), *Prime Éducation et morale de classe*. Paris and The Hague: Mouton.

Bourdieu, P. and Passeron, J. C. (1970), *La Reproduction: Éléments pour une théorie du système d'enseignement*. Paris: Les Éditions de Minuit.

Brandis, W. and Bernstein, B. (1973), *Selection and Control: A Study of Teachers' Ratings of Infant School Children*, Appendix, Routledge & Kegan Paul.

ChamboredoN, J.-C. and Prevot, J. Y. (1973), 'Le Métier d'enfant', *Définition sociale de la prime enfance et fonctions différentielles de l'école maternelle*. Centre de Sociologie Européenne (basic paper).

Cremin, L. (1961), *The Transformation of the School*, New York: Knopf.

Douglas, M. (1973), *Natural Symbols*, revised edition, Allen Lane.

Durkheim, E. (1933), *The Division of Labour in Society* (translated by G. Simpson), New York: Macmillan.

Durkheim, E. (1938), *L'Évolution pédagogique en France*, Paris: Alcan.

Durkheim, E. (1956), *Education and sociology* (translated by D. F. Pocock), Cohen &West, (chapters 2 and 3).

Gardner, B. (1973), *The Public Schools*, Hamish Hamilton.

Goldthorpe, J. and Lockwood, D. (1962), 'Affluence and the Class Structure', *Sociological Review*, vol. XI.

Green, A. G. (1972), 'Theory and practice in infant education, a sociological approach and case study', M.Sc. dissertation, University of London Institute of Education Library (for discussion of 'busyness').

Halliday, M. A. K. (1973), *Exploration in the Function of Language*, Edward Arnold.

Houdle, L. (1968), *An Enquiry into the Social Factors affecting the Orientation of English Infant Education since the early Nineteenth Century*, M.A. dissertation, University of London Institute of Education Library, (excellent bibliography).

Plowden Report (1967), *Children and their Primary Schools*, a report of the Central Advisory Council for Education (England), HMSO, Vol. 1.

Shulman, L. S. and Kreislar, E. R. (eds.) (1966), *Learning by Discovery: a critical appraisal*, Chicago: Rand McNally.

Simon, B. (Ed.). (1972), *The Radical Tradition in Education in Britain*, Lawrence & Wishart.

Stewart, W. A. C. and McCann, W. P. (1967), *The Educational Innovators*, Macmillan.

Zoldany, M. (1935), *Die Entstehungstheorie des Geistes*, Budapest: Donau.

Appendix: A Note on the Coding of Objects and Modalities of Control

The Coding of Objects

The concepts of classification and frame can be used to interpret communication between objects. In other words, objects and their relationships to each other constitute a message system whose code can be stated in terms of the relationship between classification and frames of different strengths.

We can consider:

1 The strength of the rules of exclusion which control the array of objects in a space. Thus the stronger the rules of exclusion the more distinctive the array of objects in the space; that is, the greater the difference between object arrays in different spaces.

2 The extent to which objects in the array can enter into different relationships to each other.

Now the stronger the rules of exclusion the stronger the *classification* of objects in that space and the greater the difference between object arrays in different spaces. In the same way in which we discussed relationships between subjects we can discuss the relationships between object arrays in different spaces. Thus the stronger the classification the more the object arrays resemble a collection code; the weaker the classification the more the object arrays resemble an integrated code. The greater the number of Merent relationships objects in the array can enter into with each other the weaker their framing. The fewer the number of different relationships objects in the array can enter into with each other the stronger their framing. (If the objects in the array can be called lexical items, then the syntax is their relationships to each other. A restricted code is a syntax with few choices: an elaborated code a syntax which generates a large number of choices.)

We would expect the social distribution of power and the principles of control to be reflected in the coding of objects. This code may be made more delicate if we take into account:

1   The number of objects in the array;
2   The rate of change of the array.

We can have strong classification with a large *or* a small number of objects. We can have strong classification of large or small arrays where the array is fixed across time *or* where the array varies across time. Consider, for example, two arrays which are strongly classified: a late-Victorian, middle-class living-room and a mid-twentieth-century, trendy, middle-class 'space' in Hampstead. The Victorian room is likely to contain a very large number of objects, whereas the middle-class room is likely to contain a small number of objects. In one case the object array is foreground and the space background, whereas in the second case the space is a vital component of the array. The Victorian room represents both strong classification and strong framing. Further, whilst objects may be added to the array, its fundamental characteristics would remain constant over a relatively long time-period. The Hampstead room is likely to contain a small array which would indicate strong classification (strong rules of exclusion) but the objects are likely to enter into a variety of relationships with each other; this would indicate weak framing. Further, it is possible that the array would be changed across time, according to fashion.

We can now see that if we are to consider classification (C) we need to know:

1   Whether it is strong or weak;
2   Whether the array is small or large (x);
3   Whether the array is fixed or variable (y).

At the level of frame (F) we need to know: Whether it is strong or weak (p); that is, whether the coding is restricted or elaborated.

It is also important to indicate in the specification of the code the context (c) to which it applies. We should also indicate the nature of the array by adding the concept realization (r). Thus, the most abstract formulation of the object code would be as follows:

$$f\,(c,r,\,C\,(x,y),\,F\,(p))$$

The code is some unspecified function of the variables enclosed in the brackets.

It is important to note that because the classification is weak it does not mean that there is less control. Indeed, from this point of view it is not possible to talk about amount of control, only of its modality. This point we will now develop.

Classification, Frames and Modalities of Control

Imagine four lavatories. The first is stark, bare, pristine, the walls are painted a sharp white; the washbowl is like the apparatus, a gleaming white. A square block of soap sits cleanly in an indentation in the sink. A white towel (or perhaps pink) is folded neatly on a chrome rail or hangs from a chrome ring. The lavatory paper is hidden in a cover and peeps through its slit. In the second lavatory there are books on a shelf and some relaxing of the rigours of the first. In the third lavatory there are books on the shelf, pictures on the wall and perhaps a scattering of tiny objects. In the fourth lavatory the rigour is *totally relaxed*. The walls are covered with a motley array of postcards, there is a varied assortment of reading matter and curio. The lavatory roll is likely to be uncovered and the holder may well fall apart in use.

We can say that as we move from the first to the fourth lavatory we are moving from a strongly classified to a weakly classified space: from a space regulated by strong rules of exclusion to a space regulated by weak rules of exclusion. Now if the rules of exclusion are strong, then the space is strongly marked off from other spaces in the house or flat. The *boundary* between the spaces or rooms is sharp. If the rules of exclusion are strong, the boundaries well-marked, then it follows that there must be strong boundary maintainers (authority). If things are to be kept apart, then there must be some strong hierarchy to ensure the apartness of things. Further, the first lavatory constructs a space where pollution is highly visible. Inasmuch as a user leaves a personal mark (a failure to replace the towel in its original position, a messy bar of soap, scum in the washbowl, lavatory paper floating in the bowl, etc.), this constitutes pollution and such pollution is quickly perceived. Thus the criteria for competent usage of the space are both *explicit* and *specific*. So far we have been discussing aspects of classification; we shall now consider framing.

Whereas classification tells us about the structure of relationships in *space*, framing tells us about the structure of relationships in *time*. Framing refers us to inter-action, to the power relationships of inter-action; that is, framing refers us to communication. Now in the case of our lavatories, framing *here* would refer to the communication between the occupants of the space and those outside of the space. Such communication is normally strongly framed by a door usually equipped with a lock. We suggest that as we move from the strongly classified to the weakly classified lavatory, despite the potential insulation between inside and outside, there will occur a reduction in frame strength. In the case of the first lavatory we suggest that the door will always be closed and after entry will be locked. Ideally, no effects on the inside should be heard on the outside. Indeed, a practised user of this lavatory will acquire certain competencies in order to meet this requirement. However, in the case of the most weakly classified lavatory, we suggest that the door will normally be open; it may even be that the lock will not function. It would not be considered untoward for a conversation to develop or even be continued either side of the door. A practised user of this most weakly classified and weakly framed lavatory will acquire certain communicative competencies rather different from those required for correct use of the strongly classified one.

We have already noted that lavatory one creates a space where pollution is highly visible, where criteria for behaviour are explicit and specific, where the social basis of the authority maintaining the strong classification and frames is hierarchical. Yet it is also the case that such classification and frames create a *private* although impersonal space. *For providing that the classification and framing is not violated, the user of the space is beyond surveillance.*

However, when we consider lavatory four, which has the weakest classification and weakest frames, it seems at first sight that such a structure celebrates weak control. There appear to be few rules regulating what goes into a space and few rules regulating communication between spaces. Therefore it is difficult to consider what counts as a violation or pollution. Indeed, it would appear that such a classification and framing relationship facilitates the development of spontaneous behaviour. Let us consider this possibility.

Lavatory one is predicated on the rule 'things must be kept apart', be they persons, acts, objects, communication; and the stronger the classification and frames the greater the insulation, the stronger the boundaries between classes of persons, acts, objects, communications. Lavatory four is predicated on the rule that approximates to 'things must be put together'. As a consequence, we would find objects in the space that could be found in other spaces. Further, there is a more relaxed marking off of the space, and communication is possible between inside and outside. We have as yet not discovered the fundamental principles of violation.

Imagine one user, who, seeing the motley array and being sensitive to what he or she takes to be a potential of the space, decides to add to the array and places an additional postcard on the wall. It is possible that a little later a significant adult might say 'Darling, that's beautiful but it doesn't quite fit' or 'How lovely, but wouldn't it be better a little higher up?' In other words, we are suggesting that the array has a principle, that the apparently motley collection is ordered but that the principle is implicit, and although it is not easily discoverable it is capable of being violated. Indeed, it might take our user a very long time to infer the *tacit* principle, and generate choices in accordance with it. Without knowledge of the principle our user is unlikely to make appropriate choices and such choices may require a long period of socialization. In the case of lavatory one, no principle is required; all that is needed is the following of the command 'Leave the space as you found it.'

Now let us examine the weak framing in more detail. We suggest that locking the door, avoiding or ignoring communication, would count as violation; indeed anything which would offend the principle of *things must be put together*. However, inasmuch as the framing between inside and outside is weak, then it is also the case that the user is potentially or indirectly under continuous surveillance, in which case there is no privacy. Here we have a social context which at first sight appears to be very relaxed, which promotes and provokes the expression of the person, 'a do your own thing' space where highly personal choices may be offered, where hierarchy is not explicit, yet on analysis we find that it is based upon a form of implicit control which carries the potential of total surveillance. Such a form of implicit control encourages more of the person to be made manifest, yet such manifestations are subject to continuous screening and general rather than specific criteria. *At the level of classification the pollution is 'keeping things apart'; at the level of framing the violation is 'withholding'; that is, not offering, not making visible the self.*

If things are to be put together which were once set apart, then there must be some principle of the new relationships, but this principle cannot be mechanically applied and therefore cannot be mechanically learned. In the case of the rule 'things must be kept apart', then the apartness of things is something which is clearly marked and taken for granted in the process of initial socialization. The social basis of the categories of apartness is implicit, but the social basis of the authority is explicit. In the process of such socialization the insulation between things is a condensed message about the all-pervasiveness of the authority. It may require many years before the social basis of the principles underlying the category system is made fully explicit, and by that time the mental structure is well-initiated into the classification and frames. Strong classification and frames celebrate the *reproduction* of the past.

When the rule is 'things must be put together' we have an *interruption* of a previous order, and what is of issue is the authority (power relationships) which underpins it. Therefore the rule 'things must be put together' celebrates the present over the past, the subjective over the objective, the personal over the positional. Indeed, when everything is put together we have a total organic principle which covers all aspects of life *but* which admits of a vast range of combinations and re-combinations. This points to a very abstract or general principle from which a vast range of possibilities may be derived, so that individuals can both register personal choices *and* have knowledge when a combination is not in accordance with the principle. What is taken for granted when the rule is 'things must be kept apart' is *relationships* which themselves are made explicit by when the rule is 'things must be put together'. They are made explicit by the weak classification and frames. But the latter creates a form of implicit but potentially continuous surveillance and at the same time promotes the making public of the self in a variety of ways. We arrive finally at the conclusion that the conditions for the release of the person are the absence of explicit hierarchy but the presence of a more intensified form of social interaction which creates continuous but invisible screening. From the point of view of the socialized they would be offering novel, spontaneous combinations.

Empirical Note

It is possible to examine the coding of objects from two perspectives. We can analyse the coding of overt or visible arrays and we can compare the code with the codings of covert or invisible arrays (e.g. drawers, cupboards, refrigerators, basements, closets, handbags, etc.). We can also compare the coding of verbal messages with the coding of non-verbal messages. It would be interesting to carry out an empirical study of standardized spaces, e.g. LEA housing estate, middle-class suburban 'town house' estate, modern blocks of flats, formal educational spaces which vary in their architecture and in the pedagogy.

I am well aware that the lavatory may not be seen as a space to be *specially contrived* and so subject to *special regulation* in the sense discussed. Some lavatories are not subject to the principles I have outlined. Indeed some may be casually treated spaces where pieces of newspaper may be stuffed behind a convenient pipe, where the door does not close or lock, where apparatus has low efficiency and where sound effects are taken-for-granted events.

9

The Effects of Education as an Institution

JOHN W. MEYER

How does education affect society? The dominant view has it that the schools process individuals. They are organized networks of socializing experiences which prepare individuals to act in society. More direct macro-sociological effects have been given little attention. Yet in modern societies education is a highly developed institution. It has a network of rules creating public classifications of persons and knowledge. It defines which individuals belong to these categories and possess the appropriate knowledge. And it defines which persons have access to valued positions in society. Education is a central element in the public biography of individuals, greatly affecting their life chances. It is also a central element in the table of organization of society, constructing competencies and helping create professions and professionals. Such an institution clearly has an impact on society over and above the immediate socializing experiences it offers the young.

Recently, the traditional socialization view has been attacked with an argument which incorporates a more institutional conception of education, though in a very limited way. Education is seen as an allocating institution—operating under societal rules which allow the schools to directly confer success and failure in society quite apart from any socializing effects (e.g., Collins 1971; Bowles and Gintis 1976). Allocation theory leaves open the possibility that expanded educational systems have few net effects on society. The polemic controversy has obscured the fact that allocation theory (and institutional theory in general) has many unexplored implications for socialization theory and research; those implications are considered here. For instance, allocation theory suggests effects of expanded educational institutions both on those who attend and those who do not attend schools. It also can explain why completing a given level of schooling often matters much more in determining educational outcomes than do the features of the particular school attended.

But conventional allocation theory, while considering the institutional properties of educational systems, focuses mainly on the outcomes for individuals being processed. It tends to be assumed that education has no effect on the distribution of political, economic, and social positions in society. Allocation theory is thus a limited special case of a more general institutional theory—legitimation theory—which treats education as both constructing or altering roles in society and authoritatively allocating personnel to these roles. Modern educational systems involve large-scale public classification systems, defining new roles and statuses for both elites and members. These classifications are new constructions in that the newly defined persons are expected (and entitled) to behave, and to be treated by others, in new ways. Not only new types of persons but also new competencies are authoritatively created. Such legitimating effects of education transcend the effects education may have on individuals being processed by the schools. The former effects transform the behavior of people in society quite independent of their own educational experience.

In this paper, I develop the ideas of legitimation theory and propose comparative and experimental studies which could examine the effects of education on social structure, not simply on the individuals it processes. I move away from the contemporary view of educational organization as a production system constructing elaborated individuals. Modern education is seen instead as a system of institutionalized rites transforming social roles through powerful initiation ceremonies and as an agent transforming society by creating new classes of personnel with new types of authoritative knowledge.

The Traditional Socialization Model

Prevailing research on school effects is organized around a simple image of socialization in society: Schools provide experiences which instill knowledge, skills, attitudes, and values in their students. These students then have a revised and expanded set of personal qualities enabling them to demand more from, and achieve more in, the role structure of modern society. As the competence and orientation of the personnel of society are expanded and modernized, so society as a larger system is modernized and expanded.

Three general propositions are at issue here and make up a simple model, which is diagramed in Figure 9.1:

Proposition 1 (*Socialization*). Schooled persons are socialized to expanded levels of knowledge and competence and expanded levels of modern values or orientations.

Proposition 2 (Socialization and Adult Competence). Early socialization to higher levels of knowledge, competence, and modern values or orientations creates higher levels of adult status and competence.

Proposition 3 (Individual Competence and Social Progress). The expansion of the number of skilled adults expands the complexity and wealth of society and social institutions.

Research on proposition 1 is rather clear-cut. Children and youth in schools learn a good deal more, and acquire more expanded social capacities than those not in school, even when background factors are controlled (see, e.g., Holsinger 1974; Plant 1965). The main problem in the research on this subject is the finding that the particular school students attend often seems to make little difference (see Jencks et al. [1972]; or the studies reviewed in Feldman and Newcomb [1969]). I return to this issue below; the point here is that something about participation in schools creates notable effects on all sorts of socialization—from knowledge to social values to status expectations.

Little direct empirical research has been done on proposition 3—the idea that changed people produce a changed social structure—though this kind of "demographic" explanation (Stinchcombe 1968) has been a main theme of sociological theories of social change. In recent decades some doubts have arisen, with a conservative fear that "overeducated" people create more social instability and breakdown than they do social development. There is no evidence of this, but the issue remains.

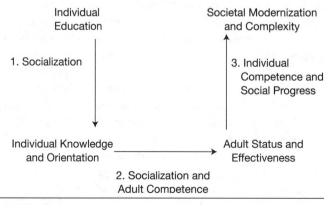

Figure 9.1 Traditional socialization theory.

Proposition 2 has been one source of doubt about the whole model. Traditional socialization theory in sociology (and child development research) becomes an adequate account of social structure only if (*a*) socialized qualities remain with the person with some stability over long periods of time, and (*b*) such qualities predict adult effectiveness in roles. But current research on personal qualities often suggests low autocorrelations over time (see the review by Mischel [1971]). Many empirical studies suggest that the personal qualities schooling creates do not effectively determine occupational success, once occupational entry has been obtained (see the polemic review by Berg [1971]). Even if socialized qualities have fair stability and offer fair predictive power, it is unlikely that the product of these effects (which amounts to a very low overall effect) explains the high correlation of education with adult status.

Thus, socialization theory, as an account of educational effects on society, has one area of success and two of failure. On the positive side, schooling does predict, with other variables held constant, many of the outcomes of socialization. On the negative side, many of the measurable socialization outcomes of schooling have little long-run staying power or predictive power.[1] Also on the negative side, variations among schools in their socialization programs show small effects on outcomes—if schools socialize through the immediate experiences they provide, schools providing different experiences should produce very different effects. The research literature provides little encouragement on this subject.[2]

Institutional Theories: Allocation Theory as a Limited Case

Traditional socialization theory defines education as an organized set of socializing experiences. It treats as peripheral the fact that modern educational systems are society-wide and state-controlled institutions. In discussions of socialization theory this property of educational settings barely appears (e.g., Wheeler 1966).

Partly in reaction to this limitation, but more in reaction to the empirical weakness of socialization theory and in polemic reaction to the earlier optimism about the socially progressive effects of education, allocation theories have been developed. It is argued that people in modern societies are allocated to adult roles on the basis of years and types of education, apart from anything they have learned in schools. Education is thus more a selector, sorter, and allocator than it is a socializer.

Education, in allocation theories, is a set of institutional rules which legitimately classify and authoritatively allocate individuals to positions in society. Allocation theories are limited in that they define only a few consequences of this system and consider effects mainly on the individuals being allocated, but they open up a broader range of institutional theories which are discussed below.

The power of the allocation idea arises from its obvious empirical validity. We all know that status positions in modern societies are assigned on the basis of education. Sometimes, as with civil service and professional positions (e.g., medicine, law, teaching), this is a matter of law. To teach in a high school one must have an educational credential. Whether one knows anything or not is less relevant. Often, rules about credentials are simply part of established organizational practice, as in the assignment of college and business-school graduates to managerial positions and of others to working-class jobs. Sometimes the whole process is informal, as in the inclination of juries and informal friendship groups to attend to the advice of their more educated members.

In any event, the relationship between education and social position—over and above socialization or learning—is quite direct. The line of research pursued by Blau and Duncan (1967) and Duncan, Featherman, and Duncan (1972) shows large direct effects of education on status attainment, sometimes with ability measures held constant. Education plays a direct causal role in occupational transition even late in the individual's career (Blau and Duncan 1967, chap. 5)—decades after any direct socialization effects must have decayed or become outmoded.

The basic idea is clear:

Proposition 4 (*Educational Allocation*). In modern societies, adult success is assigned to persons on the basis of duration and type of education, holding constant what they may have learned in school.

Educational allocation rules, that is, give to the schools social *charters* to define people as graduates and as therefore possessing distinctive rights and capacities in society (Meyer 1970a; see also Clark 1970). Thus the schools have power as an institutional system, not simply as a set of organizations processing individuals.

Impact of Allocation Rules on Socialization

The polemic contrast between socialization and allocation ideas—education as a socializing process versus education as a status competition—has concealed the fact that the two are not really inconsistent. Further, allocation theory offers interesting and useful extensions of traditional socialization ideas.

Assume that educational allocation rules in fact hold in society. Students and members of their social networks (e.g., parents, peers, teachers, and counselors) are informed members of society—not simply passive objects of educational production—and know these rules with some accuracy. Graduates, of course, experience the rules through the distinctive experiences and treatments they receive in society. Now if we assume a most elementary idea of social psychology, that people adapt and are adapted by others to their actual and expected experiences, two major propositions follow:

Proposition 5 (*Chartering*). Students tend to adopt personal and social qualities appropriate to the positions to which their schools are chartered to assign them.

Proposition 6 (*Lagged Socialization*). Adults tend to adopt qualities appropriate to the roles and expectations to which their educational statuses have assigned them.

These propositions argue that education functions for individuals as a set of initiation ceremonies of great and society-wide significance (Ramirez 1975; Garfinkel 1956). These ceremonies transform the futures and pasts of individuals, greatly enhancing their value in all sorts of social situations. On the basis of their education, individuals are expected to treat themselves, and others are expected to treat them, as having expanded rights and competencies. Given allocation rules, educational labels are of the greatest significance for the social identity of individuals.

Proposition 1 and proposition 5 parallel each other and in many instances overlap in accounting for the same findings. It is often unclear to what extent given socialization effects are generated by the immediate socializing situation in a given school and to what extent they are produced by the institutional authority in which the school is embedded.

However, proposition 5, in contrast to proposition 1, offers a direct explanation of the most puzzling general research paradox in the sociology of American education. The level of schooling achieved has substantial effects on all sorts of personal qualities. But outcome variations among schools—even though these schools differ greatly in structure and resources—are very small. This finding shows up in studies of college effects (Feldman and Newcomb 1969), high school effects, and effects at the elementary school level. If schools have their socializing effects as ritually chartered organizations (Meyer 1970a; Kamens 1971, 1974) rather than as organized collections of immediate socializing experiences, then all schools of similar ritual status can be expected to have similar effects. Since for many personnel assignment purposes all American high schools (or colleges) have similar status rights, variations in their effects should be small. But because all high schools are chartered to create "high school graduates"—a critical status in our society for college and occupational entry—all of them tend to produce marked effects on students. Proposition 5, in other words, argues that the most powerful socializing property of a school is its external institutional authority, derived from the rules of educational allocation, rather than its network of internal socializing experiences. Educators, who attend with great vigor to the accreditation of their schools, seem more aware of this process than do socialization researchers.

Thus, the educational contexts which vary substantially in the change and learning they produce in students do not usually include specific schools. They include contexts which are distinctively chartered:

1   Schooling per se. Life prospects (and hence changes in students) are vitally affected by being in an institution chartered as a school.

2   Type of school, when the types are differently chartered. Himmelweit and Swift (1969) and Kerckhoff (1975) show marked differences in outcomes for similar British students between grammar and secondary modern schools. American researchers have not looked for differences in expectations between initially similar students in general and vocational high schools. Some studies show distinct occupational effects of teachers, colleges, and engineering schools (Astin and Panos 1969).

3   Curriculum, when it is distinctively chartered. For instance, being in a college preparatory curriculum (in contrast to a vocational one) makes a considerable difference in the aspirations and expectations of American high school students (Alexander and Eckland 1975; see also Rosenbaum 1975).[3]

Proposition 6—the idea that education socializes adults by allocating them to expanded roles and role expectations—explains a second major paradoxical finding in the current sociology of education. The direct long-run effects of schools on graduates are thought to be rather moderate. But surveys of adults with regard to almost any dependent variable—attitudes, values, information, or participation—almost uniformly show that education plays a dominant role. For instance, Almond and Verba (1963) show with data on five countries that education is closely associated with political information, attitudes, and participation. Inkeles and Smith (1974) show the same result with data on six countries and are surprised to discover that the impact of education is much greater than that of work experience. Kohn's research (1969, and subsequently) shows exactly the same result, and again the author is surprised. But these findings make eminent sense. Educational allocation rules create a situation in which schooling is a fixed capital asset in the career of the individual, more durable than work or income, more stable than family life and relations, and less subject to market fluctuations than "real" property. Is it surprising that the attitudes and orientations of educated individuals continue to reflect such enhanced life prospects over long periods of time? They perceive these prospects and are surrounded by others who see them too.

Proposition 6 suggests that in explaining such long-run effects of education we do not need to look back to the details of the experience of socialization. Correlations between education and personal qualities can be maintained and increased by a structure or subsequent allocation which provides distinctive life experiences and anticipations for the educated. For instance, education can affect a person's sense of political efficacy by making him politically influential as well as by socializing him to a civic culture.

Further Implications of Allocation Theory

If taken seriously, and not simply used as a cynical critique of education, allocation theory would completely reorganize current research styles in the sociology of education. Allocation rules, unlike simple socialization effects, reign over both the students and the nonstudents, the educated and the uneducated, the graduates and those who never attended.

Research implication 1: Effects on nonstudents.—Let us examine the following hypotheses.

Hypothesis 1. The creation of social rules allocating status and competence to graduates leads to the socialization of students for expanded social roles.

Hypothesis 2. But such rules *lower* the prospects of nonstudents and, in a sense, desocialize them.

The more binding the allocation rules, the earlier and more convincingly are nonstudents committed to passive roles in society. This means that the society relying on credentials could well lower (below the previous floor) the modern competence of people of low education. Comparative contextual research is required to test this idea, since the independent variable is a property of the social system.

This argument has it that in a modern society education allocates its dropouts to failure. They (and their parents and friends) anticipate and adapt to this.

Hypothesis 3. Similarly, *subsequent* to the period of schooling, nongraduates are socialized through life experiences to the meaning of their failure just as graduates are socialized to the meaning of their success. The lagged differentials created by education should be greater the more firmly the principle of educational allocation is established.

Hypothesis 4. Those admitted to chartered educational organizations find their prospects enhanced even before attendance, while those rejected find their prospects lowered. They adapt their personal qualities in anticipation, even prior to attendance. These differentials should be greater the stronger the allocative position of the school.

For example, Benitez (1973) finds that students admitted to a national elite high school in the Philippines seem to gain in self-esteem and "competence" even before their socialization begins. Wallace's (1966) data suggest a similar interpretation.

Comparative research on effects such as these should help distinguish allocation theory from traditional socialization ideas.

Research implication 2: Aggregate effects.—A major implication of allocation theory is that inferences to the aggregate effects of education made from individual data on the basis of traditional socialization ideas are almost completely illegitimate. Researchers in the economics of education conventionally infer aggregate economic effects of education from income differentials between the educated and the less educated (see, e.g., the papers in Blaug 1968, 1969). It is assumed that these income differentials reflect real added value—the socialization gains of the educated. But if education is simply an allocation system, the gains of the educated may simply occur with equivalent losses for the uneducated. The expansion of education and educational allocation may have no effect on the aggregate product at all (Collins 1971).

Similarly, researchers on the political effects of education often infer that, because the educated occupy politically central positions, education must have helped create these positions (see the papers in Coleman 1965). But if education is simply a system of allocation, huge positional and attitudinal differences between the educated and the uneducated may exist with no aggregate effect at all. Igra (1976), in fact, shows (using Inkeles's data) that increases in the aggregate development of societies *lower* the political participation of individuals of given education (though the political information of individuals is found to be enhanced). Such "frog-pond effects" at lower levels of analysis are discussed by Davis (1966), Meyer (1970b), and Alexander and Eckland (1975).

The main arguments of allocation theory are added to those of socialization theory in Figure 9.2. Allocation ideas are discussed with some frequency in the current literature, though their implications for research remain little explored.

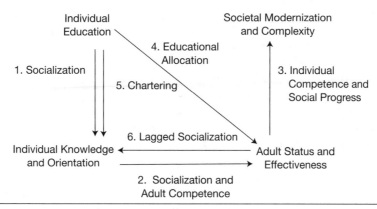

Figure 9.2 Allocation theory and its implications for socialization theory. (Pure allocation theory suggests that *3* is irrelevant. If a given set of adult competencies are simply allocated by education, no net societal gain in number of competent individuals need occur.)

The Limitations of Allocation Theory

Allocation theories, by conceiving of education as an institution, add a good deal to traditional socialization theory. But they do so in a very narrow way.

Education is seen in these theories as possessing its power because it is built into the rules and understandings which guide all sorts of personnel allocation processes in society. But its impact is considered only for those individuals being processed by the system—the students and nonstudents who are being sorted. And even this impact is denned in a limited way: these people are understood to respond only to their own role prospects as they are affected by education. Does the fact that all the other individuals around him are being magically transformed by powerful initiation ceremonies have no effect on a given student? And has it no effect on other members of society?

The problem here is that allocation theories ordinarily see education as allocating individuals to a fixed set of positions in society: a distribution of positions determined by other economic and political forces. Bowles and Gintis (1976) propose slight additional effects—education is thought to socialize people to accept as legitimate the limited roles to which they are allocated. Spence (1973) and Thurow (1975) see some marginal gains to society through more efficient selection by education. But the main development of allocation theory defines the *structure* of society as little affected by education.

Allocation theory, then, can be seen as a special case of a more general argument according to which education constructs and alters the network of positions in society in addition to allocating individuals to these positions. We simply need to abandon the assumption that the positions to which education allocates people cannot be built, expanded, and altered by education itself.

It is becoming more common to speak of education as legitimating the structure of modern society (Bowles and Gintis 1976), or of modern societies as in some essential way "schooled" (Illich 1971). If we want to understand the societal impact of education, not just its effects on the careers of individuals, we need to understand what this means.

The General Case: Legitimation Theory

Allocation theory is a special case of institutional theories of educational effects: it considers the effects of education as an institution (*a*) only on the individuals being processed and (*b*) with the structure of society held constant. We now turn to the general case: theories of the institutional impact of education on social structure itself—on the behavior of people throughout society.

Modern extended and institutionalized systems of education build into society certain rules which actors take for granted, know others take for granted, and incorporate in their decisions and actions.[4]

For instance, institutionalized educational systems create a situation in which social gatekeepers (e.g., personnel officers)—even if they read and believe Ivar Berg's book—nevertheless know that they must hire people on the basis of educational credentials.

Two closely related aspects of modern educational systems are relevant here as independent variables: (1) they are extended as systems of classification, categorizing entire adult populations by level and specialty; and (2) they are institutionalized, with their classifications often controlled by the state and enforced in daily life by rules about credentials written into law and applied in organizational practice. Almost everywhere, education is made compulsory and universal by national law, often in the national constitution (Boli-Bennett 1976). In most countries its structure is closely regulated by the nation-state (Ramirez 1973; Rubinson 1973).

Why does this occur? Whatever the economic origins of the process, the fact that it is usually accomplished and regulated by the state—unlike many aspects of economic development, which are left to individuals and subunits—suggests that its immediate origins lie in the political system: society as corporate organization (Swanson 1971) rather than as a system of exchange. *Formalized educational systems are, in fact, theories of socialization institutionalized as rules at the collective level.* The three core propositions used above to summarize traditional socialization theory *become* the structural basis of the educational system. Proposition 1—the idea that the schools teach critical skills and values—becomes institutionalized as the basic educational classification system: Education proceeds in a sequence (irreversible by ascriptive definition) from kindergarten through postdoctoral study and covers a defined series of valued substantive topics. The student is a "high school graduate" and has had compulsory units of history and English and mathematics. It is an institutionalized doctrine, since for many purposes one must treat the student as having acquired this knowledge by virtue of the units or credits completed, not by direct inspection. Proposition 2—the idea that schooled qualities are carried into adult effectiveness—is institutionalized in the basic rules for employing credentialled persons which dominate personnel allocation in modern society. If one hires an executive, a civil servant, or a teacher, one must inspect educational credentials—it is optional whether one inspects the person's competence. A teacher or a doctor who graduated from school in 1930 is still frequently treated as a socially and legally valid teacher or doctor. Proposition 3—the idea that educational allocation creates social progress—is institutionally embedded in our doctrines of progress: it consists of modernity, professionalization, and rationalization. The possession of the best certified and educated people is a main index of the advanced status of a hospital, a school, often a business organization, and indeed a society itself.

Educational systems themselves are thus, in a sense, ideologies. They rationalize in modern terms and remove from sacred and primordial explanations the nature and organization of personnel and knowledge in modern society. They are, presumably, the effects of the reorganization of modern society around secular individualism which is a main theme of Marx and Weber. Our problem here, however, is to discuss their effects.[5]

Legitimating Effects of Expanded and Institutionalized Education

Legitimating effects of education can be discussed in four general categories created by the intersection of two dichotomies. First, education functions in society as a legitimating *theory of knowledge* defining certain types of knowledge as extant and as authoritative. It also functions as a *theory of personnel*, defining categories of persons who are to be treated as possessing these bodies of knowledge and forms of authority.

Second, education validates both *elites* and *citizens*. Discussions of the legitimating function of education often emphasize only its role in supporting elites and inequality (e.g., Bowles and Gintis 1976; Carnoy 1972). But the overwhelmingly dominant kind of education in the modern world is

	Elite Education	Mass Education
Education as Theory of Knowledge	1. The Authority of Specialized Competence	3. The Universality of Collective Reality
Education as Theory of Personnel	2. Elite Definition and Certification	4. The Extension of Membership: Nation-building and Citizenship

Figure 9.3 Types of legitimating effects of education.

mass education (Coombs 1968), closely tied to the modern state and notion of universal citizenship (Marshall 1948; Bendix 1964; Habermas 1962).

These two distinctions define four types of legitimating effects of education, as specified in Figure 9.3. I discuss them in turn.

1. The Authority of Specialized Competence. Education does not simply allocate people to a fixed set of positions in society. It expands the authoritative culture and the set of specialized social positions entailed by this culture. Thus the creation of academic economics means that new types of knowledge must be taken into account by responsible actors. The creation of psychiatry means that former mysteries must now be dealt with in the social organization. The creation of academic programs in business management brings arenas of decision making from personal judgment, or luck, to the jurisdiction of rationalized knowledge. Social problems call for human-relations professionals (occasionally even sociologists). Safety or environmental problems call for industrial or environmental engineering.

The point here is that, quite apart from the immediate efficacy of these bodies of knowledge, they are authoritative and must be taken into account by actors at the risk of being judged negligent or irrational. The business manager who plans by the seat of his pants—unblessed by economic projections—has no excuse for ignoring the best advice. The political leader who sees social problems as beyond analysis or cure is reactionary and primeval. The emotionally disturbed person who rejects psychiatry is displaying irrationality.

Thus the knowledge categories of the educational system enter authoritatively into daily life. Mysteries are rationalized, brought under symbolic control, and incorporated into the social system. Society and its subunits are buffered from uncertainty (Thompson 1967):

Proposition 7. The expansion (and institutionalization) of education expands the number of functions that are brought under social control and that responsible actors must take into account.[6]

2. Elite Definition and Certification. Education as an institution creates and defines particular categories of elite personnel. This has two aspects, (a) Education consists of allocation rules and initiation ceremonies designating which persons possess the authority and competence for various elite roles. This is the core idea of allocation theory, (b) But institutionalized education also defines the nature and authority of the elite roles themselves—helping to create the categories of personnel as well as to designate the particular occupants of these categories. In this way, expanded modern educational systems function as a personnel theory in society, justifying in modern cultural terms the expansion and specialization of modern elites.

Education, that is, not only creates "economic knowledge" which must be taken into account by rational actors. It is also a structure helping to create the role of economist, to justify economists' authority claims in society, and to define precisely who is an economist. Education thus creates, not only psychiatry, but psychiatrists; not only modern management ideology, but M.B.A.s. The rational actor must take into account medical knowledge and, to do so, he must consult a doctor. Thus, the modern organizational structure of society incorporates legitimated bodies of knowledge by incorporating the designated personnel.[7]

We take too narrow a view if we see this process as involving only a few specialized occupations. The most important rules concerning credentials are more general: the set of rules which connect the educational status of *college graduate* (and *high school graduate*) with all sorts of formal and informal elite positions. These rules define a generalized body of elite knowledge and specify its legitimate carriers.

It now becomes clear why views of educational allocation as "zero-sum"—allocating a fixed set of social statuses—are wrong. Education helps *create* new classes of knowledge and personnel which then come to be incorporated in society:

> Proposition 8. The expansion (and institutionalization) of education expands the number of specialized and elite positions in society. It defines and justifies their occupancy by particular people.[8]

The point here is that institutionalized education does more than simply allocate some to success and others to failure. The educated learn to claim specialized functions and to legitimate the specialized functions of others. The less educated learn that they are part of a social world of rights and duties elaborated far beyond the traditional community. This is one of the core meanings of the modern social status *citizen*.

3. The Universality of Collective Reality. Mass education creates a whole series of social assumptions about the common culture of society and thus expands the social meaning of citizenship, personhood, and individuality (modern ideas, all). It establishes a whole series of common elements for everyone.[9] (*a*) It creates the assumption of a national language or languages and defines universal literacy, (*b*) It reifies a given national history, (*c*) It constructs a common civic order—common heroes and villains, a common constitutional and political order with some shared cultural symbols and with legitimate national participation, (*d*) It validates the existence of a common natural reality through science and a common logical structure through mathematics and in this way constructs a myth of a common culture intimately linked to world society, (*e*) It constructs broad definitions of citizen and human rights as part of the modern world view.

Regardless of what people actually learn in school about their language and culture, nationally institutionalized mass education creates the assumptions of a national culture. For many purposes, both elite and citizen actors must take them into account.

> Proposition 9. The expansion (and institutionalization) of education expands the content and jurisdiction of the elements taken for granted as part of collective reality.

4. The Extension of Membership: Nation-Building and Citizenship. Beyond defining and extending national culture, mass education defines almost the entire population as possessing this culture, as imbued with its meanings, and as having the rights implied by it. Mass education defines and builds the nation (Marshall 1948; Bendix 1964). It allocates persons to citizenship—establishing their membership in the nation over and above various subgroups. And it directly expands the definition of what citizenship and the nation mean and what obligations and rights are involved. Mass education helps create a public: as education expands, ideas about public opinion as a vital force in society rise (Habermas 1962; Bergesen 1977). Individuals come to be defined as possessing the competencies and the moral orientations to participate in an expanded collective life:

> Proposition 10. Mass education expands the number of persons seen as possessing human and citizenship responsibilities, capacities, and rights. It also expands the prevailing definitions of these roles and their associated qualities.

In expanding both the meaning of citizenship and the set of persons who are seen as citizens, education plays a dual role. Certainly it opens up new possibilities for citizens—in particular, new claims for equality which can be made on society. It also, however, redefines individuals as responsible subordinate members (and agents) of the state organization, and opens them to new avenues of control and manipulation.

Research Designs in Legitimation Theory

Legitimation ideas propose societal effects of education. They can be studied in several ways.

1 Most directly, data comparing societies over time can be examined. For instance, is it true, in comparing societies, that those with expanded mass education tend to create sooner and more completely the welfare, policing, and participatory apparatuses of citizenship?

2 The same questions can be looked at with time-series data pertaining to a single society. For example, what has been the effect of the expansion of higher education in the United States, independent of other factors, on the number of types of professionals who have privileged status (as "expert witnesses") in the courts?

3 The same questions can be studied at the individual level as well. Legitimation theory argues for the effects of the extension and institutionalization of national educational systems on the judgments, perceived realities, and actions of *given* individuals—ordinary persons, rule makers, and critical social gatekeepers. Studies can therefore compare similar individuals in societies differing in educational structure. Do persons of given education, in more schooled societies, see personal and social problems as more likely to require educated expertise? Do they see, as I argued above, a larger number of social functions as requiring explicit (and undoubtedly educated) collective social management? Comparative survey research can help examine such questions.

4 It is also possible to approach these questions experimentally. Education, it is argued, restructures social reality for given individuals. To explore this, subjects can be confronted with hypothetical societies, similar in many respects but differing in the expansion and authority of education. Would subjects be more likely to propose to use economists and other social scientists to help with business or political planning if we describe for them a society in which elite education is highly developed and institutionalized? Subjects might even attribute authority to nonexistent professions if those are described as rooted in educational programs.

These research design approaches can all be used to deal with the following central empirical hypotheses of legitimation theory.

1 Basing a particular elite in the educational system helps create and expand its authority. One can study empirically the differential rise in societies of personnel workers, social scientists, physicians, or psychiatrists as these groups are affected by differential educational institutionalization. This can be done with comparative, survey, or experimental techniques.

2 More generally, expanded elite educational systems produce and support *more* and larger elites with jurisdiction over more social functions. We can test this hypothesis by seeing whether more problems requiring collective action are denned in societies with expanded elite education, and by seeing whether the management of such problems is more likely to be reserved to educated elites in such societies.

3 Mass education expands the national culture. Both elites and masses, in societies with more mass education, should be more likely to perceive widespread literacy, attention to public

problems, information, and involvement. This should hold true even when the actual levels of these variables are held constant. Mass education is an institution, and like all institutions creates forms of pluralistic ignorance: it supports the widespread social assumption of an informed and attentive public. In expanding the national culture, mass education also creates and expands the assumption of homogeneity. In societies with more mass education, both masses and elites should be found to perceive more common interests and ideas in the population and less conflict and diversity. This should hold even when actual diversity is held constant.

4   Mass education, similarly, expands citizenship, both in size and content. Elites, in societies with more mass education, should be found to perceive masses as making more demands, having more rights, and posing more threats than in other societies. Elites planning new regimes in such societies should be found to employ more strategies of control through mobilization rather than through traditional authoritarianism. They should also attend to the creation and manipulation of "public opinion." Mass education may be one of the elements supporting the modern "activist" version of the classic military coup and regime. Again, one can study such a process comparatively, with survey data, or experimentally (presenting subjects with hypothetical societies).

These research suggestions make clear the nature of legitimation effects: Modern educational systems formally reconstruct, reorganize, and expand the socially defined categories of personnel and of knowledge in society. They expand and rationalize the social realities that enter into the choices of the socialized and the unsocialized, the allocated and the unallocated. Education is, as has often been noted, a secular religion in modern societies: as religions do, it provides a legitimating account of the competence of citizens, the authority of elites, and the sources of the adequacy of the social system to maintain itself in the face of uncertainty.[10]

The Impact of Educational Legitimation on Allocation and Socialization

The socializing impact of education as an institution is discussed above (Propositions 5 and 6) in the review of the allocation theory version of the larger idea of legitimation. The intervening discussions make necessary two extensions in the arguments presented there:

1. It is now clear that rules of educational allocation are not simply arbitrary social constructions which happen to have power over people. These rules are part of the basic institutional ideology of modern society: they represent equity, progress, and technical sophistication. As part of a larger institutional system, that is, the rules of educational allocation are highly *legitimate*, not merely instances of the exercise of power. This legitimacy intensifies the operation of rules of educational allocation, and intensifies the effects of these rules on individuals being socialized and allocated:

Proposition 11. The more institutionalized the modern system of education, the more intensified the causal relationships of allocation and socialization.

Educational allocation rules become more common, and their socializing consequences increase in intensity, under conditions of high educational institutionalization. The lagged socialization of the allocated (Proposition 6) becomes, not simply an adaptation to their increased power, but an affirmation of their authority and an account of a legitimate moral biography. Similarly, the process by which students acquire chartered qualities (Proposition 5) takes on additional meaning because of its legitimacy. Students and nonstudents are learning more than their own futures. They are also learning that the practical categories and topics of education give legitimate meaning to these futures (see also Bowles and Gintis 1976). For instance, the college student learns a little sociology because he is taught it (traditional socialization) and because he knows graduates may be expected to know a bit about it (chartering). Both processes are intensified by the legitimating reality of sociology: students (and nonstudents) learn that it *exists* as a body of knowledge and a personnel category, entirely over and above their personal acceptance of the utility of the field. Thus students acquire their sociology with a dutiful passivity which reflects the understanding that whether or not they accept this discipline, their degrees—valid throughout society—will reflect so many units of sociology.

Thus the objectified moral authority of the schools—over and above their raw power—undoubtedly intensifies socialization over and above that found in routine *training* organizations (Bidwell and Vreeland 1963).

2. In broader versions of institutional theory than allocation ideas, the effects of education are no longer fixed in sum: education may expand and alter the role structure of society. This means that there is no reason to believe that the socializing effects of allocation rules would be fixed in sum as is implied by hypotheses 1–3 above, in "Further Implications of Allocation Theory." If education expands the status order, anticipatory gains for students and their socialization consequences do not need to be balanced by losses for nonstudents. The new roles being created can simply be added to the status structure and to the socialization process. More commonly, the creation of a given new elite role also creates expanded rights and duties for others. Thus the expansion of medical authority in modern societies involves creating and expanding the role of doctor. But other people do not simply become nondoctors—they become patients. Education expands roles and sets them into proper relation with the rest of the society.

Once institutionalized education is seen as a legitimating system—not just a mechanism for allocating fixed opportunities—it can have many net consequences on both allocation and socialization of people being processed, just as on the rest of society.

The Impact of Educational Legitimation on Educational Organizations

The legitimating effect of educational organizations—but also much of their socializing and allocating power—is derived from their highly institutionalized status in society. Operating at the institutional level as an authoritative theory of personnel and knowledge in society, the schools constitute a crucial ritual system: a system of initiation ceremonies (personnel) and of classifications of information (knowledge).

This makes it clear why schools often seem to act as ritual organizations, sacrificing "effectiveness" for classificatory rigidity (Meyer and Rowan 1975; Kamens 1977). Their larger social effectiveness (and their claim to resources) inheres precisely in this ritual structure: the apparatus of classes and levels and degrees and subjects. By emphasizing their formal ritual structures, schools maximize their links to their main source of authority, their main resources, and quite possibly their main effectiveness. Dramatizing their structures as socially legitimated and legitimating initiation ceremonies informs students (and others) both about the payoffs to which they can adapt and about the fact that those payoffs are highly proper, deriving from the core meaning and values of society (Clark 1970). Ritualism, thus, by the process stated in Proposition 11, reinforces the immediate effectiveness of schools in dealing with students.

Summary of legitimation theory.—Legitimation theory suggests two general ideas concerning the effects of schooling. First, institutionalized education, as a theory of personnel and knowledge, affects society directly, apart from the training and allocation of students. Second, institutionalized education creates and intensifies the individual effects of socialization and allocation. In Figure 9.4 these two main themes are added to the explanatory structure presented earlier.

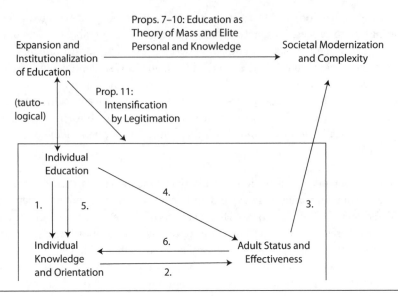

Figure 9.4 Legitimation effects of education.

Conclusion

Schools may teach people useful skills and values. Whether they do or not in particular cases, they certainly *allocate* people to positions of higher social status, and this affects the anticipations and socialization of the students (and nonstudents) as well as the experience and later socialization of the graduates (and nongraduates).

The allocating power of the schools is one aspect of their status as social institutions creating and validating categories of personnel and knowledge. The schools increase the number and legitimacy of these categories—far beyond levels possible with more primordial myths of the origins of personnel and knowledge—and thus expand the whole rationalized modern social structure. These legitimating effects of schools reconstruct reality for everyone—the schooled and the nonschooled alike. They also intensify the effects of allocating and socializing processes.

So a student is in a position of experiencing (*a*) the immediate socializing organization, (*b*) the fact that this organization has the allocating power to confer status on him, and (*c*) the broader fact that this allocation power has the highest level of legitimacy in society. The education he receives has a very special status and authority: its levels and content categories have the power to redefine him legitimately in the eyes of everyone around him and thus take on overwhelming ceremonial significance.

Research on such questions must examine the effects of education *as an institution*, considering effects of variables quite beyond the level of the classroom, the peer group, or the school as an organization. Either experimentally or with cross-societal (or time series) analyses, we need to consider the contextual effects of variations in the extension and institutionalization of education on the perspectives of students and nonstudents, graduates and nongraduates, citizens and elites. If education is a myth in modern society, it is a powerful one. The effects of myths inhere, not in the fact that individuals believe them, but in the fact that they "know" everyone else does, and thus that "for all practical purposes" the myths are true. We may all gossip privately about the uselessness of education, but in hiring and promoting, in consulting the various magi of our time, and in ordering our lives around contemporary rationality, we carry out parts in a drama in which education is authority.

Notes

1. Socialization researchers, of course, continue to pursue the grail, looking for new properties of individual socialization that are stable and that do effectively predict long-run success. The search has been going on for a long time,
2. A number of ideas have been suggested in defense of traditional theory: (1) we have not yet found or measured the relevant aspects of school structure; (2) schools tend to be random collections of teachers and thus to appear alike even though teaching is of great importance; (3) on the relevant properties—normative commitment and organization, or simply the time devoted to various topics—most schools in a country are very similar and thus have similar effects. I pursue a related, but more general, line below.
3. Intervening variables in all these effects would include the expectations of the students and those of their parents, teachers, counselors, and peers.
4. Actors may also internalize these rules as personal commitments, but this is less important—the critical aspect is that they internalize them as social facts and social realities (institutions which rely on personal beliefs, or even permit the question of personal beliefs to be relevant in social action, are less highly legitimated in important senses than are those which operate as realities).
5. The discussion which follows deals exclusively with the *effects* of institutionalized education on other aspects of society. Obviously, important causal effects also run the other way (see Meyer and Rubinson [1975] for a review). Empirically disentangling the reciprocal effects requires data on societies over time.
6. This assertion, incidentally, parallels an idea of Schumpeter (1950, chap. 12) about the way in which the intellectual optimism of modern capitalistic society generates its own institutionalization and destruction. The intellectuals rationalize more and more social functions, which are then brought under collective social and political control and removed from the market.
7. Imagine, for example, the consequences that would flow from the rise of routinely accredited university programs and degrees in astrology. Organizations would incorporate astrologers, the state would fund their programs and consult or incorporate them. Of course a justificatory literature would grow. The same basic processes have gone on with many occupational groups.
8. This proposition is impossible in conceptions of social status as simply a rank position, and thus as fixed in sum. But there is no reason to assume that the total amount of status (or for that matter power) in society is fixed. Independent of their ranks, statuses (and whole status distributions) may vary in the expansion of their substantive rights and powers. I have argued above that education expands the status rights attached to many positions in society, without necessarily altering the rank structure. This conception of status reflects Weber's original formulation.
9. I provide here a conventional list of the putative effects of mass education. But my argument is that, actual effects aside, they enter into social life as taken for granted assumptions. Many Americans are not literate in the national language. But we treat each other, expect elites to treat us, and organize our public life as if we all were. According to proposition 5, the existence of these effects as social assumptions greatly increases the likelihood that the schools actually produce them.
10. Modern education not only expands each society structurally; it also brings societies into closer organizational similarity with each other. Societies come to be made up of more and more similar elites—often in professional communication with each other—and masses with more and more shared social rights. This organizational homogeneity means that information—and exploitation—can proceed very rapidly. New ideas and techniques are not *alien*. They are the stock-in-trade of an already incorporated profession and can thus be adopted with less resistance. So, in the modern world, the presence of locally controlled, but organizationally similar, educational systems in almost all nation-states makes possible the rapid cultural penetration of techniques (and political revolution). And it makes possible new kinds of dependence (e.g., a "brain drain").

References

Alexander, K., and B. Eckland. 1975. "Contextual Effects in the High School Attainment Process." *American Sociological Review* 40 (June): 402–16.

Almond, G., and S. Verba. 1963. *The Civic Culture*. Princeton, N.J.: Princeton University Press.

Astin, A., and R. Panos. 1969. *The Educational and Vocational Development of College Students*. Washington, D.C.: American Council on Education.

Bendix, R. 1964. *Nation-Building and Citizenship*. New York: Wiley.

Benitez, J. 1973. "The Effect of Elite Recruitment and Training on Diffuse Socialization Outcomes." Doctoral dissertation, Stanford University.

Berg, I. 1971. *Education and Jobs*. Boston: Beacon.

Bergesen, A. 1977, "Political Witch Hunts: The Sacred and the Subversive in Cross-National Perspective." *American Sociological Review* 42 (April): 220–33.

Bidwell, C., and R. Vreeland. 1963. "College Education and Moral Orientations." *Administrative Science Quarterly* 8 (September): 166–91.

Blau, P. M., and O. D. Duncan. 1967. *The American Occupational Structure*. New York: Wiley.

Blaug, M., ed. 1968, 1969. *Economics of Education*. Baltimore: Penguin.

Boli-Bennett, J. 1976. "The Expansion of Constitutional Authority in Nation-States, 1870–1970: A Quantitative Assessment." Paper read at the annual meeting of the Pacific Sociological Association, San Diego, April. Mimeographed. Stanford, Calif.: Department of Sociology, Stanford University.

Bowles, S., and H. Gintis. 1976. *Schooling in Capitalist America*. New York: Basic.

Carnoy, M., ed. 1972. *Schooling in a Corporate Society*. New York: McKay.

Clark, B. 1970. "The College as Saga: Historical Inquiry in the Sociology of Education." Paper read at the annual meeting of the American Sociological Association, Washington, D.C., August. Mimeographed. New Haven, Conn.: Department of Sociology, Yale University.

Coleman, J., ed. 1965. *Education and Political Development*. Princeton, N.J.: Princeton University Press.

Collins, R. 1971. "Functional and Conflict Theories of Educational Stratification." *American Sociological Review* 36 (December): 1002–18.

Coombs, P. 1968. *The World Educational Crisis*. New York: Oxford University Press.

Davis, J. A. 1966. "The Campus as a Frog Pond." *American Journal of Sociology* 72 (July): 17–31.

Duncan, O. D., D. L. Featherman, and B. Duncan. 1972. *Socioeconomic Background and Achievement*. New York: Seminar.

Feldman, K. A., and T. H. Newcomb. 1969. *The Impact of College on Students*. San Francisco: Jossey-Bass.

Garfinkel, Harold. 1956. "Conditions of Successful Degradation Ceremonies." *American Journal of Sociology* 61 (March): 420–24.

Habermas, J. 1962. *Structurwandel der Öffentlichkeit*. Koblenz: Neuwied.

Himmelweit, H., and B. Swift. 1969. "A Model for the Understanding of School as a Socializing Agent." Pp. 154–81 in *Trends and Issues in Developmental Psychology*, edited by P. Mussen, J. Langer, and M. Covington. New York: Holt, Rinehart & Winston.

Holsinger, D. 1974. "The Elementary School as Modernizer: A Brazilian Study." Pp. 24–46 in *Education and Individual Modernity in Developing Countries*, edited by A. Inkeles and D. Holsinger. Leiden: Brill.

Igra, A. 1976. "Social Mobilization, National Context, and Political Participation." Doctoral dissertation, Stanford University.

Illich, I. 1971. *Deschooling Society*. New York: Harper & Row.

Inkeles, A., and D. H. Smith. 1974. *Becoming Modern: Individual Change in Six Developing Countries*. Cambridge, Mass.: Harvard University Press.

Jencks, C., et al. 1972. *Inequality: A Reassessment of the Effect of Family and Schooling in America*. New York: Basic.

Kamens, D. 1971. "The College 'Charter' and College Size: Effects on Occupational Choice and College Attrition." *Sociology of Education* 44 (Summer): 270–96.

———. 1974. "Colleges and Elite Formation: The Case of Prestigious American Colleges." *Sociology of Education* 47 (Summer), 354–78.

———. 1977. "Legitimating Myths and Educational Organization: The Relationship between Organizational Ideology and Formal Structure." *American Sociological Review* 42 (April): 208–19.

Kerckhoff, A. C. 1975. "Patterns of Educational Attainment in Great Britain." *American Journal of Sociology* 80 (May): 1428–37.

Kohn, M. 1969. *Class and Conformity: A Study in Values*. Homewood, Ill.: Dorsey.

Marshall, T. H. 1948. *Citizenship and Social Class*. New York: Doubleday.

Meyer, J. 1970a. "The Charter: Conditions of Diffuse Socialization in Schools." Pp. 564–78 in *Social Processes and Social Structures*, edited by W. R. Scott. New York: Holt, Rinehart & Winston.

———. 1970b. "High School Effects on College Intentions." *American Journal of Sociology* 76 (July): 59–70.

———. 1973. "Theories of the Effects of Education on Civic Participation in Developing Societies." *SEADAG Papers Series*. New York: Asia Society.

Meyer, J., and B. Rowan. 1975. "Notes on the Structure of Educational Organizations." Paper read at the annual meeting of the American Sociological Association, San Francisco, August. Mimeographed. Stanford, Calif.: Department of Sociology, Stanford University.

Meyer, J., and R. Rubinson. 1975. "Education and Political Development." *Review of Research in Education*, vol. 3, pp. 134–62.

Mischel, W. 1971. *Introduction to Personality*. New York: Holt, Rinehart & Winston.

Plant, W. 1965. "Longitudinal Changes in Intolerance and Authoritarianism for Subjects Differing in Amount of College Education over Four Years." *Genetic Psychology Monographs* 72 (November): 247–87.

Ramirez, F. 1973. "Societal Corporateness and the Nationalization and Expansion of Educational Systems." Paper read at the annual meeting of the American Sociological Association, New York, August. Mimeographed. Stanford, Calif.: Department of Sociology, Stanford University.

———. 1975. "Creating Members: A Longitudinal Cross-national Analysis." Paper read at the Comparative and International Education Society meeting, San Francisco, March. Mimeographed. San Francisco: Department of Sociology, San Francisco State University.

Rosenbaum, J. 1975. "The Stratification of Socialization Processes." *American Sociological Review* 40 (February): 48–54.

Rubinson, R. 1973. "The Political Construction of Education: Conditions for the Creation of Membership in Political Society." Paper read at the annual meeting of the American Sociological Association, New York, August. Mimeographed. Stanford, Calif.: Department of Sociology, Stanford University.

Schumpeter, J. 1950. *Capitalism, Socialism and Democracy*. New York: Harper.

Spence, M. 1973. "Job Market Signalling." *Quarterly Journal of Economics* 87 (August): 355–75.

Stinchcombe, A. 1968. *Constructing Social Theories*. New York: Harcourt.

Swanson, G. 1971. "An Organizational Analysis of Collectivities." *American Sociological Review* 36 (August): 607–23.

Thompson, J. D. 1967. *Organizations in Action*. New York: McGraw-Hill.

Thurow, L. 1975. *Generating Inequality*. New York: Basic.

Wallace, W. L. 1966. *Student Culture: Social Structure and Continuity in a Liberal Arts College*. Chicago: Aldine.

Wheeler, S. 1966. "The Structure of Formally Organized Socialization Settings." In *Socialization after Childhood*, edited by O. G. Brian, Jr., and S. Wheeler. New York: Wiley.

PART I

Suggested Readings

Aronowitz, S. and Giroux, H. (1991). *Postmodern education: Politics, culture and social criticism*. Minneapolis, MN: University of Minnesota Press.

Barton, L. (2006). *Education and society: 25 years of the British Journal of Sociology of Education*. Oxford: Routledge.

Bernstein, B. (1971). On the classification and framing of educational knowledge. In B. Bernstein, *Class, Codes, and Control* (Vol. 1, pp. 202–230, and Vol. 2, pp. 85–115). London: Routledge & Kegan Paul. (Original published in M. F. D. Young (Ed.), *Knowledge and control: New directions for the sociology of education*. London: Collier-Macmillan.)

Bernstein, B. (1977). Class and pedagogies: Visible and invisible (rev. ed.). In B. Bernstein, *Class, codes and control* (Vol. 3, pp. 116–156). London: Routledge & Kegan Paul.

Bernstein, B. (1986). On pedagogic discourse. In J. G. Richardson (Ed.), *Handbook for theory and research in the sociology of education* (pp. 205–240). New York: Greenwood. (Revised and reprinted in B. Bernstein (1990), *The structuring of pedagogic discourse* (*Class, codes and control*, Vol. 4, pp. 165–218). London: Routledge.)

Bourdieu, P. (1973). Cultural reproduction and social reproduction. In R. Brown (Ed.), *Knowledge, education, and cultural change* (pp. 71–112). London: Tavistock.

Bourdieu, P. (1973). *Outline of a theory of practice*. Cambridge, UK: Cambridge University Press.

Bourdieu, P. (1984). *Distinction: A social critique of the judgment of taste*. Cambridge, MA: Harvard University Press.

Bourdieu, P. (1986). The forms of capital. In J. G. Richardson (Ed.), *Handbook of theory and research for the sociology of education* (pp. 241–258). Westport, CT: Greenwood Press.

Bourdieu, P. & Passeron, J. C. (1977). *Reproduction in education, society and culture*. London: Sage.

Bowles, S. & Gintis, H. (1976). *Schooling in capitalist America*. New York: Basic Books.

Cole, M. (2007). *Marxism and educational theory: Origins and issues*. Oxford: Routledge.

Coleman, J. S. (1988). Social capital in the creation of human capital. *American Journal of Sociology*, 94 (Supplement), S95–S120.

Coleman, J. S. (1990). *Foundations of social theory*. Cambridge, MA: Belknap Press of Harvard University Press.

Coleman J. S., Campbell, E. Q., Hobson, C. J., McPartland, J., Mood, A. J., Weinfeld, F. D., & York, R. L. (1966) *Equality of educational opportunity*. Washington: USGPO [The Coleman Report].

Collins, R. (1971). Functional and conflict theories of educational stratification. *American Sociological Review*, 36 (6), 1002–1019.

Collins, R. (1975). *Conflict sociology*. New York: Academic Press.

Collins, R. (1978). *The credential society*. New York: Academic Press.

Davies, S. (1995). Leaps of faith: Shifting currents in critical sociology of education. *American Journal of Sociology*, 100 (6), 1448–1478.

Dreeben, R. (1994). The sociology of education: Its development in the United States. In A. M. Pallas (Ed.), *Research in sociology of education and socialization* (Vol. 10, pp. 7–52). Greenwich, CT: JAI Press.

Durkheim, E. (1956). *Education and sociology*. New York: Free Press.

Durkheim, E. (1962). *Moral education*. New York: Free Press.

Durkheim, E. (1977). *The evolution of educational thought* (P. Collins, Trans.). London: Routledge & Kegan Paul.

Giroux, H. (1981). *Ideology, culture and the process of schooling*. Philadelphia, PA: Temple University Press.

Giroux, H. (1983). *Theory and resistance in education*. South Hadley, MA: Bergin & Garvey.

Giroux, H. (1991). *Postmodernism, feminism, and cultural politics: Redrawing educational boundaries*. Albany, NY: SUNY Press.

Goffman, E. (1959). *The presentation of self in everyday life*. Garden City, NY: Doubleday.

Goffman, E. (1961). *Asylums*. Garden City, NY: Doubleday.

Goffman, E. (1963). *Stigma*. Englewood Cliffs, NJ: Prentice Hall.

Kingston, P. W. (2001). The unfulfilled promise of cultural capital theory. *Sociology of Education*, 74 (Extra Issue), 88–99.

Marx, K. (1971). *The poverty of philosophy*. New York: International Publishers.

Marx, K. and Engels, F. (1947). *The German ideology*. New York: International Publishers. (Originally published 1846.)

Meyer, J. (1977). The effects of education as an institution. *American Journal of Sociology*, 83 (1), 55–77.

Meyer, J. & Rowan, B. (1977). The structure of educational organizations. In M. Meyer & Associates (Eds.), *Environments and organizations* (pp. 78–109). San Francisco: Jossey-Bass.

Meyer, J. & Rowan, B. (1978). Institutionalized organizations: Formal structure as myth and ceremony. *American Journal of Sociology*, 83, 340–363.

Parsons, T. (1959). The school as a social system. *Harvard Educational Review*, 29, 297–318.

Pickering, W. S. F. (2009). *Durkheim: Essays on morals and education*. New York: Routledge.

Riehl, C. (2001). Bridges to the future: Contributions of qualitative research to the sociology of education. *Sociology of Education*, 74 (Extra Issue), 115–134.

Rist, R. (1970). Student social class and teacher expectations: The self fulfilling prophecy in ghetto education. *Harvard Education Review*, 40, 411–451.

Rist, R. (1973). *The urban school: Factory for failure*. Cambridge, MA: MIT Press.

Rist, R. (1977). On understanding the processes of schooling: The contributions of labeling theory. In J. Karabel & A. H. Halsey (Eds.), *Power and ideology in education* (pp. 292–305). New York: Oxford University Press.

Sadovnik, A. R. (1991). Basil Bernstein's theory of pedagogic practice: A structuralist approach. *Sociology of Education*, 64 (1), 48–63.

Sadovnik, A. R. (Ed.). (1995). *Knowledge and pedagogy: The sociology of Basil Bernstein*. Norwood, NJ: Ablex Publishing Corporation.

Sadovnik, A. R. (1995). Postmodernism and the sociology of education: Closing the rift among scholarship, research, and practice. In G. Noblit and W. Pink (Eds.). *Continuity and contradiction: The futures of the sociology of education*. Cresskill, NJ: Hampton Press.

Swartz, D. (1997). *Culture and power: The sociology of Pierre Bourdieu*. Chicago, IL: University of Chicago Press.

Weber, M. (1978). *Economy and society*, Volumes 1 and 2 (G. Roth and C. Wittich, Eds.). Berkeley, CA: University of California Press.

Weber, M. (2000). The rationalization of education and training. In R. Arum and I. Beattie (Eds.), *The structure of schooling*. Mountain View, CA: Mayfield.

Wexler, P. (1987). *Social analysis: After the new sociology*. London: Routledge & Kegan Paul.

Wexler, P. (1996). *Holy sparks: Social theory, education, and religion*. New York: St. Martin's Press.

Wexler, P. (2007). *Symbolic movement: Critique and spirituality in sociology of education*. Rotterdam: Sense Publishers.

Wexler, P. (2008). *Social theory in education primer*. New York: Peter Lang.

Young, M. F. D. (1971). *Knowledge and control: New directions for the sociology of education*. London: Collier-Macmillan.

Young, M. F. D. (2007). *Bringing knowledge back in: From social constructivism to social realism in the sociology of education*. Oxford: Routledge.

School Organization and Processes: Teaching, Learning and Curriculum

Sociologists of education analyze the way school organization and processes affect teaching and learning. The readings in Part II examine school organization and processes and focus on the relationship among teaching, learning and curriculum.

Chapter 10, "The Organizational Context of Teaching and Learning: Changing Theoretical Perspectives" by the University of Wisconsin sociologist Adam Gamoran and his colleagues Walter G. Secada and Cora B. Marrett, provides an overview of different theoretical perspectives on the organization of teaching and learning.

Chapter 11, "Is There Really a Teacher Shortage?" by the University of Pennsylvania sociologist Richard Ingersoll, provides an analysis of the alleged teacher shortage and sociological explanations of teacher supply and demand. Ingersoll examines the organizational conditions of teaching and how these relate to teacher shortages.

Chapter 12, "Whose Markets, Whose Knowledge?" by the University of Wisconsin educational theorist Michael W. Apple, provides a conflict perspective on the struggles over curriculum in the United States and how neo-conservatives and neo-liberals have dominated public discourse over the past two decades.

Questions for Reflection and Discussion

1   According to Gamoran and his colleagues, how do sociologists of education analyze the organizational contexts of teaching and learning? How do school organization and processes affect teaching and learning? If you were to reorganize your college or university to better educate its students, what insights from this article would you apply?

2   According to Richard Ingersoll, is there a teacher shortage? If there is, is the problem a supply problem or is it related to other factors inside schools? Based on his article, what policies would you implement to staff difficult-to-staff districts in urban and rural areas? What changes would you make in schools to increase retention of teachers?

3   How does Michael Apple view the organization and content of the school curriculum? Whose interests does he see reflected in what is taught? How does he see the role of different social, economic, political, and religious groups in the shaping of curriculum? How would functionalists respond to Apple's argument? How would Randall Collins?

10

The Organizational Context of Teaching and Learning

Changing Theoretical Perspectives

ADAM GAMORAN, WALTER G. SECADA, AND CORA B. MARRETT

Sociologists have a predilection for the collective. We are centrally concerned with social facts, characteristics of collectivities that give shape and motivation to individual action. Sociological research on schooling shares this interest in the collective. School resources, composition, climate, leadership, and governance, all collective attributes of schools, are often looked to as sources of influence on the outcomes of schooling for individual students.

Yet the study of school organization is marked more by failure than by success. It is especially significant that the most important contribution by sociologists to research on schooling—the famous Coleman Report of 1966—is also the most spectacular failure to connect the collective with the individual in an educational setting. Variation in school conditions was largely unrelated to differences in student outcomes, as school-level effects were dwarfed by the powerful influence of the home environment for student learning. Though policymakers drew implications from the positive impact on learning of the proportion of white students in a school, the effect of racial composition was small compared to the great importance of individual family background factors. This pattern of results, emphasizing the individual over the collective despite the sociologist's predilection for the opposite, was only to be expected given that over 80% of the variation in student learning occurs within schools, not between schools. If most of the variation in learning is internal to schools, then schoolwide characteristics cannot explain a large proportion of the variation in learning.

Despite these limitations, efforts to study school organization and student learning persist. School climate is a popular term for the normative environment of schools, and hundreds of studies have tried to document an association between climate and student learning (Anderson, 1982). Yet findings for school climate research have been weak and inconsistent, and recent authors, pointing to substantial variation within schools in perceived climate, have questioned whether the concept is meaningful (Pallas, 1988). Studies in the effective schools tradition also emphasized collective properties of schools, such as goals, leadership, and disciplinary environment (e.g., Edmonds, 1979). Although researchers have consistently reported associations between these conditions and students' achievement, this research tradition has been challenged for a lack of rigor and systematic focus in its investigations and a lack of attention to possible mechanisms through which school characteristics are supposed to influence student learning (Barr & Dreeben, 1983; Purkey & Smith, 1983).

More recent and empirically promising studies of schools and student learning also neglect important linkages. Research that documents the achievement advantages of Catholic schools has identified students' academic course taking as a key mechanism, but it is not clear whether this mechanism operates primarily at the individual or the collective level (Bryk, Lee, & Holland, 1993; Coleman &

Hoffer, 1987). A study of city high schools reported higher achievement in magnet schools than in comprehensive schools, but could not say what it was about magnet schools that led to higher achievement (Gamoran, 1996c). Research on restructured schools indicated that schoolwide restructuring may aid achievement, but many questions remain concerning what, exactly, is effective about restructuring and how school structure is linked with student learning (Lee & Smith, 1995, 1996, 1997; Newmann & Associates, 1996).

In this article, we respond to current limitations in the study of school organization and student learning. First, we take stock of research on school organization in greater detail. Second, we propose a new way of looking at the relation between the school's organizational context on the one hand, and the activities of teaching and learning on the other. Third, we present some different scenarios for teaching and learning activities and show how the organizational context of the school may play a different role in each case. Finally, we discuss the challenges of empirically verifying this new model of the organizational context of teaching and learning.

School Effects: From the Black Box to Nested Layers

Early studies of the impact of schools on student learning were exemplified by Coleman and colleagues' (1966) landmark research on equality of educational opportunity. Coleman and his colleagues estimated an economic production function in which student learning is an output that responds to various economic inputs such as expenditures, facilities, equipment, and background characteristics of teachers. In this model, the school is an unopened black box. What goes on inside the school—the production process itself—is not observed. If the production process were straightforward and predictable, the input–output production function would be a sensible way to study the impact of school resources. Yet the process of teaching and learning is complex and not fully routinized. Input–output studies do not reveal much about the effects of schools because so much depends on how the resources are used, and the use of resources is not included in the usual production function.

Scholars, educators, and politicians alike were surprised to discover that for the most part, variation in school resources bore little direct relation to variation in students' achievement, once background differences among students were taken into account (Coleman et al., 1966; Hodgson, 1975). This finding was reconfirmed in extensive reanalyses (Hanushek, 1994; Jencks et al., 1972; Mosteller & Moynihan, 1972). Most recently, a meta-analysis suggested that average resources do matter for student learning (Greenwald, Hedges, & Laine, 1996; see Hanushek, 1997, for a critique). Moreover in developing countries, where levels of resources such as trained teachers, textbooks, and facilities vary widely, the link between such resources and students' achievement tends to be stronger than it is in the United States and in other developed countries (Fuller, 1987; Fuller & Clarke, 1994; Heyneman & Loxley, 1983). In any case, it is clear that the relation between resources and outcomes is inconsistent—sometimes positive, sometimes negative, and sometimes absent—and the question of how to use resources effectively is much more important than whether average resources matter for average outcomes.

Opening the Black Box: The Nested Layers Approach

During the 1980s, sociologists of education began to open the black box of schools by studying the processes through which learning occurs. Bidwell and Kasarda (1980) distinguished between the effects of schools, the organizational context for teaching and learning, and schooling—the experiences students have in school that actually produce learning. According to this view, schools set the conditions for schooling, so that the influence of schools as organizations is always mediated by their impact on the schooling process. In this formulation, one understands the effects of schools by tracing the impact of school conditions on schooling activities and then by examining the connection between schooling activities and student learning.

Barr and Dreeben (1983) elaborated on this approach by exploring the organizational linkages among the different structural levels of school systems. In their view, outputs at one level of the organizational hierarchy (e.g., the school) become the inputs at the next level (e.g., the classroom). For example, school administrators allocate time to classroom teachers, make decisions within classrooms about how to use time, and instructional time allows teachers to cover the curriculum, which promotes student learning (Gamoran & Dreeben, 1986). This nested layers approach opened up the black box of schooling and focused attention on the technology of schooling, that is, the processes of teaching and learning within classrooms.

The theoretical foundation for the nested layers model was laid by Parsons (1963), who distinguished between the technical, managerial, and institutional levels of organization, and argued that influences tend to flow across adjacent levels. In Parsons' scheme, resource allocation was a managerial activity, and the outputs of this activity affected processes at the technical level, which in schools consists of teaching and learning. Barr and Dreeben (1983) provided concrete specification of resources allocated at the managerial level (time and materials) and activities occurring in the technical level (coverage of curricular content).

The notion of nested layers offered a valuable conceptual advance over previous work, and it has achieved some empirical success as well. Studies of the flow of resources, most notably time for instruction, show that allocations from the district and school to the classroom set constraints on teaching, which in turn influences student learning (Gamoran & Dreeben, 1986; Monk, 1992). In their analysis, Barr and Dreeben (1983) took advantage of the statistical technique of path analysis, widely known to sociologists since Blau and Duncan's (1967) seminal work on social stratification, but not previously used to examine the inner workings of school systems. Using a path model, Barr and Dreeben provided empirical documentation of the flow of resources and activities from school to classroom, from classroom to instructional group, and from group to individual student. The logic of path analysis is also evident in nested layers analyses by Alexander and Cook (1982), Rowan and Miracle (1983), Gamoran and Dreeben (1986), and others.

The nested layers model appears to have correctly identified the connections between resource allocation and the technology of teaching. However, efforts to examine a wider spectrum of school conditions have yielded inconsistent results for the nested layers model. For example, not all subjects and grade levels indicate that curricular allocations exert strong influences on student learning. Doyle (1992), summarizing the literature on the impact of curriculum on pedagogy, concluded that "curriculum is a weak force for regulating teaching" (p. 488). Although teachers tend to cover the topics reflected in the formal curriculum, they use their own discretion and may vary widely in teaching methods, in time devoted to various topics, in modes of assessment, and so on (Barr & Sadow, 1989; Freeman & Porter, 1989; Stodolsky, 1988). These findings derive from the United States, but in other countries where high-stakes tests are more closely linked to prescribed curricula, the effects of curricular allocations on teaching practices may be stronger (Stevenson & Baker, 1991; Gamoran, 1996a).

Moreover, researchers have had difficulty showing that features of schools other than resources allocated for instruction have any bearing on student learning. For example, Gamoran (1987) examined a range of high school characteristics in an attempt to identify organizational conditions that influence learning by setting the conditions for students' instructional experiences. Although Gamoran observed strong relations between instructional experiences (e.g., coursetaking) and achievement, these associations were largely unrelated to school characteristics (e.g., student body composition, availability of academic programs). Other studies of school effects have been similarly unsuccessful in tracing the influence of organizational conditions through instructional experiences to student learning (e.g., Gahng, 1993; Gamoran, Porter, & Gahng, 1995). Researchers have uncovered important effects of different types of schools, such as Catholic schools (Bryk et al., 1993; Coleman & Hoffer, 1987) and magnet schools (Gamoran, 1996c), but the organizational conditions that mattered tended to be aggregate indicators of students' instructional experiences, such as extensive academic coursetaking and orderly classrooms. Research on school types thus supports the conclusion that instructional conditions affect student learning but offers less evidence about organizational influences on instructional conditions.

Recent studies of schools and student learning have focused less on the organizational constraints of material resources and shifted the emphasis toward organizational structures and processes such as leadership, collaboration, and efficacy among educators in a school. This literature builds on the effective schools tradition (e.g., Edmonds, 1979; Purkey & Smith, 1983) that emphasized key conditions at the school level including goal consensus, high expectations for student learning, principal leadership, emphasis on basic skills, and monitoring of students' progress. Like the effective schools tradition, several recent studies show consistent associations between organizational conditions and student learning. For example, Bryk and Driscoll (1988) observed a strong positive association between students' achievement in mathematics and an index of school community—whether teachers worked together, whether the principal supported the teachers' work, and so on. Similarly, Lee and Smith (1995, 1996) showed that students' achievement is higher in high schools in which teachers perceive a greater sense of efficacy and responsibility for student learning and in schools where educators have engaged in restructuring activities, such as team teaching, changing the grouping structure, flexible scheduling, and so on.

This body of work, from research on effective schools to studies of restructuring, is limited by ambiguity in causal mechanisms and even in causal direction. If high expectations are associated with high achievement, for example, which causes which? Research on effective schools gave little attention to the actual mechanisms through which school conditions are translated into achievement. How were expectations elevated, goal consensus achieved, and so on, and how were these conditions linked to student learning? These questions were not addressed.

Current work has implicitly adopted the nested layers view as a conceptual framework. That is, the organizational context is assumed to influence student learning by constraining conditions for classroom instruction. In this framework, social conditions such as a strong sense of community promote adherence to an academic mission among teachers, which leads to enhanced teaching and greater learning. Despite the clearer conception of mechanisms, causal ambiguity remains problematic. For example, Lee and Smith (1996) argued that students achieve more when their teachers accept collective responsibility for students' learning. Lee and Smith supported their claim by showing an association between teachers' sense of responsibility and student learning. In fact, however, the causal process could run in the opposite direction: Teachers may be more apt to accept responsibility in schools where levels of learning are high.

In a study of mathematics reform, Adajian (1995) showed that teachers who participated in schoolwide professional communities engaged in more innovative mathematics teaching, including an emphasis on problem solving and on hands-on applications. This finding is consistent with the notion that a community of teachers encourages instructional innovation, which promotes greater learning. However, it is not clear from Adajian's cross-sectional data whether the professional community led to innovative teaching, or vice versa. Similarly, Lee and Smith (1997) interpreted their analysis of national data to indicate that high levels of academic coursetaking and instructional emphases on problem solving and on inquiry accounted for the benefits of restructured schools over traditionally structured schools. Yet an alternative hypothesis—that innovative instruction may lead to both school restructuring and better learning—cannot be dismissed.

Just as Barr and Dreeben (1983) took advantage of statistical advances in path analysis, current work on the relation between school conditions and student learning has also benefited from new statistical techniques, particularly multilevel modeling (or hierarchical linear modeling). The multilevel approach distinguishes group-level and individual-level effects more accurately than earlier regression methods (Bryk & Raudenbush, 1992; Goldstein, 1995). Multilevel modeling is a particularly elegant method for examining differences between groups in individual-level effects; for example, multilevel methods provide the best evidence that the effect of socioeconomic status on student learning is weaker in Catholic schools than in public schools (Bryk et al., 1993). This finding indicates that achievement is more equitably distributed in Catholic schools. However, the multilevel approach does not address the causal ambiguities of the nested layers model, nor does it offer any special benefits in the quest to identify the mechanisms through which school conditions influence student learning. On the contrary, multilevel analysts often specify individual or classroom conditions such as coursetaking and instruction as aggregate school conditions, missing the opportunity to link school conditions to student learning through the mechanism of individual or classroom-based academic experiences (Bryk et al., 1993: Lee & Smith, 1997).

The nested layers model operates well for instructionally specific resources such as time and materials and for clearly defined teaching activities such as content coverage. It seems particularly appropriate when there are clear norms about the salience of curricular topics, such as early reading instruction. It is not clear that the perspective can be applied to a broader range of school and/or classroom conditions.

The Loose-Coupling Alternative

Whereas Bidwell and Kasarda (1980) and Barr and Dreeben (1983) responded to the failure of the input–output model by specifying more carefully the technical connections between organizational resources, teaching practices, and student learning, other writers emphasized the general absence of tight connections within the school system organization. Earlier, Bidwell (1965) had recognized the structural looseness of schools, and writers such as Weick (1976) and Meyer and Rowan (1977, 1978) expanded this notion to suggest that the structural isolation of classrooms, the autonomy of teachers, and the relative absence of formal authority means that schools are loosely coupled organizations. In a loosely coupled system, decisions occurring in one segment of the organization do not reverberate in clearly patterned ways elsewhere. Thus, what occurs in one classroom may have little impact on another, and decisions made by the principal have only modest effects on what students actually experience (Weick, 1976). According to this view, schools are tightly coupled around symbolic designations such as who gets taught by whom but are loosely coupled on matters of core technology such as what gets taught in the classroom (Meyer & Rowan, 1978). Teaching practices are a result of teacher training and on-the-job socialization and are not affected much by schoolwide conditions such as resources, plans, or administrative decisions (Weick, 1982). Student learning is primarily a response to societal expectations rather than to particular school conditions or to classroom instruction (Meyer, 1977).

The reason schools are loosely coupled, according to this perspective, is that it is difficult to judge their effectiveness using a bureaucratic model of costs and outputs (Meyer & Rowan, 1977, 1978; Weick, 1976). Teaching is an uncertain technology: cause–effect relations are not well understood, and there is no consensus on the best teaching methods. Moreover, the goals of schooling are ambiguous and often conflicting, so it is hard to determine what standards to use for judging schools. Finally, the participants in schools change over time, adding further uncertainty to the complexities of teaching and the ambiguities of goals. Consequently, schools turn away from their technical cores (teaching and learning) and emphasize their symbolic attributes such as categories and certification. In schools, structures are detached from activities, and activities are disconnected from outcomes (Meyer & Rowan, 1978). A logic of confidence allows schools to appear to work when the symbolic trappings of grade-level structures, certified teachers, students progressing from grade to grade, and so on, are present (Meyer & Rowan, 1978). In this way schools avoid inspection of their technical cores and locus on legitimation in the wider society.

Metz (1989) and Hemmings and Metz (1991) provided evidence from a study of eight high schools that is strikingly consistent with the loose-coupling perspective. Despite substantial differences among the eight schools in the characteristics of their communities, all adopted the same set of structures and routines, from the arrangement of classrooms, to the organization of the curriculum, to the allocation of time. These outward attributes articulated each school's legitimacy as a "real school." Despite the similarities, students' experiences could differ dramatically from one school to the next, because students' schooling experiences bore little relation to the symbolic structural features of their schools. Moreover, the acceptance of a real school as an organizational framework limited consideration of alternate arrangements, even when the standard structures and processes were unsuccessful in promoting pupils' progress. According to Metz (1989),

> If one looks at students' learning simply as a technical system, it is quite remarkable to see situations where a technical process (or the social structure which frames it) is clearly not effective on a massive scale, but no one in the organization calls for developing alternative technical or structural approaches, (p. 79)

On the contrary, educators in schools with the least successful students were often the most insistent that their schools reflected the societal consensus on what high schools should look like.

If schools are loosely coupled, what keeps them coupled at all? How is work coordinated in a loosely coupled organization? First, as noted previously, some aspects of schools are tightly coupled: categories such as grade levels and teacher are closely monitored and used to arrange persons and positions (though not activities). Second, according to Weick (1982), teachers' common professional socialization helps coordinate work in schools. Weick argued that "even though (educators) don't communicate much with each other, they can still coordinate their actions because each person can anticipate accurately what the other person is thinking and doing" (1982, p. 675). In fact, common socialization may be the basis for the logic of confidence, that is, unexamined assumptions about who is doing what in their classrooms. For example, fourth-grade teachers may assume that third-grade teachers are introducing concepts on which they will build when they teach the same students in the following year. Similarly, teachers teaching the same subject area in different grades share a common disciplinary socialization that yields a coherent approach to teaching despite the absence of formal mechanisms of coordination (Rowan & Miskel, 1999; Stodolsky & Grossman, 1995). Shared views of subject matter probably reflect both socialization in teacher training programs and broader social definitions of subject-matter characteristics. Several writers have noted that teachers of mathematics and of foreign languages tend to see their subjects as sequentially organized in clear hierarchies, whereas language arts and social studies teachers have more flexible views of their subject matters (Gamoran & Weinstein, 1998; Loveless, 1994; Rowan, Raudenbush, & Cheong, 1993; Stodolsky & Grossman, 1995).

Meyer and Rowan (1978) acknowledged that loose coupling is probably more important in the United States than in many other countries because of the strong American tradition of decentralization and local control over education. Other countries typically have more centralized control over the curriculum, regulated through national testing, which results in tighter alignment between formal goals and outcomes than in the United States (Bishop, 1998). Formal inspections from central authorities, which rarely occur in the United States, may also serve to regulate the practice of teaching (Wilson, 1996). Thus, loose coupling as an explanatory framework may be more successful for the American case than elsewhere. Still, uncertainties that are inherent in teaching raise questions about the tightness of coupling even in more centralized educational systems than that of the United States (Benavot & Resh, 1998).

The loose-coupling model offers a strong challenge to the nested layers approach. Where nested layers is correct for the narrow conditions of resources and content coverage, could loose coupling prevail for other conditions of schooling, such as leadership, relations among teachers and between teachers and students, and so on? Loose coupling would account for the weak and inconsistent impact of school climate on teaching and on learning (Anderson, 1982). It would also explain why policy interventions often fail to reach the classroom, particularly in the United States (e.g., Pressman & Wildavsky, 1979). Further, as Meyer (1977) has argued, loose coupling is consistent with the finding of little variability between schools in student learning alongside substantial variability within schools. By and large, according to this view, schools operate similarly because they are focused on conformity to a common set of societal norms.

Moving beyond the nested layers model to confront the challenge of loose coupling requires a more nuanced analysis of the linkages between school conditions, teaching practices, and student learning. As a starting point, it is essential to rethink common assumptions about causal direction and change and to probe more deeply for the mechanisms that may connect the different elements of school organization.

Beyond Nested Layers

Building on the insights of Rowan (1990) and Newmann and Associates (1996), we suggest that the nested layers approach is limited by its assumption of a one-way relationship between organizational conditions and instructional practices. Rowan argued that when teaching is understood to be a complex, nonroutine activity, organizational support for innovation and success requires an organic relation between teaching practices and school organization, a connection that involves feedback and growth in both directions. The greater the recognition of the uncertainty and complexity of teaching, the more likely organic structures are to emerge. For example, teachers who recognize the complexities of teaching are more prone to form collegial networks for sharing information and mutual support. Rowan buttressed these claims with an insightful review of studies that indicated weak effects of collaboration and collegiality on teaching practices. Instead, organizational structures sometimes grew out of the demands of teaching. For example, Cohen, Deal, Meyer, and Scott (1979) observed that complex instructional tasks contributed to increased communication and teaming among teachers, but team teaching did not bring about complex instruction. Still, Rowan concluded that when collegial relations are intensive and embedded in a culture that emphasizes continuous improvement, the strength and quality of social relations among teachers may influence teaching practices. Although provocative, this conclusion was based on few cases, and Rowan found it difficult to provide evidence that relations among teachers substantially affect how they carry out their work in classrooms. In a subsequent empirical study, Rowan and his colleagues (1993) reported that the more teaching was viewed as a nonroutine activity, the greater the prevalence of organic management in the school. However, organic management did not result in greater amounts of ongoing learning among teachers.

Further support for the notion that organizational support for effective teaching may emerge from teachers' commitment to innovative instructional practices comes from Newmann and Associates' (1996) study of 24 highly restructured schools. This research began with the idea that there are levers at the school site that, when pressed, lead to better teaching and to more learning. What the investigators found, however, was more complex than a simple nested layers story. All 24 schools had innovative structural features, but few exhibited consistent evidence of exceptionally high-quality teaching and learning. The most successful schools were those in which educators were committed to intellectual quality in students' academic experiences and in which this commitment was the driving force behind organizational reforms. For example, teachers at Cibola High School were committed to disciplined inquiry and students' construction of knowledge. They used detracked classes to engage students in project work that resulted in high-quality instruction and high levels of learning. By contrast, teachers at Wallingford High School, who were also committed to detracking, had little notion of how their teaching might change in a detracked context. At Wallingford, researchers observed low-quality teaching and learning, mainly reflected in lectures and in a watered-down curriculum. Thus, detracking as a school organizational characteristic grew out of and supported a particular pedagogy in Cibola, whereas it was unrelated to instruction at Wallingford.

Similar conclusions emerged recently from another major study of school restructuring. Peterson, McCarthey, and Elmore (1996) reported that school structure had little consistent impact on teaching practices. Instead, teaching practices changed in response to teachers' learning, particularly when learning occurred in a community of educators. Teaching practices contributed to school conditions as much as the reverse. The authors concluded the following:

> Changing practice is primarily a problem of [teacher] learning, not a problem of organization. … School structures can provide opportunities for the learning of new teaching practices and new strategies for student learning, but structures, by themselves, do not cause learning to occur. … School structure follows from good practice not vice versa. (p. 149)

Our view of the organizational context of teaching and learning is more closely related to the nested layers model than to loose coupling. As in the nested layers view, and in contrast to loose coupling, we argue that student learning responds to instruction. This notion derives from research that documents the impact of variation in teaching on student learning, ranging from course-taking effects (Gamoran, 1987), to content coverage (Barr & Dreeben, 1983; Gamoran, Porter, Smithson, & White, 1997; Rowman & Miracle, 1983) to instructional coherence and teacher-student interaction (Gamoran, Nystrand, Berends, & LePore, 1995). Also consistent with the nested layers view, we expect that organizational resources affect student learning, but only as they are applied by teachers in classrooms. This aspect of our model has its foundation in research by Barr and Dreeben (1983; see also Gamoran & Dreeben, 1986). These studies showed that resources matter for learning when teachers apply resources in their classroom teaching. However, our model moves beyond the nested layers view in that we recognize that the relation between school conditions and classroom teaching may work in both directions and may shift over time. School conditions may respond to teaching practices, and teaching practices may be constrained or encouraged by their organizational context, as causal effects flow in both directions.

At the same time, our model draws from loose coupling the notion that teaching practices are influenced by professional socialization and training. As Peterson, McCarthey, and Elmore (1996) noted, teachers can learn to change their practice. This conclusion suggests that teachers not only respond to preservice training, as discussed by Weick (1982), but also to professional development that occurs on the job and that is a requirement for maintaining teaching certification in most states. In some cases professional development may be the sort of ritual activity that Meyer and Rowan (1978) recognized as important for legitimation but having little real significance for practice. In other cases, however, Peterson, Elmore, and McCarthey's findings suggest that professional development may result in meaningful change for teachers who participate.

Organizational Resources as the Context for Teaching and for Learning

Before elaborating on the role of professional development, we need to consider what aspects of school organization constitute salient contextual conditions for activities and outcomes. Prior research indicates that organizational resources constitute the most essential elements of the school's organizational context for teaching and for learning (Gamoran & Dreeben, 1986; Kilgore & Pendelton, 1993). We offer a broader conception of organizational resources than is found in most previous studies and as elaborated in the following sections. Resources emphasized by the input–output and the nested layers models are subsumed in our approach, and we also incorporate aspects of the school climate and school effectiveness traditions. Leadership, collaboration, and administrative support, as well as knowledge and skills, are all seen as types of resources that educators can draw on to improve their teaching. Hence, much of the past research on school effects is incorporated into our framework. However, our model does not include all aspects of school context. We focus on three categories of essential resources: material, human, and social. Other recent writers also point to the special salience of these conditions (Anderson, 1996; Newmann, 1998; Spillane & Thompson, 1997).

Material Resources

Despite inconsistent empirical support for the impact of expenditures on students' achievement, material resources constitute an important condition in the organizational context of teaching. Such resources include curriculum materials, equipment, and supplies; time available for teaching, planning and preparation; expenditures for personnel, particularly instructional staff; and the authority to expend funds for other purposes related to teaching and to learning. Material resources have no direct connection to learning because their impact depends on how they are used. Typically, educators at the school level have little discretion over the allocation of funds. According to the study of restructured schools, even when funding decisions are made at the school level, resources may not be used in ways that improve teaching (Newmann & Associates, 1996). However, some schools used resources in ways that improved instruction by allocating extra time for collaboration among teachers, by supporting professional development, and by providing tutoring sessions for students who needed extra help.

A variety of literatures support the conclusion that the effects of material resources are contingent on use. Resources devoted to instruction, not surprisingly, are more likely to pay off for student learning than resources directed in other ways (Newmann & Associates, 1996). Even when resources are allocated toward instructional needs, however, their benefits depend on how they are applied. Reducing class size, for example, may be the most common application of additional resources, yet a research literature consisting of hundreds of studies has yielded widely varying results. As Slavin (1989, 1990) has argued, reducing the number of students in a class is unlikely to yield any differences in student learning unless teachers are engaged in practices that are enhanced by working with fewer students at a time. When teachers carry out standard routines of lecture and recitation, it matters little whether there are 15, 20, or even 30 students in the class. Class size is likely to affect learning when instruction emphasizes more interactive involvement such as project work, extensive writing, and discussion, which may foster more intensive participation and feedback when there are fewer students at hand.

A similar argument can be made about time for instruction, another application of material resources. Generally, the research indicates that more time for teaching results in more learning for students (e.g., Brophy & Good, 1986). The implicit mechanism underlying the findings, as Barr and Dreeben (1983) explained, is a nested layers model: when teachers have more time available, they use it to cover the curriculum more extensively or in greater depth, and this yields enhanced learning for students. However, the pattern is not invariant. For example, when more time is allocated to first-grade teachers, they use it to advance their highest priority, the reading curriculum (Gamoran & Dreeben, 1986). They do not use additional time for other subjects, such as mathematics, science, or social studies (Gamoran, 1988). Thus time, a resource allocated by administrators to teachers, is an essential element in the context of first-grade reading instruction, but it has limited implications for first-grade teaching in other subjects. More generally, the impact of time as an organizational resource clearly depends on how that time is allocated by teachers within classrooms.

Because the impact of resources depends on how the resources are used, control over material resources is also an important consideration. According to one view, because teachers have the closest contact with students, they know best what resources are needed to meet students' needs. This perspective sees teachers as knowledgeable professionals and suggests that the greater teachers' control over the allocation of resources, the more effectively the resources will be used (Gamoran, Porter, &

Gahng, 1995). However, research to date has found little evidence for effects of teacher control over resources on teaching or learning (Park, 1998).

Human Resources

Some perspectives on schooling assume that differences among teachers in how they have been trained or in what they know have little to do with the effects of instruction on learning. Older notions of teacher-proof curricula (see Brophy & Good, 1986) have counterparts in the most extreme view of standards-based reform, which emphasizes standardized curricula as the key to successful teaching and student testing as the means of ensuring that the curriculum is taught (see Borman, Cookson, Sadovnik, & Spade, 1996). The input–output model of schooling similarly ignores the teaching process in considering the production of learning. These views are consistent with a highly bureaucratized model of schooling in which teachers adhere to standard procedures to maximize efficiency (e.g., Callahan, 1962).

Research evidence depicts teaching as an activity that, in some cases, is highly routinized. Jackson (1968) observed that teaching tends to be preactive, or scripted in advance, rather than reactive, or responsive to students. Many writers have documented the extent to which classroom life is dominated by teachers (e.g., Gamoran et al., 1995; Goodlad, 1984; McNeil, 1986). As loose-coupling theorists have shown, this attempted routinization has gaps—points at which teaching may or may not coincide with what students need for learning. Nonetheless, a logic of confidence allows teachers to proceed without being troubled by a mismatch between script and students (Hemmings & Metz, 1991; Meyer & Rowan, 1978).

Recent research on teaching, however, indicates that the logic of confidence does not always prevail and that teachers' knowledge makes a difference in the quality of instruction and, in particular, teachers' abilities to respond to students (Cohen, 1990). Drawing on findings from cognitive science, education researchers posit three types of knowledge that are essential for teaching: pedagogical knowledge, in which teachers know general strategies of teaching; content knowledge, what teachers know about their subject matters; and pedagogical content knowledge, the knowledge of how to teach a particular subject matter in a way that fosters students' understanding (Shulman, 1987). Following this argument, then, we propose that teachers' human resources—their knowledge, skills, and dispositions—constitute an important resource that may shape the quality of their teaching and their students' learning. Studies of teacher knowledge in specific areas of pedagogic content indicate that the implementation of a new instructional approach improves as teachers come to understand it more deeply (Tharp & Gallimore, 1988).

The emphasis on human resources implies a different model of change than that favored by a model focused on material resources. If human resources are important, then teacher development may be a central element of reform activities (Tharp & Gallimore, 1988). Given the high degree of teacher autonomy in the classroom, a perspective that emphasizes teachers' learning over material resources seems especially promising.

Principal leadership is another type of human resource found in schools. Research in the effective schools tradition emphasized leadership, but empirical corroboration for the salience of principal leadership for student learning is weak (Good & Brophy, 1986). A key limitation of this work is its failure to specify the mechanisms by which leadership may stimulate better learning. Current research on leadership emphasizes the principal's role in creating a community with a common purpose (Newmann & Associates, 1996). Successful principals provide a vision that sets forth a particular mission for the school and galvanizes commitment from teachers and from students. At the same time, the principal may be able to select staff members who accept the school's mission. In this way, a principal's leadership may result in a schoolwide instructional emphasis on common goals.

Interestingly, this view of leadership is more compatible with the loose-coupling model than with nested layers. Rather than viewing the allocation of resources as the key mechanism for the impact of leadership, as implied by the nested layers view, this perspective on leadership emphasizes its symbolic attributes, which are central to loose-coupling theory (Meyer & Rowan, 1978). Even though selecting staff is a technical activity, it has symbolic implications when acceptance of a common vision is a chief criterion for selection. According to loose coupling, structure and technical work are weakly connected, but rituals and symbols, including those that define the school's mission in the wider society, play an important role in pulling together and legitimizing the school in its social context. Following this view, principal leadership may affect the work of teachers by shaping a purpose for the school through selection of staff and articulation of a guiding vision.

Social Resources

Our argument about social resources comes neither from loose coupling nor from the nested layers model. Both views stress the isolation and autonomy of teachers within their classrooms, differing in that nested layers studies have shown that material resources allocated to classrooms and used by teachers can affect student learning (e.g., Gamoran & Dreeben, 1986). According to these perspectives there is little to be gained from collegiality among the faculty of a school, except perhaps the pleasures of a friendlier workplace. Similarly, these widely followed theories would lead one to expect few benefits of teacher participation in collective decisions about school policies. According to loose coupling, school policies simply have little relevance for what goes on in classrooms. According to the nested layers view, policy decisions are managerial activities whose impact occurs through the allocation of resources, regardless of how allocative decisions are made. For different reasons, neither perspective supposes that relations among teachers matter for instructional practices.

In contrast, an emerging literature about the social organization of schools suggests that under certain conditions, social relations among educators may profoundly influence teachers' classroom work and thereby affect student learning. As Rowan (1990) explained, when teaching is viewed as complex and interactive, dynamic and changing as opposed to routine, an organic system of management that relies on developing commitment rather than imposing controls may lead to more successful teaching and learning. Organic management means encouraging social relationships of trust, shared responsibility, collective decision making, and common values as mechanisms for bringing about change. When these activities are focused on student learning, they may indeed matter for instruction and for achievement (Newmann & Associates, 1996). Thus, aspects of the social environment of the school, including shared values, collaboration, and collective decision making, constitute social resources on which educators may draw to bolster their teaching.

At the same time, social resources may also emerge from experiences in the practice of teaching. Teachers who refrain from regarding instruction as a standardized, routine activity are faced with the uncertainties of finding successful ways of meeting students' needs. This uncertainty is always present in teaching, but typically it is obscured by the logic of confidence that promotes following prescribed routines that avoid being deflected by students' responses. Recognition of uncertainty may lead teachers to talk with one another—breaking down the usual isolation of teaching—as they search for better solutions to the problems of teaching and learning that appear in their classrooms. These discussions about instruction may strengthen the collective ties among teachers and teachers and in turn may help address their concerns about teaching.

Although Newmann and Associates' (1996) findings are consistent with the view that social resources matter for teaching, an alternate interpretation of the evidence cannot be rejected. Even when social relations among teachers emerge out of practical experience, these social relations may have little bearing on instruction because teachers are autonomous in their classrooms. Under this scenario, social relations would be a correlate of successful teaching but not a causal factor. Research to date cannot adjudicate among the alternative interpretations.

Professional community. One way of characterizing social resources in a school is as a professional community of educators. Several recent writers claim that a strong professional community provides the capacity for improving instruction and ultimately for enhancing student learning. Talbert and McLaughlin (1994) distinguished between professionalism and community: professionalism includes technical knowledge, an ethic of service, and commitment to the profession, and community refers to collaboration and continuous learning among teachers. Their view of professionalism is akin to our notion of human resources, except that they examine the collective, shared presence of technical knowledge, finding that teacher collaboration and learning promote a technical culture in the school. Newmann and Associates (1996) explored the contribution of professional community to authentic pedagogy, an instructional focus on disciplinary content, students' construction of knowledge, and relevance. Professional community, in their view, consists of shared purpose, a collective focus on student learning, collaboration, reflective conversations about teaching, and deprivatized practice (i.e., breaking the usual isolation of teaching by observing one another's teaching). They found more authentic pedagogy in schools with stronger professional communities. Secada and Adajian (1997), using a similar view of professional community but adding collective control over key decisions to the concept, provided a case study of an elementary school that illustrates how one schoolwide professional community helped teachers improve their teaching of mathematics.

Findings from studies of professional community are provocative, but several caveats are in order. First, the studies are based on small samples of schools. Second, particularly in the case of Newmann and Associates (1996), generalization from the evidence is difficult because the schools were selected especially for their unique features. Third, most studies of professional community have implicitly adopted the nested layers view that professional community enhances teaching and thereby improves learning; yet it is also possible that professional community is a by-product of enhanced teaching, rather than a stimulus. Secada and Adajian (1997) suggested that teachers' professional community and instructional practice may affect one another, but their empirical analysis was limited to one causal direction: the influence of professional community an instruction. Similarly, Louis, Kruse, and Marks (1996) acknowledged that the connections between social relations among teachers and classroom instruction are complex:

> [Our analysis] cannot prove that professional community causes teachers to engage in more authentic classroom practice. A skeptic could plausibly argue that teachers who are making efforts to increase authentic pedagogy are more likely to seek support for this difficult task from colleagues, thus creating professional community. (p. 184)

Social capital. We may also think of social resources in a school as a form of social capital. Social capital in a school refers to trust, expectations, shared understandings, and a sense of obligations that may characterize networks of relationships among educators (see Coleman. 1988 for a more general definition). In contrast to schools in which teachers work in isolation, teachers in some schools form relationships with one another around academic concerns of teaching and learning. These social networks constitute resources on which teachers can draw in their efforts to improve teaching (Kilgore & Pendelton, 1993). Collaboration, collegial relations, and opportunities for reflective discussion about teaching help build social capital. In such schools, teachers are likely to work together, even in the classroom; in this way, teaching becomes deprivatized and the typical isolation of teaching is overcome. Administrative support, such as advice and consultation about teaching and school policies, also builds social resources on which teachers can draw. Coleman (1988) explained that social capital can facilitate the development of human capital. In the case of schools, social capital among teachers helps them improve their knowledge and skills (i.e., their human capital) by providing a normative environment that encourages experimentation, offers a place to discuss uncertainties, and rewards improvement. This portrait differs substantially from the standard picture of schools in which teachers' activities are largely unseen by other adults and their unique contributions are unrecognized and unacknowledged.

More broadly, it is important to recognize the potential interplay between material, human, and social resources (which may also be termed economic, human, and social capital; see Spillane & Thompson, 1997). Just as social capital may promote human capital, teachers with particular knowledge and dispositions may be more likely to forge relations of social capital in the first place. Moreover, economic capital may be essential for developing both human and social capital, as teachers' learning and collaboration require infusions of time, materials, and expertise from outside the standard worklife of a school and its staff. Perhaps most important, economic resources devoted to teachers' professional development may stimulate both human and social capital as well as their interplay.

Professional Development of the Engine of Change

What is the basis for suggesting that professional development is a key mechanism for improving teaching? Surely many teachers would react to this claim with skepticism, as professional development is often regarded as a necessary job requirement without much connection to the actual work of teaching (Sparks & Loucks-Horsley, 1989). Much professional development, it seems, fails to influence practice. Workshops are typically isolated events, often unrelated to teachers' ongoing concerns. At best, a workshop is seen as useful if it provides a new tool for a teacher's toolkit—something that can be applied in an immediate and direct way (Fullan, 1991). This type of professional development does not result in meaningful change (Goldenberg & Gallimore, 1991), nor, we suspect, does it contribute to significant variation in teaching practices among teachers.

However, current research on teaching suggests an alternate possibility. Professional development that is sustained, coherent, collaborative, and reflective may lead to real changes in practice (Darling-Hammond & McLaughlin, 1996). Lieberman (1996) proposed an expanded view of professional development including direct learning through courses, through workshops, and through other avenues, informal learning in school through peer coaching, through sharing experiences, through conducting case studies, and the like, and informal learning outside of school through opportunities such as networks, partnerships, and collaboratives. According to Lieberman, "Teachers who engage in these new professional opportunities often find themselves in an exciting and powerful cycle: The more they learn, the more they open up to new possibilities and the more they seek to learn more" (pp. 189–190). Not all teachers follow this path, but those who do are profoundly influenced in their practice.

Professional development may influence organizational resources in two ways. First, it may contribute to teachers' knowledge, skills, and dispositions, that is, the human resources of a school. This is a common view of the benefits of professional development (e.g., Sparks & Loucks-Horsley, 1989), and it stands behind the regulations of many states that require teachers to participate in professional development in order to maintain their teaching licenses. Second, professional development may contribute to the social resources of a school, particularly if it is collaborative and reflective. When serious professional development is based in a school, it may help establish many of the features of a professional community, including collaboration, shared values, deprivatized practice, and reflective discussions about student learning. Thus, professional development has potential for building a school's capacity to create change in teaching and in learning (Darling-Hammond & McLaughlin, 1996; Little, 1986; Newmann & Associates, 1996; Tharp & Gallimore, 1988).

At the same time, organizational resources may affect the provision and nature of professional development. Professional development requires substantial funds, particularly if it is sustained over time and involves collaboration among teachers. Little (1986, 1990) showed that conditions for effective professional development are difficult to maintain, requiring time, leadership, and energy. Thus, the relation between organizational resources and professional development is dynamic, sometimes building momentum as noted by Lieberman (1996), but at other times faltering due to lack of resources (Little, 1990).

Not only do resources and professional development affect one another, but the impact of professional development on teaching probably depends in part on the level of resources available for implementation and for diffusion of new ideas and practices. Lotan, Cohen, and Morphew (1997) reported that teachers were more likely to engage in nonroutine behavior—a key outcome of their complex instruction professional development program—in schools where principals were more knowledgeable and supportive and where teachers obtained assistance in acquiring materials and supplies. Examining the persistence of a similar reform, Dahl (1997) found that new practices were more likely to be sustained over time when principals helped coordinate both material resources (supplies, equipment, and space) and social resources (teachers' opportunities to work together).

A key question for our formulation concerns the salience of the school's boundaries for changes in teaching and in learning. Our model assumes that resources that reach the school are of primary importance. This assumption is clearly appropriate for material and human resources because resources applied in the classroom are filtered through the school and through teachers. It is less clear whether the school is an especially important locus of social resources. If teachers find professional communities in other types of organizations or collaboratives, how much does the school really matter for their development as successful teachers? Although much of the research literature focuses on schoolwide professional communities (e.g., Newmann & Associates, 1996), it is clear from research on high schools that departments are the key organizational units (Little, 1990; Talbert, 1995). Consequently, it may be that departments rather than whole schools should be the focus of research on professional community. Middle and elementary schools, though not typically divided into departments, may have other types of subgroups in which professional communities are embedded. In addition, teacher networks that draw participants from many different schools may serve as important professional communities for some teachers (Newmann & Associates, 1996). Hence, there is no guarantee at any level that the boundaries of the professional community are the boundaries of the school.

Professional Development and Schoolwide Transformation

In some cases, professional development serves as a stimulus to change throughout a school. Humbolt Elementary School, one of the schools included in Newmann and Associates' (1996) study, joined a national organization for school reform after a few teachers became interested in its instructional approach. In-service participation by these teachers ultimately led to the adoption of a new approach by the entire school staff. In most cases, however, the schools that exhibited exceptionally high-quality teaching and learning were not so much transformed as established as new schools from the beginning. Change, moreover, was not seen as something that took place once but was regarded as a process of continuous improvement. At Careen Academy, an elementary school, key innovations included portfolio assessments, narrative reports on students' progress, and remaining with the same teacher for more than one year. Researchers concluded that "all three practices are works in progress, however, and teachers work continually to define and enrich them" (Newmann & Associates, 1996, p. 84). Similarly at Cibola High School, a teacher explained that"...every year we should get better. What we accepted as a minimum one year should be unsatisfactory the next year. It has to be that way. We have to ask for more every year. That's an ongoing thing, we'll never stop struggling over that" (Newmann & Associates, 1996, p. 131). In successful restructured schools, innovations were dynamic and adaptive, not static.

Professional development often played a key role in stimulating, supporting, and enhancing these changes. Careen Academy provides persuasive evidence of the power of professional development

(Newmann & Associates, 1996). Careen teachers participate in a summer institute lasting 1 to 3 weeks every year. They also attend four Saturday workshops, as well as a variety of activities outside the school district. Newmann and Associates (1996) also discovered that teachers were participating in three voluntary study groups on an ongoing basis. These activities contributed substantially to teachers' efforts in the classroom.

Despite these cases of wholescale development and change, other evidence indicates that most often, change efforts fall short of schoolwide transformation. Drawing on recent research, we have identified three other outcomes that commonly occur, even in the face of sustained, reflective professional development involving a number of teachers in a school: Teachers who favor change may find themselves in constant conflict with other actors in the school, due to others' resistance to change; they may compromise their ideals and moderate their teaching initiatives to avoid conflict (or adapt their technological efforts to accommodate existing circumstances); or they may create alternative structures within schools in which the new teaching practices may flourish, but not expand beyond the boundary of the alternate structure (e.g., a school-within-a-school). The outcome that finally emerges depends in part on the dynamic interplay between organizational resources and teaching practices. Research on school restructuring provides illustrations for these claims and draws attention to possible mechanisms through which the various outcomes may occur.

Constant conflict. In some cases, change efforts result in continual conflict within schools. Mechanisms that produce this conflict are varied. In Fremont High School, one of the highly restructured schools examined by Newmann and Associates (1996), a group of teachers attempted to eliminate low-level math classes and teach all students in mixed-ability classes within a subset of the school. These changes resulted in tension within the school, with teachers outside the group complaining that too much time was spent addressing affective needs and not enough was spent on academic concerns and arguing that students were not being prepared for upper division math courses. The same study found another example of constant conflict at Selway Middle School, a charter school led by a group of four teachers committed to authentic instruction. Although other teachers shared the ideal of authenticity, they resented the oligarchic control exercised by the four leading teachers and believed they had no voice in the policies and direction of the school.

In the first case, conflict occurred between two groups of teachers with competing ideas about the essential goals of math instruction and with differing views of the varied capabilities of students. In the second case, the conflict was also between groups of teachers, but it centered on control and governance issues rather than on a philosophy of teaching. In still other instances, conflict occurs between administrators and teachers or between teachers and parents. More generally, constant conflict seems to emerge under any one of three circumstances: when there are philosophical differences about what constitutes real teaching and learning; when there are competing preferences for the allocation of limited resources; or when teachers resist additional work necessary for teaching reforms. Actions that foment conflict include administrators' active opposition to change, restriction of resources to leaders of change processes, sabotage by antireform forces, and educators lining up external forces to oppose the sought-after changes.

Compromise and adaptation. Efforts to avoid internal conflict may lead to a second type of outcome, in which would-be reformers moderate their innovations as an adaptation to existing conditions. In some cases this means taking on the language of change without carrying out the activities of change. Researchers observed this situation in restructured schools where teachers "talked the talk" but did not "walk the walk"—that is, teachers spoke the rhetoric of reform but did not engage in innovative instructional practices (Gamoran, 1996b; Newmann & Associates, 1996). This outcome may result from a lack of training among teachers, from an assumption that desired changes cannot succeed, or as a consequence of pressure from other sources, such as district pressure to raise standardized test scores.

One may find that the adaptation response is an incremental step on the way toward long-term change. More commonly, however, our experience suggests that limited changes do not continue incrementally over the long term. Instead, once the boundaries of change are defined, further reforms in the same area of work do not occur.

Alternate structures. Sometimes teachers seeking change manage to avoid compromising their innovative approach to teaching and learning but are unable to diffuse their initiative to the entire school staff. In this circumstance the initiative often emerges as an alternate structure within a traditionally structured organization. An extreme example of this outcome was Island High School, in which every new idea seemingly resulted in a new structure. There were special programs for at-risk youth, for pregnant girls, for bilingual students, for low-achieving students, for technology-oriented students, and so on (Newmann & Associates, 1996). More commonly, a new initiative may result in a school-within-a-school that exists alongside and often in competition with the regular structure.

Why do innovative practices emerge through alternate structures instead of as transformations of existing institutions? Lack of organizational resources, particularly limited material and social resources, is the most likely reason. First, whereas special resources may be available for modest reforms, the new resources may be insufficient to encourage a more complete transformation. Second, teachers within schools are typically isolated from one another, separated by the boundaries of their classroom walls. They may lack opportunities to learn from one another and to teach one another. Communication among teachers around substantive issues is typically limited. Third, and probably most important, there is a strong norm of autonomy within schools, and it is considered inappropriate to criticize other teachers. Teachers are reluctant to question others' professional judgment, preferring to let others proceed as they have been and limiting the innovative practices to those who come to it on their own.

When outsiders see that reforms have been limited to alternate structures, they may take this result as a sign of the reform's failure. This perception may further inhibit growth or may lead to the reform's decline. Limitations on growth may also lead to a "circle the wagons" mentality among the leaders of change, a strong defense of a limited territory to keep the reform alive. These processes may tend to solidify the segmented character of school reforms, as Newmann and Associates (1996) observed at Island High School.

Examples of Teaching and Learning: Applying the Models

Thus far we have alluded to different views of teaching, but we have not provided many details. We noted, for example, that the uncertainties of teaching are often ignored in favor of standard routines, but sometimes uncertainties are recognized by teachers who may respond by attempting to increase their own knowledge. This example suggests that differences in conceptions of teaching may have consequences for the organizational context of teaching. That is, the aspect of the organizational context that is most salient may depend on one's conception of teaching. To explore this issue more fully, we describe three different approaches to teaching that we term teaching for understanding, conventional teaching, and core knowledge teaching. Each of these approaches calls into prominence different aspects of our dynamic model of the organizational context of teaching and learning.

Teaching for Understanding

According to Carpenter and Lehrer (1999), student understanding involves five interrelated forms of mental activity: constructing relationships, extending and applying knowledge, reflecting about experiences, articulating what one knows, and making knowledge one's own. By teaching for understanding, we mean instruction designed to stimulate these mental activities. A variety of writers have described such teaching as emphasizing students' construction of meaning and discovery of knowledge through active learning (e.g., Cohen, McLaughlin, & Talbert, 1993). Newmann and Associates (1996) had a similar concept in mind when they examined authentic pedagogy, which involves disciplined inquiry, student construction of knowledge, and relevance to students' lives beyond the school.

Teaching for understanding requires teachers to confront the uncertainties of teaching. As emphasized in loose-coupling theory, teaching is an ambiguous technology. Typically, this uncertainty is managed by focusing attention on the symbolic and ritual aspects of schooling and by avoiding inspection of the technical core. In teaching for understanding, however, the logic of confidence is not sufficient for managing uncertainty. These teachers are forced to go beyond scripted routines because they are faced with pressing questions about what students do or do not understand and what activities may improve understanding for particular students at a particular point in time. Teaching for understanding requires a means of managing uncertainty that recognizes and responds to questions rather than avoiding them. In response, teachers are likely to reach out to other teachers involved in similar efforts. Colleagues may provide moral support as well as practical suggestions. They may talk with one another, plan together, visit one another's classrooms, and so on—in short, they may begin to construct a professional community. Thus, a supportive social environment may emerge from efforts to teach for understanding. To flourish, however, this environment requires material resources, particularly time for collaboration, and human resources, some level of knowledge about fostering students' understanding, which may come from professional development. We propose that the relation between teaching for understanding and social resources in a school is dynamic, as the uncertainties of instruction, once recognized, provide the content of social relationships among educators, and these relationships in turn contribute to enhanced teaching for understanding. This conception is consistent with Bidwell, Frank, and Quiroz's (1997) finding that progressivist views of teaching are more prevalent in schools in which working conditions are more collegial.

Teaching for understanding may also call for another connection not previously recognized; feedback from student learning to teaching practices. Teachers who are focusing on students' understanding must adjust their activities in response to students' progress in learning. Thus, teaching for understanding forms a nexus between two dual processes: on the one side, the dynamic relation between teaching for understanding and social relations in the school, and on the other, a feedback loop between teaching and learning.

Conventional Teaching

By conventional teaching we mean teaching organized through a set pattern of lecture, recitation, and seatwork. This is not an abstracted ideal type; rather it accurately characterizes much of the teaching in American schools, particularly after the primary grades. A variety of studies have depicted this emotionally flat, teacher-dominated process (e.g., Goodlad, 1984). Nystrand (1997) described it as "monologic instruction," meaning that classroom life is essentially a monologue—even when students recite, they are following a script that has been laid down by the teacher. The flow of questions and answers follows a well-known pattern of initiation (teacher question), response by a student, and teacher's evaluation of the student's response (Mehan, 1979). In this type of instruction, even small-group work is prescribed by teachers (Nystrand, Gamoran, & Heck, 1993).

What are the key organizational contexts for conventional teaching? Here the flow tends to be one way, not dynamic. Consistent with the nested layers model, allocations of time and curricular materials are expected to influence teachers' coverage of curricular content. In contrast to teaching for understanding, social resources would have little impact on teachers' instructional practices. In conventional teaching, teachers work in isolation from one another, and issues of potential uncertainty are submerged beneath instructional routines. Consequently, there is little impetus for reflection about the substantive problems of teaching. Of course, teachers talk every day with their colleagues about the troubles of the job. These conversations, however, typically focus on administrative issues or on problems of specific students, rather than on new instructional approaches, on content questions, or on the intellectual quality of students' work (Newmann & Associates, 1996). We propose that the predominance of conventional teaching coupled with the marginal relevance of social resources for conventional teaching accounts for the inconsistent and generally weak effects of school-level social indicators such as collegiality and collaboration. Teachers' expectations and efficacy are exceptions to the pattern of weak school effects, but these apparent effects are better explained as responses to students' success rather than as determinants. For conventional teaching and social resources, loose coupling prevails.

Core Knowledge Teaching

Core knowledge teaching refers to teachers who emphasize the transmission of subject-matter knowledge from established authoritative sources to students. According to Hirsch (1993, 1996), this transmission of knowledge is the essential function of schooling. In contrast to teaching for understanding, where students construct meaning for themselves, core knowledge views meaning as residing outside students, within the subject matter itself. Core knowledge teaching also contrasts with conventional teaching in two important ways. First, core knowledge has explicit standards for what constitutes important knowledge (Hirsch, 1996). Second, core knowledge teaching emphasizes depth of knowledge to a much greater degree than in conventional teaching, which often introduces fragmented bits of information and ignores controversy and underlying linkages among issues (McNeil, 1986).

For core knowledge teachers, the key organizational resources are curricular materials and their own knowledge of the subject matter. Thus, material and human resources are more salient than social resources. One could imagine that core knowledge faculty might engage in substantive discussions of curricular content, and from these discussions might emerge a professional community of teachers, as in teaching for understanding. However, because the core knowledge curriculum is largely given, whereas students' understanding is highly uncertain, one would expect social relations among teachers to play a less prominent role in responding to and shaping instructional practices of core knowledge teaching as compared with teaching for understanding. Consistent with this view, Bidwell, Frank, and Quiroz (1997) reported no significant associations between the character of teachers' working relationships and their reported emphases on instructional rigor.

As in conventional teaching, we expect that student learning occurs in response to core knowledge teaching, without a meaningful feedback loop. Thus, teaching for understanding is the only case of those we have considered in which instruction responds significantly to student learning.

Conclusions: Toward a Research Agenda

In this article, we have both simplified and added complexity to conceptions of how the school as an organization provides a context for teaching and for learning. We simplified them by arguing that organizational resources are the most essential aspects of the organizational context. We subsume most of the conditions examined in previous research under our concept of resources, including such widely diverse conditions as time, materials, class size, knowledge, leadership, and collaboration. The focus on resources allowed us to trace the development of theoretical conceptions of school organization, from input–output notions, to nested layers, to our own model. In each of these perspectives, resources are the most salient features of the context of teaching and learning.

In simplifying it, we have left out some aspects of school organization. In particular, aspects of structure that are not merely a matter of resources are not found in our model. For example, structural differentiation into tracks and ability groups is usually not a matter of economic resources, yet it figures prominently as a context for teaching (Oakes, Gamoran, & Page, 1992). Interestingly, changes in differentiation policies often fail to bring about instructional improvements (Gamoran & Weinstein, 1998). Research in this area shows that structural differentiation is not an easy policy lever because of resistance to change and insufficient knowledge about teaching under new structural conditions (Wells & Serna, 1996). Indeed, research findings about structural differentiation are consistent with the general conclusions of Peterson and associates (1996), that structural conditions may facilitate teaching improvements but they are not the primary causal factors. Further research may help to specify more fully the importance of structure as a complement to resources (Newmann, 1998).

Composition of the student body is another organizational feature that does not figure prominently in our analysis. Composition, like structure, may be associated with differences in teaching and in learning but does not appear to be a driving force (Gamoran, 1992). An important question about composition is whether it operates as a contingency for organizational resources; that is, whether different types and levels of resources are needed to bring about similar changes in schools that differ in their student bodies. For example, is professional development of a certain type or quality necessary to improve teaching when the students are especially disadvantaged? This complication may also be addressed in future research.

Although we simplified it by leaving out some aspects of organization, in other ways our model is more complex than previous visions of schools and schooling because it recognizes the possibility of dynamic, multidirectional associations between organizational resources, teaching, and learning. Such complexity may not prevail in all cases, but it likely occurs in many of the reform efforts currently underway, which focus on teaching for understanding (Cohen et al., 1993), authentic pedagogy (Newmann & Associates, 1996), and dialogic instruction (Nystrand, 1997). Research on how these dynamic associations emerge is essential for learning how to provide a supportive context for new instructional approaches. Some combination of survey and qualitative research that monitors schools and districts over time is needed to trace the connections among resources, teaching, and learning.

The relation between teaching and its organizational context depends in part on what conception of teaching prevails. The importance of particular resources may also vary among and within educational systems in response to different or to changing conceptions of governance and accountability. For example, whereas loose coupling has been especially apparent in the United States until now, new accountability standards for what teachers teach and for what students learn may change the connections between allocations and outcomes. A question for future research is whether reform that emphasize new standards will be accompanied by tighter linkages between curricular allocation and students' performance, as envisioned in the nested layers view, or whether increases in professional development for teachers, rather than the pressures of curriculum and testing, may lead to changes in teaching. Yet another alternative is that longstanding norms in American education will be maintained, and educators will successfully resist pressures for greater accountability in the context of a persistently loosely coupled system. Cross-national research, as well as research that monitors trends within education systems over time, would shed light on these issues.

Research on the allocation and impact of resources has yielded clearer conclusions for some resources than for others. For some narrowly specified aspects of time, curriculum coverage, and student learning, the nested layers view has been sustained. Human resources such as teachers' knowledge also seem closely linked to teaching when teaching practices are carefully specified. Existing research offers less confidence about the impact of other human resources, such as leadership, or about social resources, particularly the relationships among educators. Research on these conditions is inconclusive, and we have argued that a more nuanced analysis of resource flows is necessary to identify their multidirectional effects.

An organization is a system of linked relationships, not simply a collection of individuals or of isolated categories. An organizational role, such as teacher, has meaning only when thought of in connection with some other role, such as student, principal, or parent. For this reason a sociological study of an organization calls for a study of relationships, centering on how relationships become ordered, how they change, and how they influence outcomes. What may prove intriguing across organizations are differences in the character of the linkages that prevail. A focus on relationships offers greater possibilities for understanding the context of teaching and learning, and thus for supporting the reform of teaching, than does a focus on the traits of organizational participants.

References

Adajian, L. B. (1995). *Teacher's professional community and the teaching of mathematics.* Unpublished doctoral dissertation, University of Wisconsin, Madison.

Alexander, K. L., & Cook, M. A. (1982). Curricula and coursework: A surprise ending to a familiar story. *American Sociological Review, 47,* 626–640.

Anderson, C. S. (1982). The search for school climate: A review of the research. *Review of Educational Research, 52,* 368–420.

Anderson, C. W. (1996). *Reform in teacher education as building systemic capacity to support the scholarship of teaching.* Paper presented at the International Workshop on Reform Issues in Teacher Education, Taipei, Taiwan.

Barr, R., & Dreeben, R. (1983). *How schools work.* Chicago: University of Chicago Press.

Barr, R., & Sadow, M. W. (1989). Influence of basal programs on fourth-grade reading instruction. *Reading Research Quarterly, 24,* 44–71.

Benavot, A., & Resh, N. (1998). *Diversity within uniformity: Conflicting pressures in the costruction of implemented school curricula.* Paper presented at the annual meeting of the American Sociological Association, San Francisco, California.

Bidwell, C. E. (1965). The school as a formal organization. In J. G. March (Ed.), *Handbook of organizations* (pp. 922–1022). Chicago: Rand McNally.

Bidwell, C. E., Frank, K. A., & Quiroz, P. A. (1997). Teacher types, workplace controls, and the organization of schools. *Sociology of Education, 70,* 285–307.

Bidwell, C. E., & Kasarda, J. D. (1980). Conceptualizing and measuring the effects of school and schooling. *American Journal of Education, 88,* 401–430.

Bishop, J. H. (1998). The effect of curriculum-based external exit exams on student achievement. *Journal of Economic Education, 29,* 171–182.

Blau, P. M., & Duncan, O. D. (1967). *The American occupational structure.* New York: Wiley.

Borman, K., Cookson, P., Sadovnik, A., & Spade, J. Z. (Eds., 1996). *Implementing federal legislation: Sociological perspectives on policy.* Norwood, NJ: Ablex.

Brophy, J., & Good, T. L. (1986). Teacher behavior and student achievement. In M. C. Wittrock (Ed.), *Handbook of research on teaching* (3rd ed., pp. 315–375). New York: Macmillan.

Bryk, A. S., & Driscoll, M. E. (1988). *The high school as community: Contextual influences, and consequences for students and teachers.* Madison, WI: National Center on Effective Secondary Schools.

Bryk, A. S., Lee, V. E., & Holland, P. B. (1993). *Catholic schools and the common good.* Cambridge, MA: Harvard University Press.

Bryk, A. S., & Raudenbush, S. W. (1992). *Hierarchical linear models.* Newbury Park, CA: Sage.

Callahan, R. (1962). *Education and the cult of efficiency.* Chicago: University of Chicago Press.

Carpenter, T. P., & Lehrer, R. (1999). Teaching and learning mathematics with understanding. In E. Fenneman & T. A. Romberg (Eds.), *Mathematics classrooms that promote understanding* (pp. 19–32). Mahwah, NJ: Lawrence Erlbaum.

Cohen, D. K. (1990). A revolution in one classroom: The case of Mrs. Oublier. *Educational Evaluation and Policy Analysis, 12,* 311–330.

Cohen, D. K., McLaughlin, M. W., & Talbert, J. E. (1993). *Teaching for understanding.* San Francisco, CA: Jossey-Bass.

Cohen, E. G., Deal, T. E., Meyer, J. W., & Scott, W. R. (1979). Technology and teaming in the elementary school. *Sociology of Education, 52,* 20–33.

Coleman, J. S. (1988). Social capital in the creation of human capital. *American Journal of Sociology, 94,* S95–S120.

Coleman, J. S., Campbell, E., Hobson, C., McPartland, J., Mood, A., Weinfield, F., & York, R. (1966). *Equality of educational opportunity.* Washington, DC: U.S. Government Printing Office.

Coleman, J. S., & Hoffer, T. (1987). *Public and private high schools: The impact of communities.* New York: Basic Books.

Dahl, R. (1997). Organizational factors and the continuation of a complex instructional technology. In E. G. Cohen & R. A. Lotan (Eds.), *Working for equity in heterogeneous classrooms: Sociological theory in practice* (pp. 260–274). New York: Teachers College Press.

Darling Hammond, L., & McLaughlin, M. W. (1996). Policies that support professional development in an era of reform. In *Teacher learning: New policies, new practices* (pp. 202–218). New York: Teachers College Press.

Doyle, W. (1992). Curriculum and pedagogy. In P. W. Jackson (Ed.), *Handbook of research on curriculum* (pp. 486–516). New York: Macmillan.

Edmonds, R. (1979). Effective schools for the urban poor. *Educational Leadership, 37,* 15–27.

Freeman, R. J., & Porter, A. C. (1989). Do textbooks dictate the content of mathematics instruction in elementary schools? *American Educational Research Journal, 26,* 403–421.

Fullan, M. G. (1991). *The new meaning of educational change.* New York: Teachers College Press.

Fuller, B. (1987). What school factors raise achievement in the Third World? *Review of Educational Research, 57,* 255–292.

Fuller, B., & Clarke, P. (1994). Raising school effects while ignoring culture? Local conditions and the influence of classroom tools, rules, and pedagogy. *Review of Educational Research, 64,* 119–157.

Gahng, T.-J. (1993). *A further search for school effects on achievement and intervening school experiences: An analysis of the Longitudinal Study of American Youth data.* Unpublished doctoral dissertation, University of Wisconsin, Madison.

Gamoran, A. (1987). The stratification of high school learning opportunities. *Sociology of Education, 60,* 135–155.

Gamoran, A. (1988). Resource allocation and the effects of schooling: A sociological perspective. In D. W. Monk & J. Underwood (Eds.). *Microlevel school finance: Issues and implications for policy* (pp. 207–232). Ninth Annual Yearbook of the American Educational Finance Association. Cambridge, MA: Ballinger.

Gamoran, A. (1992). Social factors in education. In M. Alkin (Ed.), *Encyclopedia of Educational Research* (6th ed., pp. 1222–1229). New York: Macmillan.

Gamoran, A. (1996a). Curriculum standardization and equality of opportunity in Scottish secondary education, 1984–1990. *Sociology of Education, 29,* 1–21.

Gamoran, A. (1996b). Goals 2000 in organizational perspective: Will it make a difference for states, districts, and schools? In K. Borman, P. Cookson, A. Sadovnik, & J. Z. Spade (Eds.), *Implementing federal legislation: Sociological perspectives on policy* (pp. 429–443). Norwood, NJ: Ablex.

Gamoran, A. (1996c). Student achievement in public magnet, public comprehensive, and private city high schools. *Educational Evaluation and Policy Analysis, 18,* 1–18.

Gamoran, A., & Dreeben, R. (1986). Coupling and control in educational organizations. *Administrative Science Quarterly, 31,* 612–632.

Gamoran, A., Nystrand, M., Berends, M., & LePore, P. C. (1995). An organizational analysis of the effects of ability grouping. *American Educational Research Journal, 32,* 687–715.

Gamoran, A., Porter, A. C., & Gahng, T.-J. (1995). Teacher empowerment: A policy in search of theory and evidence. In W. J. Fowler, B. Levin, & H. J. Walberg (Eds.), *Organizational Influences on Educational Productivity, Volume 5* (pp. 175–193). Greenwich, CT: JAI Press.

Gamoran, A., Porter, A. C., Smithson, J., & White, P. A. (1997). Upgrading high school mathematics instruction: Improving learning opportunities for low-income, low-achieving youth. *Educational Evaluation and Policy Analysis. 19,* 325–338.

Gamoran, A., & Weinstein, M. (1998). Differentiation and opportunity in restructured schools. *American Journal of Education, 106,* 385–415.

Goldenberg, C., & Gallimore, R. (1991, November). Changing teaching takes more than a one-shot workshop. *Educational Leadership, 49,* 69–72.

Goldstein, H. (1995). *Multilevel statistical models.* New York: Halsted Press.

Good, T. L., & Brophy, J. E. (1986). School effects. In M. C. Wittrock (Ed.), *Handbook of research on teaching* (3rd ed., pp. 570–602). New York: Macmillan.

Goodlad, J. (1984). *A place called school.* New York: McGraw-Hill.

Greenwald, R., Hedges, L., & Laine, R. D. (1996). The effects of school resources on student achievement. *Review of Educational Research, 66,* 361–396.

Hanushek, E. (1994). *Making schools work: Improving performance and controlling costs.* Washington, DC: Brookings.

Hanushek, E. (1997). Assessing the effects of school resources on student performance: An update. *Educational Evaluation and Policy Analysis, 19,* 141–64.

Hemmings, A., & Metz, M. H. (1991). Real teaching: How high school teachers negotiate societal, local community, and student pressures when they define their work. In R. N. Page & L. Valli (Eds.), *Curriculum differentiation: Interpretive studies in U.S. secondary schools* (pp. 91–112). Albany, NY: State University of New York Press.

Heyneman, S., & Loxley, W. (1983). The effects of primary-school quality on academic achievement across twenty-nine high- and low-income countries. *American Journal of Sociology, 88,* 1162–1194.

Hirsch, E. D. (1993). The core knowledge curriculum: What's behind its success? *Educational Leadership, 50,* 23–25.

Hirsch, E. D. (1996). *The schools we need and why we don't have them.* New York: Doubleday.

Hodgson, G. (1975). Do schools make a difference? In D. M. Levine & M. J. Bane (Eds.), *The inequality controversy* (pp. 24–44). New York: Basic Books.

Jackson, P. A. (1968). *Life in classrooms.* New York: Holt, Rinehart and Winston.

Jencks, C. L., Smith, M., Acland, H, Bane, M. J., Cohen, D. K., Gintis, H., Heyns, B., & Michelson, S. (1972). *Inequality: A reassessment of the effects of family and schooling in America.* New York: Basic Books.

Kilgore, S. B., & Pendleton, W. W. (1993). The organizational context of learning: Framework for understanding the acquisition of knowledge. *Sociology of Education, 66,* 63–87.

Lee, V. E., & Smith, J. B. (1995). Effects of high school restructuring and size on early gains in achievement and engagement. *Sociology of Education, 68,* 241–270.

Lee, V. E., & Smith, J. B. (1996). Collective responsibility for learning and its effects on gains in achievement for early secondary students. *American Journal of Education, 104,* 103–147.

Lee, V. E., & Smith, J. B. (1997). How high school organization influences the equitable distribution of learning in mathematics and science. *Sociology of Education, 70,* 128–150.

Lieberman, A. (1996). Practices that support teacher development: Transforming conceptions of professional learning. In *Teacher learning: New policies, new practices* (pp. 185–201). New York: Teachers College Press.

Little, J. W. (1986). Seductive images and organizational realities in professional development. In A. Lieberman (Ed.), *Rethinking school improvement* (pp. 26–45). New York: Teachers College Press.

Little, J. W. (1990). Conditions of professional development in secondary schools. In M. W. McLaughlin, J. E. Talbert, & N. Bascia, *The contexts of teaching in secondary schools: Teachers' realities* (pp. 187–223). New York: Teachers College Press.

Lotan, R. A., Cohen, E. G., & Morphew, C C. (1997). Principals, colleagues, staff developers: The case for organizational support. In E. G. Cohen & R. A. Lotan (Eds.), *Working for equity in heterogeneous classrooms: Sociological theory in practice* (pp. 223–239). New York: Teachers College Press.

Louis, K. S., Kruse, S. D., & Marks, H. M. (1996). Schoolwide professional community. In F. M. Newmann & Associates, *Authentic achievement: Restructuring schools for intellectual quality* (pp. 179–203). San Francisco, CA: Jossey-Bass.

Loveless, T. (1994). The influence of subject areas on middle school tracking policies. *Research in Sociology of Education and Socialization, 10,* 147–175.

McNeil, L. (1986). *Contradictions of control.* New York: Routledge & Kegan Paul.

Mehan, H. (1979). *Learning lessons: Social organization in the classroom.* Cambridge, MA: Harvard University Press.

Meyer, J. W. (1977). The effects of education as an institution. *American Journal of Sociology, 83,* 55–77.

Meyer, J. W., & Rowan, B. (1977). Institutionalized organizations: Formal structure as myth and ceremony. *American Journal of Sociology, 83,* 340–363.

Meyer, J. W., & Rowan, B. (1978). The structure of educational organizations. In M. Meyer & Associates, *Environments and organizations.* San Francisco, CA: Jossey-Bass.

Metz, M. H. (1989). Real school: A universal drama amid disparate experiences. *Politics of Education Association Yearbook, 1989,* 75–91.

Monk, D. H. (1992). Education productivity research: An update and assessment of is role in education finance reform. *Educational Evaluation and Policy Analysis, 14,* 307–332.

Mosteller, F. W., & Moynihan, D. P. (1972). *On equality of educational opportunity.* New York: Random House.

Newmann, F. M. (1998). How secondary schools contribute to academic success. In K. Borman & B. Schneider (Eds.), *The adolescent years: Social influences and educational challenges.* National Society for the Study of Education Yearbook 97:1. Chicago: University of Chicago Press.

Newmann, F. M., & Associates. (1996). *Authentic achievement: Restructuring schools for intellectual quality.* San Francisco, CA: Jossey-Bass.

Nystrand, M. (1997). *Opening dialogue.* New York: Teachers College Press.

Nystrand, M., Gamoran, A., & Heck, M. J. (1993). Using small groups for response to and thinking about literature. *English Journal, 82,* 14–22.

Oakes, J., Gamoran, A., & Page, R. N. (1992). Curriculum differentiation: Opportunities, outcomes, and meanings. In P. W. Jackson (Ed.), *Handbook of research on curriculum* (pp. 570–608). New York: Macmillan.

Pallas, A. (1988). School climate in American high schools. *Teachers College Record, 89,* 541–554.

Park, B. J. (1998). *Teacher empowerment and its effects on teachers' lives and student achievement in the U.S. high school.* Unpublished doctoral dissertation, University of Wisconsin, Madison.

Parsons, T. (1963). *Structure and process in modern societies.* Glencoe, IL: The Free Press.

Peterson, P. L., McCarthey, S. J., & Elmore, R. F. (1996). Learning from school restructuring. *American Educational Research Journal, 33,* 119–153.

Pressman, J. L., & Wildavsky, A. (1979). *Implementation* (2nd ed.). Berkeley, CA: University of California Press.

Purkey, S. C., & Smith, M. S. (1983). Effective schools: A review. *Elementary School Journal, 83,* 427–452.

Rowan, B. (1990). Commitment and control: Alternative strategies for the organizational design of schools. In C. Cazden (Ed.), *Review of Research in Education,* Vol., 16 (pp. 353–389). Washington, DC: American Educational Research Association.

Rowan, B., & Miracle, A. W., Jr. (1983). Systems of ability grouping and the stratification of achievement in elementary schools. *Sociology of Education, 56,* 133–144.

Rowan, B., & Miskel, C. (1999). Institutional theory and the study of educational organizations. In J. Murphy & K. S. Louis (Eds.), *Handbook of research in educational administration.* San Francisco, CA: Jossey-Bass.

Rowan, B., Raudenbush, S. W., & Cheong, Y. F. (1993). Teaching as a non-routine task: Implications for the management of schools. *Educational Administration Quarterly, 29,* 479–500.

Secada, W. G., & Adajian, L. B. (1997). Mathematics teachers' change in the context of their professional communities. In L. Fennema & B. S. Nelson (Eds.), *Mathematics teachers in transition* (pp. 193–219). Mahwah, NJ: Lawrence Erlbaum Associates.

Shulman, L. (1987). Knowledge and teaching: Foundations of the new reform. *Harvard Educational Review, 57,* 1–22.

Slavin, R. E. (1989). Class size and student achievement: Small effects of small classes. *Educational Psychologist, 24,* 99–109.

Slavin, R. E. (1990). Class size and student achievement: Is smaller better? *Contemporary Education, 62,* 6–12.

Sparks, D., & Loucks-Horsley, S. (1989). Five models of staff development for teachers. *Journal of Staff Development, 10,* 40–57.

Spillane, J., & Thompson, C. (1997). Reconstructing conceptions of local capacity: The local education agency's capacity for ambitious educational reform. *Educational Evaluation and Policy Analysis, 19,* 185–203.

Stevenson, D., & Baker, D. (1991). State control of the curriculum and classroom instruction. *Sociology of Education, 64,* 1–10.

Stodolsky, S. (1988). *The subject matters.* Chicago: University of Chicago Press.

Stodolsky, S., & Grossman, P. (1995). The impact of subject matter on curricular activity: An analysis of five academic subjects. *American Educational Research Journal, 32,* 227–249.

Talbert, J. E. (1995). Boundaries of teachers' professional communities in U. S. high schools: Power and precari-ousness of the subject department. In L. S. Siskin & J. W. Little (Eds.), *The subjects in question* (pp. 68–94). New York: Teachers College Press.

Talbert, J. E., & McLaughlin, M. W. (1994). Teacher professionalism in local school contexts. *American Journal of Education, 102,* 123–153.

Tharp, R. G., & Gallimore, R. (1988). *Rousing minds to life.* Cambridge, England: Cambridge University Press.

Weick, K. E. (1976). Educational organizations as loosely coupled systems. *Administrative Science Quarterly, 21,* 1–19.

Weick, K. E. (1982). Administering education in loosely coupled systems. *Phi Delta Kappan, 63,* 673–675.

Wells, A. S., & Serna, I. (1996). The politics of culture: Understanding local political resistance to detracking in racially mixed schools. *Harvard Educational Review, 66,* 93–118.

Wilson, T. P. (1996). *Reaching for a better standard.* New York: Teachers College Press.

11
Is There Really a Teacher Shortage?

RICHARD INGERSOLL

Few educational problems have received more attention in recent years than the failure to ensure that elementary and secondary classrooms are all staffed with qualified teachers. Severe teacher shortages, it is widely believed, are confronting our elementary and secondary schools. We have been warned repeatedly that "the nation will need to hire at least two million teachers over the next ten years" (e.g., National Commission on Teaching, 1997, pp. 15–16), and our teacher training institutions are simply not producing sufficient numbers of teachers to meet the demand. At the root of this school staffing crisis, according to the conventional wisdom, are two converging macro demographic trends—increasing student enrollments and increasing teacher turnover due to a "graying" teaching force. The resulting shortfalls of teachers, the argument continues, force many school systems to resort to lowering standards to fill teaching openings, inevitably resulting in high levels of underqualified teachers and lower school performance.

The prevailing policy response to these school staffing problems has been to attempt to increase the supply of teachers. In recent years a wide range of initiatives have been implemented to recruit new candidates into teaching. Among these are career-change programs, such as "troops-to-teachers," designed to entice professionals into mid-career switches to teaching and Peace Corps-like programs, such as Teach for America, designed to lure the "best and brightest" into understaffed schools. Some school districts have resorted to recruiting teaching candidates from overseas. Many states have instituted alternative certification programs, whereby college graduates can postpone formal education training and begin teaching immediately. Financial incentives, such as signing bonuses, student loan forgiveness, housing assistance, and tuition reimbursement have all been instituted to aid teacher recruitment (Hirsch, Koppich, & Knapp 2001; Feistritzer, 1997; Kopp, 1992). The "No Child Left Behind Act" passed in winter 2002 provides extensive federal funding for such initiatives.

Teacher shortages and subsequent teacher recruitment initiatives are not new to the K-12 education system. In the early and mid 1980s a series of highly publicized reports trumpeted an almost identical series of diagnoses and prescriptions (see, e.g., National Commission on Excellence in Education, 1983; Darling-Hammond, 1984; National Academy of Sciences, 1987; for reviews of this issue, see Boe & Gilford, 1992). Indeed, teacher shortages have been a cyclic threat for decades (Weaver, 1983).

Concern over teacher shortages in turn has spurred interest in empirical research on these issues, but until the past decade such efforts were limited by a lack of data. It was partly in order to address these data shortcomings that the U.S. Department of Education's National Center for Education Statistics conceived the Schools and Staffing Survey (SASS) and its supplement, the Teacher Followup Survey (TFS), beginning in the late 1980s (Haggstrom et al., 1988). This is now the largest and most comprehensive data source available on the staffing, occupational, and organizational aspects of schools.

Over the past decade I have undertaken a series of research projects using SASS/TFS to examine a range of issues concerned with teacher supply, demand, and quality (e.g., Ingersoll, 1995, 1999, 2001a, 2003b). In this report I will summarize what these data tell us about the realities of school staffing problems and teacher shortages. The theoretical perspective I adopt in my research is drawn from organizational theory and the sociology of organizations, occupations, and work. My operating premise is that in order to fully understand the causes and consequences of these social problems, it is necessary to examine them from the perspective of the organizations—the schools and districts—where these processes happen and within which teachers work. Employee supply, demand, and turnover are central issues in organizational theory and research. However, there have been few efforts to apply this theoretical perspective to understanding school staffing problems and policy. As I will show, by "bringing the organization back in," these school staffing problems are reframed from macro-level issues, involving inexorable societal demographic trends, to organizational issues, involving manipulable and policy-amenable aspects of particular schools. A close look at the data from this perspective, I argue, shows that the conventional wisdom concerning teacher shortages is largely a case of a wrong diagnosis and a wrong prescription.

The Data

As mentioned, the primary data source for this research is the nationally representative Schools and Staffing Survey (SASS) and its supplement, the Teacher Followup Survey (TFS), both conducted by the National Center for Education Statistics of the U.S. Department of Education. To date, four independent cycles of SASS have been completed: 1987–1988; 1990–1991; 1993–1994; 1999–2000. SASS is an unusually large survey. Each cycle of SASS administers survey questionnaires to a random sample of about 53,000 teachers, 12,000 principals, and 4,500 districts, representing all types of teachers, schools, districts, and all 50 states. In addition, one year later, the same schools are contacted again, and all those in the original teacher sample who had moved from or left their teaching jobs are given a follow-up second questionnaire to obtain information on their departures. This latter group, along with a representative sample of those who stayed in their schools, comprise the Teacher Followup Survey. The TFS sample contains about 7,000 teachers. Unlike most previous data sources on teacher turnover, the TFS is large, comprehensive, nationally representative, and includes the reasons teachers themselves give for their departures and a wide range of information on the characteristics and conditions of elementary and secondary schools. It is also unusual in that it does not solely focus on a particular subset of total separations, but includes all turnover: voluntary, involuntary, transfers, quits, retirements, etc. In this report, I present data from all four cycles of SASS and TFS (as of summer 2003, the 2000–2001 TFS had only been partially released by NCES and data presented here from that cycle are preliminary estimates).

Demand for Teachers Has Risen

What do the data tell us about school staffing problems and teacher shortages? The data show that the conventional wisdom on teacher shortages is correct in some respects. Consistent with shortage predictions, data from SASS and other NCES data sources show that demand for teachers has indeed increased in recent years. Since 1984, student enrollments have increased, most schools have had job openings for teachers, and the size of the teaching workforce (K-12) has increased, although the rate of these increases began to decline slightly in the late 1990s (Gerald & Hussar, 1998; Snyder & Hoffman, 2001, p. 11). Most importantly, many schools with teaching openings have experienced difficulties with recruitment. Overall, the data show that in the 1999–2000 school year, 58% of all schools reported at least some difficulty filling one or more teaching job openings, in one or more fields. However, the data also show that in any given field less than half of the total population of schools actually experienced recruitment problems (see Figure 11.1). For instance in 1999–2000, 54% of secondary schools had job openings for English teachers and about one half of these indicated they had at least some difficulty

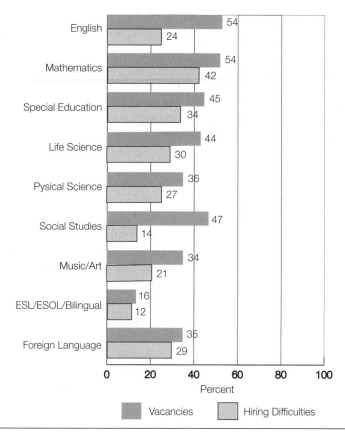

Figure 11.1 Percent secondary schools with vacancies and percent with difficulties filling those vacancies, 1999–2000.

filling these openings—representing one quarter of all secondary schools. Similarly, 54% of secondary schools had job openings for math teachers and about four fifths of these indicated they had at least some difficulty filling these math openings—representing about 40% of all secondary schools. Likewise, 45% of secondary schools had job openings for special education teachers and about three quarters of these indicated they had at least some difficulty filling these openings—representing 34% of secondary schools.[1]

How Adequate is the Supply of Teachers?

While demand has increased and many schools have had hiring difficulties, the data do not show, contrary to the conventional wisdom, that there is overall an insufficient supply of teachers being produced. National data on the overall supply of teachers trained, licensed, and certified each year are difficult to obtain. One source is NCES' Integrated Postsecondary Educational Data System (IPEDS). This source collects data on the numbers of post-secondary degree completions by field and by year. The IPEDS data indicate that, for example, at the end of the 1998–99 academic year, there were over 220,000 new recipients of education degrees at the undergraduate and graduate levels (IPEDS, 2001). But, the SASS data show that only about 86,000 of those hired for the following school year were drawn from this group of recent college graduates. Indeed, large proportions of those who train to become teachers do not ever become teachers. For example, data from the nationally representative 1993 Baccalaureate and Beyond Survey show that, of new recipients of bachelor's of education degrees who graduated in 1993, after one year out of college only 42% had taught and after four years out of college only 58% had taught. Many of those who decided not to pursue teaching indicated that they needed more education, or wanted another occupation (for a more detailed presentation of the B&B data, see Henke et al., 2000).

In short, the data appear to indicate that, overall, there are more than enough prospective teachers produced each year in the U.S. But, there are also some important limitations to these data. An overall surplus of newly trained teachers does not, of course, mean there are sufficient numbers of graduates produced in each field. A large proportion of education degree completions are in elementary education. The data are unclear on whether a sufficient quantity of teachers are produced each year in such fields as math, science, and special education.

But, on the other hand, the IPEDS database on degree completions underestimates the supply of newly qualified teachers because it does not include recipients of noneducation undergraduate degrees who also completed the requirements for certification. Moreover, newly qualified candidates, as counted in the IPEDS data, are only one source of new hires in schools. Far more of those newly hired into schools each year are from what is often referred to as the "reserve pool." These include delayed entrants—those who completed teacher training in prior years, but who have never taught, and re-entrants—former teachers who left teaching for a period to later return. The addition of these other types and sources of teachers could well mean that there are more than enough teachers produced each year.

However, from an organizational perspective, the key question is not whether the overall national supply of teachers is adequate or inadequate, instead it is which schools have staffing problems and teacher supply and demand imbalances. Even in the same jurisdiction, the degree of staffing problems varies greatly among different types of schools, and sites ostensibly drawing from the same teacher supply pool can have significantly different staffing scenarios. Some analysts have found, for example, that in the same metropolitan area in the same year some schools have extensive waiting lists of qualified candidates for their teaching job openings, while other nearby schools have great difficulty filling their teaching job openings with qualified candidates (National Commission on Teaching, 1997). Consistent with this, I have found in an analysis of variance of the SASS data that the variation in school hiring difficulties is far greater within, than between, states.[2] This suggests that to be fully understood imbalances between demand and supply must be examined at the level of the organization—an issue to which I return.

The Importance of Teacher Turnover for School Staffing Problems

There is another problem with the conventional wisdom on shortages. The data show that the demand for new teachers and subsequent staffing difficulties are not primarily due to student enrollment and teacher retirement increases, as widely believed, but these are largely due to teacher turnover—teachers moving from or leaving their teaching jobs—and most of this turnover has little to do with a graying workforce.

The TFS data show that teaching has a relatively stable annual turnover rate: 14.5% in 1988–89; 13.2% in 1991–92; 14.3% in 1994–95; 15.7% in 2000–2001 (see Figure 11.2). There are two types of total turnover included in Figure 11.2: movers—those who move to teaching jobs in other schools (often and hereafter referred to as teacher migration)—and leavers—those who leave the teaching occupation altogether (often and hereafter referred to as teacher attrition). Total teacher departures are fairly evenly split between them. Much of the existing research on teacher turnover does not include the former. Teacher cross-school migration is a form of turnover that does not decrease the overall supply of teachers because departures are simultaneously new hires. As a result, many assume that teacher migration does not contribute to the problem of staffing schools and to overall shortages. From a macro and system level of analysis, this is probably correct and for this reason educational

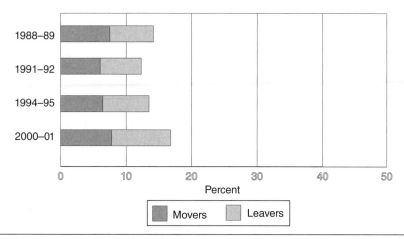

Figure 11.2 Percent annual teacher turnover.

researchers have often de-emphasized or excluded movers. However, from an organizational per-spective and from the viewpoint of those managing at the school-level, movers and leavers have the same effect—in either case it results in a decrease in staff, which usually must be replaced. Hence, research on employee turnover in other occupations and organizations almost always includes both movers and leavers—and for this reason I include them here. As illustrated in Figure 11.2, adopting a system-level or an organizational-level of analysis makes a difference—if one excludes cross-school moves, total turnover would appear far less than it is—from the viewpoint of those managing schools.

One question that naturally arises concerns how rates of teacher turnover from schools compare to those in other organizations, occupations, and industries. There has never been much empirical research on this issue. In earlier work I compared the TFS data with data from one of the better known sources of information on employee turnover in a range of occupations and organizations, the Bureau of National Affairs (2002). This comparison showed that teaching has a slightly higher annual turnover rate than the nationwide level for total employee departures—which over the past decade averaged 11.9% annually (Ingersoll, 2001a). But, this comparison provided only a crude benchmark. The BNA data represent an organizational rate of employee turnover, which ostensibly includes the whole range of employees on the payroll—from clerical staff to senior management—within a given organization. Far more informative would be comparisons of *occupational* rates of turnover, i.e., how do rates of teacher turnover compare to those in other occupations? But, such data are difficult to obtain and suffer from serious issues of measure comparability (Price, 1977, 1997).[3] In more recent work I have found that, as one might expect, teaching has higher turnover than some higher-status professions (professors at 9.3%; technology and scientific professionals from 3.6% to 9.2%), about the same as other female semi-professions (nurses at 18%) and less turnover than some lower-status, lower-skill occupations (federal clerical workers at 30%).[4]

But, from an organizational perspective the key question is not whether teaching has higher or lower turnover than other occupations, but rather is teacher turnover a problem for schools themselves. The data indicate it is. There is a strong link between teacher turnover and the difficulties schools have adequately staffing classrooms with qualified teachers—as shown in Table 11.1 which presents data on the flows in and out of schools from all four cycles of the SASS/TFS data.

Reading down the column for the 1993–94 school year, for example, Table 11.1 indicates there were just under three million teachers in the K-12 education system that year, including both public and private schools. About 377,135 of these teachers entered their schools at the beginning of the 1993–94 school year. Of these, 192,550 had not taught the prior year. This latter group included newly

Table 11.1 Trends in Teacher Flows In and Out of Schools

	1987–88 School Year	1990–91 School Year	1993–94 School Year	1999–2000 School Year
1.) Total Teaching Force – during school year	2,630,335	2,915,774	2,939,659	3,451,316
2.) Total Hires - at beginning of school year	361,649	387, 807	377, 135	534, 861
A.) Entrants	178,344	191,179	192,550	232,232
B.) Movers from other schools	183, 305	196, 628	184, 585	302,629
3.) Total Departures – by following school year	390,731	382,879	417,588	539,778
A.) Movers to other schools	218,086	208,885	204,680	252,408
B.) Leavers from occupation	172,645	173,994	212,908	287,370
Retirees	35, 179	47, 178	50,242	NA

Notes:
- Entrants: includes new, delayed, and re-entrants. This refers to those who did not teach the prior year; some did teach in the past.
- These data are calculated at the level of the school. Hence, "hires" and "departures" refer to those newly entering or departing a particular school. "Movers" includes transfers among schools within districts. Reassignments within a school are not defined as hires or as departures.
- As of summer 2003, teacher retirement data for the 2000 school year were not yet available.

qualified candidates fresh out of college, delayed entrants who had completed their training in a prior year but had not previously taught, and re-entrants who had taught previously, stopped for a while and then returned. Another 184,585 of these hires to schools had moved from another school. By the following school year, 417,588 teachers had moved from or left their school jobs. Just under half of these departures—204,680—moved to other schools to teach. Another 212,908 left the occupation altogether. Of the latter, 50,242 were retirees.

Table 11.1 documents two important points. First, the data show that the demand for new teachers is not primarily due to student enrollment increases, nor to teacher retirement increases, but to preretirement teacher turnover. That is, most of the hiring of new teachers is simply to fill spots vacated by teachers who just departed. For instance, about 191,000 individuals entered teaching at the beginning of the 1990–91 school year. However, by the following school year 12 months later, about 174,000 teachers (equivalent to 91% of those just hired) left the occupation altogether. At the beginning of the 1993–94, three years later, about 192,500 teachers entered teaching, but by the following school year, about 213,000 (equivalent to 110% of those just hired) left the occupation. At the beginning of the 1999–00, six years later, about 232,000 teachers entered teaching, but by the following school year, about 287,000 (equivalent to 124% of those just hired) left the occupation.

Second, although teacher retirements have increased in recent years, they account for only a small portion of the above total turnover. For example, from 1994 to 1995 there were about 50,000 retirees, accounting for only 24% of the 213,000 leavers and only 12% of the total turnover of 417,588 during that period. In sum, the data show that the demand for new teachers, and subsequent staffing difficulties, is not primarily due to student enrollment increases, nor to teacher retirement increases, but to preretirement teacher turnover. That is, most of the hiring of new teachers is simply to fill spots vacated by teachers who just departed. And, most of those departing are not doing so because of gray hair.

The Revolving Door

It is also important to note that teaching is a relatively large occupation—it represents 4% of the entire civilian workforce. There are, for example, over twice as many K-12 teachers as registered nurses and five times as many teachers as either lawyers or professors (U.S. Bureau of the Census, 2002).[5] The

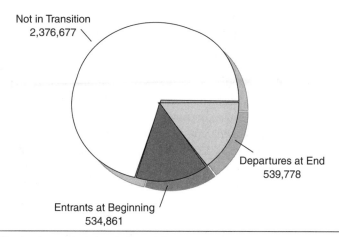

Figure 11.3 Numbers of teachers in transition before, during, and after the 1999–2000 school year.

sheer size of the teaching force combined with its relatively high annual turnover means that there are large flows in, through, and out of schools each year. The image that these data suggest is one of a "revolving door,"—which I have tried to capture in Figure 11.3. It shows that for the 1999–2000 school year, 534,861 teachers entered schools, while by the following school year an even larger number—539,778—had moved from or left their schools.[6] Hence, in a 12-month period over one million teachers—almost a third of this relatively large workforce—were in job transition into, between, or out of schools. This revolving door is a major factor behind school staffing problems.

Table 11.1 and Figure 11.3 also provide a context to interpret the widely used statistic, introduced earlier, that the nation "will need to hire at least two million teachers over the next 10 years." This statistic was drawn from an NCES analysis (Gerald & Hussar, 1998; Hussar, 1998) that projected the numbers of teachers that would need to be hired from 1998 to 2008 in order to replace those who had left teaching and to account for student enrollment increases. These analyses themselves did not examine supply, nor changes in hiring needs over time. But, a wide variety of commentators, researchers, and policy makers have interpreted this statistic to mean that hiring two million new teachers is an unusually large number and assumed to be evidence that we face an alarmingly inadequate supply of new teachers being produced. A close look at the data reveals that neither is the case.

The Importance of Teacher Turnover for Organizations

Of course, not all teacher turnover is detrimental. There is an extensive research literature on employee turnover conducted by those who study organizations and occupations in general (e.g., Price 1977, 1989; Mueller & Price, 1990; Bluedorn, 1982; Halaby & Weakliem, 1989; Horn & Griffeth, 1995; Kalleberg & Mastekaasa, 1998; March & Simon, 1958; Mobley, 1982; Steers & Momday, 1981). On the one hand, researchers in this tradition have long held that a low level of employee turnover is normal and efficacious in a well-managed organization. Too little turnover of employees is tied to stagnancy in organizations; effective organizations usually both promote and benefit from a limited degree of turnover by eliminating low-caliber performers and bringing in "new blood" to facilitate innovation. Moreover, some job and career changes are, of course, normal and inevitable in any occupation. On the other hand, researchers in this tradition have also long held that high levels of employee turnover are both cause and effect of performance problems in organizations.

Organizational analysts have also noted that the consequences of employee turnover vary among different types of employees and among different types of organizations. Labor process analysts, for instance, have argued that a major issue, from the viewpoint of organizational management, is the extent to which the organization is, or is not, dependent on particular types of employees and, hence, vulnerable to the disruption caused by their turnover (e.g., Braverman, 1974; Burawoy, 1979; Edwards, 1979). For just this reason the issue of employee "substitutability," or the ease with which organizations can replace employees, is a central concern in organizational management and a central theme in organizational research. In this perspective, employee turnover is especially consequential for work that involves uncertain and nonroutine technologies and which requires extensive interaction among participants. Such organizations are often unusually dependent upon the commitment and cohesion of employees and, hence, especially vulnerable to turnover (e.g., Burns & Stalker, 1961; Kanter, 1977; Likert, 1967; Porter, Lawler & Hackman, 1975; Turner & Lawrence, 1964; Walton, 1980).

Schools are an example of this type of organization. Education theory and research have long shown that, while education is a mass "industry" involving large complex formal organizations, in important ways schools do not fit standard input-output, economic-production models in either theory or practice (Bidwell, 1965; Lortie, 1975; Ingersoll, 2003a). The "raw materials" in schools are children and youth; the "technology" of teaching and learning is often uncertain, ambiguous, and nonroutine; and the "product" is youngsters' growth. As a result while schools in some ways resemble economic-production organizations, in other ways they resemble another kind of institution altogether—the family. Student test outcomes are one of the important output functions of school production. But not surprisingly, similar to families the presence of a positive sense of community, belongingness, communication, and cohesion among members has long been held by education theory and research to be one of the most important indicators and aspects of effective schools (e.g., Durkheim, 1925/1961; Waller, 1932; Parsons, 1959; Grant, 1988; Coleman & Hoffer, 1987; Kirst 1989; Rosenholtz, 1989).

Hence, from an organizational perspective, some teacher turnover, especially of ineffective teachers, is necessary and beneficial. But from this perspective, turnover of teachers from schools is of concern not simply because it may be an indicator of sites of potential staffing problems and so-called teacher shortages, but because of its relationship to school cohesion and, in turn, performance. Moreover, from this perspective this relationship runs both directions. That is, high rates of teacher turnover are of concern not only because they may be an outcome indicating underlying problems in how well schools function, but also because they can be disruptive, in and of themselves, for the quality of school community and performance.

Some of these costs and consequences of turnover are more easily measured and quantified than others. In contrast to the corporate sector, however, there has been very little attention paid to the costs and consequences of employee turnover in education. One notable exception was a recent attempt to quantify the costs of teacher turnover in Texas—this study concluded these costs run into the hundreds of millions of dollars each year to the state. (Texas Center for Educational Research, 2000).

Teacher and School Differences in Turnover

The data also show that the revolving door varies greatly among different kinds of teachers and different kinds of schools. As found in previous research (Murnane et al., 1991; Huling-Austin, 1990; Hafner & Owings, 1991), the SASS data show that teaching is an occupation that loses many of its newly trained members very early in their careers—long before the retirement years. I used these data to provide a rough estimate of the cumulative attrition of beginning teachers from the occupation in their first several years of teaching. The data suggest that after just five years, between 40 and 50% of all beginning teachers have left teaching altogether, (see Figure 11.4).[7] Of course, not all of this attrition results in a permanent loss of teachers. One form of this revolving door is represented by temporary attrition—teachers who leave teaching but return in later years, as discussed earlier (also see Murnane et al., 1991). But again, from the viewpoint of those managing at the school-level, temporary and permanent attrition have the same effect—in either case it results in an immediate decrease in staff, which usually must be replaced.

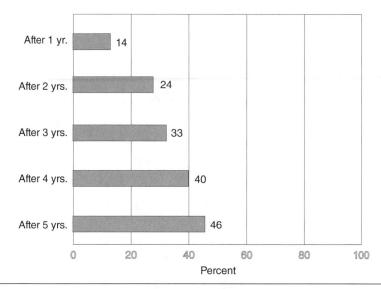

Figure 11.4 Beginning teacher attrition (cumulative percent teachers having left teaching occupation, by years of experience).

Annual teacher turnover also varies according to the teachers' main field. Math, science, and elementary special education teachers have higher rates of turnover, and social studies and English have lower rates (see Figure 11.5). Moreover, a number of studies have found that teachers with higher ability, as measured by test scores such as the SAT, the National Teacher Exam, and teacher licensure tests, are more likely to turn over (e.g., Weaver, 1983; Murnane et al., 1991; Schlecty & Vance, 1981; Stinebrickner, 2001; Henke et al., 2000).

The data also show that the revolving door varies greatly among different kinds of schools, as illustrated in Figure 11.6.[8] For example, high-poverty public schools have far higher turnover rates than

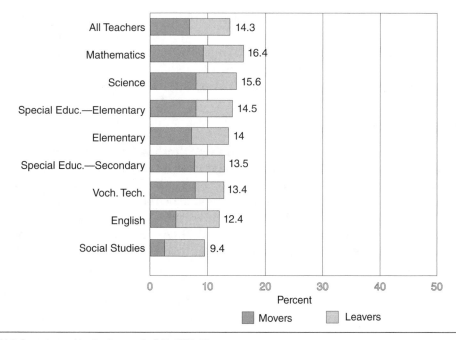

Figure 11.5 Percent annual teacher turnover, by field, 1994–95.

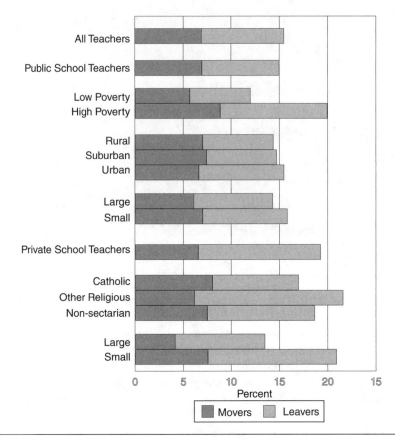

Figure 11.6 Percent annual teacher turnover, by selected school characteristics, 2000–2001.

do more affluent public schools. Urban public schools have slightly more turnover than do suburban and rural public schools. Private schools have higher turnover rates than public schools, but there are also large differences among private schools. On one end of the continuum lie larger private schools with among the lowest average turnover rate—about 13.5%. On the other end of the continuum lie smaller private schools with among the highest average levels—about 22%.

The Sources of Teacher Turnover

These data raise another important set of questions: why do teachers depart at relatively high rates and why are these rates so dramatically different among schools? To answer these questions I conducted multivariate statistical analyses of data from different cycles of SASS/TFS to determine which characteristics of teachers and schools are associated with the likelihood of teacher turnover, after controlling for background factors (Ingersoll, 2001b). I also examined data on the reasons teachers themselves give for their turnover. Such self-report data are useful because those departing are, of course, often in the best position to know the reasons for their turnover. But, such self-report data are also retrospective attributions, subject to bias and, hence, warrant caution in interpretation. Nevertheless, I found a great deal of consistency among these different types of data and from different cycles of the survey. The following section summarizes my principal findings. Along with the annual rates of turnover, Table 11.2 presents self-report data on teachers' reasons for both migration and attrition. In addition, for

Table 11.2 Percent Teacher Turnover and Percent Teachers Giving Various Reasons for Their Turnover, 1994–95.

	All	Movers	Leavers
Rates of Turnover	14.3	7	7.3
Reasons for Turnover			25
Retirement	13	–	8
School Staffing Action	20	34	44
Family or Personal	40	36	25
To Pursue other Job	27	29	25
Dissatisfaction	29	32	
Reasons for Dissatisfaction			
Poor Salary	54	49	61
Poor Administrative Support	43	51	32
Student Discipline Problems	23	22	24
Lack of Faculty Influence & Autonomy	17	18	15
Poor Student Motivation	15	12	18
No Opportunity for Professional Advancement	6	8	5
Inadequate Time to Prepare	6	5	6
Intrusions on Teaching Time	7	5	11
Class Sizes too Large	7	3	11

all teachers who departed because of job dissatisfaction, the bottom portion of the table presents data on the reasons for their dissatisfaction.[9] (definitions of these reasons can be found in the Appendix)

Contrary to conventional wisdom, retirement is not an especially prominent factor. The latter was listed by only 25% of leavers and 13% of total departures. School staffing cutbacks due to lay-offs, terminations, school closings, and reorganizations account for a larger proportion of turnover than does retirement. These staffing actions more often result in migration to other teaching jobs rather than leaving the teaching occupation altogether. But, the data also show that, overall, staffing actions, like retirement, account for only a small portion of total turnover from schools—about 20%.

A third category of turnover—that for personal reasons—includes departures for pregnancy, child rearing, health problems, and family moves. These account for more turnover than either retirement or staffing actions and they are probably common to all occupations and all types of organizations. The two final sets of reasons are directly related to the organizational conditions of teaching. Individually each of these categories accounts for more turnover than does retirement. Together these are the most prominent source of turnover. Almost half of all departures report as a reason either job dissatisfaction or the desire to pursue a better job, another career, or to improve career opportunities in or out of education.

Of those who depart because of job dissatisfaction, most often link their turnover to low salaries, lack of support from the school administration, student discipline problems, poor student motivation, and lack of teacher influence over decision-making. In general, similar kinds of dissatisfactions lie behind both teacher migration and teacher attrition. Interestingly, several factors stand out as *not major reasons* behind turnover, according to those who departed: large class sizes, intrusions on classroom time, and lack of planning time.

In sum, the data indicate that teachers depart their jobs for a variety of reasons. Retirement accounts for a relatively small number of total departures, a moderate number of departures are due to school staffing actions, a large proportion indicate they depart for personal reasons, and a large proportion also report they depart either because they are dissatisfied with their jobs or in order to seek better jobs or other career opportunities. I have found these reasons for turnover to be highly consistent across different types and cycles of the data, across different kinds of schools, and across different subsets of teacher turnover. These findings are important because of their policy implications. Unlike explanations that focus on external demographic trends "out there," these findings suggest there is a role "in here" for the internal organization and management of schools.

Implications for Policy

It is widely believed that shortfalls of teachers resulting primarily from two converging demographic trends—increasing student enrollments and increasing teacher retirements—are leading to problems staffing schools with qualified teachers and will, in turn, lower educational performance. In response school districts, states, and the federal government have developed a variety of recruitment initiatives designed to recruit more candidates into teaching.

However worthwhile these efforts may be, the data suggest that, alone, they will not solve school staffing problems. The data suggest that school staffing problems are not solely or even primarily due to teacher shortfalls resulting from either increases in student enrollment or increases in teacher retirement. In contrast, the data suggest that school staffing problems are to a large extent a result of a "revolving door"—where large numbers of teachers depart teaching for reasons other than retirement. From the framework of supply and demand theory, the data show that the problem is not primarily shortages, in the sense of an insufficient supply of teachers being recruited and trained. Some economists would still call this a shortage—in the technical sense that there is an inadequate quantity of teachers supplied—those willing to continue to offer their services at a given wage and given working conditions in given schools. This diagnostic and terminological distinction has crucial implications for prescription. It is also a distinction that is almost always overlooked in research and policy on the teacher shortage.

Supply and demand theory holds that where the quantity of teachers demanded is greater than the quantity of teachers supplied, there are two basic policy remedies: increase the quantity supplied or decrease the quantity demanded. The first approach—the traditionally dominant approach—is to increase the quantity of teachers supplied through recruitment. However, this analysis cautions that recruitment programs alone will not solve the staffing problems of schools if they do not also decrease turnover. States such as California, where class-size-reductions have strained the supply of new teachers pose exceptions. But, for just these reasons, California, like other states, must pay close attention to retention. In short, recruiting more teachers will not solve the teacher crisis if 40 to 50% of such teachers then leave within five years. The image that comes to mind is a bucket rapidly losing water because of holes in the bottom. Pouring more water into the bucket will not be the answer if the holes are not first patched.

Recruitment and other supply-side solutions may not only fail to solve the problem but could also make the situation worse. If recruitment strategies involve lowering teacher standards, or if the effect of increasing teacher supply is to deflate salaries or erode working conditions, then these measures may simply exacerbate the root factors behind school staffing problems.

This situation is analogous to aspects of management-labor conflict in industry. Critics of business practice argue that industrialists have long used labor supply recruitment as a strategy to undermine worker and union efforts to improve working conditions and wages (e.g. Braverman, 1974; Burawoy, 1979; Edwards, 1979). For example, by bringing in immigrant laborers from eastern and southern Europe at the turn of the 19th century, industrialists, the critics hold, were able to keep wages down, undermine union power, and increase profits. One of the downsides with this strategy, from a management perspective, is that it can decrease employee quality and increase employee turnover. Hence, one of the objectives behind the design of the assembly-line model of production used in industry was to increase the ease of substitutability and, hence, insulate the organization from disruption caused by employee turnover.

Similarly, social scientists have long characterized K-12 teaching as a lower status, easy-in/easy-out, high turnover occupation that has relied historically on recruitment, and not retention, to solve its staffing problems (e.g., Tyack, 1974; Lortie, 1975). Since the inception of the public school system in the late 19th century, teaching was socially defined and treated as a temporary line of work suitable for women, prior to their "real" career of child rearing. For men, teaching was socially defined as a stepping stone, prior to their "real" career in one of the male-dominated skilled blue-collar occupations or white-collar professions. Indeed, historically there was an ambivalence toward persistors in teaching, especially males—who had to account for why they continued to be "merely" a teacher. Low pre-service training standards and requirements, relatively unselective entry criteria, and front-loaded salaries that paid newcomers relatively high salaries compared to veterans all tended to favor recruitment over retention. Moreover, low pay, isolated job conditions, little professional autonomy, and a faint sense of a career ladder all undermined longer-term commitment to teaching as a career and profession. Attempts to upgrade the status of the occupation through more rigorous training and licensing standards or more selective entry gates often resulted in decreases in male entrants to teaching, who were more attracted to occupations with better rewards attached to rigorous standards (Strober & Tyack, 1980).

It appears that school districts continue to favor teacher recruitment strategies for many of the same reasons and with many of the same consequences. By widening the entry gate and increasing the quantity of teachers supplied, districts are able to control labor costs and, hence, control local property taxes. The downside of this strategy in schools, as in industry, is that it can decrease employee quality and increase employee turnover. Treating workers as interchangeable, expendable, low-skill workers cuts some expenses, but it is not cost-free. If turnover is at the root of school staffing problems and if the quality of the teaching job is a large factor behind turnover, then policies that further erode the low status of teaching, that undermine salary increases, or that undermine working conditions may simply backfire by increasing turnover.

In short, the data suggest that school staffing problems are rooted in the way schools are organized and the way the teaching occupation is treated and that lasting improvements in the quality and quantity of the teaching workforce will require improvements in the quality of the teaching job.

Conclusion: What is to Be Done?

How do schools improve the teaching job? Teachers themselves have offered some ideas. The 1994–95 TFS asked teachers who had moved from or left their teaching jobs since the prior year to suggest possible steps schools might take to encourage teachers to remain in teaching. Their responses are summarized in Figure 11.7.[10]

One strategy suggested by departed teachers to aid retention is *increasing salaries*, which are, not surprisingly, strongly linked to teacher turnover rates. But, salaries are not the only issue, which is important from a policy perspective because increasing overall salaries is expensive given the sheer size of the occupation.

Reduction of *student discipline problems* is a second factor frequently suggested by departed teachers. Multivariate analysis of the data also document that this factor is strongly tied to the rates of teacher turnover; again, not surprisingly, schools with more student misbehavior problems have more teacher turnover (Ingersoll, 2001b). But, the data also tell us that, regardless of the background and poverty levels of the student population, schools vary dramatically in their degree of student misbehavior.

One of the factors tied to both student discipline and teacher turnover is how much *decision-making influence* teachers themselves have over school policies that affect their jobs, especially those concerned with student behavioral rules and sanctions. In a separate multivariate analysis of data

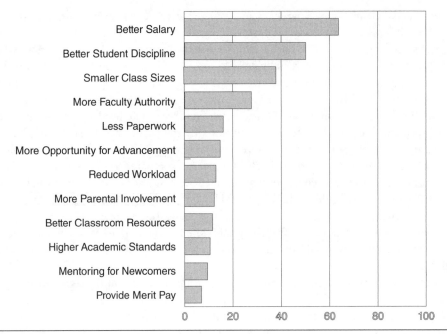

Figure 11.7 Of those teachers who moved from or left their jobs, percent giving various steps schools might take to encourage teachers to remain in teaching, 1994–95.

from SASS, I have found that, on average, teachers have little say in many of the key decisions that concern and affect their work, but schools where teachers are allowed more input into issues, such as student discipline in particular, have less conflict between staff and students and less teacher turnover (Ingersoll, 2003a). Increasing teacher decisionmaking power and authority is also, not surprisingly, suggested by teachers as a step to aid retention.

Class size reduction was also frequently suggested by teachers as a step to increase retention, although interestingly, it was not frequently given by departing teachers as one of the sources behind turnover related to dissatisfaction (Table 11.2).

Also surprising in Figure 11.7 is how few teachers suggested increasing support, such as *mentoring*, for new teachers as one of the main steps necessary for retention.

In a separate multivariate analysis of the 1999–2000 SASS data, we explored the impact of mentoring and induction programs on the turnover of new teachers. After controlling for the background characteristics of teachers and schools, we found a strong link between participation by beginning teachers in induction and mentoring programs and their likelihood of moving or leaving after their first year on the job (Smith & Ingersoll, 2003). The data showed that the predicted probability of turnover of first year, newly hired, inexperienced teachers, who did not participate in any induction and mentoring programs was 40% (see Figure 11.8). In contrast, after controlling for the background characteristics of teachers and schools, the turnover probability of beginning teachers who received what I labeled as "some" induction (had a helpful mentor from their same field; had common planning time with other teachers in their subject area; and had regularly scheduled collaboration with other teachers on issues of instruction) was 28%. Twenty-two percent of beginning teachers received just these three components. Finally, a very small number (less than 1% of beginning teachers in 1999–00) experienced what I label as a "full" induction experience that included the above three components, plus five more: participated in a general induction program; participated in a seminar for beginning teachers; had regular or supportive communication with their principal, other administrators, or department chair; participated in an external network; and had a reduced number of course preparations.

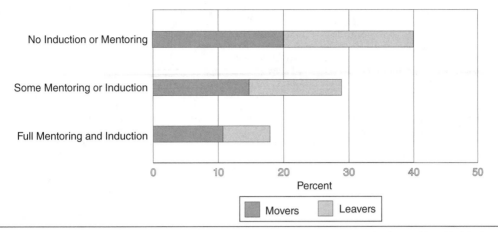

Figure 11.8 Percent turnover after first year of newly hired, inexperienced teachers, according to whether they participated in induction and mentoring programs, 2000–01.

Participation in these activities, collectively, had a very large and statistically significant impact—the probability of a departure at the end of their first year for those getting this package was less than half of those who participated in no induction activities.

It is important to recognize that none of these data suggests adopting any of the above steps will be inexpensive or easy. But, from the perspective of this analysis, the data suggest that schools are not simply victims of inexorable demographic trends and that there is a significant role for the management and organization of schools in both the genesis of, and the solution to, school staffing problems. The data suggest that improvements in the above aspects of the teaching job would contribute to lower rates of turnover, in turn, diminish school staffing problems and, hence, ultimately, aid the performance of schools.

Notes

1. The data on school hiring difficulties from the 1999–2000 SASS school questionnaire asked school officials "how difficult or easy it was to fill the vacancies for this school year" in each field. I counted as having "difficulty filling teaching vacancies" all those schools reporting either: "somewhat difficult," "very difficult," or "could not fill."
2. Using a one-way random effects ANOVA model, the data show that the variance component within states was 44 times the size of the variance component between states. Intraclass correlation = .022.
3. One example of a cross-occupational comparison that appears to have measurement shortcomings is an analysis of Baccalaureate and Beyond data by Henke et al. (2001). This analysis looked at beginning teacher attrition in comparison to other recent college grads. It followed 1993 grads who became teachers in the 1993–1994 year and then calculated how many of them were gone by April 1997. The analysis found an 18% rate of new teacher attrition for the three year span from April 1994 to April 1997. But the analysis did not appear to count all types of attrition. It appears that it only counted as attrition those who moved to full-time, nonteaching careers and jobs. It did not count those who went back to college, or those who left the workforce to, for example, do family caregiving. But other data, such as the SASS/TFS, tell us these other flows are substantial and are certainly counted as attrition in existing research. Not including them would make the overall attrition look smaller than it really is. Indeed, elsewhere in that report it appeared that 12% of new teachers left the full-time workforce for these other things; adding this 12% to the 18% attrition, the analysis did count, brings the B&B 3 year attrition rate to something close to 30% after three years—which is quite consistent with many other studies on beginning teacher attrition. It is unclear what this undercounting might mean for the cross-occupation comparisons made in the report, but it certainly casts doubt on them.
4. Data for professors are from a study sponsored by the American Association for University Professors (1989) and represent annual averages for the period from 1972 to 1989. (Ehrenberg et al. 1991) Data on technology and science professionals, such as engineers, research scientists, and software designers represent the 2000 year and are from Kochanski and Ledford (2001). Data for nurses are from the March 2000 National Sample Survey of Registered Nurses conducted by the American Hospital Association. Data for federal employees are from the Office of Personnel Management (2003).
5. The most recent data from the US Census Bureau are from 2001: 5,473,000 teachers/135,073,000 total workforce = 4.05%. "Teachers" include all Pre-K, K, Elementary, Secondary and Special education teachers. College and university instructors and professors are not counted as teachers. Counselors and librarians are not counted as teachers.

6. As in Table 11.1, the data in Figure 11.3 are calculated at the level of the school. Hence "hires" and "departures" refer to those newly entering or departing a particular school. "Movers" includes transfers among schools within districts. Reassignments within a school are not defined as hires or as departures.

7. I calculated these cumulative rates of beginning teacher attrition using preliminary data from the 2000–2001 TFS. The results are similar to what I've found using each of the other three cycles of the TFS—1988–89; 1991–92; 1994–95. It should be recognized that the data shown in Figure 11.4 are only a rough approximation. The SASS/TFS data do not follow a particular cohort of newly hired teachers to ascertain how many remain in teaching after five years. Instead I approximated the cumulative loss of beginning teachers by multiplying together the probabilities of staying in teaching for teachers with experience from 1 to 5 years, (i.e.. yr 1 probability of staying in teaching × yr. 2 probability × yr. 3 probability × yr. 4 probability × yr. 5 probability). These cumulative estimates also do not account for those who later re-enter teaching—which has been found to be as much as 25%.

8. In Figure 11.6, large schools are defined as those with 600 or more students; small schools are those with fewer than 300 students. High-poverty refers to schools with a poverty enrollment of 80% or more; low-poverty refers to schools with a poverty enrollment below 10%. Middle categories of size and poverty are omitted in the figure.

9. The data in Table 11.2 are from the 1994–95 TFS because the relevant data from the 2000–2001 TFS were not released as of summer 2003. Note that the column segments in Table 11.2 displaying percentages reporting various reasons for turnover each add up to more than 100%, because respondents could indicate up to three reasons for their departures. The same applies to the column segments displaying reasons for dissatisfaction. See Appendix for definitions of these reasons.

10. The data in Figure 11.7 are from the 1994–95 TFS, because the relevant data from the 2000–2001 TFS were not released as of summer 2003. Note that the estimates add up to more than 100%, because respondents could indicate up to three steps.

References

American Association of University Professors. (1989). The annual report on the economic status of the profession, 1988–89. *Academe, 75*(2), 3–74.

Bidwell, C. (1965). The school as a formal organization. In J. March (Ed.), *Handbook of organizations* (pp. 973–1002). Chicago, IL: Rand McNally.

Bluedorn, A. C. (1982). A unified model of turnover from organizations. *Human Relations, 35,* 135–153.

Boe, E., & Gilford, D. (1992). *Teacher supply, demand and quality.* Washington, DC: National Academy Press.

Braverman, Harry. (1974). *Labor and monopoly capitalism.* New York: Monthly Review Press.

Burawoy, Michael. (1979). *Manufacturing consent: Changes in the labor process under monopoly capitalism.* Chicago: University of Chicago Press.

Bureau of National Affairs. (2002). BNAs quarterly report on job absence and turnover. *Bulletin to Management.* Washington DC: Bureau of National Affairs.

Burns, T., & Stalker, G. M. (1961). *The management of innovation.* London: Tavistock.

Coleman, J., & Hoffer, T. (1987). *Public and private schools: The impact of communities.* New York: Basic.

Darling-Hammond, L. (1984). *Beyond the commission reports: The coming crisis in teaching.* Santa Monica, CA: Rand Corporation.

Durkheim, E. (1961/1925). *Moral education: A study in the theory and application of the sociology of education,* translated by E. K. Wilson and H. Schnurer. New York: Free Press.

Edwards, Richard. (1979). *Contested terrain.* New York: Basic Books.

Ehrenberg, R., Kasper, H., & Rees, D. (1991). Faculty turnover at American colleges and universities: Analyses of AAUP data. *Economics of Education Review, 10*(2) 99–110.

Feistritzer, E. (1997). *Alternative teacher certification: A state-by-state analysis (1997).* Washington, DC: National Center for Education Information.

Gerald, D., & Hussar, W. (1998). *Projections of education statistics to 2008.* Washington, DC: National Center for Education Statistics.

Grant, G. (1988). *The world we created at Hamilton High.* Cambridge, MA: Harvard University Press.

Hafner, A., & Owings, J. (1991). *Careers in teaching: Following members of the high school class of 1972 in and out of teaching* (NCES Report No. 91–470). Washington, DC: U.S. Department of Education, National Center for Education Statistics.

Haggstrom, G. W., Darling-Hammond, L., & Grissmer, D. (1988). *Assessing teacher supply and demand.* Santa Monica, CA: Rand Corporation.

Halaby, C., & Weakliem, D. (1989). Worker control and attachment to the firm. *American Journal of Sociology, 95,* 549–591.

Henke, R., Chen, X., & Geis, S. (2000). *Progress through the pipeline: 1992–93 college graduates and elementary/secondary school teaching as of 1997.* Washington, DC: National Center for Education Statistics.

Henke, R., Zahn, L & Carroll, D. (2001). *Attrition of new teachers among recent college graduates.* Washington, DC: National Center for Education Statistics.

Hirsch, E, Koppich, J., & Knapp, M. (2001). *Revisiting what states are doing to improve the quality of teaching: An update on patterns and trends.* Center for the Study of Teaching and Policy, University of Washington.

Hom, P., & Griffeth, R. (1995). *Employee turnover.* Cincinnati: South-Western Publishing.

Huling-Austin, L. (1990). Teacher induction programs and internships. In W. R. Houston (Ed.), *Handbook of research on teacher education.* Reston, VA: Association of Teacher Educators.

Hussar, W. (1998). *Predicting the need for newly hired teachers in the United States to 2008–09.* Washington, DC: National Center for Education Statistics.

Ingersoll, R. (1995). *Teacher supply, teacher qualifications and teacher turnover.* Washington, DC: National Center for Education Statistics.

Ingersoll, R. (1999). The problem of underqualified teachers in American secondary schools. *Educational Researcher, 28,* 26–37.

Ingersoll, R. (2001a). *Teacher turnover, teacher shortages and the organization of schools.* Center for the Study of Teaching and Policy, University of Washington.

Ingersoll, R. (2001b). Teacher turnover and teacher shortages: An organizational analysis. *American Educational Research Journal, 38*(3), 499–534.

Ingersoll, R. (2003a) *Who controls teachers' work?: Power and accountability in America's schools.* Cambridge, MA: Harvard University Press. <http://www.hup.harvard.edu/catalog/INGWHO.html>

Ingersoll, R. (2003b) Is there a shortage among mathematics and science teachers? *Science Educator 12*(1), 1–9.

Ingersoll, R. & Smith, T. (2003). The wrong solution to the teacher shortage. *Educational Leadership 60*(8), 30–33.

Integrated Postsecondary Educational Data System (IPEDS). (2001). *Data file.* Washington, DC: National Center for Education Statistics.

Kalleberg, A., & Mastekaasa, A. (1998). Organizational size, layoffs and quits in Norway. *Social Forces, 76,* 1243–73.

Kanter, R. (1977). *Men and women of the coloration.* New York: Basic.

Kirst, M. (1989). Who should control the schools? In T. J. Sergiovanni & J. Moore (Eds.), *Schooling for tomorrow.* Boston: Allyn and Bacon.

Kochanski, J. & Ledford, G. (2001). How to keep me—Retaining technical professionals. *Research-Technology Management.* May–June: 31–38.

Kopp, W. (1992). Reforming schools of education will not be enough. *Yale Law and Policy Review, 10,* 58–68.

Likert, R. (1967). *The human organization.* New York: McGraw-Hill.

Lortie, D. (1975). *School teacher.* Chicago: University of Chicago Press.

March, J., & Simon, H. (1958). *Organizations.* New York: Wiley.

Mobley, W. (1982). *Employee turnover: Causes, consequences and control.* Reading, MA: Addison-Wesley.

Mueller, C., & Price, J. (1990). Economic, psychological and sociological determinants of voluntary turnover. *Journal of behavioral economics, 19,* 321–335.

Murnane, R., Singer, J., Willett. J., Kemple, J., & Olsen, R. (Eds.). (1991). *Who will teach?: Policies that matter.* Cambridge, MA: Harvard University Press.

National Academy of Sciences. (1987). *Toward understanding teacher supply and demand.* Washington, DC: National Academy Press.

National Commission on Excellence in Education. (1983). *A nation at risk: The imperative for educational reform.* Washington, DC: Government Printing Office.

National Commission on Teaching and America's Future. (1997). *Doing what matters most: Investing in quality teaching.* New York: NCTAF.

Office of Personnel Management, (2003). *Central Personnel Data File (CPDF).* Washington, DC: OPM. <http://www.opm.gov/feddata/index.asp>

Parsons, Talcott. (1959). The school class as a social system: Some of its functions in American society. *Harvard Educational Review 29,* 297–318.

Porter, L. W., Lawler, E. E., & Hackman, J. R. (1975). *Behavior in organizations.* New York: McGraw-Hill.

Price, J. (1977). *The study of turnover.* Ames: Iowa State University Press.

Price, J. (1989). The impact of turnover on the organization. *Work and Occupations, 16,* 461–473.

Price, J. (1997). Handbook of organizational measurement. *International Journal of Manpower,* 18: no. 4–6.

Rosenholtz, S. (1989). *Teacher's workplace: The social organization of schools.* New York: Longman.

Schlecty, P., & Vance, V. (1981). Do academically able teachers leave education? The North Carolina case. *Phi Delta Kappan, 63,* 105–112.

Smith, T., & Ingersoll, R. (2003). Reducing teacher turnover: What are the components of effective induction? Paper presented at the annual meeting of the American Educational Research Association, Chicago. IL.

Snyder, T., & Hoffman, C. (2001). *The digest of education.* Washington, DC: U.S. Department of Education, National Center for Education Statistics.

Steers, R. M., & Momday, R. T. (1981). Employee turnover and the post-decision accommodation process. In B. M. Shaw and L. L. Cummings (Eds.), *Research in organizational behavior.* Greenwich: JAI Press.

Stinebrickner, T. R. (2001). A dynamic model of teacher labor supply. *Journal of Labor Economics, 19*(1), 196–230.

Strober, M., & Tyack, D (1980). Why do women teach and men manage? *Signs, 5,* 499–500.

Texas Center for Educational Research. (2000). *The cost of teacher turnover.* Austin, TX: Texas State Board for Educator Certification.

Turner, A. N., & Lawrence, P. R. (1964). *Industrial jobs and the worker.* Cambridge, MA: Harvard University Press.

Tyack, D. (1974). *The one best system.* Cambridge, MA: Harvard University Press.

U.S. Bureau of the Census. (2002). *Statistical abstract* (117th Edition). Washington, DC: U.S. Department of Commerce.

Waller, W. (1932). *The sociology of teaching.* New York: Wiley.

Walton, R. E. (1980). Establishing and maintaining high commitment work systems. In J. Kimberly & R. Miles (Eds.), *The organization life cycle.* San Francisco: Jossey-Bass.

Weaver, T. (1983). *America's teacher quality problem: Alternatives for reform.* New York: Praeger Publishers.

12

Whose Markets, Whose Knowledge?

MICHAEL W. APPLE

…We have entered a period of reaction in education. Our educational institutions are seen as total failures. High dropout rates, a decline in "functional literacy," a loss of standards and discipline, the failure to teach "real knowledge" and economically useful skills, poor scores on standardized tests, and more—all these are charges leveled at schools. And all of these, we are told, have led to declining economic productivity, unemployment, poverty, a loss of international competitiveness, and so on. Return to a "common culture," make schools more efficient, more responsive to the private sector. Do this and our problems will be solved.

Behind all of these charges is an attack on egalitarian norms and values. Although hidden in the rhetorical flourishes of the critics, in essence "too much democracy"—culturally and politically—is seen as one of the major causes of "our" declining economy and culture. Similar tendencies are quite visible in other countries as well. The extent of the reaction is captured in the words of Kenneth Baker, former British Secretary of Education and Science in the Thatcher government, who evaluated nearly a decade of rightist efforts in education by saying, "The age of egalitarianism is over."[1] He was speaking decidedly positively, not negatively.

The threat to egalitarian ideals that these attacks represent is not usually made quite this explicitly, as they are often couched in the discourse of "improving" competitiveness, jobs, standards, and quality in an educational system that is seen as in total crisis. This discourse is clearly present today in "New Labour" in the United Kingdom and in similar policies in the United States. In all too many ways, both nations' educational policies continue trends established under earlier conservative (and sometimes supposedly "liberal") governments.

It would be simplistic, however, to interpret what is happening as only the result of efforts by dominant economic elites to impose their will on education. Many of these attacks do represent attempts to reintegrate education into an economic agenda. Yet they cannot be fully reduced to that, nor can they be reduced to being only about the economy. Cultural struggles and struggles over race, gender, and sexuality coincide with class alliances and class power.

Education is a site of struggle and compromise. It serves as a proxy as well for larger battles over what our institutions should do, whom they should serve, and who should make these decisions. And, yet, by itself it is one of the major arenas in which resources, power, and ideology specific to policy, finance, curriculum, pedagogy, and evaluation in education are worked through. Thus, education is both cause and effect, determining and determined. Because of this, no one article could hope to give a complete picture of this complexity. What I hope to do instead is to provide an outline of some of the major tensions surrounding education in the United States as it moves in conservative directions. A key word here is directions. The plural is crucial to my arguments, because, as I showed, there are multiple and at times contradictory tendencies within the rightist turn.

Although my focus in this article is largely internal, it is impossible to understand current educational policy in the United States without placing it in its international context. Thus, behind the stress on higher standards, more rigorous testing, education for employment, and a much closer relationship between education and the economy in general, and so on, was the fear of losing in international competition and the loss of jobs and money to Japan, Mexico, and increasingly now the "Asian Tiger" economies such as China and elsewhere (although this has been mediated by the economic upheavals still being experienced in parts of Asia).[2] In the same way, the equally evident pressure in the United States to reinstall a (selective) vision of a common culture, to place more emphasis on the "Western tradition," on religion, on the English language, and similar emphases are deeply connected to cultural fears about Latin America, Africa, and Asia. This context provides a backdrop for my discussion.

The rightward turn has been the result of the successful struggle by the right to form a broad-based alliance. This new alliance has been so successful in part because it has been able to win the battle over common sense.[3] That is, it has creatively stitched together different social tendencies and commitments and has organized them under its own general leadership in issues dealing with social welfare, culture, the economy, and as we shall see in this article, education. Its aim in educational and social policy is what I called "conservative modernization."[4]

This alliance contains four major elements. Each has its own relatively autonomous history and dynamics, but each has also been sutured into the more general conservative movement. These elements include neoliberals, neoconservatives, authoritarian populists, and a particular fraction of the upwardly mobile professional and managerial new middle class. I pay particular attention to the first two of these groups here since they—especially neoliberals—are currently in leadership in this alliance to "reform" education. However, in no way do I want to dismiss the power of the latter two groups, and I return to them in later chapters.

Neoliberalism: Schooling, Choice, and Democracy

Neoliberals are the most powerful element within the alliance supporting conservative modernization. They are guided by a vision of the weak state. Thus, what is private is necessarily good and what is public is necessarily bad. Public institutions such as schools are "black holes" into which money is poured—and then seemingly disappears—but which do not provide anywhere near adequate results. For neoliberals, one form of rationality is more powerful than any other—economic rationality. Efficiency and an "ethic" of cost-benefit analysis are the dominant norms. All people are to act in ways that maximize their own personal benefits. Indeed, behind this position is an empirical claim that this is how *all* rational actors act. Yet, rather than being a neutral description of the world of social motivation, this is actually a construction of the world around the valuative characteristics of an efficiently acquisitive class type.[5]

Underpinning this position is a vision of students as human capital. The world is intensely competitive economically, and students—as future workers—must be given the requisite skills and dispositions to compete efficiently and effectively.[6] Furthermore, any money spent on schools that is not directly related to these economic goals is suspect. In fact, as "black holes," schools and other public services as they are currently organized and controlled waste economic resources that should go into private enterprise. Thus, for neoliberals, not only are public schools failing our children as future workers, but like nearly all public institutions they are sucking the financial life out of this society. Partly this is the result of "producer capture." Schools are built for teachers and state bureaucrats, not "consumers." They respond to the demands of professionals and other selfish state workers, not the consumers who rely on them. The increasingly virulent attacks on teachers unions and professional associations by the right is but the tip of the iceberg here.

The idea of the "consumer" is crucial here. For neoliberals, the world in essence is a vast supermarket. "Consumer choice" is the guarantor of democracy. In effect, education is seen as simply one more product like bread, cars, and television.[7] By turning it over to the market through voucher and choice plans, education will be largely self-regulating. Thus, democracy is turned into consumption practices. In these plans, the ideal of the citizen is that of the purchaser. The ideological effects of this position are momentous. Rather than democracy being a *political* concept, it is transformed into a wholly *economic* concept. The message of such policies is what might best be called "arithmetical particularism," in which the unattached individual—as a consumer—is deraced, declassed, and degendered.[8]

The metaphors of the consumer and the supermarket are actually quite apposite here. For just as in real life, there are individuals who indeed can go into supermarkets and choose among a vast array of similar or diverse products. And there are those who can only engage in what can best be called "postmodern" consumption. They stand outside the supermarket and can only consume the image.

The entire project of neoliberalism is connected to a larger process of exporting the blame from the decisions of dominant groups onto the state and onto poor people. After all, it was not the government that made the decisions to engage in capital flight and to move factories to those nations that have weak or no unions, fewer environmental regulations, and repressive governments. And it was not working-class and poor communities that chose to lose those jobs and factories, with the loss of hope and schools and communities in crisis that were among the results of these decisions. And it was neither of them who chose to lay off millions of workers—many of whom had done rather well in school—because of mergers and leveraged buyouts, trends that have again become more pronounced.

With their emphasis on the consumer rather than the producer, neoliberal policies need also to be seen as part of a more extensive attack on government employees. In education in particular, they constitute an offensive against teacher unions that are seen to be much too powerful and much too costly. Neoliberal policies, although they may not have been created as a conscious attack on women, need to be interpreted as part of a longer history of attacks on women's labor, as the vast majority of teachers in the United States—as in so many other nations—are women.[9]

Varied policy initiatives have emerged from the neoliberal segments of the new hegemonic alliance. Most have centered on either creating closer linkages between education and the economy or placing schools themselves into the market. The former is represented by widespread proposals for "school to work" and "education for employment" programs, and by vigorous cost-cutting attacks on the "bloated state." The latter initiative is no less widespread and is becoming increasingly powerful. It is represented by both national and state-by-state proposals for voucher and choice programs.[10] These include providing public money for private and religious schools (although these are highly contested proposals). Behind this is a plan to subject schools to the discipline of market competition.[11] Such "quasi-market solutions" are among the most divisive and hotly debated policy issues in the entire nation, with important court cases concerning funding for private or religious schools through voucher mechanisms having been decided or now being closely watched.[12]

Some proponents of "choice" argue that only enhanced parental "voice" and choice will provide a chance for "educational salvation" for minority parents and children.[13] Moe, for instance, claims that the best hope for the poor to gain the right "to leave bad schools and seek out good ones" is through an "unorthodox alliance."[14] Only by allying themselves with Republicans and business—the most powerful groups supposedly willing to transform the system—can the poor succeed, a set of arguments I shall take up and critically analyze later.

…Growing empirical evidence indicates that the development of "quasi-markets" in education has led to the exacerbation of existing social divisions surrounding class and race.[15] There are now increasingly convincing arguments that while the supposed overt goal of voucher and choice plans is to give poor people the right to exit public schools, among the ultimate long-term effects may be the increase of "white flight" from public schools into private and religious schools and the creation of the conditions where affluent white parents may refuse to pay taxes to support public schools that are more and more suffering from the debilitating effects of the fiscal crisis of the state. The result is even more educational apartheid, not less.[16]

In his own review of evidence from the U.S. experience, Whitty argues that although advocates of choice assume that competition will enhance the efficiency and responsiveness of schools, as well as give disadvantaged children opportunities that they currently do not have, this may be a false hope. These hopes are not now being realized and are unlikely to be realized in the future "in the context of broader policies that do nothing to challenge deeper social and cultural inequalities." As he goes on to say, "Atomized decision-making in a highly stratified society may appear to give everyone equal opportunities but transforming responsibility for decision-making from the public to the private sphere can actually reduce the scope for collective action to improve the quality of education for all."[17]

This position is ratified by Henig, who states that "the sad irony of the current education-reform movement is that, through overidentification with school choice proposals, the healthy impulse to consider radical reforms to address social problems may be channeled into initiatives that further erode the potential for collective deliberation and collective response."[18] When this effect is coupled with the fact that such neoliberal policies in practice may reproduce traditional hierarchies of class, race, and gender, these proposals should give us serious pause.[19]

There is a second variant of neoliberalism. This one *is* willing to spend more state and/or private money on schools, if and only if schools meet the needs expressed by capital. Thus, resources are made available for "reforms" and policies that further connect the education system to the project of making our economy more competitive. Two examples can provide a glimpse of this position. In a number of states, legislation has been passed that directs schools and universities to make closer links between education and the business community. In the state of Wisconsin, for instance, all teacher education programs had to include identifiable experiences on "education for employment" for all of its future teachers; and all teaching in the public elementary, middle, and secondary schools of the state had to include elements of education for employment in its formal curricula.[20]

The second example is seemingly less consequential, but in reality it is a powerful statement of the reintegration of educational policy and practice into the ideological agenda of neoliberalism. I am referring here to Channel One, a for-profit television network that is now being broadcast into schools enrolling over 40 percent of all middle and secondary school students in the nation (many of these schools are financially hard-pressed given the fiscal crisis, even though some states are currently experiencing slightly better budgets). In this "reform," schools are offered a "free" satellite dish, two VCRs, and television monitors for each of their classrooms by a private media corporation. They are also offered a free news broadcast for these students. In return for the equipment and the news, all participating schools must sign a three- to five-year contract guaranteeing that their students will watch Channel One every day.

This agreement sounds relatively benign. However, not only is the technology "hardwired" so that *only* Channel One can be received but also *mandatory advertisements* for major fast food, athletic wear, and other corporations are broadcast along with the news, which students—by contract—also must watch. Students, in essence, are sold as a captive audience to corporations. Because, by law, these students must be in schools, the United States is one of the first nations in the world to consciously allow its youth to be sold as commodities to those many corporations willing to pay the high price of advertising on Channel One to get a guaranteed (captive) audience.[21] Thus, under a number of variants of neoliberalism not only are schools transformed into market commodities, but so too now are our children.[22]

The attractiveness of conservative policies in education rests in large part on major shifts in our common sense—about what democracy is, about whether we see ourselves as possessive individuals ("consumers"), and ultimately about how we see the market working. Underlying neoliberal policies in education and their social policies in general is a faith in the essential fairness and justice of markets. Markets ultimately will distribute resources efficiently and fairly according to effort. They ultimately will create jobs for all who want them. They are the best possible mechanism to ensure a better future for all citizens (consumers).

Because of this, we of course must ask what the economy that reigns supreme in neoliberal positions actually looks like. Far from the positive picture painted by neoliberals in which technologically advanced jobs will replace the drudgery and the under- and unemployment so many people now experience if we were to only set the market loose on our schools and children, the reality is something else again. Unfortunately, markets clearly are as powerfully destructive as they are productive in people's lives.[23]

Let us take as a case in point the paid labor market to which neoliberals want us to attach so much of the education system. Even with the growth in proportion in high-tech-related jobs, the kinds of work that are and will be increasingly available to a large portion of the American population will not be highly skilled, technically elegant positions. Just the opposite will be the case. The paid labor market will increasingly be dominated by low-paying, repetitive work in the retail, trade, and service sectors. This is made strikingly clear by one fact. More cashier jobs will be created by the year 2005 than jobs for computer scientists, systems analysts, physical therapists, operations analysts, and radio-logic technicians *combined*. In fact, it is projected that 95 percent of all new positions will be found in the service sector. This sector broadly includes personal care, home health aides; social workers (many of whom are now losing or have lost their jobs because of cutbacks in social spending); hotel and lodging workers; restaurant employees; transportation workers; and business and clerical personnel. Furthermore, eight of the top ten individual occupations that will account for the most job growth in the next ten years include the following: retail salespersons, cashiers, office clerks, truck drivers, waitresses/waiters, nursing aides/orderlies, food preparation workers, and janitors. The majority of these positions obviously do not require high levels of education. Many of them are low-paid, non-unionized, temporary, and part-time, with low or no benefits. And many are dramatically linked to, and often exacerbate, the existing race, gender, and class divisions of labor. These trends are predicted to continue.[24] This is the emerging economy we face, not the overly romantic picture painted by neoliberals who urge us to trust the market.

Neoliberals argue that making the market the ultimate arbiter of social worthiness will eliminate politics and its accompanying irrationality from our educational and social decisions. Efficiency and cost-benefit analysis will be the engines of social and educational transformation. Yet among the ultimate effects of such "economizing" and "depoliticizing" strategies is actually to make it ever harder to interrupt the growing inequalities in resources and power that so deeply characterize this society. Nancy Fraser illuminates the process in the following way:

> In male dominated capitalist societies, what is "political" is normally defined contrastively against what is "economic" and what is "domestic" or "personal." Here, then, we can identify two principal sets of institutions that depoliticize social discourses: they are, first, domestic institutions, especially the normative domestic form, namely the modern restricted male-headed nuclear family; and, second, official economic capitalist system institutions, especially paid workplaces, markets, credit mechanisms, and "private" enterprises and corporations. Domestic institutions depoliticize certain matters by personalizing and/or familializing them; they cast these as private-domestic or personal-familial matters in contradistinction to public, political matters. Official economic capitalist system institutions, on the other hand, depoliticize certain matters by economizing them; the issues in question here are cast as impersonal market imperatives, or as "private" ownership prerogatives, or as technical problems for managers and planners, all in contradistinction to political matters. In both cases, the result is a foreshortening of chains of in-order-to relations for interpreting people's needs; interpretive chains are truncated and

prevented from spilling across the boundaries separating the "domestic" and the "economic" from the political.[25]

This very process of depoliticization makes it very difficult for the needs of those with less economic, political, and cultural power to be accurately heard and acted on in ways that deal with the true depth of the problem. For Fraser, this outcome occurs because of what happens when "needs discourses" get retranslated into both market talk and "privately" driven policies.

For our purposes here, we can talk about two major kinds of needs discourses: oppositional and reprivatization discourses. *Oppositional* forms of needs talk arise when needs are politicized from below and are part of the crystallization of new oppositional identities on the part of subordinated social groups. What was once seen as largely a "private" matter is now placed into the larger political arena. Sexual harassment, race and sex segregation in paid labor, and affirmative action policies in educational and economic institutions provide examples of "private" issues that have now spilled over and can no longer be confined to the "domestic" sphere.[26]

Reprivatization discourses emerge as a response to the newly emergent oppositional forms and try to press these forms back into the "private" or the "domestic" arena. They are often aimed at dismantling or cutting back social services, deregulating "private" enterprise, or stopping what are seen as "runaway needs." Thus, reprivatizers may attempt to keep issues such as, say, domestic battery from spilling over into overt political discourse and will seek to define it as purely a family matter. Or they will argue that the closing of a factory is not a political question but instead is an "unimpeachable prerogative of private ownership or an unassailable imperative of an impersonal market mechanism."[27] In each of these cases, the task is to contest both the possible breakout of runaway needs and to depoliticize the issues.

In educational policy in the United States, there are a number of clear examples of these processes. The state of California provides a well-known instance. A binding referendum that prohibited the use of affirmative action policies in state government, in university admission policies, and so on was passed overwhelmingly as reprivatizers spent an exceptional amount of money on an advertising campaign that labeled such policies as "out of control" and as improper government intervention into decisions involving "individual merit." The California referendum has spawned similar, and quite controversial, initiatives in other states. Voucher plans in education—where contentious issues surrounding whose knowledge should be taught, who should control school policy and practice, and how schools should be financed are left to the market to decide—offer another prime example of such attempts at "depoliticizing" educational needs. Finally, giving primary responsibility over the definition of important "work skills" to the private sector—an act that evacuates the possibility of criticism of the ways work is actually constructed, controlled, and paid—enables a definition of work both as a "private" matter and as purely a technical choice to go unchallenged. All these examples show the emerging power of reprivatizing discourses.

A distinction that is useful here in understanding what is happening in these cases is that between "value" and "sense" legitimation.[28] Each signifies a different strategy by which powerful groups or states legitimate their authority. In the first (value) strategy, legitimation is accomplished by actually giving people what may have been promised. Thus, the social democratic state may provide social services for the population in return for continued support. That the state will do this is often the result of oppositional discourses gaining more power in the social arena and having more power to redefine the border between public and private.

In the second (sense) strategy, rather than providing people with policies that meet the needs they have expressed, states and/or dominant groups attempt to *change the very meaning* of the sense of social need into something that is very different. Thus, if less powerful people call for "more democracy" and for a more responsive state, the task is not to give "value" that meets this demand, especially when it may lead to runaway needs. Rather, the task is to change what actually *counts* as democracy. In the case of neoliberal policies, democracy is now redefined as guaranteeing choice in an unfettered market. In essence, the state withdraws. The extent of acceptance of such transformations of needs and needs discourses shows the success of the reprivatizers in redefining the borders between public and private again and demonstrates how a people's common sense can be shifted in conservative directions during a time of economic and ideological crisis.

Neoconservatism: Teaching "Real" Knowledge

Although neoliberals largely are in leadership in the conservative alliance, I noted that the second major element within the new alliance is neoconservatism. Unlike the neoliberal emphasis on the weak state, neoconservatives are usually guided by a vision of the strong state. This is especially true surrounding issues of knowledge, values, and the body. Whereas neoliberalism may be seen as being based in what Raymond Williams would call an "emergent" ideological assemblage, neoconservatism is grounded in "residual" forms.[29] It is largely, though not totally, based in a romantic appraisal of the past, a past in which "real knowledge" and morality reigned supreme, in which people "knew their place," and where stable communities guided by a natural order protected us from the ravages of society.[30]

Among the policies being proposed under this ideological position are mandatory national and statewide curricula, national and statewide testing, a "return" to higher standards, a revivification of the "Western tradition," patriotism, and conservative variants of character education. Yet underlying some of the neoconservative thrust in education and in social policy in general is not only a call for "return." Behind it as well—and this is essential—is a fear of the "Other," fears that have been exacerbated and often cynically employed for political purposes and used to drive wedges between religious traditions since the tragedy of September 11. This is expressed in its support for a standardized national curriculum, its attacks on bilingualism and multiculturalism, and its insistent call for raising standards.[31]

That the neoconservative emphasis on a return to traditional values and "morality" has struck a responsive chord can be seen in the fact that among the best-selling books in the nation during the past decade was William Bennett's *The Book of Virtues*.[32] Bennett, a former Secretary of Education in a conservative Republican administration, has argued that for too long a period of time, "We have stopped doing the right things [and] allowed an assault on intellectual and moral standards." In opposition to this, we need "a renewed commitment to excellence, character, and fundamentals."[33] Bennett's book aims at providing "moral tales" for children to "restore" a commitment to "traditional virtues" such as patriotism, honesty, moral character, and entrepreneurial spirit. Such positions not only have entered the common sense of society in quite influential ways but also have provided part of the driving force behind the movement toward charter schools. These schools have individual charters that allow them to opt out of most state requirements and develop curricula based on the wishes of their clientele. Although in theory there is much to commend in such policies, all too many charter schools have become ways through which conservative religious activists and others gain public funding for schools—and home schooling—that would otherwise be prohibited such support.[34]

Behind much of the neoconservative position is a clear sense of loss—a loss of faith, of imagined communities, of a nearly pastoral vision of like-minded people who shared norms and values and in which the "Western tradition" reigned supreme. It is more than a little similar to Mary Douglas's discussion of purity and danger, in which what was imagined to exist is sacred and "pollution" is feared above all else.[35] We/they binary oppositions dominate this discourse and the culture of the "Other" is to be feared.

This sense of cultural pollution can be seen in the increasingly virulent attacks on multiculturalism (which is itself a very broad category that combines multiple political and cultural positions),[36] on the offering of schooling or any other social benefits to the children of "illegal" immigrants and even in some cases to the children of legal immigrants, in the conservative English-only movement, and in the equally conservative attempts to reorient curricula and textbooks toward a particular construction of the Western tradition.

In this regard, neoconservatives lament the "decline" of the traditional curriculum and of the history, literature, and values it is said to have represented.[37] Behind this worry is a set of historical assumptions about "tradition," about the existence of a social consensus over what should count as legitimate knowledge, and about cultural superiority.[38] Yet it is crucial to remember that the "traditional" curriculum whose decline is lamented so fervently by neoconservative critics "ignored most of the groups that compose the American population whether they were from Africa, Europe, Asia, Central and South America, or from indigenous North American peoples."[39] Its primary and often exclusive focus was typically only on quite a narrow spectrum of those people who came from a small number of northern and Western European nations, in spite of the fact that the cultures and histories represented in the United States were "forged out of a much larger and more diverse complex of peoples and societies." The mores and cultures of this narrow spectrum were seen as archetypes of "tradition" for everyone. They were not simply taught, but taught as superior to every other set of mores and culture.[40]

As Lawrence Levine reminds us, a selective and faulty sense of history fuels the nostalgic yearnings of neoconservatives. The canon and the curriculum have never been static. They have always been in a constant process of revision, "with irate defenders insisting, as they still do, that change would bring with it instant decline."[41] Indeed, even the inclusion of such "classics" as Shakespeare within the curriculum of schools in the United States came about only after prolonged and intense battles, ones that were the equal of the divisive debates over whose knowledge should be taught today. Thus, Levine notes that when neoconservative cultural critics ask for a "return" to a "common culture" and "tradition," they are oversimplifying to the point of distortion. What is happening in terms of the expansion and alteration of official knowledge in schools and universities today "is by no means out of the ordinary; certainly it is not a radical departure from the patterns that have marked the history of [education]—constant and often controversial expansion and alteration of curricula and canons and incessant struggle over the nature of that expansion and alteration."[42]

Of course, such conservative positions have been forced into a kind of compromise in order to maintain their cultural and ideological leadership as a movement to "reform" educational policy and practice. A prime example is the emerging discourse over the history curriculum—in particular the construction of the United States as a "nation of immigrants."[43] In this hegemonic discourse, everyone in the history of the nation was an immigrant, from the first Native American population who supposedly trekked across the Bering Strait and ultimately populated North, Central, and South America, to the later waves of populations who came from Africa, Mexico, Ireland, Germany, Scandinavia, Italy, Russia, Poland, and elsewhere, to finally the recent populations from Asia, Latin America, Africa, and other regions. Although it is true that the United States is constituted by people from all over the world—and that is one of the things that makes it so culturally rich and vital—such a perspective constitutes an erasure of historical memory. For some groups came *in chains*, with massive numbers of death in the Middle Passage, and were subjected to state-sanctioned slavery and apartheid for hundreds of years. Others suffered what can only be called bodily, linguistic, and cultural destruction.[44]

This said, however, it does point to the fact that although the neoconservative goals of national curricula and national testing are pressed for, they are strongly mediated by the necessity of compromise. Because of this, even the strongest supporters of neoconservative educational programs and policies have had to also support the creation of curricula that at least partly recognize "the contributions of the Other."[45] This is partly because there is an absence of an overt and strong national department of education and a tradition of state and local control of schooling. The "solution" has been to have national standards developed "voluntarily" in each subject area.[46] Indeed, the example I gave earlier about history is one of the results of such voluntary standards.

Because it is the national professional organizations in these subject areas—such as the National Council of Teachers of Mathematics (NCTM)—that are developing such national standards, the standards themselves are compromises and thus are often more flexible than those wished for by neoconservatives. This very process does act to provide a check on conservative policies over knowledge. However, this should not lead to an overly romantic picture of the overall tendencies emerging in educational policy. Leadership in school "reform" is increasingly dominated by conservative discourses surrounding "standards," "excellence," "accountability," and so on. Because the more flexible parts of the standards have proven to be too expensive to actually implement and have generated considerable conservative backlash,[47] standards talk ultimately functions to give more rhetorical weight to the neoconservative movement to enhance central control over "official knowledge" and to "raise the bar" for achievement. The social implications of this in terms of creating even more differential school results are increasingly worrisome.[48]

Yet it is not only in such things as the control over legitimate knowledge where neoconservative impulses are seen. The idea of a strong state is also visible in the growth of the regulatory state as it concerns teachers. There has been a steadily growing change from "licensed autonomy" to "regulated autonomy" as teachers' work is more highly standardized, rationalized, and "policed."[49] Under conditions of licensed autonomy, once teachers are given the appropriate professional certification they are basically free—within limits—to act in their classrooms according to their judgment. Such a regime is based on trust in "professional discretion." Under the growing conditions of regulated autonomy, teachers' actions are now subject to much greater scrutiny in terms of process and outcomes.[50] Indeed, some states in the United States not only have specified the content that teachers are to teach but also have regulated the only appropriate methods of teaching. Not following these specified "appropriate" methods puts the teacher at risk of administrative sanctions. Such a regime of control is based not on trust, but on a deep suspicion of the motives and competence of teachers. For neoconservatives it is the equivalent of the notion of "producer capture" that is so powerful among neoliberals. For the former, however, it is not the market that will solve this problem, but a strong and interventionist state that will see to it that only "legitimate" content and methods are taught. And this will be policed by statewide and national tests of both students and teachers. The imprint of these kinds of commitments are thoroughly visible in such policies as No Child Left Behind.

I have claimed elsewhere that such policies lead to the "deskilling" of teachers, the "intensification" of their work, and the loss of autonomy and respect. This is not surprising, as behind much of this conservative impulse is a clear distrust of teachers and an attack both on teachers' claims to competence and especially on teachers' unions.[51]

The mistrust of teachers, the concern over a supposed loss of cultural control, and the sense of dangerous "pollution" are among the many cultural and social fears that drive neoconservative policies. However, as I noted earlier, underpinning these positions as well is often an ethnocentric, and even racialized, understanding of the world. Perhaps this can be best illuminated through the example of Herrnstein and Murray's volume, *The Bell Curve*.[52] In a book that sold hundreds of thousands of copies, the authors argue for a genetic determinism based on race (and to some extent gender). For them, it is romantic to assume that educational and social policies can ultimately lead to more equal results, since differences in intelligence and achievement are basically genetically driven. The wisest thing policy makers can do would be to accept this and plan for a society that recognizes these biological differences and does not provide "false hopes" to the poor and the less intelligent, most of whom will be black. Obviously, this book has reinforced racist stereotypes that have long played a considerable part in educational and social policies in the United States.[53]

Rather than seeing race as it is—as a fully *social* category that is mobilized and used in different ways by different groups at different times[54]—positions such as those argued by Herrnstein and Murray provide a veneer of seeming scientific legitimacy for policy discourses that have been discredited intellectually many times before. The sponsored mobility given to this book, in which it is reported that the authors received large sums of money from neoconservative foundations to write and publicize the volume, speaks clearly not only to the racial underpinnings of important parts of the neoconservative agenda but also to the power of conservative groups to bring their case before the public.

The consequences of such positions are not only found in educational policies, but in the intersection of such policies with broader social and economic policies, where they have been quite influential. Here too we can find claims that what the poor lack is not money, but both an "appropriate" biological inheritance and a decided lack of values regarding discipline, hard work, and morality.[55] Prime examples here include programs such as "Learnfare" and "Workfare" in which parents lose a portion of their welfare benefits if their children miss a significant number of school days or in which no benefits are paid if a person does not accept low-paid work, no matter how demeaning or even if child care or health care are not provided by the state. Such policies reinstall earlier "workhouse" policies that were so popular—and so utterly damaging—in the United States, Britain, and elsewhere.[56]

I have spent much of my time in this section documenting the growing power of neoconservative positions in educational and social policy in the United States. Neoconservatives have forged a creative coalition with neoliberals, a coalition that—in concert with other groups—is effectively changing the landscape on which policies are argued out. Yet, even given the growing influence of neoliberal and neoconservative policies, they would be considerably less successful if they had not also brought authoritarian populist religious fundamentalists and conservative evangelicals under the umbrella of the conservative alliance. It is to this group that we now turn.

Authoritarian Populism: Schooling as God Wanted It

Perhaps more than in any other major industrialized nation, it is not possible to fully understand educational politics in the United States without paying a good deal of attention to the "Christian Right." It is exceptionally powerful and influential, beyond its numbers, in debates over public policy in the media, education, social welfare, the politics of sexuality and the body, religion, and so on. Its influence comes from the immense commitment by activists within it, its large financial base, its populist rhetorical positions, and its aggressiveness in pursuing its agenda. "New Right" authoritarian populists ground their positions on education and social policy in general in particular visions of biblical authority, "Christian morality," gender roles, and the family. The New Right sees gender and the family, for instance, as an organic and divine unity that resolves "male egoism and female selflessness."

As Hunter puts it:

Since gender is divine and natural...there is [no] room for legitimate political conflict.... Within the family women and men—stability and dynamism—are harmoniously fused when undisturbed by modernism, liberalism, feminism, and humanism which not only threaten masculinity and femininity directly, but also [do so] through their effects on children and youth.... "Real women," i.e., women who know themselves as wives *and* mothers, will not threaten the sanctity of the home by striving for self. When men or women challenge these gender roles they break with God and nature; when liberals, feminists, and secular humanists prevent them from fulfilling these roles they undermine the divine and natural supports upon which society rests.[57]

In the minds of such groups, public schooling thus is *itself* a site of immense danger. In the words of the conservative activist Tim LaHaye, "Modern public education is the most dangerous force in a child's life: religiously, sexually, economically, patriotically, and physically."[58] This is connected to the New Right's sense of loss surrounding schooling and the family.

> Until recently, as the New Right sees it, schools were extensions of home and traditional morality. Parents could entrust their children to public schools because they were locally controlled and reflected Biblical and parental values. However, taken over by alien, elitist forces, schools now interpose themselves between parents and children. Many people experience fragmentation of the unity between family, church, and school as a loss of control of daily life, one's children, and America. Indeed, [the New Right] argues that parental control of education is Biblical, for in God's plan, the primary responsibility for educating the young lies in the home and directly in the father.[59]

It is exactly this sense of "alien and elite control," the loss of biblical connections, and the destruction of "God-given" family and moral structures that drives the authoritarian populist agenda. It is an agenda that is increasingly powerful, not only rhetorically, but in terms of funding and in conflicts over what schools should do, how they should be financed, and who should control them. This agenda includes, but goes beyond, issues of gender, sexuality, and the family. It extends as well to a much larger array of questions about what is to count as "legitimate" knowledge in schools. And in this larger arena of concern about the entire corpus of school knowledge, conservative activists have had no small measure of success in pressuring textbook publishers to change what they include and in altering important aspects of state educational policy on teaching, curriculum, and evaluation. This is crucial, as in the absence of an overt national curriculum, the commercially produced *textbook*—regulated by individual state's purchases and authority—remains the dominant definition of the curriculum in the United States.[60]

The power of these groups is visible, for example, in the "self-censorship" in which publishers engage. For instance, under conservative pressure a number of publishers of high school literature anthologies have chosen to include Martin Luther King's "I Have a Dream" speech, but *only* after all references to the intense racism of the United States have been removed.[61] At the level of state curriculum policy, this is very visible in the textbook legislation in, say, Texas, which mandates texts that stress patriotism, obedience to authority, and the discouragement of "deviance."[62] Because most textbook publishers aim the content and organization of their textbooks at what will be approved by a small number of populous states that in essence approve and purchase their textbooks *statewide*, this gives states such as Texas (and California) immense power in determining what will count as "official knowledge" throughout the entire country.[63]

Thus, in concert with neoconservative elements within the conservative alliance, authoritarian populist religious activists have had a substantial influence on curriculum policy and practice. For them, only by recentering issues of authority, morality, family, church, and "decency" can schools overcome the "moral decay" so evident all around us.[64] Only by returning to inerrantist understandings of biblical teachings and fostering (or mandating) a climate in schools where such teachings are given renewed emphasis can our culture be saved.[65]

Although a number of states and school systems have been able to create mechanisms that deflect some of these pressures, the bureaucratic nature of many school systems and of the local and regional state in general has actually produced the conditions where parents and other community members who might otherwise disagree with the New Right ideologically are convinced to join them in their attacks on the content and organization of schooling.[66]

Although authoritarian populist struggles over curriculum and texts have been growing rapidly, this mistrust of public schools has also fueled considerable and intense support among them for neoliberal policies such as voucher and choice plans. The New Right, as a largely populist assemblage, has some very real mistrust of the motives and economic plans of capital. After all, such rightist populists have themselves experienced the effects of downsizing, layoffs, and economic restructuring. However, even given their partial insights into the differential effects of global competition and economic restructuring, they see in proposals for educational marketization and privatization a way in which they can use such "reforms" for their own purposes. Either through reduced school taxes, through tax credits, or through the allocation of public money to private and religious schools, they can create a set of schools organized around the more moral "imagined communities" they believe have been lost.[67] I take this up in more detail later on.

This search for the reconstitution of imagined communities points to one of the effects of reprivatization talk on the politics surrounding educational policy. In the process of denying the legitimacy of oppositional claims, reprivatization discourses may actually tend to politicize the issues even more. These issues become even more a part of public, not "domestic," contestation. This paradox—reprivatization talk may actually lead to further public discussion of breakaway needs—does not always lead to victories by oppositional groups such as feminists, racially subjected peoples, or other disempowered groups, however. Rather, such politicization can in fact lead to the growth of new social movements and new social identities whose fundamental aim is to push breakaway needs back into the economic, domestic, and private spheres. New, and quite conservative, coalitions can be formed.

This is exactly what has happened in the United States, where a set of reprivatizing discourses "in the accents of authoritarian populism" has made creative connections with the hopes and especially the fears of a range of disaffected constituencies and has united them into a tense but very effective alliance supporting positions behind reprivatization.[68] And this could not have been done if rightist groups had not succeeded in changing the very meaning of key concepts of democracy in such a way that the Christian Right could comfortably find a place under the larger umbrella of the conservative alliance.

The Professional and Managerial New Middle Class: More Testing, More Often

Although I speak somewhat more briefly about them here because of their relatively limited—but rapidly growing—power, there is a final group that provides some of the support for the policies of conservative modernization. This is a fraction of the professional new middle class that gains its own mobility within the state and within the economy based on the use of technical expertise. These are people with backgrounds in management and efficiency techniques who provide the technical and "professional" support for accountability, measurement, "product control," and assessment that is required by the proponents of neoliberal policies of marketization and neoconservative policies of tighter central control in education.

Members of this fraction of the upwardly mobile professional and managerial new middle class do not necessarily believe in the ideological positions that underpin the conservative alliance. In fact, in other aspects of their lives they may be considerably more moderate and even "liberal" politically. However, as experts in efficiency, management, testing, and accountability, they provide the technical expertise to put in place the policies of conservative modernization. Their own mobility *depends* on the expansion of both such expertise and the professional ideologies of control, measurement, and efficiency that accompany it. Thus, they often support such policies as "neutral instrumentalities," even when these policies may be used for purposes other than the supposedly neutral ends to which this class fraction is committed.[69]

Because of this situation, it is important to realize that a good deal of the current emphasis in schools on high-stakes testing, on more rigorous forms of accountability, and on tighter control is not totally reducible to the needs of neoliberals and neoconservatives. Rather, part of the pressure for these policies comes from educational managers and bureaucratic offices who fully believe that such control is warranted and "good." Not only do these forms of control have an extremely long history in education, but tighter control, high-stakes testing, and (reductive) accountability methods provide more dynamic roles for such managers, a point I noted earlier. These policies enable such actors to engage in a moral crusade and enhance the status of their own expertise.

Yet, in a time when competition for credentials and cultural capital is intense, the increasing power of mechanisms of restratification such as the return of high levels of mandatory standardization also provides mechanisms that enhance the chances that the children of the professional and managerial new middle class will have *less competition* from other children. Thus, the introduction of devices to restratify a population enhances the value of the credentials that the new middle class is more likely to accumulate, given the stock of cultural capital it already possesses.[70] I am not claiming that this is necessarily intentional, but creating such devices does *function* to increase the chances for mobility by middle-class children who depend not on economic capital but on cultural capital for advancement.

In such a situation, I believe that this group is not immune to ideological shifts to the right. Given the fear generated by the attacks on the state and on the public sphere by both neoliberals and neoconservatives, this class fraction is decidedly worried about the future mobility of its children in an uncertain economic world. Thus, they may be drawn more overtly to parts of the conservative alliance's positions, especially those coming from the neoconservative elements that stress greater attention to traditional "high-status" content, greater attention to testing, and a greater emphasis on schooling as a stratifying mechanism. This can be seen in a number of states where parents of this class fraction are supporting charter schools that will stress academic achievement in traditional subjects and traditional teaching practices. Where the majority of members of this class grouping will align in the future in the debates over policy remains to be seen. Given their contradictory ideological tendencies, it is possible that the right will be able to mobilize them under conditions of fear for the future of their jobs and children.[71]

Conclusion

Because of the complexity of educational politics in the United States, I have devoted most of this article to an analysis of the conservative social movements that are having a powerful impact on debates over policy and practice in education and in the larger social arena. I have suggested that conservative modernization in education is guided by tense coalition forces, some of whose aims partly contradict others.

The very nature of this coalition is crucial. It is more than a little possible that the alliance underpinning conservative modernization can overcome its own internal contradictions and can succeed in radically transforming educational policy and practice. Thus, although neoliberals call for a weak state and neoconservatives demand a strong state, these very evident contradictory impulses can come together in creative ways. The emerging focus on centralized standards, content, and tighter control paradoxically can be the first and most essential step on the path to marketization through voucher and choice plans.

Once statewide or national curricula and tests are put in place, comparative school-by-school data will be available and will be published in a manner similar to the "league tables" on school achievement published in England. Only when there is standardized content and assessment can the market be set free, since the "consumer" can then have "objective" data on which schools are "succeeding" and which schools are not. Market rationality, based on "consumer choice," will ensure that the supposedly good schools will gain students and the bad schools will disappear. This assemblage is embodied in many of the impulses behind No Child Left Behind, for example.

… But let me say here that one of these effects is that when the poor "choose" to keep their children in under-funded and decaying schools in the inner cities or in rural areas (given the decline and expense of urban mass transportation, poor information, the absence of time, and their decaying economic conditions, to name but a few of the realities), *they* (the poor) will be blamed individually and collectively for making bad "consumer choices." Reprivatizing discourses and arithmetical particularism will justify the structural inequalities that will be (re)produced here. In this way, as odd as it may seem, neoliberal and neoconservative policies, ones ultimately supported by authoritarian populists and even by many members of the professional middle class, that are seemingly contradictory may mutually reinforce each other in the long run.[72]

Yet, although I have argued that the overall leadership in educational policy is exercised by this alliance, I do not want to give the impression that these four elements under the hegemonic umbrella of this coalition are uncontested or are always victorious. This is simply not the case. As a number of people have demonstrated, scores of counterhegemonic programs and possibilities exist at the local level throughout the United States. Many institutions of higher education, schools, and even entire school districts have shown remarkable resiliency in the face of the concerted ideological attacks and pressures from conservative restorational groups. And many teachers, academics, community activists, and others have created and defended educational programs that are both pedagogically and politically emancipatory.[73]

Indeed, we are beginning to see cracks in the alliance's power in unanticipated ways. For example, a growing number of students in elementary, middle, and secondary schools are actively refusing to take the mandatory tests that many states have introduced. This action has been supported by groups of teachers, administrators, parents, and activists.[74] Clearly, things are bubbling up from below the surface whose effects will be "interesting" to say the least.

Having said this, however, it is important to note the obstacles in creating the conditions for large-scale movements to defend and build progressive policies. We need to remember that there is no powerful central ministry of education in the United States. Teachers' unions are relatively weak at a national level (nor is there any guarantee that teachers' unions always act progressively). There is no consensus about an "appropriate" progressive agenda in educational policy here, as there is a vast multiplicity of compelling (and unfortunately at times competing) agendas involving race/ethnicity, gender, sexuality, class, religion, "ability," and so on. Thus, it is structurally difficult to sustain long-term national movements for more progressive policies and practices.

Because of this, most counterhegemonic work is organized locally or regionally. However, there currently are growing attempts at building national coalitions around what might best be called a "decentered unity." Organizations such as the National Coalition of Educational Activists and those centered around "Rethinking Schools" are becoming more visible nationally.[75] None of these movements have the financial and organizational backing that stands behind the neoliberal, neoconservative, and authoritarian populist groups. None have the ability to bring their case before the "public" through the media and through foundations in the ways that conservative groups have been able to do. And none have the capacity or the resources to quickly mobilize a large base of nationally directed membership to challenge or promote specific policies in the ways that the members of the alliance can.

Yet, in the face of all of these structural, financial, and political dilemmas, the fact that so many groups of people have not been integrated under the alliance's hegemonic umbrella and have created scores of local examples of the very possibility of difference shows us in the most eloquent and lived ways that educational policies and practices do not go in any one unidimensional direction. Even more important, these multiple examples demonstrate that the success of conservative policies is never guaranteed. This is crucial in a time when it is easy to lose sight of what is necessary for an education worthy of its name.

Notes

1. Madeleine Arnot, "Schooling for Social Justice," unpublished paper, University of Cambridge, Department of Education, 1990.
2. William Greider, *One World, Ready or Not* (New York: Simon & Schuster, 1997).
3. See Michael W. Apple, *Cultural Politics and Education* (New York: Teachers College Press, 1996) and Michael W. Apple, *Official Knowledge*, 2d ed. (New York: Routledge, 2000).
4. I am drawing upon Roger Dale, "The Thatcherite Project in Education," *Critical Social Policy* 9 (winter 1989/1990): 4–19. Because of the size and complexity of the United States, I cannot focus on all the policy issues and initiatives now being debated or implemented. For further descriptions, see the chapters on policy research in William Pink and George Noblit, eds., *Continuity and Contradiction: The Futures of the Sociology of Education* (Cresskill, NJ: Hampton Press, 1995).
5. Apple, *Cultural Politics and Education* and Ted Honderich, *Conservatism* (Boulder: Westview Press, 1990).
6. Given the current emphasis on this by neoliberals, it may be the case that while Bowles and Gintis's book on the relationship between education and capitalism, *Schooling in Capitalist America*, was reductive, economistic, and essentializing when it first appeared in 1976, oddly it may be more accurate today. See Samuel Bowles and Herbert Gintis, *Schooling in Capitalist America* (New York: Basic Books, 1976). For criticism of their position, see Michael W. Apple, *Teachers and Texts* (New York: Routledge, 1988); Michael W. Apple, *Education and Power*, 2d ed. (New York: Routledge, 1995); and Mike Cole, ed., *Bowles and Gintis Revisited* (New York: Falmer Press, 1988).
7. See Michael W. Apple, *Ideology and Curriculum*, 3rd ed. (New York: RoutledgeFalmer, 2004).
8. Stephen Ball, *Education Reform* (Philadelphia: Open University Press, 1994) and Apple, *Cultural Politics and Education*.
9. Apple, *Teachers and Texts*, 31–78 and Sandra Acker, "Gender and Teachers' Work," in *Review of Research in Education, Volume 21*, ed. Michael W. Apple (Washington, DC: American Educational Research Association, 1995), 99–162. A number of the larger gender implications of neoliberalism in education and the economy can be seen in Jacky Brine, *Under-Educating Woman; Globalizing Inequality* (Philadelphia: Open University Press, 1992) and Madeleine Arnot, Miriam David, and Gaby Weiner, *Closing the Gender Gap: Postwar Education and Social Change* (Cambridge, England: Polity Press, 1999).
10. John Chubb and Terry Moe, *Politics, Markets, and America's Schools* (Washington, DC: The Brookings Institution, 1990). See also, Ernest House, *Schools for Sale* (New York: Teachers College Press, 1998).
11. See the discussion of these arguments in Kristen L. Buras and Michael W. Apple, "School Choice, Neoliberal Promises, and Unpromising Evidence," *Educational Policy* 19 (July 2005): 550-564.
12. See Amy Stuart Wells, *Time to Choose* (New York: Hill & Wang, 1993); Jeffrey Henig, *Rethinking School Choice* (Princeton, NJ: Princeton University Press, 1994); Kevin Smith and Kenneth Meier, eds., *The Case Against School Choice* (Armonk, NY: M. E. Sharpe, 1995); Bruce Fuller, Elizabeth Burr, Luis Huerta, Susan Puryear, and Edward Wexler, *School Choice: Abundant Hopes, Scarce Evidence of Results* (Berkeley and Stanford: Policy Analysis for California Education, University of California at Berkeley and Stanford University, 1999); and John F. Witte, *The Market Approach to Education* (Princeton, NJ: Princeton University Press, 2000).
13. Geoff Whitty, "Creating Quasi-Markets in Education," in *Review of Research in Education, Volume 22*, ed. Michael W. Apple (Washington, DC: American Educational Research Association, 1997), 17. See also Chubb and Moe, *Politics, Markets, and America's Schools* and Gary Rosen, "Are Schools Vouchers Un-American?" *Commentary* 109 (February 2000): 26–31.
14. Quoted in Whitty, "Creating Quasi-Markets in Education," 17.
15. See, for example, Geoff Whitty, Sally Power, and David Halpin, *Devolution and Choice in Education* (Philadelphia: Open University Press, 1998) and Hugh Lauder and David Hughes, *Trading in Futures: Why Markets in Education Don't Work* (Philadelphia: Open University Press, 1999).
16. See Apple, *Cultural Politics and Education*, especially Chapter 4, for a description of the ways in which many current social and educational policies often widen racial gaps.
17. Whitty, "Creating Quasi-Markets in Education," 58.
18. Henig, *Rethinking School Choice*, 22.
19. See Whitty, "Creating Quasi-Markets in Education," Lauder and Hughes, *Trading in Futures*, and Apple, *Cultural Politics and Education*.
20. Many times, however, these initiatives are actually "unfunded mandates." That is, requirements such as these are made mandatory, but no additional funding is provided to accomplish them. The intensification of teachers' labor at all levels of the education system that results from this situation is very visible. On the history of education for employment, see Herbert Kliebard, *Schooled to Work: Vocationalism and the American Curriculum, 1876–1946* (New York: Teachers College Press, 1999). For clear and thoughtful analyses of other effects on higher education, see Geoffrey White, ed., *Campus, Inc.* (Amherst, NY: Prometheus Books, 2000) and Sheila Slaughter and Larry L. Leslie, *Academic Capitalism* (Baltimore, MD: Johns Hopkins University Press, 1997).
21. For further discussion of the powerful forces of commercialism in schools, see Alex Molnar, *School Commercialism* (New York: Routledge, 2005).
22. I have engaged in a much more detailed analysis of Channel One in Apple, *Official Knowledge*, 89–112. See also Alex Molnar, *Giving Kids the Business* (Boulder: Westview Press, 1996). A good example as well is provided by financially troubled ZapMe!, which gives free computer equipment in return for demographic information on children in schools. Of course, there is a history of resistance to things such as Channel One. UNPLUG, a student-led group, has been in the forefront of contesting the commercialization of schools. Further, as I discuss in my final chapter, both conservative and progressive groups have joined forces to act against Channel One.
23. Apple, *Cultural Politics and Education*, 68–90 and Greider, *One World, Ready or Not*.

24. Ibid. See also, Christopher Cook, "Temps Demand a New Deal," *The Nation*, 27 March 2000, pp.13–19.
25. Nancy Fraser, *Unruly Practices* (Minneapolis: University of Minnesota Press, 1989), 168.
26. Ibid., 172. See also the discussion of how gains in one sphere of social life can be "transported" into another sphere in Samuel Bowles and Herbert Gintis, *Democracy and Capitalism* (New York: Basic Books, 1986) and Apple, *Teachers and Texts*. On the history of such positions in health care, see Sandra Opdycke, *No One Was Turned Away* (New York: Oxford University Press, 1999).
27. Fraser, *Unruly Practices*, 172.
28. Roger Dale, *The State and Education Policy* (Philadelphia: Open University Press, 1989).
29. For further discussion of residual and emergent ideological forms, see Raymond Williams, *Marxism and Literature* (New York: Oxford University Press, 1977).
30. See Allen Hunter, *Children in the Service of Conservatism* (Madison: University of Wisconsin, Institute for Legal Studies, 1988) and Apple, *Cultural Politics and Education*.
31. See, for example, E. D. Hirsch Jr., *The Schools We Need and Why We Don't Have Them* (New York: Doubleday, 1996). For an insightful critique of Hirsch's position, see Kristen L. Buras, "Questioning Core Assumptions: A Critical Reading of E. D. Hirsch's *The Schools We Need and Why We Don't Have Them*," *Harvard Educational Review* 69 (spring 1999): 67–93. See also Susan Ohanian, *One Size Fits Few: The Folly of Educational Standards* (Portsmouth, NH: Heinemann, 1999).
32. William Bennett, *The Book of Virtues* (New York: Simon & Schuster, 1994).
33. William Bennett, *Our Children and Our Country* (New York: Simon & Schuster, 1988), 8–10.
34. See Amy Stuart Wells, *Beyond the Rhetoric of Charter School Reform* (Los Angeles: University of California at Los Angeles, Graduate School of Education and Information Studies, 1999).
35. Mary Douglas, *Purity and Danger* (London: Routledge, 1966).
36. See, for example, Cameron McCarthy and Warren Crichlow, eds., *Race, Identity, and Representation in Education* (New York: Routledge, 1994).
37. See, for example, Diane Ravitch, *Left Back* (New York: Simon and Schuster, 2000). See my response to Ravitch in Michael W. Apple, "Standards, Subject Matter, and a Romantic Past," *Educational Policy* 15 (May 2001):7–36.
38. This is treated in greater depth in Apple, *Ideology and Curriculum*.
39. Lawrence Levine, *The Opening of the American Mind* (Boston: Beacon Press, 1996), 20.
40. Ibid.
41. Ibid., 15. See also Apple, *Ideology and Curriculum* and Herbert Kliebard, *The Struggle for the American Curriculum*, 2d ed. (New York: Routledge, 1995).
42. Levine, *The Opening of the American Mind*, 15.
43. Catherine Cornbleth and Dexter Waugh, *The Great Speckled Bird* (New York: St. Martin's Press, 1995).
44. For a counternarrative on the history of the United States, see Howard Zinn, *A People's History of the United States* (New York: HarperCollins, 1999). See also Howard Zinn, *The Howard Zinn Reader* (New York: Seven Stories Press, 1997) and Howard Zinn, *The Future of History* (Monroe, ME: Common Courage Press, 1999).
45. This is often done through a process of "mentioning" where texts and curricula include material on the contributions of women and "minority" groups but never allow the reader to see the world through the eyes of oppressed groups. Or as is the case in the discourse of "we are all immigrants," compromises are made so that the myth of historical similarity is constructed at the same time as economic divides among groups grow worse and worse. See Apple, *Official Knowledge*, 42–60.
46. Diane Ravitch, *National Standards in American Education* (Washington, DC: The Brookings Institution, 1995).
47. In the face of concerted criticism, the NCTM recently has officially voted to return to more of an emphasis on traditional mathematical concerns and methods of teaching. See Anemona Hartocollis, "Math Teachers Back Return of Education to Basic Skills," *The New York Times*, 15 April 2000, p. A16.
48. This is discussed in more detail in Michael W. Apple, *Power, Meaning, and Identity* (New York: Peter Lang, 1999) and Apple, *Cultural Politics and Education*. See also Ohanian, *One Size Fits Few*.
49. This distinction is developed in more depth in Dale, *The State and Education Policy*.
50. For a detailed critical discussion of the effects of this on curricula, teaching, and evaluation, see Linda McNeil, *Contradictions of School Reform* (New York: Routledge, 2000).
51. See Apple, *Education and Power*; Apple, *Teachers and Texts*; and Acker, "Gender and Teachers' Work." Clear gender and class antagonisms are at work here, ones that have a long history. Analyses of the ways in which race intersects with these dynamics and helps construct the history and labor process of teaching has been somewhat less developed. However, the ongoing work of Michelle Foster and Michael Fultz is quite helpful in this regard.
52. Richard Herrnstein and Charles Murray, *The Bell Curve* (New York: Free Press, 1994).
53. See Michael Omi and Howard Winant, *Racial Formation in the United States*, 2d ed. (New York: Routledge, 1994) and Steven Selden, *Inheriting Shame* (New York: Teachers College Press, 1999). Selden's book in particular demonstrates how very prevalent constructions of race were in a wide range of educational policies and practices, including many programs and individuals whose participation in, say, the popular eugenics movement is little known.
54. Ibid. See also Richard Dyer, *White* (New York: Routledge, 1997) and Cornel West, *Race Matters* (New York: Vintage Books, 1994).
55. Rebecca Klatch, *Women of the New Right* (Philadelphia: Temple University Press, 1987). For criticism of some of these positions, and especially those espoused by Herrnstein and Murray, see Joe Kincheloe, Shirley Steinberg, and Aaron D. Gresson, eds., *Measured Lies* (New York: St. Martin's Press, 1996).
56. For further discussion of this, see Apple, *Cultural Politics and Education*, 11–13.
57. Hunter, *Children in the Service of Conservatism*, 15.
58. Quoted in Ibid., 57.

59. Ibid.
60. The power of the text and its contradictory impulses have been detailed in Apple, *Teachers and Texts* and Apple, *Official Knowledge*. For more discussion of the ways in which struggles over the textbook help mobilize conservative activists, see Apple, *Cultural Politics and Education*, 42–67.
61. Delfattore, *What Johnny Shouldn't Read*, 123.
62. Ibid., 139.
63. The history and influence of the state's role in defining official knowledge and in textbooks is developed in much more depth in Apple, *Teachers and Texts* and Apple, *Official Knowledge*. See also Cornbleth and Waugh, *The Great Speckled Bird*.
64. See Alexandra S. Dimick and Michael W. Apple, "Texas and the Politics of Abstinence-Only Textbooks," *Teachers College Record*, May 02, 2005.
65. See Delfattore, *What Johnny Shouldn't Read*; Ralph Reed, *After the Revolution* (Dallas: Word Publishing, 1996); and Fritz Detwiler, *Standing on the Premises of God* (New York: New York University Press, 1999).
66. Anita Oliver and I provide an analysis of a concrete instance of this in Apple, *Cultural Politics and Education*, 42–67.
67. Although he limits himself to a discussion of the nation as an "imagined community," I am extending Benedict Anderson's metaphor to include religious communities as well since many of the attributes are the same. See Benedict Anderson, *Imagined Communities* (New York: Verso, 1991).
68. Fraser, *Unruly Practices*, 172–73.
69. Basil Bernstein makes an important distinction between those fractions of the new middle class who work for the state and those who work in the private sector. They may have different ideological and educational commitments. See Basil Bernstein, *The Structuring of Pedagogic Discourse* (New York: Routledge, 1990). For more on the ways "intermediate" classes and class fractions operate and interpret their worlds, see Erik Olin Wright, ed., *The Debate on Classes* (New York: Verso, 1998); Erik Olin Wright, *Classes* (New York: Verso, 1985); Erik Olin Wright, *Class Counts* (New York: Cambridge University Press, 1997); and Pierre Bourdieu, *Distinction* (Cambridge: Harvard University Press, 1984).
70. See Bourdieu, *Distinction;* Pierre Bourdieu, *Homo Academicus* (Stanford: Stanford University Press, 1988); and Pierre Bourdieu, *The State Nobility* (Stanford: Stanford University Press, 1996).
71. A combination of the work of Bernstein, Wright, and Bourdieu would be useful in understanding this class. A satirical, but still interesting, analysis of a segment of this class can be found in the work of the conservative commentator David Brooks. See David Brooks, *Bobos in Paradise* (New York: Simon & Schuster, 2000).
72. See Apple, *Cultural Politics and Education*, 22–41.
73. See especially Michael W. Apple and James A. Beane, eds., *Democratic Schools* (Alexandria, VA: Association for Supervision and Curriculum Development, 1995); Michael W. Apple and James A. Beane, eds., *Democratic Schools: Lessons from the Chalk Face* (Buckingham, England: Open University Press, 1999); and Gregory Smith, *Public Schools That Work* (New York: Routledge, 1993). Also of considerable interest here is the work on detracking and educational reform by Jeannie Oakes. See Jeannie Oakes, Karen H. Quartz, Steve Ryan, and Martin Lipton, *Becoming Good American Schools* (San Francisco: Jossey-Bass, 2000).
74. See Jacques Steinberg, "Blue Books Closed, Students Boycott Standardized Tests," *The New York Times,* 13 April 2000, pp. A1, A22. It remains to be seen whether this will grow. It is also unclear whether children of the poor and culturally and economically disenfranchised will participate widely in this. After all, affluent children *do* have options and can compensate for not having tests scores. This may not be the case for the children of those this society calls the "Other."
75. See, for example, the journal *Rethinking Schools*. It is one of the very best indicators of progressive struggles, policies, and practices in education. Information can be gotten from Rethinking Schools, 1001 E. Keefe Avenue, Milwaukee, WI 53212, USA or via its Web site at <www.rethinkingschools.org>.

PART II
Suggested Readings

Anyon, J. (1980). Social class and the hidden curriculum of work. *Journal of Education, 162,* 67–92.

Apple, M. W. (1978). *Ideology and curriculum.* Boston: Routledge and Kegan Paul.

Apple, M. W. (1992). The text and cultural politics. *Educational Researcher,* 21 (7), 4–11, 19.

Apple, M. W. (1993). *Official knowledge: Democratic education in a conservative age.* New York: Routledge.

Biddle, B., Good, T., & Goodson, I. (Eds.). (1996). *International handbook of teachers and teaching.* Amsterdam: Kluwer Academic Publishers.

Bidwell, C. E. (1965). The school as a formal organization. In J. G. March (Ed.), *Handbook of research on organizations* (pp. 972–1018). Chicago: Rand McNally.

Binder, A. (2002). *Contentious curricula: Afro-centrism and creationism in American public schools.* Princeton, NJ: Princeton University Press.

Boyd, D., Grossman, P. L., Hammerness, K., Lankford, R. H., Loeb, S., McDonald, M., Reininger, M., Ronfeldt, M., & Wyckoff, J. (2008). Surveying the landscape of teacher education in New York City: Constrained variation and the challenge of innovation. *Educational Evaluation and Policy Analysis,* 30, 319–343.

Boyd, D., Grossman, P. L., Lankford, R. H., Loeb, S., & Wyckoff, J. (2009). Teacher preparation and student achievement. *Educational Evaluation and Policy Analysis,* 31, 416–440.

Bryk, A., Lee, V. E., & Holland, P. B. (1993). *Catholic schools and the common good.* Cambridge, MA: Harvard University Press.

Cohen, E. G. (1994). *Designing group work: Strategies for the heterogeneous classroom.* New York: Teachers College Press.

Cohen, E. G. (1994). Restructuring the classroom: Conditions for productive small groups. *Review of Educational Research,* 64, 1–35.

Cohen, E. G., Lotan, R., & Leechor, C. (1989). Can classrooms learn? *Sociology of Education,* 62, 75–94.

Davies, S. & Quirke, L. (2007). The impact of sector on school organizations: The logics of markets and institutions. *Sociology of Education,* 80 (1), 66–89.

Dreeben, R. (1968). *On what is learned in school.* Boston: Addison-Wesley.

Dworkin, A. G. (1985). *When teachers give up: Teacher burnout, teacher turnover, and their impact on children.* Austin, TX: Hogg Foundation for Mental Health and Texas Press.

Dworkin, A. G. (1987). *Teacher burnout in the public schools: Structural causes and consequences for children.* Albany: State University of New York Press.

Gamoran, A. & Dreeben, R. (1986). Coupling and control in educational organizations. *Administrative Science Quarterly,* 31, 612–632.

Goodson, I. (1992). *Studying teachers' lives.* London: Routledge.

Goodson, I. (1993). *School subjects and curriculum change* (3rd ed.). London: Falmer Press.

Hallinan, M. T. (2008).Teacher influences on students' attachment to school. *Sociology of Education,* 81 (3), 271–283.

Hammack, F. (Ed.). (2004). *The comprehensive high school today.* New York: Teachers College Press.

Ingersoll, R. M. (1994). Organizational control in secondary schools. *Harvard Educational Review,* 64, 150–172.

Ingersoll, R. (1999). The problem of under-qualified teachers in American secondary schools. *Educational Researcher,* 28, 26–37.

Ingersoll, R. (2001). Teacher turnover and teacher shortages. *American Educational Research Journal,* 38 (3), 499–534.

Ingersoll, R. (2003). *Who controls teachers' work? Power and accountability in America's schools.* Cambridge, MA: Harvard University Press.

Johnson, S. M. (1990). *Teachers at work.* New York: Basic Books.

Lee, V. E., Dedrick, R. F., & Smith, J. B. (1991). The effect of the social organization of schools on teachers: Self-efficacy and satisfaction. *Sociology of Education,* 64, 190–208.

Lesko, N. (2001). *Act your age! A cultural construction of adolescence.* New York: Routledge.

Lortie, D. (1975). *School teacher: A sociological study.* Chicago: University of Chicago Press.

Lubeck, S. (1985). *Sandbox society: An ethnographic comparison.* London: Falmer.

Maher, F. & Tetrault, M. T. (1994). *The feminist classroom.* New York: Basic Books.

McFarland, D. (2001). Student resistance: How formal and informal organization of classrooms facilitate everyday forms of student deviance. *American Journal of Sociology,* 107, 612–678.

McLaughlin, M. & Little, J. W. (Eds.). (1993). *Teachers work: Individuals, colleagues, and contexts.* New York: Teachers College Press.

213

McLaughlin, M. W. & Talbert, J. E. (1993). *Contexts that matter for teaching and learning*. Stanford, CA: Center for Research on the Context of Secondary School Teaching.

McLaughlin, M. W. & Talbert, J. E. (1993). How the world of students and teachers challenges policy coherence. In S. H. Fuhrman (Ed.), *Designing coherent education policy: Improving the system*. San Francisco: Jossey-Bass.

McLaughlin, M. W. & Talbert, J. E. (2006). *Building school-based teacher learning communities*. New York: Teachers College Press.

Metz, M. H. (1978). *Classrooms and corridors*. Berkeley, CA: University of California Press.

Metz, M. H. (1990). How social class differences shape teachers' work. In M. W. McLaughlin, J. E. Talbert, & N. Bascia (Eds.), *The contexts of teaching in secondary schools: Teachers' realities*. New York: Teachers College Press.

Meyer, J. W., Kamens, D., Benavot, A., Cha, Y. K., & Wong, S. Y. (1992). *School knowledge for the masses: World models and national primary curriculum categories in the twentieth century*. London: Falmer.

Porter, A. C., Polikoff, M. S., & Smithson, J. (2009). Is there a de facto national intended curriculum? Evidence from state content standards. *Educational Evaluation and Policy Analysis*, 31, 238–268.

Schneider, B. & Bryk, A. (1996). *Social trust: A moral resource for school improvement*. Chicago: Center for School Improvement.

Schneider, B. & Stevenson, D. (1999). *The ambitious generation: America's teenagers, motivated but directionless*. New Haven, CT: Yale University Press.

Semel, S. F. (1996). "Yes, but . . .": Multiculturalism and the reduction of educational inequality. *Teachers College Record*, 98 (1), 153–177.

Semel, S. F. & Sadovnik, A. R. (1999). *"Schools of tomorrow," schools of today: What happened to progressive education*. New York: Peter Lang.

Stevenson, D. & Baker, D. (1991). State control of the curriculum and classroom instruction. *Sociology of Education*, 64, 1–10.

Weick, K. (1976). Educational organizations as loosely-coupled systems. *Administrative Science Quarterly*, 21, 1–19.

Whitty, G. (1985). *Sociology and school knowledge*. London: Methuen.

Wong, S. L. (1991). Evaluating the content of textbooks: Public interests and professional authority. *Sociology of Education*, 64, 11–18.

International Education

The readings in Part III examine issues in comparative and international education. The purpose of international comparisons is to explore the similarities and differences among different national systems of education in order to see to what extent there are universal processes of educational formation or to what extent schools reflect specific national cultures and characteristics.

Chapter 13, "The Political Construction of Mass Schooling: European Origins and Worldwide Institutionalization" by the Stanford University sociologist Francisco O. Ramirez and Emory University sociologist John Boli, provides an application of institutional theory to the development of mass schooling internationally. The authors examine the relationship between mass schooling, democracy, and civil society.

In Chapter 14, "Sociological Understandings of Contemporary Gender Transformations in Schooling in the UK," the Cambridge University sociologist Madeleine Arnot analyzes changes in the relationship between gender and education in in the UK in the latter part of the twentieth century. Arnot examines how the feminist movement, changes in gender roles, and changes in the global economy have affected the education of males and females and have contributed to changes in gender-based achievement gaps.

Chapter 15, "Nation versus Nation: The Race to Be the First in the World" by the Pennsylvania State sociologists David P. Baker and Gerald LeTendre, examines the worldwide competition to become first in the international student achievement rankings. The authors apply institutional theory to analyze the politics of competition, the similarities and differences among national educational systems, and the problems with the current rankings frenzy.

Questions for Reflection and Discussion

1 How do institutional theorists such as Ramirez and Boli explain the development of mass educational systems throughout the world? What would Bowles and Gintis say about their explanation? What would Randall Collins say?

2 What are the changes in the effects of education on gender that have occurred in the last half-century? What explanations does Arnot offer for these changes? How have achievement gaps between males and females changed and why have they changed? What would social-class reproduction theorists such as Bowles and Gintis say about these changes? How would functionalists explain these processes and outcomes?

3 How do Baker and LeTendre explain the competition to become ranked first on international tests? How would functionalist and conflict theorists explain this worldwide phenomenon?

13

The Political Construction of Mass Schooling

European Origins and Worldwide Institutionalization

FRANCISCO O. RAMIREZ AND JOHN BOLI

Introduction

During the late eighteenth and nineteenth centuries, national states constructed mass schooling systems that eventually came to encompass their entire populations of children. State authorization, sponsorship, funding, and control of mass education first developed in Western Europe (Collins 1977) and later became a central feature of a highly institutionalized model of national development throughout the world (Ramirez and Boli 1982). And yet, most comparative studies of education almost entirely overlook the historical origins of state systems of schooling (see the papers in Altbach, Arnove, and Kelly 1982; Kazamias 1977; Eckstein and Noah 1969), thereby ignoring the sociological significance of the successful institutionalization of this social innovation.

We examine the European origins and worldwide institutionalization of the state system of mass schooling. Our main objective is to account for the rise and legitimation of nation-states' compelling interest in mass education. We explicitly do not purport to explain the early expansion of primary school enrollments, though studies of this process are interesting in their own right (see, for instance, Craig and Spear 1983).[1] Some existing studies seek to explain early cross-national *differences* in the linkages between the state and education, such as variations in the degree of centralized control over education (Archer 1979), but we focus on transnational *similarities* in the institutional character of state educational systems. These similarities include ideological acceptance of particular goals for mass education, the adoption of compulsory school laws and constitutional provisions affirming a state interest in mass education, and the formation of national educational ministries and bureaus.

Our starting point is the observation that the development of the state's compelling interest in education was not solely a response to the needs of an industrializing economy, to class or status conflicts, nor to unique historical conjunctures in particular countries, such as the character of the central bureaucracy in Prussia (Rosenberg 1958), the revolutions and reactions in France (Gontard 1976), the power of the peasantry in Sweden (Warne 1929), or the extension of the franchise to the working classes in England (Jones 1977). These internal, societal-level factors were indeed important in shaping the particular characteristics of the various state educational systems. Our concern, however, lies in understanding the universality of state schooling: Why was the social innovation of mass state-sponsored education adopted in virtually every Western European country in the "long" nineteenth century, from Prussia (1763) to Belgium (1914), despite great variation in societal characteristics and histories?

To make sense of this phenomenon, we need to consider the broader civilizational network within which these nation-states operated. This is not an entirely novel idea: Cohen (1970, 1979) has argued that state-sponsored mass schooling systems can emerge only in a civilizational network of nation-states competing with one another, and Reisner (1922) has argued that state action in the educational domain is an outcome of European competitive processes. Here, we want to back up these views with a review of the historical evidence for a number of European countries and then develop a theoretical explanation for this phenomenon.

Our view is that European states became engaged in authorizing, funding, and managing mass schooling as part of an endeavor to construct a unified national polity (cf. Ringer 1977; Bendix 1964). Within such a polity, individuals were expected to find their primary identification with the nation, and it was presumed that state power would be enhanced by the universal participation of citizens in national projects. We show that in some cases, a military defeat or a failure to keep pace with industrial development in rival countries stimulated the state to turn to education as a means of national revitalization to avoid losing power and prestige in the interstate system. In other cases, when a nation moving toward a position of first rank in the system was challenged by rivals attempting to block its rise through military alliances and economic exertions, mass schooling was adopted as a means of achieving more comprehensive mobilization to assure continued success in the system. External challenges of these sorts were important stimuli to state action in education, not least because they exacerbated the costs associated with internal obstacles to national development and success, including such factors as the power of the clergy, state- or class-based privileges, and subunit political autonomy (Ringer 1977).

But why should mass education be invoked as a means of enhancing national unity and ensuring national success in the interstate system? Competitive rivalries and crises of national integration in prior eras had not led to the call for state-sponsored mass schooling. Nor is it correct to assume that the adoption of compulsory mass education so effectively enhanced the position of a nation-state within the broader world system that it generated imitative behavior. State interest in mass education was shaped by the political construction of mass education, that is, by its *perceived institutional character* rather than by the actual effects of compulsory mass education on nation-state structures.[2] Thus, our task is to explain why the extension of schooling to the masses through a compulsory state-sponsored system became a plausible and ultimately irresistible response to challenges from the external environment.

The explanation we develop involves two general ideas:

1   The nation-states of Europe adopted state educational systems because this organizational strategy was the course of action most consistent with *the developing Western European model of a national society*. We view this model as a set of institutionalized definitions of reality that operated as a symbolic universe (Berger and Luckman 1966) assigning meaning and legitimacy to some entities, organizational forms, and courses of action while making others unintelligible and unsupportable. The movement toward a closer union between states and schools proceeded despite sometimes profound opposition, because a state educational system increasingly became what a national society must develop when faced with challenging or adverse circumstances. The latter were increasingly interpreted not just as national crises but also as opportunities for a more comprehensive nation-building effort. Hence, the European model of a national society in the nineteenth century facilitated the establishment and success of state educational systems despite the many extinction pressures associated with the "liability of newness" (Freeman, Carroll, and Hannan 1983). As this model of the nation-state has become further institutionalized in the twentieth century, new nation-state candidates have increasingly adopted the expected educational goals and organizational forms that demonstrate the authenticity of their nation-building projects

within the established system of nation-states (cf. DiMaggio and Powell 1983; Meyer and Rowan 1977).

2 The European model of a national society emerged primarily as the product of three much-discussed and related *transformations in European culture, polity, and economy:* the Reformation and Counter-Reformation, the construction of the national state and the interstate system, and the triumph of the exchange economy. These transformations in the larger environment produced a model of the national society that emphasized both the primacy of the socializable individual (Berger, Berger, and Kellner 1973) and the ultimate authority and national responsibility of the state (Grew 1984). Thus, we contend that the union of states and schools as a nation-building process was imposed by the larger environment on its subunit states. Because the world today continues to reflect these basic features of the European experience, the European model of a nation-state is now writ worldwide. A state educational system has therefore become an institutional imperative for contemporary nation-states.

The task of this paper is to develop these ideas into a coherent explanation of the construction and institutionalization of the state educational system. First, we briefly examine the historical record, centering our discussion on five economically less developed European states—Prussia, Austria, Denmark, Sweden, and Italy—and then considering state-school linkages in the two most developed and dominant nineteenth-century powers—England and France.[3] We show that state educational systems did not originate in the most dominant countries, contrary to the widespread assumption that educational innovations inevitably start there and diffuse to less developed or less powerful countries. Rather, the most dominant powers were able to resist the systemwide pressures favoring mass education and cling to the older organizational forms associated with their earlier success in the system, even though such resistance could prove disadvantageous in the long run.

The second section of the paper develops our explanation. Focusing on Europe as a whole, we identify five institutionalized legitimating myths that underlie the European model of a national society and that justified the extension of schooling to the children of the masses and the takeover of schooling by the state. We then briefly discuss the environmental forces that shaped these legitimating myths and produced the national society model that came to dominate in nineteenth-century Europe.[4]

We conclude by briefly discussing comparative research findings that illustrate the contemporary relevance of our explanatory argument, showing that the political construction of mass schooling is a worldwide institutional undertaking legitimated by what has become the world model of a national society.

State Education Efforts to 1900: Historical Sketches

Less Developed and Less Dominant Countries

The earliest regulation proclaiming universal, compulsory education appeared in the German state of Weimar in 1619 (Thut and Adams 1964). In other countries where compulsory education was instituted early on, the rule was applied only to a very restricted class of persons, e.g., to the samurai warrior elite in Tokugawa, Japan (Dore 1964). Our historical review begins with Prussia, where the Weimarian ambition was first put into practice on a wide scale. Throughout this discussion, we rely on sources specific to each country and on Flora's (1983) dates for the various stages in the development of mass schooling and compulsory education.

Prussia. In the seventeenth century, both England and the United Provinces made great strides in economic development while the German areas stagnated (Cipolla 1974). But during this period, the relatively insignificant Electorate of Brandenburg developed into the state of Prussia, which became the nucleus of modernization of the German national state, a process completed in 1871 (see the analysis by Rosenberg [1958]). In the 1700s, Prussia was essentially a "state without a nation"; i.e., it had a strong and centralized bureaucracy that oversaw a highly fragmented polity dominated by local interests. The Prussian problem lay in creating a nation to match its state.

The starting point for examining educational development in Prussia is 1716, when Frederick William I made attendance at village schools compulsory for all children not otherwise provided with instruction. The phrase "not otherwise provided" is important; this directive was not aimed at the children of the elite, for they had private tutors or attended the Gymnasium. In 1763, Frederick II (Frederick the Great) reiterated the earlier order for compulsory education in a famous directive, "General Regulations for Village Schools" (Cubberley 1920). He pledged some financial aid from the state, which resulted in a modest increase in formal schooling in parts of Prussia.

What influenced Frederick the Great to initiate efforts in education? Marriott and Robertson (1915) argue that Frederick, following a military model of governance, tried to unify Prussia through state-directed education. All children were taught to identify with the state and its goals and purposes rather than with local polities (estates, peasant communities, regions, etc.). The timing of Frederick's regulations is highly significant: They were issued at the end of the Seven Years War, in which Prussia and England fought newly allied Austria and France. Although Prussia won the war, victory came only at great cost: enormous loss of life, exhaustion of the state treasury, and devastation of the economy. Moreover, Prussia was still surrounded by hostile enemies. Frederick faced a severe national crisis, largely because of the obdurate unwillingness of the German nobility to form a coherent territorially based national polity. Education became the means of reconstruction and renewal.

Prussia went through much the same experience only forty years later, this time on the losing end. Napoleon's triumph over the Prussians at Jena in 1806 destroyed a large part of the Prussian army and subjected Prussia to heavy French influence. The humiliating Treaty of Tilsit, imposed on Prussia by Napoleon, provoked a strong national revival movement that was epitomized by Fichte's lectures delivered in 1807 in Berlin, *Addresses to the German Nation* (Boyd and King 1975). Fichte called for patriotism to the German nation, even though that nation had yet to coalesce fully, and stressed education as the means to that end. He claimed that universal, state-directed, compulsory education would teach all Germans to be good Germans and would prepare them to play whatever role—military, economic, political—fell to them in helping the state reassert Prussian power (Marriott and Robertson 1915).

Conditions were ripe for Fichte's words to have effect. Almost immediately, a Bureau of Education was established within the Ministry of the Interior; ten years later, a separate Department of Education was created in the Ministry of Religion, Education, and Public Health. Between 1817 and 1825, under the direction of Baron von Altenstein, state administration of education was established (Rowlinson 1974). Taxes were imposed to finance the school system, and every Land was required to establish local primary and folk schools. State certification of primary school teachers and the establishment of state normal schools to provide teacher training followed later (Reisner 1922).

Some of the designers of the Prussian system were liberal reformers, but Prussian officialdom was extremely skeptical of providing the masses with too much schooling or with schooling that was too classical. Frederick the Great had clearly expressed the prevailing sentiment: "We do not confer upon the individual or upon society any benefit when we educate him beyond the bounds of his social class and vocation, give him a cultivation which he cannot make use of, and awaken in him pretensions and needs which his lot in life does not allow him to satisfy" (quoted in Reisner 1922, pp. 143–44). The reification of social divisions in Prussia went hand in hand with the reflexive association of education with religion. In 1848, when an assembly of teachers at Tivoli (near Berlin) recommended the establishment of a secular educational ministry, the government response was extremely negative: Religious instruction was more important than pedagogical theory (Alexander 1918). But two years after the Franco-Prussian War, a more unified German polity removed from the clergy the authority to inspect the schools. In 1906 the primary school system was reorganized, giving the state greater and more direct responsibility for financing education (Anderson 1970).

Some aspects of the union of state and schools in Prussia are undoubtedly unique to the German national experience, but two features of this process stand out. First, the state attempted to use mass schooling to create a more unified national citizenry and thereby consolidate state power both within the nation and relative to other national states, as enunciated explicitly by Fichte. Second, the union was sparked by a clear challenge to Prussia's position in the European state system—its defeat at the hands of the French after a period during which Prussia had managed gradually to increase its international stature and power. Prussia saw its rise in the European system blocked. Its response was state-controlled education, and the system it constructed would later be widely cited as an important element of Prussian (German) success in the state system.

Austria. In 1774, under Joseph II, Austria passed a universal compulsory education law. This law was clearly copied after Frederick the Great's work and was sparked by the dissolution of the Society of Jesus, which had controlled most of Austrian education until that time (Papanek 1962). This first effort to link schools with the state was conditioned by the defeat of Austria in the Seven Years War (1756–1763). But the full development of a system of national education was frustrated by the reactionary politics that swept Austria in the aftermath of the French Revolution and the Napoleonic era. The return of the Jesuits in 1814 ushered in an era of religious resurgence in educational matters, and after a period of state control during which the religious authorities gradually exerted more and more influence over the schools, the state signed a concordat with the Pope in 1855, returning full control to the Church.

The definitive movement toward a state educational system in Austria was triggered by Prussia's defeat of Austria in 1866 (Papanek 1962). The 1867 constitution was intended to reform Austrian government and revitalize its national power; to accomplish this nation-building goal, schools were delivered firmly into state control. Complete separation of schools from the Church was instituted in the following year. A compulsory education law followed in 1869. This movement toward the unification of schools and state took place despite vigorous opposition from a papacy that viewed state-directed education as an evil by-product of modernity.

If Prussia was upwardly mobile in the European state system between 1700 and 1870, Austria travelled the same road in reverse. The Napoleonic Wars affected Prussia and Austria in opposite ways. For Prussia, military defeat and political humiliation paved the way for the nationalization of public education; for Austria, the same experience led to a renewed commitment to the symbolic foundation of the empire—the Church (Rokkan 1980). Only after Bismarck successfully divided the moribund empire and confronted Austria with a powerful and unified Germany did Austria go the route of national state construction. At that historical juncture (1867–1868), the process of tying mass education to the state in Austria no longer differed greatly from that in Prussia. In both cases, mass public education was adopted as a means of improving national competitiveness in the interstate system.

Denmark and Sweden. Credit for the first state-managed system of compulsory mass schooling is often assigned to Denmark (Bendix 1964). As early as 1721, Frederick IV sought to build a system of schools in the royal domains, and his son Christian VI extended those efforts toward a genuine national system. But Christian could not muster the necessary resources; thus, the royal law of 1739 calling for compulsory schooling was largely a symbolic gesture that could not be realized in practice (Warne 1929). The breakthrough in forging the link between the state and education was made in 1789 under Frederick VI through the establishment of a Grand School Commission. This commission did not finish its work until 1814, when its report led to the passage of a law that set the foundations of the modern Danish school system; the specifications included compulsory education for children between the ages of seven and fourteen (Boje, Borup, and Rützebeck 1932).

Denmark's experience in establishing a state-controlled school system resembles that of Austria more than Prussia. Denmark had been a major European power in the seventeenth century, despite its small size. By 1800, however, Denmark's demise was an indisputable fact, and the loss of Norway to Sweden in 1809 symbolized its fall all too well. Denmark was prime for the appearance of its Fichte, and it found one in the person of N.F.S. Grundtvig, a clergyman who between 1807 and 1814 became the prime advocate of education as a means for Denmark to regain its spiritual and national strength (Vibaek 1964). After passage of the law of 1814, Denmark proceeded rapidly with the construction of a national system.

The development of the Swedish state educational system was influenced by changes in Sweden's position in the European system. Sweden was a major European power under Gustav Adolf in the seventeenth century, but its empire lasted only a short time as Prussia, England, and Russia struggled for control of the Baltic, enlisting Sweden and Denmark as subordinate powers in various alliances. Sweden experienced severe difficulties following several military defeats in the eighteenth century, but the conditions necessary to evoke a call for salvation through education had not yet developed in European culture. Hence, though a number of educational proposals were made before the nineteenth century, most of them were offered by reform theologians whose only concern was for religious instruction. In the middle and late eighteenth century, liberal reformers proposed educational measures to democratize the state and help Sweden regain its Great Power status, but they were defeated in the Riksdag by a coalition of the aristocracy and clergy, who feared that education would make the peasants rebellious (Warne 1929).

Sweden's involvement in the Napoleonic Wars produced further difficulties. Sweden lost Finland to Russia in 1809, receiving Norway from Denmark as a consolation prize. The ensuing upheaval resulted in a new constitution, and further turmoil and uncertainty led the Swedes to invite Jean Bernadotte, one of Napoleon's generals, to take the throne in 1810. At the same time, bourgeois liberals led a movement to develop mass schooling to provide national unity and purpose. Their efforts were defeated by the reactionary politics of the aristocracy, clergy, and new king and by the unwillingness of the peasantry to foot the bill for an educational system (Jansson 1948).

The end of the Napoleonic Wars found Sweden definitively reduced to a second-rank power. Two developments resulted. First, there was a great cultural revitalization movement, both in literature and in primarily popular religious movements. The leading figure in this movement was Esaias Tegner, Sweden's greatest poet, who (before a change of heart in the 1830s) strongly advocated the establishment of universal elementary education to unify and strengthen Sweden (Stomberg 1931). Second, a period of liberal reform swept Sweden in the 1830s and 1840s, inspired largely by the recurring revolutions in France and impeded less by aristocratic reaction in Sweden than elsewhere because of the rising power of the bourgeois class (Carlsson and Rosén 1961). Motivated partly by the desire to uplift the Swedish nation and partly by the perceived need for an educated populace in the monetarized economy that Sweden had begun to develop, the liberals pushed through a school reform bill in 1842 that founded a state system of elementary schools throughout the country. The primary model for the Swedish effort was Denmark's rapidly growing school system, but frequent reference was also made to Prussian educational progress. The 1842 law was followed in later decades by further bills that made education truly universal, and the Swedish system became in turn a model for other countries because of its efficiency and effectiveness.

In Sweden, the crisis brought about by the Napoleonic Wars was quite acute, but it did not immediately generate a state educational system, despite efforts in that direction. Detailed study of this period in Swedish history suggests that it was the resistance of the relatively powerful and independent peasantry (in conjunction with the usual resistance of the clergy and aristocracy) that slowed the movement toward state-controlled education. In any case, by mid-century, the Swedish mass schooling system was well established.

Italy. Italy constitutes a complicated case. The country's political fate was controlled by the European core powers, and national unification was not achieved until relatively late (1860). The northern Italian states were both economically and politically more developed than those in the south and more closely involved with European culture and politics. Hence, the drive for independence and unification came mostly from the north. Typically, movements in France were imitated in northern Italy, but the multiplicity of political units and the lack of an integrating national polity prevented these movements from developing effectively.

The first serious calls for state-directed schooling came in 1796, when Austria's counterattack on France seemed likely to quench the Revolution. Inspired directly by their French counterparts, the Italian Jacobins seized on education as the means to mobilize the people. They urged the construction of a secular state-operated system throughout the country (Woolf 1979), but, like the Revolution in Italy, the various proposals offered in this period came to very little.

Throughout the first half of the nineteenth century, Italian liberals and radicals organized for reform or revolution but were defeated by reactionary rulers backed by one or more of the major powers and, in the educational sphere, by the ever-present Church. Conditions favorable to Italian independence and unification finally appeared after the Crimean War, when it became clear that the balance of power formalized in the Concert of Europe had broken down (Woolf 1979). The independence movement rapidly gained strength, and by 1857, revolts, coups d'etat, and civil war raged throughout the country. In 1859, in this climate of extreme political turmoil and struggle for national entity and identity, an educational reform law was passed in Piedmont under the sponsorship of Gabrio Casati, the first Minister of Public Instruction. The law established a complete state system of education, from elementary through university level, and drastically limited the role of the Church (Tannenbaum 1974). After 1860, the law was gradually applied to the unified territories, and by 1877, the legal framework for a national system of compulsory public education was in place.

In Italy, the lag between ideological commitments to education and the implementation of organizational structure was unusually great, consistent with the ineffectiveness and fragmentation of the Italian state throughout most of its history. Thus, though the educational system was quite effectively instituted in some of the northern areas by 1880, very little was accomplished in the south before 1900, and centralizing reforms in 1904 and 1911 were necessary to begin to make the system truly universal in scope (Tannenbaum 1974). Even with these reforms, Italian elementary education developed relatively slowly until after World War II.

The Italian case offers an illuminating variant in which the state's effort in education was almost anticipatory: The Piedmontese state strove to build a national educational system even before national unification had been achieved. It was thus in the midst of its effort to enter the European state system as a unified entity that Italy initiated state-sponsored mass education. Like Prussia, Italy was upwardly mobile in the system, and education was seen as a means of increasing Italian power and prestige.

The Dominant European Powers: France and England

The dominant powers in the period up to 1850 were France and England. In France, education under the *ancien régime* consisted mainly of secondary schools run by the religious orders for the middle and upper classes. Mass schooling, to the extent that it existed, was restricted to religious instruction, and the schools were run by the Catholic Church, though they were nominally under the authority of the king. In this respect, the educational situation in England was quite similar; the principle of state supremacy over all ecclesiastical affairs (and, by implication, over the schools) had been established under Elizabeth I in the Acts of Supremacy and Unification (Thut and Adams 1964). In fact, however, these educational institutions functioned as voluntary associations with little input from the state.

Elites were their principal clientele, and the education of poor children was left to philanthropy until well into the nineteenth century.

France. The movement toward a state-managed system of compulsory primary education commenced earlier in France than in England. The Constitution of 1791 called for the establishment of a system of free public instruction common to all citizens. A series of education proposals—by Tallyrand (1791), Condorcet (1792), Lepelletier de Saint Fargeau (1793)—failed to translate the 1791 constitutional mandate into organizational reality (Furet and Ozouf 1977), and the cycle of revolution/reform/reaction that followed the Revolution prevented the permanent establishment of a national system until relatively late.

The importance of nationalizing education was not lost on Napoleon as he rose to power. In 1805 he wrote,

> Of all political questions, that [of education] is perhaps the most important. There cannot be a firmly established political state unless there is a teaching body with definitely recognized principles. If the child is not taught from infancy that he ought to be a republican or a monarchist, a Catholic or a free-thinker, the state will not constitute a nation; it will rest on uncertain and shifting foundations; and it will be constantly exposed to disorder and change. (Quoted in Reisner 1922, p. 35)

No clearer statement of the relationship of education to the formation of a national state could have been made. But in practice, Napoleon ignored primary education, concentrating instead on developing secondary and higher education, especially the Lycées and the Grandes Ecoles, with the objective of producing an effective elite to operate the military and governmental apparatus (Lynch 1974). Napoleon was still operating in accordance with the older European model of society; in his time, mass education had not yet become an ideological and social imperative. We argue, however, that he would have directed much more attention to primary schooling if he had come to power in 1850 rather than 1800.

After the defeat of Napoleon, the Church regained centrality in educational matters only to have its influence reduced anew after 1830, during the constitutional monarchy of Louis Philippe. The first serious attempt to organize a national system of primary education was generated by a law of 1833; under the direction of Guizot, an educational system, strongly influenced by the Cousin report on the Prussian primary educational-system, was established (Gontard 1976). The plan called for the establishment of schools in all but the smallest communes, state aid for poor communes, normal schools throughout the nation, and the relegation of religious instruction to an optional activity. These democratizing and secularizing trends were halted, once again, by the reaction that followed the Revolution of 1840 and the regime of Louis Napoleon in 1852. Primary school teachers in particular were targeted for repression, because they had become a vocal political force calling for free, universal, and compulsory education for the whole of France. Many teachers were dismissed, and clerical control over education was again enhanced (Lynch 1974).

The final round of the cycle occurred after the humiliating defeat by Prussia in 1870 and the establishment of the Third Republic a year later. Public debate quickly focused on primary education as a means of national renewal; one popular expression current in France at the time was that the Franco-Prussian War had been "won by the Prussian schoolmaster" (Reisner 1922). The political reconstruction of French schools rapidly became a symbol of the Third Republic. By 1881, with Jules Ferry as Minister of Public Instruction, a universal, free, compulsory primary school system had been established, and within five years of that date, very extensive state control of the educational system had been achieved (Furet and Ozouf 1977).

France offers us a fairly pure example of the nation-building perspective on education. Early demands for state involvement in elementary education were made within the context of an intense effort to reconstruct the French national polity. Identification with the national polity was achieved through the Revolution and the Napoleonic Wars, during which France found itself pitted against all of Western and Central Europe. Broadly based nationalistic sentiment, the modern alchemy through which many different individuals become one with the interests and purposes of the state, was practically invented in France during this era. But the embodiment of nationalism in education was frustrated in France by the frequent swings between revolution and reaction that occurred between 1815 and 1870. It took a decisive defeat at the hands of a unifying Germany to complete in France the nation-building project that finally resulted in a genuine national system of mass education.

England. England managed to avoid the violent revolutionary upheavals that rocked France in the eighteenth and nineteenth centuries. But the movement toward state-sponsored mass education was inhibited by the very success of England's navy and merchants in the world economy. Schooling developed slowly in private hands, and classical liberal restraints on state action kept the state out of education much longer in England than elsewhere. Hence, it is not surprising that the first attempt to extend public aid to parochial schools for the masses (the Whitehead Bill of 1807) was defeated in the House of Lords. The principle of voluntarism that had shaped the private, religious, elitist schools of England would not be easily overturned, especially in light of the global success to which it was believed these schools had contributed (Jones 1977). Though these sectarian, mostly Anglican, schools were nominally under the authority of the Crown, there was virtually no state "interference" in the schools until 1833.

The reform of 1833 was part of the liberalization process that opened Parliament to the English bourgeoisie. It was limited to a program of state grants to the schools administered by national voluntary societies that were closely tied to the churches (Jones 1977). In a short time, the Anglican educational society had won out over its Nonconformist counterpart and had gained control of most of the grants, helping to block extensive state control of the schools.

But events in the 1860s altered the situation. First, further political reform began to enfranchise the working classes (1867), and a new Liberal-Labor alliance argued strongly for compulsory mass education. The full democratization of the political realm was seen as inevitable, and education was increasingly regarded as a means to civilize the lower classes so as to "avoid anarchy" (Robert Lowe's phrase, quoted in Jones [1977, p. 50]), i.e., to teach the lower classes proper behavior in the political arena. This line of thought was more prominent in England than elsewhere, but it was also promoted in France (Furet and Ozouf 1977).

Second, the rise of Germany and the United States threatened British industrial supremacy. By 1867, Bismarck's project to unify Germany had yielded the Confederation of North German States, a brief stopping point on the way toward a fully unified Germany in 1871, and Germany's rise to major power status was accomplished. The triumph of the North in the American Civil War similarly represented a clear challenge to British world supremacy by cutting the advantageous trade relationships Britain had enjoyed with the South (Moore 1966) and by signalling that a more cohesive United States would take a more aggressive role in the world economy, especially with respect to Latin America. The threat to British dominance was clearly acknowledged both at home and abroad (Jones 1977).

A waning of national confidence was clearly reflected in the British reaction to the 1867 Paris Exhibition, a world's fair at which English products compared unfavorably with those of other countries (Royal Society of Arts 1867). The Exhibition was widely interpreted as marking the end of unchallenged British superiority in the development and manufacture of goods. As a result of all these developments, there arose a clamor for education both to improve British workmanship and to achieve greater national cohesion in order to compete in the larger system. The consequent Elementary Education (Forster) Act of 1870 mandated the provision of schooling, though it stopped short of decreeing compulsory education. A decade later, compulsory education was instituted nationwide. But it was not until 1902, when both Germany and the United States had outdistanced England in a number of dimensions of industrial production (Temin 1966), that the dual educational system (church and state schools) was unified and the role of the churches was effectively ended.

Although the law of 1902 was significant in some fundamental respects (for example, primary and secondary education were placed under a common educational authority), it did not elevate the Board of Education into a national ministry. Instead, the law created a system of local educational authorities through which much of the governance of the school system would take place. Not until 1944 did England establish a national ministry as the central educational authority. By then, the radical demise of British economic, political, and military power was conspicuous, and the United States had emerged as the new dominant power in the world.

England provides an instructive example of the limits on the power of the European model of a national society to affect the behavior of states. Because it was the dominant world power, England could exercise greater freedom from the constraints imposed by the model—constraints that bound less powerful nations more exactingly. Less dominant nations that were highly integrated into the European interstate system, such as Denmark and Prussia, conformed to the model more fully to establish their legitimacy and to mobilize their populations to compete in the system.

The Political Construction of Mass Education: European Origins

Why were state educational systems constructed throughout Europe in the late eighteenth and nineteenth centuries? Our brief historical sketches reveal that, despite much variation in level of industrialization, class structure, and political regime, the ideological and organizational responses of the various countries to challenges to state power were strikingly similar. The typical response encompassed the following elements: declaration of a national interest in mass education, legislation to make schooling compulsory, creation of a state educational ministry or department, and establishment of state authority over existing and new schools.

To understand this largely uniform response, we consider Europe as a whole, first discussing five institutionalized legitimating myths that had important implications for state-sponsored mass education. We then examine how the European model of a national society was shaped by three major transformations in European social structure and culture: the Reformation and Counter-Reformation, the rise of the national state and the interstate system, and the establishment of the exchange economy. We argue that the European states adopted a state educational system as part of a nation-building process imposed on them by the larger environment within which they competed. The state educational system became a sensible, and even imperative, organizational undertaking because it was broadly legitimated by the dominant model of a national society. The latter, in turn, was derived from and bolstered by the major transformations we shall discuss.

The European Model of a National Society

Of the many legitimating myths that arose and became institutionalized in Western Europe in the modern era, five are of primary importance for our understanding of the process by which mass schooling became a necessary part of the response to external challenges to state power. They include the legitimating myths of (1) the individual, (2) the nation as a society made up of individuals, (3) progress, (4) childhood socialization as the key to adult character, and (5) the state as guardian of the nation and guarantor of progress.

By the nineteenth century, the individual had clearly become the primary unit of action and the fundamental source of value in society, replacing the more corporate units (the family, clan, region, etc.) that had primordial importance in earlier times. Closely associated with the primacy of the individual was the institutionalized definition of the nation as an aggregate of individuals. The nation was not to be identified with the reigning household or the dominant families. Hence, national development presupposed individual development; national revitalization required individual revitalization. Moreover, national and individual development were defined as goals that could be realistically attained. Confidence in realizing a better future was at the heart of the reigning myth of progress (Nisbet 1980; Ferraroti 1985). This ideology led to a stronger emphasis on and preoccupation with the next generation—that is, with the children.

While national development was contingent on individual development, individual development itself hinged on childhood experience. This assumption presupposed continuity of personality throughout the life cycle ('the child is father to the man'), the malleability of the individual child, and the feasibility of explicit intervention in the development of the child. All of this has been referred to as the eighteenth-century discovery of socialization theory (Sommerville 1982).

This set of interrelated myths linked the development of children to the national interest: Good, loyal, and productive children would become good, loyal, and productive adults who in the aggregate would produce a better, stronger, and more developed national society. It was therefore important that children be systematically exposed to the appropriate socializing influences so that they would develop appropriate values.

The undertaking of this mandate has been discussed as a process of maintaining the social order (Dreeben 1969); thus, mass schooling was presumed to be charged with much the same mandate given to initiation ceremonies in stateless societies (Van Gennep 1960). But the myth of progress altered the mandate significantly: The emerging systems of mass schooling were expected not only to preserve the social order but also to *create the new national society*, that is, to make progress possible. The latter was expected to be accomplished via the production of the new man. Unlike initiation ceremonies, which enjoy only a generically conservative charter, the emerging systems of mass schooling were designed to achieve unity *and progress.*[5]

What agency was to assume ultimate responsibility for the socialization of children? The welfare of children had previously fallen under the authority of the family and, in some circumstances (e.g., extreme poverty or abandonment), the established churches. But once the welfare of children was linked to the national interest, the pertinent question became, What agency or organization most legitimately exercised original jurisdiction over the national domain? (See Swanson 1971.) The European model of a national society clearly allocated this jurisdiction to the state. The national interest was increasingly identified with the interests of the nation-state; in fact, the latter was expected to give substance and direction to this interest (Grew 1984). Since the national welfare was believed to be influenced by the character instilled in the nation's children, the state was impelled to play a role in the socialization of children.

The creation and intensification of the links between states and schools made sense after these myths were institutionalized in European society. These myths explain, in turn, why a range of military, political, and economic setbacks came to be classified as crises requiring national revitalization or as opportunities for upwardly mobile nation building. Given the progressive orientation to the future, national revitalization frequently centered on the establishment of a more effective school system. Given the allocation of responsibility for the nation to the state, the union of state and schools loomed large in the national revitalization movement. Thus, a state system of mass schooling became the favored strategy in the process of nation building and citizenship development (Marshall 1948; Bendix 1964, 1978) and in the homogenization of the masses (Collins 1977, 1979).[6]

Postulating the European model of a national society facilitates our understanding of the strong insistence on state control over education in this period. The nineteenth century has been depicted as both the "century of the child" (Sommerville 1982; Hughes and Klemm 1907) and the "age of nationalism" (Kohn 1962). These two seemingly unrelated depictions are in fact complementary. The words of La Chalotais, a French Republican spokesman, in 1763 capture the essence of the matter: "I claim the right to demand for the Nation an education that will depend upon the State alone; because it belongs essentially to it; because every nation has an inalienable and imprescriptible right to instruct its members; and finally, because the children of the State should be educated by the members of the State" (quoted in Bendix 1964, p. 110).

This sentiment became quite common in the nineteenth century as clerical control over education was effectively challenged throughout most of Europe. Mass schooling became national schooling, and state authority over national education became the rule. In our time, the postulation of a similar model now writ worldwide helps us understand why differences in sixth-grade scores on standardized math or science tests lead to the formation of national educational commissions and the sober rhetoric of "a nation at risk" (National Commission on Excellence in Education 1983).

Social Transformations and Development of the European Model

Institutionalized definitions of reality are grounded in the common experiences of a people (Berger and Luckman 1966). The European model of a national society reflected and codified the experiences associated with the three major transformations of culture, polity, and economy. These transformations are complex and interrelated, and we cannot escape some degree of arbitrariness in our attempt to sort out the effects of each transformation from those of the others in the exposition that follows.

The Reformation and Counter-Reformation

The contribution of the Reformation and Counter-Reformation to the union of states and schools was threefold. First, the survival of the reform movements marked the beginning of the decline of the Catholic Church's cultural hegemony in Europe. Secular powers no longer felt compelled to seek the legitimacy bestowed by the blessing of the Church. The religious movements also desacralized one another ('the whore of Rome,' 'the Protestant heathen'), thereby weakening the monopoly of all religious organizations over legitimation symbols and eventually enabling the secular powers to bypass religious authority entirely in proclaiming their legitimacy. The Reformation and Counter-Reformation thus increased the authority of national states over their populations and legitimated the authority of the interstate system (and its subunit states) over European society as a whole, creating a secular substitute for the overarching Church. The religious conflicts thus gave rise to political developments that ultimately generated the institutionalized myth of the state as the guardian of the nation.

The second important ramification of the religious movements was ontological. The Protestant emphasis on a personal relationship with God as the only means to salvation strengthened the primordial status and authority of the individual. Though individualism had earlier roots in medieval Europe (Morris 1972), the focus on the individual became much more accentuated after the Reformation (Weber 1958). The concern with education as an implication of this emphasis is easy to trace: Personal salvation required familiarity with the word of God; thus, to become a true Christian, literacy was essential (cf. Bagley 1937). The reformers expended much energy translating the Bible into vernacular languages to enhance its accessibility to all individuals (Bainton 1956), and their publication of huge numbers of pamphlets and catechetical tracts suddenly provided reading material on a broad basis, greatly stimulating literacy (Cipolla 1969).

The third outcome of the religious movements was the rapid rise of concern for childhood socialization, leading to the production of child-rearing manuals and sermons on children (Jolibert 1981). Stereotypes about Puritans notwithstanding, this early work on children was clearly progress-oriented; the earlier views of childhood, which ranged from an immodest indifference to a preoccupation with childhood innocence as a limited and fragile good that needed to be shielded from worldly assault, were replaced by the more optimistic view that children had an innate capacity for goodness that could be expanded through appropriate nurturance.

The Catholic counterattack largely embraced the individualistic and socialization ideologies implicit in the Protestant perspective (Sommerville 1982; Aries 1962). Spearheading the Counter-Reformation, the Society of Jesus, in its founding charter (1540), committed itself to work for the education of children. Moreover, Jesuit pedagogy involved an unprecedented degree of emphasis on individual learning and character formation (Durkheim 1937; Jolibert 1981). The internal states of individual children, not merely their external observance of rule and ritual, preoccupied the Jesuits and other "children-oriented" religious orders, such as the Order of Notre Dame (1628) and the Brothers of the Christian Schools (1684).

To summarize, the experiences of the reform and counter-reform movements generated myths that legitimated the primacy of individuals, the significance of childhood and childhood socialization, and the expanded authority of the state. The overarching authority of the Church was sharply diminished; it was replaced by the legitimacy and authority of more delimited social entities, in particular, the individual and the emerging national state. Both the individual and the national state were "empowered to act" in a more complete way than before, and the mobilization of individuals under state aegis became a legitimate means of pursuing the myth of progress.

The Rise of National States and the Interstate System

Much recent scholarship on the origins and development of national states in Western Europe (e.g., Lubasz 1964; Anderson 1974; Tilly 1975) has broadened our understanding of the obstacles to state building. It is evident that the major stumbling block in early state-building efforts was the pervasive authority and influence of the Church (Tierney 1964). For a millennium after the collapse of Rome, the Church was the dominant organization in Europe (Strayer 1970), and the Church both generated and monopolized the cultural symbols of legitimation that loosely integrated the European civilizational network. Within this frame, attempts by secular powers to carve for themselves spheres of original jurisdiction were inevitably thwarted. The religious wars of the fifteenth and sixteenth centuries helped the states greatly by weakening Church authority and diminishing Church resources.

The emerging state structures did not merely react against the authority of the Church. State organization was strongly aided by the Church's example of both administrative structure and claims to original sovereignty (Meyer 1980). Absolutist monarchical authority claims were secular copies of earlier Church authority (e.g., the doctrine of divine right). In the nineteenth century, states altered these authority claims by justifying them on behalf of "the nation" (Bendix 1978; Dyson 1980) and by tempering them with considerations of the rights of individuals—a legacy of the Reformation and the Enlightenment. The nineteenth-century national states were thus creatures molded both by the historical experience of Church authority and by the Reformation and Counter-Reformation.

The national states were also strongly influenced by the emerging political character of Europe, that is, by the crystallization of a European interstate system in the absence of a European political center. The religious wars led to a decline in the authority of the Church and to the erosion of the power of the Hapsburg dynasty, but the dominant European powers of the seventeenth and eighteenth centuries failed to create a political center around which Europe could be integrated. Europe was left without its prior basis for loose integration, i.e., Latin Christendom, and without a secular replacement.

However, Europe did not degenerate into an anarchic environment within which states preyed on one another in a totally unrestricted way. Instead, a new form of political structure arose: the interstate system, a set of actors and institutional rules, agreements, and conventions that validated the original sovereignty and organizational structure of the emerging national states (Ruggie 1983) and acted as a powerful constraint on the behavior of states (cf. Krasner 1983; Thomas and Meyer 1986). The interstate system evolved from a loose collection of centralizing monarchies that espoused divine-right ideologies to a highly interdependent set of national states that invoked "the nation" as the overriding justification for state action. It provided each state with a recipe for state building and its leaders with a more or less common vocabulary for articulating the national interest. As a result, state purposes and structures became strikingly uniform from the nineteenth century onwards (Boli-Bennett 1979; Grew 1984). Transforming the masses into national citizens became a standardized feature of the state-orchestrated nation-building process; utilizing state-sponsored mass schooling to achieve this political end became a routinely accepted modus operandi (Ramirez and Boli 1982).

The Rise of the Exchange Economy

In conjunction with these religious and political transformations, Europe underwent massive change in the social organization of its productive activities in the long sixteenth century. This change has been analyzed as the demise of social economy and the rise of market society (Polanyi 1944) and more recently as the emergence of the European capitalist economy (Wallerstein 1974). The new economy of exchange greatly increased the fiscal powers of the state through the taxation of commercial transactions (Lubasz 1964). It also led to legal and institutional changes—the development of contract law, the expansion of private property relations, the creation of a labor market that separated peasants from the constraints and protections of traditional serfdom and leaseholding arrangements, etc.—that were facilitated by, and in turn accelerated, the processes of individuation associated with the religious movements discussed earlier. Increasingly, the economic organization of Europe invested individuals with both the authority to conduct their own productive activities and the responsibility to support the state financially. Given the competitiveness of an economically integrating Europe, the productivity and loyalty of individuals became a central concern of state authorities.

In a related development, the entry of the educated bourgeois classes into state bureaucracies as professional administrators (Fischer and Lundgreen 1975; Rosenberg 1958) led to an increase in the social value of secular education. With the embourgeoisement of much of European society during the nineteenth century (Ellul 1967), the significance of schooling as a general means of occupational success and social mobility became broadly institutionalized.[7] In this way, there arose an economic and social ideology that supported universal education and that complemented the political ideology of state-directed schooling for purposes of national progress. Though this "human capital" theory of progress, which facilitated linkages between the state and school, originated among the bourgeoisie, the bourgeois classes fought against the expansion of schooling in the late nineteenth century (Archer 1979; Moraze 1957). However, the economic success of the bourgeoisie so greatly aided the organizational and extractive powers of the state that it was unable to contain the drive toward universal public education. The expanded state educational system was thus as much an unintended consequence of the success of the bourgeoisie as the initial ties between state and school were unplanned effects of the triumph of the Reformation.

The Political Construction of Mass Education: Worldwide Institutionalization

The world in the twentieth century remains economically integrated but politically decentralized. But as we have noted, the absence of a world state cannot be equated with the absence of worldwide understandings and conventions that legitimate some forms of social development and undermine others. A striking feature of the world in the last century has been the dramatic rise in the authority and power of the national state and the sharp increase in the civil, political, and social rights of individuals (Boli-Bennett 1981). The national state and the individual are strongly institutionalized entities within world culture, linked to one another through the institution of citizenship. The latter, in turn, presupposes an institutionalized and expanded state educational system.

Hence, the European model of a national society has evolved into a world model that strongly influences the behavior of states and societies. The extension of the world institutional framework to all territories and peoples has been achieved, standardizing the basic parameters of social ontology, purpose, and value throughout the world. Though cultural differences among national societies persist, it is increasingly taken for granted that all peoples must be organized into national units, that states must control those units, that economic development and social justice are attainable goals reflecting the highest purposes of humanity, that the state must play a central role in society if those purposes are to be realized, and that an expanded, state educational system is essential to individual and national progress. Therefore, it has become increasingly unthinkable for nation-state subunits of the world system to organize themselves in any way inconsistent with the world model.

Postulating this world model of a national society facilitates our understanding of the following research findings:

1   More recently independent states create educational ministries (Adams and Farrell 1967) and compulsory education laws (Ramirez and Boli 1982) more rapidly, symbolizing a more rapid union of states and schools.[8]

2   States are devoting an increasing proportion of funds to education and are taking a greater role in financing mass education (Inkeles and Sirowy 1983) and in regulating school admission policies, curricula, and examination structures (Ramirez and Rubinson 1979).[9]

3   Primary school enrollments in virtually all countries have rapidly expanded since the end of World War II, regardless of economic resources or political structure (Meyer et al. 1977), and this expansion has occurred faster in public schools than in private schools (World Bank 1980).

4   National and individual development have emerged as the most legitimate objectives of mass schooling (Fiala and Gordon 1986), replacing such objectives as the preservation of status distinctions, the maintenance of indigenous cultural values, and the protection of regional or subgroup interests—the types of objectives that motivated social development in earlier models of society. The emphasis on national development is clearly reflected in educational policy statements (Inkeles and Sirowy 1983), and the primacy of the individual, as distinguished from both class- and sex-related distinctions, is indicated by the nearly universal adoption of the comprehensive school and the tremendous increase in the female share of primary education (Craig 1981).

5   The quantity and quality of school-based socialization of the individual has increased. This is indicated by a great increase in the mean length of compulsory schooling during this century (Williamson and Fleming 1977) and by a universal decrease in the student/teacher ratio, symbolizing the commitment to more individualized instruction (Inkeles and Sirowy 1983).

6   The use of educational reform as an important solution to challenges to national power and prestige in the interstate system has been further institutionalized. Note the wave of educational reform triggered in the U.S. by the Soviet launching of Sputnik and, more recently, the reform generated by the growing fear of "Japan, incorporated." Other developed countries, in response to military and industrial challenges, have also used educational reform as an element of national revitalization strategies. Less developed countries have been equally enthusiastic in embracing education as a key component of their nation-building movements (Coleman 1965), more as part of their effort to attain legitimacy in the larger system than as a way of challenging for a leading position.

This perspective also helps us understand why certain states—namely, nineteenth-century England and the twentieth century United States—did not assume complete control of mass education as a tool for political mobilization. As the dominant world powers, these countries have been freer to operate at variance with the established model of national mobilization, in the familiar process whereby only those at the top of a power structure can safely deviate from convention. We find, however, that when England lost its dominant position after World War I, it also began to conform much more fully to the state-directed model of educational development. We can expect much the same sort of change in the United States in coming decades as its position as world leader comes more and more into question.

In less powerful countries, national commitments to mass schooling are more certainly imposed by the world model; indeed, such commitments are supported directly by transnational organizations such as the United Nations and the World Bank. No matter how impoverished or fragmented, every candidate national society must present itself to the world as one committed to establishing a system of mass schooling. It must provide formal access to mass schooling for all its citizens, and schooling must be rationalized around national development and individual growth goals. The production of the ideal citizen/worker is expected to have high priority on the national agenda, and the national state is held primarily responsible for this process of refining and channeling human capital.

The European model of a national society has become so deeply institutionalized as a world model that crises of the sort that occurred in the nineteenth century are no longer necessary to generate the union of states and schools. Instead, the state-formation process itself is now a sufficient condition to induce the newly independent state to devote a large proportion of its effort to constructing a secular, compulsory mass educational system. As the world model changes, we can expect to find changes in states' involvement in education as well, but in the foreseeable future, it is hard to imagine conditions (other than large-scale catastrophe) under which the insistence on state-sponsored socialization for purposes of individual and national development would be seriously weakened.

Notes

1. To some extent, more general arguments originally formulated to explain the expansion of educational systems can also be applied to the problem of state control of education: modes and levels of industrial and urban development (Katz 1968), types and degrees of class or status-group conflict (Collins 1979; Bowles and Gintis 1976), kinds of political regimes (Bendix 1964), etc.

2. We are indebted to the anonymous reviewer who suggested that we explicitly acknowledge that the state interest in mass education was stimulated not by the inherently efficacious character of mass education but by its putative institutional character.

3. Our neglect of the U.S. is motivated by two factors:
   (1) the U.S. was not well integrated into the interstate system until very late, so that our arguments about the system's importance in stimulating state-sponsored education do not apply to the U.S. in the nineteenth century;
   (2) for a variety of reasons, the central state has played a relatively weak role in education in the U.S. A different explanation must be invoked to account for the nature of the educational system here (see the very general argument developed in Boli, Ramirez, and Meyer [1985]). However, in the postwar period, our argument applies rather well even to the U.S. See footnote 6.

4. We use the terms *institutionalized definitions of reality* and *institutionalized legitimating myths* interchangeably throughout this paper, though we recognize the distinction between the cognitive and normative dimensions of the legitimation process. For an extended explication of a conceptualization of legitimation that emphasizes the extent to which both knowledge and values are socially constructed, see Berger and Luckmann (1966, pp. 92–128).

5. Both social order and cultural reproduction theories assume that mass schooling plays only a generically conservative role in society (e.g., Dreeben 1969; Bourdieu and Passeron 1970). The functionalist orientation of social order theories is well known, but Archer (in press) has convincingly argued that the same analytical orientation characterizes cultural reproduction theories. In social order theories, mass schooling "functions" to maintain social order; in cultural reproduction theories, it maintains elite rule or class dominance. Elsewhere, we have assessed the theoretical shortcomings and evidentiary problems associated with both mainstream and critical functionalist explanations of the rise of mass education (Boli et al. 1985). Suffice it to reiterate that historically, social order and class dominance have been maintained through all sorts of exclusionary and repressive mechanisms that appear to differ from the distinctively universalistic, politically incorporative, and progress-oriented mandate of mass schooling.

6. In the U.S., mass education has historically been more closely linked to the ideology of national character than to the organization of the state (Tyack 1966). Mass education is more a consequence of populist movements (Meyer et al. 1979) and status competition among ethnic groups (Collins 1979) than an outcome of state directives (see also Richardson 1986). The peculiarly decentralized character of the American state has recently been the object of much analysis (Skocpol 1980; for a discussion that specifically deals with the loose ties between state and class and the consequences for education, see Rubinson [1986]). Note, however, that a stronger state role in education was initiated after the Civil War as an attempt to integrate the South into the national polity (Bullock 1970). Expansion of state activity in education has proceeded in recent decades as well. Ideologically, the state education system in the U.S. has developed in the same direction as that in other countries, but organizationally, the level of "coupling" continues to be relatively loose.

7. We believe that status conflict theories (e.g., Collins 1979) correctly describe how varying groups attempt to use the educational system to promote their values, to advance their members, and either to retain their position of dominance or to

challenge the dominant elite. However, this perspective does not explain how mass schooling became institutionalized in the first place; it assumes that the educational realm is an important arena for group competition and social control processes without clarifying the political construction of the educational realm, that is, the agreed-upon meaning and value of mass schooling. This paper focuses on the institutionalization of mass schooling by examining the legitimating myths that facilitated its development and by considering the large-scale transformations that generated these legitimating myths. In doing so, we clarify the conditions under which the educational realm becomes the realm for competitive processes, though we emphasize competition between nation-states instead of within nation-states, since most of the literature is restricted to the latter.

8. The date of independence measure is taken from Banks (1975); the dates of compulsory education laws are found in the *World Survey of Education Handbooks* (UNESCO 1955, 71) and in Flora (1983).

9. State control over mass schooling was measured via a content analysis of detailed descriptions of educational systems reported in the *World Survey of Education Handbooks*. Seven variables capturing the degree to which the state monopolized control were coded. Over one hundred countries were classified according to this index of state control over mass schooling.

References

Adams, Don, and Joseph P. Farrell. 1967. *Education and Social Development*. Syracuse: Center for Development Education, Syracuse University.

Alexander, Thomas. 1918. *The Prussian Elementary Schools*. New York: Macmillan.

Altbach, Philip, Robert Arnove, and Gail Kelley. 1982. *Comparative Education*. New York: Macmillan.

Anderson, Eugene N. 1970. "The Prussian Volksschule in the Nineteenth Century." Pp. 261–79 in *Entstehung und Wandel der Modernen Gesellschaff*, edited by Gerhard A. Ritter. Berlin: de Gruyter.

Anderson, Perry. 1974. *Lineages of the Absolutist State*. London: New Left Books.

Archer, Margaret S. 1979. *Social Origins of Educational Systems*. Beverly Hills: Sage.

——. In press. "The Neglect of the Educational System by Bernstein and Bourdieu." *European Journal of Sociology*.

Aries, Philippe. 1962. *Centuries of Childhood*. New York: Vintage.

Bagley, William C. 1937. *A Century of the Universal School*. New York: Macmillan.

Bainton, Roland H. 1956. *The Reformation of the Sixteenth Century*. Boston: Beacon.

Banks, Arthur S. 1975. *Cross-National Time Series Data Archive*. Binghamton: Center for Comparative Political Research, SUNY-Binghamton.

Bendix, Reinhard. 1964. *Nation Building and Citizenship*. New York: Wiley.

——. 1978. *Kings or People: Power and the Mandate to Rule*. Berkeley: University of California Press.

Berger, Peter, Brigitte Berger, and Hansfried Kellner. 1973. *The Homeless Mind*. New York: Random House.

Berger, Peter, and Thomas Luckman. 1966. *The Social Construction of Reality*. Garden City, NY: Doubleday.

Boje, Andreas, Ernest Borup, and Holger Rützebeck. 1932. *Education in Denmark*. London: Oxford University Press.

Boli, John, Francisco O. Ramirez, and John W. Meyer. 1985. "Explaining the Origins and Expansion of Mass Education." *Comparative Education Review* 29:145–70.

Boli-Bennett, John. 1979. "The Ideology of Expanding State Authority in National Constitutions, 1870–1970." Pp. 222–37 in *National Development and the World System*, edited by John W. Meyer and Michael T. Hannan. Chicago: University of Chicago Press.

——. 1981. "Human Rights or State Expansion? Cross-national Definitions of Constitutional Rights, 1870–1970." Pp. 173–93 in *Global Human Rights: Public Policies, Comparative Measures, and NGO Strategies*, edited by Ved Nanda, James Scarritt, and George Shepard. Boulder. Westview.

Bourdieu, Pierre, and J. C. Passeron. 1970. *La Reproduction*. Paris: Editions de Minuit.

Bowles, Samuel, and Herbert Gintis. 1976. *Schooling in Capitalist America*. New York: Basic Books.

Boyd, William, and Edmund J. King. 1975. *The History of Western Education*. 11th ed. London: Adam and Charles Black.

Bullock, Henry Allen. 1970. *A History of Negro Education in the South*. New York Praeger.

Carlsson, Sten, and Jerker Rosén. 1961. *Svensk Historia, Vol. 2: Tiden Efter 1718*. Stockholm: Svenska Bokförlaget.

Cipolla, Carlo M. 1969. *Literacy and Development in the West*. Harmondsworth: Penguin.

——. 1974. "Introduction." Pp. 7–13 in *Fontana Economic History of Europe, Vol. 4: The Sixteenth and Seventeeth Centuries*. Glasgow: Collins.

Cohen, Yehudi. 1970. "Schools and Civilizational Systems." Pp. 55–147 in *The Social Sciences and the Comparative Study of Educational Systems*, edited by Joseph Fischer. Scranton, PA: International Textbook.

——. 1979. "The State System, Schooling, and Cognitive and Motivational Patterns." Pp. 103–40 in *Social Forces and Schooling*, edited by Nobuo Shimahara and Adam Scrupski. New York: McKay.

Coleman, James S. 1965. *Education and Political Development*. Princeton: Princeton University Press.

Collins, Randall. 1977. "Some Comparative Principles of Educational Stratification." *Harvard Educational* Review 47:1–27.

——. 1979. *The Credential Society: A Historical Sociology of Education and Stratification*. New York: Academic Press.

Craig, John. 1981. "The Expansion of Education." *Review of Research in Education* 9:151–210.

Craig, John, and Norman Spear. 1983. "Explaining Educational Expansion: An Agenda for Historical Research." Pp. 133–60 in *The Sociology of Educational Expansion: Take-Off, Growth, and Inflation in Educational Systems*, edited by Margaret S. Archer. Beverly Hills: Sage.

Cubberley, Ellwood P. 1920. *Readings in the History of Education*. Boston: Houghton Mifflin.

DiMaggio, Paul J., and Walter W. Powell. 1983. "The Iron Cage Revisited: Institutional Isomorphism and Collective Rationality in Organizational Fields." *American Sociological Review* 48:147–60.

Dore, Ronald. 1964. *Education in Tokugawa Japan*. Berkeley: University of California Press.

Dreeben, Robert. 1969. *On What is Learned in School*. Reading, MA: Addison-Wesley.

Durkheim, Emile. 1937. *L'Evolution pédagogique en France*. 2 vols. Paris: Felix Alcan.

Dyson, K. 1980. *The State Tradition in Western Europe*. New York: Oxford University Press.

Eckstein, Max, and Hans Noah. 1969. *Scientific Investigations in Comparative Education*. New York: Macmillan.

Ellul, Jacques. 1967. *Metamorphose du bourgeois*. Paris: Calmann-Levy.

Ferraroti, Franco. 1985. *The Myth of Inevitable Progress*. Westport, CT: Greenwood.

Fiala, Robert, and Audri Gordon. 1986. "Educational Ideology and the World Educational Revolution, 1950–1970." Unpublished paper, Department of Sociology, University of New Mexico.

Fischer, Wolfram, and Peter Lundgreen. 1975. "The Recruitment and Training of Administrative and Technical Personnel." Pp. 456–561 in *The Formation of National States in Western Europe*, edited by Charles Tilly. Princeton: Princeton University Press.

Flora, Peter. 1983. *State, Economy, and Society in Western Europe, 1815–1975*. 2 vols. Frankfurt: Campus Verlag.

Freeman, John, Glenn R. Carroll, and Michael T. Hannan. 1983. "The Liability of Newness: Age Dependency in Organizational Death Rates." *American Sociological Review* 48:692–710.

Furet, François, and Jacques Ozouf. 1977. *Lire et ecrire: L'Alphabetisation des Français de Calvin a Jules Ferry*. Paris: Editions de Minuit.

Gontard, Maurice. 1976. *Les Ecoles primaires de la France bourgeoise (1833–1875)*. 2d ed. Toulouse: Institut National de Recherche et de Documentation Pedagogiques.

Grew, Raymond. 1984. "The Nineteenth Century European State." Pp. 83–120 in *Statemaking and Social Movements: Essays in History and Theory*, edited by Charles Bright and Susan Harding. Ann Arbor: University of Michigan Press.

Hughes, James, and L.R. Klemm. 1907. *Progress of Education in the Century*. Toronto: Linscott.

Inkeles, Alex, and Larry Sirowy. 1983. "Convergent and Divergent Trends in National Educational Systems." *Social Forces* 62:303–34.

Jansson, Göte. 1948. *Tegner och Politiken* Uppsala: Almquist and Wiksells.

Jolibert, Bernard. 1981. *L'Enfance au XVIIe siecle*. Paris: Librairie Philosophique J. Vrin.

Jones, Donald K. 1977. *The Making of the Education System, 1851–81*. London: Routledge and Kegan Paul.

Katz, Michael B. 1968. *The Irony of Early School Reform: Educational Innovation in Mid-Nineteenth Century Massachusetts*. Cambridge, MA: Harvard University Press.

Kazamias, Andreas M., ed. 1977. "The State of the Art" (Special issue). *Comparative Education Review* 21 (2, 3).

Kohn, Hans. 1962. *The Age of Nationalism*. New York: Harper and Row.

Krasner, Steven D. 1983. *International Regimes*. Ithaca: Cornell University Press.

Lubasz, Heinz. 1964. *The Development of the Modern State*. New York: Macmillan.

Lynch, James. 1974. "Myth and Reality in the History of French Education." Pp. 1–19 in *The History of Education in Europe*, edited by T.G. Cook. London: Methuen.

Marriott, J.A.R., and G. Grant Robertson. 1915. *The Evolution of Prussia*. London: Oxford University Press.

Marshall, T.H. 1948. *Citizenship and Social Class*. New York: Doubleday.

Meyer, John W. 1980. "The World Polity and the Authority of the Nation-State." Pp. 109–37 in *Studies of the Modern World-System*, edited by Albert J. Bergesen. New York: Academic Press.

Meyer, John W., Francisco O. Ramirez, Richard Rubinson, and John Boli-Bennett. 1977. "The World Educational Revolution, 1950–1970." *Sociology of Education* 50:242–58.

Meyer, John W., and Brian Rowan. 1977. "Institutionalized Organization: Formal Structure as Myth and Ritual." *American Journal of Sociology* 83:340–63.

Meyer, John W., David Tyack, Joane P. Nagel, and Audri Gordon. 1979. "Public Education as Nation-Building in America." *American Journal of Sociology* 85:978–86.

Moore, Barrington. 1966. *Social Origins of Dictatorship and Democracy: Lord and Peasant in the Making of the Modern World*. Boston: Beacon.

Moraze, Charles. 1957. *Les Bourgeois Conquerants, XIXe siecle*. Paris: Armand Colin.

Morris, Colin. 1972. *The Discovery of the Individual, 1050–1200*. London: SPCK.

National Commission on Excellence in Education. 1983. *A Nation at Risk*. Washington, DC: National Commission on Excellence in Education.

Nisbet, Robert. 1980. *History of the Idea of Progress*. New York: Basic Books.

Papanek, Ernst. 1962. *The Austrian School Reform*. Westport, CT: Greenwood.

Polanyi, Karl. 1944. *The Great Transformation*. Boston: Beacon.

Ramirez, Francisco O., and John Boli. 1982. "Global Patterns of Educational Institutionalization." Pp. 15–38 in *Comparative Education*, edited by Philip Altbach, Robert Arnove, and Gail Kelley. New York: Macmillan.

Ramirez, Francisco O., and Richard Rubinson. 1979. "Creating Members: The Political Incorporation and Expansion of Public Education." Pp. 72–84 in *National Development and the World System*, edited by John W. Meyer and Michael T. Hannan. Chicago: University of Chicago Press.

Reisner, Edward. 1922. *Nationalism and Education Since 1789*. New York: Macmillan.

Richardson, John. 1986. "Historical Sequences and the Origins of Common Schooling in the American States." Pp. 35–63 in *Handbook of Theory and Research for the Sociology of Education*, edited by John Richardson. New York: Greenwood.

Ringer, Fritz K. 1977. *Education and Society in Modern Europe*. Bloomington: Indiana University Press.

Rokkan, Stein. 1980. "Territories, Centres, and Peripheries: Toward a Geoethnic-Geoeconomic-Geopolitical Model of Differentiation Within Western Europe." Pp. 163–204 in *Center and Periphery: Spatial Variation in Politics*, edited by J. Gothmann. Beverly Hills: Sage.

Rosenberg, Hans. 1958. *Bureaucracy, Aristocracy, and Autocracy: The Prussian Experience, 1660–1815*. Boston: Beacon.

Rowlinson, William. 1974. "German Education in a European Context." Pp. 21–35 in *The History of Education in Europe*, edited by T.G. Cook. London: Methuen.

Royal Society of Arts. 1867. *Reports of Artisans Selected by a Committee Appointed by the Council of the Society of Arts to Visit the Paris Universal Exhibition, 1867*. London: Bell and Daldy.

Rubinson, Richard. 1986 "Class Formation and Schooling in the United States." *American Journal of Sociology*, forthcoming.

Ruggie, John G. 1983. "Continuity and Transformation in the World Polity: Toward a Neorealist Synthesis." *World Politics* 36:261–85.

Skocpol, Theda. 1980. "Political Response to Capitalist Crisis: Neo-Marxist Theories of the State and the Case of the New Deal." *Politics and Society* 10:155–201.

Sommerville, John. 1982. *The Rise and Fall of Childhood*. Beverly Hills: Sage.

Stomberg, Andrew W. 1931. *A History of Sweden*. New York: Macmillan.

Strayer, Joseph. 1970. *On the Medieval Origins of the Modern State*. Princeton: Princeton University Press.

Swanson, Guy. 1971. "An Organizational Analysis of Collectivities." *American Sociological Review* 36:607–23.

Tannenbaum, Edward R. 1974. "Education." Pp. 231–53 in *Modern Italy: A Topical History Since 1861*, edited by Edward R. Tannenbaum and Emiliana P. Noether. New York: New York University Press.

Temin, Peter. 1966. "The Relative Decline of the Steel Industry, 1880–1913." Pp. 140–55 in *Industrialization in Two Systems: Essays in Honor of Alexander Gerschenkron*, edited by H. Rosovsky. New York: Wiley.

Thomas, George M., and John W. Meyer. 1986. "The Expansion of the State." *Annual Review of Sociology* 10, in press.

Thut, I.N., and Don Adams. 1964. *Educational Patterns in Contemporary Societies*. New York: McGraw-Hill.

Tierney, Brian. 1964. *The Crisis of Church and State, 1050–1300*. Englewood Cliffs: Prentice-Hall.

Tilly, Charles. 1975. *The Formation of National States in Western Europe*. Princeton: Princeton University Press.

Tyack, David. 1966. "Forming the National Character." *Harvard Educational Review* 36:29–41.

UNESCO. 1955–71. *World Survey of Education Handbook*. 5 vols. Geneva: United Nations.

Van Gennep, Arnold. 1960. *The Rites of Passage*. Chicago: University of Chicago Press.

Vibaek, Jens. 1964. *Danmarks Historie, Volume 10: Reform og Fallit, 1784–1830*. Copenhagen: Politikens Forlag.

Wallerstein, Immanuel. 1974. *The Modern World System*. Vol. 1. New York: Academic Press.

Warne, Albin. 1929. *Till Folkskolans Förhistoria i Sverige*. Stockholm: Svenska Kyrkans Diakonistyrelsens Bokförlag.

Weber, Max. 1958. *The Protestant Ethic and the Spirit of Capitalism*. Translated by Talcott Parsons. New York: Scribner's.

Williamson, J.B., and J.J. Fleming. 1977. "Convergence Theory and the Social Welfare Sector: A Cross-National Analysis." *International Journal of Comparative Sociology* 18:242–53.

Woolf, Stuart. 1979. *A History of Italy, 1700–1860: The Social Constraints of Political Change*. London: Methuen.

World Bank. 1980. *Education: Sector Policy Paper*. Washington, DC: International Bank for Reconstruction and Development.

14

Sociological Understandings of Contemporary Gender Transformations in Schooling in the UK

MADELEINE ARNOT

A new agenda is being set. New sets of gender relations are being constructed through education which are likely to work in favour of white female and male middle class students. The state is actively engaged in restoring patriarchal relations but in different form and with different consequences to those of the post-war period. Without an understanding of that project, it is unlikely that we can adequately read the significance of shifts in contemporary society.—Arnot (1993, p. 206)

In 1993, it was clear that the impact of New Right economic, educational and social reforms on gender relations would be considerable and complex. Given the contradictory agenda set by the neo-conservative and neo-liberal wings of the Conservative government under Margaret Thatcher (Arnot, 1993; Arnot, David and Weiner, 1998), it seemed likely that traditional gender relations would not simply be sustained within the new era but would also be transformed. Economic policies were likely to have differential impact on male and female patterns of employment and educational and social policies would almost certainly affect middle-class and working-class pupils in unequal ways. Central to this reform agenda was the restructuring of the pivotal relationships between schooling, families and the economy, and the role of the state within such relationships. It was probable, therefore, that the 1980s and 1990s would witness a social transformation of gender relations. As I shall argue, the restructuring of society and of schools in the late twentieth century substantially changed the modalities of gender transmission and its 'gendered' products in quite fundamental ways.

The story of gender and education in the United Kingdom, at least on the surface, appears as a story about the extraordinary success of post-war egalitarian movements. Up to sixteen years of age, a number of the major gender gaps in subject choices, examination performance and entry patterns in primary, secondary and tertiary education closed. Such is the success of girls in the school system in the United Kingdom that every summer journalists go into a frenzy as they seek to establish the latest changes in examination performances between girls and boys at sixteen (GCSE) and at eighteen (A-levels). The main focus has been the extent to which the gender balance has shifted, with girls catching up and overtaking boys in traditionally male subjects such as mathematics and science and boys continuing to perform relatively poorly in traditionally female subjects such as English and modern languages. Sociologists might ponder over this extraordinary media debate, with its incitement of government to act in the name of boys and retrieve boys' advantage. To some extent it represents a moral panic that is associated with uneven economic and political cleavages of late modernity (Epstein, Hey and Maw, 1998; Raphael Reed, 1999). But there are also other interesting questions to ask of this national phenomenon.

In this article, I consider the shifting patterns of gender performance in education through the lens of social reproduction theory.[1] From this theoretical perspective, such gender patterns of performance reflect a historical transformation of the gender codes (cf. MacDonald, 1980) of schooling—the principles which govern the production, reproduction and transmission of gender relations and gender hierarchies. I shall argue that the patterns of gender performance signify a new gender order (Connell, 1987)—a symbolic order which is embedded in the social relations of power and control in society. As Quicke argued, behind the differences in gender performance lie major political issues:

> because these [gender] differences are not 'innocent' but reflect asymmetrical power relations where men historically have been in the ascendancy. (Quicke, 1999, p. 96)

Gender patterns in education are central aspects of the relationship of education and society and transformations in society.

The structure of this article is as follows: first, I describe the changing forms of gender transmission through education by drawing upon the findings of two major reports: *Educational Reforms on Gender Equality in Schools* (Arnot, David and Weiner, 1996) commissioned by the Equal Opportunities Commission and *A Review of Recent Research on Gender and Educational Performance* (Arnot, Gray, James and Rudduck, 1998) commissioned by the UK school inspectorate (Office for Standards in Education).[2] Second, I explore the interconnections between social and educational change in the last twenty-five years, rehearsing and developing some of the main arguments put forward by Miriam David, Gaby Weiner and me in *Closing the Gender Gap: Postwar Education and Social Change* (Arnot, David and Weiner, 1998).

Shifting Gender Patterns of Educational Performance

In the period between the late 1980s and 2000, gender patterns of educational performance caught the public eye and caused consternation in relation to the maintenance of the social order. Of central significance was evidence of boys' failure to improve their performance at the same rate as girls, from very young ages. Boys' educational performance at sixteen did not seem to be improving in comparison with girls. At the same time, girls became 'space invaders'—entering into and conquering male academic space, especially in science and mathematics (Foster, 2000). Of great concern was the invasion of such public space in which male hegemonic control of women was premised. The threat of boys' disaffection and disengagement also raised the spectre of a male underclass—the so-called 'underwolves' (Wilkinson, 1994)—who would not be able to participate in the engine of social progress associated with increased performance and certification.

While public concern focuses on boys' experiences, of greater significance to sociologists is the change in gender relations represented by the divergent male and female patterns of performance. Although gender differences have been reduced in some quarters, in other sectors traditional gender divisions have been maintained, if not strengthened. The boundaries between male and female spheres have not necessarily broken down, but rather have been modified and adapted to new educational and social climates. The dominant gender codes in education have been transformed as the relations of power and control between men and women change in line with new globalised and marketised economic and social structures. These changes, as I illustrate below, are to be found primarily in the redistribution of educational credentials and the divergent modes of gender transmission found in compulsory and post-compulsory education.

The Redistribution of Educational Credentials

Examination results at sixteen and eighteen in the UK in the last twenty-five years vividly demonstrate the redistribution of educational credentials. In the 1970s, girls in the UK acquired more higher-grade qualifications at sixteen than boys (Arnot, 1986), but many failed to make the transition into post-compulsory education. Fewer girls than boys achieved the three good A-levels which would have given them access to higher education. The English educational system (especially its elite institutions) appeared reluctant to allow women access to high-status education, even though the economy required much higher numbers of scientists, engineers and skilled labour. In the 1980s, it was relatively rare for girls to study science and mathematics, to perform well in these subjects and study them at university level. Since the early 1980s, however, gender patterns of performance of sixteen-year-old school leavers have changed substantially. While the number of qualifications taken by pupils increased for the majority of pupils, by the 1990s a new pattern of female academic success was established. Girls had overcome their disadvantage and had pulled ahead. In the summer of 2001, 10 per cent more girls than boys in England and Wales achieved five GCSE with A*–C grades. Girls had turned the tide of credentialism, at least temporarily, in their favour.

Key to the shift (it not inversion) of this post-war pattern of educational performance within the period of compulsory schooling (aged five to sixteen) was a range of curriculum reforms introduced by the Conservative government under Margaret Thatcher (Arnot, Gray, James and Rudduck, 1998). The introduction in 1984 of a new common examination, the General Certificate of Secondary Education, which is now taken by nearly all pupils in England and Wales, reduced the extensive differentiation between vocational and academic courses and routes. Pupils were encouraged to take a greater range of subjects and to work with new, more flexible styles of teaching and examining. This curricular reform redistributed educational credentials not only from the elite to the masses but also, and not intentionally, in favour of girls (Arnot, David and Weiner, 1996). As Marks (2001, p. 15, figure 12) demonstrates, boys outperformed girls up to the 1960s by about 5 per cent—and for the next fifteen years boys and girls were performing at almost equivalent levels. However, from 1987 only about eighty boys to every hundred girls achieved five high grade passes at 16+. Boys had clearly lost their advantage in terms of school credentials.

A similar redistribution of educational credentials is evident in the post-compulsory sector. After sixteen, girls match (if not better) boys' performance. Marks (2001, p. 16, figure 13) demonstrates the near elimination of the difference in male and female performance at A/AS-level subjects in the last few years. Although slightly more boys than girls (taking two or more A/AS-levels) achieved the highest number of point scores in relation to their A-level grades, this gap became minimal in 1995 (boys averaged 14.5 points and girls averaged 14.1) (Arnot, Gray, James and Rudduck, 1998, p. 16). More recent statistics reveal that girls are in the lead at A-level (1.9 per cent ahead at grades A–E and 0.8 per cent ahead at grade A). The new AS-levels, which were taken for the first time in 2001, put girls ahead with a 4.2 per cent lead and a 3.2 per cent lead at grade A. This gap was larger than that for 'legacy A-levels' (the name given to the traditional A-level) (Joint Council for General Qualifications, 2001).

Girls' raised level of performance at sixteen and eighteen contributed to the rise in the number of students undertaking full-time and part-time post-sixteen courses. The figures have leapt from two-thirds (66 per cent) of the age group to around four-fifths (80 per cent) in the last decade. In 1995, three-quarters of female students were on full-time, post-sixteen courses compared with 69 per cent of boys. In the ten years after 1985, young women raised their entry on such courses from one in five (20 per cent) to around two-fifths (39 per cent) (Arnot, Gray, James and Rudduck, 1998, p. 16).

In turn, the increase in the proportion of young people staying on after sixteen has meant that numbers on full-time and part-time courses post-eighteen have more than doubled and girls now match male entry figures. In 1985, only 26 per cent of young women were in post-eighteen courses, compared with 34 per cent of young men; ten years later the figures were roughly equal (49 per cent to 47 per cent respectively). Both young men and women also more than doubled their numbers in higher education in those ten years, but here again young women overtook young men such that, in 1995, proportions entering higher education were 20 per cent and 19 per cent respectively (ibid.).

These changes in the gender distribution of educational credentials in the last twenty years have been associated with two features: the continuing strong performance of girls in English and their success in improving their results in science and mathematics. The OFSTED [Office for Standards in Education] review cites the few studies that have tracked boys and girls through primary or through secondary schools, all of which indicate that girls make better progress than boys in reading, mathematics and verbal/non-verbal reasoning (Arnot, Gray, James and Rudduck, 1998). Data collected from national assessments at the age of seven (Key Stage 1) demonstrate that girls get off to a better start at reading than boys and that the lead they establish in English is maintained at Key Stage 2 (age eleven) and Key Stage 3 (age fourteen) (Arnot, Gray, James and Rudduck, 1998). Indeed, a sizeable gap between boys and girls in reading and English is sustained throughout compulsory schooling. By 2000, approximately 15 per cent more girls than boys obtained A*–C grade in English GCSE (DfEE, 2000). The fact that boys have not reduced this female 'advantage' is one of the principal reasons why they have lost overall ground in compulsory schooling in comparison with girls.

At the same time, girls in England and Wales have caught up with boys in mathematics and science. In 1995, seven-year-old girls had a head-start in mathematics (81 per cent of girls reached the expected level compared with 77 per cent of boys) and 86 per cent of girls and 83 per cent of boys reached the expected level in science. Girls' greater success in science and mathematics at GCSE helped them invert the patterns of gender inequalities in school-leaving examinations at sixteen. The proportion of girls who achieved A*–A grades in mathematics in that year was only 2 per cent lower than the proportion of boys, and 44 per cent of girls (compared with 45 per cent of boys) reached A*–C grades. In combined science, 48 per cent of girls (compared with 47 per cent of boys) achieved A*–C grade.

In the mid- to late 1980s, the reduction of gender inequalities in performance at A/AS-level (taken at eighteen years), although not as great as that found in GCSEs, was also evident in national statistics (Arnot, Gray, James and Rudduck, 1998). Girls gradually closed the gaps in performance at A–B grades in the sciences (biology, chemistry and physics), as well as in subjects such as English and modern foreign languages. However Figure 14.1 indicates that the picture is quite complicated, since in 2000 comparatively large proportions of girls achieved high grades in biology, computer studies, geography, history and English, but a higher proportion of boys than girls performed well in chemistry, physics, mathematics and, interestingly, French.

Modalities of Gender Transmission

It would be as misleading to read these performance patterns simply as the breaking down of gender dualisms or male power as it would be to associate it simply with male 'underachievement'. There are now major differences in the patterns associated with female education in compulsory and post-compulsory education. The last two decades have demonstrated the official desegregation of subject choices in school-leaving qualifications at sixteen; on the other hand, they have been associated with the masculinisation of science and technology in the post-compulsory sector (Arnot, Gray, James and Rudduck, 1998). Thus, while within compulsory education the segregation of gender spheres and male hierarchies has been weakened, traditional gender relations in post-compulsory education have been largely strengthened. Put in Bernsteinian terms (Bernstein, 1971), there are two different 'modalities' of transmitting gender relations within the educational system—one for the majority educated up to sixteen and the other for those who proceed to further and higher education. Thus two contradictory trends in the patterns of subject choice have emerged in these data—one of which suggests the dismantling of traditional gender classifications, while the other suggests the reinforcement of male hegemony. Let us explore each in turn.

In the compulsory sector, until the early 1980s, boys and girls occupied almost completely different educational tracks. Since that time, gender boundaries between traditionally male and female subjects have been weakened, with most of these gender differences in subject take-up substantially

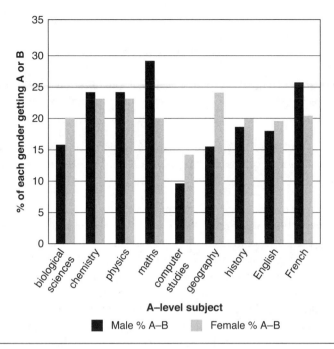

Figure 14.1 Proportion of male and female students achieving A or B grades at A-level by subject in 2000, England.

Source: http://www.standards.dfee.gov.uk/genderandachievement/2000_data_5.html

reduced. Between 1985 and 1995, the male dominance of subjects such as physics, geography, CDT [craft, design and technology] and technology decreased and a more balanced entry pattern has been sustained in English, art and design, mathematics and history. The data generated by the EOC project (Arnot, David and Weiner, 1996) showed that the gender gap in subject entry was found to be on the increase in only five of eighteen GCSE subjects (see Arnot, Gray, James and Rudduck, 1998, p. 13, table 1.2). On the whole, the picture was one of desegregation of subject choice up to sixteen.

However, Arnot et al.'s table also demonstrates that, despite the weakening of most subject boundaries, the pattern of male advantage at sixteen can still be found in the sizeable gaps in the entry into higher-status male subjects at GCSE (e.g., physics and chemistry). Far more boys than girls are among the elite minority of pupils, often in private schools, who take the single sciences at GCSE (most pupils study combined sciences). In 1995, 28,000 boys took physics GCSE compared with only 15,000 girls (the comparable figures for chemistry were 28,000 and 16,000 respectively) (ibid., p. 10). Thus, although gender boundaries between areas of knowledge have been substantially weakened for the majority, this is the not the case for elite male groups in society who start to specialise in such subjects prior to A-level.

In the post-compulsory sector, the dominance of boys in science, technology and mathematics at A-level increased further in this period. Between 1984 and 1994, many of the gender gaps in entry were sizeable. Over 30 per cent more boys than girls chose physics, mathematics, computer studies, technology, economics and CDT, and in many of these instances this gender gap had increased. Far larger proportions of girls than boys chose conventional female subjects, such as English and modern foreign languages (although here boys had made inroads), and more girls chose biology, social studies and art and design (see Arnot, Gray, James and Rudduck, 1998, p. 16, table 1.5).

These national statistics on educational performance demonstrate that, despite the near equalisation in the proportions of academically successful male and female students achieving A-levels and high grades in these examinations (and hence the pathway to university), male educational advantage was not only sustained but increased in the worlds of science and technology. Thus male students, especially after sixteen, have considerable control over these particular highly valued forms of educational knowledge.[4]

Male students' success and the 'masculinisation' of technology and the sciences at A-level also continue to be a feature of vocational and academic courses in further and higher education. Official statistics for the Advanced General National Vocational Qualification (GNVQ) demonstrate how some subjects (such as health and social care, leisure and tourism, IT [information technology]) are 'almost exclusively male or female'.[5] The OFSTED review concluded that:

> gender stereotyping in the mid-nineties among 16–19 age group in terms of the subjects studied for vocational qualifications is just as strong as at A-level. (Arnot, Gray, James and Rudduck, 1998, p. 18)

Young men are more likely to choose science and engineering in further and higher education (Cheng, Payne and Witherspoon, 1995; Felstead, Goodwin and Green, 1995; UCAS, 2000). The impressive improvement in girls' performance in science and mathematics in 16+ examinations arguably should have transformed the performance patterns of those academically able students heading for university. Instead, male dominance of the 'hard' sciences strengthened its hold.

The redistribution of educational credentials towards female students is, therefore, neither uniform nor complete. On the one hand, a higher proportion of female students achieve higher-grade qualifications in nearly all GCSE subjects. They acquire higher qualifications than boys in the period of compulsory schooling. On the other hand, the academically able boy who stays on at school to complete A-levels (used for university entrance) performs particularly well. At the same time, sex segregation in subject choice, whilst reduced in compulsory education, remains embedded in the subsequent phases. In the next section, I explore how and why such contradictory trends and complex structures of transmission came to be established in the UK.

The Challenge to Victorian Values

It would be naive to attribute these shifts in gender performance in the UK solely to educational reform. Although the 1988 Education Reform Act has been signalled as the most radical reform of the school system since the 1944 Education Act, restructuring every aspect of educational provision and practice, its political impetus in relation to gender was not necessarily new. Gender change had its roots in a far longer and more deeply embedded challenge to nineteenth-century liberal ideas concerning the role of men and women in society (Arnot, David and Weiner, 1998). Despite calls for a return to domestic, family virtues and structures, Margaret Thatcher's government failed to turn the tides of change that were symptomatic of nineteenth- and twentieth-century gender struggles. She failed, we argue, to put the genie back in the bottle (ibid.). In the second part of thus article, I describe these shifts, particularly in the relationship between the family, schooling and the state which played a key role in restructuring gender relations in education.

In *Closing the Gender Gap*, we suggest that what lies at the heart of these post-war educational changes in gender was a challenge to the hegemony of nineteenth-century (Victorian) gender values as the dominant structuring principle which shaped the selection, organisation and transmission of knowledge. The shift away from such values represents a historical break with the foundations of the modern educational system which was established in the nineteenth century and was closely associated with the historical rise of the bourgeoisie (upper middle classes) (Arnot, 1982). Key to this Victorian model of the world (its gender code of strong boundaries and hierarchies and little opportunity for negotiated identities) was the powerful ideological distinction between public and private spheres. Historians in the United Kingdom and the United States (Burstyn, 1980; Dyhouse, 1981) have provided us with excellent detailed analyses of how such a distinction functioned to shape masculinity and femininity. As Bourdieu (1977) argued, the male world was constructed around the centrifugal public world focused upon war, politics and work while the female centripetal private spheres circled around psychology, the hearth and intimacy. This distinction between public and private spheres, as feminist political theorists have reminded us, became part of the liberal democratic concept of the social contract (Arnot and Dillabough, 2000). Underlying this social contract, which defined the social order, was the disorder represented by women (Pateman, 1988). Thus women were defined as outside the social order—and as a threat to it. Further underlying the social contract was the sexual contract with women subservient to men. Women were not dominant even in their own sphere.

Such Victorian values had a deep effect on the content and structuring of female education. If women were understood to be subordinate to men both intellectually, emotionally, physically and socially, their schooling was considered to be dangerous. Women were associated with nature and emotion, men with reason and intellect. Such were the strength of these views that women were seen as incapable of learning sciences (a view that can still be found in the UK today). As a result, until well into the 1970s women were offered a domestically oriented inferior education. Education for girls was seen as supporting natural female interests, needs and choices with respect to personal/domestic life (Arnot, 1983). Even twenty years after World War II, girls in England were still being offered or being channelled into choosing subjects which prepared them for a nurturing, domestic role. Child care, domestic science and sewing were added to a diet of social sciences and humanities. It is hard to remember that, when the Sex Discrimination Act (1975) was passed, the majority of girls were sitting examinations in this narrow cluster of subjects, taught mainly by women teachers and going on to the mainly female vocational courses (beauty care, hairdressing, service work).

Such gender ideologies also involved women in supporting the developing educational system as mothers, but also critically as teachers. Thus, the educational system assumed the ready supply of female labour, with appropriate nurturing qualities, a disposition that was appropriate for the inculcation of the masses and low aspirations in terms of career development (Walkerdine, 1983). The mass educational system was built upon the labour of female citizens who, as Jo-Anne Dillabough (2000) argues, were never counted as 'productive worker citizens' but rather as public representatives of the private sphere involved in the domestication of the future generation of citizens. Female teachers and teacher educators were seen as offering an extended form of vocational domestic work in the name of the nation. They were portrayed as 'Mothers of the Nation'.

But history recounts how the imposition of this bourgeois model of family life by a liberal democratic school system was never entirely acceptable to women, even in the nineteenth century. The patterns of educational transmission and performance today are the product of counter-hegemonic struggles against, and other challenges to, such models (Arnot, 1993). Victorian gender values, we argue, were challenged by claims in the name of (a) women's rights; (b) post-war philosophies of meritocracy; (c) the second wave of the women's movement, and more specifically what has been called 'education feminism' (Stone, 1994); and (d) the individualism of the New Right. Below I outline briefly some of the arguments which we put forward in *Closing the Gender Gap* (Arnot, David and Weiner, 1998).

In the Name of Women's Rights

The challenge to Victorian domestic ideology was initiated most forcefully in nineteenth-century campaigns for women's rights. Drawing on the principles established by Mary Wollstonecraft's *Vindication of the Rights of Woman* (1792), feminist campaigners took as their central motif the humanistic claim that women would be treated and should act as autonomous beings. While clearly establishing women's right to an independent existence and indeed an education in their own name, women campaigners were nevertheless confronted with what is now called 'Wollstonecraft's dilemma' (Phillips, 1991)—should women ask for the same or different treatment to men? In educational terms, should women have equal or separate but equal education to men? In the event, the dilemma was resolved in different ways for different social classes. Historians of education remind us how one of the key campaigns was gaining access for women to high-status secondary education and to universities in the late nineteenth and early twentieth century. It was not until 1948 that the last bastions of male privilege fell and women were allowed to take the same degrees as men in Cambridge University. This battle for equal rights and equal treatment of men and women still has resonance today.

The real thrust of the educational reforms associated with the notion of women's rights affected the elite rather than the mass population. What it led to, we argued, was the rise of a *female graduate elite*—initially through private or state single-sex girls' grammar schools and also through the expansion of university places in the 1960s. Key to the rise of such an elite was the adaptation of elite girls' education to the concept of individual achievement. In the past, such girls had been educated to become the wives and mothers of the male upper middle classes (Arnot, 1983). They could rely for the reproduction of their class position on marrying into the same social class of successful men. However, by the mid-twentieth century, the status of upper-middle-class men was becoming unstable, threatened by the transformations in the economy, the rise of new scientifically based professions and the rise of credentialism (Tolson, 1977; Connell, 1997). While elite male schooling changed the class-based qualities of gentry masculinity to include elements of competitive individualism and specialist (often scientific/technological) expertise, women of this class were being educated to take responsibility for achieving and sustaining their own class position (through university education and full-time careers).

The biographies and ethnographic accounts of the schooldays of upper-class and upper-middle-class schoolgirls in the 1950s reveal the new concerns of private girls' schools to promote a notion of upper-middle-class femininity which emphasised academic success. Marriage and future domesticity were seen as poor investment for their schooling. The statistics of school performance document the growth in white middle-class girls' attainment over and above that of boys in the same social grouping, with girls taking up many of the new places in higher education and, on occasion, even surpassing men in entry in the ancient universities. However, there was a price to be paid for winning women's rights in these highly competitive male spheres: research points to the high levels of anxiety experienced by elite schoolgirls, the increased pressure from parents to deliver clusters of A-grades. It is not clear whether such short-term examination successes are matched by long-term confidence or success, especially since such women are still likely to encounter major obstacles in the labour market.

These transformations in class reproduction are associated with the internal restructuring of the professional middle classes, with women reshaping the conditions of employment and family life, challenging gender hierarchies and also economic and social forms of male control. The challenge to middle-class concepts of femininity encouraged 'a gender blind approach' to education, weakening gender boundaries and hierarchies of knowledge. As a result, the language of mass not just elite schooling was to become more gender neutral, especially when equality of the sexes was promoted within the discourses of meritocracy.

The Meritocratic Challenge

Another challenge to the structuring of the educational system in line with male interests was the promotion of meritocracy and equal opportunities, associated in the UK with the establishment of the welfare state in the post-war period. The dual repertoire of economic expansion and an egalitarian concern for social welfare which we call social democracy (1940–70s) weakened the homologous classifications of male public and female private spheres through the post-war expansion of women's work and the opening up of educational opportunities for all.

It is one of the ironies of post-war history that Victorian family values, paradoxically, were undermined at precisely the point when they were built into the nature and shape of the welfare state. The development of the health and educational systems after the war, the social security system and taxation system were premised upon models of the male head of household. Proponents of welfare stressed the value and importance of traditional families and especially the role of the mother in keeping the family cared for, educated and orderly. Mothers were held responsible for any breakdown in law and order and their children's physical, psychological or educational problems.

But while these images were being constructed, the welfare state was taking large numbers of women out of the home to work in the new welfare occupations which depended on their labour. The rise of female employment (particularly of mothers) after the war brought with it calls for child care, calls for better female education, for better conditions for female employment. Further, women started to organise politically to claim the rights invested in the concept of the welfare state. They claimed what Marshall (1950) called their social rights (over and above political and economic rights). The paradox, we argue in our book, is that the social democratic period set in train a sequence of social changes that fundamentally transformed the nature of patriarchal family life. And yet, while all this was happening, men were still encouraged to see themselves as heads of households with their main responsibility being as main wage earner. The welfare reformers asked little of fathers in terms of taking responsibility for their children (care, education). They did not ask fathers to support their wives at work, nor their children at school. The impact of the welfare state was, therefore, considerably different for each sex.

In retrospect, the principle of meritocracy had its limitations. Despite the expansion of educational opportunities and the commitment to notions of parity of esteem and equality of opportunity, the educational system in this period maintained rather than undermined a patriarchal order and gendered differences in outcomes. Gender differentiations were deep and extensive, supported as they were by school staff and management structures and a distribution of power within the educational system which gave men control over educational policy. Discriminatory practices within educational institutions and school cultures promoted what Spender (1987) called 'patriarchal educational paradigms'. Arguably these were the mechanisms by which a male hegemony and female subordination were being maintained (Arnot, 1982). Educational expansion, on its own, had not necessarily challenged the taken-for-granted cultural and disciplinary regimes of schools and their close association with the sexual division of labour.

A more substantial and critical challenge to the modernist educational project and its conventional gender codes—its boundaries between public and private, its hierarchical knowledge structures and its forms of moral surveillance—was mounted not through the state but rather through what Stone (1994) called 'education feminism'—the women's movement within the educational system. Of major significance were the counter-hegemonic actions of teachers (Weiler, 1988) caught up in this political reform movement.

Education Feminism

In the UK, education feminism took a particular form since the state had not openly challenged gender inequality. I argued that central government's approach to addressing gender inequalities had been characterised by lip-service rather than strong commitment (Arnot, 1987). Early attempts to use legislation to remove sex discrimination in education had been half-hearted and deeply problematic, based as it was on case law rather than constitutional rights. The legislation had promoted greater awareness but, given the decentralised nature of the English educational system, there was little top-down reform of schooling in the name of gender equality. Until the late 1980s, teachers were the key agents of change in the UK. They had control over the curriculum and considerable professional autonomy. Further, when social inequality became a matter of public concern, the responsibility for tackling it was delegated (or left) to teachers. Given this power and with their own experiences of discrimination themselves, women teachers were a natural audience for the ideas of the women's movement. 'Education feminism' within schools in the UK developed as a 'bottom-up' grassroots movement which captured the imagination of large numbers of women teachers, many of whom would have been on the lowest rungs of the teaching profession.

Since the influence of education feminism was patchy, leading as it did to small-scale school-based initiatives, it has appeared to have had little national impact. Moore suggests that it is highly implausible and unlikely that 'the success of girls could be attributed to the success of equal opportunities good practice' (Moore, 1996, p. 150). First, the association of changing educational practice and changing group attainment levels was not repeated elsewhere; second, the initiatives associated with this movement were not applied on a sufficient scale or for long enough to have an impact; third, there could even have been an inverse relationship of equal opportunities to school success since elite schools, which have contributed substantially to female educational success in the UK, arguably were less affected by feminist reforms. Finally, equal opportunities work was theoretically flawed and had not been evaluated properly. While not dismissing the significance of feminism for girls' success, Moore's argument sees its effects as mediated through class and racial inequalities and through 'changing occupational aspirations, labour market conditions and family structures' (ibid.). Ideological position, educational attainments and social opportunities, he argues, are related paradoxically not serially. However, this thesis fails to recognise the extent to which feminism mobilised teachers as agents of change. Connell's comment reflects precisely the stance taken by the women's movement: 'it is teachers' work as teachers that is central to the remaking of the social patterns investing education' (Connell, 1985, p. 4).

As part of a counter-hegemonic movement, feminist teachers challenged the ways in which gender categories were constructed, reproduced and transmitted through schooling. They challenged the principles of the social order—the gendered principles for the distribution of power and social control—and the framing of a unitary social identity 'woman'. Feminism had essentially destabilised the category of femininity for a generation of young women by making the process of problematisation critical to identity formation. Being female became associated not with a static class-based categorisation but with a dynamic process of 'becoming'. Women, therefore, were encouraged to become actors within a set of social relations that were described as arbitrary not given. In Bernsteinian terms, the new integrative gender code would be one of weak gender categorisations and weak framing (−C−F). Research by a range of sociologists on young women's identities and aspirations[6] provides ample evidence for the transformative effects of such feminist praxis.

In *Closing the Gender Gap*, we argue that Western feminism was able to sustain its force by its institutional adaptability. It exploited the forms of voluntarism under the conditions of social democracy when teachers were assumed to have autonomy and arenas of curriculum discretion. It manipulated, where possible, the managerialism of the Conservative government's reforms—integrating equality of opportunity notions into debates about standards, performance and good schools. Gender issues were mainstreamed into concerns about quality of teaching, about improving school management, about effectiveness in teaching and in learning, and about addressing diversity and difference. School improvement as a theme was integral to the project of egalitarianism and vice versa. Indeed, as social inclusion became the antidote to excessive competitiveness, performativity and materialism, so feminist ideas about co-operation, collaboration, therapeutic models of counselling and person-centred management also became attractive. These concepts, along with 'feminisation of work place' and work cultures (Crompton, 1993) and interest in caring concepts of citizenship, are often taken as indicative of the mainstreaming of female culture.

Interestingly, sociological ethnographies have revealed major discursive shifts in young women's thinking in this period. In contrast, there has been comparatively little evidence of such shifts recorded among young men in the UK. The voices of young men captured by ethnographers demonstrate, if anything, the importance of traditional concepts of masculinity, especially in so far as it affects male bonds and friendships. Change appeared to come to young men less through the counter-hegemonic actions of egalitarian reformers or feminist campaigners than through changes in the structural relationships between schooling and the economy, especially through the policies of the Conservative governments of the 1980s and 1990s (Haywood and Mac an Ghaill, 1996). The policies of the New Right were more likely than feminist teachers to challenge boys' traditional gender identities. Paradoxically, as I argue below, despite supporting Victorian gender structures, the Conservative government of the 1980s and 1990s undermined the male role as head of household and breadwinner and created the educational conditions for change in gender relations.

The Individualism of the New Right

Various crises throughout the 1970s—in the economy, in employment and in international competitiveness—led to a break-down in the political consensus about education in a social democracy. As we describe in our book, by the end of the 1970s there were criticisms of the welfare state and education was particularly attacked for not having helped sustain economic growth. The New Right targeted both for revision. On the one hand, they encouraged economic restructuring and, on the other, they initiated the destruction of communities based on industrial employment. Accompanying the growth of banking services and the re-emergence of the City of London as a global finance capital was a parallel decline in manufacturing industries and occupations, once central to the British economy. For example, in 1946 construction, mining and manufacturing industries provided 45 per cent of employment and service industries 36 per cent of jobs. In 1989, the three great industrial sectors made up just 25 per cent of jobs in the country, while the service sector accounted for 15 million jobs (almost 70 per cent of employment) (Arnot, David and Weiner, 1996).

The challenge to male working-class hegemony was economic. During this era, traditional working-class communities lost their soul, with high levels of male unemployment and the need for women to support the family. The effect on family life was devastating. Women were often left as single parents in families without a male head of household. Traditional middle-class male work was also undermined through the restructuring of the service sector and the traditional professions, with many industries experiencing bankruptcies and redundancies. Boys therefore had to adapt to an increasingly insecure and different economic environment where the traditional transitions between school and work were broken (Pye, Haywood and Mac an Ghaill, 1996), where collectivism was replaced by individualism and self-help. The response of boys from different social groupings to post-Fordist schools and economy has been well researched in the UK. The evidence suggests that, on the whole, boys responded by sustaining strong gender boundaries except in those cases where they choose to move in the direction of new entrepreneurial cultures where such distinctions are less clear. In these cases, boys need to cope with learning subjects and courses that traditionally had been seen as female (media studies. business and commerce, languages). But for the majority, supporting traditional class-based male identities appears to be the norm. Young black and white men in the UK have been found to hold firmly onto romantic notions of traditional family values and the male breadwinning role, even though many can now speak the language of equal opportunities and women's rights. The pressures of social change, particularly it seems the weakening of the collective economic and familial bases of traditional masculinities, appear in the investment of manhood in physique (body, sport/fitness), sexual prowess and traditional patterns of male employment (Connell, 1989, 1997; Mac an Ghaill, 1988, 1994, 1996; Sewell, 1997).

The challenge to traditional gender power relations also received considerable support, paradoxically, from educational reforms which emphasised individual choice, competition and performance. As we have seen, by restructuring the educational system, the Conservative government, unintentionally and unwittingly, also reshaped the modality of gender transmission (Arnot, 1993). New high-tech industry did not necessarily require a conventionally sex-segregated labour force and indeed the vocational courses which the Conservative government introduced into schools in the early 1980s highlighted this fact by using special funding to promote equal opportunities for both sexes.[7] The Education Reform Act intervened in gender relations by institutionalising a National Curriculum with its entitlement of nine subjects for all pupils—girls would now have to study science, mathematics and technology. A symbolic nail in the coffin for Victorian gender relations can also be found in this compulsory curriculum: it did not include domestic science for girls. In 1988, 42 per cent of girls had taken this subject—in 1993, only 15 per cent of girls were studying domestic science. The pattern from the 1970s, where boys and girls in England had almost separate educations and where boys had dominated the high-status subjects (e.g., mathematics and science), was dramatically changed. The new legislation, reinforced by the earlier introduction of the GCSE examination, appeared to remove most of the sex segregation of subjects up to sixteen from the public eye. Gender-differentiated choices were now made within subjects, through ability sets, tiered examinations and choices of modules—patterns that were hidden within individualising school practices. Statistics on male and female choices of subject components still demonstrated gender differences, but these statistics are unlikely to be part of the new public narrative around male and female education.

Gender Orders, Schooling and Society

To conclude: girls' educational performance has been read by the UK media as a major challenge to male hegemony, asserting that now 'the future is female'. At one level, such media hype is right. There is evidence of a shift in the principles which govern gender power relations and their modes of transmission. The reproduction of gender relations is no longer through the dual system of male and female education which was established in the nineteenth century and perpetuated in schooling for the masses. The principle of gender differentiation which shaped the class-divided school system is now clearly neither as explicit nor as legitimate. It is more likely to be hidden within the individualising processes of learning than to be found in the formal structures of schooling.

Paradoxically, although male educational forms were being strengthened by the introduction of a National Curriculum (which was premised upon the curricula associated with elite male education), this reform undermined the strongly gender-differentiated curriculum of the 1970s. Gender differentiation which had been shaped by nineteenth-century educational ideals of the patriarchal family was less relevant to an educational system that was focused on standards, excellence and choice. Major gender differentiations, in effect, were delayed until after the end of compulsory education when the impact of the labour market had greatest effect. Within the new National Curriculum, girls could legitimately gain an advantage in terms of the acquisition of educational credentials and, encouraged by the ethos of the women's movement, could challenge conventional notions of gender difference. Thus, although the educational codes of schooling returned to the strong classificatory practices and strong control mechanisms (+C+F), the new integrative gender codes (−C−F) encouraged the redistribution of educational credentials and the negotiation of gender identities within education. The effects were, on the one hand, the rise in female performance and, on the other, the continuing strong effects of social class and ethnic differentiation (demonstrated by Gillborn and Mirza, 2000). Put sociologically, the principles which shaped the distribution of knowledge were changed even if the gendered hierarchies of knowledge remained intact. Within a newly structured educational system which aims to inculcate individualised learning and competence, the new gender order in the UK is more likely to be found in the micro-inequalities of schooling and in the more subtle differentiated curriculum tracks (Arnot, 2000).

Elite male dominance of the sciences and technology remains within and across class and was sustained more overtly in the post-compulsory sector. Here feminist presence had historically been much less than in the secondary and primary sectors of schooling. In the post-compulsory sector, with its transitions into further study and employment, the dominant modality of gender transmission (+C+F) remained, although girls have certainly carried forward their success in improving their academic performance. This may well be a class rather than a gender factor. Here, the redistribution of educational credentials has challenged but not necessarily removed the principles of gender classification and hence power relations.

The structures and processes of gender transmission for the elite, on the whole, have been retained. Boys from the dominant social classes could sustain what Connell (1987) argued were versions of 'gentry masculinity', based on scientific expertise and credentials. Ownership of such knowledge supported closure mechanisms for entry into high-status professional work and managerial positions of authority and control. Gender classifications at the top of the social hierarchy are transmitted conventionally and with great effect. Upper-middle-class girls have proved that they can achieve in the scientific worlds, but they still choose not to enter the scientific/technological spheres of employment. The language of individualisation becomes the means by which consent is achieved to male control of the environment, scientific policy-making and government. Thus the male hegemony of dominant social classes still retains its power.

There was no evidence that the range of economic and social reforms instigated by the Conservative government of the 1980s and the New Labour policies of the 1990s have fundamentally undermined the discriminatory practices governing male and female employment. Thus, although girls appeared to be strengthening their economic and social position by gaining access to higher-status male subjects and were seen to be doing well in them in the weakened gender boundaries of the school, there was no guarantee that such academic capital could be converted and indeed would be converted into academic and economic privilege. Thus, despite media panics, despite egalitarian social movements which attempted to redistribute male power, male dominance of academic capital is still intact. The conditions for sustaining male power, although different, are still in place.

Sociological analysis can help us understand the significance of gender relations and the role of education as a means of social reproduction. It points to the complex interaction of macro- and micro-influences on education, the interconnections between family and schooling and schooling and the economy. This gendered analysis has indicated the importance of exploring the ways in which social change impinges on social relations within and across such economic categories. In many ways, gender relations are symbolic of change in the forms of social control in our society.

Acknowledgements

The first version of this paper was presented at the UK–Japan Education Forum at Waseda University, Toyko, in 2000. I am very grateful to the Forum for allowing me to publish it here. My thanks to Miriam David and Gaby Weiner for allowing me to reproduce in this article material from our co-authored book *Closing the Gender Gap*, and to John Gray, Mary James and Jean Rudduck for permission to quote material from the OFSTED report which we co-wrote. I am also grateful to Rob Moore for engaging so generously in dialogue with me. The interpretations of the material and any errors are my responsibility.

Notes

1   By social reproduction theory I mean the development of theoretical understandings of the role of education in the production, reproduction and transmission of class, race and gender relations (see MacDonald, 1980, for a fuller discussion).
2   Other reports were produced for Wales (Salisbury, 1996), Scotland (Turner, Riddell and Brown, 1995) and Australia (Collins, Kenway and McLeod, 2000; Teese et al., 1995).
4   Data for 1995, for example, suggest that at A-level boys remain top academic achievers. More male students (10 per cent) than female students (7 per cent) secured the highest number of points (30+) accrued from A-level grades in different subjects.
5   Young women frequently choose business and commerce, hairdressing and beauty and caring service courses related to the female-identified sector of the labour market. Or, at university, women choose social studies, arts and humanities degrees.

6   For example, Griffin (1985, 1989); Wallace (1987); Weis (1990); Mirza (1992); Lees (1993); Chisholm and du Bois-Reynaud (1993); Bates (1993); Sharpe (1994); Basit (1996); Skeggs (1997).
7   See, for example, Haywood and Mac an Ghaill (1996) and Pye, Haywood and Mac an Ghaill (1996) for a discussion of how male trainees experience the relationship between school and work.

References and further reading

Arnot, M. (1982) 'Male hegemony, social class and women's education', *Journal of Education,* 164, 1, pp. 64–89.
——(1983) 'A cloud over co-education: an analysis of the forms of transmission of class and gender relations', in S. Walker and L. Barton (eds) *Gender, Class and Education,* Lewes: Falmer Press.
——(1986) 'State education policy and girls' educational experiences', in V. Beechey and E. Whitelegg (eds) *Women in Britain Today,* Milton Keynes: Open University Press.
——(1987) 'Political lip-service or radical reform? Central government responses to sex equality as a policy issue', in M. Arnot and G. Weiner (eds) *Gender and the Politics of Schooling,* London: Hutchinson.
——(1993) 'A crisis in patriarchy? British feminist education politics and state regulation of gender', in M. Arnot and K. Weiler (eds) *Feminism and Social Justice in Education: international perspectives,* London: Falmer Press.
——(2000) 'Gender relations and schooling in the new century: conflicts and challenges', *Compare,* 30, 3, pp. 293–302.
Arnot, M. and Dillabough, J. (2000) (eds) *Challenging Democracy: international perspectives on gender, education and citizenship,* London: RoutledgeFalmer.
Arnot, M., David, M. and Weiner, G. (1996) *Educational Reforms and Gender Equality in Schools,* Research Discussion Series no. 17, Manchester: Equal Opportunities Commission.
——(1998) *Closing the Gender Gap: postwar education and social change,* Cambridge: Polity Press.
Arnot, M., Gray, J., James, M. and Rudduck, J. (1998) *A Review of Recent Research on Gender and Educational Performance,* OFSTED Research Series, London: The Stationery Office.
Basit, T.N. (1996) 'I'd hate to be just a housewife: career aspirations of British Muslim girls', *British Journal of Guidance and Counselling,* 24, 2, pp. 227–42.
Bates, I. (1993) 'A job which is right for me? Social class, gender and individualisation', in I. Bates and G. Riseborough (eds) *Youth and Inequality,* Buckingham: Open University Press.
Bernstein, B. (1971) 'On the classification and training of educational knowledge', in M. Young (ed.) *Knowledge and Control: new directions for the sociology of education,* London: Collier-Macmillan.
Bourdieu, P. (1977) 'The economics of linguistic exchange', *Social Science Information,* 16, 6, pp. 645–68.
Burstyn, J. (1980) *Victorian Education and the Ideal of Womanhood,* London: Croom Helm.
Burton, L. and Weiner, G. (1990) 'Social justice and the National Curriculum', *Research Papers in Education,* 5, 3, pp. 203–28.
Cheng, Y., Payne, J. and Witherspoon, S. (1995) *Science and Mathematics in Full-time Education after 16,* Youth Cohort Report no. 36, London: Department for Education and Employment.
Chisholm, L. and du Bois-Reynaud, M. (1993) 'Youth transitions, gender and social change', *Sociology,* 27, 2, pp. 259–79.
Collins, C., Kenway, J. and McLeod, J. (2000) *Factors Influencing the Educational Performance of Males and Females in School and their Initial Destinations after Leaving School,* Commonwealth Department of Education, Training and Youth Affairs, Deakin University.
Connell, R.W. (1985) *Teachers' Work,* London: Allen & Unwin.
——(1987) *Gender and Power: society, the person and sexual politics,* Cambridge: Polity Press.
——(1989) 'Cool guys, swots and wimps: the inter-play of masculinity and education', *Oxford Review of Education,* 15, 3, pp. 291–303.
——(1990) 'The state, gender and sexual politics', *Theory and Society,* 19, pp. 507–44.
——(1997) 'The big picture: masculinities in recent world history', in A.H. Halsey, H. Lander, P. Brown and A.S. Wells (eds) *Education, Culture, Economy and Society,* Oxford: Oxford University Press.
Crompton, R. (1993) *Class and Stratification: an introduction to current debates,* Cambridge: Polity Press.
DfEE (2000) http://www.standards.dfee.gov.uk/genderandachievement/2000_data_5.html
Dillabough, J. (2000) 'Women in teacher education: their struggles for inclusion as "citizen-workers" in late modernity', in M. Arnot and J. Dillabough (eds) *Challenging Democracy: international perspectives on gender, education and citizenship,* London: RoutledgeFalmer.
Dyhouse, C. (1981) *Girls Growing up in Late Victorian and Edwardian England,* London: Routledge & Kegan Paul.
Epstein, D., Elwood, J., Hey, V. and Maw, J. (eds) (1998) *Failing Boys, Issues in Gender and Achievement,* Buckingham: Open University Press.
Felstead, A., Goodwin, J. and Green, F. (1995) *Measuring up to the National Training Targets: women's attainment of vocational qualifications,* Research Report, Centre for Labour Market Studies, University of Leicester.
Foster, V. (2000) 'Is female educational "success" destabilising the male-learner citizen?', in M. Arnot and J. Dillabough (eds) *Challenging Democracy: international perspectives on gender, education and citizenship,* London: RoutledgeFalmer.
Gillborn, D. and Mirza, H.S. (2000) *Educational Inequality: mapping race, class and gender,* London: OFSTED.
Griffin, C. (1985) *Typical Girls? Young women from school to the job market,* London: Routledge & Kegan Paul.
——(1989) 'I'm not a woman's libber, but . . . Feminism, consciousness and identity', in S. Skevington and D. Baker (eds) *The Social Identity of Women,* London: Sage.
Haywood, C. and Mac an Ghaill, M. (1996) 'What about the boys? Regendered local labour markers and the recomposition of working class masculinities', *British Journal of Education and Work,* 9, 1, pp. 19–30.

Hillman, J. and Pearce, N. (1998) *Wasted Youth: raising achievement and falling social exclusion,* London: Institute for Public Policy Research.

Joint Council for General Qualifications (2001) News Releases: 'A Bumper Year for Examinations—over 1.65 million results', 15 August.

Lees, S. (1993) *Sugar and Spice: sexuality and adolescent girls,* Harmondsworth: Penguin.

Lowe, R. (1997) *Schooling and Social Change, 1964–1990,* London: Routledge.

Mac an Ghaill, M. (1988) *Young, Gifted and Black,* Buckingham: Open University Press.

——(1994) *The Making of Men: masculinities, sexualities and schooling,* Buckingham: Open University Press.

——(ed.) (1996) *Understanding Masculinities,* Milton Keynes: Open University Press.

MacDonald, M. (1980) 'Socio-cultural reproduction and women's education', in R. Deem (ed.) *Schooling for Women's Work,* London: Routledge & Kegan Paul.

Marks, J. (2001) *Girls Know Better: educational attainments of boys and girls,* London: Civitas (Institute for the Study of Civil Society).

Marshall, T.H. (1950) *Citizenship and Social Class and Other Essays,* Cambridge: Cambridge University Press.

Mirza, H. (1992) *Young, Female and Black,* London: Routledge.

Moore, R. (1996) 'Back to the future: the problem of change and the possibilities of advance in the sociology of education', *British Journal of Sociology of Education,* 17, 2, pp. 145–61.

Pateman, C. (1988) *The Sexual Contract,* Cambridge: Polity Press.

Phillips, A. (1991) *Engendering Democracy,* Cambridge: Polity Press.

Purvis, J. (1985) *The History of Women's Education,* Buckingham: Open University Press.

Pye, D., Haywood, C. and Mac an Ghaill, M. (1996) 'The training state, de-industrialisation and the production of white working class trainee identities', *International Studies in Sociology of Education,* 6, 2, pp, 133–46.

Quicke, J. (1999) *A Curriculum for Life,* Buckingham: Open University Press.

Raphael Reed, L. (1999) 'Troubling boys and disturbing discourses on masculinity and schooling: a feminist exploration of current debates and interventions concerning boys in school', *Gender and Education,* 11, 1, pp. 93–110.

Salisbury, J. (1996) *Educational Reforms and Gender Equality in Welsh Schools,* Cardiff: Equal Opportunities Commission.

Salisbury, J. and Jackson, D. (1996) *Challenging Macho Values: practical ways of working with adolescent boys,* London: Falmer Press.

Sewell, T. (1997) *Black Masculinities and Schooling,* London: Trentham Books.

Sharpe, S. (1994) *Just Like a Girl: how girls learn to be women,* 2nd edn, Harmondsworth: Penguin.

Skeggs, B. (1997) *Formations of Class and Gender,* London: Sage.

Spender, D. (1987) 'Education: the patriarchal paradigm and the response to feminism', in M. Arnot and G. Weiner (eds) *Gender and the Politics of Schooling,* London: Hutchinson.

Stone, L. (ed.) (1994) *The Education Feminism Reader,* London: Routledge.

Teese, R., Davies, M., Charlton, M. and Polesel, J. (1995) *Who Wins at School? Boys and girls in Australian secondary education,* Department of Education Policy and Management, University of Melbourne.

Tolson, A. (1977) *The Limits of Masculinity,* London: Tavistock.

Turner, E., Riddell, S. and Brown, M. (1995) *Gender Equality in Scottish Schools: the impact of recent educational reforms,* Glasgow: Equal Opportunities Commission.

UCAS (2000) http://www.ucas.ac.uk/figures/archive/gender/index.html

Walkerdine, V. (1983) 'It's only natural: rethinking child-centred pedagogy', in A.M. Wolpe and J. Donald (eds) *Is There Anyone Here from Education?,* London: Pluto.

Wallace, C. (1987) 'From girls and boys to women and men: the social reproduction of gender', in M. Arnot and G. Weiner (eds) *Gender and the Politics of Schooling,* London: Hutchinson.

Weiler, K. (1988) *Women Teaching for Change,* New York: Bergin & Harvey.

Weiner, G. (1993) 'Shell-shock or sisterhood? English school history and feminist practice', in M. Arnot and K. Weiler (eds) *Feminism and Social Justice in Education: international perspectives,* London: Falmer Press.

Weiner, G. and Arnot, M. (1987) 'Teachers and gender politics', in M. Arnot and G. Weiner (eds) *Gender and the Politics of Schooling,* London: Hutchinson.

Weis, L. (1990) *Working Class without Work: high school students in a de-industrialising economy,* New York: Routledge.

Wilkinson, H. (1994) *No Turning Back: generations and the genderquake,* London: Demos.

Wollstonecraft, M. (1792) *A Vindication of the Rights of Woman,* Harmondsworth: Penguin; reprinted 1985.

15

Nation versus Nation

The Race to Be the First in the World

DAVID P. BAKER AND GERALD LETENDRE

This article leaves the world of how schools operate and turns to the politics of how schools change across nations. Public reaction to results from international school achievement tests in many nations has heightened awareness about educational competition with other nations. For example, in the mid-1990s, after the first set of TIMSS results became public, the United States went into a kind of soul searching about its mathematics and science curricula nationwide. The release of the more recent international study on OECD nations called PISA led Germany into a national education crisis. Around the world, countries are using the results of international tests as a kind of academic Olympiad, serving as a referendum on their school system's performance. Even though these tests were never designed to assess the overall performance of an entire school system, nations and even subnational educational authorities now regularly use them for competitive assessment.

The story here is about why there is so much focus on educational problems, inventing of solutions, and implementing them across systems of schooling in nations. As with our other tales, we find a common trend among nations, one of constantly tinkering and adjusting schooling to improve achievement, social fairness, and satisfy the numerous stakeholders in formal education.

By way of illustration of the dynamics of this trend, we focus on the case of mathematics and science curricular reform policy in the United States after the first TIMSS results were released the mid-1990s, since it continues to have major implications for education policy in this nation even today. We describe how, in the middle of the last decade, American policy makers embraced an image of the international competitiveness of the nation's mathematics and science test scores that led to a rationale for curricular reform. We then present some of our own analyses of this image with the TIMSS data, and show how *underwhelming* the empirical case really was for these curricular reforms in the United States. Our analyses suggest that if there had been more thorough appreciation of how complicated the empirical relationship is between quality of curricula in nations and level of achievement of students, a more balanced set of reforms might have been developed from TIMSS. We then speculate on the institutional nature of educational reform cycles in nations and worldwide.

From Comparison to Competition to Reform

National school systems seem always to be in the shop for repairs, or for what educators boldly like to call "reforms." In an interesting volume on *The Impact of TIMSS on the Teaching and Learning of Mathematics and Science*, twenty-nine national experts report on the effect the release of TIMSS test scores results had on educational policy in particular nations (Robitaille, Beaton, and Plomp, 2000). One is struck by constant reference to the need for nations to improve mathematics. Each nation has its own story of how TIMSS brought a particular problem to light that needs to be fixed and is now being addressed in this way or that. Remarkably, this is as true for the top-scoring nations as it is for low-performing ones. For example, high-scoring South Korea sees a national gender difference in mathematics that it says needs fixing, and even top-scoring Singapore manages to admit that there is "room for improvement" in mathematics and science education.

Modern systems of public mass schooling appear to travel a continuous cycle of identifying problems, constructing solutions, and implementing new reforms, only then to start the process all over again. But this description is too orderly for what really takes place; instead, most of the time reform cycles are running at different speeds around various parts of the system all at the same time. There is simultaneously much problem identifying, solution seeking, and reform implementing happening throughout educational systems. International comparative data have often been the spark to set off a cycle of this kind. National educational crises start as easily as the common cold spreads—the right sneeze in public, so to speak, and the cycle begins.

Even though continuous reform is common in all national education systems, discussion about educational problems, solutions, and implementation takes on a particularly national tone and image. Educational problems are often discussed as though they are truly unique to a particular nation, needing unique solutions made chiefly from homegrown ideas, spread through a unique national process of implementation of solutions, all operating within a national polity made up of indigenous political enemies and champions of any particular educational reform.

But even a cursory look across nations defies the image of struggling with one's own unique problems and solutions. Although cycles of problem identification and reform are national in the simplest sense, their overall volume across nations is so large that it is likely a world trend. Furthermore, it looks irrational as a solely national enterprise; for example, top-performing nations in past international mathematics and science studies launch into reforms as frequently as do poor-performing nations, sometimes deciding on reforms that take high- and low-performing nations back toward each other without even recognizing it![1] As the TIMSS volume on national reaction illustrates, a national ministry is never heard publicly proclaiming that everything is just rosy in the nation's education system and there is no need to fix anything. To do so is political suicide, and politicians know it, since they believe in the centrality of the educational process as much as the rest of society.

In our times, educational reform is perpetual and self-reaffirming. There is remarkably little cynicism about the educational reform cycle in society; it is widely and strongly believed in. Given this, we wonder if there is not a larger institutional logic behind reform that would explain the continuous high volume in nation after nation.

The Policy Trap

Several years ago with colleagues we wrote a paper entitled "The Policy Trap," about how misinterpretation stemming from rushed and underdeveloped analyses of international test results trapped nations into misidentifying problems and aiming reform issues in less-than-productive directions (LeTendre and others, 2001). The American reaction to TIMSS on a policy level illustrates this interesting phenomenon.

To simplify and make a long story short, an initial set of reasonably good academic Olympiad standings for the United States in the TIMSS fourth grade sample were dashed by internationally mediocre eighth grade results reported some time after the fourth grade results. The main message for American education policy makers that emerged from the highly publicized results was that the mathematics and science curricula had to be raised to international standards if America's educational achievement level were to also rise internationally. Comparison of what American students learned from elementary grades to middle and high school scores was disheartening and widely covered in

TABLE 15.1 Estimated Increase Between Fourth and Eighth Grades on Science and Math

Nation	Science	Nation	Math
Iran	234	Thailand	168
Thailand	220	Singapore	159
Kuwait	213	Iceland	149
Singapore	210	Japan	148
Israel	179	New Zealand	146
Hungary	175	Hong Kong	141
Portugal	165	Norway	138
Czech Republic	164	Korea	137
Slovenia	164	Czech Republic	135
Greece	161	Iran	134
Cyprus	154	Canada	133
Netherlands	150	England	130
Norway	150	Israel	128
Ireland	149	Greece	128
England	149	Hungary	127
Iceland	148	Slovenia	127
New Zealand	147	Kuwait	125
Hong Kong	142	Australia	121
Japan	140	Austria	119
Austria	138	Ireland	116
Scotland	133	Portugal	115
Latvia	130	Scotland	115
Canada	130	Cyprus	108
Australia	127	Latvia	105
U.S.A.	113	Netherlands	103
Korea	105	U.S.A.	93

Source: Martin and others 1997.

the national media. For example, Table 15.1 shows an estimate of what students from a number of nations learn from fourth to eighth grade. The United States is at the bottom of the international rankings of how much mathematics is learned by eighth grade, although the American eighth grade mean is among average-performing nations. Results of this kind, coupled with the heated-up interest in the idea that mathematics and science education even at the most elementary level leads to national economic well-being, quickly kicked off a major cycle of problem identifying, solution inventing, and reform implementing in the United States. What happened next is what created the education policy trap we have observed in other nations as well: celebration of a solution waiting for a problem.

For some time now in the United States, mathematics and science educators have thought that what is taught across public schools in the nation is not too demanding a curriculum, and that more rigorous and better-implemented curricular materials would improve national achievement. Dating back to the 1960s' "new math" era and even before during the Sputnik crisis, there has been a long-standing wish on the part of mathematics and science curricular specialists in the United States to get a real chance at improving, strengthening, and standardizing curricula throughout the nation. This venerable interest in reform of American mathematics and science curricula was in the mid-1990s the solution waiting for a problem to attach itself to, and the media buzz about the "slump" in the TIMSS results from fourth to eighth grades became this problem—and a politically perfect one at that.

Educational reform cycles seem to occur most rapidly in the United States when there is a pending sense of educational doom (Cross, 2003). From Sputnik through the report *Nation at Risk* to the first release of the TIMSS results decades later, nothing seems to spell doom in American education quite like internationally inadequate mathematics and science education. In fact, this is probably the case in most nations.

Policy analysts and makers quickly seized on the idea that U.S. math and science curricula were "broken" and that this was the chief cause of the nation's slump in achievement compared internationally. Major national and local mathematics and science forces, such as the National Science Foundation, the U.S. Department of Education, nongovernmental organizations of curricular expert professional associations, state Departments of Education, and some local school districts, were all ready to spring into action upon hearing about this problem. Of course, they had the solution already in mind: curricular reform.

The mobilization of the American education establishment over mathematics and science curricula reform was primed by two well-established ideas about the educational performance of the nation and its economic well-being that had been widely disseminated in the media and even in scholarly works since publication of *A Nation at Risk,* in 1983. One idea was that the level of achievement of a nation in technical fields such as mathematics and science is directly linked to the nation's economic productivity. For example, two decades of concern over failing economic competition led to the national "economic threat" from superior East Asian (Japan, South Korea) national educational achievements. The other idea was that American public mass schooling was failing the nation as a producer of technically capable future workers. Both of these ideas were powerful in terms of policy, even though research on them suggests that national economic productivity is far more complicated than a one-to-one link with the performance of the school system.

By the time the TIMSS results were released in the mid-1990s, these ideas were already driving the highly ambitious federal government's "GOALS 2000" reforms. The GOALS legislation contained little in the way of concrete plans for improving education, but it laid out a clear set of lofty (if unrealistic) ambitions. The United States was to become "first in the world" in math and science by the year 2000; this was actually a goal borrowed from the George H. Bush administration. GOALS 2000 implicitly made the nation's performance on international tests a referendum on the quality of the entire educational system and promulgated the belief that a higher ranking was indicative of greater national economic competitiveness.

Note both the rhetoric of anticipation of an educational problem waiting to be solved as well as a dramatic call to reform schooling—in a press release from a powerful NGO interested in American science production. It is illustrative of the kind of statements made throughout this period:

> The American Association for the Advancement of Science (AAAS) is saddened but not surprised by the disappointing scores of U.S. high school seniors in the Third International Mathematics and Science Study (TIMSS), released today by the Department of Education.
>
> "As a country dependent on science and technology, we must see this poor performance as a call to action," said Richard Nicholson, AAAS's executive officer. "AAAS urges every community across the nation to launch into a forthright discussion about the implications of these scores and how we can improve the current system of education in science and mathematics. It will take a concerted effort by all of us—schools, parents, industry, government, and science communities—to ensure that future results are much more encouraging."
>
> February 24, 1997—Washington, D.C, AAAS Press Release

The politics behind this case of educational reform in the United States turned on two main assumptions. First, the American mathematics and science curricula were indeed broken and in need of reform as compared to other nations. Second, if we managed to fix our broken curricula we would improve the nation's educational competitiveness internationally.

Broken Curricula?

Influential reports, using past and current international data to evaluate the state of the American mathematics and science curricula, portray in dramatic terms an image of broken national mathematics and science curricula, including "a broken spiral," "an underachieving curriculum," "splintered," and "a mile wide and an inch deep" (McKnight, Crosswhite, and Dossey, 1987; Schmidt, McKnight, and Raizen, 1997). In the immediate post-TIMSS environment in the United States, the latter image—namely, that a pressing national educational problem is its "mile wide and an inch deep" mathematics and science curricula, was the main message. This image really took hold as being an identifiable problem easily described in media and accepted among influential stakeholders interested in American science and technology production. The American mathematics and science curricula at the eighth and twelfth grade levels in the 1990s were thought to cover too many topics in too superficial a manner to ensure effective learning among the nation's students. The solution, of course, was already known—reform the curricula—but how to get this across to the broad spectrum of policy makers in the highly localized American educational system?

Mathematics and science curricular experts, among them William Schmidt, the chief author of many influential and official American TIMSS reports, led a media campaign, often with the support of the National Science Foundation, to spread the broken mathematics and science curricula message throughout the nation. Here, for example, is how Schmidt and a colleague describe the broken curricula image in 1997: "These results [from TIMSS] point out that U.S. education in the middle grades is particularly troubled; the promise of our fourth-grade children (particularly in science) is dashed against the undemanding curriculum of the nation's middle schools" (Valverde and Schmidt, p. 60).

But were the U.S. mathematics and science curricula truly broken, as in being a mile wide and an inch deep? If they were broken and then fixed, would American achievement be likely to improve compared to other nations? To foreshadow a bit, neither of these key assumptions driving American policy about the mathematics and science curricula reform since the release of the initial TIMSS results is supported by the very data that are often attributed in identifying the problem in the first place.

Assessing National Curricula: Breadth, Depth, and Repetition

An abundance of international data on curriculum and what happens to it in the classroom from the 1980s onward has taken the curricular theorist out of the classroom and into the world of nations and politics. For example, many important past ideas about curriculum tended to be about classroom processes, such as the idea of a "hidden curriculum," or the things that get taught unintentionally during the classroom process (see Bowles and Gintis, 1976; Eckert, 1989; Goldman and McDermott, 1987). Even Bruner's influential ideas (1962) about effective spiraling curriculum were conceived in terms of a teacher who anchors her material around key concepts and then spirals upward as she goes through the year. Cross-national surveys, particularly the IEA-type data sets (like TIMSS), which have always been designed with considerable input from curricular experts, expanded the image of how the whole curricular process works in a nation beyond just the content or very micro ideas about teaching. It is taken for granted that curricula are organized at several levels in a nation, each level with its own name.

On the first level are national curricular guidelines and national textbooks representing the *intended* or *ideal* national curriculum. On the next level is the national *implemented* curriculum, which is what is actually taught in the nation's classrooms. Last, the national *achieved* curriculum is what is actually learned by a nation's students from the intended curriculum. An expanded notion of a nation's curriculum and the flow of international data increased policy makers' interest in international comparisons of achievement, as well as curricular explanations for any cross-national differences.

Most countries in the world create national curriculum guidelines and use standardized textbooks regarding what should be taught in their schools. In this respect, the United States is notable in lacking any national curricula or guidelines. Intended curricula in the United States are only partially the domain of individual states, with a large amount of the control of content residing at the district or even the school level. This administrative arrangement certainly contributes to the belief among American curricular experts that a lack of formal standardization in intended curricula, as well as localized and hence perhaps weak quality control over the implemented curricula in the nation's classrooms, is the cause of the nation's mediocre eighth grade and twelfth grade mathematics and science compared to many other nations.

But these strongly held beliefs among American educators have never really been put to an empirical test at the cross-national level. Our TIMSS analysis project colleague and educational psychologist Erling Boe, in a policy brief in 2001, describes the astonishing lack of evidence about the relationship between national characteristics and national achievement, including the intended and implemented curricula, in the official American TIMSS reports that caused such concern about the image of broken mathematics and science curricula in the first place:

It is not surprising, therefore, that a critic of TIMSS (Bracy, 2000, p. 5) could claim legitimately, four years after the first release of data, that publications issued by the U.S. Department of Education had not offered any explanations about which differences in national education systems have produced the differences in observed achievement. In fact, none of the official reports of TIMSS findings issued to date have contained a quantified bivariate relationship between any specific predictor variable and any national-level achievement score, nor has there been publication of any multivariate models of national differences in math or science achievement. This observation applies to all of the many reports issued [by] the TIMSS. [Boe and others, 2001, pp. 1–2]

Boe's observations are all the more ironic because the TIMSS study was specifically designed to examine claims like those of the broken American curricula argument. Consequently, using the TIMSS data for what they were partially intended for, we investigate the characteristics of the implemented American eighth grade mathematics curriculum to see if it is indeed "broken" in comparison to curricula in other nations. Then we refer to the Boe report's results about the relationship between national curricular characteristics and national achievement. Our example here is limited to just mathematics, but we find roughly the same empirical situation exists for the science curriculum as well.

In keeping with the metaphoric image of "mile wide and inch deep" put forth by American mathematics curricular experts, we examine the "breadth," "depth," and repetition (broken spiraling) of the curriculum implemented in American classrooms as compared to other nations.

Simply measured, breadth is the number of topics covered in a school year and depth is the time spent on each topic. The mile-wide-and-inch-deep image suggested American teachers try to cover too many topics, and it is often thought that if a teacher covers too much content this robs emphasis and detracts from achievement. Similarly, if too many topics are repeated there is no upward spiral of learning of mathematics concepts at a more advanced level.

Nations where teachers cover a lot of topics could be said to have a broad curriculum. So is it true that the United States has an extremely broad mathematics curriculum?

As shown in Table 15.2, the average American eighth grade teacher teaches between seventeen and eighteen mathematics topics during the eighth grade. Although the U.S. average is among those nations with broader curricula, one could hardly call it extremely broad. Most nations have relatively broad curricula; for example, high-scoring South Korea has an average of more than nineteen topics. There are only eight relatively "narrow streams" in the world of national mathematics curricula captured by these TIMSS nations. Overall, most nations are quite similar in the number of topics taught in eighth grade mathematics.

TABLE 15.2 Math Breadth for the Implemented Curriculum: Average Number of Math Topics Taught in 1994

Country	Math Breadth *Mean*	Coefficient of Variation for Math Breadth
Hungary	21.6	0.36
Greece	19.8	0.27
New Zealand	19.5	0.52
Korea	19.4	0.36
Australia	18	0.57
Slovenia	17.59	0.47
U.S.A.	**17.51**	**0.68**
Portugal	17.5	0.38
Canada	16.8	0.64
Spain	16.7	0.56
Lithuania	16.2	0.67
Romania	16.1	0.73
Belgium (Flemish)	15.9	0.47
Iran, Islamic Rep.	15.9	0.7
Colombia	15.6	0.61
Slovak Rep.	15.6	0.6
Hong Kong	15.5	0.54
Netherlands	15.3	0.61
Singapore	15.2	0.3
Belgium (French)	14	0.6
Switzerland	13.9	0.79
Austria	13.8	0.58
Germany	13.7	0.8
Iceland	13.6	0.7
Czech Rep.	13.2	0.72
Israel	11.1	0.58
Latvia	11	0.73
Sweden	10.4	0.85
Russian Federation	9.5	0.07
Thailand	7.18	1

Note: Nations in same shaded area have averages that are statistically similar.
Source: TIMSS 1995.

The second column shows an indicator of how similar or dissimilar teachers within a given country are in terms of how many mathematics topics they teach in a school year. There is some variation within many nations. For example, Greece has the least variation among teachers (.27), meaning that most teachers cover about the average of nearly twenty topics. In the United States, at .68, some teachers cover fewer topics and some teachers cover more topics than the national average of 17.5 in the school year. But this level of variation in the United States is neither very large in absolute terms nor the largest among these nations.

If we carry on with the analogy of the river that proved so useful in making the case for curricular reform among American policy makers, the U.S. curricular stream is no wider than most countries, but it has many channels and backwaters. U.S. students, depending on their teacher, may experience a broad or narrow range of topics. Conversely, students in nations such as Greece and Singapore receive a more uniformly broad mathematics curricula over the eighth grade year.

Much of the variation in the exposure to mathematics topics in classrooms arises from processes within nations more than processes between nations. To be precise, about 70 percent of the variation we see among these nations in terms of the breadth of the math curriculum from classroom to classroom comes from within the countries themselves, leaving only 30 percent being between the nations. Most cover a lot of topics, and in many nations the amount of topics varies some from teacher to teacher.

TABLE 15.3 Math Repetition for the Implemented Curriculum: Average Topics Taught in the Past Year and 1994

Country	Math Repetition Mean	Coefficient of Variation for Math Repetition
Singapore	14.4	0.35
Romania	10.8	0.89
Hungary	10.3	0.88
Lithuania	9.3	0.8
Slovak Rep.	8.8	0.85
Slovenia	8.4	0.84
Iran, Islamic Rep.	8.3	0.97
Spain	6.7	0.98
Austria	6.5	0.96
Portugal	6.4	0.95
Germany	6.1	1.18
Greece	6	1.11
Israel	6	0.92
Korea	5.7	1.2
Russian Federation	5.7	0.08
Czech Republic	5.5	1.14
Latvia	5.3	0.98
U.S.A.	5.1	**1.46**
Hong Kong	4.9	1.33
Netherlands	4.9	1.33
Australia	4.6	1.43
Colombia	4.6	1.34
Belgium (Flemish)	4.4	1.25
Canada	4.2	1.67
Switzerland	4.1	1.31
Belgium (French)	3	1.38
New Zealand	3	2.01
Iceland	2.3	2.01
Sweden	1.8	2.34
Thailand	...	...

Source: TIMSS 1995.

If the average implemented curriculum in most nations is broad, what about depth? As just one indicator of depth, we find that the average amount of instructional time given to topics did not vary greatly across these nations, and again the American implemented mathematics curriculum as a whole is not extremely shallow in its coverage. At the same time, the average American eighth grade mathematics teacher is not more prone to topic repetition than other nations' teachers are, at least not to the extent that it might create the broken spiral described in the broken curriculum literature. Actually, as Table 15.3 shows, the average U.S. teacher is less repetitious than the average teacher across the whole TIMSS sample.

So it would appear that if the implemented American eighth grade mathematics curriculum is broken, it is no more broken than in most other nations. Although there is cross-national variation on these characteristics of the curriculum, the United States is not extreme in any sense. This leads to the next question: What if nations are able to have narrower, deeper, and less repetitious mathematics intended and implemented curricula, would this mean higher national achievement?

National Curricula and National Achievement

Boe and colleagues (2001) examined this question in great detail. They looked at achievement both across the full mathematics test given by TIMSS as well as with several types of subscores that focus on several parts of mathematics achievement. They studied characteristics of the national intended curriculum using special curricular data over several grades (Schmidt, McKnight, and Raizen, 1997; Schmidt and others, 1997), as well as other curricular data. As a supplement to the Boe report, we analyzed measures of the implemented curricula broadness, depth, and repetition described earlier (national averages and within-nation variation).

In all of these analyses, on a range of characteristics of national intended and implemented curricula in both mathematics and science, virtually *no* national qualities of curricula are related to any of a range of indicators of national achievement in eighth grade. High-performing nations are not more likely to have curricula with a particular set of characteristics in terms of both intended content and implementation in the classroom. Whether it is for the full mathematics and science tests or focused subscores, or for indicators of the intended or implemented curriculum, there is no pattern of association between the qualities of national curricula and national achievement. The only exception is a moderate relationship between the coverage of algebra in nations and the cross-national level of algebra achievement.

So does this mean that curriculum is not important in the schooling process? Clearly not, but given the widely held belief that the curriculum plays a primary role in driving the national achievement level, these findings may astound some. How can they be explained?

One answer might be that curriculum really isn't important in producing the national level of achievement; another might be that the TIMSS curricular data were so flawed as to be unable to show this relationship. But we find little evidence to support either interpretation. Schmidt and others (2001) find significant correlations between curricula subtopics taught and achieved *within nations* (not among countries)—suggesting, as one would expect, that if students were not taught something they tended not to get problems of that type right on the TIMSS achievement test. Also, the TIMSS data were collected under rigorous scientific standards, so we doubt they could be so flawed as to be "hiding" major relationships between national curricula and achievement. Rather, a more global view of national curricula and national achievement helps to explain these results.

Assuming that if students are not taught something they tend to know less about it than ones who are taught, what would account for this lack of across-national association between curricula and achievement? Let's consider the intended curriculum first.

A plausible answer seems to be that every country in the TIMSS intends for its students to learn roughly the same knowledge base in mathematics and science, significantly reducing cross-national variation in the intended curriculum. A convergence of curricula means that the curricular content of eighth grade mathematics and science from one nation to the next is not large. In fact, research on historical curricular trends shows precisely this; national intended curricula continue to converge on similar content over time and across nations (see, for example, Benavot and others, 1991; McEneaney and Meyer, 2000). There has come to be much greater homogeneity in terms of recognized core knowledge—content for curricula—at least through the end of primary schooling across nations. Although nations vary with regard to the emphasis they place on numerous subtopics in the intended curriculum, virtually all nations teach mathematics and science with an increasingly standard notion of the essence and components of these subjects. In the elementary years, most students worldwide are exposed to core concepts, so it is understandable that there is no association between intended curriculum and achievement across nations. Even the one set of cross-national associations there is (those between algebra curriculum and achievement) is for a relatively distinct subtopic of mathematics that nations either do or do not teach in eighth grade. This case demonstrates what would be the case with the TIMSS data if there were significant differences in what nations intended to teach.

This isomorphic-curricular argument also explains why cross-national differences in implementation of curricula are not related to cross-national differences in achievement. We suspect there is not really much difference across nations in average implementation, particularly as compared to variation within nations. As we pointed out, considerably more variation in implemented curricula occurs among classes within nations than among nations. No nation—and certainly not the United States from the perspective of the TIMSS data—appears to have a wildly broken curriculum in terms of its average implementation. Finally, purely curricular-based reasons for national differences in achievement have been questioned for some time on the grounds that a host of curricular processes show only minor differences across nations and tend not to be significantly related to achievement (see Stevenson and Baker, 1996; see Valverde and others, 2002, for an opposite argument).

Institutionalized Policy Reform

What is interesting here beyond the specifics of this case of international educational competition and curricular reform is not just that our analysis finds little evidence for characterizing American curricula as broken, or that we find almost no evidence of an association between characteristics of national curricula and national level of achievement. Instead, the whole case illustrates how relatively easy it is for modern education systems to jump on a reform cycle. During the years that this American case unfolded, few seriously questioned the veracity of the two main assumptions about the broken American curricula and their role in national achievement. The cycle was easily launched and then wrapped in the scantiest of real evidence; there was a long-standing solution waiting for a problem, and this led to reform.

Although it may be too early to assess the long-run impact of curricular reforms in mathematics and science in the United States, we suspect that the general ideas stemming from the TIMSS case will have a significant effect on American educational policy at the national, state, and local levels for some time to come. Educational reform never happens in a vacuum; there is always some connection to past reforms, and each has some imprint on future ones. We wonder what those who will look back on the Bush administration's No Child Left Behind legislation will say about its connection to the ideas stirred up by the mathematics and science curricular reform issues of the 1990s.

Was it wrong after the release of the TIMSS initial results to be concerned about the nation's curriculum, or to have wanted to improve it to match the best in the world, or to want to try moving teachers to implement curricula in a more effective way? Of course not. Along with other professional educators, we would encourage any nation to implement the best curriculum that can be designed, and to continuously monitor it and make improvements where possible.

What we have described here is not some sort of scandal; quite the opposite. It was the result of multiple good intentions of many powerful stakeholders in educational policy in the United States. Everyone involved had the best of intentions of improving the nation's schools. We doubt that even timely, in-depth analyses of curricula and national achievement showing some of the flaws and overstatements in the original assumptions, as we show here, would have deterred this exuberant outbreak of mathematics and science curricular reform in the United States. There was just too much anticipation of the solution of reform in these areas for too long a time. What is most likely the cost of this laserlike focus on curricular reform was a chance to discuss a number of other educational problems in the United States that are identifiable with the TIMSS data—resource inequality and disadvantaged students discussed . . . being notable.

The American case is just one of many that illustrate a similar process about educational reform. We began this article with the image of a reform-crazed educational world, which often uses studies like TIMSS to adopt solutions and new approaches to prevailing concerns about a nation's schools in general. So how can we make sense of this from a more global perspective? We have already suggested that it is not just a process by which education is considered useful and everyone wants the best they can find. If this were so, it would be hard to explain why even top-performing nations are about equally prone to cycles of reform as are nations with poorer performance.

There are two productive ways to think about an educational world dripping with the political motivation for finding problems, creating solutions, and enacting reforms. One is about how education is a sector made up of many formal organizations constantly mixing with the realpolitik of social policy within a nation. The second is on a deeper institutional level, about what education has come to represent in society.

Educational Reform as an Organizational Product

As an institution, mass schooling in every nation is made up of a dense population of formal organizations of stakeholders in contrast to, say, the institution of the family, which comprises informal organizations. Schools, local education units, ministries of education, NGOs of professional educators, teachers' unions, and so forth are cast into a thick web of formal organizations, all of which have an interest and some influence in producing educational policy. As such, the institutional ideas behind education shape organizational behavior as much as they do the behavior of individuals participating in these organizations (Meyer and Jepperson, 2000). But how organizations behave is somewhat different from how individuals do, and this difference plays a role in producing the high volume of educational reform.

A relatively new and important school of thought about the interaction between formal organizations and the characteristics of the institutional sector they are in suggests some useful ways to think about constant worldwide educational reform. Observers of formal organizations from a neoinstitutional perspective (Richard Scott, John Meyer, Brian Rowan, and others) show us how constrained and even ritualistic organizations can be by the institutionalized world of common meaning and appropriate actions that they function in (Powell and DiMaggio, 1991).

As an organization, a school behaves more as the people within it think a school should behave than it does according to some unique rationalized plan of action. This is also true for governmental agencies, unions, and NGOs of all types within the educational sector. Certainly, formal organizations are bureaucracies and there are considerable rationalized processes within them, but formal organizations also conform to institutional ideas as to what they should be rational about and even how to be rational.

Taking this idea a step further, a fellow theoretical traveler of this viewpoint and organizational theorist, James March, finds that organizational processes such as problem identification, solution finding, and implementing are themselves ritualized to a degree. He convincingly argues that in real organizations, particularly large ones, each of these activities runs in a separate stream within the organization and generally does not occur in the order one would assume. Hence, organizational solutions wait for the right problems, methods of implementation wait for the right solution to spread, and so forth (March and Olsen, 1979). One needs only to ask an astute older colleague in a large organization about the history of computerization and its effect on the organization's integrating this technology to hear stories of solutions waiting for and trying to find problems, or technology waiting for applications, or implementation strategies looking for solutions to distribute, and so forth.

An insightful way to think about the American TIMSS case, as well as similar reform activity in other nations, is not to attribute the reform cycle to the actions of just one or even a few organizations (a ministry, or a union, or even the statistical branch of a ministry that helps produce studies like TIMSS). Instead, attribute the actions to a web of numerous organizations, all of which in one way or another take part in the production of problems, solutions, and implementation strategies.

As we have described, a legacy of reaction to past international studies and the image of a problematic American mathematics curriculum led expert groups of mathematics educators, federal mathematics and science policy makers, and so forth to be receptive to a curricular interpretation of the United States's placing in the academic Olympiad of TIMSS even though this interpretation is not well supported by other parts of the TIMSS data set. In the mid-1990s, use of the TIMSS international scores was really just the spark, much as Sputnik and *Nation at Risk* functioned for earlier reform cycles. The web of organizations was loaded like a compressed spring aimed at a reform cycle; American performance on international tests (which in study after study is usually in the midrange, and rarely extremely bad) released this reform energy.

The point is that institutions like education, comprising to a high degree webs of formal organizations all producing streams of problems, solutions, and implementation, are capable of generating intense motivation for collective rationalized action aimed at a specific target. For example, American organizations such as the AAAS or the NSF, made up of high-profile experts and given the public charter to monitor and recommend ways to improve American technology and science, can generate collective motivation to look for solutions, find problems, and rally around implementation of reforms. Never do we see such an organization in the United States make a public statement that all is fine with its charge.

Certainly nations differ in the exact nature in which educational policy is made and reform is started. Nations with stronger centralized political parties organize approaches to reform differently from the American system of education with its highly disconnected, localized governance system. Such political-structure variation across nations probably has some relationship to the frequency of reform cycles across them. For example, the United States, with its very high ratio of educational organizations (other than schools) to students, yields a nation often primed for reform (Tyack and Cuban, 1995). Some other nations may have slightly less frequent rounds of reform, but overall the process we describe leads to considerable reform activities worldwide. Last of all, there is evidence to suggest that, as with the case here, use of external information from other nations is more frequent when policy debates are about highly contested issues (Steiner-Khamsi, 2002; Schriewer, 1990).

Reform as an Institutional Value

The image of reform as an institutionalized value helps us think about educational policy reform as a worldwide experience that stems directly from the institutional character of mass schooling. We have discussed the power of education in modern society as an institution, how central it has become to so many important things about the future of our children and our nations. We have shown how as an institution it surpassed even the vital role of the family in many aspects of childrearing and the passing down of advantage to future generations. For better or worse, mass schooling is among a relatively small number of central institutions in modern society, and our tales so far have documented some of the things that are happening worldwide in this powerful institution. Yet when we try to explain the world trend of educational reform, we encounter a paradox.

As sociologists have long pointed out, when institutions reach their height of power and influence on human behavior, they organize meanings and norms that are highly resistant to change. However, constant educational reform seems to move in the opposite direction. The powerful institution of mass schooling appears entirely open to change.

One way out of this paradox is to suggest that reform really doesn't change much; what occurs is merely surface change, while the main values of the institution remain stable underneath. Certainly there is some truth in this image, and we don't want to equate all reform with major institutional change. Yet as various histories of educational reform in the United States have shown, reform often does lead to profound institutional change (Tyack and Cuban, 1995). Reform is not necessarily always trivial or faddish.

Perhaps a better way out of the paradox is to consider how the tendency for continuous reform cycles is built into the institutional fabric of education. Institutional theorist Meyer has thought the most about this aspect of mass schooling. In a provocative chapter (in a book celebrating the academic career of David Tyack) titled "Reflections on Education as Transcendence," he discusses how the institutional origins of mass schooling are strikingly religious in form (Meyer, 2000). This no doubt sounds like a strange thing to say about public schooling, which usually meticulously separates out religious beliefs from public instruction. But Meyer is not referring to the teaching of religion; rather, he refers to the idea that in its institutional form mass education takes on religious-like power in modern society. He points out that schooling's mission to transmit major knowledge about how the world works and its ability to transform students into "educated adults" in a universalistic fashion gives the institution transcendental qualities. It is not that public mass schooling is about religion; instead, it has powerful institutional components that make it like a religion in modern society.

Reform gets built into core values about education in modern society. The word *reform* itself, of course, derives from the idea of reforming the universal Catholic Church. Not radical restructuring but constant reform gives the institution a certain dynamic power. It is not static; it is open to some change, to the flexible exercising of basic institutional ideas in developing a better school system. This quality of schooling is what drives so much reform.

Its power as an institution is in large part derived from the belief held by many in modern society that schooling is a key component in producing the good society. Technically, morally, and civically, education is called upon to provide the masses with the right stuff to form a productive, just, and orderly world. When social problems arise, the call for an educational solution is not far behind. A powerful modern ideology is that society itself is a project, and one of the fundamental parts of the project is to use education to achieve society. Seen this way, it is no wonder that reform to improve the basic ideas, goals, and operation of mass schooling is nearly continuous and publically welcomed—exactly as it appears to be across so many nations.

Note

1. Compare, for example, how Japan, after scoring high in international studies in the 1980s, took to heart interpretations of its results that suggested too much emphasis was placed on basic computational skills and then sought reforms that put more high-order thinking in the mathematics curricula, while the United States, after scoring in the middle of the pack, sought reform for more basic skills as an interpretation of how to "catch up" with Japan.

References

Boe, E., Barkanic, G., Shin, S., May, H., Leow, C., Singleton, C., Zeng, G., and Borouch, R. *Correlates of National Differences in Mathematics and Science Achievement: Evidence from TIMSS.* (Data Analysis Report, 2001-DARI.) Philadelphia: Center for Research and Evaluation in Social Policy, University of Pennsylvania.

Bowles, S., and Gintis, H. *Schooling in Capitalist America.* New York: Basic Books, 1976.

Bracy, G. "The TIMSS 'Final Year' Study and Report: A Critique." *Educational Researcher*, 2000, 29, 4-10.

Bruner, J. *On Knowing: Lessons for the Left Hand.* New York: Antheneum, 1962.

Cross, C. *Political Education: National Policy Comes of Age.* New York: Teachers College Press, 2003.

Eckert, P. *Jocks and Burnouts.* New York: Teachers College Press, 1989.

Goldman, S., and McDermott, R. "The Culture of Competition in American Schools." In G. Spindler (ed.), *Education and Cultural Progress.* Prospect Heights, Ill.: Waveland Press, 1987.

LeTendre, G., Akiba, M., Goesling, B., Wiseman, A., and Baker, D. "The Policy Trap: National Educational Policy and the Third International Math and Science Study." *International Journal of Educational Policy, Research and Practice*, 2000, 2 (1), 45-64.

March, J., and Olsen, J. *Ambiguity and Choice in Organizations.* Bergen, Norway: Universitetsforgalet, 1979.

McKnight, C., Crosswhite, F., and Dossey, J. *The Underachieving Curriculum: Assessing U.S. Mathematics from an International Perspective.* Champaign, Ill.: Stipes, 1987.

Meyer, J. "Reflections on Education as Transcendence." In L. Cuban and D. Shipps (eds.) *Reconstructing the Common Good in Education.* Stanford, Calif.: Stanford University Press, 2000.

Meyer, J., and Jepperson, R. "The 'Actor' of Modern Society: The Cultural Construction of Social Agency." *Sociological Theory*, 2000, 18(1), 100-120.

Powell, W., and Dimaggio, P. *The New Institutionalism in Organizational Analysis.* Chicago: University of Chicago Press, 1991.

Robitaille, D., Beaton, A., and Plomp, J. *The Impact of TIMSS on the Teaching and Learning of Mathematics and Science.* Vancouver, B.C.: Pacific Education Press, 2000.

Schmidt, W., McKnight, C., and Raizen, S. *A Splintered Vision: An Investigation of U.S. Science and Mathematics Education.* Lansing, Mich.: National Research Center for the Third International Mathematics and Science Study, Michigan State University, 1997.

Schmidt, W., McKnight, C., Valverde, G., Houang, R., and Wiley, D. *Many Visions, Many Aims: A Cross-National Investigation of Curricular Intentions in School Mathematics.* Norwell, MA.: Kluwer Academic, 1997.

Schriewer, J. "The Method of Comparison and the Need for Externalization: Methodological Criteria and Sociological Concepts." In J. Schriewer and B. Holmes (eds.) *Theories and Methods in Comparative Education*. Bern, Switzerland: Lang, 1990.

Steiner-Khamsi, G. "Re-Territorializing Educational Import." In A. Novoa and M. Lawn (eds.) *Fabricating Europe: The Formation of an Education Space*. London: Kluwer Academic, 2002.

Tyack, D., and Cuban, L. *Tinkering Toward Utopia: A Century of Public School Reform*. Cambridge, Mass.: Harvard University Press, 1995.

Valverde, G., and Schmidt, W. "Refocusing U.S. Math and Science Education." *Issues in Science and Technology*, 1997, 14, 60-66.

Suggested Readings

Addi-Raccah, A. & Ayalon, H. (2008). From high school to higher education: Curricular policy and postsecondary enrollment in Israel. *Educational Evaluation and Policy Analysis, 30,* 31–50.

Apple, M. W. (2009). *Global crises, social justice, and education.* New York: Routledge.

Archer, M. S. (1979). *Social origins of educational systems.* Beverly Hills, CA: Sage.

Arnot, M. (2008). *Educating the gendered citizen: Sociological engagements with national and global agendas.* Oxford: Routledge.

Arnot, M. & Dillabough, J. (2000) *Challenging democracy: International perspectives on gender, education and citizenship.* New York: Routledge.

Ayalon, H., Grodsky, E., Gamoran, A., & Yogev, A. (2008). Diversification and inequality in higher education: A comparison of Israel and the United States. *Sociology of Education, 81* (3), 211–241.

Baker, D. P. (1993). Compared to Japan, the U.S. is a low achiever . . . really: New evidence and comment on Westbury. *Educational Researcher, 22,* 18–26.

Baker, D. P. (1994). In comparative isolation: Why comparative research has so little influence on American sociology of education. In A. M. Pallas (Ed.), *Research in Sociology of Education and Socialization* (Vol. 10, pp. 53–70). Greenwich, CT: JAI Press.

Baker, D. P. and LeTendre, G. (2005). *National differences, global similarities.* Stanford, CA: Stanford University Press.

Benavot, A. (1992). Educational expansion and economic growth in the modern world, 1913–1985. In B. Fuller and R. Rubison (Eds.), *The political construction of education.* New York: Praeger.

Boli, J., Ramirez, F., & Meyer, J. W. (1985). Explaining the origins and expansion of mass education. *Comparative Education Review, 29,* 145–170.

Bradley, K. & Ramirez, F. (1996). World polity and gender parity: Women's share of higher education, 1965–1985. *Research in Sociology of Education, 11,* 63–91.

Chudgar, A. & Luschei, T. F. (2009). National income, income inequality, and the importance of schools: A hierarchical cross-national comparison. *American Educational Research Journal, 46,* 626–658.

Collins, R. (1977). Some comparative principles of educational stratification. *Harvard Educational Review, 47* (1), 1–27.

Cookson, P. W. & Persell, C. H. (1986). English and American residential schools: A comparative study of the reproduction of elites. *Comparative Education Review, 30,* 260–270.

Cookson, P. W., Sadovnik, A. R., & Semel, S. F. (1992). *International handbook of educational reform.* Westport, CT: Greenwood.

Cummings, W. K. (2003). *The institutions of education.* Oxford: Symposium Books.

Kerckhoff, A. C. (2001). Education and social stratification process in comparative perspective. *Sociology of Education, 74* (Extra Issue), 3–18.

Kerckhoff, A. C. & Everett, D. D. (1986). Sponsored and contest education pathways in Great Britain and the United States. In A. C. Kerckhoff (Ed.), *Research in Sociology of Education and Socialization* (Vol. 6, pp. 133–163). Greenwich, CT: JAI Press.

Lewis, C. (1995). *Educating mind and heart: Rethinking the roots of Japanese education.* London: Cambridge University Press.

Meyer, J., Ramirez, F. O., Rubinson, R., & Boli, J. (1977). The world educational revolution, 1950–1970. *Sociology of Education, 50,* 242–258.

Ogbu, J. U. (1978). *Minority education and caste.* New York: Academic Press.

Paterson, L. & Iannelli, C. (2007). Social class and educational attainment: A comparative study of England, Wales, and Scotland. *Sociology of Education, 80* (4), 330–358.

Ramirez, F. & Boli, J. (1987). The political construction of mass schooling: European origins and worldwide institutionalization. *Sociology of Education, 60,* 2–17.

Torres, C. A. (2008). *Education and neoliberal globalization.* New York: Routledge.

White, M. (1987). *The Japanese educational challenge.* New York: Free Press.

Whitty, G. & Power, S. (2000). Marketization and privatization in mass education systems. *International Journal of Educational Development, 20* (2), 93–107.

Higher Education

Following World War II, access to higher education in the United States expanded. During the 1960s, liberal educational reformers demanded that groups historically denied access to higher education, such as African Americans, Latinos, women, and the working class, be given increased opportunities for postsecondary education. Compensatory higher education programs and affirmative action became institutionalized, but were challenged by conservatives who argued that opening access debased the meritocratic functions of higher education by lowering standards to many unqualified and under-prepared students. Today, although the percentage of students attending postsecondary schools in the United States is the highest in the world, there remains disagreement as to whether this expansion represents actual democratization or an expansion of secondary stratification to the postsecondary education. Functionalists argue that the development of mass higher education reflects an increase in democratic access; conflict theorists argue that, as more students attend higher education institutions, working class and minority students tend to attend two-year institutions, middle class students four-year public institutions, and upper middle-class and upper-class students elite private institutions. The following articles examine important issues and trends in higher education in the United States and provide empirical evidence regarding this debate.

Chapter 16, "College-for-All: Do Students Understand What College Demands?" by the North-western University sociologist James E. Rosenbaum, examines the effects of open admissions policies and the ideology that everyone should and can go to college. He argues that high school counselor, teacher, and student beliefs that you do not have to work hard to get into some colleges have deleteri-ous effects on working-class and minority students, who find themselves underprepared for the rigors of a college education.

Chapter 17, "It's Not Enough to Get Through the Open Door: Inequalities by Social Background in Transfer from Community Colleges to Four-Year Colleges" by the Teachers College Columbia Uni-versity sociologist Kevin J. Dougherty and American Institutes on Education researcher Gregory S. Kienzl, examines whether or not two-year colleges have provided access for their mainly working-class and minority populations to four-year colleges and universities. This chapter tests functionalist and conflict theories of higher education, the former arguing that community colleges provide increased access for educational and social mobility and the latter arguing that they extend and reproduce social class reproduction to higher education.

In Chapter 18, "Mass Higher Education and Its Critics", the City University of New York sociologists Paul Attewell and David Lavin analyze the long-term social, economic, and educational effects of City University of New York's 1969 Open Admissions Policy on the first two cohorts of female students. Using longitudinal statistical analyses, the authors argue that Open Admissions had significantly positive results for the students, their children and the City of New York. This chapter provides a defense of College-for-All.

Questions for Reflection and Discussion

1   What does Rosenbaum argue are the effects of a "college-for-all" ideology? Do you think all students should go to college? Do you think standards for admission to college should be higher?

2   According to Dougherty and Kienzl, have community colleges provided significant opportunities for low-income and minority groups to transfer to four-year colleges? If not, why do you think this has been the case? Should two-year colleges function as feeders to four-year colleges or should they have a more vocational function, preparing students for jobs when they graduate?

3   What do Attewell and Lavin argue about the effects of Open Admissions at City University of New York? Critics of this policy argued that it lowered standards and allowed underprepared students to gain admission and graduate leading to its elimination and the end of remediation at CUNY's senior colleges. What do the authors say about this? What would the authors say about Rosenbaum's argument? What would Rosenbaum say about this and Attewell and Lavin's argument?

4   How would functionalist theorists, conflict theorists, and institutional theorists explain the processes described in the three articles on higher education? How would Bowles and Gintis and Randall Collins differ? Do you think that standards have been lowered and the prestige of a college degree has been debased over the past two decades?

16

College-for-All

Do Students Understand What College Demands?

JAMES E. ROSENBAUM

Sociology has long tried to discover the ways disadvantaged backgrounds harm youth. While human capital theory in economics attributes such problems to deficiencies in individuals' ability or motivation, sociology looks at the ways societal factors block opportunity. However, reality is likely to be more complex. Societal factors do sometimes pose explicit barriers; but explicit barriers are relatively ineffective because they are so obviously unjust, readily seen, and easily attacked. Ambiguous opportunities and unclear requirements may be far more important in blocking mobility than explicit barriers (Cicourel and Kitsuse, 1963; Rosenbaum, 1978, 1989). Clark (1960) showed that the ambiguous mission of community colleges seemed to offer access to four-year colleges when, in fact, these institutions "cooled out" aspirations as students gradually realized that college was not appropriate for their abilities.

In the decades since Clark's study, community colleges have grown enormously. While four-year college enrollment roughly doubled between 1960 and 1990, public community college enrollment increased five-fold in the same period—from 200,000 to over 1,000,000 (U.S. Department of Health, Education, and Welfare, 1992, Table 169). In turn, college opportunities have dramatically increased. While 45.1% of high school graduates entered some postsecondary institution in 1960, over 62% did in 1993. Moreover, community colleges initiated open-admissions policies and remedial courses to reduce the academic barriers to college; and the Associate of Arts (AA) degree has increased in value in the labor market so that students do not need a BA to get an economic benefit from attending community college (Brint and Karabel, 1989; Grubb, 1992, 1993, 1995). Community colleges have increased access to an economically valued degree.

Have these changes created an easy route to college success, or do they merely confuse students so that they fail to prepare themselves appropriately? Studies since Clark's have continued to find substantial college attrition (Grubb, 1989) and have focussed on the factors that redirect students' plans (Karabel, 1986). Yet, rather than focus on the cooling-out process in community colleges, one must remember that "cooling out" is just the institutional mechanism for dealing with failure—not the original cause.

Clark took the term "cooling out" from Goffman's (1952) analysis of confidence swindles. The key to a swindle is to give "marks" confidence that they will gain a valuable reward at very little cost and then lure them to an "easy success" strategy. That is why a "mark" willingly hands over something of value to a swindler, and people pay for "snake oil" remedies that offer high expectations for a small price. Marks only realize that their expectations were mistaken at a later time, after the person who encouraged the expectation is no longer present.

This paper contends that the high level of community-college dropout arises because high schools offer vague promises of open opportunity for college but fail to specify the actual requirements for successful degree completion. Like Goffman's confidence schemes, students are promised college for very little effort. Lured by the prospect of easy success, students choose easy curricula and low efforts. Just as some high schools implicitly offer students an undemanding curriculum in return for non-disruptive behavior (Sedlak, Wheeler, Pullin, and Cusick, 1986), many high schools enlist students' cooperation by telling them that college is the only respectable goal and that it is easily attainable by all. Rather than community-college failure arising from an overt barrier in community colleges, the seeds of failure in community colleges may arise much earlier—when youth are still in high school.

In the current era, many high schools encourage the "college-for-all" norm which states that all students can and should attend college but which fails to tell students what they must do to attain this goal (Rosenbaum, Miller, and Krei, 1996). The college-for-all norm (CFA) is a variant of "the contest mobility norm" which says that opportunity for upward mobility should always stay open (Turner, 1960). This norm encourages youth to retain ambitions of advancement as long as possible, but it ignores barriers that limit youths' careers (Rosenbaum, 1975, 1976, 1986).

Americans are rightly proud of the CFA norm. It discourages schools from tracking students prematurely, and it encourages high expectations in youth. It argues for better instruction in schools, especially schools serving low-income youth. Without this norm, society might give up on raising the educational achievement of the most disadvantaged youth.

While it is not meant to be deceptive, the CFA norm can inadvertently encourage a deception that hurts many youth, including the disadvantaged youth it is meant to help. The CFA norm encourages all students to plan on college regardless of their past achievement. To avoid discouraging students, the CFA norm avoids focussing on requirements; but, in the process, it fails to tell students what steps they should take and does not warn them when their low achievements make their college plans unlikely to be attained. While such encouragement helps younger children, it may mislead students in their later years of high school.

Thus, while 70.9% of high school seniors in the class of 1982 planned to get college degrees, half of 12th-grade students lacked basic 9th-grade math and verbal skills (Murnane and Levy, 1997), and only about half of college entrants completed a college degree (Resnick and Wirt, 1996). The completion rate from two-year colleges is even worse. For the 1980 graduates enrolled full time in two-year public colleges in October 1980, less than 40% (38.8%) completed any degree (AA or higher) by 1986, and the rates were only 15.2% for the substantial numbers (about 25%) who were enrolled part time (U.S. Department of Health, Education, and Welfare, 1992, table 287). Students rarely attained their college plans. For the 1980 graduates who planned less than four years of college (but more than a certificate), less than 20% (19.9%) attained a college degree (AA or higher) in the next six years (U.S. Department of Health, Education, and Welfare, 1992, Table 286).

This has not always been true. The dropout rate from public two-year colleges increased sharply after 1972 (49.6% in 1980 vs. 36.0% in 1972, Grubb, 1989, Table 2). One reason for these disappointing outcomes is that school officials do not warn students about potential problems. Rather than acting as gatekeepers as they did in earlier decades (Rosenbaum, 1976), guidance counselors now urge all students to attend college but rarely warn poorly prepared students that they will have difficulty completing a degree (Rosenbaum, Miller, and Krei, 1996). Rather than hurting students by posing obstacles to their plans, counselors may now be hurting students by not informing them of potential obstacles they will face later on.

Contrary to Karabel's (1986) interpretation of community colleges as institutions which mislead students, Goffman's model suggests that deception is earlier, more subtle, and often in a different location. Indeed, "marks" go along with a swindle because their hopes are initially "heated up" to unrealistic expectations, and "cooling out" is only done late in the process. Thus, rather than focus on the "cooling out" process, one needs to examine why youth have unrealistically high expectations—the precipitating conditions for why "cooling out" is required.

This paper asserts that information is central to this process. If high school students are informed that they are poorly prepared for community college, they can either increase their efforts to prepare themselves or revise their plans to be more realistic. In either case, "cooling out" is unneeded, and youths' plans will be less likely to fail.

High schools probably do not intentionally deceive students. Rather, many schools have well-intentioned practices of raising students' expectations; but these practices may have unintended consequences. High schools encourage college plans for all students, even poorly achieving students whose subsequent failure is highly predictable even before they enter community colleges. Yet, students do not anticipate their probable failure, and they do not take actions to prepare themselves for their goals.

Such a mechanism is more subtle than the one Karabel describes. Poor information allows many students to have high hopes, to use their high school experiences poorly, and thus to seem to be personally responsible for their failures—in precisely the way that human capital theory describes. By the time students enter community college, their eventual outcomes are largely determined. Community colleges cannot be blamed for the poor preparation of their entrants. Yet, the high schools which poorly convey information about requirements are not a visible target. Indeed, they are praised for encouraging students to have "high expectations."

The above description suggests that students' perceptions of college requirements are key to their efforts in high school and to their college attainments. It can be posed as a model with several elements:

1   Many seniors believe they can attain college plans with low high school achievement.
2   Students with these beliefs, including college-bound students, exert little effort in high school.
3   Such beliefs are partly correct—students can enter college even if they have low achievement.
4   High school achievement predicts degree completion, but students' plans do not anticipate this relationship.
5   High school achievement predicts much of the lower attainment and disappointed plans of disadvantaged students.
6   Students with low high school achievement get less economic payoff for college degrees.

This paper takes these contentions as hypotheses and presents analyses to test them empirically. The analyses support these hypotheses and pose serious challenges to current practices. This paper concludes that shielding high school seniors from the realities of college demands and allowing them to hold unrealistic plans is not a kindness. It is a deception which prevents students from taking actions to improve their achievement or to revise their plans and make better use of high school. Students with unrealistic plans should be so informed. They should be encouraged to increase their efforts or to develop backup plans and preparation.

Data and Methods

This report is based on three kinds of data. First, students' perceptions are described using detailed interviews of a nonrandom sample of high school seniors in two high schools. Second, students' views are systematically analyzed using a survey administered to a random sample of 2,091 seniors classes in 12 high schools across the Chicago metropolitan area during 1992–94. The schools and sample are diverse in ethnicity and SES backgrounds and are described in detail elsewhere (Rosenbaum and Roy, 1996).

Third, students' outcomes are assessed using the recent release of the 12-year follow-up of the High School and Beyond 1980 sophomores (National Center for Educational Statistics, 1983). This national sample was first surveyed in 1980 (when respondents were sophomores) and subsequently resurveyed in 1982, 1984, 1986, and 1992. Of the original 14,825 sophomores in 1980, the survey obtained responses from 95.1% in 1982 ($n = 14,102$), and 85.3% in 1992 ($n = 12,640$). This survey provides a unique opportunity for a long-term study of the determinants of educational attainments. This paper studies the outcomes for the individuals responding in both the 1982 and 1992 surveys.

Many Seniors Believe They Can Attain College Plans with Low High School Achievement

Economic theory is a good model of our rational common sense assumptions. For instance, human capital theory explains students' achievement using two factors: students' inherent capabilities and their efforts to invest in themselves. The theory says students will invest in themselves and exert effort in school because they know there is a societal payoff.

While it is widely assumed that students believe that school efforts have a payoff, this assumption is rarely examined. Do students believe that school effort and achievement are relevant and helpful in improving their future careers? Of course teachers tell this to students, but it is clearly in teachers' own self-interest to convince students of their own importance. As parents and teachers often notice, one of the less convenient aspects of adolescence is the cognitive capacity that enables them to doubt what they are told.

Stinchcombe (1965) hypothesized that many students believed that school was not relevant to their future careers and that students' school efforts were determined, not only by their internal motivation, but also by their perceptions of schools' future relevance. While economists assume that incentives exist and are seen, Stinchcombe suggests this may not be true for work-bound students. Unfortunately, while Stinchcombe provided an intriguing model, his small sample and bivariate analyses (on a card sorter in the precomputer age) were too simple for a convincing test.

To examine these ideas, a nonrandom sample of 50 students was interviewed about how they thought about the relevance of school. Consistent with the dictum, "the more things change, the more they stay the same," these interviews in 1993 found similar sentiments to those Stinchcombe found 30 years previously. Many students reported that school was not relevant to their future careers. Yet something had changed. While Stinchcombe found that only work-bound students expressed these beliefs in 1960, these sentiments were also expressed by college-bound students in 1993. Many students who planned to attend college reported that high school achievement was not relevant to their future careers. Their comments suggested that the vast expansion of community colleges over the past 30 years contributed to their views. One student noted, "High school doesn't really matter..., because... junior college is not such a big deal to get into" (#42). Another said, "If you could apply yourself [in junior college], you'd get better grades" [regardless of how you did in high school] (#27). Many students agreed with the student who saw the "two-year college as another chance for someone who's messed up in high school" (#39). This second chance was also viewed as making high school effort less relevant. As one student said in explaining why he does not try hard in high school, "I think college is much more important than high school" (#16).

To examine Stinchcombe's hypotheses more systematically, survey items were constructed which reflected two aspects of individuals' perceptions of schools' relevance: whether students believed that high school education had relevance for their future success (hereafter "future relevance") and whether students believed that there was no penalty if they had poor school performance (hereafter "no penalty" attitude). The first variable refers to students' belief that high school can help their future careers; the second refers to beliefs that bad school performance (even if possibly relevant) is not necessarily a barrier to attaining their future careers.[1]

Surveys were recently administered to 2,091 high school seniors enrolled in 12 city and suburban high schools in a large, Midwestern metropolitan area. Just as Stinchcombe found, the survey found that many students doubted school's future relevance. This was not only true for work-bound students. Almost as many college-bound students held such beliefs. On five-point scales ranging from "strongly agree" to "strongly disagree," our analyses found that 30–40% of students did not agree with such statements as, "My courses give me useful preparation I'll need in life" (39.3% for whole sample, for college-bound respondents, 37.2%), "School teaches me valuable skills" (29.7%, college 28.2%), and "Getting a good job depends on how well you do at school" (36.6%, college 36.5%). We summed to create a scale for "future relevance."

Similar patterns appear for items concerned with lack of penalty for poor high school grades. Almost 46% of students agree with the item "Even if I do not work hard in high school, I can still make my future plans come true" (45.9%, college 44.3%). While educators want students to believe that students with bad grades rarely get college degrees or good jobs, many students disagree with the first point (regarding graduation from two-year colleges, 40.7% for whole sample, college 41.2%) and almost as many disagree with the second (getting good jobs after high school, 37.9%, college 32.9%). Most surprisingly, despite many campaigns against dropping out of high school, over 40% of seniors do not disagree with the statement "People can do OK even if they drop out of high school" (43.7%, college 40.8%). Apparently, many students see no penalty to their planned careers if they do not have high school diplomas, good grades, and work hard in school. We summed these latter items to create a scale for "no penalty."

The two scales of "future relevance" and "no penalty" are correlated, but the correlation is far from perfect ($r = .30$). Students who plan to get a college degree have a somewhat higher sense of schools' "future relevance," and a lesser sense that there is "no penalty" if they do poorly in high school, than students without college plans, but the difference is small (about 1/3 of a standard deviation). Moreover, these beliefs vary substantially within such groups, and the variation is similar within both groups (standard deviations of .61–65).

Students with These Beliefs Exert Little Effort in High School

While there is nothing wrong with students having optimistic hopes, we would be concerned if students responded to these beliefs by reducing their efforts. This section examines: what factors may determine future relevance and no penalty beliefs, what factors may determine students' school efforts, and whether these beliefs mediate the potential influence of other factors on students' school efforts and may have independent influences on students' school efforts.

The antecedents of future relevance and no penalty beliefs are first examined. The survey asked three or more items relating to locus of control, parent support, teacher help, school help, peer pro-school influences, and peer anti-school (rebellion) influences. Items were factor analyzed and scales were constructed. All had alpha coefficients over .70. The survey also asked about respondents' race, ethnicity, parents' education and occupation, and gender (for details, see Rosenbaum and Roy, 1996).

First, OLS regression analyses show that both future relevance and no-penalty are strongly explained by parent support for school, teacher help, and personal locus of control. Peers and low-SES studies also have significant coefficients but gender and being Black do not (Table 16.1, columns 1 and 2).

Second, we examine the antecedents of students' school effort. Effort is measured by a scale combining students' reports of their behaviors (how much time they spend on homework) and three other items: I just do enough to pass my classes, I try to do my best in school, I only work in school if I'm worried about failing (each coded on a five-point scale from "strongly agree" to "strongly disagree").

As in previous research (Kandel and Lesser, 1972), these analyses find that students' school efforts are explained by parent, peer, and school variables (Table 16.1, column 3). Males and having low-SES have negative coefficients, but ethnicity has no influence. Students' locus of control has a large and significant effect.

Table 16.1 Determinants of Future Relevance, No Penalty, and Effort (Standardized Coefficients)

	Future Relevance	No Penalty	Effort (step 1)	Effort (step 2)
Parental support for school	.1702**	−.2786**	.2795**	.2128**
Rebellious peers	−.0576*	.0943**	−.1369**	−.1143**
Pro-school peers	.0949**	−.0217	.1157**	.0979**
Locus of control	.1253**	−.1655**	.2060**	.1627**
Female	−.0411	−.0149	.1051**	.1094**
Low SES	−.0439*	.0828**	−.0554*	−.0366
Black	.0344	−.0202	.0006	−.0076
Hispanic	.0526*	−.0391	−.0370	−.0510*
Asian	.0660**	−.0030	−.0043	−.0149
Teacher help	.2822**	.0510*	.0893**	.0530*
School help	.1310**	−.0441	.0564**	.0300
Future relevance				.1550**
No penalty belief				−.1448**
R-squared (adjusted)	.2446	.1710	.2947	.3393

n = 2,091, * = p< .05, ** = p < .01

However, when future relevance and no-penalty are added to the analysis, we find that they mediate much of the potential influence of parents, school help, teacher help, and locus of control and reduce the negative coefficient of SES to nonsignificance. In contrast, their addition has relatively little effect on the influence of the two peer variables (see column 4). After controlling for other factors, future relevance and no-penalty also have significant independent effects on effort (standardized coefficients of .155 for future relevance, −.145 for "no penalty," column 4). Thus, these beliefs have significant and independent associations with effort, perhaps indicating strong effects in reducing students' school efforts.

These findings have implications for theory and practice. Theoretically, this study supports Stinchcombe's hypothesis. Students vary in whether they see school as relevant to their future lives, and this variable is strongly associated with their school efforts. In addition, this study identifies a second measure—the "no penalty" belief—and shows that both beliefs have significant, independent relationships with school effort.

These results imply that some youth have misread the American emphasis on opportunity. While Americans want society to provide "second chances" to youth, Stevenson and Stigler (1992) warn that youth might misinterpret this to mean that school failures never matter and effort is not needed. This study finds that many youth see little penalty to avoiding school work and little payoff to high school, and these beliefs may justify their poor effort in high school.

Of course, it is possible that causality goes in the other direction—that individuals rationalize their poor effort by denying future relevance. However, these views, whether beliefs or rationalizations, are held by 40% of students so they are not just the problems of a few individuals. Indeed, since guidance counselors do not challenge these beliefs, part of the problem arises from school practices (Rosenbaum, Miller, and Krei, 1996). Even if these views arise as rationalizations, they are not effectively challenged by schools and represent misconceptions that encourage a continuing cycle of further low effort.

Students Can Enter College Even If They Have Low Achievement

Are students wrong when they say school achievement is not relevant to their futures? Community colleges are frequently seen as "second chance" institutions for those who have done poorly before, offering open admissions, low tuition, and remedial courses. In some community college departments, remedial courses may be 40% of the courses offered. Over 40% of freshmen at public two-year colleges take one or more years of remedial coursework just to acquire the same skills they did not learn in high school (National Center for Educational Statistics, 1995).

Although sociologists have produced extensive research showing that grades are strongly related to college attendance (e.g., Kerckhoff and Campbell 1977; Porter, 1974), much of this research is based on studies from the 1960s and 1970s. Yet, college admissions have changed a great deal since 1960. As noted, the five-fold growth of community colleges has dramatically increased opportunities to go to college, and fewer students are likely to face barriers to access to college.

Moreover, community colleges have initiated open-admissions policies and remedial courses to reduce the academic barriers to college. In the past, college admission standards compelled lower-achieving students to confront their unrealistic college plans. While college admission standards were a severe barrier to college for low-achieving students in 1960, admission standards are now practically nonexistent in community colleges. For example, Illinois high school graduates can attend a community college even if they have Ds and no college-prep courses (after age 21, even a diploma is not required). In addition, a full array of remedial courses have been devised to provide high-school-level curricula in the community colleges in order to improve students' chances of success (Brint and Karabel, 1989; Dougherty, 1994; Grubb and Kalman, 1994). Open admissions policies and remedial courses have removed some academic barriers to college entrance.

Are students correct in the belief that high school performance is not relevant to their educational outcomes? The High School and Beyond data indicate that poor high school performance does not prevent college attendance. Even students with low grades (Cs or lower) can attend college. Indeed, 27% of students enrolling in two-year colleges had low grades in high school. That is only slightly less than the proportion of students with low grades who did not enroll in any postsecondary education (30%). Obviously, low grades are not a barrier to enrolling in two-year colleges. College-bound students who think high school effort is irrelevant to their future plans are partly correct—high school grades are not an obstacle to enrollment in two-year colleges.

High School Achievement Predicts Degree Completion, but Students' Plans Do Not Anticipate This Relationship

Having found that many students believe high school achievement is not relevant and, indeed, that many students with low grades can enter two-year colleges, one must wonder whether these students are correct that high school achievement is not relevant to college attainment. Or do these beliefs lead students to make plans which they will be unable to realize? This section of the paper addresses these questions with simple percentages, and the next section uses multivariate analyses.

These analyses emphasize grades because all students know their grades, so students could use this knowledge if they chose to do so. But do they choose to do so? Because most people have had a few teachers who gave arbitrary or unfair grades, grades are often dismissed as erroneous and irrelevant. Yet, knowledge of scale construction suggests that averaging grades eliminates random ideosyncracies and might make grade averages a meaningful indicator. This section examines whether students' cumulative grade point averages in high school predict college outcomes.

Our analyses of the High School and Beyond data find that many students with college plans fail to attain college degrees, and high school grades strongly predict which students fail at their college plans. Of the 12,475 seniors with complete information on plans, grades, and educational attainment, 8,795 (70.5%) planned to get a college degree (AA or higher) in their senior year in high school. Many seniors (4,103 of the 12,475) had low grades (Cs or lower), yet 50.8% of those with low grades still planned to get a college degree ($n = 2,086$).

However, low grades have a strong impact on actual educational attainment. Among all seniors with college plans, 40.3% succeed in getting a college degree (AA or higher) in the 10 years after high school (Table 16.2a). By comparison, low high school grades cut students' chances in half—only 19.6% of seniors with low grades attained their college plans.

Table 16.2 Percentage of Seniors With College Plans Who Complete College Degrees Within 10 Years

Table 16.2a. Percentage of Seniors with College Plans (AA or higher) Who Complete at Least an AA

Average high school grades	As	Bs	Cs or lower	Total
Percent attaining AA or higher	69.5	43.2	19.2	40.3
N	2007	4702	2086	8795

Table 16.2b. Percentage of Seniors with BA Plans Who Succeed in Completing at least a BA Degree

Average high school grades	As	Bs	Cs or lower	Total
Percent attaining BA or higher	70.7	46.6	20.5	49.5
N	1668	2944	916	5528

Table 16.2c. Percentage of Seniors with AA Plans Who Succeed in Completing at an AA

Average high school grades	As	Bs	Cs or lower	Total
Percent attaining AA or higher	46.6	27.1	12.6	23.9
N	339	1758	1170	3267

Note. The data displayed represent 1992 degree attainment figures for High School and Beyond respondents who were seniors in 1982.

Of all the seniors planning to get a BA or higher ($n = 5,528$), 49.5% succeed in getting that degree (Table 16.2b). However, students with As have a 70.7% chance of getting a BA or higher, and those with Bs have a 46.6% chance. Students planning BAs who have a C average or less ($n = 916$) achieve BA degrees at less than half the rate of all students with BA plans (49.5% > 20.5%). It might also be noted that 73% of those with poor grades do little homework—less than an hour per week, and low homework time decreases their BA chances to only 11%.

Since the AA is a shorter and perhaps easier degree than a BA, one might expect that students planning to get AA degrees are more likely to be successful. That is not the case. Seniors who plan to get an AA degree succeed less often than those planning a BA. Of the 3,267 seniors who plan to get an AA degree, only 23.9% succeed in getting a college degree (AA or higher) in the next 10 years; and of those with low grades (Cs or lower), only 12.6% do (Table 16.2c). The success rates are even lower for those with low grades who did little homework ($n = 248$; $p = 8\%$). Recall that these tables report students' college-degree outcomes, based only on their high school grades, and giving youth 10 years to attain any college degree (AA or higher).

Why do over half of seniors with low grades believe they can attain college degrees? Perhaps "social promotion" practices in high schools, which automatically promote students each year to the next grade regardless of their achievement, may encourage this belief. Similarly, open admissions at community colleges may contribute to this belief. Seeing these two practices, which award attainments without requiring academic achievement, students may infer a similar view of college degrees—as an award for putting in time that does not require academic achievement. This may also suggest that students view school as a credentialing process rather than a human-capital-building process.

Ironically, although colleges offering AA degrees are more accessible than BA colleges to students with low grades, the AA degree is not necessarily more available to them. Students with AA plans have lower success rates than students with BA plans, both because students with AA plans are twice as likely to have low grades and because their chances of getting the degree are very slim if they have low grades (12.6%). Multivariate analyses indicate that grades and homework time explain most of this differential success rate between those with BA and AA plans (Rosenbaum and Miller, 1998).

Newspaper stories sometimes report that students who got As in high school actually lack the academic skills to do well in college. This may explain our findings that only half (49.5%) of students with As in high school complete an AA degree or higher (although low SES seems to be more important than low test scores in explaining these failures). Yet, newspapers rarely consider the other issue, that students with Cs in high school have very little chance of completing a college degree, and their plans do not seem to recognize these risks.

In sum, many students report that they plan to get a college degree even though they have poor academic achievement. Yet, in fact, low grades predict much lower chances of attaining a degree. Within the High School and Beyond data, over 80% of students with low grades who planned to get a college degree failed to do so, and the failures were even greater for those planning an AA degree. Even without making any causal inferences, the strong predictive power of high school grades is important—it tells seniors how to place their bets. While students are correct that they can enter a college with low grades, they are usually mistaken in thinking that they can complete the degree. Their poor success rates make these outcomes a real long shot, not something students should be counting on.

High School Achievement Predicts Much of the Lower Attainment and Disappointed Plans of Disadvantaged Students

While the strong predictive power of high school grades tells seniors how to place their bets, do grades really predict educational attainment after controlling for other factors? If students want to raise their chances, they need to know whether to focus on improving grades, homework time, or track placement; and they may be worried that their future attainment is predestined by their social background (SES, ethnicity, gender) or intelligence (as test scores are sometimes interpreted). Policy makers also need to know to what extent grades or other factors predict the lower outcomes and disappointed plans of disadvantaged students.

Regression analysis is a good way to examine these issues. It allows researchers to look at simple gross associations between background characteristics and attainment and then to examine the mediating and independent predicting power of other factors such as high school achievement. We ran a series of OLS regressions on the High School and Beyond cohort who graduated in 1982 and were followed through 1992. The survey had 8,969 respondents who provided information for all variables in our model.

Our basic analyses made use of five dependent variables: students' cumulative grade point averages (Grades), tested achievement (Test), homework time (HW), educational plans (EdPlan), and educational attainment (EdYears). The first four were based on information gathered in the students' senior year, 1982; educational attainment constituted the number of years of students' educational attainments in 1992. Our independent variables included social background variables (Black, Hispanic, female, and a cumulative index of parents' SES computed in the High School and Beyond file), region of the U.S. (South, West, and Northeast regions, with the Midwest as the comparison), and school variables (private school, general, and vocational tracks, with college track as the comparison). Subsequent analyses concerned with plans and educational attainment added grade point average, tested achievement, and homework time as additional independent variables.

These analyses revealed several effects. First, Blacks, Hispanics, and low-SES students have lower grades and achievement test scores (Table 16.3, columns 1 and 3). If these coefficients indicate influences, they are partly mediated by track and private schools (columns 2 and 4). But even after controls are entered, Blacks, Hispanics, and low SES youth have lower grades and test scores.

Second, SES and being Black are associated with homework time, although in different directions (column 5), and the SES relationship is only partly diminished after controls are entered (column 6). While low-SES youth spend less time on homework than high-SES youth, Blacks spend significantly more time on homework than Whites (Hispanics spend about the same as Whites). Despite potential concerns because homework time is self-reported, Fordham and Ogbu's (1986) findings would predict that Blacks would underreport school effort (to avoid being seen as "acting White"), and these analyses find the opposite (Fordham and Ogbu's prediction was also not supported in Cook and Ludwig's, 1997, analysis). If homework time turns out to be an important predictor of educational attainment, then it may account for problems of low-SES students but is not likely to do so for Blacks.

Table 16.3 Regression Analyses for the Predictions of Grades, Tests, Homework, Educational Plans, and Attainment

	1 Grades	2 Grades	3 Test	4 Test	5 HW	6 HW	7 EdPlan	8 EdPlan	9 EdPlan	10 EdYears	11 EdYears	12 EdYears
SES	.207*	.163*	.368*	.295*	.223*	.164*	.450*	.378*	.240*	.386*	.324*	.201*
Black	−.141*	−.150*	−.212*	−.202*	.055*	.060*	.096*	.094*	.159*	−.023*	−.026*	.050*
Hispanic	−.110*	−.115*	−.201*	−.187*	−.007	.002	−.013	−.008	.060*	−.059*	−.045*	.024*
Female	.178*	.176*	−.037*	−.041*	.179*	.174*	.035*	.031*	−.014	.013	.007	−.040*
South		.020		−.055*		−.060*		−.014	.012		−.023*	−.008
West		.047*		−.007		−.017		.014	.013		−.058*	−.064*
NE		−.073*		.037*		.002		−.015	−.017		.038*	.045*
Private		−.021		.059*		.092*		.061*	.028*		.075*	.056*
Vocational		−.164		−.221*		−.119*		−.206*	−.098*		−.176*	−.075*
General		−.173		−.178*		−.172*		−.211*	−.104*		−.184*	−.085*
Test									.288*		.236*	
GPA									.126*		.221*	
HW									.200*			.105*
R^2(adj)%	12.2	16.1	27.2	33.5	7.8	12.1	19.6	25.3	41.2	16.5	22.1	36.3
n	8969	8969	8969	8969	8969	8969	8969	8969	8969	8969	8969	8969

Note. Standardized coefficients are presented. * = $p < .05$

Third, low-SES youth have lower educational plans, but Blacks have higher plans than Whites (column 7). These results remain after controls are entered for track and private schools (column 8). The SES relationship declines after controlling for grades, tests, and homework time, but the positive association for Blacks increases (column 9). Blacks have even higher plans than others with similar achievement, as previous research has noted (Jencks et al., 1972).

Fourth, Black, Hispanic, and low-SES youth have lower educational attainment (column 10). These relationships are only slightly altered after controls for track and private schools (column 11). However, these relationships are largely mediated by grades, test scores, and homework time. Indeed, when grades, test scores, and homework time are added to the analysis, the SES relationship declines substantially (from .324 to .201), although it remains statistically significant and the Black and Hispanic coefficients actually reverse and become significantly positive (column 12). Thus, students' grades, homework time, and tested achievement explain a significant part of the lower attainment of low-SES students, and Black and Hispanic students have higher attainments than Whites with similar achievement.

Finally, by adding seniors' plans to the regression, the analyses can discover which high school information predicts the disappointing attainments of disadvantaged students many years later (see Table 16.4). Since a few students (8.4%) attained more than they planned, they are removed from the analyses in Table 16.4, leaving 8,117 students in the analyses.[2] As a result, Table 16.4 shows the factors predicting which students' attainments fall short of their plans—explaining discrepancies between the 31.5% of students who attained their senior-year plans and the 60.1% who attained one or more years less than they planned. The analyses found that low-SES, Black, and Hispanic students had significantly lower attainments than they had planned (Table 16.4, column 1). However, when variables for school achievement and effort were added, the ethnic variables became insignificant and the SES coefficient became smaller (Table 16.4, column 3). Apparently, the disappointments of Black and Hispanic students are entirely predictable from their lower achievement and effort in high school.

Indeed, students' plans do not take sufficient account of their achievement. Over 58% (.142/.244) of the relationship between test scores and attainment and 78% (.173/.221) of the relationship between grades and attainment remain after controlling for plans (Table 16.4, columns 2 and 3). Less than half of these relationships are mediated by plans. Thus, consistent with the cross-tabular analyses (displayed

Table 16.4 Regression Analyses for the Predictions of Educational Attainment: All Students, Whites and Blacks

	1 EdYears	2 EdYears	3 EdYears	4 EdYears	5 EdYears	6 EdYears	7 EdYears
SES	.154*	.211*	.127*	.213*	.113*	.225*	.190*
Black	−.072*	.050*	−.008				
Hispanic	−.035*	.032*	.011				
Female	.002	−.032*	−.025*	−.048*	−.031*	.055*	.024
South	−.006	.002	−.002	−.002	−.003	−.073	−.076*
West	−.060*	−.059*	−.064*	−.066*	−.069*	−.040	−.037
NE	.041*	.041*	.046*	.046*	.052*	.012	.011
Private	.031*	.045*	.031*	.047*	.033*	.019	.008
Vocational	−.083*	−.083*	−.044*	−.089*	−.047*	−.012	.000
General	−.089*	−.093*	−.052*	−.097*	−.052*	−.044	−.024
Test		.244*	.142*	.227*	.118*	.228*	.175*
Grades		.221*	.173*	.214*	.170*	.224*	.196*
HW		.119*	.050*	.114*	.040*	.071*	.043
Plans	.483*		.354*		.383*		.201*
R2(adj)%	40.3	38.3	45.4	38.1	46.0	27.2	30.0
n	8117	8117	8117	5014	5014	996	996

Note. Standardized coefficients are presented. * = $p < .05$ Analyses cases where EdYears is less than or equal to EdPlans.

in Table 16.2), we conclude that, even after controls, seniors' college plans vastly underestimate how much their grades and test scores predict their ultimate educational outcomes.

It is noteworthy that the female coefficient on educational attainment, which is virtually zero in the early regressions (Table 16.3, column 10), becomes significantly negative after controlling for achievement (column 12). Apparently, women have roughly the same educational attainments as males, but their attainments are still below what they would be if their previous achievement were the only determinant. Females have higher grades and homework time than males (but slightly lower test scores, see Table 16.3, columns 1–6), so there should be some concern about why their attainments are lower than their achievement would predict.

Finally, while the above analyses look at simple additive effects of ethnicity, one might still wonder if some of the factors in our model have different coefficients for Blacks and Whites. One indication of bias is when Blacks get less benefit from their achievements than Whites. In the 1970s, Porter (1974) found that Blacks received less gain in educational attainment from their high school grades than did Whites. Our regression analyses for educational attainment run separately for Whites and Blacks find that grades have about the same coefficients for both (Table 16.4, columns 4 and 6—betas .224 and .214), and the same is true for test scores (.228 and .227) but slightly larger coefficients for Whites than for Blacks (.114 vs .071) when it comes to homework.[3] Thus, Blacks get roughly the same gain in attainment for increases in their test scores and grades as Whites, although they get slightly less gain for increases in their homework time. Apparently, the old pattern of discrimination in which Blacks got lower attainment benefits for increasing their grades is no longer the case. Indeed, SES, test scores, and grades are somewhat stronger predictors of attainment for Blacks than for Whites (Table 16.4, columns 5 and 7).

In sum, these results indicate that SES, ethnicity, private schools, and track are related to attainment; but grades, test scores, and homework time also have effects which tend to mediate much of the relationship between disadvantaged backgrounds and attainment. However, there are indications that many students do not realize how much high school achievement predicts future attainment. While all students probably know their grades, their plans underestimate the extent that their grades predict their later attainment—and this is true for both Black and White students. Indeed, grades are the single best predictor of the ways attainment falls short of plans, and this predictability is somewhat larger for Blacks than for Whites. If students could focus on changing one set of attributes in high school to make their plans come true, they should improve those associated with their grades.[4,5]

Thus, these analyses suggest that students are overly complacent about the ease of getting a college degree. Many students have plans that have little chance of succeeding because their plans underestimate the relationship between high school achievement and later attainment. This is particularly true for Blacks, Hispanics, and low-SES students whose attainments fall short of their plans. These disappointments are largely predicted by their high school achievements (Table 16.4, columns 1 and 3). It seems likely that these students might work harder if they realized the future relevance of their high school achievement.

Students with Low High School Achievement Get Less Economic Payoff to College Degrees

Despite these odds, some students with low high school grades get college degrees. Do they get the same earnings payoff from college as students with better grades? While Murnane, Willett, and Levy (1995) have shown additive wage payoffs of educational attainment and achievement (measured by test scores), the present analyses examine whether college degrees have lower payoffs for those with lower achievement, which is operationalized by high school grades since it more clearly indicates achievement (rather than ability) and is known by all students. The above model is used to explain the 1991 earnings of the same High School and Beyond cohort, adding dummy variables for educational attainment (AA representing those who had received the AA but no higher; BA representing those

Table 16.5 Regression Analyses for the Predictions of Earnings

	Ln(Earnings)	Ln(Earaings)
SES	.101*	.101*
Black	.040	.041
Hispanic	.026	.025
Female	−.299*	−.299*
South	−.032*	−.032*
West	−.036	−.036
NE	.097*	.099*
Private	.043*	.045*
Vocational	−.030	−.031
General	−.027	−.026
Test	.003*	.003*
Grades	.034*	.025*
HW	−.004	−.004
AA	.101*	.155*
BA	.145*	.166*
MA	−.096*	−.112*
AALoGPA		−.227*
BALoGPA		−.123*
MALoGPA		.022
c	9.657	9.695
R^2(adj.)%	13.2	13.5

Note Nonstandardized coefficients are presented.
* = p< .05 N = 8,413

who had earned the BA but no higher degree; and MA representing those who had earned an MA or higher degrees). By taking the log of annual earnings as the dependent variable, unstandardized coefficients can be interpreted as percentage increases in earnings, so these tables report unstandardized coefficients. Thus, in the first step of the analysis, the High School and Beyond data indicate that youth who earn AA and BA degrees report 10.1% and 14.5% higher earnings, respectively, than those without a degree (Table 16.5, column 1).

To see if students with low grades get the same benefits from those degrees, these analyses create a new dummy variable (AA-LoGPA) for people who got an AA degree and had low grades in high school (AA-LoGPA equals 1 if a person has an AA degree and high school grades of C or lower, 0 otherwise.), and similar variables for BA-LoGPA and MA-LoGPA. Adding these three variables into the regression, the analyses find that youth who had low high school grades got less earnings advantage for their college degrees (Table 16.5, column 2). To figure the payoff to BAs for students with Cs, the coefficients for BA and BA-LoGPA are added, so the payoff to a BA degree is 4.3% (.166 −.123 = .043), and the payoff to an AA degree is −7.2%, less than if they had not gotten the degree (.155 − .227 = −.072). While the average student gets strong earnings benefits from BA and AA degrees, students with low grades get much smaller earnings benefits from a BA degree and lower earnings from an AA degree than from no degree.[6] Previous studies have found that poor grades predict lower earnings for young adults who have only a high school diploma (Miller, 1997; Rosenbaum, Miller, and Roy, 1996). These results indicate that low grades also substantially reduce the payoffs to college degrees (cf. also Rosenbaum and Miller, 1998).

Conclusion

These analyses help elucidate the problem of disadvantaged youth. Simple gross analyses find that low-SES, Black, and Hispanic students have lower educational attainment. However, the SES coefficient declines, and the ethnic disadvantages actually reverse and become advantages when achievement variables are entered. Thus, Blacks and Hispanics have significantly higher educational attainment than Whites with the same level of high school achievement. In addition, high school grades and test scores predict many of the cases where disadvantaged youth have lower attainment than they had planned.

Looking at these results, some might blame disadvantaged youth for their failures; but another interpretation is more plausible. Students' plans are what they think they can expect in the future, and their plans are likely to influence their high school efforts. In finding that students' plans do not take sufficient account of the influence of grades on their ultimate educational attainment, one can infer that students do not realize how much high school achievement affects their actual prospects. This is consistent with the future relevance and "no penalty" beliefs noted earlier. These results may indicate that schools fail to provide clear information to these youth which is consistent with what is known about counselors' advising practices (Rosenbaum, Miller, and Krei, 1996).

What is the harm in letting students have "high expectations?" Perhaps these plans are just dreams that make students a little happier and do them little harm. As noted, guidance counselors say they do not want to disappoint young people and so they encourage all students to attend college, even students with low achievement.

Consistent with this interpretation, Manski (1989) has proposed that many youth begin community college as an "experiment," a low-cost way to discover whether they can make it in college. But is it really low cost? Manski analyzes the process from the viewpoint of a student who is already in a community college, noting that his analysis does not consider students before they enter college.

However, there are opportunity costs to any decision, and this "experiment" has some large opportunity costs to students while they are still in high school. Should students with more than an 80% chance of failing at college place *all* their bets on their college experiment? Or would it be prudent for such students to hedge their college bets?

A first opportunity cost of the college-for-all norm is that students' high expectations may inadvertently encourage them to see high school as irrelevant and thus to make poor use of high school. Our interviews and survey of high school seniors indicate that 40% of students with college plans believe that high school is irrelevant. Postponing the key test for whether one is "college-bound" until after high school may inadvertently tell students that high school achievement is not important.

A second opportunity cost of the college-for-all norm is that it may lead to a lack of effort. Human capital theory posits that people invest effort in improving their capabilities if they believe better outcomes will result. But if they believe they can get the same outcomes without added effort, they will not make the effort. If students realize that their low high school grades will be associated with blocked college plans, they might increase their efforts in high school. Yet High School and Beyond data indicate that a large majority (78.0%) of poorly achieving high school students with college plans do less than an hour a day of homework, and many (25.3%) do less than an hour in a whole week. These High School and Beyond students exert little effort, even though they have low grades (which predict an 80% failure rate). Moreover, guidance counselors let these students hold unrealistic plans because they wish to encourage "high expectations" and "second chances" (Rosenbaum, Miller, and Krei, 1996). Students are not told what level of high school achievement is needed to succeed in community college, and they are lulled into a complacency that leaves them unprepared for getting college degrees.

The third opportunity cost of the college-for-all norm is that students with little prospect for getting a college degree will fail to get vocational training. Encouraging poorly achieving students to delay their work preparation until they see the results of their college "experiment" makes it likely that they will make poor use of vocational preparation in high school, which has been shown to improve earnings (Campbell, Basinger, Dauner, and Parks, 1986; Kang and Bishop, 1986; Rosenbaum, 1996).

Indeed, students with poor grades are less likely to be in vocational courses if they have college plans than if they are not planning college (Rosenbaum, unpublished analyses), and many students with low probability of success in college have no backup plans or training. Similarly, many public schools (such as those in Chicago) have reduced or ended their vocational programs because they expect all students to delay their vocational decisions until they get to college.

Although Manski did not consider it, there is an even more inexpensive experiment to help students infer their readiness for college—high school. If the CFA norm did not focus so much on getting everyone into college, then high schools could tell students their realistic chances of attaining college degrees. If students realized that high school achievement is the first "experiment," and this "experiment" has strong predictive power, then students with poor grades would either revise their plans downwards, or they might try to correct bad habits that lead to poor achievements.

Protecting students' high expectations when they are unwarranted is not a kindness; it is a deception. Failing to challenge students to examine the plausibility of their college plans has serious opportunity costs—it prevents them from seeing the importance of high school, it prevents them from taking the additional efforts that might make their plans more likely to come true, and it prevents them from preparing for alternative outcomes. When some seniors have high school records that make their college plans highly likely to fail, schools' protection of their "high expectations" is not a kind gesture. It looks a lot more like the confidence scheme that Goffman describes, distracting the "mark" from taking other constructive actions.

Unfortunately, students understand very well the *short-term* consequences of their high school efforts—they are minor. But they assume that this means that high school achievement and effort are irrelevant and that there will be no penalty if they do badly in high school. They believe they can postpone their efforts until they get into college, and their plans will work out fine.

Students' misperceptions may arise from their limited knowledge about older cohorts. High school students can see the college enrollment of last year's seniors more easily than the college completion of much older students, and they can more easily identify with the students a year older than themselves who enter college than with the 28-year-olds who never finished the degree. As a result, perceptions are likely to be distorted. Students easily perceive college enrollment, for which high school achievements are irrelevant, but they have difficulty seeing college completion, for which high school achievements are highly relevant. Under such circumstances, students' perceptions will not improve unless policy action is taken.

Policy Implications

The community college system and its open admissions policies are rightfully a source of pride. They have created new opportunities for large numbers of youth. However, open admissions may inadvertently contribute to students' complacency. Students with low grades may not realize that they have very poor prospects of getting a degree or earnings benefits from that degree.

High schools are partly responsible for such delusions. Our research suggests that high school guidance counselors believe that open admission means that they do not have to discourage students' college expectations. They believe that "high expectations" should be encouraged, and they report that they get complaints from parents and principals if they try to discourage unrealistically high plans (Rosenbaum, Miller, and Krei, 1996). Counselors' practices may help explain why students hold these views.

While policy has focussed on opening college admissions, it has not devoted similar effort to providing clear information about community colleges (Orfield, 1997; Paul, 1997, Rosenbaum, Miller, and Krei, 1997). Indeed, many schools push the college-for-all (CFA) norm, which lulls students into a complacency, which ultimately is unwarranted. High school grades could inform students about their likelihood of attaining a college degree, but this fact is hidden from students' awareness, and perhaps even teachers' and counselors' awareness.

To return to Goffman's model, the CFA norm is highly misleading and does great harm to youth. It offers big promises to students without warning that few low-achieving students will get a college degree. Indeed, it leaves many youth worse off than before, keeping them in the dark about actual requirements so they fail to take suitable actions to prepare themselves to accomplish their plans. It also harms youth as they waste time, energy, and money on a college experience they are ill prepared to handle and that is likely to lead to failure, low self-esteem, and misused opportunities in high school. While high school counselors brag about their college enrollment rates, students will blame themselves for the failure that they did not anticipate but which was highly predictable.

The CFA norm also has big impact on policies and practices in schools. An example can be seen in the Chicago public schools in the early 1990s when Superintendent Argie Johnson urged all of the city's high schools to stress college goals. She closed or withdrew resources from many vocational programs. Even the famous Chicago Vocational School began stressing that its goal was no longer vocational, but college. Meanwhile, the Chicago schools had low achievement levels, many of their graduates lacked the academic skills needed to take college-credit courses in the city college, and the degree completion rates at the city colleges were very low. The superintendent's urging that more students attend college was politically popular because it fit the CFA norm. It stressed "high expectations," but it may have led to increased failure.

This is not to urge that one abandon "high expectations" entirely or scrap open admissions policies. But three other reforms are warranted.

First, high schools should provide more complete information on community-college success rates as a function of students' grades, test scores, and homework time. This could be aided by a universally recognized test of achievement (not aptitude or intelligence), either statewide (such as Illinois's IGAP achievement test) or national (such as Clinton's proposal for national proficiency examinations). Even if such tests are not available, grades can be used. While the grades from individual teachers are highly imperfect, grade point averages have strong predictive power. Schools and society should be stressing their importance to students. Students need to realize that "open admissions" does not mean that high school achievement is irrelevant.

Second, linkages between high schools and colleges may help improve high school students' understanding of college requirements. By seeing that many college students must repeat high school classes, high school students will learn that they can work hard now, or next year they can repeat the same class and pay tuition for it. Several recent reforms seek to improve coordination of high school and college programs which may help students see the future relevance of their current courses (e.g., tech-prep, 2 + 2 programs, and career academies; see Berryman and Bailey, 1992; Stern, Finkelstein, Stone, Latting, and Dornsife, 1995).

Finally, students must be prepared for backup career options if their college plans are unlikely to succeed. While schools can encourage all students to aim for college, this should not be an excuse to cut vocational programs. Research indicates that after controls for test scores, vocational education graduates are 10–15% more likely to be in the labor force and are paid 8–9% more than graduates of academic programs (Campbell et al., 1986; Kang and Bishop, 1986; Rosenbaum, 1996).[7] Even if students plan to attend community college, low success rates at these colleges suggest that backup plans would be prudent, particularly for students with low grades. Over 80% of such students fail to get a degree and lose time, tuition, and self-confidence in the process. After they drop out of college, they enter the labor market without the vocational skills or preparation that they might have gotten if they had not been taken in by the college-for-all rhetoric.

Notes

1. Somewhat similar beliefs have been shown to influence students' achievements (Mickelson, 1990); but since achievement is influenced by many factors besides motivation, this study has chosen to focus on the determinants of effort (cf. also Steinberg, 1996, for an excellent overview).
2. Since one would not be concerned about the disappointment of very high plans, analyses were also run using recoded versions of plans and attainments in which values higher than BA were recoded to be the same as BA = 16. This recode does not alter results very much so those results are not reported.
3. Similar results are obtained on the full sample of 8,969 individuals not shown here.
4. What determines grades? Bowles and Gintis (1976) have suggested noncognitive components which are not supported in some studies (Bills, 1983; Rosenbaum and Kariya, 1989, 1991). Miller and Rosenbaum (1998) pursue this question in greater detail.
5. Logit analyses were also run to see the determinants of who got AA or higher versus the high school graduates who got less than an AA. Using the same independent variables as the regression, the results indicate virtually the same conclusions as the above linear regression: grades, test scores, and homework all have significant influences, with grades having the largest influence. Grades have even larger influence than test scores in explaining disappointed plans. Similar findings occur in explaining who got BA or higher, although the grade influence is even greater. These tables are not reported because the results are virtually the same as those reported here.
6. Youth who did not complete high school are removed from this analysis so the constant represents all youth with high school diplomas but no college degrees. Note that the Malogpa coefficient is not significant and only 22 (4%) of MA students had low high school grades.
7. Kane and Rouse (1995) find that students get some economic benefit from the college credits they earn, even if they do not complete college degrees. However, these benefits may depend on whether the courses were vocational and on particular fields (Grubb, 1995). If the economic benefits of college courses (without a degree) arise from the vocational preparation they offer, then vocational courses in high schools or nondegree programs could possibly provide similar benefits. It is possible that the economic value of isolated college credits comes because individuals seek specific job-relevant courses, perhaps because of a job they already hold or one they know is available. Employers in some fields (tool and die, machining, etc.) require employees to obtain a few specific courses but not a certificate or degree (Rosenbaum and Binder, 1996).

   Moreover, for many students, the economic benefits of some college are negligible. Kane and Rouse (1995, p. 602) found that "40% [of two-year college dropouts] completed fewer than a semester's worth of credits" and a large number completed none, so the economic benefits of college entry were minimal for these students. Given that most of these students probably expected to get college degrees, they surely got much less academic and economic benefit from college than they anticipated and experienced relatively large psychological costs.

References

Berryman, Susan E. and Bailey, Thomas R. (1992). *The double helix: Education and the economy*. New York: Teachers College Press

Bills, David (1983). Social reproduction and the Bowles-Gintis thesis of a correspondence between school and work settings. *Research in sociology of education and socialization*. Greenwood, CT: JAI.

Bowles, Samuel and Gintis, Herbert (1976). *Schooling in capitalist America*. New York: Basic Books.

Brint, Steven and Karabel, Jerome (1989). *The diverted dream*. New York: Oxford University Press.

Campbell, Paul B., Basinger, K.S., Dauner, M.B., and Parks, M.A. (1986). *Outcomes of vocational education*. Columbus, OH: Ohio State University, National Center for Research in Vocational Education.

Cicourel, Aaron V. and Kitsuse, John I. (1963). *The educational decision-makers*. Indianapolis: Bobbs Merrill.

Clark, Burton (1960). The "cooling out" function in higher education. *American Journal of Sociology*, 65, 569–576.

Cook, Philip J. and Ludwig, Jens (1997). Weighing the burden of "acting White": Are there race differences in attitudes toward education? *Journal of Policy Analysis and Management*, 16(2), 256–278.

Dougherty, Kevin J. (1994). *The contradictory college*. Albany, NY: SUNY Press.

Fordham, Signithia and Ogbu, John (1986). Black students' school success: Coping with the burden of "acting White." *The Urban Review*, 18(3), 176–206.

Goffman, Erving (1952, November). Cooling the mark out: Some aspects of adaptation to failure. *Psychiatry*, 15, 451–163.

Grubb, W. Norton (1989). Dropouts, spells of time, and credits in postsecondary education. *Economics of Education Review*, 8(1), 49–67.

Grubb, W. Norton (1992). Postsecondary education and the sub-baccalaureate labor market. *Economics of Education Review*, 11(3), 225–248.

Grubb, W. Norton (1993). The varied economic returns of postsecondary education. *Journal of Human Resources*, 28(2), 265–282.

Grubb, W. Norton (1995). Response to comment. *Journal of Human Resources*, 30(1), 222–228.

Grubb, W. Norton and Kalman, Judy (1994, November). Relearning to earn. *American Journal of Education*, 103, 54–93.

Jencks, Christopher L., Smith, Smith, Acland, Henry, Bane, Mary Jo, Cohen, David K., Gintis, Herbert, Heyns, Barbara, and Michaelson, Stephan (1972). *Inequality*. New York: Basic Books.

Kandel, Denise and Lesser, Gerald (1972). *Youth in two worlds: United States and Denmark*. New York: Jossey-Bass.

Kane, Thomas and Rouse, Cecilia E. (1995). Labor-market returns to two- and four-year college. *American Economic Review*, 85(3), 600–614.

Kang, Suk and Bishop, John (1986). The effect of curriculum on labor market success. *Journal of Industrial Teacher Education*, 133–148.

Karabel, Jerome (1986) Community colleges and social stratification in the 1980s. In L.S. Zwerling (Ed.), *The community college and its critics*. San Francisco: Jossey-Bass, pp. 13–30.

Kerckhoff, Alan C. and Campbell, Richard T. (1977). Black-White differences in the educational attainment process. *Sociology of Education*, 50(1), 15–27.

Manski, Charles F. (1989). Schooling as experimentation. *Economics of Education Review*, 8(4), 305–312.

Mickelson, Roslyn. (1990, January). The attitude-achievement paradox among Black adolescents. *Sociology of Education*, 63, 44–61.

Miller, Shazia (1997). *Shortcut: High school grades as a signal of human capital.* Paper presented at the annual meeting of the American Sociological Association, Toronto.

Miller, Shazia and Rosenbaum, James (1998). *What do grades mean?* Unpublished manuscript, Northwestern University, Institute for Policy Research.

Murnane, Richard, Willett, John B., and Levy, Frank (1995). The growing importance of cognitive skills in wage determination. *Review of Economics and Statistics*, 77(2), 251–266.

Murnane, Richard and Levy, Frank (1997). *Teaching the new basic skills.* New York: The Free Press.

National Center for Educational Statistics (1983). *High school and beyond: 1980 senior cohort first follow-up (1982): Data file user's manual.* Chicago: National Opinion Research Center.

National Center for Educational Statistics (1983). *High school and beyond: Data file user's manual.* Chicago: National Opinion Research Center.

National Center for Educational Statistics (1995). *Remedial education at higher education institutions.* Washington, DC: U.S. Department of Education.

Orfield, Gary (1997). Going to work: Weak preparation, little help. In Kenneth K. Wong (Ed.), *Advances in educational policy* (Vol. 3). Greenwood, CT: JAI Press, pp. 3–32.

Paul, Faith (1997). Negotiated identities and academic program choice. In Kenneth K. Wong (Ed.), *Advances in educational policy* (Vol. 3). Greenwood, CT: JAI Press, pp. 53–78.

Porter, James N. (1974, June). Race, socialization and mobility in educational and early occupational attainment. *American Sociological Review*, 39, 303–316.

Resnick, Lauren B. and Wirt, John G. (1996). The changing workplace. In Lauren B. Resnick and John G. Wirt (Eds.), *Linking school and work*. San Francisco: Jossey Bass, pp. 1–22.

Rosenbaum, James E. (1975). The stratification of socialization processes. *American Sociological Review*, 40(1), 48–54.

Rosenbaum, James E. (1976). *Making inequality.* New York: Wiley.

Rosenbaum, James E. (1978). The structure of opportunity in school. *Social Forces*, 57, 236–256.

Rosenbaum, James E. (1986). Institutional career structures and the social construction of ability. In G. Richardson (Ed.), *Handbook of theory and research for the sociology of education*. Westport, CT: Greenwood Press, pp. 139–171.

Rosenbaum, James E. (1989). Organizational career systems and employee misperceptions. In Michael Arthur, Douglas T. Hall, and Barbara Lawrence (Eds.), *Handbook of career theory*. New York: Cambridge University Press, pp. 329–353.

Rosenbaum, James E. (1996, Summer). Policy uses of research on the high school-to-work transition. *Sociology of Education*, Summer, pp. 102–122.

Rosenbaum, James E. and Kariya, Takehiko (1989). From high school to work: Market and institutional mechanisms in Japan. *American Journal of Sociology*, 94(6), 1334–1365.

Rosenbaum, James E. and Kariya, Takehiko (1991). Do school achievements affect the early jobs of high school graduates in the United States and Japan? *Sociology of Education*, 64, 78–95.

Rosenbaum, James E. and Binder, Amy (1997, January). Do employers really need more educated youth? *Sociology of Education*, 70, 68–85.

Rosenbaum, James E. and Miller, Shazia (1998). The earnings payoff to college degrees for youth with poor high school achievement. * Unpublished manuscript, Northwestern University, Institute for Policy Research.

Rosenbaum, James E., Miller, Shazia, and Krei, Melinda (1996, August). Gatekeeping in an era of more open gates. *American Journal of Education*, 104, 257–279.

Rosenbaum, James E., Miller, Shazia, and Krei, Melinda (1997). What role should counselors have? In Kenneth K. Wong (Ed.), *Advances in educational policy* (Vol. 3). Greenwood, CT: JAI Press, pp. 79–92.

Rosenbaum, James E. and Roy, Kevin (1996, April). Trajectories for success in the transition from school to work. Paper presented at the annual meeting of the American Educational Research Association, New York.

Rosenbaum, James E., Miller, Shazia, and Roy, Kevin (1996, August). Long-term effects of high school grades and job placements. Paper presented at the annual meeting of the American Sociological Association, New York.

Sedlak, Michael W., Wheeler, Christopher W., Pullin, Diane C., and Cusick, Phillip A. (1986). *Selling students short*. New York: Teachers College Press.

Steinberg, Lawrence (1996). *Beyond the classroom*. New York: Simon and Shuster.

Stern, David, Finkelstein, Neal, Stone, James, Latting, John, and Dornsife, Carolyn (1995). *School to work: Research on programs in the United States*. Washington and London: Falmer Press.

Stevenson, Harold W. and Stigler, James W. (1992). *The learning gap*. New York: Simon and Shuster.

Stinchcombe, Arthur L. (1965). *Rebellion in a high school*. Chicago: Quadrangle.

Turner, Ralph (1960). Sponsored and contest mobility and the school system. *American Sociological Review*, 25, 855–867.

U.S. Department of Health, Education, and Welfare (1992). *Digest of educational statistics*. Washington, DC: U.S. Government Printing Office.

17

It's Not Enough to Get Through the Open Door

Inequalities by Social Background in Transfer from Community Colleges to Four-Year Colleges

KEVIN J. DOUGHERTY AND GREGORY S. KIENZL

From the beginning of the community college, one of its fundamental missions has been to facilitate the attainment of baccalaureate degrees by providing the early stages of a baccalaureate education and aiding transfer to four-year colleges (Brint and Karabel 1989; Cohen and Brawer 2003; Dougherty 1994). This role not only continues today but also promises to become increasingly important (Dougherty 2002; Wellman 2002).

But during the years between 1960 and 1990, the transfer mission was eclipsed. Community colleges shifted their attention to expanding occupational education and continuing education, and transfer rates declined (Brint and Karabel 1989; Dougherty 1994; Dougherty and Bakia 2000). For example, among students entering community college right out of high school, the rate of transfer to four-year colleges within four years of entering college dropped from 29% for those entering community college in 1972 to 20% for those entering community college in 1980 (Grubb 1991, 202).[1]

However, in the last 10 years, interest in the transfer function has strongly revived. The reasons are various. State governments have encouraged students eligible for the state universities to begin at community colleges and then transfer to four-year colleges because this saves the states considerable money at a time when university enrollments have been sharply rising but state finances have been badly battered by a stagnant economy (Dougherty 2002; Ignash and Townsend 2001; Mercer 1992; Wellman 2002, 4). For example, during the first decade of the new millennium, college enrollments are projected to increase 21% in California, 12% in Texas, 26% in Florida, and 20% in North Carolina (Wellman 2002, 4). Moreover, community college transfer attracted the attention of policy makers in states such as California and Texas, where affirmative action in admissions had been outlawed, but universities hoped to retain a diverse student body (Hebel 2000). Finally, advocates, scholars, and policy makers concerned about issues of social stratification have highlighted the importance of transfer, noting that minority and working-class students are increasingly relying on community colleges for access to the baccalaureate[2] because of sharply rising four-year college tuition, stagnating need-based student aid,[3] slumping incomes for less advantaged families, and the reduction of remedial education in public four-year colleges (Callan 2003; Dougherty 2002, 315–33; Lumina Foundation 2005; McPherson and Schapiro 1998, 44–46; McPherson and Schapiro 1999, 6–7, 19–24; Wellman 2002, 4–7; Young 2002).

In focusing on transfer, we are not suggesting that other outcomes of the community college are not important. Certainly, many students enter the community college interested not in transfer but in acquiring short-term training or a terminal degree, whether a certificate or an associate's degree. And in fact, students do secure valued outcomes other than transfer. For students who entered community colleges in 1995–1996, 10% had secured a certificate, and 16% had received a terminal associate's degree by June 2001 (Berkner, Ho, and Cataldi 2002, 12). And these degrees do bring significant payoffs: compared with high school graduates with similar social and academic characteristics, terminal associate degree holders enjoy a 15%–30% income advantage, and certificate degree holders a 5%–15% advantage (Grubb 2002; Kane and Rouse 1999; Kienzl 2004; Marcotte et al. 2005).

Yet transfer still remains important. Many students enter the community college with the expectation of achieving at least a baccalaureate degree. For example, an analysis of the National Education Longitudinal Study of the 8th Grade in 1988 (NELS: 88) found that among those students who graduated from high school in 1992 and entered a community college within the subsequent two years, 63% stated that they were aiming at a baccalaureate degree or higher (Hoachlander, Sikora, and Horn 2003, 10). This figure is echoed by an analysis of the most recent Beginning Postsecondary Students Longitudinal Study (BPS:96), which found that, among first-time college students entering public two-year colleges in 1995–1996, 78% planned for at least a bachelor's degree (Kojaku and Nunez 1998, 7). Clearly, there is reason to question how firm and realistic these high educational ambitions are, but they cannot simply be dismissed.[4] Moreover, there is strong warrant for community college entrants to pursue a baccalaureate degree. Although some holders of terminal occupational degrees, such as nursing, can secure incomes that exceed those of certain baccalaureate degree holders, the fact remains that on average, baccalaureate degrees still confer significantly higher economic returns than do terminal associate degrees or certificates. On average, with all other things being equal, baccalaureate degree holders enjoy a 30%–40% advantage in yearly income over high school graduates, considerably higher than the income advantage for the average terminal associate degree or certificate holder (Grubb 2002; Kane and Rouse 1999; Kienzl 2004).

This renewed importance of transfer raises the question of how equitably transfer opportunities are distributed by student background. The answer to this question carries major implications for state policies that encourage more baccalaureate aspirants to begin college at community colleges. If major differences exist in transfer rates by social background, the pursuit of equal access cannot stop simply with getting minority and working-class baccalaureate aspirants into the community college. It is also important to make sure that students have an equal chance to transfer.[5]

Review of the Literature

Transfer has been the subject of a considerable amount of study over the years.[6] The research literature is dominated by institutional studies that examine the transfer rate for a particular community college. However, a fair number of studies of national data sets exist: Velez and Javalgi's 1987 analysis of the National Longitudinal Survey of the High School Class of 1972 (NLS-72); Lee and Frank's 1990 study of High School and Beyond (HS&B); Grubb's 1991 study of both NLS-72 and HS&B; Surette's 2001 analysis of the National Longitudinal Survey of Youth (NLSY); the studies by McCormick (1997) and Bradburn, Hurst, and Peng (2001) of the Beginning Postsecondary Students Longitudinal Study (BPS:90) of 1989–1994; and the studies by Hoachlander, Sikora, and Horn (2003) of NELS:88 and the Beginning Postsecondary Students Longitudinal Study of 1995–1996 (BPS:96).

The studies of the NLS-72, HS&B, and NLSY found that for students entering community colleges in the early 1970s and early 1980s, socioeconomic status (SES), race-ethnicity, and gender all significantly affected transfer rates. Students who were female, black, or had lower-SES parents were significantly less likely to transfer than were students with the obverse characteristics (Lee and Frank 1990; Surette 2001; Velez and Javalgi 1987).

Despite the quality of these national studies, there is good reason for further analysis. For one, these studies are restricted to the 1970s and 1980s, yet the question remains as to whether the patterns found hold for the 1990s. During the late 1980s and 1990s, major efforts were made to raise the transfer rate, particularly for minority and lower-SES students. For example, the Ford Foundation sponsored the Urban Community College Transfer Opportunity Program, and several states, such as California and Florida, put extra resources into enhancing transfer rates (Dougherty 1994, 254–60; Ford Foundation 1988). Moreover, the 1990s witnessed a shift in college-going rates by gender, with women eclipsing men.

In addition, the earlier studies ignored the impact of variations in age. The surveys used by earlier studies focused on students entering college right out of high school, thus disallowing any examination of the transfer rates of students who delayed their college entrance by two or more years. Yet, the issue of the impact of age differences on transfer rates has become quite important as increasing numbers of older people enter college. To be sure, many are not first-time college entrants but returning college students. Still, many first-time college entrants are of nontraditional age. For example, among first-time college students entering community college in 1995–1996, 26% were 24 years of age and older (Kojaku and Nunez 1998, 7). Evidence that age is likely to be associated with differences in transfer comes from the Transfer and Retention of Urban Community College Students, an ongoing study of transfer in the Los Angeles Community College District. The project has found significant differences by age in transfer preparation—that is, in the taking of state-designated courses designed to prepare students for transfer (Hagedorn et al. n.d.).

All these reasons suggest the desirability of studying transfer patterns during the 1990s, particularly using data sets that allow us to examine older first-time college entrants. Two national longitudinal surveys allow us to do this. The National Educational Longitudinal Study of the 8th Grade (NELS:88) is a long-term follow-up of students who were in the eighth grade in 1988. They were subsequently followed through the year 2000. A key advantage of NELS:88 is the availability of college transcripts, which allows us to precisely measure college attendance and track transitions between postsecondary institutions. The main limitation of the NELS:88—that it cannot capture the experience of older first-time college students—is rectified by the Beginning Postsecondary Students Longitudinal Study of 1989–90 (BPS:90), which examines first-time college students of any age who entered college in 1989 and were followed up in 1994.

The data on transfer rates in the BPS:90 sample have been ably analyzed by McCormick (1997) and Bradburn, Hurst, and Peng (2001). However, neither study provides a full-blown multivariate analysis of the impact of student background on transfer. McCormick analyzed the impact of SES, gender, and age (but not race), controlling for educational aspirations, college enrollment status (full time or part time), college GPA, receipt of financial aid, and overall satisfaction with the first institution (43). These are good variables to control, but many are also left out, including racial-ethnic background, high school academic performance, marital and parental status at time of college entry, working during college, and college major. Hence, a more extensive analysis of the impact of social background on transfer and the mechanisms by which that impact is transmitted is needed.

Research Questions and Methods

The previous considerations prompted us to ask two research questions.

1   To what degree do transfer rates vary by student social background, and how have those patterns changed over time?
    Previous studies have found that SES, race-ethnicity, and gender all significantly affect transfer rates (Lee and Frank 1990; Velez and Javalgi 1987). However, these studies analyzed data from the 1970s and the 1980s (NLS-72 and HS&B, respectively). We investigated whether in the 1990s, with the renewal of interest in and support for transfer, inequality of transfer by class, race, and gender changed in its extent or form. Moreover, we also investigated the impact of a variable that those earlier studies could not examine: age.

2   How are the effects of social background transmitted?
    In this article, we focus on the impact of three sets of mediating variables: precollege personal characteristics (academic preparation in high school and educational and occupational aspirations); external demands as the student enters college (marital and parental status, extent and intensity of work, and enrollment status); and experiences during college (major or college program, degree of academic and social integration into the college).

Data

For this study, we analyzed two national data sets: the National Education Longitudinal Study of the 8th Grade (NELS: 88) and the Beginning Post-secondary Students Longitudinal Study (BPS:90). Both focus on students entering college around the same time, but they bring different strengths to this analysis. NELS:88 gives us a larger sample of community college entrants, a better measure of SES (see below), and a better set of variables that measure precollege academic preparation. However, because NELS:88 focuses on younger students, it did not allow us to examine the impact of age on transfer. Moreover, it lacks measures of academic and social integration during college. BPS:90 rectified both omissions by examining students of any age who are entering college in 1989–1990 and by providing a large number of academic and social integration variables. By analyzing these data sets together, we can get a much better sense of the extent of the impact of social background on transfer and the means by which that impact is exerted.

In the case of NELS:88, we focused on students who first entered a community college in the period between 1992 (when most of the respondents would have graduated from high school) and 1994. This allowed for a few delayers to be eligible for our analysis. All students in our NELS:88 sample responded to the 1990, 1992, 1994, and 2000 follow-ups. In the case of BPS:90, we focused on students who entered a community college in 1989 and had responded to the 1992 and 1994 follow-ups. These data sets are described in the appendix.

Dependent Variable

Our dependent variable is *transfer status*. It is a binary variable that measures whether community college entrants transferred to a four-year college at any point after their initial year in postsecondary education (PSE). For BPS:90, we used the student's primary postsecondary institution in the 1989–1990 academic year to anchor our analysis, and we restricted our sample to those stating that they attended a public two-year college as their primary institution in their first year. For the next five years, students were asked to identify their primary institution each year. If a student indicated attendance at a four-year college during any year subsequent to 1989, the student is considered to have transferred. In a small number of cases, community college students may have reported attending a four-year college and then switching back to a two-year school. We still consider them as having transferred to a four-year college. For NELS:88, we relied on transcript information to identify initial postsecondary entry and subsequent transitions between institutions. To be counted as having transferred in our NELS:88 analysis, a student's referent institution must be a public two-year college, and transfer credits must be observed on the student's four-year college transcript. Community college students who were simultaneously enrolled in a four-year college were not regarded as transfer students unless the intensity of their four-year attendance dominated in terms of credits earned in that period. Overall, students in BPS:90 had five years to transfer to a four-year college, while students in NELS:88 had, at most, eight years.

We examined the transfer status of all community college entrants, with no restriction pertaining to intentions. Much discussion has gone into what is the appropriate denominator for any measure of transfer. Many community college advocates have correctly pointed out that many students enter the community college with no intention to transfer, or if they state such an intention, it is only weakly and unrealistically held. Hence, they have called for calculating transfer rates only for those who have clearly established potential to transfer. One frequently used formula is to restrict the denominator of calculations of transfer rates to those who have accumulated 12 or more credits within four years of entering community college (Bradburn, Hurst, and Peng 2001; Cohen and Brawer 2003, 56).

Such restrictions of the denominator introduced some important distortions of analysis. First, they failed to consider as transfer eligible many students who do indeed end up transferring. For example, Bradburn and Hurst found that in the Beginning Postsecondary Students Longitudinal Study of 1989–94, 45% of those who had transferred by 1994 did not meet the 12-credit criterion proposed by Cohen and Brawer (Bradburn, Hurst, and Peng 2001, 123). Another problem with restricting the denominator to purportedly transfer-oriented students is that it hinders our ability to measure the importance of factors that affect transfer. Focusing on students with, say, baccalaureate aspirations or certain patterns of course taking hinders our ability to examine how powerfully educational aspirations or certain course-taking patterns shape whether students transfer. Moreover, measures that build transfer propensity into the denominator suggested that transfer propensity is a trait that students bring into community college and one that cannot be changed; this undercuts awareness of the possibility and desirability of changing that incoming propensity, such as by "warming up" student motivation to transfer. For all these reasons, we chose to examine the transfer status of all community college entrants regardless of incoming characteristics. We could then explicitly bring into the analysis the question of the relationship between transfer propensity and having a certain level of educational aspirations upon entering college.

Independent Variables

We examined the impact on transfer of four sets of independent variables:

- Social background: SES, race-ethnicity, gender, age
- Other precollege personal characteristics: Academic preparation in high school, educational and occupational aspirations
- External demands as the student enters college: Marital and parental status at the time of college entrance, extent and intensity of work
- Experiences during college: Enrollment status, major or college program, degree of academic and social integration into the college

Our focus is on the social background variables. In addition to establishing their total unique effects, we are interested in how much of this effect is indirect—transmitted through or mediated by the other variables in the model.

Social Background Our analysis of the impact of social background on transfer rates spotlights four background characteristics:

- Socioeconomic status (SES): In the case of NELS:88, this is an index combining the education, occupations, and incomes of parents. The scale is in centiles. Because of major deficiencies in the SES index available in BPS:90,[7] we instead use family income, in log form, and the educational level of the parent with the most education. Parental education is measured in the form of five dummy variables: less than high school, high school graduate only, some college, baccalaureate degree recipient, post-baccalaureate training.
- Gender: Binary variable, female = 1, male = 0.
- Race and ethnicity: Binary variables for black, Hispanic, and Asian backgrounds that compare the transfer rates for students of these backgrounds with those for white students. No Asian American students were in our BPS:90 community college sample.

- Age: Age at first enrollment in college, coded as four binary variables at the following intervals: 16–18, 19–20, 21–30, and 31+.

Much of the impact of social background on transfer is indirect, operating through other intervening or mediating variables. In this article, we focus on three sets of mediating variables.

Other Precollege Personal Characteristics
- Academic preparation coming out of high school: In the case of NELS:88, we used scores on reading and math tests taken in the 12th grade. The scale is in centiles. Unfortunately, BPS:90 does not have test score data for most respondents, so instead we used four other binary variables: self-rating of academic ability; whether students received a regular diploma; and whether students took remedial math or reading in college. The self-rating of academic ability was based on whether students rated themselves above average in academic ability "compared with the average person of your age."
- Educational aspirations: For both NELS.88 and BPS:90, we used a binary variable indicating whether the respondent aspired to a baccalaureate degree or higher.
- Occupational aspirations: For NELS:88, we used two variables indicating whether the respondent aspired to a professional or managerial occupation or to a lower white-collar or skilled blue-collar job. The comparison group is those aspiring to unskilled or semiskilled blue-collar jobs. Unfortunately, because a comparable question was not asked in the BPS:90 survey, we could not construct a comparable set of variables for BPS:90 and therefore relied on a single binary variable. However, as presently coded, the highest levels of occupational expectations in both data sets are roughly analogous.

External Demands as Students Enter College Students vary considerably regarding the extent of outside demands—including family obligations and work—that they encounter as they enter college. We hypothesize that the lower these demands, the more likely students are to transfer, either because they are less likely to drop out of higher education without a credential or because they are less likely to immediately work and not pursue a baccalaureate degree if they receive a sub-baccalaureate credential.

- Marital status: For both NELS.88 and BPS:90, we used whether the respondent was single, never married, at the time of college entrance. Married, separated, and divorced people were put in the excluded category. We are hypothesizing that single never-married people have fewer family obligations that may impede prolonged education or deter moving to a four-year college.
- Parental status: For both NELS:88 and BPS:90, this is defined as whether the respondent was childless at the time of college entrance. Respondents who had a child prior to college entrance were put in the excluded category.
- Work involvement during college: We hypothesize that students are more likely to transfer if they have fewer work obligations during college, either because those obligations reflect income demands incompatible with staying in college or because they provide a competing alternative to obtaining a baccalaureate degree. In both NELS:88 and BPS:90, we used a measure of work intensity that indexes the average number of hours a student worked during those weeks that he or she was working. It takes the form of three dummy variables: *no work, working 20 hours or less,* and *working between 21 and 39 hours* (NOWORK, HRSLTPT, HRSPT). The excluded category is *working 40 hours or more* (HRSFT).

Experiences During College It is not just the characteristics and experiences that students bring to college that may affect transfer but also their experiences during college. Hence, we looked at a variety of collegiate experiences. One that many observers have pointed to is the major or college program that students choose. It has been argued that students majoring in vocational subjects are considerably less likely to transfer to four-year colleges (Brint and Karabel 1989; Dougherty 1994). Moreover, because dropout interferes with transfer, we examined several different variables that have been found to affect college persistence. In particular, we focused on full-time enrollment and degree of academic and social integration into the college. The data on these within-college experiences are considerably richer in BPS:90 than NELS:88, so we rely more on the former data set at this point.

Unfortunately, we cannot capture with NELS:88 or BPS:90 data a number of other variables that have been identified as having a considerable impact on the likelihood of transfer. These include the extent to which a student's community college is highly vocationalized, its degree of commitment to transfer, whether students are accepted by four-year colleges into their preferred programs and campuses, how many credits are accepted for transfer, and how much financial aid would-be transfer students receive from four-year colleges (Dougherty 1994, 2002).

Enrollment status We hypothesize that students are more likely to persist in college and therefore are more likely to transfer the closer to full-time their student status. Full-time enrollment both betokens fewer external demands and perhaps shows a stronger commitment to college, but it also strengthens students' academic and social integration by making students more available to the academic and social influence of faculty and fellow students. In the analysis, our enrollment status variable is dichotomous, indicating whether a student was enrolled full time.

Major We hypothesize that students' majors or programs in the community colleges will affect the likelihood of transfer through differential exposure to faculty and staff who urge and facilitate transfer to four-year colleges and by shaping students' degrees of academic and social integration. In the case of NELS:88, we coded students' sell–reported major as academic, vocational, or undecided,[8] with undecided being the reference category. Unfortunately, because of peculiarities in the BPS:90 variables, we could not isolate those who were undecided. Hence, we simply coded students as academic or vocational, with the latter serving as the reference category.

Academic integration Drawing on the work of Tinto (1993) and Braxton (2000), we used several measures of a student's integration into the academic life of his or her community college during the first year of college. These include the student's GPA (as a measure of successful integration) and several measures of conditions facilitative of a commitment to the academic life: whether students talked to their academic advisors (RTALKADV), talked about academic matters with faculty outside of class (RTALKFAC), attended career related lectures (RLECTURI), and had academic contact with students in the form of participation in study groups (RSTDYGRP). In all cases, these variables were coded in binary form—that is, whether students have had the experiences in question. These measures are available only in BPS:90.

Social integration We used several different measures of students' social integration into the social life of their community colleges during the first year. These measures include whether students had informal contact with faculty outside of class (CONTACT), participated in school clubs (CLUBS), had campus friendship ties as marked by going places with friends from school (GOPLACES), and used student assistance programs on campus, such as counseling, remediation, and health programs (CENTERS). These variables, all coded in binary form, are available only in BPS:90.

See Table 17.1 for the means and standard deviations of these and other variables used in the analysis.

We estimated the impact of these characteristics on transfer via a set of logistic regressions. This set of regressions is described in Table 17.2. As can be seen, the baseline equation—Model 0—regresses transfer status on each of the four social background variables by themselves. In Model 1, we then put in all four social background variables together to give us the total unique effect of each background variable. In succeeding equations, we added various possible mediating variables, thus allowing us to explore the indirect effects of social background on transfer.

Table 17.1 Sample Means and Standard Deviations from Beginning Postsecondary Student Longitudinal Survey (BPS:90) and National Education Longitudinal Survey of 1988 (NELS:88)

Variable label	BPS:90		NELS:88	
	Mean	SD	Mean	SD
Outcome				
Transferred to four-year college	0.221	0.415	0.378	0.485
Social Background				
Female	0.512	0.500	0.503	0.500
Socioeconomic status [*x100*]			0.530	0.255
Parents with less than high school education	0.135	0.342		
Parents with high school education [*ref*]	0.377	0.485		
Parents with some college/AA	0.212	0.409		
Parents with BA education	0.179	0.384		
Parents with more than BA education	0.097	0.296		
Family income in 1988 (log)	10.016	0.983		
Black, not Hispanic	0.087	0.283	0.087	0.282
Hispanic	0.118	0.322	0.138	0.345
Asian	—	—	0.038	0.191
16 to 18 years old [*ref*]	0.439	0.497		
19 to 20 years old	0.243	0.429		
21 to 30 years old	0.186	0.390		
31 years old and higher	0.131	0.338		
High School Preparation				
12th-grade math test score [*x100*]			0.494	0.241
12th-grade reading test score [*x100*]			0.494	0.255
Received high school diploma	0.923	0.266		
No remedial math in PSE	0.889	0.314		
No remedial reading in PSE	0.896	0.305		
Above-average academic ability [*compared with others*]	0.242	0.429		
Educational Aspirations				
Aspire to complete at least a BA degree	0.705	0.457	0.708	0.455
Occupational Aspirations				
Working-class occupational expectation [*ref*]			0.034	0.182
Lower-middle-class occupational expectation			0.404	0.491
Upper-middle-class occupational expectation			0.562	0.496
Expected occupation requires at least a BA degree	0.302	0.459		
Family Status				
Single, not married	0.753	0.432	0.553	0.497
Did not have a child	0.808	0.394	0.627	0.484
Work Involvement during First PSE Year				
Did not work in first year in college	0.173	0.378	0.142	0.349
Worked 20 hours or less during first year in college	0.178	0.383	0.213	0.409
Worked 21–39 hours during first year in college	0.343	0.475	0.347	0.476
Worked 40 hours or more during first year in college [*ref*]	0.306	0.461	0.298	0.458
Enrollment Status				
Exclusively full-time enrollment during first year in college	0.482	0.500	0.779	0.415
Program of Study				
Academic major	0.345	0.476	0.325	0.469
Occupational major	0.655	0.476	0.196	0.397
Did not declare a major	—	—	0.479	0.500

(*Continued*)

Variable label	BPS:90		NELS:88	
	Mean	SD	Mean	SD
Academic Integration				
GPA in first year of college is mostly As and Bs	0.320	0.467		
Contact with advisor	0.720	0.449		
Academic contact with faculty	0.703	0.457		
Attend career events	0.435	0.496		
Study group participation	0.542	0.499		
Social Integration				
Informal faculty contact	0.473	0.500		
Campus club member	0.193	0.395		
Do things with friends on campus	0.693	0.462		
Use of student services	0.200	0.400		
Number of observations	653		2,660	

Source: Beginning Postsecondary Student Longitudinal Survey (2003) and National Education Longitudinal Survey (2003).
Note: Authors' calculations. PSE = postsecondary education.

These potential mediating variables were added in an order dictated by our judgment regarding where they fall in a causal sequence connecting social background with transfer. If the addition of one of these potential variables substantially reduces the coefficient for a background variable, we know that new variable is carrying part of the influence on transfer of that background variable.

Regression Method

Because our dependent variable is binary, we estimated the impact of these variables on transfer by means of logistic regression. The logistic model is

$$\text{prob } (y = 1) = \text{logit } (X\beta i) = \frac{e^{X\beta i}}{1+e^{X\beta i}}$$

where y is the outcome variable, transfer to a four-year college, and X is a vector of social background and educational characteristics. Unlike ordinary least squares (OLS) regression, the coefficient of a logistic regression cannot be interpreted as the probability of attaining a positive outcome—that is, the marginal effect on the dependent variable from a one-unit increase in the independent variables. Thus, in logistic regression, a separate calculation is made of the marginal effect. It is expressed as

$$[\text{prob } (y = 1)][1 - \text{prob } (y = 1)] \, \hat{\beta} i$$

and is usually reported at the mean values of the explanatory variables. This statistic is shown along with the regression coefficient, allowing a more straightforward interpretation of the impacts of the independent variables.

Findings

The Impact of Social Background

Our analysis of transfer in the 1990s using NELS:88 and BPS:90 arrived at findings about the impact of social background on transfer that both converge with and diverge from studies of transfer in the 1970s and 1980s, using the National Longitudinal Survey of the High School Class of 1972 (Velez and Javalgi 1987) and High School and Beyond (Cabrera, LaNasa, and Burkum 2001; Lee and Frank 1990).

Table 17.2 Description of Determinants Tested by Logistic Regression

Determinants	Model 0	Model 1	Model 2	Model 3	Model 4	Model 5	Model 6	Model 7
Social Background	X							
Socioeconomic status		X	X	X	X	X	X	X
Race/ethnicity		X	X	X	X	X	X	X
Gender		X	X	X	X	X	X	X
Age*		X	X	X	X	X	X	X
Other Precollege Traits								
High school preparation			X	X	X	X	X	X
Educational aspirations				X	X	X	X	X
Occupational aspirations				X	X	X	X	X
External Demands at College Entrance								
Marital status					X	X	X	X
Parental status					X	X	X	X
Average hours worked					X	X	X	X
College Experiences								
Full-time attendance						X	X	X
Major							X	X
Academic contact with faculty*								X
Talk with advisor*								X
Attend career events*								X
Join study groups*								X
Informal faculty contact*								X
Campus club member*								X
Student service use*								X
Friends on campus*								X

*Variables only available for BPS:90.
Note: Model 0 regresses transfer status on each of the background variables singly. Model 1 does so with all the background variables in at the same time.

In particular, we found, as did earlier studies, a very strongly significant impact of parental SES. We also found a powerful impact of age, a variable that the earlier studies could not address because of the nature of their data sets. However, unlike earlier studies, we did not find a statistically significant impact of gender and race-ethnicity on transfer rates.

The Impact of Socioeconomic Status Our analysis of NELS:88 and BPS:90 found that in the 1990s, as in earlier decades, the SES of the parents of students was strongly and significantly associated with whether those students transferred to four-year colleges. As can be seen in Models 0 and 1 in Tables 17.3 and 17.4, SES has a sizable and statistically significant impact on transfer rates, both before and after controlling for gender, race-ethnicity, and age. For example, in the NELS:88 analysis—comparing students who are in the top and bottom 10% in SES (87th and 16th percentiles, respectively) but of the same race, gender, and age—the gap in transfer rate is 45 percentage points (55% vs. 10%).

The Impact of Age A major benefit of analyzing the Beginning Postsecondary Students Longitudinal Study (BPS:90) is that it allowed us to examine the impact of age. Unlike NELS:88 and its predecessors (HS&B and NLS-72), BPS:90 is not built around the evolving experiences of a particular age cohort, whether 8th graders, 10th graders, or 12th graders. Rather, BPS:90 focuses on all students entering college for the first time in a given year, regardless of age.[9] Hence, it allows us to analyze students who are first entering college at much more advanced years than the traditional college-age students

Table 17.3 Determinants of Transfer to Four-Year College: Logistic Regression Analysis of National Education Longitudinal Study of 1988 (NELS:88) Data

	Model 0		Model 1		Model 2		Model 3		Model 4		Model 5		Model 6	
Variable label	Coef (std err)	dy/dx	Coef (std err)	dy/dx	Coef (std err)	dy/dx	Coef (std err)	dy/dx	Coef (std err)	dy/dx	Coef (std err)	dy/dx	Coef (std err)	dy/dx
Social Background														
Socioeconomic status [x100]	2.629** (0.286)	0.637	2.602** (0.290)	0.633	2.254** (0.363)	0.563	2.100** (0.375)	0.516	2.146** (0.396)	0.528	2.127** (0.415)	0.501	2.256** (0.460)	0.525
Female	(0.139)	-0.056	-0.030 (0.143)	-0.007	0.179 (0.166)	0.045	0.206 (0.192)	0.051	0.256 (0.198)	0.063	0.275 (0.206)	0.065	0.265 (0.214)	0.062
Race and Ethnicity														
Black, not Hispanic	-0.578 (0.375)	-0.127	-0.134 (0.371)	-0.032	0.283 (0.455)	0.070	0.334 (0.390)	0.080	0.549 (0.347)	0.129	0.364 (0.323)	0.082	0.678* (0.336)	0.143
Hispanic	-0.220 (0.272)	-0.051	0.116 (0.228)	0.028	0.420 (0.274)	0.104	0.230 (0.301)	0.056	0.390 (0.330)	0.093	0.493 (0.317)	0.109	0.746* (0.354)	0.156
Asian	0.528 (0.344)	0.130	0.465 (0.383)	0.115	0.116 (0.482)	0.029	-0.159 (0.612)	-0.039	-0.255 (0.633)	-0.063	-0.336 (0.678)	-0.081	-0.343 (0.542)	-0.082
High School Preparation														
12th-grade math test score [x100]					2.517** (0.416)	0.629	2.297** (0.455)	0.564	2.314** (0.476)	0.569	2.234** (0.486)	0.526	2.300** (0.496)	0.535
12th-grade reading test score [x100]					0.054 (0.419)	0.013	-0.226 (0.457)	-0.056	-0.489 (0.473)	-0.120	-0.339 (0.461)	-0.080	-0.515 (0.514)	-0.120
Educational Aspiration														
Aspire to complete at least a BA degree							0.948** (0.209)	0.233	0.919** (0.221)	0.226	0.945** (0.226)	0.230	0.773** (0.239)	0.187
Occupational Aspirations														
Lower-middle-class occup expectation							0.368 (0.438)	0.089	0.369 (0.388)	0.090	0.290 (0.432)	0.067	0.263 (0.452)	0.060
Upper-middle-class occup expectation							0.778 (0.424)	0.191	0.699 (0.375)	0.172	0.583 (0.421)	0.139	0.503 (0.440)	0.119
Family Status														
Single, not married									0.229 (0.206)	0.056	0.248 (0.220)	0.059	0.248 (0.218)	0.058
Did not have a child									0.871** (0.264)	0.214	0.882** (0.280)	0.213	0.777** (0.273)	0.187

(Continued)

Table 17.3 (Continued)

	Model 0		Model 1		Model 2		Model 3		Model 4		Model 5		Model 6	
Variable label	**Coef (std err)**	**dy/dx**	**Coef (std err)**	**dy/dx**	**Coef (std err)**	**dy/dx**	**Coef (std err)**	**dy/dx**	**Coef (std err)**	**dy/dx**	**Coef (std err)**	**dy/dx**	**Coef (std err)**	**dy/dx**
Work Involvement during First PSE Year														
Did not work									0.521 (0.335)	0.12	0.446 (0.340)	0.100	0.396 (0.376)	0.088
Worked 20 hours or less									1.135** (0.226)	0.259	1.059** (0.225)	0.229	0.864** (0.239)	0.188
Worked 21 to 39 hours									0.689** (0.232)	0.164	0.621** (0.238)	0.141	0.493* (0.243)	0.111
Enrollment Status														
Exclusively full-time enrollment											0.642** (0.224)	0.157	0.614* (0.240)	0.149
Program of Study														
Academic student													1.337** (0.250)	0.301
Occupational student													-0.394 (0.292)	-0.094
Constant			-1.897 (0.203)		-3.092 (0.275)		-3.879 (0.479)		-5.083 (0.490)		-5.475 (0.576)		-5.627 (0.622)	
Pseudo-R²			0.072		0.116		0.158		0.212		0.217		0.280	
Number of observations			2,574		2,052		1,705		1,631		1,523		1,523	

Source: National Education Longitudinal Survey of 1988 (2003). Authors' calculations.
Note: Coefficients marked with a single asterisk (*) are significant at the 5% level; double asterisk (**) at the 1% level. PSE = post-secondary education.

analyzed by previous studies of transfer. Analyzing BPS:90, we found that age does have a major impact on transfer. Controlling for other background characteristics, students who are older than 18 when they enter community college are significantly less likely to transfer, with the size of this negative age effect increasing as students get older. For example, students entering community college between ages 21 and 30 are 15% less likely to transfer, and students aged 31 and older are 20% less likely to transfer than are students entering college below age 19 (see Model 1 in Table 17.4).

This finding is of great importance given the growing number of students who are first entering college well after they leave high school. Although community colleges have made major efforts to facilitate the success of older students, the fact remains that they are much less likely to transfer than are younger students. This begs the question of why; this question will be addressed when we turn to analyzing the factors that transmit the influence of the social background variables on transfer.

The Impacts of Race-Ethnicity and Gender Unlike studies of transfer in the 1970s and 1980s (Lee and Frank 1990, 190; Velez and Javalgi 1987, 86), we did not find that race-ethnicity has a statistically significant impact on transfer rates in the 1990s. To be sure, compared with whites, blacks and Hispanics are less likely to transfer, and Asians are more likely to transfer. For example, in NELS:88, the transfer rates for blacks and Hispanics are, respectively, 13 and 5 percentage points lower than for whites, while that for Asians is 13 points higher (see Model 0 in Table 17.3).

However, unlike the case for data from the 1970s and 1980s, these differences are not statistically significant. Regardless of whether other background variables are controlled, blacks, Hispanics, and Asians do not demonstrate statistically significant differences in transfer rates compared with whites (see Models 0 and 1 in Tables 17.3 and 17.4). However, there is an important caveat to this finding in the case of blacks. As we note next, if we compare blacks and whites with similar educational aspirations (and high school academic preparation), the black-white gap in transfer rates grows sharply, becoming statistically significant in the BPS:90 analysis.

In the case of gender, earlier studies of transfer using national data sets found that males had a significantly higher transfer rate than females (Lee and Frank 1990, 184, 190; Velez and Javalgi 1987, 85, 88). For example, analyzing NLS-72, Velez and Javalgi found that in the 1970s, males were 18% more likely to transfer than females, even after controlling for differences in social background, academic preparation, and aspirations. However, using data from the 1990s, although we did find that women are still less likely to transfer (a gap of six percentage points), this gender gap is much smaller than before and no longer statistically significant. Gender is no longer strongly associated with transfer, whether before or after controlling for SES, race-ethnicity, and age (see Models 0 and 1 in Tables 17.3 and 17.4).

That we diverge from previous studies in not finding statistically significant impacts of race and gender on transfer rates could be attributed to peculiarities of the data that we used. However, it is noteworthy that the lack of significant impact showed up in both data sets that we analyzed. Moreover, it is important to note that the impact of race and gender on transfer was weaker in data from the 1980s (Lee and Frank 1990) compared with the 1970s data (Velez and Javalgi 1987). This suggests that a major temporal shift has occurred in the impact of race and gender to the point that they have ceased to play a major role in affecting the magnitude of transfer. This temporal shift could be due to the major efforts in the 1980s and 1990s to reduce race and gender gaps in college access and success. However, because those efforts were also directed toward reducing the social class gap in transfer, it is puzzling that the class gap remains large and statistically significant.[10]

How Are Social Background Effects Transmitted?

It is not enough to document that social class and age have a significant impact on transfer. It is important to determine how that impact is exerted. To that end, we look at three sets of possible mediating variables.

Table 17.4 Determinants of Transfer to Four-Year College: Logistic Regression Analysis of Beginning Postsecondary Student Longitudinal Survey (BPS:90) Data

	Results from Models															
	Model 0		Model 1		Model 2		Model 3		Model 4		Model 5		Model 6		Model 7	
Variable Label	Coef (std err)	dy/dx	Coef (std err)	dy/dx	Coef (std err)	dy/dx	Coef (std err)	dy/dx	Coef (std err)	dy/dx	Coef (std err)	dy/dx	Coef (std err)	dy/dx	Coef (std err)	dy/dx
Social background																
Family income in 1988 (log)	0.428** (0.127)	0.073	0.111 (0.099)	0.018	0.095 (0.109)	0.015	0.104 (0.111)	0.014	0.034 (0.117)	0.004	0.023 (0.115)	0.003	0.261 (0.160)	0.026	0.259 (0.170)	0.024
Parents with less than high school education	-1.414** (0.522)	-0.174	-1.041 (0.567)	-0.129	-0.930 (0.586)	-0.114	-0.899 (0.598)	-0.098	-0.903 (0.622)	-0.094	-1.006 (0.649)	-0.100	-0.121 (0.641)	-0.012	-0.055 (0.679)	-0.005
Parents with some college/AA	0.253 (0.258)	0.044	0.163 (0.289)	0.027	0.212 (0.302)	0.034	0.119 (0.314)	0.017	-0.023 (0.330)	-0.003	-0.113 (0.331)	-0.014	0.177 (0.454)	0.019	0.264 (0.486)	0.026
Parents with BA education	0.412 (0.262)	0.075	0.149 (0.276)	0.024	0.134 (0.281)	0.021	-0.094 (0.299)	-0.013	-0.191 (0.305)	-0.024	-0.254 (0.298)	-0.031	0.203 (0.376)	0.021	0.077 (0.409)	0.007
Parents with more than BA education	1.367** (0.345)	0.291	0.990** (0.367)	0.193	0.906* (0.375)	0.170	0.457 (0.396)	0.071	0.261 (0.420)	0.037	0.250 (0.414)	0.035	0.456 (0.528)	0.053	0.355 (0.554)	0.037
Female	-0.067 (0.184)	-0.012	0.157 (0.220)	0.025	0.253 (0.229)	0.039	0.299 (0.235)	0.041	0.490 (0.256)	0.065	0.538* (0.258)	0.070	0.700* (0.309)	0.072	0.715* (0.332)	0.067
Race and Ethnicity																
Black, not Hispanic	-0.588 (0.382)	-0.087	-0.546 (0.418)	-0.075	-0.546 (0.425)	-0.073	-0.971* (0.468)	-0.101	-1.057* (0.474)	-0.103	-1.089* (0.475)	-0.103	-2.303** (0.702)	-0.121	-2.432** (0.699)	-0.112
Hispanic	-0.006 (0.283)	-0.001	0.078 (0.349)	0.013	0.114 (0.395)	0.018	0.012 (0.388)	0.002	-0.014 (0.401)	-0.002	0.132 (0.432)	0.018	0.136 (0.580)	0.014	0.314 (0.566)	0.032
Age at First College Entrance																
19 to 20 years old	-0.847** (0.268)	-0.112	-0.759** (0.270)	-0.108	-0.692* (0.285)	-0.096	-0.703* (0.284)	-0.086	-0.681* (0.278)	-0.080	-0.658** (0.277)	-0.076	-0.286 (0.363)	-0.027	-0.295 (0.381)	-0.026
21 to 30 years old	-1.550** (0.381)	-0.173	-1.174** (0.413)	-0.147	-1.072* (0.429)	-0.133	-0.965* (0.433)	-0.107	-0.222 (0.492)	-0.028	-0.118 (0.507)	-0.015	0.049 (0.665)	0.005	-0.101 (0.685)	-0.009
31 years old and higher	-2.634** (0.539)	-0.222	-2.295** (0.706)	-0.204	-2.530** (0.735)	-0.207	-2.108** (0.778)	-0.166	-0.208 (1.032)	-0.026	0.007 (1.087)	0.001	0.807 (1.043)	0.103	0.496 (1.186)	0.054

	(1)		(2)		(3)		(4)		(5)		(6)	
High School Preparation												
Above average academic ability [*compared with others*]	0.758** (0.257)	0.130	0.622* (0.278)	0.094	0.636* (0.289)	0.093	0.673* (0.289)	0.097	0.275 (0.309)	0.029	0.209 (0.336)	0.020
Received high school diploma	1.092 (0.692)	0.124	1.166 (0.723)	0.113	0.669 (0.753)	0.072	0.692 (0.713)	0.073	0.635 (0.920)	0.052	1.918 (1.208)	0.097
No remedial math in PSE	−0.815* (0.350)	−0.150	−0.774 (0.425)	−0.128	−0.992* (0.427)	−0.167	−1.008* (0.430)	−0.167	−1.099* (0.535)	−0.150	−1.298* (0.532)	−0.174
No remedial reading in PSE	0.784 (0.482)	0.099	0.799 (0.512)	0.088	0.870 (0.524)	0.091	0.685 (0.542)	0.073	0.934 (0.699)	0.071	0.985 (0.671)	0.068
Educational Aspirations												
Aspire to complete at least a BA degree			2.213** (0.460)	0.230	2.270** (0.519)	0.225	2.280** (0.519)	0.220	2.664** (0.598)	0.192	2.805** (0.613)	0.184
Occupational Aspirations												
Expected occup requires at least a BA degree			0.093 (0.219)	0.013	0.075 (0.231)	0.010	−0.021 (0.234)	−0.003	0.238 (0.284)	0.025	0.180 (0.287)	0.017
Family Status												
Single, not married					0.564 (0.561)	0.066	0.607 (0.570)	0.069	0.797 (0.808)	0.068	0.891 (0.869)	0.068
Did not have a child					1.702* (0.764)	0.156	1.711** (0.796)	0.153	1.857* (0.864)	0.123	1.864 (0.977)	0.115
Work Involvement during First PSE Year												
Did not work					0.590 (0.446)	0.089	0.395 (0.460)	0.056	0.401 (0.602)	0.045	0.321 (0.617)	0.032
Worked 20 hours or less					0.596 (0.380)	0.089	0.422 (0.397)	0.060	0.445 (0.523)	0.050	0.434 (0.547)	0.045
Worked 21 to 39 hours					0.357 (0.392)	0.049	0.314 (0.399)	0.042	0.258 (0.519)	0.027	0.590 (0.544)	0.059
Enrollment Status												
Exclusively full-time enrollment							0.547 (0.298)	0.071	0.553 (0.364)	0.056	0.790* (0.375)	0.074
Program of Study												
Academic student											0.705* (0.293)	0.072

(Continued)

Table 17.4 (Continued)

	Results from Models														
	Model 0		Model 1		Model 2		Model 3		Model 4		Model 5		Model 6		Model 7	
Variable Label	Coef (std err)	dy/dx	Coef (std err)	dy/dx	Coef (std err)	dy/dx	Coef (std err)	dy/dx	Coef (std err)	dy/dx	Coef (std err)	dy/dx	Coef (std err)	dy/dx	Coef (std err)	dy/dx
Academic Integration																
GPA in first year of college is mostly As and Bs															0.397 (0.350)	0.039
Contact with advisor															-0.038 (0.460)	-0.004
Academic contact with faculty															-0.306 (0.435)	-0.030
Attend career events															-0.419 (0.319)	-0.038
Study group participation															0.762* (0.347)	0.068
Social Integration																
Informal faculty contact															0.312 (0.339)	0.029
Campus club member															0.290 (0.377)	0.029
Do things with friends on campus															-0.579 (0.502)	-0.060
Use of student services															-0.243 (0.383)	-0.021
Constant			-1.969 (1.027)		-3.127 (1.483)		-5.032 (1.535)		-6.359 (1.783)		-6.387 (1.774)		-10.414 (2.321)		-11.762 (2.719)	
Pseudo-R²			0.111		0.138		0.206		0.227		0.233		0.262		0.299	
Number of observations			588		570		539		506		502		382		356	

Source: Beginning Postsecondary student Longitudinal survey (2003). Authors' calculations.
Note: Coefficients marked with a single asterisk (*) are significant at the 5% level; double asterisk (**) at the 1% level. PSE = post-secondary education.

- Other precollege personal characteristics: Academic preparation in high school, educational and occupational aspirations
- External demands as students enter college: Marital and parental status at the time of college entrance, and extent and intensity of work
- Experiences during college: Enrollment status, major or college program, degree of academic and social integration into the college

As we show next, we found that these variables, with the notable exception of most of the academic and social integration variables, do substantially mediate the impact of social background on transfer.

Precollege Academic Traits We examined three sets of precollege characteristics that might mediate the impact of social background on transferring: academic preparation in high school and educational and occupational aspirations before college entrance. Models 2 and 3 in Tables 17.3 and 17.4 summarize the impact of adding these variables to the baseline social background equation. A sharp decrease in the coefficient of a background variable as another variable (such as educational aspirations) was added indicates that the new variable plays a major role in transmitting the impact of the background variable on transfer.[11]

Academic preparation coming out of high school. Our analysis found that transfer in the 1990s continued the pattern of earlier decades of transfer being strongly affected by degree of academic preparation coming out of high school (Cabrera et al. 2001, 22, 24; Lee and Frank 1990, 190; Velez and Javalgi 1987, 88). Moreover, we also found that academic preparation plays a major role in mediating the.impact of social background on transfer.

As mentioned, NELS:88 provided us with the best measures of academic preparation coming out of high school. We found that a student's score on the NELS:88 12th-grade math test has a strong impact on transfer likelihood, though reading test scores do not. In the case of BPS:90, test scores were not available for most respondents, so we used four variables to measure academic preparation: self-rating of academic ability; whether a student received a regular diploma; and whether a student took remedial math or reading in college. We found that a self-rating as *above average* in academic ability has a strongly significant positive impact on transfer. Surprisingly, however, we also found that taking remedial math increases transfer likelihood. Two possible causes could be at work. Those taking remedial math may benefit from skill improvement and therefore transfer potential. Alternatively, those taking remedial math—because a considerable element of self-selection is involved (Perin and Charron, forthcoming)—may also be those who are more motivated to begin with to achieve greater academic success and thus transfer.

The addition of academic preparation coming out of high school sharply reduces the impact of the social background variables, indicating that a considerable part of the impact of social background on transfer is indirect, operating through differences in precollege academic preparation. For example, in the NELS:88 analysis, when high school test scores are added to the social background variables, the coefficient of SES drops 15%, that of Black background drops 80%, and that of Hispanic background drops 76% (see Models 1 and 2 in Table 17.3). Clearly, a considerable part of the impact of class and racial-ethnic background on transfer is due to differences in academic preparation coming out of high school.

However, differences in high school academic preparation seem to play little role in accounting for the impact of age on transfer. In the BPS:90 analysis, we found minimal drops in the effect of the age variables when we controlled for the four high school preparation variables (see Model 2 in Table 17.4). We should not put undue weight on this finding given that the measures of academic preparation that we used in the BPS:90 analysis are less than ideal. For example, the four academic preparation variables in BPS:90 mediate much less of the influence of the SES variables (family income and parental education) on transfer than do the test score variables in NELS:88. Still, it is striking that the addition of the academic preparation variables in BPS:90 causes a much smaller drop in the coefficients for age than for the BPS.90 SES and race variables.

Educational aspirations. Educational aspirations continued in the 1990s to have the same strong impact on transfer that they did in the 1970s and 1980s (Cabrera et al. 2001, 22, 24; Lee and Frank 1990, 190; Velez and Javalgi 1987, 190). In both NELS:88 and BPS:90, educational aspirations have a large and statistically significant impact even when social background and high school academic preparation are controlled (see Model 3 in Tables 17.3 and 17.4).

Differences in educational aspirations play a key role in mediating the impact of social background on transfer. For example, in NELS:88, the addition of educational aspirations drops the coefficient for SES by another 24%. And in BPS:90, the coefficient for the oldest age group (31 and older) drops 18%, though the other coefficients for the other age variables are much less affected (see Model 3 in Tables 17.3 and 17.4).

But if class and age inequality in transfer is in part due to associated differences in educational aspirations, the opposite is the case with race. Controlling for educational aspirations does not reduce the coefficient for the black background variable but sharply increases it. In fact, in the BPS:90 analysis, the black background variable becomes statistically significant. This suggests that educational aspirations work as a suppressor variable for blacks. That is, the negative impact of black background on transfer is kept from being as big as it might otherwise be because blacks have higher educational aspirations than whites of similar social class, gender, and age.[12] But once that aspirational advantage is nullified by controlling for educational aspirations, the negative impact on transfer of being black becomes considerably larger.

Occupational aspirations. Occupational aspirations do not have a statistically significant impact on transfer in either NELS:88 or BPS:90. As a result, occupational aspirations mediate very little of the impact of SES, race-ethnicity, or age on transfer.

External Family and Work Demands as Students Enter College We have hypothesized that students are more likely to transfer if they encounter fewer external demands, whether from work or family, as they enter college. In Model 4, we add three sets of variables: marital status, parental status, and degree of involvement with work. To ease interpretation, we measured the variables in terms of the hypothesized absence of external demands—that is, we are comparing single to ever-married people; those without children to those with children; and those who do not work or work part time to those who work full time.

Being single does not have a significant impact on transfer in either NELS:88 and BPS:90. However, being childless at time of college entry has a substantially large, positive effect in both BPS:90 and NELS:88 (see Model 4 in Tables 17.3 and 17.4).

Not working or working fewer than 40 hours a week proves to have a positive impact on transfer in NELS:88 and BPS:90, but this impact is statistically significant only in NELS:88 (see Model 4 in Tables 17.3 and 17.4). Curiously, in NELS:88, though not BPS:90, working fewer than 20 hours a week has a more positive impact on transfer than not working at all.

The family status and work intensity variables substantially mediate the impact of age on transfer. In BPS:90, controlling for these variables reduces the coefficient of the age 21 to 30 variable by 78% and of the 31 years and older variable by 90%. However, the picture is less clear with regard to SES. Controlling for the external demands variables reduces the impact of family income in BPS:90 by 67%, and it substantially reduces two of the three dummy variables pertaining to students with parents with more than a high school education. But in NELS:88, controlling for the external demands variables actually increases the coefficient for SES.

Experiences During College Our three sets of measures of collegiate experiences proved to have quite mixed effects. Enrolling in an academic major proved to have a positive and significant impact on transfer. In the case of enrollment status, being enrolled full-time increased the probability that a student would transfer, with the impact being statistically significant in NELS:88 but not BPS:90. Finally, almost all the measures of academic and social integration in the BPS:90 analysis proved statistically insignificant.

Enrollment status As expected, the closer to full time a student's enrollment, the more likely he or she is to transfer. This is clearly seen in the NELS:88 analysis, in which the size of the effect is large and statistically significant. In the BPS:90 analysis, however, the magnitude of the effect is roughly half that of NELS:88, and the variable just missed being significant at the 5% level (see Model 5 in Tables 17.3 and 17.4).

Enrollment status mediated a significant portion of the impact of black background (in NELS:88 but not BPS:90) and being age 21 and older in BPS:90, as evidenced by the sharp drops in the coefficients for these variables when enrollment status was controlled (see Models 5 and 4 in Tables 17.3 and 17.4).

Major Enrolling in an academic program had a positive and significant impact (at the 0.05 level) in both NELS:88 and BPS:90. In NELS:88, the comparison group was those students who had not declared a major in the first year of college. In BPS:90, the comparison was occupational students because we were not able to isolate those students who did not have a major (see Model 6 in Tables 17.3 and 17.4).

Differences in college major appear to play a significant role in transmitting the impact of race and age on transfer. Controlling for students' college major sharply reduces the negative coefficients for those age 19 and older in BPS:90. However, choice of college major does not seem to be a significant channel through which socioeconomic background affects transfer. Controlling for major actually slightly increases the SES coefficient in NELS:88 and has inconsistent impacts on the various SES variables in BPS:90.

That enrolling in an academic program has a positive impact on transfer is important because the argument has been made that enrolling in an occupational major is no barrier to transfer. This is true if one means that it is not an absolute barrier, but it still remains an important *relative* barrier, reducing the probability that students will transfer.

Academic and Social Integration The academic and social integration variables proved to have very little impact on transfer between community colleges and four-year colleges in BPS:90. (These variables were not available in NELS.) Only one, involvement in a study group with other students, had a statistically significant impact. Moreover, several of the variables, such as academic contact with an advisor and with faculty members, had signs opposite to what we expected. Their impact on transfer was negative when we had expected positive impacts (see Model 7 in Table 17.4).

The weak effect and sometimes unexpected signs of the academic and social integration variables may be attributable to their positive impact on two different sets of students: students who go on to transfer and students who persist long enough to acquire a subbaccalaureate degree but then do not transfer. Greater contact with a faculty member or advisor may increase the persistence of both groups but promote the transfer of only the first group. Such a spread of effects across the transfer-nontransfer divide would considerably weaken the impact of the integration variables on transfer likelihood.[13]

Whatever the case, controlling for the academic and social integration variables did not affect the coefficients for the SES, race, and age variables in any clear pattern.

Summary and Conclusions

Our analysis of the National Education Longitudinal Study of the 8th Grade (NELS: 88) and the Beginning Postsecondary Students Longitudinal Study (BPS:90) arrives at findings that both validate and break with previous studies. As with earlier studies, we found that the likelihood of transfer is strongly affected by parental SES. Students whose parents have higher incomes, more advanced education, and more prestigious and remunerative jobs have a very large and statistically significant advantage in transfer over less socioeconomically favored students. A significant portion of class advantage is transmitted through differences between more or less well-off students in precollege academic preparation and educational aspirations. However, even after controlling for these differences—and differences in occupational aspirations, marital and parental status at time of college entry, enrollment status, and college major—most of the impact of socioeconomic background on transfer is still left unexplained (about 85% in NELS:88 but less in BPS:90).

With regard to race and ethnicity, we found that in the 1990s, as in the 1970s and 1980s, blacks and Hispanics had lower transfer rates than did whites and Asians. However, our study breaks with earlier studies (Lee and Frank 1990, 190; Velez and Javalgi 1987, 86) in finding that this racial-ethnic disparity is not statistically significant, particularly if we compare black and Latino students with whites of similar gender, age, and above all, SES. But there is an important caveat to be made: when we control for educational aspirations, the black-white gap in transfer rates widens considerably, becoming statistically significant in the case of BPS:90, though not of NELS:88. Blacks have higher educational aspirations than whites of the same socioeconomic background, which serves to mitigate the negative impact of being black on transfer, keeping the black disadvantage smaller than it would otherwise be.

Another key difference from studies of transfer in the 1970s and 1980s is that we did not find powerful effects of gender on transfer rates in the 1990s. Although women are slightly less likely to transfer, that difference is no longer statistically significant both before and after controlling for other background differences.

These differences in findings about the impacts of race and gender between our study of transfer in the 1990s and earlier studies of transfer in the 1980s and 1970s could be an artifact of differences in data quality or analytic technique, but we doubt this. The patterns that we found hold across two different data sets: NELS:88 and BPS:90. Moreover, transfer in the 1980s appears to have been less affected by gender and race-ethnicity than was transfer in the 1970s (Cabrera et al. 2001; Lee and Frank 1990; Velez and Javalgi 1987). Moreover, a host of programs were initiated in the 1980s to reduce class and race differences in transfer (Dougherty, 1994, 254–60; Ford Foundation 1988). Hence, we believe that the absence of statistically significant gender and race/ethnic effects that we found in Models 0 and 1 of our analyses most probably reflects temporal changes in the impact on transfer of these social background characteristics rather than artifacts of data quality or analysis technique.

Another key difference between our findings and those from studies of transfer patterns in the 1970s and 1980s is that we have been able to analyze the impact of age, a variable that earlier studies were unable to study because of the age restrictions built into the cohort structure of the NLS-72 and HS&B longitudinal surveys (Cabrera et al. 2001; Lee and Frank 1990; Velez and Javalgi 1987). We found that age at college entry has a very powerful impact on transfer. Older college entrants, especially if they are over 30 years of age, are much less likely to transfer than students who enter college right out of high school. Differences in academic preparation among different age groups seem to explain little of the age gap in transfer.[14] This gap is explained mostly by differences by age in educational aspirations (particularly for those 21 and older at college entrance), external demands (particularly having children),[15] enrollment status, and college major.

That differences in social background, particularly SES, powerfully affect whether students transfer is of great concern, especially in light of the increasing role being given to community colleges as gateways to the baccalaureate. This inequality in transfer argues that it is not enough to get baccalaureate aspirants to the community college's open door. It is also necessary to ensure equality of opportunity for community college success (Lumina Foundation 2005). To reduce or even eliminate differences in transfer rate according to social background, we need to investigate the precise channels by which social background affects transfer processes.

We have seen that differences in high school academic preparation,[16] educational aspirations,[17] having children, and college major play an important role in mediating class, age, and racial-ethnic differences in transfer. Still, we are far from exhausting our analysis of these mediating processes. We need to learn more about how precisely having children reduces the likelihood of transfer. Moreover, even with all the mediating variables that we have analyzed, most of the impact of social class on transfer is left unexplained in NELS:88. To fill in this uncharted territory, future analyses need to examine the impact of institutional variables that we have not been able to capture in our analysis of the NELS:88 and BPS:90 data—for example, the extent to which a student's community college is committed both in word and deed to transfer; the readiness with which students are accepted by four-year colleges into their preferred programs and campuses; how many credits are accepted for transfer; and how much financial aid would-be transfer students receive from four-year colleges (Dougherty, 1994, 2002).

Although much analysis remains to be done before we fully understand why inequality of opportunity in transfer exists between community colleges and four-year colleges, we already have leads that policy makers should pursue. Clearly, we need to continue to improve high school preparation not only to ensure equality of access to college but also equality of opportunity within college (Dougherty 1996; Gladieux and Swail 2000; Rosenbaum 2001; Rothstein 2004). We also need to reduce the gap in aspirations at matriculation between community college entrants who are high and low in SES and younger and older in age (McDonough 1997; Terenzini, Cabrera, and Bernal 2001). In addition, we need to find ways to reduce the transfer gap between occupational majors and academic majors. Key in this regard is finding ways of providing better transfer counseling to occupational majors and making it easier for them to secure admission, financial aid, and credit acceptance at four-year colleges (Dougherty 2002, 326–27).

Appendix
Description for Data Tests Used

National Education Longitudinal Study of the 8th Grade

(NELS:88)

NELS:88/2000 began with a nationally representative sample of eighth graders in 1988 and followed them up in 1990, 1992, 1994, and 2000. For the baseline data, questions were asked of students and their parents, teachers, and high school principals, and data such as high school transcripts were collected from school records. All dropouts were retained in the study. The 1992 follow-up occurred when most sample members were in the second term of their senior year. At that point, the NELS:88 sample was freshened by adding more respondents in order to represent the high school class of 1992, allowing trend comparisons to the high school classes of 1972 and 1980 that were studied in the National Longitudinal Survey of the High School Class of 1972 (NLS-72) and High School and Beyond (HS&B). The postsecondary transcript-based version of NELS:88/2000 allowed us to look more accurately at which colleges students entered, the college courses and program choices that students made, and transfer rates among colleges. Overall, there were more than 12,000 observations in the NELS:88 sample, but the size of the public two-year college sample is 2,660.

Beginning Postsecondary Students Survey

Based on the 1990 National Postsecondary Student Aid Study (NPSAS:90), the Beginning Postsecondary Students Longitudinal Study (BPS:90) consisted of first-time beginners (FTBs) who enrolled in a postsecondary institution at any time between July 1, 1989, and June 30, 1990. The NPSAS:90 design involved a multistage probability sample of students enrolled in postsecondary institutions. To be eligible for participation in NPSAS:90, a postsecondary institution was required to satisfy several conditions. During the 1989–1990 academic year, the institution must have offered an educational program for persons who have completed secondary education; an academically, occupationally, or vocationally oriented program of study; access to persons other than those employed by the institution; more than just correspondence courses; and at least one program lasting at least three months or 300 contact hours. A student was NPSAS:90-eligible if he or she was enrolled in an eligible institution during the 1989–1990 academic year for one or more of the following purposes: taking course(s) for credit; participating in a degree or formal award program of at least three months' duration; and taking part in a vocationally specific program of at least three months' duration. Students were excluded regardless of whether they satisfied the above conditions if they enrolled solely in a high school program at an eligible postsecondary institution, enrolled only in correspondence courses or programs of less than three months' duration, or were taking courses only for remedial or avocational purposes without receiving credit.

Initially, the BPS:90 began with around 7,200 students of all ages entering college for the first time in fall 1989. These students were then followed up in spring 1994. Complete demographic and enrollment information up to and including the 1994 follow-up is available for 83% of the sample. Data restrictions, such as institution miscodings, reduce the sample to roughly 5,600 observations. Our analysis is focused on those students who entered public two-year colleges in fall 1989. As our measure of college entered, we used the colleges that students identified as their primary institution. This yielded a sample of 653 first-time community college students.

Notes

1. Grubb analyzed the National Longitudinal Survey of the High School Class of 1972 (NLS-72) and the High School and Beyond Survey (HSB). The NLS-72 questioned 19,001 high school seniors nationwide in spring 1972 and followed them up in the fall of 1973, 1974, 1976, 1979, and 1986. The HSB study followed 10,583 high school graduates in 1982, 1984, and 1986 (Green, Duggoni, and Ingels 1995).
2. In 1981, the proportion of college entrants entering community colleges was 44.6% among students with family incomes below $20,000 and 41.4% among those with family incomes between $20,000 and $30,000. For the same groups (using inflation-adjusted constant dollars) in 1998, the percentages were 46.7% and 43.1%, respectively. At the same time, the proportion entering community colleges dropped sharply for all those with family incomes above $30,000. For example, among those with family incomes between $60,000 and $100,000 (in 1981 dollars), the proportion dropped from 31.2% to 25.7% (McPherson and Schapiro, 1999, 22–23).
3. In fiscal years 2002 and 2003, tuition at public four-year colleges rose by 10%, while state need-based aid rose only 7% (Callan 2003, 3A; Young 2002).
4. For example, in the BPS:96, only 37% of the community college entrants said that their primary purpose was transfer to a four-year college (Hoachlander, Sikora, and Horn 2003, 13). At the same time, it is important to keep in mind that even students who are focused on acquiring job skills or subbaccalaureate credentials may still harbor the desire to eventually acquire a bachelor's degree. Among BPS:96 students who had a primary intention of receiving a subbaccalaureate degree, 19% also planned to transfer (15).
5. But even if there is no difference by social background in transfer rates, there would still be the problem that baccalaureate aspirants who enter community colleges are less likely to eventually receive bachelor's degrees than comparable students (in background, high school record, and educational and occupational aspirations) entering four-year colleges. For more on this, see Dougherty (1994, 2002).
6. For reviews of the literature on the extent and determinants of transfer, see Dougherty (1994, 2002) and Pascarella and Terenzini (2005).
7. The socioeconomic variable in BPS:90 includes a measure for family income that takes a radically different form according to the student's dependency status. For students who are financially dependent on their parents, the family income value plugged in is that of the parents. But for students who are financially independent, the family income value plugged in is their own. As a result of this specification, the SES variable that emerges behaves quite oddly, showing no impact on transfer rates.

8. One of the benefits of NELS:88 is the availability of students' postsecondary transcripts, which are supposedly less prone to recall and other reporting errors inherent in self-reported information. However, there is one potential problem with using transcripts, and this drawback is magnified for community college students. Students with abbreviated or incoherent enrollment spells or who attended college but did not attain a degree, which regrettably are commonly at public two-year colleges, are coded as "nonmajors" since their program of study could not be determined clearly from transcripts.

9. It should be noted that the BPS:90 data set does exclude students in noncredit remedial and avocational programs—that is, it excludes students who are not taking courses for credit, not enrolled in a degree or formal award program of more than three months' duration, or not taking an occupational program of more than three months' duration (Bradburn, Hurst, and Peng 2001, 2).

10. One of our reviewers raised the interesting question of whether the disappearance of the gender gap in transfer rates is due to the fall in male transfer as much or more than it is due to a rise in the female transfer rate. Unfortunately, we cannot answer this question without having access to the transfer rates for each gender. We have them from our analysis of the 1990s, but the studies of transfer in the 1970s and 1980s that we have consulted do not provide gender breakdowns. However, if the gender dynamics of transfer over the last 20 years are the same as the gender dynamics of college access (U.S. National Center for Education Statistics 2002, 225), then one could argue that the erasure of the gap has been primarily due to a rise in women's transfer rates rather than in a decline in men's. A reviewer also raised the question of whether our null finding was due to the fact that, unlike previous studies, ours also controlled for age, which is correlated with gender. However, this is unlikely to be the cause of our divergence from previous studies; we did not control for age in our analysis of NELS:88 and also found a nonsignificant impact of gender in that analysis.

11. However, a sharp decrease in the coefficient of a variable may not necessarily be significant if, as in the case of gender, the baseline effect was not large to begin with.

12. When we regress educational aspirations in NELS:88 on race (black and Hispanic dummy variables), both variables are positive, though only the black variable is statistically significant. And when we control for SES, gender, and age, the coefficients stay positive and become even larger and statistically significant. This shows the degree to which blacks especially have an aspirational advantage over whites of similar social class and gender. In saying this, we do not want to gainsay the powerful argument that this aspirational advantage lies more in idealistic hopes for education than in realistic plans for securing it (Mickelson 1990). Still, it is noteworthy that controlling for these attitudes strongly changes the impact of race on transfer rates.

13. We checked to see if the small coefficients and sometimes surprising signs of these variables might be due to a high degree of collinearity. However, the highest correlation between any two academic or social integration variables was 0.39, and most correlations were well below this, with the average being around 0.17.

14. The tentative tone of our conclusion is due to the measures of academic preparation that we had available in BPS:90 not being as good as we would like and put a limit on how strongly we can say that academic preparation plays little role in accounting for age differences in transfer.

15. This is certainly the case for students in the "21 to 30" and "over 30" age groups. Not surprisingly, having children explains much less of the negative impact on transfer of being age 19 to 20 simply because most students of that age do not have children. But for older students, being a parent is much more common and imposes a myriad of obstacles—presumably of desire, time, energy, money and locational flexibility—that make it difficult to pursue a baccalaureate degree.

16. Differences in academic preparation coming out of high school play an important role in explaining class and race differences in transfer but seemingly not age differences.

17. Differences in educational aspirations play an important role in explaining class and age differences in transfer, but race does not appear to have an impact.

References

Berkner, Lutz, Shirley Ho, and Emily Forrest Cataldi. 2002. *Descriptive summary of 1995–96 Beginning Postsecondary Students: Six years later. Statistical analysis report.* NCES 2003–151. Washington, DC: National Center for Education Statistics.

Bradburn, Ellen M., David G. Hurst, and Samuel Peng. 2001. Community college transfer rates to 4-year institutions using alternative definitions of transfer. *Education Statistics Quarterly 3* (3): 119–25.

Braxton John M., ed. 2000. *Reworking the student departure puzzle.* Nashville, TN: Vanderbilt University Press.

Brint, Steven G., and Jerome B. Karabel. 1989. *The diverted dream: Community colleges and the promise of educational opportunity in America, 1900–1985.* New York: Oxford University Press.

Cabrera, Alberto F., Steven M. LaNasa, and Kurt R. Burkum. 2001. *Pathways to a four-year degree: The higher education story of one generation.* University Park, PA: Center for the Study of Higher Education, Pennsylvania State University.

Callan, Patrick. 2003. A different kind of recession. *National Crosstalk.* http://www.highereducation.org/crosstalk/ct0103/front.shtml (accessed November 21, 2005). Cohen, Arthur M., and Florence B. Brawer. 2003. *The American community college.* 4th ed. San Francisco: Jossey-Bass.

Dougherty, Kevin J. 1994. *The contradictory college: The conflicting origins, outcomes, and futures of the community college.* Albany: State University of New York Press.

Dougherty, Kevin J. 1996. Opportunity to learn standards: A sociological critique. Special issue. *Sociology of Education 68:* 40–65.

Dougherty, Kevin J. 2002. The evolving role of the community college: Policy issues and research questions. In *Higher education: Handbook of theory and research,* ed. John Smart and William G. Tierney, 295–348. Dordrecht, Netherlands: Kluwer.

Dougherty, Kevin J., and Marianne Bakia. 2000. Community colleges and contract training. *Teachers College Record 102:* 197–243.

Ford Foundation. 1988. *An assessment of Urban Community Colleges Transfer Opportunities Program. The Ford Foundation's Second Stage Transfer Opportunity Awards. Final report.* New York: Ford Foundation. ERIC ED 293573.

Gladieux, Lawrence, and W. Scott Swail. Beyond access: Improving the odds of college success. *Phi Delta Kappan 81*: 688–92.

Green, Patricia, Bernard L. Duggoni, and Steven J. Ingels. 1995. *Trends among high school seniors, 1972–1992. National Educational Longitudinal Study of 1988*. NCES 95380. Washington, DC: National Center for Education Statistics.

Grubb, W. Norton. 1991. The decline of community college transfer rates: Evidence from National Longitudinal Surveys. *Journal of Higher Education 62*: 194–217.

Grubb, W. Norton. 2002. Learning and earning in the middle, part I: National studies. *Economics of Education Review 21*: 299–321.

Hagedorn, Linda Serra, Hye Sun Moon, Scott Cypers, William E. Maxwell, and Jaime Lester, n.d. *Transfer between community colleges and four-year colleges: The all-American game*. Los Angeles: Transfer and Retention in Urban Community College Students, University of Southern California. http://www.usc.edu/dept/education/truccs/Papers/baseball.pdf (accessed November 21, 2005).

Hebel, Sara. 2000. States without affirmative action focus on community-college transfers. *Chronicle of Higher Education 46* (38): A35–37.

Hoachlander, Gary, Anna C. Sikora, and Laura Horn. 2003. *Community college students: Goals, academic preparation, and outcomes*. NCES 2003–164. Washington, DC: National Center for Education Statistics.

Ignash, Jan, and Barbara Townsend. 2001. Statewide transfer and articulation policies. In *Community colleges: Policy in the future context*, ed. Barbara Townsend and Susan Twombly, 173–92. Westport, CT: Ablex.

Kane, Thomas J., and Cecilia R. Rouse. 1999. The community college: Educating students at the margin between college and work. *Journal of Economic Perspectives 13* (1): 63–84.

Kienzl, Gregory S. 2004. *The triple helix of education and earnings: The effect of schooling, work, and pathways on the economic outcomes of community college students*. PhD diss., Teachers College, Columbia Univ.

Kojaku, Lawrence K., and Anne-Marie Nunez. 1998. *Descriptive summary of 1995–96 Beginning Postsecondary Students*. NCES 1999–030. Washington, DC: National Center for Education Statistics.

Lee, Valerie, and Kenneth Frank. 1990. Student characteristics that facilitate the transfer from two-year to four-year colleges. *Sociology of Education 63*: 178–93.

Lumina Foundation for Higher Education. 2005. *Achieving the dream: Colleges count*, http://www.luminafoundation.org/grants/atdfaqs.html (accessed November 21, 2005).

Marcotte, David E., Thomas Bailey, Carey Borkoski, and Greg S. Kienzl. 2005. The returns of a community college education: Evidence from the National Education Longitudinal Survey. *Educational Evaluation and Policy Analysis 27*: 157–75.

McCormick, Alex. 1997. *Transfer behavior among Beginning Postsecondary Students 1989–94*, NCES 97–266. Washington, DC: National Center for Education Statistics.

McDonough, Patricia. 1997. *Choosing colleges: How social class and schools structure opportunity*. Albany: State University of New York Press.

McPherson, Michael S., and Morton O. Schapiro. 1998. *The student aid game*. Princeton, NJ: Princeton University Press.

McPherson, Michael S., and Morton O. Schapiro. 1999. *Reinforcing stratification in American higher education: Some disturbing trends*. Stanford, CA: National Center for Postsecondary Improvement.

Mercer, Joye. 1992. States turn to community colleges as route to bachelor's degree as 4-year campuses fate tight budgets and overcrowding. *Chronicle of Higher Education*, May 6.

Mickelson, Roslyn Arlin. 1990. The attitude-achievement paradox among black adolescents. *Sociology of Education 63*: 44–61.

Pascarella, Ernest T., and Patrick T. Terenzini. 2005. *How college affects students*, 2nd ed. San Francisco: Jossey-Bass.

Perin, Dolores, and Carolyn Charron. Forthcoming. "Lights just click on every day": Academic preparedness and remediation in community colleges. In *Defending the community college equity agenda*, ed. Thomas Bailey and Vanessa Smith Morest. Baltimore: Johns Hopkins University. Press.

Rosenbaum, James E. 2001. *Beyond college for all: Career paths for the forgotten half*. New York: Russell Sage Foundation.

Rothstein, Richard. 2004. Class and the classroom. *American School Board Journal 191* (10): 17–21.

Surette, Brian J. 2001. Transfer from two-year to four-year college: An analysis of gender differences. *Economics of Education Review 20*: 151–63.

Terenzini, Patrick T, Alberto F. Cabrera, and Elena M. Bernal. 2001. *Swimming against the tide: The poor in American higher education*. New York: College Board.

Tinto, Vincent. 1993. *Leaving college: Rethinking the causes and cures of student attrition*. 2nd ed. Chicago: University of Chicago Press.

United States National Center for Education Statistics. 2002. *Digest of education statistics, 2002*. Washington, DC: Government Printing Office.

Velez, William, and Rajshekhar G. Javalgi. 1987. Two-year college to four-year college: The likelihood of transfer. *American Journal of Education 96*: 81–94.

Wellman, Jane V. 2002. *State policy and community college-baccalaureate transfer*. San Jose, CA: National Center for Public Policy and Higher Education.

Young, Jeffrey. 2002. Public-college tuition jumps at highest rate in 10 years. *Chronicle of Higher Education*, October 22.

18
Mass Higher Education and Its Critics

PAUL ATTEWELL AND DAVID LAVIN

In previous chapters we discussed whether going to college pays off financially for women, and whether a mother's college experience improves the educational chances of her children. We also traced out some of the mechanisms whereby maternal education benefited the children of the next generation. Along the way we considered whether racial minorities and poorer students also shared in the positive benefits of access to higher education, when they did make it as far as college. In those analyses, college going turned out to be a generally positive force, both for women and for their children.

For the last decade, however, public debate about higher education has had a different and much more negative tone than one would suspect from our largely upbeat findings. Some commentators are convinced that the United States made a terrible mistake in opening wide the doors to higher education. In their opinion, academe's efforts to become more inclusive have backfired, cheapening degrees and harming the institutions we cherish. They believe that colleges are awash with under-prepared students who have little chance of graduating or getting decent jobs. Are they right? In this chapter we will delve more deeply into those criticisms. We begin by reviewing the expansion of higher education, discussing the forces behind that growth, and noting how the demographic characteristics of undergraduates have changed over time. After providing this context, we turn to the specific criticisms of educational growth, assembling factual evidence that addresses several arguments against what has come to be called mass higher education.

The Development of Mass Higher Education

Americans have a seemingly insatiable thirst for education. Early in the twentieth century, more and more youths sought a high school diploma, at that time a mark of distinction. Over time, graduating from high school slowly changed from being something exceptional to the norm. As late as 1940, only a quarter of American adults had completed high school. By 1970, about half were high school graduates, and this portion rose to roughly three-quarters of the nation by 1990.[1] According to the U.S. Census (U.S. Census Bureau 2005), nowadays only 12 percent of young people fail to graduate from high school.[2]

Enrollment in colleges and universities similarly grew throughout the twentieth century. Under-graduate enrollments doubled from 1970 to the present. By 2005, nearly 15 million Americans were enrolled as undergraduates.[3] Currently, almost two-thirds of all high school graduates begin college in the fall semester immediately after high school,[4] but this number understates how wide the doors to college have opened, As Figure 18.1 shows, over 80 percent of a recent high school cohort had started college within about eight years of graduating from high school.[5]

Critics use the phrase "college for all" when they talk about this expansion of college access. The term is an exaggeration—not all youths go to college—but it vividly expresses the idea that the proportion of high school graduates entering college has sharply increased in recent decades, and suggests that

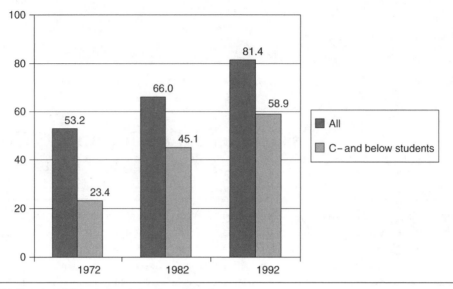

Figure 18.1 Percentage of high school graduates who went to college.

Sources: National Longitudinal Study of the High School Class of 1972 (2006), High School and Beyond (2006), National Education Longitudinal Study of 1988 (2006).

more students with weak academic skills are attending college, as seen in Figure 18.1. Unfortunately, the "for all" rhetoric also obscures substantial inequalities in college access and educational attainment associated with race and ethnicity and class and income. Recent evidence indicates that black students are about 27 percent more likely than whites to be retained in grade between kindergarten and twelfth grade[6] and that twice as many African American students, and four times as many Hispanic students, drop out of high school as whites.[7] Among students who do successfully graduate from high school, 69 percent of whites immediately transition to college, compared with 60 percent of blacks and 58 percent of Hispanics (National Center for Education Statistics 2005).[8]

Racial and ethnic gaps in college attendance have fluctuated over time; the story is not one of uninterrupted progress. From 1972 to 1977, there was no measurable gap among whites, blacks, and Hispanics in the proportion of high school graduates going on to college immediately. After 1977 enrollments continued to climb, but minority enrollments fell behind those of whites. Around 1983, the gap began to narrow again. Currently, on this measure of immediate college going, the black–white gap is roughly 9 percentage points and the Hispanic–white gap is of similar size.[9]

Income or class-based inequalities in college attendance and educational attainment are much greater than those for race and ethnicity. In 2003, students from low-income families were 77 percent as likely to graduate from high school as students from affluent families. Among those high school graduates, youths from poor families were 67 percent as likely to continue into college. Overall, the chances of a youth from a poor family earning a BA by age twenty-four are only 22 percent of the chances for a youth from an affluent family.[10]

These very large class-based differences in access to higher education have not shifted much in the last thirty years. Clifford Adelman (2004, pp. 23–24) finds "a consistent spread of 40 or more percentage points in access rates." David Ellwood and Thomas J. Kane (2000, p. 283) come to an even more pessimistic conclusion: "The role of family background . . . seems to have increased over time." Thomas G. Mortenson (2005, p. 12) identifies "a sharp deterioration in bachelor's degree completion equity for students from the bottom family income quartile since the late 1970s." The important point is that there has been little or no progress in overcoming class-based educational disadvantage, despite decades of expansion in higher education. Although lower-class students are attending college in ever-greater numbers, students from more-privileged backgrounds are outpacing them (Karen and Dougherty 2005).

Notwithstanding these important class and ethnic disparities, each generation of Americans has accumulated more years of education than the preceding one, and projections suggest that the rate of college going will continue to increase in the decades ahead (Day and Bauman 2000; Wirt et al. 2004).[11] Most scholars have viewed this expansion of higher education in a positive light, crediting the prosperity of the United States to its high levels of human capital (for example, Goldin and Katz 2001).

There is less agreement about the causes of educational expansion. One standard explanation emphasizes the changing structure of the economy, which alters the demand for different kinds of labor. As production has shifted from agriculture to manufacturing to services, the dominant trend has been toward jobs with greater skills and complexity, necessitating more highly educated workers (Attewell 1987; Berman, Bound, and Machin 1998; Levy and Murnane 2004). College enrollments have responded to that need. A related thesis is that technological change is skill-biased: in particular, the recent spread of computer technologies increases demand for, and raises the relative wages of, more-educated employees, generating greater income inequality.[12]

Some sociologists have offered a different reading of the growth of education, one that stresses competition between different social strata over access to privileged jobs, and the importance of access to education for upward mobility, both for individuals and for groups. The German sociologist Max Weber (1922/1968, 1000) viewed educational credentials as certificates that guaranteed entrance to privileged occupations, sinecures whose superior pay was governed more by status than performance. Education, in Weber's view, allows certain groups to monopolize advantageous positions and to exclude potential competitors who cannot attain sufficient education. An American sociologist, Randall Collins (1979), has updated and extended those insights, arguing that the knowledge content of formal education is arbitrary and has little to do with the jobs that credentialed employees actually do. (Real skills are learned on the job.) However, education remains critical for personal mobility because so many jobs demand a college diploma or more specific credentials. Government colludes in and reinforces this credentialism, Collins argued, by issuing licenses requiring college course work for many occupations, from hair cutting to child minding to selling real estate.

From this sociological perspective, access to college is a key resource in a contest between more- and less-privileged strata for access to better-paid jobs. The expansion of higher education reflects increased demand from competing social strata, rather than the technical needs of the economy. In the nineteenth century, as the masses recognized that better jobs required a high school diploma and agitated for free public high schools for their children, more affluent families sent their children beyond high school, to college. A century later, when the masses pushed for affordable higher education in public universities, the affluent clamored for access to private colleges, and the more prestigious jobs began requiring higher degrees: MBAs, MAs, LLBs, and so on. This contest between classes continues today: affluent families can more easily live near superior high schools or pay for private schooling, prep courses, tutoring, extracurricular activities, or other forms of educational enrichment that provide an advantage to their children when they apply to selective colleges. They can better afford to pay tuition and support their children through the many years of higher education and graduate school. This dynamic generates a never-ending game of educational catch-up, fueling enrollment growth in higher education and status competition among colleges.

Viewed in this fashion, higher education on the whole reproduces or reinforces class inequality. However, at various points in time expanded access to higher education can also facilitate social mobility for some disadvantaged individuals and groups. After World War Two, the GI Bill paid the costs of attending college for veterans. More than 2 million young men, many of whom would not otherwise have been able to afford college, took advantage of that opportunity.[13] After graduation, they swelled the ranks of an expanding middle class. Veterans' benefits have been legislated after each war since then, most recently in 2004, drawing successive cohorts into higher education. The growth of the African American middle class has similarly depended on access to higher education.[14] Since the civil rights era, the number of black students entering college each year has risen to roughly 2 million; currently about 17 percent of African American adults are college graduates (Attewell et al. 2004).

One distinctive feature of America's educational system that is especially important for social mobility is its provision of "second chance" routes to educational attainment. Students who drop out of high school may later earn a high school equivalency, the GED. High school students whose weak grades preclude entry into a four-year college have the option of attending a community college, with possible transfer to a four-year institution. Students who lack academic skills can also take remedial courses in college. Finally, course credits earned in one college or university can usually be transferred to another. Taken together, these arrangements provide students who have performed poorly in high school, or who have interrupted their college studies, with the opportunity to go back and complete their education at a later time and in a different institution. This second-chance access to college keeps hopes of social advancement alive. As a result, "Educational attainment has ceased to be fixed in early adulthood, especially among members of racial and ethnic minorities" (Day and Bauman 2000, p. 4).

In recent decades, the expanding demand for higher education has also been fueled by the insecurity of private-sector employment. Employed adults respond to the precariousness of modern careers by returning to college to develop new skills or to increase their credentials. Displaced workers retrain in college for fields where employment is expanding. Consequently, higher education is no longer the preserve of eighteen-to-twenty-five-year-olds: more than half of today's undergraduates are older than the stereotypical college student (National Center for Education Statistics 1997).

In summary, going to college has become a key part of the American dream, the most important step on the road to a rewarding job and a comfortable life. Expanded access to college offers hope of advancement to people of all ages and backgrounds: a shot at upward mobility for young people from less-advantaged families, and a route of recovery for displaced and underqualified workers. It is also central for success among young people from affluent families, where college attendance has become almost universal.

Not everyone embraces this dream. Some critics have viewed this expansion of higher education as a nightmare, a plunge into intellectual mediocrity and institutional decline. In the opinion of other commentators, the dream is a harmful fantasy, a false promise of upward mobility made to disadvantaged students who are unlikely to succeed.

What the Critics of "College for All" Say

Criticism of mass higher education is far from monolithic. All parts of the political spectrum, from the Marxist left to the conservative right, are represented. Nor is politics necessarily the motivation; sometimes nostalgia seems to be the driving force behind criticism. Several commentators, for example, bemoan the erosion of the traditional curriculum. William Bennett (1994) complains about a retreat from the study of ethical and civic virtues, mainstays of the classical liberal arts curriculum. Allan Bloom (1988) decries the decline of the "great books" approach. Both dislike the emergence of new disciplines such as sociology, the spread of vocational majors in college, and the expansion of the literary canon to include what they view as less-distinguished works by women and members of ethnic minorities.

Unfortunately, it is a short step from nostalgia to condemning the new, and another short step to blaming educational changes on the kinds of students now attending college. A widespread complaint is that the college curriculum has been "dumbed down" because colleges have admitted students who lack the skills or intelligence to cope with a rigorous curriculum (Gray and Herr 1996; Harwood 1997; MacDonald 1997, 1998, 1999; Stanfield 1997; Traub 1995). In our opinion, blaming disadvantaged students for educational change is unfair. Many of the developments that traditionalists decry—from modifications in the canon of "great books" to the spread of preprofessional majors and majors in the social and behavioral sciences to the deemphasis on moral education and the spread of postmodernism—were pioneered at elite colleges. Several of these innovations emerged during decades when student applications to those institutions were increasing, and when top colleges were becoming more selective, demanding higher intellectual standards from applicants. Those educational changes therefore had nothing to do with a decline in student quality. Nevertheless, in the popular media, curricular changes, along with grade inflation, high dropout rates, and the prevalence of remedial course work, are all read as symptoms of a malaise in higher education and are often seen to be results of lower intellectual standards caused by wider access to public universities.

If intellectual standards have been debased, and if colleges routinely graduate students who cannot write a coherent sentence, as Stanley Fish (2005) asserts, one would expect the value of a degree to be undermined That claim was made as early as 1971, when Vice President Spiro Agnew ("Bowker for Berkeley," *Time*, April 26, 1971, 81) talked disparagingly of "100,000 devalued diplomas." Others argued that the expanded production of college graduates exceeded the number of suitable job openings leading to undervalued and underemployed degree holders (Berg 1970; Freeman 1976). Indeed, economic theory would lead one to expect a fall in the economic value of a degree from oversupply or from a drop in quality. We will examine whether that devaluation actually came to pass in a following section.

As college enrollments climbed, a quite different type of criticism from the left focused on equity issues, noting that students from disadvantaged backgrounds were disproportionately found in two-year associate's degree programs at community colleges. Associate's degrees are seen as inferior to bachelor's degrees. Thus, what at first seemed a democratization of higher education was arguably transformed into a kind of academic apartheid, whereby students from poorer backgrounds were relegated to a second-class education (Brint and Karabel 1989; Clark 1960; Dougherty 1994). According to such critics, students enrolled in two-year institutions might not have understood that they might get a lesser education. It takes students several semesters in a community college before some realize that they aren't going to get as far as a BA degree. By then, their aspirations have been lowered, in a process that Burton Clark (1960) terms "cooling out."

This notion that educators are systematically misleading disadvantaged students has been reiterated over the years. In a recent version, scholars charge that poorly prepared students in community colleges don't realize that their remedial courses carry no credit toward a degree, and that college staff members fail to alert them to this fact. Thus, weak students get bogged down taking multiple remedial courses that don't advance them toward a degree, leading many to give up and drop out. Remedial education, in this view, is a hoax perpetrated by educators upon academically weak students who will be unlikely ever to graduate (Deil-Amen and Rosenbaum 2002; Rosenbaum 2001).

One striking complaint about expanded access to college is that it has undermined the work ethic of students still in high school. If any high school graduate can gain admission into college, no matter how badly he or she performs in high school, then what incentive remains for students to study hard during their school years? "Many low-achieving high school seniors believe they can attain a college degree," James Rosenbaum has written (2001, 58). "Students who believe they can attain a college degree in spite of low achievement . . . exert little effort in high school." According to Heather MacDonald (1998), "But the greatest tragedy of open admissions occurred . . . in the city's public schools. CUNY's decision to admit any breathing human being with a record of occasional high school attendance proved a deathblow to the city's schools. Already underperforming in the 1960s, the schools had no incentive to strive."

Some of these criticisms about the expansion of higher education are too subjective or complex to evaluate empirically,[15] but we can extract five hard claims concerning American higher education that can be tested against the factual record:

1   Did the value of a college degree go down as student enrollments increased?
2   Are graduation rates abysmally low, especially for students with poor high school preparation?
3   Are community colleges a dead end, academically and occupationally?
4   Does remedial education imply a lack of academic standards in college?
5   Has increased access to college undermined the work ethic of students in high school?

We will marshal evidence to answer each of these questions in the following sections.

The Changing Payoff from College Attendance

There is a broad consensus among social scientists that college degrees have a substantial payoff in terms of annual and lifetime earnings (Boesel and Fredland 1999; Card 1999; Day and Newberger 2002). College attendance paid off economically for the CUNY and NLSY populations. In this chapter we will document that college pays off for those entering college with weak high school backgrounds in addition to those who enter with straight A's; and for recipients of associate's as well as bachelor's degrees. College even pays off for students who attend but fail to graduate. As one reviewer of the literature put it, "While it is clear that investment in a college degree, especially for those students in the lowest income brackets, is a financial burden, the long-term benefits to individuals as well as to society at large, appear to far outweigh the costs" (Porter 2002).

Despite a steady growth in the proportion of high school students continuing on to college since the 1960s, and the burgeoning numbers of college students and graduates, the economic value of a BA degree has climbed over time. In Table 18.1 we summarize a thirty-year span of education and income data, drawing upon the U.S. Census Bureau's annual Current Population Surveys (CPS). The data in this table are limited to full-time year-round workers, but we also analyzed data for the years 1963 to 2003 that included part-time and part-year employees, and the same patterns prevailed. Between 1974 and 1990 the incomes of men with BAs who worked full-time year-round grew by 6.1 percent, adjusted for inflation. Between 1991 and 2003, male BA incomes increased by another 20.9 percent. The incomes of full-time working women with BAs rose even more dramatically over the same periods, reflecting ever greater numbers of women college graduates who stay in the labor force through their childbearing years and hold professional jobs.

College students who enter college but don't go as far as a BA have also experienced income growth over the last three decades. Prior to 1990, the surveys classified persons with AA degrees along with those who had some college short of a BA degree. Between 1974 and 1990, the incomes of full-time year-round male workers in this category stagnated (–0.4 percent in real dollars), although those of women grew by 16 percent. Since 1990, real incomes for men with an AA degree and those with some college short of a degree have risen by 9.5 percent and 6.8 percent, respectively.

Full-time year-round employees who were high school graduates have fared less well than college goers over the last three decades. Male incomes for these high school graduates dropped by 8.4 percent, adjusted for inflation, between 1974 and 1990, and have risen by 7.8 percent since. However, the mean income for women high school graduates who work full-time year round has grown substantially over this period.

The largest drop in income over the last four decades has occurred among men who did not complete high school. As Table 18.1 shows, the mean income for this group dropped by 16.1 percent in inflation-corrected terms between 1974 and 1990; it has declined another 1.6 percent since then. This plunge in the real income of the least-educated workers means that the gap between college-educated and the least-educated workers has widened considerably over time.

In sum, there is little empirical basis for the idea that college credentials have become devalued over the last four decades, either because more people, or less able students, were going to college.

Table 18.1 Mean Income by Educational Attainment for Male and Female Full-Time Year Round Workers, 1974 to 2003

Education Level	Percentage Mean Income Change 1974 to 1990 (Inflation-Adjusted)	Percentage Mean Income Change 1991 to 2003 (Inflation-Adjusted)	Mean Income in 2003
Men Twenty-five Years Old and Over			
Less than ninth grade	−12.1	−4.6	$23,972
Ninth to twelfth grade	−16.1	−1.6	$29,100
High school graduate (includes GED)	−8.4	7.8	$38,331
Some college or associate's degree	−0.4	—	—
Some college, no degree	—	9.5	$46,332
Associate's degree	—	6.8	$48,683
Bachelor's degree	6.1	20.9	$69,913
Women Twenty-five Years Old and Over			
Less than ninth grade	3.0	28.6	$20,979
Ninth to twelfth grade	5.2	8.7	$21,426
High school graduate (includes GED)	10.1	13.5	$27,956
Some college or associate's degree	16.0	—	—
Some college, no degree	—	10.5	$31,655
Associate's degree	—	10.8	$36,528
Bachelor's degree	25.6	23.8	$47,910

Sources: U.S. Census Bureau, Historical Income Tables P-32, P-33, P-34, and P-35 (Derived from Current Population Survey, Annual Social and Economic Survey) (U.S. Census Bureau 2004b).

Note: Owing to changes in educational attainment questions in 1991, data from 1974 to 1990 are not completely comparable with data from 1991 to 2003.

That idea emerged around the time the baby boom generation entered the labor market in the early 1970s, and indeed the earnings of college graduates did drop temporarily at that time. However, the incomes of college-educated employees recovered and they have been growing in the decades since then. Employees with college education earn considerably more today than their counterparts did in the 1960s and '70s, and the gap between the economic worth of a degree and that of a high school diploma has grown steadily wider.[16] Economic theory suggests that this pattern would not have developed if there had been a plunge in the quality of degree holders.

Nevertheless, critics of "college for all" remain convinced that many students currently attending college will not benefit economically from college. Rosenbaum (2001), for example, focuses on students with weak high school achievement, and argues vehemently that they are very unlikely to gain from going to college. As evidence, he reports that the earnings of college graduates with weak high school GPAs trail those of college students who had strong GPAs in high school. That may be true, but this is not a good yardstick for assessing the value of college attendance. A better comparison contrasts weak students who went to college with classmates with identical high school grades who never went beyond high school. Did the weak students who continued into college fare better economically than their counterparts?

In Table 18.2 we provide this contrast, analyzing national income data solely for people who graduated high school with a C average or worse. When evaluating the value of going to college, it is important to allow enough time elapse after college for people to establish their careers.[17] Fortunately, the NLSY surveys provide earnings data for full-time workers in the year 2000, by which time the people in the sample were all thirty-five or older.

Table 18.2: Long-Term Payoff to College Attendance for Students with a C Average or Worse During High School

Earnings	Estimated Value from Conventional Regression	Estimated Value from Matched Sample
Effect of college attendance, including nongraduates (log earnings)	.1290***	.1284***
Mean personal earnings (high school only)	$24,851.91	$25,766.75
Mean personal earnings (college)	$28,273.61	$29,297.10
Number of cases	N = 2,598	N = 1,514
Effect of college attendance for nongraduates only (log earnings)	.0992***	.1071***
Mean personal earnings (high school only)	$23,537.97	$26,166.62
Mean personal earnings (incomplete college)	$25,992.66	$29,124.51
Number of cases	N = 1,814	N = 992
Effect of community college attendance, including nongraduates (log earnings)	.1346***	.1550***
Mean personal earnings (high school only)	$24,478.89	$25,900.05
Mean personal earnings (community college)	$28,006.39	$30,243.27
Number of cases	N = 2,027	N = 1,032

Source: NLSY79.

Note: The log coefficients may read as percentage differences, so a .129 coefficient implies that those attending college earned on average 12.9 percent more than those who did not attend, controlling for differences in family background and high school preparation. *p < 0.05; **p < 0.01; ***p < 0.001.

These analyses assess the effects of college attendance after removing the influence of several confounding factors such as IQ, psychological orientation, race, sex, and family background.[18] In effect, we estimate the earnings of two students, both of whom had a C or below high school average and who were equivalent in intellectual and social respects, except that one went to college and the other did not.

The top panel compares academically weak students who went to college, including those who did not finish college, with otherwise-equivalent students who only completed high school. The ones who went to college earned about 13 percent more per year, on average. The middle panel of Table 18.2 compares academically weak students who attended college but failed to obtain a degree with equivalent students who only completed high school. Even these college dropouts earned about 10 percent more than equivalent high school graduates. The bottom panel examines community college attendance separately, because some critics appear especially skeptical about the economic prospects of weak students who enter community college. This contrast includes all C or worse students who attended community college, whether or not they completed a degree. On average, the C or worse students who attended community college were earning between 13 percent and 15 percent more than their counterparts who only finished high school. All these annual earnings differences are statistically significant.

These longitudinal analyses that followed students until they were thirty-five or older document that, on average, there is a substantial economic benefit when students with weak high school records attend college. This payoff is evident even among those who failed to graduate with a degree. Critics' claims that students who are "not college material" would have been better off economically had they not attended college are contradicted by these analyses.

In providing these analyses, we do not mean to downplay the problem of poor academic performance in high school. Many students with low high school GPAs have to struggle to keep up with college work, and students would progress better in college if they improved their academic performance in high school. Nevertheless, academically weak high school students are correct in believing they will gain economically from going to college. Their average income gain is impressive. Thus, contrary to critics' assertions, career counselors in high school are not doing weaker students a disservice when they encourage them to aspire to college.

Some critics argue that our nation should build new systems of vocational education, revive the apprenticeship system, or build bridges from high school to work, to better serve the career needs of high school graduates who are not academically inclined. Those are sensible proposals. At present, however, those academically weak high school students who do go to college are gaining economically by attending college. It makes no sense to discourage them from continuing to college, and it is incorrect to assert that they are wasting their time there.

College Graduation Rates

A recent front-page headline in the *New York Times* trumpets a "college dropout boom." The governor of New York State proposes rewarding colleges according to the percentage of their students who graduate from the institution on time, and advocates withholding some aid until after students graduate to encourage speedy completion.[19] The authors of such policy initiatives and others like them justify the policies by citing alarming statistics: only 53 percent of BA students nationwide are graduating from their institution within five years, and 30 percent have dropped out of college in that time period (National Center for Education Statistics 2004, p. 64).

These numbers remind us of Benjamin Disraeli's complaint: "Lies, damned lies, and statistics." They are misleading because many of those college dropouts haven't actually dropped out, and those "on time" figures are meaningless. They simply fail to capture how college going works in the twenty-first century. First, students no longer stick with one institution for their whole undergraduate career, for "roughly 60 percent of bachelor's degree recipients have attended more than one school as undergraduates since the 1970s" (Adelman 2004, p. 45). It therefore makes no sense to reward or punish a college on the basis of the percentage of its entering students who ultimately graduate from that same institution. It's not the institution's fault if students move out of state or trade up to a more prestigious alma mater.

Second, as we demonstrated in our time-to-degree analyses, many students who complete their BA take much longer than four years. Some students cannot find the right courses to fulfill all their requirements in eight semesters. Others work part-time and compensate by taking a lighter course load each semester. They are willing to trade off an extended time-to-degree for earning money, which is not surprising in an era of skyrocketing tuition at public as well as private universities. Yet other students cycle in and out of college, alternating between work or family responsibilities and going to school. (In Adelman's [1999] phrase, these are "stopouts" rather than dropouts. Sara Goldrick-Rab [2006] describes poor and working-class students as "swirling" in and out of college.) Finally, certain majors—including engineering and architecture, health sciences, and education—take longer and require more credits than in previous decades (Adelman 1999, p. 117).

This leaves us with two questions: How long should researchers wait before counting graduates? And whom should we count as a student when we calculate success rates? If one decides these questions in one direction, college graduation rates will look atrocious; if one makes different choices, graduation rates will look much healthier.

The dismal numbers on graduation rates that the media and politicians are responding to tend to measure BA graduation rates four or five years after college entry, However, a recent government study reports that only two-thirds of college graduates complete their BAs within six years, and 19 percent of students complete their BAs more than ten years after their high school graduation (National Center for Education Statistics 2003, p. 23). Thus, measuring graduation rates after five years overlooks a large number of people who do ultimately graduate. Moreover, these delayed graduates are disproportionately poorer and minority graduates, and women. Using a four- or five-year cutoff point, as most policymakers do, implies that these students have failed educationally, when they have simply graduated late.

The second issue—whom one counts as a student when calculating dropout rates—might seem straightforward, but it is not. One highly publicized claim is that only 14 percent of weak high school students ever graduate from college: an "86 percent chance of failure."[20] That remarkably high figure comes about by counting as college failures high school seniors with low grades who said they planned to attend college, but never actually enrolled. When most high school seniors report having college plans, there is a certain social pressure on the remaining seniors to say they are planning to go to college as well. But if those low-achieving seniors never set foot in an institution of higher learning, does it make sense to count them in a college failure rate? We don't think so.

At the other extreme, Adelman (2004) has argued against counting, for purposes of analyzing completion, "incidental students," those who enter college but fail to complete more than ten credits as college students. In his view, including in graduation statistics students who are just trying out college provides a misleading view of how well colleges are performing. Omitting those incidental students lifts the national BA graduation rate from 49 percent to 67 percent (Adelman 2004, p. 27). Evidently a lot of students briefly try out college and decide it is not for them.

In calculating college graduation rates for weak students, we have steered between these two extremes. We count only students who actually enrolled in college to get a degree; however, we include all college enrollees, even those whose stay in college was very brief. Use of that definition results in the graduation rates reported in Table 18.3.

Each of these surveys indicates that the proportion of weak students who complete a college degree is much larger than the 13.9 percent graduation figure that critics cite. The survey data also show that graduation rates have increased in recent years: the most recent survey, which followed the high school class of 1992, suggests somewhere between 39 percent and 52 percent of weak students who entered college earned a degree within about eight years of high school. However those figures are truncated: if those students were followed for more than eight years, their graduation rate would likely be higher. Our best estimate is that somewhere between 50 and 65 percent of C students in the class of 1992 will graduate with degrees in the longer run.[21] That strikes us as good news, especially when it is combined with the earnings data presented earlier that show that the students who fail to complete

Table 18.3 Alternative Estimates of College Graduation Rates, by Survey; Percentage of Students who Completed a College Degree (AA or Higher)

Survey		All Students	C Average or Below Students
NLSY79 survey—taken approximately twenty years after high school graduation around 1979			
1. (Self-report)	College entrants	60.9	33.9
High School and Beyond survey—taken ten years after high school graduation in 1982			
2. (Transcripts)	College entrants	58.0	25.2
3. (Self-report)	College entrants	60.7	30.3
NELS88 survey—taken approximately eight years after high school graduation in 1992			
4. (Transcripts)	College entrants	64.4	39.3
5. (Self-report)	College entrants	68.2	51.6

Source: Authors' calculations.

Note: All analyses in this table are limited to high school students who indicated their intention to complete a degree and then attended college, if only briefly. "C and below" is defined as less than or equal to a 2.0 GPA or a 75 average in twelfth grade. The 1979 to 2000 waves of the NLSY are weighted by the normalized person weight for 1979. The NELS88 analyses use a normalized panel weight for base year and fourth panel.

college still earn more than similar students who never entered college. Allowing academically weak students into college is therefore no "con game."

The Value of Community Colleges

Enrollment at public two-year institutions, often called community colleges, has grown even faster than at four-year colleges. Today about 42 percent of undergraduates begin their education at a community college (Dougherty 2002). These institutions are particularly important for the educational careers of poorer students. They are also the places where most low-achieving students enroll after high school, if they enter college at all.

As mentioned previously, community colleges were roundly criticized in the 1970s and thereafter for shunting working-class students into associate of arts, or AA, degree programs that led to less-rewarding occupations (Bowles and Gintis 1976; Brint and Karabel 1989; Dougherty 1987, 1994; Karabel 1972; Zwerling 1976). Although most community colleges provided an academic track as well as a vocational one, so that promising students could carry credits on to a four-year institution, critics argued that few students were actually following that route (Alba and Lavin 1981; Anderson 1984; Velez 1985). Some were also skeptical of the value of the sub-baccalaureate degrees that community colleges provided (Breneman and Nelson 1981; Monk-Turner 1990; Pincus 1986).

Community colleges have changed a lot since the 1970s, partly in response to earlier complaints. Many have expanded the academic channel that allows students to transfer into a BA program, urging more students to take the academic courses needed for transfer. Using national data, Adelman (2004, p. vi) reports that the transfer rate increased from 28 percent for the high school class of 1972 to 36 percent for the class of 1992. Once we control for demographic characteristics and high school preparation, we find that students who transfer from a community college into a four-year college fare just as well in terms of BA completion as similar students who started at four-year colleges (see Table 18.4).

In addition, transfers from a community college who complete the BA earn as much as graduates who spent all their college career in a four-year college (see Table 18.5). For this subgroup of transfers, there does not seem to be a disadvantage from starting at a two-year institution, other than the important fact that it takes roughly two and a half years longer to get to the BA if one starts in a junior college than if one starts in a four-year college.

Community college students who transfer into BA programs are success stories, but what about the rest of the student body at two-year colleges? Most do not transfer. At first glance, it looks as though students at community colleges are much less likely to earn a degree than students enrolled in four-year colleges: in national NLSY data, only 24 percent of community college entrants receive a degree, compared with 60 percent of students who a entered four-year college. However, community colleges teach the most economically disadvantaged students, and those with the worst high school records. When we compare the progress of students at community colleges with those at four-year colleges

Table 18.4 Percentage of Community College Transfers who Earned a BA

	Unadjusted Percentage with BA	Estimated Percentage with BA, from a Conventional Regression	Estimated Percentage with BA, from Propensity Matched Sample
Transferred from a two-year college	48.9***	56.9 n.s.	49.1 n.s.
Started at a four-year college	59.5	59.0	49.9
Number of cases	2,766	2,766	1,994

Source: NLSY79 cohort, Men and Women.

*p < 0.05; **p < 0.01; ***p < 0.001; n.s. = not statistically significant.

Table 18.5 Log Earnings for BA Recipients who Transferred from a Two-Year College, Compared with BA Recipients who Started at a Four-Year College for Full-Time Workers, NLSY Men and Women

	Unadjusted Percentage Gap in Earnings	Estimated Percentage Gap from Conventional Regression	Estimated Percentage Gap from Matched Sample
BA recipients who transferred from a two-year college	−13.1***	−3.4 n.s.	0.20 n.s.
Number of cases	917	917	342

Source: NLSY79.

*p < 0.05; **p < 0.01; ***p < 0.001; n.s. = not significant.

after adjusting for students' family background and high school preparation, the differences in educational outcomes shrink. The adjusted percentage of students who earn any degree is 46 percent for community college entrants versus 52 percent for four-year college entrants (Levey 2005). This means that although dropout rates from community colleges are very high, they are not a lot different from the dropout rates one finds for students from similar backgrounds who go to four-year institutions.

Perhaps the most telling indicator that community colleges are fairly successful is that students who enter two-year colleges earn significantly more than equivalent students who only finish high school.[22] By our estimates, those who attend community colleges earn 7.5 percent more than equivalent students who only graduated from high school.[23] Other scholars, using alternative data sources, have previously documented the payoff to sub-baccalaureate degrees.[24]

Still, an AA degree is popularly viewed as worse than a BA, and most of the time, a BA degree is indeed worth much more than an AA degree from a community college. For example, in 2003, the average male with an AA degree earned $48,683, working full-time, whereas the average male with a BA earned $69,913 (see Table 18.1). That difference is what we would expect, given that a BA graduate takes many more college credits and therefore takes much longer than an AA to complete. However, when researchers calculate the economic benefit (in terms of earning power) per credit earned in a community college compared with per credit earned at a four-year college, they find that they are about the same (Kane and Rouse 1995a). Once again, the image of community colleges as second-class institutions seems overstated.

Many, though not all, of the programs of study offered at community colleges provide skills and credentials for particular jobs. Some of these vocational AA majors result in higher average earnings than some BA majors. The field of study can greatly influence economic payoff (Jacobs 1986, 1995; Bauman and Ryan 2001). For example, AA degrees in business resulted in higher average earnings than BA degrees in education. After controlling for students' background characteristics, earnings for several AA degrees (business, natural sciences, math, computers, and health and social services) were not statistically significantly different from earnings for BA degrees in arts and humanities, social sciences, and education.

College Remediation and Academic Standards

Remedial, also called "developmental," course work in college has emerged as another highly contentious issue in higher education (Kozeracki 2002; Soliday 2002).[25] Some commentators view the existence of these courses in college as evidence that many of today's students are not academically strong enough to manage college-level work and should not have been admitted into college in the first place. The presence of remedial course work, in this view, is a demonstration of how low intellectual standards have fallen in academe (Harwood 1997; Marcus 2000; Trombley 1998). Remediation is also considered a shameful waste of money. Taxpayers paid high schools to teach skills in reading, writing, and basic math; now they are asked to pay colleges for teaching these skills all over again. Other critics focus on college students becoming bogged down taking multiple remedial courses in college, leading many to give up and drop out (Deil-Amen and Rosenbaum 2002; Rosenbaum 2001). Remediation is thus a waste of the student's time and resources as well as of taxpayers' money.

Arguments such as these have persuaded several state legislatures to remove remedial courses from public four-year universities and to redirect students in need of remediation into community colleges (Bettinger and Long 2004; Kozeracki 2002; Soliday 2002). That is insufficient, in the view of MacDonald (1999), who has argued that even community colleges should get out of the remediation business.

Many educators hold an opposite view, maintaining that remedial education is a necessary component of higher education, one with deep historical roots (Breneman and Haarlow 1998; Ignash 1997; Payne and Lyman 1996). Proponents note that many promising students combine strengths in certain subject areas with weaknesses in others, which can be addressed by skills courses. Moreover, many students enter college years after graduating from high school, and need to rebuild certain skills. Most important, proponents stress that most students who take remedial course work subsequently complete their degrees successfully (McCabe 2000; Merisotis and Phipps 2000).

Until recently, relatively little research existed about who was taking remedial courses and in what subjects, and how remedial students turned out in the long run. (The main exceptions are Adelman [1999, 2004] and Bettinger and Long [2004].) So policy debates have proceeded without much of an empirical grounding. Recently, the U.S. Department of Education remedied this by releasing college transcript data for a nationally representative sample of students in the high school class of 1992 and coding these data (in consultation with college registrars) to indicate which courses were remedial. Since we have published analyses of these data elsewhere,[26] the following section summarizes the main findings of our research. (Readers interested in the methodology, the prior literature, or who want to look at statistical results, should consult that paper.)

One theme in the controversy surrounding remediation is that students are taking many remedial courses. Our analyses show that such students do indeed exist, but they are a minority among those who take remedial courses. For example, at two-year colleges, 42 percent of students took no remediation, 44 percent took between one and three courses, and only 14 percent enrolled in more than three remedial courses. At nonselective four-year colleges, 68 percent took no remediation, 26 percent enrolled in between one and three courses, and 5 percent took more than three. At selective four-year colleges, only 2 percent of students took more than three remedial courses, and at highly selective four-year institutions almost no one attempted multiple remediation courses.

These data represent the situation that existed before many states adopted new policies that moved remediation out of four-year public colleges, reducing or eliminating its presence there. Our analyses found, however, that students who were taking more than three remedial courses (and were allegedly "bogged down") constituted at most 5 percent of traditional undergraduates at nonselective four-year colleges. That is a much smaller figure than anyone would have imagined from listening to the public debates over remedial education in four-year colleges.

The commonsense impression—that remedial courses are taken by students with poor high school preparation or very weak academic skills—has also proved inaccurate. Our analyses show that many college students with limited academic skills do not take remedial course work, whereas substantial numbers of students with strong high school backgrounds nevertheless do take some remedial courses. For example, among students who took the most advanced curriculum in high school (the top quartile), 14 percent took some remedial course work in college. In addition, 32 percent of students in the second highest quartile, who took fairly demanding courses in high school, enrolled in some remedial classes in college.

Nor is remedial course work the preserve of disadvantaged inner-city students: large proportions of students who graduated from suburban and rural high schools take remedial course work in college, as do many students from high-socioeconomic-status (high-SES) families (Adelman 1998). These empirical findings contrast with public stereotypes of remediation as a preserve of a small group of academic incompetents who have no hope of achieving success in higher education.

Critics have accused public colleges and universities of abandoning their commitment to academic standards, of granting diplomas to undeserving students. Implicit is the claim that these colleges have done this in order to accommodate academically unprepared minority students. Our analyses of national data show that public colleges are more likely than private colleges to require remedial course work for equivalently skilled students. In this context, public institutions appear to have created higher hurdles than their private-sector counterparts. In addition, black students are more likely to take remediation than white students with identical test scores and high school preparation. This is the opposite of the "soft bigotry of low expectations" that critics have claimed operates in public education.

Critics of remedial education suggest that students who need remediation will not be able to graduate. There is indeed a gap in graduation associated with taking remedial courses: 28 percent of remedial students in two-year colleges graduate within 8.5 years, compared with 43 percent of nonremedial students, and 52 percent of remedial students in four-year colleges finish B.A. degrees, compared with 78 percent of students who have not taken remedial course work. However, looked at another way, nationwide 50 percent of African American BAs and 34 percent of Hispanic BAs graduate after taking remedial course work. If those students had been deemed unsuited for college and had been denied entry to four-year institutions—as some critics have recommended—then a large proportion of the minority graduates in the high school class of 1992 would never have received degrees. (These graduation numbers would probably be considerably larger if the survey followed students beyond eight and a half years out from high school.)

Our analyses were able to distinguish the effects of a poor high school academic preparation from the effects of taking remedial courses in college, and we found that most of the gap in graduation rates has little to do with taking remedial classes in college, but instead reflects preexisting skill differences carried over from high school. In two-year colleges, we found that taking remedial classes was not associated at all with lower chances of academic success, even for students who took three or more such courses. Contra Regina Deil-Amen and James Rosenbaum's (2002) thesis, in multivariate analyses, community college students who took remedial courses were no less likely to graduate than nonremedial students with similar academic backgrounds.

In sum, students with weaker high school backgrounds are less likely to graduate from community college, but remedial courses do not pose an additional barrier for students. On the contrary, we found evidence that community college students who successfully passed remedial courses were more likely to graduate than equivalent students who never took remediation, suggesting that such courses did help those students who completed them.

The remediation situation was different among entrants to four-year colleges. At four-year institutions, taking some remedial courses did lower student chances of graduation, even after taking prior academic preparation and skills into account. Student chances of graduation were reduced between 6 and 7 percentage points. This should be a matter of concern, but this is far from saying that students in four-year colleges who take remediation are unable to graduate. In four-year colleges, the graduation rate for students who took remedial course work was about two-thirds the graduation rate of students who took no remediation. As was the case for two-year college students, these lower graduation rates predominantly reflected skill problems that students brought from high school—specifically in reading—rather than a negative consequence of taking remedial courses per se. Taking remedial course work in reading at a four-year college had a clear negative effect on graduation, even after controlling for academic skills and background. This did not occur for remedial writing courses.

The majority of colleges in the United States are nonselective: they admit any high school graduate who applies and can pay tuition. Many colleges combine open access with requirements that weaker students take remedial or college prep courses in academic areas where they have problems. Thus, remedial education acts as both a gatekeeper and as a quality control in higher education, though this function is rarely acknowledged. Students who can successfully pass these courses continue into regular college-level courses. Students who can't make it through remediation either drop out or are academically terminated. Ironically, when, in an effort to maintain academic standards, colleges require their students to demonstrate proficiency in basic skills by passing remedial courses, they are criticized for wasting the time of the students who fail to overcome these hurdles. At the same time, the provision of remedial courses is perceived by the public as indicating a lack of standards, rather than as an important mechanism for setting a basic skill standard for college graduates. Currently, college remediation functions both as a second-chance policy for poorly prepared students and as a form of institutional quality control that prevents students from graduating unless and until they demonstrate basic skills. Critics of remedial education seem to overlook the importance of remedial education for maintaining academic standards.

Access to College as Demotivator of High School Students

The next claim we will consider is that the spread of college expectations among academically weak high school students has created perverse incentives that demotivate students during high school, and lead them to reduce their work effort:

> Although there is nothing wrong with students having optimistic hopes, we would be concerned if they responded to those hopes *by reducing their effort*. (Rosenbaum 2001, p. 62; emphasis added)

> Since anyone can enter college, no matter how poorly they do in high school (because of open admissions), students believe they can wait until college to exert effort. (Rosenbaum and Person 2003, p. 12)

> What could be wrong with letting students have "high expectations"? . . . The first opportunity cost of the college-for-all norm is that students' high expectations may inadvertently encourage them to see high school as irrelevant and thus to make poor use of it . . . As a result the college-for-all norm may lead to a lack of effort. (Rosenbaum 2001, pp. 79–80)

This is a novel thesis. Previous scholars who have studied the relationship between students' college plans and their postsecondary attainment tended to stress the positive association between college plans and educational outcomes (Adelman 1999; Alexander and Cook 1979; Hauser and Anderson 1991; Kerckhoff 1977; Morgan 1998). Rosenbaum and his coauthors, in contrast, seem to be the first to argue that "high expectations" or "optimistic hopes" for college among weak students would lead to a negative outcome, a lack of effort during high school. We will call this the "effort reduction thesis."

The observation that most American high school students don't work very hard at their studies is a long-standing one that far predates the expansion of college going. In their studies of "Middletown" in the 1920s, the Lynds discovered that most high school students spent very little time doing homework or studying, even A students and those enrolled in advanced courses (Lynd and Lynd 1956, pp. 185, 195, 215). August de Belmont Hollingshead's classic study (1975), *Elmtown's Youth*, undertaken around 1941, revealed the same pattern: "The high schools' work load is so light that very few students have to study more than *an hour or two a week* outside of school hours" (Hollingshead 1975, p. 108; emphasis added).

Research carried out in 1957 for James Coleman's (1961, p. 11) famous book *Adolescent Society*, a study of Elmtown and nearby communities, argued that teachers and parents had lost "direct control over the levers they could apply to motivate children." Adolescent peer culture had taken over that motivational role. Popularity with peers came from involvement in athletics, from good looks, and from being an activities leader much more than from being an academically high-achieving student. Thus, teenage peer culture failed to reward academic effort. More recently, Laurence Steinberg (1996) attributed the causes of student disengagement and low effort in today's high schools to social promotion; to a teen culture that disparages academic success; to students' focus on part-time work; and to disengaged parents. However, none of these studies linked a lack of effort in high school to unrealistic expectations about what it takes to succeed in college.

To our knowledge, the only systematic historical survey of student effort, as measured by time spent on homework outside school, is that undertaken by Brian Gill and Steven Schlossman (2003). After analyzing survey data from the 1940s through the 1990s, they concluded, "The main historical trend over the past half-century is that of continuity. American high school students in the late 1940s and early 1950s studied no more than their counterparts did in the 1970s, 1980s, or 1990s" (p. 332).

The implication of these various community and historical studies is that a lack of academic effort among most high school students has been the norm for many decades, long predating the upswing in attendance at community colleges and other institutions with open admissions policies. What, then, led Rosenbaum to identify low academic effort with unrealistic college expectations among weak students?

Rosenbaum did not attempt a historical examination of student effort. Rather, he analyzed data from a survey of high school seniors in twelve schools in the Chicago area. Those analyses showed, for high school seniors as a whole, irrespective of achievement level, that certain beliefs are associated with lower effort at school. One belief scale included the statements "My courses give me useful preparation I'll need in life"; "School teaches me useful skills"; "Getting a good job depends on how well you do in school"; and "I need more schooling to avoid dead-end jobs." The other scale included the statements "Even if I do not work hard in school, I can still make my future plans come true"; "What I do not learn in school, I can always pick up later"; "Students with bad grades often get good jobs after high school"; and "Without a good education, it is likely that I will end up with the kind of job I want."

In our view, neither of these scales measures Rosenbaum's (2001, p. 58) assertion that "students who believe they can attain a college degree in spite of low achievement . . . exert little effort in high school." We undertake a more direct test of the effort reduction thesis. The U.S. Department of Education's National Educational Longitudinal Study (NELS), which spans the high school years of the class of 1992, allows us to test whether or not academically weak students who nevertheless believe they can graduate from college reduce their effort in high school. (A student's belief that she or he can "attain a college degree"—not just attend college—was the criterion that Rosenbaum [2001] employed, and we follow his example here.) In our analyses that follow, we select students with weak skills when they enter high school, and we compare the academic progress of weak students who nevertheless expect to graduate from college with otherwise-equivalent academically weak students who don't expect to graduate from college.

Table 18.6 presents conventional ordinary least squares (OLS) regression models predicting outcomes solely for students who had average grades of C or below from sixth through eighth grade. Each regression controls for sociodemographic characteristics of students and schools and for students' course grades when the effect of college plans is assessed. They show that, among academically weak students, those with college graduation plans were significantly less bored, spent more time on homework in the twelfth grade, increased their homework effort more between eighth and twelfth grade, had higher twelfth-grade reading/math scores, and made greater progress in test scores between eighth and twelfth grade, compared with students with similarly low grades who did not expect to graduate from college.

Table 18.6 Effects of Degree Plans on Engagement and Achievement of Weak Students (Unstandardized OLS Regression Coefficients)

	Academic Disengagement Scale (BORED)	Twelfth-Grade Homework Effort	Twelfth-Grade Homework Effort (Controlling for Eighth-Grade Effort)	Twelfth-Grade Achievement Test Score	Twelfth-Grade Achievement Test Score (Controlling for Eighth-Grade Score)
College degree plans	-0.091*	3.595***	3.575***	2.242***	1.199***
Hispanic	-0.196***	-2.188***	-2.183***	-1.025*	0.486
Black	-0.282***	-1.529*	-1.513*	-3.021***	-1.764**
Asian	-0.416***	1.923*	1.932*	1.940*	1.140
Other	-0.381***	-0.590	-0.598	-4.361***	-1.488*
Male	-0.018	0.179	0.182	1.042**	1.036***
Family SES	0.068*	0.503	0.520	2.423***	1.568***
Middle school grades	-0.226***	0.852	0.787	1.929***	0.445
Private school	-0.009	-2.146***	-2.193***	2.887***	0.660+
High-poverty school	-0.041	-0.160	-0.109	-0.336	0.190
High-minority-enrollment school	-0.096*	1.291*	1.292*	-0.648	-1.268**
Eighth-grade homework	—	—	0.050	—	—
Eighth-grade test scores	—	—	—	—	0.655***
Constant	3.036***	8.532***	8.423***	39.531***	13.022***
Pseudo R^2	0.1082	0.0525	0.1813	0.0529	0.4883
Number of cases	1,508	1,055	1,055	1,508	1,508

Source: Authors' analyses of NELS88 data.

Note: Academically weak students defined here as those having a high school GPA of C or below. *$p < 0.10$; *$p < 0.05$; **$p < 0.01$; ***$p < 0.001$.

Table 18.7 presents logistic regressions for the same low-grades group. Within this group of academically weak students, those who expected to obtain a degree were more likely to take a "new basics"[27] curriculum, to take the ACT or SAT, to earn a high school diploma, to enroll in college, and to earn a degree. In no case was there any evidence that college expectations significantly impaired engagement or effort or performance among weak students.

We also ran regression analyses using a different definition of weak student: those whose reading and math test scores placed them in the bottom quintile of their cohort during eighth grade. These again show that academically weak students with college graduation plans increased their homework hours more between eighth and twelfth grades, spent significantly more time on homework in twelfth grade, had higher twelfth-grade scores, and made more improvement on skills tests between eighth and twelfth grades than academically and demographically similar students who lacked college plans. This academically low-achieving group with college graduation plans were significantly less likely to come unprepared to class, more likely to take a "new basics" curriculum, more likely to take the ACT or SAT, and more likely to enroll in college and earn a degree than similar weak students without college plans.

In order to reduce selection biases—background differences between students with college plans and students without such plans—we next used a sample of students matched on their propensity score for having college expectations, using the same outcome measures. Table 18.8 presents the results of the "matched-sample" propensity-score models alongside probabilities obtained from the conventional OLS or logistic regression models with sociodemographic controls, for the subpopulation of grade C and below students.[28] The table shows the average probability of, say, coming to class unprepared for

Table 18.7 Effects of Degree Plans on Engagement and Achievement among Academically Weak High School Students (Unstandardized Logistic Regression Coefficients)

	Student Came to Class Unprepared	Student Took "New Basics" Curriculum	Student Took SAT or ACT Test	Student Earned High School Diploma	Student Enrolled in College	Student Earned a College Degree
College plans	−0.212+	1.055***	0.692***	0.517***	1.079***	0.332**
Hispanic	0.154	−0.498	0.474**	0.571***	0.646***	−0.595***
Black	−0.234	0.724*	0.757***	0.216	−0.185	−0.616**
Asian	0.964***	0.329	1.121***	2.460***	0.932***	−0.870***
Other	0.733*	−1.538**	0.894***	−0.777**	−0.691**	−0.949**
Male	0.440***	−0.227	−0.220**	0.175	−0.430***	0.080
Family SES	0.148*	1.977***	0.787***	0.623***	1.164***	−0.117
Middle-school grades	−0.494**	1.964***	1.225***	1.114***	−0.056	0.588***
Private school	−0.667***	−0.955**	0.026	1.523***	1.091***	0.160
High-poverty school	0.435**	0.285	−0.385**	−0.371**	0.657***	−0.098
High minority-enrollment school	−0.185	−0.308	0.394*	0.343*	−0.098	0.165
Constant	0.968***	−6.616***	−2.440***	−1.665***	0.421+	−1.559***
Pseudo R^2	0.0325	0.2877	0.1095	0.1221	0.1894	0.0302
Number of cases	1,508	1,217	1,051	1,505	1,508	1,508

Source: Authors' analyses of NELS88 data.

Note: Academically weak students defined as those with C grades or lower before eighth grade. +p < 0.10; *p < 0.05; **p < 0.01; ***p < 0.001.

Table 18.8 Effect of College Graduation Expectations on Educational Engagement and Achievement; Comparing Bivariate and Propensity Score Analyses, Students with C Grades or Lower

Outcome	Estimated Value from Conventional Regression	Estimated Value from Matched Sample
Probability of coming to class unprepared		
Eighth-grade college degree plans	0.5460+	0.5497**
No degree plans	0.5978	0.6383
Number of cases	1,508	720
Estimated score on academic disengagement scale		
Eighth-grade college degree plans	2.401*	2.420*
No degree plans	2.492	2.535
Number of cases	1,508	720
Estimated twelfth-grade homework effort		
Eighth-grade college degree plans	13.032***	12.535***
No degree plans	9.436	9.409
Number of cases	1,055	524
Estimated change in homework effort, eighth to twelfth grades		
Eighth-grade college degree plans	13.032***	12.535***
No degree plans	9.457	9.407
Number of cases	1,055	524
Probability of completing "new basics" curriculum		
Eighth-grade college degree plans	0.0345***	0.1441***
No degree plans	0.0123	0.0343
Number of cases	1,217	587
Probability of taking the ACT or SAT test		
Eighth-grade college degree plans	0.5334***	0.5495***
No degree plans	0.3640	0.4232
Number of cases	1,051	524
Estimated twelfth-grade achievement test score		
Eighth-grade college degree plans	43.744***	43.541**
No degree plans	41.501	42.207
Number of cases	1,508	720
Estimated improvement in achievement test scores, eighth to twelfth grades		
Eighth-grade college degree plans	14.221***	10.899**
No degree plans	13.022	9.959
Number of cases	1,508	720
Probability of graduating with a high school diploma		
Eighth-grade college degree plans	0.6871***	0.6943**
No degree plans	0.5671	0.5876
Number of cases	1,505	720
Probability of enrolling in college		
Eighth-grade college degree plans	0.7245***	0.7107***
No degree plans	0.4721	0.5172

Outcome	Estimated Value from Conventional Regression	Estimated Value from Matched Sample
Number of cases	1,508	720
Probability of earning a college degree		
Eighth-grade college degree plans	0.4104**	0.4077
No degree plans	0.3305	0.3527
Number of cases	1,508	720

Source: NELS88.

Note: +p < 0.10; *p < 0.05; **p < 0.01; ***p < 0.001

academically weak students who have degree expectations compared with that for similar students who did not have degree plans, controlling for students' race and ethnicity, gender, family SES, middle school grades, and several school characteristics. The overall pattern for the propensity score-matched models strongly confirms the picture previously obtained from conventional OLS and logistic models: Among students with a C average or worse, those with college degree expectations fare better academically. For one dependent variable out of eleven—the probability of earning a degree—a coefficient that was significant for the conventional model wasn't statistically significant in the propensity model. For ten other outcomes, degree plans were associated with better effort and outcomes during high school, both in conventional regression models and in propensity score-matched models that reduce selection bias. In no case were degree expectations associated with worse outcomes or greater disengagement among academically weak students.

Critics of the college-for-all norm suggest that academically weak students who, knowing that some colleges have open admissions policies, aspire to graduate from college, subsequently reduce their effort, and make little progress in high school. These critics offer very weak evidence for this claim: a cross-sectional survey of high school seniors in Chicago that links self-reported student effort in twelfth grade to opinion scales about the importance of college for life.

Previously, scholars have noted that since the 1920s, American high school students have expended little effort in high school. Survey researchers have detected no decrease in homework effort in the decades since access to college has increased. Our longitudinal analyses of the NELS follow academically weak students from the beginning of high school who nevertheless expect to complete a college degree, and compare them with similar weak students who don't expect to earn a degree. We measured low achievement in two different ways: low GPA and low math and English test scores. We found that, by either definition, academically weak students who enter high school with "high expectations" of graduating from college increase their effort and improve their performance during high school.

In conclusion, blaming open access to college for low student effort in high school is unwarranted. One may speculate that weak students might work harder if it were made more difficult to enter college, but there is no evidence of this in historical studies or elsewhere. What we can actually measure suggests that academically weak high school students with degree plans exert significantly more effort than their peers, the opposite of what the demotivation or effort reduction thesis predicts.

Conclusion

This chapter has examined several criticisms of expanded access to college. None of the critics' hard claims are convincing when compared with the empirical record. Degrees have not become devalued. College pays off quite well for most graduates, even for college goers who don't complete their degrees. College pays off economically for students with weak high school backgrounds as well as for better-prepared students.

Graduation rates are not as dire as the "86 percent failure rate" suggests. That striking number was an artifact of the way failure was defined. If one includes only students who enter college and allows that women and economically disadvantaged students take a longer time to graduate, then graduation rates look much healthier, and seem to be getting better in recent years. There is still much room for improvement, but there is no "dropout boom."

Community colleges are not the academic dead ends that commentators once feared. More students than in earlier years are in the transfer pipeline to get BAs, and after they transfer they are on average as successful as matriculants to four-year colleges. The earnings data show that getting an AA degree pays off more than entering the labor market directly after one has graduated from high school. A few vocational majors in community college pay especially well, better than certain BA majors. However, community college students do drop out and "stop out" in very high numbers. This seems to be a reflection of their family background and academic preparation. We should indeed be looking into ways of reducing dropout rates. Still, students who fail to complete a degree nevertheless do better economically than high school classmates who did not enter higher education at all.

Remedial education represents the failure of middle and high schools to impart basic skills to all students, and thus is nothing to be proud of. In fact, however, the proportion of students in four-year colleges that are "bogged down" taking remedial courses has been quite small. The political firestorm that broke out around remediation in public universities was out of proportion to the number of students affected. We believe that remediation served as a convenient scapegoat for politicians seeking to reduce state funding for higher education, push for tuition hikes, or limit enrollments.

Students in community colleges are not gravely disadvantaged by taking remedial courses, and those who get through such courses have improved chances of graduation. Most strikingly, critics of mass education fail to acknowledge that remedial course work represents an important form of quality control. Colleges that are open to all high school students do not let students advance to the degree until they show proficiency in basic skills, and they require students lacking those skils to pass remedial courses. As we showed, very large proportions of minority college graduates have taken and passed remedial courses and obtained degrees in recent years. If, as some commentators propose, remediation had no place in college, then half of African American BA recipients would have been denied the opportunity to earn a degree.

Finally, the claim that open college access has undermined the work ethic of high school students has little basis in fact. On the contrary, we found that college graduation plans motivate weak students to work harder in high school, and we documented the payoff of having college plans in terms of higher grades, better test scores, and increased effort during high school—one more reason for encouraging academically weak students to aspire to college.

Claims about booms in the number of dropouts, worthless diplomas, and bogged-down and demotivated students help persuade legislators and opinion leaders that college access has gone too far. Such arguments sway the public and embolden those who want to push institutions of higher education to be more selective and restrictive in their admissions. Unfortunately, to those who are advancing a policy agenda, it rarely matters whether their complaints are factually grounded, as long as the assertions are plausible and well publicized.

Our research suggests that the critics' main claims are factually flimsy. That does not mean that we are uncritical fans of mass higher education. There are many reasons to be worried. We share with others a deep concern that too many students are failing in high school. In addition, the current rates of "stopout" and dropout from college are undesirable, even if they are not nearly as high as critics suggest We believe that these rates are more to do with financial and family pressures and less about student's academic abilities than critics allow, but that is another story. We share with other scholars a commitment to keeping intellectual standards high in college, and we acknowledge that this is more difficult when students enter college with skills deficits. But the goal of improving mass higher education is not served by propagating fictions and exaggerations about its current functioning.

Notes

1   See U.S. Census Bureau (1993).
2   See U.S. Census Bureau (2005). A public controversy is under way regarding the proportion of students who graduate from public high schools in the United States. Critics of public education have excoriated the Census Bureau for overstating graduation rates and understating dropout rates. They claim that there is a crisis in public schooling, evidenced by very high dropout rates and academically underprepared graduates. In response, supporters of public education have argued that graduation rates have been increasing over time, and there is little evidence that students are less prepared than in previous decades. They note that larger numbers of high school students are taking more-advanced course work than a decade or two ago, and accuse the critics of provoking a public panic in order to further their political agenda of school vouchers and privatization of K-through-twelve education. Lawrence Mishel and Joydeep Roy (2006) present one side of this debate, and Jay Greene and Marcus Winters (2005) provide another. Derrick Jackson provided an account of the controversy in his column in the *Boston Globe* on June 28, 2006.
3   Two government agencies provide conflicting estimates of undergraduate enrollment nationwide: the National Center for Education Statistics (2004, table 7.1) provides the estimate cited in the text. This is a projected estimate of 14.845 million undergraduates in 2005 that is based on actual measurements through 2002. NCES's equivalent figure for 2003 was 14.46 million. These NCES numbers are derived from a survey of postsecondary educational institutions, each of which reports its enrollment in the fall.

    Using a different data set, a survey of a large representative sample of American households known as the Current Population Survey, the U.S. Census Bureau (2005, table E) reported total undergraduate enrollment of 13.4 million in October 2003, 1 million fewer students than the NCES estimates. The census reports that two-thirds of these undergraduates are enrolled in four-year institutions. Most (81 percent) students at four-year colleges attend full-time, and most are young. However, 13 percent of full-time undergraduates at four-year schools are so-called mature students aged twenty-five or older. By contrast, in two-year colleges fewer undergraduates are full-time students (58 percent) and more (27 percent) are twenty-five or older. The 2003 survey reports that among full-time college students, nearly 15 percent work full-time and another 35 percent work part-time.

    Points of contrast are that NCES reports considerably higher nationwide undergraduate enrollment (14.5 million compared with the CPS's 13.4 million). NCES also reports that 55 percent of undergraduate enrollment is in four-year colleges, whereas the CPS reports 66 percent. There is no simple way of reconciling these discrepancies.
4   See National Center for Education Statistics (2004, indicator 20).
5   This figure describes the percentage of high school graduates from three cohorts—the classes of 1972, 1982, and 1992—who entered college in the years following high school graduation. It shows that the proportion of graduates proceeding directly to college has increased each decade, to its present high of 81.4 percent. It also provides separate analyses of the proportion of high school graduates with high school GPAs of C minus or worse who went on to college. Evidently, in more recent cohorts, too, weak high school students are much more likely to enter college. These data are drawn from three separate government studies: the National Longitudinal Study of the High School Class of 1972 (NLS72), the High School and Beyond Longitudinal Study of 1980 Sophomores (HS&B), and the National Educational Longitudinal Study of 1988 (NELS88). Our analyses in Figure 18.1 are for college entrants only. Adelman (2004, p. 24) provides similar analyses, showing the same trend, but he reports college attendance percentages slightly lower than ours. We suspect the difference may occur because we limited our sample to high school graduates.
6   At the national level only an indirect measure of the number of students who have been held back a grade is available: government reports that indicate the percentage of children whose age is above the modal age of children in their grade (U.S. Census Bureau 2005). This measure combines students who have been held back a grade with students who began elementary school at an older age than the norm, possibly by parental choice (known as "red-shirting"). Examining those statistics, one finds that rate of being above modal age among blacks is 37.4 percent, compared with 29.4 percent for non-Hispanic whites.
7   Between eighteen and twenty-four, only 7 percent of whites are high school dropouts, compared with 14 percent of blacks and 28 percent of Hispanics (U.S. Census Bureau 2005). Here, a dropout is defined as someone aged eighteen to twenty-four who has not completed high school and is no longer enrolled in high school.
8   The percentage of white graduates immediately transitioning to college is reported for 2004, whereas the rates for blacks and Hispanics are three-year averages for the years 2001 to 2003. There are fewer black and Hispanic students in the survey, so that the year-to-year rates for these racial–ethnic groups fluctuate more dramatically than for whites. For this reason, I have reported the NCES's three-year averages for these two minorities. Data on this indicator are available on the web at: http://www.nces.ed.gov/_programs/coe/2006/section3/table.asp?tableID=487.
9   Longitudinal data that follow cohorts of high school graduates beyond high school graduation paint a rosier picture regarding race gaps in college attendance. For the 1992 high school cohort, Adelman (2004, 23) finds no significant differences in college access rates between whites and African Americans.
10   A poor family is defined here as one in the lowest quartile of family income and an affluent family is one in the top income quartile. The figures above are derived from October CPS data for 2003, as reported by Thomas G. Mortenson (2005). Also see the NCES figures cited in note 8.
11   One exception to this view is an essay by Pedro Carneiro and James Heckman (2003, p. 77), in which they say, "After a half century of progress, cohorts born after 1950 did not improve much, or at all, on the educational attainment of their

predecessors." They base this conclusion on cross-sectional survey data (one CPS survey for the year 2000) comparing the percentage of persons born in each year who are high school dropouts, high school graduates, or college graduates. Graphing these data gives the impression that younger cohorts have fewer years of education than older birth cohorts do. This is an error of interpretation, and not a real finding. The reason that more fifty-olds in the year 2000 survey seem to have earned college degrees than twenty- or thirty-somethings is that many of those younger people are still completing degrees during their thirties and forties. Those late degrees appear in the statistics for fifty-year-olds, but have not yet happened for the younger cohorts in Carneiro and Heckman's graph, and so go uncounted. Education is no longer complete by early adulthood. By the time younger birth cohorts reach their fifties they will have out-performed their predecessors. If one looks at longitudinal data instead of a cross-sectional survey, it is clear that more high school students are continuing to college today than in any earlier period. In addition, a larger percentage of each successive birth cohort finishes college. There has been no drop or stagnation in educational attainment over time and the growth trend continues. See Jennifer Cheeseman Day and Kurt Bauman (2000).

12 Before the 1990s, economists tended to explain increasing inequality in wages as results of institutional factors such as intensified international competition and decreased unionization, the growth and expansion of various industry sectors, a shifting occupational composition within industries, and so on (for example, Bluestone and Harrison 1988). This view was superseded by an argument that linked the spread of technology (especially computers) to wage changes. Several scholars found that people who worked with computers earned more than employees with similar education who did not use computers (Krueger 1993), and this became generalized to a thesis that technological change was skill-biased, that is, that it required more-educated workers, whose higher salaries reflected their greater skills. This idea in turn was used to explain the increased polarization of incomes that was occurring within industries and occupations (Bound and Johnson 1992; Katz and Murphy 1992; Levy and Murnane 1992). The notion of skill-biased technological change has its critics, however. David Card and John E. DiNardo (2002) suggest that the timing of the increase in wage inequality does not fit that of the spread of computer use.

13 A brief history of the GI Bill of 1944 and its consequences is provided at http://www.75anniversary.va.gov/history/gi_bill.htm.

14 African American ex-servicemen had a much harder time than white ex-servicemen in taking advantage of the educational benefits for the GI Bill of 1944, but the bill nevertheless represented an important advance. See Hilary Herbold (1995) and Ronald Roach (1997).

15 After considering various potential indicators of the quality of undergraduate education, William G. Bowen, Martin Kurzweil, and Eugene Tobin (2005, p. 64) conclude, "We see no reliable way of answering definitively either of two questions of interest: Is American undergraduate education better today than in the past? And is it better than undergraduate education outside the United States?"

16 Notwithstanding the long-term increase in the value of a degree, there are fluctuations in the value of a college credential that are linked to recessions and expansions. In a recent newspaper article, the economist Paul Krugman ("Left Behind Economics," *New York Times,* July 14, 2006) discusses evidence that except for the very richest strata, almost all Americans, including college graduates, have experienced income loss in the last year or two.

17 Neither the NELS88, which followed students for about eight and a half years after high school graduation in 1992, nor the High School and Beyond data, which followed students for ten years after high school graduation in 1982, are suitable for assessing the economic payoffs to different levels of higher education. Employees whose labor-market experience is only three or four years past completing their degree are usually far from the earning power they will have from age thirty-five on.

18 Table 18.2 reports personal earnings data in the year 2000 for full-time workers for the NLSY data set. Regression models include the following controls: race and gender dummies, age, mother's and father's highest grade completed, family income when respondent was fourteen, mother's and father's occupational prestige when respondent was fourteen, dummies indicating whether or not respondent or parent was foreign-born, dummies indicating whether or not respondent's mother and father were employed when respondent was fourteen, respondent's high school academic GPA, the total number of academic courses respondent took in high school, respondents' self-esteem and self-mastery scale scores, respondent's Armed Forces Qualification Test score, dummies indicating whether or not respondent was married or had a child before his or her eighteenth birthday. The propensity score–matched models include these controls, as well as several interaction terms, quadratics, and dummy variables to capture nonlinear effects of these predictors. In addition, the matched cases are only paired with same-race and same-gender respondents: one who went to college, the other who did not.

19 See David Leonhardt ("The College Dropout Boom," *New York Times,* May 24, 2005) and Karen Arenson ("Bonus Planned for Colleges Whose Students Finish on Time," *New York Times,* January 26, 2005, late edition, IB).

20 Rosenbaum (2001, pp. 68, 80, 82). This figure was subsequently publicized in *The American Teacher* (Rosenbaum 2004), the nation's largest-circulation journal for teachers, and also in a publication aimed at high school counselors (Rosenbaum 2003).

21 According to the National Center for Education Statistics (2003, p. 23), approximately 33 percent of BA recipients take more than six years after high school graduation to obtain their degrees, and 19 percent take more than ten years. We used this to estimate longer-term graduation rates.

22 In part, this shift in perception of the community colleges as a route for mobility depends on what yardstick is used for comparing student success. The research literature in the 1960s and 1970s tended to contrast earnings and other outcomes of community college students compared with students who graduated from four-year colleges. By that comparison, community college graduates clearly earn less. On that basis, critics viewed community college students as second-class citizens.

By contrast, current research (including our own) is more likely to compare community college students with persons of similar background who went no further than high school graduation. By that criterion, community college students clearly earn more than they would have done if they had not gone to college.

Thus, attending community college seems to be a positive step.

23   The 7.5 percent figure comes from our analyses of the NLSY (see Levey 2005).

24   See W. Norton Grubb (1993, 1995a, 1995b, 1997, 2002); Thomas Bailey, Gregory Kienzl, and David Marcotte (2004), Dougherty (1994), Thomas Kane and Celia Rouse (1995a, 1995b); U.S. Census Bureau (2004); and Card (1999).

25   This phenomenon is known popularly as remedial education, although many educators avoid that label, preferring terms such as "developmental education," "skills courses," or "college preparation" courses.

26   Paul Attewell et al. (2006).

27   In 1983, the National Commission on Excellence in Education published its well-known report, "A Nation At Risk: The Imperative for Educational Reform," which called for a major overhaul of American schools. (The report is available online at: http://www.ed.gov/pubs/NatAtRisk/index.html.) One of the report's main recommendations was to institute a "New Basics" curriculum, a set of more rigorous courses required for high school graduation. The New Basics included four years of high school English, three years of mathematics, and three years of both social studies and science. A half year of computer science was also mandated. This coursework is known as "The New Basics Curriculum." Many college-bound students go beyond this minimum, for example by taking one or more foreign languages in high school, but taking the New Basics is viewed as the mark of a well-prepared student.

28   The sample sizes for the propensity models are considerably smaller than the N's for the equivalent conventional models in this table. This shrinkage in sample size is typical in matched propensity score models, for two reasons: first, cases are lost because the technique pairs just one control case with each treated case. If fewer than half of the cases in the sample received the treatment, as is the case in this analysis, the maximum number of cases included in the analysis will be twice the number of cases in the treatment group. For example, approximately one-third of the NELS respondents with C grades or lower had college expectations. Therefore, even if every C student with college expectations was matched with a C student without college aspirations, the number of cases in the propensity analysis would shrink from approximately 1,500 to approximately 1,000. Second, sample-size shrinkage occurs in propensity models because not all students can be matched to within 0.01 on their propensity to have college graduation plans. In our analysis of the effects of college expectations for students with C grades or lower, we found suitable matches for 360 of the 519 treatment cases. The treated cases that were not matched (and therefore excluded from the matched analysis) were cases that fit the college aspirant profile so well that it was impossible to find a respondent with similar characteristics in the no-college-plans control group. Shrinkage reduces statistical power in the matched models, creating a conservative bias in significance testing, but this is worthwhile given the reduction in selection bias that propensity matching provides.

References

Adelman, Clifford. 1998. "The Kiss of Death? An Alternative View of College Remediation." *National Cross Talk* 8(3): 11.

——. 1999. *Answer on the Toolbox: Academic Intensity, Attendance Patterns, and Bachelor's Degree Attainment.* Washington: U.S. Department of Education; available at: http://www.ed.gov/pubs/Toolbox/toolbox.html (accessed October 23, 2006).

——. 2004. *Principal Indicators of Student Academic Histories in Post-Secondary Education, 1972–2000.* Washington: U.S. Department of Education, Institute of Education Sciences, Available at: http://www.ed.gov/rschstat/research/pubs/prinindicat/prinindicat.pdf.

Alba, Richard, and David Lavin. 1981. "Community Colleges and Tracking in Higher Education." *Sociology of Education* 54(4): 223–37.

Alexander, Karl, and Martha A. Cook. 1979. "The Motivational Relevance of Educational Plans: Questioning the Conventional Wisdom." *Social Psychological Quarterly* 42(3): 202–13.

Anderson, Karl 1984. "Institutional Differences in College Effects." *ERIC Digest* (ED 256204). Washington: U.S. Department of Education, Educational Research Information Center.

Attewell, Paul. 1987. "The Deskilling Controversy." *Work and Occupations* 13(3): 323–46.

Attewell, Paul, David Lavin, Thurston Domina, and Tania Levey. 2004. "The Black Middle Class: Progress, Prospects, and Puzzles." *Journal of African American Studies* 8(1–2): 6–19.

——. 2006, "New Evidence on College Remediation." *Journal of Higher Education* 77(5): 886–924.

Bailey, Thomas, Gregory Kienzl, and David Marcotte, 2004. "Who Benefits from Postsecondary Occupational Education? Findings from the 1980s and 1990s." CCRC Brief 23. New York: Columbia University, Teachers College, Community College Research Center.

Bauman, Kurt, and Camille Ryan, 2001. "What's It Worth? Field of Training and Economic Status, 1996." *Current Population Reports.* Washington: U.S. Government Printing Office, for U.S. Census Bureau.

Bennett, William. 1994. *The De-Valuing of America.* New York: Touchstone.

Berg, Ivar. 1970. *Education and Jobs: The Great Training Robbery.* New York: Praeger.

Berman, Eli, John Bound, and Stephen Machin. 1998. "Implications of Skill-Biased Technological Change: International Evidence." *Quarterly Journal of Economics* 113(4): 1245–79.

Bettinger, Eric, and Bridget Terry Long. 2004. "Shape Up or Ship Out: The Effects of Remediation on Students at Four-Year Colleges." NBER working paper 10369. Cambridge, Mass.: National Bureau of Economic Research. Available at: www.nber.org/papers/w10369.

Bloom, Allan. 1988. *The Closing of the American Mind.* New York: Simon & Schuster.

Bluestone, Barry, and Bennett Harrison. 1988. *The Great U Turn: Corporate Restructuring and the Polarization of America.* New York: Basic Books.

Boesel, David, and Eric Fredland. 1999. *College for All? Is There Too Much Emphasis on Getting a Four-Year Degree?* Washington: U.S. Department of Education, Office of Educational Research and Improvement, National Library of Education. Available at: www.ed.gov/pubs/CollegeForAll/title.html.

Bound, John, and George Johnson. 1992. "Changes in the Structure of Wages in the 1980s: An Evaluation of Alternative Explanations." *American Economic Review* 83(June): 371–92.

Bowen, William G., Martin Kurzweil, and Eugene Tobin. 2005. *Equity and Excellence in American Higher Education.* Charlottesville: University of Virginia Press.

Bowles, Samuel, and Herbert Gintis. 1976. *Schooling in Capitalist America: Educational Reform and the Contradictions of Economic Life.* New York: Basic Books.

Breneman, David W., and William N. Haarlow. 1998. *Remediation in Higher Education.* Washington, D.C.: Thomas B. Fordham Foundation.

Breneman, David W., and Susan C. Nelson. 1981. *Financing the Community College: An Economic Perspective.* Washington, D.C.: Brookings Institution.

Brint, Steven, and Jerome Karabel, 1989. *The Diverted Dream: Community Colleges and the Promise of Educational Opportunity in America, 1900–1985.* New York: Oxford University Press.

Card, David. 1999. "The Causal Effect of Education on Earnings." In *Handbook of Labor Economics,* edited by Orley Ashenfelter and David Card. Volume 3A. Amsterdam, Netherlands: North Holland.

Card, David, and DiNardo, John E. 2002. "Skill-Biased Technological Change and Rising Wage Inequality: Some Problems and Puzzles." NBER working paper 8769. Cambridge, Mass.: National Bureau of Economic Research. Available at: www.nber.org/papers/w8769.

Carneiro, Pedro, and James Heckman. 2003. "Human Capital Policy." In *Inequality in America: What Role for Human Capital Policies?,* edited by James Heckman and Alan Krueger. Cambridge, Mass.: MIT Press.

Day, Jennifer Cheeseman, and Kurt Bauman, 2000. "Have We Reached the Top? Educational Attainment Projections for the U.S. Population." Working paper 43. Washington: U.S. Census Bureau, Population Division.

Clark, Burton. 1960. "The 'Cooling Out' Function in Higher Education." *American Journal of Sociology* 65(6): 569–76.

Coleman, James S. 1961. *The Adolescent Society: The Social Life of the Teenager and its Impact on Education.* New York: Free Press.

Collins, Randall. 1979. *The Credential Society: An Historical Sociology of Education and Stratification.* New York: Academic Press.

Day, Jennifer Cheeseman, and Kurt Bauman, 2000. "Have We Reached the Top? Educational Attainment Projections for the U.S. Population." Working paper 43. Washington: U.S. Census Bureau, Population Division.

Day, Jennifer Cheeseman, and Eric Newberger. 2002. *The Big Payoff: Educational Attainment and Synthetic Estimates of Work-life Earnings.* Special studies, series P23-210. Washington: U.S. Census Bureau. Available at: http://www.census.gov/prod/2002pubs/p23-2l0.pdf.

Deil-Amen, Regina, and James Rosenbaum. 2002. "The Unintended Consequences of Stigma-Free Remediation." *Sociology of Education* 75(July): 249–68.

Dougherty, Kevin. 1987. "The Effects of Community Colleges: Aid or Hindrance to Socioeconomic Attainment?" *Sociology of Education* 60(2): 86–103.

——. 1994. *The Contradictory College: The Conflicting Origins, Impacts and Futures of the Community College.* Albany: State University of New York Press.

——. 2002. "The Evolving Role of the Community College: Policy Issues and Research Questions." In *Higher Education: Handbook of Theory and Research,* edited by John Smart and William Tierney. Volume 17. New York: Kluwer Press.

Ellwood, David, and Thomas J. Kane. 2000. "Who Is Getting a College Education? Family Background and the Growing Gaps in Enrollment." In *Securing the Future,* edited by Sheldon Danziger and Jane Waldfogel. New York: Russell Sage Press.

Fish, Stanley. 2005. "Devoid of Content." *New York Times,* May 31, 2005, p. A17.

Freeman, Richard B. 1976. *The Overeducated American.* New York: Academic Press.

Gill, Brian, and Steven Schlossman. 2003. "A Nation at Rest: The American Way of Homework." *Educational Evaluation and Policy Analysis* 25(3): 319–37.

Goldin, Claudia, and Lawrence Katz. 2001. "The Legacy of U.S. Educational Leadership: Notes on Distribution and Economic Growth in the 20th Century." *American Economic Review* 91(2): 18–23.

Goldrick-Rab, Sara. 2006. "Following Their Every Move: How Social Class Shapes Postsecondary Pathways." *Sociology of Education* 79(1; January): 61–79.

Gray, Kenneth, and Edwin L. Herr. 1996. "BA Degrees Should Not Be the 'Only Way.'" *Chronicle of Higher Education* 42, May 10, B1.

Greene, Jay, and Marcus Winters. 2005. *Public High School Graduation and College Readiness Rates in the United States.* New York: Manhattan Institute for Policy Research. Available on-line at www.manhattan-institute.org/html/ewp_08.htm.

Grubb, W. Norton. 1993. "The Varied Economic Returns to Postsecondary Education: New Evidence from the Class of 1972." *Journal of Human Resources* 28(2): 365–82.

——. 1995a. "Response to Comment." *Journal of Human Resources* 30(1): 222–28.

——. 1995b. *The Returns to Education and Training in the Sub-Baccalaureate Labor Market: Evidence from the Survey of Income and Program Participation, 1984–1990.* Berkeley: University of California, Berkeley, National Center for Research in Vocational Education.

——. 1997. "The Returns to Education and Training in the Sub-Baccalaureate Labor Market, 1984–1990." *Economics of Education Review* 16(3): 231–45.

——. 2001. "From Black Box to Pandora's Box: Evaluating Remedial/Developmental Education." CCRC Brief 11. New York: Columbia University, Teachers College, Community College Research Center.

——. 2002. "Learning and Earning in the Middle." Part I: "National Studies of Pre-Baccalaureate Education." *Economics of Education Review* 21(4): 299–321.

Harwood, Richard, 1997. "Flunking the Grade and Nobody Notices." *Washington Post, August 25,* 1997.

Hauser, Robert M., and Douglas K. Anderson. 1991. "Post High School Plans and Aspirations of Black and White High School Seniors: 1976–1986." *Sociology of Education* 64(4): 22–30.

Herbold, Hilary. 1995. "Never a Level Playing Field: Blacks and the G.I. Bill." *Journal of Blacks in Higher Education* (Winter): 104–8.

Hollingshead, August de Belmont. 1975. *Elmtown's Youth and Elmtown Revisited*. New York: John Wiley.

Ignash, Jan. 1997. "Who Should Provide Postsecondary Remedial/Developmental Education?" *New Directions for Community Colleges* 100(winter): 5–20.

Jacobs, Jerry. 1986. "Sex Segregation of Fields of Study." *Journal of Higher Education* 57(2): 135–54.

——. 1995. "Gender and Academic Specialties: Trends Among Recipients of College Degrees During the 1980s." *Sociology of Education* 57(2): 81–98.

Kane, Thomas, and Cecilia Rouse. 1995a. "Comment on W. Norton Grubb: The Varied Economic Returns to Post-secondary Education: New Evidence from the Class of 1972." *Journal of Human Resources* 30(1): 205–21.

——, 1995b. "Labor-Market Returns to Two-and Four-year Colleges." *American Economic Review* 85(3): 600–14.

Karabel, Jerome. 1972. "Community Colleges and Social Stratification." *Harvard Educational Review* 42(4): 521–62.

Karen, David, and Kevin J. Dougherty. 2005. "Necessary but Not Sufficient: Higher: Education as a Strategy of Social Mobility." In *Higher Education and the Color Line*, edited by Gary Orfield, Patricia Marin, and Catherine L. Horn. Cambridge Mass.: Harvard Education Press.

Katz, Lawrence, and Kevin Murphy. 1992. "Changes in Relative Wages 1963–1987 Supply and Demand Factors." *Quarterly Journal of Economics* 107(February) 35–78.

Kerckhoff, Alan C., and Richard T. Campbell. 1977. "Black–White Differences in the Educational Attainment Process." *Sociology of Education* 50(1): 15–27.

Kozeracki, Carol. 2002. "ERIC Review: Issues in Developmental Education." *Community College Review* 29(4): 83–100.

Krueger, Alan. 1993. "How Computers Have Changed the Wage Structure: Evidence from Microdata, 1984–1989." *Quarterly Journal of Economics* 108(February): 33–60.

Levey, Tania. 2005. "Reexamining Community College Effects: New Techniques, New Outcomes." Paper presented to the Eastern Sociological Society, Washington, D.C. (March 17).

Levy, Frank, and Richard J. Mumane. 1992. "U.S. Earnings and Earnings Inequality: A Review of Recent Trends and Proposed Explanations." *Journal of Economic Literature* 30(September): 1333–81.

——. 2004. *The New Division of Labor: How Computers Are Creating the Next Job Market*. Princeton: Princeton University Press.

Lynd, Robert S., and Helen Merrell Lynd. 1956. *Middletown: A Study in Modern American Culture*. New York: Harcourt Brace.

MacDonald, Heather. 1997. "Substandard." *The City Journal* 7(3): 11–12.

——. 1998. "CUNY Could Be Great Again." *The City Journal* 8(1): 65–70.

——. 1999. "Room for Excellence?" *The City Journal* 9(4): 6.

Marcus, Jon. 2000. "Revamping Remedial Education." *National Crass Talk* 8(1). Available at: http://www.highereducation.org/crosstalk/ct0100/front.shtml.

McCabe, R. 2000. *No One to Waste: A Report to Public Decision-Makers and Community College Leaders*. Washington, D.C.: Community College Press.

Merisotis, Jamie P., and Ronald A. Phipps. 2000. "Remedial Education in Colleges and Universities: What's Really Going On?" *The Review of Higher Education* 24(1): 67–85.

Mishel. Lawrence, and Joydeep Roy. 2006. *Rethinking High School Graduate Rates and Trends*. Washington, D.C.: Economic Policy Institute.

Monk-Turner, Elizabeth. 1990. "The Occupational Achievements of Community and Four-year College Entrants." *American Sociological Review* 55(5): 719–725.

Morgan, Stephen. 1998. "Adolescent Educational Expectations: Rationalized, Fantasized, or Both?" *Rationality and Society* 10(2): 131–62.

Mortenson, Thomas G. 2005b. "Family Income and Higher Education Opportunity 1970 to 2003." *Postsecondary Education Opportunity* 156(June). Available at: http://www.postsecondary.org.

National Center for Education Statistics. 1997. *Nontraditional Undergraduates: Trends in Enrollment from 1986 to 1992 and Persistence and Attainment Among 1989–90 Beginning Postsecondary Students*. NCES 97–578. Washington: U.S. Government Printing Office, for the U.S. Department of Education. Available at: http://nces.ed.gov/pubs/97578.pdf.

——. 2003a. *A Descriptive Summary of 1999–2000 Bachelor's Degree Recipients One Year later. With an Analysis of Time to Degree*. NCES 2003–165. Washington: U.S. Government Printing Office, for the U.S. Department of Education. Available at: http://nces.ed.gov/pubs2003/2003165.pdf.

——. 2004. *The Condition of Education 2004*, NCES 2004-077. Washington: U.S. Government Printing Office, for the U.S. Department of Education. Available at: http://nces.ed.gov/programs/coe/index.asp.

——. 2005b. *The Condition of Education 2005*. "Immediate Transition to College (Indicator 20)." Washington: U.S. Government Printing Office, for the U.S. Department of Education. Available at: http://nces.ed.gov/programs/coe/2005/section3/indicator20.asp.

Payne, Emily M., and Barbara C. Lyman. 1996. "Issues Affecting the Definition of Developmental Education." In *Defining Development Education: Theory, Research, and Pedagogy*, edited by Jeanne L. Higbee and Patricia L. Dwinell. Carol Stream, Ill.: National Association of Developmental Education. Available at: http://www.nade.net/documents/Mono96/mono96.2.pdf.

Pincus, Fred. 1986. "Vocational Education: More False Promises." *New Directions for Community Colleges* 14(2): 41–52.

Porter, Kathleen. 2002. "The Value of a College Degree." *ERIC Digest* (ED470038). Washington: U.S. Department of Education, Clearinghouse on Higher Education, Educational Research Information Center.

Roach, Ronald. 1997. "From Combat to Campus: G.I. Bill Gave a Generation of African Americans Opportunity to Pursue the American Dream." *Black Issues in Higher Education* 14(3): 26–28.

Rosenbaum, James. 2001. *Beyond College for All: Career Paths for the Forgotten Half* New York: Russell Sage Foundation.

——. 2003. "Beyond College for All: Policies and Practices to Improve Transitions into College and jobs." *Professional School Counseling* (April).

——. 2004. "It's Time to Tell the Kids: If you Don't Do Well in High School, you Won't Do Well in College (or on the Job)." *American Educator* 28(spring): 8–10.

Rosenbaum, James E., and Anne E. Person. 2003. "Beyond College for All: Policies and Practices to Improve Transitions into College and Jobs." *Professional School Counseling* 6(4): 252–60.

Soliday, Mary. 2002. *The Politics of Remediation*. Pittsburgh: University of Pittsburgh Press.

Stanfield, Rochelle L. 1997. "Overselling College." *National Journal*, April 15, 1997, 653–56.

Steinberg, Laurence. 1996. *Beyond the Classroom*. New York: Simon & Schuster.

Traub, James. 1995. *City on a Hill: Testing the American Dream at City College*. New York: Perseus.

Trombley, William. 1998. "Remedial Education Under Attack." *National CrossTalk* 6(3): 1.

U.S. Census Bureau. 1993. *We the Americans: Our Education*. Washington: U.S. Government Printing Office, for U.S. Bureau of the Census. Available at: http://www.census.gov/apsd/wepeople/we–11.pdf.

——. 2004a. "Educational Attainment in the United States 2003." *Current Population Reports*. Series P20, number 550. June. Washington: U.S. Government.

——. 2005. "School Enrollment: Social and Economic Characteristics of Students: October 2003." *Current Population Reports*. Series P20, number 554. Washington: U.S. Government Printing Office, for U.S. Bureau of the Census. Available at: http://www.census.gov/prod/2005pubs/p20-554.pdf.

Velez, William. 1985. "Finishing College: The Effects of College Type." *Sociology of Education* 58(3): 191–200.

Weber Max. 1922/1968. *Economy and Society*. New York: Bedminister Press.

Wirt John, Susan Choy, Patrick Rooney, Stephen Provasnik, Anindita Sen, and Richard Tobin. 2004. "Indicator 6: Past and Projected Undergraduate Enrollments." In *The Condition of Education 2004*. NCES 2004–077. Washington: U.S. Department of Education, National Center for Educational Statistics.

Zwerling, Steven L. 1976. *Second Best: The Crisis of the Community College*. New York: McGraw-Hill.

PART IV
Suggested Readings

Allen, W. R. (1988). Black students in U.S. higher education: Toward improved access, adjustment and achievement. *Urban Review*, 20, 165–188.

Allen, W. R. (1992). The color of success: African American college student outcomes at predominantly white and historically Black public colleges and universities. *Harvard Educational Review*, 62, 26–44.

Allen, W. R., Epps, E. G., & Haniff, N. Z. (1991). *College in Black and white: African American students in predominantly white and historically black public universities*. Albany, NY: SUNY Press.

Attewell, P. & Lavin, D. (2008). *Passing the torch: Does higher education for the disadvantaged pay off across the generations*. New York: Russell Sage Foundation

Bennett, P. R. & Lutz, A. (2009). How African American is the net black advantage? Differences in college attendance among immigrant blacks, native blacks, and whites. *Sociology of Education*, 82 (1), 70–99.

Bok, D. & Bowen, D. G. (1998). *The shape of the river*. Princeton, NJ: Princeton University Press.

Bradley, K. (2000). The incorporation of women into higher education: Paradoxical outcomes. *Sociology of Education*, 73 (1), 1–18.

Brint, S. & Karabel, J. (1989). *The diverted dream: Community colleges and the promise of educational opportunity, 1900–1985*. New York: Oxford University Press.

Canada, K. & Pringle, R. (1995). The role of gender in college classroom interactions: A social context approach. *Sociology of Education*, 68 (3), 161–186.

Conley, D. (2001) Capital for college: Parental assets and postsecondary schooling. *Sociology of Education*, 74, 59–71.

Dougherty, K. J. (1997). Mass education: What is its impetus? What is its impact? *Teachers College Record*, 99, 66–72.

Dougherty, K. J. (1991). The community college at a crossroads: The need for structural reform. *Harvard Educational Review*, 61, 311–336.

Dougherty, K. J. (1994). *The contradictory college: The conflicting origins, impacts, and futures of the community college*. Albany, NY: SUNY Press.

Dougherty, K. J. and Kienzl, G. S. (2006). It's not enough to get through the open door: Inequalities by social background in transfer from community colleges to four-year colleges. *Teachers College Record*, 108 (3), 452–487.

Fletcher, J. M. & Tienda, M. (2009). High school classmates and college success. *Sociology of Education*, 82 (4), 287–314.

Gaffikin, F. & Perry, D. C. (2009). Discourses and strategic visions: The U.S. research university as an institutional manifestation of neoliberalism in a global era. *American Educational Research Journal*, 46, 115–144.

Goldrick-Rab, S. & Pfeffer, F. T. (2009). Beyond access: Explaining socioeconomic differences in college transfer. *Sociology of Education*, 82 (2), 101–125.

Hill, L. D. (2008). School strategies and the "college-linking" process: Reconsidering the effects of high schools on college enrollment. *Sociology of Education*, 81 (1), 53–76.

Jacobs, J. A. (1995). Gender and academic specialties: Trends among recipients of college degrees in the 1980s. *Sociology of Education*, 68, 81–98.

Karabel, J. (1972). Community colleges and social stratification. *Harvard Educational Review*, 42, 521–562.

Karabel, J. (2005). *The chosen: The hidden history of admission and exclusion at Harvard, Yale, and Princeton*. New York: Houghton-Mifflin.

Karen, D. (1990). Toward a political-organizational model of gate-keeping: The case of elite colleges. *Sociology of Education*, 63, 227–240.

Karen, D. (1991). Achievement and ascription in admission to an elite college: A political-organizational analysis. *Sociological Forum*, 6, 349–380.

Karen, D. (1991). Politics of race, class, and gender: Access to higher education in the United States, 1960–1986. *American Journal of Education*, 99, 208–237.

Karen, D. (2002). Changes in access to higher education in the United States: 1980–1992. *Sociology of Education*, 75, 191–210.

Lavin, D., Alba, R., & Silberstein, D. (1981). *Right versus privilege: The open admissions experiment at City University of New York*. New York: Basic Books.

Lavin, D. & Hyllegard, D. (1996). *Changing the odds: Open admissions and the life chances of the disadvantaged*. New Haven, CT: Yale University Press.

Lee, V. E. (1985). *Access to higher education: The experience of blacks, Hispanics, and low socio-economic status whites*. Washington DC: Division of Policy Analysis and Research, American Council on Education.

Lee, V. E. & Frank, K. A. (1990). Students' characteristics that facilitate the transfer from two-year to four-year colleges. *Sociology of Education*, 63, 178–193.

Long, M. C. & Tienda, M. (2008). Winners and losers: Changes in Texas university admissions post-*Hopwood*. *Educational Evaluation and Policy Analysis*, 30, 255–280.

Long, B. T. & Kurlaender, M. (2009). Do community colleges provide a viable pathway to a baccalaureate degree? *Educational Evaluation and Policy Analysis*, 31, 30–53.

Maher, F. & Tetrault, M. K. (2006). *Diversity and privilege in the Academy*. New York: Routledge.

Massey, D. (2003). *The source of the river: The social origins of freshmen at America's selective colleges and universities*. Princeton, NJ: Princeton University Press.

McDonough, P. (1997). *Choosing colleges: How social class and schools structure opportunity*. Albany, NY: SUNY Press.

Miller-Bernal, L. (1993). Single sex versus coeducational environments: A comparison of women students' experiences at four colleges. *American Journal of Education*, 102 (1), 23–54.

Miller-Bernal, L. (1999). *Separate by degree: Women students' experiences in single-sex and coeducational colleges*. New York: Peter Lang.

Miller-Bernal, L. & Poulson, S. (2004). *Going coed: Coeducation at formerly men's colleges, 1950–2000*. Nashville, TN: Vanderbilt University Press.

Miller-Bernal, L. & Poulson, S. (2006). *Going coed: Coeducation at formerly women's colleges*. Nashville, TN: Vanderbilt University Press.

Persell, C. H., Catsambis, S., & Cookson, P. W. (1992). Differential asset conversion: Class and gender pathways to selective colleges. *Sociology of Education*, 65, 208–225.

Persell, C., Hodges, Sophia C., & Cookson, P. W. Jr. (1992). Family background, school type, and college attendance: A conjoint system of cultural capital transmission. *Journal of Research on Adolescence*, 2, 1–23.

Pincus, F. (1980). The false promises of the community college. *Harvard Educational Review*, 50, 332–361.

Riordan, C. (1992). Single- and mixed-gender colleges for women: Educational, attitudinal, and occupational outcomes. *Review of Higher Education*, 15, 327–346.

Rosenbaum, J. (1998). College-for-all: Do students understand what college demands? *Social Psychology of Education*, 2, 50–85.

Rosenbaum, J. (2001). *Beyond college for all: Career paths for the forgotten half*. New York: Russell Sage Foundation.

Rosenbaum, J. & Deil-Amen, R. (2006). *After admission: From college access to college success (with Regina)*. New York: Russell Sage Foundation.

Sadovnik, A. R. (1994). *Equity and excellence in higher education*. New York: Peter Lang.

Stearns, E., Buchmann, C., & Bonneau, K. (2009). Interracial friendships in the transition to college: Do birds of a feather flock together once they leave the nest? *Sociology of Education*, 82 (2), 173–195.

Thurston, D. (2007). Higher education policy as secondary school reform: Texas public high schools after *Hopwood*. *Educational Evaluation and Policy Analysis*, 29, 200–217.

Thurston D. (2009).What works in college outreach: Assessing targeted and schoolwide interventions for disadvantaged students. *Educational Evaluation and Policy Analysis*, 31, 127–152.

Tierney, W. (1997). The parameters of affirmative action: Equity and excellence in the academy. *Review of Educational Research*, 67 (2), 165–196.

PART V

Education and Inequality

The relationship between education and inequality has been a central concern of the sociology of education for the past forty years. Sociologists of education have examined the effects of schooling on life chances and economic outcomes, as well as the effects of race, social class, ethnicity, and gender on academic achievement. Sociological research has consistently found that family background strongly affects educational achievement, with students from higher socio-economic backgrounds achieving at higher levels than students from lower socio-economic backgrounds and white and Asian-American students achieving at higher levels than African-American, Latino, and Native American students. In addition, although women have reduced the achievement gap with men, male students still outperform women in mathematics and science, while women outperform men in reading and language arts. Moreover, women have higher high school and college graduation rates, and boys have significantly higher rates of special education placement. However, sociologists disagree about the causes of these achievement gaps and policymakers disagree about what should be done to reduce them.

A central question for sociologists of education concerns the factors that explain educational achievement and achievement gaps. Sociologists examine both school and non-school factors to explain educational inequality. School factors include curriculum and pedagogy, teacher quality, school funding, tracking and ability grouping, school leadership, and other school-level variables. Non-school factors include poverty, community, family involvement, peer group interactions, genetic differences in intelligence (a highly controversial theory), and health and environmental factors (for a detailed discussion see Riordan, 2003; Sadovnik, Cookson and Semel, 2006, chapter 9). Although some sociologists stress school factors and others stress non-school factors, it appears that the interaction of both sets of factors explains differences in educational achievement among groups. The following articles examine these complex issues.

Chapter 19 includes a debate on the functions, effects and desirability of placing students according to ability or differentiating curriculum for different groups of students, commonly referred to in the United States as tracking. "Tracking: From Theory to Practice" by the University of Notre Dame sociologist Maureen Hallinan examines the unintended consequences of tracking and the need to eliminate tracking where it is dysfunctional and improve it where required. "More than Misplaced Technology: A Normative and Political Response to Hallinan on Tracking" by the UCLA sociologist Jeannie Oakes provides a critical response to Hallinan that argues for the elimination of tracking. Following these essays, both authors respond to each other's arguments.

Chapter 20, "Invisible Inequality: Social Class and Childrearing in Black Families and White Families" by the University of Pennsylvania sociologist Annette Lareau, examines the relationship between social class and family and schooling. Through a comparison of middle-class and working-class families Lareau analyzes how different patterns of childrearing education affect social and educational outcomes. Based on a multi-year ethnographic study of black and white working-class and middle-class families, Lareau describes two different forms of childrearing and their differential effects on children from different social classes.

Chapter 21, "Collective Identity and the Burden of Acting White in Black History, Community and Education" by the late University of California Berkeley anthropologist John U. Ogbu, presents an overview of his controversial theory that Black students often have low educational achievement and attainment due to their perception that academic achievement is a characteristic of being white.

Chapter 22, "Burden of Acting Neither White nor Black: Asian American Identities and Achievement in Urban Schools" by the Rutgers University sociologist Jamie Lew, applies Ogbu's theory to Asian-American students.

Chapter 23, "Seeking Equity in the Education of California's English Learners" by the sociologist Russell W. Rumberger and social scientist Patricia Gándara, examines the achievement gap for English Language Learners (ELLs) in California. In a shorter version of a report for the *Williams v. State of California* lawsuit concerning unequal education for low-income, minority and ELL students, the authors describe the educational inequalities and the role of the state in reproducing them. Finally, they present policy recommendations for reducing these inequalities.

Chapter 24, "Gender Inequalities in the Transition to College" by the Ohio State sociologist Claudia Buchman, analyzes gender differences in the transition in higher education. She summarizes areas in which females outpace males and vice versa. She analyzes these differences and argues that we need to better understand the complex processes that are responsible for these differences in pathways and outcomes.

Questions for Reflection and Discussion

1   What are the functions of tracking? Based on the essays by Hallinan and Oakes, do you believe tracking based on ability (ability grouping) or curriculum tracking (different curricula for different groups of students) is a reasonable way of organizing instruction? What do you think Hallinan and Oakes would say about gifted and talented programs and Advanced Placement courses? Do you think all students should receive the same curriculum and teaching methods? Do you think Oakes's recommendation of heterogeneous classes for all students is practical? Do you think the problem is tracking or the way students are sorted and selected into tracks? Would a tracking system be fair if it were based on merit alone, rather than on other factors, such as race, social class, ethnicity, or gender? Is this possible? Finally, should students with learning problems or disabilities be tracked into separate special education classes or included in heterogeneous classes?

2   According to Lareau, how do working-class and middle-class family childrearing practices differ? Based on this article, do you think that working-class parents care less about their children's education? Do you think one form of childrearing practice is better than the other? Which do you think is a more powerful determinant of school achievement, social class or race?

3   According to Ogbu, why do Black students achieve at lower levels than white students? What do you think of his theory about the burden of acting white? Does Lew's research support Ogbu's theory when applied to Asian-American students? What does Lew say about the "model minority myth" concerning Asian-American students? According to Lew, how do race and social class interact to explain Asian-American student attitudes and achievement? What would Ogbu say about her conclusions? What would Coleman and Bourdieu say about Lew's conclusions?

4   What do Rumberger and Gándara say about the extent and causes of educational inequality for ELL students? What is the relationship between ethnicity and social class in explaining these differences? How has the state of California contributed to inequalities and what policies do the authors recommend to reduce them? What would Lew say about their conclusions, given that Asian-American students, whose first language is often not English, achieve at much higher levels than Hispanic students?

5   According to Buchman, what are the differences between male and female students in their transition to college? What factors account for male overrepresentation in science, mathematics, and engineering and women's higher overrepresentation in the humanities, social sciences, and the helping professions (i.e. education, nursing, and social work)? How would Arnot analyze these differences?

6   Based on the articles in this section, which do you think are more important in explaining achievement gaps, school or non-school factors? Why?

References

Riordan, C. (2003). *Equality and achievement: An introduction to the sociology of education* (2nd ed.). Saddle River, NJ: Prentice Hall.

Sadovnik, A. R., Cookson, P. W., & Semel, S. F. (2006). *Exploring education: An introduction to the foundations of education* (3rd ed.). Needham Heights, MA: Allyn and Bacon.

19
Tracking
From Theory to Practice

MAUREEN T. HALLINAN

and

More than Misplaced Technology
A Normative and Political Response to Hallinan on Tracking

JEANNIE OAKES

TRACKING: FROM THEORY TO PRACTICE

Maureen T. Hallinan

The term *tracking* refers to the practice of assigning students to instructional groups on the basis of ability. Originally, secondary school students were assigned to academic, general, or vocational tracks, with the courses within those tracks designed to prepare students for postsecondary education or careers. More recently, these track categories have been replaced by course levels, with students typically being assigned to advanced, honors, regular, or basic courses. These course levels continue to be referred to as tracks, with the regular and higher-level courses loosely equivalent to the academic track and the basic and lower courses loosely equivalent to the general and vocational tracks. Most secondary and junior high or middle schools track students for English and mathematics, and many schools track for social studies, science, language, and other courses. Tracking is an organizational practice whose aim is to facilitate instruction and to increase learning. The theory of tracking argues that tracking permits teachers to tailor instruction to the ability level of their students. A good fit between a student's ability and the level of instruction is believed to maximize the effectiveness and efficiency of the instructional process. Thus, tracking is meant to promote cognitive development; it is not designed to influence or modify students' social or emotional growth.

The practice of tracking is currently a topic of intense debate. The concern focuses on two issues pertaining to the effectiveness and equity of tracking. The first is whether tracking is more effective in promoting students' learning than are other methods of grouping. The second is whether all students benefit from tracking to the same degree.

The tracking debate is fed by conjectures and assumptions about the way tracking operates and how it affects students. Among these beliefs are that track placement is determined primarily by academic criteria, that tracks are strictly homogeneous with respect to ability, that track assignments tend to be permanent, that tracking has a negative effect on the self-esteem of low-ability students, that low-ability students are difficult to teach because they are not highly motivated to learn, and that tracking limits the college options of low-track students.

Research on Tracking

A number of fairly rigorous empirical studies, including both surveys and case studies, have provided information about how students are assigned to tracks and about the effects of track levels on students' learning. The findings of these studies are consistent with some of the commonly held beliefs about tracking, but contradict others. Empirical research supports the following conclusions about tracking.

Assignment to Tracks

1   In practice, the assignment of students to tracks is based not only on academic considerations, which would lead to strictly homogeneous groupings, but on nonacademic factors. Academic factors that influence track placement are grades, scores on standardized tests, teachers' and counselors' recommendations, prior track placement, and course prerequisites. Nonacademic considerations include course conflicts, cocurricular and extracurricular schedules, work demands, and teacher and curricular resources. A reliance on nonacademic factors increases the heterogeneity of ability groups and leads to overlapping ability distributions in adjacent tracks.

2   Schools vary in the constellation of factors on which they rely to assign students to tracks and in the weight they attach to each factor. As a result, track assignments are dependent, in part, on the schools that students attend.

3   Track assignments tend to be less permanent than is commonly believed. It is not uncommon for a student to change tracks during a school year and from one school year to the next. The flexibility of track assignments varies by school, by subject, and by grade level.

4   A greater proportion of minority and low-income students are assigned to the lower tracks. When academic achievement is controlled, the race-ethnicity and income effect on track assignment decreases, but does not disappear.

5   Higher social status is associated with placement in a higher track. The importance of track level for social status differs across schools.

Effects of Tracking

1   The quantity and quality of instruction increases with the level of the track. The curriculum and related instructional materials are more interesting and engaging in higher tracks. The amount of time spent on instruction, as opposed to administrative and disciplinary tasks, is greater in higher tracks. The relationship between track level and instructional characteristics differs among schools.

2   Students in high-ability tracks learn more and at a faster pace than do those in lower-ability tracks.

3   Tracking provides no advantage over heterogeneous grouping with respect to the achievement of students in the middle-ability range.

These conclusions indicate that tracking, as currently practiced, tends to be both inequitable and, at least for some students, ineffective. Tracking provides fewer learning opportunities for low-ability students than for those with higher ability. Since low ability is related to race, ethnicity, and socioeconomic status, tracking discriminates against students in these demographic categories. The disadvantages of tracking for low-ability students perpetuate the effects of background characteristics on achievement. Tracking also disadvantages lower-ability students by conveying on them lower social status. Differences among schools in the effectiveness and equity of tracking place additional constraints on access to learning opportunities for some students, usually those of lower ability.

In general, empirical research seems to provide the rationale for eliminating tracking as an organizational and pedagogical practice. However, the decision to detrack a school may be premature and unwarranted. To evaluate the effectiveness and equity of tracking in an effort to determine how it can be improved, rather than eliminated, it is necessary to examine its intended and unintended consequences.

Tracking as an Organizational Practice

Tracking is a way of organizing a student body. The intended purpose of tracking is to increase the effectiveness and efficiency of instruction. If tracking operated according to theory, students at all ability levels and from all backgrounds would learn more in tracked classes than in untracked ones. However, tracking produces unintended consequences that impede the attainment of its goal. Some of these consequences are inherent in the nature of tracking, whereas others are due to the failure of tracking practice to reflect tracking theory. These consequences make tracking less effective and less equitable than intended.

The task of an educational administrator who is faced with a decision about tracking is twofold: to determine whether the practice of tracking can be made more consistent with the theory and to ascertain whether negative features that are inherent in tracking can be outweighed by other school policies and practices. If the answer to these questions is affirmative, then it is reasonable to retain tracking, so teachers and students can benefit from the positive effects of the practice.

Modifying Negative Consequences

Segregation. One unintended negative consequence of tracking is the way it segregates students by race or ethnicity and socioeconomic status. Since academic achievement is related to students' background, minority and low-income students are disproportionately assigned to lower tracks. Even if the quality of instruction were the same across tracks, this segregating effect would concern educators and parents.

Although the segregation produced by tracking may be unavoidable, its negative effects can be countered by integrating students in their untracked classes and in other school activities. Ensuring that students spend a large part of their school day in integrated settings should lessen the negative effects of assignment to a small number of segregated classes. Furthermore, school authorities can create a school atmosphere that is intolerant of racism and that strongly supports positive social relations among different ethnic and racial groups.

Low social status. A second negative feature of tracking is its effects on students' social status. Tracking typically leads to a social hierarchy based on track level and academic performance. Students who are assigned to the lower tracks are apt to receive less respect from their peers and to be assigned lower status in the academic hierarchy. Lower status can have negative consequences for learning by decreasing a student's motivation and effort. In addition, rewards typically are given to higher-track students, which could further discourage or alienate lower-track students.

To counter the negative social dynamics created by tracking, school authorities need to create structures and methods to support the social and emotional experiences of lower-track students. Restructuring the reward system to broaden the bases for social recognition and respect is one way to enhance the status of low-track students.

Heterogeneous tracks. A third negative consequence of tracking results from the failure of authorities to create strictly homogeneous tracks. In practice, track levels are rarely as homogeneous as they could be. In most cases, the distribution of achievement in one track overlaps, to a surprising degree, with the distribution in adjacent tracks. Typically, students at the high end of the distribution in one track have higher achievement than do those at the low end of the distribution in the next higher track.

The degree of heterogeneity among students in a track affects teachers' ability to direct instruction to the students' ability levels. Thus, the failure of students to benefit from tracking may be due partly to the failure of schools to create homogeneous tracks.

Moreover, students develop cognitively at different rates. Even when a track structure is homogeneous at the beginning of a school year, students' different rates of growth introduce heterogeneity into the tracks during the school year. When students' track placements are permanent, either across a school year or for longer periods, allowance is not made for the heterogeneity that arises from these differential rates of growth. Heterogeneity becomes greater with time, creating a wider departure from the conditions under which tracking is expected to be effective.

What is needed is a flexible tracking policy that allows for reassignments to preserve the homogeneity of tracks. Empirical data show that track assignments in many secondary schools are flexible, both across and within school years. However, changes in tracks are often made to accommodate a student's participation in other school activities, rather than for academic reasons. These changes usually create greater heterogeneity in tracks.

Frequent reassignments of students to tracks to increase the homogeneity of tracks are desirable. Periodic evaluations of the distribution of achievement in tracks and a policy of reassigning students to different tracks, when appropriate, should ensure a good fit between students' abilities and the level of instruction.

Slower achievement of students in low tracks. The most serious, unintended negative effect of tracking is the slower growth in achievement of students in low tracks. This effect is caused, in part, by instructional inadequacies in the lower tracks. Instruction in many low tracks can be characterized by uninteresting lessons and instructional materials, by teachers' low expectations and standards for their students' performance, by low standards or teachers' performance, and by a significant number of interruptions in instruction owing to disciplinary problems.

Educational authorities have the ability to modify each of these characteristics of instruction in lower tracks. Teachers can provide more interesting instructional materials without going beyond the students' level of comprehension. They also can alter their assumptions about the learning potential of low-ability students. Recent research on the multiple facets of intelligence, as well as new developments in learning theory that have identified different learning styles, should be helpful in this regard. Teachers can raise their expectations and requirements for students' performance. Principals can devise reward systems that are aimed at improving teachers' instruction, and teachers can provide rewards that motivate students to study. The school can consistently and publicly acknowledge the accomplishments of students in all academic tracks. Principals and counselors can devise methods of dealing with disciplinary problems without infringing on the teachers' instructional time.

Negative social psychological consequences. In addition, negative social psychological processes occur in lower tracks that further jeopardize learning for lower-ability students. These processes link a student's assignment to a lower track to his or her self-esteem and social status. Students are likely to view their assignments to low tracks as evidence that teachers have a low regard for their academic abilities and as an indication that they cannot be successful in school and should not aspire to go to college. This inference leads to a loss of self-confidence and decreases their motivation to achieve academically. Discouragement usually results in students' detachment from learning and often leads to disruptive behavior or withdrawal. This negative cycle tends to be self-perpetuating.

Change or intervention can occur at any point in the negative social psychological processes that interfere with learning. The principal and faculty of a school can make a determined effort to communicate a positive message about the meaning of different track levels. Teachers can increase the academic demands they place on lower-track students and challenge these students to achieve. They can offer students frequent opportunities to succeed and provide tangible and public rewards for success and improvement. The school can adhere to a policy of flexible track assignments, motivating students to work harder to advance to higher tracks if they so choose. In short, educators can forestall or reverse the negative social psychological dynamics that often accompany placements in low tracks by fostering a more positive attitude about track placement and students' potential. When accompanied by improved instruction in the lower tracks, this attitude adjustment should generate social psychological processes that encourage, rather than obstruct, learning in the lower tracks.

A common reaction to these unintended negative consequences of tracking is to call for the abandonment of tracking as an educational practice. A more tempered response would be to improve the way tracking is practiced, so it better fits the ideal, and to counter students' negative cognitive, social psychological, or behavioral responses to being tracked. The negative effect of tracking on integration in schools can be reduced by a committed effort to eliminate racism in a school and by avoiding segregation in nontracked classes and other school activities.

Objective versus Subjective Criteria

The effectiveness and equity of tracking are also influenced by the way students are assigned to track levels. Schools differ in the criteria they use to determine students' placements in tracks. Within a school, differences also occur in the criteria for assigning students to different track levels.

Assignments to tracks that are based strictly on objective, academic criteria, such as standardized test scores, academic grades, and prerequisites for courses, produce the most academically homogeneous groups. When more arbitrary criteria are applied, such as counselors' and teachers' recommendations, parents' and students' preferences, and schedule conflicts with other academic courses or with cocurricular and extracurricular activities, tracks tend to be more heterogeneous.

Secondary schools seem to use more objective criteria in assigning students to higher tracks and more arbitrary criteria in assigning students to lower tracks. This tendency creates greater homogeneity in the upper tracks, implying that students who are assigned to the upper tracks enjoy a more optimal instructional environment than do those assigned to the lower tracks. Although subjective criteria may yield a more accurate assessment of students' potential than may objective measures, they usually do not because limitations on counselors' time leads to cursory evaluations, resulting in inappropriate assignments.

Schools differ in the criteria on which they base their decisions on track placements. Some schools rely heavily on objective measures; others use indicators of a student's improvement. Whether a school makes track placements on the basis of absolute, relative, or self-mastery standards has a direct impact on the track level to which a student is assigned. Differences in criteria among schools represent one way that tracking can transmit unequal learning opportunities to students.

School-district administrators, principals, and counselors establish their schools' criteria for placing students in tracks. Their challenge is to determine the most effective and equitable set of criteria to ensure the success of tracking. Most criteria that are defined at the district level are based on objective measures of ability or achievement, usually grades and standardized test scores. These are suitable measures generally, assuming that they correlate with students' ability, because they tend to create a fair degree of within-track homogeneity. Nevertheless, modifications of and exceptions to these criteria may be required to reduce heterogeneity further.

Although the use of objective measures of achievement as criteria for track placements increases the homogeneity of tracks, it creates other problems. Standardizing criteria for achievement results in the assignment of disproportionately fewer students to the upper tracks than to the lower tracks in some schools. Research has found that schools in which a small number of students qualify for admission to advanced tracks tend to lower their standards for admission to those tracks to increase the number of students in the advanced courses to a desire level. Thus, criteria for track placements may have to be defined at the school, rather than the district, level to take the characteristics of a school's population into account. Under these circumstances, careful counseling is called for when students change from one school to another.

A more serious consequence of standardizing criteria for admission to tracks and of basing admission primarily on objective measures of achievement is related to the equity of tracking. Administrators avoid setting objective criteria because doing so results in the assignment of fewer minority students to the higher tracks and disproportionately more minority students to the lower tracks. Since most administrators deplore this segregative aspect of tracking, they tend to prefer less objective measures of ability. To resolve this dilemma, it is necessary to compromise between the two desired goals of effectiveness and equity. In addition, however, schools need to make systematic, concerted efforts to improve the performance of low-ability students, so these students can meet the criteria for admission to higher tracks.

Conclusion

Tracking clearly has many shortcomings. Some of them, such as its segregative aspect and its effects on students' social status, are difficult to eliminate. However, schools have a number of opportunities to reduce these negative effects of tracking by ensuring that nontracked classes and other school activities are integrated and by expanding the bases of social status to include nonacademic talents.

Other shortcomings of tracking result not from the organizational technique itself, but from the way tracking is practiced in schools. Efforts to reform the practice should be directed toward improving the quantity and quality of instruction at all track levels, particularly the lower ones, to eliminate the instructional disadvantages of tracking that some students experience. Schools also need to guard against lessening the motivation of lower-track students by providing support mechanisms and reward systems for all students, including those in the lower tracks.

Finally, to ensure that tracking works as intended, great care is needed in making initial track assignments and in permitting students to change tracks when their original placements are no longer appropriate. Improving the fit of track assignments is a complex task. It requires school authorities to choose criteria that are valid measures of students' abilities and that reduce the likelihood of inappropriate placements. In the design of a student's schedule, track placement must take priority over other scheduling considerations. However, deviation from a rigid admissions policy is appropriate if it attains another objective, such as the integration of tracks, without having a major negative effect on the homogeneity of tracks.

In general, many of the criticisms leveled against tracking can be avoided by improving, rather than eliminating, tracking. The compelling advantage of retaining tracking, at least in certain subjects, is that it facilitates instruction and learning. The many teachers who favor tracking have concluded, from pedagogical experience, that teaching heterogeneously grouped students without additional resources, such as teacher aides and supplementary material, is a formidable task. Moreover, the outcome of detracking in less-than-ideal circumstances may be as unsatisfactory as that of tracking that is not practiced according to principle. If educators are willing to put serious efforts into creating a tracking system that attempts to maximize effectiveness and equity, the results should benefit students at all levels of ability.

MORE THAN MISAPPLIED TECHNOLOGY: A NORMATIVE AND POLITICAL RESPONSE TO HALLINAN ON TRACKING

Jeannie Oakes

After responding to tracking advocates' distortions of the research, I am gratified to see that Maureen Hallinan has the facts straight. But, then again, Hallinan cannot be said to be an advocate of tracking or can she? As a critic of tracking, she offers a reasonable definition of tracking, correctly identifies its explicit purposes, rightly recounts the widespread assumptions about how tracking works and how it affects students, and accurately summarizes research findings on the way students are assigned to tracks and tracking's actual effects on learning. Hallinan concludes her review of the research, as most other scholars do, by saying that the evidence on tracking adds up to a rationale for eliminating the practice, particularly since lower ability is associated with race, ethnicity, and social-class status, and, tracking, thereby, places low-status students at a considerable educational disadvantage. So far, so good.[1]

At this point in Hallinan's essay, something odd happens. She offers conclusions and a rationale that are indistinguishable from the new generation of tracking *advocates*. Hallinan asserts that it is not only premature, but likely to be unwarranted, to consider "detracking" schools! Like supporters of tracking, few of whom argue that tracking is currently done well, she contends that "a more tempered response" to the overwhelmingly negative evidence is for schools to make tracking practice more consistent with tracking theory and to balance the inherently negative features of tracking with countervailing policies and practices.

I find the disjuncture between Hallinan's review of the evidence and the implications she draws astonishing. Having spent the past three years studying 16 racially mixed secondary schools that have taken the tracking research seriously and responded with "detracking" reforms, my own conclusions depart dramatically from Hallinan's.[2] In what follows, I juxtapose Hallinan's position with my own thinking about tracking, which is based partly on the experiences of these and other schools.

Hallinan argues that tracking is essentially an organizational technique with intended and unintended consequences. Tracking's unintended consequences, she contends, are what impede tracking's intended goal of enabling students at all levels to learn more than they would in mixed-ability classes. Some of these unintended consequences are inherent in tracking, whereas others represent the failure of implementation—that is, schools do not properly enact tracking theory. This line of argument treats tracking itself as a disembodied practice, a technical matter that is far more a product of organizational structure than of the humans who enact it. It also renders tracking susceptible to tinkering—that is, to fixing the technology without altering its structural and cultural underpinnings.

In striking contrast, my work finds the structure of tracking to be embedded in cultural and political contexts, replete with good intentions, bad intentions, and messy human decision making. Consequently, I have come to believe that attempts to understand tracking apart from its normative and political content are sorely inadequate. For example, Hallinan characterizes the debate about tracking as a concern with issues of effectiveness and equity in relation to cognitive outcomes—learning. The folks who are working to detrack the schools I am studying would agree, but they also view tracking as being centrally concerned with students' life chances, including the transfer of social, economic, and political privilege, and racial and social-class discrimination.

Most educators cannot imagine tracking as a technical, neutral organizational practice that is unrelated to personal, societal, or vocational purposes. Tracking in real schools is connected to a deeply held conviction that schools are expected to contribute to a wide array of goals, only some of which are strictly cognitive, and the specific form that tracking takes reflects educators' efforts to juggle all these goals. It is no accident, for example, that students in lower-track academic classes are nearly always simultaneously being given vocational or child care training or are taught a general curriculum that is designed to prepare them for responsible citizenship and personal growth.

The history of tracking exemplifies schools' efforts to address social, personal, and workforce needs, as well as cognitive ones. At the turn of the century, G. Stanley Hall's notions about the proclivities and emotional needs of adolescents provided the intellectual underpinnings for giving most students a more practical, nonscholarly secondary school curriculum. At about the same time, Lewis Terman proclaimed that even though minority students could not be expected to have the mental capacity to master abstractions, they were well suited to separate classes that could train them to be "efficient workers." In 1908 the superintendent of Boston's schools supported tracking by heralding the new "sorting function" of schools. No more than a decade later, the National Association of Manufacturers and the AFL-CIO added their support because tracking enabled schools to act as sites for non-partisan job training. Each of these individuals and groups may be said to have been acting on good intentions.

Asserting the good intentions of educators and the neutrality of tracking as an organizational technology, Hallinan softens the evidence about the disproportionately negative impact of tracking on low-income students and minority students. She argues that the racial and social-class segregation that occurs may be inevitable, given the unfortunate coincidence of "low ability" with low-income and minority status, but that the diminished outcomes that accompany this segregation are unintended consequences. Hallinan bases this latter judgment partly on her confidence that the only "correct" purpose of tracking—to foster cognitive development—is the only operational purpose and partly on her conviction that the well-documented negative effects of tracking result from educators' failure to enact its theory faithfully (in ways that benefit students in all tracks). Hallinan then contends that tracking's segregative effects can be counterbalanced by mixing students by race and social class in their untracked classes and by creating a nonracist school atmosphere. She claims that tracking's lamentable impact on students' social status—including low-track students' diminished motivation and effort—can be circumvented if schools alter their reward structures in ways that extend higher status to low-track students. She asserts that the educational discrepancies among tracks can be remedied with a beefed-up low-track curriculum.

Hallinan's ameliorative strategies are recognized by educators who are grappling with tracking's negative consequences as tried-and-false methods of the past. First, they see that few students miss the clear status message carried by racially identifiable tracking in high-status academic classes. Even if lower-status classes and extracurricular activities are more evenly mixed racially, students and adults in all but the most extraordinary schools have their stereotypes and prejudices reinforced by racially identifiable high- and low-track classes. Educators who have tried know the limits—even impossibility—of creating a climate of intolerance for racism and for the promotion of positive inter-group relations, as long as school structures institutionalize racist conceptions of intellectual capacity. A school may become calmer around racial issues with human relations efforts, but it cannot embody egalitarianism or social justice without deeper changes in tracking structures and the norms and political relations these structures enact.

Nearly all educators are well aware that low-track students consistently have lower-quality opportunities to learn than do their peers in higher tracks. They also recognize that these differences are not appropriate modifications of curriculum and instruction to differences in the abilities of students in various groups, but that they take the form of gross inequalities in access to knowledge, instructional resources, and well-qualified teachers. Many educators have spent their careers trying to beef up the low-track curriculum, to adopt a more positive disposition toward the capacities of low-track students, and to alter the reward systems that work against these students. These educators would undoubtedly find insulting the suggestion that an "attitude adjustment" (Hallinan's phrase) would enable them to be persuasive in communicating a positive message about the meaning of different track levels and would effectively cancel out low-track students' accurate perceptions that schools have a low regard for their abilities and prospects for success in school.

In addition to salutary efforts to integrate students, to enhance low-track students' feelings of worth outside tracked classrooms, and to improve the low-track curriculum, Hallinan suggests that tracking could be vastly improved if educators more faithfully enacted tracking theory by making tracks more homogeneous. To accomplish this greater uniformity within tracks, she recommends two changes. First, schools should base track assignments on the most "objective" measures of ability and achievement. Second, schools should employ more flexible placement practices, such as frequent reassessments and reassignments to other tracks.

Hallinan is absolutely correct when she asserts that most tracks are not highly homogeneous ability groups; the ranges of ability in tracks are wide and, in many schools, overlap considerably with those in other tracks. Where she goes wrong is in suggesting that this phenomenon results from a faulty application of technology—sloppy assessment or failure to account for students' differential rates of growth. And her recommendation for reassessment and reassignment ignores the political realities of tracking.

Track assignments stem from more than the cognitive criteria and the structural constraints (such as scheduling conflicts and limited resources) that Hallinan lists. Although these factors are important, there is consistent evidence that background factors, including the discriminatory placement of minority students in low tracks, also come into play. Neither the negative impact of minority status nor discriminatory placement practices are obvious in analyses of large-scale survey data, particularly when the data are aggregated across school systems. Such analyses tend to obscure between-system differences in track assignments resulting from the composition of the student population in the schools. And their measures are usually too gross to detect differential placement practices within schools.

Let me explain this a bit more. Senior high schools in low-income, high-minority communities are similar in structure to those in White and wealthy suburban areas. That is, in both types of communities the schools strive to be "comprehensive" and to offer both college preparatory and non-college preparatory programs and courses. Teachers and students in both settings have no difficulty pointing out which programs are designed for high-, average-, and low-ability students. However, such communities and schools are not so similar in how well students score on traditional measures of academic ability and achievement. Differences in the typical "ability" composition of schools (with students in White and wealthy schools scoring higher, on average) mean that many minority students attending schools in predominantly minority communities demonstrate ability levels—as measured by test scores—that would not be high enough to qualify them for academic tracks in whiter and wealthier communities. However, because their schools need to fill a requisite number of academic track "slots," some of these students are enrolled in the academic tracks at their schools. Consequently, when data about two such communities are aggregated, one finds a pattern of track placement that appears to give a slight advantage to African American students (after controlling for ability) of being assigned to academic tracks. This aggregation can mask considerable discrimination against minority students in high-track placements in both such systems.

When analyses of the relationship among race, ability, and placements within particular schools and school systems are performed, a different understanding results. For example, I recently analyzed the relationship between race and track placement (controlling for achievement) within schools in five medium-size city school systems with racially mixed student populations.[3] In each of these schools and systems, I found clear evidence of discriminatory placements, with Whites and Asians considerably (and statistically significantly) more likely to be placed in academic classes than comparably achieving African American and Latino students. In these systems the average achievement of African American and Latino students was lower than that of Whites and Asians. However, substantial discrimination against even high-scoring minorities skewed the racial composition of classes beyond what would have been the case had track placements been made by an unfailingly strict adherence to achievement as the criteria.

When one looks carefully at such systems, one finds that much of the heterogeneity within tracks comes about precisely because powerful parents are able to secure high-track placements for their unqualified children. This represents a type of political pressure that is not likely to respond to appeals to fairness. When a status preference exists, savvy parents of high socioeconomic status (SES) will use their considerable political capital on behalf of their children. Lower SES and minority students, whose ascribed characteristics work against them in their initial track placements, tend to have families who are precluded from such political maneuvering by their ignorance of schools' frequent acquiescence to parental pressure or by their timidity about exercising such pressure. Parents of students who are currently in the higher tracks would surely resist the reassignment of their children to lower tracks with even greater vehemence than they resist the dismantling of the track system itself.

Within schools, factors related to students' race and social class shape educators' perceptions of appropriate class placements. Educators value being able to exercise their professional judgment to make exceptions to rigid tracking practices for students who "work hard but don't test well," for those whose parents promise to provide support with private tutoring, and so on. The fact that such students are disproportionately White and middle class will do little to persuade educators that such exceptions are not "fair."

In the end, Hallinan's suggestions simply beg the question, arguing that schools can solve the inequities of tracking by solving the inequities of tracking—as if the norms, politics, and practices of schools are pieces of separate games to be played independently. My work has persuaded me that the inequalities of tracking are nothing other than the normative and political guises of tracking itself.

Hallinan argues that if tracking were fixed, it could benefit students at all ability levels. But, she also acknowledges that there is no empirical evidence that such benefits accrue. I can only speculate, based on years and years of discussion with advocates of tracking, why Hallinan resists "detracking" as a way to confront the problems of tracking. These reasons often include (1) a wish to circumvent comprehensive changes in other school regularities that schools must make when they move to heterogeneous ability grouping (such as changing staffing patterns, redistributing resources, reconceptualizing the curriculum and instruction, restructuring grading practices, and more), (2) a wish to avoid scrutiny of long-standing norms underlying schools' definition and evaluations of intelligence and learning (including such constructs as high-, average-, and low ability), and (3) a wish to avoid the often-nasty political contentiousness (not the least of which is the threat of "bright flight") that "detracking" reforms often bring. It may also be the case that Hallinan, like some other social scientists, believes that her role is simply to observe social phenomena without altering them and thus takes a highly conservative stance on reform.

I have come to believe, from studying educators as they struggle firsthand with detracking reforms (many with surprising success), that heterogeneity, in itself, may be the necessary lever to ensure that low-status students have access to a high-quality curriculum, teachers, and learning experiences—to say nothing of seats next to their advantaged White peers and the increased status that comes with them. Furthermore, although tracking places a *disproportionate* burden on low-income, minority children, the group that is *numerically* most affected by tracking are low- and middle-SES White children who are identified as something other than "high track." As long as students view themselves as "low," and they are concentrated in classes where teachers expect them to act as such, rich, multidimensional educational opportunities are unlikely to come their way.

Without a doubt, "detracking" is an extraordinary reform to undertake, and those in schools that are attempting it would be the first to agree. Yet, these educators believe, often with firsthand experience that is backed by a growing body of research, that they can teach all students well. Together. And, as dramatic as it may seem, they also believe that it is their professional and moral obligation to try.

FURTHER THOUGHTS ON TRACKING

Maureen T. Hallinan

To have a meaningful discussion, it is necessary to define tracking and detracking. Tracking, or homogeneous grouping, is the organization of students for instruction, based on their ability and achievement. The practice is based on the belief that it promotes learning by providing a good fit between the level of instruction and students' learning needs. *Detracking*, or heterogeneous grouping, is the arrangement of students for instruction into groups that include students with a wide range of abilities. The rationale for detracking is the belief that cognitive diversity can be an effective teaching technique.

Both tracking and detracking, as Oakes notes, occur in a specific normative and political milieu. The school milieu can support the positive features of a school's organizational structure and promote learning, or it can undermine the pedagogical effectiveness of an organizational structure and obstruct learning. Typically, it is the school's climate and political and social agenda, not the practice of tracking or detracking, that accounts for a school's success or failure.

Most of the negative consequences of tracking can be attributed to a school environment that fails to provide the support needed to make tracking effective. Tracking itself is not designed to be a political tool, nor is it meant to influence the normative climate of a school. To assert that tracking is a failure because it is associated with a set of negative norms or a discriminatory political or social climate is a misplaced criticism. A tracked school's failure to provide students with equal opportunities to learn is not due to tracking, but to the absence of the school's commitment to equality. The negative impact of the segregation created by tracking is caused by the failure to embed tracking in an atmosphere that would counter this situation.

Remedying the deficiencies of tracking requires improving the social and political fabric of the school. It may involve changing teachers' and students' attitudes and behaviors, altering the reward structure of the school, and reorganizing the curriculum. It also may require modifying teachers' philosophies of education and political persuasions. The resulting positive school climate will enable students to take advantage of the benefits of tracking to increase their academic achievement.

When Oakes and others advocate detracking, they usually imply more than heterogeneous grouping. Proponents of detracking describe schools that have an ideal social and political climate. They refer to the use of pedagogical techniques that support lower-ability students, a curriculum that is tailored to a child's learning needs, the employment of teacher aides to assist teachers, diverse curricular assignments and projects, and an underlying respect for various manifestations of intelligence. These descriptions place heterogeneous grouping in a culture and political climate that is nondiscriminatory and that aims to accommodate the unique learning needs of each student. It is likely that this positive normative climate and support structure, rather than heterogeneous grouping, is responsible for the success of detracked schools. Homogeneous grouping may be equally effective in the same kind of environment, whereas heterogeneous grouping may be less successful than tracking in schools with a negative social climate.

The results of empirical research on the effects of ability and nonability groups on students' learning underscore the importance of separating a grouping practice from the environment in which it is practiced to evaluate its effectiveness. The studies show that the major differences between homogeneously and heterogeneously grouped schools lies in the variance, rather than the mean, of the student achievement distribution. On average, students do equally well in grouped and ungrouped instructional arrangements. But in ability grouped schools, the high-ability students tend to learn more, and the low-ability students tend to learn less than in heterogeneously grouped schools. This consistent finding implies either that ability grouping is inherently detrimental to low-ability students (and advantageous to high-ability students) or that intervening factors modify the effects of ability grouping on students who differ in ability. Both survey and ethnographic data indicate the latter.

The intervening factors that researchers identify as reducing the effectiveness of tracking for low-ability students undoubtedly are reflections of a school's normative, social, and political climate. Consequently, it is likely that a school's context, rather than its grouping practices, should be the object of reform. Replacing tracking with detracking without changing the climate of the school is unlikely to improve students' learning. On the other hand, changing a school's climate may eliminate the need to abandon tracking.

Critics of tracking seem to suggest that tracking exists only in schools that at least tolerate discrimination and inequality. Those who remain cautious about abandoning tracking note that studies of detracking seem to be conducted only in schools that are strongly dedicated to equal opportunity for all students. What is needed is rigorous empirical research on the effects of homogeneous and heterogeneous grouping in schools that vary in the several dimensions of school context to determine the impact of the organization of students on learning.

ONE MORE THOUGHT

Jeannie Oakes

Forty years ago this month, the Supreme Court ruled that school segregation was unconstitutional because separate is *inherently* unequal. It was clear to the Warren Court that in the 60 years since *Plessy*, school segregation had proved to be neither a neutral practice nor one that was separable from the negative racial norms and the discriminatory political context in which it was embedded. The Court recognized that the practice of racial separation was both a cause and an effect of a social climate of discrimination and inequality. By *definition*, racial segregation existed in communities that at least tolerated discrimination and inequality, and, in contrast, those communities that voluntarily initiated school desegregation were places committed to equal opportunity for all students. Thus, the Court did not rule that the harms of segregation could be remedied by changing philosophies or political persuasions. Neither did it ask Kenneth Clark to repeat his doll studies on Black and White children in communities with more positive racial climates to assess whether the negative responses he obtained from Black children stemmed from the practice of segregation itself or from the absence of a commitment to equality in their communities. The *Brown* ruling recognized that, although for convenience and analysis, sociologists may talk about structures, norms, and politics as components of society, these components are not distinct or separable.

Tracking is partly, but not only, about race. Whereas African American and Latino children disproportionately wind up in lower-track classes, most of the children who are disadvantaged by tracking are poor and working-class Whites. The segregative mechanism of tracking, at least ostensibly, is ability. However, like racial segregation, tracking builds inequalities into schools that both devalue and materially disadvantage those groups who are least able to defend themselves. Ability, like race, is a social construction that leads schools to define and treat children from powerless groups—Black, Brown, and White—as expendable. Thus, like racial segregation, tracking carries with it class-based damage that can neither be avoided nor compensated for. Tracking's supporters, much like opponents of the *Brown* ruling, argue otherwise, claiming that separate could be equally effective if school and classroom environments were good. They ask that institutionalized segregation by ability be left in place because the real culprits are attitudes, behaviors, reward structures, philosophies, political persuasions, culture, and normative climate. I find little to support their position, either in the empirical evidence or in principle.

Notes

1. Hallinan's piece rests heavily on empirical studies, but none are cited. For a comprehensive review of this literature, see Jeannie Oakes, Adam Gamoran, and Reba N. Page, "Curriculum Differentiation: Opportunities, Outcomes, and Meanings," in Philip Jackson, ed., *Handbook of Research on Curriculum* (New York: Macmillan, 1992). Although several later studies have added to this data base, they have not altered its fundamental conclusions.

2. Ten of these schools are currently participating in a three-year study, Beyond Sorting and Stratification: Creating Alternatives to Tracking in Racially-Mixed Secondary Schools, which I codirect at UCLA with Amy Stuart Wells under the sponsorship of the Lilly Endowment. The other six are part of a larger sample of schools that I am studying, under the sponsorship of the Carnegie Corporation of New York, that are attempting to reform the middle grades. Because both studies are still in progress, I offer only preliminary reflections about these schools here.

3. See Jeannie Oakes, Molly Selvin, Lynn Karoly, and Gretchen Guiton, *Educational Matchmaking: Academic and Vocational Tracking in Comprehensive High Schools* (Santa Monica, CA: RAND, 1992); and Jeannie Oakes, reports prepared in conjunction with two recent federal desegregation cases, *People Who Care v. Rockford Illinois Public Schools* and *Vasquez v. San Jose Unified School District*, 1993

20

Invisible Inequality

Social Class and Childrearing in Black Families and White Families

ANNETTE LAREAU

In recent decades, sociological knowledge about inequality in family life has increased dramatically. Yet, debate persists, especially about the transmission of class advantages to children. Kingston (2000) and others question whether disparate aspects of family life cohere in meaningful patterns. Pointing to a "thin evidentiary base" for claims of social class differences in the interior of family life, Kingston also asserts that "class distinguishes neither distinctive parenting styles or distinctive involvement of kids" in specific behaviors (p. 134).

One problem with many studies is that they are narrowly focused. Researchers look at the influence of parents' education on parent involvement in schooling *or* at children's time spent watching television *or* at time spent visiting relatives. Only a few studies examine more than one dynamic inside the home. Second, much of the empirical work is descriptive. For example, extensive research has been done on time use, including patterns of women's labor force participation, hours parents spend at work, and mothers' and fathers' contributions to childcare (Hertz and Marshall 2001; Jacobs and Gerson 1998; Menaghan 1991). Time parents spend with children also has been examined (Bianchi 2000; Bianchi and Robinson 1997; Marsiglio 1991; Presser 1989; Zick and Bryant 1996), as well as patterns of children's time use (Hofferth and Sandberg 2001b; Juster and Stafford 1985; Sandberg and Hofferth 2001). But these works have not given sufficient attention to the meaning of events or to the ways different family contexts may affect how a given task is executed (but see Daley 2001; Rubin 1976; Thorne 2001).

Third, researchers have not satisfactorily explained how these observed patterns are produced. Put differently, *conceptualizations* of the *social processes* through which families differ are underdeveloped and little is known about how family life transmits advantages to children. Few researchers have attempted to integrate what is known about behaviors and attitudes taught inside the home with the ways in which these practices may provide unequal resources for family members outside the home. A key exception is the work by Kohn and colleagues (e.g., Kohn and Schooler 1983), where the authors argue that middle-class parents value self-direction while working-class parents place a premium on "conformity to external authority." These researchers did not investigate, however, how parents go about translating these beliefs into actions.

Fourth, little is known about the degree to which children adopt and enact their parents' beliefs. Sociologists of the family have long stressed the importance of a more dynamic model of parent-child interaction (Skolnick 1991), but empirical research has been slow to emerge (but see Hess and Handel 1974). Ethnographers' efforts to document children's agency have provided vivid but highly circumscribed portraits (Shehan 1999; Waksler 1991), but most of the case studies look at only one social class or one ethnic group. Moreover, ethnographers typically do not explicitly examine how social class advantages are transmitted to children.

I draw on findings from a small, intensive data set collected using ethnographic methods. I map the connections between parents' resources and their children's daily lives. My first goal, then, is to challenge Kingston's (2000) argument that social class does not distinguish parents' behavior or children's daily lives. I seek to show empirically that social class does indeed create distinctive parenting styles. I demonstrate that parents differ by class in the ways they define their own roles in their children's lives as well as in how they perceive the nature of childhood. The middle-class parents, both white *and* black, tend to conform to a cultural logic of childrearing I call "concerted cultivation." They enroll their children in numerous age-specific organized activities that dominate family life and create enormous labor, particularly for mothers. The parents view these activities as transmitting important life skills to children. Middle-class parents also stress language use and the development of reasoning and employ talking as their preferred form of discipline. This "cultivation" approach results in a wider range of experiences for children but also creates a frenetic pace for parents, a cult of individualism within the family, and an emphasis on children's performance.[1]

The childrearing strategies of white and black working-class and poor parents emphasize the "accomplishment of natural growth."[2] These parents believe that as long as they provide love, food, and safety, their children will grow and thrive. They do not focus on developing their children's special talents. Compared to the middle-class children, working-class and poor children participate in few organized activities and have more free time and deeper, richer ties within their extended families. Working-class and poor parents issue many more directives to their children and, in some households, place more emphasis on physical discipline than do the middle-class parents. These findings extend Kohn and Schooler's (1983) observation of class differences in parents' values, showing that differences also exist in the *behavior* of parents *and* children.

Quantitative studies of children's activities offer valuable empirical evidence but only limited ideas about how to conceptualize the mechanisms through which social advantage is transmitted. Thus, my second goal is to offer "conceptual umbrellas" useful for making comparisons across race and class and for assessing the role of social structural location in shaping daily life.[3]

Last, I trace the connections between the class position of family members—including children—and the uneven outcomes of their experiences outside the home as they interact with professionals in dominant institutions. The pattern of concerted cultivation encourages an *emerging sense of entitlement* in children. All parents and children are not equally assertive, but the pattern of questioning and intervening among the white and black middle-class parents contrasts sharply with the definitions of how to be helpful and effective observed among the white and black working-class and poor adults. The pattern of the accomplishment of natural growth encourages an *emerging sense of constraint*. Adults as well as children in these social classes tend to be deferential and outwardly accepting in their interactions with professionals such as doctors and educators. At the same time, however, compared to their middle-class counterparts, white and black working-class and poor family members are more distrustful of professionals. These are differences with potential long-term consequences. In a historical moment when the dominant society privileges active, informed, assertive clients of health and educational services, the strategies employed by children and parents are not equally effective across classes. In sum, differences in family life lie not only in the advantages parents obtain for their children, but also in the skills they transmit to children for negotiating their own life paths.

Methodology

Study Participants

This study is based on interviews and observations of children, aged 8 to 10, and their families. The data were collected over time in three research phases. Phase one involved observations in two third-grade classrooms in a public school in the Midwestern community of "Lawrenceville."[4] After conducting observations for two months, I grouped the families into social class (and race) categories based on information provided by educators. I then chose every third name, and sent a letter to the child's home asking the mother and father to participate in separate interviews. Over 90 percent of parents agreed, for a total of 32 children (16 white and 16 African American). A black graduate student and I interviewed all mothers and most fathers (or guardians) of the children. Each interview lasted 90 to 120 minutes, and all took place in 1989–1990.

Phase two took place at two sites in a northeastern metropolitan area. One school, "Lower Richmond," although located in a predominantly white, working-class urban neighborhood, drew about half of its students from a nearby all-black housing project. I observed one third-grade class at Lower Richmond about twice a week for almost six months. The second site, "Swan," was located in a suburban neighborhood about 45 minutes from the city center. It was 90 percent white; most of the remaining 10 percent were middle-class black children.[5] There, I observed twice a week for two months at the end of the third grade; a research assistant then observed weekly for four more months in the fourth grade.[6] At each site, teachers and parents described their school in positive terms.[7] The observations took place between September 1992 and January 1994. In the fall of 1993, I drew an interview sample from Lower Richmond and Swan, following the same method of selection used for Lawrenceville. A team of research assistants and I interviewed the parents and guardians of 39 children. Again, the response rate was over 90 percent but because the classrooms did not generate enough black middle-class children and white poor children to fill the analytical categories, interviews were also conducted with 17 families with children aged 8 to 10. (Most of these interviews took place during the summers of 1996 and 1997.)[8] Thus, the total number of children who participated in the study was 88 (32 from the Midwest and 56 from the Northeast).

Family Observations

Phase three, the most intensive research phase of the study, involved home observations of 12 children and their families in the Northeast who had been previously interviewed (see Table 20.1).[9] Some themes, such as language use and families' social connections, surfaced mainly during this phase. Although I entered the field interested in examining the influence of social class on children's daily lives, I incorporated new themes as they "bubbled up" from the field observations. The evidence presented here comes mainly from the family observations, but I also use interview findings from the full sample of 88 children where appropriate.[10]

Nine of the 12 families came from the Northeastern classroom sample. The home observations took place, one family at a time, from December 1993 to August 1994. Three 10-year-olds (a black middle-class boy and girl and a white poor boy) who were not part of the classroom sample were observed in their homes during the summer of 1995.[11]

The research assistants and I took turns visiting the participating families daily, for a total of about 20 visits to each home, often in the space of one month.[12] The observations went beyond the home: Fieldworkers followed children and parents as they participated in school activities, church services and events, organized play, visits to relatives, and medical appointments. Observations typically lasted three hours, but sometimes much longer (e.g., when we observed an out-of-town funeral, a special extended family event, or a long shopping trip). Most cases also involved one overnight visit. We often carried tape recorders and used the audiotapes for reference in writing field notes. Writing field notes usually required 8 to 12 hours for each two- or three-hour home visit. Participating families each were paid $350, usually at the end of the visits.

We worked in teams of three. One field-worker visited three to four times per week; another visited one to two times per week; and I visited once or twice per week, except for the two families for which I was lead fieldworker. The research teams' composition varied with the race of the family. Two white graduate students and I (a middle-aged white woman) visited the white families; for the black families,

Table 20.1 Frequency Distribution of Children in the Study by Social Class and Race

Social Class	White	Black	Total
Middle class [a]	18	18	36
	(Garrett Tallinger)	(Alexander Williams)	
	(Melanie Handlon)	(Stacey Marshall)	
Working class [b]	14	12	26
	(Billy Yanelli)	(Tyrec Taylor)	
	(Wendy Driver)	(Jessica Irwin)[c]	
Poor[d]	12	14	26
	(Karl Greeley)	(Harold McAllister)	
	(Katie Brindle)	(Tara Carroll)	
Total sample	44	44	88

Note: The names in each cell of the table indicate the children selected to take place in the family-observation phase of the study.

[a] Middle-class children are those who live in households in which at least one parent is employed in a position that either entails substantial managerial authority or that draws upon highly complex, educationally certified skills (i.e., college-level).

[b] Working-class children are those who live in households in which neither parent is employed in a middle-class position and at least one parent is employed in a position with little or no managerial authority and that does not draw on highly complex, educationally certified skills. This category includes lower-level white-collar workers.

[c] An inter-racial girl who has a black father and a white mother.

[d] Poor children are those who live in households in which parents receive public assistance and do not participate in the labor force on a regular, continuous basis.

the teams included one white graduate student, one black graduate student, and me. All black families with male children were visited by teams that included a black male fieldworker. A white male field-worker observed the poor family with the white boy; the remaining white field workers were female. Team members met regularly to discuss the families and to review the emerging analytic themes.

Our presence altered family dynamics, especially at first. Over time, however, we saw signs of adjustment (e.g., yelling and cursing increased on the third day and again on the tenth). The children, especially, seemed to enjoy participating in the project. They reported it made them feel "special." They were visibly happy to see the fieldworkers arrive and reluctant to let them leave. The working-class and poor black boys were more comfortable with the black male field-workers than with the white female ones, especially at first.[13] Overall, however, family members reported in exit interviews that they had not changed their behavior significantly, or they mentioned very specific alterations (e.g., "the house got cleaner").

A Note on Class

I undertook field observations to develop an intensive, realistic portrait of family life. Although I deliberately focused on only 12 families, I wanted to compare children across gender and race. Adopting the fine-grained differentiations characteristic of current neo-Marxist and neo-Weberian empirical studies was not tenable.[14] Further limitations were imposed by the school populations at the sites I selected. Very few students were children of employers or of self-employed workers. I decided to focus exclusively on those whose parents were employees. Authority in the workplace and "credential barriers" are the criteria most commonly used to differentiate within this heterogeneous group. I assigned the families to a working-class or middle-class category based on detailed information that each of the employed adults provided about the work they did, the nature of the organization that employed them, and their educational credentials. I also included a category traditionally excluded from class groupings: families not involved in the labor market. In the first school I studied, many children were from households supported by public assistance. Omitting them would have restricted the scope of the study arbitrarily.[15]

The three class categories conceal important internal variations. The Williams family (black) and the Tallinger family (white) have very high incomes, both in excess of $175,000; the median income among the middle-class parents was much lower.[16] Income differences among the middle-class families were not associated with differences in childrearing methods. Moreover, no other data in the study showed compelling intraclass divisions. I consider the use of one term—middle class—to be reasonable.

Concerted Cultivation and Natural Growth

The interviews and observations suggested that crucial aspects of family life *cohered*. Within the concerted cultivation and accomplishment of natural growth approaches, three key dimensions may be distinguished: the organization of daily life, the use of language, and social connections. ("Interventions in institutions" and "consequences" are addressed later in the paper.) These dimensions do not capture all important parts of family life, but they do incorporate core aspects of childrearing (Table 20.2). Moreover, our field observations revealed that behaviors and activities related to these dimensions dominated the rhythms of family life. Conceptually, the organization of daily life and the use of language are crucial dimensions. Both must be present for the family to be described as engaging in one childrearing approach rather than the other. Social connections are significant but less conceptually essential.

All three aspects of childrearing were intricately woven into the families' daily routines, but rarely remarked upon. As part of everyday practice, they were invisible to parents and children. Analytically, however, they are useful means for comparing and contrasting ways in which social class differences shape the character of family life. I now examine two families in terms of these three key dimensions. I "control" for race and gender and contrast the lives of two black boys—one from an (upper) middle-class family and one from a family on public assistance. I could have focused on almost any of the other 12 children, but this pair seemed optimal, given the limited number of studies reporting on black middle-class families, as well as the aspect of my argument that suggests that race is less important than class in shaping childrearing patterns.

Table 20.2 Summary of Differences in Childrearing Approaches

	Childrearing Approach	
Dimension Observed	**Concerted Cultivation**	**Accomplishment of Natural Growth**
Key elements of each approach	Parent actively fosters and assesses child's talents, opinions, and skills	Parent cares for child and allows child to grow
Organization of daily life	Multiple child leisure activities are orchestrated by adults	Child "hangs out" particularly with kin
Language use	Reasoning/directives Child contestation of adult statements Extended negotiations between parents and child	Directives Rare for child to question or challenge adults General acceptance by child of directives
Social connections	Weak extended family ties Child often in homogenous age groupings	Strong extended family ties Child often in heterogeneous age groupings
Interventions in institutions	Criticisms and interventions on behalf of child Training of child to intervene on his or her own behalf	Dependence on institutions Sense of powerlessness and frustration Conflict between childrearing practices at home and at school
Consequences	Emerging sense of entitlement on the part of the child	Emerging sense of constraint on the part of the child

Developing Alexander Williams

Alexander Williams and his parents live in a predominantly black middle-class neighborhood. Their six-bedroom house is worth about $150,000.[17] Alexander is an only child. Both parents grew up in small towns in the South, and both are from large families. His father, a tall, handsome man, is a very successful trial lawyer who earns about $125,000 annually in a small firm specializing in medical malpractice cases. Two weeks each month, he works very long hours (from about 5:30 A.M. until midnight) preparing for trials. The other two weeks, his workday ends around 6:00 P.M. He rarely travels out of town. Alexander's mother, Christina, is a positive, bubbly woman with freckles and long, black, wavy hair.[18] A high-level manager in a major corporation, she has a corner office, a personal secretary, and responsibilities for other offices across the nation. She tries to limit her travel, but at least once a month she takes an overnight trip.

Alexander is a charming, inquisitive boy with a winsome smile. Ms. Williams is pleased that Alexander seems interested in so many things:

> Alexander is a joy. He's a gift to me. He's very energetic, very curious, loving, caring person, that, um…is outgoing and who, uh, really loves to be with people. And who loves to explore, and loves to read and…just do a lot of fun things.

The private school Alexander attends[19] has an on-site after-school program. There, he participates in several activities and receives guitar lessons and photography instruction.

Organization of daily life Alexander is busy with activities during the week and on weekends (Table 20.3). His mother describes their Saturday morning routine. The day starts early with a private piano lesson for Alexander downtown, a 20-minute drive from the house:

> It's an 8:15 class. But for me, it was a tradeoff. I am very adamant about Saturday morning TV. I don't know what it contributes. So…it was…um…either stay at home and fight on a Saturday morning [laughs] or go do something constructive.…Now Saturday mornings are pretty booked up. You know, the piano lesson, and then straight to choir for a couple of hours. So, he has a very full schedule.

Ms. Williams's vehement opposition to television is based on her view of what Alexander needs to grow and thrive. She objects to TV's passivity and feels it is her obligation to help her son cultivate his talents.

Sometimes Alexander complains that "my mother signs me up for everything!" Generally, however, he likes his activities. He says they make him feel "special," and without them life would be "boring." His sense of time is thoroughly entwined with his activities: He feels disoriented when his schedule is not full. This unease is clear in the following field-note excerpt. The family is driving home from a Back-to-School night. The next morning, Ms. Williams will leave for a work-related day trip and will not return until late at night. Alexander is grumpy because he has nothing planned for the next day. He wants to have a friend over, but his mother rebuffs him. Whining, he wonders what he will do. His mother, speaking tersely, says:

> You have piano and guitar. You'll have some free time. [Pause] I think you'll survive for one night. [Alexander does not respond but seems mad. It is quiet for the rest of the trip home.]

Alexander's parents believe his activities provide a wide range of benefits important for his development. In discussing Alexander's piano lessons, Mr. Williams notes that as a Suzuki student,[20] Alexander is already able to read music. Speculating about more diffuse benefits of Alexander's involvement with piano, he says:

I don't see how any kid's adolescence and adulthood could not but be enhanced by an awareness of who Beethoven was. And is that Bach or Mozart? I don't know the difference between the two! I don't know Baroque from Classical—but he does. How can that not be a benefit in later life? I'm convinced that this rich experience will make him a better person, a better citizen, a better husband, a better father—certainly a better student.

Ms. Williams sees music as building her son's "confidence" and his "poise." In interviews and casual conversation, she stresses "exposure." She believes it is her responsibility to broaden Alexander's worldview. Childhood activities provide a learning ground for important life skills:

Sports provide great opportunities to learn how to be competitive. Learn how to accept defeat, you know. Learn how to accept winning, you know, in a gracious way. Also it gives him the opportunity to learn leadership skills and how to be a team player.... Sports really provides a lot of really great opportunities.

Table 20.3 Participation in Activities Outside of School: Boys

Boy's Name/Race/Class	Activities Organized by Adults	Informal Activities
Middle Class		
Garrett Tallinger (white)	Soccer team Traveling soccer team Baseball team Basketball team (summer) Swim team Piano Saxophone (through school)	Plays with siblings in yard Watches television Plays computer games Overnights with friends
Alexander Williams (black)	Soccer team Baseball team Community choir Church choir Sunday school Piano (Suzuki) School plays Guitar (through school)	Restricted television Plays outside occasionally with two other boys Visits friends from school
Working Class		
Billy Yanelli (white)	Baseball team	Watches television Visits relatives Rides bike Plays outside in the street Hangs out with neighborhood kids
Tyrec Taylor (black)	Football team Vacation Bible School Sunday school (off/on)	Watches television Plays outside in the street Rides bikes with neighborhood boys Visit relatives Goes to swimming pool
Poor		
Karl Greeley (white)	Goes to swimming pool Walks dogs with neighbor	Watches television Plays Nintendo Plays with siblings
Harold McAllister (black)	Bible study in neighbor's house (occasionally) Bible camp (1 week)	Visits relatives Plays ball with neighborhood kids Watches television Watches videos

Alexander's schedule is constantly shifting; some activities wind down and others start up. Because the schedules of sports practices and games are issued no sooner than the start of the new season, advance planning is rarely possible. Given the sheer number of Alexander's activities, events inevitably overlap. Some activities, though short-lived, are extremely time consuming. Alexander's school play, for example, requires rehearsals three nights the week before the opening. In addition, in choosing activities, the Williamses have an added concern—the group's racial balance. Ms. Williams prefers that Alexander not be the only black child at events. Typically, one or two other black boys are involved, but the groups are predominantly white and the activities take place in predominantly white residential neighborhoods. Alexander is, however, part of his church's youth choir and Sunday School, activities in which all participants are black.

Many activities involve competition. Alex must audition for his solo performance in the school play, for example. Similarly, parents and children alike understand that participation on "A," "B," or "All-Star" sports teams signal different skill levels. Like other middle-class children in the study, Alexander seems to enjoy public performance. According to a field note, after his solo at a musical production in front of over 200 people, he appeared "contained, pleased, aware of the attention he's receiving."

Alexander's commitments do not consume *all* his free time. Still, his life is defined by a series of deadlines and schedules interwoven with a series of activities that are organized and controlled by adults rather than children. Neither he nor his parents see this as troublesome.

Language use Like other middle-class families, the Williamses often engage in conversation that promotes reasoning and negotiation. An excerpt from a field note (describing an exchange between Alexander and his mother during a car ride home after summer camp) shows the kind of pointed questions middle-class parents ask children. Ms. Williams is not just eliciting information. She is also giving Alexander the opportunity to develop and practice verbal skills, including how to summarize, clarify, and amplify information:

As she drives, [Ms. Williams] asks Alex, "So, how was your day?"
Alex: "Okay. I had hot dogs today, but they were burned! They were all black!"
Mom: "Oh, great. You shouldn't have eaten any."
Alex: "They weren't *all* black, only half were. The rest were regular."
Mom: "Oh, okay. What was that game you were playing this morning?..."
Alex: "It was [called] 'Whatcha doin?'"
Mom: "How do you play?"
Alexander explains the game elaborately—fieldworker doesn't quite follow. Mom asks Alex questions throughout his explanation, saying, "Oh, I see," when he answers. She asks him about another game she saw them play; he again explains.... She continues to prompt and encourage him with small giggles in the back of her throat as he elaborates.

Expressions of interest in children's activities often lead to negotiations over small, home-based matters. During the same car ride, Ms. Williams tries to adjust the dinner menu to suit Alexander:

Alexander says, "I don't want hot dogs tonight."
Mom: "Oh? Because you had them for lunch."
Alexander nods.
Mom: "Well, I can fix something else and save the hot dogs for tomorrow night."
Alex: "But I don't want any pork chops either."
Mom: "Well, Alexander, we need to eat something. Why didn't you have hamburgers today?"
Alex: "They don't have them any more at the snack bar."

Mom asks Alexander if he's ok, if he wants a snack. Alexander says he's ok. Mom asks if he's sure he doesn't want a bag of chips?

Not all middle-class parents are as attentive to their children's needs as this mother, and none are *always* interested in negotiating. But a general pattern of reasoning and accommodating is common.

Social connections Mr. and Ms. Williams consider themselves very close to their extended families. Because the Williams's aging parents live in the South, visiting requires a plane trip. Ms. Williams takes Alexander with her to see his grandparents twice a year. She speaks on the phone with her parents at least once a week and also calls her siblings several times a week. Mr. Williams talks with his mother regularly by phone (he has less contact with his stepfather). With pride, he also mentions his niece, whose Ivy League education he is helping to finance.

Interactions with cousins are not normally a part of Alexander's leisure time. (As I explain below, other middle-class children did not see cousins routinely either, even when they lived nearby.) Nor does he often play with neighborhood children. The huge homes on the Williams's street are occupied mainly by couples without children. Most of Alexander's playmates come from his classroom or his organized activities. Because most of his school events, church life, and assorted activities are organized by the age (and sometimes gender) of the participants, Alexander interacts almost exclusively with children his own age, usually boys. Adult-organized activities thus define the context of his social life.

Mr. and Ms. Williams are aware that they allocate a sizable portion of time to Alexander's activities. What they stress, however, is the time they *hold back*. They mention activities the family has chosen *not* to take on (such as traveling soccer).

Summary Overall, Alexander's parents engaged in concerted cultivation. They fostered their son's growth through involvement in music, church, athletics, and academics. They talked with him at length, seeking his opinions and encouraging his ideas. Their approach involved considerable direct expenses (e.g., the cost of lessons and equipment) and large indirect expenses (e.g., the cost of taking time off from work, driving to practices, and foregoing adult leisure activities). Although Mr. and Ms. Williams acknowledged the importance of extended family, Alexander spent relatively little time with relatives. His social interactions occurred almost exclusively with children his own age and with adults. Alexander's many activities significantly shaped the organization of daily life in the family. Both parents' leisure time was tailored to their son's commitments. Mr. and Ms. Williams felt that the strategies they cultivated with Alexander would result in his having the best possible chance at a happy and productive life. They couldn't imagine themselves not investing large amounts of time and energy in their son's life. But, as I explain in the next section, which focuses on a black boy from a poor family, other parents held a different view.

Supporting the Natural Growth of Harold McAllister

Harold McAllister, a large, stocky boy with a big smile, is from a poor black family. He lives with his mother and his 8-year-old sister, Alexis, in a large apartment. Two cousins often stay overnight. Harold's 16-year-old sister and 18-year-old brother usually live with their grandmother, but sometimes they stay at the McAllister's home. Ms. McAllister, a high school graduate, relies on public assistance (AFDC). Hank, Harold and Alexis's father, is a mechanic. He and Ms. McAllister have never married. He visits regularly, sometimes weekly, stopping by after work to watch television or nap. Harold (but not Alexis) sometimes travels across town by bus to spend the weekend with Hank.

The McAllister's apartment is in a public housing project near a busy street. The complex consists of rows of two- and three-story brick units. The buildings, blocky and brown, have small yards enclosed by concrete and wood fences. Large floodlights are mounted on the corners of the buildings, and wide concrete sidewalks cut through the spaces between units. The ground is bare in many places; paper wrappers and glass litter the area.

Inside the apartment, life is humorous and lively, with family members and kin sharing in the daily routines. Ms. McAllister discussed, disdainfully, mothers who are on drugs or who abuse alcohol and do not "look after" their children. Indeed, the previous year Ms. McAllister called Child Protective Services to report her twin sister, a cocaine addict, because she was neglecting her children. Ms. McAllister is actively involved in her twin's daughters' lives. Her two nephews also frequently stay with her. Overall, she sees herself as a capable mother who takes care of her children and her extended family.

Organization of daily life Much of Harold's life and the lives of his family members revolve around home. Project residents often sit outside in lawn chairs or on front stoops, drinking beer, talking, and watching children play. During summer, windows are frequently left open, allowing breezes to waft through the units and providing vantage points from which residents can survey the neighborhood. A large deciduous tree in front of the McAllister's apartment unit provides welcome shade in the summer's heat.

Harold loves sports. He is particularly fond of basketball, but he also enjoys football, and he follows televised professional sports closely. Most afternoons, he is either inside watching television or outside playing ball. He tosses a football with cousins and boys from the neighboring units and organizes pick-up basketball games. Sometimes he and his friends use a rusty, bare hoop hanging from a telephone pole in the housing project; other times, they string up an old, blue plastic crate as a makeshift hoop. One obstacle to playing sports, however, is a shortage of equipment. Balls are costly to replace, especially given the rate at which they disappear—theft of children's play equipment, including balls and bicycles, is an ongoing problem. During a field observation, Harold asks his mother if she knows where the ball is. She replies with some vehemence, "They stole the blue and yellow ball, and they stole the green ball, and they stole the other ball."

Hunting for balls is a routine part of Harold's leisure time. One June day, with the temperature and humidity in the high 80's, Harold and his cousin Tyrice (and a fieldworker) wander around the housing project for about an hour, trying to find a basketball:

> We head to the other side of the complex. On the way ... we passed four guys sitting on the step. Their ages were 9 to 13 years. They had a radio blaring. Two were working intently on fixing a flat bike tire. The other two were dribbling a basketball.
> Harold: "Yo! What's up, ya'll."
> Group: "What's up, Har." "What's up? "Yo."
> They continued to work on the tire and dribble the ball. As we walked down the hill, Harold asked, "Yo, could I use your ball?"
> The guy responded, looking up from the tire, "Naw, man. Ya'll might lose it."

Harold, Tyrice, and the fieldworker walk to another part of the complex, heading for a makeshift basketball court where they hope to find a game in progress:

> No such luck. Harold enters an apartment directly in front of the makeshift court. The door was open.... Harold came back. "No ball. I guess I gotta go back."

The pace of life for Harold and his friends ebbs and flows with the children's interests and family obligations. The day of the basketball search, for example, after spending time listening to music and looking at baseball cards, the children join a water fight Tyrice instigates. It is a lively game, filled with laughter and with efforts to get the adults next door wet (against their wishes). When the game winds down, the kids ask their mother for money, receive it, and then walk to a store to buy chips and soda. They chat with another young boy and then amble back to the apartment, eating as they walk. Another afternoon, almost two weeks later, the children—Harold, two of his cousins, and two children from the neighborhood—and the fieldworker play basketball on a makeshift court in the street (using the fieldworker's ball). As Harold bounces the ball, neighborhood children of all ages wander through the space.

Thus, Harold's life is more free-flowing and more child-directed than is Alexander Williams's. The pace of any given day is not so much planned as emergent, reflecting child-based interests and activities. Parents intervene in specific areas, such as personal grooming, meals, and occasional chores, but they do not continuously direct and monitor their children's leisure activities. Moreover, the leisure activities Harold and other working-class and poor children pursue require them to develop a repertoire of skills for dealing with much older and much younger children as well as with neighbors and relatives.

Language use Life in the working-class and poor families in the study flows smoothly without extended verbal discussions. The amount of talking varies, but overall, it is considerably less than occurs in the middle-class homes.[21] Ms. McAllister jokes with the children and discusses what is on television. But she does not appear to cultivate conversation by asking the children questions or by drawing them out. Often she is brief and direct in her remarks. For instance, she coordinates the use of the apartment's only bathroom by using one-word directives. She sends the children (there are almost always at least four children home at once) to wash up by pointing to a child, saying one word, "bathroom," and handing him or her a washcloth. Wordlessly, the designated child gets up and goes to the bathroom to take a shower.

Similarly, although Ms. McAllister will listen to the children's complaints about school, she does not draw them out on these issues or seek to determine details, as Ms. Williams would. For instance, at the start of the new school year, when I ask Harold about his teacher, he tells me she is "mean" and that "she lies." Ms. McAllister, washing dishes, listens to her son, but she does not encourage Harold to support his opinion about his new teacher with more examples, nor does she mention any concerns of her own. Instead, she asks about last year's teacher, "What was the name of that man teacher?" Harold says, "Mr. Lindsey?" She says, "No, the other one." He says, "Mr. Terrene." Ms. McAllister smiles and says, "Yeah. I liked him." Unlike Alexander's mother, she seems content with a brief exchange of information.

Social connections Children, especially boys, frequently play outside. The number of potential playmates in Harold's world is vastly higher than the number in Alexander's neighborhood. When a field-worker stops to count heads, she finds 40 children of elementary school age residing in the nearby rows of apartments. With so many children nearby, Harold could choose to play only with others his own age. In fact, though, he often hangs out with older and younger children and with his cousins (who are close to his age).

The McAllister family, like other poor and working-class families, is involved in a web of extended kin. As noted earlier, Harold's older siblings and his two male cousins often spend the night at the McAllister home. Celebrations such as birthdays involve relatives almost exclusively. Party guests are not, as in middle-class families, friends from school or from extra-curricular activities. Birthdays are celebrated enthusiastically, with cake and special food to mark the occasion; presents, however, are not offered. Similarly, Christmas at Harold's house featured a tree and special food but no presents. At these and other family events, the older children voluntarily look after the younger ones: Harold plays with his 16-month-old niece, and his cousins carry around the younger babies.

The importance of family ties—and the contingent nature of life in the McAllister's world—is clear in the response Alexis offers when asked what she would do if she were given a million dollars:

Oh, boy! I'd buy my brother, my sister, my uncle, my aunt, my nieces and my nephews, and my grandpop, and my grandmom, and my mom, and my dad, and my friends, not my friends, but mostly my best friend—I'd buy them all clothes…and sneakers. And I'd buy some food, and I'd buy my mom some food, and I'd get my brothers and my sisters gifts for their birthdays.

Summary In a setting where everyone, including the children, was acutely aware of the lack of money, the McAllister family made do. Ms. McAllister rightfully saw herself as a very capable mother. She was a strong, positive influence in the lives of the children she looked after. Still, the contrast with Ms. Williams is striking. Ms. McAllister did not seem to think that Harold's opinions needed to be cultivated and developed. She, like most parents in the working-class and poor families, drew strong and clear boundaries between adults and children. Adults gave directions to children. Children were given freedom to play informally unless they were needed for chores. Extended family networks were deemed important and trustworthy.

The Intersection of Race and Class in Family Life

I expected race to powerfully shape children's daily schedules, but this was not evident (also see Conley 1999; Pattillo-McCoy 1999). This is not to say that race is unimportant. Black parents were particularly concerned with monitoring their children's lives outside the home for signs of racial problems.[22] Black middle-class fathers, especially, were likely to stress the importance of their sons understanding "what it means to be a black man in this society" (J. Hochschild 1995). Mr. Williams, in summarizing how he and his wife orient Alexander, said:

[We try to] teach him that race unfortunately is the most important aspect of our national life. I mean people look at other people and they see a color first. But that isn't going to define who he is. He will do his best. He will succeed, despite racism. And I think he lives his life that way.

Alexander's parents were acutely aware of the potential significance of race in his life. Both were adamant, however, that race should not be used as "an excuse" for not striving to succeed. Mr. Williams put it this way:

I discuss how race impacts on my life as an attorney, and I discuss how race will impact on his life. The one teaching that he takes away from this is that he is never to use discrimination as an excuse for not doing his best.

Thus far, few incidents of overt racism had occurred in Alexander's life, as his mother noted: Those situations have been far and few between.…I mean, I can count them on my fingers.

Still, Ms. Williams recounted with obvious pain an incident at a birthday party Alexander had attended as a preschooler. The grandparents of the birthday child repeatedly asked, "Who is that boy?" and exclaimed, "He's so dark!" Such experiences fueled the Williams's resolve always to be "cautious":

We've never been, uh, parents who drop off their kid anywhere. We've always gone with him. And even now, I go in and—to school in the morning—and check [in].… The school environment, we've watched very closely.

Alexander's parents were not equally optimistic about the chances for racial equality in this country. Ms. Williams felt strongly that, especially while Alexander was young, his father should not voice his pessimism. Mr. Williams complained that this meant he had to "watch" what he said to Alexander about race relations. Still, both parents agreed about the need to be vigilant regarding potential racial problems in Alexander's life. Other black parents reported experiencing racial prejudice and expressed a similar commitment to vigilance.

Issues surrounding the prospect of growing up black and male in this society were threaded through Alexander's life in ways that had no equivalent among his middle-class, white male peers. Still, in fourth grade there were no signs of racial experiences having "taken hold" the way that they might as Alexander ages. In terms of the number and kind of activities he participated in, his life was very similar to that of Garrett Tallinger, his white counterpart (see Table 20.3). That both sets of parents were fully committed to a strategy of concentrated cultivation was apparent in the number of adult-organized activities the boys were enrolled in, the hectic pace of family life, and the stress on reasoning in parent-child negotiations. Likewise, the research assistants and I saw no striking differences in the ways in which white parents and black parents in the working-class and poor homes socialized their children.

Others (Fordham and Ogbu 1986) have found that in middle school and high school, adolescent peer groups often draw sharp racial boundaries, a pattern not evident among this study's third- and fourth-grade participants (but sometimes present among their older siblings). Following Tatum (1997:52), I attribute this to the children's relatively young ages (also see "Race in America," *The New York Times,* June 25, 2000, p. 1). In sum, in the broader society, key aspects of daily life were shaped by racial segregation and discrimination. But in terms of enrollment in organized activities, language use, and social connections, the largest differences between the families we observed were across social class, not racial groups.

Differences in Cultural Practices Across the Total Sample

The patterns observed among the Williams and McAllister families occurred among others in the 12-family subsample and across the larger group of 88 children. Frequently, they also echoed established patterns in the literature. These patterns highlight not only the amount of time spent on activities but also the quality of family life and the ways in which key dimensions of childrearing intertwine.

Organization of Daily Life

In the study as a whole, the rhythms of family life differed by social class. Working-class and poor children spent most of their free time in informal play; middle-class children took part in many adult-organized activities designed to develop their individual talents and interests. For the 88 children, I calculated an average score for the most common adult-directed, organized activities,[23] based on parents' answers to interview questions.[24] Middle-class children averaged 4.9 current activities ($N = 36$), working-class children averaged 2.5 activities ($N = 26$), and poor children averaged 1.5 ($N = 26$).[25] Black middle-class children had slightly more activities than white middle-class children, largely connected to more church involvement, with an average of 5.2 ($N = 18$) compared with 4.6 activities for whites ($N = 18$). The racial difference was very modest in the working-class group (2.8 activities for black children [$N = 12$] and 2.3 for white children [$N = 14$]) and the poor group (1.6 activities for black children [$N = 14$] and 1.4 for white children [$N = 12$]). Middle-class boys had slightly more activities than middle-class girls (5.1 versus 4.7, $N = 18$ for both) but gender did not make a difference for the other classes. The type of activity did however. Girls tended to participate in dance, music, and Scouts, and to be less active in sports. This pattern of social class differences in activities is comparable to other, earlier reports (Medrich et al. 1982). Hofferth and Sandberg's (2001a, 2000b) recent research using a representative national sample suggests that the number of children's organized activities increases with parents' education and that children's involvement in organized activities has risen in recent decades.

The dollar cost of children's organized activities was significant, particularly when families had more than one child. Cash outlays included paying the instructors and coaches who gave lessons, purchasing uniforms and performance attire, paying for tournament admission and travel to and from tournaments, and covering hotel and food costs for overnight stays. Summer camps also were expensive. At my request, the Tallingers added up the costs for Garrett's organized activities. The total was over $4,000 per year. Recent reports of parents' expenditures for children's involvement in a single sport (e.g., hockey) are comparably high (Schemari 2002). Children's activities consumed time as well as money, co-opting parents' limited leisure hours.

The study also uncovered differences in how much time children spent in activities controlled by adults. Take the schedule of Melanie Handlon, a white middle-class girl in the fourth grade (see Table 20.4). Between December 8 and December 24, Melanie had a piano lesson each Monday, Girl Scouts each Thursday, a special Girl Scout event one Monday night, a special holiday musical performance at school one Tuesday night, two orthodontist appointments, five special rehearsals for the church

Table 20.4 Participation in Activities Outside of School: Girls

Girl's Name/Race/Class	Activities Organized by Adults	Informal Activities
Middle Class		
Melanie Handlon (white)	Girl Scouts	Restricted television
	Piano	Plays outside with neighborhood kids
	Sunday school	Bakes cookies with mother
	Church	Swims (not on swim team)
	Church pageant	Listens to music
	Violin (through school)	
	Softball team	
Stacey Marshall (black)	Gymnastics lessons	Watches television
	Gymnastic teams	Plays outside
	Church	Visits friends from school
	Sunday school	Rides bike
	Youth choir	
Working Class		
Wendy Driver (white)	Catholic education (CCD)	Watches television
	Dance lessons	Visits relatives
	School choir	Does housework
		Rides bike
		Plays outside in the street
		Hangs out with cousins
Jessica Irwin (black father/ white mother)	Church	Restricted television
	Sunday school	Reads
	Saturday art class	Plays outside with neighborhood kids
	School band	Visit relatives
Poor		
Katie Brindle (white)	School choir	Watches television
	Friday evening church group (rarely)	Visits relatives
		Plays with Barbies
		Rides bike
		Plays with neighborhood kids
Tara Carroll (black)	Church	Watches television
	Sunday school	Visits relatives
		Plays with dolls
		Plays Nintendo
		Plays with neighborhood kids

Christmas pageant, and regular Sunday commitments (an early church service, Sunday school, and youth choir). On weekdays she spent several hours after school struggling with her homework as her mother coached her step-by-step through the worksheets. The amount of time Melanie spent in situations where her movements were controlled by adults was typical of middle-class children in the study.

The schedule of Katie Brindle, a white fourth-grader from a poor family, contrasts sharply, showing few organized activities between December 2 and 24. She sang in the school choir. This involved one after-school rehearsal on Wednesdays; she walked home by herself after these rehearsals. Occasionally, Katie attended a Christian youth group on Friday nights (i.e., December 3). Significantly, all her activities were free. She wanted to enroll in ballet classes, but they were prohibitively expensive. What Katie did have was unstructured leisure time. Usually, she came home after school and then played outside with other children in the neighborhood or watched television. She also regularly visited her grandmother and her cousins, who lived a few minutes away by bus or car. She often spent weekend nights at her grandmother's house. Overall, Katie's life was centered in and around home. Compared with the middle-class children in the study, her life moved at a dramatically less hectic pace. This pattern was characteristic of the other working-class and poor families we interviewed.

In addition to these activities, television provided a major source of leisure entertainment. All children in the study spent at least some free time watching TV, but there were differences in when, what, and how much they watched. Most middle-class parents we interviewed characterized television as actually or potentially harmful to children; many stressed that they preferred their children to read for entertainment. Middle-class parents often had rules about the amount of time children could spend watching television.[26] These concerns did not surface in interviews with working-class and poor parents. Indeed, Ms. Yanelli, a white working-class mother, objected to restricting a child's access to television, noting, "You know, you learn so much from television." Working-class and poor parents did monitor the content of programs and made some shows off-limits for children. The television itself, however, was left on almost continuously (also see Robinson and Godbey 1997).

Language Use

The social class differences in language use we observed were similar to those reported by others (see Bernstein 1971; Hart and Risley 1995; Heath 1983). In middle-class homes, parents placed a tremendous emphasis on reasoning. They also drew out their children's views on specific subjects. Middle-class parents relied on directives for matters of health and safety, but most other aspects of daily life were potentially open to negotiation: Discussions arose over what children wore in the morning, what they ate, where they sat, and how they spent their time. Not all middle-class children were equally talkative, however. In addition, in observations, mothers exhibited more willingness to engage children in prolonged discussions than did fathers. The latter tended to be less engaged with children overall and less accepting of disruptions (A. Hochschild 1989).

In working-class and poor homes, most parents did not focus on developing their children's opinions, judgments, and observations. When children volunteered information, parents would listen, but typically they did not follow up with questions or comments. In the field note excerpt below, Wendy Driver shares her new understanding of sin with the members of her white working-class family. She is sitting in the living room with her brother (Willie), her mother, and her mother's live-in boyfriend (Mack). Everyone is watching television:

Wendy asks Willie: "Do you know what mortal sin is?"
Willie: "No."
Wendy asks Mom: "Do you know what mortal sin is?"
Mom: "What is it?"

Wendy asks Mack: "Do you know what it is?"

Mack: "No."

Mom: "Tell us what it is. You're the one who went to CCD [Catholic religious education classes]."

Wendy: "It's when you know something's wrong and you do it anyway."

No one acknowledged Wendy's comment. Wendy's mother and Mack looked at her while she gave her explanation of mortal sin, then looked back at the TV.

Wendy's family is conversationally cooperative, but unlike the Williamses, for example, no one here perceives the moment as an opportunity to further develop Wendy's vocabulary or to help her exercise her critical thinking skills.

Negotiations between parents and children in working-class and poor families were infrequent. Parents tended to use firm directives and they expected prompt, positive responses. Children who ignored parental instructions could expect physical punishment. Field notes from an evening in the home of the white, working-class Yanelli family capture one example of this familiar dynamic. It is past 8:00 P.M. Ms. Yanelli, her son Billy, and the fieldworker are playing *Scrabble*. Mr. Yanelli and a friend are absorbed in a game of chess. Throughout the evening, Billy and Ms. Yanelli have been at odds. She feels Billy has not been listening to her. Ms. Yanelli wants her son to stop playing *Scrabble*, take a shower, and go to bed.

Mom: "Billy, shower. I don't care if you cry, screams."

Billy: "We're not done with the *Scrabble* game."

Mom: "You're done. Finish your homework earlier." That evening, Billy had not finished his homework until 8:00 P.M. Billy remains seated.

Mom: "Come on! Tomorrow you've got a big day." Billy does not move.

Mom goes into the other room and gets a brown leather belt. She hits Billy twice on the leg.

Mom: "Get up right now! Tomorrow I can't get you up in the morning. Get up right now!"

Billy gets up and runs up the steps.

Ms. Yanelli's disciplinary approach is very different from that of the middle-class parents we observed. Like most working-class and poor parents we observed, she is directive and her instructions are nonnegotiable ("Billy, shower" and "You're done."). Using a belt may seem harsh, but it is neither a random nor irrational form of punishment here. Ms. Yanelli gave Billy notice of her expectations and she offered an explanation (it's late, and tomorrow he has "a big day"). She turned to physical discipline as a resource when she felt Billy was not sufficiently responsive.[27]

Social Connections

We also observed class differences in the context of children's social relations. Across the sample of 88 families, middle-class children's involvement in adult-organized activities led to mainly weak social ties. Soccer, photography classes, swim team, and so on typically take place in 6 to 8 week blocks, and participant turnover rates are relatively high. Equally important, middle-class children's commitment to organized activities generally pre-empted visits with extended family. Some did not have relatives who lived nearby, but even among those who did, children's schedules made it difficult to organize and attend regular extended-family gatherings. Many of the middle-class children visited with relatives only on major holidays.[28]

Similarly, middle-class parents tended to forge weak rather than strong ties. Most reported having social networks that included professionals: 93 percent of the sample of middle-class parents had a friend or relative who was a teacher, compared with 43 percent of working-class parents and 36 percent of poor families. For a physician friend or relative, the pattern was comparable (70 percent versus

14 percent and 18 percent, respectively).[29] Relationships such as these are not as deep as family ties, but they are a valuable resource when parents face a challenge in childrearing.

Working-class and poor families were much less likely to include professionals in their social networks but were much more likely than their middle-class counterparts to see or speak with kin daily. Children regularly interacted in casually assembled, heterogeneous age groups that included cousins as well as neighborhood children. As others have shown (Lever 1988), we observed gender differences in children's activities. Although girls sometimes ventured outside to ride bikes and play ball games, compared with boys they were more likely to stay inside the house to play. Whether inside or outside, the girls, like the boys, played in loose coalitions of kin and neighbors and created their own activities.

Interactions with representatives of major social institutions (the police, courts, schools, and government agencies) also appeared significantly shaped by social class. Members of white *and* black working-class and poor families offered spontaneous comments about their distrust of these officials. For example, one white working-class mother described an episode in which the police had come to her home looking for her ex-husband (a drug user). She recalled officers "breaking down the door" and terrifying her eldest son, then only three years old. Another white working-class mother reported that her father had been arrested. Although by all accounts in good spirits, he had been found dead in the city jail, an alleged suicide. Children listened to and appeared to absorb remarks such as these.

Fear was a key reason for the unease with which working-class and poor families approached formal (and some informal) encounters with officials. Some parents worried that authorities would "come and take [our] kids away." One black mother on public assistance interviewed as part of the larger study was outraged that school personnel had allowed her daughter to come home from school one winter day without her coat. She noted that if *she* had allowed that to happen, "the school" would have reported her to Child Protective Services for child abuse. Wendy Driver's mother (white working-class) complained that she felt obligated to take Wendy to the doctor, even when she knew nothing was wrong, because Wendy had gone to see the school nurse. Ms. Driver felt she had to be extra careful because she didn't want "them" to come and take her kids away.[30] Strikingly, no middle-class parents mention similar fears about the power of dominant institutions.

Obviously, these three dimensions of childrearing patterns—the organization of daily life, language use, and social connections—do not capture all the class advantages parents pass to their children. The middle-class children in the study enjoyed relatively privileged lives. They lived in large houses, some had swimming pools in their backyards, most had bedrooms of their own, all had many toys, and computers were common. These children also had broad horizons. They flew in airplanes, they traveled out of state for vacations, they often traveled an hour or two from home to take part in their activities, and they knew older children whose extracurricular activities involved international travel.

Still, in some important areas, variations among families did *not* appear to be linked to social class. Some of the middle-class children had learning problems. And, despite their relatively privileged social-class position, neither middle-class children nor their parents were insulated from the realities of serious illness and premature death among family and friends. In addition, some elements of family life seemed relatively immune to social class, including how orderly and tidy the households were. In one white middle-class family, the house was regularly in a state of disarray. The house was cleaned and tidied for a Christmas Eve gathering, but it returned to its normal state shortly thereafter. By contrast, a black middle-class family's home was always extremely tidy, as were some, but not all, of the working-class and poor homes. Nor did certain aspects of parenting, particularly the degree to which mothers appeared to "mean what they said," seem linked to social class. Families also differed with respect to the presence or absence of a sense of humor among individual members, levels of anxiety, and signs of stress-related illnesses they exhibited. Finally, there were significant differences in temperament and disposition among children in the same family. These variations are useful reminders that social class is not fully a determinant of the character of children's lives.

Impact of Childrearing Strategies on Interactions with Institutions

Social scientists sometimes emphasize the importance of reshaping parenting practices to improve children's chances of success. Explicitly and implicitly, the literature exhorts parents to comply with the views of professionals (Bronfenbrenner 1966; Epstein 2001; Heimer and Staffen 1998). Such calls for compliance do not, however, reconcile professionals' judgments regarding the intrinsic value of current childrearing standards with the evidence of the historical record, which shows regular shifts in such standards over time (Aries 1962; Wrigley 1989; Zelizer 1985). Nor are the stratified, and limited, possibilities for success in the broader society examined.

I now follow the families out of their homes and into encounters with representatives of dominant institutions—institutions that are directed by middle-class professionals. Again, I focus on Alexander Williams and Harold McAllister. (Institutional experiences are summarized in Table 20.2.) Across all social classes, parents and children interacted with teachers and school officials, healthcare professionals, and assorted government officials. Although they often addressed similar problems (e.g., learning disabilities, asthma, traffic violations), they typically did not achieve similar resolutions. The pattern of concerted cultivation fostered an *emerging sense of entitlement* in the life of Alexander Williams and other middle-class children. By contrast, the commitment to nurturing children's natural growth fostered an *emerging sense of constraint* in the life of Harold McAllister and other working-class or poor children. (These consequences of childrearing practices are summarized in Table 20.2.)

Both parents and children drew on the resources associated with these two childrearing approaches during their interactions with officials. Middle-class parents and children often customized these interactions; working-class and poor parents were more likely to have a "generic" relationship. When faced with problems, middle-class parents also appeared better equipped to exert influence over other adults compared with working-class and poor parents. Nor did middle-class parents or children display the intimidation or confusion we witnessed among many working-class and poor families when they faced a problem in their children's school experience.

Emerging Signs of Entitlement

Alexander Williams's mother, like many middle-class mothers, explicitly teaches her son to be an informed, assertive client in interactions with professionals. For example, as she drives Alexander to a routine doctor's appointment, she coaches him in the art of communicating effectively in healthcare settings:

> Alexander asks if he needs to get any shots today at the doctor's. Ms. Williams says he'll need to ask the doctor.... As we enter Park Lane, Mom says quietly to Alex: "Alexander, you should be thinking of questions you might want to ask the doctor. You can ask him anything you want. Don't be shy. You can ask anything."
> Alex thinks for a minute, then: "I have some bumps under my arms from my deodorant."
> Mom: "Really? You mean from your new deodorant?"
> Alex: "Yes."
> Mom: "Well, you should ask the doctor."

Alexander learns that he has the right to speak up (e.g., "don't be shy") and that he should prepare for an encounter with a person in a position of authority by gathering his thoughts in advance.

These class resources are subsequently *activated* in the encounter with the doctor (a jovial white man in his late thirties or early forties). The examination begins this way:

Doctor: "Okay, as usual, I'd like to go through the routine questions with you. And if you have any questions for me, just fire away." Doctor examines Alex's chart: "Height-wise, as usual, Alexander's in the ninety-fifth percentile."
Although the physician is talking to Ms. Williams, Alexander interrupts him:

Alex: "I'm in the what?" Doctor: "It means that you're taller than more than ninety-five out of a hundred young men when they're, uh, ten years old."
Alex: "I'm not ten."
Doctor: "Well, they graphed you at ten . . . they usually take the closest year to get that graph."
Alex: "Alright."
Alexander's "Alright" reveals that he feels entitled to weigh-in with his own judgment.

A few minutes later, the exam is interrupted when the doctor is asked to provide an emergency consultation by telephone. Alexander listens to the doctor's conversation and then uses what he has overheard as the basis for a clear directive:

Doctor: "The stitches are on the eyelids themselves, the laceration? . . . Um . . . I don't suture eyelids . . . um . . . Absolutely not! . . . Don't even touch them. That was very bad judgment on the camp's part. . . . [Hangs up.] I'm sorry about the interruption."
Alex: "Stay away from my eyelids!"

Alexander's comment, which draws laughter from the adults, reflects this fourth grader's tremendous ease interacting with a physician.

Later, Ms. Williams and the doctor discuss Alexander's diet. Ms. Williams freely admits that they do not always follow nutritional guidelines. Her honesty is a form of capital because it gives the doctor accurate information on which to base a diagnosis. Feeling no need for deception positions mother and son to receive better care:

Doctor: Let's start with appetite. Do you get three meals a day?"
Alex: "Yeah."
Doctor: "And here's the important question: Do you get your fruits and vegetables too?"
Alex: "Yeah."
Mom, high-pitched: "Ooooo. . . . "
Doctor: "I see I have a second opinion." [laughter]
Alex, voice rising: "You give me bananas and all in my lunch every day. And I had cabbage for dinner last night."
Doctor: "Do you get at least one or two fruits, one or two vegetables every day?"
Alex: "Yeah."
Doctor: "Marginally?"
Mom: "Ninety-eight percent of the time he eats pretty well."
Doctor: "OK, I can live with that. . . . "

Class resources are again activated when Alexander's mother reveals she "gave up" on a medication. The doctor pleasantly but clearly instructs her to continue the medication. Again, though, he receives accurate information rather than facing silent resistance or defiance, as occurred in encounters between healthcare professionals and other (primarily working-class and poor) families. The doctor acknowledges Ms. Williams's relative power: He "argues for" continuation rather than directing her to execute a medically necessary action:

> Mom: "His allergies have just been, just acted up again. One time this summer and I had to bring him in."
> Doctor: "I see a note here from Dr. Svennson that she put him on Vancinace and Benadryl. Did it seem to help him?"
> Mom: "Just, not really. So, I used it for about a week and I just gave up." Doctor, sitting forward in his chair: "OK, I'm actually going to argue for not giving up. If he needs it, Vancinace is a very effective drug. But it takes at least a week to start...."
> Mom: "Oh. OK...."
> Doctor: "I'd rather have him use that than heavy oral medications. You have to give it a few weeks...."

A similar pattern of give and take and questioning characterizes Alexander's interaction with the doctor, as the following excerpt illustrates:

> Doctor: "The only thing that you really need besides my checking you, um, is to have, um, your eyes checked downstairs."
> Alex: "Yes! I love that, I love that!"
> Doctor laughs: "Well, now the most important question. Do you have any questions you want to ask me before I do your physical?"
> Alex: "Um.... only one. I've been getting some bumps on my arms, right around here [indicates underarm]."
> Doctor: "Underneath?"
> Alex: "Yeah."
> Doctor: "OK.... Do they hurt or itch?"
> Alex: "No, they're just there."
> Doctor: "OK, I'll take a look at those bumps for you. Um, what about you—um..."
> Alex: "They're barely any left."
> Doctor: "OK, well, I'll take a peek.... Any questions or worries on your part? [Looking at the mother]
> Mom: "No.... He seems to be coming along very nicely."[31]

Alexander's mother's last comment reflects her view of him as a project, one that is progressing "very nicely." Throughout the visit, she signals her ease and her perception of the exam as an exchange between peers (with Alexander a legitimate participant), rather than a communication from a person in authority to his subordinates. Other middle-class parents seemed similarly comfortable. During Garrett Tallinger's exam, for example, his mother took off her sandals and tucked her legs up under her as she sat in the examination room. She also joked casually with the doctor.

Middle-class parents and children were also very assertive in situations at the public elementary school most of the middle-class children in the study attended. There were numerous conflicts during the year over matters small and large. For example, parents complained to one another and to the teachers about the amount of homework the children were assigned. A black middle-class mother whose daughters had not tested into the school's gifted program negotiated with officials to have the girls' (higher) results from a private testing company accepted instead. The parents of a fourth-grade boy drew the school superintendent into a battle over religious lyrics in a song scheduled to be sung as part of the holiday program. The superintendent consulted the district lawyer and ultimately "counseled" the principal to be more sensitive, and the song was dropped.

Children, too, asserted themselves at school. Examples include requesting that the classroom's blinds be lowered so the sun wasn't in their eyes, badgering the teacher for permission to retake a math test for a higher grade, and demanding to know why no cupcake had been saved when an absence prevented attendance at a classroom party. In these encounters, children were not simply complying with adults' requests or asking for a repeat of an earlier experience. They were displaying an emerging sense of entitlement by urging adults to permit a customized accommodation of institutional processes to suit their preferences.

Of course, some children (and parents) were more forceful than others in their dealings with teachers, and some were more successful than others. Melanie Handlon's mother, for example, took a very "hands-on" approach to her daughter's learning problems, coaching Melanie through her homework day after day. Instead of improved grades, however, the only result was a deteriorating home environment marked by tension and tears.

Emerging Signs of Constraint

The interactions the research assistants and I observed between professionals and working-class and poor parents frequently seemed cautious and constrained. This unease is evident, for example, during a physical Harold McAllister has before going to Bible camp. Harold's mother, normally boisterous and talkative at home, is quiet. Unlike Ms. Williams, she seems wary of supplying the doctor with accurate information:

> Doctor: "Does he eat something each day—either fish, meat, or egg?"
> Mom, response is low and muffled: "Yes."
> Doctor, attempting to make eye contact but mom stares intently at paper: "A yellow vegetable?"
> Mom, still no eye contact, looking at the floor: "Yeah."
> Doctor: "A green vegetable?" Mom, looking at the doctor: "Not all the time." [Fieldworker has not seen any of the children eat a green or yellow vegetable since visits began.]
> Doctor: "No. Fruit or juice?"
> Mom, low voice, little or no eye contact, looks at the doctor's scribbles on the paper he is filling out: "Ummh humn."
> Doctor: "Does he drink milk everyday?" Mom, abruptly, in considerably louder voice: "Yeah."
> Doctor: "Cereal, bread, rice, potato, anything like that?"
> Mom, shakes her head: "Yes, definitely." [Looks at doctor.]

Ms. McAllister's knowledge of developmental events in Harold's life is uneven. She is not sure when he learned to walk and cannot recall the name of his previous doctor. And when the doctor asks, "When was the last time he had a tetanus shot?" she counters, gruffly, "What's a tetanus shot?"

Unlike Ms. Williams, who urged Alexander to share information with the doctor, Ms. McAllister squelches eight-year-old Alexis's overtures:

> Doctor: "Any birth mark?"
> Mom looks at doctor, shakes her head no.
> Alexis, raising her left arm, says excitedly: "I have a birth mark under my arm!"
> Mom, raising her voice and looking stern: "Will you cool out a minute?" Mom, again answering the doctor's question: "No."

Despite Ms. McAllister's tension and the marked change in her everyday demeanor, Harold's whole exam is not uncomfortable. There are moments of laughter. Moreover, Harold's mother is not consistently shy or passive. Before the visit begins, the doctor comes into the waiting room and calls

Harold's and Alexis's names. In response, the McAllisters (and the fieldworker) stand. Ms. McAllister then beckons for her nephew Tyrice (who is about Harold's age) to come along *before* she clears this with the doctor. Later, she sends Tyrice down the hall to observe Harold being weighed; she relies on her nephew's report rather than asking for this information from the healthcare professionals.

Still, neither Harold nor his mother seemed as comfortable as Alexander had been. Alexander was used to extensive conversation at home; with the doctor, he was at ease initiating questions. Harold, who was used to responding to directives at home, primarily answered questions from the doctor, rather than posing his own. Alexander, encouraged by his mother, was assertive and confident with the doctor. Harold was reserved. Absorbing his mother's apparent need to conceal the truth about the range of foods he ate, he appeared cautious, displaying an emerging sense of constraint.

We observed a similar pattern in school interactions. Overall, the working-class and poor adults had much more distance or separation from the school than their middle-class counterparts. Ms. McAllister, for example, could be quite assertive in some settings (e.g., at the start of family observations, she visited the local drug dealer, warning him not to "mess with" the black male fieldworker).[32] But throughout the fourth-grade parent-teacher conference, she kept her winter jacket zipped up, sat hunched over in her chair, and spoke in barely audible tones. She was stunned when the teacher said that Harold did not do homework. Sounding dumbfounded, she said, "He does it at home." The teacher denied it and continued talking. Ms. McAllister made no further comments and did not probe for more information, except about a letter the teacher said he had mailed home and that she had not received. The conference ended, having yielded Ms. McAllister few insights into Harold's educational experience.[33]

Other working-class and poor parents also appeared baffled, intimidated, and subdued in parent-teacher conferences. Ms. Driver, who was extremely worried about her fourth-grader's inability to read, kept these concerns to herself. She explained to us, "I don't want to jump into anything and find it is the wrong thing." When working-class and poor parents did try to intervene in their children's educational experiences, they often felt ineffectual. Billy Yanelli's mother appeared relaxed and chatty in many of her interactions with other adults. With "the school," however, she was very apprehensive. She distrusted school personnel. She felt bullied and powerless. Hoping to resolve a problem involving her son, she tried to prepare her ideas in advance. Still, as she recounted during an interview, she failed to make school officials see Billy as vulnerable:

Ms. Yanelli: I found a note in his school bag one morning and it said, "I'm going to kill you...you're a dead mother-f-er...." So, I started shaking. I was all ready to go over there. [I was] prepared for the counselor.... They said the reason they [the other kids] do what they do is because Billy makes them do it. So they had an answer for everything.
Interviewer: How did you feel about that answer?
Ms. Yanelli: I hate the school. I hate it.

Working-class and poor children seemed aware of their parents' frustration and witnessed their powerlessness. Billy Yanelli, for example, asserted in an interview that his mother "hate[d]" school officials.

At times, these parents encouraged their children to resist school officials' authority. The Yanellis told Billy to "beat up" a boy who was bothering him. Wendy Driver's mother advised her to punch a male classmate who pestered her and pulled her ponytail. Ms. Driver's boyfriend added, "Hit him when the teacher isn't looking."

In classroom observations, working-class and poor children could be quite lively and energetic, but we did not observe them try to customize their environments. They tended to react to adults' offers or, at times, to plead with educators to repeat previous experiences, such as reading a particular story, watching a movie, or going to the computer room. Compared to middle-class classroom interactions, the boundaries between adults and children seemed firmer and clearer. Although the children often resisted and tested school rules, they did not seem to be seeking to get educators to accommodate their own *individual* preferences.

Overall, then, the behavior of working-class and poor parents cannot be explained as a manifestation of their temperaments or of overall passivity; parents were quite energetic in intervening in their children's lives in other spheres. Rather, working-class and poor parents generally appeared to depend on the school (Lareau 2000a), even as they were dubious of the trustworthiness of the professionals. This suspicion of professionals in dominant institutions is, at least in some instances, a reasonable response.[34] The unequal level of trust, as well as differences in the amount and quality of information divulged, can yield unequal *profits* during a historical moment when professionals applaud assertiveness and reject passivity as an inappropriate parenting strategy (Epstein 2001). Middle-class children and parents often (but not always) accrued advantages or profits from their efforts. Alexander Williams succeeded in having the doctor take his medical concerns seriously. Ms. Marshall's children ended up in the gifted program, even though they did not technically qualify. Middle-class children expect institutions to be responsive to *them* and to accommodate their individual needs. By contrast, when Wendy Driver is told to hit the boy who is pestering her (when the teacher isn't looking) or Billy Yanelli is told to physically defend himself, despite school rules, they are not learning how to make bureaucratic institutions work to their advantage. Instead, they are being given lessons in frustration and powerlessness.

Why Does Social Class Matter?

Parents' economic resources helped create the observed class differences in childrearing practices. Enrollment fees that middle-class parents dismissed as "negligible" were formidable expenses for less affluent families. Parents also paid for clothing, equipment, hotel stays, fast food meals, summer camps, and fundraisers. In 1994, the Tallingers estimated the cost of Garrett's activities at $4,000 annually, and that figure was not unusually high.[35] Moreover, families needed reliable private transportation and flexible work schedules to get children to and from events. These resources were disproportionately concentrated in middle-class families.

Differences in educational resources also are important. Middle-class parents' superior levels of education gave them larger vocabularies that facilitated concerted cultivation, particularly in institutional interventions. Poor and working-class parents were not familiar with key terms professionals used, such as "tetanus shot." Furthermore, middle-class parents' educational backgrounds gave them confidence when criticizing educational professionals and intervening in school matters. Working-class and poor parents viewed educators as their social superiors.

Kohn and Schooler (1983) showed that parents' occupations, especially the complexity of their work, influence their childrearing beliefs. We found that parents' work mattered, but also saw signs that the experience of adulthood itself influenced conceptions of childhood. Middle-class parents often were preoccupied with the pleasures and challenges of their work lives.[36] They tended to view childhood as a dual opportunity: a chance for play, and for developing talents and skills of value later in life. Mr. Tallinger noted that playing soccer taught Garrett to be "hard nosed" and "competitive," valuable workplace skills. Ms. Williams mentioned the value of Alexander learning to work with others by playing on a sports team. Middle-class parents, aware of the "declining fortunes" of the middle class, worried about their own economic futures and those of their children (Newman 1993). This uncertainty increased their commitment to helping their children develop broad skills to enhance their future possibilities.

Working-class and poor parents' conceptions of adulthood and childhood also appeared to be closely connected to their lived experiences. For the working class, it was the deadening quality of work and the press of economic shortages that defined their experience of adulthood and influenced their vision of childhood. It was dependence on public assistance and severe economic shortages that most shaped poor parents' views. Families in both classes had many worries about basic issues: food shortages, limited access to healthcare, physical safety, unreliable transportation, insufficient clothing. Thinking back over their childhoods, these parents remembered hardship but also recalled times without the anxieties they now faced. Many appeared to want their own youngsters to concentrate on being happy and relaxed, keeping the burdens of life at bay until they were older.

Thus, childrearing strategies are influenced by more than parents' education. It is the interweaving of life experiences and resources, including parents' economic resources, occupational conditions, and educational backgrounds, that appears to be most important in leading middle-class parents to engage in concerted cultivation and working-class and poor parents to engage in the accomplishment of natural growth. Still, the structural location of families did not fully determine their childrearing practices. The agency of actors and the indeterminacy of social life are inevitable.

In addition to economic and social resources, are there other significant factors? If the poor and working-class families' resources were transformed overnight so that they equaled those of the middle-class families, would their cultural logic of childrearing shift as well? Or are there cultural attitudes and beliefs that are substantially independent of economic and social resources that are influencing parents' practices here? The size and scope of this study preclude a definitive answer. Some poor and working-class parents embraced principles of concerted cultivation: They wished (but could not afford) to enroll their children in organized activities (e.g., piano lessons, voice lessons), they believed listening to children was important, and they were committed to being involved in their children's schooling. Still, even when parents across all of the classes seemed committed to similar principles, their motivations differed. For example, many working-class and poor parents who wanted more activities for their children were seeking a safe haven for them. Their goal was to provide protection from harm rather than to cultivate the child's talents per se.

Some parents explicitly criticized children's schedules that involved many activities. During the parent interviews, we described the real-life activities of two children (using data from the 12 families we were observing). One schedule resembled Alexander Williams's: restricted television, required reading, and many organized activities, including piano lessons (for analytical purposes, we said that, unlike Alexander, this child disliked his piano lessons but was not allowed to quit). Summing up the attitude of the working-class and poor parents who rejected this kind of schedule,[37] one white, poor mother complained:

> I think he wants more, I think he doesn't enjoy doing what he's doing half of the time (light laughter). I think his parents are too strict. And he's not a child.

Even parents who believed this more regimented approach would pay off "job-wise" when the child was an adult still expressed serious reservations: "I think he is a sad kid," or, "He must be dead-dog tired."

Thus, working-class and poor parents varied in their beliefs. Some longed for a schedule of organized activities for their children and others did not; some believed in reasoning with children and playing an active role in schooling and others did not. Fully untangling the effects of material and cultural resources on parents and children's choices is a challenge for future research.[38]

Discussion

The evidence shows that class position influences critical aspects of family life: time use, language use, and kin ties. Not all aspects of family life are affected by social class, and there is variability within class. Still, parents do transmit advantages to their children in patterns that are sufficiently consistent and identifiable to be described as a "cultural logic" of childrearing. The white and black middle-class parents engaged in practices I have termed "concerted cultivation"—they made a deliberate and sustained effort to stimulate children's development and to cultivate their cognitive and social skills. The working-class and poor parents viewed children's development as spontaneously unfolding, as long as they were provided with comfort, food, shelter, and other basic support. This commitment, too, required ongoing effort; sustaining children's natural growth despite formidable life challenges is properly viewed as an accomplishment.

In daily life, the patterns associated with each of these approaches were interwoven and mutually reinforcing. Nine-year-old middle-class children already had developed a clear sense of their own talents and skills, and they differentiated themselves from siblings and friends. They were also learning to think of themselves as special and worthy of having adults devote time and energy to promoting them and their leisure activities. In the process, the boundaries between adults and children sometimes blurred; adults' leisure preferences became subordinate to their children's. The strong emphasis on reasoning in middle-class families had similar, diffuse effects. Children used their formidable reasoning skills to persuade adults to acquiesce to their wishes. The idea that children's desires should be taken seriously was routinely realized in the middle-class families we interviewed and observed. In many subtle ways, children were taught that they were entitled. Finally, the commitment to cultivating children resulted in family schedules so crowded with activities there was little time left for visiting relatives. Quantitative studies of time use have shed light on important issues, but they do not capture the interactive nature of routine, everyday activities and the varying ways they affect the texture of family life.[39]

In working-class and poor families, parents established limits; within those limits, children were free to fashion their own pastimes. Children's wishes did not guide adults' actions as frequently or as decisively as they did in middle-class homes. Children were viewed as subordinate to adults. Parents tended to issue directives rather than to negotiate. Frequent interactions with relatives rather than acquaintances or strangers created a thicker divide between families and the outside world. Implicitly and explicitly, parents taught their children to keep their distance from people in positions of authority, to be distrustful of institutions, and, at times, to resist officials' authority. Children seemed to absorb the adults' feelings of powerlessness in their institutional relationships. As with the middle class, there were important variations among working-class and poor families, and some critical aspects of family life, such as the use of humor, were immune to social class.

The role of race in children's daily lives was less powerful than I had expected. The middle-class black children's parents were alert to the potential effects of institutional discrimination on their children. Middle-class black parents also took steps to help their children develop a positive racial identity. Still, in terms of how children spend their time, the way parents use language and discipline in the home, the nature of the families' social connections, and the strategies used for intervening in institutions, white and black middle-class parents engaged in very similar, often identical, practices with their children. A similar pattern was observed in white and black working-class homes as well as in white and black poor families. Thus my data indicate that on the childrearing dynamics studied here, compared with social class, race was less important in children's daily lives.[40] As they enter the racially segregated words of dating, marriage, and housing markets, and as they encounter more racism in their interpersonal contact with whites (Waters 1999), the relative importance of race in the children's daily lives is likely to increase.

Differences in family dynamics and the logic of childrearing across social classes have long-term consequences. As family members moved out of the home and interacted with representatives of formal institutions, middle-class parents and children were able to negotiate more valuable outcomes than their working-class and poor counterparts. In interactions with agents of dominant institutions, working-class and poor children were learning lessons in constraint while middle-class children were developing a sense of entitlement.

It is a mistake to see either concerted cultivation or the accomplishment of natural growth as an intrinsically desirable approach. As has been amply documented, conceptions of childhood have changed dramatically over time (Wrigley 1989). Drawbacks to middle-class childrearing, including the exhaustion associated with intensive mothering and frenetic family schedules and a sapping of children's naivete that leaves them feeling too sophisticated for simple games and toys (Hays 1996), remain insufficiently highlighted.

Another drawback is that middle-class children are less likely to learn how to fill "empty time" with their own creative play, leading to a dependence on their parents to solve experiences of boredom. Sociologists need to more clearly differentiate between standards that are intrinsically desirable and standards that facilitate success in dominant institutions. A more critical, and historically sensitive, vision is needed (Donzelot 1979). Here Bourdieu's work (1976, 1984, 1986, 1989) is valuable.

Finally, there are methodological issues to consider. Quantitative research has delineated population-wide patterns; ethnographies offer rich descriptive detail but typically focus on a single, small group. Neither approach can provide holistic, but empirically grounded, assessments of daily life. Multi-sited, multi-person research using ethnographic methods also pose formidable methodological challenges (Lareau 2002). Still, families have proven themselves open to being studied in an intimate fashion. Creating penetrating portraits of daily life that will enrich our theoretical models is an important challenge for the future.

Notes

1. In a study of mothers' beliefs about child-rearing, Hays (1996) found variations in how working-class and middle-class mothers sorted information, but she concluded that a pattern of "intensive mothering" was present across social classes. My study of behavior found class differences but, as I discuss below, in some instances working-class and poor parents expressed a desire to enroll their children in organized activities.
2. Some significant differences between the study's working-class and poor families (e.g., only the poor children experienced food shortages) are not highlighted here because, on the dimensions discussed in this paper, the biggest differences were between middle-class and non-middle-class families. See Lareau (forthcoming) for a more elaborate discussion as well as Lamont (2000) for distinctions working-class families draw between themselves and the poor; see McLanahan and Sandefur (1994) regarding family structure and children's lives.
3. Case studies of nonrandom samples, such as this one, have the limitation that findings cannot be generalized beyond the cases reported. These examples serve to illustrate conceptual points (Burawoy et al. 1991) rather than to describe representative patterns of behavior. A further limitation of this study is that the data were collected and analyzed over an extended period of time, (see the "Methodology" section).
4. All names of people and places are pseudonyms. The Lawrenceville school was in a white suburban neighborhood in a university community a few hours from a metropolitan area. The student population was about half white and half black; the (disproportionately poor) black children were bused from other neighborhoods.
5. Over three-quarters of the students at Lower Richmond qualified for free lunch; by contrast, Swan did not have a free lunch program.
6. At both sites, we attended school events and observed many parent-teacher conferences. Also, I interviewed the classroom teachers and adults involved in the children's organized activities. These interview data are not presented here.
7. Both schools had computer labs, art programs, and music programs, but Swan had many more resources and much higher average achievement scores. Graffiti and physical confrontations between students were common only at Lower Richmond. At these two sites and in Lawrenceville, white faculty predominated.
8. I located the black middle-class parents through social networks; the white poor families were located through flyers left at welfare offices and social service programs, and posted on telephone poles. Ten white poor families (only) were paid $25 per interview.
9. Of 19 families asked to participate in the intensive study, 7 declined (a response rate of 63 percent). I tried to balance the observational phase sample by gender, race, and class, and to "mix and match" the children on other characteristics, such as their behavior with peers, their relationships with extended family, and their parents' level of involvement in

their education. The aim was to lessen the chance that observed differences in behavior would reflect unknown variables (e.g., church attendance or parents' participation at school). Last, I deliberately included two families (Irwins, Greeleys) who had some "middle-class" traits but who lived in a working-class and poor area, respectively. Including these unusual families seemed conceptually important for disentangling the influences of social class and environment (neighborhood).

10. I analyzed the data for the study as a whole in two ways. I coded themes from the interviews and used Folio Views software to help establish patterns. I also relied on reading the field notes, thinking about similarities and differences across families, searching for disconfirming evidence, and re-reading the field notes.

11. Recruitment to complete the sample was difficult as children needed to be a specific age, race, and class, and to be part of families who were willing to be observed. The white poor boy was recommended by a social service program manager; the black middle-class children were located through extended social networks of mine.

12. We did 12 to 14 observations of the Handlon and Carroll families before settling on the 20-visit pattern. In Alexander Williams's case, the visits occurred over a year. To observe unusual events (e.g., a family reunion), we sometimes went back after formal observations had ended.

13. Families developed preferences, favoring one fieldworker in a team over another. But these preferences were not stable across families, and the field notes did not differ dramatically between fieldworkers. Notes were much more similar than they were different.

14. Wright (1997) uses 12 categories in his neo-Marxist approach. Goldthorpe, a neo-Weberian, operationalizes his class schema at levels of aggregation ranging from 3 to 11 categories (Erikson and Goldthorpe 1993:38–39).

15. Here "poor" refers to the source of income (i.e., government assistance versus labor market) rather than the amount of income. Although lower class is more accurate than poor, it is widely perceived as pejorative. I might have used "underclass," but the literature has defined this term in racialized ways.

16. Dollar figures are from 1994–1995, unless otherwise noted. Income was not used to define class membership, but these data are available from the author.

17. Mr. and Ms. Williams disagreed about the value of their home; the figure here averages what each reported in 1995. Housing prices in their region were lower—and continue to be lower today—than in many other parts of the country. Their property is now worth an estimated $175,000 to $200,000.

18. Alexander's mother goes by Christina Nile at work, but Mrs. Williams at church. Some other mothers' last names also differ from their children's. Here I assign all mothers the same last names as their children.

19. I contacted the Williams family through social networks after I was unable to recruit the black middle-class families who had participated in the classroom observation and interview phase. As a result, I do not have data from classroom observations or parent-teacher conferences for Alexander.

20. The Suzuki method is labor intensive. Students are required to listen to music about one hour per day. Also, both child and parent(s) are expected to practice daily and to attend every lesson together.

21. Hart and Risley (1995) reported a similar difference in speech patterns. In their sample, by about age three, children of professionals had larger vocabularies and spoke more utterances per hour than the *parents* of similarly aged children on welfare.

22. This section focuses primarily on the concerns of black parents. Whites, of course, also benefited from race relations, notably in the scattering of poor white families in working-class neighborhoods rather than being concentrated in dense settings with other poor families (Massey and Denton 1993).

23. Activities coded as "organized" are Scouts/ Brownies, music lessons, any type of sports lesson (e.g., gymnastics, karate), any type of league-organized sports (e.g., Little League), dance lessons, choir, religious classes (excluding religious primary school), arts and crafts classes, and any classes held at a recreation center.

24. As other studies have found, the mothers in my sample were far more knowledgeable than the fathers about their children's daily lives and spent more time caring for children (Crouter et. al. 1999; Thompson 1999). Family observations showed fathers playing a very important role in family dynamics, however, especially by contributing laughter and humor (Lareau 2000b).

25. Some data are missing. The list of activities was so long we sometimes shortened it to conserve time (we always asked respondents, however, whether there were any activities their children had experienced that were not covered in the list). On average, middle-class parents were not queried concerning 2.5 of the approximately 20 items on the list; working-class parents were not asked about 3.0 items; and poor parents were not asked about 2.0 items. Since the sample is non-random, inferential procedures are not applicable. At a reviewer's request, I carried out a Scheffe post hoc test of group differences and found significant differences (at the $p < .001$ level) between the middle-class children and the working-class and poor children. The difference between working-class and poor children is non-significant (at the $p < .05$ level). Statistically significant differences do not occur across racial groups or by gender; nor are there significant interactions between race or gender and class

26. Recent time-diary data suggest that middleclass parents' reports of how much time their children spend watching television are significantly lower than their children's actual viewing time (Hofferth 1999). There is no comparable gap shown in national data for less educated parents.

27. During an interview, Ms. Yanelli estimated that during the previous two weeks, she had used the belt twice, but she noted that her use varied widely. Not all working-class and poor parents in the study used physical punishment, but the great majority did rely heavily on directives.

28. Interviews were open-ended; respondents' varied answers preclude summarizing the data in a single scale that would accurately measure differences in kinship ties by class. For details regarding social class and kin group contact, see Fischer (1982).

29. The overall sample included 36 middle-class, 26 working-class, and 26 poor families. For the question on teachers, there were responses from 31 middle-class parents, 21 working-class parents, and 25 poor parents. For the question on doctors,

the responses by class numbered 26, 21, and 22. Similar results were found for knowing a psychologist, family counselor, or lawyer (data available from the author). Race did not influence the results.

30. How misguided parents' suspicions might be is hard to assess. The counselor at Lower Richmond, who regularly reported children to the Department of Human Services as victims of neglect, maintained that she did so only in the gravest cases and only after repeated interventions had failed. The working-class and poor parents, however, generally saw "the school's actions" as swift, capricious, and arbitrary.

31. Not all professionals accommodated children's participation. Regardless of these adults' overt attitudes, though, we routinely observed that middle-class mothers monitor and intervene in their children's interactions with professionals.

32. Ms. McAllister told me about this visit; we did not observe it. It is striking that she perceived only the black male field-worker as being at risk.

33. Middle-class parents sometimes appeared slightly anxious during parent-teacher conferences, but overall, they spoke more and asked educators more questions than did working-class and poor parents.

34. The higher levels of institutional reports of child neglect, child abuse, and other family difficulties among poor families may reflect this group's greater vulnerability to institutional intervention (e.g., see L. Gordon 1989).

35. In 2002, a single sport could cost as much as $5,000 annually. Yearly league fees for ice hockey run to $2,700; equipment costs are high as well (Halbfinger 2002).

36. Middle-class adults do not live problem-free lives, but compared with the working class and poor, they have more varied occupational experiences and greater access to jobs with higher economic returns.

37. Many middle-class parents remarked that forcing a child to take piano lessons was wrong. Nevertheless, they continued to stress the importance of "exposure."

38. Similarly, whether concerted cultivation and the accomplishment of natural growth are new historical developments rather than modifications of earlier forms of childrearing cannot be determined from the study's findings. The "institutionalization of children's leisure" seems to be increasing (Corsaro 1997). Hays (1996) argues that families increasingly are "invaded" by the "logic of impersonal, competitive, contractual, commodified, efficient, profit-maximizing, self-interested relations" (p. 11). In addition to evidence of a new increase in children's organized activities (Sandberg and Hofferth 2001), none of the middle-class parents in the study reported having childhood schedules comparable to their children's. Change over time in parents' intervention in education and in the amount of reasoning in middle-class families also are difficult to determine accurately. Kohn and Schooler's (1983) study suggests little change with regard to reasoning, but other commentators insist there has been a rise in the amount of negotiating between parents and children (Chidekel 2002; Kropp 2001). Such debates can not be resolved without additional careful historical research.

39. The time-use differences we observed were part of the taken-for-granted aspects of daily life; they were generally unnoticed by family members. For example, the working-class Yanellis considered themselves "really busy" if they had one baseball game on Saturday and an extended family gathering on Sunday. The Tallingers and other middle-class families would have considered this a slow weekend.

40. These findings are compatible with others showing children as aware of race at relatively early ages (Van Ausdale and Feagin 1996). At the two sites, girls often played in racially segregated groups during recess; boys tended to play in racially integrated groups.

References

Aries, Philippe. 1962. *Centuries of Childhood: A Social History of the Family.* Translated by R. Baldick. London, England: Cape.

Bernstein, Basil. 1971. *Class, Codes, and Control: Theoretical Studies towards a Sociology of Language.* New York: Schocken Books.

Bianchi, Suzanne M. 2000. "Maternal Employment and Time with Children: Dramatic Change or Surprising Continuity." *Demography* 37:401–14.

Bianchi, Suzane and John Robinson. 1997. "What Did You Do Today? Children's Use of Time, Family Composition, and Acquisition of Social Capital." *Journal of Marriage and the Family* 59:332–44.

Bourdieu, Pierre. 1976. "Marriage Strategies as Strategies of Social Reproduction." Pp. 117–44 in *Family and Society,* edited by R. Forster and O. Ranum. Baltimore, MD: Johns Hopkins University Press.

———. 1984. *Distinction: A Social Critique of the Judgment of Taste.* Cambridge, MA: Harvard University Press.

———. 1986. "The Forms of Capital." Pp. 241–58 in *Handbook of Theory and Research for the Sociology of Education,* edited by J. C. Richardson. New York: Greenwood.

———. 1989. *The State Nobility: Elite Schools in the Field of Power.* Stanford, CA: Stanford University Press.

Bronfenbrenner, Urie. 1966. "Socialization and Social Class through Time and Space." Pp. 362–77 in *Class, Status and Power,* edited by R. Bendix and S. M. Lipset. New York: Free Press.

Burawoy, Michael, Alice Burton, Ann Arnett Ferguson, and Kathryn J. Fox, eds. 1991. *Ethnography Unbound: Power and Resistance in the Modern Metropolis.* Berkeley, CA: University of California Press.

Chidekel, Dana. 2002. *Parents in Charge.* New York: Simon and Schuster.

Conley, Dalton. 1999. *Being Black, Living in the Red: Race, Wealth, and Social Policy in America.* Berkeley, CA: University of California Press.

Corsaro, William A. 1997. *The Sociology of Childhood.* Thousand Oaks, CA: Pine Forge.

Crouter, Ann C, Heather Helms-Erikson, Kimberly Updegraff, and Susan M. McHale. 1999. "Conditions Underlying Parents' Knowledge about Children's Daily Lives in Middle Childhood: Between—and within—Family Comparisons." *Child Development* 70:246–59.

Daley, Kerry J. 2001. "Deconstructing Family Time: From Ideology to Lived Experience." *Journal of Marriage and the Family* 63:238–94.

Donzelot, Jacques. 1979. *The Policing of Families*. Translated by R. Hurley. New York: Pantheon.

Epstein, Joyce. 2001. *Schools, Family, and Community Partnerships*. Boulder, CO: Westview.

Erikson, Robert, and John H. Goldthorpe. 1993. *The Constant Flux: A Study of Class Mobility in Industrial Societies*. Oxford, England: Clarendon.

Fischer, Claude. 1982. *To Dwell among Friends*. Chicago: University of Chicago Press.

Fordham, Signithia and John U. Ogbu. 1986. "Black Students' School Success: Coping with the 'Burden of Acting White.'" *The Urban Review* 18:176–206.

Gordon, Linda. 1989. *Heroes of Their Own Lives: The Politics and History of Family Violence*. New York: Penguin.

Halbfinger, David M. 2002. "A Hockey Parent's Life: Time, Money, and Yes, Frustration." *New York Times*, January 12, p. 29.

Hart, Betty and Todd Risley. 1995. *Meaningful Differences in the Everyday Experience of Young American Children*. Baltimore, MD: Paul Brooks.

Hays, Sharon. 1996. *The Cultural Contradictions of Motherhood*. New Haven, CT: Yale University Press.

Heath, Shirley Brice. 1983. *Ways with Words*. London, England: Cambridge University Press.

Heimer, Carol A. and Lisa Staffen. 1998. *For the Sake of the Children: The Social Organization of Responsibility in the Hospital and at Home*. Chicago, IL: University of Chicago Press.

Hertz, Rosanna and Nancy L. Marshall, eds. 2001. *Working Families: The Transformation of the American Home*. Berkeley, CA: University of California Press.

Hess, Robert and Gerald Handel. 1974. *Family Worlds: A Psychosocial Approach to Family Life*. Chicago, IL: University of Chicago Press.

Hochschild, Arlie Russell. 1989. *The Second Shift: Working Parents and the Revolution at Home*. New York: Viking.

Hochschild, Jennifer L. 1995. *Facing Up to The American Dream*. Princeton, NJ: Princeton University Press.

Hofferth, Sandra L. 1999. "Family Reading to Young Children: Social Desirability and Cultural Biases in Reporting" (Working paper no. 005-99, May 13, 1999). Institute for Survey Research, Center for Ethnography of Everyday Life, University of Michigan, Ann Arbor, MI. (http://www.ethno.isr.umich.edu/06papers. html).

Hofferth, Sandra and John Sandberg. 2001a. "Changes in American Children's Time, 1981–1997." Pp. 193–232 in *Advances in Life Course Research*, vol. 6, *Children at the Millennium: Where Have We Come From, Where Are We Going?*, edited by S. Hofferth and T. Owens. Oxford, England, Eslevier Science Ltd.

———. 2001b. "How American Children Spend Their Time." *Journal of Marriage and the Family* 63:295–308.

Jacobs, Jerry and Kathleen Gerson. 1998. "Who Are the Overworked Americans?" *Review of Social Economy* 56:442–59.

Juster, F. Thomas and Frank P. Stafford, eds. 1985. *Time, Goods, and Well-Being*. Ann Arbor, MI: Survey Research Center, Institute for Social Research.

Kingston, Paul. 2000. *The Classless Society*. Stanford, CA: Stanford University Press.

Kohn, Melvin and Carmi Schooler, eds. 1983. *Work and Personality: An Inquiry into the Impact of Social Stratification*. Norwood, NJ: Ablex.

Kropp, Paul. 2001. *I'll Be the Parent, You Be the Child*. New York: Fisher Books.

Lamont, Michele. 2000. *The Dignity of Working Men: Morality and the Boundaries of Race, Class, and Immigration*. Cambridge, MA: Harvard University Press.

Lareau, Annette. Forthcoming. *Unequal Childhood: Class, Race, and Family Life*. Berkeley, CA: University of California Press.

———. 2002. "Doing Multi-Person, Multi-Site 'Ethnographic' Work: A Reflective, Critical Essay." Department of Sociology, Temple University, Philadelphia, PA. Unpublished manuscript.

———. 2000a. *Home Advantage: Social Class and Parental Intervention in Elementary Education*. 2d ed. Lanham, MD: Rowman and Littlefield.

———. 2000b. "My Wife Can Tell Me Who I Know: Methodological and Conceptual Issues in Studying Fathers." *Qualitative Sociology* 23:407–33.

Lever, Janet. 1988. "Sex Differences in the Complexity of Children's Play and Games." Pp. 324–44 in *Childhood Socialization*, edited by G. Handel. New York: Aldine de Gruyter.

Marsiglio, William. 1991. "Paternal Engagement Activities with Minor Children." *Journal of Marriage and the Family* 53:973–86.

Massey, Douglas and Nancy Denton. 1993. *American Apartheid*. Cambridge, MA: Harvard University Press.

McLanahan, Sara and Gary Sandefur. 1994. *Growing Up with a Single Parent: What Hurts, What Helps*. Cambridge, MA: Harvard University Press.

Medrich, Elliot, Judith Roizen, Victor Rubin, and Stuart Buckley. 1982. *The Serious Business of Growing Up*. Berkeley, CA: University of California Press.

Menaghan, Elizabeth G. 1991. "Work Experiences and Family Interaction Processes: The Long Reach of the Job?" *Annual Review of Sociology* 17:419–44.

Newman, Kathleen. 1993. *Declining Fortunes: The Withering of the American Dream*. New York: Basic Books.

Pattillo-McCoy, Mary 1999. *Black Picket Fences: Privilege and Peril among the Black Middle-Class*. Chicago, IL: University of Chicago Press.

Presser, Harriet B. 1989. "Can We Make Time for Children? The Economy, Work Schedules, and Child Care." *Demography* 26:523–43.

Robinson, John P. and Geoffry Godbey. 1997. *Time for Life: The Surprising Ways Americans Use Their Time*. University Park, PA: The Pennsylvania State Press.

Rubin, Lillian 1976. *Worlds of Pain: Life in a Working-Class Family*. New York: Basic Books.

Sandberg, John F. and Sandra L. Hofferth. 2001. "Changes in Children's Time with Parents, U.S., 1981–1997." *Demography* 38:423–36.

Shehan, Constance L., ed. 1999. *Through the Eyes of the Child: Re-Visioning Children as Active Agents of Family Life*. New York: JAI Press.

Schemari, James. 2002. "Practice Makes Perfect (and Poorer Parents)." *The New York Times,* January 27, p. 11).

Skolnick, Arlene. 1991. *Embattled Paradise: The American Family in an Age of Uncertainty.* New York: Basic Books.

Tatum, Beverly Daniel. 1997. *Why Are All the Black Kids Sitting Together in the Cafeteria? And Other Conversations about Race.* New York: Basic Books.

Thompson, Shona M. 1999. *Mother's Taxi: Sport and Women's Labor.* Albany, NY: SUNY Press.

Thorne, Barrie. 2001. "Growing Up in Oakland: Orbits of Class, 'Race,' and Culture." Paper presented at the annual meeting of the American Sociological Association, August 19, Anaheim, CA.

Van Ausdale, Debra and Joe R. Feagin. 1996. "Using Racial and Ethnic Concepts: The Critical Case of Very Young Children." *American Sociological Review* 61:779–93.

Waksler, Frances. 1991. *Studying the Social Worlds of Children.* Bristol, England: Falmer.

Waters, Mary. 1999. *Black Identities: West Indian Immigrant Dreams and American Realities.* New York: Russell Sage Foundation.

Wright, Erik Olin. 1997. *Class Counts: Comparative Studies in Class Analysis.* Cambridge, England: Cambridge University Press.

Wrigley, Julia. 1989. "Do Young Children Need Intellectual Stimulation? Experts' Advice to Parents, 1900–1985." *History of Education* 29:41–75.

Zelizer, Vivianna. 1985. *Pricing the Priceless Child: The Changing Social Value of Children.* New York: Basic Books.

Zick, Cathleen D. and W. Keith Bryant. 1996. "A New Look at Parents' Time Spent in Child Care: Primary and Secondary Time Use." *Social Science Research* 25:260–80.

21

Collective Identity and the Burden of "Acting White" in Black History, Community, and Education

JOHN U. OGBU

Introduction

Having conducted comparative research on minority education for more than 15 years, I came to the conclusion that discrimination in society and school as well as minority responses to the discrimination, though significant, are not enough to explain why there are differences in the school performance among minority groups. My comparative study suggested that two additional factors from the dynamics in minority communities also contributed to the school performance differences. In a joint publication with Dr. Signithia Fordham in 1986, we stated that the two additional factors were *collective identity* or *fictive kinship* and *cultural frame of reference* (Fordham and Ogbu, 1986). We also reported a study of Capital High students in Washington, D. C. where we found that the two factors played a major role in the school performance of Black adolescents.

The joint article has generated responses from the academic community beyond what we anticipated. It is the subject of dissertation studies (Carter, 1999; O'Connor, 1996; Taylor, 2001), several publications (Ainsworth-Darnell and Downey, 1998; Bergin and Cooks, 2002; Cook and Ludwig, 1997) and organized sessions at professional meetings (Epstein, 2003; Horvat and O'Connor, 2001). During the past 2 years, I have reviewed more than a dozen book and journal manuscripts on oppositional culture and schooling for publishers. Although it is gratifying to see the impact of the joint article on the academic community, the potential contributions of these activities to scholarship are limited by misinterpretations of the problem, replacing the thesis, and making a different conclusion.

One of the shortcomings of current scholarship is the failure to distinguish among three different perspectives on collective identity, cultural frame of reference, and the schooling of Black adolescents. This has resulted in the translating of my cultural–ecological framework into a single-factor hypothesis of *oppositional culture*. In effect, critics construct and study a different problem than the one we laid out in the joint article.

An equally serious problem is that there is no evidence that authors are aware that throughout their history Black Americans have experienced the "burden of 'acting White'" because of their oppositional collective identity and cultural frame of reference. Lacking this knowledge, critics ignore the historical and community contexts of Black students' behavior and focus almost exclusively on the transactions between the students and their school. Basing their analysis on data collected at the level of student–school transactions, it is not surprising that some critics accuse Fordham and myself of assigning a race label ("acting White") to a common ridicule, namely, teasing and harassment, endured by academically achieving adolescents or "nerds." They also believe that we have read too much into a "concept that they themselves manufactured."

The purpose of this paper is to correct these misinterpretations. I will start with the meaning of collective identity and how it differs from other identity concepts used in discussing Black students' experiences. This will be followed by a brief account of the evolution of Black American collective identity, a presentation of my study of Black American experience with the "burden of 'acting White'" in contemporary United States, and conclude with an exploration of a possible continuity between Black historical and community experiences with the "burden of 'acting White'" and the experience of Black students that I and my students have studied in Stockton (1968–70), Oakland (1989–93), San Francisco (1991–92), and Shaker Heights (1997).

What Is Collective Identity?

Some Perspectives on Identity

Psychologists have examined the development and school experience of minority children from a number of interesting perspectives as it relates to identity. Among them are (a) *the Ericksonian ego identity* (Hauser, 1972), (b) *ethnic identity* based on Erickson's theory (Phinney and Rosenthal, 1992; Phinney and Rotheram, 1987); (c) *racial identity* as measured by racial attitudes (Branch, 1999); and (d) *underclass oppositional identity* (Cross, Strauss and Fhagen-Smith, 1999, pp. 29–30). Among non-psychologists some have proposed (a) *negotiated identity* (Yon, 2000), and (b) *circumstantial/marketable identity or politics of recognition* (Cornell and Hartman, 1998). These are useful and interesting ways of looking at identity and minority status. But they have to be distinguished from collective identity as used in this paper.

What Is Collective Identity?

Collective identity refers to people's sense of who they are, their "we-feeling" or "belonging." People express their collective identity with emblems or cultural symbols which reflect their attitudes, beliefs, feelings, behaviors, and language or dialect. The persistence of a group's collective identity depends on the continuity of the external (historical and structural) forces that contributed to its formation. It also depends on the continuity of responses of the group (Castile and Kushner, 1981; DeVos, 1995; Spicer, 1966, 1971).

Collective identity usually develops because of people's collective experience or series of collective experiences. Warfare, conquest, colonization, forced labor, mass emigration, imposition of an outcast status, and enslavement are examples of the collective experience that leads to the formation of collective identity (Castile and Kushner, 1981; DeVos, 1995; Spicer, 1967). Usually, the collective identity of an oppressed minority group is created and maintained by two sets of factors: status problems and minority response to status problems.

Status Problems

Status problems are external forces that mark a group of people as a distinct segment from the rest of the population. A group so created is usually bounded and named. For example, the Emperor of Japan, by proclamation, created the Burakumin as an outcast group from the Japanese people when Japan established a four-rigid, caste-like stratification system placing the Burakumin as the outcast group during the Edoera in the 17th century. Before the establishment of the status groups, the people in the outcast category, the Burakumin, had been, like other Japanese, warriors, peasants, and artisans. Designated as an outcast, the Burakumin (people of special hamlet or residential area) were assigned the role of slaughtering animals and executing criminals, functions which the general public perceived as "polluting functions" under Buddhist and Shintoist beliefs. Their social ostracism and discrimination have continued even after they were emancipated in 1871 (DeVos, 1967; Hirasawa and Nabeshima, 1995). Similarly, White Americans created Black Americans as a separate and an enduring segment of the United States society through enslavement. Status problems are collective problems which members of the subordinate group find difficult if not impossible to solve within the existing system of majority–minority relations. They include the following.

1   *Involuntary incorporation into society:* Usually these minorities do not become minorities by choice. Rather they are forced into minority status against their will by conquest, colonization, enslavement (e.g., Black Americans) or arbitrary subjection to the status of a pariah caste (e.g., the Burakumin of Japan).

2   *Instrumental discrimination:* e.g., denial of equal access to good jobs, education, political participation, and housing.

3   *Social subordination:* e.g., residential and social segregation, hostility and violence; prohibition of intermarriage; requirement of the offsprings of intergroup mating to affiliate with one group with no choice. In some cases oppressed minorities are forced against their will to assimilate into the dominant group, although this assimilation usually results in marginalization.

4   *Expressive mistreatment:* e.g., cultural, language, and intellectual denigration.

Dominant group members stigmatize minorities' food, clothing, music, values, behaviors, and language or dialect as bad and inferior to theirs. These four mechanisms are used by the dominant group to create and maintain the collective identity of the minorities; i.e., to "carve them out" and maintain them as a separate segment of society with a distinct identity. The existence of the minorities with distinct collective identity remains as long as these mechanisms or mistreatment of the minorities remain (Ogbu, 2000).

The Response of Minorities to Status Problems

Both minorities as a group and as individuals feel the impact of status problems. The minorities experience their mistreatment regardless of their individual differences in education and ability, in status, physical appearance, or place of residence. They know fully well that they do not have the option of membership in the dominant group; they also know that they cannot easily escape from their more or less ascribed membership in a subordinate and disparaged group. Individuals who "pass" physically or culturally often find that the social and psychological costs are very high. Oppressed minorities are bitter for being forced into minority status and subjected to oppression. They usually hold the dominant group responsible for their "troubles" (e.g., their inferior economic and political status, demeaning social positions, poor health and housing, and stigmatized cultures and languages or dialects). Under this circumstance, involuntary minorities respond collectively as a group and they also respond as individuals in ways that reinforce their separate existence and collective identity. Furthermore, their response often makes their oppositional collective identity vis-a-vis their perceptions of the collective identity of the dominant group. That is, their very attempts to solve their status problem lead them to develop a new sense of who they are, that is in opposition to their understanding of who the dominant group members are.

Cultural and Language Frames of Reference

Closely related to their sense of collective identity is the way minorities interpret the cultural and language or dialect differences between them and the dominant group. We use the term 'cultural frame of reference' to refer to the correct way of behaving and 'language or dialect frame of reference' to refer to the correct way of talking from the point of view of the minorities. Cultural and language frames of reference are closely tied to collective identity, so that we can speak of them as the cultural identity and the language identity of the minorities. Where the latter is oppositional, the former is usually oppositional. Furthermore, where that is the case, we can regard the situation as one of oppositional culture and oppositional language or dialect. The relationship—oppositional or non-oppositional—between the cultural and language frames of reference of the minorities and that of the dominant group, determines to some degree the difficulty individual members of the minority group have in crossing cultural and language boundaries or learning to behave and talk like White people. However, this does not mean that all members of the minority group respond to the culture and language of the dominant group in opposition. As we shall see, minorities usually develop some strategies to deal with the demands that they behave and talk like dominant group members in order to achieve self-betterment in situations controlled by members of the dominant group.

The Case of Black Americans

Black American oppositional collective identity began to form before emancipation and has remained to the present. We have more information on the subject for more recent than earlier periods.

Pre-Emancipation Period

Status Problems

Enslavement and mistreatment under slavery: Black Americans became involuntary minorities when they were enslaved by White Americans. For more than 200 years they were denied basic human rights, exploited economically, politically, socially, and expressively. They were tightly controlled by White slave owners who forced them to behave like slaves. They were forbidden to behave in certain ways considered White prerogatives and were punished if they disobeyed. For example, they were punished for learning to read and write, where slaves were forbidden these activities (Haley, 1976). Punishment was sometimes extended to all slaves on the plantation, not just limited to the slave who committed the offence. This collective punishment was important in the creation of Black collective identity.

The treatment of Blacks following Nat Turner's "insurrection" is a good example of the collective blame and punishment which increased their sense of being a separate people with a collective identity. A slave, Nat Turner, led an "insurrection" in Southampton, Virginia in 1831. Following this incident, the movement of *all* Black people throughout the United States was restricted. Blacks were forbidden to assemble among themselves. The restriction even applied to children. For example, Black children in Washington, DC. were no longer allowed to attend Sunday School with White children as they did previously for no other reason than that they were Black (Fordham, 1984; Styron, 1966).

Instrumental discrimination: During slavery, Blacks were excluded by law and custom from economic, political, and other opportunities open to Whites.

Social discrimination: Non-reciprocal social interaction between Blacks and Whites was instituted during slavery. According to Starker (1971; pp. 6), the ritual of social interaction required Blacks and Whites to behave toward each other in certain prescribed ways. For example, they had to use certain prescribed forms of address that expressed the "ritual." Blacks addressed White slave owners as master (*massa*), mistress (*mistis*), miss (*missy*), boss or *buckra,* with or without given names. Slave owners addressed Blacks as aunt, uncle, mammy, sometimes daddy, boy (Starker, 1971; pp. 6). The etiquette also required slaves to behave in a certain manner when he or she was spoken to by Whites. For example, the slave had to "stand attentively, respond politely, bow servilely to the extent, at times, of extreme evasion and deceit" (Starker, 1971; pp. 7).

Expressive Discrimination: Expressive discrimination refers to White Americans' beliefs that Black slaves were culturally, linguistically and intellectually inferior to them; it also refers to the treatment of Blacks based on such beliefs. Historically, the overarching ideology of White American was that Black Americans belonged to a race that was inferior to the White race biologically, culturally, and socially.

White denigration of Black culture began during slavery, with the myth that the slaves came from the "dark continent" of Africa that had not produced civilizations like other continents (Becknell, 1987). They forced the slaves to give up their African cultures and to adopt superior White culture. White cultural values, behaviors, and speech were presented as correct or proper; in contrast, Black cultural values, behaviors, and speech were presented as incorrect and improper.

In the case of language, slave owners took deliberate steps to rid the slaves of their indigenous African languages. There appeared to be a policy not to have several slaves speaking the same language on a plantation for fear that they would teach others their language, and that speaking the same language would make it easy for slaves to plan an escape or a slave revolt. To avoid such incidents, the slaves were forced to speak English. The language situation during slavery, especially the evolution of Black English dialects, contributed to the creation of Blacks as a separate and enduring people with a distinct collective identity.

Intellectual denigration was (and is) an expressive exploitation because it makes White people feel good to think that they are more intelligent than Blacks.

Black Response to Status Problems During Slavery

Response to forced incorporation: Black Americans began to develop their sense of collective identity and of belonging together during slavery. Collective experience of oppression and exploitation caused them to develop the sense of a Black community which embodied their collective racial identity. It has been suggested that racial identity was more important than class or gender identity for the slaves because they knew only too well that all of them, regardless of class or gender, could be punished for an offence of one slave; and they could also be rewarded because of the good deed of one (Green, 1981; Rawick, 1972). The racial identity formed during slavery has continued to influence Black perceptions of and responses to White treatment to this day. In my ethnographic research in Black communities, I have often found that regardless of social class and gender, Black Americans tend to code their experiences with White Americans and with social institutions in terms of race, and not class or gender.

The expressive response of Blacks was particularly important in their construction and maintenance of oppositional collective identity. As noted earlier, White people forced Blacks to give up their African cultures and languages. Under oppression, Blacks developed a new culture and an English dialect different from and oppositional to the White way of behaving and talking (Green, 1981). Another area of expressing opposition was religion. Black religion evolved to satisfy slave master's expectations that this would make it easier to control Blacks, but it turned out to be the opposite of those expectations. Reverend Calvin Marshall described this paradox as follows:

> (T)he (White)man systematically killed your (i.e., Black) language, killed your culture, tried to kill your soul, tried to blot you out—but somewhere along the way he gave us Christianity and gave it to use to enslave us. But it freed us because we understood things about it and we made it work for us in ways that it never worked for him (Holt 1972).

Black music was yet another aspect of cultural evolution for expressing difference and opposition to White domination and White ways. Blacks used their music not only to entertain, lighten the burden of their labor and other sufferings but also as a means of communication, especially the transmission of messages they did not want White people to understand. For example, when Harriet Tubman sang "Steal Away, Steal Away, Steal Away to Jesus" she was not pleading for Blacks to convert to Christianity. Rather, she was telling them to run away through the Underground Railroad to the North of the United States or to Canada (Baer, 1984; Becknell 1987; pp. 45–49).

The development of the Black English dialect was yet another means of expressing differences, toward collective identity. Blacks developed their dialect because, as noted earlier, slave owners forbaded them to speak indigenous African languages and required them to speak the English dialect. The slaves developed an English dialect that the slave masters did not and could not understand (Becknell, 1987; Holt, 1972).

Black American English dialect differs from White American Standard English in phonology, morphology, and syntax. But these differences are not as important for oppositional collective identity as are differences due to secondary meanings. The secondary meanings arose from dialect inversions. The inversion was that Blacks assigned to words, phrases, or statements reverse meanings or changed their functions from what they mean to White people. Thus, the same words appearing in both White English and Black English may have different and, often, opposite meanings. For example, the word "bad" which always means "bad" in White peoples' English sometimes means "good" in Black English.

According to Holt (1972) Black slaves developed their linguistic opposition because they recognized that to use English like their White masters would mean submitting to an identity defeat. That is, it would mean that they accepted definitions of their slave or caste status built into the White semantic system. Language inversion "emerged during slavery to fight both linguistic and psychological entrapment" (Holt, 1972; pp. 154).

The Burden of Acting White During Slavery

Black Americans became bi-cultural and bi-dialectical during slavery because they lived and worked in two different worlds which expected them to think, act, and react in a particular way, depending on where they found themselves. In the Black community and among themselves, most Blacks felt at ease to talk and do things they would never attempt in a White environment. Conversely, in a White environment, Blacks talked and behaved as White people expected, which would be inappropriate among the Black community (Becknell, 1987; pp. 30).

As noted earlier, the ritual of social interaction between Blacks and Whites established during slavery required the two groups to behave toward each other in certain prescribed ways. Blacks were expected to act and react the way Whites wanted them to, otherwise, they would be punished or even put to death. As survival was the name of the game for Blacks, they talked and behaved the way Whites wanted.

Note, however, that Whites did not require Blacks to talk and behave the same way that White people actually talked and behaved; i.e., White slave owners did not require Blacks to "act White." In fact, Blacks were forbidden to talk like Whites; e.g., they were forbidden to learn to read and write. What the Whites wanted was for Blacks to talk and behave according to White people's construction of Black speech and cultural behavior. When in front of White people, Blacks tried to talk and behave out of compliance to what White people were demanding. But when they were among themselves, they acted according to their cultural ways that White people hardly observed.

The same situation existed with regard to speech. White English dialect was portrayed by Whites and Blacks as proper, correct, good, and standard. Black English dialect, by contrast, was stigmatized as improper, incorrect, flat, country, slangish, and bad. Although White people required Blacks to speak in a particular way, the requirement was not for Blacks to talk like White people actually talked; i.e., White people did not require Black slaves to speak "correct" or "standard English." Rather, they wanted Blacks to talk according to the White construction of Black speech based on Black "improper English." Blacks talked the way Whites wanted them to talk when with Whites out of compliance, but talked "Black" among themselves.

The burden of "acting White" before emancipation was how to comply with the White demand that Blacks should behave and talk like Blacks the way Whites thought that Blacks talked and behaved. It was not that Blacks should choose between behaving and talking the way White people actually behaved and talked and the way they themselves preferred to behave and talk.

There was no uniformity in Black response to this conflicting demand before emancipation. Rather, they evolved several strategies of coping with the "burden of 'acting White.'" This is evident in the variety of stock characters portrayed in novels, plays, drama, short stories and films of and about that era (Bogle, 1989; Nestby, 1982; Starker, 1971). The characters included accommodatative slaves, rebellious slaves, clowns, tragic mulattoes. Black mammies and coons. These characters represented different responses to the "burden of 'acting White.'" The accommodative slave (toms, servile Negro), for e.g., accepted his place as defined by Whites; and behaved and talked according to the White definition. The rebellious slave or "bad Negro" defied the law and the ritual of non-reciprocal social interaction. Black mammies were the nurturers of White offspring.

Black Collective Identity After Emancipation

Status Problems

Blacks continued to face status problems after emancipation. Instrumentally, they were subjected to extreme economic exploitation. They were denied free and fair competition with Whites in employment, wages, promotion and entrepreneurship (Moore, 1981; Norgren and Hill, 1964; Novak, 1978). Before 1960, about the only places where Blacks could get jobs based on formal education and ability were segregated educational and health institutions serving the Black community (Frazier, 1957; Marshall, 1967; Ross, 1967).

Although school credentials were a requirement for employment in the wider society, White employers used a job ceiling to deny them access to jobs, promotion, and wages commensurate with their qualifications.

In the social domain, residential, sexual, social, and school segregation continued. Black people were residentially segregated by statute, regulatory authorities, and custom (Ogbu and Margold, 1986). School segregation followed suit. In many states sexual relationship between white women and Black men was forbidden and severely punished when the taboo was violated (Johnson, 1943, p. 220; Myrdal, 1944). Until the year 2000, there was a culturally sanctioned rule backed by statutes in many states, namely, that biracial children should be defined as Black and should affiliate with Blacks (Rockquemore and Brunsma, 2002; Wright, 2001).

Ritual non-reciprocal social interaction continued. White people continued to believe that Blacks were inferior to them. These beliefs were expressed in their treatment of Blacks' jokes, novels, short stories, drama, and movies (Johnson, 1931, p. 100). The beliefs aroused White aversion to Blacks and this, in turn, led to another White belief, namely, that Black Americans were not assimilable. Whites did not mean by this that Blacks were not capable of acquiring the education, economic status, and lifestyle of the White middle class. Rather, what they meant was that it was not desirable or acceptable to assimilate Blacks into White society to share their collective identity because they were colored and inferior (Myrdal, 1944, p. 54, 100).

Whites continued to make Blacks collectively responsible for the offence of a single Black person. For example, in Rosewood, Florida in January, 1923, about 1,500 white men from Rosewood and surrounding communities went to the Black neighborhood in Rosewood and killed 40 black men, women, and children in retaliation for an alleged rape of a White woman by a Black man (CBS Television Magazine, 60 Minutes (August 5, 1984).

The threats of violence, punishment, and the prevalence of lynching led Blacks to petition the United Nations in 1951 to intervene on their behalf (Patterson, 1951). Blacks suffered because Whites used them as scapegoats in times of economic hardships and political crisis (Frazier, 1957, p. 155–156;

Shapiro, 1988). They were denied political power through disenfranchisement in the Southern states and through gerrymandering in the North.

Black Response to Status Problems after Emancipation

Blacks tried both as a group and as individuals to solve their status problems after emancipation. Blacks firmly believed that they were treated differently and badly because of their race and history. This interpretation of their social reality further motivated them to forge collective solutions to their collective status problems that reinforced their oppositional identity. Their collective solutions included the following:

Instrumental solutions: Blacks accepted the criteria of getting good jobs, decent wages, and upward social mobility through education and hard work like Whites. But they soon realized that there was a job ceiling which prevented them from achieving these goals by merely meeting the criteria or rules that worked for White people. For this reason, they developed folk theories of getting ahead in spite of the job ceiling. As a group, they came to believe that they had to meet additional requirements, which included collective struggle at group level and clientship or uncle tomming, as individuals. The various forms of collective struggle up to the 1960s constituted modes of coping with the instrumental aspect of their status problems. They included the following:

Accommodation: Booker T. Washington's idea of accommodation under the caste-like system of the old South was advocated. He believed that Black Americans could achieve economic self-sufficiency through industrial education and vocational training for the Black masses and through independent business enterprise for the higher classes. He emphasized working within mutually separate collective identities for Blacks and Whites (Hall, 1979).

Integration with equality of opportunity: W. E. B. DuBois and the National Association for the Advancement of Colored People (NAACP) disagreed with Washington's view. By contrast, they demanded equality of opportunity with Whites and full acceptance by White people. Actually, some version of this strategy was initiated during slavery by free Blacks like Delany and Douglas. In the 1930s its advocates picketed and boycotted White business in Black communities that discriminated against Blacks (Drake and Cayton, 1970, Hall, 1979; p. 99). This strategy increased the tension and mistrust between Blacks and Whites. More importantly, however, they increased Black Americans' sense of oppositional collective identity (Becknell, 1987).

The third strategy was separatism. The separatists did not believe that it was possible to achieve a satisfactory solution to Black status problems within the American social and economic system. They believed that the solution was for Blacks to leave the United States society both physically and spiritually, while heading for places like Africa, Mexico, Latin America, or a part of the United States set aside for Blacks. The best known separatist movement was led by Marcus Garvey. It appealed to many Blacks, whether or not they formally belonged to it, because the movement promoted Black pride and collective identity (Hall, 1979; Redkey, 1969; Sygnnerstvedt, 1972, p. 133). Another influential separatist movement, especially in its early phase, was the Black Muslim Movement.

Social response: It took about 50 years for the social response to the post-emancipation status problems to crystallize. Locke (1925, p. 631) reports that during the first 50 years, "the minds of Blacks were burrowed in trenches of the Civil War and Reconstruction." But underneath this was a psychological development that eventually enabled Blacks to liberate themselves from "the tyranny of intimidation and implied inferiority" (Locke, 1925, p. 631). The new era arrived in the mid-1920s when Blacks began to demand changes in their representation in the White minds or social image. Until then, the prevailing social image was expressed in the ritualized non-reciprocal interaction and forms of address carried over from slavery, as well as other renditions created by the Civil War (Locke, 1925, p. 631–632). By the 1920s, e.g., "Tom and Sambo" were no longer acceptable. Locke (1925, p. 632) notes that "The Negro today wishes to be known for what he is, even in his faults and shortcomings; (He) scorns a craven and even precarious survival at the price of seeming to be what he is not." Locke quotes an apt passage from a poem by Claude MacKay about the outlook of the *New Negro:*

> Mine is the future, grinding down today
> Like a great landship moving to the sea,
> Where the green hungry waters restlessly
> Heap mammoth pyramids and bark and roar
> Their eerie challenge to the crumbling shore.
> (Locke, 1925; p. 633).

Collective struggle against social discrimination went beyond ending non-reciprocal social interaction. Black Americans demanded social justice and acceptance by White Americans as social equals. Their strategies for achieving these goals included boycotts, protests, riots, civil disobedience, law suits, and lobbying for legislation (Berry, 1971; Weisbrodt, 1991). White Americans, of course, resisted the Black collective struggle for social justice and inclusion. This resistance, in turn, made Blacks more disappointed and mistrustful of White people, a situation that further increased their sense of oppositional collective identity.

Black fear and experience of physical violence also promoted their sense of oppositional collective identity and group loyalty. Group loyalty was also necessary because White violence was often indiscriminate (Fordham, 1985). The Rosewood incident described earlier was an example of White indiscriminate violence after the emancipation period.

Expressive responses: The emergence of the Harlem Renaissance and *The New Negro* also brought changes in the post-emancipation expressive adaptations of Black Americans. New interpretation of the *Negro Spirituals* is a case in point. Before the first quarter of the 20th century, *Negro Spirituals* were not accepted as original creations of folk hymns by Blacks. Instead, they were regarded as imitations of White Wesleyan hymns. Blacks were ashamed of this interpretation, but by the 1920s they were courageous enough to reject the White interpretation that their hymns were not original. Equally important is that Blacks began to express their collective identity at this time in poetry, Jazz Art, and culture (Hayes, nd; p. 666–677).

The Burden of "Acting White" After Emancipation

The burden of "acting White after emancipation, was different from the burden of "acting White" before emancipation. Recall that before emancipation "acting White" was that out of compliance Blacks had to behave and talk in the manner defined for them by the Whites to satisfy White people's expectations. Again, White people did not require that Blacks should behave and talk the way White people themselves actually behaved and talked.

However, after emancipation, Blacks were required to behave and talk the way White people actually behaved and talked: (a) in situations requiring the mastery of certain White knowledge, behaviors, and speech, such as for formal education, upward social mobility, and participation in societal institutions controlled by White people, while (b) Blacks were also now required to behave and to talk like White people to gain social acceptance and to be treated as social equals by White people. Blacks, therefore, now had to master two sets of cultural and dialect frames of reference: (1) Black ways of behaving and talking among themselves; and (2) White ways of behaving and talking in

White-controlled situations. The co-existence of Black and White frames of reference, of course, has had a dynamic relationship and changed over time. What was not required of Blacks was to assume White people's collective identity.

But there was one additional problem: Blacks were often not rewarded or accepted as equal by Whites when they successfully learned to behave and talk like Whites or had obtained stipulated educational qualification.

Coping with the Burden of "Acting White" after Emancipation

After emancipation, Black Americans did not abandon their oppositional cultural and dialect frames of reference to embrace the White cultural frame of reference for education and upward social mobility. However, they accepted the need to behave and talk like White people (to "act White") for education, upward social mobility, equality and acceptance by White people. This was a dilemma for Black people. How they responded to this dilemma, i.e., resolved the tension between the demands that they act according to White frames of reference, rather than the Black frames of reference in situations controlled by White people, constituted their coping with the "burden of acting White." They developed five identifiable coping strategies.

Cultural and linguistic assimilation: Some Black people, after emancipation, chose to assimilate in culture and language. They tried very hard to emulate White people in behavior, speech, and thought because they believed that their chances of success in education, employment in the corporate economy, and in being socially accepted by White people would be better if they abandoned Black frames of reference and emulated White people. Becknell (1987) has described some techniques such Blacks used to assimilate: they straightened their hair with scalp-brushing chemicals because Black people's hair was stigmatized as "bad;" bleached their skin to look more White; some even stopped drinking coffee because coffee made a person "black;" pinched their nose to make it more pointed instead of flat; learned to talk like White people, including going for special coaching to talk more "properly;" distanced themselves socially from other Black people; and joined White churches.

Accommodation without assimilation: Another coping strategy for some was to more or less live in two worlds at different times: Black and White. Within the Black community they behaved and talked according to the Black frames of reference. In the White world, like school, work, and among White people, they behaved and talked like White people required. This category of Blacks could "go home again," according to Becknell (1987).

Ambivalence: The third coping strategy was ambivalence. Ambivalent Blacks knew, for instance, that "proper English" was necessary for school success and for getting good jobs. However, they also knew that no matter how hard a Black person tried to talk like White people, he or she would still sound Black. So, for them, trying to "talk proper" was only "puttin' on" or pretending to be White (Ogbu, 1999), Similarly, some ambivalents believed that the obstacles facing Blacks in employment, wages, promotion, and education were racial; the fact that they were Black, not because they did not behave or talk like White people, was the key (Ogbu, 1999). I will give a concrete example later in the paper.

Resistance or opposition: Some Blacks opposed adopting White cultural and language frames of reference or "acting White" anywhere because they believed or feared that this would mean giving up their Black ways. It would also mean accepting White people's interpretation of the cultural and dialect differences between the two races. From their point of view, White people defined White ways as good and defined Black ways as bad. One informant in Oakland, California, gave a historical explanation of this resistance to "acting White" in the Black community. He said that, since slavery, White Americans have tried to get Black people to replace their inferior culture and dialect with superior White culture and language before White people would accept them. It began with teaching house slaves to imitate their White masters to make them different and superior over field hands. After emancipation, White people established "finishing schools" and "special education" to improve Black speech, manners and behaviors. These programs assumed that Black speech, manners, and behaviors were bad and should be replaced with good White speech, manners, and behaviors. A similar reason was given by some Black parents during ethnographic interviews in San Francisco for not wanting to speak standard English (Luster, 1992).

Encapsulation: Finally, some Blacks were more or less encapsulated in Black cultural and dialect frames of reference. They did not behave or talk like White people because they did not know how to rather than because they were opposed to doing so.

I have limited data on social sanctions or peer pressures against Blacks who chose any of these coping strategies to resolve the conflicting demands. Nor do we have data on how people handled or coped with the social sanctions. But there must have been consequences. More research is needed in this area.

Post-Civil Rights Era Black Responses to "Acting White"

Status Problems

Significant changes have occurred in the status problems of Blacks since the civil rights movement of the 1960s. These changes were most evident in the economic and political sectors. The factors that raised the job ceiling for Blacks included (a) executive orders (e.g., President Kennedy's Committee on Equal Employment Opportunity in 1961); (b) federal legislation (e.g., Title VIII of the Civil Rights Act of 1964); (c) the war on poverty; and (d) pressures from civil-rights organizations (Burkey, 1971; Ferman, Kornbluh and Miller, 1968). Although the changes have benefited mainly college-educated Blacks, not the Black masses, college-educated Blacks in the White establishments have complained of a glass ceiling. They say that they lag behind their White peers in promotion because of their race (Benjamin, 1991; Case, 1995).

Social discrimination: This has decreased but has not been entirely eliminated. Hostility and violence are still directed against Blacks and other minorities in times of economic recession, such as during the 1980s (State of California, 1982). The definition of inter-racial children as Black and their affiliation with Blacks continued until the census of 2000. Children can now choose their affiliation. Residential and school integration is now more or less a matter of economic status, but segregation remains because of "White flight."

Expressive discrimination: Many Whites probably no longer believe that Blacks are inferior to Whites but the residue of this belief remains. A poll conducted by the *Newsweek* magazine in 1978 found that about one quarter of the Whites (25%) still believed that Blacks had less intelligence than Whites, and about 15% thought that Blacks were inferior to White people (Newsweek, February 26, 1979, p. 48). The publication of *The Bell Curve* by Herrnstein and Murray (1994) is a reminder that the Whites' belief in the inferiority of Blacks still exist even in White "scientific" circles. After a recent report in the *San Francisco Chronicle* about my research on Black academic performance, one reader sent me statistics on standardized test performance along with a lengthy letter on the genetic basis of the low score of Blacks. The debate goes on about Black genetic endowment for intelligence (The Gene Media Forum, 2002). As this goes to press, Black culture and language are still stigmatized.

Black Response to Status Problems in Post Civil Rights Era

The civil rights mobilization of the 1960s reinforced Black collective identity, especially with the emergence of the Black Power Movement. For Blacks, the ideology and strategies of the movement removed the stigma attached to being Black, increased race pride and provided a shared slogan that "Black is Beautiful." Thus, their response to the status problems complemented their collective identity as we find it today.

Oppositional Collective Identity in Contemporary Black Community

Black Americans have always aspired to succeed like White Americans, but they have always been aware of the obstacles facing them because of their status or race (Ferman, Kornbluh and Miller, 1968; Myrdal, 1944; Ogbu, 1978; Rowan, 1967; Sochen, 1972). Another obstacle is the "burden of 'acting White.'" Before and after emancipation, as well as after the civil rights movement, they responded to this obstacle with one of the five culturally patterned strategies or copings described earlier: assimilation, accommodation without assimilation, ambivalence, resistance of opposition, and encapsulation. Clearly, resistance or opposition has always been just one of the coping responses. It is probably by no means the most prevalent coping strategy during any of the periods.

Even though it is just one of the strategies for coping with the "burden of acting White," I focus on it in this section to show that oppositional collective identity or oppositional culture exists in the contemporary Black community or post-civil rights movement and provides the context for understanding why Black students label and avoid some attitudes and behaviors as "White."

In the 1980s, I studied the collective identity and frames of reference in the Black community by reviewing ethnographic and other literature (Ogbu and Margold, 1986). The latter included more than 50 Black American autobiographies (Ogbu and Simons, 1998). I discovered in this research six recurring identity themes: (1) oppositional collective identity; (2) oppositional cultural frame of reference;(3) strategies for coping with the burden of "acting White;" (4) interpretations of the coping strategies; (5) social sanctions or peer pressures against some coping strategies; and (6) coping strategies against the social sanctions. I will revisit each of these now.

Oppositional Collective Identity

One indicator of a sense of collective identity among contemporary Black Americans is the frequency that Black authors cite the passage about "double consciousness" from DuBois' (1982/1903) *Souls of Black Folks.* In the second half of the 20th century, a number of events have reinforced this double consciousness. Among them are the civil rights mobilization, the Black Power Movement. and the Black Muslim Movement. As noted earlier, the Black Power Movement was particularly important in reinforcing the oppositional collective identity. Its ideology and tactics removed the stigma attached to being Black and increased race pride and provided an appealing slogan "Black is Beautiful." These practices removed the fear, shame. and stigma as well as the social costs of being Black for those who wanted to express the outward symbols of Black collective identity. They began to display openly what they had always felt covertly, namely, that they were proud to be Black. The new public and psychological acknowledgement and the expression of Black collective identity have not been limited to activists or poor Blacks. They have reached every segment of the Black America. They have permeated the works of Black artists, performers. and scholars (Becknell, 1987). They have been embraced by Black professionals and the Black middle class in general.

This development was taking place during my ethnographic research in Stockton, California, 1968 and 1970, the hey day of the movement. Thus, I had a chance to observe identity transformations among both poor and middle-class Blacks first-hand. The transformation included shifts in identity labels from "Negro" to "Colored" to "Black;" changes in identity symbols, such as from processed to natural hair style; and changes in organizational membership, such as Black teachers in Stockton who refusal to join Black Teachers' Alliance in 1969 (because the term Black was bad and militant) to 100% membership by the same teachers in the Black Teachers' Alliance in 1972. The changes continued. During my research in Oakland in the early 1990s, a conference was organized in New Orleans by Blacks to change their collective identity label to African Americans. We also studied the response to this label change by Blacks in Oakland.

The strongest evidence of oppositional collective identity among contemporary Black Americans is linguistic. For example, Blacks use positive labels among themselves, such as "soul" (implying eternity, spirituality and transcendence); "brother and sister" (implying some of the closest of kin) and "bloods" (referring to the very stuff of life). In contrast, they label White people, particularly White men, "Ofays" (i.e., enemies, foes). According to Johnson (1972, p. 172), Blacks have only one positive label for White men, namely, "blue-eyed soul brother" which was usually reserved for "hippies" in the 1960s.

Oppositional Frames of Reference

The literature review provided evidence that Black and White cultural and dialect frames of reference are different and oppositional. For example, both Smitherman (1977, p. 75) and Boykin (1986, p. 63) describe Black culture as characterized by spirituality, harmony with nature, and being "in time" rather than "on time." Boykin (1986, p. 63) adds other areas in which Black and White cultures are also oppositional. For example, Blacks use more organic metaphors, have more preference for expressive movement, place more emphasis on inter-connectedness, and have a richer oral tradition. The two cultures differ in cognitive modes and non-verbal discourse (Shade, 1984); styles of walking, talking and gesturing (Folb, 1980:45), in attitudes (Davis and Watson 1985, p. 113; Folb, 1980, p. 45; Weis, 1985, p. 35). The strongest evidence of oppositional frame is in language use or communication (Boykin, 1986, p. 58; Daiby, 1972; Folb, 1980; p. 227–260; Holt, 1972; Smitherman, 1977). According to Daiby (1972, p. 175) Black Americans believe that they have to be "one jump ahead" of White people in verbal communication. He goes on to say that the function of Black vernacular English has been to "strengthen the in-group solidarity of Black Americans to the exclusion of Whites, and to deceive, confuse and conceal information from White people in general" (Daiby 1972, p. 172).

Interpretations of Adoption of "White" Culture and Dialect Frames

An important clue as to how Black Americans interpret the adoption of White cultural and language frames of reference or "acting White" for professional success comes from a description in *Black Rage* of the dilemma of successful Black Professionals in White business. As the authors put it:

> The only way out, if indeed it can be so considered, is a poor one at best and the price paid for success is terribly high. *We speak of those Negroes who make it by emulating the White man. They accept as a fact that Negroes are not so smart as White people and decided to reject their blackness and, insofar as possible, embrace whiteness.* They identify with White men in every way and add to that contempt for black people. In the process they gain some of the "White man's magic." They acquire some of the superior qualities they attribute to him. They may as a result feel more competent, but it is a direct function of the feeling that "other Negroes" are incompetent. In this way they develop a contempt for themselves, because, however much they avoid it, they remain black, and there are things about themselves that will yet remind them of their blackness and those reminders will evoke feeling of self hatred and self-depreciation (Grier and Cobbs, 1968; *Emphasis added*).

Many authors state explicitly that they themselves and/or Black Americans in general see successful participation in White institutions (e.g., school, the corporate economy) as an assimilation, a one way acculturation or a subtractive process, that takes away their Black identity (Baker, 1987; Campbell, 1982; Davis and Watson, 1985; Mitchell, 1982; Steele, 1992; Taylor, 1973). Based on her ethnographic findings in a community college, Weis (1985) suggests that the students more or less interpreted mastering academic work as a one-way acculturation. A Black professor told the researcher that "a lot of Black students see (the academic world) as a White world... (If I) tell students, 'you're going to be excellent...' often times excellence means being... White.... (and) that kind of excellence is negative here" (Weis 1985, p. 100–101). Labov (1972, p. 135) asserts that it is apparent to some Black youth "that accepting... School values (is) equivalent to giving up self-respect."

Some Black professionals in the corporations, according to Taylor (1973; p. 13), find that it is in their best interest to embrace, overtly the behaviors of Whites. He goes on to say that "the flight into the White role behavior is...at a high cost." This is because for a minority person to be accepted into the top echelons of the corporations, he or she (the minority professional) must "think, manage, behave like a majority group member and be White except in external appearance." (Taylor, 1973; pp. 16–17). Campbell concluded from her study of Black female executives that they are forced to pull away from their Black cultural identity, and to consciously modify their speech, their laughter, their walk, their mode of dress, and their choice of car to conform to mainstream requirements. Thus, as Black executive women move up, they become isolated from those in their old world (Campbell, 1982; pp. 68–69, 70). Davis and Watson (1985) repeatedly mention the "phenomenal estrangement of corporate Blacks" from Black cultural traditions from their own families and communities, and even from their own pre-corporate life styles, ways of dressing, and sense of humor (see also Baker, 1987; Mitchell, 1982).

Coping Today with the "Burden of Acting White"

In the context of oppositional collective identity and cultural frame of reference as well as negative interpretation of "acting White," contemporary Blacks adopt definite strategies to cope with the demand that they adopt certain "White" attitudes and behaviors in White institutions and establishments. The strategies they use to resolve the tension between meeting the demands of the White controlled situations and the demands to conform to the Black ways are similar to the coping strategies of Blacks after emancipation. They include the following.

Assimilation or Emulation of Whites

Contemporary Black professionals in this category choose to abandon Black cultural and dialect frames of reference to behave and talk primarily according to White frames of reference. Like their predecessors they believe that their choice is more likely to help them succeed in education, upward social mobility in the wider society and acceptance by White people. Some other Blacks think that the assimilating Blacks not only reject Black dialect but also appear have a kind of linguistic self-hatred. Assimilationists try very hard to talk like White people. Some go for special coaching to "talk better" in order to keep their job or get promoted. Some send their children to private school where they will learn to "talk better" or to ensure that they learn to "speak White" when they have to, such as at school, on the job, and in the company of "better class of people."

A strong evidence of the assimilation strategy can be found in studies based on William Cross' theory of negrescence (Cross, 1991) described earlier. Before being influenced by the Black Power Movement (1968–75), these professionals and well-educated Blacks had developed a negative self-image of themselves as Black people. However, when they became involved in the Black Power Movement they underwent a transformation from their pre-involvement identity (a non-Afro-centric identity) to a new identity that is Afro-centric (Cross, 1991; p. 190).

Accommodation Without Assimilation

Another strategy is accommodation without assimilation. Blacks in this category adopt White-cultural and language frames of reference where they have to in order to succeed in school or in other White controlled institutions that are evaluated by White criteria. They do not, however, give up their Black identity or cultural and language frames of reference. They learn and follow the standard practices for success in White Americans in their institutions, without giving up their racial identity and ways of behaving or talking (Haynes, 1985; Sowell, 1974). Marva Collins on (60 Minutes, Hewitt, 1979) will serve as a good example of accommodation without assimilation. She is a Black educator who realizes that Black colloquial language is "not considered good enough" when applying for a job. Her solution was to teach Black children to master and use standard English.

Some Black autobiographers mention two important functions of accommodation: (a) it helps Blacks to maintain their sanity in a racist society, and (b) it helps them get ahead in White establishments. It is in this vein that Wiederman (1985) writes of the "seventh sense" that Blacks need in order to stay sane in America:

> It was a trick I learned early on. A survival mechanism as old as slavery. If you re born Black in America you must quickly teach yourself to recognize the invisible barriers disciplining the space in which you may move. This seventh sense you must activate is imperative for survival and sanity. Nothing is what it seems. You must always take second readings, decode appearances, pick out the abstractions erected to keep you in your place. Then work around them. What begins as a pragmatic reaction to race prejudice gradually acquires the force of an instinctive response (Wiederman, 1985, p. 222).

Edwards (1980, p. 120) sees the need to learn standard English and code-switch for upward mobility:

> My father always had a way of changing his voice when he was talking to White folks. We used to say that he could sound more like them than they could sound like themselves. He was just a regular every day "Blood" right up until a White person came on the scene. And then you never heard so many "gushes" and "golly, gee whizzes" in your life.

Ambivalence

I noted earlier that, after emancipation, some Blacks were ambivalent about adopting White behavior and talk in order to achieve success because they did not believe that the reason Black people are not as successful as White people was because they did not know how to behave or talk like White people. This was brought home to me in 1969 when I was attending a workshop on Black history and culture at the University of California, Los Angeles. One of my teachers narrated a story about a Black applicant enrolled in a program for training minority technicians in the Hollywood movie industry. The applicant was turned down because she did not speak "correct English." My teacher offered a different explanation; she said that until the late 1960s, Blacks could not work, rent, or buy homes in Westwood or Hollywood even when they spoke perfect English. She said that the applicant was turned down because of racism.

Resistance or Opposition

Some are afraid that mastering proper English will cause them to lose their Black dialect identity. They do think that they should not give up their dialect because their collective identity requires them to talk like Black people, not like White people. Several Black women in San Francisco considered "talking proper" an attempt to dissociate oneself from the Black race, to show that one is superior to other Blacks and an act of betrayal (Luster, 1992). The women "consciously resisted learning and using standard English because they believed that it is a White imposition on Blacks."

Encapsulation

Some are encapsulated in Black cultural and dialect frames of reference and do not behave or talk like White people anywhere. The reason may be that they have not learned to behave or speak proper English.

Social Sanctions (Peer Pressures) Against "Act White" Today

The belief that adopting White attitudes, behaviors, and communication style as a one-way assimilation or abandonment of Black identity and frames of reference leads to social sanctions against potential assimilation. Accommodators without assimilation are also potential targets of sanctions. Other Blacks are opposed to individuals in these categories who are perceived as trying to behave or talk like Whites in certain situations because such individuals are seen not merely as "acting White" but also as trying to betray the cause of Black people or trying to "join the enemy." The sanctions are both psychological and social.

Psychologically, some individuals trying to 'act White' may experience psychological stress or what DeVos (1967) calls affective dissonance. That is, because individual Blacks share the group's sense of oppositional racial identity, the would-be assimilationists may feel that by behaving or talking like White people they are, indeed, abandoning or betraying their own people.

There was evidence in the literature of both psychological and social sanctions against "acting White." Some Black professionals not only fear that they are being co-opted by the White world, but also experience social pressures from the Black community. Take the case of Mitchell (1983, p. 22–23). Reflecting on her position as a Black professor at a major research university, she describes the dilemma for Black academics: "the Black community rates service to the community high and research low... also the type of research that the community regards as worthwhile is that which advocates change, helps to get money and speaks in plain language." In contrast, the university regards this type of research as particularistic and subjective.

The sanctions experienced most commonly by Blacks striving for academic and professional success are (a) accusation of Uncle Tomism or disloyalty to the Black cause or Black community (Petroni, 1970, p. 263); (b) threat of personal embarrassment and humiliation (Mitchell, 1983, p. 22–23); and (c) fear of losing friends and/or a sense of community (Abdul-Jabba and Knobles, 1983; Labov, 1972; Weis, 1985). The individual also feels the need to perform a social cost/benefit analysis of his or her chances for making it (Davis and Watson, 1985, p. 51; Mitchell, 1982, p. 35). He or she may experience intense frustration and the perception of a closing down of options (Davis and Watson, 1985, p. 74). In some cases, the latter has led to suicide, while some individuals suffer from self-doubts, guilt, alienation, and paranoia (Luster, 1992).

Reports by Becknell (1987), Kochman (1987), and Luster (1992) as well as my own study in Oakland, California (Ogbu, 1999) provide evidence of contemporary community pressures against "acting White," especially against "talking proper in the community" because it would mean denying and ultimately losing one's Black identity. Becknell (1987, p. 36) talks about the pressure this way:

> When I encounter a group of Blacks on the street in my home community, I can't go up to them and say "Good afternoon, gentlemen. How are you doing today?" (i.e., greet them in Standard English). They would laugh at me and then feel sorry for me. They'd think, "Poor Charles, when he left here for college, he was OK. (That is, he talked appropriately like us and maintained his Black identity). But now, look what they've done (i.e., White people or White educational institutions) to him!" (i.e., he has learned to "talk proper" or "act White").

According to Kochman (1987, p. 228):

Black intonation patterns function as an inside (ethnic) boundary marker; those who do not manifest the distinctive Black intonation in their speech regularly acknowledge the adverse criticism they receive from other Blacks, the substance of which characterizes them as being "assimilation-oriented" or "acting White." I have observed often the nonverbal criticisms directed at these Blacks by other Blacks who do manifest such intonations (a criticisms also often verbalized about them later on, when the person is no longer present). The accused are often called upon to demonstrate the extent of their group affiliation in other ways, and may be further tested for their "Blackness" before the final judgment is rendered. (See also Ogbu, 1999).

Luster tells us that among Black women (and many were parents) who were attending a community school in San Francisco to get their GED, that the biggest opposition was against speaking standard English:

> There is a continual delineation and reinforcement of behaviors, practices, and attitudes that are "Black" (and appropriate) versus those that are "White" (and inappropriate)... "Acting White" is an acknowledged and identifiable practice within the community. The women who were both observed for more than a year and then interviewed consider "speaking proper" or using the Standard English is an attempt to disassociate oneself from the race; an attempt to demonstrate superiority, an act of betrayal. It angered and disgusted the community. The women consciously resisted learning and using the Standard English because it would mean accepting what the White society defines as "right" or "White" to replace what the same White society defines as "wrong" or "Black." (Luster, 1992, p. 202)

I also found that talking proper was a strong signifier of "acting White" in Oakland, California. The parents I studied believed that talking proper in the community was pretentious because, no Black person could really talk like a White person. Talking proper was not natural for Blacks. There was yet another reason for the opposition: Talking proper signified adopting White people's attitude of superiority toward Blacks. Here is how the community would treat a person trying to talk proper, according to my informants:

Parent 1: You know, talkin' all–you know, talkin' like White people.
Interviewer: Oh, talking–so people would not be interested in that...
Parent 1. No.
Interviewer: Ok. Well, how would they treat them?
Parent 1: Probably standoffish...Ignore them... Because they're trying to (show that they are) better than they are...Maybe that type of attitude.
Parent 2. People in the community will say, "He thinks he's smarter than everyone else, or he thinks he's White." We don't want to listen to this. I don't want to listen to this thing or that.
Parent 3: They (other Lafayette Blacks) would probably tend to be somewhat prejudicial of someone speaking very proper English, and they would probably make an assessment on that person's character as being "uppity" or... she is trying to be White, or something like that, you know.

Coping with Social Sanctions Against "Acting White" Today

Contemporary Blacks who must "act White" for whatever reason know full well that their behavior is not endorsed by the community. There are cultural ways of handling or shielding them from the social sanctions. The strategies found in both the literature and my ethnographic studies include the following:

Camouflaging: Involvement in the Black Struggle

This requires activities that give other Blacks the impression that one is for Black people, not for White people. Active participation in the civil rights struggle is a good way to camouflage. Middle class

Blacks are expected to be involved in the collective struggle against White oppression. They have to demonstrate their concern for and loyalty to the "race" through "the struggle" to be accepted as good role models for Black youth. Some Black professionals I interviewed reported that they were accused on many occasions of not being for the race because they were "not involved". This is how one Oakland parent describes the attitude of the community toward a professional suspected of abandoning the community. This is followed by a Stockton school administration's description of the dilemma of Black professionals:

Parent 5L: By now they've (i.e., successful Black professionals) gone somewhere else to live in a totally different neighborhood. So, you know, it's really hard to...

Interviewer: That's right. So, they've moved away from the community

Parent 5L: That's right.

School Administrator: Let me tell you something else about this community, about the Black people, that they don't have a lot of trust in each other, either you know.... The Black people who live in north Stockton, professionals).... if they came to the Black community Council they would be literally attacked by the people from south Stockton (Black ghetto resident). They (from south Stockton Blacks) feel that they (north Stockton Blacks) have abandoned them for having moved up there. So, once you have become a professional, and successful, and others who are not, sort of cast dispersion on you because of it. It's a difficult thing to go back and serve, to help when people are challenging you every step of the way you know (interview, 1970).

Accommodation Without Assimilation

Convincing others that one is able to behave and talk like White people in White-controlled environments and yet behave and talk like Black people in the Black community is another way to handle social sanction. Some Blacks learn to live alternately in the Black world and in the White World (Becknell, 1987). Some Black parents in Oakland recognized the importance of code-switching behavior. One mother said that she mastered proper English to disguise her racial identity, minimize racial discrimination, and increase her chances of getting a good job.

Parent: (Talking proper) is not a problem for me because I can change my tone of voice and speak in a different (way). Well, I appear to speak in a different–with an accent. Certain (White) people don't really know who they're talking to.

Interviewer: Okay.

Parent: Whereas if they were to see me, they would not (have agreed to what I said or wanted)...because of the Afro.

Support Group or Mentorship

Black professional organizations or associations function to provide needed support to Blacks. Getting a mentor helps Black professionals succeed in the mainstream. One function of the mentor is to serve as a stabilizing force against peer pressures and self-doubt. Mentors are very important even in professional sports, as can be seen in the experience of Abdul-Jabbar. Early in his professional sports career, a mentor provided him with tips on how to play. One of two other mentors who gave him emotional support, was a Muslim. His Muslim mentor admonished him to both take his religion seriously and affirm his U.S. citizenship and get all his rights as a citizen (Abdul-Jabbar and Knobles, 1983). However, the literature indicates that mentorship is not frequently available to Black achievers. According to Davis and Watson (1985, p. 89), mentoring is limited by a lack of structural opportunity. They note that, "In the early 60's...Blacks always had a 'godfather' or corporate mentor who would look out for them. But that did not mean that the mentor would help Black employees rise through the ranks" (Davis and Watson 1985, p. 29–30).

Coping with the Burden of "Acting White" at School

I have discussed at length the collective identity and frames of reference among Blacks in contemporary United States because critics of the Fordham–Ogbu thesis focus almost exclusively and atomistically on Black students attitudes and behaviors in the school context, divorced from Black history and community. But Black students are products of Black history and members of contemporary Black community. They face the same dilemma, due to the same oppositional collective identity and frames of reference characteristics, as members of their community. Therefore, in examining the students' conduct, I will not repeat the above discussions of the dilemma of "acting White" among contemporary Black Americans. Suffice it to say that at school, students responded to required attitudes and behaviors labeled "White" like adult Blacks in White institutions and corporate America. Among the students, as among adults, there are assimilationists, accommodators without assimilation, ambivalents, resisters and the encapsulated. It is important to bear in mind that although Black collective identity and cultural frame of reference are oppositional, only one of the five categories of Blacks among both adults and students is explicitly opposed to adopting White attitudes, behaviors, and speech. In my own study, I have generally found that there are relatively few students who reject good grades because it is "White." On the contrary, they want to make good grades and many report that they are well received by their close friends when they get good grades, such as when they get an A (Ogbu and Simons, 1994a, 95).

What the students reject that hurt their academic performance are "White" attitudes and behaviors conducive to making good grades (Ogbu and Simons, 1998). In Shaker Heights, for example, they include speaking standard English, enrollment in Honors and AP classes, being smart during lessons, and having too many White friends. In Oakland, they include talking proper, studying a lot or doing homework everyday, having mostly White friends, taking hard/advanced placement courses, acting like a nerd, taking mathematics and science classes, spending a lot of time in the library and reading a lot. Black students experience peer pressures from other Black students to discourage them from adopting such White attitudes and behaviors. Black students also experience peer pressures for other reasons than "acting White." In Shaker Heights, these include non-academic priorities like pressure to work too many hours on part-time jobs to pay-off credit card debts, as well as maintaining a certain lifestyle. Oakland students are pressured to sell drugs, smoke weed, cut classes, to hang out with friends and to believe that school does not matter. It is important to note that all peer pressures that hurt students' grades are not for preventing students from "acting White."

Coping with Social Sanctions Against Peer Pressures at School

Like the adults, Black students have strategies for coping with peer pressures. It is difficult to separate strategies for handling pressures against "acting White" from strategies for peer pressures for other reasons. Shaker Heights students reported three major ways they handled peer pressures. One was family upbringing and continued parental supervision, including screening their friends and monitoring their school work. The second was a student's own initiative, whereby he or she carefully chooses Black friends who are serious about school and about making good grades. Finally, some students interpret peer pressures as distractions from their goal of school success and take necessary steps to avoid them.

In Shaker Heights, the school made a significant indent into the peer pressures by establishing an academic identity program for achieving Black students, called The (Minority Achievement Committee

Scholar) MAC Scholars. Academically promising students are invited to join the program. The scholars meet periodically to discuss how they can handle peer pressures and improve their school performance. They also have an annual award ceremony for academic improvement. Equally important is that they wear special symbols identifying them as MAC scholars and greet one another in a special way. Both of these express their pride in academic achievement. The MAC Scholars are generally admired as good role models by other Black students (Ogbu, 2003, p. 125–126).

The most common strategy in Oakland is camouflaging. A good example of this is to be highly involved or to excel in Black activities and avoid "White" activities. Another common strategy is to help friends with their home-work or let them copy one's assignments. Some students act dumb in class or as class clowns. Some study in secret and their good grades, achieved "without studying," are attributed to the fact that they are "naturally smart." A few students get "bullies" to protect them in exchange for helping the latter with assignments. There seem to be more students in Oakland than in Shaker Heights, however, who "give in" to friends or yield to peer pressures and "let their grades suffer."

There are several things to be stressed as a conclusion. First, Black students face the same burden of "acting White" that Black Americans have faced throughout their history and still face in contemporary United States. Under this circumstance, they have developed culturally patterned ways of coping with the dilemma or the burden of "acting White" which one finds both in the contemporary Black community and among the students. Second, in the course of their history, Black Americans have had to cope with peer or community pressures against "acting White" and they have also developed strategies to handle such pressures. The social sanctions or pressures and the coping strategies still exist in contemporary Black community and are shared by Black students. Third, Black students experience peer pressures for other reasons than for "acting White." The peer pressures unrelated to the burden of "acting White" also contribute to their low school performance. Lastly, other and even more important contributors to their low school performance are societal, school and other community forces that discourage academic engagement (Ogbu, 2002, 2003; Ogbu and Simons, 1998).

References

Abdul-Jabbar, K. and Knobles, P. (1983). *Giant Steps; The Autobiography of Kareem Abdul-Jabbar.* New York: Bantam Books.

Ainsworth-Darnell, J. W. and Downey, D. B. (1998). Assessing the oppositional culture explanation for racial/ethnic differences in school performance. *American Sociological Review* 63:536–553.

Alba, R. (1990). *Ethnic Identity: The Transformation of White Americans.* New Haven, CN: Yale University Press.

Baer, H. A. (1984). *The Black Spiritual Movement: A Religious Response to Racism.* Knoxville, TN: The University of Tennessee Press.

Baker, H. A. Jr. (1987). *Modernism and the Harlem Renaissance.* Chicago, IL: University of Chicago Press.

Becknell, C. F. (1987). *Blacks in the Work-force: A Black Manager's Perspective.* Albuquerque, NM: Horizon Communications.

Benjamin, L. (1991). *The Black Elite: Facing the Color Line in the Twilight of the Twentieth* Century. Chicago, IL: Nelson Hail.

Bennett, L. Jr. (1996). 10 Most dramatic events in African-American history. In J. A. Kromkowski (Ed.), *Race and Ethnic Relations: Annual Edition* (pp. 31–32). Sluice Dock, Guilford, CT: Dushkin Publication.

Bergin, D. A. and Cooks, H. C. (2002). High school students of color talk about accusations of "acting white. *The Urban Review* 34(2):113–134.

Berry, M. F. (1971). *Black Resistance! White Law: A History of Constitutional Racism in America.* New York: Appleton-Century-Crofts.

Bethel, E. R. (1997). *The Roots of African American Identity: Memory and History in the Antebellum Free Communities.* New York: St. Martin's.

Bogle, D. (1989). *Toms, Coons, Mulattoes, Mammies, & Bucks: An Interpretive History of Blacks in American Films.* New York: Continuum.

Boykin, A. W. (1986). The Triple Quandary and the Schooling of Afro-American Children. In U. Neisser (Ed.). *The School Achievement of Minority Children: New Perspectives,* (pp. 57–92). Hillsdale, NJ: Lawrence Erlbaum.

Branch, C. W. (1999). Race and human development. In R. H. Sheets and E. R. Hollins (Eds.), *Racial and Ethnic Identity in School Practices: Aspects of Human Development* (pp. 7–28). Mahwah, NJ: Lawrence Erlbaum.

Burkey, R. M. (1971). *Racial Discrimination and Public Policy in the United States.* Cambridge, MA: D. C. Heath.

Campbell, F. (1982). Black executive and corporate stress. *The New York Times Magazine* 12:1–42.

Carter, P. (1999). *Balancing 'Acts': Issues of Identity and Cultural Resistance in the Social and Educational Behaviors of Minority Youth.* Ph.D. Dissertation, Department of Sociology, Columbia University, New York, NY.

Carter, R. I. and Goodwin, A. L. (1994). Racial identity and education. In L. Darling-Hammond (Ed.), *Review of Research in Education* (pp. 291–336). Washington, D.C: American Educational Research Association.

Castile, G. P. and Kushner, G. (1981). *Persistent Peoples: Cultural Enclaves in Perspective*. Tucson, AZ: University of Arizona Press.

CBS Television Network (1984). The Rosewood massacre. *60 Minutes XVI* (47): 16–22.

Cone, J. H. (1972). *The Spirituals and the Blues*. San Francisco, CA: Harper and Row.

Case, E. (1995). *The Rage of the Privileged Class: Why are Middle-class Blacks Angry? Why Should America Care?* New York: Harper Collins.

Cook, P. J. and Ludwig, J. (1997). Weighing the "burden of acting white." Are there differences in attitudes towards education. *Journal of Policy Analysis and Management,* 16(2):256–278.

Cornell, S. E. and Hartman, D. (1998). *Ethnicity and Race: Making Identities in a Changing World*. Thousand Oaks, CA: Pine Forge Press.

Cross, W. E. Jr. (1991). *Shades of Black: Diversity in African American Identity*. Philadelphia, PA: Temple University Press.

Cross, W. E., Strauss, L. and Fhagen-Smith, P. (1999). African American identity development across the life span: educational implications. In R. H. Sheets and E. R. Hollins (Eds.), *Racial and Ethnic Identity in School Practices: Aspects of Human Development* (pp. 29–47). Mahwah, NJ: Lawrence Erlbaum.

Daiby, D. (1972). The African element in American English. In T. Kochman (Ed.), *Rappin' and 'Stylin' Out: Communication in Urban Black America* (pp. 170–188). Urbana, IL: University of Illinois Press.

Davis, G. and Watson, C. (1985). *Black Life in Corporate America: Swimming in the Mainstream*. Garden City, NY: Anchor Books.

DeVos, G. A. (1992). *Ethnic Persistence and Role Degradation: Koreans in Japan*. Boulder, CO: West View Press.

DeVos, C. A. (1967). *Japan's Invisible Race*. Berkeley, CA: University of California Press.

DeVos, G. A. (1995). Ethnic pluralism: conflicts and accommodation. In L. Romanucci-Ross and G. A. DeVos (Eds.), *Ethnic Identity: Creation, Conflict, and Accommodation* (pp. 15–41). Walnut Creek, CA: Altimira Press.

Drake, St. C. and Cayton, H. R. (1970). *Black Metropolis: A Study of Negro Life in a Northern City,* Vol. 1, 2. New York: Harcourt.

DuBois, W. B. (1982, originally 1903). *The Souls of Black Folks*. New York: The New American Library.

Edwards, H. (1980). *The Struggle that must be: An Autobiography*. New York: Macmillan.

Epstein, T. (2003). Adolescent Racial/Ethnic Identity and Academic Achievement Revisited. Paper presented at the AERA Annual Meeting, Chicago, April 21–24, 2003.

Ferman, L. A., Kornbluh, J. L. and Miller, J. A. (Eds.) (1968). *Negroes and Jobs. A Book of Reading*. Ann Arbor, MI: The University of Michigan Press.

Folb, E. A. (1980). *Runnin' Down Some Lines: The Language and Culture of Black Teenagers*. Cambridge, MA: Harvard University Press.

Fordham, S. (1985). Black Students' School Success as Related to Fictive Kinship. Final Report to the National Institute of Education, Washington, D.C.

Fordham, S. (1984). Ethnography in a High School: Learning not to be A Native. A paper presented at the 83rd Annual Meeting of the American Anthropological Association, Denver, CO, November 14–18.

Fordham, S. and Ogbu, J. (1986). Black students' school success: coping with the burden of 'acting white'. *Urban Review* 18(3):176–206.

Frazier, E. F. (1957). *The Negro in the United States* (Rev. Edn.). New York: Macmillan.

Gans, H. (1979). Symbolic ethnicity: The future of ethnic groups and cultures in America." *Ethnic and Racial Studies* 2:1–20.

The Gene Media Forum (2002). *Race, Genes and Intelligence*. New York: The Gene Media Forum.

Green, V. M. (1981). Blacks in the United States: the creation of an enduring people. In G. P. Castile, and G. Kusher (Eds.), *Persistence Peoples: Cultural Enclaves in Perspective* (pp. 69–77). Tucson, AZ: University of Arizona Press.

Grier, W. H. and Cobbs, P. M. (1968). *Black Rage*. New York: Basic Books.

Haley, A. (1976). *Roots: The Saga of an American Family*. New York: Dell.

Hall, R. L. (1979). *Black Separatism in the United States:* Hanover, NH: The New England University Press.

Hauser, S. T. (1972). Black and White identity development: aspects and perspectives. *Journal of Youth and Adolescence* 1(2):113–130.

Hayes, R. (Nd). *Harlem, Mecca of the New Negro, March 1925* (pp. 631–635). Baltimore, MD: Black Classic Press.

Haynes, R. L. (1985). *Minority Strategies for Success*. Unpublished Manuscript, Department of Anthropology, University of California, Berkeley. Special Project.

Herrnstein, R. J. and Murray, C. (1994). *The Bell Curve: Intelligence and Class Structure in American Life*. New York: The Free Press.

Hewitt, D. (Executive Producer). (1979, November 11). *60 Minutes* [Television Broadcast]. New York, NY: CBS Broadcasting Inc.

Hirasawa, Y. and Nabeshima, Y. (1995). *Dowa Education: Educational Challenge Toward a Discrimination-free Japan*. Osaka, Japan: Buraku Liberation Research Institute.

Holt, G. S. (1972). Inversion in Black communication. In T. Kochman (Ed.), *Rappin and Stylin' Out: Communication in Urban Black America* (pp. 152–159). Chicago, IL: University of Illinois Press.

Horvat, E. Mc. and O'Connor, C. (2001). *The Black–White Achievement Gap and Black Cultural Opposition to Acting White: Where do we go from Here?* American Sociological Association, 97th Annual Meeting, Chicago.

Johnson, C. S. (1931). *The Negro in American Civilization*. London, England: Constable and Co.

Johnson, C. S. (1943). *Backgrounds to Patterns of Negro Segregation*. New York: Crowell-Collier.

Johnson, K. (1972). The Vocabulary of Race. In T. Kochman (Ed.). *Rappin' and 'Stylin' out. Communication in Urban Black America,* (p. 140–151). Urbana, IL: University of Illinois Press.

Keyes, C. F. (1981). *Ethnic Change*. Seattle, WA: University of Washington Press.

Kochman, T. (1981). *Black and White Styles in Conflict*. Chicago, IL: University of Chicago Press.

Kochman, T. (1987). The ethnic component in Black language and culture. In J. S. Phinney and M. J. Rotheram (Eds.), *Children's Ethnic Socialization: Pluralism and Development* (pp. 117–133). Beverly Hills, CA: Sage.

Labov, W. (1972). *Language in the Inner City: Studies in the Black English Vernacular.* Philadelphia, PA: University of Pennsylvania Press.

Locke, A. (1925). Enter the New Negro. In Hayes, R. (Nd). *Harlem, Mecca of the New Negro, March 1925* (pp. 631–635). Baltimore, MD: Black Classic Press.

Luster, L. (1992). *Schooling, Survival, and Struggles, Black Women and the GED.* Unpublished Doctoral Dissertation, School of Education, Stanford University.

Marshall, R. (1967). *The Negro Workers.* New York: Random House.

Mitchell, J. (1983). Visible, vulnerable, and viable: emerging perspectives of a minority professor. In J. H. Cones, J. F. Noonan and D. Janha (Eds.), *Teaching Minority Students: New Directions for Teaching and Learning,* No. 16. (pp. 17–28). San Francisco, CA: Jossey-Bass.

Mitchell, J. (1982). Reflections of a Black social scientist: some struggles, some doubts, some hopes. *Harvard Educational Review* 52(1):27–44.

Moore, J. T. Jr. (1981). *A Search for Equality: The National Urban League, 1910–1961.* University Park, PA: The University of Pennsylvania Press.

Myrdal, G. (1944). *An American Dilemma: The Negro Problem and Modern Democracy,* Vol. 1. New York: Harper.

Nestby, J. P. (1982). *Black Images in American Films, 1896–1954: The Interplay Between Civil Rights and Film Culture.* New York: State University of New York Press.

Norgren, P. H. and Hill, S. E. (1964). *Toward Fair Employment.* New York: Columbia University Press.

Novak, D. A. (1978). *The Wheel of Servitude: Black Forced Labor After Slavery.* Lexington, KY: The University of Kentucky Press.

O'Connor, C. (1996). *Optimism Despite Limited Opportunity: Schooling Orientation and Agency Beliefs Amongst Low-income African American Students.* Unpublished Dissertation, University of Chicago, Chicago, IL.

Ogbu, J. (1978). *Minority Education and Caste: The American System in Cross-Cultural Perspective.* New York: Academic Press.

Ogbu, J. (1998). *Community Forces and Minority Educational Strategies: The Second Part of the Problem.* Berkeley, CA: Department of Anthropology, University of California.

Ogbu, J. (1999). Beyond language: ebonics, proper english, and identity in a Black-American speech community. *American Educational Research Journal* (Summer) 36(2).

Ogbu, J. (2000). Collective Identity and Schooling. In H. Fujita and K. Shimizu (Eds.), *Education, Knowledge and Power.* Tokyo: Shinyosha Ltd (English version).

Ogbu, J. (2002). Black-American students and the academic achievement gap: What else you need to know. *Journal of Thought.* 37(4):9–33.

Ogbu, J. (2003). *Black Students in an Affluent Suburb: A Study of Academic Disengagement.* Hillsdale, NJ: Lawrence Erlbaum.

Ogbu, J. and Margold, J. (1986). *A Summary of Literature Review On Black Oppositional Identity And Cultural Frame of Reference.* Unpublished Manuscript, Survey Research Center, University of California, Berkeley, CA.

Ogbu, J. and Simons, F. (1988). *Black Autobiographies: A Search for Cultural Model of Minority Status and American Society.* Unpublished Manuscript, Survey Research Center, University of California, Berkeley, CA

Ogbu, J. and Simons, H. D. (1994). *Cultural Models of School Achievement: A Quantitative Test of Ogbu's Theory.* Final Report. Graduate School of Education, National Center for the Study of Writing, University of California, Berkeley, CA.

Ogbu, J. and Simons, H. D. (1998). Voluntary and involuntary minorities: a cultural-ecological theory of school performance with some implications for Education. *Anthropology and Education Quarterly* 29(2):155–188.

Patterson, W. L. (1951). *We Charge Genocide.* New York: International Publishers.

Petroni, F. A. (1970). 'Uncle toms': White stereotypes in the Black Movement. *Human Organization* 29(4):260–266.

Phinney, J. S. and Rotheram, M. J. (1987). Children's ethnic socialization: Themes and implications. In J. S. Phinney and M. J. Rotheram (Eds.), *Children's Ethnic Socialization: Pluralism and Development.* Newbury Park, CA: Sage Publications.

Phinney, J. S. and Rosenthal, D. A. (1992). Ethnic identity in adolescent: Process, context and outcome. In G. R. Adams, R. P. Gullotta and R. Montemayor (Eds.), *Adolescent Identity Formation* (pp. 145–172). Newbury Park, CA: Sage Publications.

Rawick, G. P. (1972). *From Sundown to Sunup: The Making of the Black Community.* Westport, CT: Greenwood Publishing Co.

Redkey, E. S. (1969). *Black Exodus: Black Nationalist and Back-to-Africa Movements, 1890–1910.* New Haven, CN: Yale University Press.

Rockquemore, K. A. and Brunsma, D. L. (2002). *Beyond Black: Biracial Identity in America.* Thousand Oaks, CA: Sage.

Ross, A. M. (1967). The Negro in the American economy. In A. M. Ross and H. Hill (Eds.), *Employment, Race and Poverty: A Critical Study of the Advantaged Status of Negro Workers from 1865 to 1965* (pp. 3–48). New York: Harcourt.

Rowan, C. T. (1967). The Negro's Place in the American Dream. In J. D. Harrison and A. B. Shaw (Eds.), *The American Dream: Vision and Reality.* San Francisco, CA: Canfield Press.

Shade, B. (1984). Personal traits of educationally successful black children. *Negro Educational Review* 32(2):6–11.

Shapiro, H. (1988). *White Violence and Black Response: From Reconstruction to Montgomery.* Amherst, MA: The University of Massachusetts Press.

Smitherman, G. (1977). *Talkin' and Testifyin':The Language of Black American.* Detroit, MI: Wayne State University Press.

Sochen, J. (1972). *The Unbridgeable Gap: Blacks and their Quest for the American Dream.* Chicago, IL: Rand McNally.

Sowell, T. (1974). Black excellence: the case of Dunbar High School. *The Public Interest* (Spring):5–7, 10–11, 12.

Spicer, E. H. (1966). The Process of Cultural Enclavement in Middle America." 36th Congress of International de Amerianistas, Seville, vol. 3:267–279.

Spicer, E. H. (1967). *Cycles of Conquest.* Tucson, AZ: University of Arizona Press.

Spicer, E. H. (1971). Persistent cultural systems: a comparative study of identity systems that can adapt to contrasting environments. *Science* 174:795–800.

Starker, C. J. (1971). *Black Portraiture in American Fiction: Stock Characters, Archetypes, and Individuals.* New York: Basic Books.

Steele, C. (1992). Race and the Schooling of Black Americans. *The Atlantic Monthly* (April), 68–73.

Stuckey, S. (1987). *Slave Culture: Nationalist Theory & The Foundations of Black America.* New York: Oxford University Press.

Styron, W. (1966). *The Confessions of Nat Turner.* New York: Random House.

Sygnnerstvedt, S. (1972). *The White Response to Black Emancipation: Second-Class Citizenship in the United States since Reconstruction.* New York: Macmillan.

Taylor, S. A. (1973). Some funny things happened on the way up. Contact 5(1):12–17.

Taylor, B. L. (2001). *Navigating Knowing/Complicating Truth: African American Learners Experiencing Oral History as Real Education.* Unpublished Dissertation, Louisiana State University and Agricultural Mechanical College.

Weis, L. (1985). *Between Two Worlds: Black Students in an Urban Community College.* London: Rutledge.

Weisbrodt, R. (1991). *Freedom Bound: A History of America's Civil Rights Movement.* New York: A Plumer Book.

Wiederman, J. E. (1985). *Brothers and Keepers.* New York: Penguin Books.

Wright, L. (1996). One drop of blood. In J. A. Kromkowski (Ed.), *Race and Ethnic Relations.* Annual Edition, (pp. 10–16). Sluice Dock, Guilford, CT: Dushkin Publication.

Wright, M. A. (2001). *I'm Chocolate, You're Vanilla: Raising Healthy Black and Biracial Children in a Race-Conscious World.* San Francisco, CA: Jossey Bass.

Yon, D. A. (2000). *Elusive Culture: Schooling, Race, and Identity in Global Times.* New York: State University of New York Press.

22

Burden of Acting Neither White Nor Black

Asian American Identities and Achievement in Urban Schools

JAMIE LEW

A growing body of research has challenged Ogbu's theory of the "burden of acting white" and to what extent cultural explanations account for black students' schooling experience and outcome. Emerging studies show that Ogbu's cultural explanations may be limited when examining variability of school achievement among black and white students, and that other social forces, such as class, peer networks, and school context may play a significant role in their schooling aspirations and achievement (Cook & Ludwig, 1998; Downey & Ainsworth-Darnell, 2002; Ferguson, 2001; Tyson, 2002; Tyson, Darity, & Castellino, 2005). In short, variability of school performance among black and white students, for instance, should take into account not only issues of race and culture but also how these processes may be fluid and salient depending on the changing social and school contexts.

These studies are important in light of the widening black and white achievement gap and the prevailing cultural discourse often used to explain school achievement. However, in the midst of this on-going debate, there is a limited understanding of how, if at all, theory of "acting white" plays a role for racial groups other than black and white students. By extending the discussion beyond a black-and-white discourse, researchers may be able to complicate and expand our understanding of the role of culture in school achievement and how it intersects with various structural forces, such as class and schools.

One of the more invisible racial groups discussed in this debate is Asian Americans. Stereotyped as model minorities, Asian American students' negotiation of multiple identities, varied schooling experiences, and racialization process are often ignored (Fong & Shinangawa, 2000; Lee, 1996; Lew, 2006; Nakanishi & Nishida, 1995; Pang & Cheng, 1998; Park, Goodwin, Lee, 2003). However, Asian American status as model minorities—a stereotype that often conflates them with whiteness—plays an important ideological role in perpetuating ideals of individual meritocracy, especially for poor minority students. Such ideals of "American dream" predicated on cultural explanations place both reward and blame on individuals without adequately taking into account important structural factors, such as race, class, and schools. Therefore, stereotype images of Asian "success" or black "failure" cannot be predicated solely on cultural explanations, but has to take into account the changing social contexts.

In order to address such limitations, this study will examine some of these timely issues by asking the following research questions: How do Asian American students in different social and economic contexts negotiate their racial and ethnic identities, and how does this process impact their academic aspirations and achievements? In what ways do peer networks and race relations in schools affect students' negotiation of identities? How do high-achieving Asian Americans who are typically viewed as model minorities negotiate their racial minority status? How is this process similar and different from those Asian American students who are low-achieving or dropping out of high schools? In what ways does this research challenge our understanding of "acting white," and the ways in which students negotiate power relations inherent in the polarized notions of blackness and whiteness?

As a way to answer some of these questions, this study compares experiences of two groups of Korean American students—both high- and low-achieving—in New York City urban schools. I compare experiences of high-achieving middle-class students attending a competitive academic magnet high school with working-class low-achieving high school dropouts attending a community-based GED (General Educational Development) program. The findings indicate that the two groups of Korean American students experienced their racial minority status and adopted different racial strategies depending on their socioeconomic backgrounds, peer networks, and school contexts. For instance, the high-achieving middle-class Korean students, in the school context of academic peer culture attended predominantly by middle-class white and Asian students were more likely to associate and identify with their ethnic backgrounds. Similar to previous studies on Hispanic and children of immigrants, the high-achieving Korean students highlighted their bicultural backgrounds and bilingual ability when noting their experiences as both Korean and American.

On the other hand, the low-achieving Korean American high school dropouts, in the context of urban schools fraught with academic failure and increasing dropout rates that consist predominantly of poor and working-class minorities, were more likely to identify themselves as "minorities." As such, the Korean high school dropouts in this study were careful to disassociate themselves from the "wealthy" and "studious" Koreans and other Asian Americans. It is important to note that neither the high- nor the low-achieving students identified themselves with whiteness; however, the two groups negotiated and interpreted their racial minority status and accompanying marginalization differently depending on their given opportunity structure at home and schools.

This research is particularly timely given the on-going debate of Ogbu's theory of "burden of acting white" and the role of culture on school achievement. It argues that academic achievement among Asian American students involves a complex relationship between culture, class, race, and schools. Asian Americans in schools face conflicting messages regarding their racial minority status: On the one hand, as racial minorities, they are often excluded from whiteness, while on the other hand, they are also stereotyped as model minorities that align them with whiteness. Asian Americans in the context of a black and white racial discourse prevalent in our society learn to negotiate their race and ethnic identities differently from black and white students—a process that is largely shaped by changing social contexts. Although neither the high- nor the low-achieving Korean American students aligned themselves with whiteness, the two groups in different economic and school contexts, learned to interpret their minority status and opportunity structure differently. The findings support earlier studies that note the significance of school structure—peer relations, racial and class composition, and academic culture—and show how these structural factors may play an integral role in fulfilling academic aspirations and achievement among minority students. In so doing, it challenges the prevalent stereotype based on cultural discourse to explain Asian "success" and black "failure." It underscores the significance of examining these processes across and within various ethnic and racial groups, while highlighting the salience of race as well as the relational nature of identities in various school and economic contexts.

"Burden of Acting White" and Oppositional Cultural Frame of Reference

For the past few decades, Ogbu's (1987) seminal research on voluntary and involuntary immigrants has helped educators examine the critical role of race and culture in academic achievement. By making a clear distinction between voluntary and involuntary immigrant experiences, he pointed to the significance of minority students' cultural frame of reference and their interpretation of economic, social, and political barriers. Ogbu and colleagues have argued that involuntary minorities, such as African American students adopt low-school performance as a form of adaptation to their limited social and economic opportunity in adult life. It is argued that involuntary minorities who were forcefully incorporated into the United States tend to attribute academic success with "whiteness" and thus reject school success with their own ethnic and racial identities. Therefore, as a means of developing survival strategies to endure structural barriers such as inferior schooling, job ceiling, and racial discrimination, African Americans form an oppositional cultural frame of reference and oppositional social identity to dominant white society (Fordham, 1988; Fordham & Ogbu, 1986; Labov, 1982; Matute-Bianchi, 1986; Villejas, 1986).

Fordham and Ogbu (1986) argued that this oppositional cultural frame of reference lead African American students who are doing well in school to be associated with and to be labeled as "acting white." For Ogbu, the growing black and white educational gap persists mainly because of this "burden of acting white" and institutionalized racial stratification inherent in our schools and society at large: "school performance gap persists because the forces of racial stratification—white treatment and black responses—that created it continue to some degree" (Ogbu, 1994, p. 264). Ogbu criticizes those scholars who talk about black and white inequality in terms of class stratification, pointing to the "temporality of class membership in contrast to the permanence of racial group membership" (p. 267). He argues that despite class variability among black communities, middle-class blacks continue to perform less academically than middle-class whites, as a result of their oppositional cultural frame of reference and resistance to "acting white."

For Ogbu, black students' attitudes and behaviors in school cannot be separated from the larger historical oppression and systemic racism that African Americans have faced in the United States. In the last article he wrote before his untimely death, Ogbu (2004) defended his position by arguing that many of his critics have misinterpreted his cultural-ecological theory simply as an oppositional culture theory (p. 1). In this last article, he articulated the various types of coping strategies that African Americans have developed in response to the White dominant society: in doing so, he pays particular attention to the processes of oppositional collective identity and cultural frame of reference in the context of African American history. Some of these coping strategies that have developed as a result of historical White oppression include processes such as assimilation, accommodation without assimilation, ambivalence, resistance or opposition, and encapsulation (pp. 21–23). Despite these various coping strategies, however, he illustrates how the strategies aforementioned are largely shaped by history of oppression, giving rise to a collective black experience and the "burden of acting white" that generally frame their attitudes, experiences, and identities (2004).

Despite the significance of Ogbu's theory of "burden of acting white," other studies have criticized Ogbu by pointing to the significance of class, ethnicity, and school context when noting the relationship between race and school achievement (Ainsworth-Darnell & Downey, 1998; Carter, 2003; Cook & Ludwig, 1998; Downey & Ainsworth-Darnell, 2002; Ferguson, 2001; Tyson, 2002; Tyson et al., 2005). For instance, Tyson and colleagues (2005) argued that Ogbu's theory of "burden of acting white" among black students may be more of a problem related to school structure than culture. They found that both black and white students were generally achievement oriented and that racialized peer pressure against high achievement was not prevalent in all schools. Similarly, Ferguson (2001) challenged the black oppositional cultural theory by arguing that depending on the family backgrounds, both blacks and whites shared similar interests and aspiration toward schooling. Carter (2003) also pointed out that low-income black youths exhibit both "dominant" and "nondominant" cultural capital and how they negotiate these cultural expectations in school may be an important factor in analyzing school stratification and achievement.

Flores-Gonzalez (1999), in her research on a group of high-achieving Puerto Rican high school students, found that despite their involuntary immigrant status, these students did not associate school success with "whiteness." These middle-class students were academically successful while maintaining their ethnic identity. In the context of a school culture that embraced academic achievement, these students did not believe that doing well in school was associated with whiteness, but instead, achieving in school was very much in line with their ethnic background. In other words, the students associated achieving in school with their Puerto Rican identity, rather than rejecting their racial minority status as a barrier to their achievement. Therefore, Flores-Gonzalez (1999) highlighted the importance of ethnicity, class, and school context when examining minority student achievement.

Studies of post-1965 immigrants and their second-generation children have also complicated the dichotomous notion of voluntary and involuntary immigrants by pointing out that voluntary black immigrants from countries in the West Indies, for instance, are also likely to adopt oppositional cultural frame of reference from their peers. Portes and Zhou (1993) have argued that certain immigrant groups are more vulnerable to downward mobility depending on the immigrant group's neighborhood incorporation, strength of ethnic networks, and mode of adaptation.

For instance, according to Portes and Rumbaut (1996), the first-generation Haitian American community in Miami, Florida, had strong national identity and solidarity with fellow ethnic Haitian immigrants. However, their national pride and achievement orientation conflicted with the children's everyday experience in school. Little Haiti, located in Miami, is adjacent to Liberty City, which is the main black inner-city area of Miami. Haitian adolescents attended predominantly inner-city schools and were labeled by other native black youths as docile or subservient to whites. They were denigrated for their French, Creole, and Haitian accents. Consequently, second-generation children faced conflicting ideas and values: "To remain Haitian, they would have to face social ostracism and continuing attacks in school; to become American—Black American in this case—they would have to forgo their parents' dreams of making it in America on the basis of ethnic solidarity and preservation of traditional values" (p. 81). Since adversarial stance toward the white mainstream is common among inner-city minority youths, many Haitian second-generation youths were given messages by their peers in their school and community that devalued education as a means for social advancement. This message directly contradicts the first-generation parents' expectations. For many of these students, to be fully assimilated means assimilating into the values and norms of the poor inner-city rather than mainstream middle-class. In the process, the solidarity and support rooted in the Haitian ethnic community dissipates (Portes & Rumbaut, 1996).

Similarly, in Waters' research of black immigrant from the West Indies in Brooklyn, New York, she argues that the high achieving black immigrants were embedded in strong ethnic networks, such as church and community organizations, whereby first-generation parents and other immigrant adults provided important educational and employment information and resources for their second-generation children. By instilling immigrant values of education and ideals of achievement, the high-achieving black immigrant students tend to adopt their ethnic identities and immigrant status, while resisting assimilation into the cultures of their black peers of the inner-city neighborhoods where they resided. On the other hand, the low-achieving black immigrant students, in the context of residing in isolated neighborhoods with limited support from ethnic networks, were more likely to reject their ethnic identities and immigrant status, while adopting oppositional cultural frame of reference from their black peers in schools and neighborhoods.

Gibson (1988) also found that the second-generation Punjabi children in California are able to succeed in schools by sustaining strong ethnic identity and not assimilating to the dominant working-class white culture surrounding them. She noted this process as "accommodation without assimilation" and argued that through selective accommodation, Punjabis learn the skills necessary to succeed in schools but are able to keep from being culturally assimilated.

Similarly, Lew's (2004, 2006) research on Korean American high school students supported earlier findings. She argues that although culture is important, issues of class, race, and school context play an integral role in academic achievement among Asian American students. Although both high-and low-achieving students experienced racism and noted their racial minority status, the two groups adopted different strategies to negotiate such institutional barriers, and hence their racial and ethnic identities. She found that compared to the middle-class high-achievers, the poor and working-class low-achievers, in the context of urban high school that is fraught with increasing school violence and high school dropout rates, are more likely to disassociate from their ethnic identities and adopt oppositional cultural frame of reference from their peers as a way to resist their limited opportunities at home, communities, and school (2006). This finding indicates that resistance to school achievement may not be specific to involuntary immigrant groups, such as African Americans, but may be generalizable beyond specific student groups. Although students' race and sociocultural backgrounds play an important role, factors of class, peer relations, and school structure may also play an integral role when taking into account school achievement among minority students (Lew, 2006).

Research Site and Methods

In order to collect information on social processes, such as intergenerational negotiations, racial and ethnic identity construction, and schooling aspirations, the research is based on in-depth interviews and participant observations. This research took place in the New York City public school and a community-based GED program. A total of 72 Korean American students were interviewed: 42 in the academic magnet high school and 30 high school dropouts in the GED program. Both 1.5-generation (born in Korea but raised in the United States) and second-generation (born and raised in the United States) Korean American students were interviewed.

Although most of the students grew up and lived in Queens, New York—the borough with the largest ethnic enclaves of Korean Americans in the New York metropolitan area—they came from different socioeconomic and family backgrounds. Compared to the Korean high school dropouts, the magnet high school students came from higher socioeconomic backgrounds with a greater number of two-parent households. For instance, 36% of the academic students were eligible for reduced and free lunch, compared to 80% of the dropout students. Furthermore, when we consider their schooling context, we see an important distinction.

As one of the most competitive elite high school in New York City, the magnet high school (MH) prides itself on student academic achievement paralleled by few public high schools. According to the annual school report (NYC Board of Assessment, 2002–2003), approximately 2,700 students were enrolled, and since entrance to the school was based on a competitive standardized exam, students commute to the school from all five of New York City's boroughs. Almost half of the students were Asian (46.5%), while 37% were White, 9.1% Hispanic, and 7.4% black. Only about 1% consists of recent immigrants to the United States (those who immigrated within the last three years).

The Youth Community Center (YCC) is a nonprofit community-based organization in Queens, New York. Its education and outreach programs provide students and adults with counseling, tutoring, classes on the Test of English as a Foreign Language (TOEFL), English-as-a-second language (ESL) classes, and preparatory classes for the GED exam. All of the Korean students in the GED program had officially dropped out of their respective neighborhood public high schools in New York City, most of which had a record of low student academic performance and high school dropout rates, as well as a disproportionate number of poor minority students and recent immigrants, and had been referred to the program by teachers, counselors, parents, community members, and peers.

Findings

Middle-Class and High-Achieving Students: Race, Class, and Schools

At MH the students were steeped in a competitive college-bound curriculum taught by teachers and administrators who are certified in their fields. Students were also surrounded predominantly by middle-class White and Asian American peers who were immersed in the school culture that fostered academic achievement and excellence; thus, the Korean American students at MH were likely to associate with peers of similar socioeconomic status, education background, and academic expectations. Even for those Korean American students at MH whose families were of lower socioeconomic backgrounds, they were more likely to be exposed to and associate with other students of higher socioeconomic backgrounds.

Moreover, by attending a high school where second-generation Asian Americans represented nearly half (46.5%) of the student population, the Korean American students were likely to reinforce old or establish new friendships with other Asian and Korean American peers who also shared similar experiences growing up as children of immigrant parents. In this respect, institutional characteristics of the school played an important role in strengthening peer relations and helping second-generation youths negotiate their ethnic and racial identities.

According to the high-achieving students in the interview, this regular contact with Korean Americans in school and community formed the basis for an important set of shared experiences—growing up with immigrant parents and maintaining close ties to ethnic communities at home and school—which reinforced their ethnic identities. Susan explains:

> The Korean community of my age group, everyone knows everyone in some way. Like, either you're friends with someone that knows this other person…it's like everything is sort of related into one big circle…I started hanging out with Koreans, and then more other Korean friends came along…church especially, tae kwon do, neighborhood, they are all part of this big circle.

By being embedded in such networks at home, community, and school, the high-achieving students also reinforced their Korean language skill. For instance, John spoke about the importance of learning to speak Korean, and how bilingual skill is an important part of identifying with and reinforcing their Korean ethnic background:

> How do you identify yourself?
> Korean American. I have a lot of Korean pride. If I see a Korean kid who can't speak Korean at all, I'd just be like, you gotta learn Korean you know, you are Korean.

Helen also highlighted her ethnicity, identifying herself as a Korean American. However, she was careful to point out that she saw herself as both Korean and American. Her comments illustrate that social constructs such as race and ethnic identity are subject to change, contradiction, and variability within specific determinate contexts. When I asked her how she identified herself, she replied:

> Korean American. I was born here, so I am definitely American in some way, but I am, of course, Korean…Even if I am born here, I look definitely Asian or Korean or whatever and like the way my parents live and the way we are—we are not Americanized…if I compare myself to some of my friends, I am more American. They were born there [Korea] and raised there.

As illustrated, the process of identity construction is relative, filled with contradictions and inconsistencies. However, the students were also keenly aware of their racial minority status and associated becoming American with whiteness. Yet, as Helen noted, in a school context that has such a large number of Asian American students, she takes pride in being identified as "Asian."

I would never consider myself just American. Sometimes, if someone teased me or something, I just wanted and would've been happier if I was American, if I looked American. You know how Asians, they look totally different. So I guess if I looked American, no one would tease me and stuff...Now, since I am going to this school, and a lot of people are Asians, so I think being Asian is good. I would never want to be like someone else.

If the school context reinforced their ethnic and racial identity, their parents also played an important role. For instance, Beth comments that her parents reminded her that regardless of whether she was born and raised in the United States, most people would not accept her as an American because of her minority racial status:

When I think of Americans, I think of white people. My parents always told me that even though you are born here and can speak English as well as them, they won't really think of you as American. I don't completely believe that, but I think there is some basis truth in that. I think that if they look at you, they are going to say, you are Asian—and then attach the American thing after. So, the first impression that people will have of me will not be that she is American, but that she is Asian.

As illustrated, despite the students identification with ethnic backgrounds, the high-achieving Korean American students at MH were also painfully aware of how their racial minority status may be used to label them as foreigners or non-American by outsiders, despite their having been born and raised in the United States. Therefore, as much as the students identified with their ethnicity, this process is also framed by exclusion and marginalization.

According to the students, in order to address such marginalization, their parents emphasized the importance of using education to compensate for their racial barriers. Underlying this advice was a firm belief that to compensate for their racial-minority status, they had to work even harder and excel in school. Therefore, embedded in strong social support at home, communities, and school, the high-achieving Korean students learned to use education as a means to, in part, withstand the stigma accompanying their racial minority status. Yun Shin at MH, reiterated her mother's advice:

My mom would want me to be Americanized and get education, since there is so much racism against Asians and stuff, but she wants me to keep my Korean culture. Being American never entered my mind. It's not that I don't want to be, but it's just that I've never been accepted as one, never been considered one, so I never thought of myself as one. Because I am always surrounded by Asians, being American never entered my mind. You know, if I say, "I am American," they would say, "No, you are not. You are Asian."

The students' responses also echo findings from earlier studies that have shown how children of immigrants who maintain close ties to their ethnic communities are more likely to reinforce their ethnic identity toward excelling in school (Caplan, Choy, & Whitmore, 1991; Gibson, 1988; Lew, 2006, Portes & Rumbaut, 1996; Suarez-Orozco & Suarez-Orozco, 1995, 2001; Zhou & Bankston III, 1996, 1998). Gibson (1988) describes this as a strategy of accommodation or selective assimilation—a process whereby the children in Punjabi community learned skills necessary to be competitive in American society but resisted assimilating with the lower-socioeconomic white community in which they resided. Other studies on Southeast Asian refugee students also indicate that their academic success was primarily attributable to their close ties to their first-generation parental ethnic networks, and their ability to resist downward assimilation into their surrounding poor minority communities (Zhou & Bankston III, 1996, 1998).

Poor and Working-Class High School Dropouts: Race, Class, and Schools

Expanding on Ogbu's (1987) theory of oppositional cultural frame of reference and "acting white," an increasing number of studies have complicated the dichotomy of voluntary and involuntary groups' experiences by illustrating how members of both groups learn to adopt oppositional cultural frames of reference (Portes & Rumbaut 1996, 2001; Waters 1994, 1999). These studies show that children of immigrants who live in poor, isolated neighborhoods without the protection of strong immigrant networks and social capital are likely to assimilate the cultures and norms of their poor minority peers and adopt an oppositional cultural frame of reference that may not be conducive to schooling success.

The working-class Korean American dropouts not only struggled financially at home, but faced limited support in school. These urban schools mostly populated by poor minorities and recent immigrants, were fraught with violence and high dropout rates. In this school context, the low-income Korean American dropouts rarely came into contact with wealthy whites. Rather, most of their peers were working-class and poor Asians, Blacks, and Hispanics. The racial and economic isolation of these youngsters, therefore, perpetuated their distrust of and alienation from wealthy whites. Henry, who was born in Korea but raised in the United States, explained that he and his friends had very little contact with wealthy whites, either in school or in their neighborhoods, and that they saw whites largely through an oppositional lens:

> I feel closer to Blacks and Hispanics than whites. I think most Koreans are closer to black culture. It's not like I hate whites, but I don't like them either. When I see a white person, I don't see them as just a person. I see them as a white person. When I see them, I think, "I don't know you, I don't know what you do, and I don't want to get to know you." My friends don't like whites either, 'cause we sometimes get into fights with whites and the way they talk about white people. When I see a white person, the first thing I think about is that they are rich and educated, and most of Koreans like me are not educated and rich. So when I see them, I think they are from another planet.

It is important to note, however, that my participants also distinguished themselves from the "wealthy" Korean and other Asian Americans who grew up in middle-class homes and privileged neighborhoods. For instance, Emily explained how such "wealthy" Korean Americans from better neighborhoods would not understand her experience and struggles of growing up in housing projects populated by poor Blacks and Hispanics:

> This Korean girl I know at church was brought up in Bayside, which is mostly white and Asian. If she was brought up in Philadelphia, it would be different. For me, where I lived, majority of the people were Hispanics and Blacks. She doesn't know the environment I grew up in. I know their culture and the way they work. She only knows what she knows. It's mixed, but they are wealthier, and they live in houses. We struggled, and she grew up more comfortable. You know, where I grew up, everybody worked to make a living, the houses were dirty, lived in one bedroom with four people in it. You know, that's how I lived. One bedroom with my mother, father, brother, and me.

Emily continued to explain that her low social and economic status represented a kind of collective "minority" experience that distinguished her from the wealthier and privileged whites and Asians:

> We went through a lot living in that environment. She [wealthy Korean American friend] doesn't know a lot about that. She is more to the whites and Asians, and I am more to the Blacks and Hispanics, more toward the minority.

Similarly, Lee (2004) in her study of second-generation Korean American adults in New York City also found that middle-class Koreans touted their ethnicity and model minority status as reasons for their achievement. However, working-class Koreans interpreted their experiences as shaped largely by their class position. In the context of an ethic community that is predominantly middle-class and socially mobile, the working-class Korean Americans, in order to "save face" from being "looked down" upon, tend to distance themselves somewhat from Korean communities at large and downplay their ethnicity (Lee, 2004).

Interestingly enough, as the Korean American high school dropouts distinguished themselves from their co-ethnic peers along class lines, they also distinguished themselves from more educated or "studious" Koreans. Ken explained that he had many Korean American friends whom he had met in Korean churches, clubs, or schools. But he carefully distinguished himself from the "studious" Koreans. He noted that while his Korean American friends "hang out" after church, the "studious" Koreans go home after school with their family:

I don't hang out with anyone else but Koreans. I used to hang out at the Elmhurst Park a lot. I used to play basketball there, and when you play sports there you meet people, and then you meet their friends. The basketball thing was always after the [church] service. Those kinds of people, you know, the studious people who don't go out much, would leave right after the service. So, you know who they are.

Ken continued to explain how he aligned "studious" and "wealthy" Koreans with whiteness because of the way they spoke, dressed, and succeeded in school:

They [studious Koreans] live a different world. Totally different. When I look at them, I never had a friend like them, so I don't know. When I see them, it's like I am seeing a white person. They never cut school, they use a different language, they use proper language, and I use slangs. They dress more simple; some try to show off, but they don't care what other people think. Their hairstyles are different. Most of them are like whites because they don't know this kind of life, and they hang out with whites, and most of the time they don't hang out anyway.

The findings show that in addition to distinguishing themselves from wealthy whites, the low-status dropouts also distinguished themselves from socially mobile Koreans and other Asians whom they deemed "wealthy and studious"—attributes of "success" they associated with whiteness. In the process, most of the dropouts aligned their shared experiences of racism and low socioeconomic status with those of their low-income minority peers—Blacks, Hispanics, and Asians (Lew, 2004, 2006).

In a society based on a polarized discourse of success and failure, rich and poor, and Black and white, it is no surprise that students struggled to make sense of their distinctive experience, one marked by low socioeconomic and racial-minority status. Their comments represent their negotiation within a polarized racial discourse that tolerates Asians as either "near-whites" or invisible minorities, and whose experiences are often de-racialized and de-contextualized. Within the Black and white racial paradigm, Asians, American Indians, and Latinos are defined in relation to acting either white or Black. As Okihiro (1994) notes, racial paradigm of being "near-whites" or "just like Blacks" is historically and socially constructed, where Asian Americans have been marginalized throughout U.S. history, as the labels of "near-Blacks" in the past or "near-whites" in the present demonstrate.

Meanwhile, embedded in the students' comments is also the implicit marginalization they experience *within* the Korean community (Lew, 2005, 2006). To be poor and uneducated within a community that is predominantly middle class, college educated, and upwardly mobile also means being looked down on and being excluded. As a means of developing survival strategies to endure and resist such marginalization within their own co-ethnic communities, as well as withstand institutional barriers such as inferior schooling, economic limitation, and racial discrimination within the larger society, the working-class Korean American high school dropouts formed cultural frames of reference and social identities in opposition to the dominant society.

Conclusion

To summarize, both groups of Korean students negotiated their racial and ethnic identities differently according to the changing social and economic context. The high-achieving Korean American students in the context of an academic high school with a significant number of middle-class white and Asian student body, were more likely to identify with their ethnicity. They often described themselves as both Korean and American noting the varied ways in which this process is filled with contradictions. Despite the fluidity of identities, however, the students also saw their racial identities ascribed to them in the form of exclusionary stereotypes and false constructs of homogeneity. As illustrated, the high-achieving Korean American students typically associated being "American" with whiteness and pointed out that because of their racial minority status, they would not be accepted as "American" despite being born and raised in the United States.

In order to resist this racial minority status and marginalization that accompanies it, the middle-class and high-achieving students are more likely to use education as a racial strategy. That is, they firmly uphold the belief that as racial minorities, they would have to work even harder in school to obtain the economic parity with white Americans. This predicament highlights multiple and situational meanings associated with being American, the salience of race, as well as the integral and complex relationship between race and class in the United States.

On the other hand, the Korean high school dropouts in the context of poor urban schools fraught with academic failure and populated by poor minority students, adopted a different mode of adaptation. The Korean dropouts were less likely to identify with their ethnicity. By distinguishing themselves from wealthy and educated Koreans and Asians who symbolically represent whiteness, they identified themselves with other "minorities"—a collective term symbolizing downward mobility and struggles with racism and poverty. In order to negotiate and resist such institutional barriers in their homes, schools, and communities, these low-income Korean American students dropped out of high school and adopted behaviors that were not conducive to school achievement.

The findings poignantly illustrate how social class intersects with identity and school achievement. It shows how middle-class high-achieving students, compared to the poor and working-class high school dropouts, have greater access to educational resources and social capital at their respective schools and ethnic communities—institutional resources that are pivotal for students to achieve academically (Lew, 2004; 2006; in press). The middle-class Korean students in the study, compared to poor and working-class Korean students, are more likely to gain access to teachers, counselors, and peers who can provide important schooling resources toward achieving in school. Therefore, even though both groups of Korean American students bring with them their distinct cultural capital and forge important relationships with fellow peers in schools and communities, the social and cultural resources available to middle-class high-achieving students are more likely to be rewarded by the mainstream school system.

Moreover, the findings point to the importance of noting class variability within ethnic communities and the implications this may have in negotiation of racial and ethnic identities. For instance, as beneficial as ethnic networks can be, depending on the background of the member, it can also serve to exclude: that is, in the context of an ethnic community that is predominantly middle-class and socially mobile, the middle-class and high-achieving Korean Americans are more likely to benefit from their ethnic communities and align themselves with their ethnic backgrounds. However, the poor and working-class high school dropouts, often facing exclusion from their own ethnic communities are less likely to benefit from their ethnic communities and disassociate themselves from their ethnic backgrounds.

The findings also complicate earlier understandings of oppositional cultural frames of reference and "acting white": In the context of a binary Black and white racial discourse, as well as the prevalent model minority stereotype that conflates Asian Americans with whiteness, the findings in this study illustrate how Asian American students in different social and economic contexts negotiate their racial minority status and social class backgrounds. To that end, it is important to distinguish the variability of social class and peer relations, highlight the fluidity of multiple identities, and examine institutional factors and schooling contexts when accounting for students' negotiation of identities and interpretation of opportunity structure.

Moreover, the stereotype of Asian "success" much like Black "failure" cannot be explained solely on their cultural orientation. Although race and cultures play an important role in students' outlook and negotiations of their opportunity structure, this process changes and adapts to given social and school contexts. Through expanding the current debate across and within racial/ethnic lines, this research shows that culture is significant and race remains salient; however, in order to examine academic aspirations and achievement among minority students, researchers may benefit by examining race relations beyond a Black and white discourse, and how students' racial and ethnic identities intersect with culture, class, race, and school context.

References

Ainsworth-Darnell, J. W., & Downey, D. B. (1998). Assessing the oppositional culture explanation for racial/ethnic differences in school performance. *American Sociological Review, 63*(4), 536–553.

Caplan, N., Choy, M. H., & Whitmore, J. K. (1991). *Children of the boat people: A study of educational success.* Ann Arbor: University of Michigan Press.

Carter, Prudence. (2003). "Black" cultural capital, status positioning, and schooling conflicts for low-income African American youth. *Social Problems, 50*(1), 136–155.

Cook, P. J., & Ludwig, J. (1998). The Burden of acting white: Do black adolescents disparage academic achievement. In Jencks, C. & Phillips, M. (Eds.), *The black-white test score gap* (pp. 375–400). Washington D.C.: Brookings Institute Press.

Downey, D. B., & Ainsworth-Darnell, J. W. (2002). The search for oppositional culture among black students. *American Sociological Review, 67*(1), 156–164.

Espiritu, Y. L. (1994). The intersection of race, ethnicity, and class: The multiple identities of second-generation Filipinos. *Identities, 9,* 249–273.

Ferguson, R. (2001). A diagnostic analysis of black-white GPA disparities in Shaker Heights, Ohio. In Ravitch, D. (Ed.), *Brookings Paper on Education Policy 2001* (pp. 347–414). Washington D.C.: Brookings Institute Press.

Flores-Gonzales, N. (1999). Puerto Rican high achievers: An example of ethnic and academic identity compatibility. *Anthropology and Education Quarterly, 30*(3), 343–362.

Fordham, S., & Ogbu, J. U. (1986). Black student's school success: Coping with the "burden of 'acting white.'" *The Urban Review, 18,* 176–204.

Kibria, N. (2002). *Becoming Asian American: Second-generation Chinese and Korean American identities.* Baltimore, MD: Johns Hopkins University Press.

Lew, J. (2004). The "Other" Story of Model Minorities: Korean American High School Dropouts in an Urban Context. *Anthropology and Education Quarterly, 35*(3), 297–311.

Lew, J. (2006). *Asian Americans in Class: Charting the Achievement Gap Among Korean American Youth.* New York: Teachers College Press.

Ogbu, J. U. (1987). Variability in minority school performance: A problem in search of an explanation. *Anthropology & Education Quarterly, 18,* 312–334.

Ogbu, J. U., & Matute-Bianchi, M. E. (1986). Understanding sociocultural factors: Knowledge, identity, and school adjustment. In *Beyond language: Social and cultural factors in schooling language minority students.* Los Angeles: California State University, Evaluation, Dissemination, and Assessment Center.

Ogbu, J. U. (1994). Racial Stratification and Education in the United States: Why Inequality Persists. *Teachers College Record, 96*(2), 264–298.

Okihiro, G. (1994). *Margins and mainstreams: Asians in American history and culture.* Seattle, WA: University of Washington Press.

Omi, M., & Winant, H. (1994). *Racial formation in the United States: From the 1960s to the 1990s.* London: Routledge.

Portes, A. (Ed.) (1996). *The new second generation.* New York: Russell Sage Foundation.

Portes, A., & Rumbaut, R. G. (1996). *Immigrant America: A portrait.* Berkeley: University of California Press.

Portes, A., & Rumbaut, R. G. (2001). *Legacies: The Story of the immigrant second-generation.* Berkeley: University of California Press.

Portes, A., & Zhou, M. (1993). The new second generation: Segmented assimilation and its variants. *Annals of the American Academy, 530,* 74–96.

Suárez-Orozco, C., & Suárez-Orozco, M. (1995). Transformations: Immigration, family, life, and achievement motivation amonz Latino adolescents. Stanford, CA: Stanford University Press.

Suárez-Orozco, C., & Suárez-Orozco, M. (2001). *Children of immigration.* Cambridge, MA: Harvard University Press.

Tyson, K. (2002). Weighing in: Elementary-Age students and the debate on attitudes toward school among black students. *Social Forces, 80*(4), 1157–1189.

Tyson, K, Darity, W. Jr., & Castellino, D. R. (2005). It's not "a black Thing": Understanding the burden of acting white and other dilemmas of high achievement. *American Sociological Review, 70*(4), 582–605.

Waters, M. C. (1999). *Black identities: West Indian immigrant dreams and American realities.* Cambridge, MA: Harvard University Press.

Zhou, M., & Bankston III, C. L. (1996). Social capital and the adaptation of the second generation: The case of Vietnamese youth in New Orleans. In A. Portes (Ed.), *The new second generation* (pp. 197–220). New York: Russell Sage Foundation.

Zhou, M., & Bankston III, C. L. (1998). *Growing up American: How Vietnamese children adapt to life in the United States.* New York: Russell Sage Foundation.

23

Seeking Equity in the Education of California's English Learners

RUSSELL W. RUMBERGER AND PATRICIA GÁNDARA

Forty percent of California's public school children speak a language other than English and 25% are identified as English learners, meaning they are not proficient in English (California Department of Education, 2003). California is home to one-third of the nation's 4.4 million English learners, more than three-quarters of whom are Spanish-speaking (Kindler, 2002). Despite their large numbers and a widespread recognition of their special educational needs, California has largely failed both to monitor the educational opportunities of English learners and, more importantly, to guarantee that English learners have the appropriate teachers, curriculum, instruction, assessment, support services, and general learning conditions they need to successfully meet the high academic standards the state has set for all its students. Moreover, even when the state has become aware of specific substandard learning conditions for English learners, it has failed to act effectively to correct these problems. In other ways—such as the ill-planned class size reduction program and the poorly articulated implementation of Proposition 227—the state has worsened the learning conditions for these students.

This article provides a brief summary of the larger report prepared for the lawsuit, *Williams v. State of California*, which provides extensive support for these claims (Gándara & Rumberger, 2003; Gándara, Rumberger, Maxwell-Jolly, & Callahan, 2003).[1] The report first examines the achievement gap for English learners in California. Second, it reviews evidence in seven areas in which these students receive a substantially inequitable education vis-à-vis their English-speaking peers, even when those peers are similarly economically disadvantaged. Third, it documents the state's role in creating and perpetuating existing inequities. Finally, it describes a series of remedies that the state could pursue to reduce these inequities.

Academic Achievement of English Learners

Data from a variety of sources reveal that the academic achievement of English learners lags considerably behind the achievement of English background students. We examined the achievement of English learners using a number of different measures and data sets. Although we disagree with the state's decision to administer and use English only tests with students who do not speak sufficient English to understand them, we analyzed the achievement of English learners vis-à-vis their English-speaking peers using these same test scores, as they are routinely reported as accountability measures in the state.

Rather than simply examine achievement differences at one point in time, we examined differences in achievement growth over time. Gauging the educational progress of English learners over time is complicated by the fact that, as English learners become proficient in English, they are reclassified as Fluent English Proficient (R-FEP). Failing to account for the reclassified English learner students can create the mistaken impression that English learners are performing more poorly as a group than they actually are. In order to address this problem Parrish and his colleagues (2002) compared English-only students with a weighted average of current English learners and former English learners who were reclassified as Fluent English Proficient (R-FEP). They examined changes in reading scale scores[2] between the years 1998 and 2001 using the Stanford Achievement Test, Version 9 (SAT9)—a national, norm-referenced, English-only achievement test[3]—for three cohorts of students:[4] (1) a cohort of students who were enrolled in Grade 2 in 1998, Grade 3 in 1999, Grade 4 in 2000, and Grade 5 in 2001; (2) a cohort of students who were enrolled in Grade 4 in 1998, Grade 5 in 1999, Grade 6 in 2000, and Grade 7 in 2001; and (3) a cohort of students who were enrolled in Grade 8 in 1998, Grade 9 in 1999, Grade 10 in 2000, and Grade 11 in 2001. To compare nonoverlapping cohorts, we replaced the second cohort with one that began when students were enrolled in Grade 5 in 1998. Thus, this analysis is both more accurate and a fairer test of these students' improvement in educational achievement over time.

The results show a sizeable achievement gap between English-only students and current/former English learners. Both groups show more achievement growth in the early years than in the later years, which reflect the increasing difficulty of learning higher levels of more academic English (Scarcella & Rumberger, 2000). The data show a slight narrowing of the achievement gap across all three cohorts, as Parrish et al. (2002) note in their evaluation study (page III–15). For example, the achievement level of English-only students in the Grade 2 cohort improved from 581 points in Grade 2 to 658 points in Grade 5, an increase of 77 points, while the achievement level of English learners and former English learners improved 80 points. As a result, this achievement gap narrowed by 3 points. Among all three cohorts and three subjects (reading, language, and math), the 227 evaluation team found that the achievement gap narrowed by 1 to 8 points (Parrish et al., 2002, Exhibits 10, 13, 16).

It is interesting to note, however, that the greatest achievement growth for the Grade 2 cohorts occurred in schools that offered bilingual instruction before Proposition 227 or continued to offer bilingual instruction after Proposition 227 (Gándara & Rumberger, 2003, Figure 3). In addition, the slight narrowing of the achievement gap between English only and EL and former EL students noted above was due to reductions in the achievement gap in those two types of schools, while in schools that never offered bilingual education, there was no reduction in the achievement gap.

Despite these minor improvements, the achievement gap is sizeable at all grade levels and puts English learners further and further behind their English-only counterparts. In Grade 5, for example, when many students have completed elementary school, current and former English learners are reading at the same level as English-only students between Grades 3 and 4, a gap of about 1.5 years. By Grade 8, when most students have completed middle school, current and former English learners are reading at the same level as English-only students in Grade 6, a gap of about 2 years. By Grade 11, current and former English learners are reading at the same level as English-only students between Grades 6 and 7, a gap of about 4.5 years. This is especially striking given that many of the poorest scoring English learners have already dropped out of school by the 11th grade.[5] Although the increase in the achievement gap across grades can be attributed to the fact that average test score performance gets closer together in the higher grades, nonetheless, the average performance of English learners at the end of secondary school never exceeds that of English-only students at the beginning of secondary school.

Other data show similar patterns. Beginning in 2006, all students in the state must pass the California High School Exit Exam (CHSEE), a standards-based, criterion referenced test. Although the need for improving the education provided by California's high schools is undeniable, there is early evidence that the CHSEE presents exceptionally high stakes for English learners. After two opportunities to pass the CHSEE, only 19% of English learners from the graduating class of 2004 had passed, compared to 48% of all students (California Department of Education, 2002, Attachment 1).[6]

One reason for the underachievement of English learners is that they begin school significantly behind their English-speaking peers. Data from the Early Childhood Longitudinal Study (ECLS) show that about half of California kindergartners from English speaking backgrounds scored above the 50th percentile in fall assessments of language, mathematics, and general knowledge, whereas no more than 17% of kindergartners from non-English speaking backgrounds scored above the 50th percentile (Gándara & Rumberger, 2003, Figure 4). Many English learners begin school without a sufficient understanding of oral English that English background students acquire naturally in their home environment and this clearly affects their test scores. According to the ECLS data, more than 60% of English learners who entered California kindergartens in the fall of 1998 did not understand English well enough to be assessed in English.[7] And even after 1 year of school, 38% of the students were still not proficient enough in English to be assessed accurately.

Not only do English learners begin school considerably behind their English background peers, their low test scores make them more likely to be placed in remedial education, even though such a placement is unlikely to help students close the educational gap with their mainstream peers because the pace of instruction is slower and the curriculum to which they are exposed is often impoverished (Gottlieb, Alter, Gottlieb, & Wishner, 1994; Skirtic, 1991).

Conditions of Inequity for English Learners

The achievement gap between English learners and their English-only counterparts can be attributed, in part, to seven inequitable conditions that affect their opportunities to learn.

1. Inequitable Access to Appropriately Trained Teachers

English learners require teachers with specialized training. The current state of the art of teaching EL students employs three central methodologies for English learner instruction. The first strategy, specially designed academic instruction in English (SDAIE), is defined as "a set of systematic instructional strategies designed to make grade-level and advanced academic curriculum comprehensible to English learners with intermediate English language proficiency" (California Commission on Teacher Credentialing, 2001, p. 2). A second means of teaching EL students is through their primary language. Although the principle goal is to provide access to the core curriculum, in reality, this involves a continuum of strategies, from using the student's primary language solely for clarification of concepts presented in English to actually providing academic instruction in the primary language. A third strategy is English language development (ELD). It is "systematic" instruction of English language that is designed to (1) promote the acquisition of English—listening, speaking and reading and writing skills by students whose primary language is other than English, and (2) provide English language skills at a level that will enable equitable access to the core curriculum for English learners once they are presented with academic content (California Teacher Commission, 2001, p. 3). This second goal is often referred to as the "catch up" strategy: once students have sufficient command of English, the assumption is that they will be able to catch up to their English-only peers with respect to mastery of academic content.

English learners in California are more likely than any other children to be taught by teachers who are not fully credentialed. Whereas 14 percent of teachers statewide were not fully credentialed in 2001–02, 25 percent of teachers of ELs were not fully certified (Rumberger, 2002). Figure 23.1, based on data from two years earlier, shows that as the concentration of ELs in a California school increased, so too did the percentage of teachers without full credentials. In as much as Figure 23.1 holds poverty constant, we would expect to see a flat line if the discrepancy in credentialed teachers were purely a function of poverty. These data show that English learners are significantly less likely to have a fully credentialed teacher than other low-income non-EL students.

In the larger report, we demonstrate that the shortage of qualified teachers was largely a problem of uneven *distribution* of qualified teachers among California's schools and classrooms. By examining

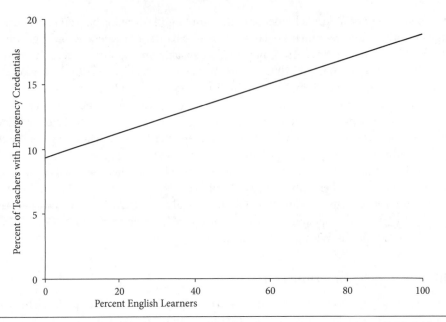

Figure 23.1 The relationship between the percent of English learners and the percent of teachers without full credentials, holding constant the percent of students on free or reduced lunch, California Schools, 1999–2000.

Source: 1999–2000 API Growth Data File. Retrieved October 4, 2000 from WWW: http://api.cde.ca.gov/datafiles.html

Note: Relationship estimated from the regression equation: 3.553 + .119*LUNCH + .095*ELL (N=6039), with LUNCH = 48.6 (sample mean).

statewide data on California teachers for the year 1999–2000, we found that there are actually more fully authorized EL teachers in the state per EL student than there are fully credentialed (non-EL) teachers per non-EL student. But when we examined the distribution of teachers by schools, we found that more than 390,000 English learners in California—one out of every four—attended a school with fewer than half the state average of teachers with specialized authorizations to teach them. As a result, many English learners are taught by unqualified teachers. Data from the 2000 Class Size Reduction (CSR) teacher survey reveal that only 53% of all English learners enrolled in Grades 1–4 in California in the 1999–2000 school year were taught by a teacher with any specialized training to teach them (Gándara & Rumberger, 2003, Table 4).[8] Ironically, a study of California's costly class size reduction effort found that schools with the most English learners benefited the least from class-size reduction, at least in terms of access to fully credentialed teachers (Stecher & Bohrnstedt, 2002).

There is reason for the concern about the low percentage of teachers who are well prepared to teach English learners. An increasingly large body of research has established that teachers with good professional preparation make a difference in students' learning (Darling-Hammond, 2002; Haycock, 1998; Sanders & Horn, 1995; Sanders & Rivers, 1996). At the same time that EL students are less likely than others to have a qualified teacher, the challenges associated with teaching them are even greater than for the typical student. The large number of English learners who are immigrants frequently come from circumstances in which their early lives and education have been disrupted by war, loss or estrangement of family members, poverty, and residential mobility (Ruiz de Velasco & Fix, 2000; Olsen, 1997). As such, teachers must know how to intervene educationally with students whose personal and educational backgrounds are significantly different from the mainstream English-speaking student. Moreover, the age and grade placements of these students in U.S. schools often do not match their skill levels because of varying educational experiences in their countries of origin (Ruiz-de-Velasco & Fix, 2000).

Many newly certified teachers report that they do not have sufficient training to work with English learners and their families. For example, one-fourth of the 1999–2000 graduates of teacher credential programs in the California State University system reported that they felt they were only "somewhat prepared" or "not at all prepared" to teach English learners (California State University, Office of the Chancellor, 2002).[9] In another study, 23% of teachers of English learners who held CLAD credentials reported that they had a hard time communicating with parents of English learners about their children's educational progress and needs. In yet another study, one that investigated of the implementation of Proposition 227 in the Los Angeles Unified School District (LAUSD), researchers noted that the largest concern reported by non-English speaking parents was lack of communication with teachers (Hayes, Salazar, & Vuckovic, 2002).

2. Inadequate Professional Development Opportunities to Help Teachers Address the Instructional Needs of English Learners

The instructional demands placed on teachers of English learners are intense. Teachers must provide instruction in English language development while simultaneously or sequentially attempting to ensure access to the core curriculum. Yet, in the state of California they have been provided very little support for these activities. Data collected for the State Department of Education's Class Size Reduction Study (Stecher & Bohrnstedt, 2000) show that even where teachers are teaching a majority of English learners, the professional development they receive that is dedicated to helping them instruct these students is minimal. The percentage of professional development time that teachers reported focusing on the instruction of English learners in 1999–2000 was about 7%, and even for teachers with more than 50% English learners in their classrooms it was only 10% (Gándara & Rumberger, 2003, Table 12).

These data are corroborated by several other recent studies. Hayes and Salazar (2001), in their study of 177 classrooms in the LAUSD, noted that teachers discussed "the problematic lack of resources and training to assist them to provide quality services to ELLs" (p. 23). A report on the results of a California Department of Education survey of every California school district during the first year of Proposition 227 implementation showed that professional development to help teachers with English learner instruction was one of the most significant unmet needs in the aftermath of the passage of the proposition (California Department of Education, 1999). The later, more ambitious, CDE-sponsored study of the implementation of Proposition 227 being conducted by American Institutes for Research (AIR; Parrish et al., 2001, 2002) likewise reports a similar theme emerging from their investigation. The study documents a significant lack of guidance from the state about the nature of the instruction that should occur in the Structured English Immersion classrooms. Parrish et al. (2001) note "teachers were not provided appropriate materials or guidance on how to use materials appropriately" (p. 36). Again, in the most recent report of this 5-year study, the researchers concluded that "Barriers to the implementation of the Proposition include insufficient guidance for implementing regulations in the law; confusion over what the law requires and allows; and lack of a clear operational definition for the various instructional approaches for EL students. In particular, educators lack clarity on what constitutes best practice within structured English immersion instruction" (Parrish, et al., 2002, p. ix).

The state funded the University of California to provide professional development for teachers through Professional Development Institutes (CPDIs). This is not the only professional development activity in the state; in fact, many districts sponsor extensive professional development programs, but it is the largest state-wide effort, with more than 45,000 teachers participating in these workshops in 2000–01. In that same year, a total of $50,866,000 was provided for this purpose. Of this amount, only $8,358,104 was earmarked for professional development in the area of English Language Development (University of California Office of the President, 2002). This constituted about 16% of the professional development budget, although English learners constitute fully 25% of the students in the state and are arguably the most educationally disadvantaged of all students. The AIR study of the implementation of Proposition 227 in California found that only 18% of the teachers in their sample had even heard of the ELD CPDIs, and only 8% had attended one or more (AIR, 2002, pp. IV–40), suggesting that relatively little is being done to disseminate information about resources that may be available to teachers of English learners.

3. Inequitable Access to Appropriate Assessment to Measure EL Achievement, Gauge their Learning Needs, and Hold the System Accountable for their Progress

While English learners must be incorporated into the state's accountability system in order to ensure that their educational needs are being met, the current system is of little value for monitoring their academic progress. The reason is that the only measures of achievement for English learners are tests administered in English.

The current state accountability practice for English learners is as follows:

- All EL students in Grades 2–11 must take both a nationally norm-referenced test that measures general subject matter knowledge and a standards-based achievement test aligned to California's grade-level content standards administered in English unless parents or a guardian provides a written request for a waiver;
- English learners who have been in the district for 12 months or more may not use nonstandard accommodations (e.g., using a parallel form of the same test content in the native language, translating directions, using word lists or dictionaries—see National Research Council, 1999, p. 218) unless they have individualized education plans (IEPs) or other exemptions that allow accommodations;[10]
- Test scores for English learners who have been in a district for less than one year (except for entering ninth graders in high school districts as of 2000) are excluded from the Academic Performance Index (API), which is used to measure each school's performance and to reward and sanction schools;[11]
- Spanish-speaking English language learners who had been enrolled in California public schools less than 12 months when testing began [are] required to take the SABE/2 in addition to taking the English-based tests, even though the results are not used to judge student or school performance;[12]
- Finally, beginning in 2006 English learners and other students with exceptional needs must pass the California High School Exit Exam to receive a high school diploma, despite that many such students are never taught the curriculum on which it is based (Wise et al., 2002).

According to several research and professional organizations, testing students in a language in which they are not yet proficient is both invalid and unethical. According to the National Academy of Sciences, "when students are not proficient in the language of the assessment (English), their scores on a test in English will not accurately reflect their knowledge of the subject being assessed" (National Research Council, 1999, p. 214). Therefore such assessments provide neither accurate data for accountability purposes, nor do they help teachers to enhance their instruction. These tests can, moreover, have serious negative effects on the schooling of English learners in at least two ways: (1) positive changes in test scores over time can give the inaccurate impression that students have gained subject matter knowledge when, in fact, they may have simply gained proficiency in English. This misperception that EL students are making academic progress can lead schools to continue providing a curriculum that fails to emphasize comprehensible subject matter; (2) on the other hand, consistently low scores on tests can lead educators to believe that students need remedial or even special education, when in fact, they may have mastered the curriculum in another language, but are unable to express these competencies through an English language test. As the National Research Council noted, "if a student is not proficient in the language of the test, her performance is likely to be affected by construct-irrelevant variance—that is, her test score is likely to underestimate her knowledge of the subject being tested" (NRC, 1999, p. 225).

The exclusive reliance on an English-language norm-referenced achievement test for EL students is not only inappropriate for these students,[13] it violates several standards established by the authoritative AERA/APA/ NCME, Standards for Educational and Psychological Testing. Research on second language acquisition shows that it takes English learners on average between four to seven years to meet various standards of English proficiency (Hakuta, Butler, & Witt, 2000; Thomas & Collier, 2002). The burden is on the state to demonstrate that test scores for English learners who have been in the United States for less than four years are valid, yet the state has not made any attempt to obtain information to shed light on this question.[14] The only cautionary statement by the CDE on the interpretation of standardized test scores appears on a web page and says: "Since the Stanford 9 norming sample was representative of the United States as a whole, it does not necessarily match California's student population."[15] Since the test scores are reported with respect to the national percentile rank (NPR), failure to issue an explicit warning with respect to Hispanics and to English learners is a clear violation of this standard.

4. Inadequate Instructional Time to Accomplish Learning Goals

There is a significant body of research that shows a clear relationship between increased time engaged in academic tasks and increased achievement;[16] however, there are many ways in which English learners experience less time on academic tasks than other students:

First, with the passage of Proposition 227, English learners who enroll in a California school for the first time must remain in a structured English immersion program for at least 30 days before being assigned to a permanent classroom. In a recent study of schools implementing the proposition, many teachers complained that they did not know what to do with students during this interim period and that a great deal of instructional time was lost trying to accommodate students who would not be continuing on in the same classroom. Particularly where parents had sought a waiver to have their child attend a bilingual classroom, teachers reported not knowing how to instruct these students. They lacked the necessary curricula and materials for the 30 days of all-English instruction before they began what would be their bilingual program for the remainder of the school year (Gándara et al., 2000).

Second, a common way that elementary schools organize instruction for English learners is to take them out of their regular classes for English language development. This strategy has been demonstrated to create further inequities in the education of "pulled out" students because they miss the regular classroom instruction (Cornell, 1995; Fleishman & Hopstock, 1993; Anstrom, 1997). Nevertheless, the practice continues to be relatively routine for English learners. There is generally no opportunity for students to acquire the instruction they have missed during the pull out period (Lucas, 1997; Ovando & Collier, 1998).

Third, as we elaborate later, English learners attending secondary schools are often assigned to multiple periods of English as a Second Language (ESL) classes while other students are taking a full complement of academic courses. When not enough courses are available, students are often given shortened day schedules, resulting in significantly less time devoted to academic instruction (Olsen, 1997).

Fourth, classrooms with large numbers of English learners also have fewer assistants in them to help the teacher provide individualized time for the students (see Table 23.1). While the district is apt to provide more bilingual aide time for classrooms with high percentages of English learners, there is significantly less time spent in these classrooms by parents or other adults. The result is that classrooms with no or few English learners enjoy a lower student-to-adult ratio, which means that

Table 23.1 Hours of Assistance on Instructional Activities in Classrooms of Teachers in Grades 1–4 by Type and Classroom Concentration of English Learners, 1999–2000 (Mean Hours)

Percent English Learners in the Classroom	Regular Aides	Special Education Aides	LEP or Bilingual Aides	Parents or Adults	Students	Other Specialists	Total
0	3	2	< 1	4	1	1	11
1–25	3	1	< 1	2	1	1	8
26–50	2	< 1	2	1	1	< 1	7
51–100	3	< 1	2	< 1	1	1	7
Total	2	1	1	2	1	1	8

Source: 2000 Class Size Reduction Teacher Survey (N = 774).

Note: Results are weighted.

they will receive more individualized instructional attention, exacerbating the gaps in instruction and achievement outcomes between English learners and English speakers. While it is not necessarily the school's or the district's "fault" that some schools enjoy more parent participation, it is a fact that must be considered in distributing resources among schools. Furthermore, bilingual teachers are often provided much less paraprofessional assistance than their non-bilingual colleagues who are seen as being in greater need of such support. In the view of many bilingual teachers this constitutes "penalizing" the most prepared teachers, and their students, for their extra expertise.

Finally, English learners are also more likely to be assigned to Concept 6 year round schools—a schedule in which students attend school for only 163 days per year, instead of the 180 mandated by state law.[17] English learners comprise fully half of the students assigned to Concept 6 schools (Gándara & Rumberger, 2003, Table 14). Students on the Concept 6 calendar attend school for 4 months twice a year, with two month breaks in between. This provides English learners less time to assimilate critical academic material and to be exposed to English language models. Just as important, however, is the loss of learning that occurs with a 2-month breaks in school every 4 months. A significant body of research has now established that low income children (and English learners) are more disadvantaged by these lengthy breaks from school than middle income children, and that there is a demonstrably negative effect on their achievement (Cooper et al., 1996). Thus, the very students who need the most exposure to schooling, to English language models, and to opportunities to "catch up" to their English speaking peers are more likely to be assigned to school calendars that provide them with fewer school days than other students and less exposure to English in a school setting.

5. Inequitable Access to Instructional Materials and Curriculum

All students need appropriate instructional materials, but English learners need additional materials in two areas. First, all English learners need developmentally appropriate texts and curriculum to learn English and to master English Language Development standards. Second, English learners receiving primary language instruction need appropriate texts and curriculum in their native language. However, the evidence suggests that many are not gaining access to such materials. In the second year report of the AIR study, researchers reported that 75% of the teachers surveyed said they "use the same textbooks for my English learner and English-only students" and fewer than half (46%) reported using any supplementary materials for EL students (Parrish et al., 2002, pp. IV–34). This raises the question of how much EL students can be expected to learn without materials adapted to their linguistic needs. It is not particularly surprising then that only 41% of teachers reported they are "able to cover as much material with EL students as with EO students" (Parrish et al., 2002, pp. IV–35). There is ample evidence in the research literature that when students cover less material than their peers, their skills decline relative to other students and they are prone to be placed in low academic groupings or tracks where educational opportunities are limited (Barr & Dreeben, 1983; Oakes, 1985; Gamoran, 1992; Goodlad, 1984).

The quality of instructional materials appears to differ by concentration of English learners in the school as well. Data from a statewide survey of California teachers[18] show that teachers with high percentages of English learners are less likely than teachers with low percentages of English learners to have access to appropriate textbooks and instructional materials, in general, and materials needed by English learners in particular. Almost half of teachers with high percentages of English learners reported that the textbooks and instructional materials at their schools were only fair or poor compared to 29% of teachers with low percentages of English learners. Teachers with high percentages of English learners were also almost twice as likely as teachers with low percentages of English learners to report that the availability of computers and other technology was only fair or poor. Moreover, almost two-thirds of teachers with high percentages of ELs in their classes reported not enough or no reading materials in the home language of their children, and more than one quarter reported that they did not have any or enough reading materials at students' reading levels in English.

In addition to inadequate instructional materials, English learners are often shortchanged because of the lack of appropriate course offerings in their schools. In secondary schools, for example, English learners are often assigned to multiple periods of ESL or ELD classes while other students are taking a full complement of academic courses. Commonly, when not enough courses are available in either SDAIE or other formats, students are given shortened day schedules (Olsen, 1997). We investigated this issue further by selecting a random sample of transcripts of secondary English learners from two different northern California districts. We found many instances where secondary English learners, even those with college preparatory coursework in their countries of origin, were assigned to nonacademic and remedial courses, and shortened days in their high schools. Because the state does not effectively monitor the quality of instruction that English learners receive, or the amount of time they spend in Structured English Immersion settings, we do not know to what extent the educational services provided for these students meet high standards of quality. We can guess at this figure, given the large number of unprepared teachers who teach them. It is worth noting, however, that more than 82,000 English learners in California receive no special instruction whatsoever.

The persistent and pervasive inequities in access to well-prepared teachers, school resources and facilities, appropriate assessment and time to accomplish learning goals result in large and growing gaps in achievement for English learners vis-à-vis their English speaking peers, and ultimately for some misplacement into special education classes. In the consent decree resulting from the *Diana v. California State Board of Education* (U. S. D. C., ND, Cal. 1970), a class action suit on behalf of English learners inappropriately placed in special education, the state agreed to address this problem. Thirty years hence the state of California has still not acted to implement the consent decree with respect to the development of appropriate assessment for English learners that could stem the overdiagnosis and placement of these students in special education. Nor does California keep reliable data on the numbers of EL students in special education. A recent study based on data from eleven school districts and over 700,000 students in the Los Angeles area for the 1998–1999 school year found that "ELs are over-represented in special education, particularly in specific learning disabilities (SLD) and language and speech impairment classes (SLI), especially at the secondary grade level where language support is minimal" (Artiles, Rueda, Salazar, & Higareda, 2002). As was the case with the 1982 report by the National Academy of Sciences (Heller, Holtzman & Messick, 1982), the study found that where few, if any, primary language support services are offered, special education misdiagnosis and misplacement occurs at higher rates. Placement in special education, especially when it is not warranted, can have devastating effects on students' access to opportunities later in life. Evidence has existed for years documenting the massive rates of high school non-completion, underemployment, poverty, and adult marginalization of special education students after they leave high school (Guy, Hasazi, & Johnson, 1999). Placed in a special education track, it is unlikely for students to rejoin the mainstream. Robert Peckham, the presiding judge for the *Diana* case, summarized the evidence on the effectiveness of California's special education program, calling it a "dead-end educational program" (*Crawford v. Honig*, 1988).

6. Inequitable Access to Adequate Facilities

Teachers of English learners are more apt than teachers of English speakers to respond that they do not have facilities that are conducive to teaching and learning. In the Harris survey close to half of teachers in schools with higher percentages of English learners reported the physical facilities at their schools were only fair or poor, compared to 26% of teachers in schools with low percentages of English learners (Table 23.2). Teachers in schools with high percentages of English learners were 50% more likely to report bathrooms that were not clean and open throughout the day and to have seen evidence of cockroaches, rats, or mice.

ECLS data show the same picture with regard to facilities. More than a third of principals in schools with higher concentrations of English learners reported that their classrooms were never or often not adequate, compared to 8% of principals with low concentration of EL students (Gándara & Rumberger, 2003, Table 19).[19]

In addition to poor facilities, schools with high concentrations of English learners have poorer working conditions for teachers, such as more overcrowded classrooms, less parental involvement, and more neighborhood crime (Gándara & Rumberger, 2003, Table 10). Given the opportunity, teachers will relocate to schools with more favorable working conditions. In fact, recent research suggests that working conditions influence teachers' decisions about where to teach more than salaries (Hanushek, Kain, & Rivkin, 2001; Loeb & Page, 2000).

7. Intense Segregation into Schools and Classrooms that Place them at High Risk for Educational Failure

English learners are highly segregated among California's schools and classrooms. While most schools have some English learners, the vast majority of these students attend a relatively small percentage of public schools. Thus, English learners are much more likely than their English-only peers to attend

Table 23.2 Schools, Students, and English Learners by Concentration of English Learners and School Level, 1999–2000 (Percent Distribution)

Percent English Learners	Elementary			Middle			High		
	Schools	Students	ELs	Schools	Students	ELs	Schools	Students	ELs
0	6	1	0	1	1	0	8	2	0
1–25	51	48	15	65	62	30	73	76	49
26–50	24	26	30	26	28	44	17	21	46
51–100	19	25	55	8	9	25	1	1	5
Total percent	100	100	100	100	100	100	100	100	100
Total number	5,306	3,124,107	979,854	1,158	1,059,767	232,481	909	1,538,617	237,129

Note: ELs = English learners.

Source: CBEDS and Language Census.

schools with large concentrations of EL students. As shown in Table 23.2, whereas 25% of all students in California attend elementary schools in which a majority of the students are English learners, 55% of all English learners are enrolled in such schools. Although middle and high schools do have such high concentrations of English learners, English learners are nonetheless more likely to attend such schools. Thus, the distribution of English learners across schools is uneven and these students tend to be clustered in a relatively small percentage of schools. English learners are even more concentrated at the classroom level. Data from a representative sample of California teachers in Grades 1–4 in 2000 show that almost two-thirds of English learners attended classrooms in which more than 50% of their fellow students were English learners (Gándara & Rumberger, 2003, Table 21).

The concentration of California English learners in classrooms and schools compromises their opportunity to receive an education that is comparable in quality and scope to that of their English background peers because: (1) the lack of peer English language models limits the development of English, (2) the lack of models of children who are achieving at high or even moderate levels inhibits academic achievement, (3) the inequitable environmental conditions and resources of segregated classrooms and schools, and (4) the lack of highly qualified, experienced, teachers in these particular classrooms depress learning.

The first two sources of inequity stem directly from the segregation itself—English learners are *more likely* to attend classes and schools surrounded by other students who are not proficient in English and *less likely* to be surrounded by peers who excel in school. The first condition hurts English learners' ability to become proficient in English because research has shown that the composition (relative numbers of English-language learners and fluent English speakers) and structure (opportunities for interaction) of the classroom can inhibit meaningful second language acquisition (Hornberger, 1990; Rumberger & Arellano, 2003; Wong Fillmore, 1991). The second condition, evidenced by data showing that classrooms with high concentrations of English learners also have a higher number of students who are below grade level in reading and math (Gándara & Rumberger, 2003, Table 22), hurts English learners' ability to achieve academically because research has shown that the academic achievement of peers influences students' own academic achievement, in part, because students learn from each other (Epstein & Karweit, 1983; Hanushek, Kain, Markman, & Rivkin, 2001; Hoxby, 2001; Mounts & Steinberg, 1995; Hurd, 2004). Thus, the concentration of English learners in California's schools and classrooms not only makes it more difficult for them to learn English, it also makes it more difficult for them to achieve academically.

If students were clustered into these classrooms to provide core academic instruction in the primary language and mainstreamed for part of the day to receive instruction in English (preferably in highly interactive and non-high stakes settings like arts, music, physical education), the segregation of EL students would not only be defensible, but would constitute a valid educational treatment. However, in the wake of Proposition 227, most English learners are simply segregated into classrooms populated disproportionately by other English learners where the opportunity to learn both English and academic content is compromised by the lack of appropriate models and instruction targeted to their linguistic strengths.

In addition to the effects of peers, as shown earlier, the segregation of English learners is accompanied by more challenging classroom conditions, by a lack of resources, and by a lack of appropriately trained teachers. Moreover, these conditions are not independent, but rather highly interrelated and cumulative, and exacerbated by segregation.

In the full report, we argue that the state has played a major role in both creating and perpetuating these inequities through the lack of suitable policies (1) to recruit, train, and certify teachers who can effectively work with English learners; (2) to provide valid assessments of the academic skills of English learners; (3) to address the poor and inequitable schooling conditions for English learners;

and (4) to monitor the nature of the instruction and educational experiences of English learners in California schools.

Remedies

There are many things that the state could do to create a more equitable education for English learners. Among these are:

- The state should provide all English learners with qualified teachers who have the appropriate skills to teach them.
- The state should ensure that the CTC standards are sufficiently high to guarantee that EL teachers are qualified to teach these students.
- The state should provide appropriate professional development for teachers of English learners focusing on strategies for developing early literacy and closing the achievement gap with English-speaking peers.
- The state should provide materials and instruction for students and their parents in English, and in the primary language, to the extent possible, to strengthen emergent literacy skills.
- The state should provide real opportunities for non-English-speaking parents to become involved in their children's education.
- The state should provide preschool educational opportunities for English learners.
- The state should provide more time during the school year to learn English and close the educational gap with their English-speaking peers.
- The state should eliminate placements in Concept 6 schedules for English Learners.
- To the extent the state is using test-based accountability vis-à-vis English learners, it should develop valid and meaningful assessments geared to the needs of these students.
- The state should monitor the administration of primary language tests where they are currently mandated, and mandate that this information be used to help design appropriate curriculum for these test-takers.
- The state should provide support and incentives for school districts to develop high quality, dual language programs that develop proficiency in two languages for both English learners and English speakers and can help reduce economic and linguistic segregation in schools.
- The state should guarantee that teachers have appropriate materials for teaching English learners.
- The state should guarantee that every child has a safe, adequate (clean, functioning bathrooms, adequate classroom space, outdoor space to exercise, heating, cooling, lighting, electrical outlets that work, and access to technology) facility in which to learn. English learners, too, deserve this.
- The state needs to collect data at the classroom level so that it is possible to know which teachers are assigned to which children, and to know what type of materials and curriculum to which students are exposed.
- The state should provide more effective monitoring of special education placements of English learners.

Conclusions

Most English learners are immigrants or the children of immigrants. There is mounting evidence that immigrant students, and the children of immigrants are more academically ambitious than native-born students (see, for example, Suárez-Orozco & Suárez-Orozco, 1996). This suggests that there is a critical window of opportunity in which to affect these children's academic futures. If we seize the opportunity and apply the resources while they are in the public schools, we may be able to set these young people on a solid upward trajectory. On the other hand, if we allow this opportunity to slip by, the challenge will be greater in succeeding generations. English learners in California, and in the nation, represent a potentially rich social and economic resource. It is up to the education system to tap it.

Notes

1 The report informed an expert report prepared for the lawsuit by Kenji Hakuta (2002).
2 Scale scores show growth in achievement over time based on a common metric.
3 Beginning in 1999, the state augmented the SAT9 with a test more closely aligned with the state's academic content standards (see http://star.cde.ca.gov/).
4 Because of migration and mobility, the cohorts are not necessarily composed of the same students each year.
5 Although neither California nor the federal government produces dropout rates by language background, most English learners are Latino and Latino dropout rates in October 2000 were 28% or three times the rate for white students (U.S. Department of Education, 2001, Table 3).
6 Students from the class of 2004 were originally required to pass the test, but in the summer of 2003 the State Board of Education postponed the requirement until the class of 2006.
7 Spanish-speaking students were given the math assessment in Spanish.
8 The survey did not identify teachers who had authorizations acquired through SB1969 or SB395.
9 The Chancellor's Office of the California State University reports that 70% of its credential graduates completed either a CLAD or BCLAD credential.
10 Standardized Testing and Reporting (STAR) Spring 2001 STAR Administration: Frequently Asked Questions (http://www.cde.ca.gov/statetests/star/qanda/smar212001.html).
11 Academic Performance Index Home Page (http://www.cde.ca.gov/psaa/api/).
12 About STAR 2001 (http://star.cde.ca.gov/star2001/help/AboutSTAR.html).
13 Standard 11.22 of the AERA/APA/NCME Standards for Educational and Psychological Testing, for example, note that "When circumstances require that a test be administered in the same language to all examinees in a linguistically diverse population, the test user should investigate the validity of the score interpretations for test takers believed to have limited proficiency in the language of the test."
14 The United States Department of Education, Office of Educational Research and Improvement has recently commissioned ARC Associates to conduct a study using San Francisco Unified School District data to help answer this question. We would hope that the findings from this study will inform California testing policy.
15 See score explanations: http://star.cde.ca.gov/star2001/help/ScoreExplanations.html.
16 There is a long literature on the importance of "time on task" for learning. Carroll (1963) devised the classic model that showed learning is a function of the amount of time needed to learn something divided by the amount of time allotted to learn it. Karweit (1989) showed that "engaged time" on task was more important than simply the time allotted.
17 School districts manage to stay within the law by adding a few minutes at the end of each day to total the same number of hours as students who are on 180-day schedules.
18 This survey, conducted in 2002 by the Lou Harris Polling group, included 1,071 California teachers, both randomly and representatively sampled to approximate a profile of all the state's teachers; 27% were male; 84% were White (See Harris, 2002).
19 It is interesting to note that 19 percent of all principals in California reported that their classrooms were never or often not adequate, compared to 9 percent of principals in the rest of the United States.

References

American Educational Research Association, American Psychological Association, National Council on Measurement in Education. (1999). *Standards for educational and psychological testing.* Washington, DC: American Educational Research Association.

Anstrom, K. (1997). *Academic achievement for secondary language minority students: Standards, measures, and promising practices.* Washington, DC: National Clearinghouse for Bilingual Education.

Artiles, A. J., Rueda, R., Salazar, J.J., & Higareda, I. (2002). English language learner representation in special education: in *California Urban School Districts* (pp. 117–136). Cambridge, MA: Harvard Education Publishing Group.

Barr, R., & Dreeben, R. (1983). *How schools work.* Chicago: University of Chicago Press.

California Commission on Teacher Credentialing. (1998). *Standards of quality and effectiveness for multiple and single subject credentials: Handbook for teacher educators and accreditation team members.* Sacramento, CA: Author.

California Department of Education. (2003). *Dataquest.* Retrieved April 9, 2003, from http:// data1.cde.ca.gov/dataquest/

California Department of Education. (2002). *Easton releases Spring 2002 California High School Exit Exam Results.* Retrieved January 23, 2003, from http://www.cde.ca.gov/news/ releases2002/rel30.asp

California Department of Education. (1999). *Proposition 227 survey: Interim report.* Sacramento, CA: Author.

California Education Code Chapter, Sections 60850–60859. *High School Exit Examination.*

California State University, Office of the Chancellor. (2001). *First systemwide evaluation of teacher education programs in the California State University: Summary report.* Long Beach, CA: Author.

Carroll, J. B. (1963). A model of school learning. *Teachers College Record, 64*, 723–733.

Cooper, H., Nye, B., Charlton, K., Lindsay, J. J., & Greathouse, S. (1996). The effects of summer vacation on achievement test scores: A narrative and meta-analytic review. *Review of Educational Research, 66*, 227–268.

Cornell, C. (1995). Reducing failure of LEP students in the mainstream classroom and why it is important. *The Journal of Education Issues of Language Minority Students*, 15.

Crawford v. Honig, No. C-89-0014(N.D.Cal.).RFP

Darling-Hammond, L. (2002). *Access to quality teaching: An analysis of inequality in California's public schools. Expert report prepared for Williams v. State of California*. Retrieved March 8, 2003, from http://www.mofo.com/decentschools/expert_reports/darling-hammond_report. pdf

Diana v. California Board of Education, No. C-70-37. (N.D. Calif. 1970). *Diana v. California Board of Education*, Complaint for Injunction and Declaratory Relief (Civil Rights), 1973.

Epstein, J. L., & Karweitt, N. (Eds.). (1983). *Friends in school: Patterns of selection and influence in secondary schools*. New York: Academic Press.

Fleishman, H. L., & Hopstock, P. J. (1993). *Descriptive study of services to limited English proficient students*. Arlington, VA: Development Associates.

Gamoran, A. (1992). The variable effects of high school tracking. *American Sociological Review, 57*, 812–828.

Gándara, P., Maxwell-Jolly, J., García, E., Asato, J., Gutiérrez, K., Stritikus, T., & Curry, J. (2000). *The initial impact of Proposition 227 on the instruction of English Learners*. Davis, CA: UC Linguistic Minority Research Center Education Policy Center.

Gándara, P., & Rumberger, R. W. (2003). *The inequitable treatment of English learners in California's public schools. Revised report prepared for the lawsuit, Williams v. State of California*. Retrieved April 25, 2003, from http://idea.gseis.ucla.edu/publications/williams

Gándara, P., Rumberger, R. W., Maxwell-Jolly, J., & Callahan, R. (2003). English learners in California schools: Unequal resources, unequal outcomes. *Educational Policy Analysis Archives*, 11. Retrieved November 19, 2003, from: http://epaa.asu.edu/epaa/v11n36/

Goodlad, J. I. (1984). *A place called school: Prospects for the future*. New York: McGraw-Hill.

Gottlieb, J., Alter, M., Gottlieb, B. W., & Wishner, J. (1994). Special education in urban America: It's not justifiable for many. *The Journal of Special Education, 27*, 453–465.

Guy, B., Hasazi, S. B., & Johnson, D. R. (1999). Transition from school to adult life. In M. J. Coutinho & A. C. Repp (Eds.), *Inclusion: The integration of students with disabilities*. Belmont, CA: Wadsworth.

Hakuta, K. (2002). *English language learner access to basic educational necessities in California: An analysis of inequities*. Retrieved November 19, 2003, from http://www.mofo.com/decentschools/expert_reports/hakuta_report.pdf

Hakuta, K., Butler, Y. G., & Witt, D. (2000). *How long does it take English learners to attain proficiency?* (Policy Report 2000-1). Santa Barbara: University of California Linguistic Minority Research Institute.

Hanushek, E. A., Kain, J. F., Markman, J. M., & Rivkin, S. G. (2001). *Does peer ability affect student achievement?* (NBER Working Paper No. w8502). Cambridge, MA: National Bureau of Economic Research.

Hanushek, E. A., Kain, J. F., & Rivkin, S. G. (2001). *Why public schools lose teachers* (Working paper 8599). Cambridge, MA: National Bureau of Economic Research.

Harris, L. (2002). *A survey of the status of equality in public education in California: A survey of a cross-section of public school teachers*. San Francisco: Public Advocates, Inc.

Haycock, K. (1998). Good teaching matters: How well-qualified teachers can close the gap. *Thinking, K–16, 3*, 1–17.

Hayes, K., & Salazar, J. J. (2001). *Evaluation of the structured English Immersion Program. Final Report: Year 1*. Program Evaluation and Research Branch, Los Angeles Unified School District. Retrieved July 26, 2004, from http://www.lausd.k12.ca.us/lausd/offices/perb/files/reports/ RPT%20SEI%20Y1.pdf

Hayes, K., Salazar, J. J., & Vuckovic, G. (2002). *Evaluation of the Structured English Immersion Program. Final Report: Year 2*. Program Evaluation and Research Branch, Los Angeles Unified School District. Retrieved July 26, 2004, from http://www.lausd.k12.ca.us/lausd/offices/perb/ files/reports/RPT%20SEI%20Y2.pdf

Heller, K. A., Holtzman, W. H., & Messick, S. (1982). *Placing children in special education: A strategy for equity*. Washington, DC: National Academy Press.

Hornberger, N. H. (1990). Creating successful learning contexts for bilingual literacy. *Teachers College Record, 99*, 212–229.

Hoxby, C. (2000). *Peer effects in the classroom: Learning from gender and race variation* (NBER Working Paper No. w7867). Cambridge, MA: National Bureau of Economic Research.

Hurd, C. (2004). English proficiency limited: The interpersonal politics of learning English among Mexican-Descent students. In G. G. Gibson, P. P. Gándara, & J. P. Koyama (Eds.), *School connections: Peers, achievement, and U.S. Mexican youth* (pp. 63–86). New York: Teachers College Press.

Loeb, S., & Page, M. E. (2000). Examining the link between teacher wages and student outcomes: The importance of alternative labor market opportunities and non-pecuniary variation. *The Review of Economics and Statistics, 82*, 393–408.

Lucas, T., Henze, R., & Donato, R. (1990). Promoting the success of Latino language minority students: An exploratory study of six high schools. *Harvard Educational Review, 60*, 315–340.

Mounts, N. S., & Steinberg, L. (1995). An ecological analysis of peer influence on adolescent grade point average and drug use. *Developmental Psychology, 31*, 915–922.

National Research Council, Committee on Appropriate Test Use. (1999). *High stakes: Testing for tracking, promotion, and graduation*. Washington, DC: National Academy Press.

Oakes, J. (1985). *Keeping track: How schools structure inequality*. New Haven, CT: Yale University Press.

Olsen, L. (1997). *Made in America: Immigrant students in our public schools*. New York: New Press.

Ovando, C., & Collier, V. (1998). *Bilingual and ESL classrooms: Teaching in multicultural contexts* (2nd ed.). Boston: McGraw-Hill.

Parrish, T. B., Linquanti, R., Merickel, A., Quick, H. E., Laird, J., & Esra, P. (2001). *Effects of the Implementation of Proposition 227 on the Education of English Learners, K–12. Year 1 Report*. Palo Alto, CA: American Institutes for Research.

Parrish, T. B., Linquanti, R., Merickel, A., Quick, H. E., Laird, J., & Esra, P. (2002). *Effects of the Implementation of Proposition 227 on the Education of English Learners, K–12: Year 2 Report*. Palo Alto, CA: American Institutes for Research.

Ruiz-de-Velasco, J., & Fix, M. (2000). *Overlooked and underserved: Immigrant students in U.S. secondary schools*. Washington, DC: The Urban Institute.

Rumberger, R. W., & Arellano, B. (2003). *Understanding and addressing the Latino achievement gap in California*. Berkeley, CA: UC Latino Policy Institute.

Rumberger, R. W., & Gándara, P. (2000). The schooling of English Learners. In E. Burr, G. Hayward, & M. Kirst (Eds.), *Crucial issues in California education* (pp. 23–44). Berkeley: Policy Analysis for California Education.

Sanders, W. L., & Horn, P. (1995). The Tennessee value-added assessment system (TVAAS): Mixed model methodology in educational assessment. In D. Schinkfield (Ed.), *Teacher evaluation: Guide to effective practice* (pp. 337–350). Boston: Kluwer Academic Publishers.

Sanders, W. L., & Rivers, C. (1996). *Cumulative and residual effects of teachers on future student academic achievement*. Knoxville: University of Tennessee Value-Added Research and Assessment Center.

Scarcella, R., & Rumberger, R. W. (2000). Academic English key to long-term success in school. *UC Linguistic Minority Research Institute Newsletter*, 9, 1–2.

Skirtic, T. M. (1991). The special education paradox: Equity as a way to excellence. *Harvard Educational Review*, 61, 148–206.

Stecher, B. M., & Bohrnstedt, G. W. (Eds.). (2002). *Class size reduction in California: Findings from 1999–00 and 2000–01*. Sacramento, CA: California Department of Education.

Suárez-Orozco, M., & Suárez-Orozco, C. (1996). *Trans-formations: Migration, family life, and achievement motivation among Latino adolescents*. Stanford, CA: Stanford University Press.

Thomas, W. P., & Collier, V. P. (2002). *A national study of school effectiveness for language minority students' long-term academic achievement*. Santa Cruz: University of California, Santa Cruz, Center for Research on Education, Diversity & Excellence.

U.S. Department of Education, National Center for Education Statistics. (2001). *Dropout rates in the United States: 2000*. Washington, DC: Author.

University of California Office of the President. (UCOP). (2002). *Report to the legislature on California Professional Development Institutes*. Oakland, CA: Author.

Wise, L. L., Sipes, D. E., DeMeyer Harris, C., George, C. E., Ford, J. P., & Sun, S. (2002). *Independent evaluation of the California High School Exit Examination (CAHSEE): Analysis of the 2001 administration*. Alexandria, VA: Human Resources Research Organization.

Wong-Fillmore, L. (1991). Second-language learning in children: A model of language learning in social context. In E. Bialystok (Ed.), *Language processing in bilingual children* (pp. 49–69). New York: Cambridge University Press.

24

Gender Inequalities in the Transition to College

CLAUDIA BUCHMAN

One of the most striking features of statistics on college-going in recent years is the growing gap between men and women. In terms of high school graduation, college entry, and persistence to earning a degree, young women consistently outperform their male peers. Trend statistics in the United States demonstrate a striking reversal of a gender gap in college completion that once favored males. In 1960, 65% of all bachelor's degrees were awarded to men, but women reached parity in 1982. From then onward, the proportion of bachelor's degrees awarded to women continued to climb; by 2003, women received 58% of all bachelor's degrees (National Center for Education Statistics [NCES] 2005) and constituted 55% of all college students.

The reversal from a male to female advantage in college enrollment and completion is an important topic of study both in its own right and because of its potential impacts on gender gaps in wages, labor force participation, and a host of other labor market outcomes (Bernhardt, Morris, and Handcock 1995). The rising proportion of college-educated women relative to men could also alter trends in educational assortative mating as more women marry down, delay marriage, or forgo marriage altogether (Lewis and Oppenheimer 2000). These changes, in turn, may impact family formation and parenting (Bianchi and Casper 2000).

Changing gender inequalities in higher education raise important questions for policy makers, researchers, and educators who want to understand how to improve the educational attainment of all youth and for institutions of higher education striving to respond to their students' needs. For example, the female advantage in college enrollment is causing concern among college administrators, who worry that the gender imbalance is detrimental to campus diversity (Thompson 2003), and among admissions officers, who are considering affirmative action for male applicants (Greene and Greene 2004).

Over a decade ago, Jacobs (1996) noted that the literature on gender inequality in education "often treats all aspects of education as disadvantaging women" (156). This tendency remains true today; most research addresses aspects of education where women trail men, such as women's underrepresentation at top-tier institutions and in science and engineering programs. The paucity of research on realms where women outpace men, namely college enrollment and completion, constitutes a gap in the literature. This article provides an overview of gender inequalities in the transition to college and in college experiences by examining the ways that women are advantaged in higher education and the arenas where they still trail men. It also discusses theoretical perspectives useful in assessing the causes of gender inequality and then suggests how future research could advance our understanding of the complex nature of gender inequality in higher education.

The Transition from High School to College and Beyond

From early childhood through adulthood, education plays a central role in individuals' lives. Gender inequalities in early and middle childhood are likely linked to gendered experiences and educational inequalities occurring later in life; thus, they are important topics for future research. Because this article primarily focuses on the transition from high school to college, it excludes a discussion of gender differences from the earliest stages of life through the adolescent years.

High School Completion

In the United States, the first step to gaining access to postsecondary education is the completion of high school, but a substantial number of youth do not do so. Since 1990, the status dropout rate—the percentage of people aged 16–24 who are not enrolled in high school and have not earned a high school diploma, GED, or other certificate of completion—for females has been lower than rate for males. In 2004, 11.6% of males aged 16–24 were dropouts, compared with 9% of females (NCES 2005).

High school dropout rates vary widely by race, ethnicity, and immigrant status (Grodsky and Jackson 2009), but the male dropout rate is higher than the female rate within all ethnic groups. In 2004, male dropout rates for whites, blacks, and Hispanics were 7.1%, 13.5%, and 28.5%, respectively, compared with female rates of 6.4%, 10.2%, and 18.5%, respectively (NCES 2005). The high dropout rates for Hispanics, as well as the larger gender gap in dropout rates for this group, are especially striking and surely play some role in the low college enrollment rates of Hispanic males. Foreign-born youth are especially vulnerable to dropping out of high school for reasons such as language difficulties, lower rates of parental education, and poor quality schooling in their country of birth (Hirschman 2001; Driscoll 1999). While only 8% of the nation's teens are foreign born, nearly 25% of high school dropouts are foreign born, of whom roughly 40% are recent immigrants who interrupted their schooling before coming to the United States (Fry 2005).

Transition to College

Among students who do complete high school, many factors are related to whether they enroll in college and to the great variations in their post-secondary experiences. Research indicates that students who enroll in college directly after high school have higher rates of overall college enrollment, persistence in college, and graduation (Horn and Premo 1995; Bozick and DeLuca 2005). While men used to be more likely than women to enroll in college directly after high school, since 1996, the reverse has been true; in 2000, 66% of women, compared with 60% of men, did so (Freeman 2004).

Data from the National Educational Longitudinal Study (NELS) of the high school class of 1992 indicate that the female advantage in immediate college enrollment holds for all socioeconomic status (SES) groups, though it is smaller for those of high SES backgrounds. Inspecting bivariate relationships between SES, race, and enrollment, King (2000) found that low-SES white and African American students were half as likely as their upper SES peers to make the transition to college immediately after high school. But in another analysis of the same data, Bozick and DeLuca (2005) showed that after controlling for academic achievement and SES, Hispanics and blacks are *more* likely than whites to enroll in college immediately after completing high school (but recall the high dropout rates of Hispanics). Males are substantially more likely to decline to enroll or to delay enrollment in college than females, net of controls. Not surprisingly, students from higher socioeconomic backgrounds are significantly more likely to enroll in college immediately after high school than their disadvantaged counterparts.

The proportion of both men and women enrolling in college has increased since the 1970s, but, as Figure 24.1 shows, the increase for women has been much more substantial (NCES 2006). In 2004, women constituted 55.6% of all students in institutions of higher education and 57.2% of all students at degree-granting institutions (NCES 2005, table 170). In addition to being more likely to enter college immediately after completing high school, women are more likely than men to return to college after age 30. In fact, more women than men attend college in every age group. According to October Current Population Survey (CPS) data of the U.S. Census, for every 100 18–19-year-old men enrolled in college in the year 2000, there were 129 women enrolled; among those age 35 and older, there were 173 women enrolled in college per 100 men (see Figure 24.2; Sum et al. 2003).

College Experiences and Persistence to Degree

Once enrolled, women are more likely than men to persist in college to obtain a degree, as evidenced by the fact that women currently earn 58% of all bachelor's degrees awarded in the United States. The female advantage exists for all racial groups, but there are important variations by race and ethnicity in the size of the gap: Women earn 67% of all bachelor's degrees awarded to blacks; the figures are 61% for Hispanics, 61% for Native Americans, 54% for Asians, and 57% for whites (NCES 2004, table 263). Note that the especially large gender gap for blacks constitutes a continuation of a long-favorable female

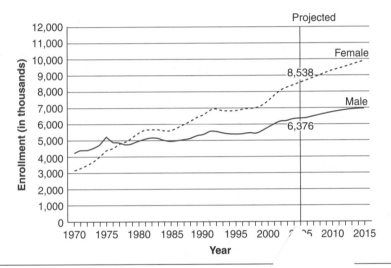

Figure 24.1 Male and female undergraduate enrollment in degree granting postseconda⌐ ⌐s, 1970–2015.

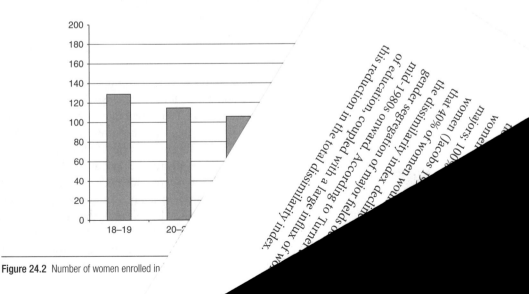

Figure 24.2 Number of women enrolled in

trend. As early as 1954, when the great majority of black college students were enrolled in historically black colleges and universities (HBCUs), women constituted 58% of students enrolled in HBCUs.

Women also earn their degrees in a more timely manner than men, and this difference relates to their higher rates of overall degree receipt. Analysis of the Beginning Postsecondary Student Survey found that among students who entered college in the 1995–1996 academic year, by 2001, 66% of women had completed a bachelor's degree, compared with 59% of men. While 50% of black and Hispanic women had completed a BA or BS degree in this period, only 37% of black men and 43% of Hispanic men had done so (Freeman 2004).

One important question for research regards differences in the college experiences of men and women and their implications for the returns on education. For example, are women concentrated in less prestigious institutions and in less-remunerated fields of study? Do they achieve a similar return to the degree as men with similar qualifications? Are there variations in these experiences by class and race/ethnicity?

Types of Institutions Attended

Higher education institutions can be ranked with respect to their duration, rigor, and social status. Charles and Bradley (2002) refer to these distinctions as the "vertical dimension of gender segregation in higher education" (574). Gender differences in fields of study represent distinctions more of kind than of level, or the horizontal dimension of segregation. As college-going becomes ever more common among the U.S. population, the importance of the prestige of the institution attended increases apace (Kingston and Lewis 1990; Karen 2002). For example, research indicates that relative to degree holders from less prestigious institutions, bachelor's degree recipients from elite institutions garner higher earnings, are more likely to pursue graduate or professional education, and enjoy more successes in the world of work (Bowen and Bok 1998).

Historically, men and women have attended very different postsecondary institutions. Many of the most prestigious universities and colleges in the United States only began to admit women in the late 1960s (Jacobs 1999). Through the 1970s and 1980s, women gained greater access to elite schools (Karen 1991), but by the mid-1990s, women were still slightly more likely to attend less prestigious schools with lower tuition rates and fewer resources (Jacobs 1996, 1999; Davies and Guppy 1997). Jacobs (1999) attributes the small but persistent gender gap in institutional prestige to the relative scarcity of women in schools with large engineering programs and the greater tendency of women to enroll in school part time (higher-status schools are less likely to accept part-time students). At any rate, today, the degree of gender segregation in the types of institutions attended is smaller than the degree of gender segregation that exists across fields of study.

Fields of Study

Not long ago, women college students were concentrated in a very narrow range of fields of study. In the early 1960s, more than 70% of female undergraduates majored in only six fields: education, English, fine arts, nursing, history, and home economics (Jacobs 1996). The degree of gender segregation across majors can be measured by the index of dissimilarity, which captures the percentage of _____ who would have to change majors in order for there to be gender parity in the distribution of _____ % indicates complete segregation, and 0% indicates identical distributions for men and _____ 95). In 1965, the dissimilarity index calculated across all fields of study indicated _____ ld have had to change major fields in order to achieve gender parity; by 1995, _____ d to 19% (Turner and Bowen 1999). Importantly, the declines in the _____ ccurred most dramatically during the 1970s and slowed from the _____ and Bowen (1999), a substantial movement of women out _____ men into business programs, accounted for much of

Gender desegregation in the fields of science and engineering has been less dramatic, but some changes are noteworthy. In these fields, gender segregation declined until 1975 but then increased and stabilized (Turner and Bowen 1999). Still, the number of women undergraduate science and engineering majors has increased consistently since 1966; by 2001, women garnered slightly more than half of all bachelor's degrees in science and engineering (National Science Foundation, Division of Science Resources Statistics 2004). Inspection of specific fields within the broad category of science and engineering reveals great variation in women's representation. Figure 24.3 shows that women now constitute the majority of students in the biological sciences and in the social sciences, with the exception of economics (National Science Foundation, 2004). They are approaching parity in chemistry but remain the minority in nearly all other sciences. Their underrepresentation in all fields within engineering is particularly striking and remains a cause for concern.

In a comprehensive book, Xie and Shauman (2003) assessed the most commonly asserted causes for women's underrepresentation. They concluded that it is not due to gender differences in math ability or math training in high school, as these gaps have closed. Nor is it due to girls' lower participation in high school math and science coursework (with the exception of physics). Male high school students are twice as likely as female students to expect to major in science and engineering in college; however, women, once in college, are more likely to change to a science major after beginning as a non–science major. Xie and Shauman concluded, therefore, that gender segregation within the sciences (e.g., biology vs. physics) and familial roles are the key barriers to women's successful career trajectories in science and engineering.

Beyond studies that focus specifically on women in science and engineering, research attempting to understand the reasons for gender differences in major choices have tended to focus on either differences in skill, such as academic performance, or differences in preferences and socialization. For example, Turner and Bowen (1999) examined the degree to which gender differences in college major are associated with gender differences in precollege math performance as measured by math SAT scores. Based on their findings that differences in SAT scores account for less than half of the total gender gap in major choice, they maintained that differences in academic preparation constitute a small part of the explanation for the persistence of gender segregation in majors; other forces, "including differences in preferences, labor market expectations, gender-specific effects of college experience and unmeasured aspects of academic preparation account for the main part of today's gender gaps in choice of academic major" (309).

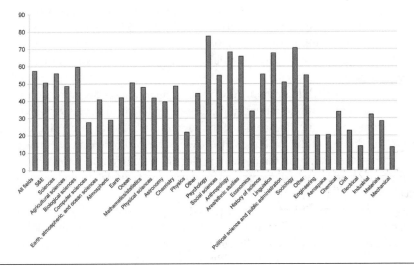

Figure 24.3 Female share of bachelor's degress in various science and engineering fields, 2001.

Other researchers have focused on the environment of undergraduate institutions in explaining students' major choices. For example, Solnick (1995) found that women at women's colleges were more likely to enter traditionally male-dominated fields than women enrolled at coeducational institutions and argued that cultural and academic environments in women's colleges facilitate women's entry into the sciences.

Gender Differences in College Outcomes and Returns to Postsecondary Education

Much research provides evidence of the beneficial effects of higher education for women's wage labor opportunities, earnings, and standard of living. When considered without regard to major field, the earnings gain from a college degree relative to a high school degree is higher for women than it is for men (DiPrete and Buchmann 2006). At the same time, the gender gap in earnings is actually larger among college-educated workers. In 2004, among all workers over 25 years of age, women earned 78.7 cents to every dollar earned by men. Among college-educated workers over 25 years of age, women earn only 75.2 cents for every dollar earned by men (Bureau of Labor Statistics 2005).

To what degree can the gender gap in earnings among college-educated workers be explained by the gender segregation of college majors? Shauman (2006) found a link between major choice and earnings: 11–17% of the gap in the likelihood of employment in relatively high-paying occupations is due to gender differences in major choice. But she further found that women and men with a bachelor's degree in the same major tend to enter different types of occupations. Gender differences in the distribution of workers across occupational characteristics, coupled with the differential remuneration of these characteristics, explained as much as 41% of the sex differences in the odds of employment in high-paying occupations.

With the important exception of the literature on wage returns, there is little research on the returns to education on a range of outcomes for women relative to men. The impact of education on union dissolution has received extensive attention in the demographic literature (Faust and McKibben 1999; Teachman, Tedrow, and Crowder 2000; Teachman 2002). Teachman (2002) documented a negative relationship between a woman's education and divorce; the risk of divorce drops 6% for each additional year of schooling. This is due in part to the fact that more educated individuals marry at later ages and in part to marital homogamy. College-educated women are more likely to marry college-educated men, who have substantially lower rates of divorce than high school-educated men, perhaps because men with a college education are less likely to initiate divorce. Moreover, after 1980, divorce rates fell among college-educated women while they continued to rise for less-educated women (Martin 2004).

Higher educational attainment is also linked to fertility rates; college-educated women tend to have fewer children than women with a high school education or less. Moreover, college-educated women are much less likely to bear children outside of marriage than are less educated women (Ellwood and Jencks 2004; McLanahan 2004). Nonmarital child-bearing is a central predictor for a low standard of living for a woman and her children.

While some recent research has examined whether gender differences in the returns to a college degree are part of the explanation for the rising college enrollment and completion rates for women (see the next section), many questions remain for future research. For example, if returns to a college degree vary by the prestige of the institution attended, research should examine how gender differences in the status of the institution can explain gender differences in returns to a college degree, net of controls for field of study. Such differences may constitute one understudied source of the gender gap in wages.

In sum, we know that the gender gap in wages is due in part to the differences in the educational attainment rates of the economically active population of men and women. Thus, it is reasonable to expect that as the trend in higher rates of college completion for women continues, the female–male earnings gap will continue to decline over the next decade (see, e.g., Loury 1997). At the same time, since occupational sex segregation also contributes to the wage gap (Blau and Kahn 1997), the fact that gender segregation in fields of study and in occupations has been slower to decline (Bradley 2000; Bobbitt-Zeher 2007) suggests that the gender gap in earnings will not be completely eradicated. Bobbitt-Zeher (2007) found that even if college-educated men and women had similar education credentials, standardized test scores, and fields of study, the gender gap in wages would be reduced but remain substantial, underscoring the point that other non-education-related factors would also have to change before the wage gap would become negligible.

Explaining Gender Gaps in Higher Education

This section focuses on both individual and institutional explanations for the rising female advantage in higher education generally. Because of the small body of conclusive research in this area, I discuss the plausibility of a variety of explanations that have yet to be examined empirically, in addition to discussing the findings of existing research.

Individual-Level Factors

Status attainment and rational choice perspectives focus on primarily individuallevel explanations for variations in postsecondary enrollment. Status attainment theory examines differences in access to resources, broadly defined, related to attending and completing college. Rational choice perspectives consider how incentives and constraints shape decisions regarding whether to pursue higher education: individuals consider both the costs and the benefits of attending college, and those for whom the benefits of attending college exceed the costs, including opportunity costs, should be those most likely to enroll.

Effects of Parental Education

A large body of research in the fields of sociology, much of it in the status attainment tradition (Blau and Duncan 1967; Sewell, Haller, and Portes 1969; Jencks 1972) and in economics (Becker 1991), demonstrates the importance of parental education and other family-related resources to an individual's educational attainment. Resources related to family background exert their influence at each level of educational attainment, partly through academic performance and partly through educational transitions. Resources such as financial capital, social capital, access to role models and mentors, access to information on the college admission process, individual attitudes (especially aspirations), and prior academic performance are likely all important in understanding disparities in the transition to college generally, and patterns of gender inequality specifically.

For enrollment in colleges and universities with noncompetitive admissions, financial resources, a high school diploma or GED, and the motivation to attend college may be prerequisites. But for access to more selective institutions with competitive admission processes, additional prerequisites are required that are related to high school course-taking and academic performance, scores on standardized achievement tests, extracurricular activities, and other factors that admissions officers consider.

Even when girls and boys share the same household, family resources may not be equally distributed between sons and daughters. For example, socialization arguments emphasize the importance of role modeling: children model their parents as they determine their own educational and occupational aspirations and attainment. Some scholars have argued that role modeling is sex specific, with girls looking more to their mothers and boys more to their fathers as they develop educational and occupational aspirations (Downey and Powell 1993). According to gender role socialization arguments, after controlling for the overall educational level of the parents, daughters should do relatively better in households where the mother is better educated than in households where the father is better educated.

Using data from the General Social Surveys, Buchmann and DiPrete (2006) found that the relationship between family background and college completion changed for men and women over the second half of the 20th century. In cohorts born before the mid-1960s, daughters were able to reach parity with sons only in the minority of families where both parents were college educated. Parents with less education appeared to favor sons over daughters, and the gender gap in college completion favoring males was largest among these less-educated families. But this pattern changed for cohorts born after the mid-1960s; the male advantage declined and even reversed in households with less educated parents or those with an absent father. The significant change in the effects of family background over time produced a situation where the female advantage remained largest in families with absent or high school-educated fathers, but extended to all family types. Males, especially black males, gain a differential advantage when they have a father in the home with some college education but lose the advantage when their father has only a high school education or is absent. These results offer little support for the gender role socialization perspective, which predicts a larger or growing impact of maternal status on daughters as compared with sons. Rather, most of the shift stems from the growing vulnerability of boys with absent fathers or fathers with only a high school education.

Buchmann and DiPrete (2006) suggested (but could not test definitively) some explanations for the pattern they found. One potential source of change relates to a cultural shift in factors of family life that are linked to father's education. Back in 1940, a high school-educated father was rather high in the educational hierarchy of the American adult population, where, according to data from the General Social Survey, fewer than 20% of fathers had some college education. Many of these fathers were first- or second-generation immigrants who, by many accounts, had a strong mobility orientation for their children (Hirschman 1983). In contrast, high school-educated fathers of the most recent cohorts are lower in the educational hierarchy and may differ in their mobility orientation from their counterparts from the 1940s.

Academic Performance

Gender differences related to academic performance and behaviors in high school also play some part in explaining gender differences in college enrollment and completion, as academic ability is highly predictive of college attendance (Baker and Velez 1996). Early research using survey data for high school students in the 1950s and 1960s found that girls received higher grades than boys, had higher class standing than boys, and, by the early 1970s, took as rigorous courses as did boys (Alexander and Eckland 1974; Alexander and McDill 1976; Thomas, Alexander, and Eckland 1979). In fact, much prior research on gender differences in educational attainment sought to explain the anomaly of women's lower rates of college enrollment and completion, in light of their superior academic performance relative to men (Alexander and Eckland 1974; Mickelson 1989; Jacobs 1996).

While girls have long been outperforming boys academically, it is possible that gender gaps in academic performance have grown over time. With data from six U.S. national probability samples from 1960 to 1992, Hedges and Nowell (1995) found a larger variance in test scores for males than females on some achievement tests, a gradual reduction of the male advantage in math and science tests, and no reduction in the female advantage on tests of reading and writing ability. To the best of my knowledge, there are not more recent analyses on changing gender differences in academic performance that update Hedges and Nowell's work, nor do we know whether there are variations in the gender gaps in test scores by race, ethnicity, immigrant status, or SES.

Girls have also come to outpace boys in terms of the number of college preparatory courses and the number of Advanced Placement (AP) examinations they take in high school (Bae et al. 2000; Freeman 2004). In 1998, female high school graduates were more likely than males to have taken biology and chemistry courses and were as likely to have taken other math and science courses. Since 1990, more females than males have taken AP examinations. Girls are also more involved in extracurricular activities than boys during their high school years, with the notable exception of participation on athletic teams (Bae et al. 2000).

These gender differences in high school behaviors are likely related to the female advantage in college enrollment and completion, but the causal relationship is unclear and probably complex. For example, do female students' higher aspirations to attend college drive their greater college preparation efforts? Some evidence supports this argument. Data from the Monitoring the Future Study indicates that in 1980, more male than female high school seniors (60% vs. 54%) expected to graduate from a four-year college, but by 2001, 82% of female high school seniors, compared with 76% of male high school seniors, expected to do so (Freeman 2004). At the same time, other factors, such as developmental differences between boys and girls or sex-role socialization in early childhood, might also underlie both gender differences in high school behaviors and college enrollment. Extensively-detailed longitudinal data sets that follow the educational experiences of individuals from early childhood into young adulthood would make it possible for researchers to answer these questions definitively.

Other research indicates that girls, compared with boys, possess higher levels of "noncognitive" abilities, such as attentiveness and organizational skills, that facilitate academic achievement and increase their probability of college enrollment (Jacob 2002). For example, teachers consistently rate girls as putting forth more effort and as being less disruptive than boys in high school (Downey and Vogt Yuan 2005).

Females' better academic performance in college does play a large role in producing the female advantage in college completion. In their analysis data from the National Educational Longitudinal Study (NELS) of the high school class of 1992, Buchmann and DiPrete (2006) found that while girls performed better in eighth grade and high school in terms of GPA and high school rank, their performance did not translate into higher rates of enrollment in four-year colleges. But they found that, especially for white women, superior academic performance in college was strongly related to women's greater likelihood of completing college. This relationship remained net of controls for a wide range of factors, including high school behaviors, college major, and the selectivity of the institution attended.

Incentives and Returns to College

Differences in the returns to attending and completing college also may play an important role in shaping individual decisions about how much education to acquire. In light of the research that documents high returns to college education in terms of earnings and marital status as well as in other realms, one plausible reason for the rising rates of women's college enrollment and completion is that the returns to college have been rising more for women than for men. Some research that has examined this question found no evidence of a female-favorable trend in the wage returns to higher education, however (Averett and Burton 1996; Perna 2003; Charles and Luoh 2003). Women's wage returns to higher education have indeed increased, but male returns have increased even more rapidly because of declining opportunities for high-wage, male-dominated manufacturing jobs for high school-educated workers.

Most recently, DiPrete and Buchmann (2006) argued that wage returns constitute too narrow a basis for evaluating the relative returns to higher education for men and women. They therefore assessed whether the growing female advantage in college completion is related to changes in the returns to higher education for women and men in terms of wages, the probability of getting and staying married, the family standard of living, and insurance against poverty. Conducting a trend analysis of the value of higher education for each of these outcomes measured against the baseline value of a high school education using 39 years of data from the Current Population Survey (CPS), they found that standard-of-living and insurance-against-poverty returns to higher education for women appear to have risen faster than for men. Thus, it is plausible that the female-favorable trend in college completion may be related at least in part to gender-specific changes in the value of higher education.

DiPrete and Buchmann (2006) noted that such gender-specific incentives are only part of the explanation for the female-favorable trend in higher education. Gender-specific trends in the value of education would likely have to persist for some time before they would become the basis for educational decisions; the initial female-specific rise may have had other causes. Furthermore, there is no reason to believe that the same explanation would apply across the socioeconomic hierarchy or across different racial or ethnic groups. The literature has demonstrated that many individual factors predict the likelihood of college attendance, and many of them begin shaping an individual's educational career at an early age, before he or she is aware of even the gross characteristics of labor or marriage markets, let alone trends in these markets. Trends in incentives nonetheless can have a powerful affect on the margin and thus may well be an important cause of the growing female advantage in college completion.

Although the value of a college education has not risen as fast for men as for women, DiPrete and Buchmann (2006) showed that the returns have indeed risen for men. The returns to education in the labor market have risen for men, and the earnings value of a spouse to men has risen as female earnings have risen and the financial vulnerability of men to divorce has risen (McManus and DiPrete 2001). Arguably, one puzzling aspect of the reversal of the gender gap in college completion is the slow pace of growth in men's rates of college completion even in the face of rising returns to college for men. Research suggests a socialization-based disadvantage for males that is relatively stronger in families with less-educated or absent fathers (Buchmann and DiPrete 2006). But whether this disadvantage plays out through a lack of knowledge about the value of postsecondary education and the way to convert it to success in the labor market, through a lower priority placed on education relative to other perhaps short-term goals, or through some other mechanism is not yet clear.

Institutional-Level Factors

Institutional-level factors also likely shape gendered patterns of college access and success. They include sociocultural changes in gender roles and expectations about life course trajectories for women and men and declining gender discrimination in the labor market. Shifts in the structure of the labor market and occupational sex segregation also impact individual incentives to attend college, as do changes in institutions of higher education themselves, such as the growth of community colleges, the rising costs of higher education, and changes in financial aid regulations. We also need to consider the role of institutions such as the military that may compete with higher education for young adults, especially young men, in shaping gender-specific patterns of participation in higher education.

Gender Role Attitudes

In the United States, there have been large changes in gender role attitudes in recent decades, with the clear trend of a declining number of Americans expressing support for traditional gender roles and a far greater number expressing more egalitarian views (Brewster and Padavic 2000; Brooks and Bolzendahl 2004). Changes in gender role attitudes are also related to the rising college attendance of young women, but in complex ways and coupled with other factors (DiPrete and Buchmann 2006; Goldin 2006). Goldin's research examines women's changing expectations regarding their labor force participation, social norms concerning women's families and careers, and factors related to women's life satisfaction over the last century in detail. For example, Goldin, Katz, and Kuziemko (2006) showed that young women's rising expectations for future employment encouraged them to attend and complete college, but they also noted that the median age of first marriage among college graduates rose by several years in recent decades. As they married later, women could take college more seriously and form their identities before getting married and having a family (Goldin 2006). Women's access to reliable contraception in the form of the birth control pill positively impacted their college attendance and a host of related factors, including their age at first marriage, professional labor force participation, and age at first birth (Goldin and Katz 2002; Goldin 2006).

Labor Markets

Important changes in the labor market in recent decades also have undoubtedly impacted women's choices to attend college. Between the 1970s and 1990s, the gender wage gap declined. While women in all segments of the earnings distribution saw increases in their wages, women with high levels of human capital (in terms of education and labor force experience) saw the greatest increase (Spain and Bianchi 1996; Morris and Western 1999). Moreover, research indicates that returns to labor force experience increased by a larger amount for women than for men during this period (Blau and Kahn 1997) because of rising levels of women's human capital and because of the passage and enforcement of antidiscrimination laws (Goldin 2006). Occupational sex segregation also fell between 1970 and 1990, although the rate of decline slowed in the second decade (Morris and Western 1999). This means that more women entered prestigious and often better-paid positions in occupational sectors such as law, business, and the sciences (Goldin 2006). All these factors are related to women's rapidly rising rates of college enrollment and completion from the 1980s onward; however, we still need to understand why the college enrollment and completion rates of men have grown much more slowly, especially in light of the fact that returns to higher education have risen for men, albeit not as rapidly as for women (DiPrete and Buchmann 2006).

Educational Institutions and Environments

Changes in higher education institutions also may have altered the access or pathways to college in gender-specific ways. The second half of the 20th century witnessed the dramatic expansion of both the community college system and the four-year college system. If community college serves as a springboard to enrollment in and graduation from a four-year college, the expansion of the community college system may have been responsible, in part, for the female-favorable trend in college completion. But Buchmann and DiPrete (2006) found little evidence that community colleges serve as a pathway to increased college completion for women. Via a decomposition analysis, they showed that while females enroll in two-year colleges at a slightly higher rate than males, the female advantage in two-year college attendance has only a small impact on their advantage in four-year college completion.

Other major changes in higher education have been the rising cost of tuition, declining levels of grant-based financial aid, and increases in student loans (Alon 2007). Cursory evidence suggests that women receive as much financial support from their families for college as do men (Jacobs 1999), but it is possible that changes in financial aid and the increasing cost of college are affecting men and women differently. This is an important topic for further research.

There is an ongoing, contentious debate about whether male and female teachers have biases in how they treat boys and girls in the classroom. Research based on classroom observation in the early 1990s talked about *How Schools Shortchange Girls* (American Association of University Women 1992) and maintained that teachers favored boys, called on them more frequently, and were more likely to praise them (Sadker and Sadker 1994; American Association of University Women 1992), only to be followed more recently by arguments that schools favor girls and contribute to a *War Against Boys* (Sommers 2000).

Unfortunately, empirical evidence on whether teachers are gender biased and whether such bias plays a role in causing gender differences in educational outcomes is quite limited. In their review of small-scale studies of teachers' gender bias in college classrooms, Jones and Dindia (2004) concluded that evidence supports the idea that the teacher's gender does shape gender equity in postsecondary classrooms. Most recently, Dee (2005, 2006) examined whether a teacher's gender shapes gender differences in achievement among middle school students. Using NELS data, he found that in the subjects of science, social studies, and English, having a female teacher instead of a male teacher raised the achievement of girls by 4% of a standard deviation and lowered the achievement of boys by roughly the same amount, producing an overall gender gap of 8% of a standard deviation (Dee 2006). He argued that these estimates suggest that the effects of a year with a teacher of a particular gender are quite large relative to the gender gaps in achievement found in the National Assessment of Educational Progress (NAEP). Dee (2006) noted that although the adverse effects of teacher gender have an impact on both boys and girls, the effect falls more heavily on the male half of the population in middle school, since most middle school teachers are female. Dee's findings are sure to generate much-needed future research on the role of gender in teacher–student interactions in the classroom. For example, while Dee offers some potential explanations for his findings, definitive assessments of why teacher gender matters for students' achievement are important tasks for future research.

Military Service: Competing with or Enhancing College Enrollment?

Finally, we must assess the degree to which the military competes with higher education for young adults, especially young men. The armed forces of the U.S. military recruit about 200,000 enlisted personnel each year, almost all of whom are high school graduates. In 2004, there were 1.4 million active duty personnel, or about one half of 1% of the total population. The size of the military population has not fluctuated much in the past 20 years; since 1975, it has constituted less than 1% of the total population. Eighty-five percent of active duty personnel in the armed forces are men (Segal and Segal 2004). Because the population of enlisted personnel is disproportionately young (with more than 50% under the age of 25), the military may compete with college as a destination for young adults, especially young men. It is too simplistic, however, to view military enlistment and college enrollment as mutually exclusive events. Many young people who enlist after high school cite the educational benefits available to them, either during or after their military service, as a primary motivation to enlist (Segal and Segal 2004). Thus, for some, military service may make enrolling in college possible, albeit at a later point in life.

Further, the armed forces commissions 15,000–20,000 officers each year, and nearly all officers are college graduates; about 40% received their commission through participation in a college or university Reserve Officer Training Corps (ROTC) program (Segal and Segal 2004). For this group, military enlistment occurs after completing college.

Nonetheless, research finds that men who serve in the military receive less education than those who do not serve (Cohen, Warner, and Segal 1995; MacLean 2005). In a study of high school graduates who served in the armed forces during the peacetime cold war, MacLean (2005) found that veterans were less likely to get a college education than were nonveterans at all levels of SES. Even among men who reported that they planned to go to college, military service reduced the odds of postsecondary education. This finding accords with the idea that military service may compete with higher education for young men who enter military service after completing high school. To the best of my knowledge, no research has examined the relationship between military service and educational attainment for women, and questions remain about whether the effects of military service found for older cohorts remain the same for military personnel today, especially during the period of the war in Iraq. These are important questions for future research. It would also be informative for future research to map out the trajectories of young people who enlist in the military and examine precisely the range and degree to which military service alters college enrollment pathways.

Implications and Future Research

The terrain of gender inequality in the transition to college has been the site of much change, with young women gaining advantages over young men in ways that could not have been anticipated just two decades ago. Females are less likely to drop out of high school than males. Men are now more likely than women to forgo college or delay college enrollment. Once enrolled in college, women tend to get better grades and have higher rates of persistence to obtain a degree. The advantages to females in all these domains are largest among blacks, Hispanics, and Native Americans. Males still retain a slight advantage in the prestige of the colleges they attend. After declining steadily in the 1970s and early 1980s, the gender segregation of major fields stabilized such that today, more men than women still attain degrees in the most lucrative fields, especially in engineering.

The future promises to bring more change than stability to the arena of gender inequality in the transition to college. It remains to be seen, for example, whether women will achieve parity with men in terms of the prestige of the institutions of they attend. The degree to which higher rates of college completion among women will reduce the gender wage gap also remains to be seen, as current evidence on this issue is mixed. Throughout this article, I have highlighted some of the potential pathways for future research to advance our understanding of the complex nature of gender inequalities in higher education: Why have men's rates of college completion apparently not kept pace with the rising returns to college for men? Among men who do enroll in college, what factors lead many of them to delay enrollment for more than a year after high school? How have gender gaps in academic performance changed in the past decade since Hedges and Nowell (1995) analyzed this question? What are the patterns of gender differences in test scores for different race, ethnic, immigrant, and SES groups today? In addition to these and other pressing research questions, I believe that there are three related domains of research that would prove especially useful in advancing our understanding of gender inequalities in the transition to college.

First, future research needs to examine gender inequalities in education early in the life course: female-favorable trends in college enrollment and completion and possible female-favorable trends in high school performance are likely partly due to gender differences in childhood experiences. For example, gender differences in problem behaviors or academically productive use of time in early to middle childhood may be linked to later differences in cognitive performance in elementary school. If so, these factors may be one of the root causes of female advantages in high school performance, either alone or in interaction with particular parenting styles. Richly detailed data pertaining to these issues are available through two new longitudinal data sets, the Early Childhood Longitudinal Study, Kindergarten Class of 1998–99 (ECLS-K) and the Early Childhood Longitudinal Study of children born in 2001 (ECLS-B). These data sets allow researchers to examine a wide range of factors, including children's health, development, care, and education during the formative years, from birth through kindergarten entry and into the elementary and middle school years. I expect that they will be used extensively to investigate questions pertaining to gender differences in early childhood experiences. Their release coincides with recent important knowledge advances in biology, psychology, and other arenas (Kimura 1999; Halpern 2000; Cahill 2005; Spelke 2005) that shed light on gender differences in cognitive and motor skills development and noncognitive abilities in early childhood. More than ever, the study of gender differences in early childhood must be an interdisciplinary enterprise, with connected efforts by social scientists, policy makers, biologists, and child development specialists.

Second, future research must investigate gender differences by race, ethnicity, SES, and immigrant status. Such research should attend to gender differences within vulnerable segments of the population who may be particularly at risk for not attending higher education. A rare example of such work is Lopez's (2003) ethnographic study of 66 low-income second-generation Dominican, West Indian, and Haitian young adults who grew up in New York City during the 1970s–1990s. Through her interviews, Lopez found that the discriminatory treatment that these young men experienced in their schools and communities generally led them to doubt their ability to succeed in school and overcome society's negative stereotypes of them. She also demonstrated how gendered norms within their families, which provided strong social controls and responsibilities for daughters but more lax regulations and too much independence for sons, could put sons and daughters within the same family on very different educational pathways. Other important evidence on how gender differences may be conditioned by race and SES comes from the work of Entwisle, Alexander, and Olson (2007) who found that in the beginning of first grade, the early reading skills of boys from disadvantaged backgrounds were weaker than those of their female counterparts, but among nondisadvantaged elementary school students, boys' and girls' reading skills were about the same. These studies should serve as exemplars for future research.

Third, there is a great need for research on how the structure and practices of schooling relate to gender differences in educational outcomes. For example, the National Association for Single-Sex Public Education reported that, as of April 2006, at least 223 public schools in the United States were offering gender-separate educational opportunities, up from just 4 in 1998. Most of these cases involved coeducational schools with single-sex classrooms, but 44 were wholly single-sex schools (Dee 2006). It would not be surprising to learn that this rise in single-sex schooling has developed in response to growing public concern about boys' poor academic performance, as reflected by magazine covers, bestselling books, and television programs, such as the PBS program based on the bestselling book, *Raising Cain: Protecting the Emotional Lives of Boys* (Kindlon and Thompson 2000). While single-sex schooling may well be a reasonable policy response to the underachievement of boys, implementing such massive changes in our educational system without a careful empirically based assessment of the consequences of such changes is risky and irresponsible.

In sum, understanding the nature, causes, and consequences of the changing gender gaps in the transition to college and beyond is an important task for future research. The rapidly shifting terrain of gender inequalities in higher education raises important questions for policy makers, researchers, and educators who want to understand how to improve the educational performance and attainment of all youth—males and females alike—and for institutions of higher education striving to respond to the needs of their students. Clearly, much work remains to be done.

References

Alexander, Karl L., and Bruce E. Eckland. 1974. Sex differences in the educational attainment process. *American Sociological Review* 39:668–82.

Alexander, Karl L., and Edward McDill. 1976. Selection and allocation within schools: Some causes and consequences of curriculum placement. *American Sociological Review* 41:963–80.

Alon, Sigal. 2007. The influence of financial aid in leveling group differences in graduating from elite institutions. *Economics of Education Review* 26:296–311.

American Association of University Women. 1992. *How schools shortchange girls*. Washington, DC: AAUW Educational Foundation.

Averett, Susan, and Mark L. Burton. 1996. College attendance and the college wage premium: Differences by gender. *Economics of Education Review* 15:37–49.

Bae, Yupin, Susan Choy, Claire Geddes, Jennifer Sable, and Thomas Snyder. 2000. *Trends in educational equity of girls and women.* U.S. Department of Education, National Center for Education Statistics. Washington, DC: U.S. Government Printing Office.

Baker, Theresa, and William Velez. 1996. Access to and opportunity in postsecondary education in the United States: A review. *Sociology of Education* 69, extra issue, 82–101.

Becker, Gary. 1991. *A treatise on the family*. Cambridge, MA: Harvard Univ. Press.

Bernhardt Annette, Martina Morris, and Mark S. Handcock. 1995. Women's gains or men's losses? A closer look at the shrinking gender gap in earnings. *American Journal of Sociology* 101:302–28.

Bianchi, Suzanne M., and Lynne M. Casper. 2000. American families. *Population Bulletin* 55, no. 4. Washington, DC: Population Reference Bureau.

Blau, Francine D., and Lawrence M. Kahn. 1997. Swimming upstream: Trends in the gender wage differential in the 1980s. *Journal of Labor Economics* 15:1–42.

Blau, Peter M., and Otis D. Duncan. 1967. *The American occupation structure*. New York: John Wiley.

Bobbitt-Zeher, Donna. 2007. The gender income gap and the role of education. *Sociology of Education* 80:1–22.

Bowen, William, and Derek Bok. 1998. *The shape of the river: The long term consequences of considering race in college and university admissions*. Princeton, NJ: Princeton Univ. Press.

Bozick, Robert, and Stefanie DeLuca. 2005. Better late than never? Delayed enrollment in the high school to college transition. *Social Forces* 84:527–50.

Bradley, Karen. 2000. The incorporation of women into higher education: Paradoxical outcomes. *Sociology of Education* 73:1–18.

Brewster, Karen, and Irene Padavic. 2000. Change in gender-ideology, 1977–1996: The contributions of intracohort change and population turnover. *Journal of Marriage and the Family* 62:477–87.

Brooks, Clem, and Catherine Bolzendahl. 2004. The transformation of U.S. gender role attitudes: Cohort replacement, social-structural change and ideological learning. *Social Science Research* 33:106–33.

Buchmann, Claudia, and Thomas A. DiPrete. 2006. The growing female advantage in college completion: The role of parental resources and academic achievement. *American Sociological Review* 71:515–41.

Bureau of Labor Statistics. 2005. *Highlights of women's earnings in 2004*. Washington, DC: Bureau of Labor Statistics.

Cahill, Larry. 2005. His brain, her brain. *Scientific American* 292:40–47.

Charles, Kerwin Kofi, and MingChing Luoh. 2003. Gender differences in completed schooling. *Review of Economics and Statistics* 85:559–77.

Charles, Maria, and Karen Bradley. 2002. Equal but separate? A cross-national study of sex segregation in higher education. *American Sociological Review* 67:573–99.

Cohen, Jere, Rebecca L. Warner, and David R. Segal. 1995. Military service and educational attainment in the all-volunteer force. *Social Science Quarterly* 76:88–104.

Davies, Scott, and Neil Guppy. 1997. Fields of study, college selectivity and student inequalities in higher education. *Social Forces* 75:1417–38.

Dee, Thomas. 2005. A teacher like me: Does race, ethnicity or gender matter? *American Economic Review* 95:158–65.

Dee, Thomas. 2006. The why chromosome: How a teacher's gender affects boys and girls. *Education Next,* Fall, 69–75.

DiPrete, Thomas A., and Claudia Buchmann. 2006. Gender-specific trends in the value of education and the emerging gender gap in college completion. *Demography* 43:1–24.

Downey, Douglas B., and Brian Powell. 1993. Do children in single-parent households fare better living with same-sex parents? *Journal of Marriage and the Family* 55:55–71.

Downey, Douglas B., and Anastasia S. Vogt Yuan. 2005 Sex differences in school performance during high school: Puzzling patterns and possible explanations. *Sociological Quarterly* 46:299–321.

Driscoll, Anne. 1999. Risk of high school dropout among immigrant and native Hispanic youth. *International Migration Review,* Winter, 857–75.

Ellwood, David T., and Christopher Jencks. 2004. The uneven spread of single-parent families: What do we know? Where do we look for answers? In *Social inequality,* ed. Kathryn Neckerman, 3–77. New York: Russell Sage Foundation.

Entwisle, Doris R., Karl L. Alexander, and Linda S. Olson. 2007. Early schooling: The handicap of being poor and male. *Sociology of Education* 80:114–38.

Faust, K., and J. McKibben. 1999. Marital dissolution: Divorce separation, annulment, and widowhood. In *Handbook of marriage and the family,* 2nd ed., ed. M. Sussman, S. Steinmetz, and G. Peterson, 475–99. New York: Plenum.

Freeman, Catherine E. 2004. *Trends in the educational equity of girls and women: 2004.* U.S. Department of Education, National Center for Education Statistics. Washington, DC:

U.S. Government Printing Office. Fry, Richard. 2005. *The higher dropout rate of foreign-born teens: The role of schooling abroad.* Washington DC: The Pew Hispanic Center.

Goldin, Claudia. 2006. The quiet revolution that transformed women's employment, education, and family. *American Economic Review* 96:1–21.

Goldin, Claudia, and Lawrence F. Katz. 2002. The power of the pill: Oral contraceptives and women's career and marriage decisions. *Journal of Political Economy* 11:730–70.

Goldin, Claudia, Lawrence F. Katz, and Ilyana Kuziemko. 2006. The homecoming of American college women: The reversal of the college gender gap. *Journal of Economic Perspectives* 20:133–56.

Greene, Howard, and Matthew Greene. 2004. The widening gender gap: Shifting student demographics will have significant impact on college admissions. *University Business* 7:27–29.

Grodsky, Eric, and Erika Jackson. 2009. Social stratification in higher education. *Teachers College Record* 111(10).

Halpern, Diane. 2000. *Sex differences in cognitive abilities.* Mahwah, NJ: Erlbaum.

Hedges, Larry V., and Amy Nowell. 1995. Sex differences in mental test scores, variability, and numbers of high scoring individuals. *Science* 269:41–45.

Hirschman, Charles. 1983. America's melting pot reconsidered. *Annual Review of Sociology* 9:397–423.

Hirschman, Charles. 2001. Educational enrollment of Hispanic youth: A test of the segmented assimilation hypothesis. *Demography* 38:317–36.

Horn, L. J., and M. D. Premo. 1995. *Profile of undergraduates in U.S. postsecondary education institutions: 1992–93, with an essay on undergraduates at risk* (NCES 96237). Washington, DC: National Center for Education Statistics, U.S. Government Printing Office.

Jacob, Brian A. 2002. Where the boys aren't: Non-cognitive skills, returns to school and the gender gap in higher education. *Economics of Education Review* 21:589–98.

Jacobs, Jerry A. 1995. Gender and academic specialties: Trends among college degree recipients in the 1980s. *Sociology of Education* 68:81–98.

Jacobs, Jerry A. 1996. Gender inequality and higher education. *Annual Review of Sociology* 22:153–85.

Jacobs, Jerry A. 1999. Gender and the stratification of colleges. *Journal of Higher Education* 70:161–87.

Jencks, Christopher. 1972. *Inequality: A reassessment of the effect of family and schooling in America.* New York: Basic.

Jones, Susanne M., and Kathryn Dindia. 2004. A meta-analytic perspective on sex equity in the classroom. *Review of Educational Research* 74:443–71.

Karen, David. 1991. The politics of class, race and gender: Access to higher education in the United States, 1960–1986. *American Journal of Education* 99:208–37.

Karen, David. 2002. Changes in access to higher education in the United States: 1980–1992. *Sociology of Education* 75:191–210.

Kimura, Doreen. 1999. *Sex and cognition.* Cambridge, MA: MIT Press.

Kindlon, Dan, and Michael Thompson. 2000. *Raising Cain: Protecting the emotional life of boys.* New York: Ballantine Books.

King, Jacqueline. 2000. *Gender equity in higher education.* Washington, DC: American Council on Education.

Kingston, Paul E., and L. S. Lewis. 1990. *The high status track.* Albany: SUNY Press.

Lewis, Susan K., and Valerie K. Oppenheimer. 2000. Educational assortative mating across marriage markets: Non-Hispanic whites in the United States. *Demography* 37:29–40.

Lopez, Nancy. 2003. *Hopeful girls, troubled boys: Race and gender disparity in urban education.* New York: Routledge.

Loury, Linda Datcher. 1997. The gender earnings gap among college-educated workers. *Industrial and Labor Relations Review* 50:580–93.

MacLean, Alair. 2005. Lessons from the Cold War: Military service and college education. *Sociology of Education* 78:250–66.

Martin, Steven P. 2004. Growing evidence of a divorce divide? Education and marital rates since the 1970s. Working Paper, Russell Sage Foundation, New York.

McLanahan, Sara S. 2004. Diverging destinies: How children are faring under the second demographic transition. *Demography* 41:607–27.

McManus, Patricia, and Thomas A. DiPrete. 2001. Losers and winners: The financial consequences of divorce for men. *American Sociological Review* 66:246–68.

Mickelson, Roslyn Arlin. 1989. Why does Jane read and write so well? The anomaly of women's achievement. *Sociology of Education* 62:47–63.

Morris, Martina, and Bruce Western. 1999. Inequality in earnings at the close of the twentieth century. *Annual Review of Sociology* 25:623–57.

National Center for Education Statistics. 2004. *Digest of educational statistics*. Washington, DC: National Center for Education Statistics.

National Center for Education Statistics. 2005. *Digest of educational statistics*. Washington, DC: National Center for Education Statistics.

National Center for Education Statistics. 2006. *The condition of education*. Washington, DC: National Center For Education Statistics.

National Science Foundation, Division of Science Resources Statistics. 2004. *Women, minorities and persons with disabilities in science and engineering*. Publication number 04317. Arlington, VA: National Science Foundation, Division of Science Resources Statistics.

Perna, Laura W. 2003. The private benefits of higher education: An examination of the earnings premium. *Research in Higher Education* 44:451–72.

Peter, Karen, and Laura Horn. 2005. *Gender differences in participation and completion of undergraduate education and how they have changed over time*. U.S. Department of Education, National Center for Education Statistics. Washington, DC: U.S. Government Printing Office.

Sadker, Myra, and David Sadker. 1994. *Failing at fairness: How our schools cheat girls*. New York: Touchstone.

Segal, David R., and Mady Wechsler Segal. 2004. America's military population. *Population Bulletin* 59, no. 4. Washington, DC: Population Reference Bureau.

Sewell, William H., A. O. Haller, and Alejandro Portes. 1969. The educational and early occupational attainment process. *American Sociological Review* 34:82–92.

Shauman, Kimberlee A. 2006. Occupational sex segregation and the earnings of occupations: What causes the link among college educated workers? *Social Science Research* 35:577–619.

Solnick, Sara. 1995. Changes in women's majors from entrance to graduation and women's and coeducational colleges. *Industrial and Labor Relations Review* 31:498–508.

Sommers, Carol Hoff. 2000. *The war against boys: How misguided feminism is harming our young men*. New York: Simon and Schuster.

Spain, Daphne, and Bianchi, Suzanne M. 1996. *Balancing act: Motherhood, marriage and employment among American women*. New York: Russell Sage.

Spelke, Elizabeth. 2005. Sex differences in intrinsic aptitude for math and science? A critical review. *American Psychologist* 60:950–58.

Sum, Andrew, Neeta Fogg, Paul Harrington (with Ishwar Khatiwada), Sheila Palma, Nathan Pond, and Paulo Tobar. 2003. The growing gender gaps in college enrollment and degree attainment in the U.S. and their potential economic and social consequences. Working paper prepared for the Business Roundtable, Center for Labor Market Studies, Northeastern University, Boston, MA.

Teachman, Jay. 2002. Stability across cohorts in divorce risk factors. *Demography* 39:331–51.

Teachman, Jay, L. Tedrow, and Kyle Crowder. 2000. The changing demography of America's families. *Journal of Marriage and the Family* 51:259–67.

Thomas, Gail E., Karl L. Alexander, and Bruce K. Eckland. 1979. Access to higher education: The importance of race, sex, social class and academic credentials. *School Review* 87:133–56.

Thompson, S. 2003. Male students' college achievement gap brings concern. *Washington Post*. August 31.

Turner, Sarah E., and William G. Bowen. 1999. Choice of major: The changing (unchanging) gender gap. *Industrial and Labor Relations Review* 52:289–313.

Xie, Yu, and Kimberlee A. Shauman. 2003. *Women in science: Career processes and outcomes*. Cambridge, MA: Harvard Univ. Press.

PART V
Suggested Readings

Alexander, K., Bozick, R., & Entwisle, D. (2008).Warming up, cooling out, or holding steady? Persistence and change in educational expectations after high school. *Sociology of Education*, 81 (4), 371–396.

Arnot, M. (2002). *Reproducing gender: Selected critical essays on educational theory and feminist politics*. London: Falmer.

Arnot, M., David, M., & Weiner, G. (1999). *Closing the gender gap: Postwar education and social change*. Cambridge: Polity.

Attewell, P. (2001) The winner-take-all high school: Organizational adaptations to educational stratification. *Sociology of Education*, 74, 267–296.

Attewell, P. & Thurston, D. (2008). Raising the bar: Curricular intensity and academic performance. *Educational Evaluation and Policy Analysis*, 30, 51–71.

Baker, D. P. & Stevenson, D. L. (1986). Mothers' strategies for children's school achievement: Managing the transition to high school. *Sociology of Education*, 59, 156–166.

Becker, H. S. (1952). Social-class variations in the teacher–pupil relationship. *Journal of Educational Sociology*, 8, 451–465.

Belfield, C. & Levin, H. (2007). *The price we pay: Economic and social consequences of inadequate education*. Washington, DC: Brookings.

Berends, M., Lucas, S. R., & Peñaloza, R. V. (2008). How changes in families and schools are related to trends in black–white test scores. *Sociology of Education*, 81 (4), 313–344.

Bloomfield Cucchiara, M. & McNamara Horvat, E. (2009). Perils and promises: Middle-class parental involvement in urban schools. *American Educational Research Journal*, 46, 974–1004.

Bobbitt-Zeher, D. (2007). The gender income gap and the role of education. *Sociology of Education*, 80 (1), 1–22.

Borman, G. & Dowling, M. (2010). Schools and inequality: A multilevel analysis of Coleman's equality of educational opportunity data. *Teachers College Record*, 112 (5), 1–2. Retrieved January 31, 2010, from http://www.tcrecord.org. ID Number: 15664.

Braddock, J. H., II. (1990). Tracking the middle grades: National patterns of grouping for instruction. *Phi Delta Kappan*, 71, 445–449.

Braddock, J. H. & Dawkins, M. P. (1993). Ability grouping, aspirations, and attainments: Evidence from the National Educational Longitudinal Study of 1988. *Journal of Negro Education*, 62, 324–336.

Braddock, J. H., II, & McPartland, J. M. (1990). Alternatives to tracking. *Educational Leadership*, 47 (7), 76–79.

Buchman, C. (2009). Gender inequalities in the transition to college. *Teachers College Record*, 111 (10), 2320–2346.

Catsambis, S. (1994). The path to math: Gender and racial–ethnic differences in mathematics participation from middle school to high school. *Sociology of Education*, 67, 199–215.

Cicourel, A. V. & Kitsuse, J. I. (1963). *The educational decision makers*. New York: Bobbs-Merrill.

Coleman, J. S. & Hoffer, T. (1987). *Public and private schools: The impact of communities*. New York: Basic Books.

Coleman, J. S., Campbell, E. Q., Hobson, C. J., McPartland, J., Mood, A. J., Weinfeld, F. D., & York, R. L. (1966). *Equality of educational opportunity*. Washington, DC: U.S. Government Printing Office.

Coleman, J. S., Hoffer, T., & Kilgore, S. (1982). *High school achievement: Public, Catholic and private schools compared*. New York: Basic Books.

Cookson, P. W. & Persell, C. H. (1985). *Preparing for power: America's elite boarding schools*. New York: Basic Books.

Crul, M. & Holdaway, J. (2009). Children of immigrants in schools in New York and Amsterdam: The factors shaping attainment. *Teachers College Record*, 111 (6), 1476–1507.

Darling-Hammond, L. (2004). Inequality and the right to learn: Access to qualified teachers in California's public schools. *Teachers College Record*, 106 (10), 1936–1966.

Darling-Hammond, L. (2010). *The flat world and education: How America's commitment to equity will determine our future*. New York: Teachers College Press.

Datnow, A. & Hubbard, L. (2002). *Gender in policy and practice*. New York: Routledge/Falmer.

DiMaggio, P. (1982). Cultural capital and school success. *American Sociological Review*, 47, 189–201.

DiMaggio, P. & Mohr, J. (1985). Cultural capital, educational attainment, and marital selection. *American Journal of Sociology*, 90, 1231–1261.

Dougherty, K. J. (1996). Opportunity-to-learn standards: A sociological critique. *Sociology of Education* (Special Issue on Sociology and educational policy: bringing scholarship and practice together), 40–65.

Downey, D. B. (2008). Black/white differences in school performance: The oppositional culture explanation. *Annual Review of Sociology*, 34, 107–126.

Downey, D. B., von Hippel, P., & Broh, B. (2004). Are schools the great equalizer? Cognitive inequality during the summer months and the school year. *American Sociological Review*, 69, 613–635.

Downey, D. B., Ainsworth, J. W., & Qian, Z. (2009). Rethinking the attitude–achievement paradox among blacks. *Sociology of Education*, 82 (1), 1–19.

Dumais, S. A. (2002). Cultural capital, gender, and school success: The role of habitus. *Sociology of Education*, 77, 44–68.

Eder, D. (1995). *School talk*. New Brunswick, NJ: Rutgers University Press.

Eder, D. & Parker, S. (1987). The cultural reproduction of gender: The effect of extracurricular activities on peer-group culture. *Sociology of Education*, 60, 200–213.

Entwisle, D. R. & Alexander, K. L. (1992). Summer setback: Race, poverty, school composition, and mathematics achievement in the first 2 years of school. *American Sociological Review*, 57, 72–84.

Entwisle, D. R., Alexander, K. L., & Olson, L. S. (1997). *Children, schools and inequality*. Boulder, CO: Westview.

Entwisle, D. R., Alexander, K. L., & Olson, Linda S. (2007). Early schooling: The handicap of being poor and male. *Sociology of Education*, 80 (2), 114–138.

Farkas, G. (1996). *Human capital or cultural capital: Ethnicity and poverty groups in an urban school district*. New York: Aldine DeGruyter.

Ferguson, A. (2001). *Bad boys*. Ann Arbor, MI: University of Michigan Press.

Fordham, S. (1997). *Blacked out: Dilemmas of race and identity and success at Capital High*. Chicago, IL: University of Chicago Press.

Fordham, S. & Ogbu, J. U. (1986). Black students' school success: Coping with the "burden" of acting white. *Urban Review*, 18 (3), 176–206.

Gamoran, A. (1987). The stratification of high school learning opportunities. *Sociology of Education*, 60: 135–155.

Gamoran, A. (1993). Alternative uses of ability grouping in secondary schools: Can we bring high-quality instruction to low-ability classes? *American Journal of Education*, 101, 1–22.

Gamoran, A. (1996). Curriculum standardization and equality of opportunity in Scottish secondary education, 1984–1990. *Sociology of Education*, 29, 1–21.

Gamoran, A. & Berends, M. (1987). The effects of stratification in secondary schools: Synthesis of survey and ethnographic research. *Review of Educational Research*, 57, 415–435.

Gamoran, A. & Mare, R. D. (1989). Secondary school tracking and educational inequality: Enforcement, compensation, or neutrality? *American Journal of Sociology*, 94, 1146–1183.

Gamoran, A., Nystand, M., Berends, M., & LePore, P. (1995). An organizational analysis of the effects of ability grouping. *American Educational Research Journal*, 32, 59–87.

Gartner, A. & Lipsky, D. K. (1987). Beyond special education: Toward a quality system for all students. *Harvard Educational Review*, 57, 367–395.

Gillborn, D. (2008). *Racism and education: Coincidence or conspiracy?* Oxford: Routledge.

Hallinan, M. T. (1987). Ability grouping and student learning. In M. T. Hallinan (Ed.), *The social organization of schools: New conceptualizations of the learning process* (pp. 41–69). New York: Plenum.

Hallinan, M. T. (1994). School differences in tracking effects on achievement. *Social Forces*, 72, 799–820.

Hallinan, M. T. (1994). Tracking: From theory to practice. *Sociology of Education*, 67, 79–84.

Hallinan, M. T. (2001). Sociological perspectives on Black–White inequalities in American schooling. *Sociology of Education*, 74 (Extra Issue), 50–70.

Harris, A. L. & Robinson, K. (2007). Schooling behaviors or prior skills? A cautionary tale of omitted variable bias within oppositional culture theory. *Sociology of Education*, 80 (2), 139–157.

Herman, M. R. (2009). The Black–White–other achievement gap: Testing theories of academic performance among multiracial and monoracial adolescents. *Sociology of Education*, 82 (1), 20–46.

Hoffer, T. B. (1992). Middle school ability grouping and student achievement in science and mathematics. *Educational Evaluation and Policy Analysis*, 14, 205–227.

Horvat, E. M. (2003). Reassessing the burden of 'acting White': The importance of peer groups in managing academic success. *Sociology of Education*, 76, 265–280.

Jencks, C. & Phillips, M. (Eds.) (1998). *The Black–White achievement gap*. Washington, DC: Brookings.

Kelly, S. (2008). What types of students' effort are rewarded with high marks? *Sociology of Education*, 81 (1), 32–52.

Kelly, S. (2009). The Black–White gap in mathematics course taking. *Sociology of Education*, 82 (1), 47–69.

Kerckhoff, A. (1986). The effects of ability grouping. *American Sociological Review*, 51, 842–858.

Kilgore, S. (1991). The organizational context of tracking in schools. *American Sociological Review*, 56, 189–203.

Lareau, A. (1987). Social class differences in family–school relationships: The importance of cultural capital. *Sociology of Education*, 60, 73–85.

Lareau, A. (1989). *Home advantage: Social class and parental intervention in elementary education*. New York: Falmer Press.

Lareau, A. (2002). Invisible inequality: Social class and childrearing in Black families and white families. *American Sociological Review*, 67 (5), 747–776.

Lareau, A. (2003). *Unequal childhood: Class, race and family life*. Berkeley, CA: University of California Press.

Lareau, A. & Horvat, E. M. (1999). Moments of social inclusion and exclusion: Race, class, and cultural capital in family–school relationships. *Sociology of Education*, 72, 37–53.

Lee, V. E. & Burkham, D. (2002). *Inequality at the starting gate: Social background differences in achievement as children begin school*. Washington, DC: Economic Policy Institute.

Lee, V. E., Marks, H. M., & Byrd, T. (1994). Sexism in single-sex and coeducational independent secondary school classrooms. *Sociology of Education*, 67, 92–120.

Lew, J. (2005). *Asian Americans in class: Charting the achievement gap among Korean American youth*. New York: Teachers

College Press.

Lewis, A. (2003). *Race in the schoolyard: Negotiating the color line in classrooms and communities.* New Brunswick, NJ: Rutgers University Press.

Lipman, P. (2003). *High stakes education: Inequality, globalization, and urban school reform.* New York: RoutledgeFalmer.

Lleras, C. (2008). Race, racial concentration, and the dynamics of educational inequality across urban and suburban schools. *American Educational Research Journal,* 45, 886–912.

Losen, D. & Orfield, G. (Eds.). (2002). *Racial inequity in special education.* Cambridge, MA: Harvard Education Publishing Group.

Lucas, S. R. (1999). *Tracking inequality: Stratification and mobility in American high schools.* New York: Teachers College Press.

Lucas, S. R. (2001). Race, class, and tournament track mobility. *Sociology of Education,* 74, 139–156.

Lucas, S. R. (2002). Socio-demographic diversity, correlated achievement, and de facto tracking. *Sociology of Education,* 75, 328–348.

Macloud, J. (1995). *Ain't no makin' it: Aspirations and attainment in a low income neighborhood.* Boulder, CO: Westview.

Maher, F. & Tetrault, M. K. (2001, expanded edition). *The feminist classroom.* Lanham, MD: Rowman and Littlefield.

Mangino, William. (2009). The downside of social closure: Brokerage, parental influence, and delinquency among African American boys. *Sociology of Education,* 82 (2), 147–172.

McDermott, R. P. (1977). Social relations as contexts for learning. *Harvard Educational Review,* 47, 198–213.

McDermott, R. P. (1994). More than misapplied technology: A normative and political response to Hallinan on tracking. *Sociology of Education,* 67, 84–89.

McDermott, R. P. & Varenne, H. (1995). Culture as disability. *Anthropology and Education Quarterly,* 26 (3), 324–348.

McDonaugh, P. (1994). Buying and selling higher education: The social construction of the college applicant. *Journal of Higher Education,* 65 (4), 427–445.

Mickelson, R. A. (1990). The attitude–achievement paradox among Black adolescents. *Sociology of Education,* 63, 44–61.

Mickelson, R. A. (2003). Gender, Bourdieu, and the anomaly of women's achievement redux. *Sociology of Education,* 75, 373–375.

Mickelson, R. A. (2003). When are racial disparities in education the result of racial discrimination? A social science perspective. *Teachers College Record,* 105 (6): 1080–1114.

Mickelson, R. A. & Ray, C. A. (1994). Fear of falling from grace: The middle class, downward mobility, and school desegregation. *Research in Sociology of Education and Socialization,* 10, 207–238.

Morgan, Stephen L. & Todd, Jennifer J. (2009). Intergenerational closure and academic achievement in high school: A new evaluation of Coleman's conjecture. *Sociology of Education,* 82 (3), 267–285.

Neckerman, K. (2006). *Schools betrayed: Roots of failure in inner-city education.* Chicago: University of Chicago Press.

Noguera, P. A. (2004) Social capital and the education of immigrant students: Categories and generalizations. *Sociology of Education,* 77, 180–184.

Oakes, J. (2006). *Keeping track: How schools structure inequality* (2nd ed.). New Haven, CT: Yale.

Oakes, J. (1994). More than misapplied technology: A normative and political response to Hallinan. *Sociology of Education,* 67, 84–88.

Ogbu, J. U. (1987). Variability in minority school performance: A problem in search of an explanation. *Anthropology and Education Quarterly,* 10 (1), 312–334.

Ogbu, J. U. (with Gibson, M. A.) (1992). *Minority status and schooling: A comparative study of immigrants and involuntary minorities.* New York: Garland.

Ogbu, J. U. (1999). Beyond language: Ebonics, proper English, and identity in a Black-American speech community. *American Education Research Journal,* 36 (2), 147–184.

Ogbu, J. (2003). *Black American students in an affluent suburb: A study of academic disengagement.* Mahwah, NJ: Lawrence Erlbaum.

Ogbu, J. U. (2004). Collective identity and the burden of acting white in black history, community and education. *Urban Review,* 36 (1), 1–35.

Orfield, G. (2004) *Dropouts in America: Confronting the graduate rate crisis.* Cambridge, MA: Harvard University Press.

Orfield, G. & Lee, C. (2002) *Why segregation matters: Poverty and educational inequality.* Cambridge, MA: The Civil Rights Project, Harvard University.

Page, R. N. (1991). *Lower-track classrooms: A curricular and cultural perspective.* New York: Teachers College Press.

Pallas, A. M., Entwisle, D. R., Alexander, K. L., & Stluka, M. F. (1994). Ability group effects: Instructional, social, or institutional. *Sociology of Education,* 67, 27–46.

Persell, C. H. (1997). *Education and inequality.* New York: Free Press.

Persell, C. H. and Cookson, P. W. (1985). Chartering and bartering: Elite education and social reproduction. *Social Problems,* 33 (2), 114–129.

Plank, S. B., DeLuca, S., & Estacion, A. (2008). High school dropout and the role of career and technical education: A survival analysis of surviving high school. *Sociology of Education,* 81 (4), 345–370.

Power, S., Warren, S., Gillborn, D., Clark, A., Thomas, S., & Coate, K. (2001). *Education in deprived areas.* London: Institute of Education, University of London.

Ream, R. K. & Palardy, G. J. (2008). Reexamining social class differences in the availability and the educational utility of parental social capital. *American Educational Research Journal,* 45, 238–273.

Ream, R. K. & Rumberger, R. W. (2008). Student engagement, peer social capital, and school dropout among Mexican American and non-Latino white students. *Sociology of Education,* 81 (2), 109–139.

Reardon, S. F. (2001). Suburban racial change and suburban school segregation: 1987–96. *Sociology of Education,* 74, 79–101.

Riordan, C. (1985). Public and Catholic schooling: The effects of gender context policy. *American Journal of Education,* 93, 518–540.

Riordan, C. (1990). *Girls and boys in school: Together or separate?* New York: Teachers College Press.

Rosenbaum, J. (1976). *Making inequality: The hidden curriculum of tracking.* New York: Wiley.

Rumberger, R. W. & Gandara, P. (2004). Seeking equity in the education of California's English learners. *Teachers College Record,* 106 (10), 2032–2056.

Salomone, R. (2003). *Same, different, equal: Rethinking single-sex schooling.* New Haven, CT: Yale University Press.

Shavit, Y. & Blossfeld, H. P. (Eds.). (1993). *Persistent inequalilty: Changing educational attainment in thirteen countries.* Boulder, CO: Westview Press.

Spade, J., Columba, L., & Vanfossen, B. E. (1997). Tracking in mathematics and science: Courses and course-selection procedures. *Sociology of Education,* 70 (2), 108–127.

Stanton-Salazar, R. D. (2001). *Manufacturing hope and despair: The school and kin support networks of U.S.-Mexican youth.* New York: Teachers College Press.

Stanton-Salazar, R. D. & Dornbusch, S. M. (1995). Social capital and the reproduction of inequality: Information networks among Mexican-origin high school students. *Sociology of Education,* 68 (2), 116–135.

Stanton-Salazar, R., Chavez, L., & Tai, L. (2001). The help-seeking orientation of Latino and non-Latino urban high school students: A critical-sociological investigation. *Social Psychology of Education,* 5, 49–82.

Stevenson, D. L., Schiller, K. S., & Schneider, B. (1994). Sequences of opportunities for learning. *Sociology of Education,* 67, 184–198.

Stewart, E. B., Stewart, E. A., & Simons, R. L. (2007). The effect of neighborhood context on the college aspirations of African American adolescents. *American Educational Research Journal,* 44, 896–919.

Suad Nasir, N., McLaughlin, M. W. & Jones, A. (2009). What does it mean to be African American? Constructions of race and academic identity in an urban public high school. *American Educational Research Journal,* 46, 73–114.

Thorne, B. (1993). *Gender play: Girls and boys in school.* New Brunswick, NJ: Rutgers University Press.

Tyson, K. (2003). Notes from the back of the room: Problems and paradoxes in the schooling of young Black students. *Sociology of Education,* 76, 326–343.

Useem, E. L. (1991). Student selection into course selection sequences in mathematics: The impact of parent involvement and school policies. *Journal of Research on Adolescence,* 1, 231–250.

Useem, E. L. (1992). Getting on the fast track in mathematics: School organizational influences on math track assignment. *American Journal of Education,* 100 (3), 325–353.

Useem, E. L. (1992). Middle schools and math groups: Parents' involvement in children's placement. *Sociology of Education,* 65, 263–279.

Valenzuela, A. (1999). *Subtractive schooling: U.S. Mexican youth and the politics of caring.* Albany, NY: SUNY Press.

Vanfossen, B. E., Jones, J. D., & Spade, J. Z. (1987). Curriculum tracking and status maintenance. *Sociology of Education,* 60, 104–122.

Van Hook, J. (2002). Immigration and African American educational opportunity: The transformation of minority schools. *Sociology of Education,* 75, 169–189.

Velez, W. (1989). High school attrition among Hispanic and non-Hispanic white youths. *Sociology of Education,* 62, 119–133.

Walters, P. B. (2001). Educational access and the state: Historical continuities and discontinuities in racial inequality in American education. *Sociology of Education,* 74 (Extra Issue), 35–45.

Weis, L. (1985). *Between two worlds: Black students in an urban community college.* Boston: Routledge & Kegan Paul.

Weis, L. (1992). *Working class without work.* Albany, NY: SUNY Press.

Weis, L. (1993). White male working-class youth: An exploration of relative privilege and loss. In L. Weis and M. Fine (Eds.), *Beyond Silenced Voices* (pp. 237–258). Albany, NY: State University of New York Press.

Weis, L. (2004). *Class reunion: The remaking of the American white working class.* New York: Routledge.

Weis, L. & Fine, M. (2000). *Construction sites: Excavating race, class and gender among urban youth.* New York: Teachers College Press.

Wells, A. S. (1995). Reexamining social science research on school desegregation: long-versus short-term effects. *Teachers College Record,* 96, 691–706.

Wells, A. S. & Serna, I. (1996). The politics of culture: Understanding local political resistance to de-tracking in racially mixed schools. *Harvard Educational Review,* 66, 93–118.

Wells, A. S. & Crain, R. L. (1997). *Stepping over the color line: African-American students in white suburban schools.* New Haven, CT: Yale UniversityPress.

Wenglinsky, H. (1997). How money matters: The effect of school district spending on academic achievement. *Sociology of Education,* 70, 221–237.

Wexler, P. (1992). *Becoming somebody.* London: Falmer Press.

Willis, P. (1981). *Learning to labor: How working class students get working class jobs.* New York: Columbia University Press.

Wrigley, J. (Ed.). (1992). *Education and gender equality.* London: Falmer.

Yaffe, D. (2007). *Other people's children: The battle for justice and equality in New Jersey's schools.* New Brunswick, NJ: Rutgers University Press.

Young, Michael. (1958). *The rise of the meritocracy, 1870–2033: An essay on education and equality.* London: Thames and Hudson.

PART **VI**

Educational Reform and Policy

From the 1980s, standards-based reform has dominated educational policy. In 1983, the National Commission on Educational Excellence's report *A Nation at Risk* argued that U.S. schools were mediocre at best and that as a nation we faced falling behind the Japanese and Germans, whose students performed better on international examinations of reading, science, and mathematics. Following this report, state and national educational policies stressed higher standards for all students. By the beginning of the twenty-first century, the concern of the 1960s and 1970s for equity began to reemerge, with President George W. Bush's 2001 No Child Left Behind Act (NCLB) requiring the elimination of the achievement gap among different groups by 2014. Today, educational policymakers are concentrating on setting high academic standards for all children and ensuring that all children can meet them. Although most policymakers support the goal of eliminating the achievement gaps, there is disagreement as to whether this can be done and, if so, how. A critical question is whether non-school factors such as poverty, family dysfunction, or health and environmental problems make the elimination of the gap, especially for poor children, unrealistic, or whether these factors are simply excuses for ineffective schools. The following readings examine different types of educational reforms and provide empirical evidence for considering this difficult question.

Chapter 25, "Refusing to Leave Desegregation Behind: From Graduates of Racially Diverse Schools to the Supreme Court" by the Columbia University sociologist Amy Stuart Wells and her colleagues Jacquelyn Duran and Terrenda White, examines the June 2007 U.S. Supreme Court decision in the Louisville and Seattle voluntary school desegregation cases, which made it more difficult for district officials to racially balance their schools. The authors present an analysis of prior research on the long-term effects of attending racially diverse schools on their adult graduates as well as new data from interviews with graduates of desegregated schools in Louisville and Seattle. Based on their findings, the authors argue that the court decision was shortsighted given the effects of segregation and the experiences of the graduates of the two systems.

Chapter 26, "False Promises: The School Choice Provisions in No Child Left Behind" by the University of North Carolina, Chapel Hill, sociologist Douglas Lauen, examines the limits and possibilities of the public school choice provision in NCLB to improve educational opportunities for children in low-performing schools. Through an overview of the school choice debates and the implementation of the choice provision under NCLB, Lauen provides a sociological analysis of the effects of educational reform policies.

Chapter 27, "Our Impoverished View of Educational Reform" by the Arizona State University educational psychologist David C. Berliner, provides a critical sociological analysis of the limits of school reform. Berliner examines the pernicious effects of poverty on the lives of low-income families and the failure of educational reform to address these effects.

Questions for Reflection and Discussion

1   According to Wells and her colleagues, what are the long-term consequences of school segregation? Based on this research and the interviews they conducted with Louisville and Seattle graduates, do you agree with the Supreme Court's decision in the Louisville and Seattle voluntary school desegregation cases?

2   According to Lauen, what are the arguments in favor of and against public and private school choice? Do you think that all parents should have the right to send their children to a school of their choice? Do you think that low-income families should receive publicly funded vouchers to send their children to private and religious schools? Based upon Lauen's findings, do you think that the reauthorization of NCLB should include a private school choice option for children in failing public schools, funded with public dollars?

3   According to Berliner, can school reform succeed in eliminating the achievement gaps in the United States? Why or why not? Do you think schools have the potential to reduce these gaps, without the types of economic policies discussed by Berliner? How do you think teachers and principals in schools with low-income children would respond to Berliner's argument?

References

National Commission on Excellence in Education. (1983). *A Nation at Risk*. Washington, DC: U.S. Department of Education.

25

Refusing to Leave Desegregation Behind

From Graduates of Racially Diverse Schools to the Supreme Court

AMY STUART WELLS, JACQUELYN DURAN, AND TERRENDA WHITE

We have rid the world of Jim Crow, but in its place we have produced a new world of inequality. And we have created an elaborate system of doctrines in order to rationalize and justify it as being entirely consistent with everyone being equal before the law.—Balkin, "Plessy, Brown and Grutter: A Play in Three Acts," p. 1729

In June 2006, the U.S. Supreme Court agreed to hear two cases—*Parents Involved in Community Schools v. Seattle School District No. 1* and *Meredith v. Jefferson Country Board of Education*—challenging the constitutionality of local school districts' voluntary efforts to racially balance their schools. In June 2007, a 5–4 majority of the Supreme Court declared these integration plans in Louisville, Kentucky, and Seattle, Washington, unconstitutional based on the districts' use of "racial classifications" as one factor in assigning students to schools in a parental choice program. The ruling, therefore, significantly narrowed the options officials have to integrate schools and left educators, parents, and students across the country wondering what impact this decision will have on public education in our increasingly diverse society.

In the year between the Court's decision to hear these cases and its ruling, hundreds of social scientists and lawyers presented evidence to the nine justices on the harms of racial segregation and the benefits of integration. Indeed, the research-based evidence supporting the Louisville and Seattle officials' pursuit of greater racial balance across their schools is strong and credible (Brief of 553 Social Scientists, 2006; Lynn & Welner, 2007), even if it was eventually ignored or dismissed by four of the five Justices who comprised the majority in this decision.

The last of the five-justice majority—Justice Kennedy—wrote a separate opinion that acknowledged the implications of some of this research and was thus supportive of the districts' "compelling interest" in fashioning racial diverse schools. Still, Kennedy concluded that school officials must use more limited measures than Louisville and Seattle did to achieve their integration goals. Such possible measures, he wrote, include locating new school sites between racially distinct neighborhoods, redrawing school attendance zones, or targeting recruitment of students or faculty to schools of choice—measures that social science research suggests would be far less effective in overcoming racial segregation than the plans that were struck down.

In short, the reams of social science research supporting the two school districts' policies in these cases (known as the *Parents Involved* cases) did not play as central a role in the final outcome as many would have hoped, even though Justice Breyer's impassioned dissent relied heavily on research. Given the makeup of the Court and the evolution of its rulings on race-conscious policies, we should not be surprised. Still, we argue that researchers must continue to inform the debate on how we move forward as a nation from this decision. In fact, as school officials and communities across the country decipher their options, we think they ought to at least consider the evidence presented to the Court. This research can both help explain the costs of this decision and fuel the search for viable alternatives.

In this article, we present one important segment of the vast body of social science evidence made available to the Court via Amicus, or friend of the court, briefs. Here we focus on the research assessing the long-term effects of attending racially diverse public schools on adults years after they have graduated from high school. This "long-term effects of school desegregation" literature provides a window into the kind of long-range impact this decision could have on future generations and the broader society.

Yet perhaps what is most significant about this body of research on the long-term impact of attending racially diverse schools is that it speaks to two significant themes that have emerged from the social science research on racial segregation (in schools and the communities that surround them) and cut through the central legal issues in these cases. These two themes are:

1   Racial discrimination and its legacies still exist in the form of "structural inequality"—namely, segregation and unequal opportunities in housing, income, wealth, health, and education. Race-conscious policies, such as school desegregation, are often needed to overcome these legacies, which are often perpetuated across generations—even if the majority of Whites do not harbor overtly discriminatory views.
2   The "diversity rationale," or the argument that racial integration in schools and universities helps prepare future generations for a more diverse society, a global economy, and more racially/ethnically integrated adult lives.

Not only does much of the social science research support one or both of these themes, but some of this research, especially the work described in this article, demonstrates the ways in which these two themes are intertwined. For instance, we know the benefits of racial integration would not be so great if the legacies of racial discrimination were not so acute. As Justice Kennedy wrote in his opinion, "That the school districts consider these plans to be necessary should remind us our highest aspirations are yet unfulfilled" (Kennedy's Opinion, *Parents Involved*, 2007, p. 1). In other words, that housing segregation remains a prominent feature of our society means that inequality across separate communities and thus public schools is perpetuated from one generation to the next unless some policy or program breaks that cycle. Meanwhile, the research suggests that efforts to overcome this segregation often have profound effects, in part by dispelling stereotypes and myths on both sides of the color line. The so-called diversity rationale, therefore, is not only about students of different racial and ethnic backgrounds learning to get along, but it is also about a more hopeful future in which the structures of racial segregation and inequality can be dismantled by more enlightened voters, parents, and home owners.

This article, then, is part review of prior research and part presentation of new data collected for an Amicus brief we wrote for these two cases. In both the prior and the new research on the long-term effects of school desegregation on the people who lived through it—those who refuse to leave desegregation behind—it is clear that these two central themes are strong and interrelated, even as judges have tried to separate and distinguish them while relying more heavily on the diversity rationale and increasingly ignoring the historical and structural view of race in America today. In an effort to create a dialogue between these themes spelled out in the research and the jurisprudence in the area of racial segregation and inequality, we begin with a brief overview of the legal background of the *Parents Involved* cases and then discuss the relationship between the law and the evidence.

The Legal Background of the Louisville and Seattle Cases

More than 50 years ago, the U.S. Supreme Court ruled in *Brown v. Board of Education* that state and district policies segregating children based solely on their race violated the Fourteenth Amendment rights of African Americans to equal protection under the law. In 2007, the Court ruled in the *Parents Involved* cases that the decision of school officials to use race as one factor in their voluntary efforts to create more integrated public schools violated the Fourteenth Amendment rights of White students who did not get into their first-choice school assignments. According to the majority opinions written by Justices Roberts and Thomas in the *Parents Involved* cases, their ruling on the rights of White plaintiffs was wholly consistent with the spirit of *Brown*, which, they say, is about separating opportunity from race. The dissenting justices strongly opposed this argument and regarded the majority opinion as antithetical to *Brown's* vision of allowing for the use of race to remedy structural or systemic racial inequality resulting from not only de jure or state-sanctioned segregation but also the legacies of such segregation as well as other ongoing forms of discrimination—an argument that carried no weight with the majority.

How and why the majority of Supreme Court justices came to see the rulings in *Brown* and the two current cases as in sync with one another is the story of the evolving conservative jurisprudence in American law—an evolution that does not bode well for the role of research-based evidence in pivotal court cases in the near future.

From Milliken to Grutter: Narrowing What Courts Can Remedy in Terms of Race

For the last three decades, the Supreme Court has stated in a series of rulings on race-conscious policies—including school desegregation, affirmative action, or set-aside programs for minority contractors—that the research on structural inequality (i.e., housing discrimination and segregation, income and wealth gaps by race, or the lack of infrastructure and supports in high poverty communities) and its intergenerational effect does not carry much legal weight. Absent a specific and blatant act of de jure or state-sponsored discrimination tied directly to the institution or persons involved in the court cases—namely, a university, municipal government, or public school board (Balkin, 2005)—the courts are unwilling to consider the broader effects of historical and societal discrimination on students of color who are applying to universities or trying to gain access to more integrated K–12 public schools.

The logical conclusion to such an interpretation of discrimination is an understanding of the U.S. Constitution as "colorblind," meaning that once state-imposed segregation has been eliminated and remedied, the government must not use racial classifications at all (see Balkin, 2005; Lindsay, 2006; Verdun, 2005). Such an interpretation implies that any effort to classify people by race for any reason—even to prepare children for a diverse society (the "diversity rationale") or to assure that children of color who have had limited educational opportunities in our society gain access to better schools—will be unconstitutional.

This journey toward a colorblind argument, which is all but complete with the *Parents Involved* decisions, began in earnest in 1974, when the Supreme Court ruled in *Milliken v. Bradley* that suburban Detroit school districts could not be forced to participate in a metropolitan-wide school desegregation remedy unless it was established that school officials in these districts – and not the housing market that envelopes the districts—had conducted racially discriminatory acts that then led to the pervasive cross-district segregation. Furthermore, the Court ruled in *Milliken* that Black plaintiffs, who had already proved that both the Detroit Public Schools and the state of Michigan had discriminated against Black children for years, would have to prove that the suburban school district boundary lines had been deliberately drawn on the basis of race.

In other words, despite ample evidence of racial discrimination on the part of government and private entities in the suburban housing market in Detroit and elsewhere, the burden placed on the African American plaintiffs after *Milliken* was far too onerous. They would need specific, well-documented proof that each and every suburban district in a metropolitan area had purposefully discriminated against Black families and their children in order to gain a metropolitan-wide remedy. And by 1974, such urban-suburban desegregation plans were necessary to achieve any meaningful integration because race was such a salient factor in deciding where people would live and who would be kept out via zoning ordinances, steering, or intimidation.

Thus, the first powerful theme from the research evidence—the legacies of prior discrimination and how they maintain structural inequality and disadvantages for Black children—was soundly rejected by the Supreme Court in *Milliken* as a Constitutional claim to a meaningful desegregation remedy. Still, since then, many federal judges have supported the second research-based theme by ruling that universities and school districts have "a compelling state interest" in promoting racial integration or the diversity rationale. (NAACP Legal Defense Fund, 2005).

One of the most notable post-*Milliken* race-conscious policy cases was the 1978 *Regents of University of California v. Bakke* higher education affirmative action case involving the University of California at Davis medical school. In this case, the Court rejected the use of race-conscious preferences as a means of remedying the past societal racial discrimination that had compromised the educational opportunities of students of color for generations. Instead of supporting a *racial equality* goal in this case, the Court relied almost solely on the diversity rationale when upholding the limited use of racial classifications in higher education admissions policies.

Twenty-five years later, the Court's majority opinion in *Grutter v. Bollinger*, written by Justice O'Connor, "reaffirms that the Fourteenth Amendment prohibits a public university from employing race-conscious means for the purpose of promoting racial equality, and insists that the university's interest in attaining a diverse student body rests exclusively in its First Amendment right of 'educational autonomy'" (Lindsay, 2006, p. 136).

The *Grutter* case, therefore, established that the university has a "compelling interest" in admitting a diverse student body that is supported by its First Amendment right to further its educational mission and goals. Policies to accomplish that goal are OK as long as they are devised "narrowly" enough to achieve only that particular goal.

Thus, the central legal issue had shifted from what it was in *Brown*—namely the Fourteenth Amendment rights of African Americans who had suffered the consequences of racial discrimination in our society—to the First Amendment rights of the universities. This evolution of case law regarding race-conscious policies has been criticized for ignoring or denying the ongoing racial inequality in the United States. According to Lindsay (2006), the *Grutter* majority refused to afford any formal legal status to the goal of remediating historical discrimination that still exists today, albeit often in more subtle forms, and instead relegated all critical issues to the netherworld of the diversity rationale. "In doing so, it relieves the Court, and the rest of the nation, from having to confront directly the question of why, fifty years after *Brown* and forty years after the 1964 [Civil Rights] Act, race-conscious public policy remains necessary to attain meaningful racial integration" (Lindsay, pp. 140–141).[1]

Yet as problematic as the *Grutter* decision may be in its failure to acknowledge the ongoing racial inequality that is well documented in the research literature and that makes policies such as affirmative action still necessary, it is not nearly as problematic as the majority opinion in the *Parents Involved* cases. When the Supreme Court agreed to hear the Louisville and Seattle cases in the summer of 2006, the post-*Grutter* case law suggested that in order to uphold the use of race in a student assignment or admissions policy, a majority of justices had to find that (1) the *goals* of such a plan comprised a "compelling state interest" that could be justified via one or both of the research-based themes described above and (2) that the *means* of achieving the goals are "narrowly tailored" enough to achieve *only* the compelling-interest goals. Given this legal precedent at the time, we and hundreds of other social scientists thought that perhaps our Amicus briefs describing the body of research supporting local school districts' "compelling state interest" in avoiding racial segregation could make a difference in these cases.

From Grutter to Meredith—Moving Closer to "Colorblindness"

By the early 2000s, the Jefferson County Public Schools in Louisville and the Seattle Public Schools had both shifted from old-fashioned desegregation policies that assigned students to schools to achieve racial integration to newer, choice-oriented policies that allowed parents and students to apply to their favorite schools. The districts then considered applicants' race as one factor in assigning them to one of their top-choice schools. This practice allowed local officials to maintain some degree of racial balance within specified guidelines that reflected the makeup of the district as a whole, while still providing families school choices (Greenhouse, 2006; NAACP Legal Defense Fund, 2005).

Both court cases were initiated when parents of White students denied their first-choice schools under these policies sued the school districts, claiming that the use of race as a factor in assigning students to schools was discriminatory. The districts responded to these claims by presenting evidence that, among other things, the vast majority of students of all races got their first- or second-choice schools (93% in Louisville) and that school officials had a "compelling state interest" in assuring that the public schools remained racially integrated after years of school desegregation efforts had yielded many positive results.

For instance, the Seattle School Board argued that diversity in public schools "fosters racial and cultural understanding, which is particularly important in a racially and culturally diverse society such as ours" (*Parents Involved v. Seattle*, 2005, p. 21). The Jefferson County Board of Education provided extensive evidence of the positive correlation between school desegregation and better student outcomes (*Meredith v. Jefferson County Board of Education*, 2006). Because neither Louisville's nor Seattle's student assignment plans were court-ordered remedies (although Louisville once had such an order), the central issue for the Supreme Court to decide in these two cases was whether locally elected school boards are allowed to racially integrate schools on their own accord, absent a court order or recent evidence of state-mandated or de jure racial segregation.

In other words, the question answered in this ruling was whether school officials had a "compelling state interest" to voluntarily address the legacies of prior discrimination—state-sanctioned or not—which continue to shape housing patterns and thus school enrollments. Furthermore, the Court was asked whether the race-conscious student assignment plans were "narrowly tailored" to achieve the compelling interest.

The answer from the Court was complicated on the first "compelling interest" issue because of Kennedy's separate opinion. But on the second issue, on whether the Louisville and Seattle plans were narrowly tailored to accomplish that goal without infringing on the rights of White students, the majority of the Court, including Justice Kennedy, clearly said "no."

Furthermore, the *Parents Involved* decision was striking in its shift toward a "colorblind" interpretation of the Constitution, rendering any race-conscious policy problematic. Taking the conservative legal argument about race described above to its logical conclusion, four of the justices implied that race-conscious policies are permissible only as a short-term remedy to dismantle de jure or Jim Crow segregation and not as a remedy for the legacies of that entrenched segregation or other forms of discrimination. In fact, except for Justice Kennedy's effort to keep the "compelling interest" window open slightly via the "diversity rationale," the majority of the Court appeared ready to dismiss it in the K–12 context.

Obviously, when the Supreme Court's jurisprudence moves so far away from the social science evidence on the issues at hand, which in this case not only strongly supported the compelling state interest argument but also the tailoring of the Louisville and Seattle plans, researchers have to wonder what our role can and will be in critical court cases. In the following section of this article, we speak more broadly about the connections between the evolving legal issues in these cases and the social science research. We then consider these issues more specifically in reference to the growing body of research evidence on the long-term effects of school desegregation as it becomes increasingly clear just how large the rift between the research and the recent Supreme Court ruling is.

Legal Questions and Social Science Evidence

The research evidence on racial segregation and desegregation provides complicated answers to a complicated set of questions about ongoing racial inequality in the United States—how it came to be, why it is perpetuated, and how to interrupt it. Indeed, as we noted above, when we examine the research on both the causes and consequences of racial segregation, we see two important themes emerge from the analyses.

1   Racial discrimination and its legacies still exist in the form of "structural inequality"—namely segregation and unequal opportunities in housing, income, wealth, health, and education. Thus, race-conscious policies, such as school desegregation, are often needed to overcome these legacies, which are often perpetuated across generations—even if the majority of Whites do not harbor discriminatory views.
2   The "diversity rationale," or the argument that racial integration in schools and universities helps prepare future generations for a more diverse society, a global economy and more integrated lives.

There is a body of solid research that strongly suggests that ongoing racial segregation, especially in housing and thus public schools, has not happened by accident; there are "structural" or societal reasons why they still exist (Sethi & Somanathan, 2004). In fact, for the last century, many public policies—federal, state, and local—have facilitated the development of separate and unequal neighborhoods and schools, and many current policies maintain this inequality. For instance, although we no longer have Jim Crow laws or blatant mandated separation of the races, we do allow local communities, homeowners, realtors, and lenders to maintain a great deal of control over who has access to what neighborhoods. The vast majority of poor people and people of color still lack access to the most desirable neighborhoods and thus the most desirable public schools (Drier, Mollenkopf, & Swanstrom, 2004). Furthermore, Blacks and Latinos who have faced such discrimination firsthand or know of family members or friends who have had such experiences are less likely to try to move into predominantly White and more affluent communities. They may lack information about such communities and their better resourced public schools when looking for a place to live because of their segregated social networks (de Souza Briggs, 2005)

This complicated web of factors is the present-day legacy of historical racial discrimination and its intergenerational effect on poor students of color. According to the Amicus brief filed in the Louisville and Seattle cases by the Caucus for Structural Equality, "Racial inequality is perpetuated by the interaction of numerous institutions, and does not require purposeful racism or malicious state action to continue. These dynamics, undisturbed, will persist because they operate in a vicious, reinforcing circle of causation" (Brief for the Caucus for Structural Equality as *Amici Curiae*, 2006).

Research on school desegregation strongly suggests that these policies help break that cycle of segregation and create greater social mobility for African Americans by allowing them access to more prestigious schools (see for example, Wells & Crain, 1994, 1997). Furthermore, there is ample evidence that the Black-White achievement gap closed more quickly during the years of racial integration of public schools than during any other period in the nation's history. This strongly suggests that providing Black and Latino students greater access to predominantly White schools helped to dismantle part of that structure of racial inequality (Grissmer, Flanagan, & Williamson, 1998).

Social science research strongly supports the conclusion that racial integration is better than racial segregation for the society as a whole. Overall, it improves intergroup relations and cross-racial understanding and acceptance. It also is more likely to reduce racial prejudice and fear or distrust of people from different backgrounds by enabling students to understand people of different races. Therefore, the research findings consistently demonstrate that racial diversity in K–12 public schools helps to prepare children of all racial backgrounds for our increasingly diverse society and global economy (Brief of 553 Social Scientists, 2006; Wells, Holme, Revilla, & Atanda, in press). Research evidence such as this constitutes what some legal scholars have dubbed the "diversity rationale" in cases regarding affirmative action and school desegregation (Balkin, 2005; Lindsay, 2006).

In other words, the research to date on school desegregation clearly supports the efforts of the two school districts in these cases. Research findings on both structural inequality and the diversity rationale demonstrate that these school districts not only had a compelling state interest in implementing their voluntary desegregation plans, but also that they needed to tailor the plans the way they did to achieve their goals and stabilize each school in the district over time (see Wells and Frankenberg, 2007). What is more, this evidence suggests that these two research themes – structural inequality and the diversity rationale—are not distinct or separate, but intertwined and connected and that giving credence to both would imply a different interpretation of the Fourteenth Amendment than that of the "colorblind" perspective. The Amicus brief that we filed with the Supreme Court for these two cases presented new social science evidence from graduates of diverse schools in Louisville and Seattle and a brief review of prior research on desegregation's graduates. In refusing to leave desegregation behind, adult graduates of school desegregation speak to the central legal issue in these cases – namely the districts' "compelling state interest" as it is reflected in both of the intertwined research themes discussed above—the "diversity rationale" and "structural inequality" as a legacy of prior and on-going racial discrimination. In the following sections of this article, we illustrate these themes across the prior and current research on the generation of Americans who experienced school desegregation firsthand.

What We Already Knew: An Overview of the Long-Term Effects Research

The research literature on the long-term effects of attending a racially mixed public school suggests that many of the effects of such an experience are not realized until long after students have graduated from high school. As adults, former students can better assess ways in which their school experiences influenced their lives as employees, homeowners or renters, parents, and friends (Eaton, 2001; Wells, Holme, Revilla, & Atanda, 2004, in press). Therefore, although the bulk of research on school desegregation examines what is happening to students while they are still in school and their immediate academic outcomes (see Crain & Mahard, 1978; Wells, 1995), we believe that the long-term-effects literature is also highly significant, especially as it speaks to the two intertwined research themes discussed above.

Indeed, these studies on adult graduates of racially diverse public schools reveal the many ways their experiences speak to both the diversity rationale and the structural inequality findings that have emerged from other research on racial inequality and school desegregation. In terms of the diversity rationale, for instance, one of the strongest findings to emerge from research on graduates of desegregated schools is the extent to which their school experiences prepared them to be better citizens, workers, and community members in an increasingly multiethnic society. In terms of the structural inequality, it is clear that the school desegregation plans that these adults participated in as children provided the one, and often only, opportunity for them to cross the color lines that divided their neighborhoods and perpetuated the racial inequality in their communities. Thus, it also increased the likelihood that they would cross these boundaries as adults even as the structures remained in tact.

The following section of this article describes the theoretical framework, originating in the 1950s, that explains why integrated schools should, in theory, have a lifelong impact on students and the inequality in which they grew up. This is followed by a description of the original research on the long-term outcomes of racially mixed schools, which is primarily survey based and focused almost exclusively on the life opportunities of African American graduates of diverse schools. The second body of research on the long-term effects of desegregation is more recent and is a mixture of quantitative and qualitative work that examines how attending a diverse school changed people—their racial attitudes and understandings, and, in some cases, their life opportunities.

Why Going to School Together Should Matter: The Contact Hypothesis

In 1954, just months before the Supreme Court's ruling in *Brown v. Board of Education,* Harvard University psychologist Gordon W. Allport published a groundbreaking book titled *The Nature of Prejudice.* His basic premise was that one reason people become and remain prejudiced against those of different racial, ethnic, and religious backgrounds is that they lack meaningful contact with such people. Allport described various forms of contact and how they affect people's thinking about members of "out groups." He concluded that certain forms of intergroup contact are far more effective at helping people overcome their stereotypes than other forms. More specifically, Allport "challenged the notion that simple encounters among different people would be sufficient to reduce prejudice" (see Nagda, Tropp, & Paluck, 2006, p. 440). Instead, Allport (1954) wrote, "contact must reach below the surface in order to be effective in altering prejudice. Only the type of contact that leads people to *do* things together is likely to result in changed attitudes" (p. 276).

Allport (1954) noted that contact in schools or on athletic teams, for example, engenders solidarity and allows people to overlook differences and eventually overcome stereotypes. Schools, teams, and activities in which students of different races come together from separate and unequal neighborhoods and are asked to work cooperatively across racial and ethnic lines, Allport stated, can foster similar understandings and lessen prejudice. In particular, he noted that intergroup contact for children at a young age would be most helpful in overcoming prejudice because children are more impressionable than adults and have not yet formed static views. Such experiences early in life, he argued, would lead to lifelong comfort levels with people of different backgrounds.

Allport's theory about the optimal conditions of intergroup contact became known in the social science literature as the "contact hypothesis" (see Pettigrew, 1998). The basic tenets of this hypothesis are that prejudice reduction across groups is most likely to happen when intergroup contact is marked by the following four conditions: (1) participants have equal status, (2) a set of common goals transcends groups, (3) intergroup cooperation instead of competition is fostered, and (4) the contact has the support of authority, law, or custom (Pettigrew). Allport's contact hypotheses, therefore, provided the central argument for the creation of more integrated public schools, where, it was believed, such conditions could more easily exist than in other settings (Aronson, 1954; Towles-Schwen & Fazio, 2001).

At the time that Allport wrote *The Nature of Prejudice,* his contact hypothesis was a well-reasoned theory, but the research evidence on what happens to people who actually experience such intergroup contact, particularly in schools, was sparse. Fifty-two years later, social scientists have documented the veracity of Allport's hypothesis, particularly as it pertains to the long-term effects of attending racially diverse public schools, where, in most instances, at least some of the four conditions exist in one form or another. For example, on the athletic teams or other extracurricular activities in diverse public schools, students of different racial or ethnic groups often find themselves working together cooperatively toward a common goal while maintaining fairly equal status for all group members (see Wells et al., in press). This was not always the case in the academic realm of such schools, however, where students of color were often designated to unequal tracks and classrooms that reflected the larger inequality in the society (see Oakes, 1985; Wells & Serna, 1996; Wells et al., in press). Thus, the public schools and the desegregation orders that they faced provided some of the best settings for testing the contact hypothesis and its limitations—both in terms of the diversity rationale and structural inequalities that were sometimes reproduced within the schools.

Early Research on the Long-Term Effects of Racially Diverse Schools Suggests Intergroup Contact Increased the Opportunities of African Americans

The original body of research examining the long-term effects of racially diverse schools comprises several quantitative studies analyzing survey and other outcome data from African American graduates of desegregated schools. Conducted mainly in the 1970s and 1980s, this work explored the ways in which the racial balance of a graduate's school correlated with various postsecondary variables such as aspirations, expectations, college attendance, and career and housing choices. Overall, this body of research demonstrates that once Black students become accustomed to racially diverse settings in school, they have far more confidence in their ability to navigate and succeed in such settings as adults, leading to greater social mobility. In other words, the evidence from this literature strongly suggests that African Americans' experiences in racially diverse schools help them to navigate some of the structural barriers that perpetuate racial inequality. In this way, this research provides an excellent example of how the diversity rationale—or the benefit of learning to get along with people of different backgrounds—is intertwined with individual efforts to overcome structural inequality and the impact school desegregation can have on that complicate process.

The theoretical framework that best explains this process is called "perpetuation theory," derived by sociologists Braddock and McPartland as a way of explaining how Black graduates from desegregated schools moved into more racially integrated adult settings. Drawing in part on Allport's argument about the significance of interracial contact in overcoming prior attitudes (see Braddock, 1980; McPartland & Braddock, 1981), McPartland and Braddock added a structural element to perpetuation theory to explain how segregation tends to repeat itself "across the stages of the life cycle and across institutions when individuals have not had sustained experiences in desegregated settings earlier in life" (p. 149).

In fact, much of this early long-term-effects research focused on whether African Americans were more likely to choose, when available, more integrated environments as adults. Such findings could infer the extent to which African Americans with desegregated school experiences had learned not to overestimate the degree of hostility they would encounter in such settings or underestimate their skill at coping with strains in interracial situations (Braddock, 1980). Overall, the research showed that Black graduates of integrated secondary and elementary schools were more confident in their ability to navigate and succeed in racially diverse settings (Braddock; Braddock, Crain, & McPartland, 1984). Thus, as adults, they tended to challenge the structural barriers to mobility by attending predominantly White colleges, moving into more racially integrated neighborhoods and accessing jobs in diverse settings that few Blacks had occupied in the past (Braddock, Crain, McPartland, & Dawkins, 1986; Braddock & McPartland, 1987; Dawkins & Braddock, 1994; Wells & Crain, 1994). These findings and the perpetuation theory that supports them suggest that attending a desegregated school is highly correlated with African American graduates' ability to overcome both some of the structural inequality in the society by gaining access to higher status schools and thus better jobs and so on, and to become more comfortable in interacting with Whites—findings that support both themes discussed above (see Wells & Crain, 1994, for a review).

Wells and Crain (1994) concluded that much of the long-term outcome data on Black graduates of racially mixed schools suggest that they are much more likely than their segregated counterparts to have access to, and to make choices that place them in, integrated and more advantageous environments for the rest of their lives. Overall, this early body of research on the long-term effects of desegregation on Blacks empirically supports the argument that interracial contact in school helps Blacks to overcome perpetual segregation (Braddock, 1980; McPartland & Braddock, 1981).

More Recent Research on Graduates of Racially Mixed Schools Demonstrates Greater Cross-Racial Understanding and Fewer Structural Barriers

In just the last decade, a small but growing body of social science research has questioned the relationship between racially diverse school attendance and adult attitudes toward members of other racial groups. This work draws heavily on Allport's (1954) theories of contact as it has broadened the focus of the long-term-effects research from African American mobility and life opportunities—important structural issues—and racial attitudes to the impact of diverse schools on adults of all racial backgrounds, especially as it relates to the diversity rationale. Indeed, as many researchers have noted, there is now a large body of psychological and social psychological research that supports the legitimacy of the "contact hypotheses" in predicting the type of conditions that lead to more positive racial attitudes and a reduction in prejudice (see Pettigrew & Tropp, 2000, for a meta-analysis). What had been missing from the literature until recently was solid evidence of the long-term effects of such interracial interactions in childhood on adults of all races and ethnicities who experienced them many years prior. This more recent research—both quantitative survey studies and qualitative interviews—strongly suggests that such contact in schools has a long-lasting positive effect on former students' racial attitudes, making them less prejudiced, on average, than adults who did not have such experiences.

Recent Survey-Based Research on Long-Term Effects of Desegregation on Adults of All Races

Two quantitative survey-based studies that examined the long-term impact of desegregated school experiences concluded that adults of different racial backgrounds who experienced intergroup contact in childhood have more positive racial attitudes. The first such study, by Wood and Sonleitner (1996), examined the impact of White children's interracial contact in desegregated schools on their adult stereotype adherence and traditional anti-Black prejudice. They set out to question whether Allport's "equal-status contact" in a school environment, "particularly during the formative years, would engender more positive racial attitudes among young persons that would endure into adulthood" (Wood & Sonleitner, p. 1).

Analyzing survey data from 292 White adults in Oklahoma City, Wood and Sonleitner (1996) found that childhood interracial contact in schools and neighborhoods not only "disconfirmed negative racial stereotypes, but had a direct, significant effect on levels of adult antiblack prejudice even controlling for other relevant factors" (p. 1). These findings are especially significant because the sample of White adults who were surveyed included those who had had very little exposure to Blacks as children, thus providing a control group for the purpose of comparison. Even after controlling for many other factors, including family income and education level, Wood and Sonleitner (1996) found that childhood contact with Blacks in their schools or neighborhoods appeared to have the strongest effect on the White adults' attitudes.

In another recent study of adult racial attitudes in relation to childhood contact with members of other racial/ethnic groups, Towles-Schwen and Fazio (2001) found that for college undergraduates of different racial backgrounds, racial attitudes were correlated with their intergroup contact when they were children. They found a significant relationship between White students' positive interactions with Blacks in school and more positive racial attitudes once they were in college. Towles-Schwen and Fazio also asked these undergraduates about their parents' racial prejudice and found that "early positive experiences with Blacks are critical to overcome the awkwardness and anxiety felt by people whose parents are prejudiced" (pp. 170–171). Indeed, it was the nature and quality of the interaction that mattered, and not just the frequency. This theme is also present in the more recent, qualitative research on the long-term effects of desegregation.

The findings of these two studies on the long-term effect of racial integration on adults' racial attitudes speak most directly to the diversity rationale themes in the research, and yet, they also suggest that important structural changes—for example, greater housing integration—may be more likely to occur in a society populated by adults who have had such intergroup experiences as children.

Qualitative Research on the Long-Term Impact of Desegregation on Adults
As helpful as the quantitative research findings are, this mostly survey-based research tells us very little about how or why these outcomes occurred among graduates of desegregated schools. Two additional studies of the long-term effects of school desegregation employed qualitative methods—in-depth interviews with graduates of racially mixed public schools—and thus produced more detailed findings on how these adults' school experiences shaped and influenced their lives. The first such study was conducted by Eaton (2001) and entailed in-depth interviews with 65 African American graduates of an urban-suburban voluntary transfer program in Boston known as METCO. These adult graduates of the METCO program had, as children of color growing up in Boston, chosen to attend predominantly White and mostly affluent suburban schools. This study explained, through the eyes of the adults who lived through it, how and why this educational journey from Boston to the suburbs was meaningful and why it resulted in them leading more integrated lives.

Eaton's (2001) findings echoed and extended some of the central tenets of perpetuation theory and the earlier long-term-effects literature described above. For instance, she found that METCO graduates felt far more comfortable in racially diverse and predominantly White settings than their friends and family members who lacked such desegregated experiences. She also found that the METCO graduates tapped into powerful social networks in their suburban schools and that information about postsecondary school experiences, including the college application process and job opportunities, flowed through these networks.

The African American graduates in Eaton's (2001) study also talked about the downsides of participating in METCO, including the racial discrimination they faced in the suburban schools, the assumptions many White students and educators made about their families and backgrounds, and a sense of disconnection from their own communities. Still, overall, only 4 out of the 65 adults interviewed—or 6%—said that they would not repeat their METCO experiences if they had the chance. Such decisions, Eaton (2001)wrote, were influenced by "their discoveries that the exposure they had in suburbia comprised fair approximations and decent preparation for life as blacks in white-dominated America" (p. 21).

Once again, we see how the effects of school desegregation on structural inequality—access to institutions and networks—and on the racial attitudes and outlook of those who lived through it are intertwined and not either-or. In fact, this more in-depth, qualitative analysis of how desegregation changed the people who lived through it strongly suggests that attitudes change only as the structural inequality shifts in a cyclical manner. Thus, to suggest, as the Supreme Court has done, that we can separate the ongoing structural inequality from the diversity rationale, seems, as Allport (1954) himself realized, quite at odds with how people experience race in our society.

The second major qualitative study that informs the long-term effects literature within school desegregation research was conducted by Wells et al. (2004, 2009) from 1999 to 2004. This study entailed in-depth case studies of six high schools within school districts that had undergone some form of desegregation—either voluntary or court ordered—by the late 1970s. It explored how African American, White, and Latino members of the class of 1980 from these six schools understood their school experience and its effect on their lives—their racial attitudes, educational and professional opportunities, personal relationships, and social networks. As far as we know, this is the first comprehensive qualitative study of White graduates' view of school desegregation.

Wells et al. (2004, 2009) conducted nearly 550 interviews—between 80 and 100 per site—with graduates from each school and with the educators and policy makers who worked in or with the schools at that time. Clearly, one of the most powerful themes to emerge was that, looking back as adults, the 1980 graduates all valued their experiences in racially mixed schools more so than they realized when they were still in high school (see Holme, Wells, & Revilla, 2005). As adults, these graduates—White, Black, and Latino—realized that getting along with people of different racial/ethnic backgrounds was essential to their success in a global economy and increasingly diverse society. For instance, one graduate interviewed noted, "I just learned a lot by being around so many different kinds of people . . . you learn something different from them without them teaching it to you in a book or writing it down, you just absorb so many different things" (see Wells et al., 2009).

Still, the ways that the graduates made sense of desegregation and how and why it was "worth it" differed somewhat across racial lines. White graduates tended to emphasize an Allport-like view of how their experiences in racially mixed high schools had made them more open-minded and more accepting of people of other racial/ethnic backgrounds than other White people they knew. As for the graduates of color, African American graduates in particular, they noted that their experiences validated perpetuation theory because racially mixed schools made them feel less intimidated by, fearful of, or subservient toward Whites (see Holme et al., 2005).

In addition to the findings on changes in racial attitudes, the Wells et al. (2009) research also provides powerful evidence of the ways in which structural inequality–namely, racial segregation—was challenged and how this process was, in turn, affected by the shifting racial attitudes and perceptions. As the Wells et al. (2009) book, *Both Sides Now*, demonstrates, the promise and possibilities of this structural change were curtailed abruptly in the 1980s when political priorities shifted abruptly. Still, Wells et al. (2004; 2009) argue that the potential for greater change remains in the hearts and minds of hundreds of thousands of graduates of desegregated schools. For instance, one of their findings was that many, but certainly not all, White graduates of the six schools they studied said that they were more empathetic with the disadvantages many people of color face in a society with such pervasive structural inequality. In other words, these findings provide clear examples of how the research themes above—structural inequality and the diversity rationale—are intertwined and interconnected.

The studies discussed in this section are part of a second wave of long-term-effects research that continues to grow as more researchers embark on similar research projects. For instance, in our research in Louisville and Seattle, we discovered both new and old themes and much support for the theories of Allport and Braddock—both the diversity rationale and issues of structural inequality.

Graduates of Racially Diverse Schools in Louisville and Seattle: Weaving the Diversity Rationale and Structural Inequity Together across Their Lives

Knowing that prior research on the long-term effects of school desegregation spoke to the central legal issue in the cases before the Supreme Court, we wanted to explore the two prominent themes from that literature—structural inequality and the diversity rationale—as they related to the life experiences of Louisville and Seattle graduates of racially diverse schools.[2] Thus, we interviewed 42 graduates—classes of 1985 and 1986—of six high schools: Central, Fern Creek, and Louisville Male high schools in Louisville, and Franklin, Garfield, and Ingraham high schools in Seattle. These six schools were selected because in each city, they represented a wide range of student experiences given their different geographic locations in the districts, their curricular programs, and the social class and racial make-up of their student bodies by the mid-1980s. Still, in each of these schools, no one ethnic group made up more than 75% of the student body at the time these graduates attended them.

Because of the short time frame of this research (August and September 2006), we were not able to conduct the type of purposive sampling for diverse perspectives that was employed by Wells et al. (2009). Instead, graduates from Louisville and Seattle were sampled randomly in two different ways in the two sites because of differential access to listings of high school graduates in these two cities.

In Louisville, we had access to lists of all the 1986 graduates from these three high schools through the 20th reunion organizers. This allowed us to sample the graduates randomly from each list. In Seattle, the reunion organizers either did not respond to our numerous requests for class lists or would not give us the lists of their classmates. We ended up working with members of the alumni associations for each school. They agreed to send out messages about our study on the e-mail lists for the classes of 1985 and 1986, asking who would be willing to be interviewed. From the many respondents to those e-mails, we randomly sampled people to interview and ended up talking with people from a wide range of backgrounds. Still, the reality is that the Louisville graduates we interviewed were sampled and contacted out of the blue, having no idea who we were or what we were doing. The Seattle graduates we interviewed had all agreed beforehand to be interviewed for this study and had volunteered their contact information.

We interviewed a total of 19 graduates from the three Louisville high schools and 23 graduates from the Seattle high schools. In terms of the racial/ethnic identities of these 42 graduates from the six high schools, 22 identified themselves as White, 14 as African Americans, 4 as Asian/Pacific Islanders, and 2 as mixed race, including one who was half Latino and half White.

In each of these cities, students who graduated from high school in the mid-1980s first experienced desegregation when they were in elementary school—for most, beginning in the fourth or fifth grade. From that point on, until they graduated from high school, these students were either reassigned to schools outside their neighborhoods or attended schools in which other students were bused in from other parts of the city or metro area.

Seven of these interviews were conducted in person in Louisville, and the rest were conducted via telephone. Each interview lasted approximately 45 minutes—although they varied in length from 20 minutes to more than an hour—and was tape-recorded and transcribed verbatim. The transcripts were coded for themes that emerged from the interviewees' responses across schools and context, and the following findings emerged as the most salient experiences of graduates across the six schools.

Graduates of Racially Mixed Schools in Louisville and Seattle Said They Learned to Be More Accepting of and Comfortable with People of Other Racial Backgrounds

Like their counterparts in the six cities of the Wells et al. (2009) study, the Louisville and Seattle graduates we interviewed said they believe that their day-to-day experiences attending diverse public schools as children and adolescents did indeed change them in an Allportian way, making them more open-minded and thus more accepting of people who differ from them racially and in terms of their background and culture.

Louisville and Seattle graduates of all racial/ethnic backgrounds said that going to school with people of different races allowed them to dispel negative racial stereotypes and realize the similarities across groups—that people are people—while at the same time appreciating and enjoying the cultural difference. This was clearly the most powerful and overwhelming theme to emerge from this systematically collected interview data, and it speaks directly to the diversity rationale of *Bakke* and *Grutter*. Yet, as we illustrate below, it also speaks to the theme about structural inequality and how separate and unequal the lives of these graduates were before their schools brought them together and provided a space in which they could cross significant boundaries.

For instance, a White graduate of Franklin High School in Seattle noted that if he had not gone to a racially diverse school,

I just think that I wouldn't be as comfortable as I am with people of a variety of races. That's just plain and simple. I think that growing up, going to schools, high school and before, that were racially diverse, helped you to be comfortable with people of different backgrounds, and makes you more accepting of differences in the world.

What is most compelling about this finding as it relates to public K–12 schools is that the graduates of these schools and others like them explained that they had to *be there*—that what they learned about getting along with people of other backgrounds could not be learned from textbooks or films. They said they had to be in these schools on a daily basis, walking through the halls and experiencing the kind of intergroup contact that Allport wrote about.

For instance, echoing many of the other former students we interviewed, a White male graduate of Garfield High School in Seattle described his involvement in extracurricular activities as a place where equal-status interactions would occur and thus where racial stereotypes were dispelled and meaningful friendships developed. He said that activities such as band, drama, and any kind of sports team provided the settings in which students came together across racial lines and it didn't "matter where you come from."

He explained, based on his own experiences and those of his classmates, that

there's a camaraderie that builds rather quickly when you play sports or if you're part of a band or whatever. That seems to be the tangible thing that really breaks down the racial barrier because if you can hang on the field or in the band room, you definitely can hang with those different backgrounds, and I think that was probably why, or probably how that all worked out.

This Garfield graduate spoke for virtually every Louisville and Seattle graduate we interviewed when he explained how these contacts in his public schools changed him:

I think it was very, very, very influential and very important, and I think I'm a stronger person for having dealt with such a diverse background and having friends of all different backgrounds. I think I just feel more well rounded, I feel stronger as an individual, and I feel definitely more confident every day that I walk around in any kind of area.

Feeling "stronger," more "confident," and more "comfortable" in an increasingly diverse society was a powerful theme across these interviews. Yet, as with the Wells et al. (2009) research on graduates from six high schools, these experiences did play out somewhat differently across racial lines; African American graduates in particular explained their increased sense of efficacy when they found themselves in predominantly White settings. This finding resonates with the perpetuation theory described in the first section of this article and in the survey-based research on African American graduates of racially diverse schools. It reiterates the prior findings from other studies showing that African American graduates of diverse schools stated that they learned to feel more comfortable in predominantly White settings because they knew they could compete in such settings. In this way, the Louisville and Seattle data also imply the ways in which school desegregation policies begin to chip away at more entrenched structural inequalities that were developed and maintained over years of racial inequality. In other words, by crossing the color lines that were clear and rigid in these two cities, these students gained access to different networks and opportunities as they learned to be more comfortable outside their own segregated communities.

As an African American graduate of Fern Creek High School in Louisville explained, the "beauty" of attending desegregated schools is that it taught him about different cultures and "how to be a chameleon." He said,

I think if you're able to deal with it positively, it makes you a much more well-rounded person, because you learn about other people and . . . I think, I think it makes you a really strong person. And the great thing now is that I can, I'm really, I have friends from so many different cultures, and I could just about talk to anyone and I have no fear.

Some Racial Separation Still Apparent but Not Predetermined

The strong positive reactions that these graduates had to their experiences in diverse schools should not imply that their experiences were always easy or ideal. In fact, some of the same complications that we see emerge from the literature on desegregated schools across the country were woven throughout these graduates' stories, including the logistical challenges of attending a school far from their homes, occasional racial tensions, and some degree of resegregation of students across classrooms because of tracking practices, although this varied tremendously across the schools. These challenges of being the first generation to live through desegregated schooling led to personal hardships and sacrifices.

Furthermore, graduates from these and other racially diverse schools were quick to point out that in most instances, there were some social divisions by race, with cliques and close friendships at least loosely shaped by racial differences. However, it is also true that at all the schools attended by the graduates we interviewed, cross-racial friendships were not uncommon and that diverse cliques did form on a regular basis—especially those related to certain activities, such as athletic teams or clubs.

As one African American woman who graduated from Franklin High School in Seattle explained it, "I think most of my real close friends were Black, but I mean, I think people had no problems getting together during lunch time or doing projects together because they would try to get you into different groups, and I don't remember it ever being a big problem."

In fact, for the most part, 20 years after they graduated from high school, these adults see the barriers and challenges as lessons learned and remain more focused on the long-term benefits of attending diverse schools—benefits they say they did not fully realize until they graduated from high school and entered the workforce.

Louisville and Seattle Graduates and the Diversity Rationale: Desegregated Public Schools Prepared Them for a Global Economy and Society

Preparation for working in a diverse setting—the "diversity rationale"—was, for these graduates, by far the most obvious and pragmatic outcome of their experiences in diverse public schools. We learned that as adults, the graduates' work environments tend to be the most diverse settings in which they find themselves on a regular basis. Thus, the vast majority of graduates we interviewed in Louisville and Seattle said that at work in particular, they draw on the skills they learned in their desegregated public schools, skills of getting along and feeling comfortable with people of divergent backgrounds and cultures.

According to another African American male graduate of Fern Creek High School in Louisville,

Being with people, once you do get out into the real world, you know, the work world, being able to like to know that you grew up with different cultures and know how people interact and how they think and feel and so forth, versus . . . say if I were White and worked around all White people, and then went to an environment that was predominantly Black, it would be—I would feel uncomfortable and wouldn't know how to interact with them and . . . comfortable on my job and so forth.

Another way that graduates understand the relationship between their school experiences and their ability to navigate diverse and complex work environments is to talk about how their intergroup contacts as young people changed their "worldview"—their outlook on how to interact with members of different races, and the parts of the city, country, or globe where other racial groups live. White graduates, for instance, talked about being comfortable in jobs that take them to places where few White people frequent.

As a White woman who graduated from Garfield High School in Seattle and now works as a social worker in that city explained,

> I definitely think that being at Garfield, in a very racially diverse school, impacted my whole sort of worldview, and it's something I look back at all the time, and I feel like it, um, gave me lots of benefits that people I know who were in, um um, racially less diverse schools don't have.

Her distinct worldview, this graduate explained, had a strong impact on the choices she has made since. For instance, she said that her high school experience influenced her decision to become a social worker and has made her more effective in her profession. She explained,

> I think it impacted what I chose and I also think that because as a social worker, I've worked with a lot of African American families, I felt like that was an easier adjustment to me than a lot of my colleagues. It felt comfortable and I sort of understood the culture in a different way than people who just maybe had read about working with African Americans.

At a more global level, this worldview of graduates who attended racially diverse schools allows those who work for international corporations to cross multiple cultural boundaries. The world, these graduates tell us, is getting smaller, and their jobs involve traveling that world and interacting with people of racial and ethnic backgrounds uncommon in the United States. The lessons learned crossing domestic U.S. racial and ethnic boundaries, even in schools that enrolled only Black and White students, serve these graduates well when they are called upon to cross other cultural divides.

A White male graduate of Franklin High School in Seattle explained his job for a global corporation as one in which he managed workers in 60 different countries. He said he would travel to these different countries, where he would have to supervise and train workers from a wide range of backgrounds. He said that it was "hugely important" for him to be able to understand and relate to cultural difference beyond the different ethnicities living in America."

And yet, he noted that attending Franklin High School, with its mix of Asians, Blacks, and Whites, still provided a "step down that path of being comfortable with people of a variety of races."

Overcoming Structural Inequality: Without Diverse Public Schools, Most Graduates Would Have Grown Up in Racial Isolation

In a society in which housing patterns, places of worship, and social circles are often segregated by race, diverse public schools have been, for many students, the only institutions in which cross-racial interaction and understanding can occur. They have also too often been historically the only institutions in our society in which students of color can gain access to predominantly White and prestigious institutions.

We know from social science research on segregation that U.S. housing patterns are, and have been for several decades, highly divided along racial lines, with African American residents the most segregated population (see Cutler, Glaeser, & Vigdor, 1999; Farley & Squires, 2005). These segregated patterns peaked nationally in the 1970s, as the class of 1986 entered the public school system. Since then, segregation in housing has decreased only slightly—far less than would be predicted given the growth of the Black middle class over the last 40 years (Sethi & Somanathan, 2004). Furthermore, churches and other places of worship and social circles have also remained highly segregated over much the 20th century (Correspondents of the New York Times, 2001).

It is not surprising, therefore, that we learned from our research in Louisville and Seattle, as well as the six other cities examined in the earlier study, that the public schools were the only—or almost the only—institutions in which these former students had any meaningful interactions with people of other races. The public schools were often the only institutions trying to address the structural inequality along racial lines in the society.

A White graduate of Louisville's historically Black high school, Central High, explained that if the Jefferson County Public Schools had not created racially diverse schools, she would have grown up in a virtually all-White environment, and she would have always thought of downtown Louisville as a crime-ridden place where White people did not go. Had she not attended her urban high school, she said, she

would have been much more apprehensive about people . . . not just African Americans, but of any other race. I certainly would have been much more sheltered because, you know, living in this area, everything that you need is right here, so there would never be any reason for me to have a lot of interaction with anyone who wasn't middle class and White.

On the other side of town, this White Central High graduate's classmate, an African American woman, described the neighborhood where she grew up as almost exclusively Black. "I think there was only one White [pause], there was one, an older White lady there. We talked to her, but there was only one." Of her interactions with people of other races, she said, "mostly it was at school."

Meanwhile, on the other side of the country, a White graduate of Seattle's Ingraham High School explained that he would not have had "any" exposure to people of other races growing up if it had not been for "the desegregation of the schools at the time." He reflected on the degree to which he learned to dismiss racial stereotypes in his high schools and noted, "I would have had no other way of knowing. I would-n't have had any, any uh, interaction. I mean, the whole north end of the city, even now, is still probably way more White than it is anything else."

An Asian American classmate of this Ingraham graduate said that if she had not been in a racially diverse public school,

I can't say I would have had a lot of Black friends because . . . I lived in a very White community and I had Asian American friends that lived in the south end, so I really probably would not have known that many Black people. And ironically, my closest friends at my own high school, I'd say, were three quarters Black and one quarter White.

As an African American graduate of Garfield High School explained,

Overall, on a scale of one to a hundred, I would say attending an interracial school, a mixed school, 80% of it is . . . what helped me. Yeah. Because if I didn't have it coming up, I wouldn't have known how to handle it . . . getting along with people, understanding them and their culture, their ways, their style of dress, who they are, you know, whatever, whatever it was, it was definitely from my growing up, my schooling in Seattle.

These quotes represent a sample of what graduates shared with us in interview after interview, namely how their schools contrasted with other realms of their lives that were far more segregated. Recent research on these other realms of students' lives today—for example, housing and social institutions—suggests that the same is true for U.S. children growing up in the 21st century. Given the lack of public policies in place to address ongoing segregation in housing in the United States, efforts to allow children to cross racial boundaries—structural borders that grew out of a history of racial inequality—to go to school together have been, and continue to be, the closest we have come as a society to trying to break down these barriers.

Louisville and Seattle Graduates Also Noted That it Was Important to Have These Experiences in Diverse Schools When They Were Young School-Age Children
It was not only the experiences in diverse public schools that changed these graduates, they will tell you, but it was also the timing of these experiences in their lives. Many of the graduates we interviewed were adamant that it was important for them to have the interracial exposure at a young, impressionable age. They needed to grow up in such a school environment; they needed for diversity to become their "norm" in order to enjoy the full benefit of the diversity rationale of desegregated schools.

As an African American female graduate from Seattle explained, her experience at Ingraham High School, "because those were my formative years, was exceptional . . . it helped me to learn and deal with diversity and do it second nature, not as if I had to make a conscious effort or a focus." She added, "I think to have a racially balanced makeup and life in your formative years is key to success in society as a whole."

Similarly, a White graduate of Louisville Male High School said that he was well prepared to work with his computer company's diverse clientele because of his exposure to African Americans at an early age. He noted, "It's easier for kids to experience the diversity and accept it than it is to throw them in after they're 20, 25 years old and say, 'Here you are! Now everybody's different, now deal with it.'"

In terms of public policy, one of the African American Franklin High School graduates quoted above stated firmly that she believes

> it would help with racial relations if you start with kids when they're young. So I think exposing kids when they're young before they have the preconceived notions that we all develop as we get older, I think it would be a great thing and definitely something that I would advocate.

Louisville and Seattle Graduates Compare Themselves with their Parents or Peers Who Did Not Have Similar Integrated Experiences as Evidence that their Public School Experiences Shaped their Worldviews
Some social scientists argue that much of the research on the long-term effects of school desegregation on adults' racial attitudes is biased because of self-selection, meaning that only graduates who did not flee diverse schools are studied. In addition to the quantitative analyses cited above, which prove otherwise, and the less than voluntary nature of the desegregation plans that many of these graduates participated in, we add here a third form of rebuttal. The graduates we interviewed from Louisville and Seattle frequently compared themselves with other people in their lives who did not experience racial integration. These graduates, along with many others from Wells et al.'s (2009) study, were quick to realize profound differences between their racial attitudes and those of their more segregated family members and peers.

Many of the graduates contrasted themselves with their parents who had led, in most instances, far more segregated lives. For instance, a White graduate of Ingraham High School in Seattle compared herself with her parents' generation and to her own parents more specifically. She noted that although they are not "racist in any way," they lacked the life experiences that she had attending racially diverse public schools. As a result, she said, they were far less comfortable than she in settings with many people of color. She said that her education

> definitely expanded my sense of um, what my world is, and it's still that way. Like I can travel up and down the Pacific Northwest into the Puget Sound Corridor and feel comfortable just about anywhere. Whereas, you know, if I ask my Mom to drive south of the major freeway, she freaks out.

This same White Ingraham High School graduate married a White man who grew up in a "primarily White" school district outside the city. She said he wasn't exposed to people of other colors until he joined the Navy:

> And then he said he really put his foot in his mouth several times and [laughs] got in trouble a couple of times, unintentionally, trying to fit in with people of other colors, and not doing it skillfully because he had no, um, he had no roadmap for how to talk or how to act or what to say or what he shouldn't say or, he just was—he said he just was not experienced at all.

A White Louisville Male High School graduate also married someone who had little experience in racially diverse settings. He explained that his wife had attended all-White private schools growing up as he was matriculating through desegregated public schools in Louisville. He recalled,

> You know, when we first got married, she was scared to go downtown, and she still is, okay? She, you know, it's—and it's not that she's, it's not that she's prejudiced against Black people, but they're just different, and she doesn't, she doesn't know how to handle it . . . and I go down there today . . . I walk down any street downtown, and I feel fine because I know that they're just different people, and I know how everybody is.

Even more casual acquaintances who are uncomfortable around people of other races lead graduates of racially diverse schools to recognize their own exceptional worldviews. For instance, an African American graduate of Franklin High School in Seattle commented that attending a diverse public school allowed her to have an open mind: "Whereas I know some people who are African American, they just don't feel comfortable if they were going into a situation where there were all Asians."

As one White graduate of Garfield High School in Seattle explained,

> I don't know if I would be the same person if I did not have those experiences . . . that I had back then, I think I'd be a completely different person. . . . And that's just my own kind of analysis . . . I've just noticed that people who haven't been exposed to that, they're not as comfortable. . . . That's just the thing I find now later on in life that has helped me deal with people of different backgrounds . . . it's almost second nature just 'cause I grew up with it.

Clearly, this finding speaks to the diversity rationale theme that has so informed the Supreme Court's thinking about affirmative action in higher education. But it also speaks clearly to the ways in which life experiences tend to perpetuate themselves across the life course to either reinforce structural inequality and segregation along racial lines, or to begin to break it down. Graduates of desegregated schools in this and other studies believe that they are more likely to be racial border crossers than are other adults they know who grew up in more segregated circumstances. Their comfort levels within racially diverse spaces make them more likely to challenge the separate and unequal structures that perpetuate racial inequality. This analysis also relates to these graduates' understanding of what is good for their own children and the boundaries they are willing to cross to accomplish their goals. In other words, the voices of these graduates help us see what the majority of the U.S. Supreme Court refuses to acknowledge: how intertwined the structures of inequality and the attitudes about diversity continue to be.

The Louisville and Seattle Graduates, Echoing National Opinion Polls, Say They Want their Children to Attend Racially Diverse Schools and They Want Some Degree of School Choice
The graduates of racially mixed schools know firsthand what the short-and long-term benefits of such diversity are, and they tend to have very strong opinions, couched in their own experiences, about

the importance of school diversity for their children. Thus, their opinions about what they want for their own children tend to be even more strongly in favor of school-level diversity than those of the public as a whole. Indeed, the vast majority of today's parents, no matter what their race or ethnicity, say that it is either very important or somewhat important for their children to attend racially diverse public schools (see Metropolitan Center for Urban Education, 2005). In one survey, the results showed that the vast majority of parents—66% of White parents and 80% of Black parents—said this (Public Agenda, 1998).

The graduates we interviewed reflected such sentiment, only more vociferously. For instance, the White Louisville Male High School graduate discussed above whose wife attended a mostly White school said that he would be "uncomfortable" if their children were in such an all-White school:

> I want them to realize that there, you know, are different people . . . I want them to realize that everybody doesn't think alike, and everybody doesn't do things the exact same way . . . I don't want them to grow up to think that, well, see, you know, if you don't think like me, then you're not worth talking to, that kind of thing.

Echoing this sentiment and the views of many of the graduates we interviewed, an African American woman who attended Fern Creek High School in Louisville explained why she wanted her son to attend a racially diverse school:

> There's a mixture, and that's what they need. If you don't have that in a school, then that person is setting theirself up for the fall, 'cause they're not learning nothing, they're not learning to cope or deal with people in the long run. You kind of . . . you see where I'm going?

Such a perspective often leads these graduates to critique other parents who place their children in more homogeneous school settings. As one black Ingraham High School graduate from Seattle explained,

> I would like my child to have a real view of what the world is—the world is not really made of one race. And you know, I have friends whose kids do go to predominantly Black schools and they just don't, to me they act different, and, I shouldn't say act different, but they're not really used to be being around other people of other races or other cultures, and they're not being exposed to a whole lot. I think it makes for a more well-rounded child when they are exposed to different cultures.

And yet, these graduates are not naïve about the interaction between the ongoing structural inequality in our society and their longing for their children to learn to get along in a diverse society. They see the barriers they face in finding racially diverse schools in an era of fewer school desegregation polices and unceasing neighborhood segregation. In fact, one Garfield High School graduate, the White woman who is a social worker now, said that diversity is so central to what she wants for her own daughter that she and her husband moved from a predominantly White neighborhood to a more racially diverse neighborhood "so that she could grow up in that environment." Thus, this couple was forced to address the structural inequalities in order to gain the benefits of diverse public schools for their child.

Furthermore, the White Franklin High School graduate quoted above who once oversaw workers in 60 different factories argued from his global corporate perspective that it is fundamentally important for his son to attend a diverse school:

> I think it's very valuable and it's important, because the country's not getting any less diverse too. So to wall yourself off in a high-end private community and private schools, so you don't

see folks like there. If you want your child to be a leader in the world some day, they have to have those experiences.

In addition to this strong support for diversity for their own children, the graduates also agree that mandatory reassignment of students was far too problematic and that they wanted some degree of choice in terms of which racially diverse schools their children attend. Here, in the midst of these preferences, is where the ongoing structural inequality in our society makes things far more complicated. As a White Ingraham High School graduate explained, "in the United States, everybody wants a choice for something."

A White classmate, also from Ingraham High School's class of 1986, noted that in recent years, the debates have sometimes gotten quite heated on the north side of Seattle about which students will get to go to one of the neighborhood high schools. This graduate has a niece who went to high school at that time, and the graduate said that she was torn about what she wanted most for her niece. She admitted that she wanted her niece to go to school close to where she lived and that she would hate for that school to become an all-White north end school. In the end, she said, "I'm glad that she had a similar experience in high school where there was a wide range of diversity. So I guess that's a very long answer to say that, um, I hope they keep some kind of either choice or, you know, some type of desegregation program."

Thus, for the most part, this graduate and the others we interviewed do believe that the government has a role to play in creating policies that can both offer parents and students choices and assure that schools are racially diverse even as the neighborhoods are not. As one White Garfield graduate, echoing the sentiments of many of his classmates in Seattle and across the country, explained,

> I think that if the government can do anything, that's the one thing they have to do, is create always a diverse society and have people of different backgrounds learn together, because obviously we don't get along with certain religions and obviously we don't get along with certain colors because we're not diverse, we don't really understand things about other people, and it's just kind of tragic actually. . . . I think growing up in Seattle, going through the educational system, that idea of being exposed to all these different groups, it's just been the best lesson I've ever learned in my life

Conclusion

This article is both about the role of school desegregation—past and present—in the United States and about the possible future of our increasingly diverse society under a legal precedent that mandates colorblind public policies and thus the end to many effective measures to achieve integration. The focus of the Wells et al. Amicus brief (Brief for Amy Stuart Wells et al., 2006) to the U.S. Supreme Court, which included the research from our Louisville and Seattle data collection described above, was designed to help convince the Supreme Court of the local schools districts' compelling state interest in creating racially diverse public schools via voluntary, choice-oriented policies. Whether we examine quantitative studies of African American mobility from the 1970s or 1980s, or in-depth interviews with high schools graduates conducted in 2006, the social science evidence overwhelmingly supports the diversity rationale and thus the need for narrowly tailored race-conscious policies for public schools in the 21st century.

Beyond the diversity rationale, however, there is a historical legacy of racial inequality in our society that is still visible today in everything from census data and gated communities to school district demographics and the achievement gap. Although the U.S. Supreme Court strongly curtailed efforts to address this legacy directly a long time ago, there are many voluntary and unassuming ways in which school desegregation and affirmative action policies within educational institutions had been, since the 1970s, quietly chipping away at those structures. Although we are not naïve enough to suggest that educational policies will ever be enough to dismantle the larger inequality in our society, it is highly problematic that the U.S. Supreme Court has decided to curtail this one countervailing force—voluntary school desegregation. Although hundreds of local school district officials will continue to try and stem racial segregation in their public schools, their hands have now been tied considerably tighter than they were before this decision.

We argue, based on our research and that of many others, that in an era when technology and free trade are breaking down physical and economic barriers across cultures and traditions, to not prepare our children to embrace and accept differences to the extent possible—the diversity rationale—is shortsighted and irresponsible. But even more important, we need to question how we can maintain a healthy democracy in a society so strongly divided by race, social class, and ideology now that the Supreme Court's decision has made it increasingly difficult to challenge such structural inequality, in spite of a compelling rationale for greater school-level diversity.

According to an African American graduate of Ingraham High School in Seattle, who was answering a question about the importance of racially diversity in public schools:

> For me, I think that um, that is something that really needs to be [sighs] promoted, um, across the board in every city, in every state, as much as possible, so there won't be, you know, the individuals that are not necessarily accepting or understanding of the differences between . . . people.

Notes

1 In fact, Lindsay (2006) and others admitted that in the *Grutter* majority opinion, Justice O'Connor did reintroduce the concept of racial inequality, not "as an argument per se for the constitutionality of racial preferences, but rather as a valuable and relevant experiential aspect of our nation's diversity" (p. 138). In other words, Justice O'Connor alluded to the disparate relationships that students of different racial backgrounds have with historical racial discrimination in this country. According to the ruling, however, such different experiences only add to the degree of diversity that they will encounter on a racially diverse college campus (*Grutter v. Bollinger,* 2003).

2 This work was funded by the Ford Foundation. The views expressed in this article are those of the authors and not necessarily those of the Foundation.

References

Allport, G. (1954). *The nature of prejudice.* Reading, MA: Addison-Wesley.

Aronson, S. H. (1954). Review of the nature of prejudice. *Social Problems, 2*(2), 113–114.

Balkin, J. M. (2005). Plessy, Brown and Grutter: A play in three acts. *Cardozo Law Review, 26,* 1689–1730.

Braddock, J. H. (1980). The perpetuation of segregation across levels of education: A behavioral assessment of the contact-hypothesis. *Sociology of Education, 53,* 178–186.

Braddock, J. H., Crain, R. L., & McPartland, J. M. (1984, December). A long-term view of school desegregation: Some recent studies of graduates as adults. *Phi Delta Kappan,* 259–264.

Braddock, J. H., II, Crain, R. L., McPartland, J. M., & Dawkins, M. P. (1986). Applicant race and job placement decisions: A national survey experiment. *International Journal of Sociology and Social Policy, 6,* 3–24.

Braddock, J. H., II, & McPartland, J. M. (1987). How minorities continue to be excluded from equal employment opportunities: Research on labor market and institutional barriers. *Journal of Social Issues, 43,* 5–39.

Brief for Amy Stuart Wells et al. as Amici Curiae Supporting respondents in Parents Involved in Community Schools v. Seattle School District No. 1 and Crystal D. Meredith v. Jefferson County Board of Education. (2006). Retrieved December 18, 2006, from http://www.naacpldf.org/content/pdf/voluntary/both_parties/Amy_Stuart_Wells_et_ al._Brief.pdf

Brief for the Caucus for Structural Equality as *Amici Curiae,* Supporting respondents in *Parents Involved in Community Schools v. Seattle School District No. 1 and Crystal D. Meredith v. Jefferson County Board of Education* (2006) Retrieved December 6, 2006, from http://www.naacpldf.org/content/pdf/voluntary/both_parties/Caucus_for_Structura l_Equity_Brief.pdf

Brief of 553 Social Scientists. (2006). *Parents Involved in Community Schools v. Seattle School District No 1, et al.,* and *Meredith v. Jefferson County Board of Education, et al.* In the Supreme Court of the United States. Amici Curiae in Support of Respondents. Retrieved October 11, 2006, from http://www.naacpldf.org/content/pdf/voluntary/social_scientists/Brief_of_553_Social_Scientists.pdf

Correspondents of the New York Times. (2001). *How race is lived in America.* New York: Times Books.

Crain, R. L., & Mahard, R. E. (1978). Desegregation and Black achievement: A review of the research. *Law and Contemporary Problems, 42*(3), 17–55.

Cutler, D. M., Glaeser, E. L., & Vigdor, J. L. (1999). The rise and decline of the American ghetto. *Journal of Political Economy, 107,* 455–507.

Dawkins, M., & Braddock, J. H. (1994). The continuing significant of desegregation: School racial composition and African American inclusion in American society. *Journal of Negro Education, 63,* 394–405.

de Souza Briggs, X. (Ed.). (2005). *The geography of opportunity: Race and housing choice in metropolitan America.* Washington, DC: Brookings Institution Press.

Drier, P., Mollenkopf, J., & Swanstrom, T. (2004). *Place matters: Metropolitics for the twenty-first century.* Lawrence: University Press of Kansas.

Eaton, S. F. (2001). *The other Boston busing story.* New Haven, CT: Yale University Press.

Farley, J. E., & Squires, G. D. (2005). Fences and neighbors: Segregation in 21st-century America. *Contexts, 4*(1), 33–39.

Greenhouse, L. (2006, June 6). Court to weigh race as factor in school rolls. *The New York Times.* Retrieved June 6, 2006, from http://www.nytimes.com

Grissmer, D., Flanagan, A., & Williamson, S. (1998). Why did the Black–White score gap narrow in the 1970s and 1980s? In C. Jencks & M. Phillips (Eds.), *The Black–White test score gap* (pp. 182–226). Washington, DC: Brookings Institution Press.

Grutter v. Bollinger, 539 U.S. 306 (2003)

Holme, J. J., Wells, A.S., & Revilla, A. T. (2005). Learning through experience: What graduates gained by attending desegregated high schools. *Equity and Excellence in Education, 38*(1), 14–24.

Lindsay, M. J. (2006). How antidiscrimination law learned to live with racial inequality. *University of Cincinnati Law Review, 75,* 87–141.

Linn, R. L., & Welner, K. G. (Eds.). (2007). *Race-conscious policies for assigning students to schools: Social science research and the Supreme Court cases.* Washington, DC: National Academy of Education.

McPartland, J. M., & Braddock, J. H. (1981). Going to college and getting a good job: The impact of desegregation. In W. D. Hawley (Ed.), *Effective school desegregation: Equality, quality and feasibility* (pp. 141–154). London: SAGE.

Meredith v. Jefferson County Board of Education on Writ of Certiorari to the United States Court of Appeals for the Sixth Circuit. Joint Appendix. No. 05-915 (2006).

Metropolitan Center for Urban Education. (2005). *"With all deliberate speed": Achievement, citizenship and diversity in American education.* New York: Steinhart School of Education, New York University.

Milliken v. Bradley. 418 U.S. 717 (1974).

NAACP Legal Defense and Educational Fund et al. (2005). *Looking to the future: Voluntary K12 school integration.* Retrieved July 18, 2006, from http://www.naacpldf.org

Nagda, B. (Ratnesh) A., Tropp, L. R., & Paluck, E. L. (2006). Looking back as we look ahead: Integrating research, theory and practice on intergroup relations. *Journal of Social Issues, 62,* 439–451.

Oakes, J. (1985). *Keeping track: How schools structure inequality.* New Haven, CT: Yale University Press.

Parents Involved in Community Schools v. Seattle School District No. 1 and Crystal D. Meredith v. Jefferson County Board of Education 551 U.S.

____ (2007). Justice Kennedy's Opinion.

Parents Involved v. Seattle School District No. 1. U.S. Court of Appeals for the Ninth Circuit. No. 01-35450. D.C. No. CV-00-01205-BJR (2005).

Pettigrew, T. F. (1998). Intergroup contact theory. *Annual Review of Psychology, 49,* 65–85.

Pettigrew, T., & Tropp, L. R. (2000). Does intergroup contact reduce prejudice: Recent meta-analytic findings. In S. Oskamp (Ed.), *Reducing prejudice and discrimination: The Claremont Symposium on Applied Social Psychology* (pp. 93–114). Mahwah, NJ: Erlbaum.

Public Agenda. (1998). *Time to move on: African-American and White parents set an agenda for public school.* New York: Author.

Regents of University of California v. Bakke, 438 U. S. 265 (1978).

Sethi, R., & Somanathan, R. (2004). Inequality and segregation. *Journal of Political Economy, 112,* 1296–1322.

Towles-Schwen, T., & Fazio, R. H. (2001). On the origins of racial attitudes: Correlates of childhood experiences. *Personality and Social Psychology Bulletin, 27,* 162–175.

Verdun, V. (2005). The big disconnect between segregation and integration. *Negro Educational Review 56,* 67–83.

Wells, A. S. (1995). Re-examining social science research on school desegregation: Long-versus short-term effects. *Teachers College Record, 96,* 691–706.

Wells, A. S., & Crain, R. L. (1994). Perpetuation theory and the long-term effects of school desegregation. *Review of Educational Research, 64,* 531–555.

Wells, A. S., & Crain, R. L. (1997). *Stepping over the color line: African American students in White suburban schools.* New Haven, CT: Yale University Press.

Wells, A.S. & Frankenberg, E. (2007) "Creating Racially Diverse Public Schools After the Supreme Court Decision in the Louisville and Seattle Cases: What to do When the 'End' is Justified, but the 'Means' are Not." *Phi Delta Kappan.*

Wells, A. S., Holme, J. J., Revilla, A. T., & Atanda, A. K. (2004). *How desegregation changed us: The effects of racially mixed schools on students and society* (Final report from the Understanding Race and Education Study). New York: Teachers College, Columbia University.

Wells, A. S., Holme, J. J., Revilla, A. J., & Atanda, A. K. (2009). *Both sides now: The story of desegregation's graduates.* Berkeley: University of Califorrnia Press.

Wells, A. S., & Serna, I. (1996). The politics of culture: Understanding local political resistance to detracking in racially mixed schools. *Harvard Educational Review, 66,* 93–118.

Wood, P. B., & Sonleitner, N. (1996). The effect of childhood interracial contact on adult antiblack prejudice. *International Journal of Intercultural Relations, 20*(1), 1–17.

26

False Promises

The School Choice Provisions in No Child Left Behind

DOUGLAS LAUEN

Stratification and Equality of Educational Opportunity

Scholars have long debated the extent to which education enhances mobility chances or simply maintains existing patterns of inequality. On the one hand, social scientists have argued that mobility based on achievement, rather status maintenance, is a hallmark of the U.S. social system (Blau & Duncan, 1967). The U.S. educational system has been characterized as one with "contest," rather than "sponsored" mobility. Unlike the British system, in which elites induct a select group of youth at an early age to groom them for high-status positions, youth in the U.S. compete in multiple contests, with every effort taken to keep students in the game (Turner, 1960). Alternative views argue that through hidden curriculum and tracking, the U.S. system "cools out" the mobility aspirations of disadvantaged students, thereby reinforcing, rather than overturning, existing patterns of stratification (Rosenbaum, 1976; MacLeod, 1995; Oakes, 1985).

If the United States is indeed characterized by mobility through achievement, one must consider the rules of the game. To establish the legitimacy of contest mobility regimes and maintain social control, participants must believe that differential outcomes, and the rewards that flow from these outcomes, are due not to differential access to the resources necessary to compete in the contest, but rather to effort and merit. Stated in terms of education in particular, in order for success in school to be viewed as an effective mechanism to attain the rights and privileges of high status, all students must have access to high quality teachers, curricula, and schools.

Throughout the 19th and 20th centuries, promoting equality of educational opportunity has been a persistent goal of U.S. education policy. Expanding access has taken various forms over time, from extending schooling in rural areas, to ensuring that immigrants attended common schools in urban areas, to school desegregation, and, as some have argued, expanding school choice. Though expansion of educational opportunity has been a hallmark of the U.S. system, structural inequality and entrenched power dynamics have made providing students the same starting point a highly contentious area of public policy. Due to the relatively high level of inequality in American society and the decentralized nature of the educational system, efforts to use education policy to reduce inequality have faced political opposition and myriad policy implementation difficulties. While there is often widespread agreement among the public and policymakers that students *should* receive equal access to education, implementing reform has often foundered on entrenched interests seeking to maintain their advantages (Hochschild & Scovronick, 2003).

The expansion of school choice through vouchers, charter schools, and NCLB has been framed by advocates as a way to enhance equality of educational opportunity; critics claim that school choice would reduce, rather than increase, educational opportunities for disadvantaged students. The stakes of this debate have been raised now that school choice is being funded and encouraged through federal policy. The D.C. Opportunity Scholarship program, begun in the 2004-2005 school year, currently serves about 1,700 students who each receive up to $7,500 of federal funds to attend one of 68 private schools (about two-thirds of which are religiously affiliated) (Wolf et al., 2006). A policy that affects many more students and schools is the school choice provision in NCLB, which requires that students in schools that have failed to make adequate yearly progress (AYP) in consecutive years be given the option of transferring to a school that has done so. The implication of this provision is that because states and local school districts have failed to provide adequate access to educational resources to low-income children, the federal government must use its authority to regulate student enrollment policy.

In order to justify what has become a significant incursion of federal government power into educational policy since the original ESEA law was passed in 1965, the president and Congressional leaders sought to instill in the public and other members of Congress a sense that urgent reform was required to fix a dysfunctional educational system. The image of "freeing" students from "failing" schools was central in this effort. For example, upon introducing his educational agenda on January 23, 2001, President George W. Bush said: "American children must not be left in persistently dangerous or failing schools. When schools do not teach and will not change, parents and students must have other meaningful options."[1]

Not surprisingly, the exertion of federal authority over student enrollment policy has proved controversial and implementation of these provisions has been uneven across local school districts. In fact, one could argue that the school choice provisions have been remarkably ineffective. Despite the fact that 3.3 million students were eligible for NCLB transfers in the 2003–04 school year, only 31,500, or 1%, of eligible students actually transferred to a school that was making AYP (United States Government Accountability Office, 2004).

The purpose of this chapter is to assess the extent to which public school choice either through local or federal policy is likely to expand equality of educational opportunity. I begin by outlining some important design principles for school choice programs. I then discuss some different modes of school choice policy, with careful consideration of NCLB choice and its relationship to other forms of school choice. Though very little research exists on NCLB choice in particular, I review what social scientific research says about the potential risks and benefits of various choice policies. With the broader context of school choice research understood, I discuss the challenges local districts have faced when attempting to comply with the NCLB transfer mandates. I conclude by drawing implications for NCLB's 2007 reauthorization and for future research on NCLB choice.

The Promises and Perils of School Choice

The most common and least controversial policy of assigning students to schools is by geographic catchment area, with all students in a given set of neighborhoods going to the same neighborhood school. This policy is the norm in American education, in which local school district officials determine which students attend which schools through drawing attendance area boundaries. Neither parents nor school principals have much choice over enrollment decisions.[2] School choice advocates criticize this type of school enrollment policy for creating monopolistic conditions in which students are essentially a captive clientele. This view holds that these monopolistic conditions stifle both diversity of educational approach and educational excellence. In 2003, about 74% of students in grades 1–12 attend an assigned public school (Wirt et al., 2004). Ten years previously, in 1993, about 80% of students attended an assigned neighborhood school, one indication of the erosion of support for assigned public schools through the 1990s and early 2000s.

School choice advocates seek to replace the neighborhood-based school with a wide variety of schools tailored to fit the needs and interests of various student groups. Advocates argue that school choice can help parents both find a school that better fits their child's educational needs and potentially leverage school reform by promoting competition among schools for students. For example, a cultural divide between teachers and poor parents has been identified as a barrier to school improvement (Lareau, 1989; Comer, 1988). A goal of school choice policy, therefore, is to bridge this divide by allowing schools to recruit parents aligned with their educational approaches. This should promote parent satisfaction and trust if teachers and administrators adhere to these approaches and serve the needs of the students (Bryk & Schneider, 2002). Moreover, some have argued that schools in which educational values are aligned among staff, parents, and students may produce more functional learning communities (Coleman & Hoffer, 1987; Bryk et al., 1993). Therefore, choice has the potential to raise parent satisfaction, student engagement, and improve the incentives that influence school leaders.

Choice, if paired with deregulation of curricular foci, could promote a better match between family values and school mission. Promoting innovation of educational approach increases the likelihood of a match between student and family interests and a school's educational approach. If one assumes that the needs of students and families vary too much to be served by one type of school, a goal of school choice policy is to subvert the common school ideal, which promotes a unitary conception of educational values. In its place, choice policy promotes a wide variety of schools, each tailored to a particular conception of educational values, with the ability to attract students and families based on shared values: the "interests of children are best served in a decentralized polity giving maximum scope to free, chosen, communal relationships that are generally organized on a small scale" (Coons & Sugarman, 1978, 2). School choice advocates have argued that it is not the state's place to enforce conformity to one set of values: "Our problem today is not to enforce conformity; it is rather that we are threatened with an excess of conformity. Our problem is to foster diversity, and the alternative [vouchers] would do this far more effectively than a nationalized system" (Friedman, 1962, 97).

Education organized around a plurality of value commitments raises the possibility that school choice might harm social cohesion. While some voucher proponents have advocated reforms to create a system of pluralistic value competition—education as a "marketplace of ideas" (Coons & Sugarman, 1978, 102)—the fact that education is a public good paid for by tax dollars makes political contestation over curricular content inevitable. As controversies over the teaching of evolution suggest, matters of curriculum involve deeply held value commitments. Because schools are one of society's most important institutions of socialization and national identity, school curricula are fiercely contested.

From an egalitarian standpoint, therefore, school choice is problematic because it threatens the common school ideal of educating children of many different social, racial, and achievement backgrounds in the same institution. It has been argued that the common school has benefits for social cohesion and perhaps even peer effects on test scores if low ability and high ability students share classrooms. Therefore, allowing students to exercise school choice to attend schools that better suit their values, racial/ethnic preferences, or abilities, would harm social cohesion and may have negative spill-over effects on the students who remain in neighborhood schools. Expanding school choice could promote "creaming" (i.e., more advantaged students would be more likely to take advantage of school choice and leave less advantaged students in failing schools). Given that the social isolation of disadvantaged groups has been shown to harm student outcomes (Hanushek et al., 2002), one could predict that school choice could increase inequality in test scores, college enrollment rates, and incomes over time.

From a meritocratic standpoint, on the other hand, school choice could promote equity. The fact that highly motivated parents and children are able to gain access to alternatives to their neighborhood schools can be viewed as unproblematic assuming the admission rules are fair. In other words, in its ideal form school choice replaces the current system of school stratification based on race and class with one governed by merit, measured by test scores, effort, grades, or some other criterion. This could improve the incentives for families to seek out schools that serve their interests and for schools to attract and hold students who place a high value on learning (Coleman, 1992). Therefore, access to high ability peers becomes a result of a fair process rather than some combination of ascriptive characteristics.

While my characterizations of these two divergent viewpoints may be roughly hewn, these perspectives are critical to understanding whether expanding school choice will increase or decrease social inequality through changes in access to educational opportunities. I now turn to the particular policies that have attempted to expand educational opportunity through school choice, with particular attention to NCLB's public school choice provision.

Varieties of School Choice

As we might expect from decentralized educational system in the U.S., choice policy varies somewhat across the country. Most areas of the country allow some degree of choice within school districts, most states allow charter schools, and vouchers are quite rare. NCLB choice, which has largely been implemented within (rather than across) school districts can be viewed as a form of intradistrict choice that has been mandated by the federal government onto local school districts. Before summarizing the features of the NCLB choice provisions, I outline the other varieties of choice to provide a context for understanding the policy environment into which NCLB choice is being implemented.

Intradistrict Choice

A major change to the traditional mode of catchment area student assignment came with busing, or mandatory student assignment in the 1960s. Busing, imposed by federal judges as a remedy for school segregation, proved to be very unpopular with politicians and many community groups (Orfield & Eaton, 1996). While busing has been largely abandoned as a remedy for segregation, voluntary student assignment programs, such as magnet schools, have proven to be longer lived. These programs encourage racial integration by creating enriched learning environments in minority schools to attract white (and now Asian-American) students to enroll. Concurrently with efforts to promote racial integration, school districts also responded to the desire of parents for separate learning environments for students with unique needs. The addition of these types of programs increased the options available for most students, but within certain limits. Students generally had to meet certain criteria to be admitted to such schools, and the schools were subject to many of the same regulations and collective bargaining agreements as other schools. There are currently 1,736 magnet schools in 28 states (Kafer, 2005).

More recently, other forms of public school choice have greatly expanded the options available to American students. Intradistrict choice allows students to attend traditional neighborhood schools or specialized programs within larger schools. Selection criteria vary across districts, schools, and programs, but these options often involve interest in specialized curriculum or educational approaches, such as occupationally-focused curriculum, military academies, international baccalaureate academics, foreign language academics, and the like. Intradistrict choice can provide a relatively high degree of both density and diversity of schooling choices, but student selection criteria can be highly regulated, requiring a certain level of test score achievement, grades, and lack of disciplinary problems.

Interdistrict Choice

Interdistrict choice, student transfers across school district boundaries, was held up as a remedy for school desegregation in the 1970s (Orfield & Eaton, 1996). While some urban districts (e.g., Boston and St. Louis) have been able to negotiate agreements with surrounding suburban districts to accept minority student transfers, suburban districts are under no obligation to enter into such agreements due to a 1974 Supreme Court decision (Milliken v. Bradley). Consequently, this type of school choice is relatively rare. Furthermore, because most school district funds come from local property taxes, not state income taxes, wealthy suburban school districts are unlikely to accept students from poorer urban school districts without compensation from state funds.

Charter School Choice

Since 1991, charter schools have emerged as one of the fastest growing forms of alternative governance in American education. Run by independent groups, charter schools are granted a fixed term performance contract by public authorities, usually local school districts. Currently, 40 states have laws authorizing charter schools (Kafer, 2005), though the extent to which charter schools are allowed to penetrate the educational marketplace varies widely. Most states allow only a limited number of charters in a small set of locales and allow local school districts to reject charter school proposals as they see fit. These laws tend to produce what might be considered "pilot" schools that do little to expand options for most students in the state. These schools are usually subject to desegregation laws and student testing programs, but have a great deal more autonomy over hiring, procurement, and curriculum decisions. In return, school charters may be revoked for failing to perform adequately. Unlike traditional schools, charter schools face a stronger form of accountability from above (in the sense that schools that fail to perform can be more easily shut down than traditional public schools) and from below (in the sense that all parents are clients who can vote with their feet). There are currently 3,400 charter schools in the United States (ibid).

States with more liberal charter school laws allow either multiple authorizing entities or charter districts. While most state laws allow only local school districts to approve charter applications, at least 11 states and the District of Columbia allow multiple public entities to authorize charter school applications (Allen & Marcucio, 2005). This tends to expand the density and diversity of choice options because local school district officials often view charter schools as a threat to the public schools under their authority. Student selection regulations are typically consistent across authorizing entities, with enrollment by lottery typically the method to handle over-subscription. The locus of accountability is more complicated in mixed authority charter states, with some charter schools accountable to local school boards, some to universities, and others to the state board of education or a state-level charter school authorizing entity. In rare cases, state laws provide for charter-only districts, most often in cases in districts subject to state take-over due to chronic under-performance or fiscal mismanagement.

Choice through Vouchers

Finally, parents in some parts of the country have the ability to receive a school voucher. Unlike charter school laws, states or local school districts do not directly contract for educational services, but instead provide parents with funds for use in a public or private school. In general, this form of educational governance provides for more autonomy and less accountability to public entities, though like charter schools, vouchers provide for more accountability to parents. Most publicly funded voucher programs are targeted to low-income students. The NCLB Act's choice provisions were, in fact, modeled after Florida's A++ Plan (Levin, 2004), which unlike programs in Cleveland, Milwaukee, and the District of Columbia does not means-test by income level. This plan provides "Opportunity Scholarships" to students in schools that fail to meet state benchmarks twice in a four-year period. In the 2003–04 school year, 650 students received such scholarships. In January 2006, Florida's Supreme Court ruled that this plan violated the state's constitutional provision to provide a "uniform" system of public schools. Florida Governor Jeb Bush's attempt to pass an amendment to the Florida constitution through the Republican-controlled legislature failed in May of 2006.

NCLB Choice

NCLB choice is a form of intradistrict choice mandated by federal law and implemented by local school districts. The NCLB school transfer provisions, which only apply to schools receiving Title I funds, are designed as a negative incentive for under-performing schools. They are triggered when a high poverty school fails to make "adequate yearly progress" (AYP) for two years in a row. AYP applies to standards set by states (and subject to the approval of the U.S. Department of Education) in reading and math. AYP describes an improvement trajectory leading to 100% proficiency in both subjects for all students by the 2013–2014 school year, measured by testing results from students in grades 3–8. A school can be judged as not making adequate yearly progress for failing to meet performance targets or for failing to test 95% of their students. In addition, schools can miss AYP for not testing at least 95% of students in a number of subgroups—major ethnic/racial groups, the economically disadvantaged, limited English proficient students, and students with disabilities—or if the average subgroup score fails meet a certain threshold.[3] If a school fails to make AYP in two consecutive years, it must offer students the opportunity to attend another public school in the same district or one nearby that is making AYP.[4] A school forced to provide NCLB transfers must do so until it succeeds in meeting AYP in two consecutive years. Students who transfer to a receiving school must be allowed to stay through the highest grade offered in the school. In implementing school transfer policies, the act requires that local school districts (LEAs) give low-income and low-achieving students priority to school transfers in the event that not enough spaces in eligible schools are available.

Based in part on comments to regulation and additional questions to the U.S. Department of Education, in February of 2004 the department provided additional guidance to states attempting to implement the laws requirements (U.S. Department of Education, 2004). While additional funding would provide a positive incentive for schools receiving NCLB transfer students, the law does not require Title I funds to "follow the child."[5] LEAs must spend an amount equal to 20% of its Title I allocation on choice-related transportation and/or tutoring, with no less than 5% of this allocation going to either transportation or tutoring. LEAs may delimit student transfer options to designated transportation zones to reduce costs. However, LEAs are not required to provide transportation to students whose original school is no longer in improvement status.

LEAs are not required to change admission requirements in schools with specialized missions (like arts magnets, science and math academies, and selective enrollment schools) even if these schools are the only ones identified by the district as eligible to receive transfers. They may, however, give NCLB transfer students priority in charter school lotteries. LEAs must not use lack of capacity to deny students the transfer option, but may take capacity under consideration in deciding which choices to make available. LEAs with a lack of capacity must create new capacity for NCLB transfers by building new classroom space, erecting portables, building new schools, starting charter schools, developing distance learning programs, sending students to another school district, or contracting with private schools. Finally, LEAs subject to desegregation orders are not exempt from the NCLB transfer provisions. They must attempt to comply with both the dictates of the order and the transfer provisions.

In summary, the NCLB choice provision is explicitly linked to school accountability, requires LEAs to use Title I funds for transportation, and forbids overcrowding from preventing student transfers. I now turn to what research says about the potential benefits and costs of policy reforms aimed expanding educational choice for families.

What Does Research Say About School Choice?

Because school choice advocates have proposed radical transformations of the educational system, the amount of research on school choice, competition in the educational sector, and similar topics is vast. Instead of summarizing the entire corpus of existing research, I will focus this review on the aspects of school choice research that seem the most relevant to understanding both the policy context of NCLB and the implementation difficulties school policymakers have faced since its passage. Unfortunately, either because NCLB choice is a recent phenomenon, or because participation rates have been so low, the extant research base on the implementation and outcomes of NCLB choice is quite thin. Therefore, I focus this review on research about other types of choice programs. I will review the few studies that exist on NCLB choice in the next section.

School choice research can be organized by at least three hypotheses: the liberation hypothesis, the competition hypothesis, and the stratification hypothesis. I begin with research that addresses the extent to which choice in education will "free" students from "failing" schools.

The Liberation Hypothesis

To understand the policy context in which NCLB was proposed and debated, it is critical to examine how school choice advocates have framed their claims. The school choice provisions in NCLB were proposed by a Republican president, George W. Bush, who like his father before him, had championed school choice as a policy issue in the presidential campaign. President Bush and many other school choice advocates align their cause with what Gunnar Myrdal called the American Creed (Myrdal et al., 1944), which espouses liberty, equality of opportunity, and civil rights. Such advocates argue that expanding school choice promotes equity by allowing students in bad schools to escape to either private schools, or public schools in better neighborhoods. This perspective, dubbed the "liberation" hypothesis by Archbald (2004), argues that wealthy families are able to reproduce their values by shopping for the appropriate school for their children, whereas poor families are captives of professional elites in school systems that are increasingly unable to serve their needs (Coons & Sugarman, 1978; Tyack, 1974). National data confirm that parents with higher levels of education, for example, are more likely to report moving to their current neighborhood for the school system (Wirt et al., 2004). School choice programs provide more educational options to parents blocked from exercising "choice through mortgage" by resource constraints or practices of racial exclusion.

School choice advocates point to the Milwaukee public voucher experiment and four private school voucher experiments in New York City, Washington, D.C., Charlotte, and Dayton (all of which employed random assignment research designs) as the best evidence on the promise of choice to reform education policy in the United States. Evidence from these studies is highly contested due to the threat vouchers present to the cherished American notion of the public and community based, common school. An initial study of the Milwaukee experiment by the state's own evaluator claimed that there was no consistent positive effect of using a voucher on educational outcomes (Witte, 2000). A group of scholars analyzed the voucher study data with a different comparison group and claimed to find consistently positive results for voucher children (Green et al., 1997). Another scholar analyzed the same data a third time and found effects for math achievement, but not in reading (Rouse, 1998). Studies of private voucher programs in five other cities are similarly contested, with scholars reporting modest effects for low income black males in a few grade levels (Gill, 2001). In a reanalysis of a private voucher experiment in New York City, Krueger & Zhu (2004) found that claims of test score gains to black students were not statistically significant when students with missing baseline scores were included in the analysis and when both mother's and father's race were taken into account when coding student's race.

In summary, school- and program-level studies offer no resounding endorsement of school choice. Treatment effects across studies are mixed, with some students in some grades and on some outcomes showing positive results, while students in other grades and on other outcomes showing null results. Studies on particular schools or programs provide what economists call "partial equilibrium" results. In other words, they tell us about the intention-to-treat effect or the average effect on the treated, but not about the effect on an entire district from school choice. To examine the general equilibrium effect of choice on student outcomes, one must expand the level of analysis from the school/program level to the district level.

The Competition Hypothesis

School choice advocates argue that school choice, by promoting competition, could transform low-performing school districts, thereby reducing inequality between poor and non-poor districts. In other words, by expanding school choice in areas, such as central cities, where access to high quality schools is severely constrained and residential mobility options are also constrained, average achievement in such areas would increase to levels approaching areas, such as affluent suburbs, where affluent middle class residents have chosen to live in part because of the quality of the schools.

If school choice produces benefits from competition, the concern that students left behind in low performing schools would be harmed by the exodus of highly motivated students abandoning their assigned schools becomes less salient. In what might be called the "competition hypothesis," advocates argue that choice might be the "tide that lifts all boats" (Hoxby, 2003). Competition can emerge from three sources: choice between private and public schools (sectoral choice), choice between public school districts (Tiebout, or interdistrict choice), or choice among public schools in the same district (intradistrict choice) (Belfield & Levin, 2002). Educational productivity has been defined as "achievement per dollar spent, controlling for incoming achievement differences of its students" (Hoxby, 2003, 287). Therefore, this hypothesis predicts that in areas with larger private school sectors, public schools would be forced to improve for fear of losing enrollment to private schools. Similarly, in areas with more extensive public school choice programs, or in areas where it is easier to move between school districts, school productivity would be higher because the consequence of under-performance would be lost enrollment.

There is some empirical support for the competition hypothesis. A meta-analysis of peer-reviewed studies testing the competition hypothesis found that a majority of studies report that increased competition positively predicts test scores and graduation rates, while at the same time increasing teacher salaries and decreasing student-teacher ratios (Belfield & Levin, 2002). This review also notes that the effect of competition on school spending is mixed. For example, a study of the effect of private school competition on public school performance and spending finds that public school students in states with larger private school sectors tended to have higher test scores than those with smaller private school sectors (Arum, 1996). This author uses resource dependency theory (Pfeffer & Salancik, 1978) to argue that the improved performance of students in states with more private school competition is due not to increased efficiency, but to higher public funding spurred by the threat of competition from the private sector.

A contrasting view is offered by a study of the competition engendered by interdistrict public school choice. Hoxby (2000) uses an instrumental variables approach to estimate the effect of public school competition on student outcomes and productivity net of the selection effects of parents of high achieving children selecting into more productive school districts. This study finds that metropolitan areas with more public school competition (which in this case is operationalized as the number of school districts in the area), tend to beget higher test scores and *lower* spending, thus producing higher productivity.[6] Positive results from competition have also been shown by Hoxby (2003) schools in Milwaukee facing voucher threats and in Arizona and Michigan among schools facing charter school threats.

Perhaps the ideal research design for studying the impact of school choice on student outcomes is to conduct an experiment. This would involve randomly assigning districts (in the simplest case) to two treatment conditions: 1) school choice, and 2) no school choice and tracking student outcome differences between treated and control districts. Assuming adequate samples of treatment and control districts, compliance with treatment condition, and fidelity of implementation, it is at least theoretically possible to estimate a district-level causal effect of school choice based on average student outcomes. Due to the political and logistical complexities of conducting an experiment on such a broad scale, a more feasible design would be to exploit the natural experiment of policy variation across districts. One would take one or more districts, each of which implemented a comparable form of school choice at roughly the same time. Student outcomes would be measured before and after the imposition of the school choice policy of interest. A subsample of control districts would provide a comparative baseline to interpret any changes in student outcomes. Because school choice policies and comparable before and after measures vary a great deal across districts, however, such studies have been difficult to design.

In sum, the policy context in which the NCLB choice provisions were proposed and debated was informed by an ideological commitment to two ideas, both backed up with some evidence, that promoting school choice would both enhance educational opportunities for low-income students and promote competition in a sector that was perceived to be under-performing.

While school choice advocates place faith in the market to generate overall benefits, school choice critics argue that relying on market incentives to deliver educational services will worsen inequities in an already stratified school system. The family's role in school selection is central due to the decentralized nature of the U.S. educational system. Middle-class parents jockey for positions in early childhood programs, schedule every spare minute of the child's day with extracurricular activities, and advocate on behalf of their children for favorable course and school placements (Lareau, 2002). Educational transition points—such as those between kindergarten and primary school and between primary and secondary school—are times when the family's role in reproducing class become particularly salient (Baker & Stevenson, 1986). Research has found, for example, that parents who exert a high degree of control over the management of their children's educational careers are more likely to successfully place them in nonneighborhood schools and keep them there once enrolled (Wells & Crain, 1997). Therefore, school choice critics focus on the role race and class play in the causes of school selections and potential consequences of school choice programs.

The Stratification Hypothesis

Though school choice programs are targeted at low-income students, research shows that this is precisely the population that is hardest to serve by school choice. In what might be called the "stratification critique," this perspective holds that marketization will compound racial and class inequality by failing to compensate for the inability of disadvantaged families to negotiate the school choice process. A relatively consistent finding in school choice research is that the most disadvantaged families seem to be less likely to exercise school choice. For example, one study found that lower income and minority parents are less aware of magnet programs (Henig, 1995). Another found that among low-income parents, those with higher education levels are more likely to exercise school choice for their children (Lee et al., 1996). A third study found that higher SES and white parents are more likely to exercise school choice (Teske & Schneider, 2001).

One reason disadvantaged families may be less likely to exercise school choice is that minority and low income parents may have less access to useful information about schools through their social networks (ibid.). More advantaged parents, on the other hand, are embedded in social networks which provide knowledge more relevant to choosing schools (Archbald, 2000) and about objective measures of school quality (Schneider et al. 1998). Another reason the disadvantaged may be less likely to attend nonneighborhood schools may be that middle class white parents, by virtue of their cultural capital, face an advantage when negotiating educational bureaucracies and in relating to teachers (Lareau, 1989).

Researchers have also questioned whether parents choose schools based on school quality or on racial/ethnic composition (Wells & Crain, 1997; Saporito, 2003; Saporito & Lareau, 1999; Glazerman, 1998).

Most studies rely on inferences drawn from the end result of a choice process, such as those provided by an intra- or interdistrict choice program. Studies of "revealed preferences" do not necessarily prove that racial preferences are driving ethnic separation since they do not directly measure preferences, but rather are the end result of a complex social process. Ideally we want to study the same-race and different-race preferences of families, something hard to measure due to the (now) widespread unacceptability of racist views. One study has attempted to directly measure preferences. By examining the online search patterns of parents interested in schools of choice in the District of Columbia, this study found that characteristics of the student body were among the most frequently searched attributes of schools (Schneider & Buckley, 2002), a finding that supports the results in revealed preference studies. Such studies call into question a central claim of school choice advocates. If parents define school quality purely in terms of poverty rates and racial composition, then schools face no incentive to improve since they are not being held accountable by parents for academic performance.

The possibility that school choice reforms would worsen segregation is a concern because since the civil rights era, federal policy has sought to mitigate between-school racial segregation. The implication of this line of research is that school choice programs must be carefully designed and regulated to avoid worsening segregation. This is particularly critical because studies have found that unrestricted choice programs worsen between-school segregation by racial/ethnic and class background (Fiske & Ladd, 2000). In the United States, there is some evidence suggesting that charter schools, which face much lower levels of government oversight, may contribute, rather than mitigate between-school segregation. A study found that Arizona's charter schools are more racially homogeneous than nearby schools (Cobb & Glass, 1999).[7] A nationwide study finds that in more integrated districts, charter schools tend to enroll higher proportions of white students, thereby worsening between-school segregation in otherwise relatively integrated districts (Renzulli & Evans, 2005). On the other hand, scholars have found that the U.K.'s country-wide choice program, in which students may attend any public school in the country, has contributed to social class integration (Gorard & Fitz, 2000; Gorard, 2000).

In sum, while research shows that school choice presents some promise as an educational reform effort, policymakers must contend with class disparities in uptake, and the potential that the effort to improve schools through choice and competition may worsen segregation. Keeping in mind the literature about how choice policy should be designed, I now turn to how it has been actually implemented by states and local school districts.

NCLB Choice Implementation

I begin my discussion of NCLB choice implementation by first providing a nation-wide overview of the difficulties school districts have had with implementing the transfer provisions of the Act. Following this, I describe in some detail what is known about Chicago's implementation of the transfer provisions. To place Chicago's compliance with federal mandates into perspective, I draw on research I conducted on the history and current operation of school choice programs in Chicago (Lauen, 2006).

Nationwide Overview

The NCLB transfer provisions have been called among the hardest provisions in the Act for local school districts to implement (Casserly, 2004). They require districts to identify schools that have failed to make AYP for two consecutive years, identify schools that are both eligible to accept transfers under the Act and have the space available for student transfers, notify parents of their eligibility for a school choice transfer, set up a selection process to assign students to schools in the event that more students apply for transfers than can be accommodated, and provide transportation for transferring students. In some districts, this process is relatively straightforward and involves very few students. Three cities in Texas, for example, Houston, Dallas, and Austin, had no schools that were in "school improvement" status in 2003–04,[8] so these districts did not have to create a transfer process. Philadelphia, on the other hand, had 74% of the schools in improvement status, and was forced by NCLB to set up an elaborate transfer program (ibid).

Nationwide, about 1% of eligible students in both the 2003–04 and 2004–05 school years actually switched schools through NCLB choice (Center for Education Policy, 2005; United States Government Accountability Office, 2004). About 15% of school districts had schools designated to offer NCLB transfers in 2004–05, and large urban districts tended to have more schools facing this sanction (Center for Education Policy, 2005). In large urban districts, NCLB transfers have been a small, but rising, percentage of the overall student population. Based on a survey of the 50 largest urban districts in 2003–04, 44,373, or 3.8%, of eligible students requested a NCLB transfer (Casserly, 2004). Of these requests, 17,879, or 40.3%, were granted. For comparison purposes, the number of NCLB transfer requests granted by these large urban districts in 2002–03 was 5,661 (ibid).

According to a survey of state and school district officials, finding enough space in schools meeting AYP to satisfy requests, identifying eligible families in a timely manner, and communicating with parents were the most challenging barriers to implementing the choice provisions (Center for Education Policy, 2005). Capacity constraints were particularly severe in some rural districts with only one school and in overcrowded urban districts and large proportions of schools in improvement status. Interdistrict choice is a potential solution to this problem, but virtually no districts have been willing or able to create cross-district agreements to allow interdistrict NCLB transfers (Brown, 2004).

Notifying families of their options in a timely manner has been a particular challenge due to testing, data cleaning, and reporting schedules. Given the high stakes attached to testing results, the complex NCLB achievement and testing participation criteria for each subgroup, and recent scandals involving mistakes in test scoring (see, for example, Duchesne (2000)), states must carefully scrutinize student, subgroup, and school test scores to ensure accuracy. While NCLB has increased the demand for accuracy, there has been a concurrent demand for results to be processed more rapidly. To ensure that testing results reflect what students have learned in a school year, students are typically tested as late in the spring as possible. Providing adequate notification to families eligible for NCLB transfers, however, requires results to be processed in a matter of months, before the next school year. This presents problems for most school districts. According to a survey of large urban districts, no district had testing results processed by the end of the 2002–03 school year, and more than half did not have results by the beginning of the next school year (Casserly, 2004).

Lack of adequate notification is one barrier that contributes to the broader challenge of parent participation in the NCLB transfer program. While NCLB is designed to serve disadvantaged families, it is precisely these families that are the least likely to know whether they are eligible for a transfer. A survey in Massachusetts found that most parents whose children qualify for an NCLB transfer do not know whether their child's school is in improvement status and is thus required to offer their child a transfer. Specifically, only one in four parents of eligible children correctly identified the improvement status of their school (Howell, 2004).

Evidence suggests that uptake for NCLB transfers has been low because parents have strong commitments to local schools and may be getting conflicting signals from the overlapping federal, state, and district accountability regimes. Opinion surveys consistently indicate that public school parents think highly of the schools their children attend, but not highly of schools in general. For example, in 2004 more than two-thirds of public school parents gave the school their oldest child attends a grade of "A" or a "B." Less than one-quarter of public school parents, however, gave public schools in the nation as a whole a grade of "A" or "B" (Rose & Gallup, 2004). This suggests that parents might be willing to support efforts like those called for in NCLB to reform schools in general, but may resist efforts to punish or reform their own child's school. Despite high levels of parent satisfaction among those whose children attend schools of choice (Gill, 2001, 128–37), most parents prefer reforming the existing school system to creating expanding school choice. Poll figures suggest that even if their child's school was in NCLB improvement status, only a small minority of parents would opt to exercise school choice. The vast majority (85%) of parents preferred that instead of choice, additional efforts should be made to improve their neighborhood school (ibid).[9]

Some evidence also suggests that parents do not believe the alternatives to their home school are markedly better. In some cases, this is understandable because state and federal quality designations sometimes vary. In some cases, states may recognize a school as being a school of excellence, but because of the under-performance of one subgroup, or because of the test participation rate of a particular subgroup, the school may miss AYP standards. In other cases, it may be that districts identify schools as NCLB transfer options that are only marginally better than the sending schools themselves.

Scholars have questioned the effectiveness of relying on an accountability program that can lead to an overly broad definition of school failure. In other words, if large majorities of schools are deemed to be "failures" by NCLB rules, then the stigmatizing effect of the label may be limited. If, however, only a small proportion of schools are deemed as failing to meet a more relaxed set of standards, then arguably the stigmatizing effect would be more likely to lead to productivity improvements. For example, in 2003 75% of Florida's elementary schools were deemed as failing to meet AYP, whereas only 10% of schools in 2002 received failing marks under the state's A++ accountability plan (which, as noted above, offered vouchers to students in failing schools) (West & Peterson, 2006). A study of Florida's A++ program found that schools facing, or at risk of facing, the voucher threat produced positive impacts on school performance; schools at risk of facing sanctions through NCLB, however, did not produce similar effects (ibid). This provides some evidence supporting the hypothesis that targeted sanctions work better than overly broad ones. Further study is needed to determine the extent to which 1) the proportion of schools facing a sanction, 2) the type of choice offered (public versus private), or 3) the extent of state and local commitment to providing teeth to negative sanctions through policy implementation are the most effective at bringing about school improvement through stigmatization and negative sanctions.

In summary, the low NCLB transfer rates stem from several sources: 1) capacity constraints, 2) the logistical hurdles inherent in meeting both annual testing and notification requirements, 3) strong commitment to local schools, 4) race and class disparities in access to information about school quality and 5) the fact that federal and state accountability regimes send conflicting signals about the quality of local schools. To provide more institutional detail and a sense of how policy implementation can evolve over time, I now turn to a more in-depth examination of one case.

Chicago Case Study

Chicago is a highly segregated city with a predominantly low income and minority student population. Its schools were once decried by William Bennett (former Secretary of Education under President Reagan) as the "worst in the nation" (Johnson, 1987). While some strides have been made to reform schools and improve student achievement, large numbers of the city's schools remain on academic probation and are deemed under-performing by local and federal standards. The District is currently identified by NCLB as being in "improvement" status for failing to meet goals in math.

Chicago has a large intra-district high school choice program in which public or private school choice is the norm. About half of secondary students exercise public school choice and almost one-fifth attend private high school (see Figure 26.1). Public alternatives include career academies, selective enrollment college preparatory high schools, magnet schools and programs, charter schools, and military academies; private alternatives are predominantly Catholic schools. Only about one-third of secondary students in Chicago attend an assigned public school. The district also runs a liberal open enrollment transfer program which allows high school students to attend any high school in the district on a space-available basis.

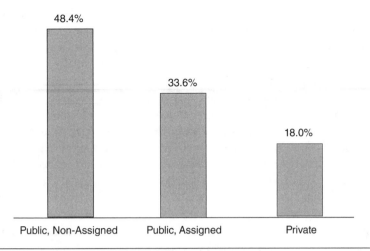

Figure 26.1 Chicago Secondary School Enrollment, by School Type, 2000. *Note*: Data on private school enrollment is from author calculations of 2000 IPUMS data. Data on nonneighborhood public school enrollment is from author calculations of CPS administrative data.

The Emergence of School Choice from Desegregation Chicago's history with school choice began as a response to the problem of school segregation. Though Chicago formally desegregated its school system in 1874, due to real estate practices, public housing policy that situated projects in black neighborhoods, and a neighborhood schools policy, Chicago's schools were segregated de facto (Hess, 1984). Despite calls for action from community groups, policy recommendations in reports by academic experts, student boycotts, and the constant threats of federal civil rights enforcement, the Chicago school board refused to implement any substantial school desegregation policy between 1960 and 1980 (Peterson, 1976). Unlike in the South, where national guard troops escorted black students through the hallways of Little Rock high school, the federal role in enforcing civil rights in Chicago was minimal. After passage of the Civil Rights Act in 1964, Chicago became an early test case in enforcement of the act's provisions. When the Office of Education withheld federal education funds from Chicago due to the board's inaction on school integration, Mayor Daley complained to President Johnson, who quickly intervened on Chicago's behalf. The funds were quickly released (Peterson, 1976; Hess, 1984). Johnson's intervention set a precedent. At least in key Democratic strongholds like Chicago and other northern cities, the federal role in enforcement would be an empty threat until 1980, the turning point for both the history of desegregation and school choice in Chicago.

To avoid a federal lawsuit, in 1980 the District negotiated a consent decree with the U.S. Department of Justice to create a voluntary transfer program called "Options for Knowledge" to entice students away from segregated schools. Creating and maintaining integrated schools was a central goal of this program, so transfer requests were evaluated to determine the impact of a student transfer on the racial composition of the sending and receiving schools. Applications to schools under this program were sorted by grade, race, and gender. Students were chosen by lottery if schools or programs were oversubscribed. The plan established a standard to guide student reassignment and transfers: if a school was more than 70% of one race or ethnicity, then it was considered segregated and was subject to student reassignment policies including boundary changes and racial/ethnic quotas on incoming student transfers. Therefore, what emerged in Chicago was a program that sought to expand school choice, while also regulating schools' racial mix.

Mayoral Takeover and a Turn Towards Selectivity During the mid to late 1990s, Mayor Richard M. Daley, Jr. used authority granted to him by a school reform law in 1995 to close chronically under-performing schools and open new schools.[10] In Chicago and other cities during the 1990s, professional discretion and union control gave way to a business-led movement to give authority to big city mayors who then hired technocrats, businessmen, and military leaders to run schools. The reform act was passed by a Republican legislature and informed by extensive input from the Chicago United and the Civic Committee of the Commercial Club, both influential Chicago-based business organizations (Klonsky, 1995). The mayor, and Paul Vallas, the mayor's former budget director (who was himself not a professional educator) tightened accountability for both students and schools. They put an end to social promotion, the practice of promoting students from one grade to the next whether or not students performed at grade level on standardized tests. In 1997, for example, 11,000 students were retained in the 3rd, 6th, and 8th grades due to poor performance on standardized tests in reading and math (Roderick et al., 1999). Vallas also used his expanded authority to use standardized test scores as a basis for evaluating schools and closing them for chronic under-performance.

Neighborhood schools, which had not fared well under the "Options for Knowledge" program, were further stigmatized by rising academic standards. One study found that schools on probation for low test score performance lost the highest proportion of their attendance area student enrollment to schools of choice (Duffrin, 2001). As neighborhood high schools gained poor reputations, families with the information and ability to negotiate the school choice process (or pay for private schooling) sent their children elsewhere. Those students who had fewer options or special needs became disproportionately represented in neighborhood high schools. In South Shore High School, once a school with a good reputation in an integrated middle class neighborhood, for example, a reporter found that a typical classroom of 28 students had 10-12 students with learning disabilities or behavior disorders (ibid).

Given the poor reputation of many neighborhood schools in Chicago, the Daley regime sought to close dysfunctional schools, open new schools in their place, and build new school buildings. Between 1995 and 2004, 22 schools were closed and 53 schools opened. Of those that opened, only 16 had attendance areas, and 37 were schools of choice such as charters, magnets, and selective enrollment high schools. One objective in creating these new schools was to change the image of the Chicago Public Schools from one of fraud, mismanagement, and failure to one of performance and innovation. Daley and Vallas sought to keep more middle class families in the city and attract students from the private sector to the district's selective enrollment schools and programs. The administration built eight new selective enrollment high schools, expanded International Baccalaureate programs (a selective high school program leading to a high school diploma set to worldwide standard), and created Math/Science/Technology academies in schools with large outflows of attendance area students. In addition, the school district created fee-based preschool programs and neighborhood set-asides in gentrifying neighborhoods in an effort to entice young professionals to consider sending their children to the public schools.[11]

Features of the Existing System Several features of Chicago's existing school choice regime are worth noting before exploring the District's implementation of the NCLB transfer provisions. At least in part because most high schools have an application process to admit some or all of their students, students with social and academic advantages are more likely to participate in public school choice programs in Chicago. Students with higher prior achievement, and students with parents who had successfully negotiated the elementary school choice process, are more likely to attend a private or public alternative to their assigned public high school (Figure 26.2). Poor students (measured by whether the student was eligible for a free or reduced priced lunch), on the other hand, are less likely to exercise private or public high school choice.[12]

There is also evidence that, consistent with prior research (Schneider & Buckley, 2002; Saporito & Lareau, 1999; Glazerman, 1998), parents in Chicago choose schools based on race. Net of assigned

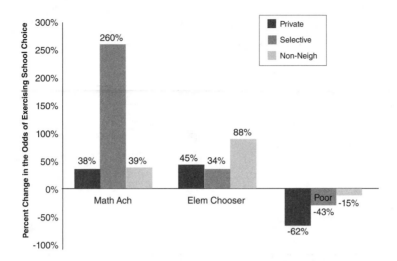

Figure 26.2 Effect of Measures of Student Social and Academic Status on High School Choice, 2000. Source: Lauen (2006). 2000–2001 Chicago Public Schools Administrative Data. 9th grade destinations of 8th Grade Public School Students Only. Effects shown control for gender, race/ethnicity, special education status, age, number of previous school moves, and measures of elementary school context.

high school average achievement, non-black families tend to avoid neighborhood high schools with high percentages of black students (Figure 26.3). This suggests that high minority schools, no matter how productive, may be at a disadvantage in Chicago's system of school choice.

Ideally, we would like to be able to separate parent racial and class preferences from their preferences for high performing schools. It could be that parents assume that schools serving disadvantaged student populations are of low quality. The evidence from Chicago is that parents prefer high schools with high compositional quality, defined as a composite of aggregate achievement, safety, mobility,

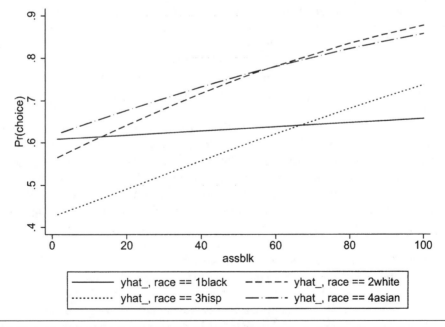

Figure 26.3 Effect of Percentage Black Students on Propensity to Exercise School Choice, by Race/Ethnicity, 2000. Source: Lauen (2006). 2000–2001 Chicago Public Schools Administrative Data. Eighth Grade Public School Students Only. Effects shown control for student-level covariates such as prior achievement, poverty, and race-ethnicity, and neighborhood high school average achievement.

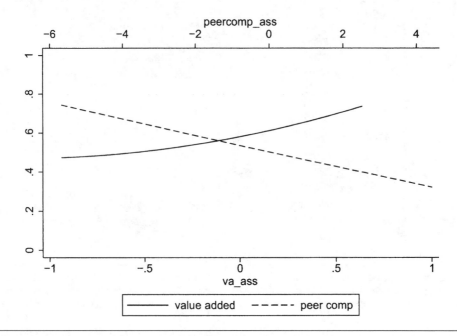

Figure 26.4 Effect of Assigned School Peer Composition and Productivity on Propensity to Exercise School Choice, by Poverty Level, 2000. Source: Lauen (2006). 2000–2001 Chicago Public Schools Administrative Data. Eighth Grade Public School Students Only. Effects shown control for student-level covariates such as prior achievement, poverty, and race-ethnicity. Peer composition is a principal components measure of assigned high school characteristics such as percent poor, mobility rate, and average achievement. Productivity is defined as the average residual 8th to 9th grade test score gain, controlling for student background and elementary school quality.

poverty, motivation, and attainment measures. (These school-level measures are all highly correlated.) The evidence also suggests, however, that parents are also likely to avoid enrolling their children in highly productive assigned high schools. This could be because parents are unaware that, controlling for student background, prior educational experiences, and elementary school quality, disadvantaged high schools in Chicago tend to produce higher 8th to 9th grade test score gains.[13] Figure 26.4 displays the opposite effects of compositional quality and productivity.

In summary, Chicago's existing system of school choice emerged from school desegregation. At first, policymakers focused on expanding educational opportunities for black students in segregated schools. After a mayoral takeover of the school system in the mid-1990s, however, the focus of school choice policy shifted somewhat to expand educational opportunities for high achieving students. By the year 2000, choice of high school in Chicago was designed as a "winner-take-all" system, with high achieving students receiving a disproportionate share of the benefits of school choice (Lauen, 2006). There is evidence to support the hypothesis that parents are sensitive to school quality differences; unfortunately, whether due to lack of access to school quality information or due to assumptions that schools serving disadvantaged students are of low quality, families seem to be avoiding schools with relatively high productivity levels.

Chicago and NCLB Choice Elected and appointed officials have been openly critical of NCLB and the transfer provisions. Mayor Daley has been quoted as arguing that NCLB should have given schools more time to improve before they were subject to the transfer threat: "it's 'ridiculous' to think schools can improve 'overnight.' ... 'Many of the schools are not performing. Everybody knows that,' Daley said. 'We know it. Where are you going to go? To another nonperforming school? You can't.'" (Rossi & Spielman, 2002). Arne Duncan, the CEO of the Chicago Public School system (CPS), has expressed doubt that NCLB would improve student learning and was "burdensome ...complex and impractical" (Rossi, 2003b).

The U.S. Department of Education official responsible for overseeing the transfer provisions of NCLB, Nina Reece, said, "Based on every single news report and discussion we've had with the city of Chicago, we feel, when it comes to choice, they are not looking at creative ways to extend capacity and meet the needs of students in low-performing schools" (Rossi, 2003a). Two options for complying with federal mandates include providing trailers for students on the grounds of schools making AYP and creating inter-district agreements for transfers across district lines. Duncan has been quoted as saying that CPS has no funds to purchase trailers and that he hasn't asked neighboring districts to accept CPS transfers because, "I don't think yellow school buses from Chicago would be well-received" (ibid.).

From these exchanges in the newspapers, it seems fair to characterize the attitude of important elected and appointed officials as being hostile to the transfer provisions of NCLB. This is perhaps understandable given that the federal share of funding is low, federal requirements under NCLB are extensive, and that NCLB labels large portions of Chicago's schools as in need of improvement, a problem that policymakers had been attempting to address in various ways for at least the past 10–15 years.

According to data provided by the Illinois State School Board, in the 2003–04 school year, three-quarters of elementary schools and 90% of high schools failed to make AYP. In subsequent years, the proportion of elementary schools failing to make AYP fell to two-thirds; the high school proportion fell and then increased to 94% (Table 26.1). By the 2005–06 school year, 64% of elementary school students and 94% of high school students attended schools that failed to make AYP according to federal guidelines. Approximately 256,000 students were eligible by federal regulation to transfer to a school making AYP in 2005–06.[14] In a district with approximately 436,000 students enrolled in the fall of 2005 eligible for a transfer under NCLB, it is clear that CPS faces implementation problems; short of shutting down all schools that missed AYP, it is impossible for the district to find spaces for all students eligible for an NCLB transfer under federal guidelines.

For 2003–04, the first year of NCLB choice implementation, CPS determined that 1,100 spaces would be made available by lottery to eligible students, which for this year was determined to be 270,000 students. Approximately 19,000 students entered the lottery. Lottery winners were given

Table 26.1 Selected NCLB Statistics, Chicago, 2003-2006.

	School Year		
	03-04	04-05	05-06
Panel A, Federal Definitions			
Elementary			
% of Schools that Failed AYP	75%	65%	64%
% of Students in Schools that Failed AYP	80%	70%	64%
High School			
% of Schools that Failed AYP	90%	84%	92%
% of Students in Schools that Failed AYP	90%	84%	94%
Panel B, Chicago Implementation of NCLB Transfers			
Eligible students (As Defined by CPS)	270,757	2,500	1,100
Applications	19,246	5,933	267
Spaces Made Available	1,100	440	550

Source: Percent of schools failing AYP from author calculations of data provided by the Illinois State Board of Education. Chicago implementation of choice transfer policy from newspaper reports, e-mail communication with CPS officials, and Center on Education policy reports (Center for Education Policy, 2005, 2006).

one day to decide whether to accept a choice seat (Rossi, 2003b). For the 2004–05 school year, CPS changed eligibility rules and determined that about 2,500 students were eligible for 440 slots. About 5,933 students applied for these slots (Center for Education Policy, 2006). It is clear that the decline in the number of students eligible for a choice transfer was due not to a large decline in the number of schools subject to the choice sanction, to a redefinition of eligibility by local officials. In 2005-06, the definition of eligibility was further restricted to students in three schools that both missed AYP and had been identified for closure under CPS' accountability regime. 550 slots were made available to students in these three schools, but only 267 students applied for an NCLB transfer to one of 20 schools that were making AYP.[15] This left more than 800 students who chose to attend schools in neighborhood adjacent to their old schools, none of which were making AYP (Grossman, 2005). The number of students applying for NCLB transfers has been falling (Table 26.1). No high school students were given opportunity to exercise NCLB choice during the 2004–05 and 2005–06 school years.

In addition to capacity constraints, CPS has had difficulty identifying schools that were significantly better than those subject to the choice sanction. Students in Chicago could only choose from schools that had, on average, very high poverty levels. The average proficiency level of the receiving schools in Chicago, while generally higher than the sending schools, was significantly below the average proficiency level of the pool of potential receiving schools (Kim & Sunderman, 2004). Of the 11 schools slated to be receiving schools of students affected by school closures in the spring of 2002, however, six were identified as needing improvement and eligible for choice in the fall of 2002 (Rossi & Spielman, 2002). In some cases, receiving schools had worse test scores than some of the sending schools (Rossi, 2003b). In at least one case, this was the case because the receiving school had not been in existence long enough to be subject to the choice sanction.

Illinois state law prevents local school districts from complying with some federal mandates. Though federal regulations state that local school districts must allow NCLB transfers even to overcrowded schools, Illinois state law forbids such an action. State law also prevents NCLB transfer students from taking precedence in admissions to academically selective schools (Center for Education Policy, 2006).

In summary, Chicago is a large and diverse urban school system that has been struggling for many years to improve student learning. NCLB choice is but a small portion of the choice transfers that exist in a district in which 30% of elementary school students and 60% of public school students attend a public school of choice. Despite the fact that NCLB was perhaps designed with school districts like Chicago in mind, the ability of federal officials to force compliance with the laws dictates has been limited. For four years local officials have been largely free to craft policies that severely constrain the number of NCLB transfer slots and limit the pool of eligible students that has little, if any, resemblance to federal regulations.

Implications for Reauthorization

Rather than encouraging the rise of new school forms that could expand educational opportunity, the NCLB transfer provisions are a blunt system of negative sanctions. Without careful attention to mid-course modifications informed by additional research in exactly how school choice leads to benefits to students, NCLB choice is likely to hold an empty promise to American school children.

To be most effective, school choice policy must encourage innovation, reform, and productivity while also promoting (or at least not harming) social cohesion, accountability, and equity (National Working Commission on Choice in K-12 Education, 2003; Levin, 2004). Policy aimed at promoting a diverse array of educational options must, therefore, regulate enough to maintain social cohesion and ensure that public dollars are being put to productive use, but not so much that schools cannot innovate, take risks, and reach populations aligned with their mission. If enough new (or reconstituted) schools enter the market, policy must also create a level playing field to foster competition between new entrants and existing schools (National Working Commission on Choice in K-12 Education, 2003). This involves providing both new and old schools adequate and equitable funding, budgetary control, and the flexibility to hire and fire teachers aligned with reform objectives. The goal of policy would be to allow teachers and families to focus on a shared mission and the technical core of education—teaching and learning—while also fostering competition among educational providers and ensuring quality standards.

In short, the state must use its powers at the federal, state, and local levels to ensure innovation and competition in education while also holding schools accountable, promoting social cohesion, and protecting the rights of students to gain access to equal access to educational opportunity. Some of these powers include maintaining an adequate and equitable flow of funding to schools, providing or paying for transportation to schools outside of a student's neighborhood, providing extra funds to schools with harder to serve student populations, funding parent information centers and social marketing campaigns to facilitate an efficient and equitable school-to-parent matching process, promoting a mix of schools with a variety of selectivity criteria and lotteries for student admission, holding schools accountable for their "value added" (the achievement gain for the students who remain in the school long enough to produce a treatment effect), widely disseminating the performance measurement results, and closing schools with persistent failure records or records of financial malfeasance.

It would be hard to conclude from the early phase of NCLB choice that the policy as currently implemented is living up to the rhetoric of "liberation" used by the framers of the act. The choice provisions are difficult for many, if not most, districts to implement, give struggling schools only one year to improve before facing sanctions, and penalize too many schools for the sanction to be effective. The vast majority of students who desire a school transfer are not being allowed one. Testing schedules, capacity constraints, the large variation in state standards, and the high between-district variation in access to high quality alternatives represent substantial barriers to the prospect of NCLB transfers actually improving the plight of students in low-performing, high-poverty schools.

Absent significant changes in the implementation of the transfer provisions, and perhaps regulatory and legislative action, NCLB choice will probably have very little effect on educational reform. Because local school districts have a great deal of latitude in designing transfer programs, those districts that want to use the negative sanction will have legislative cover to do so and those that do not will be able to design programs that render the negative sanction impotent. Until state and local officials see evidence that negative sanctions work and that school choice is directly related to educational achievement, state and local resistance is also likely to remain strong.

The implementation difficulties of the NCLB school choice provisions likely stem from several sources. First, school choice is a flash-point issue in American educational policy. It threatens the interests of powerful actors in the educational system, such as teacher unions and school boards. There is ample evidence that the NCLB transfer provisions have been resisted by powerful local actors. Second, school choice threatens the cherished notion of the common school ideal. NCLB school choice may have had such a limited impact because of strong parental loyalty to neighborhood schools. Third, the potential costs and benefits of school choice are poorly understood. As a consequence, it is not clear what system of regulation and incentives should be employed to achieve the appropriate balance of educational equity and efficiency. This suggests that the NCLB transfer policy has been ineffective simply because it was poorly conceived and implemented. Finally, it could be that the federal role in education policy is too limited to present a credible threat to local entities that ignore legal mandates. Further research is needed to test the tenability of these propositions.

NCLB dramatically alters the balance of governmental authority in education, away from local control and toward state and federal control. While it fails to set national standards and test these standards with a national test, it provides a common set of negative sanctions. Based on local and state resistance to NCLB, the limits of this expanded federal role are being severely tested. The fact that the federal share of education spending was 8% in 2003 indicates that the federal role is limited. Furthermore, because this federal share varies across states (from 4% to 18%), the leverage federal power can exert over education at the local level may also vary.[16]

A good indication of the limits of federal power in education, and a substantial limitation of the NCLB Act, is the inability of the federal government to set national standards and hold states accountable to these standards with a national test. The wide fluctuation of standards across the states results in the problem that cities with high proportions of schools in need of improvement are not necessarily those cities with the lowest NAEP scores (Casserly, 2004).[17] Therefore, while NCLB is informed by the "liberation" hypothesis, in which students are to be freed from failed schools, the federal government cannot ensure the quality of standards across states, much less the quality of particular schools slated by local districts to accept NCLB transfers. To ensure comparability of educational opportunity across states, federal policymakers should carefully scrutinize state standards. As it stands now, the easiest way to ensure that maximum number of schools in a state meets AYP is to water down state academic standards and tests.

This suggests that the ability of federal authority to enforce compliance is sharply limited. Compliance with NCLB offers a good case study of the difficulty of enforcing federal accountability provisions in a loosely coupled educational system (Meyer & Rowan, 1977). It is clear in Chicago at least that local officials are seeking to maintain the charade of minimal compliance with federal mandates to continue receiving federal funds.

There is some evidence that the Bush administration is using low transfer rates under NCLB as justification for a nationwide voucher program. Margaret Spellings, Secretary of the U.S. Department of Education, recently touted the Bush administrations $100 million "Opportunity Scholarship" program at a Christian school in New York:[18]

> In some districts, public school choice is non-existent because no public schools are meeting state standards and waiting lists for charter schools are out the door. I've heard stories about parents cramming into rooms like this one to draw numbers to see which students will make it off the waiting list. You shouldn't need to win the lottery to send your child to a high-performing school …More than 1,700 schools around the country have failed to meet state standards for five or six years in a row. And many of these schools are in districts where public school choice isn't a real option. We're proposing a new $100 million Opportunity Scholarship Fund to help thousands of low-income students in these schools attend the private school of their choice or receive intensive one-on-one tutoring after school or during the summer.

If passed by the Congress, the scholarship program would be offered to students in the restructuring phase of NCLB. The fact that private schools would become options could increase participation rates (Howell, 2004), but given the mixed results from voucher experiments and studies of private schools (Neal, 1997; Lubienski & Lubienski, 2006), substantially improved student outcomes are not likely. In addition, providing vouchers to private schools would raise the question of whether private schools funded in part by public funds should be subject to the same accountability framework as public schools. This is not likely to be something private schools would accept; without this, however, public and private schools would not be on an even playing field, and vouchers could lose support if funds were spent without appropriate evaluation and accountability.

Implications for Research

The research base about the NCLB transfer provision is surprisingly thin. For example, I am aware of no peer-reviewed studies that address the causal effect of receiving an NCLB transfer on educational outcomes. With reauthorization of NCLB slated for 2007, there is an urgent need for policy-relevant research addressing the effects of the NCLB transfer policy on students and schools. Researchers will no doubt be hampered by low participation rates in NCLB choice programs, though it may be possible to conduct studies in urban districts with relatively large transfer programs.

The liberation hypothesis predicts that those who exercise choice through an NCLB transfer would outperform students who remain in schools failing to meet AYP. Fortunately, the provisions of the Act itself provides an opportunity to exploit a research design to estimate causal effects. Specifically, because the act gives priority to low-achieving students, we may be able to employ a regression discontinuity design to examine treatment effects. This design examines the change in the slope of a treatment effect just below and just above a cutoff point. In this case, the cutoff point would be a point in a test score distribution. The logic of this approach is similar to a randomized design. While a student's test score is not as random as a flip of a coin, once we compare students just above and just below a cutoff, we can narrow our attention to a range of students whose score on a test may approximate a random difference that assigns students to two different treatment conditions. Of course, this research design may not be feasible in particular districts, It may be that the number of students transferring between two schools is too small to produce statistically significant results. If sample sizes are adequate and transfer slots are, in fact, distributed on the basis of student prior achievement, this research design provides a promising approach to estimating the causal effect of receiving an NCLB transfer opportunity.

A skeptical view of the NCLB choice sanction is that shuffling students among a number of dysfunctional urban schools will do more harm than good. The nightmare scenario goes like this: Once schools become stigmatized as nonimproving, families flee with or without an NCLB transfer and the school eventually closes. The mostly low-income students attend different schools in the same area. These new schools struggle to compensate for inadequate early childhood experiences and elementary school teaching and are soon themselves subject to sanctions, thereby encouraging yet more student mobility.

The competition hypothesis suggests that the threat of exit will force schools to do a better job serving students. If this hypothesis is correct, therefore, we could predict that rather than simply shuffling students from one school to the other, NCLB transfers could have a positive general equilibrium effect on student achievement. Thus, research could address whether, and under what conditions, the NCLB transfer provision forces school improvement through the negative sanction of being labeled as a school "in need of improvement" and by losing students under a transfer program. As shown by West and Peterson (2006), schools subject to an overly broad stigmatizing sanction may not force school improvement. It is possible, however, to test an alternative hypothesis. Specifically, that schools facing larger transfer outflows would improve more than those facing smaller transfer outflows. In other words, one might be able to design a "dose response" study to examine the effects of the NCLB transfer program where the treatment is a continuous variable—the proportion of the student body that exits the school with an NCLB transfer.

The stratification hypothesis predicts that school choice only worsens educational stratification and inequality in student outcomes. This perspective focuses attention on inequality in who benefits from choice and the social process through which education produces a stratified social order. With respect to NCLB choice in particular, research might address race and class disparities in who transfers under the act and what types of schools are made available to students wishing to transfer. While the act specifies that low achieving and poor students should get priority for transfers, it could be that few low achieving and poor students apply for transfers. The act specifies that overcrowding should not be used as an excuse to exclude students from higher quality schools; in practice it appears that in Chicago most students eligible for a transfer under NCLB are not able to attend schools with substantially lower poverty rates and substantially higher quality. Finally, the stratification hypothesis would predict that students who transfer under the act would not become integrated into the academic and social life of their receiving schools. Specifically that NCLB transfer students would be stigmatized outsiders, tracked into low ability classrooms, and, like refugees from New Orleans, part of a separate subculture.

In closing, a major methodological barrier to assessing school choice is identifying the mechanisms linking school choice with student outcomes. Any effects of school choice on student outcomes, like the effects of schools themselves, are necessarily indirect. "Choice is not a teacher, a classroom, or an instructional resource. If choice affects what students learn, it works indirectly, by leading to changes in what students experience, read, and hear" (National Working Commission on Choice in K-12 Education, 2003, 10). The effects of schooling work largely through teacher-student interaction and peer effects. To the extent that school choice can alter these processes to promote better academic achievement and attainment, it will only do so by altering what goes on in the classroom and the relationships between and among teachers and students. So the question then becomes, how does NCLB choice affect patterns of interaction among students and teachers? For example, we might expect that in schools with large outflows of students and strong professional communities, the choice sanction may spark critical dialogue about teaching practices, which could then, in turn, result in changes in teaching practices and improved student achievement. By contrast, in schools with weak professional communities, we might expect large outflows to prompt a worsening of ties between teachers.

Conclusion

NCLB represents a dramatic shift in federal education policy aimed at expanding equal access to educational opportunity for poor students. While the initial ESEA legislation focused on infusing federal funds into poor schools to address resource inequalities, NCLB focuses on the issue of school quality and whether poor children and those from traditionally under-served populations are learning what they need to know to succeed. The Act assumes that schools can spur complete proficiency in all students, including the disadvantaged and those with special educational needs. This, while it may be impossible without dramatic improvements in early childhood education system, parent participation, and anti-poverty programs, is a laudable goal.

Unfortunately, NCLB relies on blunt negative sanctions on low performing schools and must rely on local school districts to implement what is in many districts across the country an unworkable set of transfer policies. Schools are given only one year after being labeled as at-risk of facing the choice sanction to make changes in practice and improve student achievement in all the necessary subgroups. The elaborate formula used to define whether or not a school is meeting AYP labels so many schools as "in need of improvement" that the sanction becomes meaningless.

This chapter has summarized three primary hypotheses that inform a great deal of school choice research. For decades, scholars have debated the promises and perils to educational opportunity of expanding school choice policies. Scholars informed by the *liberation* hypothesis (Archbald, 2004), argue that school choice has the potential to free students from "failing" schools. Studies informed by the *competition* hypothesis claim that when parents are given greater latitude to choose alternatives to their neighborhood schools, school systems tend to become more competitive. On the other hand, sociologists of education have offered a *stratification* critique. Scholars from this tradition argue that schools choice tends to worsen inequality in an already stratified social system.

With the 2007 reauthorization of NCLB fast approaching, more research is urgently needed to test the tenability of these hypotheses with particular attention to whether and how NCLB choice promotes educational opportunity for those who transfer and encourages competition among schools. Research is also needed to determine the extent to which families offered a transfer receive the information and time to make an informed choice, receive opportunities to transfer to qualitatively better schools, and become integrated into the academic and social life of their receiving schools.

Notes

1. Quote is from a White House press conference transcript: http://www.whitehouse.gov/news/releases/2001/01/20010123-2.html, last accessed on May 26, 2006.
2. Many parents do, however, take school quality into consideration when determining where to live. National estimates suggest that about one-quarter of parents report moving to their current neighborhood for the schools (Wirt *et al.*, 2004).
3. Exceptions to this rule are made if there are too few students in a subgroup to provide statistically reliable results. The minimum subgroup size is determined by each state.
4. Schools that fail to meet AYP for three years in a row must allow students free after-school tutoring. Schools failing to make AYP for five years face school restructuring. School restructuring may include conversion to a charter school or contracting out to private management organizations.
5. Of course, if enough poor students enter a new school, it is possible that the receiving school could become eligible for Title I funds. This would then make the school subject to school choice transfer provisions, however.
6. It should be noted that the robustness of Hoxby's results have been called into question by Rothstein (2005). The instrumental variable in Hoxby's study is the number of streams of various lengths running through an area (areas with streams running through them tend to be broken into more jurisdictions, which creates an exogenous source of variation school district size). Rothstein finds that effect of choice on productivity is highly sensitive to how the lengths of streams is coded. See also Hoxby's response (2005).
7. Arizona has the highest concentration of charter schools in the country and is considered by charter school advocates to be a model for other states to follow.
8. "School improvement" status is the designation for schools that fail to make AYP in two consecutive years.
9. This 2001 Phi Delta Kappa poll found that 54% of parents oppose vouchers to choose private schools at public expense, while 42% favor them. There is some evidence, however, that those who favor vouchers care more about this issue than those who oppose them. When asked whether knowing that a candidate for a national office supports vouchers, 43%. said that this position would make supporting that candidate more likely, while only 37% said that this position would make supporting that candidate less likely (Rose & Gallup, 2004).
10. The mayoral takeover occurred just seven years after a radical decentralization reform plan passed the legislature in 1988.
11. Some analysis indicates that this policy has yet to bear fruit. In neighborhoods with the highest levels of gentrification, white enrollment in the school system has decreased rather than increased. As one observer noted, "Yuppies don't have kids, they have dogs" (Weissman, 2002).
12. Figures are from multilevel models that control for a number of student- and school-level models. See Lauen (2006, Chapter 5) for tables and more details.
13. School productivity is defined as the average student-level residual from the following OLS test score gain model: $9thGr\ Read_{ij} = \beta 0 + \beta 1\ (8thGr\ Road)_{ij} + \beta 2 X_{ij} + \sum_{j=1}^{J-1} Ej\alpha j + e_{ij}$, where $9thGr\ Read_{ij}$ is the 9th grade reading test score (in grade-equivalent units) for student i who attended elementary school j in 8th grade; $8thGr\ Read_{ij}$ is the ith student's 8th grade reading test score (in grade-equivalent units); X_{ij} is a vector of student background characteristics such as poverty, gender, and race/ethnicity; $\sum_{j=1}^{J-1} Ej\alpha j$ is a vector of elementary school fixed effects to control for prior school quality differences; and e_{ij} is the student-specific error component of test score gain. High school k's value added measure. $\hat{V}_k$, is defined as the within-high-school average of the student-level residual: $\hat{V}_k = \frac{\sum e_{ik}}{N_k}$. This specification of the value added model was proposed by Cullen *et al.* (2005). Defining and measuring school productivity is a contentious area of educational policy; further research is needed to determine the validity of this particular specification of the productivity of Chicago's neighborhood high schools.
14. This figure is the result of author calculations based on data provided by the state. It is not shown in the table because comparable figures are not available for previous years.
15. CPS later offered the unaccounted for slots to students in 15 other of the lowest performing schools. Data on the number of students who applied for transfers from this group are unavailable.
16. Figures are from author calculations of state-level federal funding shares and are based on 2003 Census Bureau statistics. (U.S. Census Bureau, 2005)
17. NAEP, or the National Assessment of Educational Progress, is a national test that is "low stakes." In other words, states are not currently held accountable for sub-par performance on NAEP.
18. Remarks published online at www.ed.gov/news/pressreleases/2006/04/04052006.html. Last accessed on May 26, 2006.

References

Allen, J., & Marcucio, A. V. 2005. *The simple guide to charter school laws.* Tech. rept. Center for Education Reform.

Archbald, D. A. 2000. School choice and school stratification: Shortcomings of the stratification critique and recommendations for theory and research. *Educational Policy*, 14(2), 214–240.

Archbald, D. A. 2004. School choice, magnet schools, and the liberation model: An empirical study. *Sociology of Education*, 77, 283–310.

Arum, R. 1996. Do private schools force public schools to compete? *American Sociological Review*, 61(1), 29–46.

Baker, D. P., & Stevenson, D. L. 1986. Mothers' strategies for children's school achievement: Managing the transition to high school. *Sociology of Education*, 59(3), 156–166.

Belfield, C. R., & Levin, H. M. 2002. The effects of competiton between schools on educational outcomes: A review for the United States. *Review of Educational Research*, 72(2), 279–341.

Blau, P. M., & Duncan, O. D. 1967. *The American occupational structure*. New York: Wiley.

Brown, C. G. 2004. *Choosing better schools: A report on student transfers under the No Child Left Behind Act*. Tech. rept. Citizen's Commission on Civil Rights.

Bryk, A., Lee, V. E., & Holland, P. B. 1993. *Catholic Schools and the Common Good*. Cambridge, MA: Harvard University Press.

Bryk, A. S., & Schneider, B. L. 2002. *Trust in schools: a core resource for improvement*. New York: Russell Sage Foundation.

Casserly, M. 2004. Choice and supplemental services in America's greatcity schools. In F. M. Hess & C. E. Finn (Eds.), *Leaving no child behind? Options for kids in failing schools* (pp. 191–211). New York: Palgrave Macmillan.

Center for Education Policy. 2005. *From the capital to the classroom: Year 3 of the No Child Left Behind Act*. Tech. rept. Center for Education Policy.

Center for Education Policy. 2006. *From the capital to the classroom: Year 4 of the No Child Left Behind Act*. Tech. rept. Center for Education Policy.

Cobb, C. D., & Glass, G. V. 1999. Ethnic segregation in Arizona charter schools. *Education Policy Analysis Archives*, 7(1), Retrieved June 23, 2005 (http://epaa.asu.edu/epaa/v7nl/).

Coleman, J. S. 1992. Some points on choice in education. *Sociology of Education*, 65(4), 260–262.

Coleman, J. S., & Holler, T. 1987. *Public and private high schools: the impact of communities*. New York: Basic Books.

Comer, J. P. 1988. Educating poor minority children. *Scientific American*, 259(5), 42–48.

Coons, J. E., & Sugarman, S. D. 1978. *Education by choice: The case for family control*. Berkeley: University of California Press.

Cullen, J. B, Jacob, B. A., & Levitt, S.. 2005. *The effect of school choice on student outcomes: Evidence from randomized lotteries*. NBER Working Paper.

Duchesne, P. D. 2000. 8,000 Passed test after all: Scoring firm blamed for basic-skills test error that kept hundreds from graduating. *Star Tribune* (Minneapolis, MN), July 29, 1A.

Duffrin, E. 2001. Why Kids Flee. *Catalyst Chicago*, December Edition.

Fiske, E. B., & Ladd, H. F. 2000. *When schools compete: A cautionary tale*. Washington, D.C.: Brookings Institution Press.

Friedman, M. 1962. *Capitalism and freedom*. Chicago: University of Chicago Press.

Gill, B. P. 2001. *Rhetoric versus reality: What we know and what we need to know about vouchers and charter schools*. Santa Monica, CA: Rand Education.

Glazeman, S. 1998. *Determinants and consequences of parental school choice*. Doctoral, University of Chicago.

Gorard, S. 2000. Questioning the crisis account: a review of evidence for increasing polarization in schools. *Education Research*, 42(3), 309–21.

Gorard, S., & Fitz, J. 2000. Markets and stratification: A view from England and Wales. *Educational Policy*, 14(3), 405–428.

Green, J. P., Peterson, P. E., & Du, J. 1997. *Effectiveness of school choice: The Milwaukee Experiment*. Tech. rept. Harvard University Program in Education Policy and Governance, Cambridge, MA.

Grossman, K. 2005. Parents declining to send children to top schools: Only a quarter of kids from closing schools apply for open schools. *Chicago Sun-Times*, April 27, News, 34.

Hanushek, E. A., Kain, J. F., & Rivkin, S. G. 2002. *New Evidence about Brown v. Board of Education: The Complex Effects of School Racial Composition on Achievement*. NBER Working Paper No. 8741, January 2002.

Henig, J. R. 1995. Race and choice in Montgomery County, Maryland, Magnet Schools. *Teachers College Record*, 96(4), 729–734.

Hess, G. A. 1984. Renegotiating a multicultural society: Participation in desegregation planning in Chicago. *Journal Of Negro Education*, 53(2), 132–146.

Hochschild, J. L., & Scovronick, N. B. 2003. *The American dream and the public schools*. New York: Oxford University Press.

Howell, W. 2004. Fumbling for an exit key: Parents, choice, and the future of NCLB. In F. M. Hess & C. E. Finn (Eds.), *Leaving no child behind? Options for kids in failing schools* (pp. 161–190). New York: Palgrave Macmillan.

Hoxby, C. M. 2000. Does competition among public schools benefit students and taxpayers? *American Economic Review*, 90(5), 1209–1238.

Hoxby, C. M. 2005 (Mar.). *Competition among public schools: A reply to Rothstein (2004)*. Tech. rept. 11216. National Bureau of Economic Research, Inc. available at http://ideas.repec.org/p/nbr/nberwo/11216.html.

Hoxby, C. M. 2003. School choice and School productivity: Could school choice be a tide that lifts all boats? In C. M. Hoxby (Ed.), *The economics of school choice* (pp. 287–341). Chicago: University of Chicago Press.

Johnson, D. 1987. Chicago leads aay in city school woe. *The New York Times*, December 9, Late City Final Edition, 7.

Kafer, K. 2005. *Choices in Education: 2005 Progress Report*. Tech. rept. 1848. The Heritage Foundation.

Kim, J., & Sunderman, G. 2004. *Does NCLB provide good choices for students in low-performing schools*. Tech. rept. The Civil Rights Project at Harvard University.

Klonsky, M. 1995. GOP clears field, Daley runs with the ball. *Catalyst Chicago*, September Edition.

Krueger, A. B., & Zhu, P. 2004. Another look at the New York City school voucher experiment. *American Behavioral Scientist*, 47(5), 658–698.

Lareau, A. 1989. *Home advantage: social class and parental intervention in elementary education*. Education policy perspectives. Social analysis series. London; New York: Falmer Press.

Lareau, A. 2002. Invisible inequality: Social class and childrearing in black families and white families. *American Sociological Review*, 67(5), 747–776.

Lauen, D. L. 2006. *Opportunity for all? The hidden causes and consequences of school choice in Chicago*. Doctoral, University of Chicago.

Lee, V. E., Croninger, R. G., & Smith, J. B. 1996. Equity and choice in Detroit. In B. Fuller & R. F. Elmore (Eds.), *Who chooses? Who loses?* (pp. 70–94). New York: Teachers College Press.

Levin, H. 2004. Multiple choice questions: The road ahead. In N. Epstein (Ed.), *Who's in charge here? the tangled web of school governance and policy* (pp. 228–255). Denver Washington, D.C.: Education Commission of the States; Brookings Institution Press.

Lubienski, C., & Lubienski, S. T.. 2006. *Charter, private, public schools and academic achievement: New evidence from NAEP Mathematics Data.* Tech. rept. National Center for the Study of Privatization in Education.

MacLeod, J. 1995. *Ain't no makin' it: aspirations and attainment in a low-income neighborhood.* Boulder: Westview Press.

Meyer, J. W., & Rowan, B. 1977. Institutionalized organizations: Formal structure as myth and ceremony. *American Journal of Sociology*, 83(2), 340–363.

Myrdal, G., Sterner, R. M. E., & Rose, A. M. 1944. *An American dilemma; the Negro problem and modern democracy.* New York and London: Harper.

National Working Commission on Choice in K-12 Education. 2003. *School choice doing it the right way makes a difference.* Tech. rept. Brookings Institution.

Neal, D. 1997. The effects of catholic schooling on educational achievement. *Journal of Labor Economics*, 15, 98–123.

Oakes, Je. 1985. *Keeping track: how schools structure inequality.* New Haven: Yale University Press.

Orfield, G., & Eaton, S. E. 1996. *Dismantling desegregation: the quiet reversal of Brown v. Board of Education.* New York: New Press: Distributed by W.W. Norton and Company.

Peterson, P. E. 1976. *School politics, Chicago style.* Chicago: University of Chicago Press.

Pfeffer, J., & Salancik, G. R. 1978. *The external control of organizations: a resource dependence perspective.* New York: Harper and Row.

Renzulli, L. A., & Evans, L. 2005. School choice, charter schools, and white flight. *Social Problems*, 52(3), 398–418.

Roderick, M., Bryk, A. S., Jacob, B. A., Easton, J. Q., & Allensworth, E. 1999. *Ending social promotion.* Tech. rept. Consortium on Chicago Schools Research, Chicago.

Rose, L. C., & Gallup, A. M. 2004. The 36th annual Phi Delta Kappa/Gallup Poll of the public's attitudes toward the public schools. *Phi Delta Kappa*, 86(1), 41–52.

Rosenbaum, J. E. 1976. *Making inequality: The hidden curriculum of high school tracking.* New York: Wiley.

Rossi, R. 2003a. Feds: City falling short of school transfer goals. *Chicago Sun-Times*, October 27, News Special Edition, 10.

Rossi, R. 2003b. To Duncan, No Child Left Behind Law is 'burdensome' and 'tmpractical'. *Chicago Sun-Times*, August 29, News Special Edition, 12.

Rossi, R., & Spielman, F. 2002. Daley protests student transfers. *Chicago Sun-Times*, July 17, News Special Edition, 5.

Rothstein, J. 2005 (Mar.). *Does competition among public schools benefit students and taxpayers? A Comment on Hoxby (2000).* Tech. rept. 11215. National Bureau of Economic Research, Inc. available at http://ideas.repec.org/p/nbr/nberwo/11215.html.

Rouse, C. E. 1998. Private school vouchers and student achievement: An evaluation of the Milwaukee Parental Choice Program. *Quarterly Journal of Economics*, 113(2), 553–602.

Saporito, S. 2003. Private choices, public consequences: Magnet school choice and segregation by race and poverty. *Social Problems*, 50(2), 181–203.

Saporito, S., & Lareau, A. 1999. School selection as a process: The multiple dimensions of race in framing educational choice. *Social Problems*, 46(3), 418–439.

Schneider, M., Teske, P., Marschall, M., & Roch, C. 1998. Shopping for schools: In the land of the blind, the one-eyed parent may be enough. *American Journal of Political Science*, 42(3), 769–793.

Schneider, M., & Buckley, J. 2002. What do parents want from schools? Evidence from the Internet. *Educational Evaluation and Policy Analysis*, 24(2), 133–44.

Teske, P., & Schneider, M. 2001. What research can tell policymakers about school choice. *Journal of Policy Analysis and Management*, 20(4), 609–631.

Turner, R. H. 1960. Sponsored and contest mobility and the school-system. *American Sociological Review*, 25(6), 855–867.

Tyack, D. B. 1974. *The one best system: a history of American urban education.* Cambridge, MA: Harvard University Press.

United States Government Accountability Office. 2004. *No Child Left Behind Act: Education needs to provide additional technical assistance and conduct implementation studies for school choice provision: report to Secretary of Education.* Washington, D.C.: United States Government Accountability Office.

U.S. Census Bureau. 2005. *Public education finances, 2003.* Tech. rept. U.S. Census Bureau.

U.S. Department of Education. 2004. *Public school choice: Non-regulatory Guidance.*

Weissman, D. 2002. Gentrifiers slow to buy CPS. *Catalyst Chicago*, Februaury Edition.

Wells, A. S., & Crain, R. L. 1997. *Stepping over the color line: African-American students in white suburban schools.* New Haven: Yale University Press.

West, M. R., & Peterson, P. E. 2006. The efficacy of choice threats within School accountability systems: Results from legislatively induced eExperiments. *The Economic Journal*, 116(March), C46–C62.

Wirt, J., Choy, S., Rooney, P, Provasnik, S., Sen, A., & Tobin, R. 2004. *The condition of education 2004.* Tech. rept. U.S. Department of Education.

Witte, J. F. 2000. *The market approach to education.* Princeton University Press.

Wolf, P., Butmann, B., Puma, M., & Silverberg, M.. 2006. *Evaluation of the D.C. Opportunity Scholarship Program: Second year report on participation.* Washington, D.C.: U.S. Government Printing Office. U.S. Department of Education, Institute of Education Sciences.

Our Impoverished View of Educational Reform

DAVID C. BERLINER

Over the last three years, I have co-authored three reports about the effects of high-stakes testing on curriculum, instruction, school personnel, and student achievement (Amrein & Berliner, 2002; Nichols & Berliner, 2005; Nichols, Glass & Berliner, 2006). They were all depressing. My co-authors and I found high-stakes testing programs in most states ineffective in achieving their intended purposes, and causing severe unintended negative effects, as well. We believe that the federal No Child Left Behind (NCLB) law is a near perfect case of political spectacle (Smith, 2004), much more theater than substance. Our collectively gloomy conclusions led me to wonder what would really improve the schools that are not now succeeding, for despite the claims of many school critics, only some of America's schools are not now succeeding (Berliner, 2004).

I do not believe that NCLB is needed to tell us precisely where those failing schools are located, and who inhabits them. We have had that information for over a half century. For me, NCLB is merely delaying the day when our country acknowledges that a common characteristic is associated with the great majority of schools that are most in need of improvement; it is this common characteristic of our failing schools that I write about, for by ignoring it, we severely limit our thinking about school reform.

This is an essay about poverty and its powerful effects on schooling. So these musings could have been written also by Jean Anyon, Bruce Biddle, Greg Duncan, Jeanne Brooks-Gunn, Gary Orfield, Richard Rothstein, and many others whose work I admire and from whom I borrow. Many scholars and teachers understand, though many politicians choose not to, that school reform is heavily constrained by factors that are outside of America's classrooms and schools. Although the power of schools and educators to influence individual students is never to be underestimated, the out-of-school factors associated with poverty play both a powerful and a limiting role in what can actually be achieved.

In writing about these issues, I ask for the tolerance of sociologists, economists, child development researchers, and others who read this essay because I discuss variables that are the subject of intense debate within the disciplines. Although scholars dispute the ways we measure the constructs of social class, poverty, and neighborhood, we all still manage to have common enough understandings of these concepts to communicate sensibly. That will suffice for my purposes. In this essay it is not important to argue about the fine points at which poverty is miserable or barely tolerable, or whether a person is stuck in the lowest of the social classes or merely belongs to the working poor, or whether families are poor at the federal poverty level or at 200% of the federal poverty level (which is still poor by almost everyone's standards). We know well enough what we mean when we talk of poverty, communities of poverty, the very poor, and the like. We also know that the lower social classes and the communities in which they live are not at all homogeneous. It is a simplification, and therefore a mistake, to treat a group as if the individuals who comprise that group were the same. I also ask for my readers' tolerance for ignoring these distinctions in what follows.

The Basic Problem of Poverty and Educational Reform

It seems to me that in the rush to improve student achievement through accountability systems relying on high-stakes tests, our policy makers and citizens forgot, or cannot understand, or deliberately avoid the fact, that our children live nested lives. Our youth are in classrooms, so when those classrooms do not function as we want them to, we go to work on improving them. Those classrooms are in schools, so when we decide that those schools are not performing appropriately, we go to work on improving them, as well. But both students and schools are situated in neighborhoods filled with families. And in our country the individuals living in those school neighborhoods are not a random cross section of Americans. Our neighborhoods are highly segregated by social class, and thus, also segregated by race and ethnicity. So all educational efforts that focus on classrooms and schools, as does NCLB, could be reversed by family, could be negated by neighborhoods, and might well be subverted or minimized by what happens to children outside of school. Improving classrooms and schools, working on curricula and standards, improving teacher quality and fostering better use of technology are certainly helpful. But sadly, such activities may also be similar to those of the drunk found on his hands and knees under a street lamp. When asked by a passerby what he was doing, the drunk replied that he was looking for his keys. When asked where he lost them, the drunk replied "over there," and pointed back up the dark street. When the passerby then asked the drunk why he wasn't looking for the keys where they were located, the drunk answered "the light is better here!"

I believe we need to worry whether the more important keys to school reform are up the block, in the shadows, where the light is not as bright. If we do choose to peer into the dark we might see what the recently deceased sociologist Elizabeth Cohen saw quite clearly: That poverty constitutes the unexamined 600-pound gorilla that most affects American education today (cited in Biddle, p. 3, 2001).

When I think about that gorilla it immediately seems ludicrous to me that most of what we try to do to help poor youth is classroom and school based. Education doesn't just take place in our schools, a point that Pulitzer prize-winning historian Lawrence Cremin tried to make as the reform movement gained momentum in the late 1980s (Cremin, 1990). It is a fact of contemporary American life that many of the poorest of the children who come to our schools have spent no time at all in school-like settings during the first five years of their life. And then, when of school-age, children only spend about 30 of their waking hours a week in our schools, and then only for about two-thirds of the weeks in a year. You can do the arithmetic yourselves. In the course of a full year students might spend just over 1,000 hours in school, and almost 5 times that amount of time in their neighborhood and with their families.

For all youth those 5,000 hours require learning to be a member of one or more cultural groups in that community, learning to behave appropriately in diverse settings, learning ways to get along with others, to fix things, to think, and to explain things to others. These are natural and influential experiences in growing up. But for poor kids, ghetto kids, what is learned in those settings can often be unhelpful. It was Jean Anyon, among others, who some time ago alerted us to the fact that many of the families in those impoverished neighborhoods are so poorly equipped to raise healthy children, that the schools those children attend would have a hard time educating them, even if they weren't also so poorly organized and run. Anyon (1995) said

> It is has become increasingly clear that several decades of educational reform have failed to bring substantial improvements to schools in America's inner cities. Most recent analyses of unsuccessful school reform (and prescriptions for change) have isolated educational, regulatory, or financial aspects of reform from the social context of poverty and race in which inner city schools are located. (p. 69)

...the structural basis for failure in inner-city schools is political, economic, and cultural, and must be changed before meaningful school improvement projects can be successfully implemented. Educational reforms cannot compensate for the ravages of society. (p. 88)

More recently Anyon (2005, p. 69) bluntly evaluated the pervasive failure of school reform. She says:

Currently, relatively few urban poor students go past ninth grade: The graduation rates in large comprehensive inner-city high schools are abysmally low. In fourteen such New York City schools, for example, only 10 percent to 20 percent of ninth graders in 1996 graduated four years later. Despite the fact that low-income individuals desperately need a college degree to find decent employment, only 7 percent obtain a bachelors degree by age twenty-six. So, in relation to the needs of low-income students, urban districts fail their students with more egregious consequences now than in the early twentieth century.

Oakland, California, where my grandson goes to school, announced recently that its high-school graduation rate is 48% (Asimov, 2005). Oakland has been reforming its schools at least since 1973 when I first started working there. Oakland's educators are not ignorant or uncaring, and neither are Oakland's parents. But no one has been able to fix Oakland's public schools. In Oakland and elsewhere, is that because we are looking for the keys in the wrong place?

As educators and scholars we continually talk about school reform as if it must take place inside the schools. We advocate, for the most part, for adequacy in funding, high-quality teachers, professional development, greater subject matter preparation, cooperative learning, technologically enhanced instruction, community involvement, and lots of other ideas and methods I also promote. Some of the most lauded of our school reform programs in our most distressed schools do show some success, but success often means bringing the students who are at the 20th percentile in reading and mathematics skills up to the 30th percentile in those skills. Statistical significance and a respectable effect size for a school reform effort is certainly worthy of our admiration, but it just doesn't get as much accomplished as needs to be done.

Perhaps we are not doing well enough because our vision of school reform is impoverished. It is impoverished because of our collective views about the proper and improper roles of government in ameliorating the problems that confront us in our schools; our beliefs about the ways in which a market economy is supposed to work; our concerns about what constitutes appropriate tax rates for the nation; our religious views about the elect and the damned; our peculiar American ethos of individualism; and our almost absurd belief that schooling is the cure for whatever ails society. These well-entrenched views that we have as a people makes helping the poor seem like some kind of communist or atheistic plot, and it makes one an apostate in reference to the myth about the power of the public schools to affect change.

James Traub (2000) writing in the New York Times said this all quite well a few years ago. He noted that it was hard to think of a more satisfying solution to poverty than education. School reform, as opposed to other things we might do to improve achievement, really involves relatively little money and, perhaps more importantly, asks practically nothing of the nonpoor, who often control a society's resources. Traub also noted that school reform is accompanied by the good feelings that come from our collective expression of faith in the capacity of the poor to overcome disadvantage on their own. Our myth of individualism fuels the school reform locomotive.

On the other hand, the idea that schools *cannot* cure poverty by themselves sounds something like a vote of no confidence in our great American capacity for self-transformation, a major element in the stories we tell of our American nation. Traub notes that when we question the schools' ability to foster transformation we seem to flirt with the racial theories expressed by Charles Murray and

Richard Herrnstein, who argued in *The Bell Curve* (1994) that educational inequality has its roots in biological inequality. But an alternative explanation to Herrnstein and Murray, "is that educational inequality is rooted in economic problems and social pathologies too deep to be overcome by school alone. And if that's true, then there really is every reason to think about the limits of school" (Traub, 2000, p. 54). Schooling alone may be too weak an intervention for improving the lives of most children now living in poverty.

Those who blame poor children and their families, like Herrnstein and Murray, or those who blame the teachers and administrators who serve those kids and families in our public schools, like Rod Paige, Jeanne Allen, Checker Finn, William Bennett, and dozens of other well-known school critics, are all refusing to acknowledge the root problem contended with by too many American schools, namely, that there is a 600-pound gorilla in the school house.

The economist Richard Rothstein understands this. In his recent book *Class and Schools* (2004), he states:

> Policy makers almost universally conclude that existing and persistent achievement gaps must be the result of wrongly designed school policies—either expectations that are too low, teachers who are insufficiently qualified, curricula that are badly designed, classes that are too large, school climates that are too undisciplined, leadership that is too unfocussed, or a combination of these.
>
> Americans have come to the conclusion that the achievement gap is the fault of "failing schools" because it makes no common sense that it could be otherwise.... This common sense perspective, however, is misleading and dangerous. It ignores how social class characteristics in a stratified society like ours may actually influence learning in schools. (pp. 9–10)

Like Anyon, Rothstein goes on to note:

> For nearly half a century, the association of social and economic disadvantage with a student achievement gap has been well known to economists, sociologists and educators. Most, however, have avoided the obvious implication of this understanding—raising the achievement of lower-class children requires the amelioration of the social and economic conditions of their lives, not just school reform. (Rothstein, p. 11)

Anyon, Rothstein, and others provide the framework for the issues I raise in this essay. But first, having raised the spectre of the gorilla, let me provide information on the magnitude of the American problem. I can do that by benchmarking American rates of childhood poverty against the rates in other industrialized nations.

America's Poverty Problem

The UNICEF report from the Innocenti Foundation (UNICEF, 2005), which regularly issues reports on childhood poverty, is among the most recent to reliably document this problem. The entire report is summarized quite simply in one graph, presented as Figure 27.1.

In this set of rich nations, the United States is among the leaders in childhood poverty over the decade of the 1990s. The only nation with a record worse than ours is Mexico, and, contrary to UNICEF, I would not consider Mexico a rich nation. Using 2003 data to compute Gross National Income per capita (using Purchasing Power Parity [PPP] as the method of comparison), the United States ranked fourth at $37,750 per capita, while Mexico ranked 80th with $8,900 per capita (World Bank, 2005). We should not be in the same league as Mexico, but, alas, we are closer to them in poverty rate than to others whom we might, more commonly, think of as our peers.

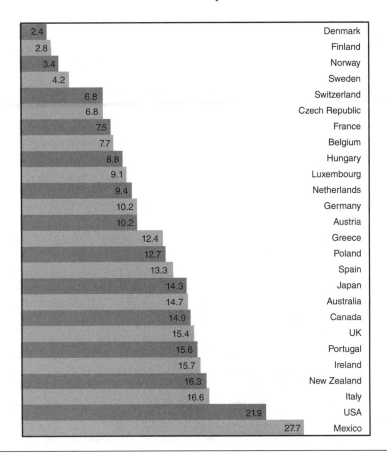

Figure 27.1 Childhood poverty rates in rich countries. (Reprinted from UNICEF, 2005, used by permission.)

Figure 27.1 informs us that we have the highest rate of childhood poverty among the rich nations, which is what other studies have shown for over a decade (Berliner and Biddle, 1995). Our rank has been remarkably steady. The United States likes to be #1 in everything, and when it comes to the percent of children in poverty among the richest nations in the world, we continue to hold our remarkable status.

One bit of good news about poverty in the United States is that over the decade of the 1990s we lowered our embarrassing rate of poverty a great deal, almost 2.5%. So in the graph presented in Figure 27.1 you are seeing a measure of childhood poverty in the United States after years of improvement! But there is also some bad news. First, the expansion of jobs and income growth in our nation stopped at the end of the 1990s, and the gains that had been made have been lost. With the sharp increase in housing prices that has occurred since then, no noticeable increases in the real wages for the poor, an economic expansion that has failed to create jobs, and a reduction in tax revenues (resulting in a reduction of aid to the poor), it is quite likely that our rate of childhood poverty is back to where it was. That would be about 2 or more percentage points higher than the figure given in this UNICEF report. Apparently this is about where we as a nation want the rate to be, since the graph makes it abundantly clear that if we cared to do something about it, we could emulate the economic policies of other industrialized nations and not have the high rate of poverty that we do.

In Figure 27.2 we note the percentage of people in the United States who are living at half the rate of those classified as merely poor (Mishel, Bernstein & Allegretto, 2005, p. 323, from data supplied

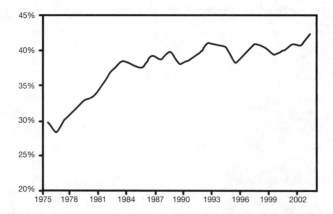

Figure 27.2 Percent of the poor living at half the official poverty rate. (Reprinted from Mishel, Bernstein and Allegretto, 2005. Used by permission of the publisher, Cornell University Press.)

by the US Bureau of the Census). These are the poorest of the poor in our nation, constituting over 40% of the tens of millions of people that are officially classified as the "poor" by our government. But I need to also note that the classification scheme used by our government is suspect. Almost all economists believe that the level of income at which the government declares a person to be poor misleads us into thinking there are fewer poor than there really are. So it is likely that there are many more very poor people than this graph suggests.

I call attention in Figure 27.2 to the overall upward trend of the desperately poor in this graph, particularly the upturn after 2000. That is why the rates given in Figure 27.1 may be an underestimate of the conditions that pertain now, in 2006. Something else needs to be noted about the poverty we see among children. It is not random. Poverty is unequally distributed across the many racial and ethnic groups that make up the American nation.

Figure 27.3 makes clear that poverty is strongly correlated with race and ethnicity (Mishel, Bernstein & Allegretto, p. 316, from data supplied by the U.S. Bureau of the Census). Note once again the

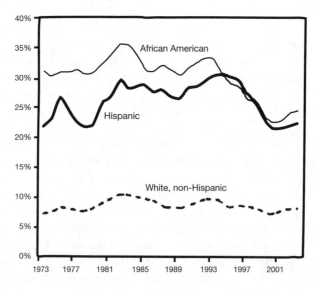

Figure 27.3 U.S. poverty rates by ethnicity. (Reprinted from Mishel, Bernstein and Allegretto, 2005, by permission of the publisher, Cornell University Press.)

upward trend for poverty among minorities after the roaring 90s ended. New immigrants, African-Americans, and Hispanics, particularly those among these groups who live in urban areas, are heavily overrepresented in the groups that suffer severe poverty. Thus, while this is a paper about poverty, it is inextricably tied to issues of race in America. I have found no way to separate the two, though here I focus on poverty, perhaps the more tractable issue.

The UNICEF report (2005, p. 8) also reminds us that there is a charter about the rights of children to which 192 United Nations members have agreed. It is sad, I know, that many member nations sign such a charter and then do little to live up to it. But still, at the very least, signing is an acknowledgment of the underlying concept and only two nations have refused to sign this treaty. One of these nations is Somalia.

Can you guess which is the other nation? You guessed correctly if you chose the United States of America. We will not sign a charter guaranteeing the rights of already born children, though we somehow managed to get a bill through our congress that guarantees the rights of unborn children. As Congressman Barney Frank was said to mutter one day, there are many people who "believe that life begins at conception, and ends at birth!" (Erbe & Shiner, 1997).

Apparently we, the American people, do not agree with such radical ideas as those expressed in article 27 of the UN charter. There it is stated that governments should "recognize the right of every child to a standard of living adequate for the child's physical, mental, spiritual, moral and social development" (UNICEF, 2005, p. 8).

Article 27 also makes clear that parents or others responsible for the child "have the primary responsibility to secure…the conditions of living necessary for the child's development," but that governments should assist parents "to implement this right and shall in case of need provide material assistance and support programs, particularly with regard to nutrition, clothing and housing" (UNICEF, 2005, p. 8).

We actually have many programs to help parents and children, but because they are fragmented, do not cover everyone eligible, are subject to variability in funding, they end up not nearly as good nor as serious in intent as those in many other countries. While school critics delight in talking about our inadequate achievement vis-à-vis other nations, it seems just as important to talk about other nations' attention to the poor and the mechanisms each has for helping people out of poverty as soon as possible. This should also be an important indicator for judging one nation's performance against another. If we do that, our country does not look good.

Table 27.1 shows that we are a leader among the rich nations of the world in terms of failing to help people exit from poverty once they have fallen into poverty (Mishel, Berstein & Allegretto, p. 409, from data supplied by the OECD). One column in this table shows the percent of individuals who became impoverished once in a three-year time period, say through illness, divorce, childbirth, or job loss—the big four poverty producers among those who had been non-poor. There we see that the U.S. rate is quite high, but not much different than that of many other nations. Poverty befalls many people, in many countries, once in a while.

Our national problem shows in the next column, displaying the percent of people who stayed poor for the entire three years after they had fallen into poverty. At a rate roughly twice that of other wealthy nations, we lead the industrialized world! Unlike other wealthy countries, we have few mechanisms to get people out of poverty once they fall into poverty.

In the last column of Table 27.1 we can see how awful it can be to stumble into poverty in the United States compared to other nations. In that column we see the percent of people who stayed below the poverty level on a relatively permanent basis. The United States likes to lead the world, and here we are, champs once again! We can claim the highest rate of the permanently poor of all the other industrialized nations! If you compare the data from Denmark, Ireland, or the Netherlands to

Table 27.1 Poverty in OECD Countries over a Three-Year Period, and Permanent Poverty, During the 1990s.

Country	Percent poor once in three years	Percent poor for all three years	Percent in nation permanently poor
United States	23.5	9.5	14.5
Denmark	9.1	0.8	1.8
Ireland	15.3	1.3	5.3
Netherlands	12.9	1.6	4.5
France	16.6	3.0	6.6
Italy	21.5	5.6	10.4
United Kingdom	19.5	2.4	6.5
Canada	18.1	5.1	8.9
Belgium	16.0	2.8	5.2
Germany	19.2	4.3	8.1
Finland	25.1	6.5	12.2
Portugal	24.2	7.8	13.4
Spain	21.3	3.7	8.7

Source: Reprinted from Mishel, Bernstein and Allegretto, 2005. Used by permission of the publisher, Cornell University Press.

that of the United States, it is easy to see the difference between societies that abhor poverty, and one such as ours, that accepts poverty as a given.

Poverty and Student Achievement

I have now pointed out that in the United States the rates of childhood poverty are high, poverty is racialized, and that those who once get trapped in poverty have a hard time getting out of poverty. But what does this mean for us in terms of student achievement? There are, of course, thousands of studies showing correlations between poverty and academic achievement. Nothing there will surprise us, though I do wonder why, after hundreds of studies showing that cigarettes were related to a great number of serious illnesses we eventually came to believe that the relationship between smoking and cancer, or smoking and emphysema, was causal. And yet when we now have research establishing analogous connections between poverty and educational attainment we ignore them. Instead we look for other causal mechanisms, like low expectations of teachers, or the quality of teachers' subject matter knowledge, to explain the relationship. Of course the low expectations of teachers and their subject matter competency are important. But I keep thinking about that 600-pound gorilla out there asking for more attention than it is getting. That big ape may be causal in the relationships we consistently find between poverty and achievement.

Since the relationship is well known, let us look briefly at how U.S. poverty is related to student achievement in just the international studies, since it is our international competitiveness that worries so many in industry and government, and it is those worries that kindled the reform movement in education. We can start with the recent Trends in International Mathematics and Science Study, known as TIMSS 2003, released at the end of 2004 (Gonzales, Guzmán, Partelow, Pahlke, Jocelyn, Kastenberg, & Williams, 2004). Table 27.2 presents data on mathematics and science scores for American 4th and 8th grade youth disaggregated by the degree of poverty in the schools they attend.

In this table three aspects of our performance with regard to other nations are instructive. First, our scores in both subject areas and at both grade levels were correlated perfectly with the percent of poor students who attend a school. In the five categories presented, schools with the wealthier students had the highest average score, the next wealthier set of schools had students who had the next highest average score, and so forth, until we see that the schools with the poorest students had the students who scored the lowest. This pattern is common.

Table 27.2 Fourth and Eighth Grade Mathematics and Science Scores from TIMMS 2003

Poverty level of school (percent free or reduced lunch)	Fourth grade math scores	Fourth grade science scores	Eighth grade math scores	Eighth grade science scores
Less than 10% in poverty (schools with wealthy students)	567	579	547	571
10%–24.9% in poverty	543	567	531	554
25%–49.9% in poverty	533	551	505	529
50%–74.9% in poverty	500	519	480	504
75% or more in poverty (schools with poor students)	471	480	444	461
U.S. Average Score	518	536	504	527
International Average Score	495	489	466	473

Source: Gonzales et al., 2004.

The second thing to note is that the average scores for the schools with less than 50% of their students in poverty exceeded the US average score, while the average scores for the schools with greater than 50% of their students in poverty fell below the US average score. This tells us who is and who is not succeeding in the United States.

The third thing to notice pertains to the schools that serve the most impoverished students, where 75% or more of the students are eligible for free or reduced lunch. That is, almost all the students in these schools live in extreme poverty and those are the students that fall well below the international average obtained in this study. In general, Table 27.2 informs us that our poor students are not competitive internationally while our middle classes and wealthy public school children are doing extremely well in comparison to the pool of countries that made up TIMSS 2003.

As we go through these data and learn that poor students are not doing well in international competitions, the question we seem unable to raise and debate intelligently is this: Why do we put so much of our attention and resources into trying to fix what goes on inside low-performing schools when the causes of low performance may reside outside the school? Is it possible that we might be better off devoting more of our attention and resources than we now do toward helping the families in the communities that are served by those schools? That would certainly be a competitive strategy for solving the problem of low academic performance if it is simply poverty (along with its associated multitude of difficulties) that prevents most poor children from doing well.

There are more international data to examine. The OECD has instituted a three-year cycle for looking at reading, mathematics, and science for 15-year-olds, called the PISA studies—the Program for International Student Assessment (Lemke, Calsyn, Lippman, Jocelyn, Kastberg, Liu, Roey, Williams, Kruger, & Bairu, 2001). Unfortunately PISA doesn't do a very good job of breaking down the data by social class. So I report on ethnicity and race to discuss the effects of poverty on achievement. Given the high inter-correlations between poverty, ethnicity, and school achievement in our country, it is (sadly) not inappropriate to use ethnicity as a proxy for poverty.

Tables 27.3, 27.4, and 27.5 display the performance in 2000 of US 15-year-olds in mathematics, literacy, and science, in relation to other nations. What stands out first is a commonly found pattern in international studies of achievement, namely, that US average scores are very close to the international average. But in a country as heterogeneous and as socially and ethnically segregated as ours, mean scores of achievement are not useful for understanding how we are really doing in international comparisons. Such data must be disaggregated. I have done that in each of the three tables presenting

Table 27.3 Mathematics Scores (mean 500) from PISA 2000

Country	Score
Japan	557
Korea, Republic of	547
New Zealand	537
Finland	536
Australia	533
Canada	533
United States Average Score for White Students	**530**
Switzerland	529
United Kingdom	529
Belgium	520
France	517
Austria	515
Denmark	514
Iceland	514
Sweden	510
Ireland	503
Norway	499
Czech Republic	498
United States Average Score	**493**
Germany	490
Hungary	488
Spain	476
Poland	470
Italy	457
Portugal	454
Greece	447
Luxembourg	446
United States Average Score for Hispanic Students	**437**
United States Average Score for African American Students	**423**
Mexico	387

Source: Lemke et al., 2001.

PISA data. From those tables we see clearly that our white students (without regard for social class) were among the highest performing students in the world. But our African American and Hispanic students, also undifferentiated by social class, were among the poorest performing students in this international sample.

Looking at all three tables reveals something very important about inequality in the United States. If the educational opportunities available to white students in our public schools were made available to all our students, the United States would have been the 7th highest scoring nation in mathematics, 2nd highest scoring nation in reading, and the 4th highest scoring nation in science. Schooling for millions of US white children is clearly working quite well. On the other hand, were our minority students "nations," they would score almost last among the industrialized countries of the world.

Given these findings, and a scientific attitude, we should be asking what plausible hypotheses might differentiate the education of white, African American, and Hispanic students from one another? Segregated schooling seems to be one obvious answer. Orfield and Lee (2005) in their recent report on school segregation make clear how race and schooling are bound together, as is shown in Table 27.6.

Orfield and Lee's data suggests that segregation is an overriding contributor to the obvious scoring disparities that exist between races. Only 12% of white children go to schools where the majority of the students are not white. And only 1% of white students go to schools that are over 90% minority. Eighty-eight percent of white children are attending schools that are majority white. In contrast,

Table 27.4 Literacy Scores (mean 500) from PISA

Country	Score
Korea, Republic of	552
Japan	550
United States Average Score for White Students	**538**
Finland	538
United Kingdom	532
Canada	529
New Zealand	528
Australia	528
Austria	519
Ireland	513
Sweden	512
Czech Republic	511
France	500
Norway	500
United States Average Score	**499**
Hungary	496
Iceland	496
Belgium	496
Switzerland	496
Spain	491
Germany	487
Poland	483
Denmark	481
Italy	478
Greece	461
Portugal	459
United States Average Score for Hispanic Students	**449**
United States Average Score for African American Students	**445**
Luxembourg	443
Mexico	422

Source: Lemke et al., 2001.

almost all African American and Latino students, usually poorer than their white age-mates, are in schools where there are students very much like them racially and socioeconomically. Latinos and African Americans are as segregated by poverty as they are by race and ethnicity, which may be the more important issue with which our schools have to deal.

In the 2003 PISA studies that came out at the end of 2004, the US position relative to other OECD nations slipped. No one is sure why this happened, and we will have to see if this holds up when the 2006 PISA results are analyzed. But relative positions of white, African American, and Hispanic students remained the same and quite discrepant. For example, Table 27.7 presents the PISA 2003 scores in mathematics literacy, the latest international scores we have. These data are disaggregated by both race and social class (Lemke, Sen, Pahlke, Partelow, Miller, Williams, Kastberg, & Jocelyn, 2004).

The pattern of results in Table 27.7 looks familiar, regardless of whether we examine race or social class. White students (disregarding social classes) and upper-income students (of all races) score well. Their test scores in mathematics literacy are significantly above the international average. But lower social class children of any race and black or Hispanic children of all social classes are not performing well. They score significantly below the international average. Clearly those who are poor do not have the mathematical skills to compete internationally, and those particular children are often African American and Hispanic. Poverty, race, and ethnicity are inextricably entwined in the United States.

One more study is informative in this brief look at poverty and the performance of US students in international comparisons. This is the PIRLS study (Ogle, Sen, Pahlke, Jocelyn, Kastberg, Roey, &

Table 27.5 Science Scores (mean 500) from PISA 2000

Country	Score
Korea, Republic of	552
Japan	550
Finland	538
United States Average Score for White Students	**535**
United Kingdom	532
Canada	529
New Zealand	528
Australia	528
Austria	519
Ireland	513
Sweden	512
Czech Republic	511
France	500
Norway	500
United States Average Score	**499**
Hungary	496
Iceland	496
Belgium	496
Switzerland	496
Spain	491
Germany	487
Poland	483
Denmark	481
Italy	478
Greece	461
Portugal	459
Luxembourg	443
United States Average Score for Hispanic Students	**438**
United States Average Score for African American Students	**435**
Mexico	422

Source: Lemke et al., 2001.

Williams, 2003). PIRLS stands for Progress in International Reading Literacy, a reading assessment administered to 9- and 10-year-olds in 35 nations. The data from this comparison are presented in Table 27.8. The United States did quite well. Our nation ranked ninth, though statistically, we tied with others at third place. This is quite heartening since these data prove our President and former Secretary of Education wrong in their belief that teachers in the United States cannot teach reading.

But PIRLS revealed more than the fact that for the second time in about a decade US 9-year-olds showed remarkably high literacy skills. For instance, the mean score of US white children, without any concern about their social class status, was quite a bit higher than that of the Swedish children who, it should be noted, are also a very white group, and in this study the leading nation in the world.

Table 27.6 Minority Makeup of Schools Attended by Different Racial/Ethnic Groups

	Minority make-up of school		
	50–100%	90–100%	99–100%
White Students	12	1	0
Latino Students	77	38	11
Black Students	73	38	18

Source: Orfield & Lee, 2005.

Table 27.7 Mathematical Literacy Scores in PISA 2003, by both Race and Social

Race	**White**	**512**
	African American	**417**
	Hispanic	**443**
Social class	Q1 (Lowest SES)	448
By quartile	Q2	477
	Q3	497
	Q4	530

Source: Lemke et al., 2001.

Once again we see that millions of US white children are doing well against international benchmarks. Further, when we take social class into consideration by looking at the scores of students who attend schools where there are few or no children of poverty, we learn that this group of public school children performed quite well. In fact, these higher social class children from the United States walloped the Swedes, scoring 585, an average of 24 points higher than the average score obtained by Swedish students. Public school students by the millions, from US schools that do not serve many poor children, are doing fine in international competition.

But the scores obtained by students attending schools where poverty is prevalent are shockingly low. The mean score in literacy in schools where more than 75% of the children are on free and reduced lunch was 485, 100 points below the scores of our wealthy students, and well below those of many nations that are our economic competitors. The PIRLS study also informed us that, compared to other nations, the United States had the largest urban/suburban score difference among the competing nations. In that finding, as in the segregation data, we see a contributor to many of our nations' educational problems. The urban/suburban social class differences in the United States result in de facto segregation by race and ethnicity. Middle- and upper-class white families in the suburbs live quite separately from the poor and ethnically diverse families of the urban areas. School and community resources differ by social class, and therefore differ also by race and ethnicity.

From these recent international studies, and from literally thousands of other studies both domestic and international, we learn that the relationship between social class and test scores is positive, high, and well embedded in theories that can explain the relationship. This suggests a hypothesis that is frightening to hear uttered in a capitalist society, namely, that if the incomes of our poorest citizens were to go up a bit, so might achievement scores and other indicators that characterize a well-functioning school. Sometimes a correlation exists precisely because causation exists.

Table 27.8 Highest Scoring Nations in Reading Literacy for Nine- and Ten-years-olds in 35 Countries

Rank	Country	Scorer
1	Sweden	561
2	Netherlands	554
3	England	553
4	Bulgaria	550
5	Latvia	545
6	Canada	544
7	Lithuania	543
8	Hungary	543
9	United States	542
10	Italy	541

Source: PIRLS 2001; Ogle et al., 2003.

How Poverty Affects Achievement

Can a reduction of poverty improve the achievement of the poor and the schools they are in? I will only mention a few of the many studies that have caught my attention while thinking about this issue. One that impressed me greatly demonstrated that poverty, pure and simple, prevents the genes involved in academic intelligence to express themselves (Turkheimer, Haley, Waldron, D'Onofrio, & Gottesman, 2003).

We all have heard of the occasional feral child, or about the child kept locked in a closet for some years. We learned from those cases that under extreme environmental conditions whatever genetic potential for language, height, or intellectual functioning a child had, that potential was unable to be expressed. The powerful and awful environment in which such children lived suppressed the expression of whatever genes that child had for complete mastery of language, for full height, for complete intellectual functioning, for competency in social relationships, and so forth.

This is the same point made by evolutionary biologist Richard Lewontin (1982), who discussed how two genetically identical seeds of corn planted in very different plots of earth would grow to very different heights. In the plot with good soil, sufficient water, and sunshine, genetics accounts for almost all of the noticeable variation in the plants, while environment is much less of a factor in the variation that we see. On the other hand, when the soil, water, and sun are not appropriate, genetics do not account for much of the noticeable variation among the lower-growing and often sickly plants that are our harvest. Genes do not have a chance to express themselves under poor environmental conditions.

Lewontin's example now has a human face. There is strong evidence that the influence of genes on intelligence is quite dependent on social class. For example, Turkheimer and his colleagues determined the hereditability of IQ for those who were and were not economically advantaged. The total sample studied began with almost 50,000 women, followed from pregnancy on, in the National Collaborative Perinatal Project. These women gave birth to hundreds of twins, both mono- and di-zygotic. At the lowest end of the socioeconomic spectrum were families with a median income of $17,000 a year in 1997 dollars. One in five of these mothers was younger than 21, one-third of them were on public assistance, and more than one-third did not have a husband. These were the most impoverished of the family groupings studied, the kind of people that we ordinarily refer to as very poor. Unlike most other studies of hereditability in twins, there were enough of these families in the sample to do a separate estimate of the hereditability of IQ in their children. Wechsler IQ was measured for the twins when they were 7 years old, old enough to get a good fix on what their adult IQ was likely to be. The findings are clear and presented in Figure 27.4.

Figure 27.4 presents the smoothed curve of the relationship between genotype and phenotype, between hereditability and its expression. It shows that at the low end of the 100 point scale that was used to measure socioeconomic status, the heritability of IQ was found to be about 0.10 on a scale of zero (no hereditability) to one (100% heritable, as is eye-color); at the other end of the SES scale, we see that for families of the highest socioeconomic status, the heritability was estimated to be 0.72.

That is, among the lowest social classes, where the mean IQ is quite a bit lower than that of those in the higher social classes, only 10% of the variation we see in measured IQ is due to genetic influences. Thus, the environment accounts for almost all the variation in intelligence that we see. Just as in Lewontin's corn growing example, genetic variation in intelligence in these impoverished environments is not being expressed in the measures we use to assess intelligence. And also as in Lewontin's example, at the top end of the SES scale, almost three quarters of the variation we see in measures of intelligence is due to genetic influences. These findings suggest a number of things.

First, put bluntly, poverty sucks. Among the poor the normal variation we see in academic talent has been sucked away, like corn growing in bad soil.

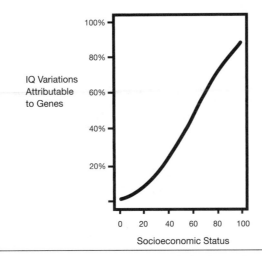

Figure 27.4 Percentage of variation in IQ attributable to genes, for various levels of socioeconomic status (Turkheimer et al., 2003, used by permission of the authors).

Second, all charges of genetic inferiority in intelligence among poor people, minorities or not, have little basis. Genes are not accounting for much of their phenotypic IQ. Environment is the overwhelming influence on measured IQ among the poor. This suggests that unless environments for the most impoverished improve we will not see the expression of the normal human genetic variation in intelligence that is expected. The problem we have, however, is that we don't yet know with much certainty how to improve those environments, because we don't yet know what it is about those environments that is so debilitating. However, Occam's razor suggests that the simplest explanation should be given precedence when attempting to explain any phenomenon. The simplest explanation available is that poverty, and all it entails, causes a restriction of genetic variation in intelligence. We do not need to wait until we understand the micro environments of the poor to know that the macro environment of the poor needs to be changed if we desire to let all the genetic talent that exists among the poor flower.

A third thought arises from this study, and others like it. That is, if genes are not accounting for a great deal of variation in IQ among the poor, and environment is, then environmental interventions for poor people are very likely to change things. In fact, environmental changes for poor children might be predicted to have much bigger effects than similar changes made in the environments for wealthier children. This often appears to be the case, a conclusion reached by Duncan and Brooks-Gunn (2001) using different data. When I look at the studies of the effects of small class size for the poor, or the effects of early childhood education for the poor, or the effects of summer school programs for the poor, the largest effects are found among the poorest children. Thus it seems to me that Turkheim et al. bring us remarkably good news from their study of genetic influences on IQ. The racism and pessimism expressed in *The Bell Curve* by Herrnstein and Murray (1994) can now be seen as completely unjustified because among the very poor genes are not very powerful influences on intelligence, while environments are.

Point four arising from this study is derived from Figure 27.5, also taken from the Turkheimer et al. study. This graph informs us that most of the variation in IQ at the bottom of the SES ladder is due to the environments shared by family members, and that the family's role in the expression of intelligence is less and less important as you go up in social class standing.

Figure 27.5 is the inverse of what was presented in Figure 27.4. Here we see that the variance in intelligence that is due to shared family factors is four times larger among the poor than it is among

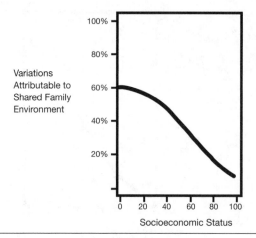

Figure 27.5 Percentage of variation in IQ attributable to shared family environment, across various levels of socioeconomic status (Turkheimer et al., 2003, used by permission of the authors).

the rich. This is another way of saying that environments matter a lot more in the determination of IQ for poor children than they do for wealthier children. After a certain point of environmental adequacy is achieved by means of economic sufficiency, it apparently doesn't much matter what gets added to the environment. A healthy childhood environment supported by adequate family economics is an amalgam of many factors, but probably includes a regular supply of nutritious food, stability in feelings of security, quick medical attention when needed, high-quality child-care, access to books and exposure to rich language usage in the home, and so forth.

Children with these kinds of environments were planted in good soil, and under those conditions the variation we see is mostly genetic and not environmental, however counterintuitive that seems. But the flip side of this is that positive changes in environments for the poor, say high-quality child-care, are expected to have much bigger effects on outcomes we value than they would have when provided to middle-class and wealthier students. That is why high-quality child-care, good nutrition, and medical attention don't just matter for the poor: They matter a lot!

School reformers are doing their best. But they are often planting in poor soil. While you can eke out a living doing that, and occasionally you even see award-winning crops come from unlikely places, we all know that the crops are consistently better where the soil is richer. Healthy trees do not often grow in forests that are ailing, though there are always some resilient ones that thrive, making us forget that most do not. Resilient children and the occasionally exemplary school that exists amidst poverty should be lauded and supported. But the focus of our attention must be on the fact that most children in poverty and most schools that serve those children are not doing well.

The simplest way to get a healthier environment in which to raise children is to provide more resources for parents to make those changes for themselves. Despite the shortcomings of many parents at every level of social class, I still believe the proper place to begin solving the problem of low achievement among poor families is by making those families less poor. I am not talking about a government giveaway. I seek only employment that can supply families with the income that gives them the dignity and hope needed to function admirably, allowing them to raise their children well.

How Money Affects School Achievement

How would a bit more income per family influence educational attainment? The two answers that immediately spring to mind are about health and neighborhood, which I address next.

Health Issues Affecting the Poor

The many medical problems that are related to social class provide obvious and powerful examples of problems affecting school achievement that are remediable with a little extra money. For example, at the simplest level are medical problems such as otitis media and those associated with vision.

Otitis media is a simple and common childhood ear infection, frequently contracted by rich and poor children alike between birth and 3 years of age. In a number of studies, recurring otitis media in the first 3 years of life has been related to hearing impairments, and thus to language development, and thus to reading problems in school, and therefore to deficits on tests such as the Stanford-Binet intelligence test. Otitis media is also implicated in the development of ADHD (see, for example, Agency for Healthcare Research and Quality, 2005; Hagerman & Falkenstein, 1987; Knishkowy, Palti, Adler 8c Tepper, 1991; Luotonen, Uhari, Aitola, Lukkaroinen, Luotonin, Uhari, & Korkeamaki, 1996). This literature makes clear that poor children have more untreated cases of otitis media than do those that are financially better off, especially those with medical insurance. The cause of otitis media may not be directly linked to poverty, but its prevalence and lack of treatment in children is quite clearly affected by poverty.

For example, recurrent otitis media as well as other childhood diseases before age 3 are found to be strongly and negatively related to breastfeeding—the less breast-feeding, the greater the rate of a number of childhood diseases. But breast-feeding of infants in America is done significantly less frequently by women who are poor (Centers for Disease Control, 2005). Breast-feeding is also done significantly less often by those who only have high school degrees or have not finished high school and by those mothers who are under 19 and who are not married (Centers for Disease Control, 2005).

In other words, poverty affects otitis media and other childhood diseases indirectly through home practices that are more common among the poor and less common in the middle class. Another example makes this point as well. The relationship to recurring odds media is also strongly positive for pacifier use (Niemela, Pihakari, Pokka, Uhari, & Uhari, 2000). Pacifiers are used more commonly, and for longer periods of time, among the lower social classes.

In the final analysis, while otitis media isn't a disease of the poor, the characteristics of child rearing and of home environment among the poor of all races and ethnicities leads to more medical problems for the children of the poor. And then, since the poor often lack proper medical insurance, they have a much greater chance of having hearing handicaps at the stage of their lives where language is being developed. In just a few years those handicaps will emerge as reading problems in the classroom.

Otitis media is precisely the kind of problem that is likely not to be much of a factor if the poor were a little richer and in possession of adequate health insurance. Note also that the norms regarding breast-feeding and pacifier use influence all who live in middle-class neighborhoods in a positive way, while the neighborhood norms for these same factors result in negative effects on children in the communities of the poor. A little more money in the lives of the poor would buy them neighborhoods with healthier norms for behavior, as well as medical insurance.

Vision is another simple case of poverty's effects on student behavior outside the teachers' control. For example, two different vision screening tests, one among the urban poor in Boston and one among the urban poor in New York, each found that over 50% of the children tested had some easily correctable vision deficiency, but most such cases were not followed up and corrected (Gillespie, 2001).

An optometrist working with poor children notes that the mass screening vision tests that schools typically use rarely assess the ability of children to do close-up work—the work needed to do reading, writing, arithmetic, and engage in computer mediated learning (Gould & Gould, 2003). What optometrists point out is that a better set of mathematics standards seems less likely to help these students improve in school than does direct intervention in their health and welfare, perhaps most easily accomplished by ensuring that the families of these children earn adequate incomes and are provided medical insurance.

The complexity of the medical problems increases when we discuss asthma. Asthma has now has reached epidemic proportions among poor children. One survey in the South Bronx found a fourth grade teacher where 12 of his 30 students have asthma and 8 of those have to bring their breathing pumps to school every day (Books, 2000). Seven years ago, according to the National Institutes of Health, asthma alone resulted in 10 million missed school days a year, with many individual children missing 20 to 40 school days a year (National Institutes for Health, 1998, cited in Books, 2000). This year, however, a survey puts missed school days due to asthma at 21 million (Children & Asthma in America, 2005). Asthma is simply preventing millions of children of all social classes from attending school and studying diligently. But asthma's effects on children from middle-income families are not nearly as severe as they are on the children of low-income families. Time-on-task, as we all know, is one of the strongest predictors of learning in schools. So it is no great leap of logic to point out that poor children, compared to their middle-class counterparts, will be missing a lot more school because of asthma, and thus will be learning a lot less.

Another level up in the seriousness of the medical problems that afflict the poor has to do with the effects of lead on mental functioning. Michael Martin (2004) of the Arizona School Boards Association has convinced me that this is much more of a problem than I had thought. No one I could find in the medical profession disputes the fact that very small amounts of lead can reduce intellectual functioning and diminish the capacity of a child to learn. The damage that lead does is almost always permanent. The good news is that lead poisoning is in decline. The bad news is that the Centers for Disease Control still estimates that some 450,000 children in the United States between 1 and 5 years of age show levels of lead in their blood that are high enough to cause cognitive damage (Centers for Disease Control, 2004). A simple extrapolation gives us a K–6 schooling population of another half million students with levels of lead in the blood high enough to cause neurological damage. The epidemiological data suggests that another half million brain-damaged students are enrolled in our middle and high schools. The effects of lead poisoning may be small or large, but whatever damage is done by the lead in the system, it is usually permanent.

Do the millions of children affected in small and big ways by lead poisoning have anything in common? They sure do. They are mostly poor and mostly children of color. The poor live in older inner-city buildings where lead contamination from paint, and lead dust from many other sources, is prevalent. But the poor cannot move and cannot afford the paint removal costs since they do not have the income to do so.

Figure 27.6 presents data from California showing the age of the school and the lead that children are exposed to. It is likely to be the case that the relationship shown in Figure 27.6 holds for all states. Essentially what is demonstrated there is that children attending schools built since 1980 are not being exposed to lead in the schools or in the soil around the schools, while the children in older schools are exposed to toxic levels of this dangerous metal. The children who attend new and old schools are not a random selection of children from the population. The poor are exposed to lead's toxicity many times more than the rich.

The literature on the symptoms of lead poisoning remind me of the problems new teachers tell me about when they teach in schools that serve the poor. A lead-damaged nervous system is associated with a variety of problems including learning disabilities, ADHD, increased aggression, and lower intelligence, and those symptoms among older children are also linked with drug use and a greater likelihood of criminal behavior (see reviews by Books, 2000; and Rothstein, 2004).

Though a reduction of, say, 4 or 5 IQ points is not disastrous in a single poisoned child, that IQ reduction in a population will increase by 50% the number of children who qualify for special education, just about what we see in the schools serving the poor. Bailus Walker, a member of both the National Academy of Sciences and the Institute of Medicine says:

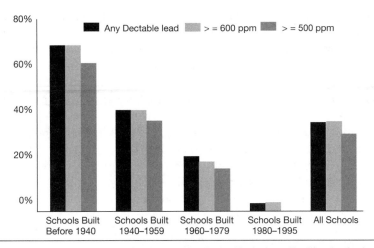

Figure 27.6 Percent of California public elementary schools with various levels of lead paint and lead deterioration, by age of school. (U.S. Environmental Protection Agency, 2003, based on data from the late 1990s.)

The education community has not really understood the demensions of this because we don't see kids falling over and dying of lead poisoning in the classroom. But there's a very large number of kids who find it difficult to do analytical work or [even] line up in the cafeteria because their brains are laden with lead. (cited in Martin, 2004)

Space limitations do not allow me to discuss mercury poisoning—a terribly powerful neurotoxin that gets into the air around medical waste disposal plants and coal fired power plants. But just ask yourselves who lives in the vicinity of the big urban medical waste fascilities or are downwind of a coal-fired power plant? The answer, of course, is that poor families, mostly Hispanics and African Americans, are those who live closest to these toxic facilities. That is the basis for charges about environmental racism.

Perhaps it is even more accurate to call it environmental classism, because the poor feel the brunt of these problems regardless of ethnicity. What is clear is that poor children and their parents are getting more lead and more mercury in their systems than their wealthier kin.

What is also important to note is that the symptoms presented by lead and mercury exposure, like ADHD, irritability, problems of concentration, and the like, are problems that display degrees of impairment. It is not like being pregnant, where a woman either is or is not. So if the lower classes suffer from exposure to lead and mercury more than those in the higher social classes, then there will be more impairments that are slight, as well as those that are more obviously noticeable. In fact at least one recent study of lead effects claims that there is absolutely no safe level for lead. It *always* causes negative cognitive and behavioral effects (Lanphear, Dietrich, Auinger, & Cox, 2000). These invisible medical problems often translate into misbehavior in school, probably resulting in more poor children receiving punishment and having negative school experiences than might their healthier middle-class peers.

The set of environmentally caused problems, both small and large, become teacher and school problems that cannot be fixed by administrators and teachers. Yet we have many politicians who worry little about environmental pollution but are quick to blame educators for the poor achievement of some schools, although that poor achievement may be, in part, a result of problems they could help to solve. I believe that more politicians need to turn their attention to the outside-of-school problems that affect inside-of-school academic performance.

There is another medical problem that is directly related to poverty. Premature births and low birth weight children are much more common problems among the poor. Neural imaging studies show that premature and low birth weight children are several times more likely to have an atomic brain abnormalities than do full-term, full birth weight controls (Peterson, Anderson, Ehrenkranz, Staib, Tageldin, Colson, Gore, Duncan, Makuch & Mendt 2003). Quantitative comparisons of brain volumes in 8-year-old children born prematurely and age-matched full-term control children also found that brain volume was less in the prematurely born. The degree of these morphologic abnormalities was strongly and inversely associated with measures of intelligence (Peterson, Vohr, Staib, Cannistraci, Dolberg, Schneider, Katz, Westerveld, Sparrow, Andersobn, Duncan, Makuch, Gore, & Mendt, 2000). Unfortunately social class and birth defects have been found to be significantly correlated in hundreds of studies. Some of the relationships seem associated with lifestyle problems (drug and alcohol use, vitamin deficiencies), while some seem neighborhood related (waste sites, lead, pesticides). But in either case, the children will still go to public schools five years later.

How Neighborhoods Affect the Poor

Neighborhoods communicate norms for behavior, such as in the case of drugs and alcohol, breast-feeding or pacifier use, and achievement. For example, Garner and Raudenbush (1991) looked at student achievement in literacy in 16 secondary schools and in 437 neighborhoods in a set of school districts. The neighborhoods were scaled to reflect sociodemographic characteristics, precisely the kinds of things that make one choose to live in (or not live in) a neighborhood. These included overall unemployment rate, youth unemployment rate, number of single-parent families, percent of low-earning wage earners, overcrowding, and permanently sick individuals. When Hierarchical Linear Modeling was used to analyze these data, significant school-to-school variance was found even when controlling for family background and neighborhood. Happily, this tells us that we should continue working on making schools better. This study and many others demonstrate that school effects are real and powerful: Schools do exert positive influences on the lives of the poor.

But the analysis did not stop there. The neighborhood deprivation variable showed a negative effect on educational attainment even after variation in the individual students and the schools they attend were stringently controlled. This was not a trivial statistical finding. For two students with identical prior background in achievement, with identical family backgrounds, and even with identical school membership, the differences in their educational attainment as a function of their neighborhood deprivation was estimated to be a difference of between the 10th and the 90th percentile on an achievement test.

More recently sociologists Catsambis and Beveridge, verified these finding using NELS 88 data with mathematics achievement as the outcome (2001). They found that neighborhood had significant direct and indirect effects on achievement, often by depressing parental practices that were usually associated with better student achievement.

The combination of home circumstances, neighborhood, and school are powerful influences on a secondary students' life circumstances. But independent of the other factors, neighborhood deprivation showed powerful effects on its own. Tragically, good parents too frequently lose their children to the streets: neighborhood effects are strong. Families who have enough money to move out of a dysfunctional neighborhood do so. On the other hand, poverty traps people in bad neighborhoods that affect their children separately from the effects of home and school.

Jeanne Brooks-Gunn and her colleagues (Brooks-Gunn, Duncan, Klebanov, & Sealand, 1993) also found that neighborhood effects rival family effects in influencing child development. In addition they found that the absence of more affluent neighbors is more important than the presence of low-income neighbors (Brooks-Gunn, Duncan, Klebanov, & Sealand, 1993). This means that well-functioning adult role models are needed in low-income neighborhoods, and that such positive role models count for a lot in the lives of poor children.

In sum, zip codes matter. Zip codes can determine school achievement as much or more than does the influence of a persons' family, and they often have more power then the quality of the school a child attends. While family involvement and school improvement programs are each to be supported, and some have garnered success (Comer, 2004), they cannot be expected to do all that needs to be done. Most low-performing schools serve poor children who live in neglected neighborhoods and we pay a price for our communal neglect.

We all know that urban segregation of the poor, along with segregation of language minorities and ethnic groups, is the reason that zip codes matter. Since the end of World War II there has been a gradual decline of white middle- and upper-class families in large metropolitan centers. As those families moved to suburbs or small cities, the white middle-class students in the schools of the central cities were replaced by large concentrations of black and Latino students. As Orfield and Lee point out (2005), these minority and poor communities had to cope with inadequate and decaying housing, weak and failing urban infrastructures, shortages of jobs, and perhaps among the most important of these problems, a critical lack of mentors for urban youth. As Rumberger (1987) noted some time ago, without strong positive peer influences, children attending high poverty schools are not likely to achieve well. Zip codes do matter. They determine who is around to exert an influence during a child's formative years.

The zip codes of the middle class have influence too. Several empirical studies have found that attending a middle-class school exposes minority students to higher expectations and more educational and career options. One team of researchers studied voluntary transfer policies in metropolitan St. Louis (Wells & Crain, 1997). They observed that minority students who attend middle- and upper-class schools had higher educational achievement and college attendance rates than their peers in schools where poverty was concentrated. Studies of Boston students who attended suburban public schools revealed that they had access to knowledge and networks of knowledge that their peers in inner-city Boston lacked (Eaton, 2001). These experiences increased their educational and professional opportunities. The famous Gautreaux study of Chicago made this plain years ago (Rubinowitz & Rosenbaum, 2000). In that natural experiment a random set of families received vouchers to move from the 'hood to the 'burbs. Their children succeeded much better than did an equivalent control group. The Gautreaux study provides convincing evidence of the power of neighborhood, and the schools available to those neighborhoods, to influence our nation's youth.

Although we have no idea what the micro elements of a middle-class culture are, when such a culture is well entrenched in a neighborhood, it is the best insurance that the schools in that neighborhood will have the quality and the student norms of behavior that lead to better academic achievement. Perhaps it is because middle-class and residentially stable neighborhoods often manifest a collective sense of efficacy and that, in turn, determines the ways that youth in those neighborhoods are monitored as they grow up (Sampson, Raudenbush & Earls, 1997).

On the other hand, neighborhoods that perpetuate the culture of poverty cannot help but have that culture spill over into the schools their children attend. Obviously, one way to help the American schools achieve more is to weave low-income housing throughout more middle-class zip codes. This would provide more low-income people with access to communities where stability exists, efficacy is promoted, and children have access to a variety of role models. But we are an economically segregated country, a condition perpetuated in various ways by the more affluent and powerful in the nation. So this is not likely to happen.

Yet another way to harness neighborhood effects on achievement is ensuring that low-income people have access to better-paying jobs so they can make and spend more on decent housing. Poverty is what drives families into zip codes that are not healthy for children and other living things. And all those unhealthy things they experience end up, eventually, being dealt with inside the school house.

I could go on. The rates of hunger among the poor continue to be high for an industrialized nation (Nord, Andrews & Carlson, 2004). In 2003 about 12.5 million households, around 36 million people, suffered food insecurity. About 4 million of those households, or around 9.5 million people, actually went hungry some time in that year. And sadly, one-third of this group experienced *chronic* hunger. Seventeen percent of the households with food insecurity have children, and these children do not ordinarily learn well. Perhaps equally unfortunate is the fact that the neighborhood norms for people who are poor promote non-nutritional foods and diets that lead to medical problems. Anemia, vitamin deficiencies, obesity, diabetes, and many other conditions that affect school learning help to keep the academic achievement of poor children lower than it might otherwise be.

The lack of high-quality affordable day care and quality early childhood learning environments is a problem of poverty that has enormous effects on later schooling. The early childhood educational gap between middle-class and poor children is well documented by Valerie Lee and David Burkham in their book *Inequality at the Starting Gate* (2002). More recent studies of the economic returns to society of providing better early childhood education for the poor have looked at the most famous of the early childhood programs with longitudinal data. From projects such as the Perry Preschool, the Abecedarian Project, the Chicago Child-Parent Centers, and the Elmira Prenatal/Early Infancy Project, scholars find that the returns to society range from $3 to almost $9 for every dollar invested. Grunewald and Rolnick (2004, p. 6) of the Minneapolis Federal Reserve noted that when expressed as a rate of return "the real (adjusted for inflation) internal rates of return on these programs range from about seven percent to above 16 percent annually" (see also Lynch, 2004, for a similar argument). Thus, since the return on investment to society for making high-quality early childhood programs available to all of our nation's children is remarkably large, why are we *not* making those investments? A plausible answer is that we won't invest in poor children's futures, nor our own, due to simple mean-spiritedness. It is clearly not due to economics!

Income also plays a role in determining the learning opportunities that are available to children during the summer months. Children of the poor consistently show greater learning losses over summer than do children of the middle class (Cooper, Nye, Charlton, Lindsay & Greathouse, 1996). Middle-class children apparently get a more nutritious cultural and academic diet during the summer than the poor. This results in middle-class children gaining in reading achievement over the summer, while lower-class children lose ground. Every summer the gap between the affluent and the poor that shows up on the first day of kindergarten gets larger and larger.

The effects of smoking, alcohol and other drugs, lack of adequate dental and medical care, increased residential mobility, fewer positive after-school groups in which to participate, and many other factors all take their toll on the families and children of the poor. While these factors all interact with the quality of the teachers and the schools that poor children attend, these social, educational, medical, and neighborhood problems are also independent of the schools, and thus beyond their control. Poverty severely limits what our schools can be expected to accomplish.

Let me take stock here so my argument is clear. I have provided reliable information that a) we have the largest percentage of poor children in the industrialized world, b) people stay poor longer in the United States than elsewhere in the industrialized world, c) poverty is negatively related to school achievement and poverty's effects on our international competitiveness appear to be serious, d) poverty has powerful effects on individuals that limit the expression of genetic diversity as well as strongly influencing the health and place of residence in which children are raised, and e) improvement in the school achievement of students from low-income families will have to come as much from improvements in their outside-of-school lives as from their inside-of school lives.

Because the out-of-school environment is so important an influence on the academic attainment of poor people, there is every reason to suspect that changes in the income of poor families will lead to changes in the school-related behavior and achievement of their children. So let us now examine my thesis, namely, that the simplest way to deal with poverty's effects on achievement is to increase the income of poor people so that they are less poor.

How Increased Family Income Affects Student Behavior and School Achievement

Two studies from a growing number about the effects of income growth on families and children have impressed me. First is the study by Dearing, McCartney, and Taylor (2001), who used as a measure of poverty the ratio of income available to the needs faced by a family. A ratio of 1.00 means that the family is just making it, that their family income and their needs such as housing, food, transportation, and so forth, are matched. A ratio of 3.00 would be more like that of a middle-class family, and a ratio of .8 would indicate poverty of some magnitude. A large and reasonably representative sample of poor and non-poor families were followed for three years and their income-to-needs ratios computed regularly, as were their children's scores on various social and academic measures. What was found was that as poor families went from poor to a lot less poor, for whatever reasons, their children's performance began to resemble that of the never poor children with whom they were matched.

Figure 27.7 presents data illustrating the performance of poor children on a measure of school readiness, as the income of poor and non-poor children changed over these three years. The mean change in income-to-needs ratios over the time period of the study is where the lines cross. That is, the mean change in income-to-needs was a positive 73, though some families went up more and some families lost ground over this time period. Plotted against a measure of school readiness, the slope of the non-poor children is seen to hardly have changed at all. Whether family income-to-need ratios went up or went down seemed unrelated to the school readiness scores of the non-poor. But the slope of the poor children showed quite a large change. Poor children in families experiencing loss of income over the three years lost ground to the non-poor on this measure of academic readiness. But children in families whose income improved showed growth in school readiness over the three years. Most interesting of all, the poor children in families whose income went up ended up scoring as well as the students who had never been poor. This was true even though the set of families who were not poor earned considerably more money than those who had been poor. Although there are many possible explanations for this, a reasonable one is that rising incomes provide families with dignity and hope, and these in turn promote greater family stability and better childcare.

An almost identical relationship was found when plotting change in income-to-needs ratios against other academic-like outcome measures such as measures of a child's expressive language, or of their receptive language. And in Figure 27.8 we see the same relationship shown for a measure of social behavior, a non-academic measure that identifies children whose presence in classes will promote or impede the work of their teachers.

Figure 27.8 illustrates that as income-to-need ratios changed for the poor and the non-poor, the poor again showed significant slope changes and the non-poor once again did not. Furthermore, poor children in families experiencing growth in income over the three years once again ended up scoring as well in social behavior as the children who had never been poor.

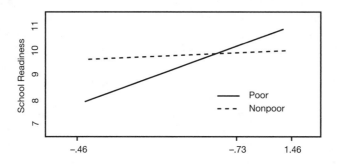

Figure 27.7 The relationship between school readiness and income change among poor and non-poor families (reprinted from Dearing, McCartney, & Taylor, 2001, used by permission of the authors).

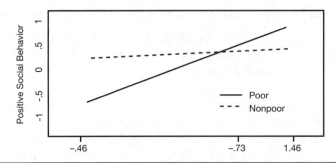

Figure 27.8 The relationship between positive social behavior and income change among poor and non-poor families (reprinted from Dearing, McCartney, & Taylor, 2001, used by permission of the authors).

As noted earlier, bigger changes are expected to occur for the poor than the non-poor as positive changes in their environments occur. We see that here. Also worth noting is that Duncan and Brooks-Gunn (2001) found that the greatest impact of family income on children's academic outcomes is when they are the youngest, and this was a study of children from birth to three years of age.

In an interesting follow-up to the original study, these researchers went on to estimate the effect size of making permanent the income changes that had occurred in the sample of poor families, and comparing that effect size to those that the Department of Health and Human Services estimates for the early head start program (Taylor, Dearing & McCartney, 2004). Both in the Head Start study and this one, the same Mental Development Index was used to look at intellectual functioning and both studies measured students' negative behavior, as well. Those interesting findings are presented as Table 27.9.

In the first row of Table 27.9 we see that Head Start researchers estimate that children enrolled in that program increased between 12% and 15% of a standard deviation on the Mental Development Index. These children also showed a decline of 10% to 11% percent of a standard deviation in their negative behavior. Those outcomes are socially significant and large enough to claim effectiveness for the gigantic head start apparatus. The second row of this table are Taylor, Dearing & McCartney's (2004) estimates of what would happen were the income of the poor families in their study increased one standard deviation, or about $13,000 per year. This estimate shows that the children for low-income families would have had gains in IQ of about 15% of a standard deviation, and that the children would decline in negative behavior about 20% of a standard deviation.

The success brought about by an increase in the incomes of poor families apparently matches or exceeds the success our nation obtains from running a giant program like Head Start, that enrolls only about 60% of those who are eligible. Equally intriguing in this study was that raising the income of families to improve the lives of poor children was actually a bit less expensive than the annual cost per-child of attending Head Start. It is impossible not to speculate about what the results might be for our society if we combined both approaches to school improvement, providing both high-quality early childhood programs and better incomes for the poor!

Table 27.9 Comparison of the Effects of Traditional Head Start and Simple Growth in Family Income on Children's Cognitive and Affective Behavior

	Mental Development Index (percent of a standard deviation)	Negative Behavior Index (percent of a standard deviation)
Head Start Program	Up 12–15 percent	Down 10–11 percent
Income Growth Study	Up 15 percent	Down 20 percent

Source: Reprinted from Taylor, Dearing, & McCartney, 2004, by permission of the authors.

The second study of income change and school success is from North Carolina and is almost a natural experiment in income redistribution (Costello, Compton, Keeler, & Angold, 2003). A Duke University team noticed that their study of psychiatric disorders and drug abuse within a rural community included a group of people who had risen out of poverty because of the income derived from a recently opened gaming casino. During these changes the researchers had been giving annual psychiatric assessments to about 1,400 children, 350 of them American Indians, and they did so over an eight-year period. The children ranged in age from 9 to 13 and were in three distinct groups: those who had never been poor, those who had been persistently poor, and a group that had been poor until the casino came to the reservation.

The researchers discovered that moving out of poverty was associated with a decrease in frequency of psychiatric symptoms over the ensuing four years. In fact, by the fourth year, the psychiatric symptom level was the same among children whose families moved out of poverty as it was among children whose families were never in poverty. A small replication of the findings was available for a group of non-Indians who also moved out of poverty over this same time period. Once again, as in the Dearing, McCartney and Taylor (2001) study, and in the main part of this study, negative psychiatric symptoms disappeared as income rose. The researchers offered an explanation for these findings, namely, that relieving poverty appeared to increase the level of parental supervision of children. One last finding of interest from this study is that additional income for the families of the never-poor had no effect on frequency of behavioral or emotional symptoms. As is common in this area of research, and noted earlier, improving the income of the very poor has large effects, while improving the income of the less poor has negligible effects.

Although the literature is not voluminous, these are not the only studies to show that a lessening of poverty helps young children succeed better at school and in life. The negative income tax was studied 20 years ago and it revealed that increases in family income resulted in increased school attendance and better school achievement for the families that gained in income (Salkind & Haskins, 1982). The work assistance programs of the 1990s have also been examined and again there is some evidence that as family income went up, the achievement and behavior of children in those families improved (Huston, Duncan, Granger, Bos, McLoyd, Mistry, Crosby, Gibson, Magnuson, Romich, & Ventura, 2001). The evidence of the positive influence on student achievement when families are able to leave poverty is consistent and replicable, suggesting that inside-of-school reform needs to begin with outside-of-school reform. Otherwise, like the drunk in the allegory I began with, we will be looking for our keys in the wrong place.

What We Need To Do

Poverty, through its many connections to other parts of people's lives, is an obstacle that is not easy for most educators to overcome. Poverty in a community almost ensures that many of the children who enter their neighborhood schools cannot maximally profit from the instruction provided there. Helping to eliminate some of that poverty is not just morally appropriate, though it is that, first of all. But to a convincing degree finding ways to reduce poverty to improve schooling is evidence based: It takes no great wisdom to realize that families with increasing fortunes have more dignity and hope, and are thus able to take better care of their children, than do families in more dire straights, where anxiety and despair are the more common emotional reactions.

So when we push for higher qualifications for the teachers of the poor, as we should, we also may need to push ourselves and others to stop shopping at companies like Wal-Mart. The logic of this is simple: if we want to primarily hold our teachers responsible for increasing their students' educational attainment, then we need at a minimum to provide those teachers with children who enter their classrooms healthy and ready to learn. Twenty years ago this was one of our national goals, to be reached by the year 2000. But one of the impediments to reaching that goal was Wal-Mart, now the largest employer in the United States. Wal-Mart and companies like them do not provide the great majority of their employees the income, medical insurance, or retirement plans needed to promote healthy families or raise healthy children. Wal-Mart and companies like it have a terrible record in its treatment of woman with children, a group who make up a big share of the poor households in this country (Shulman, 2003). Thus Wal-Mart is an impediment to school reform and although it is not usually noted, Wal-Mart is one reason we did not reach our national goal.

There are so many other problems we need to address, as well. When we push for more rigorous standards in our schools, we should also push for a raise in the minimum wage, or better yet, for livable wages. If we do not do this then we will ensure that the vast majority of those meeting the increasingly rigorous requirements for high school graduation will be those students fortunate enough to be born into the right families. If we really want a more egalitarian set of educational outcomes, our nation needs a more equalitarian wage structure.

For these same reasons when we push for more professional development for teachers and mentoring programs for new teachers, we need also to demand that women's wages be set equal to those of men doing comparable work, since it is working women and their children who make up a large percentage of America's poor.

When we push for advanced placement courses, or college preparatory curricula for all our nation's students, we must simultaneously demand universal medical coverage for all our children. Only then will all our children have the health that allows them to attend school regularly and learn effectively, instead of missing opportunities to learn due to a lack of medical treatment.

When we push for all-day kindergarten, or quality early childhood care, or de-tracked schools we need also to argue for affordable housing throughout our communities, so neighborhoods have the possibility of exerting more positive influences on children and people can move from lead and mercury polluted areas to those that are less toxic, and thus less likely to cause birth defects. This goal requires educators, parents, and other concerned citizens to be in the forefront of the environmental fight. To fight for clean air and water, and for less untested chemicals in all our food products, is a fight to have more healthy children for our schools to educate. The psychological and financial costs on families and the broader society because of students needing special education can be markedly reduced by our demands for a healthier environment.

In my estimation we will get better public schools by requiring of each other participation in building a more economically equitable society. This is of equal or greater value to our nation's future well-being than a fight over whether phonics is scientifically based, whether standards are rigorous enough, or whether teachers have enough content knowledge.

Conclusion

All I am saying in this essay is that I am tired of acting like the schools, all alone, can do what is needed to help more people achieve higher levels of academic performance in our society. As Jean Anyon (1997, p. 168) put it, "Attempting to fix inner city schools without fixing the city in which they are embedded is like trying to clean the air on one side of a screen door."

To clean the air on both sides of the screen door we need to begin thinking about building a two-way system of accountability for contemporary America. The obligation that we educators have accepted to be accountable to our communities must become reciprocal. Our communities must also be accountable to those of us who work in the schools, and they can do this by creating social conditions for our nation that allow us to do our jobs well. Accountability is a two-way process; it requires a principal and an agent. For too long schools have thought of themselves only as agents who must meet the demands of the principal, often the local community, state, or federal government. It is time for principals (and other school leaders) to become principals. That is, school people need to see communities as agents as well as principals and hold communities to standards that ensure all our children are accorded the opportunities necessary for growing well.

It does take a whole village to raise a child, and we actually know a little bit about how to do that. What we seem not to know how to do in modern America is to raise the village to promote communal values that ensure that all our children will prosper. We need to face the fact that our whole society needs to be held as accountable for providing healthy children ready to learn, as our schools are for delivering quality instruction. One-way accountability, where we are always blaming the schools for the faults that we find, is neither just nor likely to solve the problems we want to address.

I am tired, also, of those among us who say the poor are not really bad off, as claimed recently in a lengthy research report from the Heritage Foundation (Rector & Johnson, 2004). Our poor today, they say, are really much better oil than the poor in other countries, or compared to the immigrant poor at the turn of the 20th century. Because of refrigerators, televisions, and automobiles, the poor in America today actually might live as well or better than royalty did in the 13th century. But that completely fails to capture what poverty is like for poor children. As a reminder about the reality of poverty, and to shame the Heritage Foundation and all who vote to keep income inequality as it is, I want to close this essay with the introduction *to Amazing Grace,* by Jonathan Kozol (1995). In doing this 1 move away from the analytic and quantitative ways to think about poverty and its effects, and move to the only way we might actually comprehend the reality of poverty for our young, through the use of narrative.

The number 6 train from Manhattan to the South Bronx makes nine stops in the 18-minute ride between East 59th Street and Brook Avenue. When you enter the train, you are in the seventh richest congressional district in the nation. When you leave, you are in the poorest.

The 600,000 people who live here and the 450,000 people who live in Washington Heights and Harlem, which are separated from the South Bronx by a narrow river, make up one of the largest racially segregated concentrations of poor people in our nation.

Brook Avenue, which is the tenth stop on the local, lies in the center of Mott Haven, whose 48,000 people are the poorest in the South Bronx. Two thirds are Hispanic, one third black. Thirty-five percent are children. In 1991, the median household income of the area, according to *The New York Times,* was $7,600.

St. Ann's Church, on St. Ann's Avenue, is three blocks from the subway station. The children who come to this small Episcopal Church for food and comfort, and to play, and the mothers and fathers who come here for prayer, are said to be the poorest people in New York. "More than 95 percent are poor," the pastor says—"the poorest of the poor, poor by any standard I can think of."

At the elementary school that serves the neighborhood across the avenue, only seven of 800 children do not qualify for free school lunches. "Five of those seven," says the principal, "get reduced-price lunches, because they are classified as only 'poor,' not 'destitute.'"

In some cities, the public reputation of a ghetto neighborhood bears little connection to the world that you discover when you walk the streets with children and listen to their words. In Mott Haven, this is not the case. By and large, the words of the children in the streets and schools and houses that surround St. Ann's more than justify the grimness in the words of journalists who have described the area.

Crack-cocaine addiction and the intravenous use of heroin, which children I have met here call "the needle drug," are woven into the texture of existence in Mott Haven. Nearly 4,000 heroin injectors, many of whom are HIV-infected, live here. Virtually every child at St. Ann's knows someone, a relative or neighbor, who has died of AIDS, and most children here know many others who are dying now of the disease. One quarter of the women of Mott Haven who are tested in obstetric wards are positive for HIV. Rates of pediatric AIDS, therefore, are high.

Depression is common among children in Mott Haven. Many cry a great deal but cannot explain exactly why.

Fear and anxiety are common. Many cannot sleep.

Asthma is the most common illness among children here. Many have to struggle to take in a good deep breath. Some mothers keep oxygen tanks, which children describe as "breathing machines," next to their children's beds.

The houses in which these children live, two thirds of which are owned by the City of New York, are often as squalid as the houses of the poorest children I have visited in rural Mississippi, but there is none of the greenness and the healing sweetness of the Mississippi countryside outside their windows, which are often barred and bolted as protection against thieves.

Some of these houses are freezing in the winter. In dangerously cold weather, the city sometimes distributes electric blankets and space heaters to its tenants. In emergency conditions, if space heaters can't be used, because substandard wiring is overloaded, the city's practice is to pass out sleeping bags.

"You just cover up . . . and hope you wake up the next morning," says a father of four children, one of them an infant one month old, as they prepare to climb into their sleeping bags in hats and coats on a December night.

In humid summer weather, roaches crawl on virtually every surface of the houses in which many of the children live. Rats emerge from holes in bedroom walls, terrorizing infants in their cribs. In the streets outside, the restlessness and anger that are present in all seasons frequently intensify under the stress of heat.

In speaking of rates of homicide in New York City neighborhoods, the *Times* refers to the streets around St. Ann's as "the deadliest blocks" in "the deadliest precinct" of the city. If there is a deadlier place in the United States, I don't know where it is.

In 1991, 84 people, more than half of whom were 21 or younger, were murdered in the precinct. A year later, ten people were shot dead on a street called Beekman Avenue, where many of the children I have come to know reside. On Valentine's Day of 1993, three more children and three adults were shot dead on the living room floor of an apartment six blocks from the run-down park that serves the area.

In early July of 1993, shortly before the first time that I visited the neighborhood, three more people were shot in 30 minutes in three unrelated murders in the South Bronx, one of them only a block from St. Ann's Avenue. A week later, a mother was murdered and her baby wounded by a bullet in the stomach while they were standing on a South Bronx corner. Three weeks after that, a minister and elderly parishioner were shot outside the front door of their church, while another South Bronx resident was discovered in his bathtub with his head cut off. In subsequent days, a man was shot in both his eyes and a ten-year-old was critically wounded in the brain.

What is it like for children to grow up here? What do they think the world has done to them? Do they believe that they are being shunned or hidden by society? If so, do they think that they deserve this? What is it that enables some of them to pray? And when they pray, what do they say to God?[1]

Notes

1. My thanks to Jonathan Kozol for permission to use this lengthy quote. His insightful and poignant writing has educated and moved so many of us, but as is clear, not yet enough of us.

References

Agency for Healthcare Research and Quality (2005). Archived Clinical Practices Guidelines, National Library of Methcine. No. 12. *Otitis metha with effusion in young children,* Retrieved May 17, 2005 from http://www.ncbi.nlm.nih.gov

Arnrein, A. L., & Berliner, D. C. (2002, March 28). High-stakes testing, uncertainty, and student learning. *Education Policy Analysis Archives, 10*(18), Retrieved May 15, 2005 from http:// epaa.asu.edu/epaa/v10n18/

Anyon, J. (1995). Race, social class, and educational reform in an inner city school. *Teachers College Record, 97,* 69-94.

Anyon, J. (1997). Ghetto schooling. *A political economy of urban school reform.* New York: Teachers College Press.

Anyon, J. (2005). What "Counts" as Educational Policy? Notes toward a New Paradigm. *Harvard Educational Review, 75*(1), 65–88.

Asimov, N. (2005, April 5). Study puts Oakland dropout rate at 52%, Mayor decries crisis—district questions research accuracy. *San Francisco Chronicle,* Retrieved May 15, 2005 from http://sfgate.com/

Berliner, D. C (2004). If the underlying premise for No Child Left Behind is false, how can that act solve our problems? In K. Goodman, P. Shannon, Y. Goodman, & R. Rapoport (Eds.), *Saving our schools.* Berkeley, CA: RDR Books.

Berliner, D. C, & Biddle, B. J. (1995). *The manufactured crisis. Myth, fraud, and the Attack on America's Public Schools.* Reathng, MA: Adthson-Wesley.

Biddle, B. J. (Ed.) (2001). *Social class, poverty, and education.* New York: RoutlegeFarmer.

Books, S. (2002). Poverty and environmentally induced damage to children, in V. Polakow (Ed.), *The public assault on America's children: Poverty, violence, and juvenile injustice.* New York:Teachers College Press.

Brooks-Gunn, J., Duncan, G. J., Klebanov, P. K., & Sealand, N. (1993). Do neighborhoods influence child and adolescent development? *American Journal of Sociology, 99,* 353–395.

Catsambis, S., & Beveridge, A. W. (2001). Does neighborhood matter? Family, neighborhood, and school influences on eighth grade mathematics achievement. *Sociological Focus, 34(4),* 435–457.

Centers for Disease Control (2004). *Children's blood lead levels in the United States.* Retrieved May15, 2005 from http://www.cdc.gov/

Centers for Disease Control (2005). *Breastfeeding Practices: Results from the 2003 National Immunization Survey.* Retrieved May 17, 2005 from http://www.cdc.gov

Children & Asthma in America (2005). Retrieved May 15, 2005 from http://www.asthmainamerica.com/

Comer, J. P. (2004). *Leave no child behind: Preparing today's youth for tomorrow's world.* New Haven, CT: Yale University Press.

Cooper, H., Nye, B., Charlton, K., Lindsay,J., & Greathouse, S. (1996). The effects of summer vacation on achievement test scores: a narrative and meta-analytic review. *Review of Ed-ucatumal Research, 66*(3), 227–268.

Costello, E. J., Compton, S. N., Keeler, G., & Angold, A. (2003). Relationships between poverty and psychopathology: A natural experiment. *Journal of the American Medical Association, 290,* 2023–2029.

Cremin, L. A. (1990). *Popular education and its discontents.* New York: Harper & Row.

Dearing, E., McCartney, K., & Taylor, B. A. (2001). Change in family income-to-needs matters more for children with less. *Child Development,* 72(6), 1779–1793.

Duncan, G. J., & Brooks-Gunn, J. (1997). *Consequences of growing up poor.* New York: Russell Sage Foundation.

Duncan, G. J., & Brooks-Gunn, J. (2001). Poverty, welfare reform, and children's achievement (49–75). In B. J. Biddle (Ed.), *Social class, poverty, and achievement.* New York: Routlage-Farmer.

Eaton, S. (2001). *The other Boston busing story: What's won and lost across the boundary line.* New Haven, CT: Yale University Press.

Erbe, B, & Shiner, J. (1997, March 29). What Kate for the 'Partial-Birth' Bill. *Washington Times* p. 1.

Garner, C. L., & Raudenbush, S. W. (1991). Neighborhood effects on educational attainment: A multilevel analysis. *Sociology of Education, 64,* 251–262.

Gillespie, K. (2001). *How vision impacts literacy: An educational problem that can be solved.* Harvard Graduate School of Education News, 17 April 2001. Retrieved May 15, 2005 from http:// www.gse.harvard.edu/

Gonzales, P., Guzmán, J. C, Partelow, L., Pahlke, E, Jocelyn, L., Kastberg, D., & Williams, T. (2004). *Highlights from the Trends in International Mathematics and Science Study (T1MSS) 2003. (NCES 2005–005).* U.S. Department of Education, National Center for Education Statistics. Washington, D.C.: U.S. Government Printing Office. Retrieved May 15, 2005 from http:// nces.ed.gov/pubs2005/2005005.pdf

Gould, M., & Gould, H. (2003). A clear vision for equity and opportunity. *Phi Delta Kappan, 85(4),* 324–328.

Grunewald, R, & Rolnick, A. (2004). *A proposal for achieving high returns on early childhood Development.* Minneapolis, MN: Federal Reserve Bank of Minneapolis. Retrieved May 16, 2005 from http://minneapolisfed.org/research/studies/earlychild/draft_ecd_proposal.pdf

Hagerman, R. J., & Falkenstein, A. R. (1987). An association between recurrent otitis media in infancy and later hyperactivity. *Clinical Pethatrics, 26(5),* 253–257.

Herrnstein, R. J., & Murray, C. (1994). *The bell curve: intelligence and class structure in American life.* New York: The Free Press.

Huston, A. C, Duncan, G. J., Granger, R., Bos, J., McLoyd, V., Mistry, R., Crosby, D., Gibson, C, Magnuson, K., Romich, J., & Ventura, A. (2001). Work-based antipoverty programs for parents can enhance the school performance and social behavior of children. *Child Development,* 72, 318–336.

Knishkowy, B., Palti, H., Adler, B., & Tepper D,. (1991). Effect of otitis media on development: a community-based study. *Early Human Development, 26(2),* 101–111.

Kozol, J. (1995). *Amazing grace: The lives of children and the conscience of a nation.* New York: Crown.

Lanphear, B. P., Dietrich, K., Auinger, P., & Cox, C. (2000). Subclinical lead toxicity in U.S. children and adolescents. *Public Health Reports, 115,* 521–529 Retrieved May 15, 2005 from http://www.nmic.org/

Lee, V. E., & Burkam, D. T. (2002). *Inequality at the starting gate.* Washington, D.C.: Economic Policy Institute.

Lemke, M., Calsyn, C, Lippman, L., Jocelyn, L., Kastberg, D., Liu, Y. Y., Roey, S., Williams, T., Kruger, X, & Bairu, G. (2001). *Outcomes of Learning: Results from the 2000 Program for International Student Assessment of 15-year-olds in reading, mathematics, and science literacy, NCES 2002-115.* Washington, D.C.: U.S. Department of Education, National Center for Education Statistics.

Lemke, M., Sen, A., Pahlke, E., Partelow, L., Miller, D., Williams, T., Kastberg, D., & Jocelyn, L. (2004). *International outcomes of learning in mathematics literacy and problem solving: PISA 2003, results from the U.S. perspective* (NCES 2005–003). Washington, D.C.: U.S. Department of Education, National Center for Education Statistics.

Lewontin, R. (1982). *Human diversity.* New York: Freeman.

Luotonen, M., Uhari, M., Aitola, L., Lukkaroinen, A., Luotonen, J., Uhari, M., & Korkeamaki, R-L. (1996). Recurrent otitis media during infancy and linguistic skills at the age of nine years. *Pethatric Infectious Disease Journal, 15(10),* 854–858.

Lynch, R. G. (2004). *Exceptional Returns: Economic, Fiscal, and Social Benefits of Investment in Early Childhood Development.* Washington, D.C.: Economic Policy Institute.

Martin, M. (2004). *A strange ignorance: The role of lead poisoning in "failing schools".* Retrieved May 15, 2005 from http://www.azsba.org/lead.htm

Mishel, L., Bernstein, J., & Allegretto, S. (2005). *The state of working America 2004/2005.* A publication of the Economic Policy Institute, Washington, D.C.. Ithaca, NY: Cornell University Press.

Nichols, S. N., & Berliner, D. C. (2006). *The inevitable corruption of indicators and educators through high-stakes testing.* Tempe, AZ: College of Education, Education Policy Studies Laboratory Report EPSL-0503–101-EPRU. Retrieved May 15, 2005 from http://www.asu.edu

Nichols, S. N., Glass, G.V, & Berliner, D. C. (2005). High-Stakes Testing and Student Achievement: Does accountability pressure increase student learning? *Education Policy Analysis Archives,* (14)1. Retrieved April 3, 2006, from http://epaa.asu.edu/epaa/vi4nl/.

Niemela, M., Pihakari, O., Pokka, T., Uhari, M., & Uhari, M. (2000). Pacifier as a risk factor for acute otitis media: A randomized, controlled trial of parental counseling. *Pediatrics,106*(3), 483–488.

Nord, M., Andrews, M., & Carlson, S. (2004). *Household food security in the United States, 2003.* Food Assistance and Nutrition Research Report No. (FANRR42). Washington, D.C.: Economic Research Service, United States Department of Agriculture. Retrieved May 16, 2005 from: http://www.ers.usda.gov/publications/fanrr42/

Ogle, L., Sen, A., Pahlke, E., Jocelyn, L., Kastberg, D., Roey, S., & Williams, T. (2003). *International comparisons in fourth-grade reading literacy: findings from the Progress in International Reading Literacy Study (PIRLS) of 2001* (NCES 2003–073). U.S. Department of Education, National Center for Educational Statistics. Washington, D.C.: U.S. Government Printing Office.

Orfield, G., & Lee, C. (2005). *Why segregation matters: Poverty and educational inequality.* Cambridge, MA: Harvard University The Civil Rights Project. Retrieved May 15, 2005 from http://www.civilrightsproject.harvard.edu

Peterson, B. S., Anderson, A. W., Ehrenkranz, R., Staib, L. H., Tageldin, M., Colson, E., Gore, J. C, Duncan, C. C, Makuch, R., & Mendt, L. (2003). Regional brain volumes and their later neurodevelopmental correlates in term and preterm infants. *Pediatrics, 111(5),* 939–948.

Peterson B, S., Vohr, B., Staib, L. H., Cannistraci, C. J., Dolberg, A., Schneider, K. C, Katz, K. H., Westerveld, M., Sparrow, S., Anderson, A. W., Duncan, C. C, Makuch, R. W., Gore, J. C, & Ment, L. R. (2000). Regional brain volume abnormalities and long-term cognitive outcome in preterm infants. *Journal of the American Medical Association, 284,* 1939–1947.

Rector, R. E., & Johnson, K. A. (2004). *Understanding poverty in America.* Washington, D.C.: Heritage Foundation Backgrounder #1713. Retrieved May 15, 2005 from http://www.her-itage.org/

Rothstein, R. (2004). *Class and schools: Using social, economic, and educational reform to close the black-white achievement gap.* Washington, DC: Economic Policy Institute.

Rubinowitz, L. S., & Rosenbaum, J. E. (2000). *Crossing the class and color lines: from public housing to white suburbia.* Chicago: University of Chicago Press.

Rumberger, R. (1987). High school dropouts: A review of issues and evidence. *Review of Educnational Research,* 57(2), 101–121.

Salkind, N. J., & Haskins, R. (1982). Negative income tax: The impact on children from low-income families. *Journal of family Issues, 3,* 165–180.

Sampson, R. J., Raudenbush, S. W., & Earls, F. (1997). Neighborhoods and violent crime: A multilevel study of collective efficacy. *Science, 277,* 918–924.

Shulman, B. (2003). *The Betrayal of Work: How Low-Wage Jobs Fail 30 Million Americans.* New York: New Press.

Smith, M. L. (2004). *Political spectacle and the fate of American schools.* New York: Routledge-Farmer.

Taylor, B. A., Dearing, E., & McCartney, K. (2004). Incomes and Outcomes in Early Childhood. *Journal of Human Resources, 39(4),* 980–1007.

Traub, J. (2000, January 16). What no school can do. *New York Times Magazine.* Retrieved May 19, 2005, from http://www.augsburg.edu/

Turkheimer, E., Haley, A., Waldron, M., D'Onofrio, B., & Gottesman, 1. (2003). Socioeconomic status modifies hereditability of IQ in young children. *Psychological Science, 14(6),* 623–628.

UNICEF (2005). *Child poverty in rich countries, 2005.* Innocenti Report Card No. 6. Florence, Italy: UNICEF Innocenti Research Centre. Retrieved May 16, 2005 from www.unicef.org/ ire and www.unicef-irc.org

U.S. Environmental Protection Agency 2003. America's children and the environmental measures contaminants, body burdens, and illnesses. Washington, D.C.: Author. Retrieved July 23, 2005 from http://www.epa.gov

Wells, A., & Crain, R. (1997). *Stepping over the color line: African-American students in white, suburban schools.* New Haven, CT: Yale University Press.

World Bank (2005). World Development Indicators database. Retrieved May 15, 2005 from http ://www. worldbank.org

Suggested Readings

Allensworth, E., Nomi, T., Montgomery, N., & Lee, V. E. (2009). College preparatory curriculum for all: Academic consequences of requiring algebra and English I for ninth graders in Chicago. *Educational Evaluation and Policy Analysis*, 31, 367–391.

Anyon, J. (1997). *Ghetto schooling: A political economy of urban educational reform*. New York: Teachers College Press.

Anyon, J. (2005). *Radical possibilities: Public policy, urban education and a new social movement*. New York: Routledge.

Anyon, J. (2005). What "counts" as educational policy? Notes toward a new paradigm." *Harvard Educational Review*, 75 (1), 65–88.

Apple, M.W. (2006). *Educating the "right" way*. New York: Routledge.

Balfanz, R., Legters, N., West, T. C., & Weber, L. M. (2007). Are NCLB's measures, incentives, and improvement strategies the right ones for the nation's low-performing high schools? *American Educational Research Journal*, 44, 559–593.[

Belfield, C. R. & Levin H. M. (2002). The effects of competition between schools on educational outcomes: A review for the United States. Review of Education Research, 272–279.

Berends, M., Bodilly, S., & Kirby, S. (2002). Looking back over a decade of whole-school reform: The experience of new American schools. *Phi Delta Kappan*, 84 (2), 168–175.

Berends, M., Springer, M. G., & Walberg, H. J. (2007). *Charter school outcomes*. New York: Routledge.

Berliner, D. (2006). Our impoverished view of educational reform. *Teachers College Record*, 108 (6), 949–995

Berliner, D. & Biddle, B. (1996). *The manufactured crisis*. New York: Longman.

Bifulco, R., Cobb, C. D., & Bell, C. (2009). Can interdistrict choice boost student achievement? The case of Connecticut's interdistrict magnet school program. *Educational Evaluation and Policy Analysis*, 31, 323–345.

Binder, A. J. (2000). Why do some curricular challenges work while others do not? The case of three Afrocentric challenges. *Sociology of Education*, 73, 69–91.

Borman, K. M., Cookson, P. W., Jr., Sadovnik, A. R., & Spade, J. Z. (1996). *Implementing educational reform: Sociological perspectives on educational policy*. Wesport, CT: Ablex.

Borman, G., Hewes, G., Overman, L., & Brown, S. (2003). Comprehensive school reform and student achievement: A meta-analysis. *Review of Educational Research*, 73 (2), 125–230.

Borman, K. M., Kersaint, G., Boydston, T., Lee, R., Cotner, B., Uekawa, K., Baber, G., Kromrey, J., & Katzenmeyer, W. (2004). Meaningful urban education reform: Confronting the learning crises in mathematics and science. Albany, NY: SUNY Press.

Borman, K. and Associates. (2005). *Meaningful urban education reform: Confronting the learning crisis in mathematics and science*. Albany, NY: SUNY Press.

Bryk, A. S., Sebring, P. B., Allensworth, E., & Luppescu, S. (2010). *Organizing schools for improvement: Lessons from Chicago*. Chicago, IL: University of Chicago Press.

Bulkley, K., & Wohlstetter, P. (eds.) (2004). Taking account of charter schools: What's happened and what's next. New York: Teachers College Press.

Carnoy, M., Jacobsen, R., Mishal, L., & Rothstein, R. (2005). *The charter school dust-up: Examining the evidence on enrollment and achievement*. New York: Teachers College Press.

Coburn, C. E. & Russell, J. L. (2008). District policy and teachers' social networks. *Educational Evaluation and Policy Analysis*, 30, 203–235.

Darling-Hammond, L. (1996). The right to learn and the advancement of teaching: Research, policy, and practice for democratic education. *Peabody Journal of Education*, 67 (3), 123–154.

Darling-Hammond, L. (1997). *The right to learn: A blueprint for creating schools that work*. San Francisco, CA: Jossey-Bass.

Datnow, A. & Stringfield, S. (2000). Working together for reliable school reform. *Journal of Education for Students Placed at Risk*, 5 (1–2), 183–204.

Datnow, A., Borman, G., Stringfield, S., Overman, L., & Castellano, M. (2003). Comprehensive school reform in culturally and linguistically diverse contexts: Implementation and outcomes from a four-year study. *Educational Evaluation and Policy Analysis*, 25 (2), 25–54.

Diamond, J. B. (2007). Where the rubber meets the road: Rethinking the connection between high-stakes testing policy and classroom instruction. *Sociology of Education*, 80 (4), 285–313.

Downey, D. B., von Hippel, P. T., & Hughes, M. (2008). Are "failing" schools really failing? Using seasonal comparison to evaluate school effectiveness. *Sociology of Education*, 81 (3), 242–270.

Edmonds, R. (1979). Effective schools for the urban poor. *Educational Leadership*, 37, 15–27.

Edmonds, R. (1982). Programs of school improvement: An overview. *Educational Leadership*, 40, 4–11.

Elmore, R. (2004). *School reform from the inside out: Policy, practices and performance*. Cambridge, MA: Harvard Education Press.

Epstein, J. (2001). *School, family and community partnerships: Preparing educators and improving schools*. Boulder, CO: Westview Press.

Fine, M. (Ed.). (1994). *Chartering urban school reform*. New York: Teachers College Press.

Finnigan, K. S. & Gross, B. (2007). Do accountability policy sanctions influence teacher motivation? Lessons from Chicago's low-performing schools. *American Educational Research Journal*, 44, 594–630

Fruchter, N. (2007). *Urban schools, public will*. New York: Teachers College Press.

Fullan, M. G. & Stiegelbauer, S. (1991). *The new meaning of educational change*. New York: Teachers College Press.

Fuller, B. (2000). *Inside charter schools*. Cambridge, MA: Harvard Ecucation Press.

Gamoran, A. (1996). Student achievement in public magnet, public comprehensive, and private city high schools. *Educational Evaluation and Policy Analysis*, 18 (1), 1–18.

Gross, B., Booker, T. K., & Goldhaber, D. (2009). Boosting student achievement: The effect of comprehensive school reform on student achievement. *Educational Evaluation and Policy Analysis*, 31, 111–126.

Henig, J. (1994). *Rethinking school choice: Limits of the market metaphor*. Princeton, NJ: Princeton University Press.

Hess, G. Alfred, Jr. (1995). *Restructuring urban schools: A Chicago perspective*. New York: Teachers College Press.

Hubbard, L., Stein, M. K., & Mehan, H. (2006). *Reform as learning: When school reform collides with school culture and community politics*. New York: Routledge.

Hursh, D. (2007). Assessing No Child Left Behind and the rise of neoliberal education policies. *American Educational Research Journal*, 44, 493–518.

Jennings, J. L. & Beveridge, A. A. (2009). How does test exemption affect schools' and students' academic performance? *Educational Evaluation and Policy Analysis*, 31, 153–175.

Kahne, J. E., Sporte, S. E., de la Torre, M., & Easton, J. Q. (2008). Small high schools on a larger scale: The impact of school conversions in Chicago. *Educational Evaluation and Policy Analysis*, 30, 281–315.

Lauen, D. L. (2007).Contextual explanations of school choice. *Sociology of Education*, 80 (3), 179–209.

Lauen, D. L. (2008). The false promises of school choice in NCLB. In A. R. Sadovnik, J. A. O'Day, G. Bohrnstedt, & K. Borman (Eds.), *No Child Left Behind and the reduction of the achievement gap: Sociological perspectives on federal educational policy* (pp. 203–226). New York: Routledge.

Lauen, D. L. (2009). To choose or not to choose: High school choice and graduation in Chicago. *Educational Evaluation and Policy Analysis*, 31, 179–199.

Lee, V. L. & Ready, D. (2006). *Schools within schools: Possibilities and pitfalls of high school reform*. New York: Teachers College Press.

Lee, V. E. & Smith, J. B. (1995, October). Effects of high school restructuring and size on gains in achievement for early secondary school students. *Sociology of Education*, 68 (4), 241–270.

Lee, V. E. & Smith, J. B. (2001). *Restructuring high schools for equity and excellence: What works*. New York: Teachers College Press.

Lipman, P. (1998). *Race, class and power in school restructuring*. New York: State University of New York Press.

Lipman, P. (2003). *High stakes education: Inequality, globalization, and urban school reform*. New York: Routledge.

Lubienski, C. (2001). Redefining "public" education: Charter schools, common schools, and the rhetoric of reform. *Teachers College Record*, 103 (4), 634–666.

Lubienski, C. (2003). Innovation in education markets: Theory and evidence on the impact of competition and choice in charter schools. *American Educational Research Journal*, 40 (2), 394–443.

Lubienski, C. (2005). Public schools in marketized environments: Shifting incentives and unintended consequences of competition-based educational reforms. *American Journal of Education*, 111 (4), 464–486.

Lubienski, C. (2005). School choice as a civil right: District responses to competition and equal educational opportunity. *Equity & Excellence in Education*, 38 (4), 331–341.

Lubienski, C. & Lubienski, S. T. (2006). Charter schools, academic achievement and NCLB. *Journal of School Choice*, 1 (3), 55–62.

Lubienski, C., Weitzel, P., & Lubienski, S. T. (2009). Is there a "consensus" on school choice and achievement? Advocacy research and the emerging political economy of knowledge production. *Educational Policy*, 23 (1), 161–193.

Lubienski, S. T. & Lubienski, C. (2006). School sector and academic achievement: A multi-level analysis of NAEP mathematics data. *American Educational Research Journal*, 43 (4), 651–698.

Lubienski, S. T., Lubienski, C., & Crane, C. C. (2008). Achievement differences and school type: The role of school climate, teacher certification and instruction. *American Journal of Education*, 115 (1), 97–138.

McNeil, L. M. 2000. *Contradictions of school reform: Educational costs of standardized testing*. New York: Routledge.

Mickelson, R. A. (1999). International business machinations: A case study of corporate involvement in local educational reform. *Teachers College Record*, 100 (3), 476–512.

Mickelson, R. A. (2001). Subverting swan: First- and second-generation segregation in the Charlotte-Mecklenburg school. *American Educational Research Journal*, 38 (2), 215–252.

Mickelson, R. A. (2008). Segregation and the SAT. *Ohio State Law Review*, 67, 156–199.

Moore, R., Arnot, M., Beck, J., & Daniels, H. (2010). *Knowledge, power and educational reform: Applying the sociology of Basil Bernstein*. Oxford: Routledge.

Noguera, P. A. (2003). *City schools and the American dream: Reclaiming the promise of public education*. New York: Teachers College Press.

Oakes, J. (2004). Investigating the claims in *Williams v. the State of California*: An unconstitutional denial of education's basic tools. *Teachers College Record*, 106 (10), 1889–1906.

O'Day, J. A. (2002). Complexity, accountability, and school improvement. *Harvard Educational Review*, 72 (3), 293–329.

O'Day, J. A. & Smith, M. S. (1992). Systemic reform and equal educational opportunity. In S. H. Fuhrman (Ed.), *Designing*

Coherent Education Policy (pp. 250–312). San Francisco: Jossey-Bass.

Odden, A. (1993). School finance reform in Kentucky, New Jersey and Texas. *Journal of Education Finance*, 18, 293–317.

Orfield, G. & Ashkinaze, C. (1991). *The closing door: Conservative policy and Black opportunity*. Chicago: University of Chicago Press.

Orfield G. & Easton, S. (1996). *Dismantling segregation: The quiet reversal of* Brown v. Board of Education. New York: New Press.

Orfield, G. & Yun, J. T. (1999). *Resegregation in American schools*. Cambridge, MA: The Civil Rights Project, Harvard University. Retrieved August 12, 2006, from http://www.civilrightsproject.harvard.edu/research/deseg/reseg_schools99.php.

Orfield, G. & Lee, J. (2004). *Brown at 50: King's dream or Plessy's nightmare?* Retrieved August 12, 2006, from http://www.civilrightsproject.harvard.edu/research/deseg/reseg_schools99.php.

Payne, C. (2008). *So much reform, so little change: The persistence of failure in urban schools*. Cambridge, MA: Harvard Education Press.

Powers, J. M. (2004) High-stakes accountability and equity: Using evidence from California's Public Schools Accountability Act to address the issues in *Williams v. State of California*. *American Educational Research Journal*, 41 (4), 763–795.

Powers, J. M. (2009). *Charter schools: From reform imagery to reform reality*. New York: Palgrave.

Powers, J. M. & Cookson, P. W., Jr. (1999). School choice as a political movement. *Educational Policy*, 13 (1–2), 104–122.

Ravitch, D. (2010). *The death and life of the great American school system: How testing and choice are undermining education*. New York: Basic Books.

Ray, C. A. & Mickelson, R. A. (1993). Restructured students for restructured work: The economy, school reform, and noncollege-bound youth. *Sociology of Education*, 66, 1–23.

Ready, D. G., Lee, Valerie E., & Welner, K. (2004). Educational equity and social structure: School size, overcrowding, and school-within-schools. *Teachers College Record*, 106 (10), 1989–2014.

Rofes, E. & Stulberg, L. (2006). *The emancipatory promise of charter schools*. Albany, NY: SUNY Press.

Rosenbaum, J. E. (2001). *Beyond college for all: Career paths for the forgotten half*. New York: Russell Sage Foundation.

Rothstein, R. (2004). *Class and schools: Using social, economic, and educational reform to close the Black–White achievement gap*. New York: Teachers College Press.

Rowan, B. & Miller, R. J. (2007). Organizational strategies for promoting instructional change: implementation dynamics in schools working with comprehensive school reform providers. *American Educational Research Journal*, 44, 252–297.

Sadovnik, A. R., O'Day, J. A., Bohrnstedt, G., & Borman, K. M. (Eds.). (2007). *No Child Left Behind and the reduction of the achievement gap: Sociological perspectives on federal educational policy*. New York: Routledge.

Sanders, M. (2009). Collaborating for change: How an urban school district and a community-based organization support and sustain school, family, and community partnerships. *Teachers College Record*, 111 (7), 1693–1712.

Scott, J. (2005). *School choice and diversity: What the evidence says*. New York: Teachers College Press.

Semel, S. F & Sadovnik, A. R. (2008). Small schools and the history of education: Lessons from the history of progressive education. *Teachers College Record*, 110 (9), 1774–1771.

Smerdon, B. A. & Borman, K. M. (2009). *Saving America's high schools*. Washington, DC: Urban Institute Press.

Valli, L. & Buese, D. (2007). The changing roles of teachers in an era of high-stakes accountability. *American Educational Research Journal*, 44, 519–558

Van Dunk, E. & Dickman, E. (2003). *School choice and the question of accountability*. New Haven, CT: Yale University Press.

Vasquez Heilig, J. & Darling-Hammond, L. (2008). Accountability Texas-style: The progress and learning of urban minority students in a high-stakes testing context. *Educational Evaluation and Policy Analysis*, 30, 75–110.

Warren, J. R., Grodsky, E., & Lee, J. C. (2008). State high school exit examinations and postsecondary labor market outcomes. *Sociology of Education*, 81 (1), 77–107.

Wells, A. S. (1993). *Time to choose: America at the crossroads of school choice policy*. New York: Hill and Wang.

Wells, Amy, Artiles, L., Carnochan, S., Cooper, C., Grutzik, C., Holme, J., Lopez, A., Scott, J., Slayton, J., & Vasuveda, A. (1998). *Beyond the rhetoric of charter school reform: A study of ten California districts*. Los Angeles: UCLA.

Wells, A. S., Holme, J. J., Tijerina Revilla, A., & Korantemaa Atanda, A. (2009). *Both sides now: The story of school desegregation's graduates*. Berkeley, CA: University of California Press.

Wells, A. S., Duran, J., & White, T. (2008). Refusing to leave desegregation behind: From graduates of racially diverse schools to the Supreme Court. *Teachers College Record*, 110 (12), 2532–2570.

Wechsler, H. S. (2001). *Access to success in the urban high school: The middle college movement*. New York: Teachers College Press.

Whitty, G. (1997). Creating quasi-markets in education: A review of recent research on parental choice and school autonomy in three countries. *Review of Research in Education*, 22 (1), 3–47.

Witte, J. F. (2000). *The market approach to education*. Princeton, NJ: Princeton University Press.

Wohlstetter, P., Malloy, C., Chau, D., & Polhemus, J. (2003). Improving schools through networks: A new approach to urban school reform. *Educational Policy*, 17 (4), 399–430.

Permissions

Durkheim, Emile, "On Education and Society" from *The Evolution of Educational Thought: Lectures of the formation and development of secondary education in France*, pp. 92–105. Reprinted with permission from Routledge, a member of Taylor & Francis Group.

Collins, Randall, "Functional and Conflict Theories of Educational Stratification" from *American Sociological Review*, Vol. 36, No. 6 (Dec. 1971), pp. 1002–1019, ©1971. Reprinted with permission of the American Sociological Association.

Bowles, Samuel and Gintis, Herbert, "Broken Promises: School Reform in Retrospect" from *Schooling in Capitalist America*, pp. 18–41, ©1976 by Basic Books. Reprinted with permission of Perseus Books Group.

Rist, Ray C., "On Understanding the Processes of Schooling: The Contributions of Labeling Theory" from *Power and Ideology* (1997), pp. 292–305, ©1997. Reprinted with permission of Oxford University Press, Inc.

Bourdieu, Pierre, "The Forms of Capital Pierre Bourdieu" from John Richardson, *Handbook of Theory and Research for the Sociology of Education*, John Richardson, ©1986. Reprinted with permission of Greenwood Publishing Group, Inc., Westport, CT.

Coleman, James S., "Social Capital in the Creation of Human Capital" from The American Journal of Sociology, Vol. 94, No. S1 (1988), pp. S95–S120, ©1988. Reprinted with permission of The University of Chicago Press.

Bernstein, Basil, "Class and Pedagogies: Visible and Invisible," from *Basil Bernstein: Class, Codes and Control*, pp. 116–145, ©2003. Reprinted with permission from Routledge, a member of Taylor & Francis Group.

Meyer, John W., "The Effects of Education as an Institution" from *American Journal of Sociology*, Vol. 85, No. 1 (1977), pp. 55–77, ©1977. Reprinted with permission of The University of Chicago Press.

Gamoran, Adam, Secada, Walter G., and Marrett, Cora B., "The Organizational Contexts of Teaching and Learning: Changing Theoretical Perspectives" from Maureen Hallinan, *Handbook of the Sociology of Education*, pp. 37–64 (Gamoran et al.), ©2000. Reprinted with permission of Springer Science and Business Media.

Ingersoll, Richard, "Is there Really a Teacher Shortage?" from *Center for the Study of Teaching and Policy*, pp. 1–32, ©2003. Reprinted with permission of The University of Washington.

Apple, Michael W., "Whose Markets, Whose Knowledge" from Michael Apple, *Educating the "Right" Way*, 2nd Ed., ©2006. Reprinted with permission of Routledge, a member of Taylor & Francis Group.

Ramirez, Francisco and Boli, John, "The Political Construction of Mass Schooling: European

Index